The Broadview Anthology of Drama:
Plays from the Western Theatre

VOLUME II

The Nineteenth and Twentieth Centuries

The Broadview Anthology of Drama: Plays from the Western Theatre

VOLUME II

The Nineteenth and Twentieth Centuries

Jennifer Wise and Craig S. Walker

EDITORS

broadview press

National Library of Canada Cataloguing in Publication

The Broadview anthology of drama : plays from the western theatre / edited by Jennifer Wise and Craig S. Walker.

Contents: v. 1. From antiquity through the eighteenth century
— v. 2. The nineteenth and twentieth centuries
ISBN 1-55111-139-X (v. 1).—ISBN 1-55111-582-4 (v. 2)

1. Drama—Collections.   I. Wise, Jennifer, 1959-   II. Walker, Craig Stewart, 1960-

PN6112.B76 2003   808.82   C2003-902439-3

Broadview Press Ltd. is an independent, international publishing house, incorporated in 1985. Broadview believes in shared ownership, both with its employees and with the general public; since the year 2000 Broadview shares have traded publicly on the Toronto Venture Exchange under the symbol BDP.

We welcome comments and suggestions regarding any aspect of our publications–please feel free to contact us at the addresses below or at broadview@broadviewpress.com.

North America
PO Box 1243,
Peterborough, Ontario
Canada K9J 7H5
3576 California Road,
Orchard Park, NY, USA 14127
Tel: (705) 743-8990;
Fax: (705) 743-8353
email: customerservice@broadviewpress.com

UK, Ireland, and continental Europe
Plymbridge Distributors Ltd.
Estover Road
Plymouth
United Kingdom PL6 7PY
Tel: +44 (0) 1752 202301;
Fax: +44 (0) 1752 202333
email: orders@plymbridge.com

Australia and New Zealand
UNIREPS,
University of New South Wales
Sydney, NSW, 2052
Australia
Tel: 61 2 9664 0999;
Fax: 61 2 9664 5420
email: info.press@unsw.edu.au

www.broadviewpress.com

Broadview Press Ltd. gratefully acknowledges the financial support of the Government of Canada through the Book Publishing Industry Development Program for our publishing activities.

PRINTED IN CANADA

Contents

—

VOLUME II

Contents of the companion volume
The Broadview Anthology of Drama: Plays from the Western Theatre
Volume I: From Antiquity Through the Eighteenth Century

⌐

⌐

Molière
Tartuffe (1669)
> Richard Wilbur, trans.
> Craig S. Walker, ed.

Jean-Baptiste Racine
Phèdre (1677)
> William Packard, trans.
> Craig S. Walker, ed.

4 The Enlightenment Stage

Aphra Behn
The Rover (1667)
> Anne Russell, ed.

William Wycherley
The Country Wife (1675)
> Peggy Thompson, ed.

William Congreve
The Way of the World (1700)
> Richard Kroll, ed.

Susannah Centlivre
A Bold Stroke for a Wife (1718)
> Nancy Copeland, ed.

Carlo Gozzi
Turandot (1761)
> Albert Bermel & Ted Emery, trans.
> Jennifer Wise, ed.

Beaumarchais
The Marriage of Figaro (1778-1784)
> John Van Burek & Jennifer Wise, trans.
> Jennifer Wise, ed.

Friedrich Schiller
The Robbers (1778-1782)
> F.J. Lamport, trans.
> Jennifer Wise, ed.

Acknowledgements

We wish to extend our heartfelt thanks and appreciation to all the delightful people at Broadview Press: to president Don LePan, for his always cheerful encouragement; to Betsy Struthers, for her rights and permissions work; to Kathryn Brownsey, for her exacting inputting and proofreading; to Eileen Eckert, for her meticulous typesetting, copyediting and page layout, as well as for her excellent judgement and patience; and lastly but perhaps above all to Tammy Roberts, who kept us all going.

Jennifer Wise and Craig S. Walker

Introduction

Dramatic writing is designed to be spoken out loud, relished on the tongues of actors, and experienced as something close to music by a listening audience—which may be why plays so often do double duty as great poems. The works included in this anthology are no exception: many are regarded as the pinnacles of literary achievement in their respective languages. But the fact remains that drama, despite its literary pre-eminence, is not a purely literary genre. More than any other language art, drama is also a concrete social activity. It is the lasting manifestation of a tangible (if ephemeral) social practice, the theatre, whose business it is to assemble real living audiences in real public places in real time. Tied in this way to an interactive social event rooted in a precise, unrepeatable moment, drama cannot help but be marked by the extra-literary realities and contingencies of life. Theatre production is an occasion for staging plays, but it is also necessarily an exercise in finance and economics, a response to prevailing laws, an immediate casualty of and contributor to volatile political environments. Often in complete disregard of the literary intentions of the playwright, plays become intertwined through performance with prevailing religious practices and taboos; with the facts of urban planning and architectural design; with interruptions in the flow of goods, services and people because of wars and natural disasters; and with the prejudices and current concerns of the particular group of people who happen to have assembled on a given day to see it. Realism itself is actually very rare in drama and theatre in general, with most plays being constructed according to the logic of the dream, the fantasy, the wish-fulfillment and the cautionary tale. Indeed, playwrights create and transform reality more often than they endeavour simply to "represent" it. But all plays, even the least realistic, are forced nevertheless to contend with the ineluctable substratum of real bodies and things out of which theatre constitutes itself. As a type of real production in real historical time, theatre in consequence does not merely represent but always, to some extent, actually embodies the real world, its changing habits of dress, food and drug consumption, leisure, sex, gender differentiation, deportment, hygiene, marriage, civil disobedience, public speech, and political participation.

Our first principle in assembling this anthology has therefore been to acknowledge drama's special generic status as a type of literature in which meaning is inseparable from real moments in historical time. In practical terms this has meant accompanying each play with plenty of historical background in the form of context-rich introductory essays and detailed explanatory notes. But the principle has also guided our selection of plays. In choosing this particular handful of works to represent a vast literature that spreads over 2,500 years, thirteen different countries and almost as many languages, we aimed to do more than isolate forty-something "great plays" and arrange them in chronological order. Instead, we have tried to tell, as accurately as is possible with such a small sample, the ongoing story of Western theatre and drama—which, when properly understood, is the story of Western civilization. We have therefore chosen plays according to criteria that are not always, strictly speaking, literary. For example, the standard dramatic version of *Uncle Tom's Cabin*—included here for the first time in any major drama anthology—may appear to be a work of dubious quality when judged by literary standards alone. But as an event in world theatre history and in the history of slavery and racism, the play has enormous significance. Besides bringing unprecedented public attention to the atrocity of American slavery, *Uncle Tom's Cabin* was probably the most successful American play ever performed and certainly the most successful melodrama. Since melodrama remains the dominant form of storytelling around the world today and clearly retains its hold on our narrative imagination, it demands its place within any study of Western drama, despite its low reputation as a literary form.

This is not to say that inherent literary quality was not our primary requirement, as will be clear from our inclusion of such acknowledged masterpieces as *Oedipus*, *Hamlet*, *Phèdre*, *Tartuffe*, *The Way of the World*, *The Cherry Orchard*, and many others. But attention was also paid to the context of each play's creation and performance, its effects on audiences or later playwrights, and its role within the "big picture" of drama production generally. We were guided, in short, by a determination to include works whose historical significance was as demonstrable as their literary excellence. And by this we mean demonstrable not only for the country that produced it but internationally, within the whole of the Western theatrical tradition.

Our desire to give students an accurate picture of Western drama overall is also reflected in our inclusion of more plays from non-English-speaking nations than is customary in English-language anthologies. Representative plays from France, Germany, Italy, Spain, Russia, Norway, and Sweden, as well as ancient Greece and Rome, appear here, many in new translations commissioned especially for this anthology.

We were also keen to include a representative sample of plays by women from the pre-modern period. Seventeenth- and eighteenth-century playwrights such as Aphra Behn and Susannah Centlivre were among the most successful playwrights of their time; women have in fact been writing plays since the early Middle Ages, some of which, like the plays of Hroswitha and Hildegard, were among the only dramatic works being written at the time by anybody. Along with recognized gems of medieval drama such as *Everyman* and *The Second Shepherds' Play*, we have also included lesser-known works from the apparent inventors of two of the medieval theatre's most important genres, the saint's play and the morality play.

While hoping to moderate the gender imbalance that must to some degree characterize all historical anthologies such as these, we have also aimed to rectify a common generic imbalance: the preference within university textbooks for "serious" over comic plays. Long gone, we trust, is the old puritanical prejudice against laughter, with its unreasoned assumption that important ideas and experiences are not likely to coexist with amusement. Admittedly, comedy, so dependent on topical references and current events, on ephemeral scandals and passing fashions, even on brand- and street-names, can be a challenging genre to appreciate out of context, and previous anthologizers have understandably tended to shy away from it in favour of more universalist, metaphysical tragedies and "straight" plays. But the resulting picture of Western drama has been a distorted one. If anything, audiences throughout history show a slight preference for laughter over tears, and nothing is more revealing of a person's (or a period's) character than a look at what he or she laughs at. Comedy is the social form *par excellence* within a highly social art, and we have tried to restore it to its proper place by including a number of rarely anthologized comedies, each sufficiently well annotated to ensure that everybody gets all the jokes.

The general orientation of this book ideally suits it for use in theatre history surveys, as well as in literature courses at the undergraduate or graduate level that take a context-sensitive approach to drama. But at the same time, the book was designed with an eye to the needs of multi-genre English courses that approach literary texts thematically. In addition to its other merits, each play was selected for the opportunities it affords for cross-cultural, comparative readings of differing reflections on similar themes. Revenge and forgiveness, master/slave relations, *femmes fatales*, forbidden sex, passion vs. reason, the construction of self within marginalized social groups, the "angry young man," gender stereotyping, marriage, women's empowerment, tyranny and rebellion in the family and the state, law, commerce, role-playing and identity, and the transformative power of theatre itself—these and other perennial dramatic and literary themes can be found in at least two and sometimes several plays. Plays were also selected to ensure representation of a wide range of dramatic sub-genres: tragedy, political satire, situation comedy, morality, farce, tragi-comedy, romance, comedy of manners, fairytale, melodrama, naturalist drama, and allegory.

The anthology consists of six chronologically organized chapters: The Ancient Theatre, Medieval Drama, The Renaissance, and The Enlightenment Stage (Volume One); The Nineteenth Century, and The Twentieth Century: Modernism and After (Volume Two). Each chapter begins with a general introduction that sketches in the main currents of thought and literary practice, as well as the changing trends in theatre production, audience behaviour, and economic and political life that characterize the period. Individual plays are then preceded by their own introduction which locates them more narrowly within the biography and literary output of their author, explains relevant details in their production history, and provides interpretive assistance in approaching them today. As for explanatory footnotes, we have tried to strike a balance between helpfulness and unobtrusiveness, a balance that is more difficult to achieve with some plays than others. Having taught these plays for many years in the classroom, we were guided above all by the needs of our students; in all our annotations, we have tried to anticipate frequently asked questions, to illuminate obscure allusions, and provide translations and glosses that have enriched students' reading experience of these plays in the past.

The Roman theorist Horace famously said that drama's purpose is to delight and instruct. We hope this book does likewise. We dedicate it to all our students, past, present, and future.

CHAPTER FIVE

The Nineteenth Century

For the first thirty years of the nineteenth century, the most significant cultural trend in Europe continued to be the Romantic movement, which had begun in the closing decades of the eighteenth century (and which, accordingly, was represented in the first volume of this anthology by Friedrich Schiller's play *The Robbers*). By the 1830s, Romantic drama had begun to decline in most places (although in France it actually peaked with Victor Hugo's *Hernani*). However, the effects of Romanticism continued to be evident in many aspects of Western theatre.

Perhaps the most significant of these was the tradition of "great acting," which was associated with many of the Romantic values, such as the celebration of "feeling" over "reason" and the idea of the actor as a divinely inspired natural genius. In England, this emphasis on the personality of the actor was most obvious in comments made about Edmund Kean (1789–1833): "To see him act," said the Romantic poet Samuel Taylor Coleridge, "is like reading Shakespeare by flashes of lightning." Other English actors, such as Sarah Siddons (1755–1831), her brother John Philip Kemble (1757–1823), and William Charles Macready (1793–1873), were also renowned for the depth of feeling conveyed by their larger-than-life performances. A similar cult of personality arose in the United States, where the powerful Edwin Forrest (1806–1872) and the dignified black Shakespearean actor Ira Aldridge (1807–1867) were acclaimed in comparable terms, and in continental Europe, where the French actors Talma (1763–1826), Duchenois (1777–1835), Frederick Lemaitre (1800–1876), and Rachel (1820–1858), and, later in the century, Sarah Bernhardt (1844–1923) and the Italian star, Eleonora Duse (1858–1924), were all beneficiaries of the Romantic emphasis on the personality of the great artist.

Naturally, the dramatic repertoire was affected by the immense box office appeal of such performers, in that plays were often chosen for their suitability as "star vehicles." Because the Romantic style of acting appeared to best effect in plays with larger-than-life characters and stories, classical plays (especially Shakespearean tragedies) and melodramas with juicy starring roles were popular. Thus, while a series of reactions against Romanticism were making themselves felt throughout much of literature, such a reaction was at first not much visible on the stage. To be sure, the earliest play in this chapter, Georg Büchner's *Woyzeck* (1837), was written partially in reaction against the excesses of Romanticism, but it is extremely unlikely that a play of its kind ever would have been accepted for performance by the star-centred theatres of the time; indeed, *Woyzeck* was not performed until the twentieth century. Büchner has on occasion been classed among the Romantics because of his depiction of natural life erupting through the strictures of a hyper-rational society. However, the Romantic label seems finally inappropriate in his case, because his work resists the Romantic tendency to idealize and inflate the nobility of the protagonist in unrealistic ways. In this respect, Büchner's play represents a step toward Realism and Naturalism, which would become major forces in drama by the end of the nineteenth century.

In the meantime, the most important social force affecting theatre and drama throughout most of the nineteenth century was the inexorable rise in the size and power of the middle and lower-middle classes, a transformation chiefly driven by the Industrial Revolution. Generally speaking, theatre has usually represented the ideology of the social class that is financing it. Accordingly, as larger numbers of lower- and middle-class people attended theatre, more dramas began to depict class struggle and to embrace bourgeois morality as opposed to aristocratic virtue. Of course, there were differences in programming depending upon the character of a given theatre. In London, for example, the major West End theatres such as Drury Lane, Covent Garden, and the Haymarket tended to cater chiefly to the middle to upper-middle classes, whereas the music halls and East End theatres catered to the lower and lower-middle classes. At any rate, the changes in the economic conditions of the general public certainly affected the dramatic representation of notions of fate or fortune. For, in a society that recognized the growing power of money to change social status, and also recognized the possibility that the fortunes of individuals might rise to wealth or decline to poverty in a matter of a few years, social stature began to be regarded as accidental rather than as the outward symbol of inherent worth. Hence, the idea that a protagonist's central struggle might have more to do with external circumstances than with some struggle within his own divided character began to grow in popularity. One of the expressions of this new outlook was melodrama, which became the most popular form of drama in the Western hemisphere during the nineteenth century.

The term *mélodrame*—"music drama"—was first used by Rousseau to describe his *Pygmalion* (1766), a play comprising spoken dialogue underscored with music. Perhaps the genre might not have become so popular had not government licensing policy in France and England created a split between the so-called "legitimate" theatres (i.e., theatres licensed to produce spoken drama) and the "illegitimate" (i.e., theatres that did not have such licenses, but were allowed to present "musical" entertainment). When managers of the "illegitimate" Boulevard theatres in Paris realized that underscored dramas like Rousseau's provided a means of circumventing the regulations, such plays became more common and quickly became popular in their own right. René Charles Guilbert de Pixérécourt (1773–1844) perfected the form in France at the turn of the century, and soon melodrama began to win favour all over Europe and North America. Eventually, as the licensing question became less pressing, the musical aspect of melodrama became rather less prominent, although underscoring remained a feature of the plays. However, the term "melodrama" gradually came to be associated more with the conventions of plot and character common to these plays than with the musical aspect of their presentation.

George Aiken's dramatic adaptation of Harriet Beecher Stowe's *Uncle Tom's Cabin* (1852) was the most popular stage melodrama of the nineteenth century, and it is typical in many ways of the genre. Melodrama nearly always features the following:

(a) a simplified moral world of purely good versus purely evil characters, corresponding to particular types, such as:

   (i) a scheming villain, who is usually wealthy (e.g., Simon Legree);

   (ii) a morally pure heroine and/or hero, who are usually poor (e.g., Tom, George, and Eliza);

   (iii) one or more comic lower-class characters of some colourful ethnic type, who usually assist the heroine or hero (e.g., Topsy, Phineas Fletcher, and Gumption Cute—the last character an addition made by George Aiken for the stage version of *Uncle Tom's Cabin*);

(b) an episodic plot structure, consisting of a series of narrow escapes from the villain, and marked by spectacular scenes of violence and crisis (e.g., a big attraction of *Uncle Tom's Cabin* was Eliza's escape across the ice floes, which by the 1880s was "enhanced" with the addition of live bloodhounds);

(c) scenes of tearful sentimentality (e.g., the death of Little Eva);

(d) the resolution of the play, often at the last minute, in a happy ending (e.g., the come-uppance of the villain Simon Legree, and the final reunion of Tom and Eva in heaven; given the popularity of the novel, Aiken had little choice but to have these characters die).

As melodramas drew larger and larger audiences, enormous new theatres were built—many of which held between three and four thousand spectators—and these huge new auditoriums made arduous physical demands upon performers. Partly in response to these conditions, actors resorted to a number of conventionalized, broad, pantomimic gestures that could be instantly deciphered as representing a particular emotion, even by those sitting at the back of the house. Such acting served to simplify the genre's moral and emotional universe even further by reducing performances to a selection of stock clichés. When silent film arrived, actors retained many of these conventions, even when being filmed in close-up. The incongruousness of the result was not widely apparent for a time, however ludicrous some of these performances may seem to us in retrospect. As a dramatic genre, melodrama has now largely disappeared from the stage. However, its legacy lives on today in many a popular Hollywood movie which, notwithstanding a veneer of contemporary sophistica-tion, still exhibits many of the features listed above.

The highly conventionalized world of melodrama is perhaps not what we would call "realistic," and yet it is nevertheless true that popular melodramas were increasingly accompanied by the thrust toward more realistic stage design that was taking place at the same time. During the eighteenth century, a number of steps had been taken to increase the realism of set designs. Yet, the work of designers such as de Loutherbourg (who created a number of brilliant designs for David Garrick's productions at Drury Lane in London) was somewhat constrained by the poor lighting sources avail-able to him. In 1817, however, theatrical lighting took a great step forward when gas lighting was introduced at Drury Lane; this was followed by arc lighting and eventually by electrical lighting, each of which not only allowed more of the stage to be illuminated more brightly, but also allowed for considerably greater control and flexibility in the positioning and the intensity of the lighting instruments. Naturally, the improvements in lighting expanded the possibilities for stage design and inevitably contributed to improving the overall quality of theatrical illusion.

Advances in stage design took place throughout the century under the hands of many differ-ent managers all over Europe and North America. For example, in the area of spectacular effects, the playwright-director-producer Pixérécourt provided climaxes for his melodramas with realisti-cally staged large natural disasters, such as floods and volcanic eruptions. In England, Dion Boucicault (1822–1890) similarly used fires, collapsing buildings, and snowstorms. And in the United States, Augustin Daly (1836–1899) created such famous sensational effects as showing the heroine in a melodrama tied to the railroad tracks in the path of an approaching train. On a more modest level of theatrical illusion, Madame (Lucia) Vestris (1797–1856), who ran the Olympia

Theatre in London, introduced the box-set (invented in Italy during the Renaissance) to the English theatre as part of her effort to improve the realism of settings and costumes for domestic dramas. A parallel development in theatrical design was antiquarianism, wherein the clothing and architecture of the historical period in which plays were set were researched and recreated on the stage. The antiquarian movement was seen early in the century in the Shakespearean productions of John Philip Kemble and his younger brother, Charles (1775–1854); however, it would attain its most impressive heights in the late nineteenth century at the hands of the Meiningen Players, a company from the court of the tiny duchy of Saxe Meiningen (in what is now Germany), who achieved international fame for the breathtaking visual realism of their historical productions of plays by Shakespeare and Schiller.

Yet, there remained a certain inconsistency between the highly realistic detail in the design elements of many productions and the psychologically or socially unrealistic dramas often performed in these realistic environments. One theory that purported to resolve this discrepancy was Naturalism. The words "naturalism" and "realism" are often used as if they were synonyms, but, while the two terms are closely related, there is a useful distinction to be made. Realism refers to the general tendency toward creating an illusion of the real world, whether through costumes, set, a plausible story and behaviour, or accurate depiction of social circumstances. Naturalism, by contrast, refers to a specific movement founded upon a specific theory, which was first articulated by Emile Zola with reference to the novel, but which was quickly adapted to the stage. The essential proposition of the theory is that character is determined by environment and heredity. A ready example of this concept lies in the general assumption that a life of privation, cruelty, and violence is more likely to beget criminal behaviour than a life of plenty, comfort, and tenderness. So, whereas earlier drama had often seemed to represent human beings as autonomous agents—influencing, but not influenced by their environment—in Naturalist drama the setting of plays ceased to stand as mere background and became rather the embodiment of destiny.

The number of dramas explicitly proclaimed as "Naturalist" by their authors was never enormous—Emile Zola's *Thérèse Raquin* (1873) and August Strindberg's *Miss Julie* (1888) are the most frequently cited—yet the influence of Naturalist theory on the theatre was extensive. For example, it encouraged the efforts of directors such as André Antoine, director of the Théâtre Libre in Paris, to unify theatrical elements into a more coherent *mise en scène* by harnessing the new developments in realistic set design to plays written in a realistic style. Its impact was also felt in the standards by which acting came to be judged: the exaggerated and highly conventionalized performances which had been the norm began to be criticized as inauthentic and untruthful (though it would not be until early in the twentieth century, after extensive personal experience in the new realistic theatre, that Konstantin Stanislavski would develop a systematic approach to the problems that confronted an actor working within a naturalistic setting). And yet Naturalism did beget some excesses of its own. While at the heart of Zola's Naturalism lay a quasi-scientific interest in exposing the diseases of society by depicting human beings as if they were specimens in a case study—and Strindberg had, in *Miss Julie*, built from these ideas a subtle and powerfully affecting psychological drama—there were a number of subsequent works, such as the bitterly ironic and frequently gruesome plays known as *comédies rosses*, which showed less enthusiasm for Naturalism's project of exposing sociological truths with scientific rigour than for the simple shock value found in portraying sordid acts on the stage. For instance, August Linert's *Christmas Story* was notorious for a scene in which the corpse of a murdered child is thrown to the pigs to the accompaniment of carol singing.

Nevertheless, Naturalism, in a modified form, was to have a decisive, positive effect on the development of realistic drama. In its pure form, Naturalism's insistence that human behaviour is determined by environmental and biological factors seemed to allow no room for the idea of personal agency. Hence, characters conceived in purely Naturalistic terms could easily appear to be little more than ciphers for sociological forces. However, a highly effective response to the ideas of Naturalism came from the Norwegian playwright Henrik Ibsen in a series of realistic plays such as *A Doll's House* (1879), *Ghosts* (1881), and *An Enemy of the People* (1882). In these plays Ibsen explored the theme of resistance to environmental and social determinism, showing characters recognizing, reacting, and struggling self-consciously against the environment in which they find themselves rather than merely allowing themselves to be determined by it. The socially realistic drama developed by Ibsen not only became an aesthetically dominant dramatic style, it also came to be regarded as a vehicle of social reform, on the reasoning that where there was a faithful reproduction of social truths, the dissolution of social prejudices and injustice must follow. Of particular importance was Ibsen's *Ghosts*, a play in which a son's discovery that he is trapped within a world created through his late father's hypocrisy is symbolized by his suffering from hereditary venereal disease. As it was produced in one major city after another—Paris, Berlin, London—*Ghosts* became a sort of cannonball that advocates for a revolutionary new world as it is fired across the decks of the old. After a time, Ibsen began to move on from the "social problem" play, and with *Hedda Gabler* (1890), which is reproduced in this anthology, Ibsen presents us with a highly complex psychological portrait in which no one simple relationship of causation or resistance between nature or social environment and character can be delineated, though many are implied. Later still, Ibsen's dramatic style would lean toward symbolism; however, Ibsen's integration of aspects of Naturalism into his own brand of realism during the 1880s represented an important watershed in theatre history, and the influence of his work from this period would have an incalculable effect on subsequent world drama.

No sooner had realism established itself as the dominant trend in drama than efforts to resist it began to emerge. There was a sense among many people that much of the beauty, the mystery, and the imaginative elements of the theatre, including its ability to represent alternative worlds and past times, had been forsaken in favour of a dismal sordid preoccupation with the failures of the present day. One form of resistance to realism is evident in the revival of Romanticism, as seen in Edmond Rostand's *Cyrano de Bergerac* (1898), a play about a larger-than-life seventeenth-century poet and swordsman, who transcends life's ugliness as embodied in his enormous nose through sheer force of imagination. Another response was the "Art-for-Art's sake" movement, which repudiated the utilitarian view that art's only real worth lies in its use as a vehicle for instruction and social improvement. The great dramatic masterpiece exemplifying this outlook is undoubtedly Oscar Wilde's *The Importance of Being Earnest* (1895), which, in a dazzling display of dramaturgical craft and wit, creates a world not quite like any that has existed in reality.

A related movement, though in a much more sombre vein, was the Symbolist theatre based in France. The symbolists eschewed detailed realistic representations in favour of symbolic, almost hallucinatory, evocations of life's mysteries. The chief venue of the Symbolists was the Théâtre de l'Oeuvre in Paris; it was at this same theatre that a play sharing the anti-realist tendencies of the Symbolists but otherwise antithetical to their work, was produced: *Ubu Roi* [King Ubu] (1896), the often puerile but compellingly unorthodox and remarkably vital satire by the young Alfred Jarry. Unlike Wilde, Rostand, and the Symbolists, Jarry's complaint with realism had far less to do with the loss of beauty than with what he regarded as the pompous earnestness, the fatuous self-regard, and the complacent faith in reason that were typical of realism's adherents. Notwithstanding its many humorous qualities, Jarry's play constituted a sort of act of violence—a deliberate assault on the world of the Victorian middle class that, in retrospect, was also a harbinger of many of the changes that would occur in drama during the century that followed.

[C.S.W.]

GEORG BÜCHNER

Woyzeck

On June 21, 1821, in Leipzig, Johann Christian Woyzeck, a thirty-eight-year-old unemployed ex-soldier, sometime barber and apprentice wig-maker, stabbed a woman to death in a jealous rage. She was Johanna Woost, a widow in her forties, who had been Woyzeck's mistress at one point. More recently, however, she had been consorting with a number of soldiers who were garrisoned in Leipzig. Woyzeck was brought to trial for murder, but because there were reports that he had been raving for some time, a Dr. Clarus was called in to examine the defendant and assess whether he was mentally competent to stand trial. Clarus's investigation revealed extensive evidence of what today would be called schizophrenia, but he concluded that, despite numerous delusions, Woyzeck was still capable of reason. Moreover, he declared that "a stronger exercise of free will" would have prevented Woyzeck's descent into moral degeneracy and violence. Clarus's assessment only fueled the public debate, prompting numerous rebuttals, which in turn forced further examinations by Clarus. The end came at last for the real Woyzeck when he was found guilty and executed by public decapitation on August 27, 1824. His case, however, continued to be a focal point for the discussion of the treatment of the criminally insane for years to come.

Georg Büchner (1813–1837) was only ten years old at the time of Woyzeck's execution, so he was relying chiefly on court and medical documents for his information when, at twenty-three and a doctor himself, he sat down to begin a play inspired by the historical Woyzeck case. He would never finish it. He died that winter in Zurich during a typhus epidemic, leaving two finished plays—*Danton's Death*, a brilliant historical drama about one of the leaders of the French Revolution, and *Leonce and Lena*, an unusual romantic comedy in the *commedia dell'arte* tradition; a fragment of a novel, *Lenz*; a revolutionary manifesto, called *The Hessian Courtier*; and the untitled collection of manuscripts that we know as *Woyzeck*.

The *Woyzeck* manuscripts were left in the care of Georg's brother, Ludwig, and remained virtually unknown until 1879, when, having been recovered by Karl Emil Franzos, they were published in a volume of Büchner's works. But it was to be another thirty years before a production was attempted. Thus, a play originally conceived in the first half of the nineteenth century, having lain dormant for nearly three-quarters of a century, became one of the seminal works of twentieth-century drama. Just how close what we have is to what Büchner intended remains an open question. Not only were the manuscripts left in an unfinished state, they were difficult to decipher. The ink had faded, so Franzos chemically treated the paper in a way that made the writing temporarily more legible (though in the long run the chemicals worsened the deterioration of the manuscript). Even then, because Büchner wrote in such a small, cramped style, a number of errors were made: for instance, the central character's name was at first thought to be "Wozzeck" (hence the title of the opera by Alban Berg which is based on the play). Still more crucial was the question of the order Büchner had intended for the scenes. For example, of the four groups of manuscripts, it appears likely that the scenes in one were intended to more or less dovetail with the scenes in another, but this is by no means a certain matter, and in the other two groups of manuscripts there appear isolated scenes that could fit almost anywhere at all. Hence, there are several different versions of *Woyzeck* in circulation, a fact which forces any new editor, and any director, to decide individually about the most felicitous order in which to place the scenes. It is often truly remarked, then, that, in a sense, there is really no such thing as "Büchner's *Woyzeck*."

However, inchoate though *Woyzeck* may be, it is no exaggeration to call the play one of the most important works in the history of dramatic literature. The play was startling and tremendously influential when it received its first production at the beginning of the twentieth century. We can only imagine what the effect would have been had it been known to the public at the time of its composition, three-quarters of a century earlier. Indeed, it is a little difficult to name a major current of modern drama that *Woyzeck* does not anticipate in some respect: realism, naturalism, expressionism, existentialism, epic drama, absurdism, political satire, black comedy, working-class tragedy—something of each of these is present in this short play. And the list of playwrights who claim Büchner as a direct influence includes most of the outstanding names in twentieth-century drama.

Of course, the value of *Woyzeck* is by no means limited to its influence on subsequent literature. It remains an extraordinarily suggestive drama, as evinced by the great number of productions it still receives around the world. Nor should the play be regarded merely as a sort of treatise on the question of the sanity of its unfortunate historical namesake. Indeed, part of the uncanny power of the play lies in our perception that Woyzeck may escape the confines of his specific environment to stand for all of us to some degree: a sort of modern everyman figure, alienated from and driven mad by the world in which he lives. Still fresh and disturbing despite all the subsequent imitations, *Woyzeck* continues to challenge us as an enigmatic and haunting reflection on the ineffaceable tension between human nature and society.

[C.S.W.]

GEORG BÜCHNER

Woyzeck

translated by Carl Richard Mueller[1]

CHARACTERS

WOYZECK
MARIE
CAPTAIN
DOCTOR
DRUM MAJOR
SERGEANT
ANDRES
MARGRET
PROPRIETOR OF THE BOOTH
CHARLATAN
OLD MAN WITH BARREL-ORGAN
JEW
INNKEEPER
APPRENTICES
KATHY
KARL THE TOWN IDIOT
GRANDMOTHER
POLICEMAN
SOLDIERS, STUDENTS, YOUNG MEN and
    GIRLS, CHILDREN, JUDGE, COURT CLERK,
    PEOPLE

SCENE 1 — AT THE CAPTAIN'S[2]

THE CAPTAIN in a chair. WOYZECK shaving him.

CAPTAIN: Not so fast, Woyzeck, not so fast! One thing at a time! You're making me dizzy. What am I to do with the ten extra minutes that you'll finish early today? Just think, Woyzeck: you still have thirty beautiful years to live! Thirty years! That makes three hundred and sixty months! And days! Hours! Minutes! What do you think you'll do with all that horrible stretch of time? Have you ever thought about it, Woyzeck?

WOYZECK: Yes, sir, Captain.

CAPTAIN: It frightens me when I think about the world ... when I think about eternity. Busyness, Woyzeck, busyness! There's the eternal: that's eternal, that is eternal. That you can understand. But then again it's not eternal. It's only a moment. A mere moment. Woyzeck, it makes me shudder when I think that the earth turns itself about in a single day! What a waste of time! Where will it all end? Woyzeck, I can't even look at a mill wheel any more without becoming melancholy.

WOYZECK: Yes, sir, Captain.

CAPTAIN: Woyzeck, you always seem so exasperated! A good man isn't like that. A good man with a good conscience, that is. Well, say something, Woyzeck! What's the weather like today?

WOYZECK: Bad, Captain, sir, bad: wind!

CAPTAIN: I feel it already. Sounds like a real storm out there. A wind like that has the same effect on me as a mouse. [*Cunningly.*] I think it must be something out of the north-south.

WOYZECK: Yes, sir, Captain.

CAPTAIN: Ha! Ha! Ha! North-south! Ha! Ha! Ha! Oh, he's a stupid one! Horribly stupid! [*Moved.*] Woyzeck, you're a good man, but [*With dignity*] Woyzeck, you have no morality! Morality, that's when you have morals, you understand. It's a good word. You have a child without the blessings of the Church, just like our Right Reverend Garrison

---

1 This translation was first published in Georg Büchner, *Complete Plays and Prose,* ed. Carl Richard Mueller (New York: Hill and Wang, 1963).

2 SCENE 1] This scene is not always placed first; some versions place it about a third of the way into the play.

Chaplain says: "Without the blessings of the Church." It's not *my* phrase.

WOYZECK: Captain, sir, the good Lord's not going to look at a poor worm just because they said Amen over it before they went at it. The Lord said: "Suffer little children to come unto me."3

CAPTAIN: What's that you said? What kind of strange answer's that? You're confusing me with your answers!

WOYZECK: It's us poor people that … You see, Captain, sir … Money, money! Whoever hasn't got money … Well, who's got morals when he's bringing something like me into the world? We're flesh and blood, too. Our kind is miserable only once: in this world and in the next. I think if we ever got to Heaven we'd have to help with the thunder.4

CAPTAIN: Woyzeck, you have no virtue! You're not a virtuous human being! Flesh and blood? Whenever I rest at the window, when it's finished raining, and my eyes follow the white stockings along as they hurry across the street … Damnation, Woyzeck, I know what love is, too, then! I'm made of flesh and blood, too. But, Woyzeck: Virtue! Virtue! How was I to get rid of the time? I always say to myself: "You're a virtuous man [*Moved*], a good man, a good man."

WOYZECK: Yes, Captain, sir: Virtue. I haven't got much of that. You see, us common people, we haven't got virtue. That's the way it's got to be. But if I could be a gentleman, and if I could have a hat and a watch and a cane, and if I could talk refined, I'd want to be virtuous, all right. There must be something beautiful in virtue, Captain, sir. But I'm just a poor good-for-nothing!

CAPTAIN: Good, Woyzeck. You're a good man, a good man. But you think too much. It eats at you. You always seem so exasperated. Our discussion has affected me deeply. You can go now. And don't run so! Slowly! Nice and slowly down the street.

SCENE II — AN OPEN FIELD. THE TOWN IN THE DISTANCE.5

WOYZECK and ANDRES cut twigs from the bushes. ANDRES whistles.

WOYZECK: Andres? You know this place is cursed? Look at that light streak over there on the grass. There where the toadstools grow up. That's where the head rolls every night. One time somebody picked it up. He thought it was a hedgehog. Three days and three nights and he was in a box. [*Low.*] Andres, it was the Freemasons, don't you see, it was the Freemasons!6

ANDRES [*sings*]:
  Two little rabbits sat on a lawn
  Eating, oh, eating the green green grass …7

WOYZECK: Quiet! Can you hear it, Andres? Can you hear it? Something moving!

ANDRES [*sings*]: Eating, oh, eating the green green grass
Till all the grass was gone.

---

3 Suffer little children] "But Jesus said, Suffer little children, and forbid them not, to come unto me: for of such is the kingdom of heaven" (Matthew 19:14); see also Mark 10:14 and Luke 18:16.

4 I think … thunder] a paraphrase of the closing lines from a 1785 poem by Gottlieb Konrad Pfeffel called "Jostens Zweifel" (Jost's Doubt): "Made haggard with indulging his / Gentle sovereign, Jost lay / Upon the rotten moss. A pious preacher / Brought him comfort in his last struggle: / Soon, he said, God will relieve you / Of this yoke that has oppressed you: / The peace you have never yet known, / Friend, you will find in Heaven. / Oh, Lord! Jost cried out in a voice as hollow as the grave, / Who can ever say what lies beyond ? / If we poor peasants ever make it to Heaven / We may be forced to help with the thunder."

5 SCENE II] Some versions of the play begin with this scene.

6 Freemasons] the world's largest secret society, which assumed its current form in the seventeenth and eighteenth centuries, having developed out of the guilds of stonemasons and builders who worked on medieval cathedrals. Although the Freemasons are pledged to charity, morality and lawfulness, because of its quasi-religious but nonorthodox nature, the society has frequently met with opposition from organized religion; moreover, its members have been repeatedly demonized in the popular imagination and accused of conspiring to control business and politics.

7 Two little rabbits …] This and the other songs in the play are based on popular nineteenth-century German folk songs.

WOYZECK: It's moving behind me! Under me! [*Stamps on the ground.*] Listen! Hollow! It's all hollow down there! It's the Freemasons! 15

ANDRES: I'm afraid.

WOYZECK: Strange how still it is. You almost want to hold your breath. Andres! 20

ANDRES: What?

WOYZECK: Say something! [*Looks about fixedly.*] Andres! How bright it is! It's all glowing over the town! A fire's sailing around the sky and a noise coming down like trumpets. It's coming closer! 25 Let's get out of here! Don't look back! [*Drags him into the bushes.*]

ANDRES [*after a pause*]: Woyzeck? Do you still hear it?

WOYZECK: It's quiet now. So quiet. Like the world's dead.[8] 30

ANDRES: Listen! I can hear the drums inside. We've got to go!

SCENE III — THE TOWN

MARIE with her CHILD at the window. MARGRET. The Retreat passes, THE DRUM MAJOR at its head.

MARIE [*rocking THE CHILD in her arms*]: Ho, boy! Da-da-da-da! Can you hear? They're coming! There!

MARGRET: What a man! Built like a tree!

MARIE: He walks like a lion. [*THE DRUM MAJOR salutes MARIE.*] 5

MARGRET: Oh, what a look he threw you, neighbor! We're not used to such things from you.

---

8 moving behind me ... fire ... trumpets ... world's dead] "And the angel took the censer, and filled it with fire of the altar, and cast it into the earth: and there were voices, and thunderings, and lightnings, and an earthquake. And the seven angels which had the seven trumpets prepared themselves to sound. The first angel sounded, and there followed hail and fire mingled with blood, and they were cast upon the earth: and the third part of trees was burnt up, and all green grass was burnt up. And the second angel sounded, and as it were a great mountain burning with fire was cast into the sea: and the third part of the sea became blood; And the third part of the creatures which were in the sea, and had life, died ..." (Revelation 8:5–9).

MARIE [*sings*]: Soldiers, oh, you pretty lads ...

MARGRET: Your eyes are still shining. 10

MARIE: And if they are? Take *your* eyes to the Jew's and let him clean them for you. Maybe he can shine them so you can sell them for a pair of buttons!

MARGRET: Look who's talking! Just look who's 15 talking! If it isn't the Virgin herself! I'm a respectable person. But you! Everyone knows you could stare your way through seven layers of leather pants!

MARIE: Slut! [*Slams the window shut.*] Come, boy! 20 What's it to them, anyway! Even if you are just a poor whore's baby, your dishonorable little face still makes your mother happy! [*Sings.*]

I have my trouble and bother
But, baby dear, where is your father? 25
Why should I worry and fight
I'll hold you and sing through the night:
Heio popeio, my baby, my dove
What do I want now with love?

[*A knock at the window.*] Who's there? Is it you, 30 Franz? Come in!

WOYZECK: Can't. There's roll call.

MARIE: Did you cut wood for the Captain?

WOYZECK: Yes, Marie.

MARIE: What is it, Franz? You look so troubled? 35

WOYZECK: Marie, it happened again, only there was more. Isn't it written: "And there arose a smoke out of the pit, as the smoke of a great furnace"?[9]

MARIE: Oh, Franz!

WOYZECK: Shh! Quiet! I've got it! The Freemasons! 40 There was a terrible noise in the sky and everything was on fire! I'm on the trail of something, something big. It followed me all the way to the town. Something that drives us mad. What'll come of it all? 45

MARIE: Franz!

---

9 written ... furnace] The passage, from the Book of Revelation, describes the results following the trumpet of the fifth of seven angels heralding the Apocalypse. "And he opened the bottomless pit; and there arose a smoke out of the pit, as the smoke of a great furnace; and the sun and the air were darkened by reason of the smoke of the pit" (Revelation 9:2).

WOYZECK: Don't you see? Look around you! Everything hard and fixed, so gloomy. What's moving back there? When God goes, everything goes. I've got to get back. 50

MARIE: And the child?

WOYZECK: My God, the boy! — Tonight at the fair! I've saved something again.

[*He leaves.*]

MARIE: That man! Seeing things like that! He'll go mad if he keeps thinking that way! He frightened 55 me! It's so gloomy here. Why are you so quiet, boy? Are you afraid? It's growing so dark. As if we were going blind. Only that street lamp shining in from outside. [*Sings.*]

> And what if your cradle is bad 60
> Sleep tight, my lovey, my lad.

I can't stand it! It makes me shiver! [*She goes out.*]

SCENE IV — FAIR BOOTHS. LIGHTS. PEOPLE

OLD MAN with a CHILD, WOYZECK, MARIE, CHARLATAN, WIFE, DRUM MAJOR, and SERGEANT.

OLD MAN [*sings while THE CHILD dances to the barrel-organ*]:

> There's nothing on this earth will last,
> Our lives are as the fields of grass,
> Soon all is past, is past.

WOYZECK: Ho! Hip-hop there, boy! Hip-hop! Poor man, old man! Poor child, young child! Trouble 5 and happiness!

MARIE: My God, when fools still have their senses, then we're all fools. Oh, what a mad world! What a beautiful world!

They go over to THE CHARLATAN who stands in front of a booth, his WIFE in trousers, and a monkey in costume.

CHARLATAN: Gentlemen, gentlemen! You see here 10 before you a creature as God created it! But it is nothing this way! Absolutely nothing! But now look at what Art can do. It walks upright. Wears coat and pants. And even carries a saber. This monkey here is a regular soldier. So what if he *isn't* 15 much different! So what if he *is* still on the bottom rung of the human ladder! Hey there, take a bow!

That's the way! Now you're a baron, at least. Give us a kiss! [*The monkey trumpets.*] This little customer's musical, too. And, gentlemen, in here 20 you will see the astronomical horse and the little lovebirds. Favorites of all the crowned heads of Europe. They'll tell you anything: how old you are, how many children you have, what your ailments are. The performance is about to begin. And at the 25 beginning. The beginning of the beginning!

WOYZECK: You know, I had a little dog once who kept sniffing around the rim of a big hat, and I thought I'd be good to him and make it easier for him and sat him on top of it. And all the people 30 stood around and clapped.

GENTLEMEN: Oh, grotesque! How really grotesque!

WOYZECK: Don't you believe in God either? It's an honest fact I don't believe in God. — You call that grotesque? I like what's grotesque. See that? That 35 grotesque enough for you? — [*To MARIE.*] You want to go in?

MARIE: Sure. That must be nice in there. Look at the tassels on him! And his wife's got pants on! [*They go inside.*] 40

DRUM MAJOR: Wait a minute! Did you see her? What a piece!

SERGEANT: Hell, she could whelp a couple regiments of cavalry!

DRUM MAJOR: And breed drum majors! 45

SERGEANT: Look at the way she carries that head! You'd think all that black hair would pull her down like a weight. And those eyes!

DRUM MAJOR: Like looking down a well … or up a chimney. Come on, let's go after her! 50

SCENE V — INTERIOR OF THE BRIGHTLY LIGHTED BOOTH

MARIE, WOYZECK, PROPRIETOR OF THE BOOTH, SERGEANT, and DRUM MAJOR.

MARIE: All these lights!

WOYZECK: Sure, Marie. Black cats with fiery eyes.

PROPRIETOR OF THE BOOTH [*bringing forward a horse*]: Show your talent! Show your brute reason! Put a human society to shame! Gentlemen, this 5 animal you see here, with a tail on its torso, and standing on its four hoofs, is a member of all the learnèd societies — as well as a professor at our university where he teaches students how to ride and fight. But that requires simple intelligence. Now think with your double reason! What do you do when you think with your double reason? Is there a jackass in this learnèd assembly? [*The nag shakes its head.*] How's that for double reasoning? That's physiognomy for you. This is no dumb animal. This is a person! A human being! But still an animal. A beast. [*The nag conducts itself indecently.*] That's right, put society to shame. As you can see, this animal is still in a state of Nature. Not ideal Nature, of course! Take a lesson from him! But ask your doctor first, it may prove highly dangerous! What we have been told by this is: Man must be natural! You are created of dust, sand, and dung. Why must you be more than dust, sand, and dung? Look there at his reason. He can figure even if he can't count it off on his fingers. And why? Because he cannot express himself, can't explain. A metamorphosed human being. Tell the gentlemen what time it is! Which of you ladies and gentlemen has a watch? A watch?

SERGEANT: A watch? [*He pulls a watch imposingly and measured from his pocket.*] There you are, my good man!

MARIE: I want to see this. [*She clambers down to the first row of seats; THE SERGEANT helps her.*]

DRUM MAJOR: What a piece!

SCENE VI — MARIE'S ROOM

MARIE with her CHILD.

MARIE [*sitting, her CHILD on her lap, a piece of mirror in her hand*]: He told Franz to get the hell out, so what could he do? [*Looks at herself in the mirror.*] Look how the stones shine! What kind are they, I wonder? What kind did he say they were? Sleep, boy! Close your eyes! Tight! Stay that way now. Don't move or he'll get you! [*Sings.*]

> Hurry, lady, close up tight
> A gypsy lad is out tonight
> And he will take you by the hand
> And lead you into gypsyland.

[*Continues to look at herself in the mirror.*] They must be gold! I wonder how they'll look on me at the dance? Our kind's only got a little corner in the world and a piece of broken mirror. But my mouth is just as red as any of the fine ladies with their mirrors from top to bottom, and their handsome gentlemen that kiss their hands for them! I'm just a poor common piece! [*THE CHILD sits up.*] Quiet, boy! Close your eyes! There's the sandman! Look at him run across the wall! [*She flashes with the mirror.*] Eyes tight! Or he'll look into them and make you blind!

WOYZECK enters behind her. She jumps up, her hands at her ears.

WOYZECK: What's that?

MARIE: Nothing.

WOYZECK: There's something shiny in your hands.

MARIE: An earring. I found it.

WOYZECK: I never have luck like that! Two at a time!

MARIE: Am I human or not?

WOYZECK: I'm sorry, Marie. — Look at the boy asleep. Lift his arm, the chair's hurting him. Look at the shiny drops on his forehead. Everything under the sun works! We even sweat in our sleep. Us poor people! Here's some money again, Marie. My pay and something from the Captain.

MARIE: God bless you, Franz.

WOYZECK: I've got to get back. Tonight, Marie! I'll see you tonight! [*He goes off.*]

MARIE [*alone, after a pause*]: I *am* bad, I *am!* I could run myself through with a knife! Oh, what a life, what a life! We'll all end up in hell, anyway, in the end: man, woman, and child!

SCENE VII — AT THE DOCTOR'S

THE DOCTOR and WOYZECK.

DOCTOR: I don't believe it, Woyzeck! And a man of your word!

WOYZECK: What's that, Doctor, sir?

DOCTOR: I saw it all, Woyzeck. You pissed on the street! You were pissing on the wall like a dog! And here I'm giving you three groschen a day plus board![10] That's terrible, Woyzeck! The world's becoming a terrible place, a terrible place!

---

10 groschen] a small coin of very little value, like a penny.

WOYZECK: But, Doctor, sir, when Nature …

DOCTOR: When Nature? When Nature? What has Nature to do with it? Did I or did I not prove to you that the *musculus constrictor vesicae* is controlled by your will?[11] Nature! Woyzeck, man is free! In Mankind alone we see glorified the individual's will to freedom! And you couldn't hold your water! [*Shakes his head, places his hands behind the small of his back, and walks back and forth.*] Have you eaten your peas today, Woyzeck?[12] Nothing but peas! *Cruciferae!*[13] Remember that! There's going to be a revolution in science! I'm going to blow it sky-high! *Urea Oxygen.*[14] Ammonium hydrochloride hyperoxidic.[15] Woyzeck, couldn't you just *try* to piss again? Go in the other room and make another try.

WOYZECK: Doctor, sir, I can't.

DOCTOR [*disturbed*]: But you could piss on the wall. I have it here in black and white. Our contract is right here! I saw it with these very eyes. I had just stuck my head out the window, opening it to let in the rays of the sun, so as to execute the process of sneezing. [*Going toward him.*] No, Woyzeck, I'm not going to vex myself. Vexation is unhealthy. Unscientific. I'm calm now, completely calm. My pulse is beating at its accustomed sixty, and I am speaking to you in utmost cold-bloodedness. Why should I vex myself over a man, God forbid! A man! Now if he were a proteus, it would be worth the vexation![16] But, Woyzeck, you really shouldn't have pissed on the wall.

WOYZECK: You see, Doctor, sir, sometimes a person's got a certain kind of character, like when he's made a certain way. But with Nature it's not the same, you see. With Nature [*he snaps his fingers*], it's like *that!* How should I explain, it's like—

DOCTOR: Woyzeck, you're philosophizing again.

WOYZECK [*confidingly*]: Doctor, sir, did you ever see anything with double nature? Like when the sun stops at noon, and it's like the world was going up in fire? That's when I hear a terrible voice saying things to me![17]

DOCTOR: Woyzeck, you have an *aberratio!*[18]

WOYZECK [*places his finger at his nose*]: It's in the toadstools, Doctor, sir, that's where it is. Did you ever see the shapes the toadstools make when they grow up out of the earth? If only somebody could read what they say!

DOCTOR: Woyzeck, you have a most beautiful *aberratio mentalis partialis* of a secondary order![19] And so wonderfully developed! Woyzeck, your salary is increased! *Idée fixe* of a secondary order and with a generally rational state.[20] You go about your business normally? Still shaving the Captain?

WOYZECK: Yes, sir.

DOCTOR: You eat your peas?

---

11 *musculus constrictor vesicae*] (Latin) the muscle controlling the bladder.

12 peas] have a high nitrogen content, and thus abet the production of urea (see below).

13 *cruciferae*] (Latin) a family of plants (comprising cabbage and mustard, but not, in fact, peas); the word also means "carriers of the cross."

14 *Urea Oxygen*] oxygen in urea, which is a nitrogenous substance found in urine, produced by the metabolic breakdown of proteins. As a chemical, urea is used in various ways, chiefly as a fertilizer. In the early nineteenth century, urea was the subject of a number of scientific studies; it had been isolated from urine in 1773, and was the first organic substance to be synthesized from inorganic compounds, in Germany, in 1828.

15 Ammonium hydrochloride] "colourless crystals … used as an antioxidant, photographic developer, and a reagent in synthesis" —*Academic Press Dictionary of Science and Technology*; hyperoxidic] In German, Büchner uses "*Hyper-oxydul,*" which may be a variation of *hippur-oxydul,* a compound derived in the course of experiments conducted around this time by Justus von Liebig (1803–73), using the urine of soldiers who were fed a lot of peas.

16 proteus] not the character from Greek mythology who could assume any form at will, but an amphibious creature, like a chameleon, named after him.

17 sun … voice] Cf. "And I saw an angel standing in the sun; and he cried with a loud voice, saying to all the fowls that fly in the midst of heaven, Come and gather yourselves together unto the supper of the great God" (Revelation 19:17).

18 *aberratio*] (Latin) aberration, derangement.

19 *aberratio mentalis partialis*] (Latin) partial mental disorder.

20 *Idée fixe*] (French) literally, a "fixed idea"—i.e., an obsession.

WOYZECK: Just as always, Doctor, sir. My wife gets   65
the money for the household.
DOCTOR: Still in the army?
WOYZECK: Yes, sir, Doctor.
DOCTOR: You're an interesting case. Patient
Woyzeck, you're to have an increase in salary. So   70
behave yourself! Let's feel the pulse. Ah yes.

SCENE VIII — MARIE'S ROOM

DRUM MAJOR and MARIE.

DRUM MAJOR: Marie!
MARIE [*looking at him, with expression*]: Go on, show
me how you march! — Chest broad as a bull's and
a beard like a lion! There's not another man in the
world like that! And there's not a prouder woman   5
than me!
DRUM MAJOR: Wait till Sunday when I wear my
helmet with the plume and my white gloves!
Damn, that'll be a sight for you! The Prince always
says: "My God, there goes a real man!"   10
MARIE [*scoffing*]: Ha! [*Goes toward him.*] A man?
DRUM MAJOR: You're not such a bad piece yourself!
Hell, we'll plot a whole brood of drum majors!
Right? [*He puts his arm around her.*]
MARIE [*annoyed*]: Let go!   15
DRUM MAJOR: Bitch!
MARIE [*fiercely*]: You just touch me!
DRUM MAJOR: There's devils in your eyes.
MARIE: Let there be, for all I care! What's the
difference?   20

SCENE IX — STREET

*CAPTAIN and DOCTOR. THE CAPTAIN comes panting
along the street, stops; pants and looks about.*

CAPTAIN: Ho, Doctor, don't run so fast! Don't pad-
dle the air so with your stick! You're only courting
death that way! A good man with a good conscience never walks as fast as that. A good man …
[*He catches him by the coat.*] Doctor, permit me to   5
save a human life!
DOCTOR: I'm in a hurry, Captain, I'm in a hurry!
CAPTAIN: Doctor, I'm so melancholy. I have such
fantasies. I start to cry every time I see my coat
hanging on the wall.   10

DOCTOR: Hm! Bloated, fat, think neck: apoplectic
constitution.[21] Yes, Captain, you'll be having
apoplexia cerebria any time now.[22] Of course you
could have it on only one side. In which case you'll
be paralyzed down that one side. Or if things go   15
really well you'll be mentally disabled so that you
can vegetate away for the rest of your days. You
may look forward to something approximately like
that within the next four weeks! And, furthermore,
I can assure you that you give promise of being a   20
most interesting case. And if it is God's will that
only one half of your tongue become paralyzed,
then we will conduct the most immortal of
experiments.
CAPTAIN: Doctor, you mustn't scare me that way!   25
People are said to have died of fright. Of pure,
sheer fright. I can see them now with lemons in
their hands. But they'll say: "He was a good man,
a good man." You devil's coffinnail-maker!
DOCTOR [*extending his hat toward him*]: Do you   30
know who this is, Captain? This is Sir Hollowhead,
my most honorable Captain Drilltheirassesoff!
CAPTAIN [*makes a series of folds in his sleeve*]: And do
you know who this is, Doctor? This is Sir
Manifold, my dear devil's coffinnail-maker! Ha!   35
Ha! Ha! But no harm meant! I'm a good man, but
I can play, too, when I want to, Doctor, when I
want to …

*WOYZECK comes toward them and tries to pass in a
hurry.*

CAPTAIN: Ho! Woyzeck! Where are you off to in
such a hurry? Stay awhile, Woyzeck! Running   40
through the world like an open razor, you're liable
to cut someone. He runs as if he had to shave a
castrated regiment and would be hung before he
discovered and cut the longest hair that wasn't
there. But on the subject of long beards … What   45
was it I wanted to say? Woyzeck, why was I
thinking about beards?

---

[21] apoplectic constitution] a physiology likely to result in
a stroke.
[22] *apoplexia cerebria*] (Latin) an embolism or hemorrhage
in the brain.

DOCTOR: The wearing of long beards on the chin, remarks Pliny, is a habit of which soldiers must be broken —23

CAPTAIN [*continues*]: Ah, yes, this thing about beards! Tell me, Woyzeck, have you found any long hairs from beards in your soup bowl lately? Ho, I don't think he understands! A hair from a human face, from the beard of an engineer, a sergeant, a … a drum major? Well, Woyzeck? But then he's got a good wife. It's not the same as with the others.

WOYZECK: Yes, sir, Captain! What was it you wanted to say to me, Captain, sir?

CAPTAIN: What a face he's making! Well, maybe not in his soup, but if he hurries home around the corner I'll wager he might still find one on a certain pair of lips. A pair of lips, Woyzeck. Look at him, he's white as chalk!

WOYZECK: Captain, sir, I'm just a poor devil. And there's nothing else I've got in the world but her. Captain, sir, if you're just making a fool of me …

CAPTAIN: A fool? Me? Making a fool of you, Woyzeck?

DOCTOR: Your pulse, Woyzeck, your pulse! Short, hard, skipping, irregular.

WOYZECK: Captain, sir, the earth's hot as coals in hell. But I'm as cold as ice, cold as ice. Hell is cold. I'll bet you. I don't believe it! God! God! I don't believe it!

CAPTAIN: Look here, you, how would you … how'd you like a pair of bullets in your skull? You keep stabbing at me with those eyes of yours, and I'm only trying to help. Because you're a good man, Woyzeck, a good man.

DOCTOR: Facial muscles rigid, taut, occasionally twitches. Condition strained, excitable.

WOYZECK: I'm going. Anything's possible. The bitch! Anything's possible. — The weather's nice, Captain, sir. Look, a beautiful, hard, gray sky. You'd almost like to pound a nail up there and hang yourself on it. And only because of that little dash

---

23 Pliny] Perhaps the Doctor is thinking of Pliny the Younger, the Roman author and administrator who left many letters commenting on Roman life and manners; but the only such known injunction came from Alexander the Great, as reported by Plutarch.

between Yes and Yes again … and No. Captain, sir: Yes and No: did No make Yes or Yes make No? I must think about that.

He goes off with long strides, slowly at first, then faster and faster.

DOCTOR [*shouting after him*]: Phenomenon! Woyzeck, you get a raise!

CAPTAIN: I get so dizzy around such people. Look at him go! Long-legged rascals like him step out like a shadow running away from its own spider. But short ones only dawdle along. The long-legged ones are the lightning, the short ones the thunder. Haha … Grotesque! Grotesque!

SCENE X — MARIE'S ROOM

WOYZECK and MARIE.

WOYZECK: [*looks fixedly at her and shakes his head*]: Hm! I don't see it! I don't see it! My God, why can't I see it, why can't I take it in my fists!

MARIE [*frightened*]: Franz, what is it? — You're raving, Franz.

WOYZECK: A sin so swollen and big — it stinks to smoke the angels out of Heaven! You have a red mouth, Marie! No blisters on it? Marie, you're as beautiful as sin. How can mortal sin be so beautiful?

MARIE: Franz, it's your fever making you talk this way!

WOYZECK: Damn you! Is this where he stood? Like this? Like this?

MARIE: While the day's long and the world's old a lot of people can stand in one spot, one right after the other. — Why are you looking at me so strange, Franz! I'm afraid!

WOYZECK: It's a nice street for walking, uh? You could walk corns on your feet! It's nice walking on the street, going around in society.

MARIE: Society?

WOYZECK: A lot of people pass through this street here, don't they! And you talk to them — to whoever you want — but that's not my business! — Why wasn't it me!

MARIE: You expect me to tell people to keep off the streets — and take their mouths with them when they leave?

WOYZECK: And don't you ever leave your lips at

home, they're too beautiful, it would be a sin! But then I guess the wasps like to light on them, uh? 30

MARIE: And what wasp stung you? You're like a cow chased by hornets!

WOYZECK: I saw him!

MARIE: You can see a lot with two eyes while the sun shines! 35

WOYZECK: Whore! [*He goes after her.*]

MARIE: Don't you touch me, Franz! I'd rather have a knife in my body than your hands touch me. When I looked at him, my father didn't dare lay a hand on me from the time I was ten. 40

WOYZECK: Whore! No, it should show on you! Something! Every man's a chasm. It makes you dizzy when you look down in. It's got to show! And she looks like innocence itself. So, innocence, there's a spot on you. But I can't prove it — can't 45 prove it! Who can prove it? [*He goes off.*]

SCENE XI — THE GUARDHOUSE

WOYZECK and ANDRES.

ANDRES [*sings*]:
> Our hostess she has a pretty maid
> She sits in her garden night and day
> She sits within her garden …

WOYZECK: Andres!

ANDRES: Hm? 5

WOYZECK: Nice weather.

ANDRES: Sunday weather. — They're playing music tonight outside the town. All the whores are already there. The men stinking and sweating. Wonderful, uh? 10

WOYZECK [*restlessly*]: They're dancing, Andres, they're dancing!

ANDRES: Sure. So what? [*Sings.*]
> She sits within her garden
> But when the bells have tollèd
> Then she waits at her garden gate 15
> Or so the soldiers say.

WOYZECK: Andres, I can't keep quiet.

ANDRES: You're a fool!

WOYZECK: I've got to go out there. It keeps turning 20 and turning in my head. They're dancing, dancing! Will she have hot hands, Andres? God damn her, Andres! God damn her!

ANDRES: What do you want?

WOYZECK: I've got to go out there. I've got to see 25 them.

ANDRES: Aren't you ever satisfied? What's all this for a whore?

WOYZECK: I've got to get out of here! I can't stand the heat! 30

SCENE XII — THE INN

The windows are open. Dancing. Benches in front of the inn. APPRENTICES.

FIRST APPRENTICE [*sings*]:
> This shirt I've got on, it is not mine
> And my soul it stinketh of brandywine …

SECOND APPRENTICE: My soul, my soul stinketh of brandywine! — And even money passeth into decay! Forget me not, but the world's a beautiful 5 place! Brother, my sadness could fill a barrel with tears! I wish our noses were two bottles so we could pour them down one another's throats.

THE OTHERS [*in chorus*]:
> A hunter from the Rhine 10
> Once rode through a forest so fine
> Hallei-hallo, he called to me
> From high on a meadow, open and free
> A hunter's life for me.

WOYZECK stands at the window. MARIE and THE DRUM MAJOR dance past without noticing him.

WOYZECK: Both of them! God damn her! 15

MARIE [*dancing past*]: Don't stop! Don't stop!

WOYZECK [*seats himself on the bench, trembling, as he looks from there through the window*]: Listen! Listen! Ha, roll on each other, roll and turn! Don't stop, don't stop, she says! 20

IDIOT: Pah! It stinks!

WOYZECK: Yes, it stinks! Her cheeks are red, red, why should she stink already? Karl, what is it you smell?

IDIOT: I smell, I smell blood. 25

WOYZECK: Blood? Why are all things red that I look at now? Why are they all rolling in a sea of blood, one on top of the other, tumbling, tumbling! Ha, the sea is red! — Don't stop! Don't stop! [*He starts up passionately, then sinks down again onto the* 30 bench.] Don't stop! Don't stop! [*Beating his hands together.*] Turn and roll and roll and turn! God, blow out the sun and let them roll on each other in their lechery! Man and woman and man and beast! They'll do it in the light of the sun! They'll do it in the palm of your hand like flies! Whore! That whore's red as coals, red as coals! Don't stop! Don't stop! [*Jumps up.*] Watch how the bastard takes hold of her! Touching her body! He's holding her now, holding her … the way I held her once. [*He slumps down in a stupor.*] 35 40

FIRST APPRENTICE [*preaching from a table*]: I say unto you, forget not the wanderer who standeth leaning against the stream of time, and who giveth himself answer with the wisdom of God, and saith: What is Man? What is Man? Yea, verily I say unto you: How should the farmer, the cooper, the shoemaker, the doctor, live, had not God created Man for their use? How should the tailor live had not God endowed Man with the need to slaughter himself? And therefore doubt ye not, for all things are lovely and sweet! Yet the world with all its things is an evil place, and even money passeth into decay. In conclusion, my belovèd brethren, let us piss once more upon the Cross so that somewhere a Jew will die! 45 50 55

Amid the general shouting and laughing WOYZECK wakens. PEOPLE are leaving the inn.

ANDRES: What are you doing there?
WOYZECK: What time is it?
ANDRES: Ten.
WOYZECK: Is that all it is? I think it should go faster — I want to think about it before night. 60
ANDRES: Why?
WOYZECK: So it'd be over.
ANDRES: What?
WOYZECK: The fun. 65
ANDRES: What are you sitting here by the door for?
WOYZECK: Because it feels good, and because I know — a lot of people sit by doors, but they don't know — they don't know till they're dragged out of the door feet first. 70
ANDRES: Come with me!
WOYZECK: It feels good here like this — and even better if I laid myself down …

ANDRES: There's blood on your head.
WOYZECK: *In* my head, maybe. — If they all knew what time it was they'd strip themselves naked and put on a silk shirt and let the carpenter make their bed of wood shavings. 75
ANDRES: He's drunk.

Goes off with the others.

WOYZECK: The world is out of order! Why did the street-lamp cleaner forget to wipe my eyes — everything's dark. Devil damn you, God! I lay in my own way: jump over myself. Where's my shadow gone? There's not safety in the kennels any more. Shine the moon through my legs again to see if my shadow's here. [*Sings.*] 80 85

Eating, oh, eating the green green grass
Eating, oh, eating the green green grass
Till all the grass was go-o-one.

What's that lying over there? Shining like that? It's making me look. How it sparkles. I've got to have it. [*He rushes off.*] 90

SCENE XIII — AN OPEN FIELD

WOYZECK.

WOYZECK: Don't stop! Don't stop! Hishh! Hashh! That's how the fiddles and pipes go. — Don't stop! Don't stop! — Stop your playing! What's that talking down there? [*He stretches out on the ground.*] What? What are you saying? What? Louder! Louder! Stab? Stab the goat-bitch dead? Stab? Stab her? The goat-bitch dead? Should I? Must I? Do I hear it there, too? Does the wind say so, too? Won't it ever stop, ever stop? Stab her! Stab her! Dead! Dead! 5

SCENE XIV — A ROOM IN THE BARRACKS. NIGHT

ANDRES and WOYZECK in a bed.

WOYZECK [*softly*]: Andres! [*ANDRES murmurs in his sleep. Shakes ANDRES.*] Andres! Hey, Andres!
ANDRES: Mmmmm! What do you want?
WOYZECK: I can't sleep! When I close my eyes everything turns and turns. I hear voices in the fiddles: Don't stop! Don't stop! And then the walls start to talk. Can't you hear it? 5

ANDRES: Sure. Let them dance! I'm tired. God bless us all, Amen.

WOYZECK: It's always saying: Stab! Stab! And then when I close my eyes it keeps shining there, a big, broad, knife, on a table by a window in a narrow, dark street, and an old man sitting behind it. And the knife is always in front of my eyes.

ANDRES: Go to sleep, you fool!

WOYZECK: Andres! There's something outside. In the ground. They're always pointing to it. Don't you hear them now, listen, now, knocking on the walls? Somebody must have seen me out the window. Don't you hear? I hear it all day long. Don't stop. Stab! Stab the—

ANDRES: Lay down. You ought to go to the hospital. They'll give you a schnapps with a powder in it. It'll cut your fever.

WOYZECK: Don't stop! Don't stop!

ANDRES: Go to sleep!

He goes back to sleep.

SCENE XV — THE DOCTOR'S COURTYARD

STUDENTS and WOYZECK below. THE DOCTOR in the attic window.

DOCTOR: Gentlemen, I find myself on the roof like David when he beheld Bathsheba.[24] But all I see are the Parisian panties of the girls' boarding school drying in the garden. Gentlemen, we are concerned with the weighty question of the relationship of the subject to the object. If, for example, we were to take one of those innumerable things in which we see the highest manifestation of the self-affirmation of the Godhead, and examine its relationship to space, to the earth, and to the planetary constellations … Gentlemen, if we were to take this cat and toss it out the window: how would this object conduct itself in conformity with its own instincts towards its *centrum graviationis*?[25] Well, Woyzeck? [*Roars.*] Woyzeck!

WOYZECK [*picks up the cat*]: Doctor, sir, she's biting me!

DOCTOR: Damn, why do you handle the beast so tenderly! It's not your grandmother! [*He descends.*]

WOYZECK: Doctor, I'm shaking.

DOCTOR [*utterly delighted*]: Excellent, Woyzeck, excellent! [*Rubs his hands, takes the cat.*] What's this, gentlemen? The new species of rabbit louse! A beautiful species … [*He pulls out a magnifying glass; the cat runs off.*] Animals, gentlemen, simply have no scientific instincts. But in its place you may see something else. Now, observe: for three months this man has eaten nothing but peas. Notice the effect. Feel how irregularly his pulse beats! And look at his eyes!

WOYZECK: Doctor, sir, everything's going dark! [*He sits down.*]

DOCTOR: Courage, Woyzeck! A few more days and then it will all be over with. Feel, gentlemen, feel! [*They fumble over his temples, pulse, and chest.*]

DOCTOR: Apropos, Woyzeck, wiggle your ears for the gentlemen! I've meant to show you this before. He uses only two muscles. Let's go, let's go! You stupid animal, shall I wiggle them for you? Trying to run out on us like the cat? There you are, gentlemen! Here you see an example of the transition into a donkey: frequently the result of being raised by women and of a persistent usage of the Germanic language. How much hair has your mother pulled out recently for sentimental remembrances of you? It's become so thin these last few days. It's the peas, gentlemen, the peas!

SCENE XVI — THE INN

WOYZECK. THE SERGEANT.

WOYZECK [*sings*]:
    Oh, daughter, my daughter
    And didn't you know

---

24 David … Bathsheba] "It happened, late one afternoon, when David arose from his couch and was walking upon the roof of the king's house, that he saw from the roof a woman bathing; and the woman was very beautiful. And David sent and inquired about the woman. And one said, 'Is not this Bathsheba, the daughter of Eliam, the wife of Uriah the Hittite?' So David sent messengers, and took her; and she came to him, and he lay with her" (2 Samuel 11:2–4).

25 *centrum graviationis*] (Latin) centre of gravity.

That sleeping with coachmen
Would bring you low?

What is it that our Good Lord God cannot do? 5
What? He cannot make what is done undone. Ha!
Ha! Ha! — But that's the way it is, and that's the
way it should be. But to make things better is to
make things better. And a respectable man loves
his life, and a man who loves his life has no 10
courage, and a virtuous man has no courage. A
man with courage is a dirty dog.

SERGEANT [*with dignity*]: You're forgetting yourself
in the presence of a brave man.

WOYZECK: I wasn't talking about anybody, I wasn't 15
talking about anything, not like the Frenchmen do
when they talk, but it was good of you. — But a
man with courage is a dirty dog.

SERGEANT: Damn you! You broken mustache cup!
You watch or I'll see you drink a pot of your own 20
piss and swallow your own razor!

WOYZECK: Sir, you do yourself an injustice! Was it
you I talked about? Did I say *you* had courage?
Don't torment me, sir! My name is science. Every
week for my scientific career I get half a guilder. 25
You mustn't cut me in two or I'll go hungry. I'm a
Spinosa pericyclia; I have a Latin behind.[26] I am a
living skeleton. All Mankind studies me. — What
is Man? Bones! Dust, sand, dung. What is Nature?
Dust, sand, dung. But poor, stupid Man, stupid 30
Man! We must be friends. If only you had no
courage, there would be no science. Only Nature,
no amputation, no articulation. What is this?
Woyzeck's arm, flesh, bones, veins. What is this?
Dung. Why is it rooted in dung? Must I cut off 35
my arm? No, Man is selfish, he beats, shoots, stabs
his own kind. [*He sobs.*] We must be friends. I wish
our noses were two bottles that we could pour
down each other's throats. What a beautiful place
the world is! Friend! My friend! The world! 40
[*Moved.*] Look! The sun coming through the

clouds — like God emptying His bedpan on the
world. [*He cries.*]

SCENE XVII — THE BARRACKS YARD

WOYZECK. ANDRES.

WOYZECK: What have you heard?
ANDRES: He's still inside with a friend.
WOYZECK: He said something.
ANDRES: How do you know? Why do I have to be
the one to tell you? Well, he laughed and then he 5
said she was some piece. And then something or
other about her thighs — and that she was hot as
a red poker.
WOYZECK [*quite coldly*]: So, he said that? What was
that I dreamed about last night? About a knife? 10
What stupid dreams we get!
ANDRES: Hey, friend! Where you off to?
WOYZECK: Get some wine for the Captain. Andres,
you know something? There aren't many girls like
she was. 15
ANDRES: Like who was?
WOYZECK: Nothing. I'll see you. [*Goes off.*]

SCENE XVIII — THE INN

DRUM MAJOR, WOYZECK, and PEOPLE.

DRUM MAJOR: I'm a man! [*He pounds his chest.*] A
man, you hear? Anybody say different? Anybody
who's not as crocked as the Lord Himself better
keep off. I'll screw his nose up his own ass! I'll …
[*To WOYZECK.*] You there, get drunk! I wish the 5
world was schnapps, schnapps! You better start
drinking! [*WOYZECK whistles.*] Son-of-a-bitch, you
want me to pull your tongue out and wrap it
around your middle? [*They wrestle; WOYZECK loses.*]
You want I should leave enough wind in you for 10
a good old lady's fart? Uh! [*Exhausted and
trembling, WOYZECK seats himself on the bench.*] The
son-of-a-bitch can whistle himself blue in the face
for all I care. [*Sings.*]
Brandy's all my life, my life 15
Brandy gives me courage!
A MAN: He sure got more than he asked for.
ANOTHER: He's bleeding.
WOYZECK: One thing after another.

---

26 *Spinosa pericyclia*] (Latin) A pericycle is the outer portion
of an organic structure containing vascular tissues; *spinosa*
refers to spinal; accordingly, Woyzeck may be defining
himself as living tissue surrounding a spinal cord.

SCENE XIX — PAWNBROKER'S SHOP

WOYZECK and THE JEW.

WOYZECK: The pistol costs too much.
JEW: So you want it or not? Make up your mind.
WOYZECK: How much was the knife?
JEW: It's straight and sharp. What do you want if for? To cut your throat? So what's the matter? You get it as cheap here as anywhere else. You'll die cheap enough, but not for nothing. What's the matter? It'll be a cheap death.
WOYZECK: This'll cut more than bread.
JEW: Two groschen.
WOYZECK: There! [*He goes out.*]
JEW: There, he says! Like it was nothing! And it's real money! — Dog!

SCENE XX — MARIE'S ROOM

THE IDIOT. THE CHILD. MARIE.

IDIOT [*lying down, telling fairy tales on his fingers*]: This one has the golden crown. He's the Lord King. Tomorrow I'll bring the Lady Queen her child. Bloodsausage says: Come, Liversausage …
MARIE [*paging through her Bible*]: "And no guile is found in his mouth."27 Lord God, Lord God! Don't look at me! [*Paging further.*] "And the Scribes and the Pharisees brought unto him a woman taken in adultery, and set her in the midst … And Jesus said unto her: Neither do I condemn thee; go, and sin no more."28 [*Striking her hands*

---

27 no guile … mouth] The phrase appears twice in the Bible: "For even hereunto were ye called: because Christ also suffered for us, leaving us an example, that ye should follow his steps: Who did no sin, neither was guile found in his mouth" (1 Peter 2:21–22), and "These are they which were not defiled with women; for they are virgins. These are they which follow the Lamb whithersoever he goeth. These were redeemed from among men, being the first fruits unto God and to the Lamb. And in their mouth was found no guile: for they are without fault before the throne of God" (Revelation 14: 4–5).

28 Scribes … no more] from the passage in which Jesus suggests that "He that is without sin among you, let him first cast a stone" (John 8: 3–11).

together.] Lord God! Lord God! I can't. Lord God, give me only so much strength that I may pray. [*THE CHILD presses himself close to her.*] The child is a sword in my heart. [*To THE IDIOT.*] Karl! — I've strutted it in the light of the sun, like the whore I am — my sin, my sin! [*THE IDIOT takes THE CHILD and grows quiet.*] Franz hasn't come. Not yesterday. Not today. It's getting hot in here! [*She opens the window and reads further.*] "And stood at his feet weeping, and began to wash his feet with tears, and did wipe them with the hairs of her head, and anointed them with ointment."29 [*Striking her breast.*] Everything dead! Saviour! Saviour! If only I might anoint Your feet!

SCENE XXI — AN OPEN FIELD

WOYZECK.

WOYZECK [*buries the knife in a hole*]: Thou shalt not kill. Lay here! I can't stay here! [*He rushes off.*]

SCENE XXII — THE BARRACKS

ANDRES. WOYZECK rummages through his belongings.

WOYZECK: Andres, this jacket's not part of the uniform, but you can use it, Andres.
ANDRES [*replies numbly to almost everything with*]: Sure.
WOYZECK: The cross is my sister's. And the ring.
ANDRES: Sure.
WOYZECK: I've got a Holy Picture, too: two hearts — they're real gold. I found it in my mother's Bible, and it said:

O Lord with wounded head so sore
So may my heart be evermore.

My mother only feels now when the sun shines on her hands … that doesn't matter.
ANDRES: Sure.

---

29 And stood … ointment] "And, behold, a woman in the city, which was a sinner, when she knew that Jesus sat at meat in the Pharisee's house, brought an alabaster box of ointment, and stood at his feet behind him weeping, and began to wash his feet with tears, and did wipe them with the hairs of her head, and kissed his feet, and anointed them with the ointment" (Luke 7:37–38).

WOYZECK [*pulls out a paper*]: Friedrich Johann Franz   15
Woyzeck. Soldier. Rifleman, Second Regiment,
Second Battalion, Fourth Company. Born: the
Feast of the Annunciation, twentieth of July. Today
I'm thirty years old, seven months and twelve days.

ANDRES: Go to the hospital, Franz. Poor guy, you've   20
got to drink some schnapps with a powder in it.
It'll kill the fever.

WOYZECK: You know, Andres — when the carpenter
puts those boards together, nobody knows who it's
made for.   25

SCENE XXIII — THE STREET

MARIE with little GIRLS in front of the house door.
GRANDMOTHER. Later WOYZECK.

GIRLS [*singing*]:
>   The sun shone bright on Candlemas day
>   And the corn was all in bloom
>   And they marched along the meadow way
>   They marched by two and two.
>   The pipers marched ahead   5
>   The fiddlers followed through
>   And their socks were scarlet red …

FIRST CHILD: I don't like that one.

SECOND CHILD: Why do you always want to be   10
different?

FIRST CHILD: You sing for us, Marie!

MARIE: I can't.

SECOND CHILD: Why?

MARIE: Because.

SECOND CHILD: But *why* because?   15

THIRD CHILD: Grandmother, *you* tell us a story!

GRANDMOTHER: All right, you little crab apples! —
Once upon a time there was a poor little girl who
had no father and no mother. Everyone was dead,
and there was no one left in the whole wide world.   20
Everyone was dead. And the little girl went out and
looked for someone night and day. And because
there was no one left on the earth, she wanted to
go to Heaven. And the moon looked down so
friendly at her. And when she finally got to the   25
moon, it was a piece of rotten wood. And so she
went to the sun, and it was a faded sunflower. And
when she got to the stars, they were little golden
flies, stuck up there as if they were caught in a

spider's web. And when she wanted to go back to   30
earth, the earth was an upside-down pot. And she
was all alone. And she sat down there and she
cried. And she sits there to this day, all alone.[30]

WOYZECK [*appears*]: Marie!

MARIE [*startled*]: What!   35

WOYZECK: Let's go. It's getting time.

MARIE: Where to?

WOYZECK: How should I know?

SCENE XXIV — A POND BY THE
EDGE OF THE WOODS

MARIE and WOYZECK.

MARIE: Then the town must be out that way. It's so
dark.

WOYZECK: You can't go yet. Come, sit down.

MARIE: But I've got to get back.

WOYZECK: You don't want to run your feet sore.   5

MARIE: What's happened to you?

WOYZECK: You know how long it's been, Marie?

MARIE: Two years from Pentecost.[31]

WOYZECK: You know how much longer it'll last?

MARIE: I've got to get back. Supper's not made yet.   10

WOYZECK: Are you freezing, Marie? And still you're
so warm. Your lips are hot as coals! Hot as coals,
the hot breath of a whore! And still I'd give up
Heaven just to kiss them again. Are you freezing?
When you're cold through, you won't freeze any   15
more. The morning dew won't freeze you.

MARIE: What are you talking about?

WOYZECK: Nothing. [*Silence.*]

MARIE: Look how red the moon is! It's rising.

WOYZECK: Like a knife washed in blood.[32]   20

---

30 The story appears to be original, but compare "The
Seven Ravens" or "The Lilting, Leaping Lark" in *Grimms'*
Tales.

31 Pentecost] the fiftieth day after Easter, commemorating
the descent of the Holy Spirit upon the disciples of Jesus.

32 red … moon … blood] "The sun shall be turned into
darkness, and the moon into blood, before the great and
terrible day of the LORD come" (Joel 2: 31); cf. Acts
2:20 and Revelation 6:12.

MARIE: What are you going to do? Franz, you're so pale. [*He raises the knife.*]

MARIE: Franz! Stop! For Heaven's sake! Help me! Help me!

WOYZECK [*stabbing madly*]: There! There! Why can't you die? There! There! Ha, she's still shivering! Still not dead? Still not dead? Still shivering? [*Stabbing at her again.*] Are you dead? Dead! Dead! [*He drops the knife and runs away.*]

Two MEN approach.

FIRST MAN: Wait!

SECOND MAN: You hear something? Shh! Over there!

FIRST MAN: Whhh! There! What a sound!

SECOND MAN: It's the water, it's calling. It's a long time since anyone drowned here. Let's go! I don't like hearing such sounds!

FIRST MAN: Whhh! There it is again! Like a person, dying.

SECOND MAN: It's uncanny! So foggy, nothing but gray mist as far as you can see — and the hum of beetles like broken bells. Let's get out of here!

FIRST MAN: No, it's too clear, it's too loud! Let's go up this way! Come on! [*They hurry on.*]

SCENE XXV — THE INN

WOYZECK, KATHY, INNKEEPER, IDIOT, and PEOPLE.

WOYZECK: Dance! Everybody! Don't stop! Sweat and stink! He'll get you all in the end! [*Sings.*]
> Oh, daughter, my daughter
> And didn't you know
> That sleeping with coachmen
> Would bring you low?

[*He dances.*] Ho, Kathy! Sit down! I'm so hot, so hot! [*Takes off his coat.*] That's the way it is: the devil takes one and lets the other get away. Kathy, you're hot as coals! Why, tell me why? Kathy, you'll be cold one day, too. Be reasonable. — Can't you sing something?

KATHY [*sings*]:
> The Swabian land I cannot bear[33]

And dresses long I will not wear
> For dresses long and pointed shoes
> Are clothes a chambermaid never should choose.

WOYZECK: No shoes, no shoes! We can get to hell without shoes.

KATHY [*sings*]:
> To such and like I'll not be prone
> Take back your gold and sleep alone.

WOYZECK: Sure, sure! What do I want to get all bloody for?

KATHY: Then what's that on your hand?

WOYZECK: Me? Me?

KATHY: Red! It's blood! [*PEOPLE gather round him.*]

WOYZECK: Blood? Blood?

INNKEEPER: Blood!

WOYZECK: I think I cut myself. Here, on my right hand.

INNKEEPER: Then why is there blood on your elbow?

WOYZECK: I wiped it off.

INNKEEPER: Your right hand and you wiped it on your right elbow? You're a smart one!

IDIOT: And then the Giant said: "I smell, I smell the flesh of Man." Pew, it stinks already!

WOYZECK: What do you want from me? Is it your business? Out of my way or the first one who … Damn you! Do I look like I murdered somebody? Do I look like a murderer? What are you looking at? Look at yourselves! Look! Out of my way! [*He runs off.*]

SCENE XXVI — AT THE POND[34]

WOYZECK, alone.

WOYZECK: The knife! Where's the knife? I left it here. It'll give me away! Closer! And closer! What is this place? What's that noise? Something's moving! It's quiet now. — It's got to be here, close to her. Marie? Ha, Marie! Quiet. Everything's quiet! Why are you so pale, Marie? Why are you wearing those red beads around your neck? Who

---

33 Swabian land] Swabia or Schwaben, a region in south-western Germany.

34 Some versions of the play end with this scene; others make the speech part of the last scene, but continue with the exchange between two men which, in this version, appears at the end of Scene XXIV.

was it gave you that necklace for sinning with him? Your sins made you black, Marie, they made you black! Did I make you so pale? Why is your hair uncombed? Did you forget to twist your braids today? The knife, the knife! I've got it! There! [*He runs toward the water.*] There, into the water! [*He throws the knife into the water.*] It dives like a stone into the black water. No, it's not out far enough for when they swim! [*He wades into the pond and throws it out farther.*] There! Now! But in the summer when they dive for mussels? Ha, it'll get rusty, who'll ever notice it! Why didn't I break it first! Am I still bloody? I've got to wash myself. There, there's a spot, and there's another … [*He goes farther out into the water.*]

SCENE XXVII — THE STREET

CHILDREN.

FIRST CHILD: Let's go find Marie!
SECOND CHILD: What happened?
FIRST CHILD: Don't you know? Everybody's out there. They found a body!
SECOND CHILD: Where?
FIRST CHILD: By the pond, out in the woods.
SECOND CHILD: Hurry, so we can still see something. Before they bring it back. [*They rush off.*]

SCENE XXVIII — IN FRONT OF MARIE'S HOUSE

IDIOT. CHILD. WOYZECK.

IDIOT [*holding THE CHILD on his knee, points to WOYZECK as he enters*]: Looky there, he fell in the water, he fell in the water, he fell in the water!
WOYZECK: Boy! Christian!
IDIOT [*looks fixedly*]: He fell in the water.
WOYZECK [*wanting to embrace THE CHILD tenderly, but it turns from him and screams*]: My God! My God!
IDIOT: He fell in the water.
WOYZECK: I'll buy you a horsey, Christian. There, there. [*THE CHILD pulls away. To the IDIOT.*] Here, buy the boy a horsey! [*THE IDIOT stares at him.*] Hop! Hop! Hip-hop, horsey!
IDIOT [*shouting joyously*]: Hop! Hop! Hip-hop, horsey! Hip-hop, horsey!

He runs off with THE CHILD. WOYZECK is alone.

SCENE XXIX — THE MORGUE

JUDGE, COURT CLERK, POLICEMAN, CAPTAIN, DOCTOR, DRUM MAJOR, SERGEANT, IDIOT and others. WOYZECK.

POLICEMAN: What a murder! A good, genuine, beautiful murder! Beautiful a murder as you could hope for! It's been a long time since we had one like this!

WOYZECK stands in their midst, dumbly looking at the body of MARIE; he is bound, the dogmatic atheist, tall, haggard, timid, good-natured, scientific.[35]

---

[35] This stage direction is written not by Büchner but the translator, C.R. Mueller. It is, however, the only line in this version of the play which was not originally written by Büchner, in contrast to some other versions, which contain work written by Karl Emil Franzos, one of the early editors of the manuscripts.

GEORGE AIKEN/HARRIET BEECHER STOWE

Uncle Tom's Cabin

"So this is the little lady who made this big war," Abraham Lincoln is said to have joked upon meeting Harriet Beecher Stowe in 1862. The story may be apocryphal, but it lingers in the popular imagination in part because of its plausibility. The circumstances that led Americans into the Civil War were complex, but it is not incorrect to say that the war had, at root, one main cause: slavery. And while abolitionist arguments had been expressed by many voices over many years, *Uncle Tom's Cabin* was by far the single most obvious factor in the crystallization of the anti-slavery sentiment among Americans.

Uncle Tom's Cabin was the most widely read and controversial novel of the nineteenth century. Stowe (1811–1896) began writing it in response to the Fugitive Slave Act of 1850, in which, to maintain peace in the union, the North (which had abolished slavery years before) agreed to capture and return runaway slaves to the South. As the novel began to appear serially in 1851 in the anti-slavery journal, *The Nation*, Stowe's searing indignation at the craven moral abdication by the political leaders of the North made itself felt on page after page. Readership began to snowball. Upon the novel's completion, it was immediately republished; American sales passed 300,000 before the year was out; in England, 1,000 copies per week were being sold by August of 1852. By the end of the century, it had sold more than 2,000,000 copies. The only book to outsell it was the Bible.

However, even more Americans—it is impossible to tell exactly how many, but several million—encountered the story of *Uncle Tom's Cabin* through the novel's adaptation for the stage by actor-playwright George Aiken (1830–1876). Although his was not the first dramatization of Stowe's novel, Aiken's was by far the most successful. After running a record 100 performances in its first production, in Troy, New York (where it played to a total audience of 25,000 in a town with a population of 30,000), it went on to Broadway, where it ran three performances a day for a year, then on to productions all over the world, becoming the most popular play of the century. In 1879, there were forty-nine professional touring companies of *Uncle Tom's Cabin* in North America; in the 1890s there were more than 400; as late as 1927, there were still a dozen. Indeed, it seems that the first year in which there was not a professional production of the play was 1930. From 1903 on, the story was filmed twelve times.

It should be said that none of the dramatizations of *Uncle Tom's Cabin*, including Aiken's, ever secured Stowe's approval. In response to one such request, Stowe refused on the grounds that Christians might endanger their souls by attending the theatre: "If the barrier which now keeps young people of Christian families from theatrical entertainments is broken down by the introduction of respectable and moral plays, they will then be open to all the temptations of those who are not such, as there will be, as the world now is, five bad plays to one good." However, if Stowe's novel was dramatized against her will and without payment, neither did it make the fortunes of its adaptor, George Aiken. Aiken had written his unauthorized adaptation for a flat commission from his cousin-in-law, theatre producer George C. Howard, and he received no further royalties.

For all the success of his end product, Aiken's method of adaptation was surprisingly simple: he took the dialogue from Stowe's novel and, with a minimum of extra linking, set it in playscript format. His first attempt, written in a week, produced a three-hour, fifteen-minute version that took the story only as far as the death of Little Eva. Two months later, he wrote a second part, then, a month after that, combined and reduced these scripts into the popular six-act version first published in 1852 and reproduced here.

Despite Stowe's honourable intentions, her novel is still clearly racist in many respects. For example, though the most despicable characters in Stowe's novel are certainly Caucasian, she renders the shades of pigmentation among her slave characters so that the most dignified and intelligent are pale-skinned people of mixed race and the coarsest are very dark-skinned people of purely African ancestry. Furthermore, the model of submissiveness suggested by Uncle Tom himself can itself be seen as a degrading stereotype. In the 1960s, the name "Uncle Tom" became an insulting epithet used by blacks of other blacks who seemed overly concerned about ingratiating themselves with whites. Another point of controversy is Stowe's advocacy in the book of resettling emancipated slaves in an African homeland—though, in Stowe's defence, it should be said that during her own time and for years afterward, many blacks, including a number of prominent black leaders, also embraced that concept. At any rate, these probably unconscious racist elements were ultimately secondary to the power of Stowe's novel to impress the readers of her time with a profound sense of the wrongfulness of slavery, and even today's readers often find that the novel is rather more complex than its reputation had led them to believe.

Alas, one of the principal causes of the degradation of the novel's reputation is the very play that follows. The fact that Aiken took not only the dialogue of the play but the schematic arrangement of its characters (the saintly Little Eva at one end, the satanic Simon Legree at the other) from Stowe's novel may suggest that Stowe should be regarded as the play's principal author. But in condensing the material for the stage, Aiken removed most of the bitterly ironic commentary that made Stowe's novel so explosive in readers' imaginations. Unencumbered by nuance and commentary, and performed by white actors in blackface, Stowe's characters became indistinguishable from the stock figures of melodrama. This coarsening of the story continued as various novelties were introduced in many theatrical productions of the play, including minstrel versions, all-children's troupes, and "double Toms"—two casts performing side by side on the same stage. By the 1870s, one observer commented that the play was "half a minstrel show and half a circus." Still, notwithstanding its dubious literary merits, the historical importance of this stage version of *Uncle Tom's Cabin* is indisputable, both for the huge popularity it once enjoyed and as a prime example of melodrama. It is for these reasons we have included it in this anthology.

[C.S.W.]

Adapted by GEORGE AIKEN from the novel by HARRIET BEECHER STOWE

Uncle Tom's Cabin

DRAMATIS PERSONÆ

UNCLE TOM	SAMBO
GEORGE HARRIS	QUIMBO
GEORGE SHELBY	DOCTOR
ST. CLARE	WAITER
PHINEAS FLETCHER	HARRY, a child
GUMPTION CUTE	EVA
MR. WILSON	ELIZA
DEACON PERRY	CASSY
SHELBY	MARIE
HALEY	OPHELIA
SIMON LEGREE	CHLOE
TOM LOKER	TOPSY
MARKS	

ACT I

SCENE I

Plain Chamber.[1] *Enter ELIZA, meeting GEORGE.*

ELIZA: Ah! George, is it you? Well, I am so glad you've come. [*GEORGE regards her mournfully.*] Why don't you smile, and ask after Harry?

GEORGE: [*Bitterly.*] I wish he'd never been born! I wish I'd never been born myself! 5

ELIZA: [*Sinking her head upon his breast and weeping.*] Oh George!

GEORGE: There now, Eliza, it's too bad for me to make you feel so. Oh, how I wish you had never seen me—you might have been happy! 10

ELIZA: George! George! How can you talk so? What dreadful thing has happened, or is going to happen? I'm sure we've been very happy till lately.

GEORGE: So we have, dear. But, oh, I wish I'd never seen you, nor you me. 15

ELIZA: Oh, George! How can you?

GEORGE: Yes, Eliza, it's all misery, misery! The very life is burning out of me! I'm a poor, miserable, forlorn drudge![2] I shall only drag you down with me, that's all! What's the use of our trying to do 20 anything—trying to know anything—trying to be anything? I wish I was dead!

ELIZA: Oh, now, dear George, that is really wicked. I know how you feel about losing your place in the factory, and you have a hard master; but pray 25 be patient—

GEORGE: Patient! Haven't I been patient? Did I say a word when he came and took me away—for no earthly reason—from the place where everybody was kind to me? I'd paid him truly every cent of 30 my earnings, and they all say I worked well.

ELIZA: Well, it *is* dreadful; but, after all, he is your master, you know.

GEORGE: My master! And who made him my master? That's what I think of. What right has he 35 to me? I'm as much a man as he is. What right has he to make a dray-horse of me?[3] To take me from things I can do better than he can, and put me to work that any horse can do? He tries to do it; he says he'll bring me down and humble me, 40 and he puts me to just the hardest, meanest and dirtiest work, on purpose.

ELIZA: Oh, George, George! You frighten me. Why, I never heard you talk so. I'm afraid you'll do something dreadful. I don't wonder at your feelings 45

---

1 *Plain Chamber*] a simple room; the first scenes are set in Kentucky.

2 drudge] a menial servant.

3 dray-horse] a horse that pulls a low cart used for especially heavy loads.

at all, but oh, do be careful—for my sake, for
Harry's.

GEORGE: I have been careful, and I have been
patient, but it's growing worse and worse—flesh
and blood can't bear it any longer. Every chance 50
he can get to insult and torment me he takes. He
says that though I don't say anything, he sees that
I've got the devil in me, and he means to bring it
out; and one of these days it will come out, in a
way that he won't like, or I'm mistaken. 55

ELIZA: Well, I always thought that I must obey my
master and mistress, or I couldn't be a Christian.

GEORGE: There is some sense in it in your case. They
have brought you up like a child—fed you, clothed
you and taught you, so that you have a good 60
education—that is some reason why they should
claim you. But I have been kicked and cuffed and
sworn at, and what do I owe? I've paid for all my
keeping a hundred times over. I won't bear it! No,
I *won't!* Master will find out that I'm one whipping 65
won't tame. My day will come yet, if he don't look
out!

ELIZA: What are you going to do? Oh, George, don't
do anything wicked; if you only trust in heaven
and try to do right, it will deliver you. 70

GEORGE: Eliza, my heart's full of bitterness. I can't
trust in heaven. Why does it let things be so?

ELIZA: Oh, George! We must all have faith. Mistress
says that when all things go wrong to us, we must
believe that heaven is doing the very best. 75

GEORGE: That's easy for people to say who are sitting
on their sofas and riding in their carriages; but let
them be where I am—I guess it would come some
harder. I wish I could be good; but my heart burns
and can't be reconciled. You couldn't, in my place, 80
you can't now, if I tell you all I've got to say; you
don't know the whole yet.

ELIZA: What do you mean?

GEORGE: Well, lately my master has been saying that
he was a fool to let me marry off the place—that 85
he hates Mr. Shelby and all his tribe—and he says
he won't let me come here any more, and that I
shall take a wife and settle down on his place.

ELIZA: But you were married to *me* by the minister,
as much as if you had been a white man. 90

GEORGE: Don't you know I can't hold you for my

wife if he chooses to part us? That is why I wish
I'd never seen you—it would have been better for
us both—it would have been better for our poor
child if he had never been born. 95

ELIZA: Oh, but my master is so kind.

GEORGE: Yes, but who knows? He may die, and then
Harry may be sold to nobody knows who. What
pleasure is it that he is handsome and smart and
bright? I tell you, Eliza, that a sword will pierce 100
through your soul for every good and pleasant
thing your child is or has. It will make him worth
too much for you to keep.

ELIZA: Heaven forbid!

GEORGE: So, Eliza, my girl, bear up now; and good 105
bye, for I'm going.

ELIZA: Going, George! Going where?

GEORGE: To Canada;[4] and when I'm there I'll buy
you. That's all the hope that's left us. You have a
kind master, that won't refuse to sell you. I'll buy 110
you and the boy—heaven helping me, I will!

ELIZA: Oh, dreadful! If you should be taken?

GEORGE: I won't be taken, Eliza—I'll *die* first! I'll
be free, or I'll die.

ELIZA: You will not kill yourself? 115

GEORGE: No need of that; they will kill me, fast
enough. I will never go down the river alive.

ELIZA: Oh, George! For my sake, do be careful. Don't
lay hands on yourself, or anybody else. You are
tempted too much, but don't. Go, if you must, but 120
go carefully, prudently, and pray heaven to help you!

GEORGE: Well, then Eliza, hear my plan. I'm going

---

4 To Canada] Slavery was officially abolished in Canada (as
in the rest of the British Empire) in 1834. Moreover, it
had been in sharp decline since 1793, when John Graves
Simcoe had challenged its legality in Upper Canada and
established a program of gradual emancipation. In the
United States, although all the states north of Maryland
had abolished slavery between 1777 and 1804, the Fugitive Slave Act of 1793 allowed courts to decide the status of, and order returned, any alleged fugitive slave. That
law was widely ignored in the North, so, in order to ap-
pease Southern states, a much stricter version of the Fugitive Slave Act was passed in 1850, which denied
fugitives the right to testify on their own behalf, made it
a crime to aid a fugitive, and imposed heavy penalties on
marshals who refused to enforce the law.

home quite resigned, you understand, as if all was
over. I've got some preparations made, and there
are those that will help me; and in the course of a
few days I shall be among the missing. Well, now: 125
good bye.

ELIZA: A moment—our boy.

GEORGE: [*Choked with emotion.*] True, I had
forgotten him; one last look, and then farewell! 130

ELIZA: And heaven grant it be not forever! [*Exeunt.*]

SCENE II

*A dining room. Table and chairs. Dessert, wine, etc.,
on table. SHELBY and HALEY discovered at table.*

SHELBY: That is the way I should arrange the matter.

HALEY: I can't make trade that way—I positively
can't, Mr. Shelby. [*Drinks.*]

SHELBY: Why, the fact is, Haley, Tom is an
uncommon fellow! He is certainly worth that sum 5
anywhere—steady, honest, capable, manages my
whole farm like a clock!

HALEY: You mean honest, as niggers go. [*Fills glass.*]

SHELBY: No; I mean, really. Tom is a good, steady,
sensible, pious fellow. He got religion at a camp- 10
meeting, four years ago, and I believe he really *did*
get it.[5] I've trusted him since then, with everything
I have—money, house, horses, and let him come
and go round the country, and I always found him
true and square in everything. 15

HALEY: Some folks don't believe there is pious
niggers, Shelby; but I *do*. I had a fellow, now, in
this yer last lot I took to Orleans—'twas as good
as a meetin' now, really, to hear that critter pray![6]
And he was quite gentle and quiet like. He fetched 20
me a good sum, too, for I bought him cheap of a
man that was 'bliged to sell out, so I realized six
hundred on him. Yes, I consider religion a

valeyable thing in a nigger, when it's the genuine
article and no mistake. 25

SHELBY: Well, Tom's got the real article, if ever a fellow
had. Why last fall I let him go to Cincinnati alone,
to do business for me and bring home five hundred
dollars. "Tom," says I to him, "I trust you, because
I think you are a Christian—I know you wouldn't 30
cheat." Tom comes back sure enough; I knew he
would. Some low fellows, they say, said to him—
"Tom, why don't you make tracks for Canada?" "Ah,
master trusted me, and I couldn't," was his answer.
They told me all about it. I am sorry to part with 35
Tom, I must say. You ought to let him cover the
whole balance of the debt—and you would, Haley,
if you had any conscience.

HALEY: Well, I've got just as much conscience as any
man in business can afford to keep, just a little, 40
you know, to swear by, as twere; and then I'm ready
to do anything in reason to 'blige friends, but this
yer, you see, is a leetle too hard on a fellow—a
leetle too hard! [*Fills glass again.*]

SHELBY: Well, then, Haley, how will you trade? 45

HALEY: Well, haven't you a boy or a girl that you
could throw in with Tom?

SHELBY: Hum…! None that I could well spare. To
tell the truth, it's only hard necessity makes me
willing to sell at all. I don't like parting with any 50
of my hands, that's a fact. [*Harry runs in.*] Hulloa!
Jim Crow![7] [*Throws a bunch of raisins towards him.*]
Pick that up now! [*Harry does so.*]

HALEY: Bravo, little 'un! [*Throws an orange, which
Harry catches. He sings and dances around the stage.*] 55
Hurrah! Bravo! What a young 'un! That chap's a
case, I'll promise.[8] Tell you what, Shelby, fling in
that chap, and I'll settle the business. Come, now,
if that ain't doing the thing up about the rightest!

*Eliza enters. Starts on beholding Haley, and gazes
fearfully at Harry, who runs and clings to her dress,
showing the orange, etc.*

---

5 Stowe based the character of Uncle Tom on the Rev.
Josiah Henson (1789–1883), who published his autobiography in 1876 as *Uncle Tom's Story of his Life*. Henson's
life story, including this early conversion, roughly parallel Tom's story up to the events which close Act Four;
shortly after that, Henson actually escaped to Canada.

6 yer] i.e., "here" (though it is also used elsewhere for
"your").

7 Jim Crow] the stage name used beginning in 1828 by the
most famous "Negro impersonator" in minstrel shows,
Thomas Dartmouth Rice (1808–1860). The name became a derogatory epithet for blacks.

8 a case] (slang) an unusual character.

SHELBY: Well, Eliza? 60

ELIZA: I was looking for Harry, please, sir.

SHELBY: Well, take him away, then.

Eliza grasps the child eagerly in her arms, and casting another glance of apprehension at Haley, exits hastily.

HALEY: By Jupiter! There's an article, now. You might make your fortune on that ar gal in Orleans any day.[9] I've seen over a thousand in my day, paid 65 down for gals not a bit handsomer.

SHELBY: I don't want to make my fortune on her. Another glass of wine. [*Fills the glasses.*]

HALEY: [*Drinks and smacks his lips.*] Capital wine— first chop.[10] Come, how will you trade about the 70 gal? What shall I say for her? What'll you take?

SHELBY: Mr. Haley, she is not to be sold. My wife wouldn't part with her for her weight in gold.

HALEY: Ay, ay! Women always say such things, 'cause they hain't no sort of calculation.[11] Just show 'em 75 how many watches, feathers and trinkets one's weight in gold would buy, and that alters the case, I reckon.

SHELBY: I tell you, Haley, this must not be spoken of—I say no, and I mean no. 80

HALEY: Well, you'll let me have the boy tho'; you must own that I have come down pretty handsomely for him.[12]

SHELBY: What on earth can you want with the child?

HALEY: Why, I've got a friend that's going into this 85 yer branch of the business—wants to buy up handsome boys to raise for the market. Well, what do you say?

SHELBY: I'll think the matter over and talk with my wife. 90

HALEY: Oh, certainly, by all means; but I'm in a devil of a hurry and shall want to know as soon as possible, what I may depend on.

Rises and puts on his overcoat, which hangs on a chair. Takes hat and whip.

SHELBY: Well, call up this evening, between six and seven, and you shall have my answer. 95

HALEY: All right. Take care of yourself, old boy! [*Exit.*]

SHELBY: If anybody had ever told me that I should sell Tom to those rascally traders, I should never have believed it. Now it must come for aught I see, 100 and Eliza's child too. So much for being in debt, heigho! The fellow sees his advantage and means to push it. [*Exit.*]

SCENE III

Snowy landscape. Uncle Tom's Cabin. Snow on roof. Practicable door and window.[13] Dark stage. Music. Enter ELIZA hastily, with HARRY in her arms.

ELIZA: My poor boy! they have sold you, but your mother will save you yet!

Goes to Cabin and taps on window. AUNT CHLOE appears at window with a large white night-cap on.

CHLOE: Good Lord! What's that? My sakes alive if it ain't Lizy![14] Get on your clothes, old man, quick! I'm gwine to open the door.[15] 5

The door opens and CHLOE enters followed by UNCLE TOM in his shirt sleeves holding a tallow candle.

TOM: [*Holding the light towards ELIZA.*] Lord bless you! I'm skeered to look at ye. Lizy! Are ye tuck sick, or what's come over ye?

ELIZA: I'm running away, Uncle Tom and Aunt Chloe—carrying off my child! Master sold him! 10

TOM & CHLOE: Sold him!

ELIZA: Yes, sold him! I crept into the closet by mistress's door tonight and heard master tell mistress that he had sold my Harry and you, Uncle

---

9 ar] there; Orleans] New Orleans (a city notorious at that time for its brothels).

10 first chop] (slang) at first taste.

11 hain't] haven't.

12 tho'] a contraction for "though," then properly pronounced with a subtly longer "o," like that heard in "soul."

13 *Practicable ... window*] Onstage doors and windows in this period would usually be merely painted on a backdrop.

14 sakes alive] (slang) euphemism for "saints alive," a mild blasphemy.

15 gwine] (dialect) going.

Tom, both, to a trader, and that the man was to take possession to-morrow. 15

CHLOE: The good lord have pity on us! Oh! it don't seem as if it was true. What has he done that master should sell *him?*

ELIZA: He hasn't done anything—it isn't for that. 20
Master don't want to sell, and mistress—she's always good. I heard her plead and beg for us, but he told her 'twas no use—that he was in this man's debt, and he had got the power over him, and that if he did not pay him off clear, it would end in 25
his having to sell the place and all the people and move off.

CHLOE: Well, old man, why don't you run away, too? Will you wait to be toted down the river, where they kill niggers with hard work and starving?[16] 30
I'd a heap rather die than go there, any day! There's time for ye, be off with Lizy—you've got a pass to come and go any time.[17] Come, bustle up, and I'll get your things together.

TOM: No, no—I ain't going. Let Eliza go—it's her 35
right. I wouldn't be the one to say no—'taint in natur' for her to stay; but you heard what she said? If I must be sold, or all the people on the place, and everything go to rack, why, let me be sold. I s'pose I can bar it as well as any one. Mas'r always 40
found me on the spot—he always will. I never have broken trust, nor used my pass no ways contrary to my word, and I never will. It's better for me to go alone, than to break up the place and sell all. Mas'r ain't to blame, and he'll take care of you and 45
the poor little 'uns! [*Overcome.*]

CHLOE: Now, old man, what is you gwine to cry for? Does you want to break this old woman's heart? [*Crying.*]

ELIZA: I saw my husband only this afternoon, and I 50
little knew then what was to come. He told me he was going to run away. Do try, if you can, to get word to him. Tell him how I went and why I went, and tell him I'm going to try and find

Canada. You must give my love to him, and tell 55
him if I never see him again on earth, I trust we shall meet in heaven!

TOM: Dat is right, Lizy, trust in the Lord—he is our best friend—our only comforter.

ELIZA: You won't go with me, Uncle Tom? 60

TOM: No; time was when I would, but the Lord's given me a work among these yer poor souls, and I'll stay with 'em and bear my cross with 'em till the end. It's different with you—it's more'n you could stand, and you'd better go if you can. 65

ELIZA: Uncle Tom, I'll try it!

TOM: Amen! The lord help ye!

Exit ELIZA and HARRY.

CHLOE: What is you gwine to do, old man! What's to become of you?

TOM: [*Solemnly.*] Him that saved Daniel in the den 70
of lions, that saved the children in the fiery furnace, Him that walked on the sea and bade the winds be still: He's alive yet![18] And I've faith to believe he can deliver me.

CHLOE: You is right, old man. 75

TOM: The Lord is good unto all that trust him, Chloe. [*Exeunt into cabin.*]

SCENE IV

Room in a tavern by the river side.[19] *A large window in flat, through which the river is seen, filled with floating ice. Moon light. Table and chairs brought on. Enter PHINEAS.*

PHINEAS: Chaw me up into tobaccy ends! How in the name of all that's onpossible am I to get across that yer pesky river? It's a reg'lar blockade of ice! I promised Ruth to meet her to-night, and she'll be into my har if I don't come. [*Goes to window.*] 5
Thar's a conglomerated prospect for a loveyer! What in creation's to be done? That thar river looks like a permiscuous ice-cream shop come to an awful state of friz. If I war on the adjacent bank, I

---

16 down the river] i.e., down the Mississippi River, to the deep South, where slaves were used for the brutal work of the cotton plantations.

17 pass] permit to travel off the master's property on business.

18 Daniel … fiery furnace … sea] Cf. Dan. 3:23–27; Dan. 6:16–22; Mat. 14:26–29.

19 *river*] the Ohio River, which marks the northern boundary of Kentucky.

wouldn't care a teetotal atom. Rile up, you old 10
varmit, and shake the ice off your back!

Enter ELIZA and HARRY.

ELIZA: Courage, my boy—we have reached the river.
Let it but roll between us and our pursuers, and
we are safe! [*Goes to window.*] Gracious powers! The
river is choked with cakes of ice! 15

PHINEAS: Holloa, gal!—what's the matter? You look
kind of streaked.

ELIZA: Is there any ferry or boat that takes people
over now?

PHINEAS: Well, I guess not; the boats have stopped 20
running.

ELIZA: [*In dismay.*] Stopped running?

PHINEAS: Maybe you're wanting to get over—
anybody sick? Ye seem mighty anxious.

ELIZA: I—I—I've got a child that's very dangerous. 25
I never heard of it till last night, and I've walked
quite a distance to-day, in hopes to get to the ferry.

PHINEAS: Well, now, that's onlucky. I'm re'lly
consarned for ye. Thar's a man, a piece down here,
that's going over with some truck this evening, if 30
he duss to; he'll be in here to supper to-night, so
you'd better set down and wait. That's a smart little
chap. Say, young'un, have a chaw tobaccy? [*Takes
out a large plug and a bowie-knife.*]

ELIZA: No, no! not any for him. 35

PHINEAS: Oh, he don't use it, eh? Hain't come to it
yet? Well, I have. [*Cuts off a large piece, and returns
the plug and knife to pocket.*] What's the matter with
the young 'un? He looks kind of white in the gills!

ELIZA: Poor fellow! He is not used to walking, and 40
I've hurried him on so.

PHINEAS: Tuckered, eh? Well, there's a little room
there, with a fire in it. Take the baby in there, make
yourself comfortable till that thar ferryman shows
his countenance—I'll stand the damage. 45

ELIZA: How shall I thank you for such kindness to
a stranger?

PHINEAS: Well, if you don't know how, why, don't
try; that's the teetotal. Come, vamose![20] [*Exit,
ELIZA and HARRY.*] Chaw me into sassage meat, if 50

that ain't a perpendicular fine gal! she's a reg'lar A
number one sort of female! How'n thunder am I
to get across this refrigerated stream of water? I
can't wait for that ferryman. [*Enter MARKS.*]
Halloa! what sort of a critter's this? [*Advances.*] Say, 55
stranger, will you have something to drink?

MARKS: You are excessively kind: I don't care if I do.

PHINEAS: Ah, he's a human. Holloa, thar! Bring us
a jug of whisky instantaneously, or expect to be
teetotally chawed up! Squat yourself, stranger, and 60
go in for enjoyment. [*They sit at table.*] Who are
you, and what's your name?

MARKS: I am a lawyer, and my name is Marks.

PHINEAS: A land shark, eh? Well, I don't think no
worse on you for that. The law is a kind of 65
necessary evil; and it breeds lawyers just as an old
stump does fungus. Ah, here's the whisky. [*Enter
WAITER, with jug and tumblers. Places them on
table.*] Here, you—take that shin-plaster. [*Gives
bill.*] I don't want any change—thar's a gal 70
stopping in that room—the balance will pay for
her—d'ye hear?—Vamose! [*Exit WAITER. Fills
glass.*] Take hold, neighbor Marks—don't shirk the
critter. Here's hoping your path of true love may
never have an ice-choked river to cross! [*They 75
drink.*]

MARKS: Want to cross the river, eh?

PHINEAS: Well, I do, stranger. Fact is, I'm in love
with the teetotalist pretty girl, over on the Ohio
side, that ever wore a Quaker bonnet. Take another 80
swig, neighbor. [*Fills glasses, and they drink.*]

MARKS: A Quaker, eh?

PHINEAS: Yes—kind of strange, ain't it? The way of
it was this. I used to own a grist of niggers—had
'em to work on my plantation, just below here. 85
Well, stranger, do you know I fell in with that
gal—of course I was considerably smashed—
knocked into a pretty conglomerated heap—and
I told her so. She said she wouldn't hear a word
from me so long as I owned a nigger![21] 90

MARKS: You sold them, I suppose?

---

21 Quakers had been speaking out against slavery since the
late eighteenth century.

PHINEAS: You're teetotally wrong, neighbor. I gave them all their freedom and told 'em to vamose!

MARKS: Ah, yes—very noble, I dare say, but rather expensive. This act won you your lady-love, eh? 95

PHINEAS: You're off the track again, neighbor. She felt kind of pleased about it, and smiled, and all that; but she said she could never be mine unless I turned Quaker! Thunder and earth! What do you think of that? You're a lawyer—come, now, what's 100 your opinion? Don't you call it a knotty point?

MARKS: Most decidedly. Of course you refused.

PHINEAS: Teetotally; but she told me to think better of it, and come tonight and give her my final conclusion. Chaw me into mince meat, if I haven't 105 made up my mind to do it!

MARKS: You astonish me!

PHINEAS: Well, you see, I can't get along without that gal. She's sort of fixed my flint, and I'm sure to hang fire without her. I know I shall make a queer sort of 110 Quaker, because you see, neighbor, I ain't precisely the kind of material to make a Quaker out of.

MARKS: No, not exactly.

PHINEAS: Well, I can't stop no longer. I must try to get across that candaverous river some way. It's 115 getting late—take care of yourself, neighbor, lawyer. I'm a teetotal victim to a pair of black eyes. Chaw me up to feed hogs, if I'm not in a ruinatious state! [*Exit.*]

MARKS: Queer, genius, that, very! [*Enter TOM* 120 *LOKER.*] So you've come at last.

LOKER: Yes. [*Looks into jug.*] Empty! Waiter, more whisky!

WAITER enters, with jug, and removes the empty one.
Enter HALEY.

HALEY: By the land! If this yer ain't the nearest, now, to what I've heard people call Providence! Why, 125 Loker, how are ye?

LOKER: The devil! What brought you here, Haley?

HALEY: [*Sitting at table.*] I say, Tom, this yer's the luckiest thing in the world. I'm in a devil of a hobble, and you must help me out! 130

LOKER: Ugh! Aw, like enough. A body may be pretty sure of that when you're glad to see 'em, or can make something off of 'em. What's the blow now?

HALEY: You've got a friend here—partner, perhaps?

LOKER: Yes, I have. Here, Marks—here's that ar 135 fellow that I was with in Natchez.[22]

MARKS: [*Grasping HALEY's hand.*] Shall be pleased with his acquaintance. Mr. Haley, I believe?

HALEY: The same, sir. The fact is, gentlemen, this morning I bought a young 'un of Shelby up above 140 here. His mother got wind of it, and what does she do but cut her lucky with him; and I'm afraid by this time that she has crossed the river, for I tracked her to this very place.

MARKS: So, then, ye're fairly sewed up, ain't ye? He! 145 he! he! It's neatly done, too.

HALEY: This young 'un business makes lots of trouble in the trade.

MARKS: Now, Mr. Haley, what is it? Do you want us to undertake to catch this gal? 150

HALEY: The gal's no matter of mine—she's Shelby's— it's only the boy. I was a fool for buying the monkey.

LOKER: You're generally a fool!

MARKS: Come now, Loker, none of your huffs; you 155 see, Mr. Haley's a-puttin' us in a way of a good job. I reckon: just hold still—these yer arrangements are my forte. This yer gal, Mr. Haley—how is she? What is she?

ELIZA appears, with HARRY, listening.

HALEY: Well, white and handsome—well brought 160 up.[23] I'd have given Shelby eight hundred or a thousand, and then made well on her.

MARKS: White and handsome—well brought up! Look here now, Loker: a beautiful opening. We'll do a business here on our own account. We does 165 the catchin'; the boy, of course, goes to Mr. Haley—we takes the gal to Orleans to speculate on. Ain't it beautiful? [*They confer together.*]

ELIZA: Powers of mercy, protect me! How shall I escape these human blood-hounds? Ah! The window—the 170 river of ice! That dark stream lies between me and liberty! Surely the ice will bear my trifling weight. It is my only chance of escape—better sink beneath

---

22 Natchez] city in Mississippi.

23 white] i.e, relatively; Eliza is pale-skinned, being of mixed race.

the cold waters, with my child locked in my arms, then have him torn from me and sold into bondage. He sleeps upon my breast. Heaven, I put my trust in thee! [*Gets out of window.*] 175

MARKS: Well, Tom Loker, what do you say?

LOKER: It'll do!

Strikes his hand violently on the table. ELIZA screams. They all start to their feet. ELIZA disappears. Music, chord.

HALEY: By the land, there she is now! [*They all rush to the window.*] 180

MARKS: She's making for the river!

LOKER: Let's after her!

Music. They all leap through the window. Change.

SCENE V

Snow. Landscape. Music. Enter ELIZA, with HARRY, hurriedly.

ELIZA: They press upon my footsteps—the river is my only hope. Heaven grant me strength to reach it, ere they overtake me! Courage, my child! We will be free—or perish! [*Rushes off. Music continued.*]

Enter LOKER, HALEY, and MARKS.

HALEY: We'll catch her yet; the river will stop her! 5

MARKS: No, it won't, for look! She has jumped upon the ice! She's a brave gal, anyhow!

LOKER: She'll be drowned!

HALEY: Curse that young 'un! I shall lose him, after all. 10

LOKER: Come on, Marks, to the ferry!

HALEY: Aye, to the ferry! A hundred dollars for a boat!

Music. They rush off.

SCENE VI

The entire depth of stage, representing the Ohio River filled with Floating Ice. Set bank on right and in front. ELIZA appears, with HARRY, on a cake of ice, and floats slowly across to left. HALEY, LOKER, and MARKS, on bank right, observing. PHINEAS on opposite shore.

ACT II

SCENE I

A Handsome Parlor.
MARIE discovered reclining on a sofa.

MARIE: [*Looking at a note.*] What can possibly detain St. Clare? According to this note he should have been here a fortnight ago. [*Noise of carriage without.*] I do believe he has come at last.

EVA runs in.

EVA: Mamma! [*Throws her arms around Marie's neck, and kisses her.*] 5

MARIE: That will do—take care, child—don't you make my head ache! [*Kisses her languidly.*]

Enter ST. CLARE, OPHELIA, and TOM nicely dressed.

ST. CLARE: Well, my dear Marie, here we are at last. The wanderers have arrived, you see. Allow me to present my cousins; Miss Ophelia, who is about to undertake the office of our housekeeper. 10

MARIE: [*Rising to a sitting posture.*] I am delighted to see you. How do you like the appearance of our city? 15

EVA: [*Running to OPHELIA.*] Oh! is it not beautiful? My own darling home!—is it not beautiful?

OPHELIA: Yes, it is a pretty place, though it looks rather old and heathenish to me.

ST. CLARE: Tom, my boy, this seems to suit you? 20

TOM: Yes, mas'r, it looks about the right thing.

ST. CLARE: See here, Marie, I've brought you a coachman, at last, to order. I tell you, he is a regular hearse for blackness and sobriety, and will drive you like a funeral, if you wish. Open your eyes, now, and look at him. Now, don't say I never think about you when I'm gone. 25

MARIE: I know he'll get drunk.

ST. CLARE: Oh! no he won't. He's warranted a pious and sober article. 30

MARIE: Well, I hope he may turn out well; it's more than I expect, though.

ST. CLARE: Have you no curiosity to learn how and where I picked up Tom?

EVA: *Uncle* Tom, papa; that's his name. 35

ST. CLARE: Right, my little sunbeam!

TOM: Please, mas'r, that ain't no 'casion to say nothing bout me.

ST. CLARE: You are too modest, my modern Hannibal.[24] Do you know, Marie, that our little Eva took a fancy to Uncle Tom—whom we met on board the steamboat—and persuaded me to buy him. 40

MARIE: Ah! She is so odd.

ST. CLARE: As we approached the landing, a sudden rush of the passengers precipitated Eva into the water— 45

MARIE: Gracious heavens!

ST. CLARE: A man leaped into the river, and, as she rose to the surface of the water, grasped her in his arms, and held her up until she could be drawn on the boat again. Who was that man, Eva? 50

EVA: Uncle Tom! [*Runs to him. He lifts her in his arms. She kisses him.*]

TOM: The dear soul!

OPHELIA: [*Astonished.*] How shiftless![25] 55

ST. CLARE: [*Overhearing her.*] What's the matter now, pray?

OPHELIA: Well, I want to be kind to everybody, and I wouldn't have anything hurt, but as to kissing—

ST. CLARE: Niggers? That you're not up to, hey? 60

OPHELIA: Yes, that's it—how can she?

ST. CLARE: Oh, bless you, it's nothing when you are used to it!

OPHELIA: I could never be so shiftless!

EVA: Come with me, Uncle Tom, and I will show you about the house. [*Crosses with TOM.*] 65

TOM: Can I go, mas'r?

ST. CLARE: Yes, Tom; she is your little mistress—your only duty will be to attend to her! [*TOM bows and exits.*] 70

MARIE: Eva, my dear!

EVA: Well, mamma?

MARIE: Do not exert yourself too much!

EVA: No, mamma! [*Runs out.*]

OPHELIA: [*Lifting up her hands.*] How shiftless! 75

ST. CLARE sits next to MARIE on sofa. OPHELIA next to ST. CLARE.

ST. CLARE: Well, what do you think of Uncle Tom, Marie?

MARIE: He is a perfect behemoth![26]

ST. CLARE: Come, now, Marie, be gracious, and say something pretty to a fellow! 80

MARIE: You've been gone a fortnight beyond the time!

ST. CLARE: Well, you know I wrote you the reason.

MARIE: Such a short, cold letter!

ST. CLARE: Dear me! The mail was just going, and it had to be that or nothing. 85

MARIE: That's just the way; always something to make your journeys long and letters short!

ST. CLARE: Look at this. [*Takes an elegant velvet case from his pocket.*] Here's a present I got for you in New York—a Daguerreotype of Eva and myself.[27] 90

MARIE: [*Looks at it with a dissatisfied air.*] What makes you sit in such an awkward position?

ST. CLARE: Well, the position may be a matter of opinion, but what do you think of the likeness? 95

MARIE: [*Closing the case snappishly.*] If you don't think anything of my opinion in one case, I suppose you wouldn't in another.

OPHELIA: [*Sententiously, aside.*] How shiftless!

ST. CLARE: Hang the woman! Come, Marie, what do you think of the likeness? Don't be nonsensical now. 100

MARIE: It's very inconsiderate of you, St. Clare, to insist on my talking and looking at things. You know I've been lying all day with the sick headache, and there's been such a tumult made ever since you came, I'm half dead! 105

OPHELIA: You're subject to the sick headache, ma'am?

MARIE: Yes, I'm a perfect martyr to it!

OPHELIA: Juniper-berry tea is good for sick headache; at least, Molly, Deacon Abraham Perry's wife, used to say so; and she was a great nurse. 110

ST. CLARE: I'll have the first juniper-berries that get ripe in our garden by the lake brought in for that especial purpose. Come, cousin, let us take a stroll in the garden. Will you join us, Marie? 115

---

24 Hannibal] courageous Carthaginian (i.e., African) general (247–181 B.C.E.).

25 shiftless] a malapropism—the word means lacking resourcefulness or self-motivation.

26 behemoth] a legendary monster (v. Job 40:15–24, probably describing a hippopotamus).

27 Daguerreotype] an early type of photograph.

MARIE: I wonder how you can ask such a question, when you know how fragile I am. I shall retire to my chamber, and repose till dinner time. [*Exit.*]

OPHELIA: [*Looking after her.*] How shiftless! 120

ST. CLARE: Come, cousin! [*As he goes out.*] Look out for the babies! If I step upon anybody, let them mention it.

OPHELIA: Babies under foot! How shiftless! [*Exeunt.*]

SCENE II

A Garden. TOM discovered, seated on a bank, with EVA on his knee—his button-holes are filled with flowers, and EVA is hanging a wreath around his neck. Music at opening of scene. Enter ST. CLARE and OPHELIA, observing.

EVA: Oh, Tom! you look so funny.

TOM: [*Sees ST. CLARE and puts EVA down.*] I begs pardon, mas'r, but the young missis would do it. Look yer, I'm like the ox, mentioned in the good book, dressed for the sacrifice.[28] 5

ST. CLARE: I say, what do you think, Pussy? What do you like the best—to live as they do at your uncle's, up in Vermont, or to have a house-full of servants, as we do?

EVA: Oh! of course our way is the pleasantest. 10

ST. CLARE: [*Patting her head.*] Why so?

EVA: Because it makes so many more round you to love, you know.

OPHELIA: Now, that's just like Eva—just one of her odd speeches. 15

EVA: Is it an odd speech, papa?

ST. CLARE: Rather, as this world goes, Pussy. But where has my little Eva been?

EVA: Oh! I've been up in Tom's room, hearing him sing. 20

ST. CLARE: Hearing Tom sing, hey?

EVA: Oh, yes! He sings such beautiful things, about the new Jerusalem, and bright angels, and the land of Canaan.[29]

ST. CLARE: I dare say, it's better than the opera, isn't it? 25

EVA: Yes; and he's going to teach them to me.

ST. CLARE: Singing lessons, hey? You are coming on.

EVA: Yes, he sings for me, and I read to him in my Bible, and he explains what it means. Come, Tom. [*She takes his hand and they exit.*] 30

ST. CLARE: [*Aside.*] Oh, Evangeline! Rightly named; hath not heaven made thee an evangel to me?[30]

OPHELIA: How shiftless! How can you let her?

ST. CLARE: Why not? 35

OPHELIA: Why, I don't know; it seems so dreadful.

ST. CLARE: You would think no harm in a child's caressing a large dog even if he was black; but a creature that can think, reason and feel, and is immortal, you shudder at. Confess it, cousin. I 40 know the feeling among some of you Northerners well enough. Not that there is a particle of virtue in our not having it, but custom with us does what Christianity ought to do: obliterates the feelings of personal prejudice. You loathe them as you 45 would a snake or a toad, yet you are indignant at their wrongs. You would not have them abused but you don't want to have anything to do with them yourselves. Isn't that it?

OPHELIA: Well, cousin, there may be some truth in 50 this.

ST. CLARE: What would the poor and lowly do without children? Your little child is your only true democrat. Tom, now, is a hero to Eva; his stories are wonders in her eyes; his songs and 55 Methodist hymns are better than an opera, and the traps and little bits of trash in his pockets a mine of jewels, and he the most wonderful Tom that ever wore a black skin. This is one of the roses of Eden that the Lord has dropped down 60 expressly for the poor and lowly, who get few enough of any other kind.

OPHELIA: It's strange, cousin; one might almost think you was a *professor*, to hear you talk.

ST. CLARE: A professor? 65

OPHELIA: Yes, a professor of religion.[31]

---

28 ox … good book] Jer. 11:19.

29 Canaan] the homeland of the Israelites under King David after defeating the Philistines.

30 evangel] a messenger of Christ.

31 professor of religion] i.e., not in the specific sense of a university position, but the more general sense of someone who avows knowledge of and commitment to religion.

ST. CLARE: Not at all; not a professor as you town folks have it, and, what is worse, I'm afraid, not a *practicer,* either.

OPHELIA: What makes you talk so, then? 70

ST. CLARE: Nothing is easier than talking. My forte lies in talking, and yours, cousin, lies in doing. And speaking of that puts me in mind that I have made a purchase for your department. There's the article, now. Here, Topsy! [*Whistles.*] 75

TOPSY runs on.

OPHELIA: Good gracious! What a heathenish, shiftless looking object! St. Clare, what in the world have you brought that thing here for?

ST. CLARE: For you to educate, to be sure, and train in the way she should go. I thought she was rather 80 a funny specimen in the Jim Crow line. Here, Topsy, give us a song, and show us some of your dancing. [*TOPSY sings a verse and dances a breakdown.*32]

OPHELIA: [*Paralyzed.*] Well, of all things! If I ever saw 85 the like!

ST. CLARE: [*Smothering a laugh.*] Topsy, this is your new mistress—I'm going to give you up to her. See now that you behave yourself.

TOPSY: Yes, mas'r. 90

ST. CLARE: You're going to be good, Topsy, you understand?

TOPSY: Oh, yes, mas'r.

OPHELIA: Now, St. Clare, what upon earth is this for? Your house is so full of these plagues now, that 95 a body can't set down their foot without treading on 'em. I get up in the morning and find one asleep behind the door, and see one black head poking out from under the table—one lying on the door mat, and they are moping and mowing and 100 grinning between all the railings, and tumbling over the kitchen floor! What on earth did you want to bring this one for?

ST. CLARE: For you to educate—didn't I tell you? You're always preaching about educating, I thought 105 I would make you a present of a fresh caught

specimen, and let you try your hand on her and bring her up in the way she should go.

OPHELIA: I don't want her, I am sure; I have more to do with 'em now than I want to. 110

ST. CLARE: That's you Christians, all over. You'll get up a society, and get some poor missionary to spend all his days among just such heathens; but let me see one of you that would take one into your house with you, and take the labor of their 115 conversion upon yourselves.

OPHELIA: Well, I didn't think of it in that light. It might be a real missionary work. Well, I'll do what I can. [*Advances to TOPSY.*] She's dreadful dirty and shiftless! How old are you, Topsy? 120

TOPSY: Dunno, missis.

OPHELIA: How shiftless! Don't know how old you are? Didn't anybody ever tell you? Who was your mother?

TOPSY: [*Grinning.*] Never had none. 125

OPHELIA: Never had any mother? What do you mean? Where was you born?

TOPSY: Never was born.

OPHELIA: You musn't answer me in that way. I'm not playing with you. Tell me where you was born, and 130 who your father and mother were?

TOPSY: Never was born, tell you; never had no father, nor mother, nor nothin'. I war raised by a speculator, with lots of others. Old Aunt Sue used to take care on us. 135

ST. CLARE: She speaks the truth, cousin. Speculators buy them up cheap, when they are little, and get them raised for the market.

OPHELIA: How long have you lived with your master and mistress? 140

TOPSY: Dunno, missis.

OPHELIA: How shiftless! Is it a year, or more, or less?

TOPSY: Dunno, missis.

ST. CLARE: She does not know what a year is; she don't even know her own age. 145

OPHELIA: Have you heard anything about heaven, Topsy? [*TOPSY looks bewildered and grins.*] Do you know who made you?

TOPSY: Nobody, as I knows on, he, he, he! I spect I growed. Don't think nobody never made me. 150

OPHELIA: The shiftless heathen! What can you do? What did you do for your master and mistress?

---

32 *breakdown*] a fast, shuffling dance.

TOPSY: Fetch water—and wash dishes—and rub knives—and wait on folks—and dance break-downs. 155

OPHELIA: I shall break down, I'm afraid, in trying to make anything of you, you shiftless mortal!

ST. CLARE: You find virgin soil there, cousin; put in your own ideas—you won't find many to pull up. [*Exit, laughing.*] 160

OPHELIA: [*Takes out her handkerchief. A pair of gloves falls. TOPSY picks them up slyly and puts them in her sleeve.*] Follow me, you benighted innocent!

TOPSY: Yes, missis.

As OPHELIA turns her back to her, she seizes the end of the ribbon she wears around her waist, and twitches it off. OPHELIA turns and sees her as she is putting it in her other sleeve. OPHELIA takes ribbon from her.

OPHELIA: What's this? You naughty, wicked girl, you've been stealing this? 165

TOPSY: Laws! Why, that ar's missis' ribbon, a'nt it? How could it got caught in my sleeve?

OPHELIA: Topsy, you naughty girl, don't you tell me a lie—you stole that ribbon! 170

TOPSY: Missis, I declare for't, I didn't—never seed it till dis yer blessed minnit.

OPHELIA: Topsy, don't you know it's wicked to tell lies?

TOPSY: I never tells no lies, missis; it's just de truth I've been telling now and nothing else. 175

OPHELIA: Topsy, I shall have to whip you, if you tell lies so.

TOPSY: Laws missis, if you's to whip all day, couldn't say no other way. I never seed dat ar—it must a got caught in my sleeve. [*Blubbers.*] 180

OPHELIA: [*Seizes her by the shoulders.*] Don't you tell me that again, you barefaced fibber! [*Shakes her. The gloves fall on stage.*] There you, my gloves too—you outrageous young heathen! [*Picks them up.*] Will you tell me, now, you didn't steal the ribbon? 185

TOPSY: No, missis; stole de gloves, but didn't steal de ribbon. It was permiskus.[33]

OPHELIA: Why, you young reprobate! 190

TOPSY: Yes—I's knows I's wicked!

OPHELIA: Then you know you ought to be punished. [*Boxes her ears.*] What do you think of that?

TOPSY: He, he, he! De Lord, missus; dat wouldn't kill a 'skeeter.[34] [*Runs off laughing. OPHELIA follows indignantly.*] 195

SCENE III

The Tavern by the river. Table and chairs. Jug and glasses on table. On flat is a printed placard, headed: "Four Hundred Dollars Reward—Runaway—George Harris!" PHINEAS is discovered, seated at table.

PHINEAS: So yer I am; and a pretty business I've undertook to do. Find the husband of the gal that crossed the river on the ice two or three days ago. Ruth said I must do it, and I'll be teetotally chawed up if I don't do it. I see they've offered a reward for him, dead or alive. How in creation am I to find the varmint? He isn't likely to go round looking natural, with a full description of his hide and figure staring him in the face. [*Enter MR. WILSON.*] I say, stranger how are ye? [*Rises and comes forward.*] 5, 10

WILSON: Well, I reckon.

PHINEAS: Any news? [*Takes out plug and knife.*]

WILSON: Not that I know of.

PHINEAS: [*Cutting a piece of tobacco and offering it.*] Chaw? 15

WILSON: No, thank ye—it don't agree with me.

PHINEAS: Don't, eh? [*Putting it in his own mouth.*] I never felt any the worse for it.

WILSON: [*Sees placard.*] What's that? 20

PHINEAS: Nigger advertised. [*Advances towards it and spits on it.*] There's my mind upon that.

WILSON: Why, now, stranger, what's that for?

PHINEAS: I'd do it all the same to the writer of that ar paper, if he was here. Any man that owns a boy like that, and can't find any better way of treating him, than branding him on the hand with the letter H, as that paper states, *deserves* to lose him. Such papers as this ar' a shame to old Kaintuck! That's my mind right out, if anybody wants to know. 25, 30

---

33 permiskus] promiscuous (in the sense of casual, non-deliberate).

34 skeeter] mosquito.

WILSON: Well, now, that's a fact.

PHINEAS: I used to have a gang of boys, sir—that was before I fell in love—and I just told em:— "Boys," says I, "run now! Dig! put! jest when you want to. I never shall come to look after you!" That's the way I kept mine. Let 'em know they are free to run any time, and it jest stops their wanting to. It stands to reason it should. Treat 'em like men, and you'll have men's work. 35 40

WILSON: I think you are altogether right, friend, and this man described here is a fine fellow—no mistake about that. He worked for me some half dozen years in my bagging factory, and he was my best hand, sir. He is an ingenious fellow, too; he invented a machine for the cleaning of hemp—a really valuable affair; it's gone into use in several factories. His master holds the patent of it. 45

PHINEAS: I'll warrant ye; holds it, and makes money out of it, and then turns round and brands the boy in his right hand! If I had a fair chance, I'd mark him, I reckon, so that he'd carry it *one* while! 50

Enter GEORGE HARRIS, disguised.

GEORGE: [*Speaking as he enters.*] Jim, see to the trunks. [*Sees WILSON.*] Ah! Mr. Wilson here?

WILSON: Bless my soul, can it be? 55

GEORGE: [*Advances and grasps his hand.*] Mr. Wilson, I see you remember me: Mr. Butler, of Oaklands. Shelby county.

WILSON: Ye—yes—yes—sir.

PHINEAS: Holloa! there's a screw loose here some-where. That old gentlemen seems to be struck into a pretty considerable heap of astonishment. May I be teetotally chawed up! if I don't believe that's the identical man I'm arter. [*Crosses to GEORGE.*] How are ye, George Harris? 60 65

GEORGE: [*Starting back and thrusting his hands into his breast.*] You know me?

PHINEAS: Ha, ha, ha! I rather conclude I do; but don't get riled, I an't a bloodhound in disguise.

GEORGE: How did you discover me? 70

PHINEAS: By a teetotal smart guess. You're the very man I want to see. Do you know I was sent after you?

GEORGE: Ah! by my master?

PHINEAS: No; by your wife. 75

GEORGE: My wife! Where is she?

PHINEAS: She's stopping with a Quaker family over on the Ohio side.

GEORGE: Then she is safe?

PHINEAS: Teetotally! 80

GEORGE: Conduct me to her.

PHINEAS: Just wait a brace of shakes and I'll do it. I've got to go and get the boat ready. 'Twon't take me but a minute—make yourself comfortable till I get back. Chaw me up! but this is what I call doing things in short order. [*Exit.*] 85

WILSON: George!

GEORGE: Yes, George!

WILSON: I couldn't have thought it!

GEORGE: I am pretty well disguised, I fancy; you see I don't answer to the advertisement at all. 90

WILSON: George, this is a dangerous game you are playing; I could not have advised you to it.

GEORGE: I can do it on my own responsibility.

WILSON: Well, George, I suppose you're running away—leaving your lawful master, George. I don't wonder at it. At the same time, I'm sorry, George; yes, decidedly. I think I must say that it's my duty to tell you so. 95

GEORGE: Why are you sorry, sir? 100

WILSON: Why to see you, as it were, setting yourself in opposition to the laws of your country.

GEORGE: *My* country! What country have *I*, but the grave? And I would to heaven that I was laid there!

WILSON: George, you've got a hard master, in fact he is … well, he conducts himself reprehensibly. I can't pretend to defend him. I'm sorry for you, now; it's a bad case—very bad; but we must all submit to the indications of providence. George, don't you see? 105 110

GEORGE: I wonder, Mr. Wilson, if the Indians should come and take you a prisoner away from your wife and children, and want to keep you all your life hoeing corn for them, if you'd think it your duty to abide in the condition in which you were called? I rather imagine that you'd think the first stray horse you could find an indication of providence, shouldn't you? 115

WILSON: Really, George, putting the case in that somewhat peculiar light—I don't know—under those circumstances—but that I might. But it 120 seems to me you are running an awful risk. You can't hope to carry it out. If you're taken, it will be worse with you than ever; they'll only abuse you, and half kill you, and sell you down river. 125

GEORGE: Mr. Wilson, I know all this. I *do* run a risk, but—[*Throws open coat and shows pistols and knife in his belt.*] There! I'm ready for them. Down South I never *will* go! No, if it comes to that, I can earn myself at least six feet of free soil—the first and last I shall ever own in Kentucky! 130

WILSON: Why, George, this state of mind is awful—it's getting really desperate. I'm concerned. Going to break the laws of your country?

GEORGE: My country again! Sir, I haven't any 135 country any more than I have any father. I don't want anything of *your* country, except to be left alone—to go peaceably out of it; but if any man tries to stop me, let him take care, for I am desperate. I'll fight for my liberty, to the last breath 140 I breathe! You say your fathers did it; if it was right for them, it is right for me!

WILSON: [*Walking up and down and fanning his face with a large yellow silk handkerchief.*] Blast 'em all! Haven't I always said so—the infernal old cusses! 145 Bless me! I hope I an't swearing now! Well, go ahead, George, go ahead. But be careful, my boy; don't shoot anybody, unless—well, you'd *better* not shoot—at least I wouldn't *hit* anybody, you know.

GEORGE: Only in self-defense. 150

WILSON: Well, well. [*Fumbling in his pocket.*] I suppose, perhaps, I an't following my judgment—Hang it, I *won't* follow my judgment. So here, George. [*Takes out a pocket-book and offers GEORGE a roll of bills.*] 155

GEORGE: No, my kind, good sir, you've done a great deal for me, and this might get you into trouble. I have money enough, I hope, to take me as far as I need it.

WILSON: No; but you must, George. Money is a 160 great help everywhere; can't have too much, if you get it honestly. Take it, *do* take it, *now* do, my boy!

GEORGE: [*Taking the money.*] On condition, sir, that I may repay it at some future time, I will.

WILSON: And now, George, how long are you going 165 to travel in this way? Not long or far I hope? It's well carried on, but too bold.

GEORGE: Mr. Wilson, it is *so bold*, and this tavern is so near, that they will never think of it; they will look for me on ahead, and you yourself wouldn't 170 know me.

WILSON: But the mark on your hand?

GEORGE: That is a parting mark of Mr. Harris's regard. Looks interesting, doesn't it? [*Puts on glove again.*] 175

WILSON: I declare, my very blood runs cold when I think of it—your condition and your risks!

GEORGE: Mine has run cold a good many years; at present, it's about up to the boiling point.

WILSON: George, something has brought you out 180 wonderfully. You hold up your head, and move and speak like another man.

GEORGE: [*Proudly.*] Because I'm a *freeman!* Yes, sir; I've said "master" for the last time to any man. *I'm free!* 185

WILSON: Take care! You are not sure; you may be taken.

GEORGE: All men are free and equal *in the grave*, if it comes to that, Mr. Wilson

Enter PHINEAS.

PHINEAS: Them's my sentiment, to a teetotal atom, 190 and I don't care who knows it! Neighbor, the boat is ready, and the sooner we make tracks the better. I've seen some mysterious strangers lurking about these diggings, so we'd better put.

GEORGE: Farewell, Mr. Wilson, and heaven reward 195 you for the many kindnesses you have shown the poor fugitive!

WILSON: [*Grasping his hand.*] You're a brave fellow, George. I wish in my heart you were safe through, though—that's what I do. 200

PHINEAS: And ain't I the man of all creation to put him through, stranger? Chaw me up if I don't take him to his dear little wife, in the smallest possible quantity of time. Come, neighbor, let's vamose.

GEORGE: Farewell, Mr. Wilson 205

WILSON: My best wishes go with you, George. [*Exit.*]

PHINEAS: You're a trump, old Slow-and-Easy.[35]

GEORGE: [*Looking off.*] Look! look!

---

35 trump] (slang) good man.

PHINEAS: Consarn their picters, here they come! We can't get out of the house without their seeing us. We're teetotally treed! 210

GEORGE: Let us fight our way through them!

PHINEAS: No, that won't do; there are too many of them for a fair fight—we should be chawed up in no time. [*Looks round and sees trap door.*] Holloa! 215 here's a cellar door. Just you step down here a few minutes, while I parley with them. [*Lifts trap.*]

GEORGE: I am resolved to perish sooner than surrender! [*Goes down trap.*]

PHINEAS: That's your sort! [*Closes trap and stands on* 220 *it.*] Here they are!

Enter HALEY, MARKS, LOKER and three Men.

HALEY: Say, stranger, you haven't seen a runaway darkey about these parts, eh?

PHINEAS: What kind of a darkey?

HALEY: A mulatto chap, almost as light- 225 complexioned as a white man.

PHINEAS: Was he a pretty good-looking chap?

HALEY: Yes.

PHINEAS: Kind of tall?

HALEY: Yes. 230

PHINEAS: With brown hair?

HALEY: Yes.

PHINEAS: And dark eyes.

HALEY: Yes.

PHINEAS: Pretty well dressed? 235

HALEY: Yes.

PHINEAS: Scar on his right hand?

HALEY: Yes, yes.

PHINEAS: Well, I ain't seen him.

HALEY: Oh, bother! Come, boys, let's search the 240 house. [*Exeunt.*]

PHINEAS: [*Raises trap.*] Now, then, neighbor George. [*George enters up trap.*] Now's the time to cut your luck.

GEORGE: Follow me, Phineas. [*Exit.*]³⁶ 245

PHINEAS: In a brace of shakes. [*Is closing trap as HALEY, MARKS, LOKER, etc. re-enter.*]

HALEY: Ah! he's down in the cellar. Follow me, boys! [*Thrust PHINEAS aside, and rushes down trap, followed by the others. PHINEAS closes trap and stands on it.*] 250

---

³⁶ *Exit*] i.e., by the door, not the trap.

PHINEAS: Chaw me up! but I've got 'em all in a trap. [*Knocking below.*] Be quiet, you pesky varmints! [*Knocking.*] They're getting mighty oneasy. [*Knocking.*] Will you be quiet, you savagerous critters! [*The trap is forced open. HALEY and MARKS* 255 *appear. PHINEAS seizes a chair and stands over trap—picture.*] Down with you or I'll smash you into apple-fritters! [*Tableau—closed in.*]

SCENE IV

A Plain chamber.

TOPSY: [*Without.*] You go 'long. No more nigger dan you be! [*Enters, shouts and laughter without—looks off.*] You seem to think yourself white folks. You ain't nerry one—black *nor* white. I'd like to be one or turrer. Law! you niggers does you know you's 5 all sinners? Well, you is—everybody is. White folks is sinners too—Miss Feely says so—but I 'spect niggers is the biggest ones. But Lor! ye ain't any on ye up to me. I's so awful wicked there can't nobody do nothin' with me. I used to keep old 10 missis a-swarin' at me ha' de time. I 'spects I's de wickedest critter in de world. [*Song and dance introduced. Enter EVA.*]

EVA: Oh, Topsy! Topsy! you have been very wrong again. 15

TOPSY: Well, I 'spects I have.

EVA: What makes you do so?

TOPSY: I dunno; I 'spects it's cause I's so wicked.

EVA: Why did you spoil Jane's earrings?

TOPSY: 'Cause she's so proud. She called me a little 20 black imp, and turned up her pretty nose at me 'cause she is whiter than I am. I was gwine by her room, and I seed her coral earrings lying on de table, so I threw dem on de floor, and put my foot on 'em, and scrunches 'em all to little bits—he! 25 he! he! I's so wicked.

EVA: Don't you know that was very wrong?

TOPSY: I don't car'! I despises dem what sets up for fine ladies, when dey ain't nothing but cream-colored niggers! Dere's Miss Rosa—she gives me 30 lots of 'pertinent remarks. T'other night she was gwine to a ball. She put on a beau'ful dress dat missis give her—wid her har curled, all nice and pretty. She hab to go down de back stairs—dem

am dark—and I puts a pail of hot water on dem, 35
and she put her foot into it, and den she go
tumbling to de bottom of de stairs, and de water
go all ober her, and spile her dress, and scald her
dreadful bad! He! he! he! I's so wicked!

EVA: Oh! how could you! 40

TOPSY: Don't dey despise me cause I don't know
nothing? Don't dey laugh at me 'cause I'm brack,
and dey ain't?

EVA: But you shouldn't mind them.

TOPSY: Well, I don't mind dem; but when dey are 45
passing under my winder, I trows dirty water on
'em, and dat spiles der complexions.

EVA: What does make you so bad, Topsy? Why won't
you try and be good? Don't you love anybody,
Topsy? 50

TOPSY: Can't recommember.

EVA: But you love your father and mother?

TOPSY: Never had none, ye know, I telled ye that,
Miss Eva.

EVA: Oh! I know; but hadn't you any brother, or 55
sister, or aunt, or—

TOPSY: No, none on 'em—never had nothing nor
nobody. I's brack—no one loves me!

EVA: Oh! Topsy, I love you! [*Laying her hand on
TOPSY's shoulder.*] I love you because you haven't 60
had any father, or mother, or friends. I love you, I
want you to be good. I wish you would try to be
good for my sake. [*TOPSY looks astonished for a
moment, and then bursts into tears.*] Only think of
it, Topsy—*you* can be one of those spirits bright 65
Uncle Tom sings about!

TOPSY: Oh! dear Miss Eva—dear Miss Eva! I will try—
I will try. I never did care nothin' about it before.

EVA: If you try, you will succeed. Come with me.
[*Crosses and takes TOPSY's hand.*] 70

TOPSY: I will try; but den, I's so wicked! [*Exit EVA
followed by TOPSY, crying.*]

SCENE V

Chamber. Enter GEORGE, ELIZA, and HARRY.

GEORGE: At length, Eliza, after many wanderings,
we are united.

ELIZA: Thanks to these generous Quakers, who have
so kindly sheltered us.

GEORGE: Not forgetting our friend Phineas. 5

ELIZA: I do indeed owe him much. 'Twas he I met
upon the icy river's bank, after that fearful, but
successful attempt, when I fled from the slave-
trader with my child in my arms.

GEORGE: It seems almost incredible that you could 10
have crossed the river on the ice.

ELIZA: Yes, I did. Heaven helping me, I crossed on
the ice, for they were behind me—right behind—
and there was no other way.

GEORGE: But the ice was all in broken-up blocks, 15
swinging and heaving up and down in the water.

ELIZA: I know it was—I know it; I did not think I
should get over, but I did not care—I could but
die if I did not! I leaped on the ice, but how I got
across I don't know; the first I remember, a man 20
was helping me up the bank—that man was
Phineas.

GEORGE: My brave girl! you deserve your freedom—
you have richly earned it!

ELIZA: And when we get to Canada I can help you 25
to work, and between us we can find something
to live on.

GEORGE: Yes, Eliza, so long as we have each other,
and our boy. Oh, Eliza, if these people only knew
what a blessing it is for a man to feel that his wife 30
and child belong to *him!* I've often wondered to
see men that could call their wives and children
their own, fretting and worrying about anything
else. Why, I feel rich and strong, though we have
nothing but our bare hands. If they will only let 35
me alone now, I will be satisfied—thankful!

ELIZA: But we are not quite out of danger; we are
not yet in Canada.

GEORGE: True, but it seems as if I smelt the free air,
and it makes me strong! 40

Enter PHINEAS, dressed as a Quaker.

PHINEAS: [*With a snuffle.*] Verily, friends, how is it
with thee?—hum!

GEORGE: Why, Phineas, what means this metamor-
phosis?

PHINEAS: I've become a Quaker, that's the meaning 45
on't.

GEORGE: What—you?

PHINEAS: Teetotally! I was driven to it by a strong

argument, composed of a pair of sparkling eyes, rosy cheeks, and pouting lips. Them lips would persuade a man to assassinate his grandmother! [*Assumes the Quaker tone again.*] Verily, George, I have discovered something of importance to the interests of thee and thy party, and it were well for thee to hear it.

GEORGE: Keep us not in suspense!

PHINEAS: Well, after I left you on the road, I stopped at a little, lone tavern, just below here. Well, I was tired with hard driving, and after my supper I stretched myself down on a pile of bags in the corner, and pulled a buffalo hide over me—and what does I do but get fast asleep.

GEORGE: With one ear open, Phineas?

PHINEAS: No, I slept ears and all for an hour or two, for I was pretty well tired; but when I came to myself a little, I found that there were some men in the room, sitting round a table, drinking and talking; and I thought, before I made much muster, I'd just see what they were up to, especially as I heard them say something about the Quakers. Then I listened with both ears and found they were talking about you. So I kept quiet, and heard them lay off all their plans. They've got a right notion of the track we are going to-night, and they'll be down after us, six or eight strong. So, now, what's to be done?

ELIZA: What *shall* we do, George?

GEORGE: I know what I shall do! [*Takes out pistols.*]

PHINEAS: Ay-ay, thou seest, Eliza, how it will work—pistols—phitz—poppers!

ELIZA: I see; but I pray it come not to that!

GEORGE: I don't want to involve any one with or for me. If you will lend me your vehicle, and direct me, I will drive alone to the next stand.

PHINEAS: Ah! well, friend, but thee'll need a driver for all that. Thee's quite welcome to do all the fighting thee knows; but I know a thing or two about the road that thee doesn't.

GEORGE: But I don't want to involve you.

PHINEAS: Involve me! Why, chaw me—that is to say—when thee does involve me, please to let me know.

ELIZA: Phineas is a wise and skillful man. You will do well, George, to abide by his judgment. And,

oh! George, be not hasty with these—young blood is hot! [*Laying her hand on pistols.*]

GEORGE: I will attack no man. All I ask of this country is to be left alone, and I will go out peaceably. But I'll fight to the last breath before they shall take from me my wife and son! Can you blame me?

PHINEAS: Mortal man cannot blame thee, neighbor George! Flesh and blood could not do otherwise. Woe unto the world because of offenses, but woe unto them through whom the offense cometh! That's gospel, teetotally!

GEORGE: Would not even you, sir, do the same, in my place?

PHINEAS: I pray that I be not tried; the flesh is weak—but I think my flesh would be pretty tolerably strong in such a case; I ain't sure, friend George, that I shouldn't hold a fellow for thee, if thee had any accounts to settle with him.

ELIZA: Heaven grant we be not tempted.

PHINEAS: But if we are tempted too much, why, consarn 'em! let them look out, that's all.

GEORGE: It's quite plain you was not born for a Quaker. The old nature has its way in you pretty strong yet.

PHINEAS: Well, I reckon you are pretty teetotally right.

GEORGE: Had we not better hasten our flight?

PHINEAS: Well, I rather conclude we had; we're full two hours ahead of them, if they start at the time they planned; so let's vamose. [*Exeunt.*]

SCENE VI

A Rocky Pass in the Hills. Large set rock and platform.

PHINEAS: [*Without.*] Out with you in a twinkling, every one, and up into these rocks with me! run *now*, if you *ever* did run! [*Music, PHINEAS enters, with HARRY in his arms. GEORGE supporting ELIZA.*] Come up here; this is one of our old hunting dens. Come up. [*They ascend the rock.*] Well, here we are. Let 'em get us if they can. Whoever comes here has to walk single file between those two rocks, in fair range of your pistols—d'ye see?

GEORGE: I do see. And now, as this affair is mine, let me take all the risk, and do all the fighting.

PHINEAS: Thee's quite welcome to do the fighting, George; but I may have the fun of looking on, I suppose. But see, these fellows are kind of debating down there, and looking up, like hens when they are going to fly up onto the roost. Hadn't thee better give 'em a word of advice, before they come up, just to tell 'em handsomely they'll be shot if they do.

LOKER, MARKS, and three Men enter.

MARKS: Well, Tom, your coons are fairly treed.

LOKER: Yes, I see 'em go up right here; and here's a path—I'm for going right up. They can't jump down in a hurry, and it won't take long to ferret 'em out.

MARKS: But, Tom, they might fire at us from behind the rocks. That would be ugly, you know.

LOKER: Ugh! Always for saving your skin, Marks. No danger, niggers are too plaguy scared!

MARKS: I don't know why I shouldn't save my skin, it's the best I've got; and niggers do fight like the devil sometimes.

GEORGE: [*Rising on the rock.*] Gentlemen, who are you down there and what do you want?

LOKER: We want a party of runaway niggers. One George and Eliza Harris, and their son. We've got the officers here, and a warrant to take 'em too. D'ye hear? An't you George Harris, that belonged to Mr. Harris, of Shelby county, Kentucky?

GEORGE: I am George Harris. A Mr. Harris, of Kentucky, did call me his property. But now I'm a freeman, standing on heaven's free soil! My wife and child I claim as mine. We have arms to defend ourselves and we mean to do it. You can come up if you like, but the first one that comes within range of our bullets is a dead man!

MARKS: Oh, come—come, young man, this ar no kind of talk at all for you. You see we're officers of justice. We've got the law on our side, and the power and so forth; so you'd better give up peaceably, you see—for you'll certainly have to give up at last.

GEORGE: I know very well that you've got the law on your side, and the power; but you haven't got us. We are standing here as free as you are, and by the great power that made us, we'll fight for our

liberty till we die! [*During this MARKS draws a pistol, and when he concludes fires at him. ELIZA screams.*] It's nothing, Eliza; I am unhurt.

PHINEAS: [*Drawing GEORGE down.*] Thee'd better keep out of sight with thy speechifying; they're teetotal mean scamps.

LOKER: What did you do that for, Marks?

MARKS: You see, you get jist as much for him dead as alive in Kentucky.

GEORGE: Now, Phineas, the first man that advances I fire at; you take the second and so on. It won't do to waste two shots on one.

PHINEAS: But what if you don't hit?

GEORGE: I'll try my best.

PHINEAS: Creation! chaw me up if there a'nt stuff in you!

MARKS: I think I must have hit some on'em. I heard a squeal.

LOKER: I'm going right up for one. I never was afraid of niggers, and I an't a going to be now. Who goes after me?

Music. LOKER dashes up the rock. GEORGE fires. He staggers for a moment, then springs to the top. PHINEAS seizes him. A struggle.

PHINEAS: Friend, thee is not wanted here! [*Throws LOKER over the rock.*]

MARKS: [*Retreating.*] Lord help us—they're perfect devils!

Music. MARKS and Party run off. GEORGE and ELIZA kneel in an attitude of thanksgiving, with the Child between them. PHINEAS stands over them exulting. Tableau.

ACT III

SCENE I

Chamber. Enter ST. CLARE, followed by TOM.

ST. CLARE: [*Giving money and papers to TOM.*] There, Tom, are the bills, and the money to liquidate them.

TOM: Yes, mas'r.

ST. CLARE: Well, Tom, what are you waiting for? Isn't all right there?

TOM: I'm 'fraid not, mas'r.

ST. CLARE: Why, Tom, what's the matter? You look as solemn as a judge.

TOM: I feel very bad, mas'r. I allays have thought that mas'r would be good to everybody.

ST. CLARE: Well, Tom, haven't I been? come, now, what do you want? There's something you haven't got, I suppose, and this is the preface.

TOM: Mas'r allays been good to me. I haven't nothing to complain of on that head; but there is one that mas'r isn't good to.

ST. CLARE: Why, Tom what's got into you? Speak out—what do you mean?

TOM: Last night, between one and two, I thought so. I studied upon the matter then—mas'r isn't good to *himself*.

ST. CLARE: Ah! now I understand; you allude to the state in which I came home last night. Well, to tell the truth, I *was* slightly elevated—a little more champagne on board than I could comfortably carry. That's all, isn't it?

TOM: [*Deeply affected—clasping his hands and weeping.*] All! Oh, my dear young mas'r, I'm 'fraid it will be *loss of all—all*, body and soul. The good book says "it biteth like a serpent and stingeth like an adder," my dear mas'r.[37]

ST. CLARE: You poor, silly fool! I'm not worth crying over.

TOM: Oh, mas'r! I implore you to think of it before it gets too late.

ST. CLARE: Well, I won't go to any more of their cursed nonsense, Tom—on my honor, I won't. I don't know why I haven't stopped long ago; I've always despised *it*, and myself for it. So now, Tom, wipe up your eyes and go about your errands.

TOM: Bless you, mas'r. I feel much better now. You have taken a load from poor Tom's heart. Bless you!

ST. CLARE: Come, come, no blessings; I'm not so wonderfully good, now. There, I'll pledge my honor to you, Tom, you don't see me so again. [*Exit TOM.*] I'll keep my faith with him, too.

OPHELIA: [*Without.*] Come along, you shiftless mortal!

ST. CLARE: What new witchcraft has Topsy been brewing? That commotion is of her raising, I'll be bound.

Enter OPHELIA, dragging in TOPSY.

OPHELIA: Come here now; I will tell your master.

ST. CLARE: What's the matter now?

OPHELIA: The matter is that I cannot be plagued with this girl any longer. It's past all bearing; flesh and blood cannot endure it. Here I locked her up and gave her a hymn to study; and what does she do but spy out where I put my key, and has gone to my bureau, and got a bonnet-trimming and cut it all to pieces to make dolls' jackets! I never saw anything like it in my life!

ST. CLARE: What have you done to her?

OPHELIA: What have I done? What haven't I done? Your wife says I ought to have her whipped till she couldn't stand.

ST. CLARE: I don't doubt it. Tell me of the lovely rule of woman. I never saw above a dozen women that wouldn't half kill a horse or servant, either, if they had their own way with them—let alone a man.

OPHELIA: I am sure, St. Clare, I don't know what to do. I've taught and taught—I've talked till I'm tired; I've whipped her, I've punished her in every way I could think of, and still she's just what she was at first.

ST. CLARE: Come here, Tops, you monkey! [*TOPSY crosses to ST. CLARE, grinning.*] What makes you behave so?

TOPSY: 'Spects it's my wicked heart—Miss Feely says so.

ST. CLARE: Don't you see how much Miss Ophelia has done for you? She says she has done everything she can think of.

TOPSY: Lord, yes, mas'r! old missis used to say so, too. She whipped me a heap harder, and used to pull my ha'r, and knock my head agin the door; but it didn't do me no good. I 'spects if they's to pull every spear of ha'r out o' my head, it wouldn't do no good neither—I's so wicked! Laws! I's nothin' but a nigger, no ways! [*Goes up.*]

OPHELIA: Well, I shall have to give her up; I can't have that trouble any longer.

ST. CLARE: I'd like to ask one question.

---

[37] it biteth … adder] Proverbs 23:31–32.

OPHELIA: What is it?

ST. CLARE: Why, if your doctrine is not strong enough to save one heathen child, that you can have at home here, all to yourself, what's the use of sending one or two poor missionaries off with it among thousands of just such? I suppose this girl is a fair sample of what thousands of your heathen are. 95 100

OPHELIA: I'm sure I don't know; I never saw such a girl as this.

ST. CLARE: What makes you so bad, Tops? Why won't you try and be good? Don't you love any one, Topsy? 105

TOPSY: [*Comes down.*] Dunno nothing 'bout love; I loves candy and sich, that's all.

OPHELIA: But, Topsy, if you'd only try to be good, you might.

TOPSY: Couldn't never be nothing but a nigger, if I was ever so good. If I could be skinned and come white, I'd try then. 110

ST. CLARE: People can love you, if you are black, Topsy. Miss Ophelia would love you, if you were good. [*TOPSY laughs.*] Don't you think so? 115

TOPSY: No, she can't b'ar me, 'cause I'm a nigger— she'd's soon have a toad touch her. There can't nobody love niggers, and niggers can't do nothin'! I don't car'! [*Whistles.*]

ST. CLARE: Silence, you incorrigible imp, and begone! 120

TOPSY: He! he! he! didn't get much out of dis chile! [*Exit.*]

OPHELIA: I've always had a prejudice against negroes, and it's a fact—I never could bear to have that child touch me, but I didn't think she knew it. 125

ST. CLARE: Trust any child to find that out, there's no keeping it from them. but I believe all the trying in the world to benefit a child, and all the substantial favors you can do them, will never excite one emotion of gratitude, while that feeling of repugnance remains in the heart. It's a queer kind of a fact, but so it is. 130

OPHELIA: I don't know how I can help it—they are disagreeable to me, this girl in particular. How can I help feeling so? 135

ST. CLARE: Eva does, it seems.

OPHELIA: Well, she's so loving. I wish I was like her. She might teach me a lesson.

ST. CLARE: It would not be the first time a little child has been used to instruct an old disciple, if it were so.[38] Come, let us seek Eva, in her favorite bower by the lake. 140

OPHELIA: Why, the dew is falling, she musn't be out there. She is unwell, I know. 145

ST. CLARE: Don't be croaking, cousin—I hate it.

OPHELIA: But she has that cough.

ST. CLARE: Oh, nonsense, of that cough—it is not anything. She has taken a little cold, perhaps.

OPHELIA: Well, that was just the way Eliza Jane was taken—and Ellen— 150

ST. CLARE: Oh, stop these hobgoblin, nurse legends. You old hands get so wise, that a child cannot cough or sneeze, but you see desperation and ruin at hand. Only take care of the child, keep her from the night air, and don't let her play too hard, and she'll do well enough. [*Exeunt.*] 155

SCENE II

The flat represents the lake. The rays of the setting sun tinge the waters with gold. A large tree. Beneath this a grassy bank, on which EVA and TOM are seated side by side. EVA has a Bible open on her lap. Music.

TOM: Read dat passage again, please, Miss Eva?

EVA: [*Reading.*] "And I saw a sea of glass, mingled with fire."[39] [*Stopping suddenly and pointing to lake.*] Tom, there it is!

TOM: What, Miss Eva? 5

EVA: Don't you see there? There's a "sea of glass mingled with fire."

TOM: True enough, Miss Eva. [*Sings.*]

Oh, had I the wings of the morning,
I'd fly away to Canaan's shore; 10
Bright angels should convey me home,
To the New Jerusalem.[40]

EVA: Where do you suppose New Jerusalem is, Uncle Tom?

TOM: Oh, up in the clouds, Miss Eva. 15

EVA: Then I think I see it. Look in those clouds, they

---

38 child … disciple] Matthew 18:1–5.
39 And I saw … fire] Revelations 15:2.
40 from an old Methodist hymn, "The Wings of the Morning."

look like great gates of pearl; and you can see
beyond them—far, far off—it's all gold! Tom, sing
about "spirits bright."

TOM: [*Sings.*]

    I see a band of spirits bright,　　　　20
    That taste the glories there;
    They are all robed in spotless white,
    And conquering palms they bear.

EVA: Uncle Tom, I've seem *them*.

TOM: To be sure you have, you are one of them　　25
yourself. You are the brightest spirit I ever saw.

EVA: They come to me sometimes in my sleep—
those spirits bright—

    They are all robed in spotless white,
    And conquering palms they bear.　　　30
Uncle Tom, I'm going there.

TOM: Where, Miss Eva?

EVA: [*Pointing to the sky.*] I'm going *there*, to the
spirits bright, Tom; I'm going before long.

TOM: It's jest no use tryin' to keep Miss Eva here;　　35
I've allays said so. She's got the Lord's mark in her
forehead. She wasn't never like a child that's to
live—there was always something deep in her eyes.
[*Rises and comes forward. EVA also comes forward,
leaving Bible on bank.*]　　　　　　40

Enter ST. CLARE.

ST. CLARE: Ah! my little pussy, you look as blooming
as a rose! You are better now-a-days, are you not?

EVA: Papa, I've had things I wanted to say to you a
great while. I want to say them now, before I get
weaker.　　　　　　45

ST. CLARE: Nay, this is an idle fear, Eva; you know
you grow stronger every day.

EVA: It's all no use, papa, to keep it to myself any
longer. The time is coming that I am going to leave
you, I am going, and never to come back.　　50

ST. CLARE: Oh, now, my dear little Eva! you've got
nervous and low spirited; you mustn't indulge such
gloomy thoughts.

EVA: No, papa, don't deceive yourself, I am *not* any
better; I know it perfectly well, and I am going　　55
before long. I am not nervous—I am not low
spirited. If it were not for you, papa, and my
friends, I should be perfectly happy. I want to go—
I long to go!

ST. CLARE: Why, dear child, what has made your　　60
poor little heart so sad? You have everything to
make you happy that could be given you.

EVA: I had rather be in heaven! There are a great
many things here that makes me sad—that seem
dreadful to me; I had rather be there; but I don't　　65
want to leave you—it almost breaks my heart!

ST. CLARE: What makes you sad, and what seems
dreadful, Eva?

EVA: I feel sad for our poor people; they love me
dearly, and they are all good and kind to me. I　　70
wish, papa, they were all *free!*

ST. CLARE: Why, Eva, child, don't you think they are
well enough off now?

EVA: [*Not heeding the question.*] Papa, isn't there a way
to have slaves made free? When I am dead, papa,　　75
then you will think of me and do it for my sake?

ST. CLARE: When you are dead, Eva? Oh, child, don't
talk to me so. You are all I have on earth!

EVA: Papa, these poor creatures love their children
as much as you do me. Tom loves his children. Oh,　　80
do something for them!

ST. CLARE: There, there, darling; only don't distress
yourself, and don't talk of dying, and I will do
anything you wish.

EVA: And promise me, dear father, that Tom shall　　85
have his freedom as soon as—[*Hesitating.*]—I am
gone!

ST. CLARE: Yes, dear, I will do anything in the
world—anything you could ask me to. There,
Tom, take her to her chamber, this evening air is　　90
too chill for her. [*Music. Kisses her. TOM takes EVA
in his arms, and exits. Gazing mournfully after EVA.*]
Has there ever been a child like Eva? Yes, there has
been; but their names are always on grave-stones,
and their sweet smiles, their heavenly eyes, their　　95
singular words and ways, are among the buried
treasures of yearning hearts. It is as if heaven had
an especial band of angels, whose office it is to
sojourn for a season here, and endear to them the
wayward human heart, that they might bear it　　100
upward with them in their homeward flight. When
you see that deep, spiritual light in the eye when
the little soul reveals itself in words sweeter and
wiser than the ordinary words of children, hope
not to retain that child; for the seal of heaven is　　105

on it, and the light of immortality looks out from its eyes! [*Music. Exit.*]

SCENE III

A corridor. Proscenium doors on. Music.
Enter TOM, he listens at door and then lies down.
Enter OPHELIA, with candle.

OPHELIA: Uncle Tom, what alive have you taken to sleeping anywhere and everywhere, like a dog, for? I thought you were one of the orderly sort, that liked to lie in bed in a Christian way.

TOM: [*Rises. Mysteriously.*] I do, Miss Feely, I do, but now—   5

OPHELIA: Well, what now?

TOM: We mustn't speak loud; Mas'r St. Clare won't hear on't; but Miss Feely, you know there must be somebody watchin' for the bridegroom.   10

OPHELIA: What do you mean, Tom?

TOM: You know it says in Scripture, "At midnight there was a great cry made, behold, the bridegroom cometh!"[41] That's what I'm spectin' now, every night, Miss Feely, and I couldn't sleep out of hearing, noways.   15

OPHELIA: Why, Uncle Tom, what makes you think so?

TOM: Miss Eva, she talks to me. The Lord, he sends his messenger in the soul. I must be thar, Miss Feely; for when that ar blessed child goes into the kingdom, they'll open the door so wide, we'll all get a look in at the glory!   20

OPHELIA: Uncle Tom, did Miss Eva say she felt more unwell than usual tonight?   25

TOM: No; but she told me she was coming nearer—thar's them that tells it to the child, Miss Feely. It's the angels—it's the trumpet sound afore the break o' day!

OPHELIA: Heaven grant your fears be vain! Come in, Tom [*Exeunt.*]   30

SCENE IV

EVA's Chamber. EVA discovered on a couch.
A table stands near the couch with a lamp on it.
The light shines upon EVA's face, which is very pale.
Scene half dark. UNCLE TOM is kneeling near the
foot of the couch, OPHELIA stands at the head,
ST. CLARE at back. Scene opens to plaintive music.
After a strain enter MARIE, hastily.

MARIE: St. Clare! Cousin! Oh! what is the matter now?

ST. CLARE: [*Hoarsely.*] Hush! she is dying!

MARIE: [*Sinking on her knees, beside TOM.*] Dying!   5

ST. CLARE: Oh! if she would only wake and speak once more. [*Bending over EVA.*] Eva, darling! [*EVA uncloses her eyes, smiles, raises her head, and tries to speak.*] Do you know me, Eva?

EVA: [*Throwing her arms feebly about his neck.*] Dear papa. [*Her arms drop and she sinks back.*]   10

ST. CLARE: Oh heaven! this is dreadful! Oh! Tom, my boy, it is killing me!

TOM: Look at her, mas'r. [*Points to EVA.*]

ST. CLARE: [*A pause.*] She does not hear. Oh Eva! tell us what you see. What is it?   15

EVA: [*Feebly smiling.*] Oh! love! joy! peace! [*Dies.*]

TOM: Oh! bless the Lord! it's over, dear mas'r, it's over.

ST. CLARE: [*Sinking on his knees.*] Farewell, beloved child! the bright eternal doors have closed after thee. We shall see thy sweet face no more. Oh! woe   20 for them who watched thy entrance into heaven when they shall wake and find only the cold, gray sky of daily life and thou gone forever. [*Solemn music, slow curtain.*]

ACT IV

SCENE I

A street in New Orleans. Enter GUMPTION CUTE,
meeting MARKS.

CUTE: How do ye dew?

MARKS: How are you?

CUTE: Well, now, squire, it's a fact that I am dead broke and busted up.

MARKS: You have been speculating, I suppose!   5

CUTE: That's just it and nothing shorter.

---

41 At midnight … cometh] from the parable of the Wise and Foolish Virgins (Matthew 24:1–13).

MARKS: You have had poor success, you say?

CUTE: Tarnation, bad, now I tell you. You see I came to this part of the country to make my fortune.

MARKS: And you did not do it?

CUTE: Scarcely. The first thing I tried my hand at was keeping school. I opened an academy for the instruction of youth in the various branches of orthography, geography, and other graphies.

MARKS: Did you succeed in getting any pupils?

CUTE: Oh, lots on 'em! and a pretty set of dunces they were too. After the first quarter, I called on the repectable parents of the juveniles, and requested them to fork over. To which they politely answered—don't you wish you may get it?

MARKS: Why did you do then?

CUTE: Well, I kind of pulled up stakes and left those diggins. Well then I went into Spiritual Rappings for a living.[42] That paid pretty well for a short time, till I met with an accident.

MARKS: An accident?

CUTE: Yes; a tall Yahoo called on me one day, and wanted me to summon the spirit of his mother— which, of course, I did.[43] He asked me about a dozen questions which I answered to his satisfaction. At last he wanted to know what she died of—I said, Cholera. You never did see a critter so riled as he was. "Look yere, stranger," said he, "it's my opinion that you're a pesky humbug! for my mother was blown up in a *Steamboat!*" With that he left the premises. The next day the people furnished me with a conveyance, and I rode out of town.

MARKS: Rode out of town?

CUTE: Yes; on a rail!

MARKS: I suppose you gave up the spirits, after that?

CUTE: Well, I reckon I did; it had such an effect on my spirits.

MARKS: It's a wonder they didn't tar and feather you.

CUTE: There was some mention made of that, but when they said *feathers*, I felt as if I had wings, and flew away.

MARKS: You cut and run?

CUTE: Yes; I didn't like their company and I cut it. Well, after that I let myself out as an overseer on a cotton plantation. I made a pretty good thing of that, though it was dreadful trying to my feelings to flog the darkies; but I got used to it after a while, and then I used to lather 'em like Jehu.[44] Well, the proprietor got the fever and ague and shook himself out of town. The place and all the fixings were sold at auction and I found myself adrift once more.

MARKS: What are you doing at present?

CUTE: I'm in search of a rich relation of mine.

MARKS: A rich relation?

CUTE: Yes, a Miss Ophelia St. Clare. You see, a niece of hers married one of my second cousins—that's how I came to be a relation of hers. She came on here from Vermont to be housekeeper to a cousin of hers, of the same name.

MARKS: I know him well.

CUTE: The deuce you do!—well, that's lucky.

MARKS: Yes, he lives in this city.

CUTE: Say, you just point out the locality, and I'll give him a call.

MARKS: Stop a bit. Suppose you shouldn't be able to raise the wind in that quarter, what have you thought of doing?

CUTE: Well, nothing particular.

MARKS: How should you like to enter into a nice, profitable business—one that pays well?

CUTE: That's just about my measure—it would suit me to a hair. What is it?

MARKS: Nigger catching.

CUTE: Catching niggers! What on airth do you mean?

MARKS: Why, when there's a large reward offered for a runaway darkey, we goes after him, catches him, and gets the reward.

CUTE: Yes, that's all right so far—but s'pose there ain't no reward offered?

MARKS: Why, then we catches the darkey on our own account, sells him, and pockets the proceeds.

---

42 Spiritual Rappings] i.e., spiritualist seances at which the dead are allegedly contacted and communicate by rapping on the table.

43 Yahoo] a human being of bestial type (from Swift's *Gulliver's Travels*).

44 Jehu] a legendary charioteer who drove his horses hard.

CUTE: By chowder, that ain't a bad speculation!

MARKS: What do you say? I want a partner. You see, I lost my partner last year, up in Ohio—he was a powerful fellow. 90

CUTE: Lost him! How did you lose him?

MARKS: Well, you see, Tom and I—his name was Tom Loker—Tom and I were after a mulatto chap, called George Harris, that run away from Kentucky. We traced him though the greater part of Ohio, and come up with him near the Pennsylvania line. He took refuge among some rocks, and showed fight. 95 100

CUTE: Oh! then runaway darkies show fight, do they?

MARKS: Sometimes. Well, Tom—like a headstrong fool as he was—rushed up the rocks, and a Quaker chap, who was helping this George Harris, threw him over the cliff. 105

CUTE: Was he killed?

MARKS: Well, I didn't stop to find out. Seeing that the darkies were stronger than I thought, I made tracks for a safe place. 110

CUTE: And what became of this George Harris?

MARKS: Oh! he and his wife and child got away safe into Canada. You see, they will get away sometimes though it isn't very often. Now what do you say? You are just the figure for a fighting partner. Is it a bargain? 115

CUTE: Well, I rather calculate our teams won't hitch, no how. By chowder, I hain't no idea of setting myself up as a target for darkies to fire at—that's a speculation that don't suit my constitution. 120

MARKS: You're afraid, then?

CUTE: No, I ain't, it's against my principles.

MARKS: Your principles—how so?

CUTE: Because my principles are to keep a sharp lookout for No. 1. I shouldn't feel wholesome if a darkie was to throw me over that cliff to look after Tom Loker. [*Exeunt arm-in-arm.*] 125

SCENE II

Gothic Chamber. Slow music. ST. CLARE discovered, seated on sofa. TOM at left.

ST. CLARE: Oh! Tom, my boy, the whole world is as empty as an egg shell.

TOM: I know it, mas'r, I know it. But oh! if mas'r could look up—up where our dear Miss Eva is—

ST. CLARE: Ah, Tom! I do look up; but the trouble is, I don't see anything when I do. I wish I could. It seems to be given to children and poor, honest fellows like you, to see what we cannot. How comes it? 5

TOM: Thou hast hid from the wise and prudent, and revealed unto babes; even so, Father, for so it seemed good in thy sight. 10

ST. CLARE: Tom, I don't believe—I've got the habit of doubting—I want to believe and I cannot.

TOM: Dear mas'r, pray to the good Lord: "Lord, I believe; help thou my unbelief." 15

ST. CLARE: Who knows anything about anything? Was all that beautiful love and faith only one of the ever-shifting phases of human feeling, having nothing real to rest on, passing away with the little breath? And is there no more Eva—nothing? 20

TOM: Oh! dear mas'r, there is. I know it; I'm sure of it. Do, do, dear mas'r, believe it!

ST. CLARE: How do you know there is, Tom? You never saw the Lord. 25

TOM: Felt Him in my soul, mas'r—feel Him now! Oh, mas'r! when I was sold away from my old woman and the children, I was jest a'most broken up—I felt as if there warn't nothing left—and then the Lord stood by me, and He says, "Fear not, Tom," and He brings light and joy into a poor fellow's soul—makes all peace; and I's so happy, and loves everybody, and feels willin' to be jest where the Lord wants to put me. I know it couldn't come from me, 'cause I's a poor, complaining creature—it comes from above, and I know He's willin' to do for mas'r. 30 35

ST. CLARE: [*Grasping TOM's hand.*] Tom, you love me!

TOM: I's willin' to lay down my life this blessed day for you. 40

ST. CLARE: [*Sadly.*] Poor, foolish fellow! I'm not worth the love of one good, honest heart like yours.

TOM: Oh, mas'r! there's more than me loves you— the blessed Saviour loves you. 45

ST. CLARE: How do you know that, Tom?

TOM: The love of the Saviour passeth knowledge.

ST. CLARE: [*Turns away.*] Singular! that the story of a man who lived and died eighteen hundred years ago can affect people so yet. But He was no man. [*Rises.*] No man ever had such long and living power. Oh! that I could believe what my mother taught me, and pray as I did when I was a boy! But, Tom, all this time I have forgotten why I sent for you. I'm going to make a freeman of you so have your trunk packed, and get ready to set out for Kentucky.

TOM: [*Joyfully.*] Bless the Lord!

ST. CLARE: [*Dryly.*] You haven't had such very bad times here, that you need be in such a rapture, Tom.

TOM: No, no, mas'r, 'tain't that; it's being a *freeman*—that's what I'm joyin' for.

ST. CLARE: Why, Tom, don't you think, for your own part, you've been better off than to be free?

TOM: No, *indeed*, Mas'r St. Clare—no, indeed!

ST. CLARE: Why, Tom, you couldn't possibly have earned, by your work, such clothes and such living as I have given you.

TOM: I know all that, Mas'r St. Clare—mas'r's been too good; but I'd rather have poor clothes, poor house, poor everything, and have 'em *mine*, than have the best, if they belong to somebody else. I had *so*, mas'r; I think it's natur', mas'r.

ST. CLARE: I suppose so, Tom; and you'll be going off and leaving me in a month or so—though why you shouldn't no mortal knows.

TOM: Not while mas'r is in trouble. I'll stay with mas'r as long as he wants me, so as I can be any use.

ST. CLARE: [*Sadly.*] Not while I'm in trouble, Tom? And when will my trouble be over?

TOM: When you are a believer.

ST. CLARE: And you really mean to stay by me till that day comes? [*Smiling and laying his hand on TOM's shoulder.*] Ah, Tom! I won't keep you till that day. Go home to your wife and children, and give my love to all.

TOM: I's faith to think that day will come—the Lord has a work for mas'r.

ST. CLARE: A work, hey? Well, now, Tom, give me your views on what sort of a work it is—let's hear.

TOM: Why, even a poor fellow like me has a work; and Mas'r St. Clare, that has larnin', and riches, and friends, how much he might do for the Lord.

ST. CLARE: Tom, you seem to think the Lord needs a great deal done for him.

TOM: We does for him when we does for his creatures.

ST. CLARE: Good theology, Tom. Thank you, my boy; I like to hear you talk. But go now, Tom, and leave me alone. [*Exit TOM.*] That faithful fellow's words have excited a train of thoughts that almost bear me, on the strong tide of faith and feeling, to the gates of that heaven I so vividly conceive. They seem to bring me nearer to Eva.

OPHELIA: [*Outside.*] What are you doing there, you limb of Satan? You've been stealing something, I'll be bound.

OPHELIA drags in TOPSY.

TOPSY: You go 'long, Miss Feely, 'tain't none o' your business.

ST. CLARE: Heyday! what is all this commotion?

OPHELIA: She's been stealing.

TOPSY: [*Sobbing.*] I hain't neither.

OPHELIA: What have you got in your bosom?

TOPSY: I've got my hand dar.

OPHELIA: But what have you got in your hand?

TOPSY: Nuffin'.

OPHELIA: That's a fib, Topsy.

TOPSY: Well, I 'spects it is.

OPHELIA: Give it to me, whatever it is.

TOPSY: It's mine—I hope I may die this bressed minute, if it don't belong to me.

OPHELIA: Topsy, I order you to give me that article; don't let me have to ask you again. [*TOPSY reluctantly takes the foot of an old stocking from her bosom and hands it to OPHELIA.*] Sakes alive! what is all this? [*Takes from it a lock of hair, and a small book, with a bit of crape twisted around it.*]

TOPSY: Dat's a lock of ha'r dat Miss Eva give me—she cut if from her own beau'ful head herself.

ST. CLARE: [*Takes book.*] Why did you wrap *this* [*pointing to crape*] around the book?

TOPSY: 'Cause—'cause—'cause 'twas Miss Eva's. Oh! don't take 'em away, please! [*Sits down on stage, and, putting her apron over her head, begins to sob vehemently.*]

OPHELIA: Come, come, don't cry; you shall have them. 140

TOPSY: [*Jumps up joyfully and takes them.*] I wants to keep 'em, 'cause dey makes me good; I ain't half so wicked as I used to was. [*Runs off.*]

ST. CLARE: I really think you can make something of that girl. Any mind that is capable of a *real* 145 *sorrow* is capable of good. You must try and do something with her.

OPHELIA: The child has improved very much; I have great hopes of her.

ST. CLARE: I believe I'll go down the street, a few 150 moments, and hear the news.

OPHELIA: Shall I call Tom to attend you?

ST. CLARE: No, I shall be back in an hour. [*Exit.*]

OPHELIA: He's got an excellent heart, but then he's so dreadful shiftless! [*Exit.*] 155

SCENE III

Front Chamber. Enter TOPSY.

TOPSY: Dar's somethin' de matter wid me—I isn't a bit like myself. I haven't done anything wrong since poor Miss Eva went up in de skies and left us. When I's gwine to do anything wicked, I tinks of her, and somehow I can't do it. I's getting to be 5 good, dat's a fact. I 'spects when I's dead I shall be turned into a little brack angel.

Enter OPHELIA.

OPHELIA: Topsy, I've been looking for you; I've got something very particular to say to you.

TOPSY: Does you want me to say the catechism? 10

OPHELIA: No, not now.

TOPSY: [*Aside.*] Golly! dat's one comfort.

OPHELIA: Now, Topsy, I want you to try and understand what I am going to say to you.

TOPSY: Yes, missis, I'll open my ears drefful wide. 15

OPHELIA: Mr. St. Clare has given you to me, Topsy.

TOPSY: Den I b'longs to you, don't I? Golly! I thought I always belong to you.

OPHELIA: Not till to-day have I received any authority to call you my property. 20

TOPSY: I's your property, am I? Well, if you say so, I 'spects I am.

OPHELIA: Topsy, I can give you your liberty.

TOPSY: My liberty?

OPHELIA: Yes, Topsy. 25

TOPSY: Has you got 'um with you?

OPHELIA: I have, Topsy.

TOPSY: Is it clothes or wittles?

OPHELIA: How shiftless! Don't you know what your liberty is, Topsy? 30

TOPSY: How should I know when I never seed 'um.

OPHELIA: Topsy, I am going to leave this place; I am going many miles away—to my own home in Vermont.

TOPSY: Den what's to become of dis chile? 35

OPHELIA: If you wish to go, I will take you with me.

TOPSY: Miss Feely, I doesn't want to leave you no how, I loves you I does.

OPHELIA: Then you shall share my home for the rest of your days. Come, Topsy. 40

TOPSY: Stop, Miss Feely; does dey hab any oberseers in Varmount?

OPHELIA: No, Topsy.

TOPSY: Nor cotton plantations, nor sugar factories, nor darkies, nor whipping nor nothing? 45

OPHELIA: No, Topsy.

TOPSY: By Golly! de quicker you is gwine de better den.

Enter TOM, hastily.

TOM: Oh, Miss Feely! Miss Feely!

OPHELIA: Gracious me, Tom! what's the matter? 50

TOM: Oh, Mas'r St. Clare! Mas'r St. Clare!

OPHELIA: Well, Tom, well?

TOM: They've just brought him home and I do believe he's killed?

OPHELIA: Killed? 55

TOPSY: Oh dear! what's to become of de poor darkies now?

TOM: He's dreadful weak. It's just as much as he can do to speak. He wanted me to call you.

OPHELIA: My poor cousin! Who would have thought 60 of it? Don't say a word to his wife, Tom; the danger may not be so great as you think; it would only distress her. Come with me; you may be able to afford some assistance. [*Exeunt.*]

SCENE IV

Handsome Chamber. ST. CLARE discovered seated on sofa. OPHELIA, TOM and TOPSY are clustered around him. DOCTOR back of sofa feeling his pulse. Scene opens to slow music.

ST. CLARE: [*Raising himself feebly.*] Tom—poor fellow!

TOM: Well, mas'r?

ST. CLARE: I have received my death wound.

TOM: Oh, no, no, mas'r!   5

ST. CLARE: I feel that I am dying—Tom, pray!

TOM: [*Sinking on his knees.*] I do, pray, mas'r! I do pray!

ST. CLARE: [*After a pause.*] Tom, one thing preys upon my mind—I have forgotten to sign your   10 freedom papers. What will become of you when I am gone?

TOM: Don't think of that, mas'r.

ST. CLARE: I was wrong, Tom, very wrong, to neglect it. I may be the cause of much suffering to you   15 hereafter. Marie, my wife—she—oh!—

OPHELIA: His mind is wandering.

ST. CLARE: [*Energetically.*] No! it is coming *home* at last! [*Sinks back.*] At last! at last! Eva, I come! [*Dies. Music—slow curtain.*]   20

ACT V

SCENE I

An Auction Mart. UNCLE TOM and EMMELINE at back. ADOLF, SKEGGS, MARKS, MANN, and various spectators discovered. MARKS and MANN come forward.

MARKS: Hulloa. Alf! what brings you here?

MANN: Well, I was wanting a valet, and I heard that St. Clare's valet was going; I thought I'd just look at them.

MARKS: Catch me ever buying any of St. Clare's   5 people. Spoiled niggers every one—impudent as the devil.

MANN: Never fear that; if I get 'em, I'll soon have their airs out of them—they'll soon find that they've another kind of master to deal with than   10 St. Clare. 'Pon my word, I'll buy that fellow—I

like the shape of him. [*Pointing to ADOLF.*]

MARKS: You'll find it'll take all you've got to keep him—he's deucedly extravagant.

MANN: Yes, but my lord will find that he *can't* be   15 extravagant with *me*. Just let him be sent to the calaboose a few times, and thoroughly dressed down, I'll tell you if it don't bring him to a sense of his ways. Oh! I'll reform him, up hill and down, you'll see. I'll buy him; that's flat.   20

Enter LEGREE, he goes up and looks at ADOLF, whose boots are nicely blacked.

LEGREE: A nigger with his boots blacked—bah! [*Spits on them.*] Halloa, you! [*To TOM.*] Let's see your teeth. [*Seizes TOM by the jaw and opens his mouth.*] Strip up your sleeves and show your muscle. [*TOM does so.*] Where was you raised?   25

TOM: In Kintuck, mas'r.

LEGREE: What have you done?

TOM: Had care of mas'r's farm.

LEGREE: That's a likely story. [*Turns to EMMELINE.*] You're a nice-looking girl enough. How old are   30 you? [*Grasps her arm.*]

EMMELINE: [*Shrieking.*] Ah! you hurt me.

SKEGGS: Stop that, you minx! No whimpering here. The sale is going to begin. [*Mounts the rostrum.*] Gentlemen, the next article I shall offer you to-   35 day is Adolf, late valet to Mr. St. Clare. How much am I offered? [*Various bids are made. ADOLF is knocked down to MANN for eight hundred dollars.*] Gentlemen, I now offer a prime article—the quadroon girl, Emmeline, only fifteen years of age,   40 warranted in every respect.[45] [*Business as before. EMMELINE is sold to LEGREE for one thousand dollars.*] Now, I shall close to-day's sale by offering you the valuable article known as Uncle Tom, the most useful nigger ever raised. Gentlemen in want of an   45 overseer, now is the time to bid.

Business as before. TOM is sold to LEGREE for twelve hundred dollars.

LEGREE: Now look here, you two belong to me. [*TOM and EMMELINE sink on their knees.*]

---

45 quadroon] a person of one-quarter black ancestry.

TOM: Heaven help us, then!

Music. LEGREE stands over them exulting. Picture—closed in.

SCENE II

The Garden of Miss Ophelia's House in Vermont. Enter OPHELIA and DEACON PERRY.

DEACON: Miss Ophelia, allow me to offer you my congratulations upon your safe arrival in your native place. I hope it is your intention to pass the remainder of your days with us?

OPHELIA: Well, Deacon, I have come here with that 5 express purpose.

DEACON: I presume you were not over-pleased with the South?

OPHELIA: Well, to tell you the truth, Deacon, I wasn't; I liked the country very well, but the people 10 there are so dreadful shiftless.

DEACON: The result, I presume, of living in a warm climate.

OPHELIA: Well, Deacon, what is the news among you all here? 15

DEACON: Well, we live on in the same even jog-trot pace. Nothing of any consequence has happened— Oh! I forgot. [*Takes out handkerchief.*] I've lost my wife; my Molly has left me. [*Wipes his eyes.*]

OPHELIA: Poor soul! I pity you, Deacon. 20

DEACON: Thank you. You perceive I bear my loss with resignation.

OPHELIA: How you must miss her tongue!

DEACON: Molly certainly was fond of talking. She always would have the last word—heigho! 25

OPHELIA: What was her complaint, Deacon?

DEACON: A mild and soothing one, Miss Ophelia: she had a severe attack of the lockjaw.

OPHELIA: Dreadful!

DEACON: Wasn't it? When she found she couldn't 30 use her tongue, she took it so much to heart that it struck to her stomach and killed her. Poor dear! Excuse my handkerchief; she's been dead only eighteen months.

OPHELIA: Why, Deacon, by this time you ought to 35 be setting your cap for another wife.

DEACON: Do you think so, Miss Ophelia?

OPHELIA: I don't see why you shouldn't—you are still a good-looking man, Deacon.

DEACON: Ah! well, I think I do wear well—in fact, 40 I may say remarkably well. It has been observed to me before.

OPHELIA: And you are not much over fifty?

DEACON: Just turned of forty, I assure you.

OPHELIA: Hale and hearty? 45

DEACON: Health excellent—look at my eye! Strong as a lion—look at my arm!! A number one constitution—look at my leg!!!

OPHELIA: Have you no thoughts of choosing another partner? 50

DEACON: Well, to tell you the truth, I have.

OPHELIA: Who is she?

DEACON: She is not far distant. [*Looks at OPHELIA in an anguishing manner.*] I have her in my eye at this present moment. 55

OPHELIA: [*Aside.*] Really, I believe he's going to pop. Why, surely, Deacon, you don't mean to—

DEACON: Yes, Miss Ophelia, I do mean; and believe me, when I say—[*Looking off.*] The Lord be good to us, but I believe there is the devil coming! 60

TOPSY runs on, with bouquet. She is now dressed very neatly.

TOPSY: Miss Feely, here is some flowers dat I hab been gathering for you. [*Gives bouquet.*]

OPHELIA: That's a good child.

DEACON: Miss Ophelia, who is this young person?

OPHELIA: She is my daughter. 65

DEACON: [*Aside.*] Her daughter! Then she must have married a colored man off South. I was not aware that you had been married, Miss Ophelia?

OPHELIA: Married! Sakes alive! what made you think I had been married? 70

DEACON: Good gracious, I'm getting confused. Didn't I understand you to say that this— somewhat tanned—young lady was your daughter?

OPHELIA: Only by adoption. She is my adopted daughter. 75

DEACON: O-oh! [*Aside.*] I breathe again.

TOPSY: By Golly! dat old man's eyes stick out of 'um head dre'ful. Guess he never seed anything like me afore.

OPHELIA: Deacon, won't you step into the house and refresh yourself after your walk? 80

DEACON: I accept your polite invitation. [*Offers his arm.*] Allow me.

OPHELIA: As gallant as ever, Deacon. I declare, you grow younger every day. 85

DEACON: You can never grow old, madam.

OPHELIA: Ah, you flatterer! [*Exeunt.*]

TOPSY: Dar dey go, like an old goose and gander. Guess dat ole gemblemun feels kind of confectionary—rather sweet on my old missis. By Golly! she's 90 been dre'ful kind to me ever since I come away from de South; and I loves her, I does, 'cause she takes such car' on me and gives me dese fine clothes. I tries to be good too, and I's gettin 'long 'mazin' fast. I's not so wicked as I used to was. 95 [*Looks out.*] Halloa! dar's some one comin' here. I wonder what he wants now. [*Retires, observing.*]

Enter GUMPTION CUTE, very shabby, a small bundle, on a stick, over his shoulder.

CUTE: By chowder, here I am again. Phew, it's a pretty considerable tall piece of walking between here and New Orleans, not to mention the wear 100 of shoe-leather. I guess I'm about done up. If this streak of bad luck lasts much longer, I'll borrow sixpence to buy a rope, and hang myself right straight up! When I went to call on Miss Ophelia, I swow if I didn't find out that she had left for 105 Vermont; so I kind of concluded to make tracks in that direction myself and as I didn't have any money left, why I had to foot it, and here I am in old Varmount once more. They told me Miss Ophelia lived up here. I wonder if she will 110 remember the relationship. [*Sees TOPSY.*] By chowder, there's a darkey. Look here, Charcoal!

TOPSY: [*Comes forward.*] My name isn't Charcoal—it's Topsy.

CUTE: Oh! your name is Topsy, is it, you juvenile 115 specimen of Day & Martin?[46]

TOPSY: Tell you I don't know nothin' 'bout Day & Martin. I's Topsy and I belong to Miss Feely St. Clare.

CUTE: I'm much obleeged to you, you small extract 120 of Japan, for your information.[47] So Miss Ophelia lives up there in the white house, does she?

TOPSY: Well, she don't do nothin' else.

CUTE: Well, then, just locomote your pins.

TOPSY: What—what's dat? 125

CUTE: Walk your chalks!

TOPSY: By Golly! dere ain't no chalk 'bout me.

CUTE: Move your trotters.

TOPSY: How you does spoke! What you mean by trotters? 130

CUTE: Why, your feet, Stove Polish.

TOPSY: What does you want me to move my feet for?

CUTE: To tell your mistress, you ebony angel, that a gentleman wishes to see her.

TOPSY: Does you call yourself a gentleman! By Golly! 135 you look more like a scar'crow.

CUTE: Now look here, you Charcoal, don't you be sassy. I'm a gentleman in distress; a done-up speculator; one that has seen better days—long time ago—and better clothes too, by chowder! My 140 creditors are like my boots—they've no soles. I'm a victim to circumstances. I've been through much and survived it. I've taken walking exercise for the benefit of my health; but as I was trying to live on air at the same time, it was a losing speculation, 145 'cause it gave me such a dreadful appetite.

TOPSY: Golly! you look as if you could eat an ox, horns and all.

CUTE: Well, I calculate I could, if he was roasted—it's a speculation I should like to engage in. I have 150 returned like the fellow that run way in Scripture; and if anybody's got a fatted calf they want to kill, all they got to do is fetch him along. Do you know, Charcoal, that your mistress is a relation of mine?

TOPSY: Is she your uncle? 155

CUTE: No, no, not quite so near as that. My second cousin married her niece.

TOPSY: And does you want to see Miss Feely?

CUTE: I do. I have come to seek a home beneath her roof, and take care of all the spare change she don't 160 want to use.

TOPSY: Den just you follow me, mas'r.

---

46 Day & Martin] a manufacturer of "blacking" (i.e., boot polish).

47 extract of Japan] perhaps a reference to black iodine, extracted from Japanese seaweed.

CUTE: Stop! By chowder, I've got a great idee. Say, you Day & Martin, how should you like to enter into a speculation? 165

TOPSY: Golly! I doesn't know what a spec—spec—eu—what-do-you-call-'um am.

CUTE: Well, now, I calculate I've hit upon about the right thing. Why should I degrade the manly dignity of the Cutes by becoming a beggar— 170 expose myself to the chance of receiving the cold shoulder as a poor relation? By chowder, my blood biles as I think of it! Topsy, you can make my fortune, and your own, too. I've an idea in my head that is worth a million of dollars. 175

TOPSY: Golly! is your head worth dat? Guess you wouldn't bring dat out South for de whole of you.

CUTE: Don't you be too severe, now, Charcoal; I'm a man of genius. Did you ever hear of Barnum?[48]

TOPSY: Barnum! Barnum! Does he live out South? 180

CUTE: No, he lives in New York. Do you know how he made his fortin?

TOPSY: What is him fortin, hey? Is it something he wears?

CUTE: Chowder, how green you are! 185

TOPSY: [Indignantly.] Sar, I hab you to know I's not green; I's brack.

CUTE: To be sure you are, Day & Martin. I calculate, when a person says another has a fortune, he means he's got plenty of money, Charcoal. 190

TOPSY: And did he make the money?

CUTE: Sartin sure, and no mistake.

TOPSY: Golly! now I thought money always growed.

CUTE: Oh, git out! You are too cute—you are cuterer than I am—and I'm Cute by name and cute by 195 nature. Well, as I was saying, Barnum made his money by exhibiting a *woolly* horse; now wouldn't it be an all-fired speculation to show you as the woolly gal?

TOPSY: You want to make a sight of me? 200

CUTE: I'll give you half the receipts, by chowder!

TOPSY: Should I have to leave Miss Feely?

CUTE: To be sure you would.

TOPSY: Den you hab to get a woolly gal somewhere else, Mas'r Cute. [*Runs off.*] 205

CUTE: There's another speculation gone to smash, by chowder! [*Exit.*]

SCENE III

A Rude Chamber. TOM is discovered, in old clothes, seated on a stool. He holds in his hand a paper containing a curl of EVA's hair. The scene opens to the symphony of "Old Folks at Home."[49]

TOM: I have come to de dark places; I's going through de vale of shadows. My heart sinks at times and feels just like a big lump of lead. Den it gits up in my throat and chokes me till de tears roll out of my eyes; den I take out dis curl of little 5 Miss Eva's hair, and the sight of it brings calm to my mind and I feels strong again. [*Kisses the curl and puts it in his breast—takes out a silver dollar, which is suspended around his neck by a string.*] Dere's de bright silver dollar dat Mas'r George 10 Shelby gave me the day I was sold away from old Kentuck, and I've kept it ever since. Mas'r George must have grown to be a man by this time. I wonder if I shall ever see him again.

Song. "Old Folks at Home." Enter LEGREE, EMMELINE, SAMBO AND QUIMBO.

LEGREE: Shut up, you black cuss! Did you think I 15 wanted any of your infernal howling? [*Turns to EMMELINE.*] We're home. [*EMMELINE shrinks from him. He takes hold of her ear.*] You didn't ever wear earrings?

EMMELINE: [*Trembling.*] No, master. 20

LEGREE: Well, I'll give you a pair, if you're a good girl. You needn't be so frightened; I don't mean to make you work very hard. You'll have fine times with me and live like a lady; only be a good girl.

EMMELINE: My soul sickens as his eyes gaze upon 25 me. His touch makes my very flesh creep.

48 Barnum] P.T. Barnum (1810–1891), American show-man who exhibited freaks and curiosities in his American Museum (he did not enter the circus business until the 1870s). This section of the play was probably added by Aiken after Barnum's American Museum began running a version of *Uncle Tom's Cabin* in competition with Aiken's own.

49 *Old Folks at Home*] minstrel song written by Stephen Foster in 1851 ("Way down upon the Swanee River").

LEGREE: [*Turns to TOM, and points to SAMBO and QUIMBO.*] Ye see what ye'd get if ye'd try to run off. These yer boys have been raised to track niggers and they'd just as soon chaw one on ye up as eat their suppers; so mind yourself. [*To EMMELINE.*] Come, mistress, you go in here with me. [*Taking EMMELINE's hand, and leading her off.*]

EMMELINE: [*Withdrawing her hand, and shrinking back.*] No, no! let me work in the fields; I don't want to be a lady.

LEGREE: Oh! you're going to be contrary, are you? I'll soon take all that out of you.

EMMELINE: Kill me, if you will.

LEGREE: Oh! you want to be killed, do you? Now come here, you Tom, you see I told you I didn't buy you jest for the common work; I mean to promote you and make a driver of you, and to-night ye may jest as well begin to get yer hand in. Now ye jest take this yer gal, and flog her; ye've seen enough on't to know how.

TOM: I beg mas'r's pardon—hopes mas'r won't set me at that. It's what I a'nt used to—never did, and can't do—no way possible.

LEGREE: Ye'll larn a pretty smart chance of things ye never did know before I've done with ye. [*Strikes TOM with whip, three blows. Music chord each blow.*] There! now will yet tell me ye can't do it?

TOM: Yes, mas'r! I'm willing to work night and day, and work while there's life and breath in me; but his yer thing I can't feel it right to do, and, mas'r, I *never* shall do it, *never!*

LEGREE: What! ye black beast! tell *me* ye don't think it right to do what I tell ye! What have any of you cussed cattle to do with thinking what's right? I'll put a stop to it. Why, what do ye think ye are? May be ye think yer a gentleman, master Tom, to be telling your master what's right and what a'nt! So you pretend it's wrong to flog the gal?

TOM: I think so, mas'r; 'twould be downright cruel, and it's what I never will do, mas'r. If you mean to kill me, kill me; but as to raising my hand agin any one here, I never shall—I'll die first!

LEGREE: Well, here's a pious dog at last, let down among us sinners—powerful holy critter he must be. Here, you rascal! you make believe to be so pious, didn't you never read out of your Bible,

"Servants, obey your masters"?[50] An't I your master? Didn't I pay twelve hundred dollars, cash, for all there is inside your cussed old black shell? An't you mine, body and soul?

TOM: No, no! My soul a'nt yours, mas'r; you haven't bought it—ye can't buy it; it's been bought and paid for by one that is able to keep it, and you can't harm it!

LEGREE: I can't? we'll see, we'll see! Here, Sambo! Quimbo! give this dog such a breaking in as he won't get over this month!

EMMELINE: Oh, no! you will not be so cruel—have some mercy! [*Clings to TOM.*]

LEGREE: Mercy? you won't find any in this shop! Away with the black cuss! Flog him within an inch of his life!

Music. SAMBO and QUIMBO seize TOM and drag him up stage. LEGREE seizes EMMELINE, and throws her round. She falls on her knees, with her hands lifted in supplication. LEGREE raises his whip, as if to strike TOM. Picture closed in.

SCENE IV

Plain Chamber. Enter OPHELIA, followed by TOPSY.

OPHELIA: A person inquiring for me, did you say, Topsy?

TOPSY: Yes, missis.

OPHELIA: What kind of a looking man is he?

TOPSY: By golly! he's very queer looking man, anyway; and den he talks so dre'ful funny. What does you think?—yah! yah! he wanted to 'zibite me as de wooly gal! yah! yah!

OPHELIA: Oh! I understand. Some cute Yankee, who wants to purchase you, to make a show of—the heartless wretch!

TOPSY: Dat's just him, missis; dat's just his name. He told me dat it was Cute—Mr. Cute Specula-shum—dat's him.

OPHELIA: What did you say to him, Topsy?

TOPSY: Well, I didn't say much, it was brief and to the point—I tole him I wouldn't leave you, Miss Feely, no how.

50 Servants … masters] Colossians 3:22.

OPHELIA: That's right, Topsy; you know you are very comfortable here—you wouldn't fare quite so well if you went away among strangers. 20

TOPSY: By golly! I know dat; you takes care on me, and makes me good. I don't steal any now, and I don't swar, and I don't dance breakdowns. Oh! I isn't so wicked as I used to was. 25

OPHELIA: That's right, Topsy; now show the gentleman, or whatever he is, up.

TOPSY: By golly! I guess he won't make much out of Miss Feely. [*Crosses and exits.*]

OPHELIA: I wonder who this person can be? Perhaps 30 it is some old acquaintance, who has heard of my arrival, and who comes on a social visit.

Enter CUTE.

CUTE: Aunt, how do ye do? Well, I swar, the sight of you is good for weak eyes. [*Offers his hand.*]

OPHELIA: [*Coldly drawing back.*] Really, sir, I can't 35 say that I ever had the pleasure of seeing you before.

CUTE: Well, it's a fact that you never did. You see I never happened to be in your neighborhood afore now. Of course you've heard of me? I'm one of the 40 Cutes—Gumption Cute, the first and only son of Josiah and Maria Cute, of Oniontown, on the Onion River in the north part of this ere State of Varmount.

OPHELIA: Can't say I ever heard the name before. 45

CUTE: Well then, I calculate your memory must be a little ricketty. I'm a relation of yours.

OPHELIA: A relation of mine! Why, I never heard of any Cutes in our family.

CUTE: Well, I shouldn't wonder if you never did. 50 Don't you remember your niece, Mary?

OPHELIA: Of course I do. What a shiftless question!

CUTE: Well, you see my second cousin, Abijah Blake, married her. So you see that makes me a relation of yours. 55

OPHELIA: Rather a distant one, I should say.

CUTE: By chowder! I'm *near* enough, just at present.

OPHELIA: Well, you certainly are a sort of connection of mine.

CUTE: Yes, kind of sort of. 60

OPHELIA: And of course you are welcome to my house, as long as you wish to make it your home.

CUTE: By chowder! I'm booked for the next six months—this isn't a bad speculation.

OPHELIA: I hope you left all your folks well at home? 65

CUTE: Well, yes, they're pretty comfortably disposed of. Father and mother's dead, and Uncle Josh has gone to California. I am the only representative of the Cutes left.

OPHELIA: There doesn't seem to be a great deal of 70 *you* left. I declare, you are positively in rags.

CUTE: Well, you see, the fact is, I've been speculating—trying to get banknotes—specie-rags, as they say—but I calculate I've turned out rags of another sort. 75

OPHELIA: I'm sorry for your ill luck, but I am afraid you have been shiftless.

CUTE: By chowder! I've done all that a fellow could do. You see, somehow, everything I take hold of kind of bursts up. 80

OPHELIA: Well, well, perhaps you'll do better for the future; make yourself at home. I have got to see to some house-hold matters, so excuse me for a short time. [*Aside.*] Impudent and shiftless. [*Exit.*]

CUTE: By chowder! I rather guess that this specula- 85 tion will hitch. She's a good-natured old critter; I reckon I'll be a son to her while she lives, and take care of her valuables arter she's a defunct departed. I wonder if they keep the vittles in this ere room? Guess not. I've got extensive accommodations for 90 all sorts of eatables. I'm a regular vacuum, throughout—pockets and all. I'm chuck full of emptiness. [*Looks out.*] Holloa! who's this elderly individual coming up stairs? He looks like a compound essence of starch and dignity. I wonder if he isn't 95 another relation of mine. I should like a rich old fellow now for an uncle.

Enter DEACON PERRY.

DEACON: Ha! a stranger here!

CUTE: How d'ye do?

DEACON: You are a friend to Miss Ophelia, I 100 presume?

CUTE: Well, I rather calculate that I am a leetle more than a friend.

DEACON: [*Aside.*] Bless me! what can he mean by those mysterious words? Can he be her—no I don't 105 think he can. She said she wasn't—well, at all events, it's very suspicious.

CUTE: The old fellow seems kind of stuck up.

DEACON: You are a particular friend to Miss Ophelia, you say? 110

CUTE: Well, I calculate I am.

DEACON: Bound to her by any tender tie?

CUTE: It's something more than a tie—it's a regular double-twisted knot.

DEACON: Ah! just as I suspected. [*Aside.*] Might I 115 inquire the nature of that tie?

CUTE: Well, it's the natural tie of relationship.

DEACON: A relation—what relation?

CUTE: Why, you see, my second cousin, Abijah Blake, married her niece, Mary. 120

DEACON: Oh! is that all?

CUTE: By chowder, ain't that enough?

DEACON: Then you are not her husband?

CUTE: To be sure I ain't. What put that ere idee into your cranium? 125

DEACON: [*Shaking him vigorously by the hand.*] My dear sir, I'm delighted to see you.

CUTE: Holloa! you ain't going slightly insane, are you?

DEACON: No, no fear of that; I'm only happy, that's 130 all.

CUTE: I wonder if he's been taking a nipper?

DEACON: As you are a relation of Miss Ophelia's, I think it proper that I should make you my confidant; in fact, let you into a little scheme that 135 I have lately conceived.

CUTE: Is it a speculation?

DEACON: Well, it is, just at present; but I trust before many hours to make it a surety.

CUTE: By chowder! I hope it won't serve you the way 140 my speculations have served me. But fire away, old boy, and give us the prospectus.

DEACON: Well, then, my young friend, I have been thinking, ever since Miss Ophelia returned to Vermont, that she was just the person to fill the 145 place of my lamented Molly.

CUTE: Say, you, you couldn't tell us who your lamented Molly was, could you?

DEACON: Why, the late Mrs. Perry, to be sure.

CUTE: Oh! then the lamented Molly was your wife? 150

DEACON: She was.

CUTE: And now you wish to marry Miss Ophelia?

DEACON: Exactly.

CUTE: [*Aside.*] Consarn this old porpoise! if I let him do that he'll Jew me out of my living. By chowder! 155 I'll put a spoke in his wheel.

DEACON: Well, what do you say? will you intercede for me with your aunt?

CUTE: No! bust me up if I do!

DEACON: No? 160

CUTE: No, I tell you. I forbid the bans. Now, ain't you a purty individual, to talk about getting married, you old superannuated Methuselah specimen of humanity! Why, you've got one foot in etarnity already, and t'other ain't fit to stand on. 165 Go home and go to bed! have your head shaved, and send for a lawyer to make your will, leave your property to your heirs—if you hain't got any, why leave it to me—I'll take care of it, and charge nothing for the trouble. 170

DEACON: Really, sir, this language to one of my standing, is highly indecorous—it's more, sir, than I feel willing to endure, sir. I shall expect an explanation, sir.

CUTE: Now, you see, old gouty toes, you're losing 175 your temper.

DEACON: Sir, I'm a deacon; I never lost my temper in all my life, sir.

CUTE: Now, you see, you're getting excited; you had better go; we can't have a disturbance here! 180

DEACON: No, sir! I shall not go, sir! I shall not go until I have seen Miss Ophelia. I wish to know if she will countenance this insult.

CUTE: Now keep cool, old stick-in-the-mud! Draw it mild, old timber-toes! 185

DEACON: Damn it all, sir, what—

CUTE: Oh! only think, now, what would people say to hear a deacon swearing like a trooper?

DEACON: Sir—I—you—this is too much, sir.

CUTE: Well, now, I calculate that's just about my 190 opinion, so we'll have no more of it. Get out of this! start your boots, or by chowder! I'll pitch you from one end of the stairs to the other.

Enter OPHELIA.

OPHELIA: Hoity toity! What's the meaning of all these loud words? 195

CUTE: [*Together.*] Well, you see Aunt—

DEACON: Miss Ophelia, I beg—

CUTE: Now, look here, you just hush your yap! How can I fix up matters if you keep jabbering?

OPHELIA: Silence! for shame, Mr. Cute. Is that the way you speak to the deacon? 200

CUTE: Darn the deacon!

OPHELIA: Deacon Perry, what is all this?

DEACON: Madam, a few words will explain everything. Hearing from this person that he was your nephew, I ventured to tell him that I cherished hopes of making you my wife, whereupon he flew into a violent passion, and ordered me out of the house. 205

OPHELIA: Does this house belong to you or me, Mr. Cute? 210

CUTE: Well, to you, I reckon.

OPHELIA: Then how dare you give orders in it?

CUTE: Well, I calculated that you wouldn't care about marrying old half a century there.

OPHELIA: That's enough; I will marry him; and as for you [points], get out. 215

CUTE: Get out?

OPHELIA: Yes; the sooner the better.

CUTE: Darned if I don't serve him out first though.

Music. CUTE makes a dash at DEACON, who gets behind OPHELIA. TOPSY enters, with a broom and beats CUTE around stage. OPHELIA faints in DEACON's arms. CUTE falls, and TOPSY butts him kneeling over him. Quick drop.

ACT VI

SCENE I

Dark landscape. An old, roofless shed. TOM is discovered in shed, lying on some old cotton bagging. CASSY kneels by his side, holding a cup to his lips.

CASSY: Drink all ye want. I knew how it would be. It isn't the first time I've been out in the night, carrying water to such as you.

TOM: [*Returning cup.*] Thank you, missis.

CASSY: Don't call me missis. I'm a miserable slave like yourself—a lower one than you can ever be! It's no use, my poor fellow, this you've been trying to do. You were a brave fellow. You had the right on your side; but it's all in vain for you to struggle. You are in the Devil's hands; he is the strongest, and you must give up. 10

TOM: Oh! how can I give up?

CASSY: You see *you* don't know anything about it; I do. Here you are, on a lone plantation, ten miles from any other, in the swamps; not a white person here who could testify, if you were burned alive. There's no law here that can do you, or any of us, the least good; and this man! There's no earthly thing that he is not bad enough to do. I could make one's hair rise, and their teeth chatter, if I should only tell what I've seen and been knowing to here; and it's no use resisting! Did I *want* to live with him? Wasn't I a woman delicately bred? and he!—Father in Heaven! what was he and is he? And yet I've lived with him these five years, and cursed every moment of my life, night and day. 15 20 25

TOM: Oh heaven! have you quite forgot us poor critters?

CASSY: And what are these miserable low dogs you work with, that you should suffer on their account? Every one of them would turn against you the first time they get a chance. They are all of them as low and cruel to each other as they can be; there's no use in your suffering to keep from hurting them? 30

TOM: What made 'em cruel? If I give out I shall get used to it and grow, little by little, just like 'em. No, no, Missis, I've lost everything, wife, and children, and home, and a kind master, and he would have set me free if he'd only lived a day longer—I've lost everything in *this* world, and now I can't lose heaven, too: no I can't get to be wicked besides all. 35 40

CASSY: But it can't be that He will lay sin to our account; he won't charge it to us when we are forced to it; he'll charge it to them that drove us to it. Can I do anything more for you? Shall I give you some more water? 45

TOM: Oh missis! I wish you'd go to Him who can give you living waters!

CASSY: Go to him! Where is he? Who is he? 50

TOM: Our Heavenly Father!

CASSY: I used to see the picture of him, over the altar, when I was a girl but *he isn't here!* there's nothing here but sin, and long, long despair! There, there, don't talk any more, my poor fellow. Try to sleep, if you can. I must hasten back, lest my absence be noted. Think of me when I am gone, Uncle Tom, and pray, pray for me. 55

Music. Exit CASSY. TOM sinks back to sleep.

SCENE II

Street in New Orleans. Enter GEORGE SHELBY.

GEORGE: At length my mission of mercy is nearly finished. I have reached my journey's end. I have now but to find the house of Mr. St. Clare, re-purchase old Uncle Tom, and convey him back to his wife and children, in old Kentucky. Some one approaches; he may, perhaps, be able to give me the information I require. I will accost him. [*Enter MARKS.*] Pray, sir, can you tell me where Mr. St. Clare dwells?

MARKS: Where I don't think you'll be in a hurry to seek him.

GEORGE: And where is that?

MARKS: In the grave!

GEORGE: Stay, sir! You may be able to give me some information concerning Mr. St. Clare.

MARKS: I beg pardon, sir, I am a lawyer; I can't afford to *give* anything.

GEORGE: But you would have no objections to selling it?

MARKS: Not the slightest.

GEORGE: What do you value it at?

MARKS: Well, say five dollars, that's reasonable.

GEORGE: There they are. [*Gives money.*] Now answer me to the best of your ability. Has the death of St. Clare caused his slaves to be sold?

MARKS: It has.

GEORGE: How were they sold?

MARKS: At auction—they went dirt cheap.

GEORGE: How were they bought—all in one lot?

MARKS: No, they went to different bidders.

GEORGE: Was you present at the sale?

MARKS: I was.

GEORGE: Do you remember seeing a Negro among them called Tom?

MARKS: What, Uncle Tom?

GEORGE: The same—who bought him?

MARKS: A Mr. Legree.

GEORGE: Where is his plantation.

MARKS: Up in Louisiana, on the Red River; but a man never could find it, unless he had been there before.

GEORGE: Who could I get to direct me there?

MARKS: Well, stranger, I don't know of any one just at present 'cept myself, could find it for you; it's such an out-of-the-way sort of hole; and if you are a mind to come down handsome, why, I'll do it.

GEORGE: The reward shall be ample.

MARKS: Enough said, stranger; let's take the steamboat at once. [*Exeunt.*]

SCENE III

A Rough Chamber. Enter LEGREE. Sits.

LEGREE: Plague on that Sambo, to kick up this yer row between Tom and the new hands. [*CASSY steals on and stands behind him.*] The fellow won't be fit to work for a week now, right in the press of the season.

CASSY: Yes, just like you.

LEGREE: Hah! you she-devil! You've come back, have you? [*Rises.*]

CASSY: Yes, I have; come to have my own way, too.

LEGREE: You lie, you jade! I'll be up to my word. Either behave yourself or stay down in the quarters and fare and work with the rest.

CASSY: I'd rather, ten thousand times, live in the dirtiest hole at the quarters, than be under your hoof!

LEGREE: But you are under my hoof, for all that, that's one comfort; so sit down here and listen to reason. [*Grasps her wrist.*]

CASSY: Simon Legree, take care! [*LEGREE lets go his hold.*] You're afraid of me, Simon, and you've reason to be; for I've got the Devil in me!

LEGREE: I believe to my soul you have. After all, Cassy, why can't you be friends with me, as you used to?

CASSY: [*Bitterly.*] Used to!

LEGREE: I wish, Cassy, you'd behave yourself decently.

CASSY: *You* talk about behaving decently! And what have you been doing? You haven't even sense enough to keep from spoiling one of your best hands, right in the most pressing season, just for your devilish temper.

LEGREE: I was a fool, it's fact, to let any such brangle come up. Now when Tom set up his will he had to be broke in.

CASSY: You'll never break *him* in.

LEGREE: Won't I? I'd like to know if I won't? He'd be the first nigger that ever came it round me! I'll break every bone in his body but he shall give up. [*Enter SAMBO, with a paper in his hand, stands bowing.*] What's that, you dog? 40

SAMBO: It's a witch thing, mas'r.

LEGREE: A what?

SAMBO: Something that niggers gits from witches. Keep 'em from feeling when they's flogged. He had it tied round his neck with a black string. 45

LEGREE takes the paper and opens it. A silver dollar drops on the stage, and a long curl of light hair twines around his finger.

LEGREE: Damnation. [*Stamping and writhing, as if the hair burned him.*] Where did this come from? Take it off! burn it up! burn it up! [*Throws the curl away.*] What did you bring it to me for? 50

SAMBO: [*Trembling.*] I beg pardon, mas'r; I thought you like to see um.

LEGREE: Don't you bring me any more of your devilish things. [*Shakes his fist at SAMBO who runs off. LEGREE kicks the dollar after him.*] Blast it! where did 55 he get that? If it didn't look just like—whoo! I thought I'd forgot that. Curse me if I think there's any such thing as forgetting anything, any how.

CASSY: What is the matter with you, Legree? What is there in a simple curl of fair hair to appall a man 60 like you—you who are familiar with every form of cruelty.

LEGREE: Cassy, tonight the past has been recalled to me—the past that I have so long and vainly striven to forget. 65

CASSY: Has aught on this earth power to move a soul like thine?

LEGREE: Yes, for hard and reprobate as I now seem, there has been a time when I have been rocked on the bosom of a mother, cradled with prayers and 70 pious hymns, my now seared brow bedewed with the waters of holy baptism.

CASSY: [*Aside.*] What sweet memories of childhood can thus soften down that heart of iron?

LEGREE: In early childhood a fair-haired woman has 75 led me, at the sound of Sabbath bells, to worship and to pray. Born of a hard-tempered sire, on whom that gentle woman had wasted a world of unvalued love, I followed in the steps of my father. Boisterous, unruly and tyrannical, I despised all her 80 counsel, and would have none of her reproof, and, at an early age, broke from her to seek my fortunes on the sea. I never came home but once after that; and then my mother, with the yearning of a heart that must love something, and had nothing else 85 to love, clung to me, and sought with passionate prayers and entreaties to win me from a life of sin.

CASSY: That was your day of grace, Legree; then good angels called you, and mercy held you by the hand.

LEGREE: My heart inly relented; there was a conflict, 90 but sin got the victory, and I set all the force of my rough nature against the conviction of my conscience. I drank and swore, was wilder and more brutal than ever. And one night, when my mother, in the last agony of her despair, knelt at 95 my feet, I spurned her from me, threw her senseless on the floor, and with brutal curses fled to my ship.

CASSY: Then the fiend took thee for his own.

LEGREE: The next I heard of my mother was one night when I was carousing among drunken 100 companions. A letter was put in my hands. I opened it, and a lock of long, curling hair fell from it, and twined about my fingers, even as that lock twined but now. The letter told me that my mother was dead, and that dying she blest and 105 forgave me! [*Buries his face in his hands.*]

CASSY: Why did you not even then renounce your evil ways?

LEGREE: There is a dread, unhallowed necromancy of evil, that turns things sweetest and holiest to 110 phantoms of horror and afright. That pale, loving mother,—her dying prayers, her forgiving love,— wrought in my demoniac heart of sin only as a damning sentence, bringing with it a fearful looking for of judgment and fiery indignation. 115

CASSY: And yet you would not strive to avert the doom that threatened you.

LEGREE: I burned the lock of hair and I burned the letter; and when I saw them hissing and crackling in the flame, inly shuddered as I thought of 120 everlasting fires! I tried to drink and revel, and swear away the memory; but often in the deep night, whose solemn stillness arraigns the soul in forced communion with itself, I have seen that pale

mother rising by my bed-side, and felt the soft 125
twining of that hair around my fingers, 'till the
cold sweat would roll down my face, and I would
spring from my bed in horror—horror! [*Falls in
chair—After a pause.*] What the devil ails me? Large
drops of sweat stand on my forehead, and my heart 130
beats heavy and thick with fear. I thought I saw
something white rising and glimmering in the
gloom before me, and it seemed to bear my
mother's face! I know one thing; I'll let that fellow
Tom alone, after this. What did I want with his 135
cussed paper? I believe I am bewitched sure
enough! I've been shivering and sweating ever
since! Where did he get that hair? It couldn't have
been that! I *burn'd* that up, I know I did! It would
be a joke if hair could rise from the dead! I'll have 140
Sambo and Quimbo up here to sing and dance of
their dances, and keep off these horrid notions.
Here, Sambo! Quimbo! [*Exit.*]

CASSY: Yes, Legree, that golden tress was charmed;
each hair had in it a spell of terror and remorse 145
for thee, and was used by a mightier power to bind
thy cruel hands from inflicting uttermost evil on
the helpless! [*Exit.*]

SCENE IV

*Street. Enter MARKS meeting CUTE, who enters dressed
in an old faded uniform.*

MARKS: By the land, stranger, but it strikes me that
I've seen you somewhere before.

CUTE: By chowder! Do you know now, that's just
what I was a going to say?

MARKS: Isn't your name Cute? 5

CUTE: You're right, I calculate. Yours is Marks, I
reckon.

MARKS: Just so.

CUTE: Well, I swar, I'm glad to see you. [*They shake
hands.*] How's your wholesome? 10

MARKS: Hearty as ever. Well, who would have
thought of ever seeing you again. Why, I thought
you was in Vermont?

CUTE: Well, so I was. You see I went there after that
rich relation of mine—but the speculation didn't 15
turn out well.

MARKS: How so?

CUTE: Why, you see, she took a shine to an old
fellow—Deacon Abraham Perry—and married him.

MARKS: Oh, that rather put your nose out of joint 20
in that quarter.

CUTE: Busted me right up, I tell you. The Deacon
did the hand-some thing though, he said if I would
leave the neighborhood and go out South again,
he'd stand the damage. I calculate I didn't give him 25
much time to change his mind, and so, you see,
here I am again.

MARKS: What are you doing in that soldier rig?

CUTE: Oh, this is my sign.

MARKS: Your sign? 30

CUTE: Yes, you see, I'm engaged just at present in
an all-fired good speculation, I'm a Fillibusterow.

MARKS: A what?

CUTE: A Fillibusterow! Don't you know what that
is? It's Spanish for Cuban Volunteer; and means a 35
chap that goes the whole perker for glory and all
that ere sort of thing.

MARKS: Oh! you've joined the order of the Lone
Star![51]

CUTE: You've hit it. You see I bought this uniform 40
at a second hand clothing store, I puts it on and
goes to a benevolent individual and I says to him
—appealing to his feeling—I'm one of the fellows
that went to Cuba and got massacred by the
bloody Spaniards. I'm in a destitute condition— 45
give me a trifle to pay my passage back, so I can
whop the tyrannical cusses and avenge my brave
fellow soger what got slewed there.

MARKS: How pathetic!

CUTE: I tell you it works up the feelings of 50
benevolent individuals dreadfully. It draws tears
from their eyes and money from their pockets. By
chowder, one old chap gave me a hundred dollars
to help on the cause.

MARKS: I admire a genius like yours. 55

CUTE: But I say, what are you up to?

MARKS: I am the traveling companion of a young
gentleman by the name of Shelby, who is going to

_____

51 order of the Lone Star] a secret society formed in 1851,
the goal of which was to incorporate Cuba into the U.S.
and thus forestall the abolition of slavery in Cuba, an
event which would affect the U.S. South.

the plantation of a Mr. Legree of the Red River, to buy an old darkey who used to belong to his father. 60

CUTE: Legree—Legree? Well, now, I calculate I've heard that ere name afore.

MARKS: Do you remember that man who drew a bowie knife on you in New Orleans?

CUTE: By chowder! I remember the circumstance just 65 as well as if it was yesterday; but I can't say that I recollect much about the man, for you see I was in something of a hurry about that time and didn't stop to take a good look at him.

MARKS: Well, that man was this same Mr. Legree. 70

CUTE: Do you know, now, I should like to pay that critter off!

MARKS: Then I'll give you an opportunity.

CUTE: Chowder! how will you do that?

MARKS: Do you remember the gentleman that 75 interfered between you and Legree?

CUTE: Yes—well?

MARKS: He received the blow that was intended for you, and died from the effects of it. So, you see, Legree is a murderer, and we are only witnesses of 80 the deed. His life is in our hands.

CUTE: Let's have him right up and make him dance on nothing to the tune of Yankee Doodle!

MARKS: Stop a bit! Don't you see a chance for a profitable speculation? 85

CUTE: A speculation! Fire away, don't be bashful, I'm the man for a speculation.

MARKS: I have made a deposition to the Governor of the state on all the particulars of that affair at Orleans. 90

CUTE: What did you do that for?

MARKS: To get a warrant for his arrest.

CUTE: Oh! and have you got it?

MARKS: Yes; here it is. [Takes out paper.]

CUTE: Well, now, I don't see how you are going to 95 make anything by that bit of paper?

MARKS: But I do. I shall say to Legree, I have got a warrant against you for murder; my friend, Mr. Cute, and myself are the only witnesses who can appear against you. Give us a thousand dollars, and 100 we will tear the warrant and be silent.

CUTE: Then Mr. Legree forks over a thousand dollars, and your friend Cute pockets five hundred of it, is that the calculation.

MARKS: If you will join me in the undertaking. 105

CUTE: I'll do it, by chowder!

MARKS: Your hand to bind the bargain.

CUTE: I'll stick by you thro' thick and thin.

MARKS: Enough said.

CUTE: Then shake. [They shake hands.] 110

MARKS: But I say, Cute, he may be contrary and show fight.

CUTE: Never mind, we've got the law on our side, and we're bound to stir him up. If he don't come down handsomely we'll present him with a neck- 115 tie made of hemp!

MARKS: I declare you're getting spunky.

CUTE: Well, I reckon, I am. Let's go and have something to drink. Tell you what, Marks, if we don't get *him*, we'll have his hide, by chowder! 120 [*Exeunt, arm in arm.*]

SCENE V

Rough Chamber. Enter LEGREE, followed by SAMBO.

LEGREE: Go and send Cassy to me.

SAMBO: Yes, mas'r. [*Exit.*]

LEGREE: Curse the woman! she's got a temper worse than the devil; I shall do her an injury one of these days, if she isn't careful. [*Re-enter SAMBO, frightened.*] 5 What's the matter with you, you black scoundrel?

SAMBO: S'help me, mas'r, she isn't dere.

LEGREE: I suppose she's about the house somewhere?

SAMBO: No, she isn't, mas'r; I's been all over de house and I can't find nothing of her nor Emmeline. 10

LEGREE: Bolted, by the Lord! Call out the dogs! Saddle my horse. Stop! are you sure they really have gone?

SAMBO: Yes, mas'r; I's been in every room 'cept the haunted garret and dey wouldn't go dere. 15

LEGREE: I have it! Now, Sambo, you jest go and walk that Tom up here, right away! [*Exit SAMBO.*] The old cuss is at the bottom of this yer whole matter; and I'll have it out of his infernal black hide, or I'll know the reason why! I *hate* him—I *hate* him! 20 And isn't he *mine*? Can't I do what I like with him? Who's to hinder, I wonder? [*TOM is dragged on by SAMBO and QUIMBO, LEGREE grimly confronting TOM.*] Well, Tom, do you know I've made up my mind to *kill* you? 25

TOM: It's very likely, Mas'r.

LEGREE: *I—have—done—just—that—thing*, Tom, unless you'll tell me what do you know about these yer gals? [*TOM is silent.*] D'ye hear? Speak!

TOM: I han't got anything to tell you, mas'r.

LEGREE: Do you dare to tell me, you old black rascal, you don't know? Speak! Do you know anything?

TOM: I know, mas'r; but I can't tell anything. *I can die!*

LEGREE: Hark ye, Tom! ye think, 'cause I have let you off before, I don't mean what I say; but, this time, I have made *up my mind*, and counted the cost. You've always stood it out agin me; now, I'll *conquer ye or kill ye!* one or t'other. I'll count every drop of blood there is in you, and take 'em, one by one, 'till ye give up!

TOM: Mas'r, if you was sick, or in trouble, or dying, and I could save you, I'd *give* you my heart's blood; and, if taking every drop of blood in this poor old body would save your precious soul, I'd give 'em freely. Do the worst you can, my troubles will be over soon; but if you don't repent yours won't never end.

LEGREE strikes TOM down with the butt of his whip.

LEGREE: How do you like that?

SAMBO: He's most gone, mas'r!

TOM: [*Rises feebly on his hands.*] There an't no more you can do. I forgive you with all my soul. [*Sinks back, and is carried off by SAMBO and QUIMBO.*]

LEGREE: I believe he's done for finally. Well, his mouth is shut up at last—that's one comfort. [*Enter GEORGE SHELBY, MARKS and CUTE.*] Strangers! Well what do you want?

GEORGE: I understand that you bought in New Orleans a negro named Tom?

LEGREE: Yes, I did buy such a fellow, and a devil of a bargain I had of it, too! I believe he's trying to die, but I don't know as he'll make it out.

GEORGE: Where is he? Let me see him?

SAMBO: Dere he is. [*Points to TOM.*]

LEGREE: How dare you speak? [*Drives SAMBO and QUIMBO off. GEORGE exits.*]

CUTE: Now's the time to nab him.

MARKS: How are you, Mr. Legree?

LEGREE: What the devil brought you here?

MARKS: This little bit of paper. I arrest you for the murder of Mr. St. Clare. What do you say to that?

LEGREE: This is my answer! [*Makes a blow at MARK, who dodges, and CUTE receives the blow—he cries out and runs off, MARKS fires at LEGREE, and follows CUTE.*] I am hit!—the game's up! [*Falls dead. QUIMBO and SAMBO return and carry him off laughing.*]

GEORGE SHELBY enters, supporting TOM. Music. They advance and TOM falls, centre.

GEORGE: Oh! dear Uncle Tom! do wake—do speak once more! look up! Here's Master George—your own little Master George. Don't you know me?

TOM: [*Opening his eyes and speaking in a feeble tone.*] Mas'r George! Bless de Lord! it's all I wanted! They hav'n't forgot me! It warms my soul; it does my old heart good! Now I shall die content!

GEORGE: You shan't die! you mustn't die, nor think of it. I have come to buy you, and take you home.

TOM: Oh, Mas'r George, you're too late. The Lord has bought me, and is going to take me home.

GEORGE: Oh! don't die. It will kill me—it will break my heart to think what you have suffered, poor, poor fellow!

TOM: Don't call me, poor fellow! I *have* been poor fellow; but that's all past and gone now. I'm right in the door, going into glory! Oh, Mas'r George! *Heaven has come!* I've got the victory, the Lord has given it to me! Glory be to His name! [*Dies.*]

Solemn music. GEORGE covers UNCLE TOM with his cloak, and kneels over him. Clouds work on and conceal them, and then work off.

SCENE VI

Gorgeous clouds, tinted with sunlight. EVA, robed in white, is discovered on the back of a milk-white dove, with expanded wings, as if just soaring upward. Her hands are extended in benediction over ST. CLARE and UNCLE TOM who are kneeling and gazing up to her. Expressive music. Slow curtain.

END

HENRIK IBSEN

Hedda Gabler

When Henrik Ibsen (1828–1906) was eight years old, his father, a merchant in Skien, a small logging port in the north of Norway, went bankrupt. The event brought the family not only the misery and shame of poverty, but also (what was evidently more painful) a terrible sense of public scandal, personal disgrace, and bitter recrimination, from which the young Ibsen fled as soon as he could, leaving home at fifteen.

It is comforting to imagine that, later in life, Ibsen may have felt partially compensated for the unhappiness of his childhood by the quality which that experience seems to have bestowed upon his character: his unusual power of identifying and exploring unpleasant and complex truths about human nature and society. Although Ibsen would carry a morbid fear of personal scandal throughout the rest of his life, at the same time, he maintained a professional fascination with the process by which real or anticipated scandals were able to draw out aspects of character and moral dilemmas that otherwise lay below the surface of ordinary life. By repeatedly exposing the dark corners of contemporary life to the light of reason, Ibsen's plays became a major force in transforming the European imagination. For audiences used to a theatrical diet consisting, for the most part, of facile melodramas and sentimental comedies, the corrosive force of Ibsen's so-called "social problem" plays—which included *Pillars of Society* (1877), *A Doll's House* (1879), *Ghosts* (1881), *An Enemy of the People* (1882), and *The Wild Duck* (1884)—was felt keenly. And though such works were bound to raise widespread objections in the short run, they gradually earned their author extensive praise. With these plays of his middle career Ibsen became famous throughout Europe (and eventually the rest of the world). Because of their remorseless exposure of personal dishonesty, moral hypocrisy, and social injustice, his reputation became established as—depending on who was speaking—an indecent muckraker or a sort of moralist prophet who inveighed against the sins of modern civilization.

Naturally, however, the truth about Ibsen is much more complex than either of those caricatures will allow. Ibsen had been writing for many years before at last achieving fame in his fifties. His first play, *Cataline* (1850), was a historical drama set in ancient Rome. Like most first plays, it is not an outstanding work, but it is at least competent, and was enough to secure Ibsen a post as a resident playwright of the Norske Teatret in Bergen. Several years and several plays later, he became Artistic Director of the Norske Teatret in Christiana, where he continued to write and direct. During these years, Ibsen was prolific, writing several verse dramas in a progressively more assured style which culminated in *The Pretenders* (1863), and involving himself with the productions of some two hundred plays by others. However, excepting the presence of Ibsen himself, Norwegian theatre was not particularly strong in those years, relying on out-of-date methods and a largely uninspired and hackneyed repertoire; so it was perhaps a blessing in disguise that Ibsen's theatre eventually went bankrupt, leaving him free, in 1864, to embark on a tour of Italy on a travel grant. He would not return to Norway for nearly thirty years.

Freedom from the practical demands of running a theatre seems to have unshackled Ibsen's literary imagination. During his first years in exile he wrote two enormous, brilliant works of drama which he intended to be read rather than staged, and which accordingly paid little heed to any conventional stage demands. *Brand* (1866) is about a preacher who is so sternly single-minded and uncompromising in his pursuit of a higher calling that he alienates all human affection. *Peer Gynt* (1867) is about a character who is the polar opposite: an aimless, unprincipled, opportunistic (though charming) adventurer, who only discovers some meaning to his life when faced with death. In these two plays with their opposite characters, many of the themes of Ibsen's subsequent work are foreshadowed. Still, those who had read *Brand* and *Peer Gynt* could not have felt fully prepared for the series of realistic plays with their merciless criticisms of society which Ibsen began to write in the late 1870s. By the same token, however, those who remembered these plays may have been somewhat less surprised some years later when, with the last of the "social problem" plays, *The Wild Duck*, Ibsen began to turn away from the theme of the individual in conflict with society and toward a greater focus on the individual's yearning for self-fulfillment. The change was certainly evident in *Rosmersholm* (1886) and *The Lady from the Sea* (1888), but became most pronounced in the four last poetic prose dramas: *The Master Builder* (1892), *Little Eyolf* (1894), *John Gabriel Borkman* (1896), and *When We Dead Awaken* (1899).

Nestled in just before those last four plays is *Hedda Gabler* (1890), a play that does not make much overt use of symbolism, but does show a tendency toward self-analysis comparable with that found in the last plays. Were we to sum up the play in a phrase, we might, as Wilson Knight suggests, call it "the study of an exasperated woman." As for the reasons that Hedda is so exasperated, we certainly find some of them in the social conditions in which she must live. But to rest solely upon such answers is to ignore much that is most interesting in this play. For Hedda is not so clearly a victim of patriarchy as was, say, Nora in Ibsen's *A Doll's House*. Part of Hedda's problem is that she is a romantic who is waiting for something unknown to bring meaning into her life. Her various attempts to seize on likely objects of inspiration lead invariably to frustration, and her efforts to overcome this syndrome lead eventually to self-destruction. When *Hedda Gabler* first appeared it was greeted with much bafflement. Even sophisticated audience members who could comprehend the frustrated protagonists of novels like Tolstoy's *Anna Karenina* or Flaubert's *Madame Bovary* were perhaps unprepared to recognize a similar portrait on the stage. In our age, however, we may have become more used to reading through dialogue to recognize a hidden psychological portrait. Perhaps this is the reason that *Hedda Gabler* seems to hold pride of place today as Ibsen's most admired play.

[C.S.W.]

HENRIK IBSEN
Hedda Gabler

A new version by Craig S. Walker,

based on the original English translation by William Archer & Edmund Gosse.

This adaptation has been created by modernizing the language of the original translation.

CHARACTERS IN THE PLAY

GEORGE TESMAN
HEDDA TESMAN, *his wife*
MISS JULIANA TESMAN, *his aunt*
MRS. ELVSTED
JUDGE BRACK
EILERT LÖVBORG
BERTA, *a servant*

THE SETTING IS TESMAN'S VILLA, IN THE
WEST END OF CHRISTIANIA [NOW OSLO],
NORWAY.

ACT I.

A large, attractive, and tastefully furnished drawing-room, decorated in dark colours. In the back, a wide doorway with curtains drawn open leads into a smaller room decorated in the same style as the drawing-room. In the right-hand wall of the front room, a folding door leads to the hall. In the opposite wall, on the left, is a glass door, also with curtains drawn open. Through the panes can be seen part of a veranda and trees covered with autumn foliage. An oval table covered with a table-cloth and surrounded by chairs is towards the front. Downstage, by the wall on the right, is a wide dark porcelain stove and a high-backed arm-chair, a cushioned foot-rest, and two footstools. A settee, with a small round table in front of it, is in the upper right-hand corner. Downstage, not far from the wall on the left, is a sofa. Further back than the glass doors is a piano. On either side of the doorway at the back are whatnots with terra-cotta and majolica ornaments.[1] *Against the back wall of the inner room is a sofa, with a table, and one or two chairs. Hanging above the sofa is the portrait of a handsome elderly man in a General's uniform. There is a hanging lamp with an opal glass shade over the table. Several bouquets of flowers are arranged about the drawing-room, in vases. Others lie upon the tables. The floors in both rooms are covered with thick carpets. The morning sun shines in through the glass door.*

MISS JULIANA TESMAN, wearing a hat and carrying a parasol, comes in from the hall, followed by BERTA, who carries yet another bouquet wrapped in paper. MISS TESMAN is a pleasant-looking lady of about sixty-five. She is nicely but simply dressed in a gray walking-outfit. BERTA is a middle-aged woman of plain and somewhat rural appearance.

MISS TESMAN: [*Steps close to the door, listens, and says softly.*] Honestly! I don't believe they're so much as stirring yet!

BERTA: [*Also softly.*] I told you so, Miss. Remember how late the boat got in last night. Then, when they got home, Lord, what a huge lot of stuff the young mistress had to unpack before she could get to bed.

MISS TESMAN: Well—let them have their sleep. But let's see they get a good breath of fresh air when they do appear.

---

[1] *whatnots*] a stand with shelves for bric-a-brac; *majolica*] decoratively coloured white earthenware.

She goes to the glass door and throws it open.

BERTA: [*Beside the table, at a loss what to do with the bouquet in her hand.*] There isn't really a decent bit of room left for these. I guess I'll put them over here.

She places the bouquet on the piano.

MISS TESMAN: So, you've got a new mistress now, Berta. Heaven knows it wasn't easy for me to part with you.　15

BERTA: [*On the point of weeping.*] Well don't think it wasn't hard for me too, Miss. After all the wonderful years I been with you and Miss Rina.[2]　20

MISS TESMAN: Well, we have to make the best of it. Nothing else could be done. George can't do without you—absolutely not. He's had you to look after him since he was a little boy.

BERTA: Yes, but, Miss Julia, I can't help thinking of　25 poor Miss Rina, lying there helpless at home, with only that new girl to see to her. That one'll never learn how to take proper care of an invalid.

MISS TESMAN: Never mind, I'll manage to train her. Besides, I'll take on most of the burden myself. No　30 need to worry about my poor sister.

BERTA: Yes, but something else, Miss: I'm so afraid I won't suit the young mistress.

MISS TESMAN: Oh—there may be one or two things at first—　35

BERTA: I expect she'll be terrible grand in her ways.

MISS TESMAN: Well, there's no surprise there— General Gabler's daughter! Think of the sort of life she led in her father's time. Remember how we used to see her riding down the road with the　40 General? In that long black habit—with all those feathers in her hat?

BERTA: Yes, ma'am. Lord, I'd never have dreamt in those days that she and our Master George would pair up.　45

MISS TESMAN: Nor I. By the way, Berta—while I think of it—in future you mustn't say Master George. It's Dr. Tesman now.

BERTA: Yes, the young mistress mentioned that—last night—the moment they set foot in the house. It's　50 true then, Miss?

---

2 Rina] pronounced "Reena."

MISS TESMAN: Yes, indeed. Some foreign university has made him a doctor while he was abroad. I hadn't heard a word about it, until he told me himself at the pier.　55

BERTA: Well, he's clever enough for anything, he is. Though I'd never have guessed he'd go in for doctoring people, too.

MISS TESMAN: No, no, not that sort of doctor. [*Nods significantly.*] But let me tell you, we may have to　60 call him something still grander soon.

BERTA: Really? What's that, Miss?

MISS TESMAN: [*Smiling.*] Hm—wouldn't you like to know. [*With emotion.*] Oh, dear! If only my poor brother could look up from his grave and see　65 what's become of his little boy! [*Looks around.*] But, Berta—why in heaven's name have you taken all the chintz covers off the furniture?

BERTA: The mistress said to. Can't abide covers on chairs, she says.　70

MISS TESMAN: This is going to be their everyday sitting-room, then?

BERTA: Well that's what the mistress said to me. Master George—the doctor—he didn't say anything about it.　75

GEORGE TESMAN comes from the right, humming to himself, and carrying a large, empty trunk. He is a middle-sized, young-looking man of thirty-three, somewhat stout, with a round, open, cheerful face, fair hair and beard. He wears spectacles, and is somewhat carelessly dressed in comfortable indoor clothes.

MISS TESMAN: Good morning, good morning, George!

TESMAN: [*In the doorway between the rooms.*] Aunt Julia! Dear Aunt Julia! [*Goes up to her and shakes hands warmly.*] Come all this way—so early! Eh?　80

MISS TESMAN: Why, of course I had to come and see how you were getting on.

TESMAN: Despite not having a proper night's rest?

MISS TESMAN: Oh, that makes no difference to me.

TESMAN: Well, I suppose you got home all right　85 from the pier, eh?

MISS TESMAN: Yes, quite safely, thank goodness. Judge Brack was kind enough to see me right to my door.

TESMAN: We were awfully sorry we couldn't give you　90

a seat in the carriage. But you saw what a pile of boxes Hedda had to bring.

MISS TESMAN: Yes, she had certainly plenty of boxes.

BERTA: [*To* TESMAN.] Should I go in and see if there's something I can do for the mistress?

TESMAN: No thanks, Berta—no need. She said she'd ring if she wanted anything.

BERTA: [*Going towards the right.*] Very well.

TESMAN: Hang on, though—take this trunk with you.

BERTA: [*Taking it.*] I'll put it in the attic. [*She goes out by the hall door.*]

TESMAN: Imagine, Auntie—I had that whole trunk chock full of papers. You wouldn't believe how much I picked up from all those archives—strange old things no one has any idea about—

MISS TESMAN: Yes, George, you don't seem to have wasted any time on your honeymoon.

TESMAN: No, indeed, I haven't. But, please, take off your hat, Auntie. Here, why not let me untie the strings, eh?

MISS TESMAN: [*While he does so.*] Oh, well... It's just as if you were still at home with us.

TESMAN: [*With the hat in his hand, looks at it from all sides.*] My, that's a splendid bonnet you've got there!

MISS TESMAN: I bought it for Hedda's sake.

TESMAN: Eh? For Hedda's sake?

MISS TESMAN: So that Hedda needn't be ashamed of me if we happen to be out together.

TESMAN: [*Patting her cheek.*] You always think of everything, Aunt Julia. [*Lays the hat on a chair beside the table.*] Now, then, let's sit ourselves on the sofa and have a little chat, till Hedda comes.

They seat themselves. She places her parasol in the corner of the sofa.

MISS TESMAN: [*Takes both his hands and looks at him.*] What a delight it is to see you here again, as large as life, George! My dear brother's own boy!

TESMAN: It's a delight to see you too, Aunt Julia. You've been father and mother in one to me.

MISS TESMAN: Yes, I know you'll always keep a place in your heart for your old aunts.

TESMAN: What about Aunt Rina? No improvement, eh?

MISS TESMAN: Oh no. We really can't hope for any improvement there, poor thing. There she lies, helpless, just as she has for years. But God forbid that I lose her for a long while yet. If I did, I don't know what I'd do with myself—especially now that I haven't got you to care for any more.

TESMAN: [*Patting her back.*] There, there!

MISS TESMAN: [*Suddenly changing her tone.*] And to think that now you're a married man, George! And that you should be the one to carry off Hedda Gabler—the beautiful Hedda Gabler, who always had so many admirers!

TESMAN: [*Hums a little and smile complacently.*] Yes, I suppose I've got several friends in town who wouldn't mind being in my shoes, eh?

MISS TESMAN: And then to have such a fine long honeymoon! More than...well, nearly six months—

TESMAN: Well, for me it was a sort of research tour as well. I had to do a lot of grubbing among old records—and no end of books too.

MISS TESMAN: Oh yes, I suppose so. [*More confidentially, and lowering her voice a little.*] But listen now, George: is there nothing...*special* you have to tell me?

TESMAN: About our journey?

MISS TESMAN: Yes.

TESMAN: No, nothing except what I've already told you in my letters. I had a doctor's degree conferred on me—but I told you that yesterday.

MISS TESMAN: Yes, yes, you did. But what I mean is—haven't you any—any—expectations—?

TESMAN: Expectations?

MISS TESMAN: George, you know... I'm your old auntie.

TESMAN: Well, of course I have expectations.

MISS TESMAN: Ah!

TESMAN: I have every expectation of being a professor one of these days.[3]

MISS TESMAN: Well, yes, a professor...

TESMAN: Indeed, I may as well say that I'm certain of it. But, Auntie, you know all about that already.

MISS TESMAN: [*Laughing to herself.*] Yes, of course I do. You're quite right. [*Changing the subject.*] But

---

3 professor] Tesman is on a special research fellowship, and currently holds a lower rank, such as "lecturer."

we were talking about your journey. It must have cost a great deal of money, George?

TESMAN: Well, that big travelling grant went quite a way.

MISS TESMAN: But I don't understand how it could go far enough for two.

TESMAN: No, that *is* a bit baffling, eh?

MISS TESMAN: And especially travelling with a lady. That, I'm told, makes it ever so much more expensive.

TESMAN: Yes, of course—it would make it a little more expensive. But Hedda had to have this trip, Auntie. She really did. Nothing else would have done.

MISS TESMAN: No, no, I suppose not. A honeymoon seems to be quite indispensable nowadays. But tell me: have you had a good look through the house yet?

TESMAN: Yes, I certainly have. I've been up since dawn.

MISS TESMAN: And what do you think of it?

TESMAN: Delighted! Quite delighted! Except, I have no idea what we'll do with the two empty rooms between this room and Hedda's bedroom.

MISS TESMAN: [*Laughing.*] Oh, my dear George! I daresay you may find some use for them in time.

TESMAN: Yes, I suppose you may be right at that, Aunt Julia. You mean as my library increases, eh?

MISS TESMAN: Exactly, my dear boy. I was thinking of your books.

TESMAN: I'm especially pleased for Hedda's sake. Several times, before we were engaged, she said that she'd never want to live *anywhere* but the Falk villa.

MISS TESMAN: Yes, it was rather lucky that this very house should be put on the market just after you'd left.

TESMAN: Yes, fortune was on our side, eh?

MISS TESMAN: But the expense, George! You'll find it awfully expensive, all this.

TESMAN: [*Looks at her, a little cast down.*] Yes, I suppose I might...

MISS TESMAN: Oh, terribly!

TESMAN: How much do you think? In round numbers, eh?

MISS TESMAN: Oh, I couldn't even guess until all the accounts come in.

TESMAN: Well, fortunately, Judge Brack secured very favourable terms for me—so he said in a letter to Hedda.

MISS TESMAN: Yes, no need to be uneasy, my boy. Besides, I've given security for the furniture and all the carpets.

TESMAN: Security? You? But my dear Aunt Julia—what sort of security could you give?

MISS TESMAN: I took out a mortgage on our annuity.

TESMAN: [*Jumps up.*] What? On your—and Aunt Rina's annuity!

MISS TESMAN: Yes. I couldn't think of any other plan, you see.

TESMAN: [*Standing before her.*] Have you lost your senses, Auntie? Your annuity—that's all you and Aunt Rina have to live on.

MISS TESMAN: Well, well—no need to get so excited. It's only a formality you know—Judge Brack assured me of that. He was kind enough to arrange the whole affair for me. A mere formality, he said.

TESMAN: Yes, that may be all very well. But still—

MISS TESMAN: You'll have your own salary to depend upon now. And, good heavens, even if we did have to pay out a little—! To eke things out a bit at the start —Why, it would be nothing but a pleasure to us.

TESMAN: Oh Auntie! Will you never get tired of making sacrifices for me?

MISS TESMAN: [*Rises and lays her hand on his shoulders.*] What happiness do I have in this world if not to smooth your way for you, my boy? You've never had a father nor mother to turn to. But now we've reached the goal, George. Things may have looked black for us, at times; but, thank heaven, now you have nothing to fear.

TESMAN: Yes, it's amazing how everything has turned out for the best.

MISS TESMAN: And all those people who tried to stand in your way—now you've got them at your feet. They've all fallen away, George. Even your most dangerous rival—his fall was the worst. Now he'll just have to lie in the bed he's made for himself—poor misguided creature.

TESMAN: Have you heard anything of Eilert? Since I went away, I mean.

MISS TESMAN: Only that he's supposed to have published a new book.

TESMAN: Really? Eilert Lövborg! You mean just recently, eh? 270

MISS TESMAN: Yes, so they say. Heaven knows whether it's worth anything. Now, when *your* new book appears, George—that will be another story! What will it be about?

TESMAN: It will deal with the domestic industries of 275 Brabant during the Middle Ages.

MISS TESMAN: Imagine! Being able to write about a subject like that!

TESMAN: However, it may be some time before the book is ready. I have all these collections of 280 documents to sort out first, you see.

MISS TESMAN: Yes, collecting and sorting—no one can beat you at that. In that, you're certainly my brother's son.

TESMAN: I'm quite eager to get to work on it; 285 especially now that I have a wonderful home of my own to work in, eh?

MISS TESMAN: And, most of all, now that you have got the wife of your heart, dear George.

TESMAN: [*Embracing her.*] Oh, yes, Aunt Julia. 290 Hedda really is the best part of it all. [*Looks towards the doorway.*] I think I hear her coming.

HEDDA enters from the left through the inner room. She is a woman of twenty-nine. Her face and figure show refinement and distinction. Her complexion is pale and opaque. Her steel-gray eyes express a cold, unruffled repose. Her hair is an agreeable medium brown, but not particularly abundant. She is dressed in a tasteful, somewhat loose-fitting morning dress.

MISS TESMAN: [*Going to meet HEDDA.*] Good morning, my dear Hedda! Good morning, and a hearty welcome! 295

HEDDA: [*Holds out her hand.*] Good morning, dear Miss Tesman. So early a call. This is kind of you.

MISS TESMAN: [*With some embarrassment.*] Well— has the bride slept well in her new home?

HEDDA: Yes, thanks. Reasonably well. 300

TESMAN: [*Laughing.*] Reasonably! Oh, that's good, Hedda! You were sleeping like a log when I got up.

HEDDA: Fortunately. Of course, it always takes a little time to grow accustomed to new surroundings—one can't do it all at once, Miss Tesman. 305 [*Looking towards the left.*] Oh—the maid's gone

and opened the veranda door, and let in a whole flood of sunshine.

MISS TESMAN: [*Going towards the door.*] Well, let's shut it, then. 310

HEDDA: No, no. Tesman, why don't you draw the curtains instead. That will give a softer light.

TESMAN: [*At the door.*] All right—all right. There, Hedda, now you have both shade and fresh air.

HEDDA: Yes, we'll certainly need the fresh air, with 315 all these stacks of flowers—. But, Miss Tesman— won't you sit down?

MISS TESMAN: No, thank you. Now that I've seen that everything is all right here—thank heaven— I must be getting home again. My sister is lying 320 waiting for me, poor thing.

TESMAN: Give her my very best love, Auntie; and say I shall look in and see her later in the day.

MISS TESMAN: Yes, yes, I'll tell her. Oh, by the way, George—[*Feeling in her dress pocket.*]—I'd almost 325 forgotten—I have something for you.

TESMAN: What's that, Auntie? Eh?

MISS TESMAN: [*Produces a flat parcel wrapped in newspaper.*] Here you are, my dear boy.

TESMAN: [*Opening the parcel.*] Well, my word!—You 330 really saved them for me, Aunt Julia! Hedda! Isn't this touching, eh?

HEDDA: [*Beside the whatnot on the right.*] Well, what is it?

TESMAN: My old morning-shoes! My slippers. 335

HEDDA: Indeed. I remember you spoke of them quite often while we were away.

TESMAN: Yes, I missed them terribly. [*Goes up to her.*] Now you can have a look at them, Hedda.

HEDDA: [*Going towards the stove.*] Thanks, I'm not 340 really that interested.

TESMAN: [*Following her.*] Just imagine—as ill as she was, Aunt Rina embroidered these for me. You wouldn't believe how many memories cling to them. 345

HEDDA: [*At the table.*] Scarcely for me, though.

MISS TESMAN: No, of course not for Hedda, George.

TESMAN: Well, no, but now that she's part of the family, I thought—

HEDDA: [*Interrupting.*] Oh, this servant is just never 350 going to do, Tesman.

MISS TESMAN: Berta, not do?

TESMAN: My dear, why do you say that, eh?

HEDDA: [*Pointing.*] Look! She's left her old hat lying around.

TESMAN: [*In consternation, drops the slippers on the floor.*] But, Hedda—

HEDDA: Imagine, if anyone were to come in and see it.

TESMAN: But Hedda—that's—that's Aunt Julia's bonnet.

HEDDA: Is it?

MISS TESMAN: [*Taking up the hat.*] Yes, indeed it's mine. Moreover, it's not old, Madam Hedda.

HEDDA: I really didn't look closely at it, Miss Tesman.

MISS TESMAN: [*Trying on the hat.*] As a matter of fact, it's the first time I've worn it—the very first time.

TESMAN: And a very nice hat it is too—quite a beauty!

MISS TESMAN: Oh, it's no big thing, George. [*Look around her.*] My parasol—? Ah, here. [*Takes it.*] This is mine too—[*mutters*]—not Berta's.

TESMAN: A new bonnet and a new parasol! How about that, Hedda?

HEDDA: Very fine indeed.

TESMAN: Isn't it, though? Eh? But Auntie, take a good look at Hedda before you go. What a beauty she is, eh?

MISS TESMAN: Oh, my dear, there's nothing new in that. Hedda was always lovely.

She nods and goes towards the right.

TESMAN: [*Following.*] Yes, but have you noticed what a picture of health she is? How much she's filled out while we were away?

HEDDA: [*Crossing the room.*] Oh, do be quiet—!

MISS TESMAN: [*Who has stopped and turned.*] Filled out?

TESMAN: Of course, you can't notice it so much when she's got that dress on. But I see her when she's—

HEDDA: [*At the glass door, impatiently.*] Oh, you don't see anything.

TESMAN: It must be the mountain air in the Tyrol—[4]

HEDDA: [*Curtly, interrupting.*] I am exactly as I was when I left.

TESMAN: So you insist; but I'm quite certain you're not. Wouldn't you say, Auntie?

MISS TESMAN: [*Who has been gazing at her with folded hands.*] Hedda is lovely—lovely—lovely. [*Goes up to her, takes her head between both hands, draws it downwards, and kisses her hair.*] God bless and preserve Hedda Tesman—for George's sake.

HEDDA: [*Gently freeing herself.*] Oh—! Let me go.

MISS TESMAN: [*In quiet emotion.*] I shall not let a day pass without coming to see you.

TESMAN: No, you won't, Auntie, will you, eh?

MISS TESMAN: Good-bye—good-bye!

She exits through the hall door. TESMAN goes with her. The door remains half open and TESMAN can be heard repeating his message to Aunt Rina and his thanks for the slippers.

In the meantime, HEDDA paces around the room, raising her arms and clenching her hands as if in desperation. Then she flings back the curtains from the glass door, and stands there looking out.

Presently TESMAN returns and closes the door behind him.

TESMAN: [*Picks up the slippers from the floor.*] What are you looking at, Hedda?

HEDDA: [*Once more calm and mistress of herself.*] Just the leaves. They're so yellow—so withered.

TESMAN: [*Wraps up the slippers and lays them on the table.*] Well, we're well into September now.

HEDDA: [*Again restless.*] Yes, that's right isn't it? Already in...in September.

TESMAN: Did you find Aunt Julia's manner a little strange, dear? Almost solemn? You don't have any idea what was the matter with her, eh?

HEDDA: I scarcely know her. She's not often like that?

TESMAN: No, not the way she was today.

HEDDA: [*Leaving the glass door.*] Do you think she was annoyed about the hat?

TESMAN: Oh, scarcely at all. Well, maybe a little, just for a moment—

HEDDA: But what an idea, to toss her hat down in the drawing-room! No one does that sort of thing.

TESMAN: Well you may be sure Aunt Julia won't do it again.

4 Tyrol] a province in the Alps, now straddling the Austrian-Italian border.

HEDDA: In any case, I'll find some way of making peace with her. 430

TESMAN: Yes, dear, good Hedda; if only you would...

HEDDA: When you call this afternoon, you might invite her to spend the evening here.

TESMAN: Yes, I will. And there's one other thing you could do that would do her heart a world of good. 435

HEDDA: What is it?

TESMAN: If you could just manage to call her Auntie—for my sake, Hedda, eh?[5]

HEDDA: No no, Tesman—you really can't ask that of me. I've said so before. I'll try to call her Julia; 440 and you'll have to be satisfied with that.

TESMAN: Well, well. I just thought that now that you're part of the family...

HEDDA: Hm. No, I can't see why...

She goes up towards the middle doorway.

TESMAN: [*After a pause.*] Is anything the matter, 445 Hedda? Eh?

HEDDA: I'm just looking at my old piano. It doesn't go very well with all the other things.

TESMAN: The first pay-cheque I get, we'll see about exchanging it. 450

HEDDA: No, no—not an exchange. I don't want to part with it. Suppose we put it there in the inner room, and then get another for out here. When it's convenient, I mean.

TESMAN: [*A little taken aback.*] Yes—of course we 455 could do that.

HEDDA: [*Takes up the bouquet from the piano.*] These flowers weren't here last night when we arrived.

TESMAN: Aunt Julia must have brought them for you. 460

HEDDA: [*Examining the bouquet.*] A visiting-card. [*Takes it out and reads.*] "Shall return later in the day." Can you guess whose card it is?

TESMAN: No. Whose?

HEDDA: The name is "Mrs. Elvsted." 465

TESMAN: Really? [*Looking at card.*] Sheriff Elvsted's wife, eh?[6] Miss Rysing that was.

HEDDA: Exactly. The girl with the irritating hair, that she was always showing off. An old flame of yours I'm told. 470

TESMAN: [*Laughing.*] Oh, that didn't last long; and it was before I knew you, Hedda. But imagine her being in town.

HEDDA: It's odd that she'd call on us. I've scarcely seen her since we left school. 475

TESMAN: I haven't seen her either for—heaven knows how long. I wonder how she can stand living in such an out-of-the-way hole, eh?

HEDDA: [*After a moment's thought, says suddenly.*] Tesman, tell me: isn't it somewhere near there that 480 he—that—Eilert Lövborg is living?

TESMAN: Yes, he's somewhere in that part of the country.

BERTA enters by the hall door.

BERTA: That lady, ma'am, the one that brought flowers a little while ago, is here again. [*Pointing.*] 485 The flowers you have in your hand, ma'am.

HEDDA: Is she? Well, please show her in.

BERTA opens the door for MRS. ELVSTED, and goes out.—MRS. ELVSTED is a delicate woman, with pretty, soft features. Her eyes are light blue, large, round, and somewhat prominent, with a startled, inquiring expression. Her hair is remarkably light, almost flaxen, and unusually abundant and wavy. She is a couple of years younger than HEDDA. She wears a dark visiting dress, tasteful, but not quite in the latest fashion.

HEDDA: [*Receives her warmly.*] Dear Mrs. Elvsted: how do you do? Delightful to see you again.

MRS. ELVSTED: [*Nervously, struggling for self-control.*] 490 Yes, it's quite some time since we met.

TESMAN: [*Gives her his hand.*] And we too, eh?

HEDDA: Thanks for your lovely flowers—

MRS. ELVSTED: Oh, not at all. I would have come straight here yesterday afternoon; but I heard that 495 you were away—

TESMAN: Have you just come to town? Eh?

---

5 Auntie] In the original text, Tesman asks Hedda to use the intimate pronoun, *du* (rather than the formal *De*— the equivalent of *tu* versus *vous* in French).

6 Sheriff] There is no exact English equivalent for the Nor- wegian term "*fogd,*" a government official who tours a particular region administering justice, but the position of sheriff is comparable.

MRS. ELVSTED: I arrived yesterday, about noon. Oh, I was quite desperate when I heard that you weren't home. 500

HEDDA: Desperate? How so?

TESMAN: Why, my dear Miss Rysing—I mean Mrs. Elvsted—

HEDDA: I hope you're not in any trouble?

MRS. ELVSTED: Yes, I am. And I don't know another living creature here that I can turn to. 505

HEDDA: [*Laying the bouquet on the table.*] Come—let's sit here on the sofa—

MRS. ELVSTED: Oh, I'm too restless to sit down.

HEDDA: Of course you're not. Come here. 510

She draws MRS. ELVSTED down upon the sofa and sits at her side.

TESMAN: Well? What is it, Mrs. Elvsted—?

HEDDA: Has something happened at home?

MRS. ELVSTED: Yes—and no. Oh—I'm so anxious that you should not misunderstand me—

HEDDA: Then the best thing is to tell us the whole story, Mrs. Elvsted. 515

TESMAN: I suppose that's what you have come for—eh?

MRS. ELVSTED: Yes, yes—of course it is. Well then, I should tell you—if you don't already know—that Eilert Lövborg is in town, too. 520

HEDDA: Lövborg—!

TESMAN: What? Has Eilert Lövborg come back? How about that, Hedda!

HEDDA: Yes, yes—I heard. 525

MRS. ELVSTED: He's been here a week already. Imagine, a whole week, alone—in this terrible town, with temptations on all sides.

HEDDA: But, my dear Mrs. Elvsted—how does this concern you so much? 530

MRS. ELVSTED: [*Gives a startled look, and says quickly.*] He was the children's tutor.

HEDDA: Your children's?

MRS. ELVSTED: My husband's. I have none.

HEDDA: Your step-children, then? 535

MRS. ELVSTED: Yes.

TESMAN: [*Somewhat hesitatingly.*] But was he—I'm not sure how to say this—was he—regular enough in his habits to be fit for the post? Eh?

MRS. ELVSTED: For the last two years his conduct 540

has been irreproachable.

TESMAN: Has it really? How about that, Hedda!

HEDDA: I heard.

MRS. ELVSTED: Completely irreproachable, I assure you. In every respect. But still—knowing that he's 545 *here*—in a big city—with a lot of money in his hands—I can't help being terrified for him.

TESMAN: Why didn't he stay where he was? With you and your husband, eh?

MRS. ELVSTED: After his book was published he was 550 just too restless to stay with us.

TESMAN: [*To Hedda.*] Oh yes, by the way, Aunt Julia told me: he's just published a book.

MRS. ELVSTED: Yes, a big book, dealing with the progress of civilizations—in a sort of broad outline. 555 It came out about a fortnight ago, and since it's sold so well, and been so widely reviewed—and caused such a sensation—

TESMAN: Has it really? It must be something he's had sitting by since his better days, eh? 560

MRS. ELVSTED: Since long ago, you mean?

TESMAN: Yes.

MRS. ELVSTED: No, he's written it all since he's been with us—within the last year.

TESMAN: Well, that's very good news, eh, Hedda? 565 How about that!

MRS. ELVSTED: Yes, so long as it lasts.

HEDDA: Have you seen him here in town?

MRS. ELVSTED: No, not yet. I've had some difficulty finding out his address. But this morning I finally 570 discovered it.

HEDDA: [*Looks searchingly at her.*] You know, it seems a little odd that your husband...uh—

MRS. ELVSTED: [*Starting nervously.*] That my husband—what? 575

HEDDA: That he'd send you to town on such an errand, rather than coming himself to look after his friend.

MRS. ELVSTED: Oh no, no—my husband has no time. And besides, I—I had some shopping to do. 580

HEDDA: [*With a slight smile.*] Ah, well: I see.

MRS. ELVSTED: [*Rising quickly and uneasily.*] And now, Mr. Tesman, I beg you: if Eilert Lövborg comes to see you, please receive him as kindly as you can! And I'm sure he will. You were such good 585 friends in the old days. And, of course, you're both interested in the same subjects—the same discipline—as far as I can understand.

TESMAN: We used to be, at any rate.

MRS. ELVSTED: That's why I beg you—both of you—to keep a sharp eye on him. You'll promise me that, Mr. Tesman—won't you? 590

TESMAN: With pleasure, Miss Rysing—

HEDDA: Elvsted.

TESMAN: I assure you I'll do everything in my power for Eilert. You may rely on me. 595

MRS. ELVSTED: That is very, very kind of you! [*Presses his hands.*] Thank you, thank you! [*Nervously.*] You see, my husband is so fond of him.

HEDDA: [*Rising.*] You ought to write to him, Tesman. 600 He may be reluctant to come of his own accord.

TESMAN: Well, perhaps that would be the right thing to do, eh?

HEDDA: And the sooner the better. Why not right now? 605

MRS. ELVSTED: [*Imploringly.*] Oh, would you?

TESMAN: I'll write at once. Do you have his address, Miss—Mrs. Elvsted?

MRS. ELVSTED: Yes. [*Takes a slip of paper from her pocket, and hands it to him.*] Here it is. 610

TESMAN: Good, good. I'll go in—[*Looks about him.*] By the way—my slippers? Oh, here.

Takes the packet, and is about to go.

HEDDA: Be sure you write a warm, friendly letter. And a good long one too.

TESMAN: Yes, I will. 615

MRS. ELVSTED: But please, please don't say a word to show that I suggested it.

TESMAN: No, how could you think I would, eh?

He goes out to the right, through the inner room.

HEDDA: [*Goes up to MRS. ELVSTED, smiles, and says in a low voice.*] There, that's two birds with one stone. 620

MRS. ELVSTED: What do you mean?

HEDDA: You couldn't see I wanted him to go?

MRS. ELVSTED: Yes, to write the letter—

HEDDA: And so we could speak privately.

MRS. ELVSTED: [*Confused.*] About the same thing? 625

HEDDA: Precisely.

MRS. ELVSTED: [*Apprehensively.*] But there *is* nothing more, Mrs. Tesman. Nothing at all!

HEDDA: Oh, I think there is. A great deal more. Sit here—and we'll have a nice, cosy, confidential chat. 630

She forces MRS. ELVSTED into the easy-chair, and seats herself on a footstool.

MRS. ELVSTED: [*Anxiously, looking at her watch.*] But, please, Mrs. Tesman—I was really just about to leave.

HEDDA: Oh, there's no need for such a rush.—So, tell me something about your life at home. 635

MRS. ELVSTED: Well, that's the last thing I want to talk about.

HEDDA: Even to me? Weren't we schoolmates?

MRS. ELVSTED: Yes, though you were in the class above me. I was so afraid of you! 640

HEDDA: Afraid of me?

MRS. ELVSTED: Yes, dreadfully. When we met on the stairs you always pulled my hair.

HEDDA: Did I, really?

MRS. ELVSTED: Yes. And once you threatened to burn it off. 645

HEDDA: Oh, that was all nonsense, of course.

MRS. ELVSTED: Yes, but I was so silly in those days.—And since then, too, we...we've drifted so far apart from each other. Our circles have been entirely different. 650

HEDDA: Well then, we must try to drift together again. Now listen! At school we were very friendly, and called each other by our first names.[7]

MRS. ELVSTED: I'm sure you must be mistaken. 655

HEDDA: No, not at all! I remember quite distinctly. So, let's renew our old friendship. [*Draws the footstool closer to MRS. ELVSTED.*] There. [*Kisses her cheek.*] Now, you must call me Hedda.

MRS. ELVSTED: [*Press and pats her hands.*] That's very good of you. I'm not used to such kindness. 660

HEDDA: There, there, there! And I shall call you Thora, as in the old days.[8]

MRS. ELVSTED: My name is Thea.[9]

HEDDA: Of course. I meant Thea. [*Looks at her* 665

---

7 very friendly] In the original text, Hedda says they used the intimate pronoun, *du.*

8 Thora] pronounced "Tora."

9 Thea] pronounced "Taya."

compassionately.] So you're not accustomed to kindness, Thea? Not even in your own home?

MRS. ELVSTED: I only wish I really had a home! But I don't; I never have.

HEDDA: [*Looks at her for a moment.*] I almost suspected as much. 670

MRS. ELVSTED: [*Gazing helplessly before her.*] Yes—yes—yes.

HEDDA: I don't quite remember—wasn't it as a housekeeper that you first went to Mr. Elvsted's? 675

MRS. ELVSTED: I really went as governess. But his wife—his last wife—was an invalid,—and rarely left her room. So I had to do the housekeeping as well.

HEDDA: And then—at last—you became mistress of the house. 680

MRS. ELVSTED: [*Sadly.*] Yes, I did.

HEDDA: Let's see—about how long ago was that?

MRS. ELVSTED: My wedding?

HEDDA: Yes.

MRS. ELVSTED: Five years ago. 685

HEDDA: Yes, I suppose it was.

MRS. ELVSTED: Well, those five years—or at any rate, the last two or three of them! Oh, Mrs Tesman, you can't imagine—

HEDDA: [*Giving her a little slap on the hand.*] Mrs Tesman? Now, Thea! 690

MRS. ELVSTED: Yes, sorry, I'll try... Well, Hedda, if—I wish you could just imagine and understand—

HEDDA: [*Lightly.*] Eilert Lövborg has been in your neighbourhood about three years, hasn't he? 695

MRS. ELVSTED: [*Looks at her doubtfully.*] Eilert Lövborg? Yes—he has.

HEDDA: Had you known him before—here in town?

MRS. ELVSTED: Barely. I mean—I knew him by name, of course. 700

HEDDA: But you saw a good deal of him in the country?

MRS. ELVSTED: Yes, almost every day. You see, he taught the children, because in the long run I couldn't manage it all myself. 705

HEDDA: No, that's clear.—And your husband—? I suppose he's often away from home?

MRS. ELVSTED: Yes. Being sheriff, you know, he has to travel quite a bit in his district.

HEDDA: [*Leaning against the arm of the chair.*] Thea—dear, sweet Thea. Tell me everything. Tell 710 me exactly how things stand.

MRS. ELVSTED: Perhaps if you asked me questions...

HEDDA: Well, what's your husband like, Thea? I mean—you know—in everyday life. Is he kind to you? 715

MRS. ELVSTED: [*Evasively.*] I'm sure he means well.

HEDDA: I would have said he was altogether too old for you. There's at least twenty years' difference between you, isn't there? 720

MRS. ELVSTED: [*Irritably.*] Yes, it's true. It is. In fact, everything about him is repellent to me. We don't have one thought in common—not a single point of sympathy.

HEDDA: But he's fond of you just the same? In his own way? 725

MRS. ELVSTED: Oh, I don't know. I sometimes think he simply regards me as a useful piece of property. One it doesn't cost him much to keep. I'm not expensive. 730

HEDDA: That's rather stupid of you.

MRS. ELVSTED: [*Shakes her head.*] That's the only way it could be—with him. He really cares for no one but himself—perhaps a little for the children.

HEDDA: And for Eilert Lövborg? 735

MRS. ELVSTED: [*Looking at her.*] For Eilert Lövborg? Why would you think that?

HEDDA: Well, dear Thea—I'd say, when he sends you all the way to town after him— [*Smiling almost imperceptibly.*] Besides, you said so yourself, to 740 Tesman.

MRS. ELVSTED: [*With a little nervous twitch.*] Did I? Yes, I suppose I did. [*Vehemently, but not loudly.*] No—I may as well make a clean breast of it! It will all come out in any case. 745

HEDDA: What's that, my dear Thea?

MRS. ELVSTED: Well, to make a long story short: my husband had no idea I was coming.

HEDDA: Really? He didn't know?

MRS. ELVSTED: No, of course not. For that matter, 750 he's away from home right now—travelling. I couldn't stand it anymore Hedda! I really couldn't—to be so utterly alone up there...

HEDDA: Well? And so...?

MRS. ELVSTED: So I put together some of my 755 things—just the essentials—as quietly as possible. And then I left.

HEDDA: Without a word?

MRS. ELVSTED: Yes—and took the train straight to town. 760

HEDDA: My dear, Thea—I wouldn't have guessed you'd ever dare.

MRS. ELVSTED: [*Rises and paces about the room.*] What else could I do?

HEDDA: But what will your husband say when you 765 go back?

MRS. ELVSTED: [*At the table, looks at her.*] Back to him?

HEDDA: Of course.

MRS. ELVSTED: I'll never go back to him again.

HEDDA: [*Rising and going towards her.*] Then you've 770 left your home for good?

MRS. ELVSTED: Yes. There was nothing else to be done.

HEDDA: But—to run off so openly.

MRS. ELVSTED: Oh, it's impossible to keep that sort 775 of thing secret.

HEDDA: But what will people say, Thea?

MRS. ELVSTED: They may say what they like, for all *I* care. [*Seats herself wearily and sadly on the sofa.*] I've only done what I had to do. 780

HEDDA: [*After a short silence.*] And what are your plans now? What will you do?

MRS. ELVSTED: I don't know yet. I only know this, that I must live *here*, where Eilert Lövborg is—or not live at all. 785

HEDDA: [*Takes a chair from the table, seats herself beside her, and strokes her hands.*] Dear Thea—how did this—this friendship—between you and Eilert Lövborg come about?

MRS. ELVSTED: Oh—gradually. I developed a sort 790 of influence over him.

HEDDA: Oh?

MRS. ELVSTED: He gave up his old habits. Not because I asked him to—I would never dare. But, naturally, he saw how repulsive they were to me; 795 and so he dropped them.

HEDDA: [*Concealing an involuntary smile of scorn.*] So, little Thea, you have redeemed him—as the saying goes.

MRS. ELVSTED: That's what he says, at any rate. 800 And, for his part, he's made a real human being of me—taught me to think...to understand so many things.

HEDDA: He gave you lessons too?

MRS. ELVSTED: No, not exactly lessons. But he 805 talked to me, about...an infinity of things. And the time came—a lovely, happy time—when I began to share his work—he allowed me to help him.

HEDDA: Oh, did he?

MRS. ELVSTED: Yes. In fact, he never wrote anything 810 without my assistance.

HEDDA: You were two good comrades, then.

MRS. ELVSTED: [*Eagerly.*] Comrades! Yes, I suppose so, Hedda—that's the word he used.—Oh, I ought to feel happy; but I can't, because I don't know how 815 long it will last.

HEDDA: You're no surer of him than that?

MRS. ELVSTED: [*Gloomily.*] There is a woman's shadow between Eilert Lövborg and me.

HEDDA: [*Tensely.*] Who would that be? 820

MRS. ELVSTED: I don't know. Someone he knew before—in his past. Someone he's never been able to forget.

HEDDA: What has he told you about—about this?

MRS. ELVSTED: He's only alluded to it once—quite 825 vaguely.

HEDDA: And what did he say?

MRS. ELVSTED: He said that when they parted, she threatened him with a pistol.

HEDDA: [*With cold composure.*] Nonsense. No one 830 does that sort of thing here.

MRS. ELVSTED: No. That's why I think it must have been that red-headed singer he once—

HEDDA: Yes, probably.

MRS. ELVSTED: I remember hearing that *she* carried 835 loaded firearms.

HEDDA: Oh well, then it must have been her.

MRS. ELVSTED: [*Wringing her hands.*] And now I hear that this singer is in town again. Think of it, Hedda! I don't know what to do— 840

HEDDA: [*Glancing towards the inner room.*] Sh! Here comes Tesman. [*Rises and whispers.*] Thea—all this must remain between you and me.

MRS. ELVSTED: [*Springing up.*] Oh yes—yes! For heaven's sake—! 845

TESMAN, *with a letter in his hand, comes from the right through the inner room.*

TESMAN: There now: the epistle is finished.

HEDDA: Fine. Mrs. Elvsted is ready to go. Wait a minute—I'll walk you to the garden gate.

TESMAN: Do you think Berta could post the letter, Hedda dear? 850

HEDDA: [*Takes it.*] I'll tell her to.

BERTA enters from the hall.

BERTA: Judge Brack wishes to know if Mrs. Tesman will receive him.

HEDDA: Yes, ask him to come in. And here—put this letter in the post. 855

BERTA: [*Taking the letter.*] Yes, ma'am.

She opens the door for JUDGE BRACK and goes out herself. BRACK is a man of forty-five; thick-set, but well-built and agile. His face is roundish with an aristocratic profile. His hair is short, still almost black, and carefully groomed. His eyes are lively and sparkling, his eyebrows thick and his moustache is also thick, with short-cut ends. He wears a well-cut suit, a little too youthful for his age. He uses an eye-glass, which he now and then lets drop.

JUDGE BRACK: [*With his hat in his hands, bowing.*] Is it permissible for one to call so early in the day?

HEDDA: Of course one may.

TESMAN: [*Presses his hand.*] You are welcome at any time. [*Introducing him.*] Judge Brack—Miss Rysing... 860

HEDDA: Oh—!

BRACK: [*Bowing.*] Ah—delighted...

HEDDA: [*Looks at him and laughs.*] It's nice to have a look at you by daylight, Judge. 865

BRACK: You find me—altered?

HEDDA: A little younger, I think.

BRACK: Thank you very much.

TESMAN: But what do you think of Hedda—eh? Doesn't she look flourishing? She's actually— 870

HEDDA: Oh, please don't go on about me. You haven't thanked Judge Brack for all the trouble he's taken.

BRACK: Nonsense—it was a pleasure. 875

HEDDA: Yes, you are a friend indeed. But here's Thea, impatient to be off—so *au revoir*, Judge. I'll be back soon.

Mutual salutations. MRS. ELVSTED and HEDDA go out by the hall door.

BRACK: Well, is your wife tolerably satisfied—?

TESMAN: Yes, we can't thank you enough. Of course 880 she talks of doing a little rearranging here and there; and there's one or two things still needed... So we'll have to buy a few more trifles...

BRACK: Indeed.

TESMAN: But we won't trouble you with that. Hedda 885 says she'll look after what's needed herself. Shall we sit down? Eh?

BRACK: Thanks, for a moment. [*Seats himself beside the table.*] There's something I wanted to speak to you about, dear Tesman. 890

TESMAN: Oh? Ah, yes, I see! [*Seating himself.*] Here comes the serious side of all the fun now, eh?

BRACK: Oh, the money question is not so pressing; though, come to mention it, I wish we'd been a little more diligent, economically speaking. 895

TESMAN: But that wouldn't have done, you know. Think of Hedda! You know her; I couldn't possibly ask her to put up with a shabby style of living.

BRACK: No, no—that's just the difficulty.

TESMAN: But—fortunately—it can't be long til I 900 receive my appointment.

BRACK: Well, you know...these things are apt to hang fire for a time.

TESMAN: Have you heard anything definite? Eh?

BRACK: Nothing exactly definite— [*Interrupting* 905 *himself.*] But, by the way, I do have one piece of news for you.

TESMAN: Oh?

BRACK: Your old friend, Eilert Lövborg, is back in town. 910

TESMAN: Yes, I know that already.

BRACK: Indeed. How did you hear about it?

TESMAN: From that lady who just went out with Hedda.

BRACK: Really? What was her name? I didn't quite 915 catch it.

TESMAN: Mrs. Elvsted.

BRACK: Oh yes, Sheriff Elvsted's wife? Of course—he's been living up in their region.

TESMAN: And honestly—I'm delighted to hear that 920 he's reformed his ways.

BRACK: So they say.

TESMAN: Even published a new book, eh?

BRACK: Indeed he has.

TESMAN: And I hear it's made some sensation! 925

BRACK: Quite an unusual sensation.

TESMAN: Well—that's excellent news! A man of his extraordinary talents—. I hated to think he'd gone irretrievably to ruin.

BRACK: That was what everybody thought. 930

TESMAN: Can't imagine what he'll do now, though. How in the world will he ever be able to make a living, eh?

During the last words, HEDDA *has entered by the hall door.*

HEDDA: [*To* BRACK *laughing with a touch of scorn.*] Tesman is for ever worrying about how people will 935 make their living.

TESMAN: Yes, well, you see, dear—we were talking about poor Eilert Lövborg.

HEDDA: [*Glancing at him rapidly.*] Oh? [*Seats herself in the arm-chair beside the stove and asks indiffer-* 940 *ently.*] And what's the matter with him?

TESMAN: Well—he must have run through his whole inheritance ages ago; and he can scarcely write a new book every year, eh? So I really can't see what's to become of him. 945

BRACK: Perhaps I can give you some information on that point.

TESMAN: Oh, yes?

BRACK: You remember that he has relatives who have some influence. 950

TESMAN: Well, yes, but unfortunately they've entirely washed their hands of him.

BRACK: At one time they called him the hope of the family.

TESMAN: True enough. But he put an end to all that. 955

HEDDA: Who knows? [*With a slight smile.*] I hear they've reclaimed him up at Sheriff Elvsted's—

BRACK: And then this book that he's published—

TESMAN: Well, I hope to goodness they find something for him to do. I've just written and 960 asked him to come and see us—this evening.

BRACK: But, my dear Tesman, you're booked for my bachelors' party this evening. You promised last night on the pier.

HEDDA: You'd forgotten, Tesman? 965

TESMAN: Yes, I had—utterly.

BRACK: Well, it doesn't matter anyway, for you may be sure that Lövborg won't come.

TESMAN: What makes you think that, eh?

BRACK: [*With a little hesitation, rising and resting his* 970 *hands on the back of his chair.*] My dear Tesman—and you too, Mrs. Tesman—I think I'd better not keep you in the dark about something that...well, that—

TESMAN: That concerns Eilert—? 975

BRACK: Both you and him.

TESMAN: Well, my dear Judge: let's hear it.

BRACK: You should prepare yourself for the possibility that your appointment will take longer than you desired or expected. 980

TESMAN: [*Jumping up uneasily.*] Is there some hitch about it? Eh?

BRACK: The nomination may perhaps be made conditional on the result of a competition—

TESMAN: Competition! You hear that, Hedda? 985

HEDDA: [*Leans back in her chair.*] Uhuh...uhuh...

TESMAN: But who could my competitor be? Surely not...?

BRACK: Yes, precisely: Eilert Lövborg.

TESMAN: [*Clasping his hands.*] No, no—that's 990 inconceivable! Impossible! Eh?

BRACK: Well—that is what it may come to, all the same.

TESMAN: Well but, really, Judge Brack—it would show the most incredible lack of consideration for 995 me. [*Gesticulates with his arms.*] I mean—think about it—I'm a married man! We've married on the strength of these prospects, Hedda and I. Run deep into debt, and borrowed money from Aunt Julia as well...! Good heavens, they had as good as 1000 promised me the appointment, eh?

BRACK: Well, well: no doubt you'll get the position in the end—only after a contest.

HEDDA: [*Immovable in her arm-chair.*] Think of it this way, Tesman; it means there'll be a sort of 1005 sporting interest in it.

TESMAN: Hedda, dear! How can you be so indifferent about it?

HEDDA: [*As before.*] I'm not indifferent at all. I'm really quite eager to see who wins. 1010

BRACK: Well, in any case, Mrs. Tesman, it's best that you should know how things stand. I mean—before you start making any of those little purchases I hear you've been threatening.

HEDDA: This will make no difference. 1015

BRACK: Oh? Then I shall say no more. Good-bye. [*To* TESMAN.] I'll look in on my way back from my afternoon walk, and take you home with me.

TESMAN: Oh, yes, yes... This news has shaken me a little. 1020

HEDDA: [*Reclining, holds out her hand.*] Good-bye, Judge; and be sure to drop by in the afternoon.

BRACK: Many thanks. Good-bye, good-bye!

TESMAN: [*Accompanying him to the door.*] Good-bye, my dear Judge. You'll really have to excuse me...! 1025

JUDGE BRACK goes out by the hall door.

TESMAN: [*Crosses the room.*] Oh, Hedda—one should never rush into adventures, eh?

HEDDA: [*Looks at him, smiling.*] Do you do that?

TESMAN: Yes, dear—there's no denying it—it was foolishly impetuous to go and marry and buy a 1030 new house on mere expectations.

HEDDA: Perhaps you're right there.

TESMAN: Well—at any rate, we have our delightful home, eh, Hedda? Think of it, the home we both dreamed of—the home we were in love with, you 1035 could almost say, eh?

HEDDA: [*Rising slowly and wearily.*] It was part of our agreement that we would go into society—keep open house.

TESMAN: Yes, if you only knew how I'd been looking 1040 forward to it—seeing you as hostess in an elite circle. Think of it, eh? Well, well. For the present we'll just have to get on without society—only invite Aunt Julia now and then. Oh, I really meant you to lead such an utterly different life, dear...! 1045

HEDDA: So I suppose I won't have my butler for some time.

TESMAN: Oh. Well, no—unfortunately. You can see how it would be out of the question for us to keep a manservant. 1050

HEDDA: And the horse I was to have—

TESMAN: [*Aghast.*] The horse!

HEDDA: —I suppose I mustn't think of that now.

TESMAN: Good heavens, no! That's as clear as day.

HEDDA: [*Goes up the room.*] Well, meanwhile, at least 1055 I have one thing to kill time with.

TESMAN: [*Beaming.*] Well, thank heaven. What's that, Hedda? Eh?

HEDDA: [*In the middle doorway, looks at him with covert scorn.*] My pistols, George. 1060

TESMAN: [*In alarm.*] Your pistols!

HEDDA: [*With cold eyes.*] General Gabler's pistols.

She goes out through the inner room, to the left.

TESMAN: [*Rushes up to the middle doorway and calls after her.*] No, for heaven's sake, Hedda darling—don't touch those dangerous things! For my sake, 1065 Hedda! Eh?

ACT II.

The room at TESMAN's *as in the first act, except that the piano has been removed, and an elegant little writing-table with book-shelves put in its place. A smaller table stands near the sofa on the left. Most of the bouquets have been removed.* MRS. ELVSTED's *bouquet is on the large table in front. It is afternoon.*

HEDDA, dressed to receive callers, is alone in the room. She stands by the open glass door, loading a revolver. Its mate lies in an open pistol-case on the writing-table.

HEDDA: [*Looks down the garden, and calls.*] So, you're back again, Judge.

BRACK: [*Is heard calling from a distance.*] As you see, Mrs. Tesman.

HEDDA: [*Raises the pistol and points.*] Now I'll shoot 5 you, Judge Brack.

BRACK: [*Shouting.*] No, no, no! Don't aim at me!

HEDDA: This is what comes of sneaking in the back way. [*She fires.*]

BRACK: [*Nearer.*] Are you out of your mind?! 10

HEDDA: Oh dear—did I happen to hit you?

BRACK: [*Still outside.*] I wish you'd stop these practical jokes!

HEDDA: Well then come inside, Judge.

JUDGE BRACK, dressed for a men's party, enters by the glass door. He carries a light overcoat over his arm.

BRACK: What the devil—! Haven't you had enough 15 of those games? What are you shooting at?

HEDDA: Oh, just firing into the air.

BRACK: [*Gently takes the pistol out of her hand.*] Allow me, Madam. [*Looks at it.*] Hm, I remember this pistol well. [*Looks around.*] Where's the case? Ah, 20 here. [*Lays the pistol in it, and shuts it.*] Now let's not play that little game anymore today.

HEDDA: Then what in God's name am I to do with myself?

BRACK: You've had no visitors? 25

HEDDA: [*Closing the glass door.*] Not a soul. I suppose all our crowd is still out of town.

BRACK: Tesman's not home either?

HEDDA: [*At the writing-table, putting the pistol-case in a drawer which she shuts.*] No. He rushed off to 30 his aunt's right after lunch; he didn't expect you so early.

BRACK: Hm...stupid of me not to think of that.

HEDDA: [*Turning her head to look at him.*] Why stupid? 35

BRACK: Because if I'd thought of it I'd have come a little earlier.

HEDDA: [*Crossing the room.*] Then no one would have received you; I've been in my room changing ever since lunch. 40

BRACK: And there's no sort of little chink that we could hold a parley through?

HEDDA: You've forgotten to have one put in.

BRACK: Another piece of stupidity.

HEDDA: Well, we'll just have to settle down here and 45 wait. Tesman's not likely to be back for some time.

BRACK: Never mind; I'm not impatient.

HEDDA sits in the corner of the sofa. BRACK lays his overcoat over the back of the nearest chair, and sits down, but keeps his hat in his hand. A short silence. They look at each other.

HEDDA: Well?

BRACK: [*In the same tone.*] Well?

HEDDA: I spoke first. 50

BRACK: [*Bending a little forward.*] Come, let us have a cosy little chat, Mrs. Hedda.

HEDDA: [*Leaning further back in the sofa.*] Doesn't it seem an eternity since our last talk? I mean besides those few words last night and this 55 morning.

BRACK: You mean since our last confidential talk? Our last *tête-à-tête*?

HEDDA: Well, yes, if you want to put it that way.

BRACK: Not a day has passed that I haven't wished 60 that you were home again.

HEDDA: I've longed for nothing more myself.

BRACK: You have? Really, Mrs. Hedda? And I thought you'd been enjoying your trip so much.

HEDDA: [*ironically.*] Oh, yes, absolutely. 65

BRACK: But Tesman kept saying it his letters how happy—

HEDDA: Oh, Tesman! For him, there's nothing so delightful as grubbing in libraries and making copies of old parchments, or whatever. 70

BRACK: [*With a spice of malice.*] Well, that is his vocation—or part of it at any rate.

HEDDA: Yes, of course; and no doubt when it's your vocation... But for me, my dear Mr. Brack, it has been fatally boring. 75

BRACK: [*Sympathetically.*] Really? Seriously?

HEDDA: Yes, surely you can understand that. Six whole months without meeting a soul that knew anything of our circle, or could talk about the things we're interested in. 80

BRACK: Yes, yes—I'd have felt a little deprived too.

HEDDA: But worst of all...

BRACK: Well?

HEDDA: Was being incessantly in the company of— one and the same person— 85

BRACK: [*With a nod of assent.*] Morning, noon, and night, yes—at all times and seasons.

HEDDA: As I say, "incessantly."

BRACK: Indeed. But I'd have thought, with our excellent Tesman, one could— 90

HEDDA: Tesman is...a *specialist*, dear Judge.

BRACK: True.

HEDDA: And specialists do not make amusing travelling companions. Not in the long run.

BRACK: Not even the specialist one happens to love? 95

HEDDA: Ugh—what a nauseating word!

BRACK: [*Taken aback.*] I beg your pardon...?

HEDDA: [*Half laughing, half irritated.*] You should just try it! Hearing nothing but the history of civilization morning, noon and night— 100

BRACK: Incessantly.

HEDDA: Yes, yes, exactly! And then all this about the domestic industry of the middle ages! That's what's most disgusting.

BRACK: [*Looks searching at her.*] But—if that's the 105 case, how do you explain your—uh—?

HEDDA: My accepting George Tesman, you mean?

BRACK: Yes, more or less.

HEDDA: Good God, does that really seem so strange?

BRACK: Yes and no, Mrs. Hedda.. 110

HEDDA: I had danced myself out. My day was done. [*With a slight shudder.*] Well, no—perhaps I shouldn't say that; nor think it, either.

BRACK: You certainly have no reason for it.

HEDDA: Oh, reasons... [*Watching him closely.*] 115 Anyway, George Tesman, you have to admit, is...well, the very model of rectitude.

BRACK: His correctness and respectability are beyond question, yes.

HEDDA: And I see nothing *especially* ridiculous about 120 him. Do you?

BRACK: Ridiculous? No...no, I wouldn't have said so...

HEDDA: Well...and his powers of research are untiring, at least. There's a good possibility he 125 might make something of himself, after all.

BRACK: [*Look at her hesitatingly.*] I thought that you, like every one else, expected him to attain the highest distinction.

HEDDA: [*With an expression of fatigue.*] Yes, so I did... 130 And then, since he was so very desperate to be allowed to support me...I really couldn't think of any reason why I shouldn't accept his offer.

BRACK: No...if you look at it in that light...

HEDDA: It was more than my other admirers were 135 prepared to do for me, my dear Judge.

BRACK: [*Laughing.*] Well, I can't answer for all the rest; but as for myself, you know that I've always entertained a...a certain respect for the, uh...marital bond—for marriage as an institution, Mrs. Hedda. 140

HEDDA: [*Ironically.*] Oh, I assure you I've never cherished any hopes with respect to you.

BRACK: All I require is a pleasant and intimate place, where I can make myself useful, and am free to come and go as...as a trusted friend... 145

HEDDA: Of the master of the house?

BRACK: [*Bowing.*] Frankly—of the mistress first of all; but, of course, of the master, too, in the second place. Such a triangular friendship—if I may call it that—is really a great convenience for all parties, 150 let me tell you.

HEDDA: Yes, I've many a time longed for a third on our travels. Oh—those railway-carriage *tête-à-têtes*...!

BRACK: Fortunately your wedding trip is over now.

HEDDA: [*Shaking her head.*] Not by a long, *long* way. 155 I've only arrived at a station on the line.

BRACK: Well, perhaps you should jump out and move around a little, Mrs. Hedda.

HEDDA: I never jump out.

BRACK: No? 160

HEDDA: No—because there's always some one standing there to...

BRACK: [*Laughing.*] To look at your legs?

HEDDA: Precisely.

BRACK: Well, but, really— 165

HEDDA: [*With a gesture of revulsion.*] I won't do it. I'd rather keep the seat I happen to have, and... continue the *tête-à-tête*.

BRACK: But suppose a third person jumped *in*...to join the couple. 170

HEDDA: Ah, now *that* is another matter.

BRACK: A trusted, sympathetic friend—

HEDDA: —with a fund of conversation on all sorts of lively topics—

BRACK: —and not the least bit of a specialist. 175

HEDDA: [*With an audible sigh.*] Yes, that would be a relief, indeed.

BRACK: [*Hears the front door open, and glances in that direction.*] The triangle is completed.

HEDDA: [*Half aloud.*] And on goes the train. 180

GEORGE TESMAN in a gray walking-suit, with a soft felt hat, enters from the hall. He has a number of unbound books under his arm and in his pockets.

TESMAN: [*Goes up to the table beside the corner settee.*] Ouf! What a load for a warm day—all these books. [*Lays them on the table.*] Not to put too fine a point on it, Hedda, I am soaked with sweat. Hello! You're here already, eh, Judge Brack? Berta didn't tell me. 185

BRACK: [*Rising.*] I came in through the garden.

HEDDA: What are all those books you've got?

TESMAN: [*Stands looking them through.*] Some new books on my specialty—quite indispensable.

HEDDA: On your specialty? 190

BRACK: Yes, books on his area of specialization, Mrs. Tesman.

BRACK and HEDDA exchange a confidential smile.

HEDDA: Do you need any more books on your specialty?

TESMAN: Oh yes, dear Hedda, one can never have 195
enough of them. Naturally, one must keep up with
all that's being published.

HEDDA: Yes, I suppose so.

TESMAN: [*Searching among his books.*] And look at
this—I've got a copy of Eilert Lovbörg's new book, 200
too. [*Offering it to her.*] Perhaps you'd like to glance
through it, Hedda? Eh?

HEDDA: No, thanks. Or...afterwards, perhaps.

TESMAN: I skimmed through it on the way home.

BRACK: And what do you make of it—as a specialist? 205

TESMAN: It is...remarkably well argued. He never
wrote like that before. [*Putting the books together.*]
I'll just take all these into my study. I'm longing
to cut the leaves...[10] And then I must change my
clothes. [*To BRACK.*] I suppose we don't have to 210
start just yet, eh?

BRACK: Oh, dear, no—there's not the slightest hurry.

TESMAN: Well, then, I'll take my time. [*Is going with
his books, but stops in the doorway and turns.*] By
the way, Hedda—Aunt Julia won't be coming this 215
evening.

HEDDA: No? Is it the affair of the hat that keeps her
away?

TESMAN: Oh, not at all! How could you think such
a thing of Aunt Julia? Imagine! The fact is that 220
Aunt Rina is quite ill.

HEDDA: She always is.

TESMAN: Yes, but today she's worse than usual, poor
soul.

HEDDA: Oh, well, then it's only natural that her sister 225
remain with her. I must bear my disappointment.

TESMAN: And, dear, you can't imagine how delighted
Aunt Julia seemed—just because you had come
home looking so radiant.

HEDDA: [*Half aloud, rising.*] Oh, these everlasting 230
Aunts!

TESMAN: What?

HEDDA: [*Going to the glass door.*] Nothing.

TESMAN: Oh, all right.

He goes through the inner room, out to the right.

---

10 cut the leaves] Books were then published with the full-
size paper folded and sewn into smaller pages, but with
the folds left uncut.

BRACK: What hat were you talking about? 235

HEDDA: Oh, a little episode with Miss Tesman this
morning. She'd laid down her hat on the chair
there—[*looks at him and smiles*]—and I pretended
to think it was the servant's.

BRACK: [*Shaking his head.*] Now, my dear Mrs. 240
Hedda, how could you do such a thing? And to
such a fine old lady.

HEDDA: [*Nervously crossing the room.*] Well, you
know—these impulses just suddenly come over
me, and I can't resist them. [*Throws herself down 245
in the easy-chair by the stove.*] Oh, I can't explain
it.

BRACK: [*Behind the easy-chair.*] You're not really
happy—that's what's at the bottom of it.

HEDDA: [*Looking straight before her.*] I can't think of 250
any reason why I should be—happy. Can you?

BRACK: Well, amongst other things, because you've
got exactly the home you'd set your heart on.

HEDDA: [*Looks up at him and laughs.*] Do you believe
in that myth too? 255

BRACK: There's nothing in it, then?

HEDDA: Oh, yes, there is *something* in it.

BRACK: Well?

HEDDA: There's *this* in it, that I made use of Tesman
to see me home from evening parties last summer— 260

BRACK: I, alas, had to go quite a different way.

HEDDA: That's true. You were going a different way,
last summer.

BRACK: [*Laughing.*] Now, now, Mrs. Hedda! So, you
and Tesman...? 265

HEDDA: Well, we happened to pass here one evening.
Tesman was pathetically writhing about in the
agony of having to make conversation; so I took
pity on the poor learned man—

BRACK: [*Smiles doubtfully.*] You took pity? Huh! 270

HEDDA: Yes, I really did. And so—to help him out
of his torment—I happened to say, without
thinking, that I'd like to live in this house.

BRACK: No more than that?

HEDDA: Not that evening. 275

BRACK: But afterwards?

HEDDA: Yes, my thoughtlessness had consequences,
my dear Judge.

BRACK: Unfortunately, that happens all too frequently, Mrs. Hedda. 280

HEDDA: Yes, thanks.—So you see it was this enthusiasm for Secretary Falk's villa that first forged a bond of sympathy between George Tesman and me. From that came our engagement, our marriage, our honeymoon, and all the rest of it. Ah, well, Judge Brack—as you make your bed so you must lie in it, as one might say.

BRACK: This is exquisite! And you really didn't care anything about the place the whole time?

HEDDA: No, God knows, I didn't.

BRACK: But now? Now that we've made it so homelike for you?

HEDDA: Ugh...the rooms all seem to smell of lavender and dried rose-leaves.—But perhaps Aunt Julia brought that scent with her.

BRACK: [*Laughing.*] No, I think it must be a legacy from the late Mrs. Secretary Falk.

HEDDA: Yes, there's a morbid odour about it. It reminds me of a bouquet—the day after the ball. [*Clasps her hands behind her head, leans back in her chair and looks at him.*] Oh, my dear Judge: you can't imagine how excruciatingly boring it will be for me here.

BRACK: Why shouldn't you, too, find some sort of vocation, Mrs. Hedda?

HEDDA: A vocation...that I'd find attractive?

BRACK: If possible, of course.

HEDDA: God knows what sort of a vocation that could be. I often wonder whether... [*Breaking off.*] But that would never do, either.

BRACK: Who can tell? Let's hear what it is.

HEDDA: Whether I might persuade Tesman to go into politics, I mean.

BRACK: [*Laughing.*] Tesman? No, *really*, now! Politics would never suit him—not at all in his line.

HEDDA: No, I suppose not. But I might be able to push him into it all the same?

BRACK: *Why*? What satisfaction could you possibly have in that? If he's not suited for it, why should you want to drive him into it?

HEDDA: Because I'm *bored*! That's why! [*After a pause.*] So you think it quite out of the question that Tesman could get into cabinet?

BRACK: Well...you see, Mrs. Hedda, to get into cabinet, he'd have to be at least moderately rich.

HEDDA: [*Rising impatiently.*] Yes, there we have it.

It's this genteel poverty I've managed to fall into. [*Crosses the room.*] That's what makes life so pitiable. So utterly...*ludicrous*! Because that's what it is!

BRACK: Now *I* would have said the fault lay elsewhere.

HEDDA: Where?

BRACK: You've never had any really *stimulating* experience.

HEDDA: Nothing serious, you mean?

BRACK: Yes, if you like. But now, perhaps you have one in store.

HEDDA: [*Tossing her head.*] Oh, you're thinking of the nonsense about this damned professorship. That's Tesman's affair. I assure you I won't waste a thought on it.

BRACK: No, no, I daresay not. But suppose that what people call—rather pretentiously—a "solemn responsibility" were to come to you? [*Smiling.*] A *new* responsibility, Mrs. Hedda?

HEDDA: [*Angrily.*] Be quiet! Nothing of the kind is going to happen.

BRACK: [*Warily.*] We'll speak of this again a year from now—at the very outside.

HEDDA: [*Curtly.*] I have no talent for that sort of thing, Judge Brack. No responsibilities for me.

BRACK: So, are you so little like the majority of women that you have no natural aptitude whatsoever for the duties of—?

HEDDA: [*Beside the glass door.*] Oh, be quiet! Please! I often think there's only one thing in the world I have any talent for.

BRACK: [*Drawing near to her.*] And what is that, if I may ask?

HEDDA: [*Stands looking out.*] Boring myself to death. There you have it. [*Turns, looks towards the inner room, and laughs.*] Yes, I was right. Here comes the Professor.

BRACK: [*Softly, in a tone of warning.*] Now, now, Mrs. Hedda!

GEORGE TESMAN, *dressed for the party, with his gloves and hat in his hand, enters from the right through the inner room.*

TESMAN: Hedda, has there been any message from Eilert Lövborg? Eh?

HEDDA: No.

TESMAN: Well, then, you'll see, he'll be here any moment. 370

BRACK: You really think he'll come?

TESMAN: Yes, I'm almost sure of it. What you were telling us this morning must have been an idle rumour. 375

BRACK: You think so?

TESMAN: At any rate, Aunt Julia said she didn't believe for a moment that he'd ever stand in my way again. How about that!

BRACK: Well, then, that's all right. 380

TESMAN: [*Placing his hat and gloves on a chair on the right.*] Yes, but you won't mind if I wait for him as long as possible?

BRACK: We still have plenty of time. None of my guests will be there before seven or half-past. 385

TESMAN: Then we'll keep Hedda company until then, and see what happens, eh?

HEDDA: [*Placing BRACK's hat and overcoat upon the corner settee.*] And at worst Mr. Lövborg can stay here with me. 390

BRACK: [*Offering to take his things.*] Oh, allow me, Mrs. Tesman.—What do you mean by "at worst"?

HEDDA: If he won't go with you and Tesman.

TESMAN: [*Looks dubiously at her.*] But, Hedda, dear...do you think it would be quite right for him 395 to stay with you? Eh? Remember, Aunt Julia can't come.

HEDDA: No, but Mrs. Elvsted is coming. The three of us can have a cup of tea together.

TESMAN: Oh, yes, that will be all right. 400

BRACK: [*Smiling.*] And perhaps that would be the safest plan for him.

HEDDA: How so?

BRACK: Well, you know, Mrs. Tesman, how you have chided me about my little bachelor parties in the 405 past?—declared them fit only for men of the strictest principles.

HEDDA: Well no doubt Mr. Lövborg's principles are strict enough now. A converted sinner...

BERTA appears at the hall door.

BERTA: There's a gentleman asking if you're at home, ma'am— 410

HEDDA: Well, show him in.

TESMAN: [*Softly.*] That'll be him, I'm sure. How about that!

EILERT LÖVBORG enters from the hall. He is slim and lean, about the same age as TESMAN, but looks older and somewhat worn-out. His hair and beard are blackish brown, his face long and pale, but with patches of colour on the cheek-bones. He is dressed in a well-cut black suit, quite new. He has dark gloves and a silk hat. He stops near the door, and makes a quick bow, seeming somewhat embarrassed.

TESMAN: [*Goes up to him and shakes his hand warmly.*] Well, my dear Eilert: so at last we meet again! 415

EILERT LÖVBORG: [*Speaks in a subdued voice.*] Thanks for your letter, Tesman. [*Approaching Hedda.*] Will you, too, shake hands with me, Mrs. Tesman? 420

HEDDA: [*Taking his hand.*] I am glad to see you, Mr. Lövborg. [*With a motion of her hand.*] I don't know whether you two gentlemen...?

LÖVBORG: [*Bowing slightly.*] Judge Brack, I think. 425

BRACK: [*Doing likewise.*] Yes, indeed. Quite some time now...

TESMAN: [*To LÖVBORG, with his hands on his shoulders.*] Now, please, you must make yourself entirely at home, Eilert! Mustn't he, Hedda?—I 430 hear you're going to settle in town again, eh?

LÖVBORG: Yes, I am.

TESMAN: Good, good. Listen, I've got hold of your new book, though I haven't had time to read it yet.

LÖVBORG: You might as well spare yourself the 435 trouble.

TESMAN: How so?

LÖVBORG: Because there's not much in it.

TESMAN: What? How can you say that?

BRACK: But I've heard it's been very highly praised. 440

LÖVBORG: That's what I wanted; so I put only those things into the book that everyone would agree with.

BRACK: Very wise.

TESMAN: Well, but, Eilert—! 445

LÖVBORG: Because I intend to win myself a position again—to make a fresh start.

TESMAN: [*A little embarrassed.*] Ah, is that what you intend to do, eh?

LÖVBORG: [*Smiling, lays down his hat, and draws a packet, wrapped in paper, from his coat pocket.*] But when *this one* appears, George, you'll have to read it. This is the *real* book—the book I've put my true self into.

TESMAN: Indeed? And what is it?

LÖVBORG: It's the continuation.

TESMAN: The continuation? Of what?

LÖVBORG: Of the other book.

TESMAN: Of the book just published?

LÖVBORG: Of course.

TESMAN: But, Eilert: doesn't that one come down to our own days?

LÖVBORG: Yes, it does. And this one deals with the future.

TESMAN: The future? But, good heavens, we know nothing about the future.

LÖVBORG: No, but there's a thing or two to be said about it all the same. [*Opens the packet.*] Have a look here...

TESMAN: That's not your handwriting, is it?

LÖVBORG: I dictated it. [*Turning over the pages.*] It falls into two sections. The first deals with the main forces on future civilization. And this second—[*flipping through the later pages*]—forecasts the probable line of development.

TESMAN: How odd! I'd never have dreamed of writing anything like that.

HEDDA: [*At the glass door, drumming on the pane.*] Hm...I daresay you wouldn't.

LÖVBORG: [*Replacing the manuscript in its paper and laying the packet on the table.*] I brought it thinking I might read you some of it this evening.

TESMAN: That's very good of you, Eilert. But this evening? [*Looking at BRACK.*] I'm not sure we can manage it...

LÖVBORG: Well, then, some other time. There's no hurry.

BRACK: I should tell you, Mr. Lövborg: there's a little gathering at my house this evening—mainly in honor of Tesman, you know—

LÖVBORG: [*Looking for his hat.*] Oh—then I won't detain you—

BRACK: No, but listen: won't you do me the favor of joining us?

LÖVBORG: [*Curtly and decidedly.*] No, I can't. Thanks very much.

BRACK: Oh, nonsense! Please do. We'll be quite a select little group. And I can guarantee you, it will be "animated," as Mrs. Hed—as Mrs. Tesman likes to say.

LÖVBORG: I don't doubt it. Nevertheless—

BRACK: And you could bring your manuscript with you, and read it to Tesman at my house. I'll give you a room to yourselves.

TESMAN: Yes, how about that, Eilert? Why not, eh?

HEDDA: [*Interposing.*] But, Tesman, if Mr. Lövborg would rather not... I'm sure he would much prefer to stay here and have supper with me.

LÖVBORG: [*Looking at her.*] With you, Mrs. Tesman?

HEDDA: And with Mrs. Elvsted.

LÖVBORG: Ah... [*Lightly.*] I saw her briefly this morning.

HEDDA: Did you? Well, she's coming here this evening. So you see you're almost *obliged* to remain, Mr. Lövborg, or she'll have no one to see her home.

LÖVBORG: True enough. Thanks very much, Mrs. Tesman: in that case I will stay.

HEDDA: Then I'll give one or two instructions to the maid.

She goes to the hall door and rings. BERTA enters. HEDDA talks to her in a whisper, and points towards the inner room. BERTA nods and goes out again.

TESMAN: [*At the same time, to LÖVBORG.*] Tell me, Eilert, is it this new subject—the future of civilization—that you're going to lecture about?

LÖVBORG: Yes.

TESMAN: They told me at the bookstore that you're going to give a series of lectures this autumn.

LÖVBORG: That's my intention. I hope you won't take it badly, Tesman.

TESMAN: Oh no, not in the least! But...?

LÖVBORG: I can quite understand how disagreeable it might seem to you.

TESMAN: [*Cast down.*] Oh, well, I couldn't very well expect you, out of consideration for me, to—

LÖVBORG: But I'll wait till your appointment is settled.

TESMAN: You'll wait? Yes, but...yes, but...aren't you going to compete with me for the position? Eh?

LÖVBORG: No. It's more of a moral victory I'm interested in.

TESMAN: Well, for heaven's sake...so, Aunt Julia was right after all! Yes, I knew it! Hedda! How about that—Eilert Lövborg is not going to stand in our way! 540

HEDDA: [*Curtly.*] Our way? Please, leave me out of it.

She goes up towards the inner room, where BERTA is placing a tray with decanters and glasses on the table. HEDDA nods approval, and comes forward again. BERTA goes out.

TESMAN: [*At the same time.*] So, Judge Brack—what do you say now, eh? 545

BRACK: Well, I say that a moral victory, as far as it goes, is...uh...a fine thing...

TESMAN: Yes, certainly. But all the same...

HEDDA: [*Look at TESMAN with a cold smile.*] You look thunderstruck. 550

TESMAN: Yes...so I am...just about...

BRACK: That *was* quite a thunderstorm that passed over us, Mrs. Tesman.

HEDDA: [*Pointing towards the inner room.*] Would you gentlemen care for a glass of cold punch? 555

BRACK: [*Looking at his watch.*] An early cocktail? Yes, that wouldn't be a bad idea.

TESMAN: A splendid idea, Hedda! Just the thing! Now that this weight's off my mind... 560

HEDDA: Will you join them, Mr. Lövborg?

LÖVBORG: [*With a gesture of refusal.*] No, thanks. Nothing for me.

BRACK: Well, heavens...cold punch is surely not poisonous. 565

LÖVBORG: Perhaps not for every one.

HEDDA: Well, I'll keep Mr. Lövborg company in the meantime, then.

TESMAN: Yes, Hedda dear, please do.

He and BRACK go into the inner room, seat themselves, drink punch, smoke, and carry on a lively conversation during what follows. EILERT LÖVBORG remains standing by the stove. HEDDA goes to the writing-table.

HEDDA: [*Raising her voice a little.*] Would you like to see some photographs, Mr. Lövborg? Did you 570 know Tesman and I came through Tyrol on our way home?

She picks up an album, and places it on the table beside the sofa, in the further corner of which she seats herself. EILERT LÖVBORG approaches, stops, and looks at her. Then he takes a chair and seats himself to her left, with his back towards the inner room.

HEDDA: [*Opening the album.*] You see this range of mountains, Mr. Lövborg? It's the Ortler group. Tesman's written the name underneath, there: "The Ortler group near Meran." 575

LÖVBORG: [*Who has never taken his eyes off her, says softly and slowly:*] Hedda...Gabler.

HEDDA: [*Glancing hastily at him.*] Ah. Sh! 580

LÖVBORG: [*Repeats softly.*] Hedda Gabler!

HEDDA: [*Looking at the album.*] That was my name in the old days...when we two knew each other.

LÖVBORG: And I must teach myself never to say Hedda Gabler again...never, as long as I live. 585

HEDDA: [*Still turning over the pages.*] Yes, you must. And I think you ought to get into practice. The sooner the better, I'd say.

LÖVBORG: [*In a tone of indignation.*] Hedda Gabler married? And married to...George Tesman! 590

HEDDA: Yes. That's how it is.

LÖVBORG: Oh, Hedda, Hedda...how could you throw yourself away!

HEDDA: [*Looks sharply at him.*] What? I won't allow this. 595

LÖVBORG: What do you mean?

TESMAN comes into the room and goes towards the sofa.

HEDDA: [*Hears him coming and says in an indifferent tone.*] And this is a view from the Val d'Ampezzo, Mr. Lövborg. Just look at these peaks! [*Looks affectionately up at TESMAN.*] What's the name of these peculiar peaks, dear? 600

TESMAN: Let me see. Oh, those are the Dolomites.

HEDDA: Yes, that's it. —Those are the Dolomites, Mr. Lövborg.

TESMAN: Hedda, dear, I only wanted to ask whether I should bring you a little punch after all? For yourself, at any rate, eh? 605

HEDDA: Yes, please. And perhaps a few cookies.

TESMAN: No cigarettes?

HEDDA: No. 610

TESMAN: All right.

He goes into the inner room and out to the right. BRACK sits in the inner room, and keeps an eye from time to time on HEDDA and LÖVBORG.

LÖVBORG: [*Softly, as before.*] Answer me, darling Hedda. How could you go and do this?

HEDDA: [*Apparently absorbed in the album.*] If you continue to speak to me so intimately, I can't talk to you. 615

LÖVBORG: Not even when we're alone?

HEDDA: No. Think what you like, but don't speak it out loud.

LÖVBORG: Ah, I see. It's an offence against George Tesman...whom you love. 620

HEDDA: [*Glances at him and smiles.*] Love? What an idea!

LÖVBORG: You don't love him then.

HEDDA: But I won't tolerate any sort of unfaithfulness! Remember that. 625

LÖVBORG: Hedda, answer me one thing—

HEDDA: Sh!

TESMAN enters with a small tray.

TESMAN: Here we are! Isn't this tempting?

He puts the tray on the table.

HEDDA: Why do you bring it yourself? 630

TESMAN: [*Filling the glasses.*] Because I enjoy waiting on you, Hedda.

HEDDA: But you've poured two glasses. Mr. Lövborg said he wouldn't have any.

TESMAN: No, but Mrs. Elvsted will be here soon, won't she? 635

HEDDA: Yes, that's right...Mrs. Elvsted.

TESMAN: You'd forgotten her, eh?

HEDDA: We were so absorbed in the photographs. [*Shows him a picture.*] Do you remember this little village? 640

TESMAN: Oh yes, that's the one just below the Brenner Pass. We spent the night there...

HEDDA: And met that lively group of tourists.

TESMAN: Yes, that was the place. A shame you couldn't have been with us, eh, Eilert? 645

He returns to the inner room and sits beside BRACK.

LÖVBORG: Answer just this one question, Hedda...

HEDDA: Well?

LÖVBORG: Was there no love in your friendship with me, either? Not a spark, not a tinge of love? 650

HEDDA: I wonder... As I remember it, we were like two good comrades—two devoted friends. [*Smilingly.*] You, especially, were frankness itself.

LÖVBORG: That was your doing.

HEDDA: When I look back on it, I think there was really something beautiful, something fascinating—even rather daring in that...that secret intimacy—that friendship—which no one else so much as dreamed of. 655

LÖVBORG: Yes...there was, wasn't there, Hedda? When I'd come to your father's in the afternoon...the General sitting over at the window reading the papers, his back towards us... 660

HEDDA: While we sat on the corner sofa...

LÖVBORG: Always with the same magazine in front of us... 665

HEDDA: For want of a photograph album, yes.

LÖVBORG: Yes. And when I made my confessions to you, Hedda—told you things about myself that no one else knew! I'd sit there and tell you about all my escapades—my reckless days and nights. Oh, Hedda... What power was there in you that could force me to confess such things? 670

HEDDA: A power in me?

LÖVBORG: How else can I explain it? And all those...those roundabout questions you'd ask... 675

HEDDA: Which you understood perfectly well—

LÖVBORG: How could you sit and question me like that? So frankly...

HEDDA: Though in roundabout terms, as you say. 680

LÖVBORG: Yes, but frankly nonetheless. Cross-question me about...all that sort of thing?

HEDDA: How could you answer, Mr. Lövborg?

LÖVBORG: Yes, I can't explain that at all, when I look back on it. But truly, Hedda, can you tell me there was no love at the bottom of our friendship? Did you never feel, yourself, that you might purge my stains away—if I made you my confessor? Isn't that so? 685

HEDDA: No, not quite.

LÖVBORG: Then, what was your motive? 690

HEDDA: Do you find it quite incomprehensible that a young girl—provided it could be done without any one knowing...

LÖVBORG: Well?

HEDDA: ...might want to have a peep, now and then, into a world which... 695

LÖVBORG: Which...?

HEDDA: ...which she is forbidden to know anything about?

LÖVBORG: So that was it? 700

HEDDA: Partly, yes; partly—I think.

LÖVBORG: So: comrades in the thirst for life, then. But why shouldn't that, at least, have continued?

HEDDA: Well, that was your fault.

LÖVBORG: It was you that broke with me. 705

HEDDA: Yes, when our friendship threatened to develop into something more serious. Shame upon you, Eilert Lövborg! How could you think of wronging your...your frank comrade?

LÖVBORG: [Clenching his hands.] Oh, why didn't you carry out your threat? Why didn't you shoot me? 710

HEDDA: My dread of scandal.

LÖVBORG: Yes, Hedda, you are a coward at heart.

HEDDA: A terrible coward. [Changing her tone.] But it was a lucky thing for you. And now you've found ample consolation at the Elvsteds'. 715

LÖVBORG: I know what Thea has told you.

HEDDA: And perhaps you told her something about us?

LÖVBORG: Not a word. She's too stupid to understand anything like that. 720

HEDDA: Stupid?

LÖVBORG: About matters of that kind.

HEDDA: And I'm cowardly. [Bends towards him, without looking him in the face, and says more softly.] But now I will confess something to you. 725

LÖVBORG: [Eagerly.] Well?

HEDDA: The fact that I didn't dare to shoot you...

LÖVBORG: Yes?

HEDDA: ...that was not the worst of my cowardice...that evening. 730

LÖVBORG: [Looks at her a moment, understands, and whispers passionately.] Oh, Hedda! Hedda Gabler! Now I begin to see the hidden reason behind our comradeship. You and I! So, after all, it was your craving for life— 735

HEDDA: [Softly, with a sharp glance.] Take care! Assume nothing of the kind.

Twilight has begun to fall. The hall door is opening from without by BERTA.

HEDDA: [Closes the album with a bang and calls smilingly:] Ah, at last. Darling Thea—come in! 740

MRS. ELVSTED enters from the hall. She is in evening dress. The door is closed behind her.

HEDDA: [On the sofa, stretches out her arms towards her.] My sweet Thea—you can't imagine how I've been wishing you'd come!

MRS. ELVSTED, in passing, exchanges slight salutations with the gentlemen in the inner room, then goes up to the table and gives HEDDA her hand. EILERT LÖVBORG has risen. He and MRS. ELVSTED greet each other with a silent nod.

MRS. ELVSTED: Should I go in and talk to your husband for a moment? 745

HEDDA: Oh, not at all. Leave those two alone. They'll be going soon.

MRS. ELVSTED: Are they going out?

HEDDA: Yes, to a supper-party.

MRS. ELVSTED: [Quickly to LÖVBORG.] Not you? 750

LÖVBORG: No.

HEDDA: Mr. Lövborg will remain with us.

MRS. ELVSTED: [Takes a chair and is about to seat herself at his side.] Oh, how nice it is here!

HEDDA: No, please, my little Thea! Not there. Come over here by me, please. I'll sit between you. 755

MRS. ELVSTED: Yes, as you like.

She goes around the table and sits to the right of HEDDA on the sofa. LÖVBORG sits down again on his chair.

LÖVBORG: [After a short pause, to HEDDA.] Isn't she lovely to look at?

HEDDA: [Lightly stroking her hair.] Only to look at? 760

LÖVBORG: Yes. For the two of us—she and I—we really are two comrades. We have absolute faith in each other; so we can sit and talk with perfect frankness—

HEDDA: No need to be roundabout, Mr. Lövborg? 765

LÖVBORG: Well—

MRS. ELVSTED: [*Softly clinging close to HEDDA.*] Oh, Hedda, I am so happy! Imagine, he says that I've inspired *him*, too.

HEDDA: [*Looks at her with a smile.*] Ah. Does he, dear? 770

LÖVBORG: And she is *very* brave, Mrs. Tesman.

MRS. ELVSTED: Good heavens! Brave?

LÖVBORG: Exceedingly—where your comrade is concerned. 775

HEDDA: Ah, yes—courage. If one only had that.

LÖVBORG: Then...what?

HEDDA: Then life would perhaps be livable, after all. [*With a sudden change of tone.*] But now, Thea, you really must have a glass of punch. 780

MRS. ELVSTED: No, thanks—I never take anything of that kind.

HEDDA: Well, then, you, Mr. Lövborg.

LÖVBORG: Nor I, thank you.

MRS. ELVSTED: No, he doesn't, either. 785

HEDDA: [*Looks fixedly at him.*] But if I insist?

LÖVBORG: It would be no use.

HEDDA: [*Laughing.*] Then I, poor creature, have no power over you at all?

LÖVBORG: Not in that respect. 790

HEDDA: But seriously, I think you should—for your own sake.

MRS. ELVSTED: Hedda...!

LÖVBORG: How so?

HEDDA: Or rather, on account of other people. 795

LÖVBORG: Oh?

HEDDA: Otherwise people might suspect that—in your heart of hearts—you didn't feel quite secure, quite confident in yourself.

MRS. ELVSTED: [*Softly.*] Oh, please, Hedda! 800

LÖVBORG: People can suspect what they like..for the time being.

MRS. ELVSTED: [*Joyfully.*] Yes, let them!

HEDDA: I saw it plainly in Judge Brack's face a moment ago. 805

LÖVBORG: You saw...what?

HEDDA: A contemptuous smile—when you wouldn't dare go with them into the inner room.

LÖVBORG: Wouldn't dare? I preferred to stay and talk to you. 810

MRS. ELVSTED: What could be more natural, Hedda—?

HEDDA: But the Judge wouldn't guess that. And I saw the way he smiled and glanced at Tesman when you were afraid to accept his invitation to this wretched little supper-party of his. 815

LÖVBORG: Afraid. You think I was *afraid*?

HEDDA: No, but that was what Judge Brack thought.

LÖVBORG: Well, let him.

HEDDA: So you're not going with them? 820

LÖVBORG: I'm staying here with you and Thea.

MRS. ELVSTED: Yes, Hedda—how can you doubt that?

HEDDA: [*Smiles and nods approvingly to LÖVBORG.*] Firm as a rock. Faithful to your principles, now and ever. That's how a man should be. [*Turns to MRS. ELVSTED and caresses her.*] Well, now, what did I tell you, when you came here this morning in such a state of distraction— 825

LÖVBORG: [*Surprised.*] Distraction! 830

MRS. ELVSTED: [*Terrified.*] Hedda...oh, Hedda—!

HEDDA: You see? You haven't the slightest reason to be so terrified— [*Interrupting herself.*] So! Now the three of us can enjoy ourselves.

LÖVBORG: [*Who has been startled.*] Uh...what is all this about, Mrs. Tesman? 835

MRS. ELVSTED: My God, Hedda! What are you saying? What are you doing?

HEDDA: Don't get excited. That horrible Judge Brack is watching you. 840

LÖVBORG: So she was terrified. On my account.

MRS. ELVSTED: [*Softly and piteously.*] Oh, Hedda— what have you done!

LÖVBORG: [*Stares at her. His face is distorted.*] So that was my comrade's frank confidence in me? 845

MRS. ELVSTED: [*Imploringly.*] Oh, my dear, please... let me explain...

LÖVBORG: [*Takes one of the glasses of punch, raises it to his lips, and says in a low, husky voice.*] Your health, Thea! 850

He empties the glass, puts it down, and takes the second.

MRS. ELVSTED: [*Softly.*] Oh, Hedda, Hedda—how could you?

HEDDA: How could *I*? Are you crazy?

LÖVBORG: And you, too, Mrs. Tesman. Thanks for the truth. [*Raising the glass.*] Here's to the truth! 855

He empties the glass and is about to re-fill it.

HEDDA: [*Lays her hand on his arm.*] Come, come—that's enough for now. Remember you're going out to supper.

MRS. ELVSTED: No, no!

HEDDA: Sh! They're watching.   860

LÖVBORG: [*Putting down the glass.*] Now, Thea. Tell me the truth—

MRS. ELVSTED: Yes.

LÖVBORG: Did your husband know you'd come after me?   865

MRS. ELVSTED: [*Wringing her hands.*] Oh, Hedda—listen to what he's asking!

LÖVBORG: Had the two of you arranged that you would come to town and look after me? Perhaps the Sheriff himself urged you to come? Yes...yes,   870
no doubt he needed my help in the office. Or was it at the card table he missed me?

MRS. ELVSTED: [*Softly in agony.*] Oh, Lövborg, Lövborg—!

LÖVBORG: [*Seizes a glass and is about to fill it.*] Here's   875
to the old Sheriff, too!

HEDDA: [*Preventing him.*] No more just now. Remember, you have to read your manuscript to Tesman.

LÖVBORG: [*Calmly, putting down the glass.*] It was   880
stupid of me, Thea—to take it this way, I mean. Don't be angry with me, my dear friend. You'll see—you and the others—that if I fell once, I've risen again. Thanks to you, Thea.

MRS. ELVSTED: [*Radiant with joy.*] Oh, thank   885
heaven.

BRACK *has in the meantime looked at his watch. He and* TESMAN *rise and come into the drawing room.*

BRACK: [*Takes his hat and overcoat.*] Well, Mrs. Tesman, our time has come.

HEDDA: I suppose it has.

LÖVBORG: [*Rising.*] Mine too, Judge Brack.   890

MRS. ELVSTED: [*Softly and imploringly.*] Oh, Lövborg, don't!

HEDDA: [*Pinching her arm.*] They can hear you!

MRS. ELVSTED: [*With a suppressed shriek.*] Ow!

LÖVBORG: [*To* BRACK.] You were good enough to   895
invite me.

BRACK: So, you're coming after all?

LÖVBORG: Yes, many thanks.

BRACK: I'm delighted—

LÖVBORG: [*To* TESMAN, *putting the manuscript in his*   900
pocket.] I'd like to show you one or two things before I send it to the printers.

TESMAN: Imagine that—how delightful. But, Hedda dear, how will Mrs. Elvsted get home? Eh?

HEDDA: Oh, we'll manage somehow.   905

LÖVBORG: [*Looking towards the ladies.*] Mrs. Elvsted? Of course, I'll come back for her. [*Approaching.*] At ten or thereabouts, Mrs. Tesman? Will that do?

HEDDA: Perfectly.

TESMAN: Well, then, that's all arranged. But you   910
shouldn't expect me quite so early, Hedda.

HEDDA: Oh, by all means stay—as long as you like.

MRS. ELVSTED: [*Trying to conceal her anxiety.*] Well, then, Mr. Lövborg, I'll wait here until you come.

LÖVBORG: [*With a hat in his hand.*] Please do, Mrs.   915
Elvsted.

BRACK: The train is now leaving the station, gentlemen! I hope evening will be an "animated" one, as a certain lovely lady puts it.

HEDDA: Ah, if only the lovely lady could be there   920
invisible.

BRACK: Why invisible?

HEDDA: To hear a little of your "animation" uncensored.

BRACK: [*Laughing.*] I wouldn't advise it.   925

TESMAN: [*Also laughing.*] Well, you're a fine one, Hedda! Just imagine!

BRACK: Well, good-bye, good-bye, ladies.

LÖVBORG: [*Bowing.*] About ten o'clock then.

BRACK, LÖVBORG, *and* TESMAN *go out by the hall door. At the same time,* BERTA *enters from the inner room with a lighted lamp, which she places on the drawing-room table; she goes out by the way she came.*

MRS. ELVSTED: [*Who has risen and is wandering*   930
restlessly about the room.] Hedda—Hedda—what will come of all this?

HEDDA: At ten o'clock, he'll be here. I can see him already—with vine-leaves in his hair—flushed and fearless.   935

MRS. ELVSTED: Oh, I hope so.

HEDDA: And then, you'll see, he'll have regained his self control. So, he'll be a free man forever.

MRS. ELVSTED: Oh, God, if only he would come as you say.   940

HEDDA: Oh, he will come. I have no doubt about it. [*Rises and approaches* THEA.] *You* may go on doubting him if you like, but *I* believe in him. Now, let's try—

MRS. ELVSTED: You have some hidden motive in this, Hedda. 945

HEDDA: Yes, I do. I want for once to feel the power of moulding a human destiny.

MRS. ELVSTED: You don't have that power?

HEDDA: No—and never have. 950

MRS. ELVSTED: Not over your husband?

HEDDA: Do you think *that* would be worth the trouble? You have no idea how poor I really am. Whereas fate has made you so rich. [*Embraces her.*] You know, I think I may have to burn your hair off, after all. 955

MRS. ELVSTED: Let me go! Let me go! You frighten me, Hedda.

BERTA: [*In the middle doorway.*] Tea is ready in the dining-room, ma'am.

HEDDA: Good. We'll be right there. 960

MRS. ELVSTED: No, no, no. I'd rather go home alone. Right now.

HEDDA: Nonsense! You'll have a cup of tea first, you little fool. And then at ten, Eilert Lövborg will be here. With vine-leaves in his hair. 965

She drags MRS. ELVSTED *almost by force towards the middle doorway.*

ACT III.

The TESMANS'. *The curtains are drawn over the middle doorway and also over the glass door. The lamp on the table is burning, half turned down, and with a shade over it. In the stove, the door of which is open, a fire has been burning, which is now nearly out.*

MRS. ELVSTED sits in an armchair close to the stove, wrapped in a large shawl, and with her feet on a foot-stool. HEDDA, fully dressed, lies sleeping upon the sofa, with a sofa-blanket over her.

MRS. ELVSTED: [*After a pause, suddenly sits up in her chair, and listens eagerly. Then, wearily, she sinks back again, moaning to herself.*] Not yet. Oh God, oh God—not yet!

BERTA slips in cautiously by the hall door. She has a letter in her hand.

MRS. ELVSTED: [*Turns and whispers eagerly.*] Well, Berta? Has anyone come? 5

BERTA: [*Softly.*] Yes, a girl just brought this letter.

MRS. ELVSTED: [*Quickly, holding out her hand.*] A letter? Let me have it!

BERTA: No, it's for Dr. Tesman, ma'am. 10

MRS. ELVSTED: Oh.

BERTA: It was Miss Tesman's servant that brought it. I'll leave it here.

MRS. ELVSTED: Alright.

BERTA: [*Laying down the letter.*] I'd better put out the lamp. It's smoking. 15

MRS. ELVSTED: Yes, put it out. It will be daylight soon.

BERTA: [*Putting out the lamp.*] It's daylight already, ma'am.

MRS. ELVSTED: Yes, broad daylight, and noone back yet! 20

BERTA: Lord, ma'am, I guessed this would happen.

MRS. ELVSTED: Oh?

BERTA: Yes, when I saw that a certain person had come back, and that he went off with them... We've heard plenty about that gentleman before! 25

MRS. ELVSTED: Not so loud. You'll wake Mrs. Tesman.

BERTA: [*Looks towards the sofa and sighs.*] No, no, let her sleep, poor thing. Should I put some wood on the fire? 30

MRS. ELVSTED: Thanks, not for me.

BERTA: Alright, then.

She goes softly out by the hall door.

HEDDA: [*Awakened by the shutting of the door, looks up.*] What was that? 35

MRS. ELVSTED: Just the servant.

HEDDA: [*Looking about her.*] Oh, we're here. Yes, now I remember. [*Sits up, stretches, and rubs her eyes.*] What time is it, Thea?

MRS. ELVSTED: [*Looks at her watch.*] Past seven. 40

HEDDA: When did Tesman come home?

MRS. ELVSTED: He hasn't come.

HEDDA: Not home yet?

MRS. ELVSTED: [*Rising.*] No one has come.

HEDDA: To think we sat and waited here till four in the morning... 45

MRS. ELVSTED: [*Distressed.*] And *how* I waited for him!

HEDDA: [*Yawning, her hand before her mouth.*] Well. We might have spared ourselves the trouble. 50

MRS. ELVSTED: Did you get a little sleep?

HEDDA: Oh, yes; I believe I've slept pretty well. Haven't you?

MRS. ELVSTED: Not for a moment. I couldn't, Hedda, not to save my life. 55

HEDDA: [*Rises and goes towards her.*] Now, now. There's no reason to be so worried. I know exactly what's happened.

MRS. ELVSTED: Well? Tell me what you think.

HEDDA: Well, naturally, things went very late at Judge Brack's— 60

MRS. ELVSTED: Yes, yes—that's clear enough. Nevertheless—

HEDDA: —so, of course, Tesman didn't want to come home and wake us up in the middle of the night. [*Laughing.*] Perhaps, too, he wasn't inclined to show himself right after his night out. 65

MRS. ELVSTED: But, in that case where is he?

HEDDA: Probably gone to his aunts' and slept there. They've kept his old room ready. 70

MRS. ELVSTED: No, he can't be with them; a letter has just come for him from Miss Tesman. It's right there.

HEDDA: Oh? [*Looks at the address.*] Yes, it's addressed in Aunt Julia's hand. Well, then, he's still at Judge Brack's. And as for Eilert Lövborg, he's sitting, with vine-leaves in his hair, reading his manuscript. 75

MRS. ELVSTED: Oh, Hedda, you don't believe that at all.

HEDDA: You really are a little blockhead, Thea.

MRS. ELVSTED: Yes, I suppose I am. 80

HEDDA: And you look completely worn out.

MRS. ELVSTED: Yes, I am worn out.

HEDDA: Well, then, do as I tell you. Go into my room and lie down for a little while.

MRS. ELVSTED: Oh, no, no. I'd never be able to sleep. 85

HEDDA: I am sure you would.

MRS. ELVSTED: But your husband will certainly be back soon; and I want to know right away—

HEDDA: I'll make sure to let you know when he comes. 90

MRS. ELVSTED: You promise me, Hedda?

HEDDA: Yes, rely on me. Just go in and have a sleep in the meantime.

MRS. ELVSTED: Thanks, then, I'll try to. 95

She exits through the inner door.

HEDDA goes up to the glass door and draws back the curtains. The broad daylight streams into the room. Then she takes a hand-mirror from the writing-table, looks at herself in it, and arranges her hair. Next she goes to the hall door and presses the bell.

BERTA presently appears at the hall door

BERTA: Did you want something, ma'am?

HEDDA: Yes; put some more wood in the stove. I'm shivering.

BERTA: Oh dear—I'll build the fire up right away. [*She rakes the embers together and lays a piece of wood upon them; then stops and listens.*] That was the front door, ma'am. 100

HEDDA: Then go to the door. I'll look after the fire.

BERTA: It'll be blazing in no time.

She goes out by the hall door.

HEDDA kneels on the foot-rest and puts some more wood in the stove.

After a short pause, GEORGE TESMAN enters from the hall. He looks tired and rather serious. He steals on tiptoe towards the middle doorway and is about to slip through the curtains.

HEDDA: [*At the stove, without looking up.*] Good morning. 105

TESMAN: [*Turns.*] Hedda! [*Approaching her.*] Good heavens, you're up early, eh?

HEDDA: Yes, I'm up very early this morning.

TESMAN: And I assumed you were still sound asleep! How about that! 110

HEDDA: Not so loud. Mrs. Elvsted is resting in my room.

TESMAN: Has she been here all night?

HEDDA: Yes, since no one came to fetch her. 115

TESMAN: Ah...yes, of course.

HEDDA: [*Closes the door of the stove and rises.*] Well, did you enjoy yourselves at Judge Brack's?

TESMAN: Have you worried about me? Eh?

HEDDA: No, it wouldn't occur to me to *worry*. I just asked if you'd enjoyed yourself. 120

TESMAN: Oh, yes—for once. Especially the beginning of the evening, when Eilert read me part of his book. We were more than an hour too early—

just imagine!—and Brack had all these arrangements to make—so Eilert read to me.

HEDDA: [*Seating herself by the table on the right.*] Well? Tell me, then—

TESMAN: [*Sitting on a footstool near the stove.*] Oh, Hedda, you can't imagine what a brilliant book that is going to be! I believe it's one of the most remarkable things ever written. Imagine that!

HEDDA: Yes, yes; I don't care about that—

TESMAN: I have to confess, Hedda: when he'd finished reading—a horrible feeling came over me.

HEDDA: Oh?

TESMAN: Envy. I *envied* Eilert for having it in him to write a book like that. Think of it, Hedda!

HEDDA: Yes, I am thinking.

TESMAN: And yet how pitiful that—with all his gifts—he should be so incorrigible.

HEDDA: You mean...unusually brave.

TESMAN: No, no—not at all. I mean that he's incapable of taking his pleasures in moderation.

HEDDA: So what happened, then?

TESMAN: Well, to tell the truth, Hedda, you could almost call it an orgy.

HEDDA: Oh? Did he have vine-leaves in his hair?

TESMAN: Vine-leaves? Nothing like that, no. But he made a long, rambling speech in honour of the woman who had inspired him in his work—that was his phrase.

HEDDA: Did he name her?

TESMAN: No; but I can't help thinking he meant Mrs. Elvsted. In fact, I've no doubt.

HEDDA: Well... Where did you leave him?

TESMAN: On the way to town. We broke up—the last of us at any rate—all together; and Brack came with us to get a breath of fresh air. You see, we agreed to take Eilert home. He'd had far more than he should have.

HEDDA: I imagine.

TESMAN: But here's the strange thing, Hedda; or, I should say, the sad thing. Really, I'm almost ashamed, on Eilert's account, to tell you—

HEDDA: Oh, go on!

TESMAN: Well, as we were getting near town, you see, I happened to drop a little behind the rest. Well, it was just for a minute or so. You see?

HEDDA: Yes, yes, yes. And?

TESMAN: Well, then, as I was hurrying to catch up with them, what do you suppose I found by the roadside? Eh?

HEDDA: Well, how should I know?

TESMAN: You mustn't mention it to a soul, Hedda. You hear? Promise me, for Eilert's sake. [*Draws a parcel, wrapped in paper, from his coat pocket.*] Just imagine, dear: I found this.

HEDDA: Isn't that the parcel Eilert had with him yesterday?

TESMAN: Yes, his entire, precious, irreplaceable manuscript! He'd gone and lost it, and knew nothing about it. Just imagine, Hedda. To be in such a deplorable—

HEDDA: But why didn't you give it back to him right away?

TESMAN: I wouldn't dare—not in the state he was in.

HEDDA: You didn't tell any of the others you'd found it?

TESMAN: Oh, far from it! You understand, of course, that, for Eilert's sake, I wouldn't do that.

HEDDA: So no one knows that Eilert Lövborg's manuscript is in your possession?

TESMAN: No. And no one should *ever* know.

HEDDA: Then what did you say to him afterwards?

TESMAN: I didn't talk to him again at all. Once we were into the streets, he and two or three others gave us the slip and disappeared. How about that!

HEDDA: Indeed. They must have taken him home then.

TESMAN: Yes, apparently. And Brack left us too.

HEDDA: And what have you been doing since then?

TESMAN: Well, a few of us went home with one fellow, a jovial type, and had our morning coffee with him; or perhaps I should call it night coffee— eh? But now, as soon as I've had a rest, and given poor Eilert a chance to sleep it off, I'll have to take this back to him.

HEDDA: [*Holds out her hand for the packet.*] No, don't give it to him! Not in such a hurry, I mean. Let me read it first.

TESMAN: I couldn't, Hedda, dear. No, really, I couldn't.

HEDDA: You couldn't?

TESMAN: No, because imagine how desperate he'll feel when he wakes up and realizes the manuscript is missing. He has no copy, you know. He told me so.

HEDDA: [*Looking searchingly at him.*] Couldn't he just copy it out again? Rewrite it?

TESMAN: No, I don't think so...no. It's a matter of inspiration, you see. 220

HEDDA: Yes. Yes, I suppose it *would* depend on that. [*Lightly.*] Oh, by the way, there's a letter for you.

TESMAN: Really?

HEDDA: [*Handing it to him.*] It came early this morning. 225

TESMAN: It's from Aunt Julia. I wonder what... [*He lays the packet on the other footstool, opens the letter, runs his eye through it, and jumps up.*] Oh, Hedda—she says that poor Aunt Rina is dying! 230

HEDDA: Well, we were prepared for that.

TESMAN: And that if I want to see her again, I should hurry. I'll run over there at once.

HEDDA: [*Suppressing a smile.*] You'll run, will you?

TESMAN: Oh, Hedda, my dear—if you would only agree to come with me—think how much it would mean! 235

HEDDA: [*Rises and says wearily, repelling the idea.*] No, no, don't ask me to do that. I don't want to look at sickness and death. I loathe all that sort of ugliness. 240

TESMAN: Well, then... [*Bustling around.*] My hat...my overcoat? Oh, in the hall. Oh Hedda, I do hope I won't be too late, eh?

HEDDA: Well, if you *run*... 245

BERTA appears at the hall door.

BERTA: Judge Brack is here, and wants to know if he can come in.

TESMAN: Right now? No, I can't possibly see him.

HEDDA: But I can. [*To BERTA.*] Ask Judge Brack to come in. 250

BERTA goes out.

HEDDA: [*Quickly, whispering.*] The parcel, Tesman!

She snatches it up from the stool.

TESMAN: Yes, give it to me!

HEDDA: No, no, I'll keep it till you come back.

She goes to the writing-table and places it in the bookcase. TESMAN stands in a flurry, trying to get his gloves on. JUDGE BRACK enters from the hall.

HEDDA: [*Nodding to him.*] I must say, you *are* an early bird. 255

BRACK: Yes, aren't I? [*To TESMAN.*] Are you on the move, too?

TESMAN: Yes, I have to rush off to my aunts'. It looks like the invalid one is at death's door, poor thing.

BRACK: Oh dear, is she indeed? Then on no account let me detain you. At such a moment— 260

TESMAN: Yes, I really must rush... Good-bye! Good-bye!

He hurries out by the hall door.

HEDDA: [*Approaching.*] You seem to have had a particularly "animated" night of it at your place, Judge Brack. 265

BRACK: I tell you, I haven't even had my clothes off yet, Miss Hedda.

HEDDA: Not you, either?

BRACK: No, as you may see. But what has Tesman been telling you about our night's adventures? 270

HEDDA: Oh, some tiresome story about how they went and had coffee somewhere or other.

BRACK: Yes, I heard about the coffee-party. Eilert Lövborg wasn't with them, I suppose? 275

HEDDA: No, they'd taken him home before that.

BRACK: Tesman went too?

HEDDA: No, but some of the others, he said.

BRACK: [*Smiling.*] George Tesman really is a simple creature, isn't he, Miss Hedda? 280

HEDDA: Yes, heaven knows. There's something behind all this, then?

BRACK: Yes, perhaps.

HEDDA: Well then, have a seat, my dear Judge, and tell your story in comfort. 285

She seats herself to the left of the table. BRACK sits near her, at the long side of the table.

HEDDA: Well?

BRACK: I had special reasons for keeping an eye on my guests—or at least some of my guests—last night.

HEDDA: Eilert Lövborg especially, perhaps? 290

BRACK: Frankly—yes.

HEDDA: Now you've made me really curious...

BRACK: Do you know where he and one or two of the others finished the night, Miss Hedda?

HEDDA: If it is not quite unmentionable, tell me. 295

BRACK: Oh no, it's not all unmentionable. They dropped in on a particular *soirée*.

HEDDA: Of the animated kind?

BRACK: Of the *most* animated—

HEDDA: Tell me more. 300

BRACK: Lövborg and the others had been invited in advance. I knew all about it. But he declined the invitation; for, as you know, he's become a new man.

HEDDA: Up at the Elvsteds', yes. But he went after all? 305

BRACK: Well, you see Miss Hedda, unhappily inspiration found him at my place last night.

HEDDA: Yes, I heard the spirits had entered him.

BRACK: Pretty violently. Anyway, I suppose that changed his mind. Alas, we men are not always so 310 firm in our principles as we ought to be.

HEDDA: Oh, I'm sure you are an exception, Judge Brack. But as to Lövborg—?

BRACK: To make a long story short—he ended up 315 in Mademoiselle Diana's rooms.

HEDDA: Mademoiselle Diana's?

BRACK: It was Mademoiselle Diana who was giving the soirée. For a select circle of her admirers and lady friends. 320

HEDDA: Is she a red-haired woman?

BRACK: Precisely.

HEDDA: A sort of...singer?

BRACK: Yes—in her leisure moments. But moreover, a mighty huntress of men. You've no doubt heard 325 of her. In his glory days, Eilert Lövborg was one of her great favourites.

HEDDA: So how did things end?

BRACK: Not very happily, I'm afraid. They seem to have started with a welcoming embrace, but ended 330 with blows—

HEDDA: Lövborg and she?

BRACK: Yes. He accused her or her friends of having robbed him. He insisted that his wallet was missing—and other things as well. In short, he 335 seems to have made an awful scene.

HEDDA: And what came of it?

BRACK: A general melée, involving not only the men but the ladies as well. Fortunately the police arrived at last. 340

HEDDA: The police had to be involved?

BRACK: Yes. I suspect it will prove a costly frolic for Eilert Lövborg, the madman.

HEDDA: How so?

BRACK: Apparently he resisted violently—hit one of 345 the constables on the head and tore the coat off his back. So they had to march him off to the police-station with the rest.

HEDDA: How did you hear about all this?

BRACK: From the police themselves. 350

HEDDA: [*Gazing straight before her.*] So that's what happened. No vine-leaves in his hair, then.

BRACK: Vine-leaves, Miss Hedda?

HEDDA: [*Changing her tone.*] But tell me, Judge: what is your real reason for tracking Eilert Lövborg 355 so closely?

BRACK: In the first place, it would not be a matter of complete indifference to me if it were mentioned in court that he came straight from my house. 360

HEDDA: Will it come to court then?

BRACK: Of course. Though I wouldn't have worried so much about that in itself. But I considered it my duty, as a friend of the family, to inform you and Tesman about his nocturnal exploits. 365

HEDDA: Why so?

BRACK: Because I suspect that he intends to use you as a sort of blind.

HEDDA: Now, why would you think such a thing!

BRACK: Good heavens, Miss Hedda! I have eyes to 370 see! Mark my words: this Mrs. Elvsted will be in no hurry to leave town.

HEDDA: Well, even if there were anything between them, surely there are plenty of other places they could meet. 375

BRACK: Not a single home. Henceforth, as before, every respectable house will be closed to Eilert Lövborg.

HEDDA: And so should mine, you mean?

BRACK: Yes. I confess it would be more than painful 380 to me if this man were to have the freedom of your house. It would be superfluous and intrusive, were he to force his way in—into—

HEDDA: —into the triangle?

BRACK: Precisely. It would simply mean that I would 385 be homeless.

HEDDA: [*Looks at him with a smile.*] To be the one cock of the walk—that's what you want.

BRACK: [*Nods slowly and lowers his voice.*] Yes, that's what I want. And I'll fight for it—with every weapon at my command. 390

HEDDA: [*Her smile vanishing.*] I see you are a dangerous man, when it comes down to it.

BRACK: You think so?

HEDDA: I am *beginning* to think so. And I'm rather grateful that you have no sort of hold over me. 395

BRACK: [*Laughing equivocally.*] Well well, Miss Hedda—perhaps you're right. If I had, who knows what I might be capable of?

HEDDA: Now, Judge Brack! That sounds almost like a threat. 400

BRACK: [*Rising.*] Oh, not at all! The triangle, you see, is something best developed spontaneously.

HEDDA: I agree with you there.

BRACK: Well, now: I've said all I had to say; so I'd better be getting back to town. Good-bye, Miss Hedda. [*He goes towards the glass door.*] 405

HEDDA: [*Rising.*] You're going through the garden?

BRACK: Yes, it's shorter that way.

HEDDA: And it's a back way, too. 410

BRACK: Quite so. I have no objection to back ways. At times they can be quite attractive.

HEDDA: As when there's gun practice going on?

BRACK: [*In the doorway, laughing to her.*] Oh, I don't think people shoot their tame poultry. 415

HEDDA: [*Also laughing.*] Well, no, not when there's only the one cock of the walk!

They exchange laughing nods of farewell. He goes. She closes the door behind him.

HEDDA, who has become quite serious, stands for a moment looking out then goes and looks through the curtain in the middle doorway. She goes to the writing-table, takes LÖVBORG's packet out of the bookcase, and is about to look through its contents. BERTA is heard speaking loudly in the hall. HEDDA turns and listens. She hastily locks up the packet in the drawer, and puts the key on the inkstand.

EILERT LÖVBORG, with his overcoat on and his hat in his hand, tears open the hall door. He looks confused and irritated.

LÖVBORG: I'm telling you I must come in! Let me by!

He closes the door, turns, sees HEDDA, at once regains his self-control, and bows.

HEDDA: [*At the writing-table.*] Mr. Lövborg. This is a rather late hour to call for Thea. 420

LÖVBORG: You mean rather early to call on you. I beg your pardon.

HEDDA: How do you know that she is still here?

LÖVBORG: They told me at her lodgings that she had been out all night. 425

HEDDA: [*Going to the oval table.*] Did you notice anything about the people when they said that?

LÖVBORG: [*Looks inquiringly at her.*] Notice anything?

HEDDA: I mean, did they seem to think it odd? 430

LÖVBORG: [*Suddenly understanding.*] Yes, of course! I'm dragging her down with me! But no, I didn't notice anything. Tesman isn't up yet?

HEDDA: No, I don't think so.

LÖVBORG: When did he come home? 435

HEDDA: Very late.

LÖVBORG: Did he tell you anything?

HEDDA: Yes, I gathered that you'd a rather merry time of it at Judge Brack's.

LÖVBORG: Nothing more? 440

HEDDA: I don't think so—though I was very sleepy.

MRS. ELVSTED enters through the curtains of the middle doorway.

MRS. ELVSTED: [*Going towards him.*] Ah, Lövborg! At last!

LÖVBORG: Yes, at last. And too late!

MRS. ELVSTED: [*Looks anxiously at him.*] What's too late? 445

LÖVBORG : *Everything* is too late now. It's all over for me.

MRS. ELVSTED: No, no! Don't say that!

LÖVBORG: You'll say the same when you hear just what— 450

MRS. ELVSTED: I won't hear anything!

HEDDA: Perhaps you'd prefer to talk alone? If so, I'll leave you.

LÖVBORG: No, you stay too. Please. 455

MRS. ELVSTED: Yes, but I'm telling you, I don't want to hear anything.

LÖVBORG: It is not the escapades of last night I want to talk about.

MRS. ELVSTED: What is it then? 460

LÖVBORG: I want to say that we have to part now.

MRS. ELVSTED: Part?

HEDDA: [*Involuntarily.*] I knew it!

LÖVBORG: You can be of no more use to me, Thea.

MRS. ELVSTED: How can you say that? No use to 465 you! Why wouldn't I help you now, the same as before? Are we not to go on working together?

LÖVBORG: I'm not going to do any more work.

MRS. ELVSTED: [*Despairingly.*] Then what am I to do with my life? 470

LÖVBORG: Try to live as if you'd never known me.

MRS. ELVSTED: But you know I can't do that!

LÖVBORG: Try, Thea. Go back to your home and—

MRS. ELVSTED: [*In vehement protest.*] Never in this world! Wherever you are, that is where I will be also! 475 I will not let myself be driven away like this! I will stay here and be with you when the book appears.

HEDDA: [*Half aloud, in suspense.*] Ah, yes—your book.

LÖVBORG: [*Looks at her.*] Our book—mine and 480 Thea's. It really belongs to us both.

MRS. ELVSTED: Yes, I feel that it does. And that's why I have a right to be with you when it appears! So I can see all the respect and honour you receive. And the happiness—I want to share in the 485 happiness!

LÖVBORG: Thea... Our book will never appear.

HEDDA: Ah!

MRS. ELVSTED: Will never...?

LÖVBORG: *Can* never appear. 490

MRS. ELVSTED: [*In agonized foreboding.*] Lövborg, what have you done with the manuscript?

HEDDA: [*Looks anxiously at him.*] Yes, the manuscript—?

MRS. ELVSTED: Where is it? 495

LÖVBORG: Oh Thea! Don't ask me about it!

MRS. ELVSTED: Yes, yes, I want to know. I demand to be told right now.

LÖVBORG: The manuscript... Well...I've torn the manuscript into a thousand pieces. 500

MRS. ELVSTED: [*Shrieks.*] Oh no! No—!

HEDDA: [*Involuntarily.*] But that's not...

LÖVBORG: [*Looks at her.*] Not true, you think?

HEDDA: [*Collecting herself.*] Well, of course, since you say so... But it sounded so improbable— 505

LÖVBORG: Nevertheless, it's true.

MRS. ELVSTED: [*Wringing her hands.*] Oh God. Oh God, Hedda! Torn his own work to pieces!

LÖVBORG: I've torn my own life to pieces, so why not my life-work too? 510

MRS. ELVSTED: And you did this last night?

LÖVBORG: Yes, that's what I'm telling you. Tore it into a thousand pieces, and scattered them out on the fjord. Far out. There's fresh sea-water there at least. Let them drift away on it...drift with the tide 515 and the wind. And eventually sink—deeper and deeper. As I shall do.

MRS. ELVSTED: Lövborg, Lövborg...what you've done to that book—for the rest of my life, I'll feel like you've killed a little child. 520

LÖVBORG: Yes. You're right. It is a sort of child-murder.

MRS. ELVSTED: How could you! Wasn't the child mine too?

HEDDA: [*Almost inaudibly.*] Ah, the child... 525

MRS. ELVSTED: [*Breathing heavily.*] It's all over then. Well... Well, I'll be going now, Hedda.

HEDDA: You're not leaving town?

MRS. ELVSTED: I don't know what I'll do. I can't see anything but darkness ahead of me right now. [*She 530 exits through the hall door.*]

HEDDA: [*Stands waiting for a moment.*] Aren't you going to see her home, Mr. Lövborg?

LÖVBORG: I? Through the streets? You'd have people see her walking with me? 535

HEDDA: Of course, I don't know what *else* may have happened last night. But is it so utterly irretrievable?

LÖVBORG: Oh, last night won't be the end of it. I can tell you that much. But the thing is...now I've 540 lost my taste for that sort of life, too. I can't start into all that again. She's broken my courage, you see. My power of flying in the teeth of the world.

HEDDA: [*Looking straight before her.*] So the pretty little fool has meddled with a man's destiny. [*Looks 545 at him.*] All the same, how could you treat her so heartlessly?

LÖVBORG: Look, don't say that was heartless!

HEDDA: To go and destroy what's made her life worth living these last few years—you don't call 550 that heartless!

LÖVBORG: To you, Hedda, I can tell the truth.

HEDDA: The truth?

LÖVBORG: But promise me—give me your word— that Thea shall never know this. 555

HEDDA: You have my word.

LÖVBORG: Good, then let me tell you that what I told her was a lie.

HEDDA: About the manuscript?

LÖVBORG: Yes. I didn't tear it up, or throw it into the fjord. 560

HEDDA: You didn't. But, where is it then?

LÖVBORG: I have destroyed it nevertheless. Utterly destroyed it, Hedda!

HEDDA: I don't understand. 565

LÖVBORG: Thea said that what I'd done was like murdering a child.

HEDDA: Yes, that's what she said.

LÖVBORG: But killing his own child—that's not the worst thing a father can do to it. 570

HEDDA: No?

LÖVBORG: No. I wanted to spare Thea the worst.

HEDDA: And what is the worst?

LÖVBORG: Suppose, Hedda, that a man came home early one morning to his child's mother after a 575 night of debauchery, and said to her: "Listen, I've been out—here and there, this place and that. And I took our child with me—to all those places. And I've lost him. Lost him completely. God knows whose hands he's fallen into—who has their 580 clutches in him now."

HEDDA: Well, yes. But when all is said and done, this was only a book—

LÖVBORG: Thea's pure soul was in that book.

HEDDA: Yes, I understand that. 585

LÖVBORG: Then you can understand, too, that for her and me no future together is possible now.

HEDDA: What path will you take, then?

LÖVBORG: None. Just make an end of it all—the sooner the better. 590

HEDDA: [*A step nearer him.*] Eilert Lövborg...listen to me... Will you not try to—to do it beautifully?

LÖVBORG: Beautifully? [*Smiling.*] With vine-leaves in my hair? As I was in your dreams in the old days? 595

HEDDA: No. I've lost my faith in vine-leaves. But beautifully nevertheless...this once!—Good-bye.

You must go now—and don't come here any more.

LÖVBORG: Good-bye, Mrs. Tesman. And give George Tesman my love. [*He is about to go.*] 600

HEDDA: Wait! I want to give you a memento to take with you.

She goes to the writing-table, opens the drawer and pistol-case; then returns to LÖVBORG with one of the pistols.

LÖVBORG: [*Looks at her.*] This? Is this your memento?

HEDDA: [*Nodding slowly.*] You recognize it? It was 605 aimed at you once.

LÖVBORG: You should have used it then.

HEDDA: Take it—you use it now.

LÖVBORG: [*Puts the pistol in his breast pocket.*] Thanks! 610

HEDDA: And beautifully, Eilert Lövborg. Promise me that!

LÖVBORG: Good-bye, Hedda Gabler.

He goes out by the hall door.

HEDDA listens for a moment at the door. Then she goes to the writing-table, takes out the packet of manuscript, looks under the cover, draws a few of the sheets half out, and looks at them. Next she goes and sits in the arm-chair by the stove, with the packet in her lap. After a moment, she opens the stove door, and then the packet.

HEDDA: [*Throws one of the pages into the fire and whispers to herself.*] Now I'm burning your child, 615 Thea! Burning it, curly-locks! [*Throwing one or two more pages into the stove.*] Your child and Eilert Lövborg's. [*Throws the rest in.*] I'm burning it. I am burning your child.

ACT IV

The Tesmans'. Evening. The drawing-room is in darkness. The back room is lit by the hanging lamp over the table. The curtains over the glass door are closed.

HEDDA, dressed in black, paces in the dark room. Then she goes into the back room and disappears for a moment to the left and is heard playing a few chords on the piano. Then she returns to the drawing-room.

BERTA enters from the right, through the inner room, with a lighted lamp, which she places on the table in front of the corner settee. Her eyes are red with weeping, and she has black ribbons in her cap. She goes quietly out to the right. HEDDA goes to the glass door, lifts the curtain a little aside, and looks out into the darkness.

Shortly afterwards, MISS TESMAN, dressed in mourning, with a hat and veil, enters from the hall. HEDDA goes to her and holds out her hand.

MISS TESMAN: Well, Hedda, here I am, in mourning and forlorn. My poor sister has found peace at last.

HEDDA: As you see, I've heard the news already. Tesman sent me a note.

MISS TESMAN: Yes, he promised he would. But nevertheless I thought I must go to Hedda myself to bring the tidings of death into her house of life.

HEDDA: That was very kind of you.

MISS TESMAN: Ah, Rina shouldn't have left us just now. This is no time for Hedda's house to be a house of mourning.

HEDDA: [*Changing the subject.*] She died quite peacefully, did she, Miss Tesman?

MISS TESMAN: Oh, her end was so calm, so beautiful. And, of course, she had the unspeakable happiness of seeing George once more—and saying good-bye to him. Hasn't he come home yet?

HEDDA: No. He wrote that he might be detained. But, please, sit down.

MISS TESMAN: No thank you, my dear, sweet Hedda. I'd like to, but there's so much to do. I must prepare my dear one for her rest as well as I can. She'll go to her grave looking her best.

HEDDA: Can I help you in any way?

MISS TESMAN: Oh, don't think of it! Hedda Tesman's hands mustn't be touched by death. Nor her thoughts either—not at this time.

HEDDA: One is not always mistress of one's thoughts—

MISS TESMAN: [*Continuing.*] Ah well, that's the way of the world. At home we'll be sewing a shroud. Here, I suppose there'll soon be sewing too—but of a different sort, thank God!

GEORGE TESMAN enters by the hall door.

HEDDA: Ah, thank heavens, you've come at last.

TESMAN: You're here, Aunt Julia—with Hedda? How about that.

MISS TESMAN: I was just going, my dear boy. Well, have you done everything you promised to?

TESMAN: No. I'm afraid I've forgotten half of it. I'll have to come over again tomorrow. Today my brain is all in a whirl. I can't put my thoughts together.

MISS TESMAN: But, dear George, you mustn't take it like this.

TESMAN: But...how do you mean?

MISS TESMAN: Even in your sorrow you must rejoice, as I do—rejoice that she is at rest.

TESMAN: Oh yes, yes—you're thinking of Aunt Rina.

HEDDA: You'll be feeling lonely now, Miss Tesman.

MISS TESMAN: For the first while, yes. But that won't last long, I hope. I expect I'll soon find an occupant for poor Rina's little room.

TESMAN: Oh? Who do you think will take it, eh?

MISS TESMAN: Well, there's always some poor invalid in want of nursing, unfortunately.

HEDDA: Would you really take such a burden upon yourself again?

MISS TESMAN: A burden! Bless you, child—it's never been any burden for me.

HEDDA: But with a total stranger on your hands—

MISS TESMAN: Oh, one soon makes friends with sick people. And it's just essential for me to have someone to live for. Well, heaven be praised, there may soon be something in *this* house, too, to keep an old aunt busy.

HEDDA: Oh, don't trouble yourself about anything here.

TESMAN: Yes, just imagine what a nice time we three might have together, if...

HEDDA: If...?

TESMAN: [*Uneasily.*] Oh, nothing. It will all be fine. Let's hope so, eh?

MISS TESMAN: Well well, I daresay you two want to talk to one other. [*Smiling.*] And Hedda may have something to tell you, George. Good-bye! I must go home to Rina. [*Turning at the door.*] How strange that is. Now Rina is with me and with my poor brother as well.

TESMAN: Yes, imagine that, Aunt Julia, eh? [*MISS TESMAN goes out by the hall door.*]

HEDDA: [*Watches TESMAN coldly.*] I almost believe this death affects you more than it does her. 80

TESMAN: Oh, it's not just that. It's Eilert I'm so worried about.

HEDDA: [*Quickly.*] Is there any news about him?

TESMAN: I looked in at his rooms this afternoon, intending to tell him the manuscript was in safe keeping. 85

HEDDA: You, didn't find him home?

TESMAN: No. But afterwards I met Mrs. Elvsted, and she told me that he'd been here early this morning. 90

HEDDA: Yes, just after you'd left.

TESMAN: And he said that he'd torn up his manuscript, eh?

HEDDA: Yes, so he claimed.

TESMAN: He must have been completely out of his mind! And I suppose you thought it best not to give it back to him, eh, Hedda? 95

HEDDA: No, he didn't get it.

TESMAN: But you told him we had it, of course?

HEDDA: No. [*Quickly.*] Did you tell Mrs. Elvsted? 100

TESMAN: No; I thought I'd better not. But you should have told him. Imagine, if, in his despair, he goes and does himself some injury! Give me the manuscript, Hedda; I'll take it to him right away. Where is it? 105

HEDDA: [*Cold and immovable, leaning on the armchair.*] I haven't got it.

TESMAN: Haven't got it? What on earth do you mean?

HEDDA: I burnt it. Every line of it.

TESMAN: [*Horrified.*] Burnt it? Burnt Eilert's manuscript?! 110

HEDDA: Don't shout. The servant will hear you.

TESMAN: Burnt! But, good God! No, no, no! It's impossible!

HEDDA: Nevertheless. 115

TESMAN: Do you know what you've done, Hedda? It's unlawful appropriation of lost property. Think of it! Just ask Judge Brack; he'll tell you.

HEDDA: I'd advise you not to mention it—to Judge Brack, or anyone else. 120

TESMAN: But how could you do such an outrageous thing? What put it into your head? What possessed you? Answer me! Eh?

HEDDA: [*Suppressing an almost imperceptible smile.*] I did it for your sake, George. 125

TESMAN: For my sake!

HEDDA: This morning, when you told me about what he'd read to you...

TESMAN: Yes, yes—what?

HEDDA: You admitted that you envied him his work. 130

TESMAN: But I didn't mean that literally!

HEDDA: No matter—I couldn't bear the idea that anyone would put you in the shade.

TESMAN: [*In an outburst of mingled doubt and joy.*] Hedda! Is this true? But—but—I never knew you show your love like that. How about that! 135

HEDDA: Well, I may as well tell you that...I'm going to— [*Impatiently, breaking off.*] No, no; you can ask Aunt Julia. She'll tell you, fast enough.

TESMAN: Oh, Hedda! I think I understand you! 140 [*Clasps his hands together.*] Good heavens, do you really mean it? Eh?

HEDDA: Don't shout. The servant will hear.

TESMAN: [*Laughing.*] The servant! How funny you are, Hedda. It's Berta! I'll tell her right away. 145

HEDDA: [*Clenching her hands desperately.*] Oh! It's killing me, all this—killing me!

TESMAN: What is it, Hedda? Eh?

HEDDA: [*Cold, controlled.*] Oh...all this...absurdity, George. 150

TESMAN: Absurdity? Is there anything absurd about my being overjoyed at the news? But perhaps I'd better not say anything to Berta after all.

HEDDA: No, do. Why not?

TESMAN: No, no. Not yet! But I'll certainly tell Aunt 155 Julia. And that you've called me George for the first time, too. How about that! Aunt Julia will be so happy—so happy!

HEDDA: When she hears that I've burnt Eilert Lövborg's manuscript? For your sake? 160

TESMAN: No, that's right. That business about the manuscript—of course, nobody must ever know... But that you love me so much, Hedda—Aunt Julia must really hear about that! I wonder if this sort of thing is usual in young wives, eh? 165

HEDDA: You'd better ask Aunt Julia that too.

TESMAN: I will, some time or other. [*Looks uneasy and downcast again.*] But the manuscript! Good God! I shudder to think of poor Eilert now.

MRS. ELVSTED, dressed as in the first act, with hat and cloak, enters by the hall door.

MRS. ELVSTED: [*Greets them hurriedly, and says in agitation.*] Oh, Hedda dear, please forgive my coming here again. 170

HEDDA: What's the matter, Thea?

TESMAN: Is it Eilert Lövborg again, eh?

MRS. ELVSTED: Yes—I'm dreadfully afraid something awful has happened to him. 175

HEDDA: [*Seizes her arm.*] You think so?

TESMAN: Good Lord, Mrs. Elvsted—what makes you think that?

MRS. ELVSTED: I heard them talking about him at the boarding-house as I came in. The most incredible rumours are being spread about him. 180

TESMAN: Yes...I heard too! How about that. Yet I can bear witness that he went straight home to bed last night. 185

HEDDA: Well, what did they say at the boarding-house?

MRS. ELVSTED: I couldn't make out anything clearly. Either they knew nothing definite, or else... They stopped talking when they saw me; and I didn't dare ask. 190

TESMAN: [*Fidgeting.*] We must hope...we must hope that you misunderstood them, Mrs. Elvsted.

MRS. ELVSTED: No. I'm sure it was him they were talking about. And I heard something about the hospital or— 195

TESMAN: The hospital?

HEDDA: No—surely that can't be.

MRS. ELVSTED: Oh, I was so terrified! I went straight to his lodgings and asked for him.

HEDDA: Was that altogether prudent, Thea? 200

MRS. ELVSTED: What else could I do? I really couldn't bear the uncertainty.

TESMAN: But you didn't find him there either, eh?

MRS. ELVSTED: No. And they knew nothing about him. Hadn't been home since yesterday afternoon, they said. 205

TESMAN: Yesterday? How could they say that?

MRS. ELVSTED: Oh, I'm sure something terrible has happened to him.

TESMAN: Hedda dear—how would it be if I were to go and make inquiries—? 210

HEDDA: No, no. Don't get yourself mixed up in this.

JUDGE BRACK, his hat in his hand, enters by the hall door, which BERTA has opened for him. He gravely bows in silence.

TESMAN: Oh, it's you, judge. How about that.

BRACK: Yes. It was imperative that I see you.

TESMAN: I see you've heard about Aunt Rina? 215

BRACK: Yes, that among other things.

TESMAN: Isn't it tragic, eh?

BRACK: Well, my dear Tesman, that depends on how you look at it.

TESMAN: [*Looks doubtfully at him.*] Has anything else happened? 220

BRACK: Yes.

HEDDA: [*In suspense.*] Anything unhappy, Judge Brack?

BRACK: That, too, depends on how you look at it, Mrs. Tesman. 225

MRS. ELVSTED: Oh, it's something about Eilert Lövborg!

BRACK: [*Glances at her.*] What makes you think that, Madam? Perhaps you've already heard something—? 230

MRS. ELVSTED: [*Confused.*] No, nothing, but—

TESMAN: For heaven's sake, Judge, tell us!

BRACK: [*Shrugging.*] Well, I'm sorry to say he's been taken to the hospital. He's on the verge of death. 235

MRS. ELVSTED: [*Shrieks.*] Oh God! Oh God!

TESMAN: At the hospital! And dying?

HEDDA: [*Involuntarily.*] So soon!

MRS. ELVSTED: [*Weeping.*] And we parted in anger, Hedda! 240

HEDDA: [*Whispers.*] Thea! Thea, be careful!

MRS. ELVSTED: [*Ignoring her.*] I must go to him! I must see him before he dies!

BRACK: It's useless, Madam. No one will be admitted. 245

MRS. ELVSTED: At least tell me what's happened to him? What is it?

TESMAN: You don't mean that he's tried to... Eh?

HEDDA: Yes, I'm sure he has.

TESMAN: Hedda, how can you—? 250

BRACK: [*Staring at her.*] Unfortunately you've guessed correctly, Mrs. Tesman.

MRS. ELVSTED: Oh, how horrible!

TESMAN: Did himself in! How about that!

HEDDA: Shot himself. 255

BRACK: Right again, Mrs. Tesman.

MRS. ELVSTED: [*With an effort at self-control.*] When did it happen, Mr. Brack?

BRACK: This afternoon. Between three and four.

TESMAN: But, good Lord, where? Eh? 260

BRACK: [*With some hesitation.*] Where? Well...I suppose at his lodgings.

MRS. ELVSTED: No, that can't be; I was there between six and seven.

BRACK: Well then, somewhere else. I don't know 265 exactly. I only know that he was found... He'd shot himself...in the chest.

MRS. ELVSTED: Oh, how terrible! That he should die like that!

HEDDA: [*To BRACK.*] In the chest? 270

BRACK: Yes...as I said.

HEDDA: Not in the temple?

BRACK: In the chest, Mrs. Tesman.

HEDDA: Well, well...the chest is a good place, too.

BRACK: How do you mean, Mrs. Tesman? 275

HEDDA: Oh, nothing...nothing.

TESMAN: And the wound's dangerous, is it, eh?

BRACK: Quite fatal. He's probably gone by now.

MRS. ELVSTED: Yes, yes, I feel it. It's over...all over. Oh, Hedda—! 280

TESMAN: But how did you manage to learn all this?

BRACK: [*Curtly.*] The police. A man I had some business with.

HEDDA: [*In a clear voice.*] At last, a deed worth doing! 285

TESMAN: [*Terrified.*] Good God, Hedda! What are you saying?

HEDDA: There is beauty in this.

BRACK: Hm. Mrs. Tesman—

TESMAN: Beauty? But think of it! 290

MRS. ELVSTED: Hedda, how can you speak of beauty in something like this!

HEDDA: Eilert Lövborg has settled his account with life. He had the courage to do...the one right thing.

MRS. ELVSTED: No, you can't believe that was how 295 it happened! He must have been out of his mind.

TESMAN: Driven to despair.

HEDDA: No—no, he wasn't.

MRS. ELVSTED: Yes! He was mad! Just as he was when he tore up our manuscript. 300

BRACK: [*Starting.*] The manuscript? He tore it up?

MRS. ELVSTED: Yes, last night.

TESMAN: [*Whispers softly.*] Oh, Hedda, we'll never get over this.

BRACK: Hm...extraordinary. 305

TESMAN: [*Pacing.*] To think of Eilert dying in such a way! And not leaving behind him the book that would have made his name immortal.

MRS. ELVSTED: If only it could be put together again! 310

TESMAN: Yes, if only! What I wouldn't give...!

MRS. ELVSTED: Perhaps it can, Mr. Tesman.

TESMAN: What do you mean?

MRS. ELVSTED: [*Searches in the pocket of her dress.*] Look. I've kept all the loose notes he dictated from. 315

HEDDA: [*A step forward.*] Ah—!

TESMAN: Eh? You kept them, Mrs. Elvsted?

MRS. ELVSTED: Yes, I've got them right here. I put them in my pocket when I left home. They're still here. 320

TESMAN: Let me see them!

MRS. ELVSTED: [*Hands him a bundle of papers.*] But they're in such disorder—all mixed up.

TESMAN: Imagine, though, if we could make something out of them! Perhaps if the two of us 325 put our heads together—

MRS. ELVSTED: Yes, yes...let's at least try!

TESMAN: We'll manage it. We must! I'll dedicate my life to this task.

HEDDA: You, George? Your life? 330

TESMAN: Yes, or as much time as I can spare. My own work will have to wait. Hedda...you understand, eh? I owe this to Eilert's memory.

HEDDA: Perhaps.

TESMAN: So, my dear Mrs. Elvsted: we'll give our 335 whole minds to this. No use brooding over what can't be undone, eh? We must try to control our grief as far as possible, and—

MRS. ELVSTED: Yes, Mr. Tesman; yes, I'll do my best.

TESMAN: Well...come here, then. I won't rest til we've 340 looked through the notes. Where should we sit? Here? No, in there, in the back room. Please excuse us, Judge. Come with me, Mrs. Elvsted.

MRS. ELVSTED: Oh, if only we can do it!

TESMAN and MRS. ELVSTED go into the back room. She takes off her hat and cloak. They sit together at the table under the hanging lamp, and are soon absorbed in their eager examination of the papers. HEDDA crosses to the stove and sits in the armchair. After a moment, BRACK goes up to her.

HEDDA: [*In a low voice.*] Oh, this act of Eilert Lövborg's...what a sense of freedom it gives one. 345

BRACK: Freedom, Miss Hedda? Well, it's a sort of release for *him*, of course—

HEDDA: I mean for me! It gives me a sense of freedom to know that a deed of real courage is still possible in this world—a spontaneous, beautiful act. 350

BRACK: [*Smiling.*] Hm. My dear Miss Hedda—

HEDDA: Oh, I know what you're going to say. You're a kind of specialist, too—just like... 355

BRACK: [*Looking hard at her.*] I think Eilert Lövborg meant more to you than perhaps you are willing to admit to yourself. Am I wrong?

HEDDA: I don't answer that sort of question. I only know that Eilert Lövborg has had the courage to 360 live his life in his own way. And now, this last great act, with its beauty! To have the strength, the will to turn away from life's banquet so abruptly...

BRACK: I see. I'm sorry, Miss Hedda...to disabuse you of this amiable illusion. 365

HEDDA: Illusion?

BRACK: It could not have lasted long in any case.

HEDDA: What do you mean?

BRACK: Eilert Lövborg did not shoot himself voluntarily. 370

HEDDA: Not voluntarily?

BRACK: No. The thing didn't happen quite as I said.

HEDDA: You concealed something? What?

BRACK: For poor Mrs. Elvsted's sake I idealized the facts a little. 375

HEDDA: What are the facts?

BRACK: First, that he is already dead.

HEDDA: At the hospital?

BRACK: Yes—without regaining consciousness.

HEDDA: And what else did you conceal? 380

BRACK: The event didn't take place at his lodgings.

HEDDA: Well, that makes no difference.

BRACK: It may when I tell you that he was found shot in...in Mademoiselle Diana's boudoir.

HEDDA: [*Starts to rise, but sinks back again.*] 385 Impossible! He can't have gone back there again today.

BRACK: He was there this afternoon. He went, he said, to retrieve something they had taken from him. Talked wildly about a lost child— 390

HEDDA: Ah. So that was why...

BRACK: I supposed that he meant his manuscript; but now I hear he'd destroyed that himself. So I guess it must have been his wallet.

HEDDA: Yes, no doubt. And he was found there? 395

BRACK: Yes. With a pistol in his breast-pocket, discharged. The ball had lodged in a vital part.

HEDDA: Yes...in his heart?

BRACK: No. In the bowels.

HEDDA: [*Looks up at him with an expression of* 400 *loathing.*] That, too. It's a curse; everything I touch turns ludicrous and sordid.

BRACK: There's something else, Miss Hedda. Another disagreeable matter.

HEDDA: And what is that? 405

BRACK: The pistol he was carrying...

HEDDA: [*Breathless.*] Well? What about it?

BRACK: He must have stolen it.

HEDDA: [*Leaps up.*] Stolen it? That's not true! He didn't steal it! 410

BRACK: There's no other explanation. He must have stolen it— Sh!

TESMAN and MRS. ELVSTED have risen from the table in the back room, and come into the drawing-room.

TESMAN: [*With the papers in both his hands.*] Hedda, dear, one can hardly see anything under that lamp in there. Just think! 415

HEDDA: Yes, I am thinking.

TESMAN: You wouldn't mind if we sat at your writing-table, eh?

HEDDA: If you like. [*Quickly.*] No, wait—let me clear it first. 420

TESMAN: Oh, don't bother, Hedda. There's plenty of room.

HEDDA: No, no, let me clear it. I'll take these things in and put them on the piano.

She has drawn out an object, covered with sheet music, from under the bookcase. She places several other pieces of music upon it, and carries the pile into the inner room. TESMAN lays the notes on the writing-table, and moves the lamp there from the corner table. He and MRS. ELVSTED sit down to work. HEDDA returns.

HEDDA: [*Behind MRS. ELVSTED's chair, gently ruffling* 425 *her hair.*] Well, Thea, darling? How goes it with Eilert Lövborg's monument?

MRS. ELVSTED: [*Looks dispiritedly up at her.*] It will be terribly hard to put these in order.

TESMAN: We'll manage it. I'm determined. After all, arranging the notes of other people is exactly my kind of work.

HEDDA goes over to the stove, and sits on a footstool. BRACK stands over her, leaning on the armchair.

HEDDA: [*Whispers.*] What were you saying about the pistol?

BRACK: [*Softly.*] That he must have stolen it.

HEDDA: Why?

BRACK: Because any other explanation ought to be impossible, Miss Hedda.

HEDDA: I see.

BRACK: [*Glances at her.*] Eilert Lövborg was here this morning, of course. Wasn't he?

HEDDA: Yes.

BRACK: Were you alone with him?

HEDDA: Part of the time.

BRACK: Did you leave the room while he was here?

HEDDA: No.

BRACK: Try to recall. Weren't you out of the room a moment?

HEDDA: Well...perhaps just a moment—out in the hall.

BRACK: And where was your pistol-case at that time?

HEDDA: I had it locked up, in...

BRACK: Yes?

HEDDA: The case was there on the writing-table.

BRACK: Have you looked since, to see whether both pistols are there?

HEDDA: No.

BRACK: Well, no need. I saw the pistol they found in Lövborg's pocket, and I recognized it right away. I'd seen it yesterday—and before, too.

HEDDA: Do you have it with you?

BRACK: No. The police have it.

HEDDA: What will the police do with it?

BRACK: Search for the owner.

HEDDA: Do you think they'll succeed?

BRACK: [*Bends over her and whispers.*] No, Hedda Gabler...so long as I keep quiet.

HEDDA: [*Looks nervously at him.*] And if you don't? What then?

BRACK: [*Shrugs.*] There's always the possibility that the pistol was stolen.

HEDDA: [*Firmly.*] I'd sooner die than resort to that.

BRACK: [*Smiling.*] People will say such things; but they never do them.

HEDDA: [*Without replying.*] And supposing the pistol *wasn't* stolen, and the owner *is* discovered? What then?

BRACK: Well, then, Hedda...then comes the scandal.

HEDDA: The scandal?

BRACK: Yes, scandal...of which you are so terrified. Of course, you'll have to appear in court—along with Mademoiselle Diana. She'll have to explain how the thing happened—whether it was an accidental shot or murder. Did the pistol go off as he was trying to take it out of his pocket, to threaten her? Or did she snatch the pistol, shoot him, and then put it back in his pocket? That would be quite like her. She's a most capable young woman, this Mademoiselle Diana.

HEDDA: But *I* have nothing to do with all this repulsive business.

BRACK: No. But you'll have to answer the question: Why did you give Eilert Lövborg the pistol? And what conclusions will people draw from the fact that you gave it to him?

HEDDA: [*Lets her head sink.*] That's true. I hadn't thought of that.

BRACK: Well, fortunately, there's no danger, so long as I keep quiet.

HEDDA: [*Looks up at him.*] So, I'm in your power, Judge Brack. Henceforth, you have me at your beck and call.

BRACK: [*Whispers softly.*] Dearest Hedda—believe me—I won't abuse my advantage.

HEDDA: Nevertheless, I'm in your power. Subject to your will and demands. A slave then, a sort of slave. [*Rises impetuously.*] No, I couldn't bear the thought of that! Never!

BRACK: [*Looks half-mockingly at her.*] People generally get used to the inevitable.

HEDDA: [*Returns his look.*] Yes, perhaps. [*She crosses to the writing-table. Suppressing an involuntary smile, she imitates TESMAN's intonations.*] Well? Going to manage alright are you, George? Eh?

TESMAN: Heaven knows, dear. In any case it will be months of work. 515

HEDDA: [*As before.*] How about that! [*Passes her hands softly through MRS. ELVSTED's hair.*] Doesn't it seem strange, Thea? Sitting here with Tesman— just as you used to sit with Lövborg? 520

MRS. ELVSTED: If only I could inspire your husband in the same way!

HEDDA: Oh, that will come, too—in time.

TESMAN: Yes, you know, Hedda—I really think I begin to feel something like that. But you go and sit with Judge Brack. 525

HEDDA: There's nothing I can do to help you two?

TESMAN: No, nothing at all. [*Turning his head.*] I trust you'll keep Hedda company, Judge.

BRACK: [*With a glance at HEDDA.*] It will be my pleasure. 530

HEDDA: Thanks. But I'm tired this evening. I think I'll go in and lie down on the sofa for a while.

TESMAN: Yes, do dear—eh?

HEDDA goes into the back room and draws the curtains. A short pause. Suddenly she is heard playing a wild dance on the piano.

MRS. ELVSTED: [*Startled.*] Oh! What's that? 535

TESMAN: [*Runs to the doorway.*] Hedda, please dear! No dance music tonight! Think of Aunt Rina! And Eilert, too.

HEDDA: [*Puts her head out between the curtains.*] And Aunt Julia. And the rest of them... After this, I'll be quiet. [*Closes the curtains again.*] 540

TESMAN: [*At the writing-table.*] It's not good for her to see us at this distressing work... You know what, Mrs. Elvsted? You should take the empty room at Aunt Julia's, and then I could come over in the evenings, and we could sit and work *there*—eh? 545

HEDDA: [*In the inner room.*] I hear what you're saying, Tesman. But how am *I* to get through the evenings out *here*?

TESMAN: [*Turning over the papers.*] Oh, I daresay Judge Brack will be kind enough to look in now and then while I'm out. 550

BRACK: [*In the arm-chair, calls out gaily.*] Every evening—with great pleasure, Mrs. Tesman! We'll have a fine time, the two of us! 555

HEDDA: [*Speaking loud and clear.*] Yes, I'm sure you believe we will, Judge Brack. Now that you're the one cock of the walk.

A shot is heard within. TESMAN, MRS. ELVSTED, and BRACK leap to their feet.

TESMAN: Oh! Now she's playing with those pistols again! 560

He throws back the curtains and runs in, followed by MRS. ELVSTED. HEDDA lies dead on the sofa. Confusion and shouting. BERTA enters in alarm from the right.

TESMAN: [*Shrieks to BRACK.*] She's shot herself! Shot herself in the head! How about that!

BRACK: [*Half-fainting in the arm-chair.*] But, good God! People don't do such things.

OSCAR WILDE

The Importance of Being Earnest

Near the end of the first act of *The Importance of Being Earnest*, Algernon declares: "All women become like their mothers. That is their tragedy. No man does. That's his." It would seem that the aphorism is not wholly true of Oscar Fingal O'Flahertie Wills Wilde (1854–1900) himself, whose own mother, Lady Jane Francesca Wilde, was also a poet and a journalist (she published mainly under the name Speranza). Yet there can be little doubt that Wilde's life might have been less tragic if, in one respect at least, it had been less reminiscent of his father's. Wilde's father, Sir William Wilde, was a eye doctor and Irish nationalist, but his name became notorious in 1864 when Mary Josephine Travers, a woman who had been Sir William's patient for ten years, publicly accused him of having chloroformed and raped her. As it happened, Travers was widely deemed to be neurotic and deranged, and Sir William was never formally charged on the matter. Still, a sense of scandal hung over the Wilde name for years afterward, and if it seemed to have ended in 1876 with Sir William's death, it was revived with a vengeance twenty years later, when Oscar's own life was ruined by a sex scandal of a different sort.

In the meantime, Oscar Wilde distinguished himself, first as a scholar of classics at Trinity College, Dublin and at Oxford University, then, after his graduation in 1878, as a flamboyant spokesman for Aestheticism, the late-nineteenth-century movement that advocated art for art's sake—partly in reaction to what was deemed an excessive Victorian emphasis on utility, pragmatism, and moral probity. One of the central representatives of Aestheticism was the critic Walter Pater, whom Wilde had met at Oxford. In the conclusion to his influential book, *The Renaissance*, Pater outlined a cultural outlook which became a sort of manifesto to Wilde and the other young aesthetes: "What we have to do is be for ever curiously testing new opinions and courting new impressions, never acquiescing in a facile orthodoxy... The theory or idea or system which requires of us the sacrifice of any part of this experience, in consideration of some interest into which we cannot enter, or some abstract theory we have not identified with ourselves, or of what is only conventional, has no real claim upon us." Pater also argued that "not the fruit of experience, but experience itself, is the end," and, most famously, he insisted: "To burn always with this hard, gem-like flame, to maintain this ecstasy, is success in life." Wilde quickly turned himself into the very embodiment of the "gem-like flame" Pater had exalted. With his startling wit and often outrageous clothing, he soon became a noted and seemingly ubiquitous socialite at parties in London. His fame quickly spread beyond the drawing-rooms when he was satirized in the new Gilbert and Sullivan operetta, *Patience* (1881), and he capitalized on this sudden celebrity by making a public speaking tour of the United States and Canada.

As Wilde's biographer Richard Ellmann points out, the irony in Wilde's sudden rise to fame in the 1880s was that he had as yet accomplished little beyond developing his unusual and celebrated personality. His first volume of *Poems* (1881) and his first play, *Vera; or The Nihilists* (1882), had not been well-received. In effect, Wilde had become famous merely for being famous, and many people were beginning to question whether there was anything of substance behind all his celebrity. Wilde himself was conscious that his reputation was on the line, and in the late 1880s he began energetically attempting to supply some substance to justify his celebrity.

Perhaps surprisingly, Wilde's first highly regarded works bore little relation to their author's reputation for outrageousness. *The Happy Prince and Other Tales* (1888) is a delightful collection of fairy-stories written for his two sons, a work which was startling only in that it was so uncontroversial. Next came a number of superb works of literary theory, the best known of which are probably "The Decay of Lying" (1889) and "The Critic as Artist" (1890). But Wilde's reputation as a writer really began to bloom with the publication of his only novel, *The Picture of Dorian Gray* (1891), which tells the story of a beautiful young man, the effects of whose depravity appear not in his face but in a oil portrait he has hidden away. The publication of the novel created a great *succès de scandale*, though it also made Wilde a number of enemies among the morally conservative.

Wilde then finally turned his attention intensely to what perhaps had been the most natural medium for his talents all along: stage comedy. *The Importance of Being Earnest* was the fourth of Wilde's plays to open in London's West End theatre district in a three-year period. *Lady Windermere's Fan* (1892) and *A Woman of No Importance* (1893), two comedies in a somewhat more melodramatic vein, had enjoyed moderately successful runs. Then in January 1895, *An Ideal Husband*—which, though still somewhat melodramatic, contains much more of the witty dialogue we associate with Wilde—opened to become Wilde's biggest hit to that point. A month later, when *The Importance of Being Earnest* opened at the St. James Theatre, *An Ideal Husband* was still playing to full houses a few blocks away at the Haymarket. Furthermore, during the same fruitful period, Wilde had also written *Salomé* (1894), a poetic dramatization of the biblical story of John the Baptist and Herod's stepdaughter. Though at the time it was considered too immoral for the English stage, Wilde's script has since become better known through Richard Strauss's operatic treatment.

It is widely agreed that *The Importance of Being Earnest* is Wilde's masterpiece. One of the most successful of all English comedies, it is perhaps the most often quoted play written in English by a playwright other than Shakespeare. The play holds a central place in a particular tradition of English humour that begins in the eighteenth century with writers such as William Congreve, Oliver Goldsmith, and Richard Sheridan (all Irish expatriates, like Wilde) and finds its progeny in the twentieth with the likes of Tom Stoppard, the Monty Python troupe, and Bruce Robinson, who made the film *Withnail and I*.

Of course, *The Importance of Being Earnest* is celebrated for its wit rather than its emotional depth. Wilde himself described the play as "exquisitely trivial, a delicate bubble of fancy." But, he added, "it has a philosophy: that we should treat all the trivial things of life very seriously, and all the serious things of life with sincere and studied triviality." As such, *The Importance of Being Earnest* constituted a sort of attack on the prevailing Victorian outlook, which, officially, was supposed to favour moral probity, seriousness of purpose, social good works, and sensual restraint. Naturally, for a society in which, for instance, rampant prostitution was an open secret (it has been estimated that, at the height of the Victorian era, there were as many as 80,000 prostitutes working in London, a city with a total population of 2 million), there was a great deal of hypocrisy in that prevalent attitude. Wilde playfully appealed to the unhappily repressed Victorian imagination by showing the world as a game of masks and artfully manipulated appearances, one in which the artificiality of the game is acknowledged by all. Furthermore, with this play, he seemed even to have freed himself to a degree from the struggle with his own moral conscience, a struggle that had been cryptically portrayed in earlier works.

For Wilde had himself been living a double life. In 1884, he had married Constance Lloyd, with whom he had two sons. But, however loving Wilde was with his family, married life suited him badly, and it wasn't long before he was sneaking off for sexual episodes with young men. One of these was Lord Alfred Douglas (whom Wilde called "Bosie"), a physically beautiful though breathtakingly selfish person who would become both Wilde's great love and, eventually, his downfall. By 1893, Wilde's affair with Bosie was well-established and his marriage to Constance was over. This perhaps freed Wilde somewhat of the guilty burden of hypocrisy and allowed him to look at his "double life" more playfully. At any rate, as Wilde's biographer Richard Ellmann has observed, the sense of sinfulness and guilt that haunts the protagonists of Wilde's earlier works is displaced, in *The Importance of Being Earnest,* into cucumber sandwiches and "Bunburying."

Unfortunately, homosexuality was still illegal in Britain at the time, and Wilde was running an especially great risk in that Bosie's father was the notoriously brutal and homophobic Marquess of Queensbury (best known as the author of a set of rules for boxing). When the Marquess, calling to confront Wilde at his club, left a card which accused Wilde of "posing as a Somdomite" [*sic:* a misspelling of "sodomite"], Bosie, who had a habit of baiting his father and then hiding behind Wilde for protection, persuaded Wilde into the ill-advised decision to sue the Marquess for libel. Wilde lost his case when the court was offered the testimony of various young male prostitutes with whom he had been consorting. Consequently, Wilde was ordered to stand trial. Several of his friends, including Bernard Shaw, begged him to leave England for the continent, but Wilde refused, staying even for a second trial when the first resulted in a hung jury. In the end, Wilde was found guilty and sentenced to two years of hard labour.

Though Wilde's prison sentence was to break both his spirit and his health, he did manage to create two more significant works: the poem "The Ballad of Reading Gaol" (pronounced "redding") and a moving 30,000-word letter to Bosie, which is known as "De Profundis." Upon his release from prison in 1897, Wilde moved to France, where he lived partly off the charity of friends and partly off what he could make writing a few scattered articles under the pseudonym "Sebastian Melmoth." Finally, in a squalid hotel room in Paris, on November 30, 1900, at the age of 46, he died of cerebral meningitis. Accounts of his death claim that he remained delightfully amusing to the end. His last words were said to have been: "Either this wallpaper goes or I do."

[C.S.W.]

OSCAR WILDE
The Importance of Being Earnest

THE PERSONS OF THE PLAY:
JOHN WORTHING, J.P.[1]
ALGERNON MONCRIEFF
REV. CANON CHASUBLE, D.D.[2]
MERRIMAN, a butler
LANE, a manservant
LADY BRACKNELL
HON. GWENDOLEN FAIRFAX[3]
CECILY CARDEW
MISS PRISM, a governess

THE SCENES OF THE PLAY:

Act I. Algernon Moncrieff's Flat in Half-Moon Street, W.[4]

Act II. The Garden at the Manor House, Woolton.[5]

Act III. Drawing-room at the Manor House, Woolton.

TIME: The Present

FIRST ACT

Scene: Morning-room in Algernon's flat in Half-Moon Street. The room is luxuriously and artistically furnished. The sound of a piano is heard in the adjoining room.

Lane is arranging afternoon tea on the table, and after the music has ceased, Algernon enters.

---

1 J.P.] Justice of the Peace (as were many country squires).
2 D.D.] Doctor of Divinity.
3 Hon.] "the Honourable"—a title indicating that Gwendolyn's father is either a baron or a viscount.
4 Half-Moon Street] a chic street in Central London.
5 Woolton] a fictional location.

ALGERNON. Did you hear what I was playing, Lane?

LANE. I didn't think it polite to listen, sir.

ALGERNON. I'm sorry for that, for your sake. I don't play accurately—anyone can play accurately—but I play with wonderful expression. As far as the piano is concerned sentiment is my forte. I keep science for Life.

LANE. Yes, sir.

ALGERNON. And, speaking of the science of Life, have you got the cucumber sandwiches cut for Lady Bracknell?

LANE. Yes, sir. *[Hands them on a salver.]*

ALGERNON. *[Inspects them, takes two, and sits down on the sofa.]* Oh!… by the way, Lane, I see from your book that on Thursday night, when Lord Shoreman and Mr. Worthing were dining with me, eight bottles of champagne are entered as having been consumed.

LANE. Yes, sir; eight bottles and a pint.

ALGERNON. Why is it that at a bachelor's establishment the servants invariably drink the champagne? I ask merely for information.

LANE. I attribute it to the superior quality of the wine, sir. I have often observed that in married households the champagne is rarely of a first-rate brand.

ALGERNON. Good Heavens! Is marriage so demoralizing as that?

LANE. I believe it is a very pleasant state, sir. I have had very little experience of it myself up to the present. I have only been married once. That was in consequence of a misunderstanding between myself and a young person.

ALGERNON. *[Languidly.]* I don't know that I am much interested in your family life, Lane.

LANE. No, sir; it is not a very interesting subject. I never think of it myself.

ALGERNON. Very natural, I am sure. That will do, Lane, thank you.

LANE. Thank you, sir.

Lane goes out.

ALGERNON. Lane's views on marriage seem some- 40
what lax. Really, if the lower orders don't set us a good example, what on earth is the use of them? They seem, as a class, to have absolutely no sense of moral responsibility.

Enter Lane.

LANE. Mr. Ernest Worthing. 45

[Enter Jack. Lane goes out.]

ALGERNON. How are you, my dear Ernest? What brings you up to town?

JACK. Oh, pleasure, pleasure! What else should bring one anywhere? Eating as usual, I see, Algy!

ALGERNON. *[Stiffly.]* I believe it is customary in 50
good society to take some slight refreshment at five o'clock. Where have you been since last Thursday?

JACK. *[Sitting down on the sofa.]* In the country.

ALGERNON. What on earth do you do there?

JACK. *[Pulling off his gloves.]* When one is in town 55
one amuses oneself. When one is in the country one amuses other people. It is excessively boring.

ALGERNON. And who are the people you amuse?

JACK. *[Airily.]* Oh, neighbours, neighbours.

ALGERNON. Got nice neighbours in your part of 60
Shropshire?

JACK. Perfectly horrid! Never speak to one of them.

ALGERNON. How immensely you must amuse them! *[Goes over and takes sandwich.]* By the way, Shropshire is your county, is it not? 65

JACK. Eh? Shropshire? Yes, of course. Hallo! Why all these cups? Why cucumber sandwiches? Why such reckless extravagance in one so young? Who is coming to tea?

ALGERNON. Oh! merely Aunt Augusta and Gwen- 70
dolen.

JACK. How perfectly delightful!

ALGERNON. Yes, that is all very well; but I am afraid Aunt Augusta won't quite approve of your being here. 75

JACK. May I ask why?

ALGERNON. My dear fellow, the way you flirt with Gwendolen is perfectly disgraceful. It is almost as bad as the way Gwendolen flirts with you.

JACK. I am in love with Gwendolen. I have come 80
up to town expressly to propose to her.

ALGERNON. I thought you had come up for pleasure?… I call that business.

JACK. How utterly unromantic you are!

ALGERNON. I really don't see anything romantic 85
about proposing. It is very romantic to be in love. But there is nothing romantic about a definite proposal. Why, one may be accepted. One usually is, I believe. Then the excitement is all over. The very essence of romance is uncertainty. If ever I get 90
married, I'll certainly try to forget the fact.

JACK. I have no doubt about that, dear Algy. The Divorce Court was specially invented for people whose memories are so curiously constituted.

ALGERNON. Oh! there is no use speculating on that 95
subject. Divorces are made in Heaven—

[Jack puts out his hand to take a sandwich. Algernon at once interferes.]

Please don't touch the cucumber sandwiches. They are ordered specially for Aunt Augusta.

[Takes one and eats it.]

JACK. Well, you have been eating them all the time.

ALGERNON. That is quite a different matter. She is 100
my aunt. *[Takes plate from below.]* Have some bread and butter. The bread and butter is for Gwen- dolen. Gwendolen is devoted to bread and butter.

JACK. *[Advancing to table and helping himself.]* And very good bread and butter it is too. 105

ALGERNON. Well, my dear fellow, you need not eat as if you were going to eat it all. You behave as if you were married to her already. You are not married to her already, and I don't think you ever will be.

JACK. Why on earth do you say that? 110

ALGERNON. Well, in the first place girls never marry the men they flirt with. Girls don't think it right.

JACK. Oh, that is nonsense!

ALGERNON. It isn't. It is a great truth. It accounts for the extraordinary number of bachelors that one 115
sees all over the place. In the second place, I don't give my consent.

JACK. Your consent!

ALGERNON. My dear fellow, Gwendolen is my first cousin. And before I allow you to marry her, you will have to clear up the whole question of Cecily. *[Rings bell.]*

JACK. Cecily! What on earth do you mean? What do you mean, Algy, by Cecily! I don't know anyone by the name of Cecily.

[Enter Lane.]

ALGERNON. Bring me that cigarette case Mr. Worthing left in the smoking-room the last time he dined here.

LANE. Yes, sir.

[Lane goes out.]

JACK. Do you mean to say you have had my cigarette case all this time? I wish to goodness you had let me know. I have been writing frantic letters to Scotland Yard about it. I was very nearly offering a large reward.

ALGERNON. Well, I wish you would offer one. I happen to be more than usually hard up.

JACK. There is no good offering a large reward now that the thing is found.

[Enter Lane with the cigarette case on a salver. Algernon takes it at once. Lane goes out.]

ALGERNON. I think that is rather mean of you, Ernest, I must say. *[Opens case and examines it.]* However, it makes no matter, for, now that I look at the inscription inside, I find that the thing isn't yours after all.

JACK. Of course it's mine. *[Moving to him.]* You have seen me with it a hundred times, and you have no right whatsoever to read what is written inside. It is a very ungentlemanly thing to read a private cigarette case.

ALGERNON. Oh! it is absurd to have a hard-and-fast rule about what one should read and what one shouldn't. More than half of modern culture depends on what one shouldn't read.

JACK. I am quite aware of the fact, and I don't propose to discuss modern culture. It isn't the sort of thing one should talk of in private. I simply want my cigarette case back.

ALGERNON. Yes; but this isn't your cigarette case. This cigarette case is a present from someone of the name of Cecily, and you said you didn't know anyone of that name.

JACK. Well, if you want to know, Cecily happens to be my aunt.

ALGERNON. Your aunt!

JACK. Yes. Charming old lady she is, too. Lives at Tunbridge Wells.[6] Just give it back to me, Algy.

ALGERNON. *[Retreating to back of sofa.]* But why does she call herself Cecily if she is your aunt and lives at Tunbridge Wells? *[Reading.]* From little Cecily with her fondest love.

JACK. *[Moving to sofa and kneeling upon it.]* My dear fellow, what on earth is there in that? Some aunts are tall, some aunts are not tall. That is a matter that surely an aunt may be allowed to decide for herself. You seem to think that every aunt should be exactly like your aunt! That is absurd! For Heaven's sake give me back my cigarette case.

[Follows Algernon round the room.]

ALGERNON. Yes. But why does your aunt call you her uncle? From little Cecily, with her fondest love to her dear Uncle Jack. There is no objection, I admit, to an aunt being a small aunt, but why an aunt, no matter what her size may be, should call her own nephew her uncle, I can't quite make out. Besides, your name isn't Jack at all; it is Ernest.

JACK. It isn't Ernest; it's Jack.

ALGERNON. You have always told me it was Ernest. I have introduced you to everyone as Ernest. You answer to the name of Ernest. You look as if your name was Ernest. You are the most earnest looking person I ever saw in my life. It is perfectly absurd your saying that your name isn't Ernest. It's on your cards. Here is one of them. *[Taking it from case.]* Mr. Ernest Worthing, B. 4, The Albany. I'll keep this as a proof that your name is Ernest if ever you attempt to deny it to me, or to Gwendolen, or to anyone else. *[Puts the card in his pocket.]*

JACK. Well, my name is Ernest in town and Jack in

---

6 Tunbridge Wells] a fashionable resort borough and town in Kent.

the country, and the cigarette case was given to me in the country.

ALGERNON. Yes, but that does not account for the fact that your small Aunt Cecily, who lives at Tunbridge Wells, calls you her dear uncle. Come, old boy, You had much better have the thing out at once.

JACK. My dear Algy, you talk exactly as if you were a dentist. It is very vulgar to talk like a dentist when one isn't a dentist. It produces a false impression.

ALGERNON. Well, that is exactly what dentists always do. Now, go on! Tell me the whole thing. I may mention that I have always suspected you of being a confirmed and secret Bunburyist; and I am quite sure of it now.

JACK. Bunburyist? What on earth do you mean by a Bunburyist?

ALGERNON. I'll reveal to you the meaning of that incomparable expression as soon as you are kind enough to inform me why you are Ernest in town and Jack in the country.

JACK. Well, produce my cigarette case first.

ALGERNON. Here it is. *[Hands cigarette case.]* Now produce your explanation, and pray make it improbable. *[Sits on sofa.]*

JACK. My dear fellow, there is nothing improbable about my explanation at all. In fact, it's perfectly ordinary. Old Mr. Thomas Cardew, who adopted me when I was a little boy, made me in his will guardian to his granddaughter, Miss Cecily Cardew. Cecily, who addresses me as her uncle from motives of respect that you could not possible appreciate, lives at my place in the country under the charge of her admirable governess, Miss Prism.

ALGERNON. Where is that place in the country, by the way?

JACK. That is nothing to you, dear boy. You are not going to be invited.... I may tell you candidly that the place is not in Shropshire.

ALGERNON. I suspected that, my dear fellow! I have Bunburyed all over Shropshire on two separate occasions. Now, go on. Why are you Ernest in town and Jack in the country?

JACK. My dear Algy, I don't know whether you will be able to understand my real motives. You are hardly serious enough. When one is placed in the position of guardian, one has to adopt a very high moral tone on all subjects. It's one's duty to do so. And as a high moral tone can hardly be said to conduce very much to either one's health or one's happiness, in order to get up to town I have always pretended to have a younger brother of the name of Ernest, who lives in the Albany, and gets into the most dreadful scrapes. That, my dear Algy, is the whole truth pure and simple.

ALGERNON. The truth is rarely pure and never simple. Modern life would be very tedious if it were either, and modern literature a complete impossibility!

JACK. That wouldn't be at all a bad thing.

ALGERNON. Literary criticism is not your forte, my dear fellow. Don't try it. You should leave that to people who haven't been at a University. They do it so well in the daily papers. What you really are is a Bunburyist. I was quite right in saying you were a Bunburyist. You are one of the most advanced Bunburyists I know.

JACK. What on earth do you mean?

ALGERNON. You have invented a very useful younger brother called Ernest, in order that you may be able to come up to town as often as you like. I have invented an invaluable permanent invalid called Bunbury, in order that I may be able to go down into the country whenever I choose. Bunbury is perfectly invaluable. If it wasn't for Bunbury's extraordinary bad health, for instance, I wouldn't be able to dine with you at Willis's tonight, for I have been really engaged to Aunt Augusta for more than a week.[7]

JACK. I haven't asked you to dine with me anywhere tonight.

ALGERNON. I know. You are absurdly careless about sending out invitations. It is very foolish of you. Nothing annoys people so much as not receiving invitations.

JACK. You had much better dine with your Aunt Augusta.

ALGERNON. I haven't the smallest intention of doing

---

7 Willis's] a restaurant in King Street, St. James's, often frequented by the artistic set.

anything of the kind. To begin with, I dined there on Monday, and once a week is quite enough to dine with one's own relations. In the second place, whenever I do dine there I am always treated as a member of the family, and sent down with either no woman at all, or two.[8] In the third place, I know perfectly well whom she will place me next to, tonight. She will place me next Mary Farquhar, who always flirts with her own husband across the dinner-table. That is not very pleasant. Indeed, it is not even decent… and that sort of thing is enormously on the increase. The amount of women in London who flirt with their own husbands is perfectly scandalous. It looks so bad. It is simply washing one's clean linen in public. Besides, now that I know you to be a confirmed Bunburyist, I naturally want to talk to you about Bunburying. I want to tell you the rules.

JACK. I'm not a Bunburyist at all. If Gwendolen accepts me, I am going to kill my brother, indeed I think I'll kill him in any case. Cecily is a little too much interested in him. It is rather a bore. So I am going to get rid of Ernest. And I strongly advise you to do the same with Mr.… with your invalid friend who has the absurd name.

ALGERNON. Nothing will induce me to part with Bunbury, and if you ever get married, which seems to me extremely problematic, you will be very glad to know Bunbury. A man who marries without knowing Bunbury has a very tedious time of it.

JACK. That is nonsense. If I marry a charming girl like Gwendolen, and she is the only girl I ever saw in my life that I would marry, I certainly won't want to know Bunbury.

ALGERNON. Then your wife will. You don't seem to realize, that in married life three is company and two is none.

JACK. *[Sententiously.]* That, my dear young friend, is the theory that the corrupt French Drama has been propounding for the last fifty years.[9]

ALGERNON. Yes; and that the happy English home has proved in half the time.

JACK. For heaven's sake, don't try to be cynical. It's perfectly easy to be cynical.

ALGERNON. My dear fellow, it isn't easy to be anything nowadays. There's such a lot of beastly competition about. *[The sound of an electric bell is heard.]* Ah! that must be Aunt Augusta. Only relatives, or creditors, ever ring in that Wagnerian manner.[10] Now, if I get her out of the way for ten minutes, so that you can have an opportunity for proposing to Gwendolen, may I dine with you Tonight at Willis's?

JACK. I suppose so, if you want to.

ALGERNON. Yes, but you must be serious about it. I hate people who are not serious about meals. It is so shallow of them.

Enter Lane.

LANE. Lady Bracknell and Miss Fairfax.

[Algernon goes forward to meet them. Enter Lady Bracknell and Gwendolen.]

LADY BRACKNELL. Good afternoon, dear Algernon, I hope you are behaving very well.

ALGERNON. I'm feeling very well, Aunt Augusta.

LADY BRACKNELL. That's not quite the same thing. In fact the two things rarely go together.

[Sees Jack and bows to him with icy coldness.]

ALGERNON. *[To Gwendolen.]* Dear me, you are smart!

GWENDOLEN. I am always smart! Aren't I, Mr. Worthing?

JACK. You're quite perfect, Miss Fairfax.

---

8 sent down] i.e., to the dining-room below.

9 corrupt French Drama] e.g., beginning in the 1830s and '40s, the theme is touched on in several plays by Alfred de Musset; in the 1850s, it is found in dramas by Alexandre Dumas *fils* and farces by Eugène Labiche; sub-

sequently, the theme is treated more specifically in Emile Zola's *Thérèse Raquin* (1873), in which the adulterous heroine and her lover murder her husband; by Henri Becque's *The Parisian Woman* (1885), a comedy about an adulterous society woman; by Jean Jullien's *Serenade* (1887), in which a mother and daughter share the same man; and by Georges Courteline's *Boubouroche* (1893), a farce about a cuckolded husband.

10 Wagnerian] in the manner of the operas of Richard Wagner: i.e., long and loud.

GWENDOLEN. Oh! I hope I am not that. It would leave no room for developments, and I intend to develop in many directions.

[Gwendolen and Jack sit down together in the corner.]

LADY BRACKNELL. I'm sorry if we are a little late, Algernon, but I was obliged to call on dear Lady Harbury. I hadn't been there since her poor husband's death. I never saw a woman so altered; she looks quite twenty years younger. And now I'll have a cup of tea, and one of those nice cucumber sandwiches you promised me.

ALGERNON. Certainly, Aunt Augusta. *[Goes over to tea-table.]*

LADY BRACKNELL. Won't you come and sit here, Gwendolen?

GWENDOLEN. Thanks, Mamma, I'm quite comfortable where I am.

ALGERNON. *[Picking up empty plate in horror.]* Good heavens! Lane! Why are there no cucumber sandwiches? I ordered them specially.

LANE. *[Gravely.]* There were no cucumbers in the market this morning, sir. I went down twice.

ALGERNON. No cucumbers!

LANE. No, sir. Not even for ready money.

ALGERNON. That will do, Lane, thank you.

LANE. Thank you, sir.

ALGERNON. I am greatly distressed, Aunt Augusta, about there being no cucumbers, not even for ready money.

LADY BRACKNELL. It really makes no matter, Algernon. I had some crumpets with Lady Harbury, who seems to me to be living entirely for pleasure now.

ALGERNON. I hear her hair has turned quite gold from grief.

LADY BRACKNELL. It certainly has changed its colour. From what cause I, of course, cannot say. *[Algernon crosses and hands tea.]* Thank you. I've quite a treat for you tonight, Algernon. I am going to send you down with Mary Farquhar. She is such a nice woman, and so attentive to her husband. It's delightful to watch them.

ALGERNON. I am afraid, Aunt Augusta, I shall have to give up the pleasure of dining with you tonight after all.

LADY BRACKNELL. *[Frowning.]* I hope not, Algernon. It would put my table completely out. Your uncle would have to dine upstairs. Fortunately he is accustomed to that.

ALGERNON. It is a great bore, and, I need hardly say, a terrible disappointment to me, but the fact is I have just had a telegram to say that my poor friend Bunbury is very ill again. *[Exchanges glances with Jack.]* They seem to think I should be with him.

LADY BRACKNELL. It is very strange. This Mr. Bunbury seems to suffer from curiously bad health.

ALGERNON. Yes; poor Bunbury is a dreadful invalid.

LADY BRACKNELL. Well, I must say, Algernon, that I think it is high time that Mr. Bunbury made up his mind whether he was going to live or to die. This shilly-shallying with the question is absurd. Nor do I in any way approve of the modern sympathy with invalids. I consider it morbid. Illness of any kind is hardly a thing to be encouraged in others. Health is the primary duty of life. I am always telling that to your poor uncle, but he never seems to take much notice... as far as any improvement in his ailments goes. I should be obliged if you would ask Mr. Bunbury, from me, to be kind enough not to have a relapse on Saturday, for I rely on you to arrange my music for me. It is my last reception, and one wants something that will encourage conversation, particularly at the end of the season when everyone has practically said whatever they had to say, which, in most cases, was probably not much.

ALGERNON. I'll speak to Bunbury, Aunt Augusta, if he is still conscious, and I think I can promise you he'll be all right by Saturday. Of course the music is a great difficulty. You see, if one plays good music, people don't listen, and if one plays bad music, people don't talk. But I'll run over the programme I've drawn out, if you will kindly come into the next room for a moment.

LADY BRACKNELL. Thank you, Algernon. It is very thoughtful of you. *[Rising, and following Algernon.]* I'm sure the programme will be delightful, after a few expurgations. French songs I cannot possibly allow. People always seem to think that they are improper, and either look shocked, which is vulgar, or laugh, which is worse. But German sounds a thoroughly respectable language, and indeed, I believe it is so. Gwendolen, you will accompany me.

GWENDOLEN. Certainly, Mamma.

[Lady Bracknell and Algernon go into the music-room, Gwendolen remains behind.]

GWENDOLEN. Pray don't talk to me about the weather, Mr. Worthing. Whenever people talk to me about the weather, I always feel quite certain that they mean something else. And that makes me so nervous.

JACK. I do mean something else.

GWENDOLEN. I thought so. In fact, I am never wrong.

JACK. And I would like to be allowed to take advantage of Lady Bracknell's temporary absence…

GWENDOLEN. I would certainly advise you to do so. Mamma has a way of coming back suddenly into a room that I have often had to speak to her about.

JACK. *[Nervously.]* Miss Fairfax, ever since I met you I have admired you more than any girl… I have ever met since… I met you.

GWENDOLEN. Yes, I am quite aware of the fact. And I often wish that in public, at any rate, you had been more demonstrative. For me you have always had an irresistible fascination. Even before I met you I was far from indifferent to you. *[Jack looks at her in amazement.]* We live, as I hope you know, Mr. Worthing, in an age of ideals. The fact is constantly mentioned in the more expensive monthly magazines, and has reached the provincial pulpits I am told: and my ideal has always been to love someone of the name of Ernest. There is something in that name that inspires absolute confidence. The moment Algernon first mentioned to me that he had a friend called Ernest, I knew I was destined to love you.

JACK. You really love me, Gwendolen?

GWENDOLEN. Passionately!

JACK. Darling! You don't know how happy you've made me.

GWENDOLEN. My own Ernest!

JACK. But you don't really mean to say that you couldn't love me if my name wasn't Ernest?

GWENDOLEN. But your name is Ernest.

JACK. Yes, I know it is. But supposing it was something else? Do you mean to say you couldn't love me then?

GWENDOLEN. *[Glibly.]* Ah! that is clearly a metaphysical speculation, and like most metaphysical speculations has very little reference at all to the actual facts of real life, as we know them.

JACK. Personally, darling, to speak quite candidly, I don't much care about the name of Ernest… I don't think the name suits me at all.

GWENDOLEN. It suits you perfectly. It is a divine name. It has a music of its own. It produces vibrations.

JACK. Well, really, Gwendolen, I must say that I think there are lots of other much nicer names. I think Jack, for instance, a charming name.

GWENDOLEN. Jack?… No, there is very little music in the name Jack, if any at all, indeed. It does not thrill. It produces absolutely no vibrations.… I have known several Jacks, and they all, without exception, were more than usually plain. Besides, Jack is a notorious domesticity for John! And I pity any woman who is married to a man called John. She would probably never be allowed to know the entrancing pleasure of a single moment's solitude. The only really safe name is Ernest.

JACK. Gwendolen, I must get christened at once—I mean we must get married at once. There is no time to be lost.

GWENDOLEN. Married, Mr. Worthing?

JACK. *[Astounded.]* Well… surely. You know that I love you, and you led me to believe, Miss Fairfax, that you were not absolutely indifferent to me.

GWENDOLEN. I adore you. But you haven't proposed to me yet. Nothing has been said at all about marriage. The subject has not even been touched on.

JACK. Well… may I propose to you now?

GWENDOLEN. I think it would be an admirable opportunity. And to spare you any possible disappointment, Mr. Worthing, I think it only fair to tell you quite frankly before hand that I am fully determined to accept you.

JACK. Gwendolen!

GWENDOLEN. Yes, Mr. Worthing, what have you got to say to me?

JACK. You know what I have got to say to you.

GWENDOLEN. Yes, but you don't say it.

JACK. Gwendolen, will you marry me? *[Goes on his knees.]* 535

GWENDOLEN. Of course I will, darling. How long you have been about it! I am afraid you have had very little experience in how to propose.

JACK. My own one, I have never loved anyone in the world but you. 540

GWENDOLEN. Yes, but men often propose for practice. I know my brother Gerald does. All my girlfriends tell me so. What wonderfully blue eyes you have, Ernest! They are quite, quite blue. I hope you will always look at me just like that, especially when there are other people present. 545

Enter Lady Bracknell.

LADY BRACKNELL. Mr. Worthing! Rise, sir, from this semi-recumbent posture. It is most indecorous.

GWENDOLEN. Mamma! *[He tries to rise; she restrains him.]* I must beg you to retire. This is no place for you. Besides, Mr. Worthing has not quite finished yet. 550

LADY BRACKNELL. Finished what, may I ask?

GWENDOLEN. I am engaged to Mr. Worthing, Mamma. *[They rise together.]* 555

LADY BRACKNELL. Pardon me, you are not engaged to anyone. When you do become engaged to someone, I, or your father, should his health permit him, will inform you of the fact. An engagement should come on a young girl as a surprise, pleasant or unpleasant, as the case may be. It is hardly a matter that she could be allowed to arrange for herself…. And now I have a few questions to put to you, Mr. Worthing. While I am making these inquiries you, Gwendolen, will wait for me below in the carriage. 560 565

GWENDOLEN. *[Reproachfully.]* Mamma!

LADY BRACKNELL. In the carriage, Gwendolen!

[Gwendolen goes to the door. She and Jack blow kisses to each other behind Lady Bracknell's back. Lady Bracknell looks vaguely about as if she could not understand what the noise was. Finally turns round.]

Gwendolen, the carriage! 570

LADY BRACKNELL. *[Sitting down.]* You can take a seat, Mr. Worthing.

[Looks in her pocket for note-book and pencil.]

JACK. Thank you, Lady Bracknell, I prefer standing.

LADY BRACKNELL. *[Pencil and note-book in hand.]* I feel bound to tell you that you are not down on my list of eligible young men, although I have the same list as the dear Duchess of Bolton has. We work together, in fact. However, I am quite ready to enter your name, should your answers be what a really affectionate mother requires. Do you smoke? 575 580

JACK. Well, yes, I must admit I smoke.

LADY BRACKNELL. I am glad to hear it. A man should always have an occupation of some kind. There are far too many idle men in London as it is. How old are you? 585

JACK. Twenty-nine.

LADY BRACKNELL. A very good age to be married at. I have always been of opinion that a man who desires to get married should know either everything or nothing. Which do you know? 590

JACK. *[After some hesitation.]* I know nothing, Lady Bracknell.

LADY BRACKNELL. I am pleased to hear it. I do not approve of anything that tampers with natural ignorance. Ignorance is like a delicate exotic fruit; touch it and the bloom is gone. The whole theory of modern education is radically unsound. Fortunately in England, at any rate, education produces no effect whatsoever. If it did, it would prove a serious danger to the upper classes, and probably lead to acts of violence in Grosvenor Square. What is your income? 595 600

JACK. Between seven and eight thousand a year.

LADY BRACKNELL. *[Makes a note in her book.]* In land, or in investments? 605

JACK. In investments, chiefly.

LADY BRACKNELL. That is satisfactory. What between the duties expected of one during one's lifetime, and the duties exacted from one after one's death, land has ceased to be either a profit or a pleasure. It gives one position, and prevents one from keeping it up. That's all that can be said about land. 610

JACK. I have a country house with some land, of course, attached to it, about fifteen hundred acres,

I believe; but I don't depend on that for my real income. In fact, as far as I can make out, the poachers are the only people who make anything out of it.

LADY BRACKNELL. A country house! How many bedrooms? Well, that point can be cleared up afterwards. You have a town house, I hope? A girl with a simple, unspoiled nature, like Gwendolen, could hardly be expected to reside in the country.

JACK. Well, I own a house in Belgrave Square, but it is let by the year to Lady Bloxham. Of course, I can get it back whenever I like, at six months' notice.

LADY BRACKNELL. Lady Bloxham? I don't know her.

JACK. Oh, she goes about very little. She is a lady considerable advanced in years.

LADY BRACKNELL. Ah, nowadays that is no guarantee of respectability of character. What number in Belgrave Square?

JACK. 149.

LADY BRACKNELL. [Shaking her head.] The unfashionable side. I thought there was something. However, that could easily be altered.

JACK. Do you mean the fashion, or the side?

LADY BRACKNELL. [Sternly.] Both, if necessary, I presume. What are your politics?

JACK. Well, I am afraid I really have none. I am a Liberal Unionist.[11]

LADY BRACKNELL. Oh, they count as Tories. They dine with us. Or come in the evening, at any rate. Now to minor matters. Are your parents living?

JACK. I have lost both my parents.

LADY BRACKNELL. To lose one parent, Mr Worthing, may be regarded as a misfortune; to lose both looks like carelessness. Who was your father? He was evidently a man of some wealth. Was he born in what the Radical papers call the purple of commerce, or did he rise from the ranks of aristocracy?[12]

JACK. I am afraid I really don't know. The fact is, Lady Bracknell, I said I had lost my parents. It would be nearer the truth to say that my parents seem to have lost me…. I don't actually know who I am by birth. I was… well, I was found.

LADY BRACKNELL. Found!

JACK. The late Mr. Thomas Cardew, an old gentleman of a very charitable and kindly disposition, found me, and gave me the name of Worthing, because he happened to have a first-class ticket for Worthing in his pocket at the time. Worthing is a place in Sussex. It is a seaside resort.

LADY BRACKNELL. Where did the charitable gentleman who had a first-class ticket for this seaside resort find you?

JACK. [Gravely.] In a hand-bag.

LADY BRACKNELL. A hand-bag?

JACK. [Very seriously.] Yes, Lady Bracknell. I was in a hand-bag—a somewhat large, black leather hand-bag, with handles to it—an ordinary hand-bag, in fact.

LADY BRACKNELL. In what locality did this Mr. James, or Thomas, Cardew come across this ordinary hand-bag?

JACK. In the cloak-room at Victoria Station. It was given to him in mistake for his own.

LADY BRACKNELL. The cloak-room at Victoria Station?

JACK. Yes. The Brighton Line.

LADY BRACKNELL. The line is immaterial. Mr. Worthing, I confess I feel somewhat bewildered by what you have just told me. To be born, or at any rate, bred in a hand-bag, whether it had handles or not, seems to me to display a contempt for the ordinary decencies of family life that remind one of the worst excesses of the French Revolution. And I presume you know what that unfortunate movement led to? As for the particular locality in which the hand-bag was found, a cloak-room at a railway station might serve to conceal a social indiscretion—has probably, indeed, been used for that purpose before now—but it could hardly be

birth—possibly a poor one, from which condition one would have to "rise" to wealth.

---

11 Liberal Unionist] a conservative splinter group of the Liberal party; they broke from the Liberals when the party embraced Irish Home Rule, but declined to join the Conservative party.

12 purple of commerce] having become upper-class by making "new" money, as opposed to being an aristocrat by

regarded as an assured basis for a recognized position in good society.

JACK. May I ask you then what you would advise me to do? I need hardly say I would do anything in the world to ensure Gwendolen's happiness. 700

LADY BRACKNELL. I would strongly advise you, Mr. Worthing, to try and acquire some relations as soon as possible, and to make a definite effort to produce at any rate one parent, of either sex, before the season is quite over. 705

JACK. Well, I don't see how I could possibly manage to do that. I can produce the hand-bag at any moment. It is in my dressing-room at home. I really think that should satisfy you, Lady Bracknell.

LADY BRACKNELL. Me, sir! What has it to do with 710 me? You can hardly imagine that I and Lord Bracknell would dream of allowing our only daughter—a girl brought up with the utmost care—to marry into a cloak-room, and form an alliance with a parcel? Good morning, Mr. 715 Worthing!

[Lady Bracknell sweeps out in majestic indignation.]

JACK. Good morning!

[Algernon, from the other room, strikes up the Wedding March. Jack looks perfectly furious, and goes to the door.]

For goodness' sake don't play that ghastly tune, Algy! How idiotic you are!

[The music stops, and Algernon enters cheerily.]

ALGERNON. Didn't it go off all right, old boy? You 720 don't mean to say Gwendolen refused you? I know it is a way she has. She is always refusing people. I think it is most ill-natured of her.

JACK. Oh, Gwendolen is as right as a trivet.[13] As far as she is concerned, we are engaged. Her mother 725 is perfectly unbearable. Never met such a Gorgon … I don't really know what a Gorgon is like, but I am quite sure that Lady Bracknell is one. In any case, she is a monster, without being a myth, which

is rather unfair… I beg your pardon, Algy, I sup- 730 pose I shouldn't talk about your own aunt in that way before you.

ALGERNON. My dear boy, I love hearing my relations abused. It is the only thing that makes me put up with them at all. Relations are simply 735 a tedious pack of people who haven't got the remotest knowledge of how to live, nor the smallest instinct about when to die.

JACK. Oh, that is nonsense!

ALGERNON. It isn't! 740

JACK. Well, I won't argue about the matter. You always want to argue about things.

ALGERNON. That is exactly what things were originally made for.

JACK. Upon my word, if I thought that, I'd shoot 745 myself…. *[A pause.]* You don't think there is any chance of Gwendolen becoming like her mother in about a hundred and fifty years, do you, Algy?

ALGERNON. All women become like their mothers. That is their tragedy. No man does. That's his. 750

JACK. Is that clever?

ALGERNON. It is perfectly phrased! and quite as true as any observation in civilized life should be.

JACK. I am sick to death of cleverness. Everybody is clever nowadays. You can't go anywhere without 755 meeting clever people. The thing has become an absolute public nuisance. I wish to goodness we had a few fools left.

ALGERNON. We have.

JACK. I should extremely like to meet them. What 760 do they talk about?

ALGERNON. The fools! Oh! about the clever people, of course.

JACK. What fools!

ALGERNON. By the way, did you tell Gwendolen the 765 truth about your being Ernest in town, and Jack in the country?

JACK. *[In a very patronizing manner.]* My dear fellow, the truth isn't quite the sort of thing one tells to a nice, sweet, refined girl. What extraordinary ideas 770 you have about the way to behave to a woman!

ALGERNON. The only way to behave to a woman is to make love to her, if she is pretty, and to someone else, if she is plain.

JACK. Oh, that is nonsense! 775

---

13 as right as a trivet] A trivet has three legs, and therefore is extremely steady.

ALGERNON. What about your brother? What about the profligate Ernest?

JACK. Oh, before the end of the week I shall have got rid of him. I'll say he died in Paris of apoplexy. Lots of people die of apoplexy, quite suddenly, don't they? 780

ALGERNON. Yes, but it's hereditary, my dear fellow. It's a sort of thing that runs in families. You had much better say a severe chill.

JACK. You are sure that a severe chill isn't hereditary, or anything of that kind? 785

ALGERNON. Of course it isn't!

JACK. Very well, then. My poor brother Ernest is carried off suddenly, in Paris, by a severe chill. That gets rid of him. 790

ALGERNON. But I thought you said that… Miss Cardew was a little too much interested in your poor brother Ernest? Won't she feel his loss a good deal?

JACK. Oh, that is all right. Cecily is not a silly romantic girl, I am glad to say. She has got a capital appetite, goes for long walks, and pays no attention at all to her lessons. 795

ALGERNON. I would rather like to see Cecily.

JACK. I will take very good care you never do. She is excessively pretty, and she is only just eighteen. 800

ALGERNON. Have you told Gwendolen yet that you have an excessively pretty ward who is only just eighteen?

JACK. Oh! one doesn't blurt these things out to people. Cecily and Gwendolen are perfectly certain to be extremely great friends. I'll bet you anything you like that half an hour after they have met, they will be calling each other sister. 805

ALGERNON. Women only do that when they have called each other a lot of other things first. Now, my dear boy, if we want to get a good table at Willis's, we really must go and dress. Do you know it is nearly seven? 810

JACK. [Irritably.] Oh! it always is nearly seven. 815

ALGERNON. Well, I'm hungry.

JACK. I never knew you when you weren't….

ALGERNON. What shall we do after dinner? Go to a theatre?

JACK. Oh, no! I loathe listening. 820

ALGERNON. Well, let us go to the Club?

JACK. Oh, no! I hate talking.

ALGERNON. Well, we might trot round to the Empire at ten?[14]

JACK. Oh, no! I can't bear looking at things. It is so silly. 825

ALGERNON. Well, what shall we do?

JACK. Nothing!

ALGERNON. It is awfully hard work doing nothing. However, I don't mind hard work where there is no definite object of any kind. 830

Enter Lane.

LANE. Miss Fairfax.

Enter Gwendolen. Lane goes out.

ALGERNON. Gwendolen, upon my word!

GWENDOLEN. Algy, kindly turn your back. I have something very particular to say to Mr. Worthing. 835

ALGERNON. Really, Gwendolen, I don't think I can allow this at all.

GWENDOLEN. Algy, you always adopt a strictly immoral attitude towards life. You are not quite old enough to do that. 840

Algernon retires to the fireplace.

JACK. My own darling!

GWENDOLEN. Ernest, we may never be married. From the expression on mamma's face I fear we never shall. Few parents nowadays pay any regard to what their children say to them. The old-fashioned respect for the young is fast dying out. Whatever influence I ever had over mamma, I lost at the age of three. But although she may prevent us from becoming man and wife, and I may marry someone else, and marry often, nothing that she can possibly do can alter my eternal devotion to you. 845 850

JACK. Dear Gwendolen!

GWENDOLEN. The story of your romantic origin, as related to me by mamma, with unpleasing comments, has naturally stirred the deeper fibres of my nature. Your Christian name has an 855

---

14 the Empire] a notorious variety theatre, where people would go more often than not to watch one another— and the prostitutes—rather than the shows themselves.

irresistible fascination. The simplicity of your character makes you exquisitely incomprehensible to me. Your town address at the Albany I have. What is your address in the country? 860

JACK. The Manor House, Woolton, Hertfordshire.

[Algernon, who has been carefully listening, smiles to himself, and writes the address on his shirtcuff. Then picks up the Railway Guide.]

GWENDOLEN. There is a good postal service, I suppose? It may be necessary to do something desperate. That of course will require serious consideration. I will communicate with you daily. 865

JACK. My own one!

GWENDOLEN. How long do you remain in town?

JACK. Till Monday.

GWENDOLEN. Good! Algy, you may turn round now. 870

ALGERNON. Thanks, I've turned round already.

GWENDOLEN. You may also ring the bell.

JACK. You will let me see you to your carriage, my own darling? 875

GWENDOLEN. Certainly.

JACK. *[To Lane, who now enters.]* I will see Miss Fairfax out.

LANE. Yes, sir.

[Jack and Gwendolen go off.]

[Lane presents several letters on a salver to Algernon. It is to be surmised that they are bills, as Algernon after looking at the envelopes, tears them up.]

ALGERNON. A glass of sherry, Lane. 880

LANE. Yes, sir.

ALGERNON. Tomorrow, Lane, I'm going Bunbury-ing.

LANE. Yes, sir.

ALGERNON. I shall probably not be back till Monday. You can put up my dress clothes, my smoking jacket, and all the Bunbury suits… 885

LANE. Yes, sir.

[Handing sherry.]

ALGERNON. I hope tomorrow will be a fine day, Lane. 890

LANE. It never is, sir.

ALGERNON. Lane, you're a perfect pessimist.

LANE. I do my best to give satisfaction, sir.

[Enter Jack. Lane goes off.]

JACK. There's a sensible, intellectual girl! The only girl I ever cared for in my life. *[Algernon is laughing immoderately.]* What on earth are you so amused at? 895

ALGERNON. Oh, I'm a little anxious about poor Bunbury, that is all.

JACK. If you don't take care, your friend Bunbury will get you into a serious scrape some day. 900

ALGERNON. I love scrapes. They are the only things that are never serious.

JACK. Oh, that's nonsense, Algy. You never talk anything but nonsense. 905

ALGERNON. Nobody ever does.

[Jack looks indignantly at him, and leaves the room. Algernon lights a cigarette, reads his shirtcuff, and smiles.]

Act Drop

SECOND ACT

Scene: Garden at the Manor House. A flight of grey stone steps leads up to the house. The garden, an old-fashioned one, full of roses. Time of year, July. Basket-chairs, and a table covered with books, are set under a large yew-tree.[15]

[Miss Prism discovered seated at the table. Cecily is at the back watering flowers.]

MISS PRISM. *[Calling.]* Cecily, Cecily! Surely such a utilitarian occupation as the watering of flowers is rather Moulton's duty than yours? Especially at a moment when intellectual pleasures await you. Your German grammar is on the table. Pray open it at page fifteen. We will repeat yesterday's lesson. 5

CECILY. *[Coming over very slowly.]* But I don't like German. It isn't at all a becoming language. I know perfectly well that I look quite plain after my German lesson. 10

MISS PRISM. Child, you know how anxious your guardian is that you should improve yourself in

---

15 *Basket-chairs]* outdoor wicker chairs.

every way. He laid particular stress on your German, as he was leaving for town yesterday. Indeed, he always lays stress on your German when he is leaving for town.

CECILY. Dear Uncle Jack is so very serious! Sometimes he is so serious that I think he cannot be quite well.

MISS PRISM. *[Drawing herself up.]* Your guardian enjoys the best of health, and his gravity of demeanour is especially to be commended in one so comparatively young as he is. I know no one who has a higher sense of duty and responsibility.

CECILY. I suppose that is why he often looks a little bored when we three are together.

MISS PRISM. Cecily! I am surprised at you. Mr. Worthing has many troubles in his life. Idle merriment and triviality would be out of place in his conversation. You must remember his constant anxiety about that unfortunate young man his brother.

CECILY. I wish Uncle Jack would allow that unfortunate young man, his brother, to come down here sometimes. We might have a good influence over him, Miss Prism. I am sure you certainly would. You know German, and geology, and things of that kind influence a man very much.

[Cecily begins to write in her diary.]

MISS PRISM. *[Shaking her head.]* I do not think that even I could produce any effect on a character that according to his own brother's admission is irretrievably weak and vacillating. Indeed I am not sure that I would desire to reclaim him. I am not in favour of this modern mania for turning bad people into good people at a moment's notice. As a man sows so let him reap.[16] You must put away your diary, Cecily. I really don't see why you should keep a diary at all.

CECILY. I keep a diary in order to enter the wonderful secrets of my life. If I didn't write them down I should probably forget all about them.

MISS PRISM. Memory, my dear Cecily, is the diary that we all carry about with us.

CECILY. Yes, but it usually chronicles the things that have never happened, and couldn't possibly have happened. I believe that Memory is responsible for nearly all the three-volume novels that Mudie sends us.[17]

MISS PRISM. Do not speak slightingly of the three-volume novel, Cecily. I wrote one myself in earlier days.

CECILY. Did you really, Miss Prism? How wonderfully clever you are! I hope it did not end happily? I don't like novels that end happily. They depress me so much.

MISS PRISM. The good ended happily, and the bad unhappily. That is what Fiction means.

CECILY. I suppose so. But it seems very unfair. And was your novel ever published?

MISS PRISM. Alas! no. The manuscript unfortunately was abandoned. *[Cecily starts.]* I use the word in the sense of lost or mislaid. To your work, child; these speculations are profitless.

CECILY. *[Smiling.]* But I see dear Dr. Chasuble coming up through the garden.

MISS PRISM. *[Rising and advancing.]* Dr. Chasuble! This is indeed a pleasure.

Enter Canon Chasuble.

CHASUBLE. And how are we this morning? Miss Prism, you are, I trust, well?

CECILY. Miss Prism has just been complaining of a slight headache. I think it would do her so much good to have a short stroll with you in the Park, Dr. Chasuble.

MISS PRISM. Cecily, I have not mentioned anything about a headache.

CECILY. No, dear Miss Prism, I know that, but I felt instinctively that you had a headache. Indeed I was thinking about that, and not about my German lesson, when the Rector came in.

CHASUBLE. I hope, Cecily, you are not inattentive.

CECILY. Oh, I am afraid I am.

CHASUBLE. That is strange. Were I fortunate enough to be Miss Prism's pupil, I would hang upon her lips. *[Miss Prism glares.]* I spoke metaphorically.—

---

16 As a man sows so let him reap] Galatians 6:7.

17 Mudie] a lending library that specialized in three-volume novels.

My metaphor was drawn from bees. Ahem! Mr. Worthing, I suppose, has not returned from town yet?

MISS PRISM. We do not expect him till Monday afternoon.

CHASUBLE. Ah yes, he usually likes to spend his Sunday in London. He is not one of those whose sole aim is enjoyment, as, by all accounts, that unfortunate young man his brother seems to be. But I must not disturb Egeria and her pupil any longer.[18]

MISS PRISM. Egeria? My name is Lætitia, Doctor.

CHASUBLE. *[Bowing.]* A classical allusion merely, drawn from the pagan authors. I shall see you both no doubt at Evensong?[19]

MISS PRISM. I think, dear Doctor, I will have a stroll with you. I find I have a headache after all, and a walk might do it good.

CHASUBLE. With pleasure, Miss Prism, with pleasure. We might go as far as the schools and back.

MISS PRISM. That would be delightful. Cecily, you will read your Political Economy in my absence. The chapter on the Fall of the Rupee you may omit.[20] It is somewhat too sensational. Even these metallic problems have their melodramatic side.

[Goes down the garden with Dr. Chasuble.]

CECILY. *[Picks up books and throws them back on table.]* Horrid Political Economy! Horrid Geography! Horrid, horrid German!

Enter Merriman with a card on a salver.

MERRIMAN. Mr. Ernest Worthing has just driven over from the station. He has brought his luggage with him.

CECILY. *[Takes the card and reads it.]* Mr. Ernest Worthing, B. 4 The Albany, W. Uncle Jack's brother! Did you tell him Mr. Worthing was in town?

MERRIMAN. Yes, Miss. He seemed very much disappointed. I mentioned that you and Miss Prism were in the garden. He said he was anxious to speak to you privately for a moment.

CECILY. Ask Mr. Ernest Worthing to come here. I suppose you had better talk to the housekeeper about a room for him.

MERRIMAN. Yes, Miss. *[Merriman goes off.]*

CECILY. I have never met any really wicked person before. I feel rather frightened. I am so afraid he will look just like everyone else. *[Enter Algernon, very gay and debonair.]* He does!

ALGERNON. *[Raising his hat.]* You are my little cousin Cecily, I'm sure.

CECILY. You are under some strange mistake. I am not little. In fact, I believe I am more than usually tall for my age. *[Algernon is rather taken aback.]* But I am your cousin Cecily. You, I see from your card, are Uncle Jack's brother, my cousin Ernest, my wicked cousin Ernest.

ALGERNON. Oh! I am not really wicked at all, cousin Cecily. You mustn't think that I am wicked.

CECILY. If you are not, then you have certainly been deceiving us all in a very inexcusable manner. I hope you have not been leading a double life, pretending to be wicked and being really good all the time. That would be hypocrisy.

ALGERNON. *[Looks at her in amazement.]* Oh! Of course I have been rather reckless.

CECILY. I am glad to hear it.

ALGERNON. In fact, now you mention the subject, I have been very bad in my own small way.

CECILY. I don't think you should be so proud of that, though I am sure it must have been very pleasant.

ALGERNON. It is much pleasanter being here with you.

CECILY. I can't understand how you are here at all. Uncle Jack won't be back till Monday afternoon.

ALGERNON. That is a great disappointment. I am obliged to go up by the first train on Monday morning. I have a business appointment that I am anxious… to miss!

CECILY. Couldn't you miss it anywhere but in London?

---

18 Egeria] in Roman mythology, a spirit and teacher associated with vestal virgins.

19 Evensong] evening worship.

20 Fall of the Rupee] Owing to a series of misfortunes, such as a fall-off in India's cotton trade, the devaluation of silver, and the spread of bubonic plague, the value of India's currency, the rupee, had fallen precipitously in the 1890s.

ALGERNON. No: the appointment is in London. 175

CECILY. Well, I know of course, how important it is not to keep a business engagement, if one wants to retain any sense of the beauty of life, but still I think you had better wait till Uncle Jack arrives. I know he wants to speak to you about your emigrating. 180

ALGERNON. About my what?

CECILY. Your emigrating. He has gone up to buy your outfit.

ALGERNON. I certainly wouldn't let Jack buy my outfit. He has no taste in neckties at all. 185

CECILY. I don't think you will require neckties. Uncle Jack is sending you to Australia.[21]

ALGERNON. Australia! I'd sooner die.

CECILY. Well, he said at dinner on Wednesday night, that you would have to choose between this world, the next world, and Australia. 190

ALGERNON. Oh, well! The accounts I have received of Australia and the next world are not particularly encouraging. This world is good enough for me, cousin Cecily. 195

CECILY. Yes, but are you good enough for it?

ALGERNON. I'm afraid I'm not that. That is why I want you to reform me. You might make that your mission, if you don't mind, cousin Cecily. 200

CECILY. I'm afraid I've no time, this afternoon.

ALGERNON. Well, would you mind my reforming myself this afternoon?

CECILY. It is rather Quixotic of you. But I think you should try. 205

ALGERNON. I will. I feel better already.

CECILY. You are looking a little worse.

ALGERNON. That is because I am hungry.

CECILY. How thoughtless of me! I should have remembered that when one is going to lead an entirely new life, one requires regular and wholesome meals. Won't you come in? 210

ALGERNON. Thank you. Might I have a buttonhole first? I never have any appetite unless I have a buttonhole first. 215

CECILY. A Maréchal Niel?[22] [Picks up scissors.]

ALGERNON. No, I'd sooner have a pink rose.

CECILY. Why? [Cuts a flower.]

ALGERNON. Because you are like a pink rose, Cousin Cecily. 220

CECILY. I don't think it can be right for you to talk to me like that. Miss Prism never says such things to me.

ALGERNON. Then Miss Prism is a short-sighted old lady. [Cecily puts the rose in his buttonhole.] You are the prettiest girl I ever saw. 225

CECILY. Miss Prism says that all good looks are a snare.

ALGERNON. They are a snare that every sensible man would like to be caught in.

CECILY. Oh! I don't think I would care to catch a sensible man. I shouldn't know what to talk to him about. 230

[They pass into the house. Miss Prism and Dr. Chasuble return.]

MISS PRISM. You are too much alone, dear Dr. Chasuble. You should get married. A misanthrope I can understand—a womanthrope, never![23] 235

CHASUBLE. [With a scholar's shudder.] Believe me, I do not deserve so neologistic a phrase. The precept as well as the practice of the Primitive Church was distinctly against matrimony.[24]

MISS PRISM. [Sententiously.] That is obviously the reason why the Primitive Church has not lasted up to the present day. And do you not seem to realize, dear Doctor, that by persistently remaining single, a man converts himself into a permanent public temptation. Men should be more careful; this very celibacy leads weaker vessels astray. 240 245

CHASUBLE. But is a man not equally attractive when married?

---

21 sending you to Australia] Australia, founded as a British convict colony in the late eighteenth century, still had a reputation in English society as a place to which undesirables might be exiled.

22 Maréchal Niel] a fashionable yellow rose.

23 womanthrope] A misanthrope is a hater of mankind. Miss Prism's incorrect word mixes Anglo-Saxon and Greek etymologies to describe a hater of women; the correct word is misogynist.

24 Primitive Church] the pre-Reformation (Catholic) church; as an Anglican minister, Chasuble has some leeway in the degree to which he should adhere to pre-Reformation doctrines.

MISS PRISM. No married man is ever attractive except to his wife. 250

CHASUBLE. And often, I've been told, not even to her.

MISS PRISM. That depends on the intellectual sympathies of the woman. Maturity can always be depended on. Ripeness can be trusted. Young 255 women are green. *[Dr. Chasuble starts.]* I spoke horticulturally. My metaphor was drawn from fruits. But where is Cecily?

CHASUBLE. Perhaps she followed us to the schools.

Enter Jack slowly from the back of the garden. He is dressed in the deepest mourning, with crape hatband and black gloves.

MISS PRISM. Mr. Worthing! 260

CHASUBLE. Mr. Worthing?

MISS PRISM. This is indeed a surprise. We did not look for you till Monday afternoon.

JACK. *[Shakes Miss Prism's hand in a tragic manner.]* I have returned sooner than I expected. Dr. 265 Chasuble, I hope you are well?

CHASUBLE. Dear Mr. Worthing, I trust this garb of woe does not betoken some terrible calamity?

JACK. My brother.

MISS PRISM. More shameful debts and extravagance? 270

CHASUBLE. Still leading his life of pleasure?

JACK. *[Shaking his head.]* Dead!

CHASUBLE. Your brother Ernest dead?

JACK. Quite dead.

MISS PRISM. What a lesson for him! I trust he will 275 profit by it.

CHASUBLE. Mr. Worthing, I offer you my sincere condolence. You have at least the consolation of knowing that you were always the most generous and forgiving of brothers. 280

JACK. Poor Ernest! He had many faults, but it is a sad, sad blow.

CHASUBLE. Very sad indeed. Were you with him at the end?

JACK. No. He died abroad; in Paris, in fact. I had a 285 telegram last night from the manager of the Grand Hotel.

CHASUBLE. Was the cause of death mentioned?

JACK. A severe chill, it seems.

MISS PRISM. As a man sows, so shall he reap. 290

CHASUBLE. *[Raising his hand.]* Charity, dear Miss Prism, charity! None of us are perfect. I myself am peculiarly susceptible to draughts. Will the interment take place here?

JACK. No. He seemed to have expressed a desire to 295 be buried in Paris.

CHASUBLE. In Paris! *[Shakes his head.]* I fear that hardly points to any very serious state of mind at the last. You would no doubt wish me to make some slight allusion to this tragic domestic 300 affliction next Sunday. *[Jack presses his hand convulsively.]* My sermon on the meaning of the manna in the wilderness can be adapted to almost any occasion, joyful, or, as in the present case, distressing.[25] *[All sigh.]* I have preached it at 305 harvest celebrations, christenings, confirmations, on days of humiliation and festal days. The last time I delivered it was in the Cathedral, as a charity sermon on behalf of the Society for the Prevention of Discontent among the Upper Orders. The 310 Bishop, who was present, was much struck by some of the analogies I drew.

JACK. Ah! that reminds me, you mentioned christenings, I think, Dr. Chasuble? I suppose you know how to christen all right? *[Dr. Chasuble looks 315 astounded.]* I mean, of course, you are continually christening, aren't you?

MISS PRISM. It is, I regret to say, one of the Rector's most constant duties in this parish. I have often spoken to the poorer classes on the subject. But 320 they don't seem to know what thrift is.

CHASUBLE. But is there any particular infant in whom you are interested, Mr. Worthing? Your brother was, I believe, unmarried, was he not?

JACK. Oh, yes. 325

MISS PRISM. *[Bitterly.]* People who live entirely for pleasure usually are.

JACK. But it is not for any child, dear Doctor. I am very fond of children. No! the fact is, I would like to be christened myself, this afternoon, if you have 330 nothing better to do.

CHASUBLE. But surely, Mr. Worthing, you have been christened already?

JACK. I don't remember anything about it.

---

25 manna in the wilderness] e.g., Exodus 16.

CHASUBLE. But have you any grave doubts on the subject? 335

JACK. I certainly intend to have. Of course, I don't know if the thing would bother you in any way, or if you think I am a little too old now.

CHASUBLE. Not at all. The sprinkling, and, indeed, the immersion of adults is a perfectly canonical practice.[26] 340

JACK. Immersion!

CHASUBLE. You need have no apprehensions. Sprinkling is all that is necessary, or indeed I think advisable. Our weather is so changeable. At what hour would you wish the ceremony performed? 345

JACK. Oh, I might trot round about five if that would suit you.

CHASUBLE. Perfectly, perfectly! In fact I have two similar ceremonies to perform at that time. A case of twins that occurred recently in one of the outlying cottages on your own estate. Poor Jenkins the carter, a most hard-working man. 350

JACK. Oh! I don't see much fun in being christened along with other babies. It would be childish. Would half-past five do? 355

CHASUBLE. Admirably! Admirably! *[Takes out watch.]* And now, dear Mr. Worthing, I will not intrude any longer into a house of sorrow. I would merely beg you not to be too much bowed down by grief. What seems to us bitter trials are often blessings in disguise. 360

MISS PRISM. This seems to me a blessing of an extremely obvious kind. 365

Enter Cecily from the house.

CECILY. Uncle Jack! Oh, I am pleased to see you back. But what horrid clothes you have got on! Do go and change them.

MISS PRISM. Cecily!

CHASUBLE. My child! my child! *[Cecily goes towards Jack; he kisses her brow in a melancholy manner.]* 370

CECILY. What is the matter, Uncle Jack? Do look happy! You look as if you had toothache, and I have got such a surprise for you. Who do you think is in the dining-room? Your brother! 375

JACK. Who?

CECILY. Your brother Ernest. He arrived about half an hour ago.

JACK. What nonsense! I haven't got a brother!

CECILY. Oh, don't say that. However badly he may have behaved to you in the past he is still your brother. You couldn't be so heartless as to disown him. I'll tell him to come out. And you will shake hands with him, won't you, Uncle Jack? 380

[Runs back into the house.]

CHASUBLE. These are very joyful tidings. 385

MISS PRISM. After we had all been resigned to his loss, his sudden return seems to me peculiarly distressing.

JACK. My brother is in the dining-room? I don't know what it all means. I think it is perfectly absurd. 390

[Enter Algernon and Cecily hand in hand. They come slowly up to Jack.]

JACK. Good heavens!

[Motions Algernon away.]

ALGERNON. Brother John, I have come down from town to tell you that I am very sorry for all the trouble I have given you, and that I intend to lead a better life in the future. 395

[Jack glares at him and does not take his hand.]

CECILY. Uncle Jack, you are not going to refuse your own brother's hand?

JACK. Nothing will induce me to take his hand. I think his coming down here disgraceful. He knows perfectly well why. 400

CECILY. Uncle Jack, do be nice. There is some good in everyone. Ernest has just been telling me about his poor invalid friend Mr. Bunbury whom he goes to visit so often. And surely there must be much good in one who is kind to an invalid, and leaves the pleasures of London to sit by a bed of pain. 405

JACK. Oh! he has been talking about Bunbury, has he? 410

---

26 immersion of adults] as a technique mainly used by Baptists; to a conservative Anglican minister this might seem a rather outlandish, albeit technically acceptable, practice.

CECILY. Yes, he has told me all about poor Mr. Bunbury, and his terrible state of health.

JACK. Bunbury! Well, I won't have him talk to you about Bunbury or about anything else. It is enough to drive one perfectly frantic. 415

ALGERNON. Of course I admit that the faults were all on my side. But I must say that I think that Brother John's coldness to me is peculiarly painful. I expected a more enthusiastic welcome, especially considering it is the first time I have come here. 420

CECILY. Uncle Jack, if you don't shake hands with Ernest, I will never forgive you.

JACK. Never forgive me?

CECILY. Never, never, never!

JACK. Well, this is the last time I shall ever do it. 425

[Shakes hands with Algernon and glares.]

CHASUBLE. It's pleasant, is it not, to see so perfect a reconciliation? I think we might leave the two brothers together.

MISS PRISM. Cecily, you will come with us.

CECILY. Certainly, Miss Prism. My little task of reconciliation is over. 430

CHASUBLE. You have done a beautiful action today, dear child.

MISS PRISM. We must not be premature in our judgments. 435

CECILY. I feel very happy. *[They all go off except Jack and Algernon.]*

JACK. You young scoundrel, Algy, you must get out of this place as soon as possible. I don't allow any Bunburying here. 440

Enter Merriman.

MERRIMAN. I have put Mr. Ernest's things in the room next to yours, sir. I suppose that is all right?

JACK. What?

MERRIMAN. Mr. Ernest's luggage, sir. I have unpacked it and put it in the room next to your own. 445

JACK. His luggage?

MERRIMAN. Yes, sir. Three portmanteaux, a dressing-case, two hat-boxes, and a large luncheon-basket. 450

ALGERNON. I am afraid I can't stay more than a week this time.

JACK. Merriman, order the dog-cart at once.[27] Mr. Ernest has been suddenly called back to town.

MERRIMAN. Yes, sir. 455

[Goes back into the house.]

ALGERNON. What a fearful liar you are, Jack. I have not been called back to town at all.

JACK. Yes, you have.

ALGERNON. I haven't heard anyone call me.

JACK. Your duty as a gentleman calls you back. 460

ALGERNON. My duty as a gentleman has never interfered with my pleasures in the smallest degree.

JACK. I can quite understand that.

ALGERNON. Well, Cecily is a darling.

JACK. You are not to talk of Miss Cardew like that. I don't like it. 465

ALGERNON. Well, I don't like your clothes. You look perfectly ridiculous in them. Why on earth don't you go up and change? It is perfectly childish to be in deep mourning for a man who is actually staying for a whole week with you in your house as a guest. I call it grotesque. 470

JACK. You are certainly not staying with me for a whole week as a guest or anything else. You have got to leave… by the four-five train. 475

ALGERNON. I certainly won't leave you so long as you are in mourning. It would be most unfriendly. If I were in mourning you would stay with me, I suppose. I should think it very unkind if you didn't. 480

JACK. Well, will you go if I change my clothes?

ALGERNON. Yes, if you are not too long. I never saw anybody take so long to dress, and with such little result.

JACK. Well, at any rate, that is better than being always over-dressed as you are. 485

ALGERNON. If I am occasionally a little over-dressed, I make up for it by being always immensely over-educated.

JACK. Your vanity is ridiculous, your conduct an outrage, and your presence in my garden utterly absurd. However, you have got to catch the four-five, and I hope you will have a pleasant journey 490

---

27 dog-cart] a small, two-wheeled carriage drawn by a single horse.

back to town. This Bunburying, as you call it, has not been a great success for you. 495

[Goes into the house.]

ALGERNON. I think it has been a great success. I'm in love with Cecily, and that is everything.

Enter Cecily at the back of the garden. She picks up the can and begins to water the flowers.

But I must see her before I go, and make arrangements for another Bunbury. Ah, there she is. 500

CECILY. Oh, I merely came back to water the roses. I thought you were with Uncle Jack.

ALGERNON. He's gone to order the dog-cart for me.

CECILY. Oh, is he going to take you for a nice drive?

ALGERNON. He's going to send me away. 505

CECILY. Then have we got to part?

ALGERNON. I am afraid so. It's very painful parting.

CECILY. It is always painful to part from people whom one has known for a very brief space of time. The absence of old friends one can endure 510 with equanimity. But even a momentary separation from anyone to whom one has just been introduced is almost unbearable.

ALGERNON. Thank you.

Enter Merriman.

MERRIMAN. The dog-cart is at the door, sir. 515

[Algernon looks appealingly at Cecily.]

CECILY. It can wait, Merriman… for… five minutes.

MERRIMAN. Yes, Miss.

[Exit Merriman.]

ALGERNON. I hope, Cecily, I shall not offend you if I state quite frankly and openly that you seem to me to be in every way the visible personification 520 of absolute perfection.

CECILY. I think your frankness does you great credit, Ernest. If you will allow me, I will copy your remarks into my diary.

[Goes over to table and begins writing in diary.]

ALGERNON. Do you really keep a diary? I'd give 525 anything to look at it. May I?

CECILY. Oh no. *[Puts her hand over it.]* You see, it is simply a very young girl's record of her own thoughts and impressions, and consequently meant for publication. When it appears in volume form 530 I hope you will order a copy. But pray, Ernest, don't stop. I delight in taking down from dictation. I have reached absolute perfection. You can go on. I am quite ready for more.

ALGERNON. *[Somewhat taken aback.]* Ahem! Ahem! 535

CECILY. Oh, don't cough, Ernest. When one is dictating one should speak fluently and not cough. Besides, I don't know how to spell a cough.

[Writes as Algernon speaks.]

ALGERNON. *[Speaking very rapidly.]* Cecily, ever since I first looked upon your wonderful and incompa- 540 rable beauty, I have dared to love you wildly, passionately, devotedly, hopelessly.

CECILY. I don't think that you should tell me that you love me wildly, passionately, devotedly, hopelessly. Hopelessly doesn't seem to make much 545 sense, does it?

ALGERNON. Cecily!

Enter Merriman.

MERRIMAN. The dog-cart is waiting, sir.

ALGERNON. Tell it to come round next week, at the same hour. 550

MERRIMAN. *[Looks at Cecily, who makes no sign.]* Yes, sir.

Merriman retires.

CECILY. Uncle Jack would be very much annoyed if he knew you were staying on till next week, at the same hour. 555

ALGERNON. Oh, I don't care about Jack. I don't care for anybody in the whole world but you. I love you, Cecily. You will marry me, won't you?

CECILY. You silly boy! Of course. Why, we have been engaged for the last three months. 560

ALGERNON. For the last three months?

CECILY. Yes, it will be exactly three months on Thursday.

ALGERNON. But how did we become engaged?

CECILY. Well, ever since dear Uncle Jack first 565 confessed to us that he had a younger brother who was very wicked and bad, you of course have formed the chief topic of conversation between myself and Miss Prism. And of course a man who is much talked about is always very attractive. One feels there must be something in him after all. I daresay it was foolish of me, but I fell in love with you, Ernest.

ALGERNON. Darling! And when was the engagement actually settled?

CECILY. On the 14th of February last. Worn out by your entire ignorance of my existence, I determined to end the matter one way or the other, and after a long struggle with myself I accepted you under this dear old tree here. The next day I bought this little ring in your name, and this is the little bangle with the true lover's knot I promised you always to wear.

ALGERNON. Did I give you this? It's very pretty, isn't it?

CECILY. Yes, you've wonderfully good taste, Ernest. It's the excuse I've always given for your leading such a bad life. And this is the box in which I keep all your dear letters. *[Kneels at table, opens box, and produces letters tied up with blue ribbon.]*

ALGERNON. My letters! But my own sweet Cecily, I have never written you any letters.

CECILY. You need hardly remind me of that, Ernest. I remember only too well that I was forced to write your letters for you. I always wrote three times a week, and sometimes oftener.

ALGERNON. Oh, do let me read them, Cecily!

CECILY. Oh, I couldn't possibly. They would make you far too conceited. *[Replaces box.]* The three you wrote me after I had broken off the engagement are so beautiful, and so badly spelled, that even now I can hardly read them without crying a little.

ALGERNON. But was our engagement ever broken off?

CECILY. Of course it was. On the 22nd of last March. You can see the entry if you like. *[Shows diary.]* Today I broke off my engagement with Ernest. I feel it is better to do so. The weather still continues charming.

ALGERNON. But why on earth did you break it off? What had I done? I had done nothing at all. Cecily, I am very much hurt indeed to hear you broke it off. Particularly when the weather was so charming.

CECILY. It would hardly have been a really serious engagement if it hadn't been broken off at least once. But I forgave you before the week was out.

ALGERNON. *[Crossing to her, and kneeling.]* What a perfect angel you are, Cecily!

CECILY. You dear romantic boy. *[He kisses her, she puts her fingers through his hair.]* I hope your hair curls naturally, does it?

ALGERNON. Yes, darling, with a little help from others.

CECILY. I am so glad.

ALGERNON. You'll never break off our engagement again, Cecily?

CECILY. I don't think I could break it off now that I have actually met you. Besides, of course, there is the question of your name.

ALGERNON. *[Nervously.]* Yes, of course.

CECILY. You must not laugh at me, darling, but it had always been a girlish dream of mine to love someone whose name was Ernest. *[Algernon rises, Cecily also.]* There is something in that name that seems to inspire absolute confidence. I pity any poor married woman whose husband is not called Ernest.

ALGERNON. But, my dear child, do you mean to say you could not love me if I had some other name?

CECILY. But what name?

ALGERNON. Oh, any name you like—Algernon—for instance…

CECILY. But I don't like the name of Algernon.

ALGERNON. Well, my own dear, sweet, loving little darling, I really can't see why you should object to the name of Algernon. It is not at all a bad name. In fact, it is rather an aristocratic name. Half of the chaps who get into the Bankruptcy Court are called Algernon. But seriously, Cecily… *[Moving to her.]*… if my name was Algy, couldn't you love me?

CECILY. *[Rising.]* I might respect you, Ernest, I might admire your character, but I fear that I should not be able to give you my undivided attention.

ALGERNON. Ahem! Cecily! *[Picking up hat.]* Your Rector here is, I suppose, thoroughly experienced in the practice of all the rites and ceremonials of the Church?

CECILY. Oh, yes. Dr. Chasuble is a most learned man. He has never written a single book, so you can imagine how much he knows.

ALGERNON. I must see him at once on a most important christening—I mean on most important business.

CECILY. Oh! 665

ALGERNON. I shan't be away more than half an hour.

CECILY. Considering that we have been engaged since February the 14th, and that I only met you today for the first time, I think it is rather hard that you should leave me for so long a period as half an hour. Couldn't you make it twenty minutes? 670

ALGERNON. I'll be back in no time. *[Kisses her and rushes down the garden.]*

CECILY. What an impetuous boy he is! I like his hair so much. I must enter his proposal in my diary. 675

Enter Merriman.

MERRIMAN. A Miss Fairfax has just called to see Mr. Worthing. On very important business Miss Fairfax states.

CECILY. Isn't Mr. Worthing in his library? 680

MERRIMAN. Mr. Worthing went over in the direction of the Rectory some time ago.

CECILY. Pray ask the lady to come out here; Mr. Worthing is sure to be back soon. And you can bring tea. 685

MERRIMAN. Yes, Miss. *[Goes out.]*

CECILY. Miss Fairfax! I suppose one of the many good elderly women who are associated with Uncle Jack in some of his philanthropic work in London. I don't quite like women who are interested in philanthropic work. I think it is so forward of them. 690

Enter Merriman.

MERRIMAN. Miss Fairfax.

Enter Gwendolen.

[Exit Merriman.]

CECILY. *[Advancing to meet her.]* Pray let me introduce myself to you. My name is Cecily Cardew. 695

GWENDOLEN. Cecily Cardew? *[Moving to her and shaking hands.]* What a very sweet name! Something tells me that we are going to be great friends. I like you already more than I can say. My first impressions of people are never wrong. 700

CECILY. How nice of you to like me so much after we have known each other such a comparatively short time. Pray sit down.

GWENDOLEN. *[Still standing up.]* I may call you Cecily, may I not? 705

CECILY. With pleasure!

GWENDOLEN. And you will always call me Gwendolen, won't you?

CECILY. If you wish. 710

GWENDOLEN. Then that is all quite settled, is it not?

CECILY. I hope so.

[A pause. They both sit down together.]

GWENDOLEN. Perhaps this might be a favourable opportunity for my mentioning who I am. My father is Lord Bracknell. You have never heard of papa, I suppose? 715

CECILY. I don't think so.

GWENDOLEN. Outside the family circle, papa, I am glad to say, is entirely unknown. I think that is quite as it should be. The home seems to me to be the proper sphere for the man. And certainly once a man begins to neglect his domestic duties he becomes painfully effeminate, does he not? And I don't like that. It makes men so very attractive. Cecily, Mamma, whose views on education are remarkably strict, has brought me up to be extremely short-sighted; it is part of her system; so do you mind my looking at you through my glasses? 720 725

CECILY. Oh! not at all, Gwendolen. I am very fond of being looked at. 730

GWENDOLEN. *[After examining Cecily carefully through a lorgnette.]* You are here on a short visit, I suppose.

CECILY. Oh no! I live here. 735

GWENDOLEN. *[Severely.]* Really? Your mother, no doubt, or some female relative of advanced years, resides here also?

CECILY. Oh no! I have no mother, nor, in fact, any relations. 740

GWENDOLEN. Indeed?

CECILY. My dear guardian, with the assistance of Miss Prism, has the arduous task of looking after me.

GWENDOLEN. Your guardian? 745

CECILY. Yes, I am Mr. Worthing's ward.

GWENDOLEN. Oh! It is strange he never mentioned to me that he had a ward. How secretive of him! He grows more interesting hourly. I am not sure, however, that the news inspires me with feelings 750 of unmixed delight. *[Rising and going to her.]* I am very fond of you, Cecily; I have liked you ever since I met you! But I am bound to state that now that I know that you are Mr. Worthing's ward, I cannot help expressing a wish you were—well just 755 a little older than you seem to be—and not quite so very alluring in appearance. In fact, if I may speak candidly—

CECILY. Pray do! I think that whenever one has anything unpleasant to say, one should always be 760 quite candid.

GWENDOLEN. Well, to speak with perfect candour, Cecily, I wish that you were fully forty-two, and more than usually plain for your age. Ernest has a strong upright nature. He is the very soul of truth 765 and honour. Disloyalty would be as impossible to him as deception. But even men of the noblest possible moral character are extremely susceptible to the influence of the physical charms of others. Modern, no less than Ancient History, supplies us 770 with many most painful examples of what I refer to. If it were not so, indeed, History would be quite unreadable.

CECILY. I beg your pardon, Gwendolen, did you say Ernest? 775

GWENDOLEN. Yes.

CECILY. Oh, but it is not Mr. Ernest Worthing who is my guardian. It is his brother—his elder brother.

GWENDOLEN. *[Sitting down again.]* Ernest never mentioned to me that he had a brother. 780

CECILY. I am sorry to say they have not been on good terms for a long time.

GWENDOLEN. Ah! that accounts for it. And now that I think of it I have never heard any man mention his brother. The subject seems distasteful 785 to most men. Cecily, you have lifted a load from my mind. I was growing almost anxious. It would have been terrible if any cloud had come across a friendship like ours, would it not? Of course you are quite, quite sure that it is not Mr. Ernest 790 Worthing who is your guardian?

CECILY. Quite sure. *[A pause.]* In fact, I am going to be his.

GWENDOLEN. *[Inquiringly.]* I beg your pardon?

CECILY. *[Rather shy and confidingly.]* Dearest 795 Gwendolen, there is no reason why I should make a secret of it to you. Our little county newspaper is sure to chronicle the fact next week. Mr. Ernest Worthing and I are engaged to be married.

GWENDOLEN. *[Quite politely, rising.]* My darling 800 Cecily, I think there must be some slight error. Mr. Ernest Worthing is engaged to me. The announcement will appear in the Morning Post on Saturday at the latest.

CECILY. *[Very politely, rising.]* I am afraid you must 805 be under some misconception. Ernest proposed to me exactly ten minutes ago.

[Shows diary.]

GWENDOLEN. *[Examines diary through her lorgnette carefully.]* It is certainly very curious, for he asked me to be his wife yesterday afternoon at 5.30. If 810 you would care to verify the incident, pray do so. *[Produces diary of her own.]* I never travel without my diary. One should always have something sensational to read in the train. I am so sorry, dear Cecily, if it is any disappointment to you, but I 815 am afraid I have the prior claim.

CECILY. It would distress me more than I can tell you, dear Gwendolen, if it caused you any mental or physical anguish, but I feel bound to point out that since Ernest proposed to you he clearly has 820 changed his mind.

GWENDOLEN. *[Meditatively.]* If the poor fellow has been entrapped into any foolish promise I shall consider it my duty to rescue him at once, and with a firm hand. 825

CECILY. *[Thoughtfully and sadly.]* Whatever unfortunate entanglement my dear boy may have got into, I will never reproach him with it after we are married.

GWENDOLEN. Do you allude to me, Miss Cardew, 830

as an entanglement? You are presumptuous. On an occasion of this kind it becomes more than a moral duty to speak one's mind. It becomes a pleasure.

CECILY. Do you suggest, Miss Fairfax, that I entrapped Ernest into an engagement? How dare you? This is no time for wearing the shallow mask of manners. When I see a spade I call it a spade. 835

GWENDOLEN. *[Satirically.]* I am glad to say that I have never seen a spade. It is obvious that our social spheres have been widely different. 840

Enter Merriman, followed by the footman. He carries a salver, table cloth, and plate stand. Cecily is about to retort. The presence of the servants exercises a restraining influence, under which both girls chafe.

MERRIMAN. Shall I lay tea here as usual, Miss?

CECILY. *[Sternly, in a calm voice.]* Yes, as usual.

[Merriman begins to clear table and lay cloth. A long pause. Cecily and Gwendolen glare at each other.]

GWENDOLEN. Are there many interesting walks in the vicinity, Miss Cardew?

CECILY. Oh! yes! a great many. From the top of one of the hills quite close one can see five counties. 845

GWENDOLEN. Five counties! I don't think I should like that; I hate crowds.

CECILY. *[Sweetly.]* I suppose that is why you live in town? 850

[Gwendolen bites her lip, and beats her foot nervously with her parasol.]

GWENDOLEN. *[Looking round.]* Quite a well-kept garden this is, Miss Cardew.

CECILY. So glad you like it, Miss Fairfax.

GWENDOLEN. I had no idea there were any flowers in the country. 855

CECILY. Oh, flowers are as common here, Miss Fairfax, as people are in London.

GWENDOLEN. Personally I cannot understand how anybody manages to exist in the country, if anybody who is anybody does. The country always bores me to death. 860

CECILY. Ah! That is what the newspapers call agricultural depression, is it not? I believe the aristocracy are suffering very much from it just at present. It is almost an epidemic amongst them, I 865

have been told. May I offer you some tea, Miss Fairfax?

GWENDOLEN. *[With elaborate politeness.]* Thank you. *[Aside.]* Detestable girl! But I require tea!

CECILY. *[Sweetly.]* Sugar? 870

GWENDOLEN. *[Superciliously.]* No, thank you. Sugar is not fashionable any more.

[Cecily looks angrily at her, takes up the tongs and puts four lumps of sugar into the cup.]

CECILY. *[Severely.]* Cake or bread and butter?

GWENDOLEN. *[In a bored manner.]* Bread and butter, please. Cake is rarely seen at the best houses nowadays. 875

CECILY. *[Cuts a very large slice of cake, and puts it on the tray.]* Hand that to Miss Fairfax.

[Merriman does so, and goes out with footman. Gwendolen drinks the tea and makes a grimace. Puts down cup at once, reaches out her hand to the bread and butter, looks at it, and finds it is cake. Rises in indignation.]

GWENDOLEN. You have filled my tea with lumps of sugar, and though I asked most distinctly for bread and butter, you have given me cake. I am known for the gentleness of my disposition, and the extraordinary sweetness of my nature, but I warn you, Miss Cardew, you may go too far. 880

CECILY. *[Rising.]* To save my poor, innocent, trusting boy from the machinations of any other girl there are no lengths to which I would not go. 885

GWENDOLEN. From the moment I saw you I distrusted you. I felt that you were false and deceitful. I am never deceived in such matters. My first impressions of people are invariably right. 890

CECILY. It seems to me, Miss Fairfax, that I am trespassing on your valuable time. No doubt you have many other calls of a similar character to make in the neighbourhood. 895

Enter Jack.

GWENDOLEN. *[Catching sight of him.]* Ernest! My own Ernest!

JACK. Gwendolen! Darling! *[Offers to kiss her.]*

GWENDOLEN. *[Drawing back.]* A moment! May I ask if you are engaged to be married to this young lady? *[Points to Cecily.]* 900

JACK. *[Laughing.]* To dear little Cecily! Of course not! What could have put such an idea into your pretty little head?

GWENDOLEN. Thank you. You may! *[Offers her cheek.]* 905

CECILY. *[Very sweetly.]* I knew there must be some misunderstanding, Miss Fairfax. The gentleman whose arm is at present round your waist is my dear guardian, Mr. John Worthing. 910

GWENDOLEN. I beg your pardon?

CECILY. This is Uncle Jack.

GWENDOLEN. *[Receding.]* Jack! Oh!

Enter Algernon.

CECILY. Here is Ernest.

ALGERNON. *[Goes straight over to Cecily without noticing anyone else.]* My own love! *[Offers to kiss her.]* 915

CECILY. *[Drawing back.]* A moment, Ernest! May I ask you—are you engaged to be married to this young lady? 920

ALGERNON. *[Looking round.]* To what young lady? Good heavens! Gwendolen!

CECILY. Yes! to good heavens, Gwendolen, I mean to Gwendolen.

ALGERNON. *[Laughing.]* Of course not! What could have put such an idea into your pretty little head? 925

CECILY. Thank you. *[Presenting her cheek to be kissed.]* You may. *[Algernon kisses her.]*

GWENDOLEN. I felt there was some slight error, Miss Cardew. The gentleman who is now embracing you is my cousin, Mr. Algernon Moncrieff. 930

CECILY. *[Breaking away from Algernon.]* Algernon Moncrieff! Oh!

[The two girls move towards each other and put their arms round each other's waists as if for protection.]

CECILY. Are you called Algernon?

ALGERNON. I cannot deny it. 935

CECILY. Oh!

GWENDOLEN. Is your name really John?

JACK. *[Standing rather proudly.]* I could deny it if I liked. I could deny anything if I liked. But my name certainly is John. It has been John for years. 940

CECILY. *[To Gwendolen.]* A gross deception has been practised on both of us.

GWENDOLEN. My poor wounded Cecily!

CECILY. My sweet wronged Gwendolen!

GWENDOLEN. *[Slowly and seriously.]* You will call me sister, will you not? 945

[They embrace. Jack and Algernon groan and walk up and down.]

CECILY. *[Rather brightly.]* There is just one question I would like to be allowed to ask my guardian.

GWENDOLEN. An admirable idea! Mr. Worthing, there is just one question I would like to be permitted to put to you. Where is your brother Ernest? We are both engaged to be married to your brother Ernest, so it is a matter of some importance to us to know where your brother Ernest is at present. 950 955

JACK. *[Slowly and hesitatingly.]* Gwendolen— Cecily—it is very painful for me to be forced to speak the truth. It is the first time in my life that I have ever been reduced to such a painful position, and I am really quite inexperienced in doing anything of the kind. However I will tell you quite frankly that I have no brother Ernest. I have no brother at all. I never had a brother in my life, and I certainly have not the smallest intention of ever having one in the future. 960 965

CECILY. *[Surprised.]* No brother at all?

JACK. *[Cheerily.]* None!

GWENDOLEN. *[Severely.]* Had you never a brother of any kind?

JACK. *[Pleasantly.]* Never. Not even of any kind. 970

GWENDOLEN. I am afraid it is quite clear, Cecily, that neither of us is engaged to be married to anyone.

CECILY. It is not a very pleasant position for a young girl suddenly to find herself in. Is it? 975

GWENDOLEN. Let us go into the house. They will hardly venture to come after us there.

CECILY. No, men are so cowardly, aren't they?

[They retire into the house with scornful looks.]

JACK. This ghastly state of things is what you call Bunburying, I suppose? 980

ALGERNON. Yes, and a perfectly wonderful Bunbury it is. The most wonderful Bunbury I have ever had in my life.

JACK. Well, you've no right whatsoever to Bunbury here. 985

ALGERNON. That is absurd. One has a right to Bunbury anywhere one chooses. Every serious Bunburyist knows that.

JACK. Serious Bunburyist! Good heavens!

ALGERNON. Well, one must be serious about 990 something, if one wants to have any amusement in life. I happen to be serious about Bunburying. What on earth you are serious about I haven't got the remotest idea. About everything, I should fancy. You have such an absolutely trivial nature. 995

JACK. Well, the only small satisfaction I have in the whole of this wretched business is that your friend Bunbury is quite exploded. You won't be able to run down to the country quite so often as you used to do, dear Algy. And a very good thing too. 1000

ALGERNON. Your brother is a little off colour, isn't he, dear Jack? You won't be able to disappear to London quite so frequently as your wicked custom was. And not a bad thing either.

JACK. As for your conduct towards Miss Cardew, I 1005 must say that your taking in a sweet, simple, innocent girl like that is quite inexcusable. To say nothing of the fact that she is my ward.

ALGERNON. I can see no possible defence at all for your deceiving a brilliant, clever, thoroughly 1010 experienced young lady like Miss Fairfax. To say nothing of the fact that she is my cousin.

JACK. I wanted to be engaged to Gwendolen, that is all. I love her.

ALGERNON. Well, I simply wanted to be engaged 1015 to Cecily. I adore her.

JACK. There is certainly no chance of your marrying Miss Cardew.

ALGERNON. I don't think there is much likelihood, Jack, of you and Miss Fairfax being united. 1020

JACK. Well, that is no business of yours.

ALGERNON. If it was my business, I wouldn't talk about it. *[Begins to eat muffins.]* It is very vulgar to talk about one's business. Only people like stockbrokers do that, and then merely at dinner- 1025 parties.

JACK. How you can sit there, calmly eating muffins when we are in this horrible trouble, I can't make out. You seem to me to be perfectly heartless.

ALGERNON. Well, I can't eat muffins in an agitated 1030 manner. The butter would probably get on my cuffs. One should always eat muffins quite calmly. It is the only way to eat them.

JACK. I say it's perfectly heartless your eating muffins at all, under the circumstances. 1035

ALGERNON. When I am in trouble, eating is the only thing that consoles me. Indeed, when I am in really great trouble, as anyone who knows me intimately will tell you, I refuse everything except food and drink. At the present moment I am 1040 eating muffins because I am unhappy. Besides, I am particularly fond of muffins. *[Rising.]*

JACK. *[Rising.]* Well, that is no reason why you should eat them all in that greedy way.

[Takes muffins from Algernon.]

ALGERNON. *[Offering tea-cake.]* I wish you would 1045 have tea-cake instead. I don't like tea-cake.

JACK. Good heavens! I suppose a man may eat his own muffins in his own garden.

ALGERNON. But you have just said it was perfectly heartless to eat muffins. 1050

JACK. I said it was perfectly heartless of you, under the circumstances. That is a very different thing.

ALGERNON. That may be. But the muffins are the same. *[He seizes the muffin-dish from Jack.]*

JACK. Algy, I wish to goodness you would go. 1055

ALGERNON. You can't possibly ask me to go without having some dinner. It's absurd. I never go without my dinner. No one ever does, except vegetarians and people like that. Besides I have just made arrangements with Dr. Chasuble to be christened 1060 at a quarter to six under the name of Ernest.

JACK. My dear fellow, the sooner you give up that nonsense the better. I made arrangements this morning with Dr. Chasuble to be christened myself at 5.30, and I naturally will take the name 1065 of Ernest. Gwendolen would wish it. We can't both be christened Ernest. It's absurd. Besides, I have a perfect right to be christened if I like. There is no evidence at all that I ever have been christened by anybody. I should think it extremely probable that 1070 I never was, and so does Dr. Chasuble. It is entirely different in your case. You have been christened already.

ALGERNON. Yes, but I have not been christened for years. 1075

JACK. Yes, but you have been christened. That is the important thing.

ALGERNON. Quite so. So I know my constitution can stand it. If you are not quite sure about your ever having been christened, I must say I think it 1080 rather dangerous your venturing on it now. It might make you very unwell. You can hardly have forgotten that someone very closely connected with you was very nearly carried off this week in Paris by a severe chill. 1085

JACK. Yes, but you said yourself that a severe chill was not hereditary.

ALGERNON. It usen't to be, I know—but I daresay it is now. Science is always making wonderful improvements in things. 1090

JACK. *[Picking up the muffin-dish.]* Oh, that is nonsense; you are always talking nonsense.

ALGERNON. Jack, you are at the muffins again! I wish you wouldn't. There are only two left. *[Takes them.]* I told you I was particularly fond of 1095 muffins.

JACK. But I hate tea-cake.

ALGERNON. Why on earth then do you allow tea-cake to be served up for your guests? What ideas you have of hospitality! 1100

JACK. Algernon! I have already told you to go. I don't want you here. Why don't you go!

ALGERNON. I haven't quite finished my tea yet! and there is still one muffin left.

[Jack groans, and sinks into a chair, Algernon still continues eating.]

Act Drop

THIRD ACT

Scene: Morning-room at the Manor House.

[Gwendolen and Cecily are at the window, looking out into the garden.]

GWENDOLEN. The fact that they did not follow us at once into the house, as anyone else would have done, seems to me to show that they have some sense of shame left.

CECILY. They have been eating muffins. That looks 5 like repentance.

GWENDOLEN. *[After a pause.]* They don't seem to notice us at all. Couldn't you cough?

CECILY. But I haven't got a cough!

GWENDOLEN. They're looking at us. What effrontery! 10

CECILY. They're approaching. That's very forward of them.

GWENDOLEN. Let us preserve a dignified silence.

CECILY. Certainly. It's the only thing to do now.

Enter Jack followed by Algernon. They whistle some dreadful popular air from a British Opera.

GWENDOLEN. This dignified silence seems to 15 produce an unpleasant effect.

CECILY. A most distasteful one.

GWENDOLEN. But we will not be the first to speak.

CECILY. Certainly not.

GWENDOLEN. Mr. Worthing, I have something very 20 particular to ask you. Much depends on your reply.

CECILY. Gwendolen, your common sense is invaluable. Mr. Moncrieff, kindly answer me the following question. Why did you pretend to be my guardian's brother? 25

ALGERNON. In order that I might have an opportunity of meeting you.

CECILY. *[To Gwendolen.]* That certainly seems a satisfactory explanation, does it not?

GWENDOLEN. Yes, dear, if you can believe him. 30

CECILY. I don't. But that does not affect the wonderful beauty of this answer.

GWENDOLEN. True. In matters of grave importance, style, not sincerity is the vital thing. Mr. Worthing, what explanation can you offer to me for pretend- 35 ing to have a brother? Was it in order that you might have an opportunity of coming up to town to see me as often as possible?

JACK. Can you doubt it, Miss Fairfax?

GWENDOLEN. I have the gravest doubts upon the 40 subject. But I intend to crush them. This is not the moment for German scepticism.[28] *[Moving to*

---

28 German scepticism] allusion to the proposition of Immanuel Kant (1724–1804) that our perceptions do not necessarily convey any true knowledge of things-in-themselves.

Cecily.] Their explanations appear to be quite satisfactory, especially Mr. Worthing's. That seems to me to have the stamp of truth upon it.

CECILY. I am more than content with what Mr. Moncrieff said. His voice alone inspires one with absolute credulity.

GWENDOLEN. Then you think we should forgive them?

CECILY. Yes. I mean no.

GWENDOLEN. True! I had forgotten. There are principles at stake that one cannot surrender. Which of us should tell them? The task is not a pleasant one.

CECILY. Could we not both speak at the same time?

GWENDOLEN. An excellent idea! I nearly always speak at the same time as other people. Will you take the time from me?

CECILY. Certainly. *[Gwendolen beats time with uplifted finger.]*

GWENDOLEN and CECILY. *[Speaking together.]* Your Christian names are still an insuperable barrier. That is all!

JACK and ALGERNON. *[Speaking together.]* Our Christian names! Is that all? But we are going to be christened this afternoon.

GWENDOLEN. *[To Jack.]* For my sake you are prepared to do this terrible thing?

JACK. I am.

CECILY. *[To Algernon.]* To please me you are ready to face this fearful ordeal?

ALGERNON. I am!

GWENDOLEN. How absurd to talk of the equality of the sexes! Where questions of self-sacrifice are concerned, men are infinitely beyond us.

JACK. We are.

[Clasps hands with Algernon.]

CECILY. They have moments of physical courage of which we women know absolutely nothing.

GWENDOLEN. *[To Jack.]* Darling!

ALGERNON. *[To Cecily.]* Darling!

[They fall into each other's arms.]

Enter Merriman. When he enters he coughs loudly, seeing the situation.

MERRIMAN. Ahem! Ahem! Lady Bracknell!

JACK. Good heavens!

Enter Lady Bracknell. The couples separate in alarm.

[Exit Merriman.]

LADY BRACKNELL. Gwendolen! What does this mean?

GWENDOLEN. Merely that I am engaged to be married to Mr. Worthing, mamma.

LADY BRACKNELL. Come here. Sit down. Sit down immediately. Hesitation of any kind is a sign of mental decay in the young, of physical weakness in the old. *[Turns to Jack.]* Apprised, sir, of my daughter's sudden flight by her trusty maid, whose confidence I purchased by means of a small coin, I followed her at once by a luggage train.[29] Her unhappy father is, I am glad to say, under the impression that she is attending a more than usually lengthy lecture by the University Extension Scheme on the Influence of a permanent income on Thought.[30] I do not propose to undeceive him. Indeed I have never undeceived him on any question. I would consider it wrong. But of course, you will clearly understand that all communication between yourself and my daughter must cease immediately from this moment. On this point, as indeed on all points, I am firm.

JACK. I am engaged to be married to Gwendolen, Lady Bracknell!

LADY BRACKNELL. You are nothing of the kind, sir. And now, as regards Algernon!… Algernon!

ALGERNON. Yes, Aunt Augusta.

LADY BRACKNELL. May I ask if it is in this house that your invalid friend Mr. Bunbury resides?

ALGERNON. *[Stammering.]* Oh! No! Bunbury doesn't live here. Bunbury is somewhere else at present. In fact, Bunbury is dead.

LADY BRACKNELL. Dead! When did Mr. Bunbury die? His death must have been extremely sudden.

ALGERNON. *[Airily.]* Oh! I killed Bunbury this

---

29 luggage train] a train intended to carry not passengers, but their luggage and freight.

30 University Extension Scheme] extramural courses available to the general public; continuing education.

afternoon. I mean poor Bunbury died this afternoon.

LADY BRACKNELL. What did he die of?

ALGERNON. Bunbury? Oh, he was quite exploded.

LADY BRACKNELL. Exploded! Was he the victim of a revolutionary outrage? I was not aware that Mr. Bunbury was interested in social legislation. If so, he is well punished for his morbidity.

ALGERNON. My dear Aunt Augusta, I mean he was found out! The doctors found out that Bunbury could not live, that is what I mean—so Bunbury died.

LADY BRACKNELL. He seems to have had great confidence in the opinion of his physicians. I am glad, however, that he made up his mind at the last to some definite course of action, and acted under proper medical advice. And now that we have finally got rid of this Mr. Bunbury, may I ask, Mr. Worthing, who is that young person whose hand my nephew Algernon is now holding in what seems to me a peculiarly unnecessary manner?

JACK. That lady is Miss Cecily Cardew, my ward.

[Lady Bracknell bows coldly to Cecily.]

ALGERNON. I am engaged to be married to Cecily, Aunt Augusta.

LADY BRACKNELL. I beg your pardon?

CECILY. Mr. Moncrieff and I are engaged to be married, Lady Bracknell.

LADY BRACKNELL. *[With a shiver, crossing to the sofa and sitting down.]* I do not know whether there is anything peculiarly exciting in the air of this particular part of Hertfordshire, but the number of engagements that go on seems to me considerably above the proper average that statistics have laid down for our guidance. I think some preliminary enquiry on my part would not be out of place. Mr. Worthing, is Miss Cardew at all connected with any of the larger railway stations in London? I merely desire information. Until yesterday I had no idea that there were any families or persons whose origin was a Terminus.

[Jack looks perfectly furious, but restrains himself.]

JACK. *[In a clear, cold voice.]* Miss Cardew is the granddaughter of the late Mr. Thomas Cardew of

149 Belgrave Square, S.W.; Gervase Park, Dorking, Surrey; and The Sporran, Fifeshire, N.B.

LADY BRACKNELL. That sounds not unsatisfactory. Three addresses always inspire confidence, even in tradesmen. But what proof have I of their authenticity?

JACK. I have carefully preserved the Court Guides of the period.[31] They are open to your inspection, Lady Bracknell.

LADY BRACKNELL. *[Grimly.]* I have known strange errors in that publication.

JACK. Miss Cardew's family solicitors are Messrs. Markby, Markby, and Markby.

LADY BRACKNELL. Markby, Markby, and Markby? A firm of the very highest position in their profession. Indeed I am told that one of the Mr. Markbys is occasionally to be seen at dinner parties. So far I am satisfied.

JACK. *[Very irritably.]* How extremely kind of you, Lady Bracknell! I have also in my possession, you will be pleased to hear, certificates of Miss Cardew's birth, baptism, whooping cough, registration, vaccination, confirmation, and the measles; both the German and the English variety.

LADY BRACKNELL. Ah! A life crowded with incident, I see; though perhaps somewhat too exciting for a young girl. I am not myself in favour of premature experiences. *[Rises, looks at her watch.]* Gwendolen! the time approaches for our departure. We have not a moment to lose. As a matter of form, Mr. Worthing, I had better ask you if Miss Cardew has any little fortune?

JACK. Oh! about a hundred and thirty thousand pounds in the Funds.[32] That is all. Good-bye, Lady Bracknell. So pleased to have seen you.

LADY BRACKNELL. *[Sitting down again.]* A moment, Mr. Worthing. A hundred and thirty thousand pounds! And in the Funds! Miss Cardew seems to me a most attractive young lady, now that I look at her. Few girls of the present day have any really solid qualities, any of the qualities that last, and

---

31 Court Guides] registries of the names and addresses of members of the aristocracy.

32 the Funds] low-risk government stocks.

improve with time. We live, I regret to say, in an age of surfaces. *[To Cecily.]* Come over here, dear. *[Cecily goes across.]* Pretty child! your dress is sadly simple, and your hair seems almost as Nature might have left it. But we can soon alter all that. A thoroughly experienced French maid produces a really marvellous result in a very brief space of time. I remember recommending one to young Lady Lancing, and after three months her own husband did not know her.

JACK. And after six months nobody knew her.

LADY BRACKNELL. *[Glares at Jack for a few moments. Then bends, with a practised smile, to Cecily.]* Kindly turn round, sweet child. *[Cecily turns completely round.]* No, the side view is what I want. *[Cecily presents her profile.]* Yes, quite as I expected. There are distinct social possibilities in your profile. The two weak points in our age are its want of principle and its want of profile. The chin a little higher, dear. Style largely depends on the way the chin is worn. They are worn very high, just at present. Algernon!

ALGERNON. Yes, Aunt Augusta!

LADY BRACKNELL. There are distinct social possibilities in Miss Cardew's profile.

ALGERNON. Cecily is the sweetest, dearest, prettiest girl in the whole world. And I don't care twopence about social possibilities.

LADY BRACKNELL. Never speak disrespectfully of Society, Algernon. Only people who can't get into it do that. *[To Cecily.]* Dear child, of course you know that Algernon has nothing but his debts to depend upon. But I do not approve of mercenary marriages. When I married Lord Bracknell I had no fortune of any kind. But I never dreamed for a moment of allowing that to stand in my way. Well, I suppose I must give my consent.

ALGERNON. Thank you, Aunt Augusta.

LADY BRACKNELL. Cecily, you may kiss me!

CECILY. *[Kisses her.]* Thank you, Lady Bracknell.

LADY BRACKNELL. You may also address me as Aunt Augusta for the future.

CECILY. Thank you, Aunt Augusta.

LADY BRACKNELL. The marriage, I think, had better take place quite soon.

ALGERNON. Thank you, Aunt Augusta.

CECILY. Thank you, Aunt Augusta.

LADY BRACKNELL. To speak frankly, I am not in favour of long engagements. They give people the opportunity of finding out each other's character before marriage, which I think is never advisable.

JACK. I beg your pardon for interrupting you, Lady Bracknell, but this engagement is quite out of the question. I am Miss Cardew's guardian, and she cannot marry without my consent until she comes of age. That consent I absolutely decline to give.

LADY BRACKNELL. Upon what grounds may I ask? Algernon is an extremely, I may almost say an ostentatiously, eligible young man. He has nothing, but he looks everything. What more can one desire?

JACK. It pains me very much to have to speak frankly to you, Lady Bracknell, about your nephew, but the fact is that I do not approve at all of his moral character. I suspect him of being untruthful.

[Algernon and Cecily look at him in indignant amazement.]

LADY BRACKNELL. Untruthful! My nephew Algernon? Impossible! He is an Oxonian.[33]

JACK. I fear there can be no possible doubt about the matter. This afternoon, during my temporary absence in London on an important question of romance, he obtained admission to my house by means of the false pretence of being my brother. Under an assumed name he drank, I've just been informed by my butler, an entire pint bottle of my Perrier-Jouet, Brut, '89; a wine I was specially reserving for myself.[34] Continuing his disgraceful deception, he succeeded in the course of the afternoon in alienating the affections of my only ward. He subsequently stayed to tea, and devoured every single muffin. And what makes his conduct all the more heartless is, that he was perfectly well aware from the first that I have no brother, that I never had a brother, and that I don't intend to have a brother, not even of any kind. I distinctly told him so myself yesterday afternoon.

---

33 Oxonian] a graduate of Oxford University (as was Wilde himself).

34 Perrier-Jouet, Brut, '89] a fine champagne.

LADY BRACKNELL. Ahem! Mr. Worthing, after careful consideration I have decided entirely to overlook my nephew's conduct to you.

JACK. That is very generous of you, Lady Bracknell. My own decision, however, is unalterable. I decline to give my consent.

LADY BRACKNELL. [To Cecily.] Come here, sweet child. [Cecily goes over.] How old are you, dear?

CECILY. Well, I am really only eighteen, but I always admit to twenty when I go to evening parties.

LADY BRACKNELL. You are perfectly right in making some slight alteration. Indeed, no woman should ever be quite accurate about her age. It looks so calculating…. [In a meditative manner.] Eighteen, but admitting to twenty at evening parties. Well, it will not be very long before you are of age and free from the restraints of tutelage. So I don't think your guardian's consent is, after all, a matter of any importance.

JACK. Pray excuse me, Lady Bracknell, for interrupting you again, but it is only fair to tell you that according to the terms of her grandfather's will Miss Cardew does not come legally of age till she is thirty-five.

LADY BRACKNELL. That does not seem to me to be a grave objection. Thirty-five is a very attractive age. London society is full of women of the very highest birth who have, of their own free choice, remained thirty-five for years. Lady Dumbleton is an instance in point. To my own knowledge she has been thirty-five ever since she arrived at the age of forty, which was many years ago now. I see no reason why our dear Cecily should not be even still more attractive at the age you mention than she is at present. There will be a large accumulation of property.

CECILY. Algy, could you wait for me till I was thirty-five?

ALGERNON. Of course I could, Cecily. You know I could.

CECILY. Yes, I felt it instinctively, but I couldn't wait all that time. I hate waiting even five minutes for anybody. It always makes me rather cross. I am not punctual myself, I know, but I do like punctuality in others, and waiting, even to be married, is quite out of the question.

ALGERNON. Then what is to be done, Cecily?

CECILY. I don't know, Mr. Moncrieff.

LADY BRACKNELL. My dear Mr. Worthing, as Miss Cardew states positively that she cannot wait till she is thirty-five—a remark which I am bound to say seems to me to show a somewhat impatient nature—I would beg of you to reconsider your decision.

JACK. But my dear Lady Bracknell, the matter is entirely in your own hands. The moment you consent to my marriage with Gwendolen, I will most gladly allow your nephew to form an alliance with my ward.

LADY BRACKNELL. [Rising and drawing herself up.] You must be quite aware that what you propose is out of the question.

JACK. Then a passionate celibacy is all that any of us can look forward to.

LADY BRACKNELL. That is not the destiny I propose for Gwendolen. Algernon, of course, can choose for himself. [Pulls out her watch.] Come, dear, [Gwendolen rises] we have already missed five, if not six, trains. To miss any more might expose us to comment on the platform.

Enter Dr. Chasuble.

CHASUBLE. Everything is quite ready for the christenings.

LADY BRACKNELL. The christenings, sir! Is not that somewhat premature?

CHASUBLE. [Looking rather puzzled, and pointing to Jack and Algernon.] Both these gentlemen have expressed a desire for immediate baptism.

LADY BRACKNELL. At their age? The idea is grotesque and irreligious! Algernon, I forbid you to be baptized. I will not hear of such excesses. Lord Bracknell would be highly displeased if he learned that that was the way in which you wasted your time and money.

CHASUBLE. Am I to understand then that there are to be no christenings at all this afternoon?

JACK. I don't think that, as things are now, it would be of much practical value to either of us, Dr. Chasuble.

CHASUBLE. I am grieved to hear such sentiments from you, Mr. Worthing. They savour of the heretical views of the Anabaptists, views that I have completely refuted in four of my unpublished sermons.[35] However, as your present mood seems to be one peculiarly secular, I will return to the church at once. Indeed, I have just been informed by the pew-opener that for the last hour and a half Miss Prism has been waiting for me in the vestry.[36]

LADY BRACKNELL. *[Starting.]* Miss Prism! Did I hear you mention a Miss Prism?

CHASUBLE. Yes, Lady Bracknell. I am on my way to join her.

LADY BRACKNELL. Pray allow me to detain you for a moment. This matter may prove to be one of vital importance to Lord Bracknell and myself. Is this Miss Prism a female of repellent aspect, remotely connected with education?

CHASUBLE. *[Somewhat indignantly.]* She is the most cultivated of ladies, and the very picture of respectability.

LADY BRACKNELL. It is obviously the same person. May I ask what position she holds in your household?

CHASUBLE. *[Severely.]* I am a celibate, madam.

JACK. *[Interposing.]* Miss Prism, Lady Bracknell, has been for the last three years Miss Cardew's esteemed governess and valued companion.

LADY BRACKNELL. In spite of what I hear of her, I must see her at once. Let her be sent for.

CHASUBLE. *[Looking off.]* She approaches; she is nigh.

Enter Miss Prism hurriedly.

MISS PRISM. I was told you expected me in the vestry, dear Canon. I have been waiting for you there for an hour and three quarters. *[Catches sight of Lady Bracknell who has fixed her with a stony glare. Miss Prism grows pale and quails. She looks anxiously round as if desirous to escape.]*

LADY BRACKNELL. *[In a severe, judicial voice.]* Prism! *[Miss Prism bows her head in shame.]* Come here, Prism! *[Miss Prism approaches in a humble manner.]* Prism! Where is that baby? *[General consternation. The Canon starts back in horror. Algernon and Jack pretend to be anxious to shield Cecily and Gwendolen from hearing the details of a terrible public scandal.]* Twenty-eight years ago, Prism, you left Lord Bracknell's house, Number 104, Upper Grosvenor Street, in charge of a perambulator that contained a baby of the male sex. You never returned. A few weeks later, through the elaborate investigations of the Metropolitan police, the perambulator was discovered at midnight standing by itself in a remote corner of Bayswater. It contained the manuscript of a three-volume novel of more than usually revolting sentimentality. *[Miss Prism starts in involuntary indignation.]* But the baby was not there. *[Everyone looks at Miss Prism.]* Prism! Where is that baby? *[A pause.]*

MISS PRISM. Lady Bracknell, I admit with shame that I do not know. I only wish I did. The plain facts of the case are these. On the morning of the day you mention, a day that is for ever branded on my memory, I prepared as usual to take the baby out in its perambulator. I had also with me a somewhat old, but capacious hand-bag, in which I had intended to place the manuscript of a work of fiction that I had written during my few unoccupied hours. In a moment of mental abstraction, for which I never can forgive myself, I deposited the manuscript in the bassinette, and placed the baby in the hand-bag.[37]

JACK. *[Who has been listening attentively.]* But where did you deposit the hand-bag?

MISS PRISM. Do not ask me, Mr. Worthing.

JACK. Miss Prism, this is a matter of no small importance to me. I insist on knowing where you deposited the hand-bag that contained that infant.

MISS PRISM. I left it in the cloak-room of one of the larger railway stations in London.

JACK. What railway station?

MISS PRISM. *[Quite crushed.]* Victoria. The Brighton line. *[Sinks into a chair.]*

---

35 Anabaptists] a protestant sect; the name means "re-baptizers," in reference to their belief that childhood christening or baptism was meaningless, and that only the baptism of a fully aware adult (or re-baptism) had any efficacy.

36 pew-opener] a person whose job was to open the gates to the pews of wealthy parishioners.

37 bassinette] a large, hooded perambulator.

JACK. I must retire to my room for a moment. Gwendolen, wait here for me.

GWENDOLEN. If you are not too long, I will wait here for you all my life. 460

[Exit Jack in great excitement.]

CHASUBLE. What do you think this means, Lady Bracknell?

LADY BRACKNELL. I dare not even suspect, Dr. Chasuble. I need hardly tell you that in families of high position strange coincidences are not 465 supposed to occur. They are hardly considered the thing.

[Noises heard overhead as if someone was throwing trunks about. Everyone looks up.]

CECILY. Uncle Jack seems strangely agitated.

CHASUBLE. Your guardian has a very emotional nature. 470

LADY BRACKNELL. This noise is extremely unpleasant. It sounds as if he was having an argument. I dislike arguments of any kind. They are always vulgar, and often convincing.

CHASUBLE. *[Looking up.]* It has stopped now. *[The* 475 *noise is redoubled.]*

LADY BRACKNELL. I wish he would arrive at some conclusion.

GWENDOLEN. The suspense is terrible. I hope it will last. 480

Enter Jack with a hand-bag of black leather in his hand.

JACK. *[Rushing over to Miss Prism.]* Is this the hand-bag, Miss Prism? Examine it carefully before you speak. The happiness of more than one life depends on your answer.

MISS PRISM. *[Calmly.]* It seems to be mine. Yes, here 485 is the injury it received through the upsetting of a Gower Street omnibus in younger and happier days.38 Here is the stain on the lining caused by the explosion of a temperance beverage, an

incident that occurred at Leamington. And here, 490 on the lock, are my initials. I had forgotten that in an extravagant mood I had had them placed there. The bag is undoubtedly mine. I am delighted to have it so unexpectedly restored to me. It has been a great inconvenience being without it 495 all these years.

JACK. *[In a pathetic voice.]* Miss Prism, more is restored to you than this hand-bag. I was the baby you placed in it.

MISS PRISM. *[Amazed.]* You? 500

JACK. *[Embracing her.]* Yes... mother!

MISS PRISM. *[Recoiling in indignant astonishment.]* Mr. Worthing! I am unmarried!

JACK. Unmarried! I do not deny that is a serious blow. But after all, who has the right to cast a stone 505 against one who has suffered?39 Cannot repentance wipe out an act of folly? Why should there be one law for men, and another for women? Mother, I forgive you. *[Tries to embrace her again.]*

MISS PRISM. *[Still more indignant.]* Mr. Worthing, 510 there is some error. *[Pointing to Lady Bracknell.]* There is the lady who can tell you who you really are.

JACK. *[After a pause.]* Lady Bracknell, I hate to seem inquisitive, but would you kindly inform me who 515 I am?

LADY BRACKNELL. I am afraid that the news I have to give you will not altogether please you. You are the son of my poor sister, Mrs. Moncrieff, and consequently Algernon's elder brother. 520

JACK. Algy's elder brother! Then I have a brother after all. I knew I had a brother! I always said I had a brother! Cecily,—how could you have ever doubted that I had a brother? *[Seizes hold of Algernon.]* Dr. Chasuble, my unfortunate brother. 525 Miss Prism, my unfortunate brother. Gwendolen, my unfortunate brother. Algy, you young scoundrel, you will have to treat me with more respect in the future. You have never behaved to me like a brother in all your life. 530

ALGERNON. Well, not till to-day, old boy, I admit. I did my best, however, though I was out of practice. *[Shakes hands.]*

---

38 Gower Street omnibus] a horse-drawn bus in the Bloomsbury district of London; the implication may be that it was overturned during some sort of public protest.

39 the right to cast a stone] Cf. John 8:7.

GWENDOLEN. *[To Jack.]* My own! But what own are you? What is your Christian name, now that you have become someone else? 535

JACK. Good heavens!… I had quite forgotten that point. Your decision on the subject of my name is irrevocable, I suppose?

GWENDOLEN. I never change, except in my affections. 540

CECILY. What a noble nature you have, Gwendolen!

JACK. Then the question had better be cleared up at once. Aunt Augusta, a moment. At the time when Miss Prism left me in the hand-bag, had I been christened already? 545

LADY BRACKNELL. Every luxury that money could buy, including christening, had been lavished on you by your fond and doting parents.

JACK. Then I was christened! That is settled. Now, what name was I given? Let me know the worst. 550

LADY BRACKNELL. Being the eldest son you were naturally christened after your father.

JACK. *[Irritably.]* Yes, but what was my father's Christian name? 555

LADY BRACKNELL. *[Meditatively.]* I cannot at the present moment recall what the General's Christian name was. But I have no doubt he had one. He was eccentric, I admit. But only in later years. And that was the result of the Indian climate, and marriage, and indigestion, and other things of that kind. 560

JACK. Algy! Can't you recollect what our father's Christian name was?

ALGERNON. My dear boy, we were never even on speaking terms. He died before I was a year old. 565

JACK. His name would appear in the Army Lists of the period, I suppose, Aunt Augusta.[40]

LADY BRACKNELL. The General was essentially a man of peace, except in his domestic life. But I 570 have no doubt his name would appear in any military directory.

JACK. The Army Lists of the last forty years are here. These delightful records should have been my constant study. *[Rushes to bookcase and tears the* 575 *books out.]* M. Generals… Mallam, Maxbohm, Magley, what ghastly names they have—Markby, Migsby, Mobbs, Moncrieff! Lieutenant 1840, Captain, Lieutenant-Colonel, Colonel, General 1869, Christian names, Ernest John. *[Puts book* 580 *very quietly down and speaks quite calmly.]* I always told you, Gwendolen, my name was Ernest, didn't I? Well, it is Ernest after all. I mean it naturally is Ernest.

LADY BRACKNELL. Yes, I remember now that the 585 General was called Ernest. I knew I had some particular reason for disliking the name.

GWENDOLEN. Ernest! My own Ernest! I felt from the first that you could have no other name!

JACK. Gwendolen, it is a terrible thing for a man to 590 find out suddenly that all his life he has been speaking nothing but the truth. Can you forgive me?

GWENDOLEN. I can. For I feel that you are sure to change. 595

JACK. My own one!

CHASUBLE. *[To Miss Prism.]* Lætitia! *[Embraces her.]*

MISS PRISM. *[Enthusiastically.]* Frederick! At last!

ALGERNON. Cecily! *[Embraces her.]* At last!

JACK. Gwendolen! *[Embraces her.]* At last! 600

LADY BRACKNELL. My nephew, you seem to be displaying signs of triviality.

JACK. On the contrary, Aunt Augusta, I've now realized for the first time in my life the vital Importance of Being Earnest. 605

Tableau.

Curtain.

---

40 Army Lists] a directory of all commissioned officers.

ALFRED JARRY

King Ubu

In 1888, fifteen-year-old Alfred Jarry (1873–1907) began attending a school in Rennes, France, where he discovered that his schoolmates had made a tradition of mocking their physics teacher, Monsieur Hébert, whom translator David Edney describes as "short, obese, incompetent, pompous and ineffective in imposing discipline on his unruly students." One of Jarry's schoolmates, Henri Morin, with his older brother Charles, had written a short farce called *les Polonais* (The Poles) featuring a character based on Hébert, *"le Père Ebé,"* the ridiculous King of an imaginary Poland. Jarry and Morin produced the play in their homes and, according to legend, Monsieur Hébert attended without recognizing himself. Afterwards Jarry grew more fascinated with the idea of this character, still toying with it a few years later, after he had moved to Paris. By then the name Hébert had already gone through several versions—*P.H., Père Heb, le Père Ebé,* and so on. Thus, with a little further distortion from Jarry, the character *Père Ubu* (Pa Ubu) was born.

On December 10, 1896, when Jarry was twenty-three, *Ubu Roi* (King Ubu) premiered at the avant-garde Théâtre de l'Oeuvre in Paris, where, from the first word spoken ("*merdre,*" a distortion of "*merde*": "shit"), it provoked howls of outrage and rioting. No doubt the schoolboy provenance of *King Ubu* was (and is) still apparent to audiences. However, in his reworking and expansion of the original idea, Jarry had broadened the satire considerably. His new target was the bourgeoisie itself, in all of its vulgarity and pettiness. (Jarry's notes on costuming call for Pa Ubu to appear as a middle-class businessman: "a steel-gray suit-jacket, with a cane in his right pocket, a bowler hat...and a crown on top of his hat, starting in Act II.") We may suppose by the pandemonium with which the play was received that Jarry had hit his mark; but truthfully, any bourgeois spectators probably had little more idea than had Monsieur Hébert that they themselves were being portrayed. And indeed, there were considerations beyond offended self-images here.

In fact, what seemed to be at stake was nothing less than the question of what direction theatre was to take in the modern age. The Théâtre de l'Oeuvre was run by a producer and director named Aurélien Lugné-Poë, who, in reaction to what he saw as the limited scope and tendency toward sordidness of the dominant Realist movement, had developed the concept of a Symbolist theatre of poetic, dream-like forays into the unconscious. While Jarry shared the anti-realist sentiments of the *symbolistes* in several respects, his fierce irony, his primitivism, and his enthusiasm for shocking the prudish and offending the sensitive were greatly at odds with the delicate *symboliste* aesthetic. Moreover, Jarry parodies Shakespearean works such as *Macbeth, Richard III, Julius Caesar,* and *Hamlet* (in the Buggerlas revenge plot), along with classical French works by Racine and Corneille, as if to suggest that finer ideas are untenable in the modern world. Accordingly, the feelings of the *symbolistes* about Jarry's production were mostly negative, and might be summed up in the bleak remark of the Irish poet, W.B. Yeats: "After us, the savage god."

King Ubu was to be followed by other Ubu plays—*Ubu Enchaine* and *Ubu Cocu*—which didn't meet with anything like the first play's reaction. Nevertheless, Jarry's assault on convention, etiquette, and reason was to make a lasting impression. For example, in the 1960s, the absurdist playwright Eugene Ionesco claimed Jarry's work as an inspiration (particularly Jarry's "pataphysics": the "science of exceptions," which insists that all events are unique and therefore the world is unpredictable). Indeed, with a little stretch, one might see Malcolm McLaren's creation of the Sex Pistols in the late 1970s as an emergence of further descendants of Jarry's Ubu.

[C.S.W.]

Alfred Jarry
King Ubu
Translated by David Edney

DRAMATIS PERSONÆ
PA UBU
MA UBU
CAPTAIN BORDURE
KING WENCESLAS[1]
QUEEN ROSAMUNDA
BOLESLAS, *their son*
LADISLAS, *another son*
BUGGERLAS, *another son*
GENERAL LASKY
STANISLAS LECZINSKI
JOHN SOBIESKI
EMPEROR ALEXIS
PALOTINS:[2] GYRON
          FESS
          DEXTER

CONSPIRATORS AND SOLDIERS
COMMON PEOPLE
MICHAEL FEDEROVITCH
NOBLES
MAGISTRATES
COUNCILLORS
FINANCIERS
SERVANTS OF PHYNANCE
PEASANTS
THE WHOLE RUSSIAN ARMY
THE WHOLE POLISH ARMY
MA UBU'S GUARDS
A CAPTAIN
A BEAR
THE PHYNANCE HORSE
THE DEBRAINING MACHINE
A SHIP'S CREW
THE SHIP'S CAPTAIN

1 Wenceslas] The real King Wenceslas (1361–1419) was a peace-loving but incompetent ruler of Bohemia; Jarry's source is more directly the "good King" of the Christmas carol.

2 Palotins] named *Giron, Pile* and *Cotice* in French. These names, and also *Bordure*, are heraldic terms referring to elements of a coat of arms. The English names used here are also heraldic terms. *Fess* is a band across the middle of a heraldic field (and *fesse* is the French word for buttock); *gyron* divides a coat of arms into parts (the name indicates the character's fate: he is cut in four); *pile*, a long, narrow, vertical triangle, is a phallic symbol; *bordure* is a border (and also evokes "ordure"—excrement). [*Tr. & Ed.*]

ACT I

SCENE I

Enter PA and MA UBU.

PA ABU: Shhheet.[3]

MA UBU: A nice way to talk, Pa Ubu; you're an arrant rogue.

PA UBU: Careful, or I'll bash your brains in, Ma Ubu.

MA UBU: It's not me, Pa Ubu, it's someone else you should assassinate.[4]

PA UBU: By my jolly green candle, I don't understand.

MA UBU: What do you mean, Pa Ubu; are you happy with your lot?

PA UBU: Sheet, madam, by my jolly green candle, of course I'm happy. I'm doing quite all right: captain of the dragoons, King Wenceslas' right hand man, decorated with the Order of the Red Eagle of Poland, and former King of Aragon; what more do you want?

MA UBU: What! After being King of Aragon, you're content to lead a few dozen lackeys armed with cabbage choppers, when you could be wearing the crown of Poland on your noggin?

PA UBU: What are you saying, Ma Ubu? I don't get it.

MA UBU: What a dummy!

PA UBU: By my jolly green candle, King Wenceslas is still alive; and even if he died, he has legions of children.

MA UBU: What's stopping you from butchering the lot and putting yourself in his place?

PA UBU: You dishonor me, Ma Ubu; watch it or you'll end up in the stewpot.

MA UBU: You poor fool, if I end up in the stewpot, who'll mend the seat of your pants for you?

PA UBU: So what? Don't I have a bum like any one else's?

MA UBU: If I were you, I'd want that bum to be sitting on a throne. You could be fabulously wealthy, eat all the sausage you like, and ride through the streets in a carriage.[5]

PA UBU: If I were King, I'd have a great parka built for myself like the one I had in Aragon until those Spanish buggers swiped it.

MA UBU: You could also get yourself an umbrella and a long raincoat down to your heels.

PA UBU: Ah, I yield to temptation. Crock sheet, sheet crock, if I ever run into him in a lonely corner of the forest, he'll have a bad time of it.[6]

MA UBU: That's it, Pa Ubu, now you're sounding like a real man.

PA UBU: Oh no! Me, Captain of the dragoons, assassinate the King of Poland? I'd rather die!

MA UBU: [*Aside.*] Oh, sheet! [*Aloud.*] So you'll stay as threadbare as a rat, Pa Ubu?

PA UBU: Jumpin' juniper, by my jolly green candle, I'd rather be ragged as a skinny, loyal rat than rich as a nasty fat cat.

MA UBU: And the parka? And the umbrella? And the long raincoat?

PA UBU: What of them, Ma Ubu? [*He exits, slamming the door behind him.*]

MA UBU: [*Alone.*] Fart sheet, he's a hard nut to crack, but fart sheet, I think I've shaken him. With God's help and my own, maybe in a week I'll be Queen of Poland. [*Exit MA UBU.*]

SCENE II

A room in PA UBU's house; there is a magnificently decked table. Enter MA and PA UBU.

MA UBU: Our guests are very late!

PA UBU: By my jolly green candle, that's right. And I'm starving. You're looking very ugly today, Ma Ubu. Is it because we're having company?

MA UBU: [*Shrugging her shoulders.*] Sheet.

PA UBU: [*Grabbing a roast chicken.*] Oh dear, I'm hungry. I'll have a bite of this bird. A chicken, I think. Not bad.

MA UBU: What are you doing, you wretch? What are our guests going to eat?

PA UBU: There'll be plenty. I won't touch anything else. Go to the window, Ma Ubu, and see if our guests are coming.

---

3 Shhheet] i.e., "shit," spoken in a drawl.

4 Cf. *Macbeth*, Act I.

5 sausage] An excremental and phallic symbol, this term unites three physical activities important to Ubu: eating, excreting and sex. [*Tr.*]

---

6 crock sheet] idiosyncratic profanities, as throughout the play.

MA UBU: [*Going.*] I don't see them.

PA UBU swipes a piece of veal.

MA UBU: Ah, here come Captain Bordure and his partisans. What's that you're eating, Pa Ubu? 15

PA UBU: Nothing; a bit of veal.

MA UBU: The veal! The veal! The veal! He's eaten the veal! Help!

PA UBU: By my jolly green candle, I'll tear your eyes out. 20

SCENE III

Enter CAPTAIN BORDURE and his partisans.

MA UBU: Good day, gentlemen; we couldn't wait for you to come. Sit down.

BORDURE: Good day, madam. Where is Pa Ubu?

PA UBU: Here I am, here I am! Crumps, by my jolly green candle, am I so easy to miss? 5

BORDURE: Good day, Pa Ubu. Sit down, men. [*They all sit.*]

PA UBU: Ouf, a little more, and I'd break the chair.

BORDURE: Have you got something good for us today, Ma Ubu? 10

MA UBU: Here's the menu.

PA UBU: Ah, I'm interested in this.

MA UBU: Polish soup, rastom chops, veal, chicken, dog paté, turkey pope's noses, Russian charlotte…

PA UBU: Oh, that's enough, isn't it? Is there any more? 15

MA UBU: [*Continuing.*] Ice pudding, salad, fruit, dessert, pablum, cauliflower a la sheet.

PA UBU: Hey, do you think I'm Emperor of the Orient to afford such a layout? 20

MA UBU: Don't listen to him; he's an idiot.

PA UBU: I'll sharpen my teeth on your shins.

MA UBU: Eat, Pa Ubu. Here's some Polish soup.

PA UBU: Crumps, it's awful.

BORDURE: You're right, it's not very good. 25

MA UBU: You bunch of Turks, what do you want?

PA UBU: [*Striking his forehead.*] Ah, I've got an idea. I'll be right back. [*He exits.*]

MA UBU: Gentlemen, have some veal.

BORDURE: It was very good; I've had enough. 30

MA UBU: Now for the pope's noses.

BORDURE: Exquisite! Exquisite! Long live Ma Ubu.

ALL: Long live Ma Ubu!

PA UBU: [*Coming back.*] And soon you'll be crying "Long live Pa Ubu." [*He has an unspeakable brush in his hand and throws it on the table.*][7] 35

MA UBU: What are you doing, you wretch?

PA UBU: Try that. [*Several taste it and fall down poisoned.*]

PA UBU: Ma Ubu, pass me the rastom chops, and I'll serve. 40

MA UBU: Here they are.

PA UBU: Everybody out! Captain Bordure, I want to talk to you.

OTHERS: But we haven't eaten. 45

PA UBU: What do you mean, you haven't eaten! Everybody out! Stay, Bordure. [*Nobody moves.*] Still here? By my jolly green candle, I'll brain you with rastom chops. [*He begins to throw pieces of rastom.*]

ALL: Oh! Ow! Help! Defend yourselves! Oh, damn! I'm done for! 50

PA UBU: Sheet, sheet, sheet. I said out!

ALL: Run for your lives! Damn Pa Ubu! Wretched blooming villain!

PA UBU: Ah, they've gone. Now I can breathe; but dinner was no good, I'm still hungry. Come, Bordure. [*They exit with MA UBU.*] 55

SCENE IV

Enter MA and PA UBU and BORDURE.

PA UBU: Well, Captain, how was your dinner?

BORDURE: Excellent, sir, except the sheet.

PA UBU: Ah, the sheet wasn't bad.

MA UBU: To each his own.

PA UBU: Captain Bordure, I've decided to make you Duke of Lithuania. 5

BORDURE: I thought you were stone broke, Pa Ubu.

PA UBU: In a few days, I could be King of Poland; it's up to you.

BORDURE: You're going to kill Wenceslas? 10

PA UBU: This guy's no slouch; he's figured it out.

BORDURE: If you're going to kill Wenceslas, count me in. I'm his mortal enemy, and I answer for my men.

PA UBU: [*Embracing him.*] Ah, I love you, Bordure. 15

7 brush] a toilet brush. [*Tr.*]

BORDURE: Oh, you stink, Pa Ubu. Don't you ever wash?

PA UBU: Rarely.

MA UBU: Never.

PA UBU: I'll step on your toes. 20

MA UBU: Lump of sheet.

PA UBU: Okay, Bordure, I've finished with you. But by my jolly green candle, I swear on Ma Ubu to make you Duke of Lithuania.

MA UBU: But… 25

PA UBU: Be quiet, my sweet.

They exit.

SCENE V

Enter MA and PA UBU and a messenger.

PA UBU: What do you want, sir? Buzz off, you're getting on my nerves.

MESSENGER: Sir, you are summoned by the King. [*Exit the messenger.*]

PA UBU: Oh sheet, garnidingdong, by my jolly green 5 candle, my plot's been discovered; I'll get my head chopped off. Oh dear, oh dear!

MA UBU: What a jellyfish! And time presses.

PA UBU: Ah, I've got an idea; I'll say it's Ma Ubu and Bordure. 10

MA UBU: P.U., you slob, if you do that…[8]

PA UBU: I'll go right now. [*He exits.*]

MA UBU: [*Running after him.*] Pa Ubu, Pa Ubu, I'll give you some sausage. [*She exits.*]

PA UBU: [*Off.*] Sheet! Sausage yourself. 15

SCENE VI

Enter KING WENCESLAS surrounded by his officers, BORDURE, the King's sons—BOLESLAS, LADISLAS, and BUGGERLAS. Then PA UBU.

PA UBU: [*Entering.*] It's not me, you know, it's Ma Ubu and Bordure.

KING: What's wrong with you, Pa Ubu?

BORDURE: He's drunk too much.

KING: Like me this morning. 5

PA UBU: I am a bit tipsy; it's because I drank too much French wine.

KING: Pa Ubu, I want to reward you for your many services as Captain of the dragoons; I am making you Count of Sandomir.[9] 10

PA UBU: Oh, Mr. Wenceslas, I don't know how to thank you.

KING: Don't thank me, Pa Ubu, but come tomorrow morning to the grand review.

PA UBU: I'll be there, but please accept this little 15 kazoo. [*He presents a kazoo to the KING.*]

KING: What am I to do with a kazoo at my age? I'll give it to Buggerlas.

BUGGERLAS: What a dumdum!

PA UBU: Well, I'm off. [*He falls as he turns around.*] 20 Oh, ow, help! By my jolly green candle, I've broken my gut and burst my bozo!

KING: [*Helping him up.*] Did you hurt yourself, Pa Ubu?

PA UBU: Darn right I did; I'm going to kick the 25 bucket. What'll become of Ma Ubu?

KING: We'll provide for her.

PA UBU: You're very kind. [*Exiting.*] Yes, King Wenceslas, but you'll be bumped off none the less. [*Exit all.*]

SCENE VII

PA UBU's house. Enter GYRON, FESS, DEXTER, MA and PA UBU, conspirators and soldiers, CAPTAIN BORDURE.

PA UBU: My friends, it's time to finalize our plans for the conspiracy. We want everyone's advice. I'll give mine first if you don't mind.

BORDURE: Go ahead, Pa Ubu.

PA UBU: My advice is simple: we'll poison the King 5 by putting arsenic in his lunch. When he chews his cud, he'll drop dead, and then I'll be king.

ALL: Oh, the slob.

PA UBU: What's wrong with that? All right, let's hear Bordure's advice. 10

BORDURE: My advice is to split him open from head to waist with a blow of the sword.

ALL: Yes, yes, that's brave, noble, valiant!

---

8 P.U.] i.e., Pa Ubu's initials (also an expression of distaste, as at a bad smell).

9 Sandomir] or Sandomierz, a region in the south of Poland.

PA UBU: And what if he kicks you? I remember now; for reviews he wears iron boots that really hurt. If I could, I'd go and denounce you to get myself out of this dirty business; I think he'd give me some money too.

MA UBU: Oh, the villain, the coward, the no-good scum.

ALL: Down with Pa Ubu.

PA UBU: Calm down everyone, if you don't want to end up in my knapsack. Still, I'm willing to expose myself for you. So Bordure, you'll look after splitting the King's skull.

BORDURE: Wouldn't it be better if we all rush him together, yelling and shouting? That way, we might rally the troops.

PA UBU: All right, here's what we'll do. I'll try and step on his toes; he'll resist; then I'll shout: "SHEET," and at the signal, you'll all jump him.

MA UBU: Yes, and as soon as he's dead, you'll grab his scepter and crown.

BORDURE: And I'll take my men and chase down the royal family.

PA UBU: Yes, and take special note of young Buggerlas.

They exit.

PA UBU: [*Running after them and bringing them back.*] Men, we forgot one thing: we've got to swear an oath to fight bravely.

BORDURE: How can we do that? We don't have a priest.

PA UBU: Ma Ubu will take his place.

ALL: Yes, yes, that'll be good.

PA UBU: You swear to kill the King?

ALL: Yes, we swear. Long live Pa Ubu! [*Exit all.*]

ACT II

SCENE I

The KING's palace. Enter WENCESLAS, QUEEN ROSAMUNDA, BOLESLAS, LADISLAS, and BUGGERLAS.

KING: Master Buggerlas, you were very rude this morning to Mr. Ubu, a knight in my service and Count of Sandomir. Accordingly, I forbid you to appear at the review.

QUEEN: But Wenceslas, you need your whole family to protect you.

KING: Madam, I never go back on my word. And I won't put up with any more of your whining.

BUGGERLAS: I shall obey, father.

QUEEN: Oh sire, will you really go to that review?

KING: Why not, madam?

QUEEN: I've already told you, I saw him in a dream, striking you with all his weapons and throwing you in the Vistula; then an eagle like the one on the Polish coat of arms placed the crown on his head.[10]

KING: Who?

QUEEN: Pa Ubu.

KING: What nonsense. Lord Ubu is a worthy gentleman, who would have himself drawn and quartered for me.

QUEEN: } What an error!
BUGGERLAS: }

KING: Be quiet, young ruffian. And you, madam, to show you how much I fear Mr. Ubu, I am going to the review just as I am—no sword, no weapon of any kind.

QUEEN: Fatal recklessness; I shall not see you again alive.

KING: Come Ladislas; come Boleslas.

They exit. The QUEEN and BUGGERLAS go to the window.

QUEEN: } May God and the great Saint
BUGGERLAS: } Nicholas watch over you.[11]

QUEEN: Buggerlas, come to the chapel with me to pray for your father and your brothers. [*Exit the QUEEN and BUGGERLAS.*]

SCENE II

The reviewing ground. Enter the Polish army, the KING, BOLESLAS, LADISLAS, PA UBU, CAPTAIN BORDURE and his men, GYRON, FESS, DEXTER.

KING: Noble Pa Ubu, I want you and your men beside me to inspect the troops.

---

10 Cf. Calpurnia in *Julius Caesar*, II.ii; Vistula] the largest river in Poland.

11 Saint Nicholas] patron saint of merchants, travelers, captives and schoolboys. [*Tr.*]

PA UBU: [*To his men.*] On guard, men. [*To the KING.*] Coming, sir, coming. [*PA UBU's men surround the KING.*]   5

KING: Ah, the regiment of the Danzig horse guard. How dashing they look.[12]

PA UBU: You think so? They look pretty measly to me. Look at this one. [*To the soldier.*] How long since you've had a bath, soldier?   10

KING: But this soldier is very clean. What's wrong with you, Pa Ubu?

PA UBU: There! [*He stomps on his foot.*]

KING: You wretch!

PA UBU: SHEET! Help me, men!   15

BORDURE: Hurray! Charge! [*All strike the KING; a Palotin explodes.*][13]

KING: Help! Holy Virgin, I'm dead.

BOLESLAS: [*To LADISLAS.*] What's going on? [*Drawing his sword.*] Draw your sword.   20

PA UBU: I've got the crown! Now for the others.

BORDURE: Get 'em boys!

The KING'S SONS flee; all pursue them.

SCENE III

The QUEEN and BUGGERLAS.

QUEEN: At last, I'm feeling easier.

BUGGERLAS: There's nothing to worry about.

A frightful clamor is heard off.

BUGGERLAS: Ah, what's this? My two brothers pursued by Pa Ubu and his men.

QUEEN: Oh heavens! Holy Virgin, they're losing ground.   5

BUGGERLAS: The whole army is following Pa Ubu. The King is nowhere to be seen. Oh horror! Help!

QUEEN: Boleslas has been killed! He took a bullet.

BUGGERLAS: Oh! [*LADISLAS turns.*] Defend yourself, Ladislas! Courage!   10

QUEEN: Oh, he's surrounded.

BUGGERLAS: He's done for. Bordure has cut him in two like a piece of salami.

---

12 Danzig] the German name for Gdansk, a Polish city.

13 Jarry's drawings portray the Palotins as inflatable rubber creatures. [*Tr.*]

QUEEN: Oh, the madmen are entering the palace; they're coming up the stairs!   15

The clamor grows louder.

QUEEN: ⎫ [*On their knees.*]
BUGGERLAS: ⎬ Oh God, protect us.

BUGGERLAS: Oh, that Pa Ubu! That no-good villain, if I had ahold of him…

SCENE IV

The door is broken down; PA UBU and the raging soldiers enter.

PA UBU: What would you do with me, Buggerlas?

BUGGERLAS: By God, I'll defend my mother to the death! The first one who takes a step is a dead man.

PA UBU: Oh Bordure, I'm afraid; let me out of here.

SOLDIER: [*Advancing.*] Surrender, Buggerlas.   5

BUGGERLAS: Here, you rogue, this is for you! [*He smashes his skull.*]

QUEEN: Stand firm, Buggerlas; stand firm!

OTHERS: [*Advancing.*] Buggerlas, we'll guarantee you your life.   10

BUGGERLAS: You scum, you winesacks, you mercenary villains!

He whirls his sword like a propeller and wreaks havoc.

PA UBU: I'll get the better of him yet!

BUGGERLAS: Mother, flee by the secret staircase.

QUEEN: But what of you, son?   15

BUGGERLAS: I'll follow.

PA UBU: Catch the Queen. There she goes. [*Exit the QUEEN, pursued by the soldiers.*] As for you, you wretch…! [*He advances on BUGGERLAS.*]

BUGGERLAS: Ah, thank God; here is my revenge! [*He slashes UBU's badong with a vicious blow of his sword.*] I'm coming, mother! [*He disappears down the secret staircase. Exit PA UBU.*]   20

SCENE V

A cave in the mountains. Enter young BUGGERLAS, followed by ROSAMUNDA.

BUGGERLAS: We'll be safe here.

QUEEN: Yes, I think so! Hold me, Buggerlas! [*She falls on the snow.*]

BUGGERLAS: What's wrong, mother?

QUEEN: I am not well, Buggerlas. I have no more than two hours to live.

BUGGERLAS: Has the cold got to you?

QUEEN: How can I resist so many blows? The King assassinated, our family destroyed, and you, an offspring of the noblest line that ever bore a sword, forced to flee to the mountains like a smuggler.

BUGGERLAS: And who is to blame, by God? Who is to blame? That vulgar Pa Ubu, an adventurer who crawled up from who knows where, vile scum, wretched tramp! And when I think that my father decorated him and made him a count, and the next day that villain was not ashamed to raise his arm against him.

QUEEN: Oh Buggerlas! When I remember how happy we were before Pa Ubu came along! And now, alas, all is changed!

BUGGERLAS: What do you expect? But let us not give up hope, and let us not abandon our rights.

QUEEN: That is for you, my dear child; I shall not see that happy day.

BUGGERLAS: What is wrong, mother? She is growing pale, she is falling; help! But I am in the wilderness! Oh God, her heart has stopped beating. She is dead! Is it possible? Another victim of Pa Ubu? [*He hides his face in his hands and weeps.*] Oh God, how sad to be all alone at the age of fourteen with a terrible vengeance to accomplish! [*He is overcome by the most violent despair.*]

The souls of WENCESLAS, BOLESLAS, LADISLAS, and ROSAMUNDA enter the cave; their ancestors accompany them and fill the cave. The oldest goes to BUGGERLAS and wakes him gently.

BUGGERLAS: Ah, what do I see? My whole family, my ancestors…What magic is this?

GHOST: Buggerlas, during my life, I was Lord Matthias of Koenigsberg, the first king and founder of the line. You must avenge us.[14] [*He gives him a huge sword.*] May this sword I give you now have no rest until it smites the usurper to death.

---

14 Cf. Richmond in *Richard III*, V.iii.

They all disappear; BUGGERLAS remains for a moment in an attitude of ecstasy before exiting.

SCENE VI

The palace of the KING. Enter MA and PA UBU, and CAPTAIN BORDURE.

PA UBU: No, I won't. No way! You want me to ruin myself for this trash?

BORDURE: But Pa Ubu, can't you see the people are expecting a gift to celebrate the new reign?

MA UBU: If you don't distribute food and gold, you'll be overthrown in two hours.

PA UBU: Food yes, gold no! Slaughter three old horses; that's good enough for scum like that.

MA UBU: Scum yourself! How did I get stuck with such an animal?

PA UBU: I've told you, I want to get rich, and I won't let go of one penny.

MA UBU: When you have all the treasures of Poland in your hands.

BORDURE: There's a huge treasure in the chapel; we can distribute it.

PA UBU: You wretch, if you do that…

BORDURE: But Pa Ubu, if you don't distribute anything, the people won't pay their taxes.

PA UBU: Is that true?

MA UBU: Yes, yes.

PA UBU: In that case, I agree. Get together three million, roast a hundred and fifty cows and sheep, and I'll have some too. [*They exit.*]

SCENE VII

The court at the palace full of people. Enter PA UBU wearing a crown, MA UBU, CAPTAIN BORDURE, and servants carrying platters of food.

PEOPLE: Here comes the King. Long live the King! Hurrah!

PA UBU: [*Throwing gold.*] Here, this is for you. I wasn't keen on giving you money, but Ma Ubu insisted. At least, promise to pay your taxes.

ALL: Yes, yes.

BORDURE: Look, Ma Ubu, how they're fighting over the gold. What a battle!

MA UBU: Horrible, isn't it? Peuh, that one's got his skull split open. 10

PA UBU: What a sight! Bring more chests of gold.

BORDURE: Why don't we have a race?

PA UBU: That's an idea. [*To the people.*] Friends, you see this chest of gold? It contains three hundred thousand in gold in good Polish coin. Those who 15 want to enter the race stand at the far end of the court. Start when I wave my handkerchief, and the first one here will get the chest. Those who don't win will have a consolation prize: this other chest will be shared among them. 20

ALL: Yay! Long live Pa Ubu! What a good king! We didn't see anything like this in the days of Wenceslas.

PA UBU: [*Gleefully to MA UBU.*] Listen to them.

The people line up at the far end of the court.

PA UBU: One, two three! Ready? 25

ALL: Yes, yes!

PA UBU: Go! [*They start with much shoving and stumbling. Cries and tumult.*]

BORDURE: Here they come, here they come!

PA UBU: The leader's losing ground. 30

MA UBU: No, he's pulling ahead.

BORDURE: Oh, he's lost, he's lost! It's over! It's the other one!

The one who was second finishes first.

ALL: Long live Michael Federovitch! Long live Michael Federovitch! 35

MICHAEL: Sire, I don't know how to thank your Majesty…

PA UBU: It's nothing, my friend. Take your chest home, Michael; and the rest of you share this other one; each take a coin till there's nothing left. 40

ALL: Long live Michael Federovitch! Long live Pa Ubu!

PA UBU: Friends, to dinner! Today the doors of the palace are open; come and do honor to my table!

PEOPLE: Let's go in, let's go in! Long live Pa Ubu! 45 The noblest of sovereigns!

They enter the palace. There is the sound of a great orgy, which lasts until the next day. The curtain falls.

ACT III

SCENE 1

The palace. Enter MA and PA UBU.

PA UBU: By my jolly green candle, here I am king in this country. I've already got indigestion, and they're going to bring me my great parka.

MA UBU: What is it made of, Pa Ubu? Royalty or not, we've still got to be economical. 5

PA UBU: Madam, my female, it's in lambskin with hook and harness in dogskin.

MA UBU: That's lovely, but it's even lovelier being royals.

PA UBU: Yes, you were right, Ma Ubu. 10

MA UBU: We owe a debt of gratitude to the Duke of Lithuania.

PA UBU: Who?

MA UBU: Why, Captain Bordure.

PA UBU: Please, Ma Ubu, don't talk to me of that 15 clown. Now that I don't need him any more, he can brush his belly all he wants, he's not getting his dukedom.

MA UBU: You're making a mistake, Pa Ubu; he'll turn against you. 20

PA UBU: Oh, I feel real sorry for the poor chap; I don't care about him any more than I do about Buggerlas.

MA UBU: And do you think you've heard the last of Buggerlas? 25

PA UBU: Sword of finance, of course I have! What can he do to me, a little squirt of fourteen?

MA UBU: Pa Ubu, mark my words. Try to win over Buggerlas by being good to him.

PA UBU: You want me to give away more money. Oh 30 no, not this time! You've already made me throw away twenty-two million.

MA UBU: Do as you like, Pa Ubu, he'll cook your goose.

PA UBU: Well, you'll be with me in the cooker. 35

MA UBU: Listen, young Buggerlas will win out in the end, I'm sure of it, because he has right on his side.

PA UBU: Hell, isn't wrong just as good as right? You're insulting me, Ma Ubu; I'm going to cut you into little pieces. 40

MA UBU runs away pursued by PA UBU.

SCENE II

The great hall of the palace. Enter MA and PA UBU,
officers and soldiers, GYRON, FESS, DEXTER, nobles in
chains, Financiers, Magistrates, and Bailiffs.

PA UBU: Bring the nobles' chest and the nobles'
hook, the nobles' knife and the nobles' book; then
have the nobles come forward.

The nobles are roughly pushed forward.

MA UBU: Please, Pa Ubu, control yourself.

PA UBU: I have the honor of informing you that to   5
add to the wealth of the kingdom, I'm going to
have all the nobles executed and take their money.

NOBLES: Horrors! Help! People, soldiers! Help!

PA UBU: Bring me the first noble and hand me the
nobles' hook. Those who are condemned to death   10
I'll push down the shaft; they'll fall into the Pork-
Pincer basement and the Treasure Chamber, where
they'll be debrained. [*To the noble.*] Who are you,
scum?

NOBLE: Count Vitebsk.[15]   15

PA UBU: How much are you worth?

NOBLE: Three million rixdals.[16]

PA UBU: Condemned! [*He takes the hook and pushes*
him down the shaft.]

MA UBU: What vile cruelty!   20

PA UBU: Second nobleman, who are you? [*The*
nobleman does not answer.] Will you answer, scum?

NOBLE: Grand-Duke of Posen.[17]

PA UBU: Excellent! Excellent! That's all I need to
know. Down the shaft. Third nobleman, who are   25
you? You have a nasty mug.

NOBLE: Duke of Courland, of the towns of Riga,
Revel, and Mitau.[18]

PA UBU: Good, good! Anything else?

NOBLE: Nothing.   30

PA UBU: Down the shaft then. Fourth nobleman,
who are you?

NOBLE: Prince of Podolia.[19]

PA UBU: What is your income?

NOBLE: I am ruined.   35

PA UBU: For talking so foully, down the shaft with
you. Fifth nobleman, who are you?

NOBLE: Margrave of Thorn, Palatine of Polock.[20]

PA UBU: That's not much. Nothing else?

NOBLE: It was enough for me.   40

PA UBU: Well, better a little than nothing at all.
Down the shaft. Why are you scowling, Ma Ubu?

MA UBU: You're too cruel, Pa Ubu.

PA UBU: Hey, I'm getting rich. I'm going to have MY list
of MY goods read. Bailiff, read MY list of MY goods.   45

BAILIFF: Earldom of Sandomir.

PA UBU: Start with the Princedoms, stupid!

BAILIFF: Princedom of Podolia, Grand Dukedom of
Posen, Dukedom of Courland, Earldom of
Sandomir, Earldom of Vitebsk, Palatinate of   50
Polock, Margraviate of Thorn.

PA UBU: And then?

BAILIFF: That's all.

PA UBU: What do you mean, that's all? Okay, bring
on the Nobles, and as I'll never stop getting richer,   55
I'll have all the Nobles executed, and then I'll have
all the vacant properties. Come on, down the shaft
with them. [*The nobles are piled into the pit.*] Hurry
up, faster; I want to make some laws now.

SEVERAL: Let's see what comes of this.   60

PA UBU: First I'll reform justice, and then we'll
proceed to finance.

MAGISTRATES: We oppose any changes.

PA UBU: First, magistrates will not be paid.

MAGISTRATES: What'll we live on? We're poor.   65

PA UBU: You'll get the fines you impose and the
goods of people condemned to death.

MAGISTRATE 1: Horrors.

MAGISTRATE 2: Infamy.

MAGISTRATE 3: Scandal.   70

MAGISTRATE 4: Indignity.

---

15 Vitebsk] or Vitsyebsk, a city in north-eastern Belarus.

16 rixdals] an invented currency.

17 Posen] or Poznan, a west-central province of Poland.

18 Courland] or Kurland, formerly a region on the Baltic
seacoast; Riga] now the capital of Latvia; Revel] now
called Tallinn, the capital of Estonia; Mitau] the capital
of Courland, now called Jelgava, a city in Latvia.

---

19 Podolia] a western Ukraine region.

20 Margrave] a military governor; Thorn] now Torun, in
northern Poland; Palatine] a feudal lord; Polock] or
Polotsk, city in Belarus.

ALL MAGISTRATES: We refuse to judge in conditions like that.

PA UBU: Down the shaft with the magistrates!

They resist in vain.

MA UBU: What are you doing, Pa Ubu? Now who'll   75
deliver justice?

PA UBU: I will. It'll be perfect, you'll see.

MA UBU: That'll be something to behold.

PA UBU: Shut up scumbag. And now, gentlemen,
we'll proceed to finance.   80

FINANCIERS: There's nothing to be changed.

PA UBU: What do you mean? I'm going to change
everything. First, I want to keep half the taxes for
myself.

FINANCIERS: Helps himself.   85

PA UBU: Gentlemen, we'll establish a tax of ten per
cent on property, another on commerce and
industry, a third on marriages, and a fourth on
deaths: fifteen francs a piece.

FINANCIER 1: That's crazy, Pa Ubu.   90

FINANCIER 2: It's absurd.

FINANCIER 3: It makes no sense.

PA UBU: Are you trying to make a fool of me? Down
the shaft with the financiers!

The financiers are dumped in.

MA UBU: What a king you are, Pa Ubu; putting   95
everybody to death.

PA UBU: Ah, sheet.

MA UBU: No more justice, no more finance.

PA UBU: Have no fear, my sweet; I'll go myself from
village to village to collect the taxes. [*Exit all.*]   100

SCENE III

*A peasant's house in the vicinity of Warsaw. Several
peasants are gathered.*

A PEASANT: [*Entering.*] News! News! The King is
dead the dukes too, and young Buggerlas has fled
to the mountains with his mother. What's more,
Pa Ubu has seized the throne.

2 PEASANT: I have more news. I've come from   5
Cracow, where I saw the bodies of more than three
hundred nobles and five hundred magistrates who
were killed, and it seems that taxes are going to

be doubled, and Pa Ubu is coming to collect them
himself.   10

ALL: Good God, what'll become of us? Pa Ubu is a
loathsome goon, and his family is an abomination.

A PEASANT: Listen, isn't that a knock at the door?

UBU'S VOICE: [*Off.*] Crockbadong! Open up, by my
sheet, by Saint John, Saint Peter and Saint Nicholas!   15
Open up, sabre of finance, crock finance, I've come
for the taxes! [*The door is broken down; PA UBU enters
followed by a legion of Money-Grabbers.*]

SCENE IV

PA UBU: Which of you is the oldest? [*A peasant steps
forward.*] What's your name?

PEASANT: Stanislas Leczinski.

PA UBU: Now listen to me, crockbadong, or these
fellows will cut off your ears. Are you going to   5
listen or not?

STANISLAS: But Your Excellency hasn't said anything
yet.

PA UBU: What do you mean? I've been talking for
an hour. Do you think I'm here to preach in the   10
wilderness?

STANISLAS: Never would such a thought cross my
mind.

PA UBU: Right, I've come to tell you, order you, and
inform you that you are to produce and exhibit   15
your finance at once, or else you'll be butchered.
Dastards of finance, roll up the vehicle of
phynance. [*The vehicle is brought.*]

STANISLAS: Sire, we're registered only for two
hundred and fifty-two rixdals, which we paid six   20
weeks ago on Saint Matthew's Day.

PA UBU: That may be, but I've changed the
government, and I had it put in the newspaper that
all taxes are to be paid twice, three times for those
that may be indicated later. With this system, I'll   25
soon make a fortune; then I'll kill everybody and
leave.

PEASANTS: Please, Mr. Ubu, have pity on us. We are
poor citizens.

PA UBU: I couldn't care less. Pay up.   30

PEASANTS: We can't; we have paid.

PA UBU: Pay up, or Ee'll dump you in my knapsack
after torture, unscrewing of the neck, and

decapitation! Crockbadong, I am the King, am I not?

ALL: All right, in that case, to arms! Long live Buggerlas, by the grace of God, King of Poland and Lithuania.

PA UBU: Forward, men of finance; do your duty.

Fighting breaks out, the house is destroyed, and old STANISLAS flees alone across the plain. PA UBU stays to collect the finance. Then all exit.

SCENE V

A blockhouse in the fortifications of Thorn. Enter CAPTAIN BORDURE in chains and PA UBU.

PA UBU: Well, well, citizen, so this is what it's come to; you wanted me to pay what I owed you; then you revolted because I didn't want to; you plotted against me, and now here you are in a bit of a jam. Crockfinance, this is good; so neatly done you must get a kick out of it yourself.

BORDURE: Take care, Pa Ubu. In the five days you've been king, you've committed more murders than it would take to damn all the saints in heaven. The blood of the King and the nobles cries vengeance, and the cries will be heard.

PA UBU: My friend, your tongue wags too much. If you escaped, I'm sure there'd be no end of complications, but the prison cells of Thorn have never released any of the honest chaps confined there. And so good night; I invite you to sleep on your two nears, though the rats here dance a pretty sarabande.

He exits. The turnkeys come and lock the doors, then exit.

SCENE VI

The palace in Moscow. Enter EMPEROR ALEXIS and his court, and BORDURE.

ALEXIS: Infamous adventurer, you participated in the death of our cousin Wenceslas?

BORDURE: Sire, pardon me, I was brought to it against my will by Pa Ubu.

ALEXIS: Detestable liar! Well, what do you want?

BORDURE: Pa Ubu had me imprisoned on the pretext that I plotted against him; I managed to escape, and I've ridden five days and five nights on horseback across the steppes to come and implore your gracious mercy.

ALEXIS: What have you brought as a token of your submission?

BORDURE: My adventurer's sword and a detailed map of the city of Thorn.

ALEXIS: I'll take the sword, but by Saint George, burn that map; I don't want to owe my victory to treachery.

BORDURE: One of Wenceslas' sons, young Buggerlas, is still alive; I'll do all I can to restore him to the throne.

ALEXIS: What was your rank in the Polish army?

BORDURE: I commanded the fifth regiment of dragoons of Vilna and a company of irregulars in the service of Pa Ubu.[21]

ALEXIS: Very well, I name you sub-lieutenant in the tenth regiment of Cossacks, and woe to you if you betray me. If you fight well, you will be rewarded.

BORDURE: I do not lack courage, Sire.

ALEXIS: All right, be gone.

Exit BORDURE and then the others.

SCENE VII

UBU's council chamber. MA and PA UBU and the councillors of phynance.

PA UBU: Gentlemen, the session is open; try to listen and keep still. First we'll do the finances; then we'll talk of a little system I've thought up to exorcize rain and have fine weather all the time.

COUNCILLOS: Very good, Mr. Ubu.

MA UBU: What a fool!

PA UBU: Watch it, madam sheet; I'm not putting up with any nonsense from you. As I was saying, gentlemen, the finances are not doing too badly. Tracking dogs with woolen socks take to the streets every morning, and the Dastards are doing marvels. Everywhere you can see burned houses and people bending under the weight of our phynances.

---

21 Vilna] or Vilnius, capital of Lithuania.

COUNCILLORS: What about the new taxes, Mr Ubu? How are they doing? 15

MA UBU: The pits. The tax on marriage has only produced eleven cents, even though Pa Ubu is hounding people everywhere to make them get hitched. 20

PA UBU: Sabre of finance, crock of my badong, madam financier, I have nears to talk with and you a mouth to hear me. [*Bursts of laughter.*] No, wait a minute! You've got me all mixed up, and you're the reason I'm stupid. But crock of Ubu! [*A* 25 *messenger enters.*] Oh now what? Scram, scum, or I'll bag you with decapitation and twisting of the legs. [*Exit the messenger.*]

MA UBU: And off he goes, but there's a letter.

PA UBU: Read it. Either I'm losing my mind or I 30 don't know how to read. Hurry up, villainess; it must be from Bordure.

MA UBU: That's right. He says the Czar has received him well, he's going to invade your states to restore Buggerlas, and you'll be killed. 35

PA UBU: Oh dear, oh dear! I'm afraid! I'm afraid! Ah, I'm going to die! Oh me, oh my, what will become of me? That mean man will kill me. Saint Anthony and all the saints, protect me, and I'll give you some phynance, I'll burn candles for you. Lord, 40 what will become of me? [*He weeps and sobs.*]

MA UBU: There's only one course to take, Pa Ubu.

PA UBU: What is that, my love?

MA UBU: War!!

ALL: Hurray! A noble scheme! 45

PA UBU: Yes, and I'll get hit again.

COUNCILLOR 1: Hurry, let's marshal the troops.

COUNCILLOR 2: And gather supplies.

COUNCILLOR 3: And prepare the artillery and the fortresses. 50

COUNCILLOR 4: And get money for the army.

PA UBU: Oh no you don't. Do you want to be rubbed out? I'm not giving any money. Before, I was paid to wage war, and now I have to wage it at my expense. No, by my jolly green candle, let's wage 55 war, since you're so keen on it, but without spending a red cent.

ALL: Long live war! [*Exit all.*]

SCENE VIII

A camp near Warsaw.

SOLDIERS & PALOTINS: Long live Poland! Long live Pa Ubu!

PA UBU: Ma Ubu, give me my breastplate and my little piece of wood. I'm going to be so weighed down I won't be able to walk if I'm chased. 5

MA UBU: What a coward!

PA UBU: Ah, there goes the sheetsword, and the finance hook won't stay in place!!! I'll never be ready, and the Russians are advancing; they'll kill me.

SOLDIER: Lord Ubu, the near scissors have fallen. 10

PA UBU: Ee'll butcher you with the sheethook and the facial knife.

MA UBU: How fine he looks with his helmet and breastplate: like a well-armed pumpkin!

PA UBU: Now I'll mount my horse. Gentlemen, bring 15 the phynance horse.

MA UBU: Pa Ubu, your horse won't be able to carry you. He hasn't eaten for five days, and he's on his last legs.

PA UBU: That's a good one! I have to pay twelve cents 20 a day for that nag, and he can't even carry me. Are you pulling my leg, crock of Ubu, or are you robbing me? [*MA UBU blushes and lowers her eyes.*] Bring me another animal then, but I'm damned if I'll go on foot, crockbadong! [*An enormous horse* 25 *is brought.*] I'll get on. Oh, wait till I'm seated! I'm going to fall! [*The horse starts moving.*] Stop him! Oh God, I'm going to fall off and kill myself!!!

MA UBU: What an imbecile! There he is on high! And there he is on the ground! 30

PA UBU: Physics crock, I practically killed myself! But never mind, I'm off to war, and I'm going to kill everybody. Woe to anyone who doesn't march in time. I'll put him in my knapsack, with twisting of the nose and teeth and extraction of the tongue. 35

MA UBU: Good luck, Mr. Ubu.

PA UBU: I forgot to tell you, I'm making you regent. But I have the finance book on me; too bad for you if you rip me off. I'm leaving Palotin Gyron to assist you. Goodbye, Ma Ubu. 40

MA UBU: Bye, Pa Ubu. Be sure and kill the Czar.

PA UBU: I will. I'll twist his nose and his teeth, extract his tongue, and insert the little piece of wood in his nears.

The army moves off to the sound of fanfares.

MA UBU: Now that tubby has gone, I'll get down to   45
business. I'll kill Buggerlas and grab the treasure
for myself. [*Exit MA UBU.*]

ACT IV

SCENE 1

The royal crypt in Warsaw Cathedral.

MA UBU: Now where is that treasure? There's no
hollow tile. I counted thirteen stones along the wall
from the tomb of Ladislas the Great, and there's
nothing. I've been given a bum steer. Ah, here's
something; this tile sounds hollow. To work, Ma   5
Ubu, to work. Pull up the stone. It won't budge.
I'll use the finance hook; just the thing. There!
There's the gold in with the bones of the kings.
Into our bag with it all! Oh! What's that noise?
Could there still be a living being under these   10
ancient vaults? No, it's nothing; let's be quick. I'll
take it all. It'll look better in daylight than here in
the tombs of old kings. Now back goes the stone.
Oh! That noise again. This place gives me the
creeps. I'll take the rest of the gold another time;   15
I'll come back tomorrow.
VOICE: [*Coming from the tomb of John Sigismond.*][22]
Never, Ma Ubu!

*MA UBU runs away in terror through the secret door,
carrying the stolen gold.*

SCENE II

*The central square in Warsaw. Enter BUGGERLAS and
his partisans, and a crowd of people and soldiers.*

BUGGERLAS: Forward to victory, my friend! Long
live Wenceslas and Poland! Pa Ubu, the old
blackguard, has gone; the only one left is that

---

22 John Sigismond] possibly a confusion of Sigismund III
Vasa, King of Poland (1566–1632), who *is* buried in
Warsaw, and either his contemporary, John Sigismund,
elector of Brandenburg (1572–1620) or John Sigismond,
King of Transylvania (d. 1571).

witch Ma Ubu with her Palotin. I'm ready to
march at your head, and we'll restore the race of   5
my forefathers.
ALL: Long live Buggerlas!
BUGGERLAS: We'll do away with all the taxes
imposed by Pa Ubu.
ALL: Hurray! Onward to victory! To the palace to   10
massacre that scum.
BUGGERLAS: There's Ma Ubu coming out on the
steps with her guards.
MA UBU: What do you fellows want? Oh, it's
Buggerlas!   15

The crowd throws stones.

GUARD 1: All the window panes are broken.
GUARD 2: Holy Saint George, I'm done for!
GUARD 3: Gadcrock, I'm dying!
BUGGERLAS: Throw stones, friends.
GYRON: Once more into the breach!   20

*He unsheathes his sword and rushes into the throng,
creating frightful carnage.*

BUGGERLAS: I'll take you on. Defend yourself, you
yellow belly!

They fight.

GYRON: Ah, I'm slain!
BUGGERLAS: Victory, friends! After Ma Ubu!

The sound of trumpets is heard.

BUGGERLAS: Here come the nobles! Let's catch that   25
harpy!
ALL: And then go and strangle the old bandit himself!

*MA UBU runs away pursued by all the Poles. Gunshots
and a hail of stones.*

SCENE III

The Polish army on the march in the Ukraine.

PA UBU: Judecrock, hamgad, gibbled flu, we'll never
survive; we're dying of thirst, and we're all tuckered
out. Sir Soldier, would you carry our finance
helmet, and you, sir Lancer, would you take the
sheet scissors and the physics stick to relieve us,   5
for, I repeat, we're all tuckered out.

The soldiers obey.

FESS: Isn't it strange, sir? No sign of the Russians.

PA UBU: Too bad the state of our finances doesn't permit a vehicle appropriate to our size. For fear of destroying our mount, we've made the entire journey on foot, pulling our horse by the bridle. When we're back in Poland, with our knowledge of physics and the enlightened help of our advisors, we'll invent a wind vehicle capable of transporting the whole army.

DEXTER: Here comes Nicolas Rensky in a great hurry.

PA UBU: What's up, lad?

RENSKY: All is lost, Sire. The Poles have revolted. Gyron has been killed, and Ma Ubu has fled to the mountains.

PA UBU: Bird of night, beast of doom, owl in gaiters, where did you dig up nonsense like that? A likely story! And who's responsible? Buggerlas, I bet. Where did you come from?

RENSKY: From Warsaw, My Lord.

PA UBU: Sheet-boy, if I believed you, I'd have the whole army turn round and go back. But you've got more feathers than brains, my lad, and you've been off in never-never land. Go to the advance stations, boy; the Russians are not far off, and we'll soon have to put our weapons to use: the sheet weapons, the phynance weapons, and the physics weapons.

LASKY: Pa Ubu, the Russians are in the plain.

PA UBU: That's right, the Russians! A pretty pickle I'm in. If only there was a way out, but there's not; we're on high ground, and we'll be exposed to attack on all sides.

ARMY: The Russians! The enemy!

PA UBU: All right, men, let's prepare for battle. We'll stay on top of the hill; only fools would try to go down. I'll take up position in the middle like a living citadel; the rest of you move in circles around me. Put as many bullets in your rifles as you can; eight bullets can kill eight Russians, and that's eight Russians I won't have on my back. We'll station the infantry at the foot of the hill to receive the Russians and kill them a bit, the cavalry at the rear to rush into the tumult, and the artillery around this windmill to fire into the throng. As for yours truly, we'll stay in the windmill and fire from the window with the phynance pistol; we'll bar the door with the physics stick, and if anyone tries to get in, let him watch out for the sheet hook!!!

OFFICERS: Yours orders will be executed, Sir Ubu.

PA UBU: Good, good, we'll be victorious. What time is it?

LASKY: Eleven o'clock in the morning.

PA UBU: Well, let's go and eat; the Russians won't attack before noon. General, tell the soldiers to ease themselves and to sing the Hymn to Finance.

LASKY exits.

SOLDIERS & PALOTINS: Long live Pa Ubu, our great financier! Ting, ting, ting; ting, ting, ting; ting, ting, tating!

PA UBU: What fine fellows! I adore them. [*A Russian cannonball smashes the arm of the windmill.*] Oh, I'm afraid; oh God, I'm dead! Wait, though, I'm not hit.

SCENE IV

Enter a CAPTAIN.

CAPTAIN: Sir Ubu, the Russians are attacking.

PA UBU: So? What do you want me to do about it? I'm not the one who told them to. Oh well, Men of Finance, let's get ready for battle.

LASKY: Another cannonball.

PA UBU: Oh, I can't take any more of this. It's raining lead, and our precious person could get damaged. Let's go down.

They all run down. The battle is engaged. They disappear in clouds of smoke at the foot of the hill.

RUSSIAN: [*Swinging his sword.*] For God and the Czar!

RESNKY: Ah, I'm dead.

PA UBU: Charge! Hey, you, just let me catch you, buster; you gave me a fright, you winebag, waving that dud of a shooting iron.

RUSSIAN: Oh, is that so? [*He fires a shot.*]

PA UBU: Ah! Oh! I'm hit, I'm wounded, I'm perforated, I'm administered, I'm dead and buried!

Oh, but wait. Aha, I've got him! [*He tears him apart.*] There! That'll take care of you!

LASKY: Forward, push on, to the other side of the trench. Victory is ours.

PA UBU: You think so? So far, I've got more bumps than laurels on my brow.

RUSSIAN CAVALRYMEN: Hurray! Make way for the Czar!

The CZAR arrives, accompanied by BORDURE in disguise.

A POLE: Oh lord, run for your lives! Here comes the Czar!

POLE 2: Oh God, he's crossing the trench.

POLE 3: Pif! Paf! Down go four slaughtered by that big lummox of a lieutenant.

BORDURE: You haven't had enough yet? Here's what you've been asking for, John Sobiesky! [*He knocks him senseless.*] Now for the rest! [*He massacres many Poles.*]

PA UBU: Forward, men! Catch that blighter! Make mincemeat of the Muscovites! Victory is ours. Long live the red eagle!

ALL: Forward! Hurray! Hamgad! Catch the big blighter!

BORDURE: But Saint George, I'm down.

PA UBU: [*Recognizing him.*] Ah, it's you, Bordure! Well, well! We're all so glad to see you again. I'm going to roast you over a slow fire. Men of Finance, light the fire. Oh! Ah! Ow! I'm dead. It's a cannonball at least that hit me. Oh God above, pardon me my sins. Yes, it was a cannonball.

BORDURE: It was a cap gun.

PA UBU: You're pulling my leg! Well, here's for you! Into my knapsack with you! [*He rushes at him and tears him apart.*]

LASKY: Pa Ubu, we're advancing on all sides.

PA UBU: So I see; I can't take any more, I've been kicked almost to death; I've got to sit down on the ground. Oh, my poor bottle!

LASKY: Go and take the Czar's, Pa Ubu.

PA UBU: Ah, I will. All right, sheet saber, do your thing, and you, finance hook, don't stay in the background. Let the physics stick put forth a noble effort and share with the little piece of wood the honor of massacring, gouging, and exploiting the Muscovite Emperor. And you, sir finance horse, charge! [*He rushes on the CZAR.*]

A RUSSIAN OFFICER: On guard, Majesty!

PA UBU: Here's for you, fellow! Oh! Ow! No, now! I beg your pardon, sir; don't you touch me. I didn't mean it! [*He runs away; the CZAR pursues him.*] Holy Virgin, that madman is running after me! What did I do, for heaven's sake? Uh-oh, there's still the trench to get across. I can feel him right behind, the trench in front! Courage! I'll close my eyes! [*He jumps over the trench; the CZAR falls in.*]

CZAR: I'm in for it now!

POLES: Hurray, the Czar is down!

PA UBU: Oh, I hardly dare look round. Ah, he's in it. Good, and they're hitting him. Come on, Poles, go to it. Wham, bam! Everybody take a turn; he's got a strong back, the villain. Oh, I don't dare look. But our prediction has come true; the physics stick performed miracles, and there's no doubt I would have killed him completely if a strange dread had not thwarted our courage and annulled its effects. But suddenly we had to turn tail, and if we were saved, it was only thanks to our ability as a horseman and to the solid hocks of our finance horse, whose swiftness is equaled only by his solidity, and whose lightness is legendary, and also the depth of the trench, which happened to be strategically located, under the feet of the enemy of the here present Master of Phynance. A lovely speech, but nobody's listening. Oh good grief, it's starting again!

The Russian dragoons make a charge and free the CZAR.

LASKY: This time it's a rout.

PA UBU: Ah, here's a chance to get away from the feet. All right, you Poles, forward! Or rather backward!

POLES: Run for your lives!

PA UBU: Let's get going. What a throng, what a stampede, what a multitude! How will I get out of this? [*He is jostled.*] Hey, you, watch it, or you'll experience the boiling valor of the Master of Finance. Ah, he's gone; let's get out of here, and quick, while Lasky doesn't see us. [*He leaves; then the CZAR and the Russian army can be seen pursuing the Poles.*]

SCENE V

A cave in Lithuania. It is snowing. Enter PA UBU, FESS, and DEXTER.

PA UBU: What a bitch of a day! It's enough to freeze the tail of the devil himself, and the Master of Finance is feeling the effects.

FESS: Well, Mr. Ubu, have you recovered from your terror and your running away?   5

PA UBU: Yes! I'm no longer afraid, but I still have the runs.

DEXTER: [*Aside.*] What a pig!

PA UBU: Ah, sir Dexter, how is your near?

DEXTER: As well as can be expected given the shape   10
it's in. The lead weighs it down, and I haven't been able to remove the bullet.

PA UBU: Serves you right! You were always eager to get your licks in at others. I demonstrated the greatest valor, and without placing myself in   15
danger, I massacred four of the enemy with my own hands, without counting all the ones who were already dead and whom we finished off.

DEXTER: Fess, do you know what happened to little Rensky?   20

FESS: He took a bullet in the head.

PA UBU: As the poppy and the dandelion, in the full flower of their youth are mown down by the cruel mow of the cruel mower, who cruelly mows their pitiful noggins, so was little Rensky a poppy; he   25
put up a good fight though; there were just too damn many Russians.

FESS: ⎱ Oh, sir!
DEXTER: ⎰

ECHO: Oh, shrr.

FESS: What's that? Let's take out our blades.   30

PA UBU: Oh no, a bunch of Russians again, I bet. I'm sick and tired of them! But it's simple; if they catch me, I'll stuff them in my knapsack.

SCENE VI

Enter a bear.

DEXTER: Oh, Lord of Finance!

PA UBU: Oh, look at the little doggie. What a cutie!

FESS: Watch out! A huge bear! My bullets!

PA UBU: A bear! Ah, the horrible beast! Oh, poor me,

I'll be eaten. God protect me! He's coming straight   5
for me. No, it's Dexter he's after. Ah, I can breathe again.

The bear rushes at DEXTER. FESS attacks him with his knife. UBU takes refuge on a rock.

DEXTER: Help! Fess, help me! Mr. Ubu, help!

PA UBU: Nothing doing; get out of your own jams, pal; we're saying our prayers just now. Each his   10
own turn to be eaten.

FESS: There, I've got him.

DEXTER: Keep it up, mate, he's letting go.

PA UBU: *Sanctificatur nomen tuum.*[23]

DEXTER: Damn coward!   15

FESS: Ah, he's biting me! Oh God, help me or I'm a goner.

PA UBU: *Fiat voluntas tua!*

DEXTER: I've wounded him.

FESS: Good, he's losing blood.   20

In the midst of the Palotins' cries, the bear bellows in pain, and UBU continues to mutter.

DEXTER: Keep hold of him while I get my exploding knuckles.

PA UBU: *Panem nostrum quotidianum da nobis hodie.*

FESS: Have you got him? I can't hold out any longer.   25

PA UBU: *Sicut et nos dimittimus debitoribus nostris.*

DEXTER: I've got him.

There is an explosion, and the bear falls dead.

FESS: ⎱ Victory!
DEXTER: ⎰

PA UBU: *Sed libera nos a malo.* Amen. So, is he good and dead? Can I come down from the rocks?   30

FESS: [*Scornfully.*] Whenever you like.

PA UBU: [*Climbing down.*] You can be proud of the fact that if you are still alive, and if you are still able to tread the snow of Lithuania, you owe it to the magnanimous virtue of the Master of Finance,   35
who strained, strove, and struggled to pour forth his pater nosters to save you, and who showed as much courage in wielding the spiritual sword of

---

23 *Sanctificatur ...*] "Hallowed be thy name"—the lord's prayer, in Latin.

prayer as you showed skill in manipulating the temporal exploding knuckles of the here present Palotin Dexter.[24] We even carried our devotion further, for we did not hesitate to ascend a tall rock so that our prayers would have a shorter distance to reach the heavens.

FESS: Disgusting ass.

PA UBU: That's one large animal. Thanks to me, you have something for supper. What a belly, gentlemen! The Greeks would have found more room in there than in the wooden horse, and we nearly went to verify its capacity with our own eyes.[25]

FESS: I'm starving. What is there to eat?

DEXTER: The bear!

PA UBU: My poor lads, are you going to eat it raw? We have no way to make a fire.

FESS: We have our gunflints.

PA UBU: That's right. And I think I see a little thicket over there; there should be some dry branches. Go and see, Master Dexter.

DEXTER walks off through the snow.

FESS: And now, sir Ubu, go and cut up the bear.

PA UBU: Oh no! He might not be dead. You're bitten and half eaten already; that's a job for you. I'll light the fire while we wait for him to bring some wood.[26]

FESS starts to cut up the bear.

Look out, he moved!

FESS: He's already cold.

PA UBU: Too bad; it would have been better to eat him warm. This will give the Master of Finance a stomach ache.

FESS: [*Aside.*] It's disgusting. [*Aloud.*] Give me a hand, Mr. Ubu; I can't do everything by myself.

PA UBU: I'm not doing a thing! I'm worn out.

DEXTER: [*Coming back.*] What snow! You'd think you were in Castile or at the North Pole. The light's starting to fade. In an hour it'll be dark. Let's hurry while we can still see.

PA UBU: Yes, you hear that, Fess? Get a move on. Both of you, get cracking. Put him on a spit and roast him; I'm hungry!

FESS: That's the last straw; you'll have to work, or you won't get a thing; you hear that, pig?

PA UBU: Doesn't matter to me; I'd just as soon eat it raw. And I'm sleepy!

DEXTER: What do you expect, Fess? Let's make dinner on our own. He won't get any, that's all. Or we can leave him the bones.

FESS: Right. Ah, the fire's roaring.

PA UBU: Ah, that feels good; it's warm now. But I see Russians everywhere. Oh lord, I've got to get away! Ah! [*He falls asleep.*]

DEXTER: I'd like to know if what Rensky said is true, if Ma Ubu has really been deposed. It's not impossible.

FESS: Let's finish making dinner.

DEXTER: No, we have more important things to discuss. It would be a good idea to investigate that news.

FESS: That's right, would it be better to stick with Pa Ubu or drop him?

DEXTER: Let's sleep on it. Tomorrow we'll see what's to be done.

FESS: No, it'd be better to take advantage of the dark to get away.

DEXTER: Let's go then.

They exit.

SCENE VII

PA UBU: [*Talking in his sleep.*] Ah, watch out, Mister Russian dragoon; don't fire over here, there are people. Ah, there's Bordure; how awful he looks; you'd think he was a bear.[27] And Buggerlas coming at me! The bear, the bear! Ah, he's down! My God but he's stiff! I won't do a thing! Get out of here, Buggerlas! You hear, you clown? And here come Rensky and the Czar! Oh, they're going to hit me! And the old lady! Where did you get that gold?

---

24 pater nosters] lord's prayers.

25 wooden horse] i.e., the horse in which the Greeks concealed themselves to invade Troy.

26 Lighting a fire while waiting for wood is a characteristic Ubuesque action; the laws of the physical world do not count. [*Tr.*]

---

27 The same actor played both Bordure and the bear.

You stole my gold, you bitch; you went digging 10
around in my tomb in Warsaw cathedral near the
Moon. I've been dead for ages; it's Buggerlas who
bumped me off, and I'm buried in Warsaw right
near Vladislas the Great[28] and also in Cracow near
John Sigismond, and also in Thorn in the 15
blockhouse with Bordure! There he is again. Get
away, you wretched bear. You look like Bordure.
You hear, beast from hell? No, he doesn't hear; the
Dastards have cut off his nears. Debrain, kevill, cut
off the nears, tear out the finances, and drink 20
yourself to death, that's the life of the Dastards,
that's the happy life of the Master of Finance.[29]
[*He stops talking and sleeps.*]

ACT V

SCENE I

It is dark. PA UBU *is sleeping.* MA UBU *enters without
seeing him. The darkness is complete.*

MA UBU: Safe at last! I'm all alone, nothing wrong with
that; but what a mad dash, crossing the whole of
Poland in four days! Besieged by every possible hardship. As soon as that blockhead cleared off, I go to
the crypt for the gold. Right after that I'm almost 5
stoned to death by Buggerlas and his maniacs. I lose
my escort, Palotin Gyron, who was so taken with
my charms he swooned with ecstasy whenever he
saw me, and even, they say, when he didn't see me,
which is the pinnacle of love. He'd have willingly 10
been cut in two for me, poor boy. The proof is he
was cut in four by Buggerlas. Pif, paf, poof! Ah, I
thought I was a goner. Then I take to my heels and
flee for my life, purused by an angry mob. I leave the
palace, arrive at the Vistula; all the bridges are guard- 15
ed. I swim across the river, hoping to escape my per-
secutors. Nobles gather from all parts and set off
after me. I was close to death a thousand times, surrounded by a throng of Poles bent on destroying me.
At last I evade their fury, and after four days walking 20

through the snowy fields of what was once my kingdom, I make it to this place of refuge. I've had nothing to eat or drink for four days. Buggerlas was close
on my heels...But at last I'm safe. Ah, I'm half dead
with cold and exhaustion. But I'd like to know what 25
happened to that big buffoon of mine, I mean my
most worthy husband. Did I filch his finances! Did
I rifle his rixdals! Did I make away with his moolah!
And his finance horse who was starving away; didn't
often see any oats, poor creature. What a strange 30
tale! But alas, I've lost my treasure! It's in Warsaw;
whoever wants to go and look for it can have it.

PA UBU: [*Waking up.*] Catch Ma Ubu, cut off her
nears!

MA UBU: Oh my God, where am I? I'm going crazy. 35
Oh lord no!
A vision from on high I've spied,
Pa Ubu snoring at my side.[30]
I'll suck up to him. Well, old fellow, did you sleep
well? 40

PA UBU: No, terribly. That bear was damn hard! The
voracious fought the curiacious and devoured them
completely, as you'll see when it's light; you hear,
noble Palotins?[31]

MA UBU: What's he going on about? He's crazier than 45
when he left.

PA UBU: Dexter, Fess, answer me, for sheet sake.
Where are you? Oh, I'm afraid. But somebody was
talking. Who was talking? Not the bear, I hope.
Sheet! Where are my matches? Oh, I lost them in 50
the battle.

MA UBU: [*Aside.*] I'll take advantage of the situation
and the dark; I'll pretend to be an apparition and
make him promise to pardon my pilfering.

PA UBU: Holy Saint Anthony, somebody's talking, 55
hang it.

MA UBU: [*Raising her voice.*] Yes, Mr. Ubu, some one
is talking, and the trumpet of the archangel, who
will raise the dead from their ashes and dust at the
end, would not speak any differently! Hear this 60

---

28 Vladislas] (1456–1516), King of Bohemia and Hungary,
son of Casimir IV, King of Poland.
29 kevill] an invented word: to kill in an Ubuesque way. The
French is *tudez* rather than *tuez*. [*Tr.*]

30 Cf. Racine's *Andromache* V.v.1627-8.
31 curiacious] In French, *vorace* (voracious) and *coriace*
(tough) make a play on words, alluding to Corneille's
tragedy *Horace*, in which the three Horace brothers fight
the three Curiace brothers. [*Tr.*]

severe voice. It is the voice of Saint Gabriel, who proffers good advice.

PA UBU: Oh my goodness!

MA UBU: Do not interrupt or I shall say no more, and it will be all up for you and your breadbasket. 65

PA UBU: Oh, my badong! I'll be quiet, I won't say another thing. Continue, Madam Apparition.

MA UBU: We were saying, Mr. Ubu, that you are a very fat fellow.

PA UBU: Very fat, that's true. 70

MA UBU: Be quiet, God dammit.

PA UBU: Oh, angels don't swear.

MA UBU: Sheet! [*Continuing.*] You are married, Mr. Ubu.

PA UBU: I am, to the vilest hag! 75

MA UBU: You mean to the most charming lady.

PA UBU: A horror. Talons everywhere; you don't know how to approach her.

MA UBU: With gentleness, sir Ubu; if you approach her that way, you will see that she is at least the equal of the Venus of Capua. 80

PA UBU: Kapooh-a to you-a too-a.

MA UBU: You are not listening, Mr. Ubu; please pay attention. [*Aside.*] I'll have to hurry; it's starting to get light. [*Aloud.*] Mr. Ubu, your wife is adorable and delightful; she doesn't have a single fault. 85

PA UBU: There's not a single fault she doesn't have.

MA UBU: Silence! Your wife has never been unfaithful to you.

PA UBU: Who'd fall in love with her? She's a hell-cat! 90

MA UBU: She doesn't drink!

PA UBU: Since I took away the key to the wine cellar. Before that, she was plastered by seven in the morning, and she perfumed herself with brandy. Now that she uses heliotrope she doesn't smell any worse.[32] Not that it makes any difference to me. Anyway, now I'm the only one who's well oiled! 95

MA UBU: [*Aside.*] Pompous ass! [*Aloud.*] Your wife doesn't steal your gold.

PA UBU: No, that's funny! 100

MA UBU: She doesn't lift a penny!

PA UBU: What about our noble and unfortunate phynance horse, who wasn't fed for three months and for the whole campaign had to be dragged

---

[32] heliotrope] a fragrant flower.

across the Ukraine by his bridle? Died in the effort, poor creature! 105

MA UBU: That's all a pack of lies! Your wife is a model, and you, you're nothing but a monster!

PA UBU: It's the straight truth. My wife is a scoundrel, and you, you're nothing but a fool! 110

MA UBU: Take care, Pa Ubu.

PA UBU: Oh, that's right, I forgot who I was talking to. No, I didn't say that!

MA UBU: You killed Wenceslas.

PA UBU: That's not my fault. It was Ma Ubu who wanted me to. 115

MA UBU: You had Boleslas and Ladislas put to death.

PA UBU: Too bad! They wanted to hit me.

MA UBU: You didn't keep your promise to Bordure, and then you killed him. 120

PA UBU: So that I'd be ruler in Lithuania, not him. For the moment it's neither one of us. So you see it's not my fault.

MA UBU: There is only one way you can be pardoned for all your misdeeds. 125

PA UBU: What's that? I'm ready to be a holy man; I want to be a bishop and see my name on the calendar.

MA UBU: You must pardon Ma Ubu for taking a little of your money. 130

PA UBU: Aha! I'll pardon her when she's given it all back, when she's had a good licking, and when she's brought my finance horse back to life.

MA UBU: He's obsessed with that horse! Oh, I'm in for it now, the sun's coming up. 135

PA UBU: Well anyway, I'm glad to know for sure that my dear wife was stealing from me. Now I have it from a reliable source. *Omnis a Deo scientia*, which means *Omnia*, all; *a Deo*, knowledge; *scientia*, comes from God. That's the explanation of the phenomenon. But the apparition's been rather quiet. Too bad I can't offer her any refreshment. What she was saying was very interesting. Ah, it's light! Oh lord, by my finance horse, it's Ma Ubu. 140

MA UBU: [*Boldly.*] That's not true; I'll excommunicate you. 145

PA UBU: You bitch!

MA UBU: What a way to talk!

PA UBU: That's the last straw. I can see it's you, you vixen! What the devil are you doing here? 150

MA UBU: Gyron is dead, and the Poles were after me.

PA UBU: The Russians were after me. The cream ends up together.

MA UBU: Say rather that the cream sometimes ends up with a slob! 155

PA UBU: Oh? Well now it's going to end up with a quadrupole.[33] [*He throws the bear at her.*]

MA UBU: [*Falling under the weight of the bear.*] Oh good lord, argh! Oh, I'm dying! I'm smothering! It's biting me! It's gobbling me up! It's digesting 160 me!

PA UBU: It's dead, you fool! But actually, maybe it's not! Oh lord, no, it's not, let's get out of here! [*Climbing back on his rock.*] *Pater noster qui es...*

MA UBU: [*Getting free.*] Hey, where's he gone? 165

PA UBU: Oh lord, there she is again! There's no way of getting rid of her, it seems. Is the bear dead?

MA UBU: Of course, you ass; it's stone cold. How did it get here?

PA UBU: [*Confused.*] I don't know. Oh yes, I know! 170 It tried to eat Fess and Dexter, and I killed it with a pater noster.

MA UBU: Fess, Dexter, pater noster? What's that nonsense? My financier's gone round the bend!

PA UBU: What I said is just the way it was! And you 175 are an idiot, my gargoyle!

MA UBU: Tell me about your campaign, Pa Ubu.

PA UBU: No, it'd take too long. All I know is that in spite of my undeniable valor, everybody hit me.

MA UBU: What, even the Poles? 180

PA UBU: They cried: "Long live Wenceslas and Buggerlas." I thought they were going to draw and quarter me. The maniacs! And then they killed Rensky!

MA UBU: I couldn't care less! You know that 185 Buggerlas killed Palotin Gyron!

PA UBU: I couldn't care less! And then they killed poor old Lasky!

MA UBU: I couldn't care less!

PA UBU: Now just a minute. Come here, scum! Kneel 190 before your master; [*He grabs her and throws her to the ground.*] you're going to undergo the ultimate torture.

---

33 quadrupole] Ubu confuses this word with quadruped. [*Tr.*]

MA UBU: Oh, oh, Mr. Ubu!

PA UBU: Oh, oh, oh, that's enough out of you. I'll 195 begin: twisting of the nose, tearing out of the hair, insertion of the little piece of wood in the nears, extraction of the brain through the nankles, laceration of the posterior, partial or even total suppression of the spinal marrow (if only that 200 would get rid of the spines in her character), without forgetting the opening of the swim bladder, and last but not least, a reenactment of the grand beheading of Saint John the Baptist, all taken from the Holy Scriptures, both Old and 205 New Testaments, ordered, corrected, and perfected by the here present Master of Finance! How does that suit you, clot? [*He tears her apart.*]

MA UBU: Have pity, Mr. Ubu!

A great commotion is heard at the entrance to the cave.

SCENE II

BUGGERLAS rushes into the cave with his soldiers.

BUGGERLAS: Onward, men! Long live Poland!

PA UBU: Now wait just a minute, Mister Pollack. Wait till I've finished with my other half!

BUGGERLAS: [*Striking him.*] Take that, you yellow belly, you lump of jelly, you pervert, you rogue, 5 you scoundrel, you heathen!

PA UBU: [*Fighting back.*] Take that, you piddly Pole, you old bunghole, you bum, you crumb, you slimy scum, you itch, you twitch, you son of a bitch, you rake, you snake, you belly ache! 10

MA UBU: [*Hitting him as well.*] Take that, you noxious brew, you kangaroo, you tit, you toad, you antipode!

The soldiers rush at the UBUS, who defend themselves as well as they can.

PA UBU: God, what a fiasco!

MA UBU: Watch out, you Poles, we've got feet, you 15 know.

PA UBU: By my jolly green candle, will there never be an end to this? Another one! Ah, if only I had my phynance horse!

BUGGERLAS: Keep at them! 20

VOICES OUTSIDE: Long live Pa Ubu, our great

financier!

PA UBU: Ah, there they are! Hurray! There are the Pa Ubus! Come on! This way, Men of Finance! Just in the nick of time! 25

The Palotins rush into the melee.

DEXTER: To the entrance, Poles!

FESS: We meet again, Mister Finance. Forward! Charge! Try to make it to the entrance; once we're outside, we can take to our heels.

PA UBU: Ah, that's my specialty! Look at him swing 30 that sword!

BUGGERLAS: Ah, I'm hit!

STANISLAS: It's nothing, sire.

BUGGERLAS: No, I'm only dazed.

JOHN SOBIESKI: Keep fighting; they're reaching the 35 entrance, the beggars.

DEXTER: We're making headway. All together now. I can see the sky.

FESS: Keep your courage up, Sir Ubu!

PA UBU: Oh, I'm pooping my pants. Forward, 40 crockbadong! Kevill, bleed, skin, massacre, crock of Ubu! Ah, the fighting's dying down.

DEXTER: There are only two left guarding the entrance.

PA UBU: [*Knocking them over the head with the bear.*] 45 There's one and there's two! Oof, outside at last! Let's get out of here! Follow me, gang, on the double! [*Exit all.*]

SCENE III

The province of Livonia, covered in snow.[34] *Enter the UBUS and their followers in flight.*

PA UBU: I think they've given up trying to catch us.

MA UBU: Yes, Buggerlas has gone to have himself crowned.

PA UBU: I don't envy him his crown.

MA UBU: You're right, Pa Ubu. 5

They disappear into the distance.

---

34 Livonia] a region on the eastern coast of the Baltic Sea, north of Lithuania.

SCENE IV

The deck of a ship sailing on the Baltic. PA UBU and his band are on deck.

CAPTAIN: Ah, a fine breeze!

PA UBU: Yes, we're moving at quite a clip. We must be doing at least a million knots an hour, and these knots have one advantage: once done, they never come undone. It's true that the wind is at our 5 backs.

FESS: What an imbecile!

A gust of wind blows the ship over on its side.

PA UBU: Oh lord, we're capsizing. Your boat's going screwy; it's going to fall over.

CAPTAIN: Everyone to the leeward, haul on the 10 foresail!

PA UBU: No, no! Don't all go to the same side! That's dangerous. What if the wind changes direction? Everybody'd be in the drink, and we'd be eaten by fish. 15

CAPTAIN: Lie to, keep it tight!

PA UBU: Oh no, no lying down on the job; this is time for action, not slacking off. It's your fault, Captain, if we don't make good time. We should have been there by now. Oh, I'll take command 20 myself then! Prepare to turn! It's in God's hands. Heave ho, turn to the wind, turn before the wind. Hoist the sails, pull them taut, helm up, helm down, helm to the side. You see, there's nothing to it. Take the waves broadside, and we'll be fine. 25

All are doubled up with laughter; the breeze picks up.

CAPTAIN: Strike the jib; put a reef in the topsail!

PA UBU: Good, good. You hear, Sir Crew? Strike a jig, cook some beef, and topple.

People kill themselves laughing. A big wave comes.

PA UBU: What a deluge! The result of our manoeuvres.

MA UBU: ⎱ A delightful activity navigation! 30
FESS: ⎰

A second wave comes.

FESS: [*Drenched.*] Beware of Satan with his pumps and vanities.

PA UBU: Sir boy, bring us something to drink.

[V.iv]

All prepare to drink.

MA UBU: Just think, soon we'll be back in sweet France, with our old friends and our castle of Mondragon![35]

PA UBU: Yes, it won't be long now. We're just coming under Elsinore castle.[36]

FESS: I feel rejuvenated at the thought of seeing my dear Spain again.

DEXTER: Yes, and we'll dazzle our compatriots with tales of our wonderful adventures.

PA UBU: I suppose so. And I'll get myself named Master of Finance in Paris.

MA UBU: That's right. Oh, what a jolt!

DEXTER: It's nothing; we've just rounded the point of Elsinore.

FESS: And now our sturdy vessel is bounding at full speed over the dark waves of the North Sea.

PA UBU: A wild and inhospitable sea that bathes the land called Germania, which got its name because all the inhabitants had German measles.

MA UBU: Now that's what I call erudition. They say it's a beautiful country.

PA UBU: However beautiful it is, it can't hold a candle to Poland. If there weren't a Poland, there would be no Poles!

The end.

---

[35] Mondragon] an inland town in the Rhone valley, in the south of France.

[36] Elsinore castle] Hamlet's home, in Denmark.

CHAPTER SIX

The Twentieth Century: Modernism and After

The development of theatrical realism was the nineteenth century's lasting legacy to the twentieth. Reaffirmed first by the proliferation of photography and then by the growth of the motion picture industry, realism quickly passed from being regarded as a shocking innovation to the status of the aesthetic norm from which all other stylistic variations were considered to be self-conscious departures. Rightly or wrongly, and however vaguely defined, realism came to inform the critical standards by which theatre was most often judged, and the challenges presented by realism were soon absorbed into the heart of theatrical training in virtually all disciplines.

Take acting, for example. An actor standing downstage-centre, declaiming poetic text in front of an abstract or obviously artificial backdrop, might employ a highly refined lexicon of theatrical gesture without ever needing to seem "natural," and might be quite effective nevertheless; but an actor moving within and interacting with a realistic set while speaking relatively realistic text confronts a greater necessity of appearing to be a "natural" creature within this environment. Accordingly, in 1906, after several years of experience with the new realistic theatre, Konstantin Stanislavski, the artistic director of the Moscow Art Theatre, began to develop the systematic approach to the problems of modern acting that still forms the basis of most actor training in Western theatre today. Stanislavski recognized the enormous difficulty for the actor of achieving a sense of authenticity night after night, especially in the intimate proximity to the audience inherent in the smaller, non-commercial theatres which were at the leading edge of the reform of dramatic literature. The problem, Stanislavski believed, was best approached not by actors striving to manipulate outward appearances—a crude form of deception that, he felt, must inevitably become fatiguing and false—but by creating an approximately authentic emotional life for the characters by focusing on their internal motivations within the context of the specific circumstances given by the play. It seems clear in retrospect that Stanislavski's approach to acting was part of a whole new climate of opinion—one that included the psychoanalytic theories of Sigmund Freud (whose landmark work, *The Interpretation of Dreams*, was published in 1900). To be sure, like Freud, Stanislavski remains a controversial figure; there are few acting teachers today who adopt the original Stanislavski system in an unadulterated form (a system which, in any case, even he was continually revising). Nevertheless, just as Freud's basic postulate of the unconscious has been almost universally embraced despite objections to specific theories, in the case of Stanislavski there is a widespread recognition that, whatever the worth of any given individual solution he advanced, his embrace of the central questions facing modern actors is nearly encyclopedic and that therefore his thinking should remain at least the starting point in the performance of realistic plays.

Yet if realism became, to a large extent, the tacitly agreed upon aesthetic standard, its existence certainly did not beget conformity. On the contrary, over the course of the twentieth century, virtually every aspect of realism—and indeed, every recognizable theatrical convention of any kind—was challenged by new theatrical approaches. In the first decades of the century it became evident, in the theatre as elsewhere in art, that the very spirit of scientific investigation out of which many of the advances in realism had arisen was generating a tendency toward experimentation that might easily reach *beyond* realism. And out of this impatient spirit of experimentation there ultimately arose a much broader lexicon of theatrical expression than any commitment to realism could have achieved.

Some early departures from realism were barely discernible at the time. For example, Anton Chekhov, whose plays received productions at the hands of the the Moscow Art Theatre that were regarded as milestones of theatrical realism, nevertheless infused these plays with poetry and symbolism in a way that was not always fully understood, even by those who performed them. In Chekhov's letters, and in comments made by the young actor-director Meyerhold, we find references to Stanislavski's shortcomings as a director—not because he was unable to achieve a realistic *mise en scène*, but because the very single-mindedness of his commitment to realism tended to ride roughshod over the more delicate elements of Chekhov's work. In *The Cherry Orchard,* these include the symbolism of the orchard and the sound of the breaking string, both of which lie outside the realist's mandate of empirically documenting ordinary life.

Bernard Shaw presents a comparable case. There is no doubt that Shaw had a profound affinity for the social realism of Ibsen: he was inspired by it to write *The Quintessence of Ibsenism*, one of the first important studies of the Norwegian playwright, and he energetically promoted the first English productions of Ibsen's plays. But in most of his own works, Shaw resisted the bonds of strict realism—as indeed did Ibsen himself, who, despite the realistic plays of his middle career which made his international reputation, always saw himself as a poet: his earliest plays were written in verse and his last plays are explicitly symbolic. Shaw's affinity for Shakespearean romance and his interest in melodrama and light comedy seem to have exerted a sort of gravitational pull away from realism. In *Major Barbara*, for example, we see Shaw borrowing liberally from the conventions of melodrama and, in the third act, creating a fantastic setting that has at least as much to do with the wish-fulfillment of romance as it does with hard-headed political analysis.

Few efforts to move theatre in a non-realistic direction were as moderate as Chekhov's and Shaw's. In the culture leading up to and following the First World War, there was a great impatience to throw off the yoke of tradition and create new forms of art for a new machine age. One of the most important movements to emerge in the first two decades of the century was Expressionism. The movement began in painting, where the term was used to distinguish the style from Impressionist works. Expressionist paintings were ones in which the artist *expressed* an often incoherent inner emotional experience rather than recording *impressions* of light playing upon the external world. In a sense, then, the movement can be seen to have had its origins in the same Freudian (or quasi-Freudian) ideas upon which realism itself had drawn. Expressionist drama was most common in Germany, where it often depicted the violent rebellion of young men against an oppressive patriarchy and their disavowal of its values. The theme is evident, for example, in Strindberg's *Ghost Sonata*, which, while not altogether typical, is certainly one of the most influential of all Expressionist plays. Strindberg's bizarre depiction of a turbulent inner life beneath a staid bourgeois exterior drew the attention of, and was embraced by, many subsequent playwrights. The Expressionist movement affected not only dramatic form, but also theatrical technique, for the plays made novel demands of the stage in calling for a strong dream-like control of atmosphere, spatial and temporal distortions, and the depiction of nightmarish visions.

Two movements that were related to German Expressionism, though based chiefly in France, were Dada and Surrealism. The Dada movement shared the same violent impulse toward overthrowing the past that characterized Expressionism, but departed even further from tradition in celebrating nonsense and randomness in an often aggressively confrontational manner that owed much to the work of Alfred Jarry. Surrealism, on the other hand, attempted to go beyond realism by representing the content and peculiar logic of the unconscious. As such, it shared features with both Expressionism and Dada, but was more firmly aligned with psychoanalytic theory and also with Marxism, for the Surrealists saw in Marx's ideas about the liberation of the proletariat from economic oppression a counterpart to the liberation of repressed unconscious material sought after by psychoanalysis.

Other alternatives to realism arose not out of conscious programs of resistance, but simply because they originated in different sources. A good example is the musical—arguably the most popular and certainly the most lucrative theatrical genre of the century. Of course, there is an inherent problem in trying to represent the musical in an anthology such as this one. While the scripts of most dramatic works, for better or worse, are able to some degree to stand alone as literature, the "book" of a musical almost always seems a poor thing when bereft of its score. Accordingly, we have not included any musicals in this anthology, but a few words about the genre are in order. From various nineteenth-century sources such as burlesque, pantomime, melodrama, and operetta, the American musical gradually developed from a sketch-based comic diversion into a unified, ambitious work of art. Some of the milestones in its development were provided by Jerome Kern's *Showboat* (1927), which used American styles of popular music to tell a serious story; Mark Blitzstein's *The Cradle Will Rock* (1938), an attack on capitalism; Rodgers and Hammerstein's *Oklahoma* (1943), which included a murder and a dream ballet; Lerner and Lowe's *My Fair Lady* (1956), which, using Bernard Shaw's *Pygmalion* as a source, made greater acting demands on the performers than had been made in any musical to that point; Bernstein and Sondheim's *West Side Story* (1957), which retold *Romeo and Juliet* using a complex jazz-influenced score; and Bock and Harnick's *Fiddler on the Roof* (1964), a story about the pogroms faced by East European Jews, featuring a score inspired by Ashkenazi klezmer music. While some of the most popular musicals of recent years have been written by Europeans—for example, *Cats* (1981) and *Phantom of the Opera* (1986) by Britain's Andrew Lloyd Webber, and *Les Misérables* (1980) by France's Claude-Michel Schönberg—the genre is still mainly associated with the United States. Indeed, most musical theatre scholars agree that the most important contribution to the art in the last several decades has been made by Stephen Sondheim, whose brilliant and often controversial works have included such landmarks as *A Little Night Music* (1973), *Sweeney Todd* (1979), *Sunday in the Park With George* (1984), *Into the Woods* (1986), and *Assassins* (1990).

When one considers the proliferation of theatrical styles mentioned above, and considers that these styles emerged alongside a widespread revival of works from the classical repertoire, there is little wonder that one of the most significant developments in twentieth-century theatre was the rise of the director. Whereas, in earlier periods, the broad acceptance of a limited range of theatrical conventions and resources had left little scope for directorial input, the vastly expanded resources and stylistic range of twentieth-century theatre began to make a director's contribution seem ever more essential. A good example of the creative collaboration between director and playwright is Orson Welles's 1941 production of *Native Son*, a play by Richard Wright and Paul Green based on Wright's novel. For this production, Welles drew on some of the theatrical devices associated with Expressionism—a haunting sound-scape, a suggestive, non-realistic lighting design, and a seamless flow of action from one setting to the next—but he also drew on many of the mechanical set-changing devices developed for commercial Broadway musicals, such as *Ziegfeld's Follies*. Welles deftly controlled shifts in the production from scenes of gritty realism to scenes saturated with the protagonist's paranoid imagination, thereby representing psychological aspects of Wright's novel that could not have been captured on stage through dialogue alone.

A similar case is presented by Bertolt Brecht, who directed the first productions of most of his plays. Like Richard Wright, Brecht had strong Marxist sympathies, but because he was primarily a man of the theatre and only secondarily a novelist, he expended a great deal of effort on devising a theatrical style suited to politically enlightening his audiences. At the beginning of his career in Germany, Brecht had come into extensive contact with the Expressionist theatre, which had prompted him to observe that, while watching an effect intended to induce a particular emotional state, he often found himself critically assessing the means by which the effect was achieved. This realization was an important step in Brecht's development of his *verfremdungseffekt*, or "alienation effect" theory, which asserted that the theatre should not strive to carry the viewers away in unreasoned emotion, but should rather allow them to maintain a critical distance from which they can form a rational opinion about what they are being shown. Accordingly, Brecht intentionally exposed the mechanisms of theatrical production to the audience as a way of reminding them that what they were seeing was not an objective, unalterable fact but rather a constructed point of view. As is evident in *The Caucasian Chalk Circle*, Brecht also borrowed freely from non-Western traditions—perhaps partially as a result of the influence of director Max Reinhardt, with whom Brecht had worked in Berlin, and who had vastly expanded the stylistic range of German theatre, not only by staging plays drawn from many periods and cultures, but also by reworking the theatrical conventions appropriate to each. While Brecht did not possess quite so wide a range as Reinhardt, he became an omnivorous devourer of theatrical ideas, and thus maximized the flexibility of the style he created for himself. Today, while Brecht's passion for politics remains as clear and galvanizing as ever, he is admired at least as much for his vivid grasp of style.

One of the most important factors in considering the development of last century's theatre is, of course, the growth of film and television. The relationships between these media and the theatre are extensive and complex, and include matters ranging from the competition for audiences through to intriguing shifts in content. For instance, one striking development is the way in which the configuration of character that had been typical of theatrical melodrama was appropriated by Hollywood and simultaneously abandoned by drama. The clearly identifiable villain who drove the plot on the nineteenth-century stage is now often seen in action films, whereas in modern drama, villainy has largely been internalized. While a protagonist may still have external enemies, the more important obstacles usually have to do with a schism within the protagonist's own personality—with "inner demons," so to speak.

This internalization is evident, for example, in Tennessee Williams's *Cat on a Hot Tin Roof*. While the play is often casually called a "melodrama," it is clear that Brick and Maggie are not innocent victims; that Big Daddy, who may appear to be a villain at first, actually shares a common cause with Brick; that Gooper and Mae are not finally very substantial adversaries; and that the chief problems Brick and Maggie face are lodged within their own lives and choices. In fact, if one had to choose the single most common theme found in the drama of the twentieth century, it would be the struggle to maintain a strong sense of personal agency—the ability to enact one's own wishes in the world as an integrated and autonomous being. It would appear that, as playwrights became ever more aware of all the sociological, economic, psychological and biological forces that determine human behaviour, they grew ever more likely to see their characters' dilemmas in terms of the difficulty of achieving coherent self-knowledge and taking decisive action. (It is perhaps little wonder that Hamlet is the most popular Shakespearean character of the modern age.) In Williams's work, we see that it is the characters least afflicted with self-consciousness that emerge the most negatively (e.g., Gooper in *Cat on a Hot Tin Roof*). Their simplicity represents a sort of brutal threat to the more sensitive characters, though it is clear that the chief threat facing the latter is the disintegration of identity.

Where characters are unable to attain a sense of personal agency and remain instead trapped in an atmosphere of determinism, the results are catastrophic. We see versions of such a scenario in two very different plays, Samuel Beckett's *Play* and Michel Tremblay's *Les Belles Soeurs*. While the first play appears to be a fantastic depiction of a kind of existential hell, and the second is ostensibly set within a realistic Montreal kitchen, both plays depict characters who have become collectively trapped by the interdependent dysfunctions of their personalities. A similar situation is found in Colleen Wagner's *The Monument*, which, by playing out the ramifications of vengeance within a starkly limited sampling of humanity, exposes the morbid futility of perpetuating relations based on retribution. Further variations of this theme of personal agency are evident in Wallace Shawn's *Aunt Dan and Lemon* and Tomson Highway's *The Rez Sisters*. Highway's play bears a clear resemblance to Tremblay's *Les Belles Soeurs*, and indeed, was partly inspired by that play. But unlike the static situation of Tremblay's (and, of course, Beckett's) characters, Highway's women are on a journey—both literally, to Toronto, and figuratively, to a recovery of their own sense of personal agency. With *Aunt Dan and Lemon*, however, the thrust of the story moves in quite a different direction. So much of the play is directed right at the audience that one is led inescapably to the conclusion that it is the spectator's own sense of independent thought and personal agency that is at issue in this work.

Another theme that is touched on by many of the plays in this chapter, and which became increasingly common in the latter half of the twentieth century, is the theatricalization of everyday life. The theme is especially well represented by the two plays that were partly composed using the technique of collective creation, Timberlake Wertenbaker's *Our Country's Good* and Caryl Churchill's *Mad Forest*. By involving acting ensembles in the early stages of the creation of these plays, both playwrights in effect transformed performance from a merely interpretive into a compositional art as well—just as a pianist might use the instrument to compose music as well as to perform it. In a way, this technique returns the craft of the playwright to conditions similar to those enjoyed by

Renaissance playwrights like Shakespeare and Molière, who wrote and revised their plays in close contact with their companies, conceiving particular roles for particular actors and specific scenes for specific theatrical conditions. But in another way, the rise of collective creation marks an important new stage in drama.

The first important appearance of collective creation in the twentieth century was in the United States during the 1930s, when the Federal Theatre Project supported the creation of so-called "living newspapers"—theatrical productions in which the ensembles collectively drew on documentary and journalistic techniques to dramatize important social issues for the working class. Later, the director Joan Littlewood adapted many of these techniques for her work with Theatre Workshop in England after the war, most notably in the company's satire of the British class-system, *Oh, What a Lovely War* (1963). In the late 1960s, the widespread anti-establishment sentiments evinced by the demonstrations and revolts by students in Europe and North America, along with the various experiments in communal living, helped to foment a new generation of theatre artists to whom the concept of collective creation was especially congenial. For, in part, collective creation represented an attempt to replace the formal hierarchy of director or playwright over performer with a more integrated and democratic organization. Accordingly, during the 1970s the technique thrived in an atmosphere infused with socialist and feminist consciousness, begetting many highly sophisticated theatrical productions. Of course, the idealism inherent in collective creation could and did raise problems of its own. But the new approach seemed to open up new avenues of artistic creation, and to result in plays that were often different in form from traditional, single-protagonist-based dramas, offering instead a sense of what we might call "communal protagonism." How far such a shift may transform the face of drama in the long run is impossible to predict, but it is certainly evident that the energy of collective creation has not exhausted itself yet.

[C.S.W.]

ANTON CHEKHOV

The Cherry Orchard

nton Chekhov (1860–1904) always thought of himself as a doctor first and a writer second. This is perhaps a surprising self-assessment from one of the great writers of the modern age, but from a certain perspective it makes good sense. For it is easy to believe that Chekhov's paramount concern was for the well-being of others when one considers the unusual combination of profound compassion and merciless observation that is manifest in the characters he created. Indeed, some of his early works, including "A Dreary Story" and the play *Ivanov*, have been called "clinical studies" for the way in which they explore the nature of dysfunctional personalities.

Chekhov began to achieve his reputation as an author even while he was a medical student at Moscow University, writing a series of comic sketches for popular journals as a means of supporting not only himself, but also his parents and younger siblings. Shortly after graduating from medical school, he began to turn from these comic sketches to more serious work, publishing "The Steppe" (1888), the first of many superb short stories upon which much of his reputation (especially in Russia) still rests today. His earliest forays into the theatre (excluding *Platonov*, a long play written but abandoned while he was a student) began around the same time, and a number of his one-act comedies, including *The Bear* (1888), *The Proposal* (1889), and *The Wedding* (1890), were successfully produced. However, Chekhov had much less success during this period with his more serious full-length plays, *Ivanov* (1887) and *The Wood-Demon* (1889). In 1896, even *The Seagull*, a play now universally regarded as a masterpiece, proved disastrous with the public. Admittedly, the play had received a rather weak production, but it was the last straw for Chekhov, who resolved to write no more for the stage. Fortunately, two years later, Vladimir Nemirovich-Danchenko, the literary manager of the newly founded Moscow Art Theatre (M.A.T.), was able—though only after a great deal of effort—to persuade Chekhov to allow the company to remount *The Seagull* under the direction of Konstantin Stanislavski. The resounding success of that production inaugurated a collaboration between the playwright and the theatre company that would eventually embrace all four of Chekhov's acknowledged masterpieces: *The Seagull* in 1898, *Uncle Vanya* (a much revised version of *The Wood-Demon*) in 1899, *Three Sisters* in 1901, and finally, a few months before Chekhov died of tuberculosis, *The Cherry Orchard* in 1904.

It is clear, in retrospect, that the M.A.T. needed Chekhov as much as Chekhov needed the M.A.T. For if Chekhov had not previously found a sufficiently talented ensemble and a sensitive enough director to do justice to his plays, neither had Stanislavski and Nemirovich-Danchenko, determined that their company should become renowned for high-quality realistic productions, found plays that were adequate vehicles for their purpose. Stanislavski shows great humility in describing, in *My Life in Art*, the difficulty he had at first in understanding Chekhov's plays, as both director and actor. But the very difficulty of this struggle to understand how to inhabit the world Chekhov had captured on paper would give immense impetus to the major project of Stanislavski's career: to understand the actor's art and develop a careful method through which to practice it. Whereas other plays might accommodate facile performance conventions in the service of stereotypical characters in conventional plots, Chekhov's seemingly plotless plays demanded the careful discovery and passionate apprehension of characters' inner lives and their complex and enigmatic relations with one another. Even today, Chekhov's plays represent some of the most demanding challenges an actor can face, and Stanislavski's early attempts to come to terms with these challenges have bequeathed an important legacy that is respected by students of acting all over the world.

Yet, notwithstanding the success of Stanislavski's productions of his plays, Chekhov became irritated at what he felt was Stanislavski's overly sombre treatment of his work. Accordingly, he deliberately called *The Cherry Orchard* "a comedy" to encourage the notion that it should be approached with a light touch. However, we should be wary of the sorts of anticipation this label sets up in us. This is not the sort of comedy that is especially rich in belly-laughs, and to produce it as if it were is to risk distorting those delicate observations of personality that are its main appeal. On the other hand, it would be equally heavy-handed and incorrect to ignore Chekhov's pleas and treat the play as if it were a tragedy. Indeed, the very fact that it can be treated in either way is evidence that the play is considerably more subtle than either extreme allows, that, although it embraces moments of tragedy and moments of farce, on the whole it is something quite different than either of these. *The Cherry Orchard* is comic in the way that life itself can seem comic, taken in all its variety and viewed with a particular combination of detachment and insight. But perhaps a better term for the overriding perspective represented by this play is "ironic." The philosopher Kenneth Burke described irony as "a perspective of perspectives," and this phrase certainly serves as a succinct and accurate description of Chekhov's work, comprising as it does all the various perspectives on life embodied by his flawed but sympathetic—his all too human—characters.

One might even say that the action of *The Cherry Orchard* consists principally of a series of shifts from one kind of perspective to another. This is not the sort of action one expects from most dramas, which perhaps accounts for the impression some people have that *The Cherry Orchard* is a play in which nothing really happens. To be sure, at a first reading, it may indeed seem that very little is happening; but, with greater familiarity, one begins to see that it is the very rapidity and enormity of the off-stage action that is driving the story—the transformation of the world as it enters the modern age—which creates the sense of irresolution and stasis among many of the characters.

It is worth noting that the play is organized around a series of arrivals and departures: the return of Lyubov to the estate; the preparing to go back to the house; the arrival of Gayev and Lopakhin from the auction; the final departure from the house. Life here seems to be lived in a state of continual flux. We are reminded, even in the moments of greatest apparent stillness, that hanging over everything said and done is the undeniable sense that a way of life is passing—or disintegrating—and that a different sort of life must arrive in its place. That this change is variously regarded with despair, fear, loathing, resignation, indifference, hopefulness, and relish, but that, at the same time, all these things are felt by a group of people who are convincingly shown living together, at least temporarily, with tolerance (more or less) and even some affection, is one of the most deeply affecting aspects of this remarkable play. Indeed, considered deeply enough, *The Cherry Orchard* is a work that seems to take the measure of our own sense of humanity.

[C.S.W.]

ANTON CHEKHOV

The Cherry Orchard

A Comedy in Four Acts

A new version by Craig S. Walker.

This adaptation is based on a comparison and a modernization

of the language of several earlier translations.

CHARACTERS:

MADAME RANEVSKY (LYUBOV ANDREYEVNA),
  owner of the estate
ANYA, *her daughter, aged 17*
VARYA, *her adopted daughter, aged 24*
GAYEV (LEONID ANDREYEVITCH), *brother of
  Madame Ranevsky*
LOPAKHIN (YERMOLAY ALEXEYEVITCH),
  a merchant
TROFIMOV (PYOTR SERGEYEVITCH), *a student*
SEMYONOV-PISHCHIK, *a landowner*
CHARLOTTA IVANOVNA, *a governess*
EPIHODOV (SEMYON PANTALEYEVITCH),
  a clerk
DUNYASHA, *a maid*
FIRS, *a valet, aged 87*
YASHA, *a young valet*
A STRANGER
THE STATION MASTER
A POST-OFFICE CLERK
GUESTS, SERVANTS

*THE PLAY IS SET ON THE ESTATE OF
MADAME RANEVSKY.*

ACT I.

*A room which has always been known as "the nursery."
One of the doors leads into ANYA's room. Dawn is
breaking; during the scene, the sun will rise. It is May.
The cherry trees are in bloom, but it is still cold and
there is morning frost in the orchard. The windows are
closed.*

*Enter DUNYASHA with a candle and LOPAKHIN
with a book in his hand.*

LOPAKHIN: The train's in, thank God. What time is
  it?

DUNYASHA: Nearly two. [*Puts out the candle.*] It's
  daylight already.

LOPAKHIN: So the train's late—by at least two hours.   5
  [*Yawns and stretches.*] A fine idiot I am. I make a
  special point of coming here to meet them at the
  station and then I fall asleep. Nodded off in the
  chair. Irritating. Why didn't you wake me?

DUNYASHA: I thought you'd already left. [*Listens.*]   10
  There, that's them coming now!

LOPAKHIN: [*Listens.*] No, not yet. They'll have to get
  the luggage and everything. [*Pause.*] It's five years
  that Lyubov Andreyevna's been gone. I wonder
  what she's like now. Always was a fine lady: good-   15
  natured, kind. I remember one time, when I was
  a boy of fifteen or so, my dad—dead now, but he
  ran a little shop here at that time—he punched me
  in the face and made my nose bleed. We'd come
  out here for some reason, I forget what, and we   20
  were in the yard out there. He had a few drinks
  in him. Well, Lyubov Andreyevna—I can see her
  now—just a slender young girl then—she brought

me in to wash my face, and we came in here, into the nursery. "Don't cry, little peasant," she says, "it'll be better before you know it." [*Pause.*] Huh. Little peasant. It's true, my father was a peasant.[1] But look at me now, all decked out in a white waistcoat and brown shoes… Like a pig in a pastry shop. Yes sir, I'm a rich man alright, but at bottom? Still pretty much the same peasant I always was. [*Flips the pages of the book.*] I've been trying to read this book. Can't understand a word of it. It put me to sleep. [*Pause.*]

DUNYASHA: The dogs were restless all night. They can sense that the mistress is coming.

LOPAKHIN: What's up with you, Dunyasha?

DUNYASHA: My hands are shaking. I feel like I might faint.

LOPAKHIN: Aw, you've gone soft. Spoiled. Look at you: dressed up like a lady, your hair all done. It doesn't work. You've got to know your place.

Enter EPIHODOV with a bouquet of flowers, wearing a jacket and a pair of highly polished, creaking boots. He drops the bouquet.

EPIHODOV: [*Picking up the flowers.*] Here! The gardener sent these. Says to put them in the dining-room. [*Gives DUNYASHA the flowers.*]

LOPAKHIN: And bring me some kvass.[2]

DUNYASHA: I will. [*Goes out.*]

EPIHODOV: It's chilly this morning: three degrees of frost, though the cherry trees are in bloom. I can't say much for this climate. [*Sighs.*] No. Our climate is seldom what you'd call propitious. And if you'll permit me a further observation, Yermolay Alexeyevitch, I draw your attention to this pair of boots, which, in point of fact, I purchased just the day before yesterday, and—would you believe it? [*Creaks boots.*]—they creak! It's positively intoler-

able, I assure you. Any suggestions about how I might grease them?

LOPAKHIN: Look, shut up, can't you. Leave me alone.

EPIHODOV: Not a day goes by without some new misfortune befalling me. Not that I complain. I'm altogether used to it. And: I always wear a smile.

DUNYASHA comes in, hands LOPAKHIN his kvass.

EPIHODOV: Well, I'm off. [*Bumps into a chair, knocking it over.*] Voila! [*Triumphantly.*] If you'll excuse the expression: what did I tell you? A typical example. It's actually quite remarkable. [*Goes out.*]

DUNYASHA: Well, what do you think, Yermolay Alexeyevitch. Epihodov has proposed to me.

LOPAKHIN: Oh?

DUNYASHA: I'm not sure what to do. He's nice enough, but there are times when he gets to talking, that you just can't tell what he's going on about. I mean, I guess it's all pretty impressive; but it just doesn't make any sense. But, I don't know: I sort of like him, and he's crazy about me… He's just so … unlucky. Every day it's something new. People tease him about it—they call him "The Luckless Loser."

LOPAKHIN: [*Listening.*] There! I think that's them coming now.

DUNYASHA: They're coming! What's the matter with me? I'm suddenly all shivering.

LOPAKHIN: Yes, that's them for sure. Let's go and meet them. I wonder if she'll recognize me? It's been five years since we laid eyes on one another.

DUNYASHA: [*Agitated.*] Oh my goodness, I'm going to faint… I will, I'll faint.

Two carriages are heard driving up to the house. LOPAKHIN and DUNYASHA go out quickly, leaving the stage empty. Noises are heard in the adjoining rooms. FIRS, who has met Madam Ranevsky at the station, hurries across the stage using a stick. He wears old-fashioned livery and a high hat. He mutters something to himself, but the words are indistinguishable. The offstage noises grow louder. ANYA's voice: "Let's go in this way, shall we?" Enter LYUBOV ANDREYEVNA, ANYA, and CHARLOTTA IVANOVNA with a pet dog on a chain, all in travelling outfits. VARYA, wearing an

---

1 peasant] a person of the bottom tier of society, and in this case, a former serf. Serfs were like slaves in that they were unfree workers belonging by heredity to a particular lord, though unlike slaves in that the lord did have certain obligations to them (e.g., military protection). Serfdom was abolished in Russia in 1861.

2 kvass] a mildly alcoholic Russian beverage made from rye flour or bread with malt.

*outdoor coat and a kerchief over her head, GAYEV,
SEMYONOV-PISHCHIK, LOPAKHIN, and DUNYASHA,
with a bag and a parasol, and other servants with
other articles, all enter and cross the room.*

ANYA: Yes, let's come through here. You remember
this room, don't you, Mamma?   90

LYUBOV: [*Joyfully, through her tears.*] The nursery!

VARYA: It's so cold! My hands are numb! [*To LYUBOV
ANDREYEVNA.*] Your rooms, the white one and the
lavender, are just as they always were, Mamma.

LYUBOV: The nursery! My dear, wonderful room. I   95
slept here as a little girl. [*Cries.*] And here I am,
like a child again… [*Kisses her brother and VARYA,
and then her brother again.*] Varya's exactly the same
as ever, still looks like a nun. And I recognized
Dunyasha at once. [*Kisses DUNYASHA.*]   100

GAYEV: The train was two hours late. How do you
like that for efficiency, eh?

CHARLOTTA: [*To PISHCHIK.*] My dog eats nuts, too.

PISHCHIK: [*Wonderingly.*] Remarkable!

*They all go out the other side of the nursery except
ANYA and DUNYASHA.*

DUNYASHA: We've been waiting so long for you!   105
[*Takes ANYA's hat and coat.*]

ANYA: I haven't slept the last four nights we've been
traveling, and now I'm chilled to the bone.

DUNYASHA: You started out just before Easter, when
there was snow and frost—and now? Darling   110
Anya! [*Laughs and kisses her.*] I have missed you so
much, my precious angel. I have some news to tell
you. I can't put it off another minute!

ANYA: [*Wearily.*] Oh, what now?

DUNYASHA: Epihodov—you know, the clerk?—he   115
proposed to me just after Easter!

ANYA: Unh-huh, what else is new. [*Straightening her
hair.*] Ah! I've lost all my hairpins. [*She is actually
staggering a little from exhaustion.*]

DUNYASHA: I don't know what to think, you know?   120
He really does love me—he does!

ANYA: [*Looking through the doorway of her room,
tenderly.*] Oh, look! My own room, my windows,
it's just as though I had never gone away. I'm home
at last! Tomorrow morning I'll get up and run out   125
into the garden, and… Oh, if I could just get some

sleep! I couldn't sleep the whole way back, I was
so anxious.

DUNYASHA: Oh, Pyotr Sergeyevitch arrived here the
day before yesterday.   130

ANYA: [*Joyfully.*] Petya!

DUNYASHA: He's asleep right now in the bath house.
He's settled in there. He said, "I'm afraid of being
in their way." [*Glancing at her watch.*] I was
supposed to wake him, but your sister said not to.   135
"Don't you dare wake him," she said.

VARYA comes in. She now has a bunch of keys at her waist.

VARYA: Dunyasha, coffee, quickly. Mamma's asking
for some.

DUNYASHA: I'll get it right away. [*Goes out.*]

VARYA: [*To ANYA.*] Well, thank God, you're back.   140
You're home at last. [*Petting her.*] My little darling
has come back! My precious angel has come home
again!

ANYA: It's been an awful time.

VARYA: I can imagine.   145

ANYA: We set off for Paris in Holy Week—when it
was so cold—and the whole way Charlotta
wouldn't stop talking and showing off her tricks.
Why did you have to force Charlotta on me?

VARYA: But darling, you couldn't have traveled all   150
alone. At seventeen!

ANYA: Well, we got to Paris at last, and it was cold
there too—snow. My French is appalling. Mamma
was living on the fifth floor of this place, and when
I went up to see her, there were all these French   155
people, some ladies and this old priest with a book.
The place was so uncomfortable; it absolutely
stank of tobacco… I just felt so sorry, so sorry for
Mamma, and I threw my arms round her, and I
hugged her and just wouldn't let go. Mamma was   160
really terribly sweet, and she cried…

VARYA: [*Through her tears.*] Oh Anya, don't, I can't
bear it!

ANYA: She had sold her villa at Mentone, she had
nothing left, just … nothing. And all of my money   165
was gone too—we had barely enough between us
to get back here. And Mamma just doesn't
understand! Whenever we stopped and had dinner,
she always ordered the most expensive things and
tipped the waiters a whole ruble. Charlotta's just   170

as bad. And Yasha, of course, Yasha has to have exactly the same as we do. It's horrible! You know Yasha? He's Mamma's valet now, we brought him back with us.

VARYA: Yes, I've seen him. A good-for-nothing. 175

ANYA: Well, anyway. Tell me—did you manage to pay the arrears on the mortgage?

VARYA: Where would we get the money?

ANYA: Oh, God, what a disaster!

VARYA: The estate is going to be put up for sale in 180 August.

ANYA: Oh my God!

LOPAKHIN: [*Peeps in at the door and moos like a cow.*] Mooooo! [*Disappears.*]

VARYA: [*Starting to weep.*] Oh, I could just give him 185 such a smack sometimes… [*Shakes her fist.*]

ANYA: [*Embracing VARYA, quietly.*] Varya, has he made you a proposal? [*VARYA shakes her head.*] Why? He loves you. Why can't you come to an understanding? What are you two waiting for? 190

VARYA: I don't believe that anything will ever happen between us. He's too busy to make any time for me … in fact, to take any notice of me. It's all so foolish. I'm fed up. Just the sight of him makes me miserable now. Everyone talks about us getting 195 married, offering congratulations as if it's all arranged, when there isn't anything really to it; it's all just rumour, a dream. [*In another tone.*] You've got a new brooch—like a bee.

ANYA: [*Mournfully.*] Yes, Mamma bought it. [*Goes* 200 *into her room and says in a light child-like tone.*] Did you know that in Paris I went up in a big balloon!

VARYA: My darling, sweet Anya is home again!

DUNYASHA has returned with the coffee-pot and started making coffee.

VARYA: [*Standing by the door.*] You know sweetheart, when I'm working around the house, I spend the 205 whole time daydreaming about your marrying some rich man. Then I could rest easy, go off on my own somewhere, to a convent—perhaps to Kiev or Moscow—just spend my days wandering from one holy place to another… Just wander on 210 and on… What bliss!

ANYA: You can hear the birds singing in the orchard. What time is it?

VARYA: It must be nearly three. Time you were asleep, darling. [*Enters ANYA's room.*] What bliss! 215

YASHA enters with a rug and a traveling bag.

YASHA: [*Crosses the stage, mincingly.*] Tell me, is it permitted for one to pass through here?

DUNYASHA: I wouldn't have known you, Yasha. You've changed while you were abroad.

YASHA: Hm! … And who are you? 220

DUNYASHA: At the time you left, I was no bigger than this. [*Shows height from the floor.*] I'm Dunyasha, Fyodor's daughter… You wouldn't remember me.

YASHA: Hm!… A sweet little thing! [*Looks round then* 225 *embraces her. She lets out a shriek and drops a saucer.* *YASHA hurries out.*]

VARYA: [*In the doorway, vexed.*] What now?

DUNYASHA: [*Through tears.*] I broke a saucer.

VARYA: Well … that's supposed to be good luck. 230

ANYA: [*Coming out of her room.*] Someone will have to speak to Mamma: Petya is here.

VARYA: I told them not to wake him.

ANYA: [*Thoughtfully.*] It's been six years now since father died. And it was only a month after that we 235 lost our little brother. Poor little Grisha, drowned in the river. Such a lovely boy he was, just seven years old. It was more than Mamma could bear, so she went away, just dropped everything and ran off. [*Shuddering.*] … If she only knew: I understand her 240 all too well! [*Pause.*] Petya Trofimov was Grisha's tutor; the sight of him may bring it all back.

FIRS enters, wearing a jacket and white waistcoat.

FIRS: [*Goes up to the coffee-pot, anxiously.*] The mistress will take coffee in here. [*Puts on white gloves.*] Is it ready? [*Sternly to DUNYASHA.*] You girl! 245 Where's the cream?

DUNYASHA: Oh goodness! [*Goes out quickly.*]

FIRS: [*Fussing round the coffee-pot.*] Aghh! Little moron! [*Muttering to himself.*] So they're back from Paris. Time was, the old master would go to Paris 250 … Horse and carriage, all the way. [*Laughs.*]

VARYA: What's that, Firs?

FIRS: Beg your pardon? [*Gleefully.*] Well, the mistress has come home! And I alive to see her once more! Now I can die happy. [*Weeps with joy.*] 255

Enter LYUBOV ANDREYEVNA, LOPAKHIN, GAYEV and SEMYONOV-PISHCHIK; the last dressed in a short vest made of fine cloth, and full trousers, tucked into boots. As GAYEV enters, he makes gestures with his arms and his whole body, as if he were playing billiards.

LYUBOV: How does it go again? I'm trying to remember. Ricochet into the corner pocket!

GAYEV: That's it—off the blue, into the middle! There was a time, sister, we used to sleep together in this room. And here I am, fifty-one, strange as that sounds. 260

LOPAKHIN: Yes, time marches on.

GAYEV: What do you say?

LOPAKHIN: Time—it marches on, I said.

GAYEV: What a stench of cheap perfume in here! 265

ANYA: I'm going to bed. Good-night, Mamma. [*Kisses her mother.*]

LYUBOV: My precious baby girl. [*Kisses her hands.*] Are you glad to be home? I can hardly believe it.

ANYA: Good-night, Uncle.

GAYEV: [*Kissing her face and hands.*] God bless you! 270 How like your mother you are! [*To his sister.*] You looked just like her when you were her age you know, Lyuba.

ANYA shakes LOPAKHIN's hand and PISHCHIK's, then goes out, shutting the door behind her.

LYUBOV: She's quite worn out. 275

PISHCHIK: Sure, well, it's a long trip.

VARYA: [*To LOPAKHIN and PISHCHIK.*] So, gentlemen? It's three in the morning. Time to say good-bye.

LYUBOV: [*Laughs.*] You're just the same as ever, Varya. 280 [*Draws her to herself and kisses her.*] I'll just drink my coffee and then we'll all go and sleep. [*FIRS puts a cushion under her feet.*] Thank you, my dear. I've grown so fond of coffee, I drink it day and night. Thanks, dear old fellow. [*Kisses FIRS.*] 285

VARYA: I'll just check that all the things have been brought in. [*Goes out.*]

LYUBOV: Can this really be me sitting here? [*Laughs.*] I feel like dancing around and clapping my hands! [*Covers her face with her hands.*] And I could fall 290 asleep any moment now! God knows I love my country, I love it deeply. In the train, I could hardly

see out the window, I was crying so hard. [*Through her tears.*] But I should drink my coffee. Thank you, Firs, thanks, dear old fellow. I'm so glad to 295 find you still alive.

FIRS: The day before yesterday.

GAYEV: He's a bit deaf.

LOPAKHIN: I have to go off to Harkov in just a little while—at five o'clock. It's frustrating. I wanted a 300 proper look at you... I wanted a little talk. [*Pause.*] You are just as magnificent as ever.

PISHCHIK: [*Breathing heavily.*] More beautiful still... All dressed up in your Paris fashions... You completely bowled me over, I'll tell you that. 305

LOPAKHIN: You know, Leonid Andreyevitch here, your dear brother, is always calling me a boor and a lout and all that, or saying I'm a lousy money-grubber... But it just runs right off my back. He's wasting his breath. But, you...! Well, I just hope 310 that you can believe in me like you used to. That's what I care about; to have those wonderful, lovely eyes of yours look at me the way they did in the old days. God Almighty! When I think that my father was one of your father's serfs—and your 315 grandfather's too, it's... But, you...! You've meant so much to me that I've forgotten all that. And I can even say that I love you ... just as if we were family... More, even.

LYUBOV: I can't sit still, honestly, I can't... 320

Jumps up and begins pacing in agitation.

All this happiness is just ... overwhelming... Laugh at me if you will, I know I'm being silly... Oh, my own bookcase! [*Kisses the bookcase.*] And my wee table.

GAYEV: Nanny died while you were away. 325

LYUBOV: [*Sitting down and drinking her coffee.*] Yes. God rest her soul. It was mentioned in one of your letters.

GAYEV: And Anastasy is dead too. And Petruchka?— you remember, the one who squinted—he's left me 330 and now he's working for the chief of police in town.

Takes a box of caramels out of his pocket and puts one in his mouth

PISHCHIK: Dashenka--my daughter—asked me to send her regards.

LOPAKHIN: Well, I'd like to give you a good, cheerful piece of news. [*Glancing at his watch.*] I'll have to leave in a few minutes, so there's no time to say much… Anyway, I can say it in a couple of words. Now, I don't need to tell you that your cherry orchard has got to be sold to pay your debts. The auction's all set for the twenty-second of August. But never fear, my dear lady, you can rest easy, because there is a way out! … Alright, here's my proposal. Now listen carefully. Your estate lies less than twenty miles from town. And the new railway is very close. So, if we took the cherry orchard, and the land along the river, and split the property into a series of building lots, which could then be leased out for summer cottages, I figure you would have yourself an income of at least twenty-five thousand rubles a year!

GAYEV: Oh, please. What nonsense.

LYUBOV: I'm not sure I quite follow you, Yermolay Alexeyevitch.

LOPAKHIN: Well, for each and every three-acre plot, you would get yourself a rent from summer visitors of at least twenty-five rubles a year.[3] And if you started to put the word out right now, I'd bet you wouldn't have a square foot vacant by the Fall. Every single plot would be taken. So, in short: congratulations, you're saved! With that deep river there, it's really a dream location. The only thing is, naturally, that the land would have to be cleared—all those old buildings and so on would have to go; this house too, which is really not much use at this point anyway; and the old cherry orchard, it would have to be cut down…

LYUBOV: Cut down? Oh dear, you are sweet, but I'm afraid you don't know what you are talking about. Surely, the one interesting—in fact, quite remarkable—thing in this whole province is our cherry orchard.

LOPAKHIN: Remarkable? Well … it's *big*. That's really the only remarkable thing; it's a *large* orchard. There's maybe one crop of cherries every other year, and nobody knows what to do with them. No one wants to buy them.

GAYEV: This orchard is mentioned in the *Encyclopædia*.

LOPAKHIN: [*Glancing at his watch.*] Well, we have to decide on something, and fast, because if we don't get moving, on August twenty-second the cherry orchard and all the rest of the estate is going to be auctioned off! So … make up your minds. I swear to you, it's the only way there is of saving it, and … that's all there is to it.

FIRS: In the old days—forty, fifty years ago—they used to dry the cherries, and make preserves with them. And jam too, they'd make that. And back then, they'd—

GAYEV: Do be quiet, Firs.

FIRS: Back then they'd send the cherry preserves off to Moscow and to Harkov by the wagon-load! Then the money came rolling in! And those preserved cherries were plump and juicy, back then, sweet and tasty… Yes sir, they knew just how to do the thing in those days…

LYUBOV: And where is the recipe now?

FIRS: Lost. No one remembers it.

PISHCHIK: [*To LYUBOV ANDREYEVNA.*] So, how was Paris? Eat any frogs while you were there?

LYUBOV: Oh, I ate crocodiles!

PISHCHIK: Amazing!

LOPAKHIN: Up to a few years ago, you'd only ever see the gentry or the peasants out here in the country. Now, though, we get all these *other* people coming out to spend their summers here. Every town, every little village, has some of these "summer cottages" around the outskirts. And for sure, in another twenty years, we'll be getting plenty more of these people. They'll be everywhere you look! Now, so far, most of your summer visitors don't do much but sit on the porch drinking tea. But at some point, they might start trying to do a little gardening themselves… And when *that* happens, your cherry orchard would really come to life, you know? Be something fertile, prosperous…

GAYEV: [*Indignant.*] What garbage!

Enter VARYA and YASHA.

VARYA: A couple of telegrams came for you, Mamma. [*She takes out her keys and opens the glass doors of an old-fashioned bookcase with a loud crack and takes out the telegrams.*] Here.

---

3 By Lopakhin's calculations, the estate has at least three thousand acres.

LYUBOV: From Paris [*Tears up the telegrams, without reading them.*] I've finished with Paris.

GAYEV: Lyuba, do you have any idea how old that bookcase is? Last week I pulled out the bottom drawer and saw a date branded on it. That bookcase was made exactly one hundred years ago. Isn't that something? We could celebrate its centenary. I mean, yes, it's an inanimate object, but it is a *book* case.

PISHCHIK: [*Impressed.*] A hundred years! Amazing.

GAYEV: Yes … It's quite the thing, it is… [*Gently caressing the bookcase.*] Dear, honoured, bookcase! We salute you for your one hundred years of devotion … to the noble ideals of virtue and justice. You have stood there making your … silent clarion to creative labour, without flagging once in those hundred years, bolstering … [*In tears.*] … from generation to generation, our courage and our faith in a brighter future … and fostering in us ideals of goodness and social awareness! [*Pause.*]

LOPAKHIN: Yes…

LYUBOV: You haven't changed a bit, Leonid.

GAYEV: [*A little embarrassed.*] Right bank into the corner pocket!

LOPAKHIN: [*Looking at his watch.*] Well, it's time I was going.

YASHA: [*Handing some pills to LYUBOV ANDREY-EVNA.*] Would you like to take your medicine now?

PISHCHIK: You shouldn't bother taking pills, dear lady … they don't do a thing, for better or worse. Here, let me see them, my dear madam. [*He takes the pillbox, pours all the pills into his palm, blows on them, puts them in his mouth and washes them down with a drink of kvass.*] There!

LYUBOV: [*In alarm.*] Are you insane?!

PISHCHIK: I've finished off the lot!

LOPAKHIN: You greedy pig! [*All laugh.*]

FIRS: His honour stayed with us over Easter week, ate a gallon and a half of cucumbers… [*Mutters.*]

LYUBOV: What is he saying?

YARYA: He's been muttering like that for the last few years. We've gotten used to it.

YASHA: Well, his clock's winding down!

CHARLOTTA IVANOVNA, looking gaunt and lanky, crosses the stage in a white dress, with a lorgnette in her belt.

LOPAKHIN: Charlotta Ivanovna, I'm sorry; I haven't had a chance to say hello yet. [*Tries to kiss her hand.*]

CHARLOTTA: [*Pulls her hand away.*] I let you kiss my hand, next it will be the elbow, then the shoulder…

LOPAKHIN: I guess this isn't my day! [*All laugh.*] Charlotta, do some tricks for us!

LYUBOV: Yes, please Charlotta, show us a few tricks!

CHARLOTTA: I don't feel like it. I'm ready for bed. [*Goes out.*]

LOPAKHIN: Three weeks from now, we'll meet again. [*Kisses LYUBOV ANDREYEVNA's hand.*] But for now its good-bye—I really have to go. [*To GAYEV.*] Good-bye. [*Kisses PISHCHIK.*] Good-bye. [*Shakes hands with VARYA, FIRS and YASHA.*] I wish I didn't have to leave. [*To LYUBOV ANDREYEVNA.*] Think over what I was saying about the cottages, and if you decide to go ahead, just … say the word, and I'll set you up with a loan for 50,000. Give it some serious thought.

VARYA: [*Angrily.*] Oh, just go, for heaven's sake.

LOPAKHIN: I'm going, I'm going. [*Goes out.*]

GAYEV: What an oaf! … Oh, I'm sorry, I keep forgetting that Varya is going to marry him, that he's Varya's "betrothed."

VARYA: Don't be foolish, Uncle.

LYUBOV: Well, Varya, I would be delighted. He's a fine man.

PISHCHIK: Yes, you have to admit it, he is a very good man. And my Dashenka says that too… She says that … um, says things. [*Gives a snore and then wakes up right away.*] By the way, my dear lady, would you mind lending me 240 rubles…? I've got an interest payment due on my mortgage to-morrow.

VARYA: [*Dismayed.*] No. No, we absolutely can't.

LYUBOV: Honestly, I really don't have any money.

PISHCHIK: Well … something will turn up. [*Laughs.*] I never lose hope. Just when I think its all over, that I'm bankrupt—lo and behold!—a railway comes along and has to go through my land, and I get paid for that! And something else will turn up sooner or later… Dashenka will win two hundred thousand! She's got a lottery ticket.

LYUBOV: Well, we've finished our coffee. Let's get to bed.

FIRS: [*Brushes GAYEV's clothes, reprovingly.*] You've got the wrong trousers on again! What am I to do with you?

VARYA: [*Softly.*] Anya's asleep. [*Quietly opens the window.*] The sun's risen now, it's not at all cold. Look, Mamma, the trees are just exquisite! And the air is heavenly! You can hear the starlings singing!

GAYEV: [*Opens another window.*] The orchard is entirely white now. You've not forgotten how it is, Lyuba? With that long avenue running on and on—straight as an arrow!—how it shines on a moonlit night? You remember? You haven't forgotten?

LYUBOV: [*Looking out into the garden.*] Oh, my childhood, my innocence! It was in this nursery I would sleep, and from here … I looked out into the orchard! Every morning when I awoke, happiness awoke with me! And in those days the orchard was just the same. Nothing has changed. [*Laughs with delight.*] White! All, all white! Oh, my orchard… After the dismal, dark autumn, and the cold winter; you are young once more, and full of happiness! Heaven's angels have never left you…! If I could only cast off this burden weighing on my heart… If I could forget these past years…

GAYEV: Hm… And yet now the orchard is to be sold to pay our debts. It seems strange…

LYUBOV: Look, there's Mother walking … all in white … down the avenue! [*Laughs with delight.*] There she is!

GAYEV: Where?

VARYA: Oh, really, Mamma, don't!

LYUBOV: No… There's no one there. Just my imagination. On the right there—just by the path to the arbour—there is a bent white tree, a little like a woman…

Enter TROFIMOV wearing a shabby student's uniform and spectacles.

… What a glorious orchard! All those masses of white blossom, the blue sky…!

TROFIMOV: Lyubov Andreyevna. [*She looks around at him.*] I will just pay my respects and then leave you at once. [*Kisses her hand with great warmth.*] I was told to not to come until later in the morning, but I was too impatient to wait any longer…

LYUBOV ANDREYEVNA stares at him in bewilderment.

VARYA: [*Through tears.*] This is Petya Trofimov.

TROFIMOV: Petya Trofimov. I was your Grisha's tutor… Can I have changed so much?

LYUBOV ANDREYEVNA embraces him and quietly weeps.

GAYEV: [*Disconcerted.*] There, there, Lyuba, no need to cry.

VARYA: [*Crying.*] I told you, Petya, to wait until later.

LYUBOV: Grisha… My little boy… Grisha… My son!

VARYA: It can't be helped, Mamma, it is God's will.

TROFIMOV: [*Softly through his tears.*] Please don't cry…

LYUBOV: [*Weeping quietly.*] I lost him, my little boy was … drowned. Why? Oh, why did it happen, dear Petya? [*Speaking more quietly.*] Oh … Anya is asleep in there, and here I am talking loudly … making all this noise… But, Petya? Why have you grown so unhandsome? Why do you look so old?

TROFIMOV: A woman in the train called me "mangy-looking."

LYUBOV: You were such a boy then—a lovely little student—and … and, now your hair's thin, and you have these spectacles… You can't still be a student can you? [*Goes towards the door.*]

TROFIMOV: It appears likely that I will remain a student for ever.[4]

LYUBOV: Well… [*Pause. Kisses VARYA.*] Let's be off to bed… [*Kissing her brother.*] You are older too, Leonid.

PISHCHIK: [*Rising to follow her.*] I suppose it *is* time we were asleep… Ugh! My gout! I'll spend the night here! So, Lyubov Andreyevna, my dear, if you could manage it in the morning…? That bit of money?

GAYEV: Always the same thing!

PISHCHIK: 240 rubles—you remember—to pay the interest on my mortgage?

LYUBOV: My dear man, I have no money!

---

4 At this time in Russia, it was common for a student to be refused advancement and graduation repeatedly if he had expressed political opinions deemed offensive to the Czar.

PISHCHIK: I will pay you back, my dear! It's practically spare-change!

LYUBOV: Oh, alright! Leonid will give it to you. Give him the money, Leonid.

GAYEV: *Me* give it to him! Fat chance! 595

LYUBOV: It can't be helped, give him the money. He needs it. He'll pay it back.

LYUBOV ANDREYEVNA, TROFIMOV, PISHCHIK and FIRS go out. GAYEV, VARYA and YASHA remain.

GAYEV: Well, my sister hasn't lost her habit of throwing her money away. [*To YASHA.*] Go on, be off with you, man! You smell like a barnyard! 600

YASHA: [*With a grin.*] And you, Leonid Andrey-evitch, are just the same as you always were.

GAYEV: What's that? [*To VARYA.*] What did he say?

VARYA: [*To YASHA.*] You know that your mother has come here from the village? She's been sitting there 605 in the servants' room since yesterday, waiting to see you.

YASHA: Oh, what's the matter with her!

VARYA: Shame on you!

YASHA: Well, what's the hurry? She could have waited 610 until tomorrow. [*Goes out.*]

VARYA: [*Pause.*] Mamma's the same as ever. She hasn't changed a bit! If we let her, she'd give away everything.

GAYEV: Yes. [*Pause.*] When many different remedies 615 are suggested for a disease, it means that the disease is incurable. I keep going over it, racking my brains. I've come up with all sorts of solutions— any number of them—which really means I have none. Perhaps someone would leave us some 620 money in a will... Perhaps we could marry Anya to some wealthy man... Perhaps we could go to Yaroslavl and give our old aunt, the Countess, a try...[5] *She*, you know, is very, very wealthy indeed.

VARYA: [*Weeps.*] If only God would help us. 625

GAYEV: Now, don't start blubbering...! Yes, Aunty is *very* rich. Problem is, she doesn't like us. In the first place, my sister went and married a lawyer, a non-aristocrat ... so... [*Shrugs.*]

ANYA appears in the doorway.

5 Yaroslavl] an industrial city on the Volga River, north-east of Moscow.

... And in the second, when you look at Lyubov's 630 behaviour ... well, it's not altogether virtuous. She's a decent, good-hearted, and likeable woman, and I love her very much, but ... however you try to make allowances for extenuating circumstances, there's no getting away from the fact that she's 635 immoral. You can see it in every move she makes.

VARYA: [*In a whisper.*] Anya's in the doorway.

GAYEV: What's that? [*Pause.*] How odd, it feels as if there's something wrong with my right eye. I can't see properly out of it... And then, on Thursday 640 when I was up at the district Court...

Enter ANYA.

VARYA: Why aren't you asleep, Anya?

ANYA: I can't get to sleep.

GAYEV: My pet. [*Kisses ANYA's face and hands.*] My little girl. [*Weeps.*] You are not my niece, you are 645 my angel! You are my whole world to me! Believe me, do believe me...!!

ANYA: I believe you, Uncle. Everyone loves you and respects you... But, my dear Uncle, you must keep quiet ... just keep quiet. What were you saying just 650 now about my mother, about your own sister? What made you say it?

GAYEV: Yes, yes... [*Puts his hand over his face.*] You're right, that was horrible! God help me... God! And that speech I made to the bookcase earlier ... what 655 a stupid thing! And it was only when I'd finished that I saw how stupid it was.

VARYA: It's true, Uncle, you should try to stay quiet. Just don't talk, that's all.

ANYA: If you could keep from talking, you'd feel 660 more at ease.

GAYEV: I won't speak. [*Kisses ANYA's and VARYA's hands.*] I will be silent... [*beat*] Only this is about business. On Thursday I was at the district Court. There was a large group of us there and we were 665 talking about a number of things, this and that, and it seems it might be possible to take out a loan on an I.O.U. to catch up with the mortgage payments.

VARYA: May God help us! 670

GAYEV: I'm going back on Tuesday; I'll speak to them about it again. [*To VARYA.*] Now don't go crying. [*To ANYA.*] Your Mamma will have a talk with

Lopakhin, and I'm sure he won't deny her. And once you had a chance to rest, you can go to Yaroslavl to see your great-aunt, the Countess. This way, we'll approach the thing from three directions at once, and so clinch it for sure. We'll pay off the interest we owe anyway, I'm sure of that. [*Puts a caramel in his mouth.*] I swear on my word of honour—I swear by anything you like—the estate will not be sold. [*Excitedly.*] By my own happiness, I swear it! Here's my hand, and you can call me the lowest of the low, if I let this estate be auctioned off! On my very soul I swear it! 675 680 685

ANYA: [*Her equanimity has returned, she is quite happy.*] What a good man you are, Uncle. So clever! [*Embraces her uncle.*] I feel at peace now. Quite calm and happy.

Enter FIRS.

FIRS: [*Reproachfully.*] Leonid Andreyevitch, have you no fear of God? When are you going to bed? 690

GAYEV: Right away, right away. You go ahead, Firs. I'll … yes, I'll get undressed by myself. Well, children, time for bed. We'll talk over the details tomorrow, but for now … bed. [*Kisses ANYA and VARYA.*] I'm a man of the Eighties.[6] Nowadays, that period's disparaged; but I'm telling you, I have had to suffer more than a little for my convictions! It's not for nothing that I'm loved by the peasants. Naturally, you have to know your peasant! You have to know exactly how— 695 700

ANYA: Uncle, you're at it again!

VARYA: Uncle dear, you ought to try and be quiet!

FIRS: [*Angrily.*] Leonid Andreyevitch!

GAYEV: I'm coming. I'm coming. Go to bed. Banked off the end…! There's a shot for you! A beauty! [*Goes out, FIRS hobbling after him.*] 705

ANYA: My mind feels easy now. I'd rather not go to Yaroslavl, I don't like my great-aunt. But anyway, my mind's at rest. Thanks to Uncle. [*Sits down.*] 710

---

6 the Eighties] In 1881, Czar Alexander II, who was, for a time, mildly in favour of social and political reform, was assassinated and his son, Alexander III, presided over a much more reactionary regime. The next decade in Russia was a period of counter-reform, in which domination of the nobility was reasserted.

VARYA: We must get to bed. I'm going. [*beat*] Oh, there was an unpleasant thing that happened while you were away. You know that in the old servants' quarters there's only a few of the elderly former servants now: there's Efimyushka, Polya, and Yevstigney and, uh … Karp. Well, they started letting all these tramps in to spend the night. Now, I didn't say anything. But then, all of a sudden, I heard they'd been spreading rumours—that I fed them nothing but mashed peas! That I was as stingy as that, you know…? And it was Yevstigney who was behind it. Alright, fine, I said to myself, if that's how you want it, just wait and see! So I sent for Yevstigney. [*Yawns.*] And he comes… "Well, what's all this I'm hearing?" I ask him. "How could you be so stupid as to…" [*Looking at ANYA.*] Anitchka! [*Pause.*] She's asleep. [*Puts her arm around ANYA.*] Come to bed, sweetheart. Come on. [*Leads her.*] My little darling has fallen asleep! Come on, now… [*They go.*] 715 720 725 730

Far off, beyond the orchard a shepherd plays on a pipe. TROFIMOV enters and, seeing VARYA and ANYA, stands still.

VARYA: Shhh! Asleep, asleep. Come on, my own.

ANYA: [*Half asleep.*] I'm so tired. I keep hearing these bells. Uncle … dear … Mamma and Uncle…

VARYA: Come on, my own, come on.

They go into ANYA's room.

TROFIMOV: [*Tenderly.*] My sunshine… My spring! 735

CURTAIN.

ACT II.

The open country. A decrepit little chapel, abandoned long ago and leaning badly. There is a well nearby, some large stones that were evidently once tombstones, and an old garden bench. The road leading to the estate is seen. On one side stand some dark poplars; beyond them the cherry orchard begins. In the distance is a row of telegraph poles and far, far away on the horizon is the faint outline of a large town, visible only in clear weather. It is near sunset. CHARLOTTA, YASHA and DUNYASHA are sitting on the bench. EPIHODOV stands near by, playing softly on a guitar. All of them are deep in thought. CHARLOTTA wears a man's old hunting cap; she has taken a shotgun from her shoulder and is tightening the strap buckle.

CHARLOTTA: [*Musingly.*] I don't own a real passport or anything like it. So I really have no idea how old I am. In my mind, I'm always a youngster. When I was a just little girl, my father and mother used to travel from one fair to the next, giving these shows—really quite good ones. I used to perform with them—"The Dance of Death" and a few other things. Then, when Papa and Mamma died, a German lady took me in and had me educated. So, I grew up and became a governess. But really, where I'm originally from, who I am— I've no idea… Not even who my parents were. It's unlikely that they were married… But I don't know. [*Takes a cucumber out of her pocket and eats.*] I really don't know anything at all. [*Pause.*] I have this urge to talk, but there's no one to talk to. No one at all.

EPIHODOV: [*Plays his guitar and sings.*]
    Oh, let me leave this noisy world,
    Abandon all my friends and foes…
How pleasant it is to play the mandolin!

DUNYASHA: That's a guitar, not a mandolin. [*Looks in a hand-mirror and powders her face.*]

EPIHODOV: To a man madly in love, it's a mandolin. [*Sings.*]
    And if her heart had a flame as bright,
    Then two might join in love's white light…

YASHA joins in.

CHARLOTTA: What horrible singing! Ugh! Like hyenas!

DUNYASHA: [*To YASHA.*] It must be wonderful, though, to have travelled abroad.

YASHA: Yes, indeed. You're certainly right there. [*Yawns, and lights a cigar.*]

EPIHODOV: To be sure, it's a logical preference. Other countries have long since recognized—or very nearly—their full social potential.

YASHA: Well, of course they have.

EPIHODOV: Now I'm a cultivated man, I've read all sorts of remarkable books; nevertheless, determining just precisely what my own objective now should be is a point that eludes me. To wit: shall I persist with life, or shall I shoot myself? At any rate, I maintain myself in a state of readiness by invariably carrying my revolver. See…? [*Shows revolver.*]

CHARLOTTA: Alright, enough's enough. I'm going. [*Slings her gun over her shoulder.*] Epihodov, you're very clever, and very dangerous too. You must drive the women wild. Br-r-r! [*Goes.*] The clever types are always so stupid. There really isn't a soul to speak to. Always alone, completely alone in the world… And who I am, or why I'm here on earth, I haven't the faintest idea. [*Walks slowly away.*]

EPIHODOV: Well, setting aside all other considerations and speaking quite strictly, I'd have to admit that I myself am a person whom destiny treats as mercilessly as a storm does a small boat. Let us suppose just for a moment that I am mistaken. Fine; well, why then was it that I awoke this very morning—to cite merely one example among many— only to find that there, perched upon my chest, was a spider of truly enormous proportions? Approximately this size… [*Shows with both hands.*] And should I perhaps lift a jug of kvass, let us say, to quench my thirst, inevitably there is in it something of the rankest nature—for instance, a member of the cockroach species. [*Pause.*] Have you read Buckle?[7] [*Pause.*] Might I prevail upon you, Dunyasha, to speak a word or two with you?

DUNYASHA: Well, speak.

EPIHODOV: I should prefer on the whole to speak with you alone. [*Sighs.*]

DUNYASHA: [*Embarrassed.*] Well, alright. Only would you mind bringing me my shawl first? It's hanging near the cupboard. It's a bit damp out here.

EPIHODOV: Why, certainly I'll fetch it. By all means. And now I see what I must do with my revolver. [*Exits, playing his guitar.*]

YASHA: "The Luckless Loser"! Between you and me, the man's an idiot. [*Yawns.*]

---

7 Buckle] Henry Thomas Buckle (1821–1862), who, in *History of Civilization in England*, argues that "events apparently the most irregular and capricious" are in fact "in accordance with certain fixed and universal laws" governing the development of civilization.

DUNYASHA: I hope to God he doesn't shoot himself. 80
[*Pause.*] I'm so high-strung now, always in a tizzy.
I was just a little girl when they took me in at
Madame's house, and now I've completely
outgrown my peasant background. My hands are
all white like a lady's, and I'm so delicate, so 85
sensitive, that now the least thing leaves me
shaking. I'm afraid of everything. So, Yasha, if you
betray me, my nerves will just be shattered.

YASHA: [*Kisses her.*] You're a sweetie! Of course a girl
can never forget herself. What I despise more than 90
anything is a flighty girl.

DUNYASHA: I've fallen deeply in love with you,
Yasha. You're so cultured—you can give an opinion
about anything. [*Pause.*]

YASHA: [*Yawns.*] True enough. And my opinion is 95
this: a girl who is in love with anyone is immoral.
[*Pause.*] How nice it is to smoke a cigar out in the
open. [*Listens.*] Someone's coming… It's madame
and the gentry. [*DUNYASHA embraces him impulsively.*] Head back for the house as though you'd 100
been to the river for a swim. Use that path, or else
you'll run into them and they'll guess that you were
out here with me. I don't want that happening.

DUNYASHA: [*Coughing a little.*] That cigar has given
me a headache… [*Goes off.*] 105

*YASHA remains, sitting near the shrine. Enter LYUBOV
ANDREYEVNA, GAYEV and LOPAKHIN.*

LOPAKHIN: You have to make up your minds once and
for all—there's no time left to lose. It comes down to
a pretty basic question, you know. Are you going to
lease the land to have the cottages built or not? It's a
one-word answer: yes or no? Just one word. 110

LYUBOV: Now, who has been smoking these
disgusting cigars out here? [*Sits down.*]

GAYEV: It's really very convenient that they've
brought the railway so much nearer. [*Sits down.*]
Here we sit now, having lunched graciously over 115
in town! Ricochet into the side pocket! Perhaps I'll
go back home for a game right now.

LYUBOV: Now, there's no need to rush.

LOPAKHIN: Just one word! [*Beseechingly.*] Please
answer me! 120

GAYEV: [*Yawning.*] What's that?

LYUBOV: [*Looks in her purse.*] I had a great deal of
money in here yesterday, and there's practically
nothing left today. Poor Varya tries to economize
by feeding us all on milk soup; the old folks in the 125
kitchen get nothing but mashed peas, and here I
go on, senselessly frittering money away. [*Drops
purse, scattering gold pieces.*] There, now I've
dropped the whole lot of them! [*Annoyed.*]

YASHA: Allow me to pick them up, Madame. 130
[*Collects the coins.*]

LYUBOV: Please do, Yasha… And why did I agree to
have lunch in town? That restaurant of yours is
wretched, with its music and tablecloths smelling
of soap. Is there any need to drink so much, 135
Leonid? And eat so much? And talk so much?
Today in the restaurant, you talked on and on, and
all of it so inappropriate—the era of the Seventies
and the Decadents.[8] Think about it! Talking to
waiters about the Decadents! 140

LOPAKHIN: Yes, truly.

GAYEV: [*Waving his hand dismissively.*] I'm incorrigible, that's the fact of the matter. [*Irritably to
YASHA.*] Why are you always hanging about in
front of us! 145

YASHA: [*Laughs.*] I just can't help laughing whenever
I hear your voice.

GAYEV: [*To his sister.*] Either he goes or I do.

LYUBOV: Off with you, Yasha. Go on.

YASHA: [*Gives LYUBOV ANDREYEVNA her purse.*] 150
Right away, Madame. [*Barely able to suppress his
laughter.*] This very minute… [*Exits.*]

LOPAKHIN: You know who's planning to buy your
property, do you? Deriganov, the millionaire. They
say he's coming to the sale in person. 155

LYUBOV: Where did you hear that?

LOPAKHIN: It's all over town.

GAYEV: Our aunt in Yaroslavl has promised to send
us some money. Though when it will come, and
how much it will be, we have no idea. 160

LOPAKHIN: How much will she send? A hundred
thousand? Two hundred?

---

8 Decadents] (not to be confused with the French "Deca-
dent literature" movement of the 1890s). In the 1870s,
while revolution brewed, many of the Russian nobles
were becoming much more materialist, and it became
fashionable to affect the manners of French society.

LYUBOV: Oh well!… Ten or fifteen thousand, if we're lucky.

LOPAKHIN: With all due respect, I have never met two such scatter-brained, two such bizarre, unbusiness-like people, in all my life! I tell you just as plainly as I can that your estate is about to be auctioned off, but it seems that you can't take it in.

LYUBOV: Well, what are we to do about it? Tell us that.

LOPAKHIN: I *do* tell you! *Every day* I tell you! Every day, I say the very same thing: you have *got* to lease out the cherry orchard and the rest of the estate for building lots. And you have to do it right away, just as fast as you can—the auction's right on top of us! Try to get your minds around that fact! The moment you decide on the cottages, you can raise as much money as you like, and you'll be fine.

LYUBOV: But really, cottages and tourists—excuse my saying so—it's all so vulgar.

GAYEV: I couldn't agree with you more.

LOPAKHIN: I don't know whether to weep or scream or foam at the mouth! I can't take this anymore! You're driving me insane! [*To GAYEV.*] You are a silly old maid!

GAYEV: What did you say?

LOPAKHIN: A silly old maid! [*Gets up to go.*]

LYUBOV: [*In dismay.*] No, please don't go! Stay here, my dear, I beg you! Perhaps we'll think of something.

LOPAKHIN: Think? Think of what? What is there to think of?

LYUBOV: Just don't go! Please! If nothing else, it's more cheerful with you here. [*Pause.*] I keep expecting something terrible to happen, as though the house were about to fall down around us…

GAYEV: [*Dejected, lost in thought.*] Blue into the corner, misses by a hair…

LYUBOV: I suppose we're paying for all our sins…

LOPAKHIN: Sins? You? What sins could you have to repent?

GAYEV: [*Puts a caramel in his mouth.*] People say I've squandered my fortune on candy. [*Laughs.*]

LYUBOV: Oh, my sins! Well, look at the senseless way I've always thrown my money away. And I went and married a man who could make nothing but debts. He killed himself with champagne; he was an appalling drunkard. And then I … had the misfortune to fall in love with another man, to start an affair with him… And right away came my first punishment. An awful one. It struck just near here, too, over in the river. My little boy was drowned… So I went away—ran off for ever, never to return—so I would never have to look upon that river again… I shut my eyes, and I *ran*! I was just … out of my mind. But, of course, *he* followed me … brutally, without pity. At Mentone I bought that villa, because he had fallen ill, and for the next three years, night and day, I could never rest.[9] His illness utterly wore me out. I could feel myself drying up inside, to the very soul. So then, last year, when the villa had to be sold to pay my debts, I left for Paris; and there he robbed me, left me with nothing, and abandoned me for another woman. So, I tried to poison myself… It was all so stupid, so humiliating! … But suddenly, I felt this yearning to see Russia again, to be back in my own country, with my little girl… [*Dries her tears.*] Oh God, God have mercy! Forgive my sins! Don't punish me any more! [*Takes a telegram out of her pocket.*] This came today, from Paris. He begs my forgiveness, entreats me to return. [*Tears up the telegram.*] Is that music I hear somewhere? [*Listens.*]

GAYEV: That's our famous Jewish orchestra. You remember? Four violins, a flute and a double bass.

LYUBOV: They're still playing together? We should have them out to the house some evening, and give a little dance.

LOPAKHIN: [*Listens.*] I can't quite hear them… [*Sings softly.*]

"For a bit of cash the Prussians
  Will make Frenchmen out of Russians…!"

[*Laughs.*] I saw a good play at the theatre last night, something really very funny…!

LYUBOV: I doubt there was anything funny in it at all. You people waste too much time going to plays, when you should be looking into yourselves. You lead such dull lives! And talk such nonsense.

LOPAKHIN: True enough. In all honesty, our lives *are* spent foolishly. [*Pause.*] My father was a peasant,

---

9 Mentone] on the south coast of France near the Italian border.

an ignorant idiot who understood nothing and taught me nothing; just beat me when he was drunk—and used his stick to do it, too. But the truth is, I'm no better: still just another bonehead and ignoramus. I haven't really learned anything. My handwriting's a disgrace. If anyone sees it, it's humiliating. Makes me feel like a pig.

LYUBOV: You need to get yourself married, my dear.

LOPAKHIN: Yes, you're probably right.

LYUBOV: Why not marry our Varya? She's a very nice girl.

LOPAKHIN: Yes.

LYUBOV: She's good-natured, keeps herself busy all day long—and what's more, she loves you. And you've been fond of her for ages.

LOPAKHIN: Well, sure, I've nothing against it… She *is* a nice girl. [*Pause.*]

GAYEV: Did I tell you that I'd been offered a position at the bank? 6,000 rubles a year.

LYUBOV: Imagine you in a bank! You'll stay right where you are.

Enter FIRS with overcoat.

FIRS: Sir, you'd better put this on. It's getting damp.

GAYEV: [*Putting it on.*] You're becoming a bore, old fellow.

FIRS: Well, you can't go on like this. Went off this morning without so much as a word. [*Looks him over.*]

LYUBOV: You have aged, Firs!

FIRS: What is your pleasure, Madam?

LOPAKHIN: She says you look older.

FIRS: Well, I've been alive for a long time. They were arranging my wedding before your Papa had been so much as thought of… [*Laughs.*] By the time the serfs were freed, I was already head footman. I wouldn't have any part of their emancipation. Kept my place with the old master… [*Pause.*] I remember all their celebrating and carrying on, though they didn't a clue what they were celebrating about!

LOPAKHIN: Yes, the good old days! Back when we still had flogging.

FIRS: [*Not hearing.*] That's the truth! Back then, the peasants knew their place, and the masters knew theirs. Now, they're all so much at sixes and sevens, you can't make head nor tail of it.

GAYEV: Quiet now, Firs. I have to go into town in the morning. I've been promised an introduction to a general, who might make us a loan.

LOPAKHIN: It won't come off. And you'll never pay off your arrears, either; you can bet on that.

LYUBOV: It's all nonsense anyway. There *is* no general.

Enter TROFIMOV, ANYA and VARYA.

GAYEV: Here are the girls coming.

ANYA: There's Mamma on the bench.

LYUBOV: [*Tenderly.*] Come along, come to me, my darlings! [*Embraces ANYA and VARYA.*] If you only knew how much I love both of you. Sit here beside me—right here, yes. [*All sit down.*]

LOPAKHIN: Our perpetual student is never far from the young ladies.

TROFIMOV: Look, do you mind…?

LOPAKHIN: What is he, nearly fifty, and he's still a student.

TROFIMOV: You can drop all your idiotic jokes!

LOPAKHIN: What are you getting all upset about, you oddball?

TROFIMOV: Just leave it alone.

LOPAKHIN: [*Laughs.*] Just let me ask you one thing. What exactly do you think of me?

TROFIMOV: Alright, I'll tell you what I think of you, Yermolay Alexeyevitch. You're a very rich man. Soon, you'll be a millionaire. And just as in nature, where the wild beast is of use insofar as he transforms one sort of matter into another by devouring everything in his way, you too have your use.

All laugh.

VARYA: Perhaps you'd better talk to us about the planets, instead, Petya.

LYUBOV: No, let's go back to that conversation we were having yesterday.

TROFIMOV: What was that about?

GAYEV: About pride.

TROFIMOV: That's right; we had quite a lengthy discussion yesterday, though we didn't come to any conclusion. Pride, in your conception, has something almost mystical about it. And perhaps this is quite right from your point of view. Still, if one looks at it simply, without trying to make fine distinctions—well, what place can there be for pride? what real *sense* is there in it? once we have acknowledged that man is really a rather shabby physiological specimen, and that—in the vast majority of cases—he is vulgar, stupid and miserable? This habit of self-admiration must be broken. We should devote ourselves to work, and that's all.

GAYEV: But we must all die in any case.

TROFIMOV: Do we truly know that? and what does it mean, anyway—to die? Perhaps each of us has a hundred senses, and we lose only the five we know at death, while the other ninety-five live on!

LYUBOV: How clever you are, Petya!

LOPAKHIN: [*Ironically.*] Oh, yes! Brilliant!

TROFIMOV: Humanity progresses continually; it is forever improving its powers. That which eludes us now will someday lie well within our grasp; but for this to happen, we must *work*; and we must lend all our collective strength to those among us who are searching for truth. Here in Russia there are, as yet, few *real* workers. As far as I can see, the vast majority of so-called intellectuals here aspire to nothing, accomplish nothing—they don't even really know the meaning of hard work yet. They like to refer to themselves as the intelligentsia, but they treat their servants as inferiors, and the peasants as if they were animals. They learn very little, they never read any serious literature; they do practically nothing at all! They only chatter superficially about science and they're woefully ignorant about art! Of course, they're all quite serious looking, with their solemn expressions and their discussions of important issues and their impressive abstractions... And yet, meanwhile, the vast majority of our people—perhaps ninety-nine per cent of us—live utterly savage lives: fighting like animals, eating garbage, sleeping in desolate conditions: huddled together in masses, infested with bugs and stench and damp and moral depravity... So evidently, all our fine talk is just a diversion, a way of deceiving ourselves and everyone else. I mean, where are all these hostels we hear so much about, or all these public libraries that have been built? They're something we just read about in novels; we haven't actually got any of these things. No, what we have is just vulgarity and squalor and filth! So, you see, I fear and loathe all these solemn expressions. And I distrust their serious conversations. We'd be better off just staying silent for a change.

LOPAKHIN: You know, I get up at five o'clock every morning, and I work from morning to night. And all day long, I've got money, my own and other people's, passing through my hands: so, I can see what the people around me are made of. And I'm telling you, you've only got to start in on any job at all to see for yourself just how few honest, decent folk there are around these days. Sometimes, I lie awake at night, and I think: "God has given us such huge forests, such vast plains and such ... limitless horizons, that, living in the midst of it all, we should really be giants ourselves."

LYUBOV: You want giants, do you? They're a fine thing to encounter in fairy-tales, but when they show up in real life, we find them a little daunting.

EPIHODOV passes in the background, playing on the guitar.

LYUBOV: [*Wistfully.*] There goes Epihodov.

ANYA: [*Wistfully.*] There goes Epihodov.

GAYEV: The sun has set, my friends.

TROFIMOV: Yes.

GAYEV: [*A quiet oratory.*] Nature! Oh, resplendent Nature! Radiant with the light of eternity, beautiful, but indifferent! You, whom we call mother, embrace within your bosom both life and death! Giver and destroyer of life—!

VARYA: [*Imploringly.*] Uncle!

ANYA: There you go again, Uncle!

TROFIMOV: You'd be better off sticking with ricocheting off the end into the middle pocket.

GAYEV: I'll hold my tongue. I will.

Everyone sits lost in thought. Perfect stillness. The only thing audible is the muttering of FIRS. Suddenly there is a sound in the distance, as if from the sky—the sound of a breaking string. It mournfully dies away.

LYUBOV: What was that?

LOPAKHIN: I don't know. Somewhere off in the mines, a cable broke. But it must be very far away.

GAYEV: It might have been some sort of bird—a heron, perhaps.

TROFIMOV: Or an owl.

LYUBOV: [*Shudders.*] It was eery somehow… Macabre. [*Pause.*]   425

FIRS: We had the same sort of thing before the calamity—the owl hooting and the samovar hissing all the time.

GAYEV: Before what calamity?   430

FIRS: The emancipation. [*Pause.*]

LYUBOV: Come along, everyone; let's go in. Evening is falling. [*To ANYA.*] There are tears in your eyes. What is it, darling? [*Embraces her.*]

ANYA: It's nothing, Mamma. I'm fine.   435

TROFIMOV: Somebody is coming.

The STRANGER appears in a shabby, white, peaked cap and an overcoat. He is a little drunk.

STRANGER: Excuse me for asking, but can I get to the station in this way?

GAYEV: Yes. Just take that road.

STRANGER: My heartfelt thanks to you. [*Coughing.*]   440
The weather is wonderful, isn't it. [*Declaims.*]
   "My brother, my suffering brother!…
   Come out to the Volga!
   Whose groan do you hear?…"[10]
[*To VARYA.*] Miss, could you spare thirty kopecks   445
for a starving Russian?[11]

VARYA shrieks in alarm.

LOPAKHIN: [*Angrily.*] Look, even for something likes this, there's such a thing as good manners!

LYUBOV: [*Hurriedly.*] Here, take this. [*Looks in her purse.*] Oh, I have no silver. Never mind—here's   450
some gold.

STRANGER: My heartfelt thanks! [*Goes off.*]
[*Laughter.*]

VARYA: [*Frightened.*] I'm going home—I'm going… Mamma! We can't feed the servants at home, and   455
you gave him all that money!

LYUBOV: There's nothing to be done with me. I'm so silly! When we get home, I'll give you everything I have left. Yermolay Alexeyevitch, you'll lend me some more, won't you.   460

LOPAKHIN: Of course I will.

LYUBOV: Come along then, everyone, it's time we went in. By the way, Varya, we've arranged a match for you. Congratulations!

VARYA: [*Through her tears.*] Mamma, that's not   465
something to joke about.

LOPAKHIN: "Euphelia, get thee to a nunnery!"[12]

GAYEV: My hands are shaking. It's been too long since my last game of billiards.

LOPAKHIN: "Euphelia! Nymph, in thy orisons be all   470
my sins remembered."

LYUBOV: Let's go, it will be supper-time soon.

VARYA: That man frightened me! My heart's pounding!

LOPAKHIN: Let me remind you, ladies and gentle-   475
men, that on the twenty-second of August the cherry orchard will be sold. Think about that! You must give that some thought!

All go off, except TROFIMOV and ANYA.

ANYA: [*Laughing.*] I'm indebted to that stranger! He frightened Varya and now we've been left alone.   480

TROFIMOV: Varya's so terrified that we're going to fall in love, that she won't leave us alone together for days at a time. She's too narrow-minded to grasp the fact that what we have is something above love. To eliminate all the petty vanities and   485
everything transitory which might prevent freedom and happiness—that is the goal and the purpose of our lives. Forward! On and on we march, towards that bright star shining far off in the distance. On and on we march, friends, without   490
ever lagging behind!

ANYA: [*Claps her hands.*] How beautifully you speak! [*Pause.*] It is wonderful here today, isn't it?

TROFIMOV: Yes, the weather's glorious.

ANYA: I'm not sure how you've done this, Petya, but   495
somehow I don't love the cherry orchard the way I used to. I used to love it so deeply. I thought that

---

10 My brother … hear] two fragments from two of Russia's most celebrated poets, Nikolay Alekseyevich Nekrasov (1821–1877) and Semyon Yakovlevich Nadson (1862–1887).

11 thirty kopecks] akin to asking for a quarter; there are 100 kopecks to a ruble.

12 Euphelia] Lopakhin makes a slight error in the pronunciation of Ophelia's name.

there was no better spot on earth than our garden.

TROFIMOV: All Russia is our garden. The earth is so vast and so wonderful—it is full of beautiful places. [*Pause.*] Just think of it, Anya: your grandfather, your great-grandfather, and all your ancestors were slave-owners—they *owned* living souls! And from every cherry in this orchard, from every leaf and every trunk those people are looking out at you. Can't you hear their voices? It's terrible. Your orchard is a dreadful thing. And when you walk through it at dusk or at night, and the bark is glimmering in the moonlight, the old cherry trees seem to be dreaming of all the centuries past, to be tormented by horrible visions. Owning living souls, that has infected all of you, all those who came before and all those alive today. Your mother, you, and your uncle little realized that you were living on credit—off the labour of other people, off of people who weren't so much as allowed through your front door! Yes, we are at least two hundred years behind the times. We've made almost no real progress towards the future as yet, and have developed no real understanding of the past. We just talk in abstractions, or complain about our boredom, or we drink vodka. But if we are ever to even begin to live in the present, it is clear that we must first expiate our past—break with it entirely! And this can only be achieved through suffering, through extraordinary and incessant labour. You see that, Anya.

ANYA: The house we live in has long ago ceased to be ours, and I will leave it behind, I promise you.

TROFIMOV: If you have the keys to the house, throw them into the well and walk away. Become as free as the wind.

ANYA: [*Ecstatic.*] How beautifully you put that!

TROFIMOV: Believe me, Anya, believe me! I'm still not thirty yet, I'm young, still a student, but I've lived through so much already! When the winter comes I'm always hungry, sick, weary and wretchedly poor. And I've been through some strange and violent turns of fortune! But always—every minute of every day and night—my soul has been filled with strange visions of the future. I have a foreboding of happiness, Anya, I can glimpse it already.

ANYA: [*Pensively.*] The moon is rising.

EPIHODOV is heard playing still the same mournful song on the guitar. The moon rises. Somewhere near the poplars VARYA is looking for ANYA and calling.

VARYA: [*Offstage.*] Anya? Where are you?

TROFIMOV: Yes, the moon is rising. [*Pause.*] Here it comes—happiness! Nearer and nearer it is coming. I can already hear its footsteps. And if *we* should never see it—if it is never granted to *us* to know it—what does that matter? Others, after us, will see it.

VARYA: [*Offstage.*] Anya! Where are you?

TROFIMOV: Varya again! [*Angrily.*] It's revolting!

ANYA: Well, let's go down to the river. It's lovely there.

TROFIMOV: Yes, let's go. [*They go.*]

VARYA: [*Offstage.*] Anya! Anya!

CURTAIN.

ACT III.

A drawing-room, which is divided by an arch from a large ballroom. A chandelier burns. A Jewish orchestra, the one mentioned in Act II, is heard playing in the vestibule. It is evening. In the ballroom they are dancing a grand rond.[13] *The voice of SEMYONOV-PISHCHIK is heard calling:* "Promenade à une paire!" *The dancers enter the drawing-room in couples: first PISHCHIK and CHARLOTTA IVANOVNA, then TROFIMOV and LYUBOV ANDREYEVNA, thirdly ANYA with the POST-OFFICE CLERK, fourthly VARYA with the STATION MASTER, and then other guests. VARYA is quietly weeping, wiping away her tears as she dances. In the last couple is DUNYASHA. They pass through the drawing-room. PISHCHIK calls out:* "Grand rond, balancez!" *and* "Les Cavaliers à genou et remerciez vos dames."*

FIRS, wearing tails, brings in soda-water on a tray. PISHCHIK re-enters with TROFIMOV.

PISHCHIK: I've got high blood pressure. I've already had two strokes. Dancing's hard work. But, as they say: when you run with the pack, you've got to

---

13 grand rond] a promenade.

bark with the rest. Anyway, I'm as strong as a horse. My father—he did love his little joke, God bless him—used to boast of our pedigree, that the Semyonov-Pishchiks were descended from the horse Caligula made a senator.[14] [*Sits down.*] Problem is, though, I've got no money. And hungry dog can think of nothing but meat. [*Snores, but at once wakes up.*] That's me all over… nothing but money on my mind.

TROFIMOV: Come to mention it, there is something a little horsy about you.

PISHCHIK: Well, that's alright. A horse is a fine animal—you can sell a horse.

There is the sound of billiards being played in an adjoining room. VARYA appears in the archway leading to the ballroom.

TROFIMOV: [*Teasing.*] Well, if it isn't Madame Lopakhin! Hello, Madame Lopakhin!

VARYA: [*Angrily.*] Mangy-looking man!

TROFIMOV: Yes, mangy-looking, and proud of it!

VARYA: [*Brooding bitterly.*] We've gone and hired these musicians when we have nothing to pay them! [*Goes out.*]

TROFIMOV: [*To PISHCHIK.*] You know, if all the energy you've spent over your lifetime trying to find money to pay your interest had been put into something else, you could have turned the world upside down by now.

PISHCHIK: Nietzsche, the philosopher—a great man, very famous, a brilliant mind—he says in his books that there's nothing wrong with forging money.[15]

TROFIMOV: You've read Nietzsche?

PISHCHIK: Well, actually Dashenka told me. But the fix I'm in now—forging money might be the best way out of it. The day after tomorrow I have to pay three hundred and ten rubles. So far, I've scraped together a hundred and thirty. [*Feels in his pockets, in alarm.*] The money's gone! I've lost the money! [*Through his tears.*] Where is it?! [*Gleefully.*] Oh, wait, here it is in the lining… That gave me quite a spell.

Enter LYUBOV ANDREYEVNA and CHARLOTTA IVANOVNA.

LYUBOV: [*Hums the* Lezginka.[16]] What can be keeping Leonid so long? What could he be doing in town? [*To DUNYASHA.*] Offer the musicians some tea.

TROFIMOV: Probably the auction wasn't even held.

LYUBOV: It's a bad time to have the orchestra here, and a bad time for a party. Well, never mind. [*Sits down and hums softly.*]

CHARLOTTA: [*Gives PISHCHIK a pack of cards.*] Here's a pack of cards. Think of any card you like.

PISHCHIK: All right.

CHARLOTTA: Now, shuffle the pack … that's right. Now hand them back, please, Mr. Pishchik.—*Ein, zwei, drei!*—Now look in your breast pocket. Is it there?

PISHCHIK: [*Taking the card out.*] The eight of spades! Quite right! [*Wonderingly.*] Amazing!

CHARLOTTA: [*Offering pack of cards to TROFIMOV.*] Quickly, now: what is the top card?

TROFIMOV: Uh, the queen of spades.

CHARLOTTA: So it is! [*To PISHCHIK.*] Well, which card is at the top?

PISHCHIK: The ace of hearts.

CHARLOTTA: So it is! [*Claps her hands, the cards disappear.*] Ah! Isn't this lovely weather today!

A mysterious feminine voice which seems to come from the floor answers her:

VOICE: Oh, yes, the weather's marvellous, madam!

CHARLOTTA: What a perfect creature you are!

VOICE: And you too, madam, are quite splendid.

STATION MASTER: [*Applauding.*] Bravo! The lady ventriloquist!

PISHCHIK: [*Wonderingly.*] Amazing! Quite charming, Charlotta Ivanovna. I'm quite in love with you.

---

14 Caligula] Roman Emperor, 37–41 C.E.; a notoriously cruel megalomaniac who, though he didn't actually appoint his favourite horse to the Senate, did, according to Suetonius, threaten to name the horse consul.

15 Nietzsche … money] Friedrich Nietzsche (1844–1900) didn't exactly endorse forgery, though he did suggest in *The Dawn* that the "will to power" lay as much at the heart of the creation of art and culture as it did with the most selfish of activities, such as counterfeiting.

16 Lezingka] a Caucasian dance tune.

CHARLOTTA: In love? [*Shrugging shoulders.*] What would you know of love? *Guter Mensch, aber schlechter Musikant.*[17] 75

TROFIMOV: [*Pats PISHCHIK on the shoulder.*] Poor old horse…

CHARLOTTA: Attention, please! One more trick! [*Takes a travelling rug from a chair.*] Now, here's a 80 fine rug; I'd be happy to sell it. [*Shaking it out.*] Would anyone like to buy it?

PISHCHIK: [*Wonderingly.*] Amazing!

CHARLOTTA: *Ein, zwei, drei!* [*Quickly picks up rug she has dropped; behind the rug stands ANYA; she* 85 *curtsies, runs and embraces her mother, then runs back into the ballroom amidst general enthusiasm.*]

LYUBOV: [*Applauds.*] Bravo! Bravo!

CHARLOTTA: And again…! *Ein, zwei, drei!* [*Lifts the rug; behind the rug stands VARYA, bowing.*] 90

PISHCHIK: [*Wonderingly.*] Amazing!

CHARLOTTA: And that is the end. [*Throws the rug at PISHCHIK, curtsies, runs into the ballroom.*]

PISHCHIK: [*Hurries after her.*] Bewitching creature! Amazing! [*Goes out.*] 95

LYUBOV: Still no sign of Leonid. I can't understand what could be keeping him in town all this time! Everything must be over and done with by now. Either the estate is sold, or the auction was called off. Why keep us in suspense like this? 100

VARYA: [*Trying to console her.*] Uncle's bought it. I'm sure of it.

TROFIMOV: [*Ironically.*] Sure, he has!

VARYA: Our great-aunt sent him an authorization to buy it in her name, and transfer the mortgage to 105 her. She's doing it for Anya's sake. God is merciful. Uncle will buy it.

LYUBOV: My aunt in Yaroslavl sent fifteen thousand to buy the estate in her name—she doesn't trust us—but that won't even pay the arrears. [*Hides her* 110 *face in her hands.*] My fate is being sealed today, my whole future…

TROFIMOV: [*Teasing VARYA.*] Madame Lopakhin.

VARYA: [*Angrily.*] The perpetual student! Twice now, you've been kicked out of the University. 115

---

17 *Guter … Musikant*] (German) a good man, but a rotten musician (i.e., no sense of beauty or feeling).

LYUBOV: Why so angry, Varya? He's only teasing you about Lopakhin; what does it matter? If you want to marry Lopakhin, go ahead—he's a good man, he's interesting; if you don't want to, don't! Nobody's forcing you, darling. 120

VARYA: I'll be honest with you, Mamma, I take this very seriously. He's a good man and I like him.

LYUBOV: Well, then marry him. I can't see what you're waiting for!

VARYA: Mamma! I can't very well propose to him 125 myself, can I? For the last two years, everyone's been talking to me about him. *Everyone* talks about it, except him. He says nothing at all or else makes a joke. I know what's going on. He's getting richer and richer, and he's so absorbed in business, he 130 can't spare a thought for me. If I had any money at all, even a hundred rubles, I'd give it all up and run off somewhere. I'd join a convent.

TROFIMOV: What bliss!

VARYA: [*To TROFIMOV.*] A student should have more 135 sense! [*In a soft tone , tearfully.*] You have become unattractive, Petya! And you look so old! [*To LYUBOV ANDREYEVNA, no longer crying.*] But I can't stand doing nothing, Mamma; I have to have work to do every minute of the day. 140

Enter YASHA.

YASHA: [*Barely restraining his laughter.*] Epihodov has broken a billiard cue! [*Goes out.*]

VARYA: What is Epihodov doing here? Who gave him permission to play billiards? I just can't understand these people. [*Goes out.*] 145

LYUBOV: Don't tease her, Petya. You can see that she has grief enough already without adding to it.

TROFIMOV: She's so officious. Always sticking her nose into other people's business. She hasn't given Anya and me a moment's peace all summer long 150 for fear that we'll fall in love. Well, what's it to her? Besides, I've never given her any grounds for her suspicions; I'm well beyond such trivialities. We are above love!

LYUBOV: And I suppose I am *beneath* it. [*Very* 155 *uneasily.*] Why is Leonid not here? If I could just know whether the estate is sold or not! It seems such an inconceivable calamity that I really don't know what to think. I'm at my wit's end … any minute, I'm going to scream, or something stupid. Help me, Petya. Tell me something; talk to me!

TROFIMOV: What does it matter whether the estate's sold today or not? It's all over and done with anyway. There's no turning back, now; that road is closed. Don't worry yourself, dear Lyubov Andreyevna. And don't deceive yourself, either; for once in your life you've got to face the truth!

LYUBOV: What truth? Perhaps *you* can see where the truth lies, but apparently I've lost my sight, because I can't see anything at all. You confidently offer solutions to even the biggest problems, but tell me, my dear boy, isn't that because you're still so young? That you've never yet had to suffer through one of your problems? If you can look towards the future with such confidence, then it may be that you can't really imagine anything dreadful happening to you, because your young eyes haven't seen enough of life yet. It's true that you're a bolder person—and more honest and more profound!—but think for a moment, with a bit more generosity. And ... have some pity for me. I was born here, you know; my father and mother both lived here, and my grandfather lived here. I love this house. I just can't imagine life without the cherry orchard. So if it really has to be sold, better to sell me with it. [*Pause. Embraces TROFIMOV, kisses him on the forehead.*] My little boy was drowned here! [*Weeps.*] Have some pity, my friend.

TROFIMOV: You know that I feel sorry for you with all my heart.

LYUBOV: Still, perhaps you could express yourself better than you did. [*Takes out her handkerchief, another telegram falls to the floor.*] My heart feels made of lead today. All this noise here...! Every little sound goes right through me—it's got me trembling. But I can't leave; I'm afraid to be on my own ... afraid of the silence. Oh, Petya, don't be too hard on me... You know, I love you as though you were one of the family. And I would happily have you marry Anya—truly, I would—except, my boy, you have got to finish your degree! As it is, you never actually do anything—you simply wander wherever fate takes you, from place to place. It's peculiar, really, isn't it? And I wish you would do something about that beard of yours, to make it grow somehow. [*Laughs.*] You look so comical!

TROFIMOV: [*Picks up the telegram.*] I have no desire to be a beauty.

LYUBOV: That telegram's from Paris. Every day I get one. One yesterday and another today. That mad animal is sick again; again he's in trouble. He begs me to forgive him, implores me to return...! I suppose I'll really have to go back to Paris and visit him. You look shocked, Petya. Well, what else can I do, my dear boy, what else is there to do? He's ill, he's miserable and alone, with no one to look after him, no one to save him from his own foolishness, to make sure he takes his medicine on time. And why pretend it isn't so or keep quiet about it? It's obvious that I love him. I love him! I love him! He's a millstone around my neck, and he's dragging me to the bottom with him, but I love that stone ... I can't live without it. [*Presses TROFIMOV's hand.*] Don't think badly of me, Petya, and please don't say anything; say nothing at all.

TROFIMOV: [*Through his tears.*] For God's sake forgive my bluntness, but he robbed you!

LYUBOV: No! No! No! You mustn't say things like that. [*Covers her ears.*]

TROFIMOV: The man is a pig! You're the only person who doesn't see it! He's worthless! He's completely despicable!

LYUBOV: [*Growing angry, but speaking with restraint.*] You're, what, twenty-six or seven years old, but still just a schoolboy.

TROFIMOV: So?

LYUBOV: You should be a man at your age! You should understand something about love! You ought to be in love yourself. You need to fall in love! [*Angrily.*] And yes, the truth is, you're not this pure being either; what you are is a prude, a prig, this ridiculous little freak!

TROFIMOV: [*Horrified.*] Listen to what she's saying...!

LYUBOV: "I am above love!" You're not *above* love, at all, you're just, as Firs would say, you're a moron! To be your age and not to have a mistress!

TROFIMOV: [*In horror.*] This is horrible! For her to say such things...! [*Goes quickly into the ballroom, his hands clutching his face.*] It's outrageous! I can't stand it! I'm going. [*Goes off, but at once returns.*] We are finished for ever! [*Goes off into the ante-room.*]

LYUBOV: [*Shouts after him.*] Petya! Wait a minute! You silly thing! I was only joking! Petya! [*There is a sound of someone running downstairs and falling with a crash. ANYA and VARYA scream, but there is laughter immediately afterwards.*]

LYUBOV: What happened?

ANYA runs in.

ANYA: [*Laughing.*] Oh, Petya fell down the stairs! [*Runs out.*]
LYUBOV: Such a strange boy he is!

The STATION MASTER stands in the middle of the ballroom and begins reciting Tolstoy's The Magdalene.[18] The others listen to him at first, but not long after he has begun, a waltz is struck up in the vestibule and the recital breaks off. Everyone dances. TROFIMOV, ANYA, VARYA and LYUBOV ANDREYEVNA pass through.

LYUBOV: Come here, Petya—come here, my darling boy! Forgive me, please. Let's dance together! [*Dances with PETYA.*]

ANYA and VARYA dance. FIRS comes in, rests his stick near the side door. YASHA also comes in and looks on at the dancing.

YASHA: How's it going, old timer?
FIRS: I don't feel so well. In old days, generals, barons and admirals used to come to our dances. Now, we send for the post-office clerk and the station master and even they're not overanxious to come. I'm getting feeble. The old master, their grandfather, used to give us a dose of sealing-wax whatever the complaint was. It's more than twenty years now that I've been taking sealing-wax. Perhaps that's what's kept me alive.
YASHA: You're boring me, Pops. [*Yawns.*] It's time they finished you off.

FIRS: Ah, you're nothing but a bum! [*Mutters.*]

TROFIMOV and LYUBOV ANDREYEVNA dance in from the ballroom.

LYUBOV: *Merci.* I think I'll sit for a little. [*Sits down.*] I'm tired.

Enter ANYA.

ANYA: [*Excitedly.*] There was a man in the kitchen saying that the cherry orchard was sold today!
LYUBOV: Sold to whom?
ANYA: He didn't say. He's gone now.

She dances with TROFIMOV, and they go off into the ballroom.

YASHA: It was just some old stranger gossiping.
FIRS: Where is Leonid Andreyevitch? He's still not back. And he's got nothing but a light overcoat on, so he'll catch cold no doubt. Aggh! These youngsters!
LYUBOV: I feel like I'm going to die. Yasha, go find out who bought it.
YASHA: But he's been gone ages, that old fellow. [*Laughs.*]
LYUBOV: [*Slightly vexed.*] What are you laughing at? What are you pleased about?
YASHA: Epihodov, what a clown! Totally inept. The Luckless Loser!
LYUBOV: Firs, if the estate is sold, where will you go?
FIRS: Wherever you tell me to go.
LYUBOV: Why do you look that way? Are you feeling ill? You should be in bed.
FIRS: Oh, yes. [*Ironically.*] I go off to bed and who will take care of things here? I'm the only one who can run things in the house.
YASHA: [*To LYUBOV ANDREYEVNA.*] Lyubov Andreyevna, do you mind my asking: if you go back to Paris, will you please take me with you. I just can't stay here. It's impossible. [*Looking about him; in an undertone.*] I hardly need to say it, you can see for yourself what an uncivilized country this is; the people have no morals at all. And boring? Besides, the food in the kitchen's disgusting, and then you have Firs running around you muttering and using the wrong sort of language. Please: take me with you, please!

18 Magdalene] also known as "The Sinful Woman" by Count Aleksey Tolstoy (1817–1875)—not to be confused with the novelist, Leo Tolstoy.

Enter PISHCHIK.

PISHCHIK: May I have the pleasure of a waltz, my dear lady? [*LYUBOV ANDREYEVNA goes with him.*] By the way, my enchantress, I'm afraid I have to borrow one hundred and eighty rubles from you, [*dances*] just a hundred and eighty, though. [*They pass into the ballroom.*]   320

In the ballroom, a figure in a gray top hat and in check trousers is gesticulating and jumping. Shouts of "Bravo, CHARLOTTA IVANOVNA."

DUNYASHA: [*She has stopped to powder herself.*] Miss Anya told me I should join the dancing. There are too many gentlemen, and too few ladies; but dancing makes me so dizzy and makes my heart pound like anything. Oh, Firs, the post-office clerk said something to me just now that just bowled me over.   325

Music becomes more subdued.

FIRS: What did he say?   330
DUNYASHA: He said I was "flower-like."
YASHA: [*Yawns.*] What ignorance! [*Goes out.*]
DUNYASHA: "Flower-like," he said. I'm a sensitive girl, so I do like a pretty speech.
FIRS: Your head's being turned.   335

Enter EPIHODOV.

EPIHODOV: Evidently, you have no wish to see me, Dunyasha. I'm like some insect. [*Sighs.*] There's life for you!
DUNYASHA: What do you want?
EPIHODOV: Undoubtedly, it may be that you are right. [*Sighs.*] And yet, naturally, were one to examine the matter from another point of view, if I do say so myself, it would appear that you have, to speak candidly, completely reduced me to a state. My destiny is, to be sure, all too clear. Every day brings its own new misfortune, and to this I have long since grown accustomed, to the point whereof I may smile even upon my fate. A promise was made by you to me, and though I—   340   345
DUNYASHA: Can we have this talk a little later? Please? But for now, just leave me, will you? I'm in a sort of dream at the moment. [*Plays with her fan.*]   350

EPIHODOV: Yes, indeed, every day its misfortune! And yet, I can aver, it provokes from me nothing but a smile. Perchance, at times, a laugh!   355

VARYA enters from the ballroom.

VARYA: Haven't you left yet, Epihodov? What an insolent oaf you are, really! [*To DUNYASHA.*] Run along, Dunyasha! [*To EPIHODOV.*] First you play billiards and break the cue, then you go wandering around the drawing-room as if you were a guest!   360
EPIHODOV: You really have no right, if I may say, to arraign me in this manner.
VARYA: I'm not arraigning you, I'm yelling at you! All you do is wander around aimlessly, shirking your work! We pay you to keep the accounts, but I can't think why: you're totally useless!   365
EPIHODOV: [*Offended.*] Whether I work or wander, or eat or play billiards, are matters to be decided by persons of greater wisdom and maturity than you!   370
VARYA: How dare you speak to me like that! [*Firing up.*] How dare you! Say that I don't know what I'm talking about! Get out! Get out of here this minute!   375
EPIHODOV: [*Intimidated.*] I must entreat you to express yourself with greater delicacy.
VARYA: [*Beside herself with rage.*] Right now! Get out! Out!! [*He moves towards the door, she follows.*] Luckless Loser! Get lost! Get out of my sight!   380

EPIHODOV has gone out, but from behind the door we hear his voice:

EPIHODOV: [*Offstage.*] I shall make a complaint against you!
VARYA: What! Are you coming back? [*Snatches up the stick FIRS has left near the door.*] Come here! Come on, then! I'll show you something! Oh, you're coming? Good, how do you like this! [*She swings the stick at the very moment that LOPAKHIN enters.*]   385
LOPAKHIN: Well, thank you very much!
VARYA: [*Angrily and ironically.*] Well, I beg your pardon!   390
LOPAKHIN: Not at all! Thanks very much for the warm reception!
VARYA: No need for thanks. [*Moves away, then turns and asks gently.*] I didn't hurt you, did I?

LOPAKHIN: No, no! It's fine! I'll have a pretty fair-sized bump, though! 395

VOICES FROM BALLROOM: Lopakhin has come! Yermolay Alexeyevitch!

PISHCHIK: Well, look who's here! [*Kisses LOPAKHIN.*] There's a whiff of brandy on you, my boy! We're having a fine old time here, too! 400

Enter LYUBOV ANDREYEVNA.

LYUBOV: You're here at last, Yermolay? Why have you been so long? Where's Leonid?

LOPAKHIN: Leonid Andreyevitch is with me. He's coming in a moment. 405

LYUBOV: [*In agitation.*] Well? Well? Was the auction held? Say something!

LOPAKHIN: [*Embarrassed, afraid of betraying his joy.*] The sale was over by four o'clock. We missed our train, though—had to wait till half-past nine. [*Sighing heavily.*] Ohhh! I'm a bit dizzy… 410

Enter GAYEV. In his right hand he carries packages; his left hand is wiping away his tears.

LYUBOV: Well, Leonid? What happened? [*Impatiently, tearfully.*] Hurry up, for God's sake!

GAYEV: [*Does not answer her, simply waves his hand. To FIRS, weeping.*] Here, take these; there's some anchovies, and some Kertch herrings.[19] I haven't eaten a thing all day. I've had an awful time! [*The door into the billiard room is open. The sound of a break is heard and the voice of Yasha saying "Eighty-seven." GAYEV's expression changes, he stops off weeping.*] I am horribly tired. Firs, come and help me change, will you. [*Goes to his own room across the ballroom.*] 415 420

PISHCHIK: What about the sale? For God's sake, tell us!

LYUBOV: Was the cherry orchard sold? 425

LOPAKHIN: It was.

LYUBOV: And who bought it?

LOPAKHIN: I bought it.

Pause. LYUBOV is devastated. Were she not standing near a chair and table, she would fall down. VARYA takes the house keys from her waistband, throws them on the floor in the middle of the room and goes out.

---

19 Kertch herrings] a delicacy caught in the Black Sea.

LOPAKHIN: I bought it! Oh, hang on a moment, ladies and gentlemen, please. I'm a little muddled; I can't quite speak. [*Laughs.*] We arrived at the auction and Deriganov was already there. Leonid Andreyevitch only had the fifteen thousand and straight off, Deriganov bids thirty thousand, plus the arrears. I could see the way it was, so I started bidding against him. I bid forty thousand; he bids forty-five; so I call fifty-five… And that's the way it went on, see: him raising me five thousand, me raising him ten. And then, finally, it ended. I bid ninety, plus the arrears, and … the gavel fell. So … the cherry orchard's mine. It's mine! [*Chuckles.*] My God! The cherry orchard is mine! Tell me that I'm drunk, that I'm out of my mind, say that it's all a dream! [*Stamps his feet.*] Don't laugh at me! If only my father and my grandfather could rise from their graves and see what has happened! How their Yermolay—poor, ignorant, Yermolay, who was always getting beaten, who used to run around barefoot in the snow!—how that very same Yermolay has bought this estate, the most beautiful place on earth! I have bought the same estate where my father and grandfather were slaves! where they weren't even allowed into the kitchen! I must be asleep, I must be dreaming! It can't be true! I've got to be imagining the whole thing, it's just a figment of imagination shining out of the darkness of ignorance! [*Picks up keys, smiling fondly.*] She threw away the keys—wanted to show that she won't be housekeeper here anymore. [*Jingles the keys.*] Well, never mind. [*The orchestra is heard tuning up.*] Hey, you musicians! Play something! I want to hear you. Come on, all of you, and watch, while Yermolay Lopakhin takes an axe to the cherry orchard! Watch those trees come crashing down! We'll build houses on it and our grandsons and great-grandsons will see a new life come to these parts. Music, now! Come on, play! 430 435 440 445 450 455 460 465

Music begins to play. LYUBOV ANDREYEVNA has sunk into a chair and is weeping bitterly.

LOPAKHIN: [*Reproachfully.*] Why, oh why wouldn't you listen to me? My poor friend! My dear lady, there's no way back now. [*With tears.*] Oh, I wish this could be all over and done with right now. I 470 wish that, somehow, soon, we could get beyond this rotten, misshapen life!

PISHCHIK: [*Takes him by the arm, in an undertone.*] She's crying. Let's go, now; let's leave her alone. 475 Come on. [*Takes him by the arm and leads him into the ballroom.*]

LOPAKHIN: What's going on here! Come on, musicians, play with some feeling! Everything's got to be the way I want it now! [*With irony.*] Here 480 he comes! The new master, the owner of the cherry orchard! [*Accidentally tips over a small table, almost upsetting the candelabra.*] I can pay for everything! [*Goes out with PISHCHIK. No one remains on the stage or in the ballroom except LYUBOV, who sits 485 huddled, weeping bitterly. The music plays softly. ANYA and TROFIMOV come in quickly. ANYA goes to her mother and kneels in front of her. TROFIMOV stands at the entrance to the ballroom*]

ANYA: Mamma! Mamma, you're crying? My darling, 490 lovely, kind Mamma! My precious! I love you! Bless you! The cherry orchard is sold, it is gone now. That's true; it is true! But don't cry, Mamma! Your life is still ahead of you; and you still have your good, pure heart! Let's leave, darling Mamma, let's 495 go away from this place! We'll make a new garden, even more beautiful than this one. You'll see. And when you do, you'll understand. And your heart will feel joy, a deep, full joy, descending just as serenely as a beautiful sunset! And then you'll 500 smile, Mamma! Come, darling, come with me.

CURTAIN.

ACT IV.

The same room as in Act One. There are no curtains or pictures. Only a few pieces of furniture remain, piled up in a corner as if for sale. It creates a desolate impression. Close to the outer door and in the background are trunks, travelling bags, etc. The door on the left is open, and from here the voices of VARYA and ANYA are audible. LOPAKHIN is standing waiting. YASHA holds a tray with glasses of champagne. At the front of the stage EPIHODOV is tying up a box. In the background there is the murmur from the peasants who have come to say goodbye. The voice of GAYEV is heard: "Thanks, friends, thank you very much!"

YASHA: The peasants have come to say good-bye. If you want my opinion, Yermolay Alexeyevitch, the peasants are good-natured enough, but they don't have much intelligence.

The murmur dies away. LYUBOV ANDREYEVNA and GAYEV cross the room. She is not weeping, but she is pale; her face is trembling—she cannot speak.

GAYEV: You gave them your purse, Lyuba. You can't 5 do these things, you know, you can't!

LYUBOV: I couldn't help it! I just couldn't help it!

Both go out.

LOPAKHIN: [*In the doorway, calls after them.*] You'll take a glass before you leave? Please do. I forgot to bring some with me from town, and at the 10 station I could only get the one bottle. Please, have a glass. [*Pause.*] What is it? You don't want any? [*Comes away from the door.*] If I'd known, I wouldn't have bothered. Well, I don't really want any either. [*YASHA carefully sets the tray down on a 15 chair.*] You have some, Yasha, anyway.

YASHA: *Bon voyage* to the travellers, and *bon chance* to those left behind! [*Drinks.*] I'll tell you one thing: this champagne is definitely not the real thing. 20

LOPAKHIN: Eight rubles a bottle it cost. [*Pause.*] It's damn cold in here.

YASHA: They haven't fired up the stoves today. Doesn't matter. We're leaving anyway. [*Laughs.*]

LOPAKHIN: What are you laughing about? 25

YASHA: Just for pleasure.

LOPAKHIN: It's October already, but it could be summer, it's so nice and sunny. Perfect weather for construction. [*Looks at his watch; says in doorway.*] Just want to remind you folks that the train leaves 30 in forty-seven minutes, so we'll have to leave for the station about twenty minutes from now. Better get moving!

TROFIMOV comes in from outdoors wearing an overcoat.

TROFIMOV: It's just about time to start; the horses are ready. Damn it, where have my galoshes gone? 35 I've lost them. [*In the doorway.*] Anya! My galoshes aren't here. I can't find them.

LOPAKHIN: Well, as for me, I'm off for Harkov. We'll be taking the same train. I'll be in Harkov the whole winter. I've spent so much time sitting around and gossiping with you folk, I'm itching to get to work. I don't know what to do with myself without work. Look at my hands: they flap around in this weird way as if they weren't mine.

TROFIMOV: Well, we'll be gone shortly, so you'll be able to resume your profitable labours.

LOPAKHIN: Have a glass of champagne.

TROFIMOV: No, thanks.

LOPAKHIN: So, you're off to Moscow, are you?

TROFIMOV: Yes. I'll see them as far as the town, and tomorrow I'll go to Moscow.

LOPAKHIN: Yes, I suppose the professors haven't been able to start any lectures yet. They've been waiting for you to arrive.

TROFIMOV: Well, it's none of your business.

LOPAKHIN: How many years have you been at that university now, eh?

TROFIMOV: Can't you come up with something new? You've worn that joke out. [Searches for his galoshes.] You know, there's a good chance we'll never see one another again, so allow me to give you a parting piece of advice. Don't wave your arms around when you talk—try to break that habit. And something else, this thing of building cottages and speculating how the summer visitors will eventually turn themselves into local farmers—all that calculating is also gauche. But, still, on the whole, I rather like you. You have the hands of an artist—those fine, delicate fingers—and deep down, you've got a fine, sensitive soul, too.

LOPAKHIN: [Embraces him.] Good-bye, Petya. Thanks for everything. If you want money for the journey, I'd be happy to give you some.

TROFIMOV: What for? I don't need it.

LOPAKHIN: Look, you haven't got a kopeck.

TROFIMOV: Yes, I have, thank you. I got some money for a translation. It's right here. [Anxiously.] But I still can't find my galoshes!

VARYA: [From the next room.] Oh, take the filthy things! [Flings a pair of galoshes onstage.]

TROFIMOV: What's got into you, Varya? Eh? Wait, those aren't my galoshes!

LOPAKHIN: Look, I planted three thousand acres of poppies last spring, and now I've cleared forty thousand profit on them. But those poppies were gorgeous when they were in bloom, eh? Anyway, like I say, I made an easy forty thousand from that, so I'd like to lend it to you, just because I can. No need to turn up your nose at it… I'm a peasant, so I'm a bit blunt sometimes.

TROFIMOV: Your father was a peasant, mine was a chemist, which proves exactly nothing. [LOPAKHIN takes out his wallet.] Will you stop that? Stop it! If you offered me two hundred thousand I wouldn't take it. I'm a free man. And all these things that the rest of you, whether you're rich or poor, prize so highly and hold so dear, none of it has any power over me—it's all so much fluff sailing through the breeze. I can get by without your help. I'll pass right by you. I'm strong and I'm proud. Humanity is marching towards a a much higher truth, towards the greatest happiness possible on earth, and I'm right in the vanguard.

LOPAKHIN: Will you make it there?

TROFIMOV: I'll make it. [Pause.] I'll make it, or at least show others the way.

An axe is heard striking a tree in the distance.

LOPAKHIN: Good-bye, Petya; it's time we were going. You and I might look down at one another, but meanwhile, life passes on. When I'm hard at work for a good stretch of time, my mind starts to relax, and then it starts to feel as if my existence also has some meaning. But, boy, when you think of all the people in Russia—who can say why some of them exist. Anyway, never mind; none of this is what makes the world go round. I hear that Leonid Andreyevitch has taken a position. He's going to be a clerk at the bank for 6,000 rubles a year. He'll never stick it out, though. He's way too lazy.

ANYA: [In the doorway.] Mamma begs you not to let them chop down the orchard until she's gone.

TROFIMOV: Yes, you really could have shown a little more tact. [Walks out into hall.]

LOPAKHIN: Okay, I'll take care of it, I'll speak to them. Morons! [Goes out after Petya.]

ANYA: Has Firs been taken to the hospital?

YASHA: I told them this morning. I'm sure they must have taken him.

ANYA: [*To EPIHODOV, who is passing through.*] Semyon Pantaleyevitch, would you mind asking whether Firs has been taken to the hospital? 130

YASHA: [*Offended.*] I told Yegor this morning. Why keep asking time after time?

EPIHODOV: It is my considered opinion that the elderly Firs is beyond treatment. It's time he was gathered to his fathers. As it stands, I can only envy 135 him. [*Puts a trunk down on a cardboard hat-box, crushing it.*] There you have it, naturally—I could have predicted it.

YASHA: [*Jeeringly.*] The Luckless Loser!

VARYA: [*Through the door.*] Has Firs been taken to 140 the hospital?

ANYA: Yes.

VARYA: Why wasn't the note for the doctor taken too?

ANYA: Oh, well, we'll have to send it after them. 145 [*Goes out.*]

VARYA: [*From the adjoining room.*] Where's Yasha? Tell him his mother's arrived to say good-bye to him.

YASHA: [*Waves his hand.*] They'll drive me up the wall! [*All this time, DUNYASHA has kept herself busy* 150 *with the luggage. Now that YASHA is alone, she goes up to him.*]

DUNYASHA: You might just look at me once, Yasha. You're going away. You're abandoning me. [*Sobs and throws her arms around his neck.*] 155

YASHA: What are you crying about? [*Drinks the champagne.*] Within a week, I'll be back in Paris. To-morrow we'll get on board that express train and be off in a flash. I can hardly believe it! *Vive la France!* I don't belong here at all—it's not the 160 life for me and that's all there is to it. I've seen enough stupidity here to last me a lifetime. [*Drinks champagne.*] Why all the sobbing? Be a good girl and stop it, will you.

DUNYASHA: [*Powders her face in a pocket-mirror.*] 165 Will you send me a letter from Paris? I loved you very much you know, Yasha—I loved you terribly! Yasha, I'm so soft-hearted, you know.

YASHA: Look out, they're coming!

Busies himself with the trunks, humming softly. Enter LYUBOV ANDREYEVNA, GAYEV, ANYA and CHARLOTTA IVANOVNA.

GAYEV: We ought to get going, we're almost out of 170 time. [*Looking at YASHA.*] Oh, I can smell herring!

LYUBOV: In ten minutes, we should get into the carriage. [*Casts a look around the room.*] Goodbye, dear house, dear old family home! Winter will pass and when spring comes, you will be no more. They 175 will tear you down. The things these walls have seen! [*Kisses her daughter passionately.*] My treasure, you look radiant. Your eyes are sparkling like diamonds. Are you happy? Very happy?

ANYA: Very happy! This is the beginning of a new 180 life, Mamma.

GAYEV: Yes, it's true, everything seems just fine now. Before the cherry orchard was sold, we were all worried and miserable, but afterwards, once the thing had been decided on once and for all, and 185 there was no turning back, we all felt a little easier and even cheerful. Now I've got this job at the bank—I've become a financier! Red in the corner pocket! And even you, Lyuba, have to admit that you're looking much heathier these days. 190

LYUBOV: Yes, my nerves aren't so much on edge, that's true. [*Her hat and coat are handed to her.*] And I'm sleeping better. Take my things out, please, Yasha. It's time. [*To ANYA.*] It won't be long, darling, until we see one another again. I'll be off 195 in Paris, living on the money your great-aunt in Yaroslavl sent us to buy the estate—God bless auntie!—but that won't last for long.

ANYA: You *will* come back soon, won't you Mamma? I'll be getting ready for my high school examina- 200 tion, and when I've passed that, I'll settle down and help you. We'll read all sorts of books to one an- other, won't we, Mamma? [*Kisses her mother's hands.*] We'll read away the autumn evenings—all *kinds* of books—and a new, wonderful world will 205 open up for us. [*Dreamily.*] Please come back, Mamma.

LYUBOV: I will, my precious. [*Embraces her.*]

Enter LOPAKHIN. CHARLOTTA softly hums a song.

GAYEV: Well, Charlotta's happy, singing away…

CHARLOTTA: [*Picks up a bundle that looks like a* 210 *swaddled baby.*] Rock-a-bye, my baby. [*A baby is heard crying: "Ooah! ooah!"*] Hush, hush, my pretty boy! [*Ooah! ooah!*] Poor little thing! [*Throws the bundle back*.] Please, you really must find me a situation somewhere. I can't go on like this. 215

LOPAKHIN: We'll find you one, Charlotta Ivanovna. Don't you worry.

GAYEV: Everyone's leaving us. Varya's going too. Suddenly, we're of no use to anyone.

CHARLOTTA: There's nowhere for me in town. I'll have to go away somewhere. [*Sings softly.*] 220

Oh let me leave this noisy world…

Enter PISHCHIK.

LOPAKHIN: Well, look what the cat dragged in!

PISHCHIK: [*Gasping.*] Ohh!… Let me get my breath…! I'm worn right out…! My friends—let me have some water. 225

GAYEV: Here for money, I suppose. Thanks very much, I'll stay out of the line of fire. [*Goes out.*]

PISHCHIK: It's been ages since I last came to visit, dear lady. [*To LOPAKHIN.*] And you're here too! 230 Good, glad to see it. What a brilliant man this is! Here, take this. [*Gives money to LOPAKHIN.*] Four hundred rubles. That makes eight hundred and forty I owe you.

LOPAKHIN: [*Shrugging his shoulders in amazement.*] 235 I must be dreaming. Where did you get it?

PISHCHIK: Hang on a bit. I'm so hot… An amazing thing! Some Englishmen came along. And they found this sort of … white clay in my land. [*To LYUBOV ANDREYEVNA.*] And here's four hundred 240 for you too, most lovely, gracious… [*Gives money.*] I'll give you the rest later. [*Drinks some water.*] There was this young man in the train just now. Told me how this great philosopher says everyone should jump off roof-tops. "Just make that leap!" 245 he says, "that's the only way to tackle the problem."[20] [*Wonderingly.*] Amazing, yes? More water, please.

LOPAKHIN: What Englishmen?

PISHCHIK: I've leased them the rights to dig for the 250 clay for the next twenty-four years But, excuse me, now. I've got to be off. Going to see Znoikovo, then Kardamanovo. I owe everybody. [*Drinks.*] All the best to you all. I'll pop in on Thursday.

---

[20] great philosopher … leap] a garbled version of Soren Kierkegaard's "leap of faith."

LYUBOV: We're just leaving for town. Tomorrow I 255 start for abroad.

PISHCHIK: What! [*Upset.*] Why are you going to town? Oh, I see. The furniture and the boxes… Never mind. [*Through his tears.*] Never mind. Brilliant men, these Englishmen. Never mind. 260 Keep yourselves happy, and God bless you. Never mind. Everything in the world must come to an end. [*Kisses LYUBOV ANDREYEVNA's hand.*] If you should ever hear the rumour that my end has come, please remember this old horse, and say: 265 "There once was this man, who lived in the world, known as Semyonov-Pishchik, may he rest in peace." Exceptional weather we're having, yes. [*Goes out deeply moved, but returns immediately and says from the doorway.*] Dashenka asked me to send 270 her regards. [*Goes out.*]

LYUBOV: Well, now we can be off. I'm leaving with two things still on my mind. The first is leaving when poor Firs is ill. [*Looking at her watch.*] We still have five minutes. 275

ANYA: Firs has been taken to the hospital, Mamma. Yasha sent him off this morning.

LYUBOV: My other worry is Varya. She's used to getting up early and working all day; and now, with nothing to do, she's like a fish out of water. The 280 poor girl's grown quite thin and pale, and she's always crying. [*Pause.*] You're well aware, Yermolay, that I had hopes of her marrying you, and it did indeed look as though that is just what would happen. [*Whispers to ANYA and motions to CHARLOTTA* 285 *and both go out.*] She loves you—and she seems to suit you very well. But I can never see—I don't know why it is that you two seem, almost, to avoid one another. I can't understand it.

LOPAKHIN: I have to admit that I don't understand 290 it myself. It's all very odd. If there's enough time, I'm prepared to go ahead with it now. Let's get it settled and done with right away. Without you here, I don't feel I'll be able to make the proposal.

LYUBOV: Excellent. A single moment's all that's 295 needed. I'll call her in.

LOPAKHIN: We've even got the champagne all ready. [*Looks at the glasses.*] They're all empty! Someone drank it all. [*YASHA coughs.*] That's what I call greedy. 300

LYUBOV: [*Eagerly.*] This is wonderful! We'll go out. Yasha, *allez!* I'll call her in. [*At the door.*] Varya, leave all that, and come in here. Come on! [*Goes out with YASHA.*]

LOPAKHIN: [*Looking at his watch.*] Yes.   305

Pause. Behind the door, smothered laughter and whispering, and, at last, VARYA enters.

VARYA: [*Looking a long while over the luggage.*] That's strange, I can't find it anywhere.

LOPAKHIN: What are you looking for?

VARYA: I packed it myself, and now I can't remember. [*Pause.*]   310

LOPAKHIN: Where are you going now, Varvara Mihailova?

VARYA: Me? To the Ragulins. I have arranged to move in with them and take care of the house—a sort of housekeeper.   315

LOPAKHIN: That's in Yashnovo, isn't it? A good fifty miles away. [*Pause.*] So, this is the end of life in this house.

VARYA: [*Looking among the things.*] Now where can I have put it? Perhaps the trunk. Yes, life has left   320 this house—and it won't be back.

LOPAKHIN: Well, I'm off for Harkov—on this next train. Plenty of business waiting for me there. I'm leaving Epihodov in charge here, though. I've taken him on.   325

VARYA: Is that right.

LOPAKHIN: By this time last year, it had snowed already, remember? But now, it's lovely and sunny now. A bit cold, of course—three degrees of frost.

VARYA: I haven't checked. [*Pause.*] Anyway, our   330 thermometer's broken. [*Pause.*]

Voice from the yard: "Yermolay Alexeyevitch!"

LOPAKHIN: [*As though he had long expected this summons.*] Coming!

LOPAKHIN goes out quickly. VARYA sits on the floor and lays her head on a bag of clothes, sobbing quietly. The door opens. LYUBOV ANDREYEVNA comes in cautiously.

LYUBOV: Well? [*Pause.*] We have to go.   335

VARYA: [*Has wiped her eyes and is no longer crying.*] Yes, Mamma, it's time. I'll be able to make it to the Ragulins today, so long as we don't miss the train.

LYUBOV: [*In the doorway.*] Anya, put your things on.   340

Enter ANYA, then GAYEV and CHARLOTTA IVANOVNA. GAYEV has on a warm overcoat with a hood. Servants and cabmen come in. EPIHODOV arranges the luggage.

LYUBOV: So, we're ready to embark on our travels.

ANYA: [*Joyfully.*] Our travels!

GAYEV: My friends! Dear, precious friends! As we leave this house for ever, can I remain silent? Can I refrain, at this moment of departure, from giving   345 expression to all the emotions which surge through my soul?

ANYA: [*Supplicatingly.*] Uncle!

VARYA: Uncle, please don't!

GAYEV: [*Dejectedly.*] Off the boards and into the   350 pocket… I'll be quiet.

Enter TROFIMOV and afterwards LOPAKHIN.

TROFIMOV: Well, ladies and gentlemen, it's time to go.

LOPAKHIN: Epihodov, my coat!

LYUBOV: I'll stay behind just a minute. It suddenly   355 seems as though I've never truly seen the walls and the ceilings of this house before, and now I can't get enough of them, I love them so dearly.

GAYEV: I remember being six years old and sitting in that window on Trinity Day watching Father   360 go off to church.

LYUBOV: Have all the things been taken out?

LOPAKHIN: I think so. [*Putting on overcoat, to EPIHODOV.*] Epihodov, make sure that everything is all right, will you?   365

EPIHODOV: [*In a husky voice.*] Not to worry, Yermolay Alexeyevitch.

LOPAKHIN: What's happened to your voice?

EPIHODOV: I was having a drink of water. I believe I may have swallowed something.   370

YASHA: [*Contemptuously.*] The stupidity!

LYUBOV: Once we've gone, not a soul will be left here.

LOPAKHIN: Until the spring, at any rate.

VARYA: [*Pulls a parasol out of a bundle in a way that   375 looks as though she might hit someone. LOPAKHIN ducks as though frightened.*] Oh, now stop it. That wasn't deliberate.

TROFIMOV: Ladies and gentlemen, it's time we got into the carriage. The train will be in soon.   380

VARYA: Petya, your galoshes are right over there by that box. [*With tears.*] They're filthy old things anyway!

TROFIMOV: [*Putting on his galoshes.*] Alright, friends: let's go!   385

GAYEV: [*Deeply moved, afraid of weeping.*] To the train—the station! Into the left corner, the white sinks in the right…

LYUBOV: Let's be off!

LOPAKHIN: Is everybody here, now? No one left?   390
[*Locks the sidedoor on left.*] There's some things still here, so I'll have to lock up. Right, let's go!

ANYA: Good-bye, house! Good-bye, old life!

TROFIMOV: And welcome, new life!

TROFIMOV goes out with ANYA. VARYA has a last look round the room and goes out slowly. YASHA and CHARLOTTA IVANOVNA, with her dog, go out.

LOPAKHIN: Until spring, then! Come along, friends,   395
till we meet again! [*Goes out.*]

LYUBOV ANDREYEVNA and GAYEV remain alone. They seem to have been waiting for this. They throw their arms around one another's necks, and quietly smother their sobs, afraid of being overheard.

GAYEV: [*In despair.*] Lyuba, my dear sister!

LYUBOV: Oh, my orchard! My sweet, beautiful orchard! My life, my youth, my happiness, good-bye! Good-bye!   400

ANYA: [*Offstage; calling gaily.*] Mamma!

TROFIMOV: [*Offstage; gaily, excitedly.*] Aa-oo!

LYUBOV: One last look at these walls and windows. Mother loved to walk about this room.

GAYEV: Oh my sister!   405

ANYA: [*Offstage.*] Mamma!

TROFIMOV: [*Offstage.*] Hello-oo!

LYUBOV: We're coming! [*They go out.*]

The stage is empty. There is the sound of the doors being locked up, then of the carriages driving away. Silence. In the stillness there is the dull stroke of an ax in a tree, thudding with a mournful lonely sound. Footsteps are heard. FIRS appears in the doorway on the right. He is dressed as always—in jacket and waistcoat—though with slippers on his feet. He is ill.

FIRS: [*Goes to the doors and tries the handles.*] Locked! They've gone… [*Sits down on sofa.*] They've gone   410
and forgotten me. Never mind. I'll sit here a bit. I'll bet Leonid Andreyevitch hasn't put his fur overcoat on, just gone off with his thin one on. [*Sighs anxiously.*] I should have seen to him. Youngsters… [*Mutters indistinct.*] Life has slipped   415
by just as though I hadn't lived at all. [*Lies down.*] Better lie down for a bit… There's no strength left in you, nothing left you at all—nothing! Agh! I'm good for nothing—just a moron. [*Lies motionless.*]

There is a sound in the distance, as if from the sky— the sound of a breaking string. It mournfully dies away. Then all is still again, and nothing is heard but the strokes of the ax far off in the orchard.

CURTAIN.

BERNARD SHAW

Major Barbara

"To me God does not yet exist," wrote Bernard Shaw in a 1910 letter to novelist Leo Tolstoy, "but there is a creative force constantly struggling to evolve an executive organ of godlike knowledge and power: that is, to achieve omnipotence and omniscience; and every man and woman born is a fresh attempt to achieve this object." It is no exaggeration to suggest that Shaw (1856–1950) devoted most of the waking hours of his long life to the achievement of that object, in the pursuit of which he would become one of the most prolific and learned playwrights in the modern age. In the later years of his nearly century-long life, when he had become world famous, there was scarcely a popular issue in any area about which he was not consulted for his almost invariably well-informed, revolutionary and amusing opinion. And yet Shaw received surprisingly little formal education. Along with William Shakespeare and Tom Stoppard, Bernard Shaw offers one of the outstanding examples in English drama of the extraordinary level of accomplishment that may be attained by a self-educated playwright.

Born into a state of genteel poverty in Dublin, George Bernard Shaw was named after his father, an ineffectual alcoholic about whom he felt a painful ambivalence. This may have been the reason that he detested and almost never used the name "George." It was his discovery as a child that his mother secretly despised his father for his alcoholism and hypocrisy, Bernard Shaw later wrote, that turned him into a lifelong "scoffer"—his facetious term for his commitment to challenging any popular but unexamined preconception. Shaw was perhaps too embarrassed to mention another probable source of his disillusionment: his mother's long-standing affair with a music teacher named Vandeleur Lee, an affair which was apparently conducted right in the Shaw home where Lee was a resident, provoking the all-too-plausible gossip that Lee, and not George Shaw after all, was young Bernard's father (certainly, there was a striking physical resemblance). In such circumstances, it is perhaps unsurprising that as a boy Shaw spent a good deal of time in his room, reading voraciously whatever books he could find in the house—especially Shakespeare and Dickens. Later, when at the age of nineteen he followed his sister and mother (and Vandeleur Lee) to England, he began to spend every day in the Reading Room of the British Museum, educating himself to an awe-inspiring level on an astonishing array of subjects. As Michael Holroyd relates in *Bernard Shaw: The Search for Love*, the first volume of his excellent four-volume biography of Shaw, over a period of eight years of daily visits to the library, Bernard Shaw read an average of 300 books a year, including the entire *Encyclopedia Britannica*. Ironically, the very insecurity he felt at his lack of formal education prompted him to go to far greater lengths to ensure that he was fastidiously well-informed than he might have had he enjoyed the privilege of a university degree.

The energy and discipline that Shaw put into his education were sustained when it came to building his career as a writer. This was fortunate, for he was to suffer a long series of disappointments before achieving any decisive success. Apart from music and theatre criticism (his first work was done on behalf of Vandeleur Lee, who, having secured a position of music critic but being a non-writer, simply turned the work over to young Bernard), Shaw's early efforts were chiefly expended on novels. His perseverance in the face of seemingly relentless discouragement is remarkable. At twenty-one, he began his first novel, but abandoned it immediately; the following year, he began work on another, called *Immaturity*. It was rejected by several publishers, as was his second complete novel, *The Irrational Knot*, and his third, *Love Among the Artists*, and his fourth, *Cashel Byron's Profession*, and his fifth, *An Unsocial Socialist*. However, this last was eventually picked up by a small socialist magazine (though no payment was to be made to Shaw in this arrangement), and *An Unsocial Socialist* began to appear in serial form in 1884. This event seemed to raise the interest of other publishers, for over the next few years, as Shaw became better known, his earlier novels gradually became sought after and published. In the meantime, Shaw had become heavily involved in the Fabian Society, a group that promoted non-violent socialist reform within parliamentary democracy, and his speeches and writings in support of the group were to occupy much of his time over the next few years.

However, at around the same time that *An Unsocial Socialist* was appearing serially, Shaw had been thinking of writing for the stage. He began his first play as a collaboration with the critic and translator William Archer. Archer was to supply the plot and Shaw the dialogue, but the project was shelved when, after only two acts, Shaw had used up all of the plot Archer had intended for the whole. In 1892, however, encouraged by J.T. Grein, who had produced several of Henrik Ibsen's plays in English translation, Shaw returned to the unfinished manuscript and completed it. *Widowers' Houses* was a play very much inspired by Ibsen. It exposed the hypocrisy of putatively respectable men who were secretly slumlords. If this first play was somewhat derivative, Shaw's subsequent work was ever less so, and within twenty years, he would be regarded as one of the leading and most original playwrights in the world.

This success, however, was not easily won. As he had done with his novels, Shaw weathered a quantity of discouragement that would have defeated many another writer. Sometimes he had to wait as long as twelve years before seeing a particular play produced. Undaunted by such setbacks, however, he continued to write, creating a body of work that would transform the face of English drama.

Shaw's decisive breakthrough to public recognition had to wait until the years 1904–7, when ten of his plays were presented in repertory by Granville Barker and J.E. Vedrenne at the Royal Court Theatre. From that point on, Shaw's work has never been wholly absent from the English-speaking stage. At least twelve of his plays have earned a secure place in the international repertoire (the dates reflect Shaw's completion of the plays rather than the first production dates): *Mrs Warren's Profession* (1893), *Arms and the Man* (1894), *Candida* (1894) *You Never Can Tell* (1896), *The Devil's Disciple* (1897), *Man and Superman* (1903), *Major Barbara* (1905), *Caesar and Cleopatra* (1906), *Misalliance* (1910), *Pygmalion* (1914), *Heartbreak House* (1920), and *Saint Joan* (1923). Furthermore, the ongoing rejuvenation of the theatrical viability of his work is now ensured by the fact that the second largest repertory theatre company in North America and one of the foremost theatre companies in the world, the Shaw Festival in Ontario, is dedicated to the production of the plays of Bernard Shaw and his contemporaries.

Major Barbara is certainly one of Shaw's best plays, and it provides a fine example of both Shaw's mastery of the dramatic forms of his own time and his ability to turn these familiar dramatic forms into something more substantial than had been their wont. For, however entertaining and accessible Shaw's plays are in conventional ways (his characters are vividly drawn, his dialogue witty, and his dramatic situations richly conceived), ultimately he uses each of his plays as a vehicle for working particular ideas about modern life through to their consequences. Consider, for example, the uses to which Shaw puts some of the conventions of popular melodrama: a poor mother and her children who are about to be turned out of their house by an unscrupulous rich villain; the heroine who is the embodiment of Christian piety; a drunken thug who threatens the heroine; endearing lower-class characters; the hidden circumstances of a hero's birth. All those situations make an appearance in *Major Barbara*, but they never quite turn out in the way one sees in the commercial melodramas of Shaw's age. Or, to look at Shaw's use of another sort of convention, consider the parallels between Shaw's use of settings in *Major Barbara* and Shakespeare's settings in romantic comedies such as *As You Like It* or *A Midsummer Night's Dream*. In *Major Barbara*, as in those plays, we see characters transplanted from a familiar urban setting into alleged utopias, but Shaw provides two competing utopias—the Salvation Army yard and the Undershaft cannonworks—which represent two radically different social models. Shaw's characters, like Shakespeare's, are transformed by their journey from the "real" to the "ideal" environments, and as in Shakespeare, these transformations seem to represent the inevitable revelation of a hidden true nature. (Shaw symbolically conveys this idea through Barbara's name, which recalls Saint Barbara, the patron saint of artillerymen and gunsmiths.) But in *Major Barbara* the transformations also suggest a kind of dialectic argument. Here we should recall that Shaw subtitles this play "a discussion in three acts." The resolution of this discussion, however, like Shaw's God who "does not yet exist," appears to lie a little beyond our present sight and just outside the action circumscribed by the play.

[C.S.W.]

BERNARD SHAW

Major Barbara

A Discussion in Three Acts

PREFACE TO MAJOR BARBARA

FIRST AID TO CRITICS

BEFORE dealing with the deeper aspects of *Major Barbara*, let me, for the credit of English literature, make a protest against an unpatriotic habit into which many of my critics have fallen. Whenever my view strikes them as being at all outside the range of, say, an ordinary suburban churchwarden, they conclude that I am echoing Schopenhauer, Nietzsche, Ibsen, Strindberg, Tolstoy, or some other heresiarch in northern or eastern Europe.[1]

I confess there is something flattering in this simple faith in my accomplishment as a linguist and my erudition as a philosopher. But I cannot tolerate the assumption that life and literature is so poor in these islands that we must go abroad for all dramatic material that is not common and all ideas that are not superficial. I therefore venture to put my critics im possession of certain facts concerning my contact with modern ideas.

About half a century ago, an Irish novelist, Charles Lever, wrote a story entitled *A Day's Ride: A Life's Romance*.[2] It was published by Charles Dickens in

Household Words, and proved so strange to the public taste that Dickens pressed Lever to make short work of it.[3] I read scraps of this novel when I was a child; and it made an enduring impression on me. The hero was a very romantic hero, trying to live bravely, chivalrously, and powerfully by dint of mere romance-fed imagination, without courage, without means, without knowledge, without skill, without anything real except his bodily appetites. Even in my childhood I found in this poor devil's unsuccessful encounters with the facts of life, a poignant quality that romantic fiction lacked. The book, in spite of its first failure, is not dead: I saw its title the other day in the catalogue of Tauchnitz.[4]

Now why is it that when I also deal in the tragicomic irony of the conflict between real life and the romantic imagination, no critic ever affiliates me to my countryman and immediate forerunner, Charles Lever, whilst they confidently derive me from a Norwegian author of whose language I do not know three words, and of whom I knew nothing until years after the Shavian *Anschauung* was already unequivocally declared in books full of what came, ten years later, to be perfunctorily labelled Ibsenism.[5] I was not Ibsenist even at second hand; for Lever, though he may have read Henri Beyle, alias Stendhal, certainly never read Ibsen.[6] Of the books that made Lever

---

1 Schopenhauer] Arthur Schopenhauer (1788–1860), German philosopher, often called pessimistic, who emphasized the power of will and intuition against reason and spirit; Nietzsche] Friedrich Nietzsche (1844–1900), German philosopher who exposed the concealed motives and hypocrisies of modern civilization; Ibsen] see *Hedda Gabler*; Strindberg] see *The Ghost Sonata*; Tolstoy] Count Leo Tolstoy (1828–1910), Russian author of *Anna Karenina* and *War and Peace*; heresiarch] an originator or outstanding advocate of heresy.

2 Lever] Charles James Lever (1806–1872).

3 *Household Words*] a magazine edited by Dickens that published novels in serial form.

4 Tauchnitz] *The Tauchnitz Collection of British and American Authors* (1841–1939) was a series of inexpensive reprints of previously published works.

5 *Anschauung*] (German) outlook, view.

6 Stendhal] (1783–1842), French author of *Le Rouge et le noir* and *Le Chartreuse de Parme*.

popular, such as *Charles O'Malley* and *Harry Lorrequer*, I know nothing but the names and some of the illustrations. But the story of the day's ride and life's romance of Potts (claiming alliance with Pozzo di Borgo)[7] caught me and fascinated me as something strange and significant, though I already knew all about Alnaschar and Don Quixote and Simon Tappertit and many another romantic hero mocked by reality.[8] From the plays of Aristophanes to the tales of Stevenson that mockery has been made familiar to all who are properly saturated with letters.[9]

Where, then, was the novelty in Lever's tale? Partly, I think, in a new seriousness in dealing with Potts's disease. Formerly, the contrast between madness and sanity was deemed comic: Hogarth shews us how fashionable people went in parties to Bedlam to laugh at the lunatics.[10] I myself have had a village idiot exhibited to me as something irresistibly funny. On the stage the madman was once a regular comic figure: that was how Hamlet got his opportunity before Shakespear touched him. The originality of Shakespear's version lay in his taking the lunatic sympathetically and seriously, and thereby making an advance towards the eastern consciousness of the fact that lunacy may be inspiration in disguise, since a man who has more brains than his fellows necessarily appears as mad to them as one who has less. But Shakespear did not do for Pistol and Parolles what he did for

Hamlet.[11] The particular sort of madman they represented, the romantic make-believer, lay outside the pale of sympathy in literature: he was pitilessly despised and ridiculed here as he was in the east under the name of Alnaschar, and was doomed to be, centuries later, under the name of Simon Tappertit. When Cervantes relented over Don Quixote, and Dickens relented over Pickwick, they did not become impartial: they simply changed sides, and became friends and apologists where they had formerly been mockers.[12]

In Lever's story there is a real change of attitude. There is no relenting towards Potts: he never gains our affections like Don Quixote and Pickwick: he has not even the infatuate courage of Tappertit. But we dare not laugh at him, because, somehow, we recognize ourselves in Potts. We may, some of us, have enough nerve, enough muscle, enough luck, enough tact or skill or address or knowledge to carry things off better than he did; to impose on the people who saw through him; to fascinate Katinka (who cut Potts so ruthlessly at the end of the story); but for all that, we know that Potts plays an enormous part in ourselves and in the world, and that the social problem is not a problem of storybook heroes of the older pattern, but a problem of Pottses, and of how to make men of them. To fall back on my old phrase, we have the feeling — one that Alnaschar, Pistol, Parolles, and Tappertit never gave us — that Potts is a piece of really scientific natural history as distinguished from comic story telling. His author is not throwing a stone at a creature of another and inferior order, but making a confession, with the effect that the stone hits everybody full in the conscience and causes their self-esteem to smart very sorely. Hence the failure of Lever's book to please the readers of *Household Words*. That pain in the self-esteem nowadays causes critics to raise a cry of Ibsenism. I therefore assure them that the sensation first came to me from Lever and may have come to him from Beyle, or at least out of the

---

7 Pozzo di Borgo] (1768–1842) Corsican diplomat and nobleman who was involved in various international intrigues in the years after the Napoleonic Wars.

8 Alnaschar] "the Barber's fifth brother" in *Arabian Nights*, who daydreams of a life made from the profits of his basket of glassware; Don Quixote] the deluded, but ultimately noble, hero of Cervantes' novel; Simon Tappertit] a conceited and bombastic character in Dickens' *Barnaby Rudge*.

9 Aristophanes] see *The Frogs*; Stevenson] Robert Louis Stevenson (1850–1894), Scottish author of *Treasure Island* and *Dr. Jekyll and Mr. Hyde*.

10 Hogarth] William Hogarth (1697–1764), English painter known for his satirical work; shews] one of Shaw's several spelling idiosyncrasies; Bedlam] Bethlem Royal Hospital, the first asylum for the insane in England, open to paying spectators in the seventeenth and eighteenth centuries.

---

11 Pistol] the foolish braggart of *Henry IV, Pt. 2, Henry V* and *Merry Wives*; Parolles] a cowardly fool in *All's Well That Ends Well*.

12 Pickwick] the bumbling hero of *The Pickwick Papers*, who is eventually respected.

Stendhalian atmosphere. I exclude the hypothesis of complete originality on Lever's part, because a man can no more be completely original in that sense than a tree can grow out of air.

Another mistake as to my literary ancestry is made whenever I violate the romantic convention that all women are angels when they are not devils; that they are better looking than men; that their part in courtship is entirely passive; and that the human female form is the most beautiful object in nature. Schopenhauer wrote a splenetic essay which, as it is neither polite nor profound, was probably intended to knock this nonsense violently on the head. A sentence denouncing the idolized form as ugly has been largely quoted. The English critics have read that sentence; and I must here affirm, with as much gentleness as the implication will bear, that it has yet to be proved that they have dipped any deeper. At all events, whenever an English playwright represents a young and marriageable woman as being anything but a romantic heroine, he is disposed of without further thought as an echo of Schopenhauer. My own case is a specially hard one, because, when I implore the critics who are obsessed with the Schopenhaurian formula to remember that playwrights, like sculptors, study their figures from life, and not from philosophic essays, they reply passionately that I am not a playwright and that my stage figures do not live. But even so, I may and do ask them why, if they must give the credit of my plays to a philosopher, they do not give it to an English philosopher? Long before I ever read a word by Schopenhauer, or even knew whether he was a philosopher or a chemist, the Socialist revival of the eighteen-eighties brought me into contact, both literary and personal, with Mr. Ernest Belfort Bax, an English Socialist and philosophic essayist, whose handling of modern feminism would provoke romantic protests from Schopenhauer himself, or even Strindberg.[13] At a matter of fact I hardly noticed Schopenhauer's disparagements of women when they came under my notice later on, so thoroughly had Mr. Bax familiarized me with the homoist attitude, and forced me to recognize the extent to which public

opinion, and consequently legislation and jurisprudence, is corrupted by feminist sentiment.[14]

But Mr. Bax's essays were not confined to the Feminist question. He was a ruthless critic of current morality. Other writers have gained sympathy for dramatic criminals by eliciting the alleged "soul of goodness in things evil"; but Mr. Bax would propound some quite undramatic and apparently shabby violation of our commercial law and morality, and not merely defend it with the most disconcerting ingenuity, but actually prove it to be a positive duty that nothing but the certainty of police persecution should prevent every right-minded man from at once doing on principle. The Socialists were naturally shocked, being for the most part morbidly moral people; but at all events they were saved later on from the delusion that nobody but Nietzsche had ever challenged our mercanto-Christian morality. I first heard the name of Nietzsche from a German mathematician, Miss Borchardt, who had read my Quintessence of Ibsenism, and told me that she saw what I had been reading: namely, Nietzsche's *Jenseits von Gut und Böse*.[15] Which I protest I had never seen, and could not have read with any comfort, for want of the necessary German, if I had seen it.

Nietzsche, like Schopenhauer, is the victim in England of a single much quoted sentence containing the phrase "big blonde beast." On the strength of this alliteration it is assumed that Nietzsche gained his European reputation by a senseless glorification of selfish bullying as the rule of life, just as it is assumed, on the strength of the single word Superman (*Übermensch*) borrowed by me from Nietzsche, that I look for the salvation of society to the despotism of a single Napoleonic Superman, in spite of my careful demonstration of the folly of that outworn infatuation. But even the less recklessly superficial critics seem to believe that the modern objection to Christianity as a pernicious slave-morality was first put forward by Nietzsche. It was familiar to me before I ever heard of Nietzsche. The late Captain Wilson, author of several queer pamphlets, propagandist of a metaphysi-

---

13 Bax] (1854–1926), author of *Ethics of Socialism, The Fraud of Feminism*, etc.

14 homoist] a neologism, i.e., a male-based equivalent of feminism.

15 *Jenseits … Böse*] *Beyond Good and Evil*.

cal system called Comprehensionism, and inventor of the term "Crosstianity" to distinguish the retrograde element in Christendom, was wont thirty years ago, in the discussions of the Dialectical Society, to protest earnestly against the beatitudes of the Sermon on the Mount as excuses for cowardice and servility, as destructive of our will, and consequently of our honor and manhood. Now it is true that Captain Wilson's moral criticism of Christianity was not a historical theory of it, like Nietzsche's; but this objection cannot be made to Mr. Stuart-Glennie, the successor of Buckle as a philosophic historian, who has devoted his life to the elaboration and propagation of his theory that Christianity is part of an epoch (or rather an aberration, since it began as recently as 6000 B.C. and is already collapsing) produced by the necessity in which the numerically inferior white races found themselves to impose their domination on the colored races by priestcraft, making a virtue and a popular religion of drudgery and submissiveness in this world not only as a means of achieving saintliness of character but of securing a reward in heaven.[16] Here you have the slave-morality view formulated by a Scotch philosopher long before English writers began chattering about Nietzsche.

As Mr. Stuart-Glennie traced the evolution of society to the conflict of races, his theory made some sensation among Socialists — that is, among the only people who were seriously thinking about historical evolution at all — by its collision with the class-conflict theory of Karl Marx. Nietzsche, as I gather, regarded the slave-morality as having been invented and imposed on the world by slaves making a virtue of necessity and a religion of their servitude. Mr. Stuart-Glennie regards the slave-morality as an invention of the superior white race to subjugate the minds of the inferior races whom they wished to exploit, and who would have destroyed them by force of numbers if their minds had not been subjugated. As this process is in operation still, and can be studied at first hand

not only in our Church schools and in the struggle between our modern proprietary classes and the proletariat, but in the part played by Christian missionaries in reconciling the black races of Africa to their subjugation by European Capitalism, we can judge for ourselves whether the initiative came from above or below. My object here is not to argue the historical point, but simply to make our theatre critics ashamed of their habit of treating Britain as an intellectual void, and assuming that every philosophical idea, every historic theory, every criticism af our moral, religious and juridical institutions, must necessarily be either imported from abroad, or else a fantastic sally (in rather questionable taste) totally unrelated to the existing body of thought. I urge them to remember that this body of thought is the slowest of growths and the rarest of blossomings, and that if there is such a thing on the philosophic plane as a matter of course, it is that no individual can make more than a minute contribution to it. In fact, their conception of clever persons parthenogenetically bringing forth complete original cosmogonies by dint of sheer "brilliancy" is part of that ignorant credulity which is the despair of the honest philosopher, and the opportunity of the religious impostor.

THE GOSPEL OF ST. ANDREW UNDERSHAFT.

It is this credulity that drives me to help my critics out with Major Barbara by telling them what to say about it. In the millionaire Undershaft I have represented a man who has become intellectually and spiritually as well as practically conscious of the irresistible natural truth which we all abhor and repudiate: to wit, that the greatest of evils and the worst of crimes is poverty, and that our first duty — a duty to which every other consideration should be sacrificed — is not to be poor. "Poor but honest," "the respectable poor," and such phrases are as intolerable and as immoral as "drunken but amiable," "fraudulent but a good after dinner speaker," "splendidly criminal," or the like. Security, the chief pretence of civilization, cannot exist where the worst of dangers, the danger of poverty, hangs over everyone's head, and where the alleged protection of our persons from violence is only an accidental result of the existence of a police force

---

16 Stuart-Glennie] John S. Stuart-Glennie, Scottish author of *In the Morningland; or, the law of the origin and transformation of Christianity*; Buckle] Henry Thomas Buckle (1821–1862), English author of *History of Civilization in England*.

whose real business is to force the poor man to see his children starve whilst idle people overfeed pet dogs with the money that might feed and clothe them.

It is exceedingly difficult to make people realize that an evil is an evil. For instance, we seize a man and deliberately do him a malicious injury: say, imprison him for years. One would not suppose that it needed any exceptional clearness of wit to recognize in this an act of diabolical cruelty. But in England such a recognition provokes a stare of surprise, followed by an explanation that the outrage is punishment or justice or something else that is all right, or perhaps by a heated attempt to argue that we should all be robbed and murdered in our beds if such senseless villainies as sentences of imprisonment were not committed daily. It is useless to argue that even if this were true, which it is not, the alternative to adding crimes of our own to the crimes from which we suffer is not helpless submission. Chickenpox is an evil; but if I were to declare that we must either submit to it or else repress it sternly by seizing everyone who suffers from it and punishing them by inoculation with smallpox, I should be laughed at; for though nobody could deny that the result would be to prevent chickenpox to some extent by making people avoid it much more carefully, and to effect a further apparent prevention by making them conceal it very anxiously, yet people would have sense enough to see that the deliberate propagation of smallpox was a creation of evil, and must therefore be ruled out in favor of purely humane and hygienic measures. Yet in the precisely parallel case of a man breaking into my house and stealing my wife's diamonds I am expected as a matter of course to steal ten years of his life, torturing him all the time. If he tries to defeat that monstrous retaliation by shooting me, my survivors hang him. The net result suggested by the police statistics is that we inflict atrocious injuries on the burglars we catch in order to make the rest take effectual precautions against detection; so that instead of saving our wives' diamonds from burglary we only greatly decrease our chances of ever getting them back, and increase our chances of being shot by the robber if we are unlucky enough to disturb him at his work.

But the thoughtless wickedness with which we scatter sentences of imprisonment, torture in the solitary cell and on the plank bed, and flogging, on moral invalids and energetic rebels, is as nothing compared to the stupid levity with which we tolerate poverty as if it were either a wholesome tonic for lazy people or else a virtue to be embraced as St. Francis embraced it. If a man is indolent, let him be poor. If he is drunken, let him be poor. If he is not a gentleman, let him be poor. If he is addicted to the fine arts or to pure science instead of to trade and finance, let him be poor. If he chooses to spend his urban eighteen shillings a week or his agricultural thirteen shillings a week on his beer and his family instead of saving it up for his old age, let him be poor. Let nothing be done for "the undeserving": let him be poor. Serve him right! Also — somewhat inconsistently — blessed are the poor!

Now what does this Let Him Be Poor mean? It means let him be weak. Let him be ignorant. Let him become a nucleus of disease. Let him be a standing exhibition and example of ugliness and dirt. Let him have rickety children. Let him be cheap and let him drag his fellows down to his price by selling himself to do their work. Let his habitations turn our cities into poisonous congeries of slums. Let his daughters infect our young men with the diseases of the streets and his sons revenge him by turning the nation's manhood into scrofula, cowardice, cruelty, hypocrisy, political imbecility, and all the other fruits of oppression and malnutrition. Let the undeserving become still less deserving; and let the deserving lay up for himself, not treasures in heaven, but horrors in hell upon earth. This being so, is it really wise to let him be poor? Would he not do ten times less harm as a prosperous burglar, incendiary, ravisher or murderer, to the utmost limits of humanity's comparatively negligible impulses in these directions? Suppose we were to abolish all penalties for such activities, and decide that poverty is the one thing we will not tolerate — that every adult with less than, say, £365 a year, shall be painlessly but inexorably killed, and every hungry half naked child forcibly fattened and clothed, would not that be an enormous improvement on our existing system, which has already destroyed so many civilizations, and is visibly destroying ours in the same way?

Is there any radicle of such legislation in our parliamentary system? Well, there are two measures just sprouting in the political soil, which may conceivably grow to something valuable. One is the institution of a Legal Minimum Wage. The other, Old Age Pensions. But there is a better plan than either of these. Some time ago I mentioned the subject of Universal Old Age Pensions to my fellow Socialist Mr. Cobden-Sanderson, famous as an artist-craftsman in bookbinding and printing. "Why not Universal Pensions for Life?" said Cobden-Sanderson. In saying this, he solved the industrial problem at a stroke. At present we say callously to each citizen: "If you want money, earn it," as if his having or not having it were a matter that concerned himself alone. We do not even secure for him the opportunity of earning it: on the contrary, we allow our industry to be organized in open dependence on the maintenance of "a reserve army of unemployed" for the sake of "elasticity." The sensible course would be Cobden-Sanderson's: that is, to give every man enough to live well on, so as to guarantee the community against the possibility of a case of the malignant disease of poverty, and then (necessarily) to see that he earned it.

Undershaft, the hero of *Major Barbara*, is simply a man who, having grasped the fact that poverty is a crime, knows that when society offered him the alternative of poverty or a lucrative trade in death and destruction, it offered him, not a choice between opulent villainy and humble virtue, but between energetic enterprise and cowardly infamy. His conduct stands the Kantian test, which Peter Shirley's does not.[17] Peter Shirley is what we call the honest poor man. Undershaft is what we call the wicked rich one: Shirley is Lazarus, Undershaft Dives.[18] Well, the misery of the world is due to the fact that the great mass of men act and believe as Peter Shirley acts and believes. If they

acted and believed as Undershaft acts and believes, the immediate result would be a revolution of incalculable beneficence. To be wealthy, says Undershaft, is with me a point of honor for which I am prepared to kill at the risk of my own life. This preparedness is, as he says, the final test of sincerity. Like Froissart's medieval hero, who saw that "to rob and pill was a good life," he is not the dupe of that public sentiment against killing which is propagated and endowed by people who would otherwise be killed themselves, or of the mouth-honor paid to poverty and obedience by rich and insubordinate do-nothings who want to rob the poor without courage and command them without superiority.[19] Froissart's knight, in placing the achievement of a good life before all the other duties — which indeed are not duties at all when they conflict with it, but plain wickednesses — behaved bravely, admirably, and, in the final analysis, public-spiritedly. Medieval society, on the other hand, behaved very badly indeed in organizing itself so stupidly that a good life could be achieved by robbing and pilling. If the knight's contemporaries had been all as resolute as he, robbing and pilling would have been the shortest way to the gallows, just as, if we were all as resolute and clearsighted as Undershaft, an attempt to live by means of what is called "an independent income" would be the shortest way to the lethal chamber. But as, thanks to our political imbecility and personal cowardice (fruits of poverty, both), the best imitation of a good life now procurable is life on an independent income, all sensible people aim at securing such an income, and are, of course, careful to legalize and moralize both it and all the actions and sentiments which lead to it and support it as an institution. What else can they do? They know, of course, that they are rich because others are poor. But they cannot help that: it is for the poor to repudiate poverty when they have had enough of it. The thing can be done easily enough: the demonstrations to the contrary made by the economists, jurists, moralists and sentimentalists hired by the rich to defend them, or even doing the work gratuitously out of sheer folly and abjectness, impose only on the hirers.

---

17 Kantian test] German philosopher Immanuel Kant (1724–1804) proposed that a rational act does not merely reflect one person's desires; rather, it can be willed as a universal law.

18 Lazarus, Dives] from Jesus' parable about the Rich Man (Latin: *dives*) and Lazarus, which illustrates that one cannot be the servant of two masters, God and mammon (wealth). Lazarus, a poor beggar, lay at the gate of Dives, by whom he was ignored. Lazarus is rewarded in heaven, Dives punished (Luke 16:13-31).

---

19 Froissart] Jean Froissart (1337–1410), author of *Chronicles* and *Méliador*.

The reason why the independent income-tax payers are not solid in defence of their position is that since we are not medieval rovers through a sparsely populated country, the poverty of those we rob prevents our having the good life for which we sacrifice them. Rich men or aristocrats with a developed sense of life — men like Ruskin and William Morris and Kropotkin — have enormous social appetites and very fastidious personal ones.[20] They are not content with handsome houses: they want handsome cities. They are not content with bediamonded wives and blooming daughters: they complain because the charwoman is badly dressed, because the laundress smells of gin, because the sempstress is anemic, because every man they meet is not a friend and every woman not a romance. They turn up their noses at their neighbors' drains, and are made ill by the architecture of their neighbors' houses. Trade patterns made to suit vulgar people do not please them (and they can get nothing else): they cannot sleep nor sit at ease upon "slaughtered" cabinet makers' furniture. The very air is not good enough for them: there is too much factory smoke in it. They even demand abstract conditions: justice, honor, a noble moral atmosphere, a mystic nexus to replace the cash nexus. Finally they declare that though to rob and pill with your own hand on horseback and in steel coat may have been a good life, to rob and pill by the hands of the policeman, the bailiff, and the soldier, and to underpay them meanly for doing it, is not a good life, but rather fatal to all possibility of even a tolerable one. They call on the poor to revolt, and, finding the poor shocked at their ungentlemanliness, despairingly revile the proletariat for its "damned wantlessness" (*verdammte Bedürfnislosigkeit*).

So far, however, their attack on society has lacked simplicity. The poor do not share their tastes nor understand their art-criticisms. They do not want the simple life, nor the esthetic life, on the contrary, they want very much to wallow in all the costly vulgarities from which the elect souls among the rich turn away with loathing. It is by surfeit and not by abstinence that they will be cured of their hankering after unwholesome sweets. What they do dislike and despise and are ashamed of is poverty. To ask them to fight for the difference between the Christmas number of the *Illustrated London News* and the *Kelmscott Chaucer* is silly: they prefer the *News*.[21] The difference between a stockbroker's cheap and dirty starched white shirt and collar and the comparatively costly and carefully dyed blue shirt of William Morris is a difference so disgraceful to Morris in their eyes that if they fought on the subject at all, they would fight in defence of the starch. "Cease to be slaves, in order that you may become cranks" is not a very inspiring call to arms; nor is it really improved by substituting saints for cranks. Both terms denote men of genius; and the common man does not want to live the life of a man of genius: he would much rather live the life of a pet collie if that were the only alternative. But he does want more money. Whatever else he may be vague about, he is clear about that. He may or may not prefer *Major Barbara* to the Drury Lane pantomime; but he always prefers five hundred pounds to five hundred shillings.

Now to deplore this preference as sordid, and teach children that it is sinful to desire money, is to strain towards the extreme possible limit of impudence in lying, and corruption in hypocrisy. The universal regard for money is the one hopeful fact in our civilization, the one sound spot in our social conscience. Money is the most important thing in the world. It represents health, strength, honor, generosity and beauty as conspicuously and undeniably as the want of it represents illness, weakness, disgrace, meanness and ugliness. Not the least of its virtues is that it destroys base people as certainly as it fortifies and dignifies noble people. It is only when it is cheapened to worthlessness for some, and made impossibly dear to others, that it becomes a curse. In short, it is a curse only in such foolish social conditions that life itself is

---

20 Ruskin] John Ruskin (1819–1900), celebrated English critic and artist; William Morris] (1834–1896), English designer, artist, writer and socialist who promoted beautification of the ordinary daily environment; Kropotkin] Peter Alekseyevich Kropotkin (1842–1921), Russian theorist of "anarchist communism."

21 *Illustrated London News*] a popular tabloid newspaper; *Kelmscott Chaucer*] i.e, the edition of Chaucer's works beautifully produced by Morris's Kelmscott Press.

a curse. For the two things are inseparable: money is the counter that enables life to be distributed socially: it is life as truly as sovereigns and bank notes are money. The first duty of every citizen is to insist on having money on reasonable terms; and this demand is not complied with by giving four men three shillings each for ten or twelve hours' drudgery and one man a thousand pounds for nothing. The crying need of the nation is not for better morals, cheaper bread, temperance, liberty, culture, redemption of fallen sisters and erring brothers, nor the grace, love and fellowship of the Trinity, but simply for enough money. And the evil to be attacked is not sin, suffering, greed, priestcraft, kingcraft, demagogy, monopoly, ignorance, drink, war, pestilence, nor any other of the scapegoats which reformers sacrifice, but simply poverty.

Once take your eyes from the ends of the earth and fix them on this truth just under your nose; and Andrew Undershaft's views will not perplex you in the least. Unless indeed his constant sense that he is only the instrument of a Will or Life Force which uses him for purposes wider than his own, may puzzle you. If so, that is because you are walking either in artificial Darwinian darkness, or in mere stupidity. All genuinely religious people have that consciousness. To them Undershaft the Mystic will be quite intelligible, and his perfect comprehension of his daughter the Salvationist and her lover the Euripidean republican natural and inevitable. That, however, is not new, even on the stage. What is new, as far as I know, is that article in Undershaft's religion which recognizes in Money the first need and in poverty the vilest sin of man and society.

This dramatic conception has not, of course, been attained *per saltum*.[22] Nor has it been borrowed from Nietzsche or from any man born beyond the Channel. The late Samuel Butler, in his own department the greatest English writer of the latter half of the XIX century, steadily inculcated the necessity and morality of a conscientious Laodiceanism in religion and of an earnest and constant sense of the importance of money.[23] It drives one almost to despair of Eng-

lish literature when one sees so extraordinary a study of English life as Butler's posthumous *Way of All Flesh* making so little impression that when, some years later, I produce plays in which Butler's extraordinarily fresh, free and future-piercing suggestions have an obvious share, I am met with nothing but vague cacklings about Ibsen and Nietzsche, and am only too thankful that they are not about Alfred de Musset and Georges Sand.[24] Really, the English do not deserve to have great men. They allowed Butler to die practically unknown, whilst I, a comparatively insignificant Irish journalist, was leading them by the nose into an advertisement of me which has made my own life a burden. In Sicily there is a Via Samuele Butler. When an English tourist sees it, he either asks "Who the devil was Samuele Butler?" or wonders why the Sicilians should perpetuate the memory of the author of *Hudibras*.[25]

Well, it cannot be denied that the English are only too anxious to recognize a man of genius if somebody will kindly point him out to them. Having pointed myself out in this manner with some success, I now point out Samuel Butler, and trust that in consequence I shall hear a little less in future of the novelty and foreign origin of the ideas which are now making their way into the English theatre through plays written by Socialists. There are living men whose originality and power are as obvious as Butler's; and when they die that fact will be discovered. Meanwhile I recommend them to insist on their own merits as an important part of their own business.

THE SALVATION ARMY.

When *Major Barbara* was produced in London, the second act was reported in an important northern

---

religion culminated in the autobiographical *The Way of All Flesh* (1903), describing a personal journey into pragmatism; Laodiceanism] being indifferent or lukewarm in political or religious matters, from Rev. 3:14–16: "because thou art lukewarm, and neither cold nor hot, I will spit thee out of my mouth."

[24] de Musset, Sand] French romantic writers of the early nineteenth century.

[25] *Hudibras*] a long poem written by a much earlier Samuel Butler (1612–1680).

[22] *per saltum*] (Latin) at a single bound.

[23] Samuel Butler] (1835–1902), English novelist and essayist, whose re-examination of Victorian morality and

newspaper as a withering attack on the Salvation Army, and the despairing ejaculation of Barbara deplored by a London daily as a tasteless blasphemy. And they were set right, not by the professed critics of the theatre, but by religious and philosophical publicists like Sir Oliver Lodge and Dr. Stanton Coit, and strenuous Nonconformist journalists like Mr. William Stead, who not only understand the act as well as the Salvationists themselves, but also saw it in its relation to the religious life of the nation, a life which seems to lie not only outside the sympathy of many of our theatre critics, but actually outside their knowledge of society. Indeed nothing could be more ironically curious than the confrontation *Major Barbara* effected of the theatre enthusiasts with the religious enthusiasts. On the one hand was the playgoer, always seeking pleasure, paying exorbitantly for it, suffering unbearable discomforts for it, and hardly ever getting it. On the other hand was the Salvationist, repudiating gaiety and courting effort and sacrifice, yet always in the wildest spirits, laughing, joking, singing, rejoicing, drumming, and tambourining: his life flying by in a flash of excitement, and his death arriving as a climax of triumph. And, if you please, the playgoer despising the Salvationist as a joyless person, shut out from the heaven of the theatre, self-condemned to a life of hideous gloom; and the Salvationist mourning over the playgoer as over a prodigal with vine leaves in his hair, careering outrageously to hell amid the popping of champagne corks and the ribald laughter of sirens! Could misunderstanding be more complete, or sympathy worse misplaced?

Fortunately, the Salvationists are more accessible to the religious character of the drama than the playgoers to the gay energy and artistic fertility of religion. They can see, when it is pointed out to them, that a theatre, as a place where two or three are gathered together, takes from that divine presence an inalienable sanctity of which the grossest and profanest farce can no more deprive it than a hypocritical sermon by a snobbish bishop can desecrate Westminster Abbey. But in our professional playgoers this indispensable preliminary conception of sanctity seems wanting. They talk of actors as mimes and mummers, and, I fear, think of dramatic authors as liars and pandars, whose main business is the voluptuous soothing of the tired city speculator when what he calls the serious business of the day is over. Passion, the life of drama, means nothing to them but primitive sexual excitement: such phrases as "impassioned poetry" or "passionate love of truth" have fallen quite out of their vocabulary and been replaced by "passional crime" and the like. They assume, as far as I can gather, that people in whom passion has a larger scope are passionless and therefore uninteresting. Consequently they come to think of religious people as people who are not interesting and not amusing. And so, when Barbara cuts the regular Salvation Army jokes, and snatches a kiss from her lover across his drum, the devotees of the theatre think they ought to appear shocked, and conclude that the whole play is an elaborate mockery of the Army. And then either hypocritically rebuke me for mocking, or foolishly take part in the supposed mockery!

Even the handful of mentally competent critics got into difficulties over my demonstration of the economic deadlock in which the Salvation Army finds itself. Some of them thought that the Army would not have taken money from a distiller and a cannon founder: others thought it should not have taken it: all assumed more or less definitely that it reduced itself to absurdity or hypocrisy by taking it. On the first point the reply of the Army itself was prompt and conclusive. As one of its officers said, they would take money from the devil himself and be only too glad to get it out of his hands and into God's. They gratefully acknowledged that publicans not only give them money but allow them to collect it in the bar — sometimes even when there is a Salvation meeting outside preaching teetotalism. In fact, they questioned the verisimilitude of the play, not because Mrs. Baines took the money, but because Barbara refused it.

On the point that the Army ought not to take such money, its justification is obvious. It must take the money because it cannot exist without money, and there is no other money to be had. Practically all the spare money in the country consists of a mass of rent, interest, and profit, every penny of which is bound up with crime, drink, prostitution, disease, and all the evil fruits of poverty, as inextricably as with enterprise, wealth, commercial probity, and national prosperity. The notion that you can earmark certain coins as tainted is an unpractical individualist superstition. None the less the fact that all our money is tainted gives a very severe shock to earnest young souls when some dramatic instance of the taint first makes them conscious of it. When an enthusiastic young clergyman of the Established Church first realizes that the Ecclesiastical Commissioners receive the rents of sporting public houses, brothels, and sweating dens; or that the most generous contributor at his last charity sermon was an employer trading in female labor cheapened by prostitution as unscrupulously as a hotel keeper trades in waiters' labor cheapened by tips, or commissionaire's labor cheapened by pensions; or that the only patron who can afford to rebuild his church or his schools or give his boys brigade a gymnasium or a library is the son-in-law of a Chicago meat King, that young clergyman has, like Barbara, a very bad quarter hour. But he cannot help himself by refusing to accept money from anybody except sweet old ladies with independent incomes and gentle and lovely ways of life. He has only to follow up the income of the sweet ladies to its industrial source, and there he will find Mrs. Warren's profession and the poisonous canned meat and all the rest of it.[26] His own stipend has the same root. He must either share the world's guilt or go to another planet. He must save the world's honor if he is to save his own. This is what all the Churches find just as the Salvation Army and Barbara find it in the play. Her discovery that she is her father's accomplice; that the Salvation Army is the accomplice of the distiller and the dynamite maker; that they can no more escape one another than they can escape the air they breathe; that there is no salvation for them through personal righteousness, but only through the redemption of the whole nation from its vicious, lazy, competitive anarchy: this discovery has been made by everyone except the Pharisees and (apparently) the professional playgoers, who still wear their Tom Hood shirts and underpay their washerwomen without the slightest misgiving as to the elevation of their private characters, the purity of their private atmospheres, and their right to repudiate as foreign to themselves the coarse

depravity of the garret and the slum.[27] Not that they mean any harm: they only desire to be, in their little private way, what they call gentlemen. They do not understand Barbara's lesson because they have not, like her, learnt it by taking their part in the larger life of the nation.

BARBARA'S RETURN TO THE COLORS.

Barbara's return to the colors may yet provide a subject for the dramatic historian of the future. To go back to the Salvation Army with the knowledge that even the Salvationists themselves are not saved yet; that poverty is not blessed, but a most damnable sin; and that when General Booth chose Blood and Fire for the emblem of Salvation instead of the Cross, he was perhaps better inspired than he knew: such knowledge, for the daughter of Andrew Undershaft, will clearly lead to something hopefuller than distributing bread and treacle at the expense of Bodger.

It is a very significant thing, this instinctive choice of the military form of organization, this substitution of the drum for the organ, by the Salvation Army. Does it not suggest that the Salvationists divine that they must actually fight the devil instead of merely praying at him? At present, it is true, they have not quite ascertained his correct address. When they do, they may give a very rude shock to that sense of security which he has gained from his experience of the fact that hard words, even when uttered by eloquent essayists and lecturers, or carried unanimously at enthusiastic public meetings on the motion of eminent reformers, break no bones. It has been said that the French Revolution was the work of Voltaire, Rousseau and the Encyclopedists[28] It seems to me to have been the work of men who had observed that virtuous indignation, caustic criticism, conclusive argument and

---

26 Mrs. Warren's profession] i.e., prostitution, as in Shaw's play of that title.

27 Pharisees] i.e., religious hypocrites without any sense of charity; Tom Hood shirts] Thomas Hood's (1799–1845) "Song of the Shirt" tells of a poor old woman losing her eyesight sewing a man's shirt: "It is not linen you're wearing out / But human creatures' lives!"

28 Encyclopedists] i.e., contributors to Denis Diderot's *Encyclopédie,* who, like Voltaire and Rousseau, fed radical and revolutionary opinion in eighteenth-century France.

instructive pamphleteering, even when done by the most earnest and witty literary geniuses, were as useless as praying, things going steadily from bad to worse whilst the Social Contract and the pamphlets of Voltaire were at the height of their vogue. Eventually, as we know, perfectly respectable citizens and earnest philanthropists connived at the September massacres because hard experience had convinced them that if they contented themselves with appeals to humanity and patriotism, the aristocracy, though it would read their appeals with the greatest enjoyment and appreciation, flattering and admiring the writers, would none the less continue to conspire with foreign monarchists to undo the revolution and restore the old system with every circumstance of savage vengeance and ruthless repression of popular liberties.

The nineteenth century saw the same lesson repeated in England. It had its Utilitarians, its Christian Socialists, its Fabians (still extant): it had Bentham, Mill, Dickens, Ruskin, Carlyle, Butler, Henry George, and Morris.[29] And the end of all their efforts is the Chicago described by Mr. Upton Sinclair,[30] and the London in which the people who pay to be amused by my dramatic representation of Peter Shirley turned out to starve at forty because there are younger slaves to be had for his wages, do not take, and have not the slightest intention of taking, any effective step to organize society in such a way as to make that everyday infamy impossible. I, who have preached and pamphleteered like any Encyclopedist, have to confess that my methods are no use, and would be no use if I were Voltaire, Rousseau, Bentham, Mill, Dickens, Carlyle, Ruskin, George,

Butler, and Morris all rolled into one, with Euripides, More, Moliere, Shakespear, Beaumarchais, Swift, Goethe, Ibsen, Tolstoy, Moses and the prophets all thrown in (as indeed in some sort I actually am, standing as I do on all their shoulders). The problem being to make heroes out of cowards, we paper apostles and artist-magicians have succeeded only in giving cowards all the sensations of heroes whilst they tolerate every abomination, accept every plunder, and submit to every oppression. Christianity, in making a merit of such submission, has marked only that depth in the abyss at which the very sense of shame is lost. The Christian has been like Dickens' doctor in the debtor's prison, who tells the newcomer of its ineffable peace and security: no duns; no tyrannical collectors of rates, taxs, and rent; no importunate hopes nor exacting duties; nothing but the rest and safety of having no further to fall.[31]

Yet in the poorest corner of this soul-destroying Christendom vitality suddenly begins to germinate again. Joyousness, a sacred gift long dethroned by the hellish laughter of derision and obscenity, rises like a flood miraculously out of the fetid dust and mud of the slums; rousing marches and impetuous dithyrambs rise to the heavens from people among whom the depressing noise called "sacred music" is a standing joke; a flag with Blood and Fire on it is unfurled, not in murderous rancor, but because fire is beautiful and blood a vital and splendid red; Fear, which we flatter by calling Self, vanishes; and transfigured men and women carry their gospel through a transfigured world, calling their leader General, themselves captains and brigadiers, and their whole body an Army: praying, but praying only for refreshment, for strength to fight, and for needful MONEY (a notable sign, that); preaching, but not preaching submission; daring ill-usage and abuse, but not putting up with more of it than is inevitable; and practising what the world will let them practise, including soap and water, color and music. There is danger in such activity; and where there is danger there is hope. Our present security is nothing, and can be nothing, but evil made irresistible.

---

[29] Bentham] Jeremy Bentham (1748–1832), English theoretical jurist, who expounded Utilitarianism: the theory that an action is good if it promotes the happiness of the majority; Carlyle] Thomas Carlyle (1795–1881), British historian whose *French Revolution* showed the event to be a judgement on the greed and folly of the aristocrats; Henry George] (1839–1897), American economist who toured Britain promoting his idea of a tax on landowners to be spent on humanitarian public works.

[30] Sinclair] Upton Sinclair's novel *The Jungle* grimly describes life in a Chicago meat-packing factory.

---

[31] Dickens' doctor] Doctor Haggage in *Little Dorrit*.

WEAKNESSES OF THE SALVATION ARMY.

For the present, however, it is not my business to flatter the Salvation Army. Rather must I point out to it that it has almost as many weaknesses as the Church of England itself. It is building up a business organization which will compel it eventually to see that its present staff of enthusiast-commanders shall be succeeded by a bureaucracy of men of business who will be no better than bishops, and perhaps a good deal more unscrupulous. That has always happened sooner or later to great orders founded by saints; and the order founded by St. William Booth is not exempt from the same danger. It is even more dependent than the Church on rich people who would cut off supplies at once if it began to preach that indispensable revolt against poverty which must also be a revolt against riches. It is hampered by a heavy contingent of pious elders who are not really Salvationists at all, but Evangelicals of the old school. It still, as Commissioner Howard affirms, "sticks to Moses," which is flat nonsense at this time of day if the Commissioner means, as I am afraid he does, that the Book of Genesis contains a trustworthy scientific account of the origin of species, and that the god to whom Jephthah sacrificed his daughter is any less obviously a tribal idol than Dagon or Chemosh.[32]

Further, there is still too much other-worldliness about the Army. Like Frederick's grenadier, the Salvationist wants to live for ever (the most monstrous way of crying for the moon);[33] and though it is evident to anyone who has ever heard General Booth and his best officers that they would work as hard for human salvation as they do at present if they believed that death would be the end of them individually, they and their followers have a bad habit of talking as if the Salvationists were heroically enduring a very bad

time on earth as an investment which will bring them in dividends later on in the form, not of a better life to come for the whole world, but of an eternity spent by themselves personally in a sort of bliss which would bore any active person to a second death. Surely the truth is that the Salvationists are unusually happy people. And is it not the very diagnostic of true salvation that it shall overcome the fear of death? Now the man who has come to believe that there is no such thing as death, the change so called being merely the transition to an exquisitely happy and utterly careless life, has not overcome the fear of death at all: on the contrary, it has overcome him so completely that he refuses to die on any terms whatever. I do not call a Salvationist really saved until he is ready to lie down cheerfully on the scrap heap, having paid scot and lot and something over, and let his eternal life pass on to renew its youth in the battalions of the future.[34]

Then there is the nasty lying habit called confession, which the Army encourages because it lends itself to dramatic oratory, with plenty of thrilling incident. For my part, when I hear a convert relating the violences and oaths and blasphemies he was guilty of before he was saved, making out that he was a very terrible fellow then and is the most contrite and chastened of Christians now, I believe him no more than I believe the millionaire who says he came up to London or Chicago as a boy with only three halfpence in his pocket. Salvationists have said to me that Barbara in my play would never have been taken in by so transparent a humbug as Snobby Price; and certainly I do not think Snobby could have taken in any experienced Salvationist on a point on which the Salvationist did not wish to be taken in. But on the point of conversion all Salvationists wish to be taken in; for the more obvious the sinner the more obvious the miracle of his conversion. When you advertize a converted burglar or reclaimed drunkard as one of the attractions at an experience meeting, your burglar can hardly have been too burglarious or your drunkard too drunken. As long as such attractions are relied on, you will have your Snobbies claiming to have beaten their mothers when they were as a matter of prosaic fact habitually beaten by them, and your Rummies

---

32 Jephthah's daughter] Jephtha made a vow, in exchange for victory, to sacrifice the first creature he met outside his house; this turned out to be his daughter (Judges 11:30–40); Dagon] the Philistine god whose temple in Gaza is destroyed by Samson (Judges 16); Chemosh] a god to whom the Moabites offered human sacrifices.

33 Frederick's grenadier] At Kolin, Bohemia, in 1757, Frederick the Great allegedly rallied his grenadier troops by shouting: "Rogues! Would you live forever?"

34 scot and lot] i.e., pay in full.

of the tamest respectability pretending to a past of reckless and dazzling vice. Even when confessions are sincerely autobiographic there is no reason to assume at once that the impulse to make them is pious or the interest of the hearers wholesome. It might as well be assumed that the poor people who insist on shewing appalling ulcer to district visitors are convinced hygienists, or that the curiosity which sometimes welcomes such exhibitions is a pleasant and creditable one. One is often tempted to suggest that those who pester our police superintendents with confessions of murder might very wisely be taken at their word and executed, except in the few cases in which a real murderer is seeking to be relieved of his guilt by confession and expiation. For though I am not, I hope, an unmerciful person, I do not think that the inexorability of the deed once done should be disguised by any ritual, whether in the confessional or on the scaffold.

And here my disagreement with the Salvation Army, and with all propagandists of the Cross (to which I object as I object to all gibbets) becomes deep indeed. Forgiveness, absolution, atonement, are figments: punishment is only a pretence of cancelling one crime by another; and you can no more have forgiveness without vindictiveness than you can have a cure without a disease. You will never get a high morality from people who conceive that their misdeeds are revocable and pardonable, or in a society where absolution and expiation are officially provided for us all. The demand may be very real; but the supply is spurious. Thus Bill Walker, in my play, having assaulted the Salvation Lass, presently finds himself overwhelmed with an intolerable conviction of sin under the skilled treatment of Barbara. Straightway he begins to try to unassault the lass and deruffianize his deed, first by getting punished for it in kind, and, when that relief is denied him, by fining himself a pound to compensate the girl. He is foiled both ways. He finds the Salvation Army as inexorable as fact itself. It will not punish him: it will not take his money. It will not tolerate a redeemed ruffian: it leaves him no means of salvation except ceasing to be a ruffian. In doing this, the Salvation Army instinctively grasps the central truth of Christianity and discards its central superstition: that central truth being the vanity of revenge and punishment, and that central superstition the salvation of the world by the gibbet.

For, be it noted, Bill has assaulted an old and starving woman also; and for this worse offence he feels no remorse whatever, because she makes it clear that her malice is as great as his own. "Let her have the law of me, as she said she would," says Bill: "what I done to her is no more on what you might call my conscience than sticking a pig." This shews a perfectly natural and wholesome state of mind on his part. The old woman, like the law she threatens him with, is perfectly ready to play the game of retaliation with him: to rob him if he steals, to flog him if he strikes, to murder him if he kills. By example and precept the law and public opinion teach him to impose his will on others by anger, violence, and cruelty, and to wipe off the moral score by punishment. That is sound Crosstianity. But this Crosstianity has got entangled with something which Barbara calls Christianity, and which unexpectedly causes her to refuse to play the hangman's game of Satan casting out Satan. She refuses to prosecute a drunken ruffian; she converses on equal terms with a blackguard whom no lady could be seen speaking to in the public street: in short, she behaves as illegally and unbecomingly as possible under the circumstances. Bill's conscience reacts to this just as naturally as it does to the old woman's threats. He is placed in a position of unbearable moral inferiority, and strives by every means in his power to escape from it, whilst he is still quite ready to meet the abuse of the old woman by attempting to smash a mug on her face. And that is the triumphant justification of Barbara's Christianity as against our system of judicial punishment and the vindictive villainthrashings and "poetic justice" of the romantic stage.

For the credit of literature it must be pointed out that the situation is only partly novel. Victor Hugo long ago gave us the epic of the convict and the bishop's candlesticks, of the Crosstian policeman annihilated by his encounter with the Christian Valjean.[35] But Bill Walker is not, like Valjean, romantically changed from a demon into an angel. There are millions of Bill Walkers in all classes of society to-day; and the point which I, as a professor of natural psy-

---

35 Victor Hugo's epic] *Les Miserables*.

chology, desire to demonstrate, is that Bill, without any change in his character whatsoever, will react one way to one sort of treatment and another way to another.

In proof I might point to the sensational object lesson provided by our commercial millionaires today. They begin as brigands: merciless, unscrupulous, dealing out ruin and death and slavery to their competitors and employees, and facing desperately the worst that their competitors can do to them. The history of the English factories, the American trusts, the exploitation of African gold, diamonds, ivory and rubber, outdoes in villainy the worst that has ever been imagined of the buccaneers of the Spanish Main. Captain Kidd would have marooned a modern Trust magnate for conduct unworthy of a gentleman of fortune.[36] The law every day seizes on unsuccessful scoundrels of this type and punishes them with a cruelty worse than their own, with the result that they come out of the torture house more dangerous than they went in, and renew their evil doing (nobody will employ them at anything else) until they are again seized, again tormented, and again let loose, with the same result.

But the successful scoundrel is dealt with very differently, and very Christianly. He is not only forgiven: he is idolized, respected, made much of, all but worshipped. Society returns him good for evil in the most extravagant overmeasure. And with what result? He begins to idolize himself, to respect himself, to live up to the treatment he receives. He preaches sermons; he writes books of the most edifying advice to young men, and actually persuades himself that he got on by taking his own advice; he endows educational institutions; he supports charities; he dies finally in the odor of sanctity, leaving a will which is a monument of public spirit and bounty. And all this without any change in his character. The spots of the leopard and the stripes of the tiger are as brilliant as ever; but the conduct of the world towards him has changed; and his conduct has changed accordingly. You have only to reverse your attitude towards him — to lay hands on his property, revile him, assault him, and he will be a brigand again in a moment, as ready to crush

you as you are to crush him, and quite as full of pretentious moral reasons for doing it.

In short, when Major Barbara says that there are no scoundrels, she is right: there are no absolute scoundrels, though there are impracticable people of whom I shall treat presently. Every practicable man (and woman) is a potential scoundrel and a potential good citizen. What a man is depends on his character; but what he does, and what we think of what he does, depends on his circumstances. The characteristics that ruin a man in one class make him eminent in another The characters that behave differently in different circumstances behave alike in similar circumstances. Take a common English character like that of Bill Walker. We meet Bill everywhere: on the judicial bench, on the episcopal bench, in tbe Privy Council, at the War Office and Admiralty, as well as in the Old Bailey dock or in the ranks of casual unskilled labor. And the morality of Bill's characteristics varies with these various circumstances. The faults of the burglar are the qualities of the financier: the manners and habits of a duke would cost a city clerk his situation. In short, though character is independent of circumstances, conduct is not; and our moral judgments of character are not: both are circumstantial. Take any condition of life in which the circumstances are for a mass of men practically alike: felony, the House of Lords, the factory, the stables, the gipsy encampment or where you please! In spite of diversity of character and temperament, the conduct and morals of the individuals in each group are as predicable and as alike in the main as if they were a flock of sheep, morals being mostly only social habits and circumstantial necessities. Strong people know this and count upon it. In nothing have the master-minds of the world been distinguished from the ordinary suburban season-ticket holder more than in their straightforward perception of the fact that mankind is practically a single species, and not a menagerie of gentlemen and bounders, villains and heroes, cowards and daredevils, peers and peasants, grocers and aristocrats, artisans and laborers, washerwomen and duchesses, in which all the grades of income and caste represent distinct animals who must not be introduced to one another or intermarry. Napoleon constructing a galaxy of generals and courtiers, and even of monarchs, out of his

---

[36] Captain Kidd] (c.1645–1701), legendary pirate.

collection of social nobodies; Julius Caesar appointing as governor of Egypt the son of a freedman — one who but a short time before would have been legally disqualified for the post even of a private soldier in the Roman army; Louis XI. making his barber his privy councillor: all these had in their different ways a firm hold of the scientific fact of human equality, expressed by Barbara in the Christian formula that all men are children of one father. A man who believes that men are naturally divided into upper and lower and middle classes morally is making exactly the same mistake as the man who believes that they are naturally divided in the same way socially. And just as our persistent attempts to found political institutions on a basis of social inequality have always produced long periods of destructive friction relieved from time to time by violent explosions of revolution; so the attempt — will Americans please note — to found moral institutions on a basis of moral inequality can lead to nothing but unnatural Reigns of the Saints relieved by licentious Restorations; to Americans who have made divorce a public institution turning the face of Europe into one huge sardonic smile by refusing to stay in the same hotel with a Russian man of genius who has changed wives without the sanction of South Dakota; to grotesque hypocrisy, cruel persecution, and final utter confusion of conventions and compliances with benevolence and respectability. It is quite useless to declare that all men are born free if you deny that they are born good. Guarantee a man's goodness and his liberty will take care of itself. To guarantee his freedom on condition that you approve of his moral character is formally to abolish all freedom whatsoever, as every man's liberty is at the mercy of a moral indictment, which any fool can trump up against everyone who violates custom, whether as a prophet or as a rascal. This is the lesson Democracy has to learn before it can become anything but the most oppressive of all the priesthoods.

Let us now return to Bill Walker and his case of conscience against the Salvation Army. Major Barbara, not being a modern Tetzel, or the treasurer of a hospital, refuses to sell Bill absolution for a sovereign. Unfortunately, what the Army can afford to refuse in the case of Bill Walker, it cannot refuse in the case of Bodger. Bodger is master of the situation because he holds the purse strings. "Strive as you will," says Bodger, in effect: "me you cannot do without. You cannot save Bill Walker without my money." And the Army answers, quite rightly under the circumstances, "We will take money from the devil himself sooner than abandon the work of Salvation." So Bodger pays his conscience-money and gets the absolution that is refused to Bill. In real life Bill would perhaps never know this. But I, the dramatist, whose business it is to shew the connexion between things that seem apart and unrelated in the haphazard order of events in real life, have contrived to make it known to Bill, with the result that the Salvation Army loses its hold of him at once.

But Bill may not be lost, for all that. He is still in the grip of the facts and of his own conscience, and may find his taste for blackguardism permanently spoiled. Still, I cannot guarantee that happy ending. Let anyone walk through the poorer quarters of our cities when the men are not working, but resting and chewing the cud of their reflections; and he will find that there is one expression on every mature face: the expression of cynicism. The discovery made by Bill Walker about the Salvation Army has been made by everyone of them. They have found that every man has his price; and they have been foolishly or corruptly taught to mistrust and despise him for that necessary and salutary condition of social existence. When they learn that General Booth, too, has his price, they do not admire him because it is a high one, and admit the need of organizing society so that he shall get it in an honorable way: they conclude that his character is unsound and that all religious men are hypocrites and allies of their sweaters and oppressors. They know that the large subscriptions which help to support the Army are endowments, not of religion, but of the wicked doctrine of docility in poverty and humility under oppression; and they are rent by the most agonizing of all the doubts of the soul, the doubt whether their true salvation must not come from their most abhorrent passions, from murder, envy, greed, stubbornness, rage, and terrorism, rather than from public spirit, reasonableness, humanity, generosity, tenderness, delicacy, pity and kindness. The confirmation of that doubt, at which our newspapers have been working so hard for years past, is the morality of militarism; and the justification of militarism is that circumstances may at any time make it the true morality of the moment. It is by producing such moments that we produce violent and sanguinary revolutions, such as the one now in progress in Russia and the one which Capitalism in England and America is daily and diligently provoking.

At such moments it becomes the duty of the Churches to evoke all the powers of destruction against the existing order. But if they do this, the existing order must forcibly suppress them. Churches are suffered to exist only on condition that they preach submission to the State as at present capitalistically organized. The Church of England itself is compelled to add to the thirty-six articles in which it formulates its religious tenets, three more in which it apologetically protests that the moment any of these articles comes in conflict with the State it is to be entirely renounced, abjured, violated, abrogated and abhorred, the policeman being a much more important person than any of the Persons of the Trinity. And this is why no tolerated Church nor Salvation Army can ever win the entire confidence of the poor. It must be on the side of the police and the military, no matter what it believes or disbelieves; and as the police and the military are the instruments by which the rich rob and oppress the poor (on legal and moral principles made for the purpose), it is not possible to be on the side of the poor and of the police at the same time. Indeed the religious bodies, as the almoners of the rich, become a sort of auxiliary police, taking off the insurrectionary edge of poverty with coals and blankets, bread and treacle, and soothing and cheering the victims with hopes of immense and inexpensive happiness in another world when the process of working them to premature death in the service of the rich is complete in this.

CHRISTIANITY AND ANARCHISM.

Such is the false position from which neither the Salvation Army nor the Church of England nor any other religious organization whatever can escape except through a reconstitution of society. Nor can they merely endure the State passively, washing their hands of its sins. The State is constantly forcing the consciences of men by violence and cruelty. Not content with exacting money from us for the maintenance of its soldiers and policemen, its gaolers and executioners, it forces us to take an active personal part in its proceedings on pain of becoming ourselves the victims of its violence. As I write these lines, a sensational example is given to the world.[37] A royal marriage has been celebrated, first by sacrament in a cathedral, and then by a bullfight having for its main amusement the spectacle of horses gored and disembowelled by the bull, after which, when the bull is so exhausted as to be no longer dangerous, he is killed by a cautious matador. But the ironic contrast between the bull fight and the sacrament of marriage does not move anyone. Another contrast — that between the splendor, the happiness, the atmosphere of kindly admiration surrounding the young couple, and the price paid for it under our abominable social arrangements in the misery, squalor and degradation of millions of other young couples — is drawn at the same moment by a novelist, Mr. Upton Sinclair, who chips a corner of the veneering from the huge meat packing industries of Chicago, and shews it to us as a sample of what is going on all over the world underneath the top layer of prosperous plutocracy. One man is sufficiently moved by that contrast to pay his own life as the price of one terrible blow at the responsible parties. Unhappily his poverty leaves him also ignorant enough to be duped by the pretence that the inno-

---

37 sensational example] Shaw is alluding to the news surrounding the spectacular wedding of King Alfonso XIII of Spain and his English bride, Victoria Eugenia of Battenberg, in Madrid on May 31, 1906. A young man, Mateo Morral, attempted to assassinate the royal couple by throwing from a balcony a bomb concealed in a floral arrangement. The bomb rebounded into the street, missing the couple, but killing and maiming many bystanders. Morral escaped and fled first to his employer, the anarchist theorist, editor, publisher and teacher, Francisco Ferrer (through whom it seems Morral knew of Upton Sinclair's *The Jungle*). Later, Morral killed a policeman and then himself. At the time of Shaw's writing, Ferrer, who was assumed to have instigated the assassination attempt, had been imprisoned. He would be released after a year in prison for lack of evidence, but he was to be executed on trumped-up charges after the uprisings of 1909.

cent young bride and bridegroom, put forth and crowned by plutocracy as the heads of a State in which they have less personal power than any policeman, and less influence than any chairman of a trust, are responsible. At them accordingly he launches his sixpennorth of fulminate, missing his mark, but scattering the bowels of as many horses as any bull in the arena, and slaying twenty-three persons, besides wounding ninety-nine. And of all these, the horses alone are innocent of the guilt he is avenging: had he blown all Madrid to atoms with every adult person in it, not one could have escaped the charge of being an accessory, before, at, and after the fact, to poverty and prostitution, to such wholesale massacre of infants as Herod never dreamt of, to plague, pestilence and famine, battle, murder and lingering death — perhaps not one who had not helped, through example, precept, connivance, and even clamor, to teach the dynamiter his well-learnt gospel of hatred and vengeance, by approving every day of sentences of years of imprisonment so infernal in its unnatural stupidity and panic-stricken cruelty, that their advocates can disavow neither the dagger nor the bomb without stripping the mask of justice and humanity from themselves also.[38]

Be it noted that at this very moment there appears the biography of one of our dukes, who, being Scotch, could argue about politics, and therefore stood out as a great brain among our aristocrats.[39] And what, if you please, was his grace's favorite historical episodes which he declared he never read without intense satisfaction? Why, the young General Bonaparte's pounding of the Paris mob to pieces in 1795, called in playful approval by our respectable classes "the whiff of grapeshot," though Napoleon, to do him justice, took a deeper view of it, and would fain have had it forgotten. And since the Duke of Argyll was not a demon, but a man of like passions with ourselves, by no means rancorous or cruel as men go, who can doubt that all over the world proletarians of the ducal kidney are now reveling in "the whiff of dynamite" (the flavor of the joke seems to evaporate a little, does it not?) because it was aimed at the class they hate even as our argute duke hated what he called the mob.[40]

In such an atmosphere there can be only one sequel to the Madrid explosion. All Europe burns to emulate it. Vengeance! More blood! Tear "the Anarchist beast" to shreds. Drag him to the scaffold. Imprison him for life. Let all civilized States band together to drive his like off the face of the earth; and if any State refuses to join, make war on it. This time the leading London newspaper, anti-Liberal and therefore anti-Russian in politics, does not say "Serve you right" to the victims, as it did, in effect, when Bobrikoff, and De Plehve, and Grand Duke Sergius, were in the same manner unofficially fulminated into fragments.[41] No: fulminate our rivals in Asia by all means, ye brave Russian revolutionaries; but to aim at an English princess — monstrous! hideous! hound down the wretch to his doom; and observe, please, that we are a civilized and merciful people, and, however much we may regret it, must not treat him as Ravaillac and Damiens were treated.[42] And meanwhile, since we have not yet caught him, let us soothe our quivering nerves with the bullfight, and comment in a courtly way on the unfailing tact and good taste of the ladies of our royal houses, who, though presumably of full normal natural tenderness, have been so effectually broken in to fashionable routine that they can be taken to see the horses slaughtered as helplessly as they could no doubt be taken to a gladiator show, if that happened to be the mode just now.

---

38 massacre of infants] Matt. 2:16.

39 duke] George Douglas Campbell, Eighth Duke of Argyll (1823–1900); his *Autobiography and Memoirs* was published posthumously in 1906.

40 argute] quick, sharp (play on Argyll).

41 Bobrikoff] Nikolay Bobrikoff (1839–1904), tyrannical Russian governor-general of Finland, assassinated by the son of a Finnish senator; De Plehve] Vyacheslav Konstantinovich von Plehve (1846–1904), brutal authoritarian Russian politician assassinated by a member of the Socialist Revolutionary Party; Grand Duke Sergius] ultrareactionary Governor General of Moscow, assassinated in 1905 by an revolutionary.

42 Ravaillac and Damiens] François Ravaillac, Roman Catholic assassin of Protestant King Henry IV of France in 1610, and Robert-François Damiens, who, for uncertain reasons, stabbed without killing King Louis XV in 1757; each of the regicides was tortured cruelly and then dismembered by horses.

Strangely enough, in the midst of this raging fire of malice, the one man who still has faith in the kindness and intelligence of human nature is the fulminator, now a hunted wretch, with nothing, apparently, to secure his triumph over all the prisons and scaffolds of infuriate Europe except the revolver in his pocket and his readiness to discharge it at a moment's notice into his own or any other head. Think of him setting out to find a gentleman and a Christian in the multitude of human wolves howling for his blood. Think also of this: that at the very first essay he finds what he seeks, a veritable grandee of Spain, a noble, high-thinking, unterrified, malice-void soul, in the guise — of all masquerades in the world! — of a modern editor. The Anarchist wolf, flying from the wolves of plutocracy, throws himself on the honor of the man. The man, not being a wolf (nor a London editor), and therefore not having enough sympathy with his exploit to be made bloodthirsty by it, does not throw him back to the pursuing wolves — gives him, instead, what help he can to escape, and sends him off acquainted at last with a force that goes deeper than dynamite, though you cannot make so much of it for sixpence. That righteous and honorable high human deed is not wasted on Europe, let us hope, though it benefits the fugitive wolf only for a moment. The plutocratic wolves presently smell him out. The fugitive shoots the unlucky wolf whose nose is nearest; shoots himself; and then convinces the world, by his photograph, that he was no monstrous freak of reversion to the tiger, but a good looking young man with nothing abnormal about him except his appalling courage and resolution (that is why the terrified shriek Coward at him): one to whom murdering a happy young couple on their wedding morning would have been an unthinkably unnatural abomination under rational and kindly human circumstances.

Then comes the climax of irony and blind stupidity. The wolves, balked of their meal of fellow-wolf, turn on the man, and proceed to torture him, after their manner, by imprisonment, for refusing to fasten his teeth in the throat of the dynamiter and hold him down until they came to finish him.

Thus, you see, a man may not be a gentleman nowadays even if he wishes to. As to being a Christian, he is allowed some latitude in that matter, because, I repeat, Christianity has two faces. Popular Christianity has for its emblem a gibbet, for its chief sensation a sanguinary execution after torture, for its central mystery an insane vengeance bought off by a trumpery expiation. But there is a nobler and profounder Christianity which affirms the sacred mystery of Equality, and forbids the glaring futility and folly of vengeance, often politely called punishment or justice. The gibbet part of Christianity is tolerated. The other is criminal felony. Connoisseurs in irony are well aware of the fact that the only editor in England who denounces punishment as radically wrong, also repudiates Christianity; calls his paper *The Freethinker*; and has been imprisoned for two years for blasphemy.[43]

SANE CONCLUSIONS.

And now I must ask the excited reader not to lose his head on one side or the other, but to draw a sane moral from these grim absurdities. It is not good sense to propose that laws against crime should apply to principals only and not to accessories whose consent, counsel, or silence may secure impunity to the principal. If you institute punishment as part of the law, you must punish people for refusing to punish. If you have a police, part of its duty must be to compel everybody to assist the police. No doubt if your laws are unjust, and your policemen agents of oppression, the result will be an unbearable violation of the private consciences of citizens. But that cannot be helped: the remedy is, not to license everybody to thwart the law if they please, but to make laws that will command the public assent, and not to deal cruelly and stupidly with lawbreakers. Everybody disapproves of burglars; but the modern burglar, when caught and overpowered by a householder, usually appeals, and often, let us hope, with success, to his captor not to deliver him over to the useless horrors of penal servitude. In other cases the lawbreaker escapes because those who could give him up do not consider his breach of the law a guilty action. Sometimes, even, private tribunals are formed in opposition to the official tribunals; and

---

43 editor] George W. Foote (1850–1915), founding editor of *The Freethinker*, an atheist newspaper; he was sentenced to hard labour for blasphemy, 1883 to 1884.

these private tribunals employ assassins as executioners, as was done, for example, by Mahomet before he had established his power officially, and by the Ribbon lodges of Ireland in their long struggle with the landlords.[44] Under such circumstances, the assassin goes free although everybody in the district knows who he is and what he has done. They do not betray him, partly because they justify him exactly as the regular Government justifies its official executioner, and partly because they would themselves be assassinated if they betrayed him: another method learnt from the official government. Given a tribunal, employing a slayer who has no personal quarrel with the slain; and there is clearly no moral difference between official and unofficial killing.

In short, all men are anarchists with regard to laws which are against their consciences, either in the preamble or in the penalty. In London our worst anarchists are the magistrates, because many of them are so old and ignorant that when they are called upon to administer any law that is based on ideas or knowledge less than half a century old, they disagree with it, and being mere ordinary homebred private Englishmen without any respect for law in the abstract, naively set the example of violating it. In this instance the man lags behind the law; but when the law lags behind the man, he becomes equally an anarchist. When some huge change in social conditions, such as the industrial revolution of the eighteenth and nineteenth centuries, throws our legal and industrial institutions out of date, Anarchism becomes almost a religion. The whole force of the most energetic geniuses of the time in philosophy, economics, and art, concentrates itself on demonstrations and reminders that morality and law are only conventions, fallible and continually obsolescing. Tragedies in which the heroes are bandits, and comedies in which law-abiding and conventionally moral folk are compelled to satirize themselves by outraging the conscience of the spectators every time they do their duty, appear simultaneously with economic treatises entitled "What is Property? Theft!" and with histories of "The Conflict between Religion and Science."[45]

Now this is not a healthy state of things. The advantages of living in society are proportionate, not to the freedom of the individual from a code, but to the complexity and subtlety of the code he is prepared not only to accept but to uphold as a matter of such vital importance that a lawbreaker at large is hardly to be tolerated on any plea. Such an attitude becomes impossible when the only men who can make themselves heard and remembered throughout the world spend all their energy in raising our gorge against current law, current morality, current respectability, and legal property. The ordinary man, uneducated in social theory even when he is schooled in Latin verse, cannot be set against all the laws of his country and yet persuaded to regard law in the abstract as vitally necessary to society. Once he is brought to repudiate the laws and institutions he knows, he will repudiate the very conception of law and the very groundwork of institutions, ridiculing human rights, extolling brainless methods as "historical," and tolerating nothing except pure empiricism in conduct, with dynamite as the basis of politics and vivisection as the basis of science. That is hideous; but what is to be done? Here am I, for instance, by class a respectable man, by common sense a hater of waste and disorder, by intellectual constitution legally minded to the verge of pedantry, and by temperament apprehensive and economically disposed to the limit of old-maidishness; yet I am, and have always been, and shall now always be, a revolutionary writer, because our laws make law impossible; our liberties destroy all freedom; our property is organized robbery; our morality is an impudent hypocrisy; our wisdom is administered by inexperienced or malexperienced dupes, our power wielded by cowards and weaklings, and our honor false in all its points. I am an enemy of the existing order for good reasons; but that does not make my attacks any less encouraging or helpful to people who

---

44 Mahomet] (c.570–632) the prophet (a.k.a. Muhammad), founder of Islam, who established "unofficial" power while in exile in Medina from 622; Ribbon lodges] the forerunner of the Fenian Society, established in the 1850s to protect tenants' rights against unscrupulous, but legally protected, landowners.

45 treatises, histories] e.g., Pierre-Joseph Proudhon, *What is Property?* (1840); John William Draper, *History of the Conflict Between Religion and Science* (1873).

are its enemies for bad reasons. The existing order may shriek that if I tell the truth about it, some foolish person may drive it to become still worse by trying to assassinate it. I cannot help that, even if I could see what worse it could do than it is already doing. And the disadvantage of that worst even from its own point of view is that society, with all its prisons and bayonets and whips and ostracisms and starvations, is powerless in the face of the Anarchist who is prepared to sacrifice his own life in the battle with it. Our natural safety from the cheap and devastating explosives which every Russian student can make, and every Russian grenadier has learnt to handle in Manchuria, lies in the fact that brave and resolute men, when they are rascals, will not risk their skins for the good of humanity, and, when they are sympathetic enough to care for humanity, abhor murder, and never commit it until their consciences are outraged beyond endurance. The remedy is, then, simply not to outrage their consciences.

Do not be afraid that they will not make allowances. All men make very large allowances indeed before they stake their own lives in a war to the death with society. Nobody demands or expects the millennium. But there are two things that must be set right, or we shall perish, like Rome, of soul atrophy disguised as empire.

The first is, that the daily ceremony of dividing the wealth of the country among its inhabitants shall be so conducted that no crumb shall go to any able-bodied adults who are not producing by their personal exertions not only a full equivalent for what they take, but a surplus sufficient to provide for their superannuation and pay back the debt due for their nurture.

The second is that the deliberate infliction of malicious injuries which now goes on under the name of punishment be abandoned, so that the thief, the ruffian, the gambler, and the beggar, may without inhumanity be handed over to the law, and made to understand that a State which is too humane to punish will also be too thrifty to waste the life of honest men in watching or restraining dishonest ones. That is why we do not imprison dogs. We even take our chance of their first bite. But if a dog delights to bark and bite, it goes to the lethal chamber. That seems to me sensible. To allow the dog to expiate his bite by a period of torment, and then let him loose in a much more savage condition (for the chain makes a dog savage) to bite again and expiate again, having meanwhile spent a great deal of human life and happiness in the task of chaining and feeding and tormenting him, seems to me idiotic and superstitious. Yet that is what we do to men who bark and bite and steal. It would be far more sensible to put up with their vices, as we put up with their illnesses, until they give more trouble than they are worth, at which point we should, with many apologies and expressions of sympathy, and some generosity in complying with their last wishes, place them in the lethal chamber and get rid of them. Under no circumstances should they be allowed to expiate their misdeeds by a manufactured penalty, to subscribe to a charity, or to compensate the victims. If there is to be no punishment there can be no forgiveness. We shall never have real moral responsibility until everyone knows that his deeds are irrevocable, and that his life depends on his usefulness. Hitherto, alas! humanity has never dared face these hard facts. We frantically scatter conscience money and invent systems of conscience banking, with expiatory penalties, atonements, redemptions, salvations, hospital subscription lists and what not, to enable us to contract-out of the moral code. Not content with the old scapegoat and sacrificial lamb, we deify human saviors, and pray to miraculous virgin intercessors. We attribute mercy to the inexorable; soothe our consciences after committing murder by throwing ourselves on the bosom of divine love; and shrink even from our own gallows because we are forced to admit that it, at least, is irrevocable — as if one hour of imprisonment were not as irrevocable as any execution!

If a man cannot look evil in the face without illusion, he will never know what it really is, or combat it effectually. The few men who have been able (relatively) to do this have been called cynics, and have sometimes had an abnormal share of evil in themselves, corresponding to the abnormal strength of their minds; but they have never done mischief unless they intended to do it. That is why great scoundrels have been beneficent rulers whilst amiable and privately harmless monarchs have ruined their countries by trusting to the hocus-pocus of innocence and guilt, reward and punishment, virtuous indignation and pardon, instead of standing up to the facts without either malice or mercy. Major Barbara stands up to Bill Walker in that way, with the result that the ruffian who cannot get hated, has to hate himself. To relieve this agony he tries to get punished; but the Salvationist whom he tries to provoke is as merciless as Barbara, and only prays for him. Then he tries to pay, but can get nobody to take his money. His doom is the doom of Cain, who, failing to find either a savior, a policeman, or an almoner to help him to pretend that his brother's blood no longer cried from the ground, had to live and die a murderer.[46] Cain took care not to commit another murder, unlike our railway shareholders (I am one) who kill and maim shunters by hundreds to save the cost of automatic couplings, and make atonement by annual subscriptions to deserving charities. Had Cain been allowed to pay off his score, he might possibly have killed Adam and Eve for the mere sake of a second luxurious reconciliation with God afterwards. Bodger, you may depend on it, will go on to the end of his life poisoning people with bad whisky, because he can always depend on the Salvation Army or the Church of England to negotiate a redemption for him in consideration of a trifling percentage of his profits.

There is a third condition too, which must be fulfilled before the great teachers of the world will cease to scoff at its religions. Creeds must become intellectually honest. At present there is not a single credible established religion in the world. That is perhaps the most stupendous fact in the whole world-situation. This play of mine, *Major Barbara*, is, I hope, both true and inspired; but whoever says that it all happened, and that faith in it and understanding of it consist in believing that it is a record of an actual occurrence, is, to speak according to Scripture, a fool and a liar, and is hereby solemnly denounced and cursed as such by me, the author, to all posterity.

London, June 1906.

(Shaw did not customarily include lists of characters with his published plays, because he believed that it would be better for readers to encounter characters only as they emerged in the action. The following list has been supplied by the editor.)

CHARACTERS

LADY BRITOMART UNDERSHAFT, *the daughter of the Earl of Stevenage*

STEPHEN, *her son*

SARAH, *her younger daughter*

BARBARA, *her elder daughter, a Major in the Salvation Army*

CHARLES LOMAX, *an aristocrat, engaged to Sarah*

ADOLPHUS CUSINS, *a professor of Greek, engaged to Barbara*

MORRISON, *a butler*

ANDREW UNDERSHAFT, *owner of a large munitions factory, separated from Lady Britomart*

RUMMY MITCHENS, *an impoverished woman*

SNOBBY PRICE, *an under-employed house painter*

JENNY HILL, *a Salvation Army worker*

PETER SHIRLEY, *an unemployed mill worker*

BILL WALKER, *a bully*

MRS. BAINES, *a Salvation Army Commissioner*

BILTON, *a munitions worker*

ACT I

It is after dinner on a January night, in the library in Lady Britomart Undershaft's house in Wilton Crescent.[47] *A large and comfortable settee is in the middle of the room, upholstered in dark leather. A person sitting on it (it is vacant at present) would have, on his right, Lady Britomart's writing-table, with the lady herself busy at it; a smaller writing-table behind him on his left; the door behind him on Lady Britomart's side; and a window with a window-seat directly on his left. Near the window is an armchair.*[48]

---

46 doom of Cain] Genesis 4:9–17.

---

47 *Wilton Crescent*] an extremely elegant street off Belgrave Square near Buckingham Palace, and the location of several embassies.

48 *Britomart*] a name made from the fusion of Britain and Mars, used by Edmund Spenser in *The Fairie Queene*, where Britomart is a pure figure destined to secure the future for her children.

Lady Britomart is a woman of fifty or thereabouts, well dressed and yet careless of her dress, well bred and quite reckless of her breeding, well mannered and yet appallingly outspoken and indifferent to the opinion of her interlocutors, amiable and yet peremptory, arbitrary, and high-tempered to the last bearable degree, and withal a very typical managing matron of the upper class, treated as a naughty child until she grew into a scolding mother, and finally settling down with plenty of practical ability and worldly experience, limited in the oddest way with domestic and class limitations, conceiving the universe exactly as if it were a large house in Wilton Crescent, though handling her corner of it very effectively on that assumption, and being quite enlightened and liberal as to the books in the library, the pictures on the walls, the music in the portfolios, and the articles in the papers.

Her son, Stephen, comes in. He is a gravely correct young man under 25, taking himself very seriously, but still in some awe of his mother, from childish habit and bachelor shyness rather than from any weakness of character.

STEPHEN. Whats the matter?

LADY BRITOMART. Presently, Stephen. *(Stephen submissively walks to the settee and sits down. He takes up* The Speaker.*)*[49]

LADY BRITOMART. Dont begin to read, Stephen. I shall require all your attention. 5

STEPHEN. It was only while I was waiting —

LADY BRITOMART. Dont make excuses, Stephen. *(He puts down* The Speaker.*)* Now! *(She finishes her writing; rises; and comes to the settee.)* I have not kept you waiting v e r y long, I think.[50] 10

STEPHEN. Not at all, mother.

LADY BRITOMART. Bring me my cushion. *(He takes the cushion from the chair at the desk and arranges it for her as she sits down on the settee.)* Sit down. *(He sits down and fingers his tie nervously.)* Dont fiddle with your tie, Stephen: there is nothing the matter with it. 15

STEPHEN. I beg your pardon. *(He paddles with his watch chain instead.)* 20

LADY BRITOMART. Now are you attending to me, Stephen?

---

49 Speaker] a liberal weekly newspaper.
50 v e r y] Shaw spaces out a word to indicate emphasis.

STEPHEN. Of course, mother.

LADY BRITOMART. No: it's n o t of course. I want something much more than your everyday matter-of-course attention. I am going to speak to you very seriously, Stephen. I wish you would let that chain alone. 25

STEPHEN *(hastily relinquishing the chain).* Have I done anything to annoy you, mother? If so, it was quite unintentional. 30

LADY BRITOMART *(astonished).* Nonsense! *(With some remorse.)* My poor boy, did you think I was angry with you?

STEPHEN. What is it, then, mother? You are making me very uneasy. 35

LADY BRITOMART *(squaring herself at him rather aggressively).* Stephen: may I ask how soon you intend to realize that you are a grown-up man, and that I am only a woman? 40

STEPHEN *(amazed).* Only a —

LADY BRITOMART. Dont repeat my words, please: it is a most aggravating habit. You must learn to face life seriously, Stephen. I really cannot bear the whole burden of our family affairs any longer. You must advise me: you must assume the responsibility. 45

STEPHEN. I!

LADY BRITOMART. Yes, you, of course. You were 24 last June. Youve been at Harrow and Cambridge.[51] Youve been to India and Japan. You must know a lot of things, now; unless you have wasted your time most scandalously. Well, a d v i s e me. 50

STEPHEN *(much perplexed).* You know I have never interfered in the household — 55

LADY BRITOMART. No: I should think not. I dont want you to order the dinner.

STEPHEN. I mean in our family affairs.

LADY BRITOMART. Well, you must interfere now; for they are getting quite beyond me. 60

STEPHEN *(troubled).* I have thought sometimes that perhaps I ought; but really, mother, I know so little about them; and what I do know is so painful — it is so impossible to mention some things to you — *(he stops, ashamed).* 65

---

51 Harrow] a prestigious boys' school in London; Cambridge] i.e., the university.

LADY BRITOMART. I suppose you mean your father.

STEPHEN (almost inaudibly). Yes.

LADY BRITOMART. My dear: we cant go on all our lives not mentioning him. Of course you were quite right not to open the subject until I asked you to; but you are old enough now to be taken into my confidence, and to help me to deal with him about the girls.

STEPHEN. But the girls are all right. They are engaged.

LADY BRITOMART (complacently). Yes: I have made a very good match for Sarah. Charles Lomax will be a millionaire at 35. But that is ten years ahead; and in the meantime his trustees cannot under the terms of his father's will allow him more than £800 a year.[52]

STEPHEN. But the will says also that if he increases his income by his own exertions, they may double the increase.

LADY BRITOMART. Charles Lomax's exertions are much more likely to decrease his income than to increase it. Sarah will have to find at least another £800 a year for the next ten years; and even then they will be as poor as church mice. And what about Barbara? I thought Barbara was going to make the most brilliant career of all of you. And what does she do? Joins the Salvation Army; discharges her maid; lives on a pound a week; and walks in one evening with a professor of Greek whom she has picked up in the street, and who pretends to be a Salvationist, and actually plays the big drum for her in public because he has fallen head over ears in love with her.

STEPHEN. I was certainly rather taken aback when I heard they were engaged. Cusins is a very nice fellow, certainly: nobody would ever guess that he was born in Australia; but —

LADY BRITOMART. Oh, Adolphus Cusins will make a very good husband. After all, nobody can say a word against Greek: it stamps a man at once

---

52 £800] To compare rough figures for the time, the average British worker's annual income was less than £100; a middle-class household would have over £300; the upper classes would begin at about £1000.

---

as an educated gentleman. And my family, thank Heaven, is not a pig-headed Tory one. We are Whigs, and believe in liberty. Let snobbish people say what they please: Barbara shall marry, not the man they like, but the man I like.

STEPHEN. Of course I was thinking only of his income. However, he is not likely to be extravagant.

LADY BRITOMART. Dont be too sure of that, Stephen. I know your quiet, simple, refined, poetic people like Adolphus—quite content with the best of everything! They cost more than your extravagant people, who are always as mean as they are second rate. No: Barbara will need at least £2000 a year. You see it means two additional households. Besides, my dear, y o u must marry soon. I dont approve of the present fashion of philandering bachelors and late marriages; and I am trying to arrange something for you.

STEPHEN. It's very good of you, mother; but perhaps I had better arrange that for myself.

LADY BRITOMART. Nonsense! you are much too young to begin matchmaking: you would be taken in by some pretty little nobody. Of course I dont mean that you are not to be consulted: you know that as well as I do. (Stephen closes his lips and is silent.) Now dont sulk, Stephen.

STEPHEN. I am not sulking, mother. What has all this got to do with — with — with my father?

LADY BRITOMART. My dear Stephen: where is the money to come from? It is easy enough for you and the other children to live on my income as long as we are in the same house; but I cant keep four families in four separate houses. You know how poor my father is: he has barely seven thousand a year now; and really, if he were not the Earl of Stevenage, he would have to give up society. He can do nothing for us. He says, naturally enough, that it is absurd that he should be asked to provide for the children of a man who is rolling in money. You see, Stephen, your father must be fabulously wealthy, because there is always a war going on somewhere.

STEPHEN. You need not remind me of that, mother. I have hardly ever opened a newspaper in my life without seeing our name in it. The Undershaft torpedo! The Undershaft quick firers!

The Undershaft ten inch! the Undershaft disappearing rampart gun! the Undershaft submarine! and now the Undershaft aerial battleship! At Harrow they called me the Woolwich Infant.[53] At Cambridge it was the same. A little brute at King's who was always trying to get up revivals, spoilt my Bible — your first birthday present to me — by writing under my name, "Son and heir to Undershaft and Lazarus, Death and Destruction Dealers: address, Christendom and Judea." But that was not so bad as the way I was kowtowed to everywhere because my father was making millions by selling cannons.

LADY BRITOMART. It is not only the cannons, but the war loans that Lazarus arranges under cover of giving credit for the cannons. You know, Stephen, it's perfectly scandalous. Those two men, Andrew Undershaft and Lazarus, positively have Europe under their thumbs. That is why your father is able to behave as he does. He is above the law. Do you think Bismarck or Gladstone or Disraeli could have openly defied every social and moral obligation all their lives as your father has?[54] They simply wouldnt have dared. I asked Gladstone to take it up. I asked *The Times* to take it up. I asked the Lord Chamberlain to take it up. But it was just like asking them to declare war on the Sultan.[55] They w o u l d n t. They said they couldnt touch him. I believe they were afraid.

STEPHEN. What could they do? He does not actually break the law.

LADY BRITOMART. Not break the law! He is always breaking the law. He broke the law when he was born: his parents were not married.

STEPHEN. Mother! Is that true?

LADY BRITOMART. Of course it's true: that was why we separated.

STEPHEN. He married without letting you know this!

LADY BRITOMART (*rather taken aback by this inference*). Oh no. To do Andrew justice, that was not the sort of thing he did. Besides, you know the Undershaft motto: Unashamed. Everybody knew.

STEPHEN. But you said that was why you separated.

LADY BRITOMART. Yes, because he was not content with being a foundling himself: he wanted to disinherit you for another foundling. That was what I couldnt stand.

STEPHEN (*ashamed*). Do you mean for — for — for —

LADY BRITOMART. Dont stammer, Stephen. Speak distinctly.

STEPHEN. But this so frightful to me, mother. To have to speak to you about such things!

LADY BRITOMART. It's not pleasant for me, either, especially if you are still so childish that you must make it worse by a display of embarrassment. It is only in the middle classes, Stephen, that people get into a state of dumb helpless horror when they find that there are wicked people in the world. In our class, we have to decide what is to be done with wicked people; and nothing should disturb our self-possession. Now ask your question properly.

STEPHEN. Mother: you have no consideration for me. For Heaven's sake either treat me as a child, as you always do, and tell me nothing at all; or tell me everything and let me take it as best I can.

LADY BRITOMART. Treat you as a child! What do you mean? It is most unkind and ungrateful of you to say such a thing. You know I have never treated any of you as children. I have always made you my companions and friends, and allowed you perfect freedom to do and say whatever you liked, so long as you liked what I could approve of.

STEPHEN (*desperately*). I daresay we have been the

---

53 Woolwich infant] a type of heavy gun.

54 Bismarck] Otto von Bismarck (1815–1898), Prime Minister of Prussia, founder and Chancellor of the German Empire; Gladstone] William Gladstone (1809–1898), four-time British Prime Minister; Disraeli] Benjamin Disraeli (1804–1881), British statesman and novelist.

55 Sultan] probably any of several Omani Sultans of Oman and Zanzibar, especially Sa'id ibn Sultan (1791–1856), who acquired vast areas of East Africa, including Zanzibar, and grew immensely rich and powerful from the slave trade. The British were repeatedly asked by smaller African countries to intervene but did not, because of their economically favourable agreements with the Sultan. Eventually the power of the Sultanate was broken by partitioning East Africa into protectorates.

very imperfect children of a very perfect mother; but I do beg you to let me alone for once, and tell me about this horrible business of my father wanting to set me aside for another son.

LADY BRITOMART *(amazed)*. Another son! I never said anything of the kind. I never dreamt of such a thing. This is what comes of interrupting me.

STEPHEN. But you said —

LADY BRITOMART *(cutting him short)*. Now be a good boy, Stephen, and listen to me patiently. The Undershafts are descended from a foundling in the parish of St. Andrew Undershaft in the city.[56] That was long ago, in the reign of James the First. Well, this foundling was adopted by an armorer and gun-maker. In the course of time the foundling succeeded to the business; and from some notion of gratitude, or some vow or something, he adopted another foundling, and left the business to him. And that foundling did the same. Ever since that, the cannon business has always been left to an adopted foundling named Andrew Undershaft.

STEPHEN. But did they never marry? Were there no legitimate sons?

LADY BRITOMART. Oh yes: they married just as your father did; and they were rich enough to buy land for their own children and leave them well provided for. But they always adopted and trained some foundling to succeed them in the business; and of course they always quarreled with their wives furiously over it. Your father was adopted in that way; and he pretends to consider himself bound to keep up the tradition and adopt somebody to leave the business to. Of course I was not going to stand that. There may have been some reason for it when the Undershafts could only marry women in their own class, whose sons were not fit to govern great estates. But there could be no excuse for passing over m y son.

STEPHEN *(dubiously)*. I am afraid I should make a poor hand of managing a cannon foundry.

LADY BRITOMART. Nonsense! you could easily get a manager and pay him a salary.

STEPHEN. My father evidently had no great opinion of my capacity.

LADY BRITOMART. Stuff, child! you were only a baby: it had nothing to do with your capacity. Andrew did it on principle, just as he did every perverse and wicked thing on principle. When my father remonstrated, Andrew actually told him to his face that history tells us of only two successful institutions: one the Undershaft firm, and the other the Roman Empire under the Antonines. That was because the Antonine emperors all adopted their successors. Such rubbish! The Stevenages are as good as the Antonines, I hope; and you are a Stevenage. But that was Andrew all over. There you have the man! Always clever and unanswerable when he was defending nonsense and wickedness: always awkward and sullen when he had to behave sensibly and decently!

STEPHEN. Then it was on my account that your home life was broken up, mother. I am sorry.

LADY BRITOMART. Well, dear, there were other differences. I really cannot bear an immoral man. I am not a Pharisee, I hope; and I should not have minded his merely doing wrong things: we are none of us perfect. But your father didnt exactly d o wrong things: he said them and thought them: that was what was so dreadful. He really had a sort of religion of wrongness. Just as one doesnt mind men practising immorality so long as they own that they are in the wrong by preaching morality; so I couldnt forgive Andrew for preaching immorality while he practised morality. You would all have grown up without principles, without any knowledge of right and wrong, if he had been in the house. You know, my dear, your father was a very attractive man in some ways. Children did not dislike him; and he took advantage of it to put the wickedest ideas into their heads, and make them quite unmanageable. I did not dislike him myself: very far from it; but nothing can bridge over moral disagreement.

STEPHEN. All this simply bewilders me, mother.

---

[56] foundling] an infant abandoned by its parents; St. Andrew Undershaft] a church in northeast London, so called because it was dedicated to the Apostle Andrew, and its steeple was lower than (under) a nearby maypole (shaft).

People may differ about matters of opinion, or even about religion; but how can they differ about right and wrong? Right is right; and wrong is wrong; and if a man cannot distinguish them properly, he is either a fool or a rascal: thats all. 320

LADY BRITOMART (touched). Thats my own boy (she pats his cheek)! Your father never could answer that: he used to laugh and get out of it under cover of some affectionate nonsense. And now that you understand the situation, what do you advise me to do? 325

STEPHEN. Well, what c a n you do?

LADY BRITOMART. I must get the money somehow.

STEPHEN. We cannot take money from him. I had 330 rather go and live in some cheap place like Bedford Square or even Hampstead than take a farthing of his money.

LADY BRITOMART. But after all, Stephen, our present income comes from Andrew. 335

STEPHEN (shocked). I never knew that.

LADY BRITOMART. Well, you surely didnt suppose your grandfather had anything to give me. The Stevenages could not do everything for you. We gave you social position. Andrew had to 340 contribute s o m e t h i n g. He had a very good bargain, I think.

STEPHEN (bitterly). We are utterly dependent on him and his cannons, then?

LADY BRITOMART. Certainly not: the money is 345 settled. But he provided it. So you see it is not a question of taking money from him or not: it is simply a question of how much. I dont want any more for myself.

STEPHEN. Nor do I. 350

LADY BRITOMART. But Sarah does; and Barbara does. That is, Charles Lomax and Adolphus Cusins will cost them more. So I must put my pride in my pocket and ask for it, I suppose. That is your advice, Stephen, is it not? 355

STEPHEN. No.

LADY BRITOMART (sharply). Stephen!

STEPHEN. Of course if you are determined —

LADY BRITOMART. I am not determined: I ask your advice; and I am waiting for it. I will not have 360 all the responsibility thrown on my shoulders.

STEPHEN (obstinately). I would die sooner than ask him for another penny.

LADY BRITOMART (resignedly). You mean that I must ask him. Very well, Stephen: it shall be as you 365 wish. You will be glad to know that your grandfather concurs. But he thinks I ought to ask Andrew to come here and see the girls. After all, he must have some natural affection for them.

STEPHEN. Ask him here!!! 370

LADY BRITOMART. Do n o t repeat my words, Stephen. Where else can I ask him?

STEPHEN. I never expected you to ask him at all.

LADY BRITOMART. Now dont tease, Stephen. Come! you see that it is necessary that he should 375 pay us a visit, dont you?

STEPHEN (reluctantly). I suppose so, if the girls cannot do without his money.

LADY BRITOMART. Thank you, Stephen: I knew you would give me the right advice when it was 380 properly explained to you. I have asked your father to come this evening. (Stephen bounds from his seat.) Dont jump, Stephen: it fidgets me.

STEPHEN (in utter consternation). Do you mean to say that my father is coming here to-night — that 385 he may be here at any moment?

LADY BRITOMART (looking at her watch). I said nine. (He gasps. She rises.) Ring the bell, please. (Stephen goes to the smaller writing table; presses a button on it; and sits at it with his elbows on the ta- 390 ble and his head in his hands, outwitted and overwhelmed.) It is ten minutes to nine yet; and I have to prepare the girls. I asked Charles Lomax and Adolphus to dinner on purpose that they might be here. Andrew had better see them in case 395 he should cherish any delusions as to their being capable of supporting their wives. (The butler enters: Lady Britomart goes behind the settee to speak to him.) Morrison: go up to the drawing room and tell everybody to come down here at once. 400 (Morrison withdraws. Lady Britomart turns to Stephen.) Now remember, Stephen: I shall need all your countenance and authority. (He rises and tries to recover some vestige of these attributes.) Give me a chair, dear. (He pushes a chair forward from the 405 wall to where she stands, near the smaller writing table. She sits down; and he goes to the arm-chair, into *which he throws himself.)* I dont know how Barbara will take it. Ever since they made her a major in the Salvation Army she has developed a propensity to have her own way and order people about which quite cows me sometimes. It's not ladylike: I'm sure I dont know where she picked it up. Anyhow, Barbara shant bully m e; but still it's just as well that your father should be here before she has time to refuse to meet him or make a fuss. Dont look nervous, Stephen; it will only encourage Barbara to make difficulties. I am nervous enough, goodness knows; but I dont shew it.

Sarah and Barbara come in with their respective young men, Charles Lomax and Adolphus Cusins. Sarah is slender, bored, and mundane. Barbara is robuster, jollier, much more energetic. Sarah is fashionably dressed: Barbara is in Salvation Army uniform. Lomax, a young man about town, is like many other young men about town. He is afflicted with a frivolous sense of humor which plunges him at the most inopportune moments into paroxysms of imperfectly suppressed laughter. Cusins is a spectacled student, slight, thin haired, and sweet voiced, with a more complex form of Lomax's complaint. His sense of humor is intellectual and subtle, and is complicated by an appalling temper. The lifelong struggle of a benevolent temperament and a high conscience against impulses of inhuman ridicule and fierce impatience has set up a chronic strain which has visibly wrecked his constitution. He is a most implacable, determined, tenacious, intolerant person who by mere force of character presents himself as — and indeed actually is — considerate, gentle, explanatory, even mild and apologetic, capable possibly of murder, but not of cruelty or coarseness. By the operation of some instinct which is not merciful enough to blind him with the illusions of love, he is obstinately bent on marrying Barbara. Lomax likes Sarah and thinks it will be rather a lark to marry her. Consequently he has not attempted to resist Lady Britomart's arrangements to that end.

All four look as if they had been having a good deal of fun in the drawingroom. The girls enter first, leaving the swains outside. Sarah comes to the settee. Barbara comes in after her and stops at the door.

BARBARA. Are Cholly and Dolly to come in?

LADY BRITOMART *(forcibly).* Barbara: I will not have Charles called Cholly: the vulgarity of it positively makes me ill.

BARBARA. It's all right, mother. Cholly is quite correct nowadays. Are they to come in?

LADY BRITOMART. Yes, if they will behave themselves.

BARBARA *(through the door).* Come in, Dolly, and behave yourself.

Barbara comes to her mother's writing table. Cusins enters smiling, and wanders towards Lady Britomart.

SARAH *(calling).* Come in, Cholly. *(Lomax enters, controlling his features very imperfectly, and places himself vaguely between Sarah and Barbara.)*

LADY BRITOMART *(peremptorily).* Sit down, all of you. *(They sit. Cusins crosses to the window and seats himself there. Lomax takes a chair. Barbara sits at the writing table and Sarah on the settee.)* I dont in the least know what you are laughing at, Adolphus. I am surprised at you, though I expected nothing better from Charles Lomax.

CUSINS *(in a remarkably gentle voice).* Barbara has been trying to teach me the West Ham Salvation March.[57]

LADY BRITOMART. I see nothing to laugh at in that; nor should you if you are really converted.

CUSINS *(sweetly).* You were not present. It was really funny, I believe.

LOMAX. Ripping.

LADY BRITOMART. Be quiet, Charles. Now listen to me, children. Your father is coming here this evening. *(General stupefaction.)*

LOMAX *(remonstrating).* Oh I say!

LADY BRITOMART. You are not called on to say anything, Charles.

SARAH. Are you serious, mother?

LADY BRITOMART. Of course I am serious. It is on your account, Sarah, and also on Charles's. *(Silence. Charles looks painfully unworthy.)* I hope you are not going to object, Barbara.

BARBARA. I! why should I? My father has a soul to be saved like anybody else. Hes quite welcome as far as I am concerned.

---

57 West Ham] a borough in East London.

LOMAX *(still remonstrant)*. But really, dont you know! Oh I say!

LADY BRITOMART *(frigidly)*. What do you wish to convey, Charles? 465

LOMAX. Well, you must admit that this is a bit thick.

LADY BRITOMART *(turning with ominous suavity to Cusins)*. Adolphus: you are a professor of Greek. Can you translate Charles Lomax's remarks into 470 reputable English for us?

CUSINS *(cautiously)*. If I may say so, Lady Brit, I think Charles has rather happily expressed what we all feel. Homer, speaking of Autolycus, uses the same phrase. *pukinon domon elthein* means a bit 475 thick.

LOMAX *(handsomely)*. Not that I mind, you know, if Sarah dont.

LADY BRITOMART *(crushingly)*. Thank you. Have I your permission, Adolphus, to invite my own 480 husband to my own house?

CUSINS *(gallantly)*. You have my unhesitating support in everything you do.

LADY BRITOMART. Sarah: have you nothing to say? 485

SARAH. Do you mean that he is coming regularly to live here?

LADY BRITOMART. Certainly not. The spare room is ready for him if he likes to stay for a day or two and see a little more of you; but there are 490 limits.

SARAH. Well, he cant eat us, I suppose. I dont mind.

LOMAX *(chuckling)*. I wonder how the old man will take it. 495

LADY BRITOMART. Much as the old woman will, no doubt, Charles.

LOMAX *(abashed)*. I didnt mean — at least —

LADY BRITOMART. You didnt t h i n k, Charles. You never do; and the result is, you never mean 500 anything. And now please attend to me, children. Your father will be quite a stranger to us.

LOMAX. I suppose he hasnt seen Sarah since she was a little kid.

LADY BRITOMART. Not since she was a little kid, 505 Charles, as you express it with that elegance of diction and refinement of thought that seem never

to desert you. Accordingly — er — *(impatiently)* Now I have forgotten what I was going to say. That comes of your provoking me to be sarcastic, 510 Charles. Adolphus: will you kindly tell me where I was.

CUSINS *(sweetly)*. You were saying that as Mr. Undershaft has not seen his children since they were babies, he will form his opinion of the way 515 you have brought them up from their behavior to-night, and that therefore you wish us all to be particularly careful to conduct ourselves well, especially Charles.

LOMAX. Look here: Lady Brit didnt say that. 520

LADY BRITOMART *(vehemently)*. I did, Charles. Adolphus's recollection is perfectly correct. It is most important that you should be good; and I do beg you for once not to pair off into opposite corners and giggle and whisper while I am 525 speaking to your father.

BARBARA. All right, mother. We'll do you credit.

LADY BRITOMART. Remember, Charles, that Sarah will want to feel proud of you instead of ashamed of you. 530

LOMAX. Oh I say! theres nothing to be exactly proud of, dont you know.

LADY BRITOMART. Well, try and look as if there was.

Morrison, pale and dismayed, breaks into the room in unconcealed disorder.

MORRISON. Might I speak a word to you, my 535 lady?

LADY BRITOMART. Nonsense! Shew him up.

MORRISON. Yes, my lady. *(He goes.)*

LOMAX. Does Morrison know who it is?

LADY BRITOMART. Of course. Morrison has 540 always been with us.

LOMAX. It must be a regular corker for him, dont you know.

LADY BRITOMART. Is this a moment to get on my nerves, Charles, with your outrageous expres- 545 sions?

LOMAX. But this is something out of the ordinary, really —

MORRISON *(at the door)*. The — er — Mr. Undershaft. *(He retreats in confusion.)* 550

Andrew Undershaft comes in. All rise. Lady Britomart meets him in the middle of the room behind the settee.

Andrew is, on the surface, a stoutish, easygoing elderly man, with kindly patient manners, and an engaging simplicity of character. But he has a watchful, deliberate, waiting, listening face, and formidable reserves of power, both bodily and mental, in his capacious chest and long head. His gentleness is partly that of a strong man who has learnt by experience that his natural grip hurts ordinary people unless he handles them very carefully, and partly the mellowness of age and success. He is also a little shy in his present very delicate situation.

LADY BRITOMART. Good evening, Andrew.

UNDERSHAFT. How d'ye do, my dear.

LADY BRITOMART. You look a good deal older.

UNDERSHAFT *(apologetically)*. I a m somewhat older. *(With a touch of courtship.)* Time has stood still with you.   555

LADY BRITOMART *(promptly)*. Rubbish! This is your family.

UNDERSHAFT *(surprised)*. Is it so large? I am sorry to say my memory is failing very badly in some things. *(He offers his hand with paternal kindness to Lomax.)*   560

LOMAX *(jerkily shaking his hand)*. Ahdedoo.

UNDERSHAFT. I can see you are my eldest. I am very glad to meet you again, my boy.   565

LOMAX *(remonstrating)*. No but look here dont you know — *(Overcome.)* Oh I say!

LADY BRITOMART *(recovering from momentary speechlessness)*. Andrew: do you mean to say that you dont remember how many children you have?   570

UNDERSHAFT. Well, I am afraid I —. They have grown so much — er. Am I making any ridiculous mistake? I may as well confess: I recollect only one son. But so many things have happened since, of course — er —   575

LADY BRITOMART *(decisively)*. Andrew: you are talking nonsense. Of course you have only one son.

UNDERSHAFT. Perhaps you will be good enough to introduce me, my dear.

LADY BRITOMART. That is Charles Lomax, who is engaged to Sarah.   580

UNDERSHAFT. My dear sir, I beg your pardon.

LOMAX. Notatall. Delighted, I assure you.

LADY BRITOMART. This is Stephen.

UNDERSHAFT *(bowing)*. Happy to make your acquaintance, Mr. Stephen. Then *(going to Cusins)* y o u must be my son. *(Taking Cusins' hands in his.)* How are you, my young friend? *(To Lady Britomart.)* He is very like you, my love.   585

CUSINS. You flatter me, Mr. Undershaft. My name is Cusins: engaged to Barbara. *(Very explicitly.)* That is Major Barbara Undershaft, of the Salvation Army. That is Sarah, your second daughter. This is Stephen Undershaft, your son.   590

UNDERSHAFT. My dear Stephen, I b e g your pardon.   595

STEPHEN. Not at all.

UNDERSHAFT. Mr. Cusins: I am much indebted to you for explaining so precisely. *(Turning to Sarah.)* Barbara, my dear —   600

SARAH *(prompting him)*. Sarah.

UNDERSHAFT. Sarah, of course. *(They shake hands. He goes over to Barbara.)* Barbara — I am right this time, I hope.

BARBARA. Quite right. *(They shake hands.)*   605

LADY BRITOMART *(resuming command)*. Sit down, all of you. Sit down, Andrew. *(She comes forward and sits on the settee. Cusins also brings his chair forward on her left. Barbara and Stephen resume their seats. Lomax gives his chair to Sarah and goes for another.)*   610

UNDERSHAFT. Thank you, my love.

LOMAX *(conversationally, as he brings a chair forward between the writing table and the settee, and offers it to Undershaft)*. Takes you some time to find out exactly where you are, dont it?   615

UNDERSHAFT *(accepting the chair)*. That is not what embarrasses me, Mr. Lomax. My difficulty is that if I play the part of a father, I shall produce the effect of an intrusive stranger; and if I play the part of a discreet stranger, I may appear a callous father.   620

LADY BRITOMART. There is no need for you to play any part at all, Andrew. You had much better be sincere and natural.   625

UNDERSHAFT *(submissively)*. Yes, my dear: I daresay that will be best. *(Making himself comfortable.)* Well, here I am. Now what can I do for you all?

LADY BRITOMART. You need not do anything, Andrew. You are one of the family. You can sit with us and enjoy yourself. 630

Lomax's too long suppressed mirth explodes in agonized neighings.

LADY BRITOMART *(outraged).* Charles Lomax: if you can behave yourself, behave yourself. If not, leave the room.

LOMAX. I'm awfully sorry, Lady Brit; but really, you 635 know, upon my soul! *(He sits on the settee between Lady Britomart and Undershaft, quite overcome.)*

BARBARA. Why dont you laugh if you want to Cholly? It's good for your inside.

LADY BRITOMART. Barbara: you have had the 640 education of a lady. Please let your father see that; and dont talk like a street girl.

UNDERSHAFT. Never mind me, my dear. As you know, I am not a gentleman; and I was never educated. 645

LOMAX *(encouragingly).* Nobody'd know it, I assure you. You look all right, you know.

CUSINS. Let me advise you to study Greek, Mr. Undershaft. Greek scholars are privileged men. Few of them know Greek; and none of them know 650 anything else; but their position is unchallengeable. Other languages are the qualifications of waiters and commercial travellers: Greek is to a man of position what the hallmark is to silver.

BARBARA. Dolly: dont be insincere. Cholly: fetch 655 your concertina and play something for us.

LOMAX *(doubtfully to Undershaft).* Perhaps that sort of thing isnt in your line, eh?

UNDERSHAFT. I am particularly fond of music.

LOMAX *(delighted).* Are you? Then I'll get it. *(He 660 goes upstairs for the instrument.)*

UNDERSHAFT. Do you play, Barbara?

BARBARA. Only the tambourine. But Cholly's teaching me the concertina.

UNDERSHAFT. Is Cholly also a member of the 665 Salvation Army?

BARBARA. No: he says it's bad form to be a dissenter. But I dont despair of Cholly. I made him come yesterday to a meeting at the dock gates, and took the collection in his hat. 670

LADY BRITOMART. It is not my doing, Andrew. Barbara is old enough to take her own way. She has no father to advise her.

BARBARA. Oh yes she has. There are no orphans in the Salvation Army. 675

UNDERSHAFT. Your father there has a great many children and plenty of experience, eh?

BARBARA *(looking at him with quick interest and nodding).* Just so. How did y o u come to understand that? *(Lomax is heard at the door trying 680 the concertina.)*

LADY BRITOMART. Come in, Charles. Play us something at once.

LOMAX. Righto! *(He sits down in his former place, and preludes.)* 685

UNDERSHAFT. One moment, Mr. Lomax. I am rather interested in the Salvation Army. Its motto might be my own: Blood and Fire.

LOMAX *(shocked).* But not your sort of blood and fire, you know. 690

UNDERSHAFT. My sort of blood cleanses: my sort of fire purifies.

BARBARA. So do ours. Come down to-morrow to my shelter — the West Ham shelter — and see what we're doing. We're going to march to a great 695 meeting in the Assembly Hall at Mile End.[58] Come and see the shelter and then march with us: it will do you a lot of good. Can you play anything?

UNDERSHAFT. In my youth I earned pennies, and 700 even shillings occasionally, in the streets and in public house parlors by my natural talent for stepdancing. Later on, I became a member of the Undershaft orchestral society, and performed passably on the tenor trombone. 705

LOMAX *(scandalized).* Oh I say!

BARBARA. Many a sinner has played himself into heaven on the trombone, thanks to the Army.

LOMAX *(to Barbara, still rather shocked).* Yes; but what about the cannon business, dont you know? 710 *(To Undershaft.)* Getting into heaven is not exactly in your line, is it?

LADY BRITOMART. Charles!!!

LOMAX. Well; but it stands to reason, dont it? The cannon business may be necessary and all that: we 715

---

[58] Mile End] a street and neighbourhood in London.

cant get on without cannons; but it isnt right, you know. On the other hand, there may be a certain amount of tosh about the Salvation Army — I belong to the Established Church myself — but still you cant deny that it's religion; and you cant go against religion, can you? At least unless youre downright immoral, dont you know.

UNDERSHAFT. You hardly appreciate my position, Mr. Lomax —

LOMAX *(hastily)*. I'm not saying anything against you personally, you know.

UNDERSHAFT. Quite so, quite so. But consider for a moment. Here I am, a manufacturer of mutilation and murder. I find myself in a specially amiable humor just now because, this morning, down at the foundry, we blew twenty-seven dummy soldiers into fragments with a gun which formerly destroyed only thirteen.

LOMAX *(leniently)*. Well, the more destructive war becomes, the sooner it will be abolished, eh?

UNDERSHAFT. Not at all. The more destructive war becomes the more fascinating we find it. No, Mr. Lomax: I am obliged to you for making the usual excuse for my trade; but I am not ashamed of it. I am not one of those men who keep their morals and their business in watertight compartments. All the spare money my trade rivals spend on hospitals, cathedrals and other receptacles for conscience money, I devote to experiments and researches in improved methods of destroying life and property. I have always done so; and I always shall. Therefore your Christmas card moralities of peace on earth and goodwill among men are of no use to me. Your Christianity, which enjoins you to resist not evil, and to turn the other cheek, would make me a bankrupt. M y morality — my religion — must have a place for cannons and torpedoes in it.

STEPHEN *(coldly — almost sullenly)*. You speak as if there were half a dozen moralities and religions to choose from, instead of one true morality and one true religion.

UNDERSHAFT. For me there is only one true morality; but it might not fit you, as you do not manufacture aerial battleships. There is only one true morality for every man; but every man has not the same true morality.

LOMAX *(overtaxed)*. Wold you mind saying that again? I didnt quite follow it.

CUSINS. It's quite simple. As Euripides says, one man's meat is another man's poison morally as well as physically.[59]

UNDERSHAFT. Precisely.

LOMAX. Oh, that. Yes, yes, yes. True. True.

STEPHEN. In other words some men are honest and some are scoundrels.

BARBARA. Bosh. There are no scoundrels.

UNDERSHAFT. Indeed? Are there any good men?

BARBARA. No. Not one. There are neither good men nor scoundrels: there are just children of one Father; and the sooner they stop calling one another names the better. You neednt talk to me: I know them. Ive had scores of them through my hands: scoundrels, criminals, infidels, philanthropists, missionaries, county councillors, all sorts. Theyre all just the same sort of sinner; and theres the same salvation ready for them all.

UNDERSHAFT. May I ask have you ever saved a maker of cannons?

BARBARA. No. Will you let me try?

UNDERSHAFT. Well, I will make a bargain with you. If I go to see you to-morrow in your Salvation Shelter, will you come the day after to see me in my cannon works?

BARBARA. Take care. It may end in your giving up the cannons for the sake of the Salvation Army.

UNDERSHAFT. Are you sure it will not end in your giving up the Salvation Army for the sake of the cannons?

BARBARA. I will take my chance of that.

UNDERSHAFT. And I will take my chance of the other. *(They shake hands on it.)* Where is your shelter?

BARBARA. In West Ham. At the sign of the cross. Ask anybody in Canning Town.[60] Where are your works?

UNDERSHAFT. In Perivale St. Andrews.[61] At the sign of the sword. Ask anybody in Europe.

---

59 Euripides] See *Hippolytus*.
60 Canning Town] the London district next to West Ham.
61 Perivale St. Andrews] a fusion of two place names in Ealing, a western borough of London.

LOMAX. Hadnt I better play something?

BARBARA. Yes. Give us Onward, Christian Soldiers.

LOMAX. Well, thats rather a strong order to begin with, dont you know. Suppose I sing Thourt passing hence, my brother. It's much the same tune.

BARBARA. It's too melancholy. You get saved, Cholly; and youll pass hence, my brother, without making such a fuss about it.

LADY BRITOMART. Really, Barbara, you go on as if religion were a pleasant subject. Do have some sense of propriety.

UNDERSHAFT. I do not find it an unpleasant subject, my dear. It is the only one that capable people really care for.

LADY BRITOMART (looking at her watch). Well, if you are determined to have it, I insist on having it in a proper and respectable way. Charles: ring for prayers. (General amazement. Stephen rises in dismay.)

LOMAX (rising). Oh I say!

UNDERSHAFT (rising). I am afraid I must be going.

LADY BRITOMART. You cannot go now, Andrew: it would be most improper. Sit down. What will the servants think?

UNDERSHAFT. My dear: I have conscientious scruples. May I suggest a compromise? If Barbara will conduct a little service in the drawingroom, with Mr. Lomax as organist, I will attend it willingly. I will even take part, if a trombone can be procured.

LADY BRITOMART. Dont mock, Andrew.

UNDERSHAFT (shocked — to Barbara). You dont think I am mocking, my love, I hope.

BARBARA. No, of course not; and it wouldnt matter if you were: half the Army came to their first meeting for a lark. (Rising.) Come along. Come, Dolly, Come, Cholly. (She goes out with Undershaft, who opens the door for her. Cusins rises.)

LADY BRITOMART. I will not be disobeyed by everybody. Adolphus: sit down. Charles: you may go. You are not fit for prayers: you cannot keep your countenance.

LOMAX. Oh I say! (He goes out.)

LADY BRITOMART (continuing). But you, Adolphus, can behave yourself if you choose to. I insist on your staying.

CUSINS. My dear Lady Brit: there are things in the family prayer book that I couldnt bear to hear you say.

LADY BRITOMART. What things, pray?

CUSINS. Well, you would have to say before all the servants that we have done things we ought not to have done, and left undone things we ought to have done, and that there is no health in us. I cannot bear to hear you doing yourself such an injustice, and Barbara such an injustice. As for myself, I flatly deny it: I have done my best. I shouldnt dare to marry Barbara — I couldnt look you in the face — if it were true. So I must go to the drawingroom.

LADY BRITOMART (offended). Well, go. (He starts for the door.) And remember this, Adolphus (he turns to listen): I have a very strong suspicion that you went to the Salvation Army to worship Barbara and nothing else. And I quite appreciate the very clever way in which you systematically humbug me. I have found you out. Take care Barbara doesnt. Thats all.

CUSINS (with unruffled sweetness). Dont tell on me. (He goes out.)

LADY BRITOMART. Sarah: if you want to go, go. Anything's better than to sit there as if you wished you were a thousand miles away.

SARAH (languidly). Very well, mamma. (She goes.)

Lady Britomart, with a sudden flounce, gives way to a little gust of tears.

STEPHEN (going to her). Mother: whats the matter?

LADY BRITOMART (swishing away her tears with her handkerchief). Nothing. Foolishness. You can go with him, too, if you like, and leave me with the servants.

STEPHEN. Oh, you mustnt think that, mother. I — I dont like him.

LADY BRITOMART. The others do. That is the injustice of a woman's lot. A woman has to bring up her children; and that means to restrain tbem, to deny them things they want, to set them tasks, to punish them when they do wrong, to do all the unpleasant things. And then the father, who has nothing to do but pet them and spoil them, comes in when all her work is done and steals their affection from her.

STEPHEN. He has not stolen our affection from you. It is only curiosity. 895

LADY BRITOMART (*violently*). I wont be consoled, Stephen. There is nothing the matter with me. (*She rises and goes towards the door.*)

STEPHEN. Where are you going, mother? 900

LADY BRITOMART. To the drawingroom, of course. (*She goes out. Onward, Christian Soldiers, on the concertina, with tambourine accompaniment, is heard when the door opens.*) Are you coming, Stephen? 905

STEPHEN. No. Certainly not. (*She goes. He sits down on the settee, with compressed lips and an expression of strong dislike.*)

END OF ACT I

ACT II

The yard of the West Ham shelter of the Salvation Army is a cold place on a January morning. The building itself, an old warehouse, is newly whitewashed. Its gabled end projects into the yard in the middle, with a door on the ground floor, and another in the loft above it without any balcony or ladder, but with a pulley rigged over it for hoisting sacks. Those who come from this central gable end into the yard have the gateway leading to the street on their left, with a stone horse-trough just beyond it, and, on the right, a penthouse shielding a table from the weather. There are forms at the table, and on them are seated a man and a woman, both much down on their luck, finishing a meal of bread (one thick slice each, with margarine and golden syrup) and diluted milk.[62]

The man, a workman out of employment, is young, agile, a talker, a poser, sharp enough to be capable of anything in reason except honesty or altruistic considerations of any kind. The woman is a commonplace old bundle of poverty and hard-core humanity. She looks sixty and probably is forty-five. If they were rich people, gloved and muffed and even

wrapped up in furs and overcoats, they would be numbed and miserable; for it is a grindingly cold, raw, January day; and a glance at the background of grimy warehouses and leaden sky visible over the whitewashed walls of the yard would drive any idle rich person straight to the Mediterranean. But these two, being no more troubled with visions of the Mediterranean than of the moon, and being compelled to keep more of their clothes in the pawnshop, and less on their persons, in winter than in summer, are not depressed by the cold: rather are they stung into vivacity, to which their meal has just now given an almost jolly turn. The man takes a pull at his mug, and then gets up and moves about the yard with his hands deep in his pockets, occasionally breaking into a stepdance.

THE WOMAN. Feel better arter your meal, sir?

THE MAN. No. Call that a meal! Good enough for you, praps; but wot is it to me, an intelligent workin man.

THE WOMAN. Workin man! Wot are you? 5

THE MAN. Painter.

THE WOMAN (*skeptically*). Yus, I dessay.

THE MAN. Yus, you dessay! I know. Every loafer that cant do nothink calls isself a painter. Well, I'm a real painter: grainer, finisher, thirty-eight bob a 10 week when I can get it.

THE WOMAN. Then why dont you go and get it?

THE MAN. I'll tell you why. Fust: I'm intelligent —fffff! it's rotten cold here (*he dances a step or two*) yes: intelligent beyond the station o life into which 15 it has pleased the capitalists to call me; and they dont like a man that sees through em. Second, an intelligent bein needs a doo share of appiness, so I drink somethink cruel when I get the chawnce. Third, I stand by my class and do as little as I can 20 so's to leave arf the job for me fellow workers. Fourth, I'm fly enough to know wots inside the law and wots outside it; and inside it I do as the capitalists do: pinch wot I can lay me ands on. In a proper state of society I am sober, industrious and 25 honest: in Rome, so to speak, I do as the Romans do. Wots the consequence? When trade is bad and it's rotten bad just now and the employers az to sack arf their men, they generally start on me.

THE WOMAN. Whats your name? 30

---

[62] forms] benches.

THE MAN. Price. Bronterre O'Brien Price. Usually called Snobby Price, for short.

THE WOMAN. Snobby's a carpenter, aint it? You said you was a painter.

PRICE. Not that kind of snob, but the genteel sort. 35 I'm too uppish, owing to my intelligence, and my father being a Chartist and a reading, thinking man: a stationer, too.[63] I'm none of your common hewers of wood and drawers of water; and dont you forget it. (He returns to his seat at the table, and 40 takes up his mug.) Wots y o u r name?

THE WOMAN. Rummy Mitchens, sir.

PRICE (quaffing the remains of his milk to her). Your elth, Miss Mitchens.

RUMMY (correcting him). Missis Mitchens. 45

PRICE. Wot! Oh Rummy, Rummy! Respectable married woman, Rummy, gittin rescued by the Salvation Army by pretendin to be a bad un. Same old game!

RUMMY. What am I to do? I cant starve. Them 50 Salvation lasses is dear good girls; but the better you are, the worse they likes to think you were before they rescued you. Why shouldnt they av a bit o credit, poor loves? theyre worn to rags by their work. And where would they get the money 55 to rescue us if we was to let on we're no worse than other people? You know what ladies and gentlemen are.

PRICE. Thievin swine! Wish I ad their job, Rummy, all the same. Wot does Rummy stand for? Pet 60 name praps?

RUMMY. Short for Romola.

PRICE. For wot!?

RUMMY. Romola. It was out of a new book. Somebody me mother wanted me to grow up like. 65

PRICE. We're companions in misfortune, Rummy. Both on us got names that nobody cawnt pronounce. Consequently I'm Snobby and youre Rummy because Bill and Sally wasnt good enough for our parents. Such is life! 70

RUMMY. Who saved you, Mr. Price? Was it Major Barbara?

PRICE. No: I come here on my own. I'm goin to be Bronterre O'Brien Price, the converted painter. I know wot they like. I'll tell em how I blasphemed 75 and gambled and wopped my poor old mother—

RUMMY (shocked). Used you to beat your mother?

PRICE. Not likely. She used to beat me. No matter: you come and listen to the converted painter, and youll hear how she was a pious woman that taught 80 me me prayers at er knee, an how I used to come home drunk and drag her out o bed be er snow white airs, an lam into er with the poker.

RUMMY. Thats whats so unfair to us women. Your confessions is just as big lies as ours: you dont tell 85 what you really done no more than us; but you men can tell your lies right out at the meetins and be made much of for it; while the sort o confessions we az to make az to be whispered to one lady at a time. It aint right, spite of all their piety. 90

PRICE. Right! Do you spose the Army 'd be allowed if it went and did right? Not much. It combs our air and makes us good little blokes to be robbed and put upon. But I'll play the game as good as any of em. I'll see somebody struck by lightnin, 95 or hear a voice sayin "Snobby Price: where will you spend eternity?" I'll ave a time of it, I tell you.

RUMMY. You wont be let drink, though.

PRICE. I'll take it out in gorspellin, then. I dont want to drink if I can get fun enough any other way. 100

Jenny Hill, a pale, overwrought, pretty Salvation lass of 18, comes in through the yard gate, leading Peter Shirley, a half hardened, half worn-out elderly man, weak with hunger.

JENNY (supporting him). Come! pluck up. I'll get you something to eat. Youll be all right then.

PRICE (rising and hurrying officiously to take the old man off Jenny's hands). Poor old man! Cheer up, brother: youll find rest and peace and appiness ere. 105 Hurry up with the food, miss: e's fair done. (Jenny hurries into the shelter.) Ere, buck up, daddy! shes fetchin y'a thick slice o breadn treacle, an a mug o skyblue.[64] (He seats him at the corner of the table.)

RUMMY (gaily). Keep up your old art! Never say 110 die!

63 Chartist] a member of the British working-class movement that lobbied for labour reforms in the mid-nineteenth century; stationer] bookseller.

64 treacle] molasses; skyblue] thin or watery milk.

SHIRLEY. I'm not an old man. I'm only 46. I'm as good as ever I was. The grey patch come in my hair before I was thirty. All it wants is three pennorth o hair dye: am I to be turned on the streets to starve for it?[65] Holy God! I've worked ten to twelve hours a day since I was thirteen, and paid my way all through; and now am I to be thrown into the gutter and my job given to a young man that can do it no better than me because Ive black hair that goes white at the first change?

PRICE (cheerfully). No good jawrin about it. Youre ony a jumped-up, jerked-off, orspittle-turned-out incurable of an ole workin man: who cares about you? Eh? Make the thievin swine give you a meal: theyve stole many a one from you. Get a bit o your own back. (Jenny returns with the usual meal.) There you are, brother. Awsk a blessin an tuck that into you.

SHIRLEY (looking at it ravenously but not touching it, and crying like a child). I never took anything before.

JENNY (petting him). Come, come! the Lord sends it to you: he wasnt above taking bread from his friends; and why should you be? Besides, when we find you a job you can pay us for it if you like.

SHIRLEY (eagerly). Yes, yes: thats true. I can pay you back: its only a loan. (Shivering.) Oh Lord! oh Lord! (He turns to the table and attacks the meal ravenously.)

JENNY. Well, Rummy, are you more comfortable now?

RUMMY. God bless you, lovey! youve fed my body and saved my soul, havent you? (Jenny, touched, kisses her.) Sit down and rest a bit: you must be ready to drop.

JENNY. Ive been going hard since morning. But theres more work than we can do. I mustnt stop.

RUMMY. Try a prayer for just two minutes. Youll work all the better after.

JENNY (her eyes lighting up). Oh isnt it wonderful how a few minutes prayer revives you! I was quite lightheaded at twelve o'clock, I was so tired; but Major Barbara just sent me to pray for five

_____
[65] pennorth] a penny's worth.

minutes; and I was able to go on as if I had only just begun. (To Price.) Did you have a piece of bread?

PRICE (with unction). Yes, miss; but Ive got the piece that I value more; and thats the peace that passeth hall hannerstennin.

RUMMY (fervently). Glory Hallelujah!

Bill Walker, a rough customer of about 25, appears at the yard gate and looks malevolently at Jenny.

JENNY. That makes me so happy. When you say that, I feel wicked for loitering here. I must get to work again.

She is hurrying to the shelter, when the newcomer moves quickly up to the door and intercepts her. His manner is so threatening that she retreats as he comes at her truculently, driving her down the yard.

BILL. I know you. Youre the one that took away my girl. Youre the one that set er agen me. Well, I'm goin to av er out. Not that I care a curse for her or you: see? But I'll let er know; and I'll let you know. I'm goin to give er a doin thatll teach er to cut away from me. Now in with you and tell er to come out afore I come in and kick er out. Tell er Bill Walker wants er. She'll know what that means; and if she keeps me waitin itll be worse. You stop to jaw back at me; and I'll start on you: d'ye hear? Theres your way. In you go. (He takes her by the arm and slings her towards the door of the shelter. She falls on her hand and knee. Rummy helps her up again.)

PRICE (rising, and venturing irresolutely towards Bill). Easy there, mate. She aint doin you no arm.

BILL. Who are you callin mate? (Standing over him threateningly.) Youre goin to stand up for her, are you? Put up your ands.

RUMMY (running indignantly to him to scold him). Oh, you great brute— (He instantly swings his left hand back against her face. She screams and reels back to the trough, where she sits down, covering her bruised face with her hands and rocking herself and moaning with pain.)

JENNY (going to her). Oh God forgive you! How could you strike an old woman like that?

BILL (seizing her by the hair so violently that she also

screams, and tearing her away from the old woman). You Gawd forgive me again and I'll Gawd forgive you one on the jaw thatll stop you prayin for a week. *(Holding her and turning fiercely on Price.)* Av you anything to say agen it? Eh? 195

PRICE *(intimidated)*. No, matey: she aint anything to do with me. 200

BILL. Good job for you! I'd put two meals into you and fight you with one finger after, you starved cur. *(To Jenny.)* Now are you goin to fetch out Mog Habbijam; or am I to knock your face off you and fetch her myself? 205

JENNY *(writhing in his grasp)*. Oh please someone go in and tell Major Barbara *(she screams again as he wrenches her head down; and Price and Rummy flee into the shelter).*

BILL. You want to go in and tell your Major of men do you? 210

JENNY. Oh please dont drag my hair. Let me go.

BILL. Do you or dont you? *(She stifles a scream.)* Yes or no.

JENNY. God give me strength 215

BILL *(striking her with his fist in the face)*. Go and shew her that, and tell her if she Rants one like it to come and interfere with me. *(Jenny, crying with pain, goes into the shed He goes to the form and addresses the old man.)* Here: finish your mess; and get out o my way. 220

SHIRLEY *(springing up and facing him fiercely, With the mug in his hand)*. You take a liberty with me, and I'll smash you over the face with the mug and cut your eye out. Aint you satisfied young whelps like you with takin the bread out o the mouths of your elders that have brought you up and slaved for you, but you must come shovin and cheekin and bullyin in here, where the bread o charity is sickenin in our stummicks? 225 230

BILL *(contemptuously, but backing a little)*. Wot good are you, you old palsy mug? Wot good are you?

SHIRLEY. As good as you and better. I'll do a day's work agen you or any fat young soaker of your age. Go and take my job at Horrockses, where I worked for ten year.[66] They want young men there: they 235

cant afford to keep men over forty-five. Theyre very sorry — give you a character and happy to help you to get anything suited to your years — sure a steady man wont be long out of a job. Well, let em try you. Theyll find the differ. What do you know? Not as much as how to beeyave yourself — layin your dirty fist across the mouth of a respectable woman! 240

BILL. Dont provoke me to lay it acrost yours: d'ye hear? 245

SHIRLEY *(with blighting contempt)*. Yes: you like an old man to hit, dont you, when youve finished with the women. I aint seen you hit a young one yet. 250

BILL *(stung)*. You lie, you old soupkitchener, you. There was a young man here. Did I offer to hit him or did I not?

SHIRLEY. Was he starvin or was he not? Was he a man or only a crosseyed thief an a loafer? Would you hit my son-in-law's brother? 255

BILL. Who's he?

SHIRLEY. Todger Fairmile o Balls Pond.[67] Him that won £20 off the Japanese wrastler at the music hall by standin out 17 minutes 4 seconds agen him. 260

BILL *(sullenly)*. I'm no music hall wrastler. Can he box?

SHIRLEY. Yes: an you cant.

BILL. Wot! I cant, cant I? Wots that you say *(threatening him)*? 265

SHIRLEY *(not budging an inch)*. Will you box Todger Fairmile if I put him on to you? Say the word.

BILL *(subsiding with a slouch)*. I'll stand up to any man alive, if he was ten Todger Fairmiles. But I dont set up to be a perfessional. 270

SHIRLEY *(looking down on him with unfathomable disdain)*. Y o u box! Slap an old woman with the back o your hand! You hadnt even the sense to hit her where a magistrate couldnt see the mark of it, you silly young lump of conceit and ignorance. Hit a girl in the jaw and ony make her cry! If Todger Fairmile'd done it, she wouldnt a got up inside o ten minutes, no more than you would if he got on to you. Yah! I'd set about you myself if I had a 275 280

---

66 Horrockses] the John Horrocks Company, an enormous cotton mill in Preston, Lancashire.

67 Balls Pond] a street in London.

week's feedin in me instead o two months starvation. *(He returns to the table to finish his meal.)*

BILL *(following him and stooping over him to drive the taunt in).* You lie! you have the bread and treacle in you that you come here to beg. 285

SHIRLEY *(bursting into tears).* Oh God! it's true: I'm only an old pauper on the scrap heap. *(Furiously.)* But youll come to it yourself; and then youll know. Youll come to it sooner than a teetotaller like me, 290 fillin yourself with gin at this hour o the mornin!

BILL. I'm no gin drinker, you old liar; but when I want to give my girl a bloomin good idin I like to av a bit o devil in me: see? An here I am, talkin to a rotten old blighter like you sted o givin her wot 295 for. *(Working himself into a rage.)* I'm goin in there to fetch her out. *(He makes vengefully for the shelter door.)*

SHIRLEY. Youre goin to the station on a stretcher, more likely; and theyll take the gin and the devil 300 out of you there when they get you inside. You mind what youre about: the major here is the Earl o Stevenage's granddaughter.

BILL *(checked).* Garn!

SHIRLEY. Youll see. 305

BILL *(his resolution oozing).* Well, I aint done nothin to er.

SHIRLEY. Spose she said you did! who'd believe you?

BILL *(very uneasy, skulking back to the corner of the penthouse).* Gawd! theres no jastice in this country. 310 To think wot them people can do! I'm as good as er.

SHIRLEY. Tell her so. Its just what a fool like you would do.

Barbara, brisk and businesslike, comes from the shelter with a note book, and addresses herself to Shirley. Bill, cowed, sits down in the corner on a form, and turns his back on them.

BARBARA. Good morning.

SHIRLEY *(standing up and taking off his hat).* Good 315 morning, miss.

BARBARA. Sit down: make yourself at home. *(He hesitates; but she puts a friendly hand on his shoulder and makes him obey.)* Now then! since youve made friends with us, we want to know all about you. 320 Names and addresses and trades.

SHIRLEY. Peter Shirley. Fitter.[68] Chucked out two months ago because I was too old.

BARBARA *(not at all surprised).* Youd pass still. Why didnt you dye your hair? 325

SHIRLEY. I did. Me age come out at a coroner's inquest on me daughter.

BARBARA. Steady?

SHIRLEY. Teetotaller. Never out of a job before. Good worker. And sent to the knackers like an old 330 horse!

BARBARA. No matter: if you did your part God will do his.

SHIRLEY. *(suddenly stubborn).* My religion's no concern of anybody but myself. 335

BARBARA. *(guessing).* I know. Secularist?[69]

SHIRLEY. *(hotly).* Did I offer to deny it?

BARBARA. Why should you? My own father's a Secularist, I think. Our Father — yours and mine — fulfils himself in many ways; and I daresay he 340 knew what he was about when he made a Secularist of you. So buck up, Peter! we can always find a job for a steady man like you. *(Shirley, disarmed, touches his hat. She turns from him to Bill.)* Whats your name? 345

BILL. *(insolently).* Wots that to you?

BARBARA. *(calmly making a note).* Afraid to give his name. Any trade?

BILL. Who's afraid to give his name? *(Doggedly, with a sense of heroically defying the House of Lords in the 350 person of Lord Stevenage.)* If you want to bring a charge agen me, bring it. *(She waits, unruffled.)* My name's Bill Walker.

BARBARA *(as if the name were familiar: trying to remember how).* Bill Walker? *(Recollecting.)* Oh, I 355 know: youre the man that Jenny Hill was praying for inside just now. *(She enters his name in her note book.)*

BILL. Who's Jenny Hill? And what call has she to pray for me? 360

---

68 Fitter] in this case, probably one of the many machine-fitters maintaining the looms at the cotton mill.

69 Secularist] a follower of Secularism, a movement arguing that religion is irrelevant speculation and that any belief system should be founded on reason and science. Lancashire was a hotbed of Secular societies.

BARBARA. I dont know. Perhaps it was you that cut her lip.

BILL *(defiantly)*. Yes, it was me that cut her lip. I aint afraid o y o u.

BARBARA. How could you be, since youre not afraid of God? Youre a brave man, Mr. Walker. It takes some pluck to do our work here; but none of us dare lift our hand against a girl like lit, for fear of her father in heaven.

BILL *(sullenly)*. I want none o your cantin jaw. I suppose you think I come here to beg from you, like this damaged lot here. Not me. I dont want your bread and scrape and catlap.[70] I dont believe in your Gawd, no more than you do yourself.

BARBARA *(sunnily apologetic and ladylike, as on a new footing with him)*. Oh, I beg your pardon for putting your name down, Mr. Walker. I didnt understand. I'll strike it out.

BILL *(taking this as a slight, and deeply wounded by it)*. Eah! you let my name alone. Aint it good enough to be in your book?

BARBARA *(considering)*. Well, you see, theres no use putting down your name unless I can do something for you, is there? Whats your trade?

BILL *(still smarting)*. Thats no concern o yours.

BARBARA. Just so. *(Very businesslike.)* I'll put you down as *(writing)* the man who struck poor little Jenny Hill in the mouth.

BILL *(rising threateningly)*. See here. Ive ad enough o this.

BARBARA *(quite sunny and fearless)*. What did you come to us for?

BILL. I come for my girl, see? I come to take her out o this and to break er jawr for her.

BARBARA *(complacently)*. You see I was right about your trade. *(Bill, on the point of retorting furiously, finds himself, to his great shame and terror, in danger of crying instead. He sits down again suddenly.)* Whats her name?

BILL *(dogged)*. Er name's Mog Abbijam: thats wot her name is.

BARBARA. Oh, she's gone to Canning Town, to our barracks there.

BILL *(fortified by his resentment of Mog's perfidy)*. Is she? *(Vindictively.)* Then I'm goin to Kennintahn arter her. *(He crosses to the gate, hesitates; finally comes back at Barbara.)* Are you lyin to me to get shut o me?

BARBARA. I dont want to get shut of you. I want to keep you here and save your soul. Youd better stay: youre going to have a bad time today, Bill.

BILL. Who's goin to give it to me? Y o u, praps.

BARBARA. Someone you dont believe in. But youll be glad afterwards.

BILL *(slinking off)*. I'll go to Kennintahn to be out o the reach o your tongue. *(Suddenly turning on her with intense malice.)* And if I dont find Mog there, I'll come back and do two years for you, selp me Gawd if I dont!

BARBARA *(a shade kindlier, if possible)*. It's no use, Bill. Shes got another bloke.

BILL. Wot!

BARBARA. One of her own converts. He fell in love with her when he saw her with her soul saved, and her face clean, and her hair washed.

BILL *(surprised)*. Wottud she wash it for, the carroty slut? It's red.

BARBARA. It's quite lovely now, because she wears a new look in her eyes with it. It's a pity youre too late. The new bloke has put your nose out of joint, Bill.

BILL. I'll put his nose out o joint for him. Not that I care a curse for her, mind that. But I'll teach her to drop me as if I was dirt. And I'll teach him to meddle with my judy.[71] Wots is bleedin name?

BARBARA. Sergeant Todger Fairmile.

SHIRLEY *(rising with grim joy)*. I'll go with him, miss. I want to see them two meet. I'll take him to the infirmary when it's over.

BILL *(to Shirley, With undissembled misgiving)*. Is that im you was speakin on?

SHIRLEY. Thats him.

BILL. Im that wrastled in the music all?

SHIRLEY. The competitions at the National Sportin Club was worth nigh a hundred a year to him. Hes gev em up now for religion; so hes a bit fresh for want of the exercise he was accustomed to. Hell be glad to see you. Come along.

BILL. Wots is weight?

---

70 catlap] i.e., milk.

71 judy] (slang) girlfriend.

SHIRLEY. Thirteen four.[72] (Bill's last hope expires.)

BARBARA. Go and talk to him, Bill. He'll convert you. 450

SHIRLEY. He'll convert your head into a mashed potato.

BILL (sullenly). I aint afraid of him. I aint afraid of ennybody. But he can lick me. Shes done me. (He sits down moodily on the edge of the horse trough.) 455

SHIRLEY. You aint goin. I thought not. (He resumes his seat.)

BARBARA (calling). Jenny!

JENNY (appearing at the shelter door with a plaster on the corner of her mouth). Yes, Major. 460

BARBARA. Send Rummy Mitchens out to clear away here.

JENNY. I think shes afraid.

BARBARA (her resemblance to her mother washing out for a moment). Nonsense! she must do as shes told. 465

JENNY (calling into the shelter). Rummy: the Major says you must come.

Jenny comes to Barbara, purposely keeping on the side next Bill, lest he should suppose that she shrank from him or bore malice.

BARBARA. Poor little Jenny! Are you tired? (Looking at the wounded cheek.) Does it hurt? 470

JENNY. No: it's all right now. It was nothing.

BARBARA (critically). It was as hard as he could hit, I expect. Poor Bill! You dont feel angry with him, do you?

JENNY. Oh no, no, no: indeed I dont, Major, bless his poor heart! (Barbara kisses her; and she runs away merrily into the shelter. Bill writhes with an agonizing return of his new and alarming symptoms, but says nothing. Rummy Mitchens comes from the shelter.) 475

BARBARA (going to meet Rummy). Now Rummy, bustle. Take in those mugs and plates to be washed; and throw the crumbs about for the birds. 480

Rummy takes the three plates and mugs; but Shirley takes back his mug from her, as there is still some milk left in it.

RUMMY. There aint any crumbs. This aint a time to waste good bread on birds.

PRICE (appearing at the shelter door). Gentleman come to see the shelter, Major. Says hes your father. 485

BARBARA. All right. Coming. (Snobby goes back into the shelter, followed by Barbara.)

RUMMY (stealing across to Bill and addressing him in a subdued voice, but with intense conviction). I'd av the lor of you, you flat eared pignosed potwalloper, if she'd let me. Youre no gentleman, to hit a lady in the face. (Bill, with greater things moving in him, takes no notice.) 490

SHIRLEY (following her). Here! in with you and dont get yourself into more trouble by talking. 495

RUMMY (with hauteur). I aint ad the pleasure o being hintroduced to you, as I can remember. (She goes into the shelter with the plates.)

SHIRLEY. Thats the — 500

BILL (savagely). Dont you talk to me, d'ye hear. You lea me alone, or I'll do you a mischief. I'm not dirt under your feet, anyway.

SHIRLEY (calmly). Dont you be afeerd. You aint such prime company that you need expect to be sought after. (He is about to go into the shelter when Barbara comes out, with Undershaft on her right.) 505

BARBARA. Oh there you are, Mr. Shirley! (Between them.) This is my father: I told you he was a Secularist, didnt I? Perhaps youll be able to comfort one another. 510

UNDERSHAFT (startled). A Secularist! Not the least in the world: on the contrary, a confirmed mystic.[73]

BARBARA. Sorry, Im sure. By the way, papa, what i s your religion — in case I have to introduce you again? 515

UNDERSHAFT. My religion? Well, my dear, I am a Millionaire. That is my religion.

BARBARA. Then I'm afraid you and Mr. Shirley wont be able to comfort one another after all. Youre not a Millionaire, are you, Peter? 520

SHIRLEY. No; and proud of it.

UNDERSHAFT (gravely). Poverty, my friend, is not a thing to be proud of. 525

---

72 Thirteen four] i.e., thirteen stone (a measure equal to fourteen pounds) and four pounds (186 pounds or roughly 85 kilograms).

---

73 mystic] i.e., one who claims to have a direct insight into divine truth that stands apart from any formal religion.

SHIRLEY (*angrily*). Who made your millions for you? Me and my like. Whats kep us poor? Keepin you rich. I wouldnt have your conscience, not for all your income.

UNDERSHAFT. I wouldnt have your income, not for all your conscience, Mr. Shirley. (*He goes to the penthouse and sits down on a form.*)   530

BARBARA (*stopping Shirley adroitly as he is about to retort*). You wouldnt think he was my father, would you, Peter? Will you go into the shelter and lend the lasses a hand for a while: we're worked off our feet.   535

SHIRLEY (*bitterly*). Yes: I'm in their debt for a meal, aint I?

BARBARA. Oh, not because youre in their debt; but for love of them, Peter, for love of them. (*He cannot understand, and is rather scandalized.*) There! dont stare at me. In with you; and give that conscience of yours a holiday (*bustling him into the shelter*).   540

SHIRLEY (*as he goes in*). Ah! it's a pity you never was trained to use your reason, miss. Youd have been a very taking lecturer on Secularism.   545

Barbara turns to her father.

UNDERSHAFT. Never mind me, my dear. Go about your work; and let me watch it for a while.

BARBARA. All right.

UNDERSHAFT. For instance, whats the matter with that out-patient over there?   550

BARBARA (*looking at Bill, whose attitude has never changed, and whose expression of brooding wrath has deepened*). Oh, we shall cure him in no time. Just watch. (*She goes over to Bill and waits. He glances up at her and casts his eyes down again, uneasy, but grimmer than ever.*) It would be nice to just stamp on Mog Habbijam's face, wouldnt it, Bill?   555

BILL (*starting up from the trough in consternation*). It's a lie: I never said so. (*She shakes her head.*) Who told you wot was in my mind?   560

BARBARA. Only your new friend.

BILL. Wot new friend?

BARBARA. The devil, Bill. When he gets round people they get miserable, just like you.   565

BILL (*with a heartbreaking attempt at devil-may-care cheerfulness*). I aint miserable. (*He sits down again, and stretches his legs in an attempt to seem indifferent.*)

BARBARA. Well, if youre happy, why dont you look happy, as we do?   570

BILL (*his legs curling back in spite of him*). I'm appy enough, I tell you. Why dont you lea me alown? Wot av I done to y o u? I aint smashed y o u r face, av I?   575

BARBARA (*softly: wooing his soul*). It's not me thats getting at you, Bill.

BILL. Who else is it?

BARBARA. Somebody that doesnt intend you to smash women's faces, I suppose. Somebody or something that wants to make a man of you.   580

BILL (*blustering*). Make a man o' m e! Aint I a man? eh? aint I a man? Who sez I'm not a man?

BARBARA. Theres a man in you somewhere, I suppose. But why did he let you hit poor little Jenny Hill? That wasnt very manly of him, was it?   585

BILL (*tormented*). Av done with it, I tell you. Chack it. I'm sick of your Jenny Ill and er silly little face.

BARBARA. Then why do you keep thinking about it? Why does it keep coming up against you in your mind? Youre not getting converted, are you?   590

BILL (*with conviction*). Not ME. Not likely. Not arf.

BARBARA. Thats right, Bill. Hold out against it. Put out your strength. Dont lets get you cheap. Todger Fairmile said he wrestled for three nights against his Salvation harder than he ever wrestled with the Jap at the music hall. He gave in to the Jap when his arm was going to break. But he didnt give in to his salvation until his heart was going to break. Perhaps youll escape that. You havnt any heart, have you?   595, 600

BILL. Wot d'ye mean? Wy aint I got a art the same as ennybody else?

BARBARA. A man with a heart wouldnt have bashed poor little Jenny's face, would he?   605

BILL (*almost crying*). Ow, w i l l you lea me alown? Av I ever offered to meddle with y o u, that you come naggin and provowkin me lawk this? (*He writhes convulsively from his eyes to his toes.*)

BARBARA (*with a steady soothing hand on his arm and a gentle voice that never lets him go*). It's your soul thats hurting you, Bill, and not me. Weve been through it all ourselves. Come with us, Bill. (*He looks wildly round*). To brave manhood on earth and eternal glory in heaven. (*He is on the   610, 615 *point of breaking down.*) Come. (*A drum is heard in the shelter; and Bill, with a gasp, escapes from the spell as Barbara turns quickly. Adolphus enters from the shelter with a big drum.*) Oh! there you are, Dolly. Let me introduce a new friend of mine, Mr. Bill Walker. This is my bloke, Bill: Mr. Cusins. (*Cusins salutes with his drumstick.*)

BILL. Goin to marry im?

BARBARA. Yes.

BILL (*fervently*). Gord elp im! Gawd elp im!

BARBARA. Why? Do you think he wont be happy with me?

BILL. Ive only ad to stand it for a mornin: e'll av to stand it for a lifetime.

CUSINS. That is a frightful reflection, Mr. Walker. But I cant tear myself away from her.

BILL. Well, I can. (*To Barbara.*) Eah! do you know where I'm going to, and wot I'm goin to do?

BARBARA. Yes: youre going to heaven; and youre coming back here before the week's out to tell me so.

BILL. You lie. I'm goin to Kennintahn, to spit in Todger Fairmile's eye. I bashed Jenny Ill's face; and now I'll get me own face bashed and come back and shew it to er. E'll it me ardern I it er. Thatll make us square. (*To Adolphus.*) Is that fair or is it not? Youre a genlmn: you oughter know.

BARBARA. Two black eyes wont make one white one, Bill.

BILL. I didnt ast y o u. Cawnt you never keep your mahth shut? I ast the genlmn.

CUSINS. (*refectively*). Yes: I think youre right, Mr. Walker. Yes: I should do it. Its curious: its exactly what an ancient Greek would have done.

BARBARA. But what good will it do?

CUSINS. Well, it will give Mr. Fairmile some exercise; and it will satisfy Mr. Walker's soul.

BILL. Rot! there aint no sach a thing as a soul. Ah kin you tell wether Ive a soul or not? You never seen it.

BARBARA. Ive seen it hurting you when you went against it.

BILL (*with compressed aggravation*). If you was my girl and took the word out o me mahth lawk thet, I'd give you suthink youd feel urtin, so I would. (*To Adolphus.*) You take my tip, mate. Stop er jawr;

or youll die afore your time. (*With intense expression.*) Wore aht: thets wot youll be: wore aht. (*He goes away through the gate.*)

CUSINS (*looking after him*). I wonder!

BARBARA. Dolly! (*indignant, as her mother's manner.*)

CUSINS. Yes, my dear, it's very wearing to be in love with you. If it lasts, I quite think I shall die young.

BARBARA. Should you mind?

CUSINS. Not at all. (*He is suddenly softened, and kisses her over the drum, evidently not for the first time, as people cannot kiss over a big drum without practice. Undershaft coughs.*)

BARBARA. It's all right, papa, weve not forgotten you. Dolly: explain the place to papa: I havnt time. (*She goes busily into the shelter.*)

Undershaft and Adolphus now have the yard to themselves. Undershaft, seated on a form, and still keenly attentive, looks hard at Adolphus. Adolphus looks hard at him.

UNDERSHAFT. I fancy you guess something of what is in my mind, Mr. Cusins. (*Cusins flourishes his drumsticks as if in the act of beating a lively rataplan, but makes no sound.*) Exactly so. But suppose Barbara finds you out!

CUSINS. You know, I do not admit that I am imposing on Barbara. I am quite genuinely interested in the views of the Salvation Army. The fact is, I am a sort of collector of religions; and the curious thing is that I find I can believe them all. By the way, have you any religion?

UNDERSHAFT. Yes.

CUSINS. Anything out of the common?

UNDERSHAFT. Only that there are two things necessary to Salvation.

CUSINS (*disappointed, but polite*). Ah, the Church Catechism. Charles Lomax also belongs to the Established Church.

UNDERSHAFT. The two things are —

CUSINS. Baptism and —

UNDERSHAFT. No. Money and gunpowder.

CUSINS (*surprised, but interested*). That is the general opinion of our governing classes. The novelty is in hearing any man confess it.

UNDERSHAFT. Just so.

CUSINS. Excuse me: is there any place in your religion for honor, justice, truth, love, mercy and so forth? 705

UNDERSHAFT. Yes: they are the graces and luxuries of a rich, strong, and safe life.

CUSINS. Suppose one is forced to choose between them and money or gunpowder?

UNDERSHAFT. Choose money a n d gunpowder; 710 for without enough of both you cannot afford the others.

CUSINS. That is your religion?

UNDERSHAFT. Yes.

The cadence of this reply makes a full close in the conversation. Cusins twists his face dubiously and contemplates Undershaft. Undershaft contemplates him.

CUSINS. Barbara wont stand that. You will have to 715 choose between your religion and Barbara.

UNDERSHAFT. So will you, my friend. She will find out that that drum of yours is hollow.

CUSINS. Father Undershaft: you are mistaken: I am a sincere Salvationist. You do not understand the 720 Salvation Army. It is the army of joy, of love, of courage: it has banished the fear and remorse and despair of the old hell-ridden evangelical sects: it marches to fight the devil with trumpet and drum, with music and dancing, with banner and palm, as 725 becomes a sally from heaven by its happy garrison. It picks the waster out of the public house and makes a man of him: it finds a worm wriggling in a back kitchen, and lo! a woman! Men and women of rank too, sons and daughters of the Highest. It takes 730 the poor professor of Greek, the most artificial and self-suppressed of human creatures, from his meal of roots, and lets loose the rhapsodist in him; reveals the true worship of Dionysos to him; sends him down the public street drumming dithyrambs *(he* 735 *plays a thundering flourish on the drum).*[74]

UNDERSHAFT. You will alarm the shelter.

CUSINS. Oh, they are accustomed to these sudden ecstasies of piety. However, if the drum worries you *(he pockets the drumsticks; unhooks the drum; and* 740 *stands it on the ground opposite the gateway).*

UNDERSHAFT. Thank you.

CUSINS. You remember what Euripides says about your money and gunpowder?

UNDERSHAFT. No. 745

CUSINS *(declaiming).*

"One and another
In money and guns may outpass his brother;
And men in their millions float and flow
And seethe with a million hopes as leaven; 750
And they win their will; or they miss their win;
And their hopes are dead or are pined for still;
But whoe'er can know
As the long days go
That to live is happy, has found h i s heaven." 755
My translation: what do you think of it?[75]

UNDERSHAFT. I think, my friend, that if you wish to know, as the long days go, that to live is happy, you must first acquire money enough for a decent life, and power enough to be your own master. 760

CUSINS. You are damnably discouraging. *(He resumes his declamation.)*

"Is it so hard a thing to see
That the spirit of God—whate'er it be—
The Law that abides and changes not, ages long, 765
The Eternal and Nature-born: t h e s e things be strong?
What else is Wisdom? What of Man's endeavor,
Or God's high grace so lovely and so great?
To stand from fear set free? to breathe and wait?
To hold a hand uplifted over Fate? 770
And shall not Barbara be loved for ever?"

UNDERSHAFT. Euripides mentions Barbara, does he?

CUSINS. It is a fair translation. The word means Loveliness. 775

UNDERSHAFT. May I ask — as Barbara's father — how much a year she is to be loved for ever on?

CUSINS. As Barbara's father, that is more your affair than mine. I can feed her by teaching Greek: that is about all. 780

UNDERSHAFT. Do you consider it a good match for her?

---

74 Dionysos] the Greek god of religious ecstasy, wine, irrational release, and theatre.

75 translation] from *The Bacchae* by Euripides; Shaw actually used a translation by his friend, the classicist Gilbert Murray (1866–1957), on whom he had based Cusins.

CUSINS (with polite obstinacy). Mr. Undershaft: I am in many ways a weak, timid, ineffectual person; and my health is far from satisfactory. But whenever I feel that I must have anything, I get it, sooner or later. I feel that way about Barbara. I dont like marriage: I feel intensely afraid of it; and I dont know what I shall do with Barbara or what she will do with me. But I feel that I and nobody else must marry her. Please regard that as settled. Not that I wish to be arbitrary; but why should I waste your time in discussing what is inevitable?

UNDERSHAFT. You mean that you will stick at nothing: not even the conversion of the Salvation Army to the worship of Dionysos.

CUSINS. The business of the Salvation Army is to save, not to wrangle about the name of the pathfinder. Dionysos or another: what does it matter?

UNDERSHAFT (rising and approaching him). Professor Cusins: you are a young man after my own heart.

CUSINS. Mr. Undershaft: you are, as far as I am able to gather, a most infernal old rascal; but you appeal very strongly to my sense of ironic humor.

Undershaft mutely offers his hand. They shake.

UNDERSHAFT (suddenly concentrating himself). And now to business.

CUSINS. Pardon me. We were discussing religion. Why go back to such an uninteresting and unimportant subject as business?

UNDERSHAFT. Religion is our business at present, because it is through religion alone that we can win Barbara.

CUSINS. Have you, too, fallen in love with Barbara?

UNDERSHAFT. Yes, with a father's love.

CUSINS. A father's love for a grown-up daughter is the most dangerous of all infatuations. I apologize for mentioning my own pale, coy, mistrustful fancy in the same breath with it.

UNDERSHAFT. Keep to the point. We have to win her; and we are neither of us Methodists.

CUSINS. That doesnt matter. The power Barbara wields here — the power that wields Barbara herself — is not Calvinism, not Presbyterianism, not Methodism —

UNDERSHAFT. Not Greek Paganism either, eh?

CUSINS. I admit that. Barbara is quite original in her religion.

UNDERSHAFT (triumphantly). Aha! Barbara Undershaft would be. Her inspiration comes from within herself.

CUSINS. How do you suppose it got there?

UNDERSHAFT (in towering excitement). It is the Undershaft inheritance. I shall hand on my torch to my daughter. She shall make my converts and preach my gospel —

CUSINS. What! Money and gunpowder!

UNDERSHAFT. Yes, money and gunpowder; freedom and power; command of life and command of death.

CUSINS (urbanely: trying to bring him down to earth). This is extremely interesting, Mr. Undershaft. Of course you know that you are mad.

UNDERSHAFT (with redoubled force). And you?

CUSINS. Oh, mad as a hatter. You are welcome to my secret since I have discovered yours. But I am astonished. Can a madman make cannons?

UNDERSHAFT. Would anyone else than a madman make them? And now (with surging energy) question for question. Can a sane man translate Euripides?[76]

CUSINS. No.

UNDERSHAFT (seizing him by the shoulder). Can a sane woman make a man of a waster or a woman of a worm?

CUSINS (reeling before the storm). Father Colossus — Mammoth Millionaire —

UNDERSHAFT (pressing him). Are there two mad people or three in this Salvation shelter to-day?

CUSINS. You mean Barbara is as mad as we are!

UNDERSHAFT (pushing him lightly off and resuming his equanimity suddenly and completely). Pooh, Professor! let us call things by their proper names. I am a millionaire; you are a poet; Barbara is a savior of souls. What have we three to do with the common mob of slaves and idolaters? (He sits down again with a shrug of contempt for the mob.)

---

76 sane … Euripides] Euripides has the reputation of being more willing than the other Greek tragedians to explore the irrational and dangerous side of human experience.

CUSINS. Take care! Barbara is in love with the common people. So am I. Have you never felt the romance of that love? 870

UNDERSHAFT (cold and sardonic). Have you ever been in love with Poverty, like St. Francis? Have you ever been in love with Dirt, like St. Simeon? Have you ever been in love with disease and 875 suffering, like our nurses and philanthropists? Such passions are not virtues, but the most unnatural of all the vices. This love of the common people may please an earl's granddaughter and a university professor; but I have been a common man and a 880 poor man; and it has no romance for me. Leave it to the poor to pretend that poverty is a blessing: leave it to the coward to make a religion of his cowardice by preaching humility: we know better than that. We three must stand together above the 885 common people: how else can we help their children to climb up beside us? Barbara must belong to us, not to the Salvation Army.

CUSINS. Well, I can only say that if you think you will get her away from the Salvation Army by 890 talking to her as you have been talking to me, you dont know Barbara.

UNDERSHAFT. My friend: I never ask for what I can buy.

CUSINS (in a white fury). Do I understand you to 895 imply that you can buy Barbara?

UNDERSHAFT. No; but I can buy the Salvation Army.

CUSINS. Quite impossible.

UNDERSHAFT. You shall see. All religious organi- 900 zations exist by selling themselves to the rich.

CUSINS. Not the Army. That is the Church of the poor.

UNDERSHAFT. All the more reason for buying it.

CUSINS. I dont think you quite know what the 905 Army does for the poor.

UNDERSHAFT. Oh yes I do. It draws their teeth: that is enough for me — as a man of business —

CUSINS. Nonsense. It makes them sober —

UNDERSHAFT. I prefer sober workmen. The 910 profits are larger.

CUSINS. — honest —

UNDERSHAFT. Honest workmen are the most economical.

CUSINS. — attached to their homes — 915

UNDERSHAFT. So much the better: they will put up with anything sooner than change their shop.

CUSINS. — happy —

UNDERSHAFT. An invaluable safeguard against revolution. 920

CUSINS. — unselfish —

UNDERSHAFT. Indifferent to their own interests, which suits me exactly.

CUSINS. — with their thoughts on heavenly things — 925

UNDERSHAFT (rising). And not on Trade Union-ism nor Socialism. Excellent.

CUSINS (revolted). You really are an infernal old rascal.

UNDERSHAFT (indicating Peter Shirley, who has 930 just come from the shelter and strolled dejectedly down the yard between them). And this is an honest man!

SHIRLEY. Yes; and what av I got by it? (He passes on bitterly and sits on the form, in the corner of the penthouse.) 935

Snobby Price, beaming sanctimoniously, and Jenny Hill, with a tambourine full of coppers, come from the shelter and go to the drum, on which Jenny begins to count the money.

UNDERSHAFT (replying to Shirley). Oh, your employers must have got a good deal by it from first to last. (He sits on the table, with one foot on the side form. Cusins, overwhelmed, sits down on the same form nearer the shelter. Barbara comes from the 940 shelter to the middle of the yard. She is excited and a little overwrought.)

BARBARA. Weve just had a splendid experience meeting at the other gate in Cripps's lane. Ive hardly ever seen them so much moved as they were 945 by your confession, Mr. Price.

PRICE. I could almost be glad of my past wickedness if I could believe that it would elp to keep hathers stright.

BARBARA. So it will, Snobby. How much, Jenny? 950

JENNY. Four and tenpence, Major.

BARBARA. Oh Snobby, if you had given your poor mother just one more kick, we should have got the whole five shillings!

PRICE. If she heard you say that, miss, she'd be sorry 955

I didnt. But I'm glad. Oh what a joy it will be to her when she hears I'm saved!

UNDERSHAFT. Shall I contribute the odd two-pence, Barbara? The millionaire's mite, eh? *(He takes a couple of pennies from his pocket.)*

BARBARA. How did you make that twopence?

UNDERSHAFT. As usual. By selling cannons, torpedoes, submarines, and my new patent Grand Duke hand grenade.

BARBARA. Put it back in your pocket. You cant buy your Salvation here for twopence: you must work it out.

UNDERSHAFT. Is twopence not enough? I can afford a little more, if you press me.

BARBARA. Two million millions would not be enough. There is bad blood on your hands; and nothing but good blood can cleanse them. Money is no use. Take it away. *(She turns to Cusins.)* Dolly: you must write another letter for me to the papers. *(He makes a wry face.)* Yes: I know you dont like it; but it must be done. The starvation this winter is beating us: everybody is unemployed. The General says we must close this shelter if we cant get more money. I force the collections at the meetings until I am ashamed: dont I, Snobby?

PRICE. It's a fair treat to see you work it, Miss. The way you got them up from three-and-six to four-and-ten with that hymn, penny by penny and verse by verse, was a caution. Not a Cheap Jack on Mile End Waste could touch you at it.[77]

BARBARA. Yes; but I wish we could do without it. I am getting at last to think more of the collection than of the people's souls. And what are those hatfuls of pence and halfpence? We want thousands! tens of thousands! hundreds of thousands! I want to convert people, not to be always begging for the Army in a way I'd die sooner than beg for myself.

UNDERSHAFT *(in profound irony)*. Genuine unselfishness is capable of anything, my dear.

BARBARA *(unsuspectingly, as she turns away to take the money from the drum and put it in a cash bag she carries)*. Yes, isnt it? *(Undershaft looks sardonically at Cusins.)*

CUSINS *(aside to Undershaft)*. Mephistopheles! Machiavelli![78]

BARBARA *(tears coming into her eyes as she ties the bag and pockets it)*. How are we to feed them? I cant talk religion to a man with bodily hunger in his eyes. *(Almost breaking down.)* It's frightful.

JENNY *(running to her)*. Major, dear —

BARBARA *(rebounding)*. No, dont comfort me. It will be all right. We shall get the money.

UNDERSHAFT. How?

JENNY. By praying for it, of course. Mrs. Baines says she prayed for it last night; and she has never prayed for it in vain: never once. *(She goes to the gate and looks out into the street.)*

BARBARA *(who has dried her eyes and regained her composure)*. By the way, dad, Mrs. Baines has come to march with us to our big meeting this afternoon; and she is very anxious to meet you, for some reason or other. Perhaps she'll convert you.

UNDERSHAFT. I shall be delighted, my dear.

JENNY *(at the gate: excitedly)*. Major! Major! heres that man back again.

BARBARA. What man?

JENNY. The man that hit me. Oh, I hope hes coming back to join us.

Bill Walker, with frost on his jacket, comes through the gate, his hands deep in his pockets and his chin sunk between his shoulders, like a cleaned-out gambler. He halts between Barbara and the drum.

BARBARA. Hullo, Bill! Back already!

BILL *(nagging at her)*. Bin talkin ever sence, av you?

BARBARA. Pretty nearly. Well, has Todger paid you out for poor Jenny's jaw?

BILL. No he aint.

BARBARA. I thought your jacket looked a bit snowy.

BILL. So it is snowy. You want to know where the snow come from, dont you?

BARBARA. Yes.

---

77 Cheap Jack] a smooth-talking, haggling merchant; Mile End Waste] an open market area of Mile End Road in London.

78 Mephistopheles] the devil who buys Faustus's soul; Machiavelli] Niccolò Machiavelli (1469–1527), who, in *The Prince*, advises how to deviously manipulate for political advantage.

BILL. Well, it come from off the ground in Parkinses Corner in Kennintahn. It got rubbed off be my shoulders: see? 1035

BARBARA. Pity you didnt rub some off with your knees, Bill! That would have done you a lot of good.

BILL *(with sour mirthless humor)*. I was saving 1040 another man's knees at the time. E was kneelin on my ed, so e was.

JENNY. Who was kneeling on your head?

BILL. Todger was. E was prayin for me: prayin comfortable with me as a carpet. So was Mog. So 1045 was the ole bloomin meetin. Mog she sez "O Lord break is stubborn spirit; but dont urt is dear art." That was wot she said. "Dont urt is dear art"! An er bloke — thirteen stun four! — kneelin wiv all is weight on me. Funny, aint it? 1050

JENNY. Oh no. We're so sorry, Mr. Walker.

BARBARA *(enjoying it frankly)*. Nonsense! of course it's funny. Served you right, Bill! You must have done something to him first.

BILL *(doggedly)*. I did wot I said I'd do. I spit in is eye. 1055 E looks up at the sky and sez, "O that I should be fahnd worthy to be spit upon for the gospel's sake!" e sez; an Mog sez "Glory Allelloolier!"; and then e called me Brother, an dahned me as if I was a kid and e was me mother washin me a Setterda nawt. I adnt 1060 just no show wiv im at all. Arf the street prayed; an the tother arf larfed fit to split theirselves. *(To Barbara.)* There! are you settisfawd nah?

BARBARA *(her eyes dancing)*. Wish I'd been there, Bill. 1065

BILL. Yes: youd a got in a hextra bit o talk on me, wouldnt you?

JENNY. I'm so sorry, Mr. Walker.

BILL *(fiercely)*. Dont you go bein sorry for me: youve no call. Listen ere. I broke your jawr. 1070

JENNY. No, it didnt hurt me: indeed it didnt, except for a moment. It was only that I was frightened.

BILL. I dont want to be forgive be you, or be ennybody. Wot I did I'll pay for. I tried to get me own jawr broke to settisfaw you — 1075

JENNY *(distressed)*. Oh no —

BILL *(impatiently)*. Tell y'I did: cawnt you listen to wots bein told you? All I got be it was bein made a sight of in the public street for me pains. Well, if I cawnt settisfaw you one way, I can another. 1080 Listen ere! I ad two quid saved agen the frost; an Ive a pahnd of it left. A mate o mine last week ad words with the judy e's goin to marry. E give er wotfor; an e's bin fined fifteen bob. E ad a right to it er because they was goin to be marrid; but I 1085 adnt no right to it you; so put anather fawv bob on an call it a pahnd's worth. *(He produces a sovereign.)* Eres the money. Take it; and lets av no more o your forgivin an prayin and your Major jawrin me. Let wot I done be done and paid for; 1090 and let there be a end of it.

JENNY. Oh, I couldnt take it, Mr. Walker. But if you would give a shilling or two to poor Rummy Mitchens! you really did hurt her; and shes old.

BILL *(contemptuously)*. Not likely. I'd give her anather 1095 as soon as look at er. Let her av the lawr o me as she threatened! S h e aint forgiven me: not mach. Wot I done to er is not on me mawnd — wot she *(indicating Barbara)* might call on me conscience — no more than stickin a pig. It's this Christian 1100 game o yours that I wont av played agen me: this bloomin forgivin an naggin an jawrin that makes a man that sore that in lawf's a burdn to im. I wont av its I tell you; so take your money and stop throwin your silly bashed face hup agen me. 1105

JENNY. Major: may I take a little of it for the Army?

BARBARA. No: the Army is not to be bought. We want your soul, Bill; and we'll take nothing less.

BILL *(bitterly)*. I know. It aint enough. Me an me few shillins is not good enough for you. Youre a 1110 earl's grendorter, you are. Nothin less than a underd pahnd for you.

UNDERSHAFT. Come, Barbara! you could do a great deal of good with a hundred pounds. If you will set this gentleman's mind at ease by taking his 1115 pound, I will give the other ninety-nine. *(Bill, astounded by such opulence, instinctively touches his cap.)*

BARBARA. Oh, youre too extravagant, papa. Bill offers twenty pieces of silver. All you need offer is 1120 the other ten. That will make the standard price to buy anybody who's for sale.[79] I'm not; and the

---

79 twenty pieces of silver ... the other ten] Judas took a bribe of thirty pieces of silver for betraying Christ.

Army's not. (*To Bill.*) Youll never have another quiet moment, Bill, until you come round to us. You cant stand out against your salvation.

BILL (*sullenly*). I cawnt stend aht agen music-all wrastlers and artful tongued women. Ive offered to pay. I can do no more. Take it or leave it. There it is. (*He throws the sovereign on the drum, and sits down on the horse-trough. The coin fascinates Snobby Price, who takes an early opportunity of dropping his cap on it.*)

Mrs. Baines comes from the shelter. She is dressed as a Salvation Army Commissioner. She is an earnest looking woman of about 40, with a caressing, urgent voice, and an appealing manner.

BARBARA. This is my father, Mrs. Baines. (*Undershaft comes from the table, taking his hat off with marked civility.*) Try what you can do with him. He wont listen to me, because he remembers what a fool I was when I was a baby. (*She leaves them together and chats with Jenny.*)

MRS. BAINES. Have you been shewn over the shelter, Mr. Undershaft? You know the work we're doing, of course.

UNDERSHAFT (*very civilly*). The whole nation knows it, Mrs. Baines.

MRS. BAINES. No, sir: the whole nation does not know it, or we should not be crippled as we are for want of money to carry our work through the length and breadth of the land. Let me tell you that there would have been rioting this winter in London but for us.

UNDERSHAFT. You really think so?

MRS. BAINES. I know it. I remember 1886, when you rich gentlemen hardened your hearts against the cry of the poor. They broke the windows of your clubs in Pall Mall.[80]

UNDERSHAFT (*gleaming with approval of their method*). And the Mansion House Fund went up next day from thirty thousand pounds to seventy-nine thousand![81] I remember quite well.

MRS. BAINES. Well, wont you help me to get at the people? They wont break windows then. Come here, Price. Let me shew you to this gentleman (*Price comes to be inspected*). Do you remember the window breaking?

PRICE. My ole father thought it was the revolution, maam.

MRS. BAINES. Would you break windows now?

PRICE. Oh no maam. The windows of eaven av bin opened to me. I know now that the rich man is a sinner like myself.

RUMMY (*appearing above at the loft door*). Snobby Price!

PRICE. Wot is it?

RUMMY. Your mother's askin for you at the other gate in Crippses Lane. She's heard about your confession (*Price turns pale*).

MRS. BAINES. Go, Mr. Price; and pray with her.

JENNY. You can go through the shelter, Snobby.

PRICE (*to Mrs. Baines*). I couldnt face her now, maam, with all the weight of my sins fresh on me. Tell her she'll find her son at ome, waitin for her in prayer. (*He skulks off through the gate, incidentally stealing the sovereign on his way out by picking up his cap from the drum.*)

MRS. BAINES (*with signing eyes*). You see how we take the anger and the bitterness against you out of their hearts, Mr. Undershaft.

UNDERSHAFT. It is certainly most convenient and gratifying to all large employers of labor, Mrs. Baines.

MRS. BAINES. Barbara: Jenny: I have good news: most wonderful news. (*Jenny runs to her.*) My prayers have been answered. I told you they would, Jenny, didn't I?

JENNY. Yes, yes.

BARBARA (*moving nearer to the drum*). Have we got money enough to keep the shelter open?

---

80 1886] On February 8, separate meetings of the London United Workmen's Committee and the Social Democratic Federation were scheduled to be held in Trafalgar Square. There a rally in Hyde Park was announced and a crowd of 5,000 streamed into Pall Mall, a street of expensive homes and clubs in St. James's near Buckingham Palace, where they smashed the windows of the private clubs along the way.

81 Mansion House Fund] a fund for the relief of the poor funded by the Lord Mayor of London; Mansion House is the Mayor's official residence.

MRS. BAINES. I hope we shall have enough to keep all the shelters open. Lord Saxmundham has promised us five thousand pounds —

BARBARA. Hooray! 1200

JENNY. Glory!

MRS. BAINES. — if —

BARBARA. "If!" If what?

MRS. BAINES. — if five other gentlemen will give a thousand each to make it up to ten thousand. 1205

BARBARA. Who is Lord Saxmundham? I never heard of him.

UNDERSHAFT (who has pricked up his ears at the peer's name, and is now watching Barbara curiously). A new creation, my dear. You have heard of Sir 1210 Horace Bodger?

BARBARA. Bodger! Do you mean the distiller? Bodger's whisky!

UNDERSHAFT. That is the man. He is one of the greatest of our public benefactors. He restored the 1215 cathedral at Hakington.[82] They made him a baronet for that. He gave half a million to the funds of his party: they made him a baron for that.

SHIRLEY. What will they give him for the five thousand? 1220

UNDERSHAFT. There is nothing left to give him. So the five thousand, I should think, is to save his soul.

MRS. BAINES. Heaven grant it may! Oh Mr. Undershaft, you have some very rich friends. Cant 1225 you help us towards the other five thousand? We are going to hold a great meeting this afternoon at the Assembly Hall in the Mile End Road. If I could only announce that one gentleman had come forward to support Lord Saxmundham, 1230 others would follow. Dont you know somebody? couldnt you? wouldnt you? (Her eyes fill with tears.) Oh, think of those poor people, Mr. Undershaft: think of how much it means to them, and how little to a great man like you. 1235

UNDERSHAFT (sardonically gallant). Mrs. Baines: you are irresistible. I cant disappoint you; and I

---

[82] Hakington] (or Hackington) St. Stephen's parish, which is not a cathedral but a very old church; however, Canterbury Cathedral (which would not be referred to as being in Hakington) is less than a mile away.

cant deny myself the satisfaction of making Bodger pay up. You shall have your five thousand pounds.

MRS. BAINES. Thank God! 1240

UNDERSHAFT. You dont thank m e?

MRS. BAINES. Oh sir, dont try to be cynical: dont be ashamed of being a good man. The Lord will bless you abundantly; and our prayers will be like a strong fortification round you all the days of your 1245 life. (with a touch of caution.) You will let me have the cheque to shew at the meeting, wont you? Jenny: go in and fetch a pen and ink. (Jenny runs to the shelter door.)

UNDERSHAFT. Do not disturb Miss Hill: I have 1250 a fountain pen. (Jenny halts. He sits at the table and writes the cheque. Cusins rises to make more room for him. They all watch him silently.)

BILL (cynically, aside to Barbara, his voice and accent horribly debased). Wot prawce Selvytion nah? 1255

BARBARA. Stop. (Undershaft stops writing: they all turn to her in surprise.) Mrs. Baines: are you really going to take this money?

MRS. BAINES (astonished). Why not, dear?

BARBARA. Why not! Do you know what my father 1260 is? Have you forgotten that Lord Saxmundham is Bodger the whisky man? Do you remember how we implored the County Council to stop him from writing Bodger's Whisky in letters of fire against the sky; so that the poor drink-ruined creatures on 1265 the embankment could not wake up from their snatches of sleep without being reminded of their deadly thirst by that wicked sky sign? Do you know that the worst thing I have had to fight here is not the devil, but Bodger, Bodger, Bodger, with 1270 his whisky, his distilleries, and his tied houses? Are you going to make our shelter another tied house for him, and ask me to keep it?

BILL. Rotten dranken whisky it is too.

MRS. BAINES. Dear Barbara: Lord Saxmundham 1275 has a soul to be saved like any of us. If heaven has found the way to make a good use of his money, are we to set ourselves up against the answer to our prayers?

BARBARA. I know he has a soul to be saved. Let him 1280 come down here; and I'll do my best to help him to his salvation. But he wants to send his cheque down to buy us, and go on being as wicked as ever.

UNDERSHAFT *(with a reasonableness which Cusins alone perceives to be ironical)*. My dear Barbara: alcohol is a very necessary article. It heals the sick — 1285

BARBARA. It does nothing of the sort.

UNDERSHAFT. Well, it assists the doctor: that is perhaps a less questionable way of putting it. It makes life bearable to millions of people who could 1290 not endure their existence if they were quite sober. It enables Parliament to do things at eleven at night that no sane person would do at eleven in the morning. Is it Bodger's fault that this inestimable gift is deplorably abused by less than one per cent 1295 of the poor? *(He turns again to the table; signs the cheque; and crosses it.)*

MRS. BAINES. Barbara: will there be less drinking or more if all those poor souls we are saving come tomorrow and find the doors of our shelters shut 1300 in their faces? Lord Saxmundham gives us the money to stop drinking — to take his own business from him.

CUSINS *(impishly)*. Pure self-sacrifice on Bodger's part, clearly! Bless dear Bodger! *(Barbara almost 1305 breaks down as Adolphus, too, fails her.)*

UNDERSHAFT *(tearing out the cheque and pocketing the book as he rises and goes past Cusins to Mrs. Baines)*. I also, Mrs. Baines, may claim a little disinterestedness. Think of my business! think of the 1310 widows and orphans! the men and lads torn to pieces with shrapnel and poisoned with lyddite![83] *(Mrs. Baines shrinks; but he goes on remorselessly.)* The oceans of blood, not one drop of which is shed in a really just cause! the ravaged crops! the peaceful 1315 peasants forced, women and men, to till their fields under the fire of opposing armies on pain of starvation! the bad blood of the fierce little cowards at home who egg on others to fight for the gratification of their national vanity! All this makes money for 1320 me: I am never richer, never busier than when the papers are full of it. Well, it is your work to preach peace on earth and goodwill to men. *(Mrs. Baines's face lights up again.)* Every convert you make is a vote against war. *(Her lips move in prayer.)* Yet I give you 1325 this money.

CUSINS *(mounting the form in an ecstasy of mischief)*.

The millennium will be inaugurated by the unselfishness of Undershaft and Bodger. Oh be joyful! *(He takes the drumsticks from his pockets and 1330 flourishes them.)*

MRS. BAINES *(taking the cheque)*. The longer I live the more proof I see that there is an Infinite Goodness that turns everything to the work of salvation sooner or later. Who would have thought 1335 that any good could have come out of war and drink? And yet their profits are brought today to the feet of salvation to do its blessed work. *(She is affected to tears.)*

JENNY *(running to Mrs. Baines and throwing her 1340 arms round her)*. Oh dear! how blessed, how glorious it all is!

CUSINS *(in a convulsion of irony)*. Let us seize this unspeakable moment. Let us march to the great meeting at once. Excuse me just an instant. *(He 1345 rushes into the shelter. Jenny takes her tambourine from the drum head.)*

MRS. BAINES. Mr. Undershaft: have you ever seen a thousand people fall on their knees with one impulse and pray? Come with us to the meeting. 1350 Barbara shall tell them that the Army is saved, and saved through you.

CUSINS *(returning impetuously from the shelter with a flag and a trombone, and coming between Mrs. Baines and Undershaft)*. You shall carry the flag 1355 down the first street, Mrs. Baines *(he gives her the flag)*. Mr. Undershaft is a gifted trombonist: he shall intone an Olympian diapason to the West Ham Salvation March. *(Aside to Undershaft, as he forces the trombone on him.)* Blow, Machiavelli, 1360 blow.

UNDERSHAFT *(aside to him, as he takes the trombone)*. The trumpet in Zion![84] *(Cusins rushes to the drum, which he takes up and puts on. Undershaft continues, aloud.)* I will do my best. I 1365 could vamp a bass if I knew the tune.

CUSINS. It is a wedding chorus from one of Donizetti's operas; but we have converted it. We

---

83 lyddite] a toxic high explosive.

84 trumpet in Zion] "Blow ye the trumpet in Zion, and sound an alarm in my holy mountain: let all the inhabitants of the land tremble: for the day of the LORD cometh, for it is nigh at hand" (Joel 2:1).

convert everything to good here, including Bodger. You remember the chorus. "For thee immense rejoicing — immenso giubilo — immenso giubilo."[85] *(With drum obbligato.)* Rum tum ti tum tum, tum tum ti ta — 1370

BARBARA. Dolly: you are breaking my heart.

CUSINS. What is a broken heart more or less here? Dionysos Undershaft has descended. I am possessed. 1375

MRS. BAINES. Come, Barbara: I must have my dear Major to carry the flag with me.

JENNY. Yes, yes, Major darling. 1380

CUSINS *(snatches the tambourine out of Jenny's hand and mutely offers it to Barbara).*

BARBARA *(coming forward a little as she puts the offer behind her with a shudder, whilst Cusins recklessly tosses the tambourine back to Jenny and goes to the gate).* I cant come. 1385

JENNY. Not come!

MRS. BAINES *(with tears in her eyes).* Barbara: do you think I am wrong to take the money?

BARBARA *(impulsively going to her and kissing her).* No, no: God help you, dear, you must: you are saving the Army. Go; and may you have a great meeting! 1390

JENNY. But arnt you coming?

BARBARA. No. *(She begins taking off the silver S brooch from her collar.)* 1395

MRS. BAINES. Barbara: what are you doing?

JENNY. Why are you taking your badge off? You cant be going to leave us, Major.

BARBARA *(quietly).* Father: come here. 1400

UNDERSHAFT *(coming to her).* My dear! *(Seeing that she is going to pin the badge on his collar, he retreats to the penthouse in some alarm.)*

BARBARA *(following him).* Dont be frightened. *(She pins the badge on and steps back towards the table, shewing him to the others.)* There! It's not much for £5000, is it? 1405

MRS. BAINES. Barbara: if you wont come and pray w i t h us, promise me you will pray f o r us.

BARBARA. I cant pray now. Perhaps I shall never pray again. 1410

MRS. BAINES. Barbara!

JENNY. Major!

BARBARA *(almost delirious).* I cant bear any more. Quick march! 1415

CUSINS *(calling to the procession in the street outside).* Off we go. Play up, there! I m m e n s o g i u b i l o. *(He gives the time with his drum; and the band strikes up the march, which rapidly becomes more distant as the procession moves briskly away.)* 1420

MRS. BAINES. I must go, dear. Youre overworked: you will be all right tomorrow. We'll never lose you. Now Jenny: step out with the old flag. Blood and Fire! *(She marches out through the gate with her flag.)* 1425

JENNY. Glory Hallelujah! *(fourishing her tambourine and marching).*

UNDERSHAFT *(to Cusins, as he marches out past him easing the slide of his trombone).* "My ducats and my daughter"![86] 1430

CUSINS *(following him out).* Money and gunpowder!

BARBARA. Drunkenness and Murder! My God: why hast thou forsaken me?[87]

She sinks on the form with her face buried in her hands. The march passes away into silence. Bill Walker steals across to her.

BILL *(taunting).* Wot prawce Selvytion nah? 1435

SHIRLEY. Dont you hit her when shes down.

BILL. She it me wen aw wiz dahn. Waw shouldnt I git a bit o me own back?

BARBARA *(raising her head).* I didnt take y o u r money, Bill. *(She crosses the yard to the gate and turns her back on the two men to hide her face from them.)* 1440

BILL *(sneering after her).* Naow, it warnt enough for you. *(Turning to the drum, he misses the money.)* Ellow! If you aint took it summun else az. Weres it gorn? Blame me if Jenny Ill didnt take it arter all! 1445

---

85 immenso giubilo] from Donizetti's *Lucia de Lammermoor*, Act II, Scene 2 (in which the marriage of Lucia, who is morose because she has been betrayed, is celebrated).

86 ducats … daughter] Shylock's cry in *Merchant of Venice* after his daughter, Jessica, has taken his money (ducats) and eloped.

87 My God … forsaken me] the cry of Jesus on the cross: "Eli, Eli, lama sabachthani?" (Matthew 27:46).

RUMMY *(screaming at him from the loft).* You lie, you dirty blackguard! Snobby Price pinched it off the drum wen e took ap iz cap. I was ap ere all the time an see im do it.

BILL. Wot! Stowl maw money! Waw didnt you call thief on him, you silly old mucker you? 1450

RUMMY. To serve you aht for ittin me acrost the fice. It's cost y'pahnd, that az. *(Raising a paean of squalid triumph.)* I done you. I'm even with you. Ive ad it aht o y— *(Bill snatches up Shirley's mug and hurls it at her. She slams the loft door and vanishes. The mug smashes against the door and falls in fragments.)* 1455

BILL *(beginning to chuckle).* Tell us, ole man, wot o'clock this mornin was it wen im as they call Snobby Prawce was sived? 1460

BARBARA *(turning to him more composedly, and with unspoiled sweetness).* About half past twelve, Bill. And he pinched your pound at a quarter to two. I know. Well, you cant afford to lose it. I'll send it to you. 1465

BILL *(his voice and accent suddenly improving).* Not if I was to starve for it. I aint to be bought.

SHIRLEY. Aint you? Youd sell yourself to the devil for a pint o beer; ony there aint no devil to make the offer. 1470

BILL *(unshamed).* So I would, mate, and often av, cheerful. But s h e cawnt buy me. *(Approaching Barbara.)* You wanted my soul, did you? Well, you aint got it. 1475

BARBARA. I nearly got it, Bill. But weve sold it back to you for ten thousand pounds.

SHIRLEY. And dear at the money!

BARBARA. No, Peter: it was worth more than money. 1480

BILL *(salvationproof).* It's no good: you cawnt get rahnd me nah. I dont blieve in it; and Ive seen today that I was right. *(Going.)* So long, old soupkitchener! Ta, ta, Major Earl's Grendorter! *(Turning at the gate.)* Wot prawce Selvytion nah? Snobby Prawce! Ha! ha! 1485

BARBARA *(offering her hand).* Goodbye, Bill.

BILL *(taken aback, half plucks his cap off; then shoves it on again defiantly).* Git aht. *(Barbara drops her hand, discouraged. He has a twinge of remorse.)* But thets aw rawt, you knaow. Nathink pasnl, Naow 1490

mellice. So long, Judy. *(He goes.)*

BARBARA. No malice. So long, Bill.

SHIRLEY *(shaking his head).* You make too much of him, Miss, in your innocence. 1495

BARBARA *(going to him).* Peter: I'm like you now. Cleaned out, and lost my job.

SHIRLEY. Youve youth an hope. Thats two better than me.

BARBARA. I'll get you a job, Peter. Thats hope for you: the youth will have to be enough for me. *(She counts her money.)* I have just enough left for two teas at Lockharts, a Rowton doss for you, and my tram and bus home.[88] *(He frowns and rises with offended pride. She takes his arm.)* Dont be proud, Peter: it's sharing between friends. And promise me youll talk to me and not let me cry. *(She draws him towards the gate.)* 1500 1505

SHIRLEY. Well, I'm not accustomed to talk to the like of you— 1510

BARBARA *(urgently).* Yes, yes: you must talk to me. Tell me about Tom Paine's books and Bradlaugh's lectures. Come along.[89]

SHIRLEY. Ah, if you would only read Tom Paine in the proper spirit, Miss! *(They go out through the gate together.)* 1515

END OF ACT II.

ACT III

Next day after lunch Lady Britomart is writing in the library in Wilton Crescent. Sarah is reading in the armchair near the window. Barbara, in ordinary dress, pale and brooding, is on the settee. Charles Lomax enters. Coming forward between the settee and the writing table, he starts on seeing Barbara fashionably attired and in low spirits.

---

88 Rowton doss] a place to sleep (slang: doss) in the pauper's hotel founded by Baron Montagu Rowton (1838–1903).

89 Tom Paine] (1737–1809), author of *The Rights of Man*, a defence of the French Revolution, and *The Age of Reason*, about the place of religion in society; Bradlaugh] Charles Bradlaugh (1833–1891), British atheist and freethinker.

LOMAX. Youve left off your uniform!

Barbara says nothing; but an expression of pain passes over her face.

LADY BRITOMART *(warning him in low tones to be careful)*. Charles!

LOMAX *(much concerned, sitting down sympathetically on the settee beside Barbara)*. I'm awfully sorry, Barbara. You know I helped you all I could with the concertina and so forth. *(Momentously.)* Still, I have never shut my eyes to the fact that there is a certain amount of tosh about the Salvation Army.[90] Now the claims of the Church of England—

LADY BRITOMART. Thats enough, Charles. Speak of something suited to your mental capacity.

LOMAX. But surely the Church of England is suited to all our capacities.

BARBARA *(pressing his hand)*. Thank you for your sympathy, Cholly. Now go and spoon with Sarah.[91]

LOMAX *(rising and going to Sarah)*. How is my ownest today?

SARAH. I wish you wouldnt tell Cholly to do things, Barbara. He always comes straight and does them. Cholly: we're going to the works at Perivale St. Andrews this afternoon.

LOMAX. What works?

SARAH. The cannon works.

LOMAX. What! Your governor's shop![92]

SARAH. Yes.

LOMAX. Oh I say!

Cusins enters in poor condition. He also starts visibly when he sees Barbara without her uniform.

BARBARA. I expected you this morning, Dolly. Didnt you guess that?

CUSINS. *(sitting down beside her)*. I'm sorry. I have only just breakfasted.

SARAH. But weve just finished lunch.

BARBARA. Have you had one of your bad nights?

CUSINS. No: I had rather a good night: in fact, one of the most remarkable nights I have ever passed.

BARBARA. The meeting?

CUSINS. No: after the meeting.

LADY BRITOMART. You should have gone to bed after the meeting. What were you doing?

CUSINS. Drinking.

LADY BRITOMART. Adolphus!

SARAH. Dolly!

BARBARA. Dolly!

LOMAX. Oh I say!

LADY BRITOMART. What were you drinking, may I ask?

CUSINS. A most devilish kind of Spanish burgundy, warranted free from added alcohol: a Temperance burgundy in fact.[93] Its richness in natural alcohol made any addition superfluous.

BARBARA. Are you joking, Dolly?

CUSINS. *(patiently)*. No. I have been making a night of it with the nominal head of this household: that is all.

LADY BRITOMART. Andrew made you drunk!

CUSINS. No: he only provided the wine. I think it was Dionysos who made me drunk. *(To Barbara.)* I told you I was possessed.

LADY BRITOMART. Youre not sober yet. Go home to bed at once.

CUSINS. I have never before ventured to reproach you, Lady Brit; but how could you marry the Prince of Darkness?[94]

LADY BRITOMART. It was much more excusable to marry him than to get drunk with him. That is a new accomplishment of Andrew's, by the way. He usent to drink.

CUSINS. He doesnt now. He only sat there and completed the wreck of my moral basis, the rout of my convictions, the purchase of my soul. He cares for you, Barbara. That is what makes him so dangerous to me.

BARBARA. That has nothing to do with it, Dolly. There are larger loves and diviner dreams than the fireside ones. You know that, dont you?

CUSINS. Yes: that is our understanding. I know it.

---

90 tosh] nonsense.

91 spoon] flirt, fondle, and kiss.

92 governor] (slang, in this case) father.

93 Temperance burgundy] i.e., a wine promoted by one of the temperance societies devoted to promoting moderation or abstinence in alcohol consumption.

94 Prince of Darkness] the Devil.

I hold to it. Unless he can win me on that holier ground he may amuse me for a while; but he can get no deeper hold, strong as he is. 80

BARBARA. Keep to that; and the end will be right. Now tell me what happened at the meeting?

CUSINS. It was an amazing meeting. Mrs. Baines almost died of emotion. Jenny Hill went stark mad with hysteria. The Prince of Darkness played his 85 trombone like a madman: its brazen roarings were like the laughter of the damned. 117 conversions took place then and there. They prayed with the most touching sincerity and gratitude for Bodger, and for the anonymous donor of the £5000. Your 90 father would not let his name be given.

LOMAX. That was rather fine of the old man, you know. Most chaps would have wanted the advertisement.

CUSINS. He said all the charitable institutions 95 would be down on him like kites on a battle field if he gave his name.

LADY BRITOMART. Thats Andrew all over, He never does a proper thing without giving an improper reason for it. 100

CUSINS. He convinced me that I have all my life been doing improper things for proper reasons.

LADY BRITOMART. Adolphus: now that Barbara has left the Salvation Army, you had better leave it too. I will not have you playing that drum in 105 the streets.

CUSINS. Your orders are already obeyed, Lady Brit.

BARBARA. Dolly: were you ever really in earnest about it? Would you have joined if you had never seen me? 110

CUSINS (disingenuously). Well — er — well, possibly, as a collector of religions —

LOMAX (cunningly). Not as a drummer, though, you know. You are a very clearheaded brainy chap, Cholly; and it must have been apparent to you that 115 there is a certain amount of tosh about—

LADY BRITOMART. Charles: if you must drivel, drivel like a grown-up man and not like a schoolboy.

LOMAX (out of countenance). Well, drivel is drivel, 120 dont you know, whatever a man's age.

LADY BRITOMART. In good society in England, Charles, men drivel at all ages by repeating silly formulas with an air of wisdom. Schoolboys make their own formulas out of slang, like you. When 125 they reach your age, and get political private secretaryships and things of that sort, they drop slang and get their formulas out of *The Spectator* or *The Times.* Y o u had better confine yourself to *The Times.* You will find that there is a certain 130 amount of tosh about *The Times*; but at least its language is reputable.

LOMAX (overwhelmed). You are so awfully strong-minded, Lady Brit.

LADY BRITOMART. Rubbish! (Morrison comes in.) 135 What is it?

MORRISON. If you please, my lady, Mr. Undershaft has just drove up to the door.

LADY BRITOMART. Well, let him in. (Morrison hesitates.) Whats the matter with you? 140

MORRISON. Shall I announce him, my lady; or is he at home here, so to speak, my lady?

LADY BRITOMART. Announce him.

MORRISON. Thank you, my lady. You wont mind my asking, I hope. The occasion is in a manner 145 of speaking new to me.

LADY BRITOMART. Quite right. Go and let him in.

MORRISON. Thank you, my lady. (He withdraws.)

LADY BRITOMART. Children: go and get ready. 150 (Sarah and Barbara go upstairs for their out-of-door wraps.) Charles: go and tell Stephen to come down here in five minutes: you will find him in the drawing room. (Charles goes.) Adolphus: tell them to send round the carriage in about fifteen 155 minutes. (Adolphus goes.)

MORRISON (at the door). Mr. Undershaft.

Undershaft comes in. Morrison goes out.

UNDERSHAFT. Alone! How fortunate!

LADY BRITOMART (rising). Dont be sentimental, Andrew. Sit down. (She sits on the settee: he sits 160 beside her, on her left. She comes to the point before he has time to breathe.) Sarah must have £800 a year until Charles Lomax comes into his property. Barbara will need more, and need it permanently, because Adolphus hasnt any property. 165

UNDERSHAFT (resignedly). Yes, my dear: I will see to it. Anything else? for yourself, for instance?

LADY BRITOMART. I want to talk to you about Stephen.

UNDERSHAFT *(rather wearily)*. Dont, my dear. Stephen doesnt interest me.

LADY BRITOMART. He does interest me. He is our son.

UNDERSHAFT. Do you really think so? He has induced us to bring him into the world; but he chose his parents very incongruously, I think. I see nothing of myself in him, and less of you.

LADY BRITOMART. Andrew: Stephen is an excellent son, and a most steady, capable, highminded young man. You are simply trying to find an excuse for disinheriting him.

UNDERSHAFT. My dear Biddy: the Undershaft tradition disinherits him. It would be dishonest of me to leave the cannon foundry to my son.

LADY BRITOMART. It would be most unnatural and improper of you to leave it anyone else, Andrew. Do you suppose this wicked and immoral tradition can be kept up for ever? Do you pretend that Stephen could not carry on the foundry just as well as all the other sons of the big business houses?

UNDERSHAFT. Yes: he could learn the office routine without understanding the business, like all the other sons; and the firm would go on by its own momentum until the real Undershaft — probably an Italian or a German — would invent a new method and cut him out.

LADY BRITOMART. There is nothing that any Italian or German could do that Stephen could not do. And Stephen at least has breeding.

UNDERSHAFT. The son of a foundling! nonsense!

LADY BRITOMART. My son, Andrew! And even you may have good blood in your veins for all you know.

UNDERSHAFT. True. Probably I have. That is another argument in favor of a foundling.

LADY BRITOMART. Andrew: dont be aggravating. And dont be wicked. At present you are both.

UNDERSHAFT. This conversation is part of the Undershaft tradition, Biddy. Every Undershaft's wife has treated him to it ever since the house was founded. It is mere waste of breath. If the tradition be ever broken it will be for an abler man than Stephen.

LADY BRITOMART *(pouting)*. Then go away.

UNDERSHAFT *(deprecatory)*. Go away!

LADY BRITOMART. Yes: go away. If you will do nothing for Stephen, you are not wanted here. Go to your foundling, whoever he is; and look after h i m.

UNDERSHAFT. The fact is, Biddy —

LADY BRITOMART. Dont call me Biddy. I dont call you Andy.

UNDERSHAFT. I will not call my wife Britomart: it is not good sense. Seriously, my love, the Undershaft tradition has landed me in a difficulty. I am getting on in years; and my partner Lazarus has at last made a stand and insisted that the succession must be settled one way or the other; and of course he is quite right. You see, I havnt found a fit successor yet.

LADY BRITOMART *(obstinately)*. There is Stephen.

UNDERSHAFT. Thats just it: all the foundlings I can find are exactly like Stephen.

LADY BRITOMART. Andrew!!

UNDERSHAFT. I want a man with no relations and no schooling: that is, a man who would be out of the running altogether if he were not a strong man. And I cant find him. Every blessed foundling nowadays is snapped up in his infancy by Barnardo homes, or School Board officers, or Boards of Guardians; and if he shews the least ability, he is fastened on by schoolmasters; trained to win scholarships like a racehorse; crammed with secondhand ideas; drilled and disciplined in docility and what they call good taste; and lamed for life so that he is fit for nothing but teaching.[95] If you want to keep the foundry in the family, you had better find an eligible foundling and marry him to Barbara.

LADY BRITOMART. Ah! Barbara! Your pet! You would sacrifice Stephen to Barbara.

---

95 Barnardo homes] an organization founded by Thomas John Barnardo (1845–1905), which rescued children out of poverty and set them up in homes, many in Canada; Boards of Guardians] from 1834 to 1929, the Poor Law Amendment Act decreed that boards of guardians were to be set up by parishes to deal with the poor through the management of workhouses.

UNDERSHAFT. Cheerfully. And you, my dear, would boil Barbara to make soup for Stephen.

LADY BRITOMART. Andrew: this is not a question of our likings and dislikings: it is a question of duty. It is your duty to make Stephen your successor.

UNDERSHAFT. Just as much as it is your duty to submit to your husband. Come Biddy! these tricks of the governing class are of no use with me. I am one of the governing class myself; and it is a waste of time giving tracts to a missionary. I have the power in this matter; and I am not to be humbugged into using it for your purposes.

LADY BRITOMART. Andrew: you can talk my head off; but you cant change wrong into right. And your tie is all on one side. Put it straight.

UNDERSHAFT (disconcerted). It wont stay unless its pinned (he fumbles at it with childish grimaces). Stephen comes in.

STEPHEN (at the door). I beg your pardon (about to retire).

LADY BRITOMART. No: come in, Stephen. (Stephen comes forward to his mother's writing table.)

UNDERSHAFT (not very cordially). Good afternoon.

STEPHEN (coldly). Good afternoon.

UNDERSHAFT (to Lady Britomart). He knows all about the tradition, I suppose?

LADY BRITOMART. Yes. (To Stephen.) It is what I told you last night, Stephen.

UNDERSHAFT (sulkily). I understand you want to come into the cannon business.

STEPHEN. I go into trade! Certainly not.

UNDERSHAFT (opening his eyes, greatly eased in mind and manner). Oh! in that case!

LADY BRITOMART. Cannons are not trade, Stephen. They are enterprise.

STEPHEN. I have no intention of becoming a man of business in any sense. I have no capacity for business and no taste for it. I intend to devote myself to politics.

UNDERSHAFT (rising). My dear boy: this is an immense relief to me. And I trust it may prove an equally good thing for the country. I was afraid you would consider yourself disparaged and slighted. (He moves towards Stephen as if to shake hands with him.)

LADY BRITOMART (rising and interposing). Stephen: I cannot allow you to throw away an enormous property like this.

STEPHEN (stiffly). Mother: there must be an end of treating me as a child, if you please. (Lady Britomart recoils, deeply wounded by his tone.) Until last night I did not take your attitude seriously, because I did not think you meant it seriously. But I find now that you left me in the dark as to matters which you should have explained to me years ago. I am extremely hurt and offended. Any further discussion of my intentions had better take place with my father, as between one man and another.

LADY BRITOMART. Stephen! (She sits down again; and her eyes fill with tears.)

UNDERSHAFT (with grave compassion). You see, my dear, it is only the big men who can be treated as children.

STEPHEN. I am sorry, mother, that you have forced me —

UNDERSHAFT (stopping him). Yes, yes, yes, yes: thats all right, Stephen. She wont interfere with you any more: your independence is achieved: you have won your latchkey. Dont rub it in; and above all, dont apologize. (He resumes his seat.) Now what about your future, as between one man and another — I beg your pardon, Biddy: as between two men and a woman.

LADY BRITOMART (who has pulled herself together strongly). I quite understand, Stephen. By all means go your own way if you feel strong enough. (Stephen sits down magisterially in the chair at the writing table with an air of affirming his majority.)

UNDERSHAFT. It is settled that you do not ask for the succession to the cannon business.

STEPHEN. I hope it is settled that I repudiate the cannon business.

UNDERSHAFT. Come, come! dont be so devilishly sulky: it's boyish. Freedom should be generous. Besides, I owe you a fair start in life in exchange for disinheriting you. You cant become prime minister all at once. Havnt you a turn for something? What about literature, art and so forth?

STEPHEN. I have nothing of the artist about me, either in faculty or character, thank Heaven!

UNDERSHAFT. A philosopher, perhaps? Eh?

STEPHEN. I make no such ridiculous pretension. 345

UNDERSHAFT. Just so. Well, there is the army, the navy, the Church, the Bar. The Bar requires some ability. What about the Bar?

STEPHEN. I have not studied law. And I am afraid I have not the necessary push — I believe that is 350 the name barristers give to their vulgarity — for success in pleading.

UNDERSHAFT. Rather a difficult case, Stephen. Hardly anything left but the stage, is there? *(Stephen makes an impatient movement.)* Well, 355 come! is there a n y t h i n g you know or care for?

STEPHEN *(rising and looking at him steadily)*. I know the difference between right and wrong.

UNDERSHAFT *(hugely tickled)*. You dont say so! 360 What! no capacity for business, no knowledge of law, no sympathy with art, no pretension to philosophy; only a simple knowledge of the secret that has puzzled all the philosophers, baffled all the lawyers, muddled all the men of business, and 365 ruined most of the artists: the secret of right and wrong. Why, man, youre a genius, a master of masters, a god! At twenty-four, too!

STEPHEN *(keeping his temper with difficulty)*. You are pleased to be facetious. I pretend to nothing 370 more than any honorable English gentleman claims as his birthright *(he sits down angrily)*.

UNDERSHAFT. Oh, thats everybody's birthright. Look at poor little Jenny Hill, the Salvation lassie! she would think you were laughing at her if you 375 asked her to stand up in the street and teach grammar or geography or mathematics or even drawingroom dancing; but it never occurs to her to doubt that she can teach morals and religion. You are all alike, you respectable people. You cant tell me 380 the bursting strain of a ten-inch gun, which is a very simple matter; but you all think you can tell me the bursting strain of a man under temptation. You darent handle high explosives; but youre all ready to handle honesty and truth and justice and the whole 385 duty of man, and kill one another at that game. What a country! what a world!

LADY BRITOMART *(uneasily)*. What do you think he had better do, Andrew?

UNDERSHAFT. Oh, just what he wants to do. He 390 knows nothing; and he thinks he knows everything. That points clearly to a political career. Get him a private secretaryship to someone who can get him an Under Secretaryship; and then leave him alone. He will find his natural and proper 395 place in the end on the Treasury bench.

STEPHEN *(springing up again)*. I am sorry, sir, that you force me to forget the respect due to you as my father. I am an Englishman; and I will not hear the Government of my country insulted. *(He 400 thrusts his hands in his pockets, and walks angrily across to the window.)*

UNDERSHAFT *(with a touch of brutality)*. The government of your country! I am the government of your country: I, and Lazarus. Do you suppose that 405 you and half a dozen amateurs like you, sitting in a row in that foolish gabble shop, can govern Undershaft and Lazarus? No, my friend: you will do what pays u s. You will make war when it suits us, and keep peace when it doesnt. You will find 410 out that trade requires certain measures when we have decided on those measures. When I want anything to keep my dividends up, you will discover that my want is a national need. When other people want something to keep my dividends down, 415 you will call out the police and military. And in return you shall have the support and applause of my newspapers, and the delight of imagining that you are a great statesman. Government of your country! Be off with you, my boy, and play with 420 your caucuses and leading articles and historic parties and great leaders and burning questions and the rest of your toys. I am going back to my counting house to pay the piper and call the tune.

STEPHEN *(actually smiling, and putting his hand on 425 his father's shoulder with indulgent patronage)*. Really, my dear father, it is impossible to be angry with you. You don't know how absurd all this sounds to m e. You are very properly proud of having been industrious enough to make money; 430 and it is greatly to your credit that you have made so much of it. But it has kept you in circles where you are valued for your money and deferred to for it, instead of in the doubtless very old fashioned and behind-the-times public school and university 435 where I formed my habits of mind. It is natural for you to think that money governs England; but you must allow me to think I know better.

UNDERSHAFT. And what d o e s govern England, pray?

STEPHEN. Character, father, character.

UNDERSHAFT. Whose character? Yours or mine?

STEPHEN. Neither yours nor mine, father, but the best elements in the English national character.

UNDERSHAFT. Stephen: Ive found your profession for you. Youre a born journalist. I'll start you with a high-toned weekly review. There!

Stephen goes to the smaller writing table and busies himself with his letters.

Sarah, Barbara, Lomax, and Cusins come in ready for walking. Barbara crosses the room to the window and looks out. Cusins drifts amiably to the armchair, and Lomax remains near the door, whilst Sarah comes to her mother.

SARAH. Go and get ready, mamma: the carriage is waiting. (*Lady Britomart leaves the room.*)

UNDERSHAFT (*to Sarah*). Good day, my dear. Good afternoon, Mr. Lomax.

LOMAX (*vaguely*). Ahdedoo.

UNDERSHAFT (*to Cusins*). Quite well after last night, Euripides, eh?

CUSINS. As well as can be expected.

UNDERSHAFT. Thats right. (*To Barbara.*) So you are coming to see my death and devastation factory, Barbara?

BARBARA (*at the window*). You came yesterday to see my salvation factory. I promised you a return visit.

LOMAX (*coming forward between Sarah and Undershaft*). You'd find it awfully interesting. Ive been through the Woolwich Arsenal; and it gives you a ripping feeling of security, you know, to think of the lot of beggars we could kill if it came to fighting. (*To Undershaft, with sudden solemnity.*) Still, it must be rather an awful reflection for you, from the religious point of view as it were. Youre getting on, you know, and all that.

SARAH. You dont mind Cholly's imbecility, papa, do you?

LOMAX (*much taken aback*). Oh I say!

UNDERSHAFT. Mr. Lomax looks at the matter in a very proper spirit my dear.

LOMAX. Just so. Thats all I meant, I assure you.

SARAH. Are you coming, Stephen?

STEPHEN. Well, I am rather busy — er — (*Magnanimously.*) Oh well, yes: I'll come. That is, if there is room for me.

UNDERSHAFT. I can take two with me in a little motor I am experimenting with for field use. You wont mind its being rather unfashionable. It's not painted yet; but it's bullet proof.

LOMAX (*appalled at the prospect of confronting Wilton Crescent in an unpainted motor*). Oh I s a y!

SARAH. The carriage for me, thank you. Barbara doesnt mind what shes seen in.

LOMAX. I say, Dolly old chap: do you really mind the car being a guy?[96] Because of course if you do I'll go in it. Still —

CUSINS. I prefer it.

LOMAX. Thanks awfully, old man. Come, Sarah. (*He hurries out to secure his seat in the carriage. Sarah follows him.*)

CUSINS (*moodily walking across to Lady Britomart's writing table*). Why are we two coming to this Works Department of Hell? that is what I ask myself.

BARBARA. I have always thought of it as a sort of pit where lost creatures with blackened faces stirred up smoky fires and were driven and tormented by my father? Is it like that, dad?

UNDERSHAFT (*scandalized*). My dear! It is a spotlessly clean and beautiful hillside town.

CUSINS. With a Methodist chapel? Oh d o say theres a Methodist chapel.

UNDERSHAFT. There are two: a Primitive one and a sophisticated one. There is even an Ethical Society; but it is not much patronized, as my men are all strongly religious.[97] In the High Explosives Sheds they object to the presence of Agnostics as unsafe.

CUSINS. And yet they dont object to you!

BARBARA. Do they obey all your orders?

---

96 guy] (slang) something of grotesque appearance.
97 Ethical Society] an atheist group dedicated to the discussion of ethics.

UNDERSHAFT. I never give them any orders. When I speak to one of them it is "Well, Jones, is the baby doing well? and has Mrs. Jones made a good recovery?" "Nicely, thank you, sir." And thats all.

CUSINS. But Jones has to be kept in order. How do you maintain discipline among your men? 520

UNDERSHAFT. I dont. They do. You see, the one thing Jones wont stand is any rebellion from the man under him, or any assertion of social equality between the wife of the man with 4 shillings a week less than himself, and Mrs. Jones! Of course they all rebel against me, theoretically. Practically, every man of them keeps the man just below him in his place. I never meddle with them. I never bully them. I dont even bully Lazarus. I say that certain things are to be done; but I dont order anybody to do them. I dont say, mind you, that there is no ordering about and snubbing and even bullying. The men snub the boys and order them about; the carmen snub the sweepers; the artisans snub the unskilled laborers; the foremen drive and bully both the laborers and artisans; the assistant engineers find fault with the foremen; the chief engineers drop on the assistants; the departmental managers worry the chiefs; and the clerks have tall hats and hymnbooks and keep up the social tone by refusing to associate on equal terms with anybody[98]. The result is a colossal profit, which comes to me. 525 530 535 540

CUSINS (revolted). You really are a — well, what I was saying yesterday. 545

BARBARA. What was he saying yesterday?

UNDERSHAFT. Never mind, my dear. He thinks I have made you unhappy. Have I?

BARBARA. Do you think I can be happy in this vulgar silly dress? I! who have worn the uniform. Do you understand what you have done to me? Yesterday I had a man's soul in my hand. I set him in the way of life with his face to salvation. But when we took your money he turned back to drunkenness and derision. (With intense conviction.) I will never forgive you that. If I had a child, and you destroyed its body with your explosives — if you murdered Dolly with your horrible guns — I could forgive you if my forgiveness would open the gates of heaven to you. But to 550 555

take a human soul from me, and turn it into the soul of a wolf! that is worse than any murder. 560

UNDERSHAFT. Does my daughter despair so easily? Can you strike a man to the heart and leave no mark on him?

BARBARA (her face lighting up). Oh, you are right: he can never be lost now: where was my faith? 565

CUSINS. Oh, clever clever devil!

BARBARA. You may be a devil; but God speaks through you sometimes. (She takes her father's hands and kisses them.) You have given me back my happiness: I feel it deep down now, though my spirit is troubled. 570

UNDERSHAFT. You have learnt something. That always feels at first as if you had lost something.

BARBARA. Well, take me to the factory of death, and let me learn something more. There must be some truth or other behind all this frightful irony. Come, Dolly. (She goes out.) 575

CUSINS. My guardian angel! (To Undershaft.) Avaunt![99] (He follows Barbara.) 580

STEPHEN (quietly, at the writing table). You must not mind Cusins, father. He is a very amiable good fellow; but he is a Greek scholar and naturally a little eccentric.

UNDERSHAFT. Ah, quite so. Thank you, Stephen. Thank you. (He goes out.) 585

Stephen smiles patronizingly; buttons his coat responsibly; and crosses the room to the door. Lady Britomart, dressed for out-of-doors, opens it before he reaches it. She looks round for the others; looks at Stephen; and turns to go without a word.

STEPHEN (embarrassed). Mother —

LADY BRITOMART. Dont be apologetic, Stephen. And dont forget that you have outgrown your mother. (She goes out.) 590

Perivale St. Andrews lies between two Middlesex hills, half climbing the northern one. It is an almost smokeless town of white walls, roofs of narrow green slates or red tiles, tall trees, domes, campaniles, and slender chimney shafts, beautifully situated and beautiful in itself. The best view of it is obtained from

---

98 carmen] men working on rail cars.

99 Avaunt] hence, away (traditionally spoken to the Devil).

the crest of a slope about half a mile to the east, where the high explosives are dealt with. The foundry lies hidden in the depths between, the tops of its chimneys sprouting like huge skittles into the middle distance.[100] Across the crest runs a platform of concrete, with a parapet which suggests a fortification, because there is a huge cannon of the obsolete Woolwich Infant pattern peering across it at the town. The cannon is mounted on an experimental gun carriage: possibly the original model of the Undershaft disappearing rampart gun alluded to by Stephen. The parapet has a high step inside which serves as a seat.

Barbara is leaning over the parapet, looking towards the town. On her right is the cannon; on her left the end of a shed raised on piles, with a ladder of three or four steps up to the door, which opens outwards and has a little wooden landing at the threshold, with a fire bucket in the corner of the landing. The parapet stops short of the shed, leaving a gap which is the beginning of the path down the hill through the foundry to the town. Behind the cannon is a trolley carrying a huge conical bombshell, with a red band painted on it. Further from the parapet, on the same side, is a deck chair, near the door of an office, which, like the sheds, is of the lightest possible construction.

Cusins arrives by the path from the town.

BARBARA. Well?

CUSINS. Not a ray of hope. Everything perfect, wonderful, real. It only needs a cathedral to be a heavenly city instead of a hellish one.

BARBARA. Have you found out whether they have done anything for old Peter Shirley.

CUSINS. They have found him a job as gatekeeper and timekeeper. He's frightfully miserable. He calls the timekeeping brainwork, and says he isnt used to it; and his gate lodge is so splendid that hes ashamed to use the rooms, and skulks in the scullery.

BARBARA. Poor Peter!

Stephen arrives from the town. He carries a fieldglass.

STEPHEN (enthusiastically). Have you two seen the place? Why did you leave us?

CUSINS. I wanted to see everything I was not intended to see; and Barbara wanted to make the men talk.

STEPHEN. Have you found anything discreditable?

CUSINS. No. They call him Dandy Andy and are proud of his being a cunning old rascal; but it's all horribly, frightfully, immorally, unanswerably perfect.

Sarah arrives.

SARAH. Heavens! what a place! (She crosses to the trolley.) Did you see the nursing home!? (She sits down on the shell.)

STEPHEN. Did you see the libraries and schools!?

SARAH. Did you see the ball room and the banqueting chamber in the Town Hall!?

STEPHEN. Have you gone into the insurance fund, the pension fund, the building society, the various applications of co-operation!?

Undershaft comes from the office, with a sheaf of telegrams in his hands.

UNDERSHAFT. Well, have you seen everything? I'm sorry I was called away. (Indicating the telegrams.) News from Manchuria.[101]

STEPHEN. Good news, I hope.

UNDERSHAFT. Very.

STEPHEN. Another Japanese victory?

UNDERSHAFT. Oh, I dont know. Which side wins does not concern us here. No: the good news is that the aerial battleship is a tremendous success. At the first trial it has wiped out a fort with three hundred soldiers in it.

CUSINS (from the platform). Dummy soldiers?

UNDERSHAFT. No: the real thing. (Cusins and Barbara exchange glances. Then Cusins sits on the step and buries his face in his hands. Barbara gravely lays her hand on his shoulder, and he looks up at her in a sort of whimsical desperation.) Well, Stephen, what do you think of the place?

STEPHEN. Oh, magnificent. A perfect triumph of organization. Frankly, my dear father, I have been

---

100 *skittles*] i.e., the pins for the game of that name, similar to bowling.

101 Manchuria] a province in northeast China, at the time the site of the Russo-Japanese war (1904–5).

a fool: I had no idea of what it all meant — of the wonderful forethought, the power of organization, the administrative capacity, the financial genius, the colossal capital it represents. I have been repeating to myself as I came through your streets "Peace hath her victories no less renowned than War." I have only one misgiving about it all.

UNDERSHAFT. Out with it.

STEPHEN. Well, I cannot help thinking that all this provision for every want of your workmen may sap their independence and weaken their sense of responsibility. And greatly as we enjoyed our tea at that splendid restaurant — how they gave us all that luxury and cake and jam and cream for threepence I really cannot imagine! — still you must remember that restaurants break up home life. Look at the continent, for instance! Are you sure so much pampering is really good for the men's characters?

UNDERSHAFT. Well you see, my dear boy, when you are organizing civilization you have to make up your mind whether trouble and anxiety are good things or not. If you decide that they are, then, I take it, you simply dont organize civilization; and there you are, with trouble and anxiety enough to make us all angels! But if you decide the other way, you may as well go through with it. However, Stephen, our characters are safe here. A sufficient dose of anxiety is always provided by the fact that we may be blown to smithereens at any moment.

SARAH. By the way, papa, where do you make the explosives?

UNDERSHAFT. In separate little sheds, like that one. When one of them blows up, it costs very little; and only the people quite close to it are killed.

Stephen, who is quite close to it, looks at it rather scaredly, and moves away quickly to the cannon. At the same moment the door of the shed is thrown abruptly open; and a foreman in overalls and list slippers comes out on the little landing and holds the door open for Lomax, who appears in the doorway.[102]

---

[102] *list slippers*] slippers made of thick woven cloth.

LOMAX *(with studied coolness)*. My good fellow: you neednt get into a state of nerves. Nothing's going to happen to you; and I suppose it wouldnt be the end of the world if anything did. A little bit of British pluck is what y o u want, old chap. *(He descends and strolls across to Sarah.)*

UNDERSHAFT *(to the foreman)*. Anything wrong, Bilton?

BILTON *(with ironic calm)*. Gentleman walked into the high explosives shed and lit a cigaret, sir: thats all.

UNDERSHAFT. Ah, quite so. *(To Lomax.)* Do you happen to remember what you did with the match?

LOMAX. Oh come! I'm not a fool. I took jolly good care to blow it out before I chucked it away.

BILTON. The top of it was red hot inside, sir.

LOMAX. Well, suppose it was! I didnt chuck it into any of y o u r messes.

UNDERSHAFT. Think no more of it, Mr. Lomax. By the way, would you mind lending me your matches?

LOMAX *(offering his bow)*. Certainly.

UNDERSHAFT. Thanks. *(He pockets the matches.)*

LOMAX *(lecturing to the company generally)*. You know, these high explosives dont go off like gunpowder, except when theyre in a gun. When theyre spread loose, you can put a match to them without the least risk: they just burn quietly like a bit of paper. *(Warming to the scientific interest of the subject.)* Did you know that, Undershaft? Have you ever tried?

UNDERSHAFT. Not on a large scale, Mr. Lomax. Bilton will give you a sample of gun cotton when you are leaving if you ask him. You can experiment with it at home. *(Bilton looks puzzled.)*

SARAH. Bilton will do nothing of the sort, papa. I suppose it's your business to blow up the Russians and Japs; but you might really stop short of blowing up poor Cholly. *(Bilton gives it up and retires into the shed.)*

LOMAX. My ownest, there is no danger. *(He sits beside her on the shell.)*

Lady Britomart arrives from the town with a bouquet.

LADY BRITOMART *(coming impetuously between*

Undershaft and the deck chair). Andrew: you shouldnt have let me see this place.

UNDERSHAFT. Why, my dear?

LADY BRITOMART. Never mind why: you shouldnt have: thats all. To think of all that *(indicating the town)* being yours! and that you have kept it to yourself all these years!

UNDERSHAFT. It does not belong to me. I belong to it. It is the Undershaft inheritance.

LADY BRITOMART. It is not. Your ridiculous cannons and that noisy banging foundry may be the Undershaft inheritance; but all that plate and linen, all that furniture and those houses and orchards and gardens belong to us. They belong to m e: they are not a man's business. I wont give them up. You must be out of your senses to throw them all away; and if you persist in such folly, I will call in a doctor.

UNDERSHAFT *(stooping to smell the bouquet).* Where did you get the flowers, my dear?

LADY BRITOMART. Your men presented them to me in your William Morris Labor Church.[103]

CUSINS *(springing up).* Oh! It needed only that. A Labor Church!

LADY BRITOMART. Yes, with Morris's words in mosaic letters ten feet high round the dome. NO MAN IS GOOD ENOUGH TO BE ANOTHER MAN'S MASTER. The cynicism of it!

UNDERSHAFT. It shocked the men at first, I am afraid. But now they take no more notice of it than of the ten commandments in church.

LADY BRITOMART. Andrew: you are trying to put me off the subject of the inheritance by profane jokes. Well, you shant. I dont ask it any longer for Stephen: he has inherited far too much of your perversity to be fit for it. But Barbara has rights as well as Stephen. Why should not Adolphus succeed to the inheritance? I could manage the town for him; and he can look after the cannons, if they are really necessary.

---

103 Labor Church] a number of Labour Churches were founded in the 1890s, usually as a socialist protest against a clergyman's support of the Liberal or Conservative Party. There is a Labour Church named after William Morris (see note 20) in Leek, Staffordshire.

UNDERSHAFT. I should ask nothing better if Adolphus were a foundling. He is exactly the sort of new blood that is wanted in English business. But hes not a foundling; and theres an end of it.

CUSINS *(diplomatically).* Not quite. *(They all turn and stare at him. He comes from the platform past the shed to Undershaft.)* I think — Mind! I am not committing myself in any way as to my future course — but I think the foundling difficulty can be got over.

UNDERSHAFT. What do you mean?

CUSINS. Well, I have something to say which is in the nature of a confession.

SARAH. Confession!

LADY BRITOMART. Confession!

BARBARA. Confession!

STEPHEN. Confession!

LOMAX. Oh I say!

CUSINS. Yes, a confession. Listen, all. Until I met Barbara I thought myself in the main an honorable truthful man, because I wanted the approval of my conscience more than I wanted anything else. But the moment I saw Barbara, I wanted her far more than the approval of my conscience.

LADY BRITOMART. Adolphus!

CUSINS. It is true. You accused me yourself, Lady Brit, of joining the Army to worship Barbara; and so I did. She bought my soul like a flower at a street corner; but she bought it for herself.

UNDERSHAFT. What! Not for Dionysos or another?

CUSINS. Dionysos and all the others are in herself. I adored what was divine in her, and was therefore a true worshipper. But I was romantic about her too. I thought she was a woman of the people, and that a marriage with a professor of Greek would be far beyond the wildest social ambitions of her rank.

LADY BRITOMART. Adolphus!!

LOMAX. Oh I s a y!!!

CUSINS. When I learnt the horrible truth—

LADY BRITOMART. What do you mean by the horrible truth, pray?

CUSINS. That she was enormously rich; that her grandfather was an earl; that her father was the Prince of Darkness —

UNDERSHAFT. Chut!

CUSINS. — and that I was only an adventurer trying to catch a rich wife, then I stooped to deceive her about my birth. 810

BARBARA. Dolly!

LADY BRITOMART. Your birth! Now Adolphus, dont dare to make up a wicked story for the sake of these wretched cannons. Remember: I have seen photographs of your parents; and the Agent General for South Western Australia knows them personally and has assured me that they are most respectable married people. 815 820

CUSINS. So they are in Australia; but here they are outcast. Their marriage is legal in Australia, but not in England. My mother is my father's deceased wife's sister; and in this island I am consequently a foundling. *(Sensation.)* Is the subterfuge good enough, Machiavelli? 825

UNDERSHAFT *(thoughtfully)*. Biddy: this may be a way out of the difficulty.

LADY BRITOMART. Stuff! A man cant make cannons any the better for being his own cousin instead of his proper self. *(She sits down in the deck chair with a bounce that expresses her downright contempt for their casuistry.)* 830

UNDERSHAFT *(to Cusins)*. You are an educated man. That is against the tradition. 835

CUSINS. Once in ten thousand times it happens that the schoolboy is a born master of what they try to teach him. Greek has not destroyed my mind: it has nourished it. Besides, I did not learn it at an English public school. 840

UNDERSHAFT. Hm! Well, I cannot afford to be too particular: you have cornered the foundling market. Let it pass. You are eligible, Euripides: you are eligible.

BARBARA *(coming from the platform and interposing between Cusins and Undershaft)*. Dolly: yesterday morning, when Stephen told us all about the tradition, you became very silent; and you have been strange and excited ever since. Were you thinking of your birth then? 845 850

CUSINS. When the finger of Destiny suddenly points at a man in the middle of his breakfast, it makes him thoughtful. *(Barbara turns away sadly and stands near her mother, listening perturbedly.)*

UNDERSHAFT. Aha! You have had your eye on the business, my young friend, have you? 855

CUSINS. Take care! There is an abyss of moral horror between me and your accursed aerial battleships.

UNDERSHAFT. Never mind the abyss for the present. Let us settle the practical details and leave your final decision open. You know that you will have to change your name. Do you object to that? 860

CUSINS. Would any man named Adolphus — any man called Dolly! — object to be called something else? 865

UNDERSHAFT. Good. Now, as to money! I propose to treat you handsomely from the beginning. You shall start at a thousand a year.

CUSINS *(with sudden heat, his spectacles twinkling smith mischief)*. A thousand! You dare offer a miserable thousand to the son-in-law of a millionaire! No, by Heavens, Machiavelli! you shall not cheat m e. You cannot do without me; and I can do without you. I must have two thousand five hundred a year for two years. At the end of that time, if I am a failure, I go. But if I am a success, and stay on, you must give me the other five thousand. 870 875

UNDERSHAFT. What other five thousand? 880

CUSINS. To make the two years up to five thousand a year. The two thousand five hundred is only half pay in case I should turn out a failure. The third year I must have ten per cent on the profits.

UNDERSHAFT *(taken aback)*. Ten per cent! Why, man, do you know what my profits are? 885

CUSINS. Enormous, I hope: otherwise I shall require twentyfive per cent.

UNDERSHAFT. But, Mr. Cusins, this is a serious matter of business. You are not bringing any capital into the concern. 890

CUSINS. What! no capital! Is my mastery of Greek no capital? Is my access to the subtlest thought, the loftiest poetry yet attained by humanity, no capital? My character! my intellect! my life! my career! what Barbara calls my soul! are these no capital? Say another word; and I double my salary. 895

UNDERSHAFT. Be reasonable—

CUSINS *(peremptorily)*. Mr. Undershaft: you have my terms. Take them or leave them. 900

UNDERSHAFT (*recovering himself*). Very well. I note your terms; and I offer you half.

CUSINS (*disgusted*). Half!

UNDERSHAFT (*firmly*). Half.

CUSINS. You call yourself a gentleman; and you offer me half!! 905

UNDERSHAFT. I do not call myself a gentleman; but I offer you half.

CUSINS. This to your future partner! your successor! your son-in-law! 910

BARBARA. You are selling your own soul, Dolly, not mine. Leave me out of the bargain, please.

UNDERSHAFT. Come! I will go a step further for Barbara's sake. I will give you three fifths; but that is my last word. 915

CUSINS. Done!

LOMAX. Done in the eye. Why, I only get eight hundred, you know.

CUSINS. By the way, Mac, I am a classical scholar, not an arithmetical one. Is three fifths more than 920 half or less?

UNDERSHAFT. More, of course.

CUSINS. I would have taken two hundred and fifty. How you can succeed in business when you are willing to pay all that money to a University don 925 who is obviously not worth a junior clerk's wages! — well! What will Lazarus say?

UNDERSHAFT. Lazarus is a gentle romantic Jew who cares for nothing but string quartets and stalls at fashionable theatres. He will get the credit of 930 your rapacity in money matters, as he has hitherto had the credit of mine. You are a shark of the first order, Euripides. So much the better for the firm!

BARBARA. Is the bargain closed, Dolly? Does your soul belong to him now? 935

CUSINS. No: the price is settled: that is all. The real tug of war is still to come. What about the moral question?

LADY BRITOMART. There is no moral question in the matter at all, Adolphus. You must simply 940 sell cannons and weapons to people whose cause is right and just, and refuse them to foreigners and criminals.

UNDERSHAFT (*determinedly*). No: none of that. You must keep the true faith of an Armorer, or you 945 dont come in here.

CUSINS. What on earth is the true faith of an Armorer?

UNDERSHAFT. To give arms to all men who offer an honest price for them, without respect of persons or principles: to aristocrat and republican, to 950 Nihilist and Tsar, to Capitalist and Socialist, to Protestant and Catholic, to burglar and policeman, to black man, white man and yellow man, to all sorts and conditions, all nationalities, all faiths, all 955 follies, all causes and all crimes. The first Undershaft wrote up in his shop IF GOD GAVE THE HAND, LET NOT MAN WITHHOLD THE SWORD. The second wrote up ALL HAVE THE RIGHT TO FIGHT: NONE HAVE THE 960 RIGHT TO JUDGE. The third wrote up TO MAN THE WEAPON: TO HEAVEN THE VICTORY. The fourth had no literary turn; so he did not write up anything; but he sold cannons to Napoleon under the nose of George the 965 Third.[104] The fifth wrote up PEACE SHALL NOT PREVAIL SAVE WITH A SWORD IN HER HAND. The sixth, my master, was the best of all. He wrote up NOTHING IS EVER DONE IN THIS WORLD UNTIL MEN ARE PRE- 970 PARED TO KILL ONE ANOTHER IF IT IS NOT DONE. After that, there was nothing left for the seventh to say. So he wrote up, simply, UNASHAMED.

CUSINS. My good Machiavelli, I shall certainly 975 write something up on the wall; only, as I shall write it in Greek, you wont be able to read it. But as to your Armorer's faith, if I take my neck out of the noose of my own morality I am not going to put it into the noose of yours. I shall sell 980 cannons to whom I please and refuse them to whom I please. So there!

UNDERSHAFT. From the moment when you become Andrew Undershaft, you will never do as you please again. Dont come here lusting for 985 power, young man.

CUSINS. If power were my aim I should not come here for it. Y o u have no power.

UNDERSHAFT. None of my own, certainly.

---

104 Napoleon … George the Third] when the two were adversaries in the Napoleonic Wars.

CUSINS. I have more power than you, more will. 990
You do not drive this place: it drives you. And what
drives the place?

UNDERSHAFT (enigmatically). A will of which I
am a part.

BARBARA (startled). Father! Do you know what you 995
are saying; or are you laying a snare for my soul?

CUSINS. Dont listen to his metaphysics, Barbara.
The place is driven by the most rascally part of
society, the money hunters, the pleasure hunters,
the military promotion hunters; and he is their 1000
slave.

UNDERSHAFT. Not necessarily. Remember the
Armorer's Faith. I will take an order from a good
man as cheerfully as from a bad one. If you good
people prefer preaching and shirking to buying my 1005
weapons and fighting the rascals, dont blame me.
I can make cannons: I cannot make courage and
conviction. Bah! You tire me, Euripides, with your
morality mongering. Ask Barbara: s h e understands. (He suddenly takes Barbara's hands, and looks 1010
powerfully into her eyes.) Tell him, my love, what
power really means.

BARBARA (hypnotized). Before I joined the
Salvation Army, I was in my own power; and the
consequence was that I never knew what to do 1015
with myself. When I joined it, I had not time
enough for all the things I had to do.

UNDERSHAFT (approvingly). Just so. And why was
that, do you suppose?

BARBARA. Yesterday I should have said, because I 1020
was in the power of God. (She resumes her self-
possession, withdrawing her hands from his with a
power equal to his own.) But you came and shewed
me that I was in the power of Bodger and
Undershaft. Today I feel — oh! how can I put into 1025
words? Sarah: do you remember the earthquake at
Cannes, when we were little children?[105] how little
the surprise of the first shock mattered compared
to the dread and horror of waiting for the second?
That is how I feel in this place today. I stood on 1030
the rock I thought eternal; and without a word of
warning it reeled and crumbled under me. I was
safe with an infinite wisdom watching me, an army
marching to Salvation with me; and in a moment,
at a stroke of your pen in a cheque book, I stood 1035
alone; and the heavens were empty. That was the
first shock of the earthquake: I am waiting for the
second.

UNDERSHAFT. Come, come, my daughter! dont
make too much of your little tinpot tragedy. What 1040
do we do here when we spend years of work and
thought and thousands of pounds of solid cash on
a new gun or an aerial battleship that turns out
just a hairsbreadth wrong after all? Scrap it. Scrap
it without wasting another hour or another pound 1045
on it. Well, you have made for yourself something
that you call a morality or a religion or what not.
It doesnt fit the facts. Well, scrap it. Scrap it and
get one that does fit. That is what is wrong with
the world at present. It scraps its obsolete steam 1050
engines and dynamos; but it wont scrap its old
prejudices and its old moralities and its old
religions and its old political constitutions. Whats
the result? In machinery it does very well; but in
morals and religion and politics it is working at a 1055
loss that brings it nearer bankruptcy every year.
Dont persist in that folly. If your old religion broke
down yesterday, get a newer and a better one for
tomorrow.

BARBARA. Oh how gladly I would take a better one 1060
to my soul! But you offer me a worse one. (Turning on him with sudden vehemence.) Justify yourself:
shew me some light through the darkness of this
dreadful place, with its beautifully clean workshops, and respectable workmen, and model 1065
homes.

UNDERSHAFT. Cleanliness and respectability do
not need justification, Barbara: they justify
themselves. I see no darkness here, no dreadfulness.
In your Salvation shelter I saw poverty, misery, cold 1070
and hunger. You gave them bread and treacle and
dreams of heaven. I give from thirty shillings a
week to twelve thousand a year. They find their
own dreams; but I look after the drainage.

BARBARA. And their souls? 1075

UNDERSHAFT. I save their souls just as I saved
yours.

---

105 earthquake at Cannes] Shaw is probably thinking of the
one on February 23, 1887.

BARBARA (*revolted*). Y o u saved my soul! What do you mean?

UNDERSHAFT. I fed you and clothed you and housed you. I took care that you should have money enough to live handsomely — more than enough; so that you could be wasteful, careless, generous. That saved your soul from the seven deadly sins.

BARBARA (*bewildered*). The seven deadly sins!

UNDERSHAFT. Yes, the deadly seven. (*Counting on his fingers.*) Food, clothing, firing, rent, taxes, respectability and children. Nothing can lift those seven millstones from Man's neck but money; and the spirit cannot soar until the millstones are lifted. I lifted them from your spirit. I enabled Barbara to become Major Barbara; and I saved her from the crime of poverty.

CUSINS. Do you call poverty a crime?

UNDERSHAFT. The worst of crimes. All the other crimes are virtues beside it: all the other dishonors are chivalry itself by comparison. Poverty blights whole cities; spreads horrible pestilences; strikes dead the very souls of all who come within sight, sound or smell of it. What y o u call crime is nothing: a murder here and a theft there, a blow now and a curse then: what do they matter? they are only the accidents and illnesses of life: there are not fifty genuine professional criminals in London. But there are millions of poor people, abject people, dirty people, ill fed, ill clothed people. They poison us morally and physically: they kill the happiness of society: they force us to do away with our own liberties and to organize unnatural cruelties for fear they should rise against us and drag us down into their abyss. Only fools fear crime: we all fear poverty. Pah! (*turning on Barbara*) you talk of your half-saved ruffian in West Ham: you accuse me of dragging his soul back to perdition. Well, bring him to me here; and I will drag his soul back again to salvation for you. Not by words and dreams; but by thirtyeight shillings a week, a sound house in a handsome street, and a permanent job. In three weeks he will have a fancy waistcoat; in three months a tall hat and a chapel sitting; before the end of the year he will shake hands with a duchess at a Primrose League meeting and join the Conservative Party.[106]

BARBARA. And will he be the better for that?

UNDERSHAFT. You know he will. Dont be a hypocrite, Barbara. He will be better fed, better housed, better clothed, better behaved; and his children will be pounds heavier and bigger. That will be better than an American cloth mattress in a shelter, chopping firewood, eating bread and treacle, and being forced to kneel down from time to time to thank heaven for it: knee drill, I think you call it. It is cheap work converting starving men with a Bible in one hand and a slice of bread in the other. I will undertake to convert West Ham to Mahometanism on the same terms.[107] Try your hand on m y men: their souls are hungry because their bodies are full.

BARBARA. And leave the east end to starve?[108]

UNDERSHAFT (*his energetic tone dropping into one of bitter and brooding remembrance*). I was an east ender. I moralized and starved until one day I swore that I would be a full-fed free man at all costs — that nothing should stop me except a bullet, neither reason nor morals nor the lives of other men. I said "Thou shalt starve ere I starve"; and with that word I became free and great. I was a dangerous man until I had my will: now I am a useful, beneficent, kindly person. That is the history of most self-made millionaires, I fancy. When it is the history of every Englishman we shall have an England worth living in.

LADY BRITOMART. Stop making speeches, Andrew. This is not the place for them.

UNDERSHAFT (*punctured*). My dear: I have no other means of conveying my ideas.

LADY BRITOMART. Your ideas are nonsense. You got on because you were selfish and unscrupulous.

UNDERSHAFT. Not at all. I had the strongest scruples about poverty and starvation. Your moralists are quite unscrupulous about both: they make virtues of them. I had rather be a thief than

---

106 Primrose League] a conservative organization founded by Lord Randolph Churchill in 1883, named for the favourite flower of Disraeli.

107 Mahometanism] Islam.

108 east end] i.e., the poor section of London.

a pauper. I had rather be a murderer than a slave. I dont want to be either; but if you force the alternative on me, then, by Heaven, I'll choose the braver and more moral one. I hate poverty and slavery worse than any other crimes whatsoever. And let me tell you this. Poverty and slavery have stood up for centuries to your sermons and leading articles: they will not stand up to my machine guns. Dont preach at them: dont reason with them. Kill them.

BARBARA. Killing. Is that your remedy for everything?

UNDERSHAFT. It is the final test of conviction, the only lever strong enough to overturn a social system, the only way of saying Must. Let six hundred and seventy fools loose in the street; and three policemen can scatter them. But huddle them together in a certain house in Westminster; and let them go through certain ceremonies and call themselves certain names until at last they get the courage to kill; and your six hundred and seventy fools become a government.[109] Your pious mob fills up ballot papers and imagines it is governing its masters; but the ballot paper that really governs is the paper that has a bullet wrapped up in it.

CUSINS. That is perhaps why, like most intelligent people, I never vote.

UNDERSHAFT. Vote! Bah! When you vote, you only change the names of the cabinet. When you shoot, you pull down governments, inaugurate new epochs, abolish old orders and set up new. Is that historically true, Mr. Learned Man, or is it not?

CUSINS. It is historically true. I loathe having to admit it. I repudiate your sentiments. I abhor your nature. I defy you in every possible way. Still, it is true. But it ought not to be true.

UNDERSHAFT. Ought, ought, ought, ought, ought! Are you going to spend your life saying ought, like the rest of our moralists? Turn your oughts into shalls, man. Come and make explo-

sives with me. Whatever can blow men up can blow society up. The history of the world is the history of those who had courage enough to embrace this truth. Have you the courage to embrace it, Barbara?

LADY BRITOMART. Barbara, I positively forbid you to listen to your father's abominable wickedness. And you, Adolphus, ought to know better than to go about saying that wrong things are true. What does it matter whether they are true if they are wrong?

UNDERSHAFT. What does it matter whether they are wrong if they are true?

LADY BRITOMART *(rising)*. Children: come home instantly. Andrew: I am exceedingly sorry I allowed you to call on us. You are wickeder than ever. Come at once.

BARBARA *(shaking her head)*. It's no use running away from wicked people, mamma.

LADY BRITOMART. It is every use. It shews your disapprobation of them.

BARBARA. It does not save them.

LADY BRITOMART. I can see that you are going to disobey me. Sarah: are you coming home or are you not?

SARAH. I daresay it's very wicked of papa to make cannons; but I dont think I shall cut him on that account.

LOMAX *(pouring oil on the troubled waters)*. The fact is, you know, there is a certain amount of tosh about this notion of wickedness. It doesnt work. You must look at facts. Not that I would say a word in favor of anything wrong; but then, you see, all sorts of chaps are always doing all sorts of things; and we have to fit them in somehow, dont you know. What I mean is that you cant go cutting everybody; and thats about what it comes to. *(Their rapt attention to his eloquence makes him nervous.)* Perhaps I dont make myself clear.

LADY BRITOMART. You are lucidity itself, Charles. Because Andrew is successful and has plenty of money to give to Sarah, you will flatter him and encourage him in his wickedness.

LOMAX *(unruffled)*. Well, where the carcase is, there will the eagles be gathered, dont you know. *(To Undershaft.)* Eh? What?

---

109 Westminster] i.e., the borough in London where the Palace of Westminster, site of the Houses of Parliament, is located.

UNDERSHAFT. Precisely. By the way, m a y I call you Charles?

LOMAX. Delighted. Cholly is the usual ticket.

UNDERSHAFT (to Lady Britomart). Biddy — 1255

LADY BRITOMART (violently). Dont dare call me Biddy. Charles Lomax: you are a fool. Adolphus Cusins: you are a Jesuit.[110] Stephen: you are a prig. Barbara: you are a lunatic. Andrew: you are a vulgar tradesman. Now you all know my opinion; 1260 and m y conscience is clear, at all events (she sits down again with a vehemence that almost wrecks the chair).

UNDERSHAFT. My dear: you are the incarnation of morality. (She snorts.) Your conscience is clear 1265 and your duty done when you have called everybody names. Come, Euripides! it is getting late; and we all want to get home. Make up your mind.

CUSINS. Understand this, you old demon — 1270

LADY BRITOMART. Adolphus!

UNDERSHAFT. Let him alone, Biddy. Proceed, Euripides.

CUSINS. You have me in a horrible dilemma. I want Barbara. 1275

UNDERSHAFT. Like all young men, you greatly exaggerate the difference between one young woman and another.

BARBARA. Quite true, Dolly.

CUSINS. I also want to avoid being a rascal. 1280

UNDERSHAFT (with biting contempt). You lust for personal righteousness, for self-approval, for what you call a good conscience, for what Barbara calls salvation, for what I call patronizing people who are not so lucky as yourself. 1285

CUSINS. I do not: all the poet in me recoils from being a good man. But there are things in me that I must reckon with: pity —

UNDERSHAFT. Pity! The scavenger of misery.

CUSINS. Well, love.

UNDERSHAFT. I know. You love the needy and the 1290 outcast: you love the oppressed races, the negro, the Indian ryot, the Pole, the Irishman.[111] Do you love the Japanese? Do you love the Germans? Do you love the English? 1295

CUSINS. No. Every true Englishman detests the English. We are the wickedest nation on earth; and our success is a moral horror.

UNDERSHAFT. That is what comes of your gospel of love, is it? 1300

CUSINS. May I not love even my father-in-law?

UNDERSHAFT. Who wants your love, man? By what right do you take the liberty of offering it to me? I will have your due heed and respect, or I will kill you. But your love. Damn your imperti- 1305 nence!

CUSINS (grinning). I may not be able to control my affections, Mac.

UNDERSHAFT. You are fencing, Euripides. You are weakening: your grip is slipping. Come! try your 1310 last weapon. Pity and love have broken in your hand: forgiveness is still left.

CUSINS. No: forgiveness is a beggar's refuge. I am with you there: we must pay our debts.

UNDERSHAFT. Well said. Come! you will suit me. 1315 Remember the words of Plato.

CUSINS (starting). Plato! Y o u dare quote Plato to me!

UNDERSHAFT. Plato says, my friend, that society cannot be saved until either the Professors of Greek 1320 take to making gunpowder, or else the makers of gunpowder become Professors of Greek.[112]

CUSINS. Oh, tempter, cunning tempter!

UNDERSHAFT. Come! choose, man, choose.

CUSINS. But perhaps Barbara will not marry me if 1325 I make the wrong choice.

BARBARA. Perhaps not.

CUSINS (desperately perplexed). You hear!

BARBARA. Father: do you love nobody?

UNDERSHAFT. I love my best friend. 1330

LADY BRITOMART. And who is that, pray?

UNDERSHAFT. My bravest enemy. That is the man who keeps me up to the mark.

CUSINS. You know, the creature is really a sort of poet in his way. Suppose he is a great man, after 1335 all!

---

110 Jesuit] in this case, one who embraces a questionable line of reasoning.

111 ryot] Indian peasant.

112 Plato says …] a rendering of the philosopher king concept argued in *The Republic*.

UNDERSHAFT. Suppose you stop talking and make up your mind, my young friend.

CUSINS. But you are driving me against my nature. I hate war. 1340

UNDERSHAFT. Hatred is the coward's revenge for being intimidated. Dare you make war on war? Here are the means: my friend Mr. Lomax is sitting on them.

LOMAX (springing up). Oh I say! You dont mean 1345 that this thing is loaded, do you? My ownest: come off it.

SARAH (sitting placidly on the shell). If I am to be blown up, the more thoroughly it is done the better. Dont fuss, Cholly. 1350

LOMAX (to Undershaft, strongly remonstrant). Your own daughter, you know.

UNDERSHAFT. So I see. (To Cusins.) Well, my friend, may we expect you here at six tomorrow morning? 1355

CUSINS (firmly). Not on any account. I will see the whole establishment blown up with its own dynamite before I will get up at five. My hours are healthy, rational hours: eleven to five.

UNDERSHAFT. Come when you please: before a 1360 week you will come at six and stay until I turn you out for the sake of your health. (Calling.) Bilton! (He turns to Lady Britomart, who rises.) My dear: let us leave these two young people to themselves for a moment. (Bilton comes from the shed.) I am 1365 going to take you through the gun cotton shed.

BILTON (barring the way). You cant take anything explosive in here, sir.

LADY BRITOMART. What do you mean? Are you alluding to me? 1370

BILTON (unmoved). No, maam. Mr. Undershaft has the other gentleman's matches in his pocket.

LADY BRITOMART (abruptly). Oh! I beg your pardon. (She goes into the shed.)

UNDERSHAFT. Quite right, Bilton, quite right: 1375 here you are. (He gives Bilton the box of matches.) Come, Stephen. Come, Charles. Bring Sarah. (He passes into the shed.)

Bilton opens the box and deliberately drops the matches into the fire-bucket.

LOMAX. Oh I say! (Bilton stolidly hands him the empty box.) Infernal nonsense! Pure scientific 1380 ignorance! (He goes in.)

SARAH. Am I all right, Bilton?

BILTON. Youll have to put on list slippers miss: thats all. Weve got em inside. (She goes in.)

STEPHEN (very seriously to Cusins). Dolly, old fellow, 1385 think. Think before you decide. Do you feel that you are a sufficiently practical man? It is a huge undertaking, an enormous responsibility. All this mass of business will be Greek to you.

CUSINS. Oh, I think it will be much less difficult 1390 than Greek.

STEPHEN. Well, I just want to say this before I leave you to yourselves. Dont let anything I have said about right and wrong prejudice you against this great chance in life. I have satisfied myself that 1395 the business is one of the highest character and a credit to our country. (Emotionally.) I am very proud of my father. I (Unable to proceed, he presses Cusins' hand and goes hastily into the shed, followed by Bilton.) 1400

Barbara and Cusins, left alone together, look at one another silently.

CUSINS. Barbara: I am going to accept this offer.

BARBARA. I thought you would.

CUSINS. You understand, dont you, that I had to decide without consulting you. If I had thrown the burden of the choice on you, you would sooner 1405 or later have despised me for it.

BARBARA. Yes: I did not want you to sell your soul for me any more than for this inheritance.

CUSINS. It is not the sale of my soul that troubles me: I have sold it too often to care about that. I 1410 have sold it for a professorship. I have sold it for an income. I have sold it to escape being imprisoned for refusing to pay taxes for hangmen's ropes and unjust wars and things that I abhor. What is all human conduct but the daily and hourly sale 1415 of our souls for trifles? What I am now selling it for is neither money nor position nor comfort, but for reality and for power.

BARBARA. You know that you will have no power, and that he has none. 1420

CUSINS. I know. It is not for myself alone. I want to make power for the world.

BARBARA. I want to make power for the world too; but it must be spiritual power.

CUSINS. I think all power is spiritual: these cannons will not go off by themselves. I have tried to make spiritual power by teaching Greek. But the world can never be really touched by a dead language and a dead civilization. The people must have power; and the people cannot have Greek. Now the power that is made here can be wielded by all men.

BARBARA. Power to burn women's houses down and kill their sons and tear their husbands to pieces.

CUSINS. You cannot have power for good without having power for evil too. Even mother's milk nourishes murderers as well as heroes. This power which only tears men's bodies to pieces has never been so horribly abused as the intellectual power, the imaginative power, the poetic, religious power than can enslave men's souls. As a teacher of Greek I gave the intellectual man weapons against the common man. I now want to give the common man weapons against the intellectual man. I love the common people. I want to arm them against the lawyer, the doctor, the priest, the literary man, the professor, the artist, and the politician, who, once in authority, are the most dangerous, disastrous, and tyrannical of all the fools, rascals, and impostors. I want a democratic power strong enough to force the intellectual oligarchy to use its genius for the general good or else perish

BARBARA. Is there no higher power than that (pointing to the shell)?

CUSINS. Yes: but that power can destroy the higher powers just as a tiger can destroy a man: therefore man must master that power first. I admitted this when the Turks and Greeks were last at war.[113] My best pupil went out to fight for Hellas.[114] My parting gift to him was not a copy of Plato's Republic, but a revolver and a hundred Undershaft cartridges. The blood of every Turk he shot — if he shot any — is on my head as well as on Undershaft's. That act committed me to this place

---

113 war] the Thirty Days' War of 1897.

114 Hellas] the Greek nation as conceived in its classical glory.

for ever. Your father's challenge has beaten me. Dare I make war on war? I dare. I must. I will. And now, is it all over between us?

BARBARA (touched by his evident dread of her answer). Silly baby Dolly! How could it be?

CUSINS (overjoyed). Then you—you—you— Oh for my drum! (He flourishes imaginary drumsticks.)

BARBARA (angered by his levity). Take care, Dolly, take care. Oh, if only I could get away from you and from father and from it all! if I could have the wings of a dove and fly away to heaven!

CUSINS. And leave m e!

BARBARA. Yes, you, and all the other naughty mischievous children of men. But I cant. I was happy in the Salvation Army for a moment. I escaped from the world into a paradise of enthusiasm and prayer and soul saving; but the moment our money ran short, it all came back to Bodger: it was he who saved our people: he, and the Prince of Darkness, my papa. Undershaft and Bodger: their hands stretch everywhere: when we feed a starving fellow creature, it is with their bread, because there is no other bread; when we tend the sick, it is in the hospitals they endow; if we turn from the churches they build, we must kneel on the stones of the streets they pave. As long as that lasts, there is no getting away from them. Turning our backs on Bodger and Undershaft is turning our backs on life.

CUSINS. I thought you were determined to turn your back on the wicked side of life.

BARBARA. There is no wicked side: life is all one. And I never wanted to shirk my share in whatever evil must be endured, whether it be sin or suffering. I wish I could cure you of middle-class ideas, Dolly.

CUSINS (gasping). Middle cl—! A snub! A social snub to m e! from the daughter of a foundling!

BARBARA. That is why I have no class, Dolly: I come straight out of the heart of the whole people. If I were middle-class I should turn my back on my father's business; and we should both live in an artistic drawing room, with you reading the reviews in one corner, and I in the other at the piano, playing Schumann: both very superior persons, and neither of us a bit of use. Sooner than that, I would sweep out the guncotton shed, or be one of Bodger's barmaids. Do you know what would have happened if you had refused papa's offer?

CUSINS. I wonder! 1515

BARBARA. I should have given you up and married the man who accepted it. After all, my dear old mother has more sense than any of you. I felt like her when I saw this place — felt that I must have it — that never, never, never could I let it go; only 1520 she thought it was the houses and the kitchen ranges and the linen and china, when it was really all the human souls to be saved: not weak souls in starved bodies, crying with gratitude for a scrap of bread and treacle, but fullfed, quarrelsome, 1525 snobbish, uppish creatures, all standing on their little rights and dignities, and thinking that my father ought to be greatly obliged to them for making so much money for him and so he ought. That is where salvation is really wanted. My father 1530 shall never throw it in my teeth again that my converts were bribed with bread. (She is trans-figured.) I have got rid of the bribe of bread. I have got rid of the bribe of heaven. Let God's work be done for its own sake: the work he had to create 1535 us to do because it cannot be done except by living men and women. When I die, let him be in my debt, not I in his; and let me forgive him as becomes a woman of my rank.

CUSINS. Then the way of life lies through the 1540 factory of death?

BARBARA. Yes, through the raising of hell to heaven and of man to God, through the unveiling of an eternal light in the Valley of The Shadow.[115] (Seizing him with both hands.) Oh, did you think 1545 my courage would never come back? did you believe that I was a deserter? that I, who have stood in the streets, and taken my people to my heart, and talked of the holiest and greatest things with them, could ever turn back and chatter foolishly 1550 to fashionable people about nothing in a drawing room? Never, never, never, never: Major Barbara will die with the colors. Oh! and I have my dear little Dolly boy still; and he has found me my place and my work. Glory Hallelujah! (She kisses him.) 1555

CUSINS. My dearest: consider my delicate health. I cannot stand as much happiness as you can.

BARBARA. Yes: it is not easy work being in love with me, is it? But it's good for you. (She runs to the shed, and calls, childlike) Mamma! Mamma! (Bilton 1560 comes out of the shed, followed by Undershaft.) I want Mamma.

UNDERSHAFT. She is taking off her list slippers, dear. (He passes on to Cusins.) Well? What does she say? 1565

CUSINS. She has gone right up into the skies.

LADY BRITOMART (coming from the shed and stopping on the steps, obstructing Sarah, who follows with Lomax. Barbara clutches like a baby at her mother's skirt.) Barbara: when will you learn to be 1570 independent and to act and think for yourself? I know as well as possible what that cry of "Mamma, Mamma," means. Always running to me!

SARAH (touching Lady Britomart's ribs with her finger tips and imitating a bicycle horn). Pip! pip! 1575

LADY BRITOMART (highly indignant). How dare you say Pip! pip! to me, Sarah? You are both very naughty children. What do you want, Barbara?

BARBARA. I want a house in the village to live in with Dolly. (Dragging at the skirt.) Come and tell 1580 me which one to take.

UNDERSHAFT (to Cusins). Six o' clock tomorrow morning, my young friend.

THE END

---

115 Valley of The Shadow] an allusion to Psalm 23.

AUGUST STRINDBERG

The Ghost Sonata

A udiences and critics alike were bewildered by *The Ghost Sonata* when it premiered at Strindberg's tiny Intimate Theatre in Stockholm in January 1908. If the play seems slightly less strange today than it did at its premiere nearly a century ago, this may be attributable to the enormous influence that it, and other plays by August Strindberg (1849–1912), had on subsequent drama throughout the twentieth century. For in attempting to depict the uncanny effect of a hidden, irrational inner life erupting through the naturalistic surface of everyday appearances, *The Ghost Sonata* heralded some of the main currents of modern experimental theatre—namely, expressionism, surrealism, and absurdism—movements which, in turn, have made an impact on mainstream consciousness through film. The peeling away of the ordinary material world to reveal the grotesque, nightmarish figures hidden within; the depiction of the inner fantastic life, the world of dreams, as if it were an outward reality; the deliberate distortions of time and space: all these techniques, familiar enough today, were novelties when Strindberg brought them onto the stage.

Indeed, it may be that *The Ghost Sonata* suffers a little for today's reader in comparison with the works it has begotten. Where once its fantastic elements had the power to startle audiences, now its various grotesque disclosures and long passages of peculiar dialogue may seem somewhat less sensational. Be that as it may, when we consider Strindberg's play as a product of its time, it is clear that he has done something extraordinary. The setting of the play as it begins was based on Strindberg's own observations of his neighbours in the street where he lived in Stockholm. Even the background relationship between the Old Man and the Student's late father, as it is initially revealed, is typical of Naturalism—a school of thought to which Strindberg had made a seminal contribution with his *Miss Julie*. However, having started with a basically naturalistic situation, Strindberg quickly moves off in a new direction. Rather than assuming the putatively objective scientific gaze of the naturalist playwright, Strindberg shows what is hidden beneath the surface lives of these characters, drawing on symbolism and caricature to render these darker truths.

The Ghost Sonata is remarkable not only for its technique, but also its structure. The play is one of the series of so-called "chamber plays" Strindberg wrote for the Intimate Theatre. Strindberg described these short works as "intimate in form; a simple theme treated with thoroughness; few characters; vast perspectives." In short, he was attempting to create the dramatic equivalent of chamber music, and for *The Ghost Sonata*, he was directly inspired by two chamber works by Beethoven— the Piano Sonata in D minor, Opus 31, no. 2 and the Piano Trio, Opus 70, no. 1, sometimes known as the "ghost sonata" and the "ghost trio." So, while the three parts of *The Ghost Sonata* seem only slightly related to one another in terms of plot, they comprise a clear development of a central theme in the manner of classical music: a statement, a counter-statement, and a conclusion. In the first part, the Student is obsessed with what, based on appearances, he imagines is the perfect life within the house; next we go within the house, where the illusions are stripped away to reveal the sordid truths of these lives; last, the Student and the Girl are in the inner room, the "hyacinth room," where their attempts to embrace an idealistic vision leads them only to the truth of death. In a sense, then, the play delineates the journey from the illusions of daily life through to death. Still, it hints at a truth transcending death, as Strindberg suggested in a letter to his translator, Emil Schering (April 7, 1907), declaring that he would like have "inserted into the last scene … or made visible in letters of fire" above the painting: "And God shall wipe away all tears from their eyes; and there shall be no more death, neither sorrow, nor crying, neither there be any more pain: for the former things are passed away" (Revelation 21:4).

[C.S.W.]

AUGUST STRINDBERG
The Ghost Sonata
Translated by Elizabeth Sprigge

DRAMATIC PERSONÆ

THE OLD MAN (JACOB HUMMEL), *a Company Director*

THE STUDENT, (ARKENHOLTZ)

THE MILKMAID, *an apparition*

THE CARETAKER'S WIFE

THE CARETAKER

THE LADY IN BLACK, *the daughter of the Caretaker's Wife and the Dead Man. Also referred to as the Dark Lady.*

THE COLONEL

THE MUMMY (AMELIA), *the Colonel's wife*

THE GIRL (ADÈLE), *the Colonel's daughter, actually the daughter of the Old Man*

THE ARISTOCRAT (BARON SKANSKORG), *engaged to the Lady in Black*

JOHANSSON, *the Old Man's servant*

BENGTSSON, *the Colonel's servant*

THE FIANCÉE, (BEATRICE VON HOLSTEINKRONA), *a white-haired old woman, once betrothed to the Old Man*

THE COOK

A MAIDSERVANT

BEGGARS

SCENE I

Outside the house. The corner of the façade of a modern house, showing the ground floor above, and the street in front. The ground floor terminates on the right in the Round Room, above which, on the first floor, is a balcony with a flagstaff. The windows of the Round Room face the street in front of the house, and at the corner look on to the suggestion of a side-street running toward the back. At the beginning of the scene the blinds of the Round Room are down. When, later, they are raised, the white marble statue of a young woman can be seen, surrounded with palms and brightly lighted by rays of sunshine.

To the left of the Round Room is the Hyacinth Room; its window filled with pots of hyacinths, blue, white, and pink. Further left, at the back, is an imposing double front door with laurels in tubs on either side of it. The doors are wide open, showing a staircase of white marble with a banister of mahogany and brass. To the left of the front door is another ground-floor window, with a window-mirror.[1] On the balcony rail in the corner above

---

1 *window-mirror*] a mirror set at an angle just inside a window, so those inside can see what is happening in the street, supposedly without being seen themselves.

the Round Room are a blue silk quilt and two white pillows. The windows to the left of this are hung with white sheets.[2]

In the foreground, in front of the house, is a green bench; to the right a street drinking-fountain, to the left an advertisement column.

It is a bright Sunday morning, and as the curtain rises the bells of several churches, some near, some far away, are ringing.

On the staircase the LADY IN BLACK stands motionless.

The CARETAKER'S WIFE sweeps the doorstep, then polishes the brass on the door and waters the laurels.

In a wheel-chair by the advertisement column sits the OLD MAN, reading newspaper. His hair and beard are white and he wears spectacles.

The MILKMAID comes round the corner on the right, carrying milk bottles in a wire basket. She is wearing a summer dress with brown shoes, black stockings and a white cap. She takes off her cap and hangs it on the fountain, wipes the perspiration from her forehead, washes her hands and arranges her hair, using the water as a mirror.

A steamship bell is heard, and now and then the silence is broken by the deep notes of an organ in a nearby church.

After a few moments, when all is silent and the MILKMAID has finished her toilet, the STUDENT enters from the left. He has had a sleepless night and is unshaven. He goes straight up to the fountain. There is a pause before he speaks.

STUDENT: May I have the cup? [*The MILKMAID clutches the cup to her.*] Haven't you finished yet?

The MILKMAID looks at him with horror.

OLD MAN: [*To himself.*] Who's he talking to? I don't see anybody. Is he crazy?

He goes on watching them in great astonishment.

STUDENT: [*To the MILKMAID.*] What are you staring at? Do I look so terrible? Well, I've had no sleep, and of course you think I've been making a night   5

of it...[*The MILKMAID stays just as she is.*] You think I've been drinking, eh? Do I smell of liquor? [*The MILKMAID does not change.*] I haven't shaved,   10
I know. Give me a drink of water, girl. I've earned it. [*Pause.*] Oh well, I suppose I'll have to tell you. I spent the whole night dressing wounds and looking after the injured. You see, I was there when that house collapsed last night. Now you know.   15
[*The MILKMAID rinses the cup and gives him a drink.*] Thanks. [*The MILKMAID stands motionless. Slowly.*] Will you do me a great favor? [*Pause.*] The thing is, my eyes, as you can see, are inflamed, but my hands have been touching wounds and corpses,   20
so it would be dangerous to put them near my eyes. Will you take my handkerchief—it's quite clean—and dip it in the fresh water and bathe my eyes? Will you do this? Will you play the good Samaritan?[3] [*The MILKMAID hesitates, but does as   25
he bids.*] Thank you, my dear. [*He takes out his purse. She makes a gesture of refusal.*] Forgive my stupidity, but I'm only half-awake....

The MILKMAID disappears.

OLD MAN: [*To the STUDENT.*] Excuse me speaking to you, but I heard you say you were at the scene   30
of the accident last night. I was just reading about it in the paper.

STUDENT: Is it in the paper already?

OLD MAN: The whole thing, including your portrait. But they regret that they have been unable to find   35
out the name of the splendid young student....

STUDENT: Really? [*Glances at the paper.*] Yes, that's me. Well I never!

OLD MAN: Who was it you were talking to just now?

STUDENT: Didn't you see? [*Pause.*]   40

OLD MAN: Would it be impertinent to inquire— what in fact your name is?

STUDENT: What would be the point? I don't care for publicity. If you get any praise, there's always disapproval too. The art of running people down   45

---

2 *white sheets*] a traditional Swedish symbol of mourning.

3 good Samaritan] The phrase is usually associated with the Samaritan of Jesus' parable who rescues a man left by the roadside (Luke 10:30–37), but here also evokes the woman of Samaria whom Jesus asks for water, and to whom he promises "water of everlasting life" (John 4:7–15).

has been developed to such a pitch…. Besides, I don't want any reward.

OLD MAN: You're well off, perhaps.

STUDENT: No, indeed. On the contrary, I'm very poor.　50

OLD MAN: Do you know, it seems to me I've heard your voice before. When I was young I had a friend who pronounced certain words just as you do. I've never met anyone else with quite that pronunciation. Only him—and you. Are you by any chance　55 related to Mr. Arkenholtz, the merchant?

STUDENT: He was my father.

OLD MAN: Strange are the paths of fate. I saw you when you were an infant, under very painful circumstances.　60

STUDENT: Yes, I understand I came into the world in the middle of a bankruptcy.

OLD MAN: Just that.

STUDENT: Perhaps I might ask your name.

OLD MAN: I am Mr. Hummel.　65

STUDENT: Are you the?…I remember that…

OLD MAN: Have you often heard my name mentioned in your family?

STUDENT: Yes.

OLD MAN: And mentioned perhaps with a certain　70 aversion? [*The STUDENT is silent.*] Yes, I can imagine it. You were told, I suppose, that I was the man who ruined your father? All who ruin themselves through foolish speculations consider they were ruined by those they couldn't fool.　75 [*Pause.*] Now these are the facts. Your father robbed me of seventeen thousand crowns—the whole of my savings at that time.

STUDENT: It's queer that the same story can be told in two such different ways.　80

OLD MAN: You surely don't believe I'm telling you what isn't true?

STUDENT: What am I to believe? My father didn't lie.

OLD MAN: That is so true. A father never lies. But I　85 too am a father, and so it follows…

STUDENT: What are you driving at?

OLD MAN: I saved your father from disaster, and he repaid me with all the frightful hatred that is born of an obligation to be grateful. He taught his　90 family to speak ill of me.

STUDENT: Perhaps you made him ungrateful by poisoning your help with unnecessary humiliation.

OLD MAN: All help is humiliating, sir.

STUDENT: What do you want from me?　95

OLD MAN: I'm not asking for the money, but if you will render me a few small services, I shall consider myself well paid. You see that I am a cripple. Some say it is my own fault; others lay the blame on my parents. I prefer to blame life itself, with its pitfalls.　100 For if you escape one snare, you fall headlong into another. In any case, I am unable to climb stairs or ring doorbells, and that is why I am asking you to help me.

STUDENT: What can I do?　105

OLD MAN: To begin with, push my chair so that I can read those playbills. I want to see what is on tonight.

STUDENT: [*Pushing the chair.*] Haven't you got an attendant?　110

OLD MAN: Yes, but he has gone on an errand. He'll be back soon. Are you a medical student?

STUDENT: No, I am studying languages, but I don't know at all what I'm going to do.

OLD MAN: Aha! Are you good at mathematics?　115

STUDENT: Yes, fairly.

OLD MAN: Good. Perhaps you would like a job.

STUDENT: Yes, why not?

OLD MAN: Splendid. [*He studies the playbills.*] They are doing *The Valkyrie* for the matinée.[4] That　120 means the Colonel will be there with his daughter, and as he always sits at the end of the sixth row, I'll put you next to him. Go to that telephone kiosk please and order a ticket for seat eighty-two in the sixth row.　125

STUDENT: Am I to go to the Opera in the middle of the day?

OLD MAN: Yes. Do as I tell you and things will go well with you. I want to see you happy, rich, and

---

4 *The Valkyrie*] *Die Walküre*, the second opera in the *Ring des Nibelungen* cycle by Richard Wagner (1813–1883): two children of the god Wotan, Siegmund and Sieglinde, meet and, mysteriously drawn to one another, conceive a child, unaware that they are brother and sister. Siegmund is killed by Wotan; Sieglinde later dies bearing their child.

honored. Your début last night as the brave rescuer 130
will make you famous by tomorrow and then your
name will be worth remembering.

STUDENT: [*Going to the telephone kiosk.*] What an
odd adventure!

OLD MAN: Are you a gambler? 135

STUDENT: Yes, unfortunately.

OLD MAN: We'll make it fortunately. Go on now,
telephone. [*The STUDENT goes. The OLD MAN
reads his paper. The LADY IN BLACK comes out on
to the pavement and talks to the CARETAKER'S WIFE.* 140
*The OLD MAN listens, but the audience hears
nothing. The STUDENT returns.*] Did you fix it up?

STUDENT: It's done.

OLD MAN: You see that house?

STUDENT: Yes, I've been looking at it a lot. I passed 145
it yesterday when the sun was shining on the
window-panes, and I imagined all the beauty and
elegance there must be inside. I said to my
companion: "Think of living up there in the top
flat, with a beautiful young wife, two pretty little 150
children and an income of twenty thousand
crowns a year."

OLD MAN: So that's what you said. That's what you
said. Well, well! I too am very fond of this house.

STUDENT: Do you speculate in houses? 155

OLD MAN: Mm—yes. But not in the way you mean.

STUDENT: Do you know the people who live here?

OLD MAN: Every one of them. At my age one knows
everybody, and their parents and grandparents too,
and one's always related to them in some way or 160
other. I am just eighty, but no one knows me—
not really. I take an interest in human destiny. [*The
blinds of the Round Room are drawn up. The
COLONEL is seen, wearing mufti.*[5] *He looks at the
thermometer outside one of the windows, then turns* 165
*back into the room and stands in front of the marble
statue.*] Look, that's the Colonel, whom you will
sit next to this afternoon.

STUDENT: Is he—the Colonel? I don't understand
any of this, but it's like a fairy story. 170

OLD MAN: My whole life's like a book of fairy stories,
sir. And although the stories are different, they are

held together by one thread, and the main theme
constantly recurs.

STUDENT: Who is that marble statue of? 175

OLD MAN: That, naturally, is his wife.

STUDENT: Was she such a wonderful person?

OLD MAN: Er…yes.

STUDENT: Tell me.

OLD MAN: We can't judge people, young man. If I 180
were to tell you that she left him, that he beat her,
that she returned to him and married him a second
time, and that now she is sitting inside there like
a mummy, worshipping her own statue—then you
would think me crazy. 185

STUDENT: I don't understand.

OLD MAN: I didn't think you would. Well, then we
have the window with the hyacinths. His daughter
lives there. She has gone out for a ride, but she will
be home soon. 190

STUDENT: And who is the dark lady talking to the
caretaker?

OLD MAN: Well, that's a bit complicated, but it is
connected with the dead man, up there where you
see the white sheets. 195

STUDENT: Why, who was he?

OLD MAN: A human being like you or me, but the
most conspicuous thing about him was his vanity.
If you were a Sunday child, you would see him
presently come out of that door to look at the 200
Consulate flag flying at half-mast.[6] He was, you
understand, a Consul, and he reveled in coronets
and lions and plumed hats and colored ribbons.

STUDENT: Sunday child, you say? I'm told I was
born on a Sunday. 205

OLD MAN: No, were you really? I might have known
it. I saw it from the color of your eyes. Then you
can see what others can't. Have you noticed that?

STUDENT: I don't know what others do see, but at
times…. Oh, but one doesn't talk of such things! 210

OLD MAN: I was almost sure of it. But you can talk
to me, because I understand such things.

STUDENT: Yesterday, for instance…I was drawn to
that obscure little street where later on the house

---

5 *mufti*] plain clothes, as opposed to military uniform.

6 Sunday child] According to folklore, a child born on a
Sunday is blessed with a strong sixth sense—some psy-
chic power and the ability to see ghosts.

collapsed. I went there and stopped in front of that building which I had never seen before. Then I noticed a crack in the wall.... I heard the floor boards snapping.... I dashed over and picked up a child that was passing under the wall.... The next moment the house collapsed. I was saved, but in my arms which I thought held the child, was nothing at all.

OLD MAN: Yes, yes, just as I thought. Tell me something. Why were you gesticulating that way just now by the fountain? And why were you talking to yourself?

STUDENT: Didn't you see the milkmaid I was talking to?

OLD MAN: [*In horror.*] Milkmaid?

STUDENT: Surely. The girl who handed me the cup.

OLD MAN: Really? So that's what was going on. Ah well, I haven't second sight, but there are things I can do. [*The FIANCÉE is now seen to sit down by the window which has the window-mirror.*] Look at that old woman in the window. Do you see her? Well, she was my fiancée once, sixty years ago. I was twenty. Don't be alarmed. She doesn't recognize me. We see one another every day, and it makes no impression on me, although once we vowed to love one another eternally. Eternally!

STUDENT: How foolish you were in those days! We never talk to our girls like that.

OLD MAN: Forgive us, young man. We didn't know any better. But can you see that that old woman was once young and beautiful?

STUDENT: It doesn't show. And yet there's some charm in her looks. I can't see her eyes.

The CARETAKER'S WIFE comes out with a basket of chopped fir branches.[7]

OLD MAN: Ah, the caretaker's wife! That dark lady is her daughter by the old man. That's why her husband was given the job of caretaker. But the dark lady has a suitor, who is an aristocrat with great expectations. He is in the process of getting a divorce—from his present wife, you understand. She's presenting him with a stone mansion in order to be rid of him. This aristocratic suitor is the son-in-law of the dead man, and you can see his bedclothes being aired on the balcony upstairs. It is complicated, I must say.

STUDENT: It's fearfully complicated.

OLD MAN: Yes, that it is, internally and externally, although it looks quite simple.

STUDENT: But then who was the dead man?

OLD MAN: You asked me that just now, and I answered. If you were to look round the corner, where the tradesmen's entrance is, you would see a lot of poor people whom he used to help—when it suited him.

STUDENT: He was a kind man then.

OLD MAN: Yes—sometimes.

STUDENT: Not always?

OLD MAN: No-o. That's the way of people. Now, sir, will you push my chair a little, so that it gets into the sun. I'm horribly cold. When you're never able to move about, the blood congeals. I'm going to die soon, I know that, but I have a few things to do first. Take my hand and feel how cold I am.

STUDENT: [*Taking it.*] Yes, inconceivably. [*He shrinks back, trying in vain to free his hand.*]

OLD MAN: Don't leave me. I am tired now and lonely, but I haven't always been like this, you know. I have an enormously long life behind me, enormously long. I have made people unhappy and people have made me unhappy—the one cancels out the other—but before I die I want to see you happy. Our fates are entwined through your father—and other things.

STUDENT: Let go of my hand. You are taking all my strength. You are freezing me. What do you want with me?

OLD MAN: [*Letting go.*] Be patient and you shall see and understand. Here comes the young lady.

They watch the GIRL approaching, though the audience cannot yet see her.

STUDENT: The Colonel's daughter?

OLD MAN: His daughter—yes. Look at her. Have you ever seen such a masterpiece?

STUDENT: She is like the marble statue in there.

OLD MAN: That's her mother, you know.

STUDENT: You are right. Never have I seen such a

---

7 *fir branches*] The spreading of fir branches after a death is a Swedish tradition.

woman of woman born. Happy the man who may lead her to the altar and his home.

OLD MAN: You can see it. Not everyone recognizes her beauty. So, then, it is written. 300

The GIRL enters, wearing an English riding habit. Without noticing anyone she walks slowly to the door, where she stops to say a few words to the CARETAKER'S WIFE. Then she goes into the house. The STUDENT covers his eyes with his hand.

OLD MAN: Are you weeping?

STUDENT: In the face of what's hopeless there can be nothing but despair.

OLD MAN: I can open doors and hearts, if only I find 305 an arm to do my will. Serve me and you shall have power.

STUDENT: Is it a bargain? Am I to sell my soul?

OLD MAN: Sell nothing. Listen. All my life I have *taken*. Now I have a craving to give—give. But no 310 one will accept. I am rich, very rich, but I have no heirs, except for a good-for-nothing who torments the life out of me. Become my son. Inherit me while I am still alive. Enjoy life so that I can watch, at least from a distance. 315

STUDENT: What am I to do?

OLD MAN: First go to *The Valkyrie*.

STUDENT: That's settled. What else?

OLD MAN: This evening you must be in there—in the Round Room. 320

STUDENT: How am I to get there?

OLD MAN: By way of *The Valkyrie*.

STUDENT: Why have you chosen me as your medium? Did you know me before?

OLD MAN: Yes, of course. I have had my eye on you 325 for a long time. But now look up there at the balcony. The maid is hoisting the flag to half-mast for the Consul. And now she is turning the bedclothes. Do you see that blue quilt? It was made for two to sleep under, but now it covers only one. 330 [*The GIRL, having changed her dress, appears in the window and waters the hyacinths.*] There is my little girl. Look at her, look! She is talking to the flowers. Is she not like that blue hyacinth herself? She gives them drink—nothing but pure water, and they 335 transform the water into color and fragrance. Now here comes the Colonel with the newspaper. He

is showing her the bit about the house that collapsed. Now he's pointing to your portrait. She's not indifferent. She's reading of your brave deed.... 340

I believe it's clouding over. If it turns to rain I shall be in a pretty fix, unless Johansson comes back soon. [*It grows cloudy and dark. The FIANCÉE at the window-mirror closes her window.*] Now my fiancée is closing the window. Seventy-nine years 345 old. The window-mirror is the only mirror she uses, because in it she sees not herself, but the world outside—in two directions. But the world can see her; she hasn't thought of that. Anyhow she's a handsome old woman. 350

Now the DEAD MAN, wrapped in a winding sheet, comes out of the door.

STUDENT: Good God, what do I see?

OLD MAN: What do you see?

STUDENT: Don't *you* see? There, in the doorway, the dead man?

OLD MAN: I see nothing, but I expected this. Tell me. 355

STUDENT: He is coming out into the street. [*Pause.*] Now he is turning his head and looking up at the flag.

OLD MAN: What did I tell you? You may be sure he'll count the wreaths and read the visiting cards. Woe 360 to him who's missing.

STUDENT: Now he's turning the corner.

OLD MAN: He's gone to count the poor at the back door. The poor are in the nature of a decoration, you see. "Followed by the blessings of many." Well, 365 he's not going to have my blessing. Between ourselves he was a great scoundrel.

STUDENT: But charitable.

OLD MAN: A charitable scoundrel, always thinking of his grand funeral. When he knew his end was 370 near, he cheated the State out of fifty thousand crowns. Now his daughter has relations with another woman's husband and is wondering about the will. Yes, the scoundrel can hear every word we're saying, and he's welcome to it. Ah, here 375 comes Johansson! [*JOHANSSON enters.*] Report! [*JOHANSSON speaks, but the audience does not hear.*] Not at home, eh? You are an ass. And the telegram? Nothing? Go on.... At six this evening? That's good. Special edition, you say? With his name in 380 full. Arkenholtz, a student, born…parents…That's splendid.… I think it's beginning to rain.… What did he say about it? So—so. He wouldn't? Well, he must. Here comes the aristocrat. Push me round the corner, Johansson, so I can hear what the poor are saying. And, Arkenholtz, you wait for me here. Understand? [*To JOHANSSON.*] Hurry up now, hurry up.

JOHANSSON wheels the chair round the corner. The STUDENT remains watching the GIRL, who is now loosening the earth round the hyacinths. The ARISTOCRAT, wearing mourning, comes in and speaks to the DARK LADY, who has been walking to and fro on the pavement.

ARISTOCRAT: But what can we do about it? We shall have to wait.

LADY: I can't wait.

ARISTOCRAT: You can't? Well then, go into the country.

LADY: I don't want to do that.

ARISTOCRAT: Come over here or they will hear what we are saying.

They move toward the advertisement column and continue their conversation inaudibly. JOHANSSON returns.

JOHANSSON: [*To the STUDENT.*] My master asks you not to forget that other thing, sir.

STUDENT: [*Hesitatingly.*] Look here…first of all tell me…who is your master?

JOHANSSON: Well, he's so many things, and he has been everything.

STUDENT: Is he a wise man?

JOHANSSON: Depends what that is. He says all his life he's been looking for a Sunday child, but that may not be true.

STUDENT: What does he want? He's grasping, isn't he?

JOHANSSON: It's power he wants. The whole day long he rides round in his chariot like the god Thor himself.[8] He looks at houses, pulls them down, opens up new streets, builds squares.… But he breaks into houses too, sneaks through windows,

plays havoc with human destinies, kills his enemies—and never forgives. Can you imagine it, sir? This miserable cripple was once a Don Juan—although he always lost his women.

STUDENT: How do you account for that?

JOHANSSON: You see he's so cunning he makes the women leave him when he's tired of them. But what he's most like now is a horse-thief in the human market. He steals human beings in all sorts of different ways. He literally stole me out of the hands of the law. Well, as a matter of fact I'd made a slip—hm, yes—and only he knew about it. Instead of getting me put in jail, he turned me into a slave. I slave—for my food alone, and that's none of the best.

STUDENT: Then what is it he means to do in this house?

JOHANSSON: I'm not going to talk about that. It's too complicated.

STUDENT: I think I'd better get away from it all.

The GIRL drops a bracelet out the window.

JOHANSSON: Look! The young lady has dropped her bracelet out of the window. [*The STUDENT goes slowly over, picks up the bracelet and returns it to the GIRL, who thanks him stiffly. The STUDENT goes back to JOHANSSON.*] So you mean to get away. That's not so easy as you think, once he's got you in his net. And he's afraid of nothing between heaven and earth—yes, of one thing he is—of one person rather.…

STUDENT: Don't tell me. I think perhaps I know.

JOHANSSON: How can you know?

STUDENT: I'm guessing. Is it a little milkmaid he's afraid of?

JOHANSSON: He turns his head the other way whenever he meets a milk cart. Besides, he talks in his sleep. It seems he was once in Hamburg.…

STUDENT: Can one trust this man?

JOHANSSON: You can trust him—to do anything.

STUDENT: What's he doing now round the corner?

JOHANSSON: Listening to the poor. Sowing a little word, loosening one stone at a time, till the house falls down—metaphorically speaking. You see I'm an educated man. I was once a book-seller.… Do you still mean to go away?

---

8 Thor] the god of thunder in Norse mythology, often regarded as the chief god.

STUDENT: I don't like to be ungrateful. He saved my father once, and now he only asks a small service in return.

JOHANSSON: What is that? 460

STUDENT: I am to go to *The Valkyrie*.

JOHANSSON: That's beyond me. But he's always up to new tricks. Look at him, now, talking to that policeman. He is always thick with the police. He uses them, gets them involved in his interests, 465 holds them with false promises and expectations, while all the time he's pumping them. You'll see that before the day is over he'll be received in the Round Room.

STUDENT: What does he want there? What connec- 470 tion has he with the Colonel.

JOHANSSON: I think I can guess, but I'm not sure. You'll see for yourself once you're in there.

STUDENT: I shall never be in there.

JOHANSSON: That depends on yourself. Go to *The* 475 *Valkyrie*.

STUDENT: Is that the way?

JOHANSSON: Yes, if he said so. Look. Look at him in his war chariot, drawn in triumph by the beggars, who get nothing for their pains but the 480 hint of a treat at his funeral.

The OLD MAN appears standing up in his wheelchair, drawn by one of the beggars and followed by the rest.

OLD MAN: Hail the noble youth who, at the risk of his own life, saved so many others in yesterday's accident. Three cheers for Arkenholtz! [*The BEGGARS bare their heads but do not cheer. The GIRL* 485 *at the window waves her handkerchief. The COLONEL gazes from the window of the Round Room. The OLD WOMAN rises at her window. The MAID on the balcony hoists the flag to the top.*] Clap your hands, citizens. True, it is Sunday, but the ass 490 in the pit and the ear in the corn field will absolve us.[9] And although I am not a Sunday child, I have

---

9 ass in the pit] Jesus to the Pharisees: "Which of you shall have an ox fallen into a pit, and will not straightway pull him out on the sabbath day?" (Luke 14:5); ear in the corn field] "And it came to pass, that he went through the corn fields on the sabbath day; and his disciples began, as they went, to pluck the ears of corn" (Mark 2:23).

the gift of prophecy and also that of healing. Once I brought a drowned person back to life. That was in Hamburg on a Sunday morning just like this.... 495

The MILKMAID enters, seen only by the STUDENT and the OLD MAN. She raises her arms like one who is drowning and gazes fixedly at the OLD MAN. He sits down, then crumples up, stricken with horror.

Johannson! Take me away! Quick!... Arkenholtz, don't forget *The Valkyrie*.

STUDENT: What is all this?

JOHANSSON: We shall see. We shall see.

SCENE II

Inside the Round Room. At the back is a white porcelain stove. On either side of it are a mirror, a pendulum clock, and candelabra. On the right of the stove is the entrance to the hall beyond which is a glimpse of a room furnished in green and mahogany. On the left of the stove is the door to a cupboard, papered like the wall. The statue, shaded by palms has a curtain which can be drawn to conceal it.

A door on the left leads into the Hyacinth Room, where the GIRL sits reading.

The back of the COLONEL can be seen, as he sits in the Green Room, writing.

BENGTSSON, the Colonel's servant, comes in from the hall. He is wearing livery, and is followed by JOHANSSON, dressed as a waiter.

BENGTSSON: Now you'll have to serve the tea, Johansson, while I take the coats. Have you ever done it before?

JOHANSSON: It's true I push a war chariot in the daytime, as you know, but in the evenings I go as 5 a waiter to receptions and so forth. It's always been my dream to get into this house. They're queer people here, aren't they?

BENGTSSON: Ye-es. A bit out of the ordinary anyhow. 10

JOHANSSON: Is it to be a musical party or what?

BENGTSSON: The usual ghost supper, as we call it. They drink tea and don't say a word—or else the Colonel does all the talking. And they crunch their biscuits, all at the same time. It sounds like rats in 15 an attic.

JOHANSSON: Why do you call it the ghost supper?

BENGTSSON: They look like ghosts. And they've kept this up for twenty years, always the same people saying the same things or saying nothing at all for fear of being found out. 20

JOHANSSON: Isn't there a mistress of the house?

BENGTSSON: Oh yes, but she's crazy. She sits in a cupboard because her eyes can't bear the light. [*He points to the papered door.*] She sits in there. 25

JOHANSSON: In there?

BENGTSSON: Well, I told you they were a bit out of the ordinary.

JOHANSSON: But then—what does she look like?

BENGTSSON: Like a mummy. Do you want to have 30 a look at her? [*He opens the door.*] There she is.

The figure of the COLONEL'S WIFE is seen, white and shriveled into a MUMMY.

JOHANSSON: Oh my God!

MUMMY: [*Babbling.*] Why do you open the door? Haven't I told you to keep it closed?

BENGTSSON: [*In a wheedling tone.*] Ta, ta, ta, ta. Be 35 a good girl now, then you'll get something nice. Pretty Polly.

MUMMY: [*Parrot-like.*] Pretty Polly. Are you there, Jacob? Currrrr!

BENGTSSON: She thinks she's a parrot, and maybe 40 she's right. [*To the MUMMY.*] Whistle for us, Polly.

The MUMMY whistles.

JOHANSSON: Well, I've seen a few things in my day, but this beats everything.

BENGTSSON: You see, when a house gets old, it grows mouldy, and when people stay a long time 45 together and torment each other they go mad. The mistress of the house—shut up, Polly!—that mummy there, has been living here for forty years—same husband, same furniture, same relatives, same friends. [*He closes the papered door.*] 50 And the goings-on in this house—well, they're beyond me. Look at that statue—that's her when she was young.

JOHANSSON: Good Lord! Is that the mummy?

BENGTSSON: Yes. It's enough to make you weep. 55 And somehow, carried away by her own imagination or something, she's got to be a bit like a parrot—the way she talks and the way she can't stand cripples or sick people. She can't stand the sight of her own daughter, because she's sick. 60

JOHANSSON: Is the young lady sick?

BENGTSSON: Didn't you know that?

JOHANSSON: No. And the Colonel, who is he?

BENGTSSON: You'll see.

JOHANSSON: [*Looking at the statue.*] It's horrible to 65 think that… How old is she now?

BENGTSSON: Nobody knows. But it's said that when she was thirty-five she looked nineteen, and that's what she made the Colonel believe she was—here in this very house. Do you know what that black 70 Japanese screen by the couch is for? They call it the death-screen, and when someone's going to die, they put it round—same as in a hospital.

JOHANSSON: What a horrible house! And the student was longing to get in, as if it were paradise. 75

BENGTSSON: What student? Oh, I know. The one who's coming here this evening. The Colonel and the young lady happened to meet him at the Opera, and both of them took a fancy to him. Hm. Now it's my turn to ask questions. Who is 80 your master—the man in the wheelchair?

JOHANSSON: Well, he er…Is he coming here too?

BENGTSSON: He hasn't been invited.

JOHANSSON: He'll come uninvited—if need be.

The OLD MAN appears in the hall on crutches, wearing a frock-coat and top-hat. He steals forward and listens.

BENGTSSON: He's a regular old devil, isn't he? 85

JOHANSSON: Up to the ears.

BENGTSSON: He looks like Old Nick himself.[10]

JOHANSSON: And he must be a wizard too, for he goes through locked doors.

The OLD MAN comes forward and takes hold of JOHANSSON by the ear.

OLD MAN: Rascal—take care! [*To BENGTSSON.*] Tell 90 the Colonel I am here.

BENGTSSON: But we are expecting guests.

OLD MAN: I know. But my visit is as good as expected, if not exactly looked forward to.

---

10 Old Nick] the Devil.

BENGTSSON: I see. What name shall I say? Mr. Hummel? 95

OLD MAN: Exactly. Yes. [*BENGTSSON crosses the hall to the Green Room, the door of which he closes behind him. To JOHANSSON.*] Get out! [*JOHANSSON hesitates.*] Get out! [*JOHANSSON disappears into the hall. The OLD MAN inspects the room and stops in front of the statue in much astonishment.*] Amelia! It is she—she! 100

MUMMY: [*From the cupboard.*] Prrr-etty Polly. [*The OLD MAN starts.*] 105

OLD MAN: What was that? Is there a parrot in the room? I don't see it.

MUMMY: Are you there, Jacob?

OLD MAN: The house is haunted.

MUMMY: Jacob! 110

OLD MAN: I'm scared. So these are the kind of secrets they guard in this house. [*With his back turned to the cupboard he stands looking at a portrait.*] There he is—he!

The MUMMY comes out behind the OLD MAN and gives a pull at his wig.

MUMMY: Currrr! Is it…? Currrr! 115

OLD MAN: [*Jumping out of his skin.*] God in heaven! Who is it?

MUMMY: [*In a natural voice.*] Is it Jacob?

OLD MAN: Yes, my name is Jacob.

MUMMY: [*With emotion.*] And my name is Amelia. 120

OLD MAN: No, no, no…Oh my God!

MUMMY: That's how I look. Yes. [*Pointing to the statue.*] And that's how I *did* look. Life opens one's eyes, does it not? I live mostly in the cupboard to avoid seeing and being seen…. But, Jacob, what do you want here? 125

OLD MAN: My child. Our child.

MUMMY: There she is.

OLD MAN: Where?

MUMMY: There—in the Hyacinth Room.

OLD MAN: [*Looking at the GIRL.*] Yes, that is she. [*Pause.*] And what about her father—the Colonel, I mean—your husband? 130

MUMMY: Once, when I was angry with him, I told him everything. 135

OLD MAN: Well…?

MUMMY: He didn't believe me. He just said: "That's what all wives say when they want to murder their husbands." It was a terrible crime none the less. It has falsified his whole life—his family tree too. Sometimes I take a look in the Peerage, and then I say to myself: Here she is, going about with a false birth certificate like some servant girl, and for such things people are sent to the reformatory.[11] 140

OLD MAN: Many do it. I seem to remember your own date of birth was given incorrectly. 145

MUMMY: My mother made me do that. I was not to blame. And in our crime, *you* played the biggest part.

OLD MAN: No. Your husband caused that crime, when he took my fiancée from me. I was born one who cannot forgive until he has punished. That was to me an imperative duty—and is so still. 150

MUMMY: What are you expecting to find in this house? What do you want? How did you get in? Is it to do with my daughter? If you touch her, you shall die. 155

OLD MAN: I mean well by her.

MUMMY: Then you must spare her father.

OLD MAN: No. 160

MUMMY: Then you shall die. In this room, behind that screen.

OLD MAN: That may be. But I can't let go once I've got my teeth into a thing.

MUMMY: You want to marry her to that student. Why? He is nothing and has nothing. 165

OLD MAN: He will be rich, through me.

MUMMY: Have you been invited here tonight?

OLD MAN: No, but I propose to get myself an invitation to this ghost supper. 170

MUMMY: Do you know who is coming?

OLD MAN: Not exactly.

MUMMY: The Baron. The man who lives up above—whose father-in-law was buried this afternoon.

OLD MAN: The man who is getting a divorce in order to marry the daughter of the Caretaker's wife… The man who used to be—your lover. 175

MUMMY: Another guest will be your former fiancée, who was seduced by my husband.

OLD MAN: A select gathering. 180

MUMMY: Oh God, if only we might die, might die!

---

11 Peerage] a book detailing the genealogy of the aristocracy.

OLD MAN: Then why have you stayed together?

MUMMY: Crime and secrets and guilt bind us together. We have broken our bonds and gone our own ways, times without number, but we are always drawn together again.   185

OLD MAN: I think the Colonel is coming.

MUMMY: Then I will go in to Adèle. [*Pause.*] Jacob, mind what you do. Spare him. [*Pause. She goes into the Hyacinth Room and disappears.*]   190

The COLONEL enters, cold and reserved, with a letter in his hand.

COLONEL: Be seated, please. [*Slowly the OLD MAN sits down. Pause. The COLONEL stares at him.*] You wrote this letter, sir?

OLD MAN: I did.

COLONEL: Your name is Hummel?   195

OLD MAN: It is. [*Pause.*]

COLONEL: As I understand, you have bought in all my unpaid promissory notes. I can only conclude that I am in your hands. What do you want?

OLD MAN: I want payment, in one way or another.   200

COLONEL: In what way?

OLD MAN: A very simple one. Let us not mention the money. Just bear with me in your house as a guest.

COLONEL: If so little will satisfy you…   205

OLD MAN: Thank you.

COLONEL: What else?

OLD MAN: Dismiss Bengtsson.

COLONEL: Why should I do that? My devoted servant, who has been with me a lifetime, who has   210
the national medal for long and faithful service—why should I do that?[12]

OLD MAN: That's how you see him—full of excellent qualities. He is not the man he appears to be.

COLONEL: Who is?   215

OLD MAN: [*Taken aback.*] True. But Bengtsson must go.

COLONEL: Are you going to run my house?

OLD MAN: Yes. Since everything here belongs to me—furniture, curtains, dinner service, linen…   220
and more too.

COLONEL: How do you mean—more?

OLD MAN: Everything. I own everything here. It is mine.

COLONEL: Very well, it is yours. But my family   225
scutcheon and my good name remain my own.[13]

OLD MAN: No, not even those. [*Pause.*] You are not a nobleman.

COLONEL: How dare you!

OLD MAN: [*Producing a document.*] If you read this   230
extract from *The Armorial Gazette*, you will see that the family whose name you are using has been extinct for a hundred years.

COLONEL: I have heard rumors to this effect, but I inherited the name from my father. [*Reads.*] It is   235
true. You are right. I am not a nobleman. Then I must take off my signet ring. It is true, it belongs to you. [*Gives it to him.*] There you are.

OLD MAN: [*Pocketing the ring.*] Now we will continue. You are not a Colonel either.   240

COLONEL: I am not…?

OLD MAN: No. You once held the temporary rank of Colonel in the American Volunteer Force, but after the war in Cuba and the reorganization of the Army, all such titles were abolished.[14]   245

COLONEL: Is this true?

OLD MAN: [*Indicating his pocket.*] Do you want to read it?

COLONEL: No, that's not necessary. Who are you, and what right have you to sit there stripping me   250
in this fashion?

OLD MAN: You will see. But as far as stripping you goes…do you know who you are?

COLONEL: How dare you?

OLD MAN: Take off that wig and have a look at   255
yourself in the mirror. But take your teeth out at the same time and shave off your moustache. Let Bengtsson unlace your metal stays and perhaps a certain X.Y.Z., a lackey, will recognize himself. The fellow who was a cupboard lover in a certain   260
kitchen…[*The COLONEL reaches for the bell on the table, but HUMMEL checks him.*] Don't touch that

---

12 national medal] It was common in Sweden at one time to award long-time servants with a medal.

13 scutcheon] coat of arms.

14 war in Cuba] the Spanish-American War (1898), prompted by Cuba's U.S.-backed rebellion against Spain, in which many Swedes served on the American side.

bell, and don't call Bengtsson. If you do, I'll have him arrested. [*Pause.*] And now the guests are beginning to arrive. Keep your composure and we will continue to play our old parts for a while.

COLONEL: Who are you? I recognize your voice and eyes.

OLD MAN: Don't try to find out. Keep silent and obey.

The STUDENT enters and bows to the COLONEL.

STUDENT: How do you do, sir.

COLONEL: Welcome to my house, young man. Your splendid behaviour at that great disaster has brought your name to everybody's lips, and I count it an honor to receive you in my home.

STUDENT: My humble descent, sir…Your illustrious name and noble birth…

COLONEL: May I introduce Mr. Arkenholtz—Mr. Hummel. If you will join the ladies in here, Mr. Arkenholtz—I must conclude my conversation with Mr. Hummel. [*He shows the STUDENT into the Hyacinth Room, where he remains visible, talking shyly to the GIRL.*] A splendid young man, musical, sings, writes poetry. If he only had blue blood in him, if he were of the same station, I don't think I should object…

OLD MAN: To what?

COLONEL: To my daughter…

OLD MAN: *Your* daughter! But apropos of that, why does she spend all her time in there?

COLONEL: She insists on being in the Hyacinth Room except when she is out-of-doors. It's a peculiarity of hers. Ah, here comes Miss Beatrice von Holsteinkrona—a charming woman, a pillar of the Church, with just enough money of her own to suit her birth and position.

OLD MAN: [*To himself.*] My fiancée.

The FIANCÉE enters, looking a little crazy.

COLONEL: Miss Holsteinkrona—Mr. Hummel. [*The FIANCÉE curtseys and takes a seat. The ARISTOCRAT enters and seats himself. He wears mourning and looks mysterious.*] Baron Skanskorg…

OLD MAN: [*Aside, without rising.*] That's the jewel-thief, I think. [*To the COLONEL.*] If you bring in the Mummy, the party will be complete.

COLONEL: [*At the door of the Hyacinth Room.*] Polly!

MUMMY: [*Entering.*] Currrrr…!

COLONEL: Are the young people to come in too?

OLD MAN: No, not the young people. They shall be spared.

They all sit silent in a circle.

COLONEL: Shall we have the tea brought in?

OLD MAN: What's the use? No one wants tea. Why should we pretend about it?

COLONEL: Then shall we talk?

OLD MAN: Talk of the weather, which we know? Inquire about each other's health, which we know just as well. I prefer silence—then one can hear thoughts and see the past. Silence cannot hide anything—but words can. I read the other day that differences of language originated among savages for the purpose of keeping one tribe's secrets hidden from another. Every language therefore is a code, and he who finds the key can understand every language in the world. But this does not prevent secrets from being exposed without a key, specially when there is a question of paternity to be proved. Proof in a Court of Law is another matter. Two false witnesses suffice to prove anything about which they are agreed, but one does not take witnesses along on the kind of explorations I have in mind. Nature herself has instilled in human beings a sense of modesty which tries to hide what should be hidden, but we slip into situations unintentionally, and by chance sometimes the deepest secret is divulged—the mask torn from the impostor, the villain exposed…. [*Pause. All look at each other in silence.*] What a silence there is now! [*Long silence.*] Here, for instance, in this honorable house, in this elegant home, where beauty, wealth and culture are united…. [*Long silence.*] All of us now sitting here know who we are—do we not? There's no need for me to tell you. And you know me, although you pretend ignorance. [*He indicates the Hyacinth Room.*] In there is my daughter. *Mine*—you know that too. She had lost the desire to live, without knowing why. The fact is she was withering away in this air charged with crime and deceit and falseness of every kind. That is why I looked for a friend for her in whose company she might enjoy the light and warmth of noble deeds. [*Long silence.*] That was my mission in this house: to pull up the weeds, to expose the crimes, to settle all accounts, so that those young people might start afresh in this home, which is my gift to them. [*Long silence.*] Now I am going to grant safe-conduct, to each of you in his and her proper time and turn. Whoever stays I shall have arrested. [*Long silence.*] Do you hear the clock ticking like a death-watch beetle in the wall? Do you hear what it says? "It's time, it's time, it's time." When it strikes, in a few moments, your time will be up. Then you can go, but not before. It's raising its arm against you before it strikes. Listen! It is warning you. "The clock can strike." And I can strike too. [*He strikes the table with one of his crutches.*] Do you hear?

Silence. The MUMMY goes up to the clock and stops it, then speaks in a normal and serious voice.

MUMMY: But I can stop time in its course. I can wipe out the past and undo what is done. But not with bribes, not with threats—only through suffering and repentance. [*She goes up to the OLD MAN.*] We are miserable human beings, that we know. We have erred and we have sinned, we like all the rest. We are not what we seem, because at bottom we are better than ourselves, since we detest our sins. But when you, Jacob Hummel, with your false name, choose to sit in judgment over us, you prove yourself worse than us miserable sinners. For you are not the one you appear to be. You are a thief of human souls. You stole me once with false promises. You murdered the Consul who was buried today; you strangled him with debts. You have stolen the student, binding him by the pretence of a claim on his father, who never owed you a farthing. [*Having tried to rise and speak, the OLD MAN sinks back in his chair and crumples up more and more as she goes on.*] But there is one dark spot in your life which I am not quite sure about, although I have my suspicions. I think Bengtsson knows. [*She rings the bell on the table.*]

OLD MAN: No, not Bengtsson, not him.

MUMMY: So he does know. [*She rings again. The MILKMAID appears in the hallway door, unseen by all but the OLD MAN, who shrinks back in horror. The MILKMAID vanishes as BENGTSSON enters.*] Do you know this man, Bengtsson?

BENGTSSON: Yes, I know him and he knows me. Life, as you are aware, has its ups and downs. I have been in his service; another time he was in mine. For two whole years he was a sponger in my kitchen. As he had to be away by three, the dinner was got ready at two, and the family had to eat the warmed-up leavings of that brute. He drank the soup stock, which the cook then filled with water. He sat out there like a vampire, sucking the marrow out of the house, so that we became like skeletons. And he nearly got us put in prison when we called the cook a thief. Later I met this man in Hamburg under another name. He was a usurer then, a blood-sucker. But while he was there he was charged with having lured a young girl out on to the ice so as to drown her, because she had seen him commit a crime he was afraid would be discovered....

The MUMMY passes her hand over the OLD MAN'S face.

MUMMY: *This* is you. Now give up the notes and the will. [*JOHANSSON appears in the hallway door and watches the scene with great interest, knowing he is now to be freed from slavery. The OLD MAN produces a bundle of papers and throws it on the table. The MUMMY goes over and strokes his back.*] Parrot. Are you there, Jacob?

OLD MAN: [*Like a parrot.*] Jacob is here. Pretty Polly. Currrr!

MUMMY: May the clock strike?

OLD MAN: [*With a clucking sound.*] The clock may strike. [*Imitating a cuckoo clock.*] Cuckoo, cuckoo, cuckoo....

The MUMMY opens the cupboard door.

MUMMY: Now the clock has struck. Rise, and enter the cupboard where I have spent twenty years repenting our crime. A rope is hanging there, which you can take as the one with which you strangled the Consul, and with which you meant to strangle your benefactor....Go! [*The OLD MAN goes in to the cupboard. The MUMMY closes the door.*]

Bengtsson! Put up the screen—the death-screen.
[BENGTSSON *places the screen in front of the door.*]
It is finished. God have mercy on his soul.   435
ALL: Amen. [*Long silence.*]

*The GIRL and the STUDENT appear in the Hyacinth
Room. She has a harp, on which she plays a prelude,
and then accompanies the STUDENT's recitation.*]

STUDENT: I saw the sun. To me it seemed
    that I beheld the Hidden.
Men must reap what they have sown;   440
blest is he whose deeds are good.
Deeds which you have wrought in fury,
cannot in evil find redress.
Comfort him you have distressed
with loving-kindness—this will heal.
No fear has he who does no ill.   445
Sweet is innocence.15

SCENE III

*Inside the Hyacinth Room. The general effect of the
room is exotic and oriental. There are hyacinths
everywhere, of every color, some in pots, some with the
bulbs in glass vases and the roots going down into the
water.*

*On top of the tiled stove is a large seated Buddha, in
whose lap rests a bulb from which rises the stem of a
shallot (Allium ascalonicum), bearing its globular cluster
of white, starlike flowers.*

*On the right is an open door, leading into the Round
Room, where the COLONEL and the MUMMY are seated,
inactive and silent. A part of the death-screen is also
visible.*

On the left is a door to the pantry and kitchen.

*The STUDENT and the GIRL (Adèle) are beside the
table; he is standing, she seated with her harp.*

GIRL: Now sing to my flowers.
STUDENT: Is this the flower of your soul?
GIRL: The one and only. Do you too love the
    hyacinth?
STUDENT: I love it above all other flowers—its   5
    virginal shape rising straight and slender out of the

_____
15 Based on parts of the Icelandic poem, "*Sólarlióth*" (Song
   of the Sun).

bulb, resting on the water and sending its pure
white roots down into the colorless fluid. I love
its colors: the snow-white, pure as innocence, the
yellow honey-sweet, the youthful pink, the ripe   10
red, but best of all the blue—the dewy blue, deep-
eyed and full of faith. I love them all, more than
gold or pearls. I have loved them ever since I was
a child, have worshipped them because they have
all the fine qualities I lack…. And yet…   15
GIRL: Go on.
STUDENT: My love is not returned, for these
    beautiful blossoms hate me.
GIRL: How do you mean?
STUDENT: Their fragrance, strong and pure as the   20
    early winds of spring which have passed over
    melting snows, confuses my senses, deafens me,
    blinds me, thrusts me out of the room, bombards
    me with poisoned arrows that wound my heart and
    set my head on fire. Do you know the legend of   25
    that flower?
GIRL: Tell it to me.
STUDENT: First its meaning. The bulb is the earth,
    resting on the water or buried in the soil. Then
    the stalk rises, straight as the axis of the world, and   30
    at the top are the six-pointed star-flowers.
GIRL: Above the earth—the stars. Oh, that is
    wonderful! Where did you learn this? How did you
    find it out?
STUDENT: Let me think…In your eyes. And so, you   35
    see, it is an image of the Cosmos. This is why
    Buddha sits holding the earth-bulb, his eyes
    brooding as he watches it grow, outward and
    upward, transforming itself into a heaven. This
    poor earth will become a heaven. It is for this that   40
    Buddha waits.
GIRL: I see it now. Is not the snowflake six-pointed
    too like the hyacinth flower?
STUDENT: You are right. The snowflakes must be
    falling stars.   45
GIRL: And the snowdrop is a snow-star, grown out
    of snow.
STUDENT: But the largest and most beautiful of all
    the stars in the firmament, the golden-red Sirius,
    is the narcissus with its gold and red chalice and   50
    its six white rays.
GIRL: Have you seen the shallot in bloom?

STUDENT: Indeed I have. It bears its blossoms within a ball, a globe like the celestial one, strewn with white stars. 55

GIRL: Oh how glorious! Whose thought was that?

STUDENT: Yours.

GIRL: Yours.

STUDENT: Ours. We have given birth to it together. We are wedded. 60

GIRL: Not yet.

STUDENT: What's still to do?

GIRL: Waiting, ordeals, patience.

STUDENT: Very well. Put me to the test. [*Pause.*] Tell me. Why do your parents sit in there so silently, 65 not saying a single word?

GIRL: Because they have nothing to say to each other, and because neither believes what the other says. This is how my father puts it: What's the point of talking, when neither of us can fool the other? 70

STUDENT: What a horrible thing to hear!

GIRL: Here comes the Cook. Look at her, how big and fat she is. [*They watch the COOK, although the audience cannot yet see her.*]

STUDENT: What does she want? 75

GIRL: To ask me about the dinner. I have to do the housekeeping as my mother's ill.

STUDENT: What have we to do with the kitchen?

GIRL: We must eat. Look at the Cook. I can't bear the sight of her. 80

STUDENT: Who is that ogress?

GIRL: She belongs to the Hummel family of vampires. She is eating us.

STUDENT: Why don't you dismiss her?

GIRL: She won't go. We have no control over her. 85 We've got her for our sins. Can't you see that we are pining and wasting away?

STUDENT: Don't you get enough to eat?

GIRL: Yes, we get many dishes, but all the strength has gone. She boils the nourishment out of the 90 meat and gives us the fibre and water, while she drinks the stock herself. And when there's a roast, she first boils out the marrow, eats the gravy and drinks the juices herself. Everything she touches loses its savor. It's as if she sucked with her eyes. 95 We get the grounds when she has drunk the coffee. She drinks the wine and fills the bottles up with water.

STUDENT: Send her packing.

GIRL: We can't. 100

STUDENT: Why not?

GIRL: We don't know. She won't go. No one has any control over her. She has taken all our strength from us.

STUDENT: May I get rid of her? 105

GIRL: No. It must be as it is. Here she is. She will ask me what is to be for dinner. I shall tell her. She will make objections and get her own way.

STUDENT: Let her do the ordering herself then.

GIRL: She won't do that. 110

STUDENT: What an extraordinary house! It is bewitched.

GIRL: Yes. But now she is turning back, because she has seen you.

COOK: [*In the doorway.*] No, that wasn't the reason. 115 [*She grins, showing all her teeth.*]

STUDENT: Get out!

COOK: When it suits me. [*Pause.*] It does suit me now. [*She disappears.*]

GIRL: Don't lose your temper. Practice patience. She 120 is one of the ordeals we have to go through in this house. You see, we have a housemaid too, whom we have to clean up after.

STUDENT: I am done for. *Cor in Æthere.*[16] Music!

GIRL: Wait. 125

STUDENT: Music!

GIRL: Patience. This room is called the room of ordeals. It looks beautiful, but it is full of defects.

STUDENT: Really? Well, such things must be seen to. It is very beautiful, but a little cold. Why don't you 130 have a fire?

GIRL: Because it smokes.

STUDENT: Can't you have the chimney swept?

GIRL: It doesn't help. You see that writing-desk there?

STUDENT: An unusually fine piece. 135

GIRL: But it wobbles. Every day I put a piece of cork under that leg, and every day the housemaid takes it away when she sweeps and I have to cut a new piece. The penholder is covered with ink every morning and so is the inkstand. I have to clean 140 them up every morning after that woman, as sure

---

16 *Cor in Æthere*] (Latin) lift the heart to the heavens.

as the sun rises. [*Pause.*] What's the worst job you can think of?

STUDENT: To count the washing. Ugh!

GIRL: That I have to do. Ugh!

STUDENT: What else?

GIRL: To be waked in the middle of the night and have to get up and see to the window, which the housemaid has left banging.

STUDENT: What else?

GIRL: To get up on a ladder and tie the cord on the damper to the big stove, which the housemaid has torn off.

STUDENT: What else?

GIRL: To sweep after her, to dust after her, to light the fire in the stove when all she's done is throw in some wood. To see to the damper, to wipe the glasses, to lay the table over again, to open the bottles, to see that the rooms are aired, to remake my bed, to rinse the water-bottle when it's green with sediment, to buy matches and soap which are always lacking, to wipe the chimneys and trim the wicks to keep the lamps from smoking—and so that they don't go out when we have company, I have to fill them myself....

STUDENT: Music!

GIRL: Wait. The labor comes first. The labor of keeping the dirt of life at a distance.

STUDENT: But you are wealthy and have two servants.

GIRL: It doesn't help. Even if we had three. Living is hard work, and sometimes I grow tired. [*Pause.*] Think then if there were a nursery as well.

STUDENT: The greatest of joys.

GIRL: And the costliest. Is life worth so much hardship?

STUDENT: That must depend on the reward you expect for your labors. I would not shrink from anything to win your hand.

GIRL: Don't say that. You can never have me.

STUDENT: Why not?

GIRL: You mustn't ask. [*Pause.*]

STUDENT: You dropped your bracelet out of the window....

GIRL: Because my hand has grown so thin. [*Pause.*]

The COOK appears with a Japanese bottle in her hand.

There she is—the one who devours me and all of us.

STUDENT: What has she in her hand?

GIRL: It is the bottle of coloring matter that has letters like scorpions on it. It is the soy which turns water into soup and takes the place of gravy. She makes cabbage soup with it—and mock-turtle soup too.

STUDENT: [*To COOK.*] Get out!

COOK: You drain us of sap, and we drain you. We take the blood and leave you the water, but colored...colored. I am going now, but all the same I shall stay, as long as I please.

She goes out.

STUDENT: Why did Bengtsson get a medal?

GIRL: For his great merits.

STUDENT: Has he no defects?

GIRL: Yes, great ones. But you don't get a medal for them.

They smile.

STUDENT: You have many secrets in this house.

GIRL: As in all others. Permit us to keep ours.

STUDENT: Don't you approve of candor?

GIRL: Yes—within reason.

STUDENT: Sometimes I'm seized with a raging desire to say all I think. But I know the world would go to pieces if one were completely candid. [*Pause.*] I went to a funeral the other day...in church. It was very solemn and beautiful.

GIRL: Was it Mr. Hummel's?

STUDENT: My false benefactor's—yes. At the head of the coffin stood an old friend of the deceased. He carried the mace. I was deeply impressed by the dignified manner and moving words of the clergyman. I cried. We all cried. Afterward we went to a tavern, and there I learned that the man with the mace had been in love with the dead man's son.... [*The girl stares at him, trying to understand.*] And that the dead man had borrowed money from his son's admirer. [*Pause.*] Next day the clergyman was arrested for embezzling the church funds. A pretty story.

GIRL: Oh...! [*Pause.*]

STUDENT: Do you know how I am thinking about you now?

GIRL: Don't tell me, or I shall die.

STUDENT: I must, or I shall die.

GIRL: It is in asylums that people say everything they 230
think.

STUDENT: Exactly. My father finished up in an
asylum.

GIRL: Was he ill?

STUDENT: No, he was well, but he was mad. You 235
see, he broke out once—in these circumstances.
Like all of us, he was surrounded with a circle of
acquaintances; he called them friends for short.
They were a lot of rotters, of course, as most people
are, but he had to have some society—he couldn't 240
get on all alone. Well, as you know, in everyday
life no one tells people what he thinks of them,
and he didn't either. He knew perfectly well what
frauds they were—he'd sounded the depths of their
deceit—but as he was a wise and well-bred man, 245
he was always courteous to them. Then one day
he gave a big party. It was in the evening and he
was tired by the day's work and by the strain of
holding his tongue and at the same time talking
rubbish with his guests…. [*The GIRL is frightened.*] 250
Well, at the dinner table he rapped for silence,
raised his glass, and began to speak. Then
something loosed the trigger. He made an
enormous speech in which he stripped the whole
company naked, one after the other, and told them 255
of all their treachery. Then, tired out, he sat down
on the table and told them all to go to hell.

GIRL: Oh!

STUDENT: I was there, and I shall never forget what
happened then. Father and Mother came to blows, 260
the guests rushed for the door…and my father was
taken to a madhouse, where he died. [*Pause.*]
Water that is still too long stagnates, and so it is
in this house too. There is something stagnating
here. And yet I thought it was paradise itself that 265
first time I saw you coming in here. There I stood
that Sunday morning, gazing in. I saw a Colonel
who was no Colonel. I had a benefactor who was
a thief and had to hang himself. I saw a mummy
who was not a mummy and an old maid—what 270
of the maidenhood, by the way? Where is beauty
to be found? In nature, and in my own mind,
when it is in its Sunday clothes. Where are honor

and faith? In fairy-tales and children's fancies.
Where is anything that fulfills its promise? In my 275
imagination. Now your flowers have poisoned me
and I have given the poison back to you. I asked
you to become my wife in a home full of poetry
and song and music. Then the Cook came….
Sursum Corda![17] Try once more to strike fire and 280
glory out of the golden harp. Try, I beg you, I
implore you on my knees. [*Pause.*] Then I will do
it myself. [*He picks up the harp, but the strings give
no sound.*] It is dumb and deaf. To think that the
most beautiful flowers are so poisonous, are the 285
most poisonous. The curse lies over the whole of
creation, over life itself. Why will you not be my
bride? Because the very life-spring within you is
sick…now I can feel that vampire in the kitchen
beginning to suck me. I believe she is a Lamia, one 290
of those that suck the blood of children.[18] It is
always in the kitchen quarters that the seed-leaves
of the children are nipped, if it has not already
happened in the bedroom. There are poisons that
destroy the sight and poisons that open the eyes. 295
I seem to have been born with the latter kind, for
I cannot see what is ugly as beautiful, nor call evil
good. I cannot. Jesus Christ descended into hell.
That was His pilgrimage on earth—to this
madhouse, this prison, this charnel-house, this 300
earth. And the madmen killed Him when He
wanted to set them free; but the robber they let
go. The robber always get the sympathy. Woe! Woe
to us all. Saviour of the world, save us! We perish.

*And now the GIRL has drooped, and it is seen that she
is dying. She rings.*
BENGTSSON enters.

GIRL: Bring the screen. Quick. I am dying. 305

*BENGTSSON comes back with the screen, opens it and
arranges it in front of the GIRL.*

STUDENT: The Liberator is coming. Welcome, pale
and gentle one. Sleep, you lovely, innocent,

---

17 *Sursum Corda*] (Latin) lift up your hearts.

18 Lamia] a female demon from classical mythology, originally an eater of children, but later a vampire who preyed
on young men.

doomed creature, suffering for no fault of your own. Sleep without dreaming, and when you wake again…may you be greeted by a sun that does not burn, in a home without dust, by friends without stain, by a love without flaw. You wise and gentle Buddha, sitting there waiting for a Heaven to spout from the earth, grant us patience in our ordeal and purity of will, so that this hope may not be confounded. 310 315

The strings of the harp hum softly and a white light fills the room.

I saw the sun. To me it seemed
that I beheld the Hidden
Men must reap what they have sown;
blest is he whose deeds are good. 320

Deeds which you have wrought in fury,
cannot in evil find redress.
Comfort him you have distressed
with loving-kindness—this will heal.
No fear has he who does no ill. 325
Sweet is innocence.

[*A faint moaning is heard behind the screen.*] You poor little child, child of this world of illusion, guilt, suffering and death, this world of endless change, disappointment, and pain. May the Lord of Heaven be merciful to you upon your journey. 330

The room disappears. Böcklin's picture, The Island of the Dead, *is seen in the distance, and from the island comes music, soft, sweet, and melancholy.*[19]

CURTAIN.

---

[19] *Böcklin*] Arnold Böcklin (1827–1901) was a Swiss painter known for his moody landscapes. *Die Toteninsel* (The Island of the Dead), his best known painting, depicts a foreboding mountainous island, approached by a boat containing a figure shrouded in white, who stands before a coffin. The painting inspired Sergei Rachmaninoff (1873–1943) to compose a symphonic poem of the same name. Strindberg hung a copy of the painting in the auditorium of his Intimate Theatre.

PAUL GREEN AND RICHARD WRIGHT

Native Son

Richard Wright (1908–1960) did not have much of a head start in life. He was born in the profoundly racist state of Mississippi, the grandson of slaves, was abandoned by his father at the age of five, raised in poverty, and was able to attend school only until grade nine, after which followed a period of nomadic shifting among a series of menial jobs. Thus, it would not have been surprising, perhaps, had Wright turned out to resemble his protagonist, Bigger Thomas, a great deal more than was the case. Indeed, as Wright explains in his essay "How 'Bigger' Was Born," he encountered many models for the character in his early life; beneath his gentle, controlled exterior he shared the anger and resentment of these young men. Of course, Wright was an unusually intelligent man with great literary gifts, but his autobiography, *Black Boy* (1947), shows just how narrow his escape was from the life of constant, hopeless rage and despair that was the lot of so many of his acquaintances.

As it happened, however, Wright moved north to Chicago in 1927, and began a literary career with the help of the Federal Writers' Project—a program subsidized by the American government. Wright also became a member of the Communist Party at this time, and though he later left the party for political and personal reasons, he remained committed to Marxist ideals in his work and life. Wright's first book, a collection of short stories called *Uncle Tom's Children* (1938), created a minor stir with its portraits of black people struggling to create meaningful lives in a dehumanizing nation. His next book, the novel *Native Son* (1940), made Wright famous when it became a bestseller and was unexpectedly chosen as a Book of the Month Club selection.

Paul Green's path to collaborating with Richard Wright on the dramatic adaptation of *Native Son* was very different. A white, liberal graduate of the University of North Carolina and Cornell, Green (1894–1981) had in part made his reputation as a playwright with a series of plays such as the Pulitzer Prize-winning *In Abraham's Bosom* (1927), which showed a sympathetic understanding of the difficulties faced by black Americans. Green read the novel *Native Son* shortly after it was published, and immediately sent a telegram to Wright care of his publisher, expressing his admiration for the novel and his interest in adapting it for the stage. Wright, who was in Mexico at the time, wrote back enthusiastically to Green to say that he had received a number of such offers, but preferred Green's above all the others because of his admiration for Green's work, and particularly "the manner in which you handled the Negro character in your play, *Hymn to the Rising Son*" (a hard-hitting exposé of life on the chain gangs in the south). In fact, he added, although they had never met, the two men had a sort of previous relationship based in that play. Several years before, Wright had been employed as publicity director for the Federal Negro Theatre in Chicago, and had brought *Hymn to the Rising Sun* to the attention of the company. However, having begun rehearsals, the actors suddenly refused to perform the play on the grounds that the script was "indecent." "We want a play that will make the American public love us," they added, according to Wright.

When he had been unable to persuade them that the play's worth and authenticity transcended such concerns, Wright had resigned his job in protest. Since *Native Son* was also a work that avoided sentimentalizing the lives of black Americans, Green appeared to be the right person for the job.

Thus, the two men agreed to work together on the script. Accordingly, when writer-producer-director John Houseman (later to become famous as an actor and acting teacher), who was then working off-and-on with Orson Welles as the producer of the Mercury Theater Company, contacted Wright to ask about adapting the novel himself, Wright told Houseman that an agreement had already been made with Green. Houseman reluctantly admitted that Green seemed a good choice in many ways and, contenting himself with purchasing the production rights to the play for Mercury, sat down to await its completion.

Unfortunately, despite having been founded in mutual admiration, and despite highly cordial personal relations, the professional collaboration between Green and Wright was not to prove a happy one—at least as John Houseman describes it in his first volume of memoirs, *Run-Through*. (To be sure, Houseman's account may be somewhat coloured by his resentment at not having the opportunity to write the dramatization himself, but that there was indeed a disagreement seems beyond doubt.) At base, the disagreement seems to have had to do with Green's wish to see a play that downplayed the Marxist thought Wright had invested in his novel, and that instead showed the development of civic consciousness in Bigger, thus creating a more sympathetic character for white liberal-democratic audiences and thereby producing a work that pressed for social reform. By contrast, Wright was not only Marxist but existentialist in his thinking; accordingly, he saw Bigger's act of violence itself as a crucial, self-defining action in a world that until then had alienated his character from any sense of agency in forming his own identity. The tension between Green's and Wright's ideas was perhaps most neatly represented by the initial decision to change the first name of the lawyer Max from Boris, a Russian name (which, at that time, would evoke Bolshevism), to the more common American and Christian name (and Green's own name, at that), Paul. (Perhaps because he was stung by Houseman's criticism on this point, Green would later change the character's name again, to Edward.)

At any rate, as the older, better-established, and more self-confident writer, Green's ideas about how to adapt the play tended to drive the process, and the adaptation the two men at first offered Houseman was notably more sentimental than the novel. (For example, in one version of the end of the play, Green had Bigger snatching a pistol from a prison guard, but then returning it because of his dawning sense of personal responsibility and morality.) Houseman hated it. Wright admitted to being unhappy with Green's ending himself, but he told Houseman that he had decided to keep quiet because he was reluctant to have his disagreement with Green become public, fearing that such a quarrel would be gleefully seized upon by those wishing to see this rare collaboration between a white liberal and a black intellectual fail. However, Houseman was able to persuade Wright to work with him in Green's absence to return the play to a form more closely resembling what he had written in the novel.

Orson Welles, who had then just completed his first film, *Citizen Kane*, and was anxiously awaiting its release, returned from Hollywood to direct the play. The chief difficulty with adapting *Native Son* for the stage was that the main force of the novel lies in its representation of Bigger's interior thoughts. Perhaps even more than Dostoyevsky's *Crime and Punishment*, the novel manages to fuse the reader's mind with that of its angry and guilty protagonist. In this regard, Welles's production provided a brilliant theatrical substitution for those literary effects that could not be captured in dialogue. Backed by Hollywood money, Welles had his designers create a complicated set in which a series of different wagons, flying walls, and false ceilings, all set within a brick proscenium, were operated by a crew of thirty-seven stagehands. He also used lights and (as always in his theatrical productions) sound to great effect, all the elements combining to create an ever-changing, but always oppressive, claustrophobic and menacing atmosphere that was the expressionistic equivalent of Bigger Thomas's desperate state of mind. The production was greeted with great critical acclaim and, after over 100 performances on Broadway, went on tour for another year.

For his part, though he admired Welles's direction, Green was ambivalent about the production's success. In fact, he had at first been quite angry to find that some of his work had been discarded, and had considered taking legal action against Houseman and Welles; but, since Wright was clearly on their side, he relented. "After all," he wrote in his diary, it was "his [Wright's] novel, his characters." Evidently, Green meant this, for, although he later had full control over the published script, Green made only one really significant change. He replaced the closing image, which had been created by Welles—Bigger with arms outstretched, grasping the bars of his cell in an image of crucifixion—with an ending that is arguably even closer to Wright's vision than the produced version: Bigger walking alone to his execution. Indeed, even though Green outlived Richard Wright by more than twenty years, when the play was remounted in 1978 (for a production at the theatre named after Green at the University of North Carolina), Green only slightly revised the script, continuing for the most part to cleave closely to the version that the Mercury Theater had presented in 1941 and that Wright himself had approved. It is this final version which is published here.

[C.S.W.]

PAUL GREEN AND RICHARD WRIGHT

Native Son: The Biography of a Young American[1]

A play in eleven scenes

From the novel by Richard Wright

CAST

BIGGER THOMAS, a Negro youth about twenty
    or twenty-one years old.
HANNAH THOMAS, his mother, fifty five.
VERA THOMAS, his sister, sixteen.
BUDDY THOMAS, his brother, twelve.
JACK HENSON ⎤ cronies of
GUS MITCHELL ⎟ Bigger and
"G.H." RANKIN ⎦ about his age.
ERNIE JONES, a café and night club owner.
HENRY G. DALTON, a capitalist, about fifty-five.
ELLEN DALTON, his wife, about fifty.
MARY DALTON, their daughter, twenty-two or
    twenty-three.
PEGGY MACAULIFE, the Dalton cook and maid,
    forty.
JEFF BRITTEN, a private detective and local
    politician, forty-five.
JAN ERLONE, a labour leader, twenty-eight.
JED NORRIS, a newspaper man, forty.
CLARA MEARS, Bigger's girlfriend, twenty.
MISS EMMET, a social worker, thirty-two.
DAVID A. BUCKLEY, District Attorney, forty.

EDWARD MAX, an elderly lawyer.
REVEREND HAMMOND, a fundamentalist
    preacher, fifty.
JUDGE ALVIN C. HANLEY
COURT STENOGRAPHER
REPORTERS, GUARDS

SCENES

   I.   The Thomas one-room apartment, an
      early mid-winter morning.
  II.   A street in front of Ernie's Kitchen
      Shack, later the same day.
 III.   The Dalton breakfast room, a few hours
      later.
 IV.   Mary Dalton's bedroom, late the same
      night.
  V.   The Dalton breakfast room, the
      following morning.
 VI.   The kitchenette apartment of Clara
      Mears, evening of the same day.
VII.   The basement of the Dalton home, the
      next afternoon.
VIII.   A room in a ruined apartment house,
      night, a day later.
 IX.   A hearing room in the City Court-
      house, some days later.
  X.   The Courtroom, a week later.
 XI.   The death cell, some days later.

TIME: 1939–1940
PLACE: The Black Belt of Chicago mainly

---

[1] *Native Son* was first presented as a Mercury Production by Orson Welles and John Houseman at the St. James Theater, New York City, March 24, 1941. It was directed by Welles, with Canada Lee in the role of the confused and erring Bigger Thomas. This revised version of the drama was produced by the Carolina Playmakers for the dedication of the Paul Green Theatre at the University of North Carolina, Chapel Hill, N.C., September 29, 1978.

SCENE ONE

*In the darkness of the theatre, a strident alarm clock
begins ringing. It continues a while and then dies out as
the curtain rises on a small poverty-stricken room in an
old apartment house in the crowded Black Belt of
Chicago's southside. A door at the Right leads into the
hallway, and at the Right Centre is a pallet of quilts
upon which two of the Thomas family,* BIGGER *and*
BUDDY, *sleep.*[2] *Farther back and at the Right is a rusty
iron bed upon which* VERA *and* HANNAH *sleep, and
at the Centre Rear is a small dresser with a dull and
splotched mirror. At the Left Rear, screened from view
by a cheap chintz curtain, is a corner nook with a gas
stove, a sink, and shelves for groceries. A drop leaf table,
covered with an oilcloth, is against the wall at the Left
Front. There are a couple of chairs, a box and a chest
about the room. The plastered walls are cracked and
show the lathing here and there. A few crayon likenesses
of dead relatives are on the wall —* BIGGER'S *father,
his grandfather and grandmother. And in clear
dominance above the one bed at the Right Rear is a
large coloured lithograph of Jesus Christ hanging on the
Cross, with the motto — "I am the Resurrection and
the Life." A flower pot on the sill of the window at the
Left Centre with a single red geranium is the room's one
pretense to beauty. As the curtain rises the family is busy
getting dressed and preparing breakfast. The muffled
form of* BIGGER THOMAS *lies bundled under a quilt
on the pallet. Far away in the distance the chimes of a
great clock are heard ringing.*

HANNAH: (*The middle-aged careworn mother who is
busy at the stove and still wearing her flannel
nightgown.*) You children hurry up. That old clock
done struck the half-past. Hear me, Vera?

VERA: Yes, Ma. (VERA *is a slender brown-skinned girl
of sixteen, dressed in a pink cotton nightgown.*) 5

HANNAH: And you too, Buddy. I got a big washing
on my hands today.

(BUDDY, *a dark sober little fellow of twelve, is
standing by the stove buttoning his shirt with one hand
and warming the other at the gas flame. He is
shivering from the morning chill.*)

---

2 *pallet*] straw bed.

BUDDY: Yessum.

HANNAH: And, Vera, you got to get to that sewing 10
class. (BUDDY *sneezes.*) Yes, look at that boy, caught
cold again sleeping on that old floor. Told you
better sleep with me and Vera at the bed foot.
(HANNAH *is now fastening her skirt which she has
pulled on over her nightgown.*) Turn your head, son, 15
so we can get our clothes on. (*Silently* BUDDY *turns
and looks toward the pallet where* BIGGER *lies,
buttoning his shirt the while. The sleeping* BIGGER
*turns over, muttering under his quilt, and stuffs a
pillow against his head.*) 20

VERA: Ma wants you to get up too, Bigger. Somebody'll stumble over you. (*She pulls her dress over
her head and slips her cotton nightgown off underneath it.* HANNAH *looks toward the pallet and sighs.*)

HANNAH: Get the milk from the hall, Buddy. 25

BUDDY: Yessum. (*He quickly pulls on his little old coat,
his lips blubbering from the cold.* HANNAH *pushes the
table out from the wall and begins setting a few dishes
on it.* BUDDY *goes out as* HANNAH *calls after him.*)

HANNAH: Take the empty bottle. Every time I got 30
to tell you. (*He turns back, picks up a bottle by the
door and disappears.*) And, Vera, spread up the bed.
(*She begins singing her shrill morning song as she
works.*)

Life is like a mountain railroad 35
With an engineer that's brave —
We must make the run successful
From the cradle to the grave.[3]

BIGGER: (*Muttering from his pallet.*) How the hell can
a man sleep with all this racket? 40

VERA: (*A little testily.*) Who'd want to sleep when the
rest of us have to get out and work so hard?

BIGGER: (*Growling.*) Yeah, start right in soon's I git
my eyes open! (*He covers his head with the quilt
again.*) 45

HANNAH: Let him alone, Vera.

VERA: He ought to be up looking for a job. It's the
truth, Ma.

HANNAH: Well, he's got his application down at the
relief station. 50

---

3 Life … grave] "Life is Like a Mountain Railroad," an old
folk song by Charles D. Tillman and Eliza R. Snow, had
been adapted into a Baptist hymn by M.E. Abbey.

VERA: But he ought to get out — hunt for work — maybe ask that truck man to take him back, and we'd have something for Christmas!

BIGGER: (*Sitting suddenly up.*) And that white man sassing at me? No, sir. (BIGGER *is a dark muscular young fellow of some twenty or twenty-one with deep-set eyes and sensitive heavy face. He is dressed in rumpled trousers, shirt and socks.*)

VERA: Thought it was you sassing at him?

BIGGER: You go to — (*Muttering darkly.*) They don't want no niggers driving trucks down to Florida —

HANNAH: Better get up, son.

BIGGER: Might as well — tongues clanging like fire bells. (HANNAH *goes out with her towel and is heard humming her song offstage.* BIGGER *rises and stands over his shoes, kicks one into place with his foot, and then rams his left foot down halfway into it. He stomps to get the shoe on.*) These old shoes wet from that snow four days ago. I was looking for a job then.

VERA: (*Who is now putting things on the table.*) Well, knocking the house down won't dry 'em. Every morning you get up like something mad at the world! (BIGGER *stomps his right foot to get the other shoe on.* BUDDY *enters at the Right with a bottle of milk.*)

BUDDY: (*Coming up to the table and helping* VERA.) Goody, peaches to go with them cornflakes.

VERA: And we better go slow on 'em, too. That relief box got to last till Saturday. (BUDDY *pours the milk.* BIGGER *lights a cigarette and stands smoking and staring before him.* HANNAH *returns, still singing her song.*)

HANNAH: Watch the curves, the fills, the tunnels,
Never falter, never fail.
Keep your hand upon the throttle
And your eyes upon the rail.[4]

(*She hands her towel to* VERA, *who takes it and goes out at the Right.* BUDDY *strains at the can of peaches with a large pocket knife.*)

Gimme that knife. And get away from this table until you done washed yourself. Go on. Vera's got

the towel. (BUDDY *shies away and goes out.* HANNAH *appraises the knife an instant in her hand.*) Why any human being wants to carry around a knife as big as this, I don't see. Why you give it to him, Bigger?

BIGGER: (*As he reaches out and grabs the knife.*) I didn't *give* it to him. He just wanted to tote it a little bit. (HANNAH *opens the can with a can opener.* BIGGER *sits bent over in a chair smoking and idly turning the pages of a movie magazine spread on the floor before him. She looks over at him.*)

HANNAH: Bigger, try for one time to roll that pallet up. No telling when Miss Emmet might come by.

BIGGER: (*Still lazily reading.*) That old caseworker ain't studying 'bout us.

HANNAH: She got us on relief — and kept us from starving. (VERA *comes in again.* BIGGER *rises and rushes out at the Right, bumping into somebody in the hall. A woman's high-pitched voice fills the air with a whorl of words.*)

VOICE: Heigh — you! Yeh, look at you, just look at you, Bigger Thomas, a-tromping and a-scrounging. I'm ahead of you and you knows it! Git back in line and wait your turn, boy. (BIGGER *comes back and stands angrily in the door.*)

VERA: (*With a biting little laugh.*) Reckon Sister Temple told him his manners.

BIGGER: (*Wrathfully.*) All right now, and what's so funny about that old woman with the toilet trots? (BUDDY *enters.*)

BUDDY: Here's the towel, Bigger. (BIGGER *grabs the towel, balls it up and hurls it across the room, then sits down an resumes his magazine.* VERA *and* BUDDY *help their mother at the table, passing in and out of the nook with a few dishes and food.*)

VERA: (*Coming from the stove.*) And that's another thing he ain't got — no respect.

HANNAH: Sister Temple lives with her Lord.

BIGGER: And her Epsom Salts! Eats it like oatmeal. Jack says so.

VERA: Yeh, and that Jack's breaking his grandma's heart like you're breaking Ma's.

BIGGER: I wish you'd stop being a little snot, dirting up where you don't belong.

HANNAH: (*Opening a box of cornflakes.*) That's no way to speak to your own sister, son, and her

---

4 Watch … rail] the second half of the first verse of "Life is Like a Mountain Railroad."

getting to be a young lady now. (BIGGER *flaps his magazine over irritatedly.*)

VERA: If you was the sort of man Ma always hoped you'd be, you'd not have to wait for your turn to go to the bathroom. You'd be up early and get there first. But no — you'd rather hang around Ernie's place with Jack and that low-life gang and let us live on relief.[5]

HANNAH: Hush, Vera.

BIGGER: (*Muttering.*) Relief don't say more'n forty people got to use the same toilet every morning — lining up like women to see Clark Gable.[6] (*With sudden viciousness as he flings out his arms.*) It's the way the damned white folks built these rat nests!

VERA: Now don't start cussing the white folks again.

HANNAH: They what keep us alive right this minute. (*He gets up, picks up the towel and strides into the hall.* HANNAH *wags her head dolefully.*) Now here we go again. Said to myself last night we was gonna quit fussing at him. Don't do no good.

VERA: How can we help it, Ma, and seem like some devil growing in him all the time. (*Her voice filled with angry earnestness.*) He gets more like a stranger every day. And there's that Clara woman he runs with. Here I try to make myself respectable and be somebody. He ain't never got a *smile* for nobody.

HANNAH: (*Calling contritely.*) Come on back, son. Le's try to eat in peace, Vera.

BUDDY: (*Piping up.*) Bigger says we ain't got nothing to smile about, says that's what's wrong with the niggers — always smiling, and nothing to smile about. (*He leans over, smells the peaches and wrinkles his nose in delight.*)

HANNAH: Shut yo' mouth, boy.

BUDDY: That's what he say —

HANNAH: Yeh, and he say a lot he hadn't ought to. If the white folks ever hear him talkin' 'gainst them —

VERA: And some these days they're gonna hear him. Mark my words, Ma. Some of these days he's going to sit down and cry, and he'll wish he'd made something of himself instead of just a tramp. But

it'll be too late then. (BIGGER *appears in the doorway.*)

HANNAH: Bigger needs God in him, that's what. I've prayed, and Reverend Hammond's put up special prayers for him. Yeh, God's what he needs, po' boy.

BIGGER: God! (*Flinging out a gesture, his voice rising mockingly.*) Yeh, you got him hanging on the wall there — the white folks' God! (*Mockingly.*) "I am the Resurrection and the Life."[7]

HANNAH: (*With a touch of piteousness as she looks fervently at the picture on the wall.*) Your pa lived by it — he believed in that —

BIGGER: But that white mob back in Mississippi didn't believe in it. (*Half-chanting.*) "They hung his head on the thorny cross, the red blood trickled down."

HANNAH: Bigger, stop that!

VERA: (*Quickly.*) Come on, let's eat breakfast.

BUDDY: (*Uncertainly.*) Yeh, le's eat! (*They sit to the table.*)

HANNAH: Bow your heads. (*Suddenly there comes a thin, dry rattling sound in the wall at the Rear. They all sit listening an instant.* BUDDY *calls out.*)

BUDDY: Listen! That rat again — I hear him!

BIGGER: Yeah, that's old man Dalton all right. (*Hacking a hunk of bread off from the loaf and buttering it.*) If that old rat stick his head out this time, I'm gonna scrush it for him. (*The noise in the wall is heard still again.*)

BUDDY: (*Whispering.*) That's him, aw right.

HANNAH: Bow your heads, children. (BUDDY *and* VERA *bow their heads.* BIGGER *sits munching his bread and staring moodily before him.* HANNAH'S *words rise in deep humility.*) Our Father in Heaven, we thank thee for this food you have prepared for the nourishment of our humble bodies. We thank thee for the many blessings of thy loving grace and mercy. Bless this home, this food and these children you gave me. Help me to raise them right. And thine be the power and the glory forever and ever — Amen. (*They all begin eating. Suddenly* BIGGER *springs out of his chair with a shout.*)

BIGGER: There he go! (*He lunges across the room, flings himself over the bed and begins jabbing in the corner*

---

[5] relief] welfare.

[6] Clark Gable] a very popular Hollywood star from the 1930s through the 1950s.

---

[7] I am … Life] John 11:25.

with his foot. Then springing back he seizes an old baseball bat from the floor.)

BUDDY: (*As* VERA *and* HANNAH *jump to their feet.*) Where is he? Where is he?

BIGGER: Stop up his hole! He's our meat this time. (BUDDY *lunges behind the chest and strikes a shattering blow against the floor. There is a scramble as* BUDDY *rushes across the room and peers under the bed.* BIGGER *creeps forward, his whole body tensely alive.*)

BUDDY: (*Pointing.*) Yonder — yonder —

BIGGER: (*Bending down.*) Jesus, look at them teeth! (*He grabs the end of the bed with one hand and swings it around.*) He's behind that box now. (*His voice is charged with a harsh intensity.*)

VERA: (*Half-weeping.*) Let him go, Bigger. Let him go.

HANNAH: (*Piteously.*) Unstop the hole, let him out.

BUDDY: Gimme that skillet, quick! (BUDDY *rushes over to the alcove and hands him the skillet.* BIGGER *takes aim and hurls it into the corner.*)

BUDDY: (*Excitedly.*) You hit him, you hit him!

(*A smallish young white woman, carrying a black portfolio in her hands, stands in the doorway. She looks inquiringly and then half-frightenedly at the scene before her. Now* BIGGER *creeps toward the kitchen nook.* HANNAH *and* VERA *have their arms about each other, watching him breathlessly.* BIGGER *stands waiting, poised, his hand raised.*)

BIGGER: (*His feet weaving to the Right and Left.*) Yeah, there you sit on your hind legs and gnashing them tushes at me — I'm gonna beat your brains out — Wheeooh![8] (*With a yell he jumps forward and strikes with flailing, lightning blows along the curtain edge on the floor.*)

HANNAH: Bigger, Bigger!

BIGGER: (*Lifting the rat up and holding it by the tail, a murmuring chant running from his lips.*) I got you, old man Dalton, got you this time. I done told you yo' time would come — I put out your light. You dead now — dead, dead, dead, dead —

VERA: Stop him, Ma! (*The woman in the door now stands shaken and weakly leaning against the lintel.* VERA *sees her.*) Look, Ma!

HANNAH: (*Moaning.*) Mercy sake, Bigger. Here's Miss Emmet.

BIGGER: Try to run now — try to bite me — just try it, you fat, slimy, greedy bastard! (*His words gradually die out as he looks up and sees* MISS EMMET. *She comes on into the room.*)

HANNAH: Miss Emmet! — Bigger, take that thing out of here right now!

MISS EMMET: I came a little early — before you got to work. (*She is a kindly, efficient, young woman, serious-faced and sincere.*)

BUDDY: We just killed a rat. Yessum. (*With a touch of boyish pride.*) Bigger done it. Ain't he a big one?

BIGGER: That scutter could cut your throat — the biggest one we ever killed.[9] (*Holding the rat up.*) See him Miss Emmet?

MISS EMMET: Yes, I see it. (*Drawing back.*) Better throw it away.

BIGGER: (*Feeling him.*) See how fat he is — feeding on garbage. They get more to eat than we do. Yeh, old Dalton, you're going to the incinerator and there ain't no coming back. (*He shakes the rat at* VERA *and she squeals.*)

MISS EMMET: (*Quietly.*) Why do you call it Dalton, Bigger?

BIGGER: Just call 'em that.

BUDDY: Yessum — we calls all the rats "Old Man Dalton" — the big millionaire what owns all the houses round here. Gimme heah, Bigger.

BIGGER: (*Now beginning to grow silent again, the excitement dying in him.*) Okay. (*He hands the rat to* BUDDY *who takes it proudly and goes out.* BIGGER *sits down on the chest, finishing a hunk of bread.*)

HANNAH: I said to the boys, "You might leastwise say '*Mister* Dalton.'" (*A small meek smile passes around* MISS EMMET'S *lips.*)

MISS EMMET: Yes, considering Mr. Dalton's kindness to the people of your race.

HANNAH: Sit down, ma'am. (MISS EMMET *sits down and opens her portfolio.*)

---

8 tushes] (slang) teeth, particularly canine teeth (from "tusks").

9 scutter] (slang) a creature that scuttles or scurries; a rat.

BIGGER: (*Softly.*) Kindness? 300

MISS EMMET: Yes, kindness. Think of all he does for your race — his gift of millions of dollars to coloured schools, and then that new recreation hall with the ping-pong tables —

BIGGER: Ping-pong tables. What good are they to a 305 man that's burning down? (*Mockingly.*) Yes, ma'am.

HANNAH: (*Watching* MISS EMMET *eagerly, holding her cup of coffee in her hand.*) Don't mind him, ma'am. I pray the Lord you got some good news for us, ma'am. 310

MISS EMMET: (*Now all business-like.*) I hope so.

HANNAH: Just a final question or two, Bigger, about your application. As head of the house — (*She takes out a double-leaved form sheet and unstops her fountain pen.*) 315

BIGGER: (*With a little laugh.*) We ain't got nothin' but this one room, and there ain't no head to it.

MISS EMMET: But as soon as we place you in a job, Bigger, you'll feel differently.

BIGGER: (*Fumbling with the movie magazine.*) What 320 kind of job?

MISS EMMET: Mr. Dalton is interested in placing his jobless tenants.

HANNAH: (*Happily.*) Hear that, Bigger?

BIGGER: (*With the faintest touch of a snicker.*) Yessum. 325 He wants to be sure we're able to pay the rent. (HANNAH *sets her coffee cup down and wipes her hands on her apron.* BUDDY *reappears and goes back to his bowl of cornflakes.*)

MISS EMMET: (*As she looks at her wristwatch.*) There's 330 an opening with Mr. Dalton's family itself — the job of chauffeur. You might get that place. According to the record here, you're a first-rate driver.

BUDDY: He can sure drive. And he can fix cars too. 335 I can tell you that! (*Snapping his fingers.*) She's gone from here. (*He proudly grasps an imaginary steering wheel and "drives."*) Hot dog!

MISS EMMET: But we must supply Mr. Dalton with *all* the facts. (*Sympathetically.*) Here under previ- 340 ous history you failed to mention that matter of the reform school, Bigger. (*Reading from her report.*) Three months term, ending June 15th, 1939. Metropolitan Home for the Detention of Juvenile Delinquents — Theft — Taking of three auto- 345

mobile tires from a colored garage — Is that right?[10]

BIGGER: (*With a faint touch of mockery.*) Yessum, that must be about right.

MISS EMMET: And you haven't had any other trouble 350 since, Bigger?

HANNAH: No'm. (VERA *and* BUDDY *say "No'm" too.*)

BIGGER: No'm.

MISS EMMET: (*Holding her fountain pen.*) Now please sign there. 355

BIGGER: (*With apparent reluctance as he takes the pen.*) I done signed that paper once.

MISS EMMET: Yes, but this is added material and we must follow the Washington rules.

BIGGER: Sure, if the big man in Washington say so. 360 He the boss. (*With a flourish in the air, he writes his name.*)

MISS EMMET: (*Taking the blank, breathing on it, and then giving it a little drying wave in the air.*) I'll send Mr. Dalton a confidential report recommend- 365 ing you, Bigger. In fact, I'll *take* it to him right away.

HANNAH: (*Joy breaking over her face.*) God bless you, ma'am. Bigger gonna have a good job — (*Touching her hands together evangelically.*) Bless the Lord, 370 bless the Lord. Bigger will make a new start — From now on he will, ma'am. Won't you, son? (BIGGER *is silent.*)

BUDDY: (*With fervent admiration.*) You gonna drive Mr. Dalton's big car, Bigger. (*Suddenly putting his* 375 *hands on the steering wheel of his imaginary car and driving it around the room.*) Swoos-s-sh! Look out, everybody — old cannonball coming round the curve. (*He bumps into* MISS EMMET *who stands up with a gentle little laugh.*) 380

HANNAH: Look out, boy, you 'bout to run over the lady!

BIGGER: (*Flinging up his hand and grinning as he adopts the attitude of a traffic cop, at the same time blowing a sharp whistle through his teeth.*) Hey, what 385 you mean running through that red light? Pull up heah and lemme see your license, boy. (*He scuffs* BUDDY'S *hair a bit in spontaneous friendliness. Then*

---

10 colored garage] i.e., a garage run by and for persons of color.

his face grows heavy again.) But, pshaw, I ain't gonna get that job. 390

MISS EMMET: Now good-bye, Mrs. Thomas. Good-bye, Bigger. You'll hear as soon as I contact Mr. Dalton. Keep your head up.

HANNAH: (*Following her to the door.*) Bless you, ma'am, bless you — whole soul and body! (*She turns happily about the room.*) And my prayers are answered. I knowed they'd be. (*She turns to* VERA *and hugs her, then begins piling the household wash rapidly in a sheet.*) 395

VERA: (*Coming by* BIGGER *and stopping — with deep earnestness.*) Maybe this is the real break. We are all so glad, Bigger. And we can quit living in one room like pigs. 400

BIGGER: Aw, cut it out.

VERA: Good-bye, Ma. (*She goes by her mother, gives her a little pecking kiss and then turning gives* BIGGER'S *arm an affectionate squeeze.*) And you'll help me pay for my domestic science, won't you?[11] 405

HANNAH: Sure he will.

VERA: Come on, Buddy, time you was out selling your papers. (*Jubilantly.*) This is a big day for all of us. 410

HANNAH: (*Jubilantly also.*) Ain't it the truth. Thank the Lord for the bountiful blessings of this day. (*She looks over to the picture of the religious figure.*) Now let's all hurry. (BIGGER *is now sitting at the table idly marking across the movie magazine with a pencil.*) 415

BUDDY: (*Putting on his overcoat and cap.*) 'Bye, Ma. (*Standing in front of* BIGGER.) You lemme ride in that Cadillac sometime? 420

BIGGER: (*Spreading out an imaginary document in front of him and beginning to write gravely.*) Have to examine the records of the — er — Detention Home first. How the hell I know what you been doing on the sly? 425

BUDDY: (*His face crinkling into a smile.*) Bigger, you sure a case. Look, Ma, Bigger's smiling.

BIGGER: Hell, I ain't smiling none. (BUDDY *scampers out after* VERA.) 430

HANNAH: (*Laying a coin on the table by him.*) Here, son, take this fifty cents. Run down there to the corner and get me two bars of that hard soap, a bottle of bluing, a box of starch, and a can of Red Devil lye, and make a bee-line back to the basement.[12] Sister Temple and me will be needing it for the work. (BIGGER *continues to scrawl with his pencil.*) Hear me? 435

BIGGER: Yeh.

HANNAH: (*Turning to him, her voice affectionate and serious.*) Bigger, that good white lady is right. From now on, you're the real head of the house. She gonna get you that job. I ain't gonna be with you always, trying to make a home for you children. And Vera and Buddy has got to have protection. Hear me, son? (*She lifts the bundled sheet of clothes over her shoulder.*) 440

BIGGER: Uhm —

HANNAH: I'll be too old to work soon. (*Laying a hand gently on his shoulder.*) And some day yet you'll believe like me — my boy — believe in God. In His protection I'm never afraid — never afraid. (*She indicates the religious calendar on the wall, then bends over, touches him lightly on the hair with her lips and goes silently and suddenly out. For an instant he sits stock still. His hand goes up in the air as if to feel the top of his head and then comes down on the table in a clenched fist. He looks upward at the picture of Christ on the wall. He begins to study it closely, and gradually a wry twisting smile slides around his lips.*) 450 455 460

BIGGER: (*Reading.*) "I am the Resurrection and the Life." — Uhm — (*He gets sharply up and puts on his old leather coat and cap. The chimes begin to ring again. He stands listening.*) They ringing your bells, Lord, high in the white man's tower! (*As if irritated by some inner thought, he slaps the coin down on the table.*) Heads I get your stuff, Ma, tails I don't. (*Distractedly.*) Heads — damn! (*He gives a little laugh, shakes his shoulders and spits angrily. A signal whistle comes up from outside the window at the Left. It is repeated. He stands in indecision a moment and then goes over and looks out. Finally he raises his hand in a sort of fascist salute and waves it across the pane.*) Hey, Jack. Yeh — yeh — I'll meet you at Ernie's. (*He turns back toward the bed, pulls forth a wooden* 465 470 475

---

11 domestic science] courses in home economics.

12 bluing] laundry whitener.

packing box and unlocks it. He takes out a pistol and looks at it and then up.) This here's what you didn't have, Lord — but I got it! (*He makes a movie quick-draw, then crams the pistol into his coat.* HANNAH *comes in.*)   480

HANNAH: (*To herself.*) Seem like my mind failing away. Forgot my washboard again. (*Queryingly.*) What you up to, boy? (*Without answering,* BIGGER *kicks the box back under the bed and goes quickly out. Something in his actions disturbs* HANNAH. *She gazes worriedly after him and then hurries to the door and calls.*) Bigger! (*More loudly.*) Bigger! (*But there is no answer. She hurries into the hall, calling.*) Come back here, boy! (*The chimes continue to ring. The scene fades out.*)   490

SCENE II

The chimes die away as the scene opens on a street and sidewalk in front of Ernie's Kitchen Shack, somewhere on Indiana Avenue near 47ᵗʰ Street. At the Right Front the gullet of a narrow alleyway leads back into the shadows. And at the mouth of the alleyway sits a garbage can, looking like a squat molar in its maw, across which is a staring label saying, "Keep Our City Clean." The entrance to Ernie's place of business is through a door in the Centre with windows on either side. Adjoining the "shack" is an empty building with a boarded-up window on which are posters announcing in large letters the candidacy of two men for the office of District Attorney for Cook County. One of the men depicted, David A. Buckley, is middle-aged, of imposing bearing, and declared to be "The Party's Choice for District Attorney." The other, Edward Max, is somewhat elderly, less commanding, and announced to be "The People's Choice." At the Left Front is a hydrant and near it a steel lamppost topped above with the usual globular glass. The sounds of a busy thoroughfare are heard Off at the Left — a streetcar clanging, automobile horns, now and then a tremulous roar of a heavy truck, and once or twice the siren of a police car or ambulance — a great wash of droning sound. BIGGER *enters. He stares at the posters and reads aloud to himself.*

BIGGER: "David Buckley — for District Attorney. The law is your protector." You old sonofabitch, I

bet you make a million a year already in graft. If I was in your shoes for just one day, I'd never have to worry again. (*He spits at the poster.*) Get elected   5
and no telling how much you'll steal. (*He turns toward the poster of* MAX.) And you, old crumb, they say, are a communist! — (*Mockingly.*) "The people's friend!" Wants us all to become Reds! (JACK *enters. He is a rather short, pudgy, young*   10
Negro, alert and quick-moving.)

JACK: Hiya, Bigger!

BIGGER: Hiya, Jack. (*Gesturing to the posters.*) Which of them bastards you gonna vote for?

JACK: (*In sudden and hilarious ridicule.*) Vote, you say!   15
Vote! — for the right price. (*He bows about him in laughter, slapping his thighs.*) All politicians in Chicago are crooks, you know that. That's the way white folks run things, ain't it? And we niggers got no say-so.   20

BIGGER: Yeh. (*Indulgently.*) And if you and me run things, we'd steal all we could too, wouldn't we?

JACK: Sho' God would! Last 'lection I voted twice — five bucks a crack. I was only nineteen. (*Imitatingly.*) "You twenty-one, boy?" "Oh, yessuh,   25
twenty-one my last birthday — twenty-one."[13] "Here you are." (*Pantomimically he reaches to take the money. They both laugh.*)

BIGGER: (*Looking off.*) Time G.H. was here.

JACK: He'll be here soon. Everything's jake.   30

BIGGER: Okay.

JACK: (*Softly.*) Passed old Blum's pawnshop while ago — old devil setting in there like a crab.

BIGGER: (*Looking carefully about him.*) Yeh, I seen him. Back to the door — bent over by the cash   35
register working in his books. How much you think we get?

JACK: Hundred-fifty bucks anyhow. It's a cinch.[14]

BIGGER: Cinch — and a white man. (*Shaking his head.*) Hope you're right.   40

JACK: Getting up into the big time, boy. Not like — (*With a chuckle.*) stealing tires from a nigger garage. (*He laughs.*)

---

13 twenty-one] The voting age in the United States was twenty-one until it was lowered to eighteen by constitutional amendment XXVI in 1971.

14 a cinch] (slang) an easy task.

BIGGER: (*Pulling his dollar watch from his pocket.*) Uhm — twenty minutes till. Gimme a cigarette, Jack. I done smoked out. (JACK *pulls out a pack of cigarettes and gives* BIGGER *one.*)

JACK: (*Peering at him narrowly.*) And ain't no gun in it.

BIGGER: Who said a gun? Gus say it?

JACK: Somebody get killed — then the hot seat. (*Whistling.*) Jesus! No! (BIGGER *stares at him.*)

BIGGER: That Gus Mitchell — old tongue wags at both ends. He keep mo' out of trouble just wagging one end. (*He lights his cigarette and holds the match for* JACK.)

JACK: Gus got mighty sharp eyes, though. (*After a few draws.*) Gosh, you shake like an old woman. And what your hands doing sweating so?

BIGGER: (*Throwing down the match.*) Hell, light it yourself.

(JACK *lights up.* CLARA MEARS, *an attractive, young Negro girl, comes in at the Right, carrying a package under one arm. She smiles brightly over at* BIGGER *and stops.*)

CLARA: Hi, Bigger.

JACK: Hi, Clara.

BIGGER: (*Nonchalantly.*) Hi, Clara.

CLARA: (*To* BIGGER.) Thought I'd find you here.

BIGGER: Smart girl —

CLARA: Missed you last night, honey.

BIGGER: I was busy. (*She puts out a hand and touches him affectionately on the arm.*)

CLARA: Gonna see you tonight?

BIGGER: Maybe.

JACK: (*Laughing.*) Maybe.

CLARA: The Rhinelanders got a house full of company for Christmas — but I'll get off. Maybe we'll go to a picture? (*Looking at her wristwatch and then up at the sun.*) Gee, I got to hurry. (*Giving* BIGGER'S *arm a farewell squeeze.*) It's a date.

BIGGER: (*Still nonchalantly.*) Okay. (*She gazes deep into his face and then hurries out at the Left.*)

JACK: Shucks, that gal loves the very ground you walk on.

BIGGER: It don't matter.

JACK: Uh? It better matter.

BIGGER: Love 'em and leave 'em.

JACK: Not Clara. (*They puff in silence a moment and then stare Off before them.* BIGGER *runs his fingers around inside his collar and twists his head.* JACK *looks at him.*) Kinder warm today — for December.

BIGGER: Yeh.

JACK: Be glad when summer comes and them sweet old watermelons start rolling up from the South.

BIGGER: (*Sharply.*) Summer or winter — all the same. (*He pulls out his watch again.*)

JACK: Yeh, all the same. Quit looking at that old dollar watch — time never pass. (*He chuckles.*)

BIGGER: What's so funny? (*He spits.*)

JACK: Gus say he don't want you in on the Blum job neither — too nervous, he say.

BIGGER: Lousy runt!

JACK: Say you too hair-trigger. Now keep your shirt on and quit that spitting. There he come.

(JACK *straightens up and stares Off as* GUS MITCHELL *comes cake-walking briskly into the scene. He is a small-sized Negro about* BIGGER'S *age and wears his cap turned round like a baseball catcher. As he enters, he cups his right hand to his mouth as though holding an imaginary telephone transmitter and his left to his ear as a receiver. He grins as he bows.*)

GUS: Hello — hello.

JACK: (*Responding quickly with his telephone pantomiming.*) Hello — Yes — uhm — old Gus boy —

GUS: Who's speaking?

JACK: Why — er — this is the President of the United States of America.

GUS: Oh, yes suh, Mr. President. What's on your mind?

JACK: I'm calling a cabinet meeting this afternoon at three o'clock — as Secretary of State you must be there!

BIGGER: (*Satirically.*) Hah-hah.

GUS: Well, now, Mr. President, I'm pretty busy. Bombs falling all over Europe. I'm thinking of sending that old Hitler another note.

JACK: And them Japs — they —

BIGGER: (*Pantomiming like the others.*) Hello, Mr. President. I just cut in from the sidelines and heard what you said. Better wait about that war business. The niggers is raising sand all over the country about no jobs! You better put them down first.

JACK: Oh, if it's about the niggers, Mr. Wilkie, we'll wait on the war!

BIGGER: Yes, suh. At a time like this, we Republicans and Democrats got to pull together! 125

GUS: Reckon we can do without you, Mr. Wilkie. (GUS *and* JACK *bow about in sudden and rich physical laughter, slapping their thighs, their knees easy and bent.* BIGGER *stares at them morosely.*) 130

JACK: Lawd, Lawd, Lawd —

GUS: I bet that's just how white folks talk.

JACK: Sho, it is —

(ERNIE *comes to the door at the Rear. He is a stoutish phlegmatic Negro of fifty or more.*)

ERNIE: 'Bout time to open up here, and how you 'spect me to have any customers and you all wallowing all over the pavement? 135

BIGGER: Go suck something, Ernie Jones!

ERNIE: (*Angrily.*) I don't want none of your back-talk, Bigger Thomas. Cut out the monkeyshines and move on! 140

BIGGER: Nine o'clock our zero hour — ten minutes and we go.

ERNIE: Ten minutes then 'fore I call a cop. (*He turns back into the shadow.*) You're up to devilment, I know you. (*He disappears.*) 145

BIGGER: (*Muttering.*) Sonofabitch! (*Turning toward* GUS *and staring at him with hard bright eyes.*) So you don't want Mr. Wilkie in on the deal — huh — meaning me?

GUS: Aw, I was just joking, Bigger. 150

BIGGER: You wanter live and keep doing well — so drop the joking. (*He pauses a moment, then with sudden anger.*) Where's G.H.? Goddammit, I'm ready for old Blum!

JACK: Christ, don't talk so loud. Ernie'll hear you. 155 (*They are silent for a moment.* BIGGER *tilts back his face and the sun shines full upon it.* JACK *stares up at the sky and sneezes twice.*)

GUS: That's a sign o' bad luck!

BIGGER: (*Yelling.*) Go to hell! 160

GUS: (*Doggedly.*) Grandma allus said so — double sneezes, evil seizes.

BIGGER: Superstition — you niggers — signs, wonders! Look up there — the white man's sign.

JACK: What? 165

BIGGER: That airplane — writing on the sky — like a little finger — (*They all three look up.*) So high up, looks like a little bird. (*Waving his hands.*) Sailing and looping and zooming — and that white smoke coming out of his tail — (*He walks restlessly about.*) 170

JACK: (*Reading — afar off.*) "Use Speed Gasoline" —

BIGGER: (*Exultantly.*) Yeh, Speed. That's what them white boys got — speed!

GUS: (*Whispering.*) Daredevils. 175

BIGGER: Go on, boys, fly them planes, fly 'em to the end of the world, fly 'em smack into the sun! I'm with you. Goddamn! (*He stares up, the sunlight on his face.*)

GUS: (*Unable to let well enough alone, doffing his cap* 180 *in a mock bow to* BIGGER.) Yessuh! If you wasn't *black* and if you had some *money* and if they'd *let* you go to that *aviation* school, you might could be with 'em.

JACK: Yessuh. 185

BIGGER: (*Fiercely.*) Yeh, keep on, keep on now!

JACK: (*Flexing his hands as though holding onto controls, he makes the sound of an airplane motor.*) Thrr — hu — hu — hu — hu —

BIGGER: (*Raucously, half-singingly.*) Wish I had wings 190 for to fly now!

GUS: (*Satirically.*) Reverend Hammond say God's gonna give us *all* some wings — in the judgment day.

(BIGGER *joins* JACK *in the roar of the plane, primping* 195 *his lips.* GUS *also joins in, and for a moment the sound of the motor goes on uninterruptedly. They stretch out their arms like wings and go "flying" about.* G.H., *a darkish heavy-set young Negro, comes in at the Left. He lifts one hand in a mocking "Heil* 200 *Hitler" salute, holding his nose with the other.* BIGGER *sees him and barks out an order.*)

BIGGER: You pilot!

G.H.: (*Falling in with the game.*) Yessuh, Major!

BIGGER: Give her the stick and pull right over! (*He* 205 *bends over, squinting, as if peering down through glasses from a great height.*) Machine gunner, look at that crowd down there on Michigan Avenue doing their Christmas shopping. Give 'em some hot lead. Hah, hah, hah, peace on earth! (*Making* 210 *the rat-tat-tat of a machine gun.*) Rat-tat-tat-tat-tat-

tat, rat-tat-tat-tat-tat — Look at 'em fall! (*He speaks in a half singsong as he turns with growing excitement about him — exultantly.*) Now we gonna dive-bomb that Tribune Tower. (*He leads off with the zooming roar of an airplane throttle opened at full speed. The others join in.* BIGGER *cries out wildly.*) Turn 'em loose! — The bombs! The bombs! (*He makes a kicking motion downward with his foot, and then in a high whine depicts the passage of the bombs earthward. They all make the "boom" of the explosion together.*)

GUS: (*Bent over, staring down.*) Lawd, look at that smoke!

BIGGER: A direct hit, Sergeant. (*Loudly.*) Look at the fires — things flying through the air — houses — people — streetcars — hunks of sidewalk and pavements. Goddamn! Whoom — Tracer bullets. (*Yelling.*) Look out! There come the fighter planes! (*Frantically pulling his pistol.*) Cold steel! Watch the turn — Give 'em the hot lead. (*The three boys look at him and then spring back in fear, their playful spirit suddenly gone.*)

GUS: (*Pointing.*) Look, he's got a gun. I knowed it. (BIGGER *continues to aim about him. The others mumble in half fear.*)

BIGGER: (*Hunching out his shoulder and running at* GUS *who dodges him.*) Crash him! Crash him!

GUS: (*Throwing out his hands in fear.*) Put up that gun, fool!

JACK: Bigger!

BIGGER: (*Whirling and leveling the gun at* GUS.) Ride into 'em or I'll shoot your lights out. (*He gives a high wild laugh.*)

G.H.: Bigger, for Christ's sake! Somebody'll see you!

GUS: I told you he's crazy! Now look at him!

BIGGER: (*Advancing upon* GUS *with gun leveled.*) You sonofabitch, don't you call me crazy —

GUS: (*Backing away toward the other two boys, who stare at him silently.*) He's yellow. He's scared to rob a white man, that how come he brung that gun. (*He moves behind* JACK.) I told you to leave him out of it. (BIGGER *jams his gun back into his blouse and suddenly darts out his hand, seizes* GUS *by the collar, and bangs his head against the wall.*)

BIGGER: (*His face working in violent rage, as he pulls his knife again.*) I don't need no gun. Yellow, huh?

(*Pushing the knife against* GUS'S *stomach.*) Take it back.

JACK: That ain't no way to play, Bigger.

BIGGER: Who the hell said I was playing?

GUS: Please, Bigger. I was just joking. Oh, you hurt me.

BIGGER: (*His lips snarled back over his teeth.*) Want me to cut your belly button out?

G.H.: Aw, leave him alone, Bigger.

BIGGER: Put your hands up. Way up! (GUS *swallows and stretches his hands high along the wall. He stares out with wide frightened eyes, and sweat begins to trickle down his temples. His lips hang open and loose.*) Shut them liver lips.

GUS: (*In a tense whisper.*) Bigger!

BIGGER: (*Pressing the point of the knife deeper against his belly.*) Take it back. Say, "I'm a lying sonofabitch."

GUS: (*With a moan.*) Quit!

BIGGER: Say it, say it.

G.H.: (*Staring horrified at him.*) For Christ's sake, Bigger!

BIGGER: Take it back. Say it. (GUS *begins to slump down along the wall.* BIGGER *jabs him slightly, and he straightens up quickly with a howl.*) Say "I'm a lying sonofabitch."

GUS: I'm — I'm a lying sonofabitch. (*His arm falls down and his head slumps forward.* BIGGER *releases him.*)

BIGGER: Next time you whimper on me I won't ease up — I'll kill you. (*Hissing.*) You ain't gonna be in on this robbing old Blum. I'll take your share of the haul. Now scat! (*He starts again at* GUS, *who gazes wildly around him a moment and then flies out of the scene at the Right. For a while they are all silent. The noise of the city rolls in across the scene.*) Somebody say something, Goddamit!

JACK: (*Watching him.*) Don't cuss at us.

G.H.: (*Angrily.*) Lay off! (*Somewhere from a tower a clock booms. They listen, stock still.*)

JACK: All right, zero hour.

BIGGER: I ain't going nowhere — now.

G.H.: Hundred fifty bucks waiting in that cash drawer. (*They eye him in cold silence.*) Goddamit, you scared! You scared all along.

JACK: We was gonna walk in quiet — put a piece of little hard stick against old Blum's back — "Hand over your money," we say — (*He pulls a sort of wooden peg from his pocket.*) and then back out. 305 Now, you bring along a gun and a knife — maybe kill somebody and put us in the 'lectric chair. (*Laughing harshly.*) You scared!

G.H.: You done ruint everything.

JACK: Maybe that's what you want. 310

BIGGER: You go to hell! (ERNIE *comes to the door.*)

ERNIE: For the last time, Bigger Thomas, get away from here. I done had enough of you, hear me?

BIGGER: (*Whirling on him and jerking out his knife.*) Make me! 315

ERNIE: I'll fix you this time — I'll get my gun! (*He turns around and reaches up as if to lift a hidden weapon down from above the door. But BIGGER springs forward, grabs him and jerks him out to the sidewalk. With a swipe of his knife he cuts off a piece* 320 *of* ERNIE'S *coat and holds it up, yelling.*)

BIGGER: This is a sample of the cloth. Wanta see a sample of the flesh?

G.H.: Come on. Let's get away from here.

(BUDDY *comes running into the scene carrying a bundle of papers under his arm and an envelope in his hand. He stops for an instant and looks at the scene, and then hurries forward.*)

BUDDY: Bigger — that lady come by the house — 325 sent a message for you. (BIGGER *stares at* ERNIE *and chuckles. At the same time he reaches out and takes the letter from* BUDDY. BUDDY *stands waiting to hear the contents of the letter.*)

BIGGER: You all keep quiet whilst I read my mail. 330 (*He backs off a few steps, opens the letter with a rip of his knife and looks at it.*) Good Gordon gin![15] (*The others watch him.* BIGGER *shouts out at them.*) Damn all of you now — you can all go to hell! I'm gonna be driving for a millionaire, and don't 335 you speak to me no more, none of you. Hear me? (*He laughs and spits.*) I spit in your slimy faces — a bunch of yellow cowards.

JACK: (*Placatingly, as he edges forward.*) It is a job for real, Bigger? 340

---

15 Good Gordon gin] an oath popularized by a Tampa Red blues song of that name in the late 1920s; a euphemism for "Good God in Heaven."

BIGGER: And when I go riding by in Mr. Dalton's Cadillac, tip your hats —

G.H.: (*Moving up in curiosity.*) Uhm, uhm — driving a Cadillac!

JACK: Driving for a millionaire — lawd, lawd! 345

G.H.: And maybe driving one them millionaire gals around. They say they're hot numbers. Say so, Bigger? Yeh, yeh.

JACK: Hear tell they'll go to bed with anything from a poodle dog on up. 350

G.H.: Rich, rich. I bet their mattresses is stuffed with hundred dollar bills. Soft, soft.

JACK: And they got them butlers in uniform, tiptoeing about and standing by the bed at night to turn the millionaires over when they grumble. (*He and* G.H. 355 *jiggle their feet, laugh and hug each other, then pantomime turning their masters in their beds.*)

BIGGER: Hah! Hah! Yeh, I'm finished with all you cheesy little punks — I'm on my way now. Don't ask me for time to die. (*He makes an upward gesture, then* 360 *feeling in his coat pocket, pulls out a coin and scornfully throws it at them.*) Here, take this fifty cents and buy you some hash. (*He turns and goes quickly out at the Left.* BUDDY *goes with him admiringly.*)

BUDDY'S VOICE: (*Offscene.*) Paper, mister, paper! 365

ERNIE: On his way no! (*Mopping his forehead.*) Somebody gonna kill that fool yet.

JACK: Or he's gonna kill somebody. Takes more'n a job to cure what ails him!

G.H.: (*Picking up the coin from the pavement.*) Come 370 on, let's get something to drink, Jack.

JACK: And a nickel for some canned music.

G.H.: Old boogie-woogie take the pressure off.

ERNIE: Yeh, come on in. What'll you have? (*The boys start into the café. The automatic phonograph* 375 *immediately begins playing a drumbeaten blues song and continues. The scene fades out.*)

SCENE III

As the blues music dies away, the curtain rises on the sun-filled, spotless DALTON *breakfast room, a short time later.* MR. DALTON *is seated at the table. He is about fifty-five or sixty, well-dressed and with pince-nez, beribboned glasses on the bridge of his nose.* JEFF BRITTEN, DALTON'S *private detective, sits on a sofa at the Left reading a newspaper. He is a little younger than* DALTON *and always certain and self-important in his manner.* BIGGER, *dressed as usual in his old black leather coat, is standing near* DALTON *with his cap in his hand.)*

DALTON: (*Reading in a hurried slurring tone.*) Twenty years of age — grammar school education — poor student but learns quickly when he applies himself — (*He glances at* BIGGER.) Counted as head of the house — colour complex — father killed in a race riot in Mississippi when the applicant was five years old. (*He looks up again, clearing his throat.*) Quite a lot of background factors.

BIGGER: (*Mumbling uncertainly.*) Yessuh, they wanted to put it all down.

(PEGGY, *the Irish cook and maid, refills* MR. DALTON'S *coffee cup. She is middle-aged, vivacious and efficient.*)

DALTON: (*Continuing.*) Knows how to obey orders but is of unstable equilibrium as to disposition. (*Chuckling.*) Never mind all these words, Bigger — part of the new social philosophy. Uh, what kind of car did you drive last?

BIGGER: A truck, suh.

DALTON: Got your license?

BIGGER: (*Showing it.*) Yessuh, I can drive most any kind. I can handle a Cadillac right off.

DALTON: Well, I have a Buick.

BIGGER: Yessuh.

(MRS. DALTON *enters, carefully feeling her way. She is dressed in shimmering, almost ghostly, white and carries a white pet cat in the crook of her arm.* PEGGY *gently helps her to her chair.*)

PEGGY: Let me bring you some tea, Mrs. Dalton.

MRS. DALTON: Thank-you, Peggy. (*To* DALTON.) Is someone with you?

DALTON: Yes, Ellen. This is the boy the relief sent — Bigger Thomas. (*To* BIGGER.) Now, Bigger, about this reform school business. Just forget it. I was a boy myself once, and God knows I got into plenty of jams.

MRS. DALTON: (*Softly.*) But you weren't coloured, Henry. There's a difference. (*She sips the tea* PEGGY *has provided.*)

DALTON: (*A little impatiently.*) I know, I know, Ellen, that's why I'm telling him to forget it.

BRITTEN: (*Rising and calling out.*) We'd better get started, Mr. Dalton.

DALTON: (*Rising also.*) Yes, Britten. (*To* MRS. DALTON.) They're threatening a rent strike, Ellen, over on Prairie Avenue.

BRITTEN: Left-wingers behind it, Mrs. Dalton. But we'll take care of them radicals all right. Oh, yes.

DALTON: More of that Edward Max's work. Britten here's trailing right after him. We'll see he never becomes District Attorney — we'll see to that.

BRITTEN: And that squirt of a labour leader — Jan Erlone — I've got an eye on him too. I know it worries you — him dating your daughter.

DALTON: (*Abruptly.*) Peggy, suppose you show Bigger around. Let him try his hand at that furnace. It's cantankerous as the devil at times. He suits me all right, Ellen. (*To* BIGGER.) I always leave the final decision in these matters to Mrs. Dalton. (*A buzzer sounds, and* PEGGY *turns quickly.* DALTON *calls out.*) No, you don't, Peggy. Mary will eat downstairs here.

PEGGY: (*Stopping.*) Yes, sir.

DALTON: No more of this breakfast in bed in the middle of the day. I've told her. (*He takes his overcoat and cane from* BRITTEN *who has picked them up from a chair.*)

MRS. DALTON: But she was out late last night, Henry, at the University.

DALTON: She can get up just the same. (*He bends to kiss* MRS. DALTON *on the forehead.*)

MRS. DALTON: Henry, the flowers —

DALTON: Oh yes, you wanted me to take them to the hospital.

MRS. DALTON: Yes, I'll show you. (*She rises and they go out together.* PEGGY *begins to clean up the table.* BRITTEN *comes over to* BIGGER *and takes hold of his coat sleeve.*)

BRITTEN: Where'd you get that coat, boy?

BIGGER: (*Trembling.*) From the welfare, suh. (BRITTEN'S *coat opens and reveals his badge.* BIGGER *flinches.*)

BRITTEN: (*Chuckling.*) Don't be alarmed. I'm not the law. I'm Mr. Dalton's private detective. Asking questions is my business. (*He turns and goes out after DALTON. *The buzzer sounds again, more insistently this time.*) 80

PEGGY: (*Shaking her head.*) I know — in my soft heart I want to answer it. But Mr. Dalton's right — We've got to be firm. Have one of my hot rolls.

BIGGER: No'm — no'm — I ain't hungry.

PEGGY: (*Deftly buttering a roll and sticking it out to him.*) Take it. (*He takes it with a slow hand and bites into it.*) Good? 85

BIGGER: Yessum — Sure mighty good.

PEGGY: That's one thing I can pride myself on — my bread. I always say everybody in the world's got at least one talent — it's up to him to find it and be happy. Mine's cooking and I evermore like to do it. (*Staring at* BIGGER *an instant.*) Well, you've got a talent, too. That's the way the Lord made us. Of course maybe it's a little harder for you coloured people to find yours on account of — well, but don't you get discouraged. We'll all help you. (*The sound of an automatic furnace turning itself on in a great windy draft comes up from the basement below.* BIGGER *stands listening to it.*) Oh, that's the furnace — it works by machinery. A big thing it is — has to be big to warm this old house. That'll be one of your duties — to keep it stoked up and the ashes cleaned out. 90 95 100

BIGGER: Yessum. I can learn machinery easy — always could. 105

PEGGY: Maybe that's your talent. I believe you're going to fit here. (*Still working at the table.*) Before I forget it, Miss Mary's going to Detroit tomorrow. She's visiting her grandmother for the Christmas holiday. You'll have to come early in the morning and drive her to the LaSalle Street Station. 110

BIGGER: Yessum.

PEGGY: She's not a bit like her folks. Drives her father crazy! Runs around with a wild bunch of radicals. But she's good-hearted — she'll learn better. She'll marry and settle down one of these days. 115

BIGGER: Yessum.

PEGGY: Now Mrs. Dalton — you'll like her. She's a fine lady. 120

BIGGER: She — she can't see, can she?

PEGGY: (*Pouring herself a cup of coffee and drinking from it.*) She's blind. Went blind years ago. She loves people and tries to help them — especially coloured people. Loves that cat and her piano and her flowers. (*She sets her cup down and wipes her hands on her apron.* MRS. DALTON *comes feeling her way in from the Left dressed as before and carrying the white cat.*) 125

MRS. DALTON: Have you told the young man his duties, Peggy? 130

PEGGY: Part of 'em, ma'am. I haven't spoke about the flowers yet.

MRS. DALTON: Bigger, you are to water them every morning. 135

BIGGER: Yessum.

PEGGY: I'll start the cleaning, ma'am. (MRS. DALTON *makes her way along the table and sits down.* PEGGY *goes out at the Right.* MRS. DALTON *takes one of the blossoms from the vase on the table and strokes it against her cheek.*) 140

MRS. DALTON: (*Detached.*) Flowers are wonderful creatures, Bigger. Each with a personality of its own. You'll learn to love them while you are here.

BIGGER: (*Nervously, but with respect.*) Yes, ma'am. (*He looks about him and lifts a glass of water from the little table. He drinks and watches* MRS. DALTON *over the rim.*) 145

MRS. DALTON: Bigger, we've decided to engage you. This is your new start. 150

BIGGER: Thank you, ma'am.

MRS. DALTON: Now you are one of us — a member of the family. We'll do all in our power to help you find your way in this new life. (*Her face tilted up, as if drinking in the sunlight that pours through the window.*) Bigger, I used to teach school, and I once had a coloured boy in one of my classes who was so distrustful and fearful that he carried a knife and a gun. 155

BIGGER: Huh? (*The water glass drops from his hand to the floor.*) Oh — (*He bends down in a scramble to pick up the glass, but his eyes remain on her face. He stands up again, his knees bent a little.*) I'm sorry, ma'am. I dropped one of your glasses. 160

MRS. DALTON: (*Quietly.*) That's all right — accidents will happen. (*A little strongly.*) I too have known what fear is, Bigger. But I am afraid no longer in this darkness. (*She indicates her eyes.*) I have dedicated my life to wiping out fear. We must wipe it out of you, for fear produces hate, and hate produces death and destruction. That is the woeful 165 170 lesson of this pitiful, tragic world. And if we as individuals cannot win a victory over ourselves, how can we expect the nations to?

BIGGER: (*Whispering but watching her as if fascinated.*) Yessum.

MRS. DALTON: (*Rising.*) That is all, Bigger. You have the job. You'll have your own room. Your pay will be twenty dollars a week, which will go to your mother. There will be five dollars more for yourself. You will have every second Sunday off. Is that clear? And you can start this evening.

BIGGER: Yessum.

MRS. DALTON: We have a lot of books in the library. You may read any you like.

BIGGER: No'm. Yessum.

MRS. DALTON: You don't have to read them. Peggy'll show you the rest of the routine. (*Turning.*) And if you're ever bothered about anything — about anything — come to me and we'll talk it over. (*She turns and moves slowly out at the Left.* BIGGER *stares after her as the door closes.*)

BIGGER: Uhm — queer — that old woman! Jesus! (*Shivering.*) Like I can feel her all over my skin. (*The sound of his own words seems to give him courage. He straightens up and gazes about him.*) So this the big job I been waiting for, talking about. (*Gesturing about him.*) This is the new world, Bigger. That old world gone — liquor, Clara, Ernie, them boys, even old Blum! (*He picks up a silver knife.*) Huh, solid silver. Yeh, rich folks! And me sitting in clover. This here the clover patch. Gonna eat me a belly full of it. Like a cow, yeh, like a big bull grazing in the moonlight on top of a hill. (*Fiercely and reprimandingly to himself.*) Goddammit, Bigger Thomas, here you make a new start! (*He puts the knife down.* MARY DALTON *enters from the Left, dressed in a flowing red robe opened at the bosom. It blows and trails behind her. Her hair is bunchy and tousled, and she is puffing a cigarette.* MARY *is a slender, pale-faced girl of some twenty-two or three, with wide, restless dark eyes. Her lips are rouged heavily, and her fingernails done to a deep vermillion. Her whole appearance denotes a sense of boredom and weary child-like disillusionment. She comes to the table, then stops and glances at* BIGGER. BIGGER *takes a step back.*) Yessum.

MARY: (*Quenching her cigarette on a saucer.*) I'm not going to hurt you. (BIGGER *stands with downcast eyes, saying nothing.* MARY *pours herself a cup of coffee and gulps down a couple of aspirin tablets. She gazes back at* BIGGER.) What's your name?

BIGGER: Bigger — Bigger Thomas, ma'am.

MARY: Funny name. Where'd you get it?

BIGGER: (*Without looking up.*) They just give it to me, ma'am.

MARY: (*Sitting down and picking idly at a roll.*) Our new chauffeur?

BIGGER: Yessum.

MARY: Do you belong to a union?

BIGGER: No'm — no'm, I ain't never fooled with them folks, ma'am.

MARY: Better join a union or Father'll exploit your shirt off. My name's Mary Dalton. I'm the pampered daughter and heiress to all the Dalton millions. And I've got a helluva hangover.

BIGGER: (*Uncertainly.*) Yessum.

MARY: Guess they've already told you about me though — how lazy I am and all — Peggy has, bless her sweet, dumb soul. Has Mother hired you?

BIGGER: Yessum.

MARY: Where do you live? (*Now* BIGGER *looks at her.*)

BIGGER: Over on Indiana Avenue and —

MARY: (*Bitingly.*) Ah, in one of the Dalton rat-traps. (*With a bit of energetic confiding.*) So you're on our side. Say, I'll have you meet Jan Erlone, a special friend of mine, and Edward Max and some of our friends. Max is going to be the next D.A. He knows what it's all about — a great man. We're having a rally down at party headquarters tonight.

BIGGER: Yessum.

MARY: (*Mockingly.*) Yessum — yessum — the subservience of the defeated. — You'll drive me down there —

BIGGER: Got to — got to stick to my job.

MARY: That is your job — to take me where I want to go. (*As if quoting.*) There is a new spirit abroad in the world, Bigger. People have lost their trust in the old leaders. The old security is gone. Upheavals are ripping this terrestrial ball to pieces. Young people don't know where to turn anymore. Everywhere we are searching for something to live for — to dream for — to fight for. We have been betrayed, Bigger. And we alone can save ourselves — the young people, the labouring people. And in the great struggle all are brothers — black, white, yellow or red. (BIGGER *blinks helplessly at her. She takes out a cigarette and looks around for a match.*) Match! (BIGGER *does not move.*) Father and Mother made a law-abiding punk out of our last chauffeur. He's got a job in Washington — big government pay. (*Loudly.*) Match! (BIGGER *nervously feels through his pockets, finds a book of matches and steps toward her and holds it out to her.*) Light it! (*He strikes the match and lights the cigarette. She takes a deep draw and blows out smoke.*) Have you got a girl? (BIGGER *blinks helplessly at her.*) Why don't you talk? (*He is silent.*) Bigger, how do you coloured people feel about the way you have to live? Do you ever get real mad? I'm not saying the right things, but what are the right things to say? I don't know. Bigger, say something. (*Strongly.*) How is it that two human beings can stand in a foot of each other and not speak the same language? Bigger, what are you thinking about? What are you feeling? (*He still doesn't answer.*) Do you think I'm crazy?

BIGGER: No — no, ma'am.

MARY: I appoint you a committee of one to look after me tonight. Get me home if I should happen to drink too much. Hell, I always drink too much. (*With a laugh she throws her coffee cup against the wall and breaks it.* PEGGY *comes in at the Left.*)

PEGGY: Did something break, Miss Mary?

MARY: I dropped my cup.

PEGGY: (*Sighing.*) Is your head better?

MARY: No.

PEGGY: I'll get you an aspirin.

MARY: I've already had two.

PEGGY: I wanted to bring your tray up, darlin', but your father —

MARY: I know. He's issued his orders.

PEGGY: (*After a moment, quietly.*) Come with me, Bigger, and I'll show you the furnace.

BIGGER: Yessum. (*In the distance* MRS. DALTON *begins playing a Chopin prelude on the piano.* MARY *shudders.*)

PEGGY: And then the flowers.

BIGGER: Yessum. (*He follows her out.* MARY *stands smoking and gazing before her.*)

MARY: (*Mockingly in the air.*) Yassum — yassum. (*The piano continues to play. The scene fades out.*)

SCENE IV

The bedroom of MARY DALTON *later that night. When the curtain rises, the piano stops playing. At the Left Front is a door opening into the hall, and to the Left and set at an angle from the audience is* MARY'S *bed draped in ghostly white and raised like a dais or bier. At the Centre Rear is a filmy-curtained window, and to the Right of that a huge oblong mirror, so tilted that its depths are discernible, but only a vague blur of images is reflected in it. In front of the mirror is a delicately-patterned chaise longue and stool. An entrance to the dressing-room is at the Right Front. The walls of the bedroom are cold and dead, and the whole scene is bathed in the snowy city's pallid light which glimmers through the window.*

BIGGER'S VOICE: (*In hushed anxiety.*) Please, Miss Dalton. Please, stand up and walk. Is this your room? (*Her voice, stiff-lipped and almost mechanical, is heard in the hall at the Left, drunkenly.*)

MARY'S VOICE: A great celebration, Bigger. God, I'm drunk!

BIGGER'S VOICE: (*Tense and in a hushed pleading.*) Sh-sh —

(MARY *appears in the door, her hat awry, her hair hanging down, her eyes set in a frozen stare and her face mask-like and dead. She grasps the lintel with her right hand. She has some pamphlets in her left hand.*)

MARY: And you're drunk too. It's a victory, Bigger! Hooray for the rent strike. Hooray for our side!

BIGGER: For Christ's sake! (*Still unseen, his voice a sort of moan.*) This ain't my job, Miss Dalton.

MARY: It is your job — to get me home — safe home. (*She pulls* BIGGER *on into the room. His head is lowered, his face somewhat averted from her. On his left arm he carries* MARY'S *red handbag, hung by its handle. He is dressed in his chauffeur's uniform, with overcoat.*) The people are strong, Bigger — you and me — thousands like us — Poor Father — Gimme a drink. Why don't you give me a drink? (*She reaches for her handbag.*)

BIGGER: No'm.

MARY: (*Rocking her head from right to left, mockingly.*) Yessum — yessum — My father — a landlord that walks like a man — And we had a big celebration, didn't we? Here, Bigger, I want you to read these pamphlets — "The Road to Freedom," "Share the Wealth."

BIGGER: (*Moaning again.*) Lemme go, Miss Dalton. (*Suddenly his head snaps about him as if he hears an enemy in the dark.*) I got to go — ain't my job — got to get out of here.

MARY: (*Stuffing pamphlets into* BIGGER'S *pocket.*) Here, take these! Put them in your pocket! (BIGGER *pulls away.*) What are you scared of? You don't frighten me, Bigger. I frighten you now — See, it's all turned around. Crazy world, isn't it?

BIGGER: This your room, Miss Dalton? They kill me — kill me — they find me in here. You home safe now. (*He turns away.*)

MARY: (*Insistently.*) Know what I am, Bigger?

BIGGER: (*Mumbling.*) I dunno — No'm — I dunno. Please'm, Miss Mary, you keep calling my name. Don't.

MARY: I'm what the Russians call "the penitent rich" — I feed the poor — (*Her hands go out as if scattering largesse to a begging world.*) And I'm drunk — and I'm dead — drunk and dead — inside I am — (*Giggling, as though at herself.*) I'm just a girl falling to pieces, Bigger. (*Shaking her head.*) I want to talk — Trouble with the world, Bigger — nobody to talk to — Mother and Father — they talk up to God in the sky — I talk down — way, way down to you at the bottom — (*With wild, emotional impulsiveness.*) Oh, I wish I was black — Honest, I do — black like you — down there with you — to start all over again — a new life — (*She puts out her hand toward him. He shivers and stands trembling. She touches his hair.*) Your hair is hard. Like little black wires — I know — It has to be hard — tough — to stand it — (*She touches his cheek.*)

BIGGER: (*In a whispering scream.*) Naw — naw! (*The air of his lungs hisses through his lips and dies, as it were, in an echoing supplication. His face glistens more brightly with the sweat that drenches it.*)

MARY: (*Looking at her hand.*) See, not shoe polish — it won't come off. (*Now touching her own cheek and gazing at her crooked, spread-out fingers and wagging her head hopelessly.*) There's a difference, and there's not a difference — (*His eyes are lifted, gazing blindly at her.*) Bigger, what are you thinking — what are you feeling? (*She begins to weep noiselessly.*)

BIGGER: (*Moaning, twisting his shoulders as if in the grip of some overpowering, aching pain. Gasping.*) Lemme go.

MARY: Yes, that's what I want — to break through and find you, to understand you.

BIGGER: Ain't my job — ain't my job — (*As* BIGGER *speaks,* MARY *falls, and he lifts her suddenly into his arms.*)

MARY: Your arms — hard — hurt — make me feel safe — and hurt — I want to suffer — begin all over again — home — take me home. (*Singing.*) "Swing low, sweet chariot, coming for to carry me home—"[16] That's Mother's favourite song. (*With a cry.*) Mother! (*Her eyes glare wide with fear.*) Let me go! Let me — (*But still his arms, as if against his will, hold to her.* MARY *is now staring at him coldly.*) Who are you? (*Lifting a weak hand, she strikes him blindly in the face.*) Stop — (*Shrieking.*) Stop it!

(*Wriggling like a rubber thing, queerly alive, the breath goes out of her. Her head falls back and she lies still and limp in his arms. For a moment* BIGGER *does not move. Fascinatedly he gazes at her face, his lips open and breathless. He jerks his face away from hers and lowers her feet to the floor, but the upper part of her body hangs over his arm. He looks frantically about him, then eases and half-drags her to the bed. A sob rises into his throat.*)

BIGGER: Miss Mary — Mary — Mary — Miss Dalton — (*With his head bowed, his hands reach to touch her reclining figure.*) Gotta get away — get away quick. (*Now, as if from some interminable distance deep in the house, comes the sound of* MRS. DALTON'S *gentle voice.*)

MRS. DALTON VOICE: Mary! — Is that you, Mary?

---

16 Swing … chariot] a well-known Negro spiritual.

[IV]

(BIGGER *springs up terrified. The door at the Left swings open and the blur of* MRS. DALTON'S *tall form stands there in its white dressing gown. And now, as if the calling voice had penetrated into* MARY'S *deep unconsciousness, the bed heaves and a murmur rises from it.* BIGGER'S *whole body grows taut, caught in a flooding horror of fear. He stares at* MRS. DALTON *with wide eyes, and as she moves farther into the room he backs noiselessly around the bed from her, the palms of his hands outstretched as if in piteous supplication before her unseeing vision, and his lips making a gasping, soundless cry. For an instant the scene is silent.* MRS. DALTON *clasps her long fingers in front of her and stands listening at the bed.*)

MRS. DALTON: (*In her normal voice.*) Mary? (BIGGER 100 *remains across the bed from* MRS. DALTON, *his face tilted and his eyes glued in awe upon the white figure. One of his hands is half-raised, the fingers weakly open as if an object he had been holding had just dropped from them.* MRS. DALTON *calls again.*) 105 Mary, are you asleep? (*There is no answer from the bed. The white figure turns slowly and seems to look about the room.* BIGGER *shrinks back into the shadows as if unable to face the blinding condemnation of that sightless face.* MRS. DALTON 110 *feels toward the bed, and then, as if touching* MARY *through the air itself, suddenly draws back.*) You reek of liquor. Mary, you're drunk! (BIGGER *carries his right hand to his mouth as if about to scream.*) My poor child — why do I fail you? Sleep — sleep 115 then. (*She fumbles for the coverlet, spreads it over* MARY'S *feet and turns back toward the door. A low sigh of relief passes through* BIGGER'S *lips.* MRS. DALTON *wheels about.*) What is it? (*The sleeping figure lifts a hand and mumbles as if waking up.* 120 *Quick as a flash and with an instinctive action,* BIGGER *picks up a pillow and pushes it down against* MARY'S *face. Her hands flash up in the gloom, clawing helplessly at his arms. But he holds the pillow against her, heedless of her struggle, his face turned* 125 *watchfully toward* MRS. DALTON. *She takes a step back toward the bed, then stops — in alarm.*) Mary — are you ill? (MARY'S *form on the bed moves, and there is a sound of a heavy breath. A quick, muscular tautness in* BIGGER'S *entire body indicates the* 130

enormous strength with which he is holding the pillow. The white hands continue to clutch futilely at his wrists. MRS. DALTON'S *voice calls out sharply.*) What is it, Mary? (*She listens.*) Mary! (*The white hands have fallen limp by the pillow now.*) 135 Goodnight, Mary. I'll call you early for your train.

(*She moves silently from the room. The door closes behind her. For a moment there is no sound or movement; then with a deep, short gasp of relieved tension,* BIGGER *falls to the floor, catching the weight of his body on his hands and knees. His chest heaves in and out as though he had just completed a hard foot-race. Gradually his heavy breathing subsides, and he stands slowly up looking at the door. His body is relaxed now, the burden of fear gone from him. Then he looks toward the bed, his whole attitude changing, his body becoming taut again. He takes a step forward, then stops uncertainly. He stares at the white form, his face now devoid of that former hard concentration. With a quick movement, he bends, and stares down at* MARY'S *face. Slowly his right hand goes up in the air, the fingers sensitively poised, until again he assumes the same position in which he was standing and looking when the white blur of* MRS. DALTON *first roused him. He stares anxiously at* MARY'S *face, as though a dreadful knowledge were on the threshold of his consciousness. His right hand moves timidly toward* MARY *and touches her, then is jerked rapidly away. He touches her head, gently rolls it from side to side, then puts his hands behind him as if they had suffered some strange and sudden hurt.*)

BIGGER: (*In a whisper.*) Naw — naw — (*For a moment he stands looking at the still form as though it had in some manner deeply offended him. Once more he places his hand on* MARY'S *head. This time* 140 *it remains there and his body does not move. He mumbles frenziedly.*) Naw — naw — naw — (*He is silent for an instant, then whispers.*) She's dead. (*He takes a quick step back.*) I didn't, I tell you I didn't. Wake up, wake up, Miss Dalton. (*His voice* 145 *takes on a note of pleading.*) Miss Dalton, Miss Mary — (*For a second he stands, then straightens up suddenly. He turns, walks swiftly to the door, opens it, and looks out into the darkness. All is quiet. He walks back to the Centre of the room and stands* 150

looking at the bed. He mumbles piteously.) Naw —
naw — naw — I didn't do it — I didn't do it —
(In a clear, sober, deep voice, as if all his faculties were
suddenly alive.) They'll say I done it — I'm black
and they'll say I done it. (Again he bends over the   155
bed.) It was your fault. I didn't want to come to
your room. You were too drunk to walk. You made
me come, you bitch. I hated you then — I hate
you now! Yeh. (His voice dies out. Far away in the
depths of the house, a clock booms the hour.) Seem   160
like that clock winding itself up to wake the world
and tell what I done. Got to hide her — get her
away from here — so they'll never know — can't
tell what happened — (He stops, trembling violently,
then looking back over his shoulder at the door, slides   165
his hands under MARY'S body and lifts her in his
arms. The hum of the furnace switching itself on is
heard below.) Naw, ain't nothing happened. Just a
dream — a dream — I been dreaming. (With a
smothered shriek.) It ain't no dream — it's   170
happened! Cold — cold — she's growing cold.
(Listening to the furnace draft.) Yeh, everything cold
around me — like a great tomb. That furnace
needs tending, boy. (With a moaning cry he rushes
through the door with the body of MARY in his arms.   175
The sound of the furnace draft grows louder and
continues. The scene fades out.)

SCENE V

The sound of the furnace draft dissolves gradually into
the metallic tingling of a telephone. The scene is the
DALTON breakfast room (same as Scene III), a few
hours later. MR. DALTON is using the telephone. MRS.
DALTON is sitting in a chair, bolt upright, listening.

DALTON: Now, Mother, don't get upset. We'll get
things straightened out. You know how impulsive
Mary is. She might be on a later train. I'll call you
back. (He pauses, then hangs up the receiver and
turns to MRS. DALTON.) Well, it doesn't look good,   5
Ellen, it doesn't. (Shaking his head.) I can't
understand Mary's bed not being slept in and her
trunk not packed and still in her room.
MRS. DALTON: (With a tremor in her voice.) Mary
had been drinking again last night, Henry. When   10
I came into her room — I —

DALTON: Yes, yes — maybe that Erlone fellow she
goes with knows something. He called up from the
station — seemed worried.
MRS. DALTON: Mr. Britten ought to be back any   15
minute with some news. (PEGGY comes in with a
tray at the Right Front. Her face shows signs of recent
weeping.)
PEGGY: Here's your tea, Mrs. Dalton.
MRS. DALTON: (With a gesture.) No, thank you,   20
Peggy.
PEGGY: But you must keep up your strength, ma'am.
MRS. DALTON: No, thank you. (BRITTEN comes in.)
BRITTEN: Whew, snow's pouring down all right.
Regular blizzard for old Santa Claus. Well, Mr.   25
Dalton, Buckley better get busy. That labour
crowd's talking up this fellow Edward Max for
District Attorney, and talking loud.
DALTON: I know, I know — but Buckley'll win.
We'll see to that.   30
MRS. DALTON: (Quickly.) What did you find out at
the station, Mr. Britten?
BRITTEN: Nothing. Absolutely nothing, Mrs.
Dalton. (A sob breaks from PEGGY. She goes out.)
Mmm — I don't understand her car being left out   35
there all night. Your new chauffeur says he brought
Miss Dalton home about two o'clock.
MRS. DALTON: About two-thirty this morning. I
heard the clock strike downstairs. Later I went to
her room. She was restless.   40
BRITTEN: Ahm — By the way, this coloured boy
Thomas — is he all right?
DALTON: We have his complete record. I'm sure he's
all right.

(PEGGY comes in and listens. While they are talking,
BIGGER slowly enters the conservatory at the Rear. He
has a watering can in his hand and goes about quietly
and methodically watering the flowers. But even in his
nonchalant and detached manner, we sense that he is
straining every nerve to hear the words of the group in
the breakfast room.)

BRITTEN: (To PEGGY.) And what do you think of   45
this Thomas boy? Is he polite? Does he pull off his
cap when he comes into the house?
PEGGY: Yes, sir.
BRITTEN: Does he seem to be acting at any time? I

mean, does he appear like he's more ignorant than he really is? 50

PEGGY: I don't know, Mr. Britten.

BRITTEN: I'd like to talk to him again.

PEGGY: (*Gesturing toward the rear glass door of the conservatory.*) He's out there watering the flowers. 55

MRS. DALTON: I'm sure he's all right, Mr. Britten.

BRITTEN: (*In a loud voice.*) Come in here, boy! (BIGGER *turns, opens the glass door and comes slowly through, still carrying the watering can in his hand.* BRITTEN *turns to him.*) I want to ask you some more questions! 60

BIGGER: (*Blinking and starting back.*) Yessuh.

BRITTEN: What time do you say you took Miss Dalton from here last night?

BIGGER: About eight-thirty, suh. 65

BRITTEN: You drove her to her night class at the University? (BIGGER *hangs his head and makes an answer.*) Open your mouth and talk, boy. (BRITTEN *puts out a placating hand to the* DALTONS. *They wait.*) 70

BIGGER: Well, Mister, you see — I'm just working here.

BRITTEN: You told me that before. You drove her to school, didn't you? (BIGGER *still makes no answer.*) I asked you a question, boy! 75

BIGGER: (*His face strangely alert and yet impassive.*) No, suh, I didn't drive her to school.

BRITTEN: Where did you drive her?

BIGGER: Well, suh, she told me after I got as far as the Park to turn around and take her to the Loop. 80

DALTON: (*His lips parted in surprise.*) She didn't go to school?

BIGGER: No, suh.

MRS. DALTON: Why didn't you tell us this before, Bigger? 85

BIGGER: (*Quietly.*) She told me not to, ma'am.

BRITTEN: Where did you take her, then?

BIGGER: To the Loop, suh.

BRITTEN: Whereabouts in the Loop?

BIGGER: To Lake Street. 90

BRITTEN: Do you remember the number?

BIGGER: Sixteen, I think, suh.

BRITTEN: (*Rubbing his chin.*) That's a good boy — Uhm — Sixteen Lake Street — the Labour Defenders' Office. 95

BIGGER: (*Kindly.*) Say, boy, the water is pouring out on the floor.

BIGGER: Thank you, suh. Yessuh! (*He jerks the watering can up and hugs it in front of him.*)

BRITTEN: How long was she in this place — Number Sixteen? 100

BIGGER: 'Bout half an hour, I reckon, suh.

BRITTEN: Then what happened?

BIGGER: (*Quietly.*) Then they came out.

BRITTEN: They? 105

BIGGER: Her and this — this Mr. Jan. Miss Mary said to go by there to pick him up.

DALTON: Jan Erlone — she's been dating him.

BRITTEN: (*Confirmingly.*) Uh-huh. (*He looks triumphantly around him.*) And then you drove 'em to — ? 110

BIGGER: To the speaking — to hear that man — Mr. Max —

BRITTEN: Erlone's one of his crowd, a Red. And then where did you go? 115

BIGGER: To Ernie's Kitchen Shack.

BRITTEN: And how long did they stay there?

BIGGER: We must have stayed —

BRITTEN: We? Didn't you wait outside in the car?

BIGGER: Naw, suh. You see, Mister, I did what they told me. I was only working for 'em. 120

BRITTEN: And then what did you do?

BIGGER: I didn't want to, Mister. I swear I didn't want to. They kept worrying at me until I went in and had a drink with 'em. 125

BRITTEN: (*With a placating gesture toward* MRS. DALTON.) A drink, eh? So they were drinking —

BIGGER: Christmas time and all —

DALTON: And then you brought them home here?

BIGGER: Yessuh. 130

MRS. DALTON: (*In sad but firm graciousness.*) How intoxicated was Miss Dalton, Bigger?

BIGGER: (*Not looking at her.*) She — she couldn't hardly stand up —

BRITTEN: (*Conclusively.*) And they told you to leave the car outside, huh? 135

BIGGER: Yes, suh, he told me to leave the car. And I could go on home, get my things, and come back this morning.

BRITTEN: How was this Erlone acting? Drunk, eh? 140

BIGGER: Yes, suh, I guess he was drunk. (*Suddenly*

BRITTEN *takes from his pocket a small batch of pamphlets and holds them under* BIGGER'S *nose.*)

BRITTEN: Where did you get these? I found 'em in your overcoat pocket — in the basement. Is that the coat you were wearing last night? 145

BIGGER: Yessuh.

BRITTEN: Then where did you get them?

BIGGER: Miss Dalton, she gave 'em to me, but I didn't read 'em — 150

BRITTEN: What unit are you in?

BIGGER: (*Backing away.*) Suh?

BRITTEN: (*Savagely.*) Come on, comrade. Tell me what unit you are in. (BIGGER *stares at him in speechless amazement.*) Who's your organizer? 155

BIGGER: I don't know what you mean, suh!

DALTON: Britten, he doesn't know anything about that.

BRITTEN: Didn't you know this Erlone before you came to work here? 160

BIGGER: Naw, suh, naw, suh. You got me wrong, sir. I ain't never fooled around with them folks. The ones at the meeting last night was the first ones I ever met, so help me God. (*Now* BRITTEN *comes pushing nearer to* BIGGER *till he has forced him back against the wall at the Right. He looks him squarely in the eye, then grabs him by the collar and rams his head against the wall.*) 165

BRITTEN: Come on, gimme the facts. Tell me about Miss Dalton and that Erlone. What did he do to her? 170

BIGGER: Now, suh, I ain't — I don't know — Naw, suh.

DALTON: (*Sternly.*) That's enough, Britten.

BRITTEN: Okay. I guess he's all right. (*Smiling kindly at* BIGGER.) Just playing a little, son. (BIGGER *gulps and stares at him.*) If you say he's okay, then he's okay with me, Mr. Dalton. (*To* BIGGER.) You say Erlone told you to leave the car in the drive and then he helped Miss Dalton up the steps? 175

BIGGER: Yes, suh. 180

BRITTEN: And did he go away?

BIGGER: He helped her up the steps, suh, and — uh, she was just about passed out.

BRITTEN: And he went with her into the house?

BIGGER: Yes, suh — (*He suddenly stops and stares toward the door at the Left.* JAN ERLONE *is shown in by* PEGGY. *His face is pale.*) 185

PEGGY: Mr. Erlone, sir. He insisted on seeing you.

ERLONE: What's all this about? Have you heard anything from Mary — Miss Dalton? 190

BRITTEN: (*Savagely.*) You're just in time to tell us, Erlone. (ERLONE *stares at* BIGGER, *who straightens up and gazes fearlessly before him.* ERLONE *looks around.*)

ERLONE: I don't know anything. That's why I'm here. 195 (*He turns to* BIGGER.)

DALTON: Bigger, this is the man that came home with Miss Mary last night? (ERLONE'S *lips part. He stares at* DALTON, *then at* BIGGER.)

BIGGER: (*Without flinching.*) Yes, suh. (ERLONE *stares at* BIGGER *with wide incredulous eyes.*) 200

ERLONE: I didn't come here, Bigger. Why are you saying such a thing? (*To* MRS. DALTON.) Mrs. Dalton, I'm worried too. That's why I'm here. You see — I love your daughter Mary — and — (*With strong frankness.*) she loves me — I know she does. (*Roughly to* BRITTEN.) What are you making this boy lie for? 205

BRITTEN: Where is Miss Dalton, Erlone?

ERLONE: She was supposed to go to Detroit this morning, to see her grandmother. I was at the railroad station early waiting to see her off. 210

BRITTEN: So you know your story by heart, don't you? She didn't go. Did you see Miss Dalton last night?

ERLONE: (*Hesitating.*) No.

BRITTEN: But you were with her and with this Negro boy — at Ernie's Kitchen Shack. We have his word for that. 215

ERLONE: All right then, I saw her. So what?

BRITTEN: (*Sarcastically.*) So you saw her. Where is she now? 220

ERLONE: If she's not in Detroit, I don't know where she is.

DALTON: I've just talked to her grandmother. Mary's not there.

BRITTEN: You and Miss Dalton were drunk last night. 225

ERLONE: Oh, come on! We weren't drunk. We just had a little to drink.

BRITTEN: You brought her home about two in the morning. 230

ERLONE: No, I did not. (BIGGER *is seen to take a quick step backward and his hand takes hold of the knob on the glass door.*)

DALTON: Mr. Erlone, we know my daughter was drunk last night when you brought her home here. 235

ERLONE: (*Quickly.*) I — I didn't come here last night.

MRS. DALTON: But you were with her and she was intoxicated. Do you mean you left her in that condition?

ERLONE: (*Hesitating and swallowing.*) Well, I came 240 as far as the trolley stop. I had to go to a meeting. Had to hurry. Bigger here drove her home. (ERLONE *turns to* BIGGER.) Bigger, what are you telling these people? (BIGGER *makes no answer.*)

MRS. DALTON: (*In an agitated voice.*) I'll see you in 245 my room, Henry — please. (PEGGY *comes to her, helps her up and assists her from the room. Just before she leaves,* MRS. DALTON *turns and gazes toward* ERLONE *with her sightless eyes. Then lowering her head, she goes away with* PEGGY.) 250

ERLONE: (*Beseechingly around him.*) Bigger, didn't you get Miss Dalton home safely? What's happened to her? (BIGGER *gazes stonily at him and does not answer.* ERLONE *seems to read a strange and ultimate antagonism in* BIGGER'S *face for he gradually* 255 *lowers his head and stares at the floor.*)

BRITTEN: (*Chuckling.*) So Bigger brought her home and you didn't?

ERLONE: Yes.

BRITTEN: You're a liar, Erlone. First you say you 260 didn't see her, then you did. Then you didn't bring her home, then you did. Then again you didn't. Come on, what's your game?

ERLONE: (*In a low desolate voice as he stares about him.*) I was trying to protect her. 265

BRITTEN: You're trying to protect yourself, and making a damn poor job of it.

ERLONE: I didn't come here, I tell you.

BRITTEN: You got Miss Dalton drunk, Erlone — you brought her here early this morning. You told 270 the boy to leave the car out in the driveway. You went inside and upstairs with her, and now she's disappeared. Where is she? (ERLONE *looks at him with staring, bewildered eyes.*)

ERLONE: Listen, I told you all I know. 275

DALTON: (*Stepping forward.*) Erlone, you and I don't agree on certain things. I hear that you are a communist — an enemy to this beloved country of mine. So be it. I want to know where my daughter is. That's the only thing that counts now. 280

ERLONE: I tell you I don't know, Mr. Dalton. (DALTON *throws up his hands in futile, desperate anger.*)

DALTON: We'll see you upstairs later, Britten. (*He goes out.*)

BRITTEN: (*Blocking the way to the door and glaring* 285 *at* ERLONE *as he yells.*) Get over there! (ERLONE *backs away from his menacing look.*) Now listen to me, you damn communist!

ERLONE: I tell you I don't know where Mary Dalton is!

BRITTEN: All right. You don't know now — eh? But 290 you will know, and you'll know damn soon. We'll help you remember. (PEGGY *appears in the door.*)

PEGGY: The house is getting cold. You better look after the furnace, Bigger. It needs tending.

BRITTEN: Okay. That's all I got to say now, Erlone. 295 But you know more than you're telling. (*He follows* PEGGY *out. For a moment* ERLONE *stares at the floor.* BIGGER *watches him with steady, smoldering eyes. In the street outside a chorus begins singing a Christmas carol. Slowly* BIGGER'S *hand goes up and* 300 *slides into his coat and rests there. Presently* ERLONE *looks up.*)

ERLONE: What's all this about, Bigger? Why did you tell those lies? I haven't done anything to you, have I? Where's Mary? 305

BIGGER: (*Mumbling.*) I don't want to talk to you.

ERLONE: (*Desperately.*) But what have I done to you?

BIGGER: I don't want to talk to you. (*With a sharp cry.*) Get out!

ERLONE: Listen, Bigger. If these people are bothering 310 you, just tell me. Don't be scared. We are used to this sort of persecution. Mr. Max will help you in your rights. He knows their crooked law. Listen, now. Tell me about it. Come on, we'll go out and get a cup of coffee and talk it over. (ERLONE *comes* 315 *toward him.* BIGGER *suddenly whips out his gun.* ERLONE *cries out.*) For God's sake, man, what are you doing?

BIGGER: I don't need you — that Mr. Max neither — (*Hoarsely.*) Get out! 320

ERLONE: I haven't bothered you. Don't —

BIGGER: (*His voice tense and hysterical.*) Leave me alone.

ERLONE: (*Backing away from him.*) For Christ's sake, man! 325

BIGGER: (*His voice rising almost to a scream.*) Get away from here! Now! Now! They think you the one done it — yeh! (*He points the pistol at ERLONE.*) You, you, Red!

(ERLONE *backs farther away, then turns and goes rapidly out at the Right Front, looking back over his shoulder with hurt and helpless eyes. For a moment BIGGER jerks his head up with a shudder, listening. Gradually a low moaning sound rises from his lips. For a moment he remains so, then wheeling quickly, he goes into the conservatory and passes out of sight through the flowers at the Right Rear, leaving the watering pot sitting on the floor. The singing of the carollers comes in more strongly from the street and continues. The scene fades out.*)

SCENE VI

The music of the carol singers melts into the evangelical fervour of a Negro song-service in a church across the street. The curtain rises on CLARA MEARS' one-room kitchenette apartment. A bed is at the Left Rear, a window by it, and a dresser at the Right Front next to the door. In the Right Rear are a sink and a little table. It is night, a few hours later. CLARA is standing in front of her mirror arranging her hair. She is partly dressed. BIGGER is sitting on the edge of the bed dressed in trousers and undershirt. His shoulders are hunched over. The Negro song-service dies out.

CLARA: (*Glancing over at BIGGER'S coat hanging on the chair at the Left.*) Look, puddles of water dripped all over the floor from your coat. (*She moves the chair and coat near the radiator, then goes back to the mirror.*) 5

BIGGER: (*Muttering musingly.*) Yeh, little brown doll there talking about a wet coat and puddles on the floor. Rain or snow, they don't matter. (*He flings out a clenched fist and bangs the railing of the bed. CLARA turns toward him questioningly.*) 10

CLARA: Bigger, what's wrong with you?

BIGGER: (*Musingly.*) She asks me what's wrong — yeh, what's wrong?

CLARA: You don't seem like yourself — You ain't yourself — 15

BIGGER: All right, I ain't. I'm different, then.

CLARA: (*Tripping swiftly over and dropping on her knees by him.*) Bigger, honey, don't be like that. Don't stay away from me.

BIGGER: Aw, shut up! 20

CLARA: All the time I loved you in my arms there, seemed like you full of something different.

BIGGER: You done had all you want from me now, and I better go. (CLARA *impulsively grabs his hand and kisses it.*) 25

CLARA: Please, Bigger, I don't mean to make you mad. I want to make you happy — that's all I want. I know your folks tries to turn you against me — say I ain't no good. (*Growling, he turns and seizes her roughly by the shoulders, his voice a mixture of anguish and cruelty and bitter love.*) 30

BIGGER: Goddamit, you know why I come here — 'Cause I can't help it. I wish I could help it. Now I wish I could. (*Springing up.*) I don't need you no more. You keep me from running free. You start holding me too tight, pulling at me, trying to suck me down like a swamp. 35

CLARA: (*Half-weeping.*) I don't — I don't —

BIGGER: Then I get mad, freeze on you, feel like slamming the door in your damn face, leave you out in the cold. Then I hate myself and I hate you for making me hate myself. Then it's your little soft baby-talk fumbling at my heart and then we get some likker and end up by kissing and going to bed. I hate it! I hate it! Wish it was different. *Now* I do. 40 45

CLARA: (*Echoing.*) Why you keep saying "now" all the time!

BIGGER: 'Cause things come to me clear now, like watching the sun rise over the skyscrapers. Like the folks say you feel, maybe, when you been baptized. Like Ma in her dreams seeing God riding in the clouds on high. A light busting in front of me like a big rocket showing up everything in no-man's land. (*His voice dies in his throat and he stares unseeingly in front of him. CLARA'S inquiring, begging eyes are fastened on his face. He breaks into a hoarse, raucous laughter and pounds his knees with his fists.*) 50 55

CLARA: (*Whispering.*) Why you laughing like that? (*She shudders.*) 60

BIGGER: I'm laughing — laughing at everybody —

everybody in the whole damn world. Laughing at you.

CLARA: (*Piteously.*) Please, Bigger, please. 65

BIGGER: Feel like I'm living way off by myself, nobody there but me — like I'm sailing out in space like a star. Then I come back to you and feel your arms around me. Goddamit, take 'em 'way.

CLARA: (*Her lips quivering.*) And they'd always be 70 around you, Bigger — they would. (*Frantically.*) But you talk wild, drunk-like.

BIGGER: (*Gesturing.*) That little old bottle of whiskey? Didn't even feel it.

CLARA: I'll fix you supper. You got to sleep some, 75 honey. You tired. Your po' face all tight, and yo' eyes full of blood. (*She rises and stands by his side.*)

BIGGER: (*His arms clutching around her as though suddenly doubting everything.*) You love me, Clara?

CLARA: You know that. (*She bends down and kisses* 80 *him. Her arm is tight along his side. Suddenly she draws it away with an exclamation.*) You got a gun! (*Gasping.*) Is that how you got this money you give me — rob somebody? (*She picks a wad of bills up from the dresser and turns to hand them back to him.*) 85

BIGGER: Naw, naw! Maybe they give me something in advance on my job. Yeh.

CLARA: Who? (*Looking at him sharply.*) Old white gal I seen you eating with down at Ernie's last night?

BIGGER: (*Stolidly.*) Maybe. (*Heartily.*) Yeh, she was 90 drunk, pushed that money on me — nigh a whole hundred dollars. (*Snickering.*) Something on account, she said, not a tip.

CLARA: (*In fierce jealousy.*) She's crazy. Her face say she's crazy. 95

BIGGER: Aw, don't worry 'bout her.

CLARA: Leave her alone, honey. She'll get you in trouble.

BIGGER: Nunh-unh! (CLARA *puts the money in her bosom and resumes her toilette.*) 100

CLARA: Say, Bigger, where is this you're working — the Dalton place?

BIGGER: (*Sharply.*) How come you want to know? (*He is lacing up one of his shoes.*)

CLARA: Anything has you in it I want to know. 105

BIGGER: Over on Drexel.

CLARA: Where?

BIGGER: In the forty-six hundred block.

CLARA: (*Her brush slowing.*) Oh.

BIGGER: Oh, what? 110

CLARA: Nothing much. I used to work over in that section, not too far from where the Loeb folks lived.

BIGGER: Loeb?

CLARA: Yeah, one of the fellows that killed the Franks 115 boy.[17] Remember?

BIGGER: Yeh.

CLARA: They tried to get money from the boys' family. Sent a kidnap note.

BIGGER: Yeh, yeh. And them boys — got by that old 120 'lectric chair, didn't they? They didn't burn. (*He is suddenly excited, looks off, hits his hands together. His voice rises.*) Yeh! Kidnap — they asked for plenty dough. (CLARA *comes to the bed and sits down by him. She puts her arm around him.*) 125

CLARA: Come on — we'll go out and get something to eat. (*She indicates the money in her bosom.*) I'll treat you to a steak. (*He says nothing, his mind working feverishly. She looks at him.*) We'll go to the Paris Grill. (*He says nothing.*) What's the matter, 130 Bigger?

BIGGER: Them boys asked for money. (*Staring off, twisting his hands together.*) All comes back — I remember. (*Springing up.*) Money, Goddamit! Everybody talking about it — papers with big 135 headlines, telephones ringing. Yeh, let 'em ring — ringing all over America, asking, asking about

---

17 Franks boy] On May 21, 1924, Richard Loeb and Nathan Leopold, two nineteen-year-old students from respected wealthy families, kidnapped and killed Bobby Franks, a fourteen-year-old boy from a wealthy family in the Kenwood district of Chicago. They then stowed the boy's body in a culvert and attempted to collect a ransom. In the meantime, however, the body was found, and various clues led to the questioning of Leopold and Loeb, who finally confessed that they had committed the crime for an intellectual thrill. Clarence Darrow, their celebrated lawyer, managed to have them spared the death penalty. Instead, the two were sentenced to life imprisonment at Joliet State Prison, where Loeb was stabbed to death by his cell-mate in 1936. Leopold was paroled in 1958 and moved to Puerto Rico, where he lived until his death in 1971.

Bigger. The bells ringing! They'll sound the sirens and the ambulances beat their gongs.

CLARA: Bigger! Bigger! Something wrong make you talk like that. (*He sinks down on the bed and again takes her hand.*) 140

BIGGER: Yeh, Clara, plenty wrong, and I'm going to tell you, and you stay with me.

CLARA: (*Piteously.*) I stay with you. 145

BIGGER: Cross your heart?

CLARA: Cross my heart. (*She kisses him.*)

BIGGER: Here's the dope, see. The gal where I'm working, the daughter of the old man who's a millionaire, well, she's done run off with one of them Reds. She's crazy like I told you. 150

CLARA: Eloped?

BIGGER: Yeh. They don't know where she is. I got an idea. We can make 'em think she's kidnapped. We could ask for money and get it, too. You see, we cash in, 'cause nobody else is trying to. 155

CLARA: But suppose she shows up?

BIGGER: She won't

CLARA: (*In alarm.*) Bigger, you know where that girl is? 160

BIGGER: We'll come cheap, we'll ask for ten thousand dollars.

CLARA: Bigger, you ain't done nothing to that girl, is you?

BIGGER: Say that again and I'll slap you 'crost this bed. 165

CLARA: But they'll catch you.

BIGGER: Naw, we'll outsmart 'em. It'll be easy, see? They got millions — won't miss it. We get some of it. Then you and me — we's free, Goddamit, free! You hear me? Free like them. (*He hugs her tightly for an instant. She begins to weep.*) One of them old empty buildings over there — Thirty-six Place and Michigan — a good place to hide and wait for them to drop off the money. The coast clear — you'll pick it up. 170 175

CLARA: They'll catch me, Bigger, they will. (*She sobs.*)

BIGGER: I'll write 'em a letter —

CLARA: They'll never stop looking — the white folks never stop. 180

BIGGER: Yeh, but looking for the wrong guy — one of them Reds. They already suspect him. (*Rising and pushing her arms away.*) Yeh, I'll get the pencil and paper — (*He moves to the dresser.*) write them a letter — print it. They think they sharp, huh? We see, we see. (*He gets his gloves from his coat pocket and puts them on. He chuckles.*) That dumb detective can look for fingerprints, but he won't find any. (*He gets pencil and paper from the drawer and spreads the paper out on the floor.*) 185 190

CLARA: (*Words breaking through her sobs.*) What are you doing to me, Bigger? Please, please! (*She drops to the floor by him and hugs his knees to her.* BIGGER *ponders the message he is to write, his mind far from her. Her words pour out in a dithyramb while she hugs his knees to her.*) All you ever caused me was trouble — just plain black trouble. I been a fool — just a blind, dumb, black, drunk fool, and I'll go on being a fool 'cause I love you — love you clean down to hell. I ain't never had nobody but you — nobody in my arms but you. I give all of me to you and now you do this to me! 195 200

BIGGER: Stop your whining! (*He kicks his legs loose from her.*) I got to write. Naw, I'll print it — with my left hand. Yeh, I'll sign the note, "Red." They're all scared of Reds. You see it in the newspapers. (*Exultantly.*) Won't ever think we done it. Think we too scared. (*Excitedly.*) We ain't scared, is we, Clara? Ain't scared. (*Writing.*) "Dear Sir." Ha! Ha! Naw, just "Sir." (*Cocking his head.*) Look at that word. A few more of them and the whole world turn upside-down, and we done it. Big headlines in the papers, police running around like chickens with their heads cut off — and all the time we stay back watching, waiting to pick up the dough in that old house. (*His voice rising like a croon.*) Twenty years, up and down the dark alleys, like a rat. Nobody hear you. And the white folks walking high and mighty don't even know we're alive, don't even know we want to breathe. Now they cut the pigeon wing and do the dance the way *we* say — 205 210 215 220

CLARA: (*Moaning.*) Bigger, Bigger! (*She falls sobbing on the floor.*)

BIGGER: (*His head raised, staring off, his face alight with his vision.*) Yeh, and you can feel it, you can see it — freedom — like bars falling away — like doors swinging open, and walls dropping down. And all the big cars and all the big buildings, and the finery and the marching up and down, and the 225

big churches and the big bells ringing and the 230
millionaires bowing low before their God — It
ain't God now, it's Bigger. Bigger Thomas, that's
my name — on the hot wires of the world!
(CLARA'S *sobs break hopelessly through the room.*
BIGGER *begins to write.*) "Sir: — We got your 235
daughter — say nothing to the police — the
ransom price is —" (*The Negro evangelical song-
service comes more loudly into the room from a distant
street and continues. The scene fades out.*)

SCENE VII

*The song-service dies away. The curtain rises on the
basement of the* DALTON *home, the next afternoon.*
BRITTEN *and a lynx-eyed, middle-aged newspaperman named* JED NORRIS *are looking down into the
reddish gloom.* PEGGY *is on the steps calling.*

PEGGY: Bigger Thomas! Where is that boy? (BRIT-
TEN *turns toward her.*) Oh, Mr. Britten — you
scared me.

BRITTEN: Everybody's on nerves, and no wonder.
This is my friend, old Jed Norris, Miss Peggy — 5
the best Tribune man what is — got a long nose
for news and as ornery as he's smart. (JED *lifts a
nonchalant hand to his old hat brim.* PEGGY *nods.*)

PEGGY: What do you think has happened to Mary,
Mr. Britten? (*Weeping.*) What has happened? 10

BRITTEN: We've locked up this Jan Erlone, and we're
going to find out. We will. (BIGGER *enters.*)

PEGGY: There you are.

BIGGER: I was cleaning the front walk, ma'am.

PEGGY: Well, first things first. The house is cold. Fix 15
the furnace, will you?

BIGGER: Yessum.

PEGGY: Right away — now!

BIGGER: (*Picking up the coal shovel.*) Yessum. (PEGGY
hurries off. BIGGER *makes no move to stir up the* 20
fire.)

NORRIS: (*To* BRITTEN.) I'll look around.

BRITTEN: Do, old hoss, but you won't find a thing
down here. (NORRIS *moves off into the shadows.*
BRITTEN *looks at* BIGGER.) Hear what the lady 25
said?

BIGGER: Yessuh. (*But he still makes no move to stir
up the fire.* BRITTEN *finally bends down and opens*

the furnace door. We see NORRIS *now as a vague
figure, looking back at the scene.* BIGGER *slowly raises* 30
his shovel.)

BRITTEN: No wonder the house is cold upstairs —
a big pile of ashes banked up in there. (*He
straightens suddenly up, and* BIGGER *jumps back.*)

BIGGER: Yessuh, I'm gonna fix it right away. 35
(NORRIS *strolls back into the scene. His eye is on*
BIGGER. *The action of the lifted shovel has at least
aroused his curiosity.*)

BRITTEN: This is the new chauffeur, old hoss, Bigger
Thomas. Just started work here yesterday. 40

NORRIS: I see. How are you, Mr. Thomas?

BIGGER: I — uh — okay, suh.

BRITTEN: We'll go upstairs now — get some of
Peggy's hot rolls.

NORRIS: Believe I'll hang around a bit down here. 45
Maybe I'll want to talk to er — Mr. Thomas some.

BRITTEN: He don't know nothing. (NORRIS *stares at*
BIGGER.)

BIGGER: (*Trembling.*) No, suh, I — I don't know
nothing. (BRITTEN *goes.* NORRIS'S *manner is* 50
confidential and easy.)

NORRIS: Mr. Britten says you were with Miss Dalton
last night — drove her downtown.

BIGGER: Yessuh, her and that Mr. Erlone.

NORRIS: Have a cigarette? (*He offers a cigarette.* 55
BIGGER *stares at him.*) Don't smoke?

BIGGER: Yessuh — nosuh — yessuh. (*He takes a
cigarette.* NORRIS *holds a light.* BIGGER *smokes.*)

NORRIS: You're sweating a lot — I'm cold. Why don't
you stir up the furnace? (BIGGER *shivers and still* 60
makes no move.) What do *you* think has happened
to Miss Dalton, Bigger?

BIGGER: Don't know, suh — Mebbe — mebbe —
(*His voice dies out.*)

NORRIS: Mebbe what? (BIGGER *is silent.* NORRIS 65
*coolly blows smoke at his face. A pounding sets up on
the outside basement door.* BRITTEN *hurries in.*)

BRITTEN: Goddamn reporters! Say, Bigger, you
forgot to lock that driveway gate. (*Before* BIGGER
can answer, the door at the Right opens and several 70
*newspapermen crowd their way in, some of them with
cameras.* BRITTEN *tries to stop them.*) You can't
come in. Get out and stay out.

VOICE: We're in, Mr. Britten. (BIGGER *backs slowly*

away to the wall at the Left and stands alert in the 75
shadow. As the scene progresses, NORRIS *watches*
BIGGER *closely.*)

BRITTEN: Now listen here, boys. This is Mr. Dalton's home, and Mr. Dalton's got no statement to make.

VOICES: What's the dope? Come on. What's going 80
on?

BRITTEN: Nothing!

VOICE: How about that Red they picked up?

2ND VOICE: Jan Erlone?

3RD VOICE: Was she sleeping with him? 85

VOICE: He says he didn't even come here that night. Says he's got witnesses. Says you had him arrested because he's a communist.

BRITTEN: (*Shouting.*) I don't know a thing — not a goddamn thing. (*The reporters have their pads and* 90 *pencils out. They crowd around* BRITTEN, *shooting questions at him.*)

VOICES:

When was she seen last?

Can we get a picture of her room?

Is the girl really missing? 95

Or is this a publicity stunt, Britten?

(*A flash bulb goes off in* BRITTEN'S *face. He blinks and backs away.*)

BRITTEN: Hey, steady, boys.

VOICE: What's the matter?

BRITTEN: I only work here. For Christ's sake, give me a break. (*Another flash bulb explodes in his face.*) 100

VOICE: Then talk.

BRITTEN: I could say go to hell all of you.

VOICE: (*To* BIGGER.) Say, Mike, what do you think?

BIGGER: (*In a hard, cold voice.*) My name ain't Mike.

VOICE: That's the Thomas boy. Bigger Thomas. 105

BRITTEN: The new chauffeur. Just started work here yesterday. He don't know a thing, I tell you. (*A bulb goes off in* BIGGER'S *face.* BIGGER *dodges, throwing his hands up before his eyes.*) Cut it out, will you? Listen, boys — they're worried about the 110 girl — Mrs. Dalton's ill. The whole house is upset — (*A newspaperman walks over to* BIGGER *and slips something into his hand.*)

VOICE: Come on, boy. Give us a break.

BRITTEN: (*Hurrying forward.*) No, none of that. (*He* 115 *snatches the money from* BIGGER'S *fingers and*

returns it to the newspaperman.) Take your damn money back.

(BIGGER *inches away from them, his head lowered. All fall abruptly silent as the door at the Upper Centre opens and* MR. DALTON — *old, weary, and shaken — stands framed in the light, the red shadows flickering across his wan features. He holds a white piece of paper tremblingly in his hand. The photographers begin hastily loading their cameras.*)

DALTON: Gentlemen — (*They all watch him, waiting, as he descends the steps.* BRITTEN *moves* 120 *protectively to his side. Several flash bulbs now blind the scene as* DALTON *lifts his hand, emphasizing his words.*) Please, gentlemen — just a moment. (*After a pause.*) I am ready to make a statement now. (*His voice fails. He then continues.*) I want you to listen 125 carefully. The way you gentlemen handle this will mean life or death to someone — someone very dear to me. (*The bulbs flash again, making* DALTON *blink and lose the train of his thought. Pencils are already flying over their pads.* MRS. DALTON, *dressed* 130 *in white as always, and holding the white cat in her arms, appears in the doorway and descends the stairs and stops. One photographer is on his knees, pointing his camera upwards.* BIGGER *remains silent by the wall, his right hand going now and then to his lips* 135 *in a nervous gesture.* NORRIS *is still watching him.*) Gentlemen, I have just phoned the police and requested that Mr. Jan Erlone be released immediately. I want it known and understood publicly that I have no charges to prefer against 140 him. It is of the utmost importance that this be understood. I hope your papers will carry the story. Further, I want to announce publicly that I apologize for his arrest and inconvenience. Gentlemen, our daughter, Mary Dalton — (*His* 145 *voice fails, then recovers.*) has been kidnapped. (*There is a commotion in the basement.* BRITTEN *confirms the news with a sage nod of his head as if he knew it all the time.*)

VOICE: How do you know, Mr. Dalton? 150

VOICE: When did it happen?

DALTON: (*Recovering himself.*) We think it happened early Sunday morning.

VOICE: How much are they asking?

DALTON: Ten thousand dollars. 155

VOICE: Have you any idea who they are?

DALTON: We know nothing.

VOICE: Have you received any word from your daughter, Mr. Dalton?

DALTON: No, not directly, but we *have* heard from 160 the kidnappers.

VOICE: Is that the letter there?

DALTON: Yes, this is it.

VOICE: Did it come through the mail? How did you get it? 165

DALTON: Someone left it under the door.

VOICE: When?

DALTON: An hour ago.

VOICE: Can we see it?

DALTON: The instructions for the delivery of the 170 money are here, and I have been cautioned not to make them public. But you can say in your papers that these instructions will be followed and I shall pay the ransom.

VOICE: How is the note signed? (*There is silence.*) 175

DALTON: It's signed "Red."

VOICES: Red! Do you know who it is? What does that mean?

DALTON: No.

VOICE: Do you think some communist did it, Mr. 180 Dalton?

DALTON: I don't know. I am not positively blaming anybody. If my daughter is returned, I'll ask no questions of anyone. Now that's all, gentlemen — all — (*He gives a final wave of his hand, but a chorus* 185 *of questions breaks in the air.*)

VOICES:

One minute, please, Mr. Dalton.

One more question.

When do you expect to hear from the kidnappers again? 190

Maybe Mrs. Dalton has a word.

Yes, give us a statement, Mrs. Dalton.

We haven't got our story yet.

(*The scene grows quiet, waiting.*)

DALTON: Would you like to say anything, Ellen? (*His tone of voice suggests she shouldn't. All wait.*) 195

MRS. DALTON: (*Controlling her feelings.*) These terrible things should not happen, but unfortunately they do happen. My husband and I do what good we can. But somehow it seems this is not enough, for now sorrow has come upon us — and grief is 200 in our hearts! We pray for the safe return of our daughter. (*She puts her handkerchief to her lips. DALTON escorts her off. There is a babble of noise among the newspapermen.*)

VOICES: (*Swirling around the confused BRITTEN.*) 205
Get a shot of the girl's room!
Climb a tree if you have to.
And play up Mrs. Dalton's blindness and her cat.
Get a picture of her among her flowers.

A SINGLE VOICE: Hell, this is bigger than the Loeb-Leopold case. 210

ANOTHER VOICE: We can make it just as big!

BRITTEN: (*Half-forcing, half-following the men out.*) Come on, fellows, have a heart, give the old folks a break. (*The reporters are all out now except NORRIS. BRITTEN turns to him.*) Well, old hoss, 215 got an opinion?

NORRIS: As friend Sherlock says — data, man, data — no bricks without straw. Don't mind me.

BRITTEN: Here's hoping. (*He mops his forehead and goes. NORRIS moves with him off into the shadows.* 220 *BIGGER comes tremblingly forward and stands in front of the furnace, gazing at the dull red light. PEGGY comes swiftly in.*)

PEGGY: Bigger.

BIGGER: (*Whirling.*) Huh? 225

PEGGY: For goodness' sake, get the ashes out and start the fire going. I told you.

BIGGER: Yessum.

PEGGY: Now! Mrs. Dalton's had to wear her shawl all day to keep warm. (*She picks up the shovel and* 230 *hands it to him.*) Go ahead, it won't bite you. I'll have your supper ready soon.

BIGGER: (*Taking the shovel mechanically.*) Yessum. (*She goes hurriedly away. BIGGER stands holding the shovel in his hand. He bends down, reaches to open* 235 *the furnace door, then backs off.*) Naw! Naw! (*NORRIS watches him. Once more BIGGER approaches the furnace, then turns away. NORRIS now comes strolling out of the shadows.*)

NORRIS: What's the trouble, boy? (*BIGGER springs* 240 *around, the shovel flying instinctively up in the air as if about to strike something.*)

BIGGER: (*Gasping and dropping the shovel blade against the floor.*) Nothing, suh — nothing, suh.

NORRIS: I understand you're right new here. 245

BIGGER: Yessuh.

NORRIS: And don't know how to run the furnace just yet.

BIGGER: Furnace is easy — you just take hold there — and — and — No suh — yessuh, it's kinda 250 hard to manage.

NORRIS: That's why you don't shake the ashes down like the good woman said?

BIGGER: Yessuh — yessuh. (NORRIS *smiles in a friendly manner and taps* BIGGER *kindly on the* 255 *shoulder.* BIGGER *cringes.*)

NORRIS: Have another cigarette.

BIGGER: Nawsuh, nawsuh. (NORRIS *pulls one out and lights it, then holds the package out to* BIGGER *who takes one of the cigarettes, his hand trembling* 260 *in spite of itself.* NORRIS *strikes another match and holds it for* BIGGER *as before.*)

NORRIS: Sit down, son. I want to talk with you a little more. (*He pulls a couple of seats out from the rear, sits in one and motions* BIGGER *to the other.* 265 BIGGER *sinks quietly down, breathing heavily. He sucks the smoke of the cigarette deep into his lungs and, as if through that action gaining control of himself, he lifts his face and looks directly at his questioner.*) 270

BIGGER: (*In a suddenly clear hard voice.*) What about?

NORRIS: Just a few questions. You know anything connected with this story is news. Say, what do you think of private property?

BIGGER: Suh? Naw, suh, I don't own no property. 275

NORRIS: (*Soothingly.*) Sure, sure. (*Puffing on his cigarette, his eyes crinkling into a gentle smile.*) Tell me, what do you think of Miss Dalton? I've heard she's sort of wild.

BIGGER: (*Quickly.*) Nawsuh, nawsuh. She was a 280 mighty fine lady.

NORRIS: (*Coolly blowing a ring of smoke.*) Why do you say she *was?*

BIGGER: I — uh — I mean she was fine to me.

NORRIS: Yes, the Daltons are mighty fine folks. (*As* 285 *though veering off from the subject.*) What did old Max talk about at that meeting last night?

BIGGER: Suh?

NORRIS: Some of his radical ideas? What did he say to you — well, about the rich and the poor? 290

BIGGER: Well, suh, he said that some day there'd be no more rich folks and no more poor folks, if folks could get together.

NORRIS: Here's hoping, son — especially about the poor. Go ahead. 295

BIGGER: (*With a touch of harshness.*) And he said that us black folks could all get good jobs like anybody else — and stand up high and equal some day.

NORRIS: And there wouldn't be any more lynchings?

BIGGER: Yessuh, no more lynchings. 300

NORRIS: And what did the girl, Miss Dalton, say?

BIGGER: She said so too.

NORRIS: And what did he say to you about white women?

BIGGER: Nothing, suh, nothing. 305

NORRIS: (*Sighing.*) Too bad! You know, Bigger, such things as this ought to be a warning to this country. Here was a happy family, living in peace, loving their neighbor, with one daughter — a beautiful daughter — You agree with that, don't 310 you, Bigger?

BIGGER: Yessuh.

NORRIS: Yes, it's a warning to us. You might say she was a martyr, died to help us see the error of our ways. We've got to learn to treat people better in 315 this country — raise up the oppressed, give them a chance. From what I've heard, Mary Dalton thought like that too. (BIGGER *now and then gives him a queer, questioning baffled look.*) What do you think has really happened to her? 320

BIGGER: I don't know, suh.

NORRIS: Look, that cigarette's burning your fingers. (BIGGER *drops it like a hot coal.* NORRIS *shakes his head.*) They must have killed her, don't you think?

BIGGER: (*Spasmodically.*) They must've done it, suh. 325

NORRIS: Who?

BIGGER: Them Commies — Reds, suh.

NORRIS: And then send the kidnap note with their name signed to it? That's no way to win converts to their cause. You wouldn't be that dumb, would 330 you, Bigger? (*His voice is low, cool, confidential.*)

BIGGER: Nawsuh, nawsuh.

NORRIS: (*Hunching his chair confidentially up toward* BIGGER.) Just suppose you had killed her, Bigger —

BIGGER: (*Wildly.*) Nawsuh, I didn't do it. I didn't do it! 335

NORRIS: Aw, take it easy. Just suppose I had killed her, then. Now that we both agree she's dead. Well, what would I do? (*He rises slowly out of his chair, pushes his hands into his pockets, and begins walking slowly back and forth in a weaving semicircle around* BIGGER, *his hat tilted back on his head as usual.*) Let me see. Yes, I need money. I'd write a ransom note, collect that and skedaddle before they found out she'd been murdered. Wouldn't you do it that way, Bigger? 340 345

BIGGER: Nawsuh.

NORRIS: What would you do?

BIGGER: I didn't do it.

NORRIS: I'm just imagining. Where were we? Oh, she's murdered. So now, we've got to dispose of the body — no traces — nobody ever to know. Well, what about a trunk — ship it off somewhere? Nunh-unh, that wouldn't do. In four days the smell. What about weights — sink her to the bottom of the lake? Nunh-unh, they always rise to the surface. Bury her? No, that's too difficult. Somebody see you digging. What is it that wipes away all traces, Bigger? 350 355

BIGGER: (*Hoarsely.*) Dunno, suh. 360

NORRIS: I'll tell you — fire. (*Whirling and snapping his fingers.*) Yeh, that's what I'd do — I'd burn the body up. Wouldn't you, Bigger? (*With sudden loudness.*) Go ahead and shake the ashes down, like the woman said! (BIGGER'S *head sinks lower still, his shoulders shaking. With a click the thermostat turns the furnace fan on. There is a deep, blowing draft of sound.* BIGGER *springs out of his chair.* NORRIS *looks at him wonderingly.*) Come on, now. Shake 'em down. (*Flipping a coin in his hand.*) Bet you two bits you won't. (BIGGER *bends down puppet-like and reaches for the shovel.* NORRIS *steps briskly over and lifts down an ax hanging on the wall and weighs it idly in his hand.* BIGGER *turns slowly around.* NORRIS *smiles at him.*) This is a good ax, Bigger. Old Kelly. I used to chop with one like this when I was a kid, back on the farm. And I was good at trapping in the winter too — used to catch a lot — minks, and now and then a skunk or two — in my trap! 365 370 375 380

(*And now in desperation* BIGGER *turns fiercely back to the furnace, flings open the door and plunges the shovel into the blinding bank of glowing, red-hot ashes. A puff of dust sails out and settles about the room. Then flinging the shovel down, he hysterically seizes the upright grate handle and shakes it with a great clatter.*)

BIGGER: (*Breathing deeply.*) It's all fixed now. Draws fine — everything be warmed up now. (*Yelling at the ceiling above him.*) Miss Peggy, the furnace okay now! Listen at her sing! (*Making a puffing noise with his lips.*) She's putting on the steam now! Going to town. Goddam! (*He begins singing cheerily.*) "John Henry was a little boy, sitting on his father's knee!" 385

NORRIS: (*Hanging the ax on the wall behind him and strolling over again.*) Sing on, boy, sounds mighty good. 390

BIGGER: (*Joy breaking in his voice.*) Listen to that old coal crackle on down! The old valve creeping up — soon be popping off. Hear them drivers roll. (BRITTEN *comes hurriedly down the steps at the rear.*) 395

BRITTEN: What's going on here? Hell of a time to be singing. (NORRIS *is now standing by the pile of ashes, idly stirring them with the toe of his shoe.*)

NORRIS: He's a croon-baby. Come on, baby, sing us some more. 400

BIGGER: Got to clean up now. (*He grabs a broom from behind the furnace and goes to work.*)

BRITTEN: Hell of a note. We just called up the jail and that Erlone fellow won't leave. He's raising hell — 405

NORRIS: Says this Bigger boy's been lying, don't he?

BRITTEN: How'd you know? That's just what he said. (NORRIS *lifts a charred object from the ashes.*)

NORRIS: Look here. 410

BRITTEN: What is it?

NORRIS: See this? Look — it's — (BIGGER *shudders and turns away.*) It's a piece of bone.

BRITTEN: Aw — just some garbage they're burning maybe. 415

NORRIS: And look — here's something else. (*He stoops and picks up a bit of rounded metal and examines it closely.*) It's an earring.

BRITTEN: Good God! That means —

NORRIS: Tell him what it means, Bigger.   420

BIGGER: (*With a scream.*) Let me out of here! Let me out! (*He staggers as if about to fall, then stumbles drunkenly out of the scene yelling.*) Help me! Help me!

BRITTEN: Holy smoke! What's the matter with him   425
— having a fit or something?

NORRIS: You'd better catch him. He raped and killed Mary Dalton and burned her body in that furnace!

(BRITTEN *stares at him dumbfounded an instant, then begins blowing his whistle violently as he rushes from the room. Other whistles are heard blowing. Then the sound of a police siren and distant shouts. The scene fades out. Offscene, newsboys are heard giving their high and raucous calling in the darkness.*)

NEWSBOYS:
Heiress murdered and raped!
Body of girl burned in a furnace!   430
Rapist escapes!
Read all about it!
Five thousand policemen search for the killer
Bigger Thomas!
Black chauffeur murders millionaire's daughter!
Governor offers reward for the killer!   435
Read all about it!

SCENE VIII

The sounds die away as the curtain rises on an empty room on the top floor of an abandoned apartment house. The Rear wall of the room has collapsed and gives a view of a ruined balcony at the back, with frozen rooftops, chimneys, and a stretch of night sky beyond. Part of the wall at the Right Rear leans forward, and in, to form a sort of shelter. In the shadow at the Right Front is the distorted shape of a door frame. The colour of the scene runs from thick black shadow at the Right to a diffused yellowish glare in the Centre and Back. The wind moans intermittently. From the deep canyon below comes the muffled drone of the great city, punctuated by an auto horn, a snatch of radio music, and vague wandering noises — all hushed and muted down by the thick snow enveloping the world. The room is lit up at intervals by the changing colours of what is evidently a large electric sign on a neighbouring roof. Less noticeable at first is the faint light from a revolving beacon far away.

When the curtain rises, BIGGER *is seen standing half-crouched in the shadow of the wall at the Right Rear. An old piece of rotted blanket is pulled protectively around his shoulders, and his feet are tied up in pieces of wrapped towsacking.*[18] *He is peering out toward the Rear and listening, as if some sound had just disturbed him and he is trying to discover what it is. The glint of his pistol barrel shows from beneath the blanket where he holds it in his hand. Presently he turns and begins to pace up and down, beating himself with his arms to keep from freezing. A mumble of words rises from his lips.*

BIGGER: Pshaw, nothing but that old piece of tin banging. They ain't found me yet! From the first jump I out-figure 'em. (*Stopping.*) Uhm — everything sleepy and 'way off — (*With sudden loudness.*) I ain't scared, naw. They all scared, feeling   5
me in the night, feel me walking behind 'em. And everywhere the bulls is searching them old nigger houses — Indiana, Calumet, Prairie, Wabash! Ha! But I ain't 'mong the niggers. (*Calling softly.*) Clara! (*He listens at the door at the Right.*) Why don't she   10
come on here? (*He sinks down on an old box and pulls his blanket shiveringly about him. The flopping tin bangs off at the Left. He springs instinctively and nervously up, then sits down again.*) Ain't nothing — that old tin banging again, hanging loose and   15
ready to fall. Fall on down, old tin, but I ain't gonna fall. They ain't gonna get me. (*Gazing back over his shoulder at the night sky, he chuckles with low and bitter irony.*) They smart, them white folks! Yeh, they get the niggers. But maybe not too smart   20
— (*He spits in the air. He beats his arms about him and stares out into the night.*) That's right! Flash away, old sign! "Sun-kissed oranges." Ha! I'll be in them orange groves soon with the sun on my back! (*He raises his head and sees far away, above him, the   25
revolving beam of the beacon in the sky.*) Uhmm — and look at that old Lindbergh beacon, shining

---

18 *towsacking*] rough material made of hemp, used for wrapping bales, etc.

there 'way out through the darkness — (*Musingly.*) Old Lindbergh — he knowed the way. Slashings of icy water below him, the thunder and the 30 lightning, the freezing and the hail around him. Keep on driving — riding through. (*Imitating the sound of an airplane propeller with his numbed lips.*) V-r-r-r-rh-h-h-h! V-r-r-r-ruh-uh-uh! Yes, he made it, got there. And all the people running and 35 shouting, and the headlights switching and sweeping the sky! Old Lindbergh — he made it — got home, safe home.[19] He not scared! (*Snapping his head up, his hollow eyes burning through the shadows before him.*) Aw, I ain't scared 40 neither! And when I light, ain't going to be no lot of people running to me with flowers! No! When *I* come, they run the other way! Run like hell! (*He laughs. And now from the depths of the great city below comes the sound of a siren. He springs around,* 45 *the piece of rotted blanket falling from his shoulders. He grips his gun tightly in his hand and crouching down moves swiftly to the window at the Left. Inching his head up against the sill, he peers over. The sound dies away. He turns from the window.*) Sure, nothing 50 but a' ambulance! Another fool white man done broke his neck somewhere. (*He moves back toward the box, flapping his arms like a bird to restore the circulation of his blood. A soft sound of fumbling footsteps is heard at the Right. Holding his pistol, he* 55 *backs away, keeping his eyes fastened on the door. The footsteps come nearer, then stop. He calls out softly.*) That you, Clara?

CLARA'S VOICE: (*Outside.*) Open the door. (*He springs over, unbars the door, and lets* CLARA *in.* 60 *Ramming the bar of plank back in place, he grabs a package from her.*)

BIGGER: Okay?

CLARA: (*In a low dull voice.*) Eat something, Bigger. (*With shaking, eager hands, he opens the bag of food* 65 *and begins devouring the sandwiches she has brought.*)

BIGGER: Thought you was never coming back. And me sitting here freezing to death. Things going 'round in my head! How everything look?

CLARA: Go ahead and eat — 70

BIGGER: (*His mouth full of food.*) Anybody notice you?

CLARA: Went to a new delicatessen — Thirty-ninth and Indiana.

BIGGER: And you come back under the El like I told you?[20] 75

CLARA: I come back that way.

BIGGER: Get the papers?

CLARA: Here's some liquor — you 'bout froze. (*She pulls a bottle from her pocket. He grabs it, unstops it and drinks half of it swiftly down, then lays the bottle* 80 *on the floor. She stands with her hands shoved by each other into her coat sleeves, looking at him.*)

BIGGER: Where the papers? I ask you.

CLARA: Didn't get 'em, Bigger.

BIGGER: Damn it, told you to — See what they say? 85

CLARA: They got your picture.

BIGGER: On the front page?

CLARA: On the front page.

BIGGER: Reckon they have. And big headlines — huh? 90

CLARA: Big headlines, black — (*Her mouth twists with pain.*)

BIGGER: Hmmm. Where they think I hid?

CLARA: Section down by Ernie's all surrounded.

BIGGER: Hah — knowed it. Dumb nuts. If them 95 cops' brains was dynamite, wouldn't have enough to make 'em sneeze! (*Angrily.*) Why'n hell didn't you bring me that paper? (*She stares at him with dull, dead eyes, saying nothing.*) What's the matter? What time is it? 100

CLARA: Forgot to wind my watch.

BIGGER: What the big clock down there say?

CLARA: Ten till one, it say.

BIGGER: Ten more minutes and I'm gone from here. Ten more minutes and that big old sign out there 105 goes off, and I make it 'cross that old stairway over there in the dark to the next building and down that long alley.

CLARA: (*Piteously.*) Then what, Bigger?

BIGGER: I find somebody with a car — (*With the* 110 *gun, he indicates a jab in the side.*) He drive me till I say stop. Then I catch a train to the west — Still got that money?

---

19 Lindbergh] In 1927, Charles Lindbergh was the first person to fly solo across the Atlantic Ocean.

20 the El] Chicago's elevated railway transit system (also known as "the L").

CLARA: I got it.

BIGGER: How much? 115

CLARA: 'Bout ninety dollars.

BIGGER: Gimme. (*She pulls it out of her pocket and hands it to him.*)

CLARA: Bigger, you can't make it that way — You can't. 120

BIGGER: Want me to set here and freeze stiff as a pool stick and wait for 'em to come and pick me up?[21] I got everything figured to the minute. (*Now from the city below comes the sound of the siren again. It continues longer than before. He jerks his head around.*) 125 Don't like the sound of that. Jesus, won't that sign hurry and go off?

CLARA: Bigger, you can't do it.

BIGGER: (*With a shout.*) Cut it out!

CLARA: They offer twenty-five thousand dollars 130 reward — the paper say. The coloured folks are helping to hunt for you too.

BIGGER: (*After an instant of silence.*) Uhm — they want me bad. Well, they ain't gonna get me.

CLARA: It say you killed her, Bigger. 135

BIGGER: All right, then, I killed her. I didn't mean to. (*Angrily.*) But hell, we got no time to talk about that. Got to keep my mind clear, my feet free. (*He bends down and begins unwrapping the sacking from around his feet.*) 140

CLARA: You told me you wasn't never gonna kill nobody, Bigger. (*She chokes down the sob that keeps rising up in her throat.*)

BIGGER: I tell you, I wasn't trying to kill her. It was an accident — 145

CLARA: Accident —

BIGGER: She was drunk — passed out cold — She was so drunk she didn't even know where she was.

CLARA: And what she do?

BIGGER: Nothing — I just put her on the bed, and 150 her blind ma come in — (*Shuddering.*) Blind. She come in and I got scared. Scared, I tell you. She was like all the white folks in the world had been rolled into one and I was scared of 'em. (*His voice quickening.*) Yeh, her ma come into the room — 155 had her hands stretched out like. So I just pushed the pillow hard over the gal's mouth to keep her

---

21 pool stick] billiard cue.

from talking. (*His voice drops to a low note of helpless confession.*) Then when she left, I looked at that gal and she was dead — that's all — it happened just 160 like that — (*He looks at* CLARA *as though imploring her belief.*) She was dead!

CLARA: You — you smothered her.

BIGGER: Yeh, I reckon I did — but I didn't mean to — I swear to God I didn't. (*In a hopeless tone.*) But 165 what difference do it make? Nobody'll believe me. I'm black and they'll say — (*He flings a rag savagely away.*)

CLARA: The paper say —

BIGGER: Yeah, I know what they say. They say rape. 170 But I didn't. I never touched that girl that way. (*Pause.*) And then when I see she dead, I, oh, Clara, I didn't know what to do. I took her to the basement and put her — burnt her up in that big old furnace. (CLARA *stares at him, her fist stuffed* 175 *against her mouth as if to keep herself from screaming.*) Jesus, it don't seem like I really done it now — really it don't seem like I done it. (*He looks off, his face hard and tense.*) Maybe I didn't do it. Maybe I just think I did. Maybe somebody else 180 did all that — (*His body relaxes and his shoulders slump.*) But I did. Yeh — this old house, this freezing cold makes me know it. Your face say so — and the feeling in here say so. Yeh, I hated her. I was scared but all the time I hated her and deep 185 down glad that I had killed her. Like some day I might kill you — you stand in my way. (*She gazes at him, her eyes filled with their dull nameless look of horror and despair. He picks up the bottle and takes another drink.*) 190

CLARA: (*Monotonously.*) You can't get away. You got to walk down — meet 'em — tell 'em how it happened.

BIGGER: (*With a wild laugh.*) Goddamit, I stick my head out that door, my life ain't worth a snowflake 195 in hell. They shoot me down like a dog. Jesus, that tin keeps banging! (*A strange light flares into the scene an instant and then is gone.* BIGGER *leaps to his feet with a cry.*) What the hell was that! (*He tilts the bottle again, finishes it, then throws it away into* 200 *the darkness.*) But I ain't scared now!

CLARA: Maybe you ought to be scared — Scared maybe 'cause you ain't scared.

[VIII]

BIGGER: Huh? Aw, to hell with it.

CLARA: What you gonna do? 205

BIGGER: (*With sudden rage.*) Gonna scram, I tell you. (*With rough brutality.*) And I don't need you now.

CLARA: I know — all last night and today, I know. Don't do no good now — nothing do any good. Your eyes so cold, your face so hard — like you 210 want to kill me. And my heart's all heavy like a lump of lead and — dead.

BIGGER: Yeh. Anything get in my way now, I kill it. (*Another siren sounds in the streets below, and now faintly comes the sound of mumbling voices.* BIGGER 215 *darts back into the shadow and stops.*) Listen there! (*Again as if from an unseen brilliant eye, the ruined room is illuminated in a white light.* BIGGER *draws his gun.*) Goddamn, they got a spotlight some-where. They found me. (*Whirling on* CLARA *and* 220 *seizing her by the throat.*) They seen you coming back. (*Hissing.*) I ought to kill you. You tell 'em.

CLARA: No! No! Bigger! Bigger!

BIGGER: (*His lips snarled back, his eyes cold as a snake's.*) Yeh, weak, blind — couldn't do without 225 you. You tell 'em where I am. (*He shakes her like a rag-doll. He hurls her from him against the ruined wall at the Right. She lies there in the shadows, shivering and gasping. A low, dog-like whimper rises from her. He rushes over and kicks her.*) Goddamit, 230 stop that whining. (*She crawls toward him.*) Don't you come toward me. I'll kill you. (*The noise in the streets below has increased in volume.*)

CLARA: (*Now clinging to his legs.*) Go ahead. Shoot me. Kill us both — and then, no more worry — 235 no more pain. Do it, Bigger.

(*He jerks loose from her. She falls forward on her face and lies still. The brilliant light floods into the scene again from the faraway hidden spot, and* BIGGER *stands, half-blinded, in it. He runs to the window and looks out. Suddenly the electric sign falters in its cycle of going on and off — then goes out entirely. A clock is heard striking one. In a convulsive gesture, his hand rises to his lips, then drops to his side.*)

BIGGER: Yeh, you done it. They coming along that roof over there with their saw-off guns. I see 'em! (*He rushes to the Right, starts to unbar the door when a heavy pounding sets up below. He springs back.*) They 240

coming up there, too. (*He runs over and jerks* CLARA *violently from the floor. An ooze of blood is seeping from her mouth.*) You set 'em on me, you bitch! (*Her head sways weakly from side to side, saying "no." He throws her from him again. She stands tottering and about to* 245 *fall. He runs out on the balcony at the Rear. The powerful light remains on him. He starts back with an oath, then runs wildly along the balcony toward the Left. The sound of the distant voices rises more loudly. A shot rings.* BIGGER *ducks back into the room behind* 250 *the piece of ruined wall. Another shot barks, and the sound of breaking glass is heard.* BIGGER *yells.*) Shoot! Shoot! (*The pounding at the Right increases and shouts are heard near at hand off at the Left. He grabs* CLARA *and holds her in front of him, moving swiftly over to the* 255 *Right Rear.*)

VOICES: (*At the left.*) There he is! Let him have it! We've got him!

(BIGGER *whirls now, holding* CLARA *protectingly in front of him with one hand. Her arms go up and about him in an impulsive gesture of love. Another shot rings out and she sags down in his arms. He looks at her, then lets her slide out of his arms to the floor.*)

BIGGER: Yeh. In front of me, and they shot you — All right, Goddamit, I killed you. (*Wagging his* 260 *head.*) Yeh. I said I would. I said so.

A VOICE: (*Beyond the door at the Right.*) Come on out of there, Bigger Thomas! (BIGGER *fires at the door. And now the air is permeated with a multitude of voices, as if an invisible ring of people were* 265 *squeezing the scene in a tightening circle. A voice at the Left calls out.*)

VOICE: Come on out, you black bastard!

VOICE: You're going to wish you were dead!

VOICE: Drop that gun. (*The sound of sirens from the* 270 *distance has grown to a roaring volume now. Above the tumult* BIGGER'S *voice lashes out, high and clear.*)

BIGGER: Yeh, white boys! Come on and get me! You ain't scared of me, is you? Ain't nobody but Bigger 275 in here — (*He shoots at the door.*) Bigger! Bigger! Bigger standing against the lot of you! Against your thousand — two thousand — three thousand — (*He fires again and again. The scene fades out. The sirens continue, then gradually die away.*) 280

SCENE IX

A hearing-room in the City Courthouse, some days later. In the darkness the voice of EDWARD MAX *is heard, then that of* DAVID BUCKLEY.

MAX'S VOICE: I am representing Bigger Thomas at this hearing, Mr. Buckley.

BUCKLEY'S VOICE: And I am the newly-elected state's attorney, Mr. Max, and have a right to question the defendant.   5

MAX'S VOICE: He is *my* client — (*The light comes up on a medium-sized room.* MAX *and* BUCKLEY *are in an argument.* MAX *is a man of late middle age, heavy-set, gray-haired and kindly-faced.* BUCKLEY *is younger, spryer, and bull-doggish and* 10 *wears a flower in his lapel.*) my client all the way! I'll see that his rights are protected.

BUCKLEY: And it'll be all the way too — the death house for this boy unless —

MAX: Unless what? There are always extenuating 15 circumstances, Mr. Buckley.

BUCKLEY: But not enough to save his neck. (*Two guards bring* BIGGER *in. They are armed. He is handcuffed.* BIGGER *sinks sluggishly down into a chair.*)   20

MAX: Take the cuffs off. I'm right here, Bigger. (BIGGER *says nothing. The guard unlocks the handcuffs and holds them.*)

BUCKLEY: I want to ask you a few questions, Bigger Thomas! (BIGGER *makes no reply.*)   25

MAX: Go ahead and ask them, but he needn't answer if he doesn't want to.

BUCKLEY: If he answers freely, we'll put that to his credit. How many white women have you raped besides Miss Dalton? (*No answer.* BIGGER *stares at* 30 *the floor as if he hadn't heard.*) We've got a line on you and all you ever did. How about that girl you attacked in Jackson Park last summer? While you were sleeping in your cell, we brought a woman in who identified you.   35

MAX: Don't believe him, Bigger.

BUCKLEY: (*With a half shout — to* MAX.) And sir, you be careful how you obstruct justice. (*Bending toward* BIGGER.) And Miss Ashton says you attacked her last summer by climbing through the 40 window of her bedroom. (*A raucous moan breaks*

from BIGGER'S *throat, and he shakes his head from side to side.*) Boy, let the newspapers learn what we've got on you, you're cooked. Come on now, come clean. Lying won't get you anywhere.   45

MAX: Let him talk, Bigger. (BUCKLEY *strikes his hands together angrily.* MAX *chuckles.*) He's trying to fabricate charges against you.

BUCKLEY: I'm trying to get at the truth and give him a chance by confessing to these already proved 50 crimes to possibly save his black skin. (*Pleadingly.*) Come on, boy, I'm trying to help you!

MAX: And a fine way of doing it by accusing him of still more crimes. He has already testified he did not mean to kill Mary Dalton. It —   55

BUCKLEY: (*Interrupting.*) He burnt her body in the furnace to wipe out the traces of raping her. And he murdered Clara Mears to keep her quiet forever.

MAX: It has already been proved that a policeman's bullet killed Clara Mears. (BUCKLEY *throws out his* 60 *hands in exasperation as* MR. *and* MRS. DALTON *appear, accompanied by* BRITTEN. *They wear heavy coats against the outside cold.*)

DALTON: Bigger Thomas, we want to help you. (BUCKLEY *steps back.*)   65

MRS. DALTON: (*Softly, intensely.*) Yes — to help. (*The light emphasizes* DALTON *as he moves toward* BIGGER *and stops.*)

DALTON: I'm a friend of your people still, Bigger. I've just sent a large contribution to the Southside 70 Negro Boys' Club. Hear that, Mr. Max?

MAX: (*Sharply.*) This problem, Mr. Dalton, is deeper than any money.

DALTON: (*With sudden sharpness to* BIGGER.) Why did you do this thing to us? To us, you hear, who 75 have tried so hard to help! Why, Bigger?

BUCKLEY: Speak up, boy! (*But* BIGGER *sits as if seeing nothing, hearing nothing.*)

MRS. DALTON: He doesn't want us to help him, Henry.   80

(*She,* DALTON *and* BRITTEN *move back into the shadows.* BUCKLEY *and* MAX *move with them.* GUS, JACK, *AND* G.H. *appear at the Left. They come nearer and stop.* JAN ERLONE *is with them.*)

ERLONE: We're all pulling for you, Bigger — me — and Gus and Jack and G.H. here. (*For an instant*

BIGGER *looks out, then resumes his hunched-over and lightless staring at the floor.* GUS *comes farther into the light. He is weeping.*) 85

GUS: Just want you to know, Bigger — no hard feelings anymore. (*He snivels and wipes his eyes with his hand.*) Ain't bothered old Blum neither. We quit all that.

JACK and G.H.: (*In chorus.*) Quit all that jiving around, Bigger. 90

GUS: Anything we can do, Bigger?

G.H.: They picked us up too, Bigger. But we didn't tell nothing.

JACK: Mr. Erlone got us off. 95

ERLONE: And they're helping down at headquarters. Hear, Bigger, hear that? They're learning. And I have always been your friend. (*He holds out his hand.* BIGGER *pays no attention to it.* ERLONE *and the three boys move back into the shadows and remain* 100 *there, like the* DALTONS, *"haunting" the scene. There is a noise at Right, and* HANNAH *comes in. She is accompanied by* VERA, BUDDY, *and* REVEREND HAMMOND, *an elderly, gaunt, gray-haired preacher.* BIGGER *springs up.*) 105

HANNAH: (*As* BIGGER *shrinks back.*) My po' boy! My boy!

BIGGER: (*Desperately.*) Naw, naw! Ma! Ma! (*He tries to move away but the guard stops him.*)

HANNAH: We've been praying, son, night and day, 110 praying for you.

HAMMOND: Yes, Lord, yes! God hears us!

VERA: (*Half-sobbing.*) And crying, praying and crying. (BUDDY *gets hold of one of* BIGGER'S *hands and holds it tight as he gazes piteously up at him.* 115 *His lips blubber with smothered sobs.* VERA *stuffs her handkerchief against her mouth.* BIGGER *twists his head about and looks appealingly to the guard.*)

HANNAH: It's God we're praying to, son, and he's got the power. He can save your soul. They say they're 120 gonna kill you in the 'lectric chair. The papers say it.

VERA: (*With a little scream.*) They do!

HAMMOND: Your body, only your body, son. They can't kill your soul. 125

HANNAH: Your soul! That belongs to God. But you got to open your heart, let him in.

HAMMOND: Let him in. Take Jesus as your saviour

and nothing can harm you. You'll be saved! Saved! Pray, brother, pray. 130

HANNAH: Pray!

VERA and BUDDY: (*Likewise.*) Pray! (HANNAH *flings her arms tightly around* BIGGER. VERA *and* BUDDY *hug him too. For an instant they stand so.* BIGGER'S *arms go around the three, and he hugs them to him,* 135 *then violently rebuffs them and turns away.*)

HAMMOND: Send down thy power, Heavenly Father, and purify this poor sinner.

HANNAH: Yes, Lawd, yes! Hear us, hear us! Oh, son, hear our prayers. Get right with God. I am old and 140 poor and won't be here much longer. But you and me — all of us — can meet beyond the grave and this trouble will be over. We have God's blessed promise. Get right with Him and we will be together again up in heaven, there where your pa 145 waits for us. Son! Son!

VERA and BUDDY: Yes, Bigger, yes. (REVEREND HAMMOND *falls on his knees in prayer. The rest of the family do likewise.* HANNAH *is sobbing and has her handkerchief stuffed against her mouth.*) 150

HAMMOND: (*In evangelical fervour.*) Son, son, listen to me! For thousands of years man has been praying for God to take the curse of sin off of him. God heard man and he sent his son Jesus down to earth. He put on human flesh and lived and 155 died to show us the way. (*The light tightens on the praying group, leaving the rest of the scene in shadow.*) Jesus let men crucify him. But his death was a victory. He showed us that to live in this world was to be crucified by the world. Life every day is a 160 crucifixion. There ain't but one way out, son, and that's the Jesus way, the way of love and forgiveness. Be like Jesus. Don't resist. It's love that's got to save you and bring your soul to heaven. You got to believe that God gives eternal life through the 165 love of Jesus Christ. Look at me. (*Loudly.*) Look at me! Promise you'll stop hating and let God's love come into your heart. (BIGGER *is silent.* REVEREND HAMMOND *rises and takes out a cross.*) This is the cross of the Lord Jesus Christ. Let me put it 170 around your neck — to bring his comfort unto you.

BIGGER: (*Screaming.*) Go away! Leave me! (*He jerks the cross from the preacher's hand and flings it to the*

floor.) Take your Jesus and go! I got no use for him! 175
He couldn't help my dead father. He can't help me!

(*He turns to the guards who lead him away.* HANNAH
and the others rise. REVEREND HAMMOND *picks up
the cross. The light widens, and* MRS. DALTON *and*
HANNAH *now have their arms around each other.
They all move away. The scene fades out. Far off we
hear the rainy washing sound of angry voices. It comes
nearer, then fades. In the darkness the banging of a
gavel is heard.*)

SCENE X

*The City Courtroom sometime later. On an imposing
dais at the Rear sits the* JUDGE, *draped in a long black
gown, and with a gray and heavy judicial face.
Hanging directly above him, and behind, is the picture
of an eighteenth-century statesman resembling Thomas
Jefferson and surmounted by the graceful folds of the
Stars and Stripes. Down in Front of the* JUDGE'S *desk
is an oblong table. Between the desk and the table sits
the court stenographer and to the Right and Left Rear
stand two guards. At the Right Front sit* HANNAH
THOMAS, VERA, *and* BUDDY. BUDDY *is holding
tightly to his mother's hand. In the same position at the
Left sit the* DALTONS *and* PEGGY. *The two women
wear veils and are in deep mourning. At the table,
with his back to the audience, is* BIGGER. *He seems to
pay no attention to what is going on around him. The
scene is in darkness as the curtain rises, and out of this
darkness comes the deep tumult of many voices, and
then other voices raised in argument. As if in rhythm to
the banging of the* JUDGE'S *gavel the light comes
swiftly up.* MAX *and* BUCKLEY *are on their feet in
front of the* JUDGE'S *stand.*

JUDGE: If there is another disturbance, I shall clear
the court. (*The noise subsides and* MAX *sits down.*)
Proceed, Mr. Buckley.
BUCKLEY: Your Honour, I deplore that in these cru- 5
cial times the viperous issue of race and class hatred
has been dragged forward in order to excuse a brutal and perverted crime. I shall not deign to answer
or discuss these incompetent, irrelevant and immaterial arguments. Likewise, I *could* call the long
roll of this defendant's misdemeanours and crimes 10

— could describe him as a thug, as a degenerate
who abused and cursed his Christian mother, describe him as a deep-dyed criminal, a murderer at
heart, who preyed upon innocent people, who
stalked about in the deep darkness of night, thiev- 15
ing, robbing and lying in wait — a black ape who
climbed his way into a peaceful home and
deflowered, mutilated and destroyed the light of
that home, the joy of these parents — a beautiful
girl. But I will not. For I shrink from the mere re- 20
cital of the facts connected with this most horrible
crime — a crime that has marked this defendant
in every newspaper in the land as a sub-human
killer who in his idle and leisure moments loafed
about the streets, pilfered from newsstands, robbed 25
the stores, molested women, frequented dives, attended cheap movies and chased prostitutes. A few
more words, Your Honour, and I am done. The
defendant, Bigger Thomas, pleads guilty to the
charges of the indictment — 30
MAX: Objection, Your Honour. The confession was
obtained under duress and is not allowed as
evidence.
JUDGE: Objection sustained. (BUCKLEY *bows
graciously.*) 35
BUCKLEY: The rest is simple and brief. Punishment
must follow — punishment laid down by the
sacred laws of this commonwealth, laws created to
protect that society and that social system of which
we are a part. (*With heavy judicial gravity.*) A 40
criminal is one who goes against those laws. He
attacks the laws. Therefore the law must destroy
him. If thine eye offend thee, pluck it out! And if
a branch of the tree withers and dies, it must be
cut off lest it contaminate the rest of the tree. Such 45
a tree is the State through whose flourishing and
good health we ourselves exist and carry on our
lives on this earth. I pity this diseased and ruined
defendant, but as a true surgeon looking to the
welfare of the organic body of our people, I repeat 50
that it is necessary this diseased member be cut off
— be cut off and obliterated lest it infect us all
unto death. (*Fervently.*) Your Honour, in the name
of the people of this city, in the name of truth and
in the name of Almighty God, I demand that for 55
the rape and brutal murder of beautiful and

innocent Mary Dalton this Bigger Thomas justly die in the electric chair. (*He looks to* BIGGER, *then crosses to his chair at the end of the table at the Left and sits down, with his back to the audience. The* JUDGE *recognizes* MAX *who already is on his feet.*)

JUDGE: Mr. Max.

MAX: Your Honour, night after night, I have lain without sleep trying to think of a way to picture to you, and to the world, the causes, the reason, why this boy, Bigger Thomas, sits here today — and why our city is boiling with a fever of excitement and hate. (*He gestures off.*) I have pled the cause of other criminal youths in this Court, as Your Honour well knows. And when I took this case, I thought at first it was the same old story of a boy run afoul of the law. But I am convinced it is more terrible than that — with a meaning far more reaching. Where is the responsibility? Where is the guilt? There is guilt and responsibility in the hate that inflames the crowds of people gathered in the streets below these windows. (*He turns and gestures through the air.*) What is the atmosphere that surrounds this trial? Are the citizens intent upon seeing that the majesty of the law is upheld? That retribution be dealt out in measure with the facts? That the guilty and only the guilty be caught and punished? No! (*He looks around at* BUCKLEY.) Every conceivable prejudice has been dragged into this case. The press, radio, even the authorities of the city and state have inflamed the public mind to the point where martial law is threatened in this city.

BUCKLEY: (*Rising angrily.*) I object, Your Honour.

JUDGE: Objection sustained. (BUCKLEY *sits down. The* JUDGE *looks sternly at* MAX.) Counsel will please confine his remarks to the evidence in the case!

MAX: Your Honour, for the sake of this boy I wish I could bring to you evidence of a morally worthier nature. I wish I could say that love or ambition or jealousy or the quest for adventure, or any of the more romantic emotions were back of this case. But I have no choice in this matter. Life has cut this cloth, not I. I do not claim that this boy is the victim of injustice only, but he is a victim of a way of life that has grown like a cancer into the very blood and bones of our social structure.

Bigger Thomas sits here today as a symbol of that way, and the judgment delivered upon him is a judgment delivered upon ourselves.

JUDGE: But you and I are not on trial in this court, Mr. Max. (*He gestures quietly with his hand for* MAX *to continue.*)

MAX: But in a deeper way, Your Honour, we are on trial. And if you and I, as representative citizens of this city and nation, refuse to see it, if we too are caught in the mire of blind emotion like Bigger Thomas, then this vicious evil will continue to grow, and the future of this great country and its precious institutions stand threatened by the convulsions of a destructive and bloody revolution. We are warned in time. Let us heed that warning. (*The* JUDGE *is now listening intently to* MAX.) Your Honour, it has taken me days and nights to think my way through this labyrinth of darkness and evil, but I feel I see the truth now, and I want the court to see it, in order that this chain of woeful circumstances may be broken here. Yes, I will go so far as to say that in the very evil which Bigger Thomas wrought so violently upon our society, he for the first time in his twisted and misshapen life was born into the world for awhile as a free and responsible soul. What an awful fact to contemplate!

BUCKLEY: (*Suddenly shouting out.*) He is pleading the prisoner insane, Your Honour! I will call for a trial by jury!

JUDGE: (*Rapping with his gavel.*) Silence!

MAX: I am not making that claim, Your Honour. For one time, horrible as it seems and as true as it is, Bigger Thomas acted in the full capacity of himself. In the evil of his deed he had for the first time in his life found himself. For the first time he was completely alive, and all the pent-up emotion, the frustrated urges of his life flowered into expression. Bigger Thomas is an organism which our American system has bred. He represents but a tiny aspect of a problem whose reality sprawls all over this nation — as is shown by the disturbances and crimes now shaking the land. Kill him, burn the life out of him, and still more this living death continues. In this courtroom today not only Bigger Thomas is on trial but our American civilization. (*Turning toward* MR. *and* MRS. DALTON.) I have

only sympathy for these kind-hearted and griev-
ing parents. You have their testimony, and you 150
have heard them plead for mercy for this boy. Well
may they so plead, for they too share the guilt of
this terrible crime.

BUCKLEY: (*Loudly.*) Your Honour! —

MAX: Unconsciously and against their will perhaps. 155
They intended no evil, yet they produced evil.

BUCKLEY: I object! He is impugning the character
of my witnesses. (*He stands up.*)

MAX: (*Facing him.*) I am not. I am trying to state
the facts — (*Turning toward the* JUDGE.) And 160
these are the facts, Your Honour. (BUCKLEY *reseats
himself in fuming silence.*) Mr. Dalton rents his vast
Chicago real estate holdings to hundreds, to
thousands of Negroes, and among these thousands
is the family of this Bigger Thomas. The rents in 165
those tenements, those foul ghetto buildings —

BUCKLEY: (*On his feet again.*) I object, Your Honour.

JUDGE: Objection sustained. (*Calling down to the
stenographer.*) Strike the words "foul ghetto" from
the record. 170

MAX: The conditions in those buildings are among
the worst in the city. Yet this man is held in high
esteem. Why? Because out of the profits he makes
he turns around and gives back to the Negroes a
small part of that in charity. For this he is lauded 175
in the press and held up as an example of fine
citizenship. But where do the Negroes come in?
What have they to say about how they live?
Nothing! Around the whole vicious circle they
move and act at Dalton's behest and must accept 180
the crumbs of their own bread of charity fed back
at them as this man wills or wills not. It is a form
of bribery that continues and will continue until
we see the truth and stop it.

BUCKLEY: Your Honour! (*The* JUDGE *waves him* 185
down, and MAX *goes on.*)

MAX: One word more, Your Honour, and I am
through. (*Pointing toward the Rear.*) There under
that mighty American flag is the likeness of one
of our forefathers — our forefathers who came to 190
these strange shores hundreds of years ago — men
who found a land whose tasks called forth the
deepest and best that was in them. And these men
and we who followed them built a nation mighty
and powerful, today the most powerful nation on 195
earth. But we have denied one of the basic truths
of Thomas Jefferson who said "We hope to avail
the state of those talents which nature has sown
as liberally among the poor as the rich, but which
perish without use, if not sought for and culti- 200
vated." Yes, perish or turn to crime. We have said
to those we enslaved to help us build this nation,
this is a white man's country! And we have kept it
a white man's country three hundred years. But
night and day millions of turmoiling souls, the 205
souls of our black people, are pleading — "This
is our country too. We helped build it. Give us a
part in it, a part free and hopeful and wide as the
everlasting horizon." And in this fear-crazed, guilt-
ridden body of Bigger Thomas that vast multitude 210
cries out in a mighty voice saying, "Give us our
freedom, our chance and our hope to be men!"
Your Honour, I beg you, not in the name of Almighty God, but in the name of ourselves — spare
the life of Bigger Thomas! (*The lights begin to dim.*) 215

JUDGE: Bigger Thomas, stand up! (*The scene fades
out. Somewhere deep chimes are heard sprinkling
their music over the city. They continue a moment
and fade out.*)

SCENE XI

*The light comes up on a cell on the prison death row
sometime later. Two guards are at the Rear.* BIGGER *is
standing against the wall in his cell. He is dressed in a
pair of white shorts.* HANNAH, VERA *and* BUDDY
*have said good-bye and are ready to leave. The two
women are sobbing and* BUDDY *is manfully
controlling his grief.*

BUDDY: Ma, don't, don't Ma! (*The* FIRST GUARD
leads HANNAH, VERA *and* BUDDY *away, then turns
back and takes his stand.*)

FIRST GUARD: That old woman takes it hard.

SECOND GUARD: It's her son. 5

FIRST GUARD: (*Indicating* BIGGER.) He don't seem
to care though.

SECOND GUARD: Since that time he cried all night
long, he don't say much.

FIRST GUARD: And how he cried! But that old water 10
hose stopped him. (BUDDY *comes scampering back.*)

BUDDY: Ma says don't you worry. We gonna take care of you later.

SECOND GUARD: Come on, sonny.

BUDDY: And it gonna be at Reverend Hammond's church, Bigger. And plenty of flowers and folks, Bigger. (*The* SECOND GUARD *leads* BUDDY *off. He calls back brokenly.*) Good-bye. (*Suddenly from the shadows, his voice is heard in helpless wail.*) Don't kill my brother!

FIRST GUARD: (*With meaningless comfort toward* BIGGER.) I know — the time passes slow. Ten more minutes, boy, that's all. Then eight seconds after that you won't worry. Just take a deep breath — eight seconds. (BIGGER *says nothing.*)

SECOND GUARD: (*Coming back.*) Your lawyer's here. (BIGGER *shakes his head.*)

FIRST GUARD: He'll want to walk with you, in case —

BIGGER: (*Muttering.*) Don't need nobody.

SECOND GUARD: (*Admiringly.*) Got iron in his blood all right, I'll say that. Damn, he's tough! (MAX *enters along the corridor carrying an open telegram in his hand. At a gesture from the* FIRST GUARD *he goes over to* BIGGER *and stands mopping his face, now sagging, heavy and old.*)

MAX: It's bad news. I'm sorry, Bigger. (BIGGER *reads the telegram, then crumples it up and throws it on the floor.*)

BIGGER: I know you did all you could, Mr. Max.

MAX: Mr. and Mrs. Dalton went with me to the Governor. (*He shakes his head.*) They tried very hard.

BIGGER: Wish they hadn't. Aw, I'm all right, Mr. Max. You ain't to blame for what's happening to me. I reckon — I — uh — I just had it coming.

MAX: Is there anything I can do for you, Bigger?

BIGGER: (*His voice dropping down.*) Ain't nobody ever talked to me like you before, Mr. Max. (*He breaks off and turns distractedly about him.*) How come you do it — and you a white man? (MAX *places his hand on* BIGGER'S *shoulder as he pulls away.*)

MAX: Bigger, in my work — and the work the world has ahead — there are no whites and blacks — only men. And you make me feel, Bigger, and others feel it — how badly men want to live in this world — to say here is where I once was. This was me, big and strong. You feel like that, don't you, Bigger? You felt like that?

BIGGER: Sometimes I wish you wouldn't ask me all them questions, Mr. Max. I wish you wouldn't.

MAX: I want to understand you, Bigger.

BIGGER: (*Almost whispering.*) Understand me. She said that — understand me — (*His voice dies out. The guards now stand muffled and motionless in the gloom.*)

MAX: And Mary Dalton was trying to help you, wasn't she? (*Pause.*) Don't you know she was trying to help you — in her confused way?

BIGGER: She made me feel like a dog! Yeah, that's the way all of 'em made me feel. In their big house I was all trembling and afraid. (*His voice trails off again.*) I hated her.

MAX: (*Suddenly.*) Didn't you ever love anybody, Bigger?

BIGGER: Maybe I loved my daddy. Long time ago. They killed him. (*Suddenly shouting as he begins to pace the cell.*) Goddamit, there you start again! You mix me all up! (*With a wild moan.*) You creep in on me, crowd me to the wall, smother me and I want my breath, right up till that lightning hits me. (*Wetting his lips.*) All the time I lie here thinking, beating my head against a wall, trying to see through, over it, but can't. Maybe 'cause I'm gonna die makes me want to see — know what I am maybe. How can I die like that, Mr. Max?

MAX: If we knew how to live, Bigger, we'd know how to die.

BIGGER: Yeh, people can live together but a man got to die by himself. That don't make sense. He needs something to die by more than to live by. (MAX *is silent.*) I ain't trying to dodge what's coming. But, Mr. Max, maybe I ain't never wanted to hurt nobody — for real I ain't, maybe. (*His eyes are wide as he stares ahead, straining to feel and think his way through the darkness.*)

MAX: Go on, Bigger.

BIGGER: That time I was thinking about robbing old Blum, or cutting Gus with a knife — yeh, that time I was threat'ning to carve Ernie up, I didn't really intend to at first, then all of a sudden I did intend to. And then I got sick inside, like wanting to vomit — my hands shaking and sweating like an old woman's. And when Ernie's eyes looked out at me all scared-like and begging, I felt sorry for him and while I was feeling sorry for him, that sickness went away, that vomit feeling went away. (*Shaking his head.*) It's queer, Mr. Max, all queer and strange.

MAX: (*Staring at him.*) Go on, Bigger.

BIGGER: I reckon I ain't never done nothing right the way it ought to be done. (*More quietly.*) Seem like with you here trying to help me — you so good and kind — I begin to think better. (*Shaking his head again.*) Uh, but why the folks who sent me here hate me so? That mob — I can hear 'em still — 'Cause I'm black?

MAX: (*With gentle, yearning comfort.*) No, that's not it, Bigger. Your being black just makes it easier to be singled out in a white man's world. That's all. They are men like you, like me, and they feel like you. They want the things of life just as you do, their own chance. (*He pauses.*) Bigger, the day these millions — these millions of poor men — begin to believe in themselves —

BIGGER: Yeh, reckon the workers believe in themselves all right. Let me try to get into one of them labour unions. Naw, Mr. Max. Everywhere you turn they shut the door in your face, keep you homeless as a dog. Never no chance to be your own man. That's what I always wanted to be — my own man — (*Staring at* MAX.) Honest to God, Mr. Max, I never felt like my own man till right after that happened — till after I killed her — the way you said at the trial. It's the truth, Mr. Max, after I killed that white girl, I wasn't scared no more — for a little while. (*His voice rises with feverish intensity.*) I was my own man then, I was free. Maybe it was 'cause they was after my life then. They made me wake up. That made me feel high and powerful — free! I felt like a man. (*Shouting.*) I was a man! Yeah, yeah! (*With a piteous childlike cry.*) Why, Mr. Max? Why!?

MAX: That's the answer men must find, Bigger.

BIGGER: (*Lowering his head.*) I'm all right now, Mr. Max — I'm all right. You go on. (*Whispering queerly.*) That midnight mail is flying late. (*Licking his dry lips.*) Just go and tell Ma I was all right and not to worry none — see? Tell her I was all right and not crying none. Standing up straight, see?

MAX: I'll tell her, Bigger.

BIGGER: And tell Mr. Erlone — Jan — goodbye. (MAX *nods.*) And tell Buddy I said to be a good boy. He always would listen to me. And Vera, be smart in school.

MAX: Anything else, Bigger?

BIGGER: (*His voice shaking.*) I just want to say maybe I'm glad I got to know you before I go, Mr. Max.

MAX: I — I'm glad I got to know you too, Bigger. I'll soon be going, son. But others will carry on your fight.

BIGGER: What I got to do with it?

MAX: Because of you, we will be nearer the victory — justice and freedom for men.

BIGGER: (*Staring at him.*) Me? (*With a grim chuckle.*) How come that?

MAX: You, Bigger Thomas — I know your story — its beginning, its end. I will tell it.

BIGGER: Nobody listen to that.

MAX: (*Strongly.*) They will read, they will listen! Goodbye, Bigger.

BIGGER: Good-bye, Mr. Max. (MAX *turns heavily away. Far above in the sky the sound of the night mail plane passing is heard.* BIGGER *raises his face.*)

BIGGER: (*In a high call.*) I hear you! Fly them planes, boys! Fly 'em! — Riding through — Fly 'em on to the end of the world, smack into the face of the sun! Fly 'em for Bigger — me! (*He stands listening, his face raised.*)

FIRST GUARD: Well —

SECOND GUARD: Yeh, one minute to midnight.

(*They come into the cell and assist* BIGGER *out. The door of the execution chamber at the Rear opens, and the light streams out.* BIGGER *pushes off the hands of the guards. He straightens his shoulders and moves toward the light. The guards follow. The three enter the chamber, the door closing behind them. The stage darkens. In the church tower far away the midnight chimes begin their harmonious ringing. From the death cell now comes the hum of the deadly dynamo that puts an end to* BIGGER'S *short and troubled life.*)

FADEOUT

BERTOLT BRECHT

The Caucasian Chalk Circle

Born into a comfortable middle-class family in Augsburg, a town in the Bavarian region of Germany, Bertolt Brecht (1898–1956) was a sickly child and never really enjoyed robust health (he suffered his first heart attack when he was only twelve), but, as if by way of compensation, he developed a feisty personality from an early age. He continually criticized the bourgeois values embraced by his parents, even while, ironically, relying on the financial support of his father, a paper-mill plant manager, for much of his life. Indeed, throughout his career, Brecht remained an outspoken critic of the status quo, often becoming such a gadfly to the establishment that he aroused the hostile attentions of the authorities.

The First World War had a major effect on the formulation of Brecht's political and artistic outlook. In 1916 he had enrolled as a medical student to avoid conscription. But near the end of the war, he did military service in an army hospital, where he found himself badly shaken by his contact with the wounded soldiers. The experience provoked one of his first significant works, the poem "The Ballad of the Dead Soldier," a pacifist satire of war morality in which a soldier is slaughtered at the front and then patched up to be sent to be slaughtered once again. The poem caused something of an outrage, but Brecht was unintimidated, asserting that it was the very banality of so much cultural discourse that had led Germans into the unfortunate war. Shortly afterwards, he wrote to his friend, the painter Caspar Neher: "Nothing is happening in art. I'm for closing down the theatres—for artistic reasons. There will be no art until the last theatre-goer has been hung with the guts of the last actor" (December 29, 1917).

As it happened, around that time art did begin to change rapidly in the larger urban centres of Germany. A violent change occurred throughout the entire culture as Germans, already disenchanted with the cultural ethos that had led to the war, experienced a series of economic and social upheavals, such as runaway inflation caused by their enormous national debt. (Much of this was a pre-existing debt, though the problem was certainly exacerbated by the war reparations demanded by the Treaty of Versailles—notwithstanding the fact that, in the end, only about a sixth of the total reparations were ever actually paid.) As the economy fell apart, public opinion flailed about wildly in a desperate search for any kind of solution; thus, by the 1920s, political parties from the extreme fringes were brought well into the mainstream. On the extreme right, the Nazis began to rise in popularity, while on the left were the Communists and Anarchists. As the political climate heated up, Brecht's own convictions began to acquire more definition—but only gradually.

In 1918, Brecht moved to Munich to continue his studies as a medical student, but before long he was neglecting his studies in favour of writing for local theatres and cabarets. According to his own account, he possessed no real political convictions at the time of his arrival in Munich, apart from being a vaguely anarchistic critic of philistinism, and his earliest plays bear him out in this assessment. His first full-length play, *Baal* (which he wrote in 1918, though it was not produced until 1923), shows the influence of Büchner's *Woyzeck*, telling the story of a disaffected, self-indulgent and dissolute poet, who leaves a trail of broken hearts and dead bodies in his path as he wanders about in search of some point to his life. It was most remarkable at the time for its language, which was a poeticized version of common speech, whereas most plays at the time were still written in a sort of formal literary German that was not spoken in the street. Slightly more explicitly political was his next play, *Drums in the Night* (1919), a work that sets a love story of an army deserter and his girlfriend against the backdrop of the Spartacus riots (the Spartacus League was the forerunner of the German Communist Party). In the same year, Brecht was appointed the theatre critic for a left-wing paper in his hometown of Augsburg. His criticism at this time was highly acerbic, but his theatrical notions were still rather conventional on the whole, though he did express enthusiasm for the work and style of Frank Wedekind, the politically controversial author of *Spring Awakening* and the "Lulu plays," whom Brecht would meet soon after he moved to Berlin in 1921.

Berlin was a more sophisticated and bohemian city than Munich, and Brecht's reputation grew quickly there. The caustic satire and artistic power of his new plays such as *In the Jungle of Cities* (written 1921, produced 1923) and *A Respectable Wedding* (written 1923, produced 1926), along with new productions of his earlier plays, caused him to be regarded as an artistic rebel, if not yet as much of a political activist. Brecht also began studying foreign drama, especially Shakespeare and the Elizabethans, writing an adaptation of Christopher Marlowe's *Edward II* in 1924. The structural conventions of these dramas had a liberating effect on Brecht's subsequent dramaturgy.

An even stronger influence on his work, however, stemmed from his study in 1925–26 of Karl Marx's work on history and economics. The first result of this awakening was *A Man's A Man* (1926), about a dockworker, Galy Gay, who is forced to impersonate a soldier and, in doing so, gradually loses his own identity. After that, Brecht developed his new political dramaturgy further when he was drawn into collaboration with Erwin Piscator, the Marxist director who had been working on the problem of a documentary style of theatre that would make comprehensible the connections between smaller, intimate dramatic scenes and massive social transformations. In 1928 came one of Brecht's most popular works, the musical *Threepenny Opera*, a caustic satire of corruption in the ruling class adapted from John Gay's *The Beggar's Opera*, written in collaboration with Elizabeth Hauptmann and composer Kurt Weill. Weill would again work fruitfully with Brecht on *Happy End* (1929), *The Rise and Fall of Mahagonny* (1930), and *The Seven Deadly Sins* (1933).

In the meantime, however, Adolf Hitler and the Nazi party had become more and more powerful. On February 27, 1933, the Nazis burned the Reichstag (the German legislature) and blamed the Communists, using the crisis as a pretext to seize power. Brecht, who was near the top of the Nazi hate list, fled the country, to spend the next fifteen years in exile in France, Denmark, Switzerland and the U.S.A. During this period, though he was often disconnected from the means of theatrical production, he wrote several of his finest works, including *Galileo* (written 1937–39, produced 1943); *Mother Courage and her Children* (written 1938–39, produced 1941) and *The Good Woman of Setzuan* (written 1938–41, produced 1943), both written with Margarete Steffin; *The Resistible Rise of Arturo Ui*, a play in which the rise of Hitler is told as a parable about a Chicago gangster (written 1941, but not produced until 1958); and *The Caucasian Chalk Circle* (written 1943–5, produced 1948). He also earned some money working on screenplays for Hollywood.

While living in the U.S.A. in 1948, Brecht was ordered to appear before the House Un-American

Activities Committee, through which Senator Joseph McCarthy was directing his communist witch-hunt. Brecht testified, but left for Europe the next day, and eventually settled back in Berlin, in the sector that had become a part of communist East Germany. There he founded the state-funded Berliner Ensemble, with which he spent most of the remaining years of his life developing what are regarded as the definitive productions of his most important works. Brecht died of a heart attack on August 14, 1956, and was buried close to his home and theatre. He had written forty dramatic works in his life.

Aside from the many political controversies that beset much of Brecht's life and work, there were other controversies that continue to be the subject of debate. Brecht was seemingly almost as promiscuous in his sex life as he was prolific in his professional life. His wife, actress Helene Weigel, indulged and, indeed, even encouraged these affairs, because they often were joined to fruitful working relationships. Naturally, questions have arisen as to which parts of certain works were written by Brecht and which by his collaborators/mistresses, though these questions are difficult to answer (apart from looking at each of the collaborators' work outside any given play, a method whereby Brecht certainly gains much credibility). Furthermore, Brecht always drew on a variety of sources for his work, and sometimes aroused accusations of plagiarism—as with *Jungle of the Cities*, for which he had drawn on Arthur Rimbaud's "A Season in Hell," and *Threepenny Opera*, for which he had drawn on a particular translation of the ballads of François Villon. In his defense, it may be said that Shakespeare, Molière and countless other playwrights have often relied heavily on the works of others to create their plays. But Brecht was working in an age of copyright, and so the question is more complicated in his case.

The Caucasian Chalk Circle provides a good practical example of this issue. The original source for the play is an old Chinese play, called simply *The Chalk Circle*; but Brecht also had in mind *Kreidekreis (Chalk Circle)*, a German play written in 1925 by Klabund (Alfred Henschke), which had been based on the same Chinese source, and which had already added some of the elements found in the Brecht version, such as the transference of the setting to the Caucasus and the addition of the character of the disreputable judge. Accordingly, questions of plagiarism have been raised, though closer examination reveals little foundation for the charge. In many ways, Klabund's *Chalk Circle* is quite different from Brecht's. (Ironically, the extent to which they differ is partly demonstrated by Brecht's use of several elements of Klabund's play as a source for an entirely separate work, *The Good Woman of Setzuan*.)

An instance where Brecht's use of other sources is both definite and uncontroversial, however, is in the integration of Western theatrical conventions with techniques drawn from Eastern theatrical traditions. For example, the narrator and chorus evoke the Noh theatre of Japan; and for the ingeniously simple representation of journeys, bridges, and so on, Brecht drew on traditional storytelling techniques associated with Chinese opera. When one considers that these techniques are joined to a dramaturgical framework indebted in part to Elizabethan drama, and that, furthermore, Brecht uses the sort of "flashback" associated most closely with film, one understands how it is that Brecht's work can seem, at the same time, so oddly familiar and yet somehow still unique.

[C.S.W.]

BERTOLT BRECHT

The Caucasian Chalk Circle[1]

Translated by Ralph Manheim

CHARACTERS

DELEGATES OF THE "GALINSK" GOAT BREED-
   ING KOLKHOZ: an old peasant, a peasant
   woman, a young peasant, a very young worker
MEMBERS OF THE "ROSA LUXEMBURG"
   FRUIT GROWING KOLKHOZ: an old peasant,
   a peasant woman, the woman agronomist, the
   girl tractor driver, the wounded soldier, and
   other peasants and peasant women
THE EXPERT FROM THE CAPITAL
ARKADI CHEIDZE, the singer
HIS MUSICIANS
GEORGI ABASHVILI, the governor
HIS WIFE NATELLA
THEIR SON MICHAEL
SHALVA, the aide-de-camp
ARSEN KAZBEKI, the fat prince
THE RIDER FROM THE CAPITAL
NIKO MIKADZE and MIKHA LOLADZE, doctors
SIMON CHACHAVA, a soldier
GRUSHA VACHNADZE, a kitchen maid
THREE ARCHITECTS
BROTHER ANASTASIUS, a monk
FOUR CHAMBERMAIDS: Assya, Masha, Zulika,
   Fat Nina
THE NURSE
THE WOMAN COOK

THE MAN COOK
THE STABLE HAND
SERVANTS IN THE GOVERNOR'S PALACE
IRONSHIRTS AND SOLDIERS OF THE GOVER-
   NOR AND THE FAT PRINCE
BEGGARS AND PETITIONERS
THE OLD DAIRY MAN
TWO UPPER-CLASS LADIES
THE LANDLORD
THE HOUSE SERVANT
THE CORPORAL
BLOCKHEAD, a soldier
A PEASANT WOMAN AND HER HUSBAND
THREE PEDDLERS
LAVRENTI VACHNADZE, Grusha's brother
HIS WIFE ANIKO
THEIR HIRED HAND
THE PEASANT WOMAN, for a time Grusha's
   mother-in-law
HER SON YUSSUP
THE BLACKMAILER
WEDDING GUESTS
CHILDREN
AZDAK, the village scribe
SHAUVA, a policeman
A FUGITIVE, the grand duke
THE NEPHEW OF THE FAT PRINCE
THE DOCTOR
THE INVALID
THE LAME MAN
LUDOVIKA, the landlord's daughter-in-law
A POOR OLD PEASANT WOMAN
HER BROTHER-IN-LAW IRAKILL, a bandit
THREE KULAKS
ILLO SHUBOLADZE AND SANDRO OBOLADZE,
   lawyers
THE VERY OLD COUPLE

---

[1] Brecht wrote *The Caucasian Chalk Circle* in 1944, hoping that the play would be produced on Broadway. Instead the premiere was a student production at Carleton
College in Northfield, Minnesota, in 1948. The first professional production took place later the same year at the
Hedgerow Theater in Philadelphia and was directed by
Eric Bentley.

1. PROLOGUE: THE DISPUTE OVER THE VALLEY

Amid the ruins of a war-torn Caucasian village the members of two kolkhoz villages, for the most part women and old men, but also a few soldiers, are sitting in a circle, smoking and drinking wine.[2] With them is an expert from the state reconstruction commission in the capital.

A PEASANT WOMAN, LEFT: (*pointing.*) Over there in the hills we stopped three Nazi tanks, but by that time the apple orchard was ruined.

AN OLD PEASANT WOMAN, RIGHT: Our beautiful dairy farm: nothing but rubble! 5

A GIRL TRACTOR DRIVER, LEFT: I set that fire, comrade.

(*Pause.*)

THE EXPERT: Now listen to the minutes: Delegates of the Galinsk goat-breeding kolkhoz have come to Nukha.[3] At the approach of Hitler's armies, the 10 kolkhoz, by order of the authorities, drove its goats eastward. Its members are now contemplating a return to this valley. Their delegates have inspected the village and surroundings and found much destruction. (*The delegates, right, nod.*) 15

(*Turning to those on the left.*) The adjoining Rosa Luxemburg kolkhoz grows fruit.[4] Within the framework of the reconstruction program they have put in a petition that the former territory of the Galinsk kolkhoz, a valley where the grazing is 20 poor, should be converted to orchards and vineyards.

As expert for the reconstruction commission, I call on the two kolkhoz villages to decide between them whether the Galinsk kolkhoz should return 25 here or not.

THE OLD PEASANT, RIGHT: First I wish to protest against the restriction of discussion time. It has taken us delegates of the Galinsk kolkhoz three days and three nights to get here, and now we're 30 told that only half a day has been set aside for discussion.

A WOUNDED SOLDIER, LEFT: Comrade, we haven't as many villages or as much manpower or as much time as we used to. 35

THE GIRL TRACTOR DRIVER: All pleasures have to be rationed. Tobacco and wine are rationed, and that goes for discussion too.

THE OLD PEASANT, RIGHT: (*with a sigh.*) Death to the Fascists! Very well, I'll come straight to the 40 point and explain why we want our valley back. There are many reasons, but I'll begin with the simplest. Makinä Abakidze, bring out the goat cheese.

(*A peasant women, right, takes an enormous cheese wrapped in a cloth from a basket. Applause and laughter.*)

THE OLD PEASANT, RIGHT: Help yourselves, 45 comrades. Take some.

AN OLD PEASANT, LEFT: (*distrustfully.*) Are you trying to influence us?

THE OLD PEASANT, RIGHT: (*amid laughter.*) How can I expect to influence you, Surab, you valley- 50 thief! Everybody knows you'll take the cheese and the valley too. (*Laughter.*) All I want from you is an honest answer: do you like the taste of this cheese?

THE OLD PEASANT, LEFT: The answer is yes. 55

THE OLD PEASANT, RIGHT: You do, do you? (*Bitterly.*) I ought to have known you wouldn't know anything about cheese.

THE OLD PEASANT, LEFT: Why not? I've told you I like it. 60

THE OLD PEASANT, RIGHT: Because you can't like it. Because it's not the same as in the old days. And why isn't it the same? Because our goats don't like

---

2 Caucasian] The Caucasus (in Russian: *Kavkaz*) region and mountain system was traditionally considered part of the dividing line between Europe and Asia. It lies between the Black and Azov Seas (to the west) and the Caspian Sea (to the east), and is currently occupied by Russia, Georgia and Azerbaijan; kolkhoz] a collective farm on state-owned land, run by a group of peasants working on a cooperative basis.

3 Nukha] a city in north-central Azerbaijan; its name was changed to Saki in 1968.

4 Rosa Luxemburg] This kolkhoz is named after the Polish revolutionary, one of the founders of the Spartacus League, which was the forerunner of the Communist Party of Germany. She was assassinated during the Spartacus Revolt of 1919.

the new grass the way they liked the old grass. Cheese isn't cheese because grass isn't grass, that's the trouble. Kindly put that in your minutes. 65

THE OLD PEASANT, LEFT: But your cheese is perfect.

THE OLD PEASANT, RIGHT: It is not perfect, it's barely middling. The new pasture is no good, 70 whatever the young folks may say. I say we can't live there. It doesn't even smell like morning in the morning.

(*Several laugh.*)

THE EXPERT: Let them laugh, they know what you mean. Comrades, why does a man love his home 75 country? Because the bread tastes better, the sky is higher, the air is spicier, voices ring out more clearly, the ground is softer to walk on. Am I right?

THE OLD PEASANT, RIGHT: The valley has always belonged to us. 80

THE SOLDIER: What do you mean "always"? Nothing has always belonged to anybody. When you were young, you didn't even belong to yourself, you belonged to the princes of Kazbeki.

THE OLD PEASANT, RIGHT: The valley belongs to 85 us by law.

THE GIRL TRACTOR DRIVER: The laws will have to be reexamined in any case to see if they still apply.

THE OLD PEASANT, RIGHT: Of course. I suppose 90 it doesn't make any difference what kind of tree grows outside the house where you were born? Or who you've got for a neighbour? Doesn't that make any difference? Why, one of our reasons for wanting to come back is to have you near our 95 kolkhoz, you valley-thieves. Now you can laugh again.

THE OLD PEASANT, LEFT: (*laughs.*) Then why don't you listen quietly to what your "neighbour," Kato Vachtang our agronomist, has to say about your 100 valley?

A PEASANT WOMAN, RIGHT: We haven't said half of what we've got to say about our valley. The houses aren't all gone, the foundations of the dairy are still intact. 105

THE EXPERT: You have a right to government aid in either place—you know that.

THE PEASANT WOMAN, RIGHT: Comrade expert, this isn't a matter for bargaining. I can't take your cap and give you another and say "this one is 110 better." Maybe the other is better, but you like your own best.

THE GIRL TRACTOR DRIVER: It's not the same with a piece of land as with a cap. Not in our country, comrade. 115

THE EXPERT: Don't get excited. It's true we must regard a piece of land largely as an implement for producing something useful, but it's equally true that we must recognize people's love for a particular piece of land. Before proceeding with the 120 discussion, I propose that you tell the comrades from the Galinsk kolkhoz what you are planning to do with the disputed valley.

THE OLD PEASANT, RIGHT: Agreed.

THE OLD PEASANT, LEFT: Right, give Kato the 125 floor.

THE EXPERT: Comrade agronomist!

THE AGRONOMIST, LEFT: (*stands up, she is in army uniform.*) Comrades, last winter, when we were partisans fighting in these hills, we talked about 130 the possibility of vastly increasing our fruit production once the Germans were driven out. I drew up an irrigation project. By damming our mountain lake we can irrigate three hundred acres of barren ground. That will enable our kolkhoz not only to 135 plant more fruit trees, but to put in vineyards as well. However, the project will only be worthwhile if we can include the disputed valley, now belonging to the Galinsk kolkhoz. Here are my calculations. (*She hands the expert a portfolio.*) 140

THE OLD PEASANT, RIGHT: Put it down in the minutes that our kolkhoz is planning to start breeding horses.

THE GIRL TRACTOR DRIVER: Comrades, the project was worked out in the days and nights 145 when we were hiding in the mountains, half the time without cartridges for the few rifles we had. Even a pencil was hard to get.

(*Applause on both sides.*)

THE OLD PEASANT, RIGHT: Our thanks to the comrades of the Rosa Luxemburg kolkhoz and to 150 all those who fought for our country!

(*They shake hands all around and embrace.*)

THE PEASANT WOMAN, LEFT: Our idea was that our soldiers, our men and yours, should come home to a still more fertile country.

THE GIRL TRACTOR DRIVER: As the poet Maya- 155
kovski said "The home of the Soviet people shall also be the home of reason!"[5]

(*The delegates right, except for the old peasant, have stood up and are studying the agronomist's sketches with the expert. Exclamations such as "Why a twenty-three-yard fall?"—"The rock here will be blasted."—"All they really need is concrete and dynamite!"—"They'll make the water come down here; mighty clever!".*)

A VERY YOUNG WORKER, RIGHT: (*to the old peasant, right.*) They're going to irrigate the fields between the hills. Look at that, Alleko. 160

THE OLD PEASANT, RIGHT: I won't look. I knew their project would be good. I refused to be forced at gunpoint.

THE SOLDIER, LEFT: But they're only trying to force you at pencil point. 165

(*Laughter.*)

THE OLD PEASANT, RIGHT: (*stands up gloomily and goes to look at the drawings.*) The trouble is these valley-thieves know perfectly well that nobody in this country can resist machines and projects.

THE PEASANT WOMAN, RIGHT: Alleko Bereshvili, 170
you're the worst sucker of all for new projects, everybody knows that.

THE EXPERT: How about my minutes? Can I say that you'll go back to your kolkhoz and recommend that they relinquish their old valley in the 175
interest of this project?

THE PEASANT WOMAN, RIGHT: I'll recommend it. How about you, Alleko?

THE OLD PEASANT, RIGHT: (*over the drawings.*) I request copies of the plans to take back with us. 180

THE PEASANT WOMAN, RIGHT: In that case we can sit down to eat. Once he has the plans and a

---

5 Mayakovski] Vladimir Vladimirovich Mayakovski—or, more usually, Mayakovsky—(1893–1930), a leading poet of the early Soviet period.

chance to discuss them, the matter is settled. I know him. And the rest of our people are the same.

(*The delegates embrace each other again, laughing.*)

THE OLD PEASANT, LEFT: Three cheers for the 185
Galinsk kolkhoz and good luck with your horses!

THE PEASANT WOMAN, LEFT: Comrades, in honour of the delegates from the Galinsk kolkhoz and of the expert, we have arranged to put on a play related to our problem. Arkadi Cheidze, the 190
singer, will take part.

(*Applause. The girl tractor driver has run off to get the singer.*)

THE PEASANT WOMAN, RIGHT: Comrades, your play had better be good, we're paying a valley for it.

THE PEASANT WOMAN, LEFT: Arkadi Cheidze 195
knows 21,000 lines by heart.

THE OLD PEASANT, LEFT: We've worked up the play under his direction. He's a hard man to get. You people from the planning commission should arrange to have him come north more often, 200
comrade.

THE EXPERT: Economics is more in our line.

THE OLD PEASANT, LEFT: (*smiling.*) You organize the redistribution of vineyards and tractors, why not of songs? 205

(*Led by the girl tractor operator, Arkadi Cheidze, the singer, enters the circle. He is a powerfully built man of simple ways. He is accompanied by musicians with their instruments. The artists are greeted with applause.*)

THE GIRL TRACTOR DRIVER: Arkadi, this is the comrade expert.

(*The singer greets those around him.*)

THE PEASANT WOMAN, RIGHT: I am greatly honoured to make your acquaintance. I heard about your songs when I was a little girl in school. 210

THE SINGER: This time it will be a play with songs, and almost everyone in the whole kolkhoz will take part.

THE OLD PEASANT, RIGHT: Will it be one of the old legends? 215

THE SINGER: A very old one. It is called *The Chalk Circle* and comes from the Chinese. We play it in different form, though. Shura, show them the masks. Comrades, it is an honour for us to entertain you after a difficult debate. We hope you will find that the old poet's voice still rings true, even in the shadow of the Soviet tractors. It may be wrong to mix different wines, but old and new wisdom make an excellent mixture. Well, I hope we shall all get something to eat before the play begins. That helps.   220

225

VOICES: Of course—Everybody to the club house.

(*All go gaily to dinner. As they are leaving, the expert turns to the singer.*)

THE EXPERT: How long will this story take, Arkadi? I've got to go back to Tiflis tonight.

THE SINGER: (*offhand.*) Actually there are two stories. A couple of hours.   230

THE EXPERT: (*confidentially.*) Can't you make it shorter?

THE SINGER: No.

2. THE NOBLE CHILD

(*The singer is sitting on the ground in front of his musicians. A black sheepskin cloak over his shoulders, he leafs through a worn-out copybook with slips of paper inserted.*)

In olden times, in bloody times
There ruled in this city, known as "the accursed city"
A governor by the name of Georgi Abashvili.
He was as rich as Croesus.[6]
He had a beautiful wife.   5
He had a thriving child.
No other governor in Gruznia had
So many horses in his stable
And so many beggars at his door
So many soldiers in his service   10

---

6 Croesus] The proverbially rich last King of Lydia (d. c.546 B.C.E.), he is best known through Herodotus's account of his (fictitious) meeting with Solon, the Greek law-maker.

And so many petitioners in his courtyard.
How shall I tell you the kind of man Georgi Abashvili was?
He enjoyed his life.
One Easter Sunday morning
The governor and his family went   15
To church.

(*From the archway of a palace pour beggars and petitioners, holding up emaciated children, crutches and petitions. Behind them two Ironshirts, then, splendidly attired, the Governor and his family.*)[7]

THE BEGGARS AND PETITIONERS: Mercy, your grace, the taxes are too high.—I lost my leg in the Persian War, where can I get …—My brother is innocent, your grace, a misunderstanding.—He's starving on me.—He's our last remaining son—please release him from military service.—Please, your grace, the water inspector has been bribed.   20

(*A servant collects the petitions, another hands out coins from a pouch. The soldiers push back the crowd, striking at them with heavy leather whips.*)

A SOLDIER: Back! Clear the church door.

(*Behind the Governor, his wife, and an aide-de-camp, the Governor's child is rolled out through the archway in a magnificent baby carriage. The crowd presses forward again to see him.*)

THE SINGER: (*while the crowd is whipped back.*)
That Easter the people saw the Governor's heir for the first time.   25
Two doctors never stirred from the side of the Noble Child Apple of the Governor's eye.

(*Cries from the crowd: "The child!"—"I can't see him, don't push so." "God bless you, your grace.".*)

THE SINGER:
Even the powerful Prince Kazbeki
Paid his respects to him at the church door.

(*A fat prince steps forward and greets the family.*)

THE FAT PRINCE: Happy Easter, Natella Abashvili.

---

7 Ironshirts] soldiers armoured in mail.

[II]

(*A command is heard. A dust-covered rider dashes in and holds out a roll of papers to the Governor. At a sign from the Governor, the aide-de-camp, a handsome young man, goes to the rider and holds him back. A brief pause while the fat prince looks distrustfully at the rider.*)

THE FAT PRINCE: What a beautiful day! When it rained last night, I thought to myself: gloomy holidays. But this morning, the sky was clear. I love clear skies, Natella Abashvili, and a simple heart. And little Michael, every inch a Governor. Ti-ti-ti-ti. (*He tickles the child.*) Happy Easter, little Michael, ti-ti-ti-ti.

THE GOVERNOR'S WIFE: What do you think, Arsen, Georgi has finally decided to start building the new east wing. The whole neighbourhood with its wretched shacks is being torn down to make room for the garden.

THE FAT PRINCE: That is good news after so much bad news. What do you hear about the war, brother Georgi? (*The Governor makes a gesture meaning that he doesn't wish to speak of it.*) A strategic withdrawal, I hear? Oh well, there are always these little setbacks. Good days and bad days. The fortunes of war. Not very important, is it?

THE GOVERNOR'S WIFE: He's coughing! Georgi, did you hear? (*Sharply to the two dignified doctors standing right behind the baby carriage.*) He's coughing!

FIRST DOCTOR: (*to the second.*) Permit me to remind you, Niko Mikadze, that I was opposed to that lukewarm bath. A slight error in the temperature of the bath water, your grace.

SECOND DOCTOR: (*also very polite.*) I am unable to agree with you, Mikha Loladze. The temperature of the bath water was that prescribed by our great and beloved Mishiko Oboladze. More likely a draft during the night, your grace.

THE GOVERNOR'S WIFE: But do something for him! He looks feverish, Georgi.

FIRST DOCTOR: (*over the child.*) No cause for alarm, your grace. We shall make his bath water a little warmer and it won't happen again.

SECOND DOCTOR: (*with a venomous look at him.*) I won't forget that, my dear Mikha Loladze. No cause for concern, your grace.

THE FAT PRINCE: Ai, ai, ai, ai. I always say: if my liver pains me, give the doctor fifty strokes across the soles of his feet. And that's only because the times have gone soft; in the old days it was simply: Off with his head!

THE GOVERNOR'S WIFE: Let's go inside, it's probably because of the draft out here.

(*The procession consisting of the family and their servants turns into the church door. The Fat Prince follows. The Aide-de-camp steps out of the procession and indicates the rider.*)

THE GOVERNOR: Not *before* mass, Shalva.

THE AIDE-DE-CAMP: (*to the rider.*) The Governor does not wish to be molested with reports before mass, especially if, as I presume, they are depressing. Go to the kitchen, my friend, and tell them to give you something to eat.

(*The Aide-de-camp joins the procession while the rider with a curse enters the palace gate. A soldier comes out of the palace and stops in the archway.*)

THE SINGER:
The city is silent.
Pigeons are strutting on the square.
A soldier of the palace guard
Is joking with a kitchen maid
Who is coming up from the river with a bundle.

(*A kitchen maid with a bundle wrapped in large green leaves tries to enter the archway.*)

THE SOLDIER: What's this? Not in church? Playing hooky from services, young lady?

GRUSHA: I was all dressed, but then they were missing a goose for Easter dinner and they asked me to get one, because I know about geese.

THE SOLDIER: A goose? (*With affected suspicion.*) I'd like to see that goose.

(*Grusha does not understand.*)

THE SOLDIER: You've got to watch your step with women. "I've only been getting a goose." That's what they say, when actually it's something entirely different.

GRUSHA: (*goes resolutely up to him and shows him the goose.*) Here it is. And if it isn't a good fifteen-pound goose crammed full of corn, I'll eat the feathers. 100

THE SOLDIER: A queen of a goose. The Governor himself will eat it. So you've been down by the river again? 105

GRUSHA: Yes, at the poultry farm.

THE SOLDIER: Oh, at the poultry farm down by the river? Not upstream in those willows?

GRUSHA: I only go to the willows when I wash clothes. 110

THE SOLDIER: (*pointedly.*) Exactly.

GRUSHA: Exactly what?

THE SOLDIER: (*winking.*) Exactly what I meant.

GRUSHA: Why shouldn't I wash clothes by the willows? 115

THE SOLDIER: (*with exaggerated laughter.*) "Why shouldn't I wash clothes by the willows?" That's good, really good.

GRUSHA: I don't understand you, soldier. What's good? 120

THE SOLDIER: (*slyly.*) If someone finds out what I know, hot and cold she's sure to grow.

GRUSHA: I fail to see what anybody can know about those willows. 125

THE SOLDIER: Even if there were bushes nearby, where someone can sit and see everything? Everything that goes on when a certain person "washes clothes"!

GRUSHA: What goes on, soldier? Can't you just say what you mean and be done with it? 130

THE SOLDIER: Something that someone can see.

GRUSHA: Why, soldier, you wouldn't mean that on a hot day I sometimes put my toes in the water, because that's all there is to it. 135

THE SOLDIER: There's more. Your toes and something more.

GRUSHA: What more? Well, maybe my foot.

THE SOLDIER: Your foot and a little more. (*He laughs loudly.*) 140

GRUSHA: (*angrily.*) Simon Chachava, you ought to be ashamed. Sitting in the bushes on a hot day, waiting for someone to put her leg in the water. And probably with some other soldier at that! (*She runs away.*) 145

THE SOLDIER: (*calls after her.*) Not with another soldier!

(*As the singer resumes his story, the soldier runs after Grusha.*)

THE SINGER:
  The city lies silent, but why these men in arms?
  The Governor's palace is at peace.
  Why then is it a fortress? 150

(*The Fat Prince comes quickly out of the church door, left. He stops and looks around. Two Ironshirts are waiting outside the archway to the right. The Prince sees them and passes them slowly, making a sign to them; then he goes out quickly. One Ironshirt goes through the archway into the palace; the other stays behind on guard. Muffled cries are heard from various directions in the background. "Ready!" The palace is surrounded. Church bells are heard in the distance. Out of the church door comes the Governor's family and the rest of the procession.*)

THE SINGER:
  Then the Governor returned to his palace
  And the palace was a trap.
  The goose was plucked and roasted
  But the goose was not eaten
  Noon was no longer a time for eating 155
  Noon was a time for dying.

THE GOVERNOR'S WIFE: (*passing by.*) It's really impossible to live in this hovel, but of course Georgi builds only for his little Michael, not for me. Michael is everything, everything for Michael! 160

THE GOVERNOR: Did you hear that? Brother Kazbeki wishing us a happy Easter! That's all very well, but as far as I know it didn't rain in Nushka last night. Where brother Kazbeki was, it rained. Where was brother Kazbeki? 165

THE AIDE-DE-CAMP: We must investigate.

THE GOVERNOR: Yes, immediately. Tomorrow.

(*The procession turns into the archway. The rider who has meanwhile come out of the palace steps up to the Governor.*)

THE AIDE-DE-CAMP: Excellency, won't you listen to the rider from the capital? He arrived this morning with confidential papers. 170

THE GOVERNOR: (*continuing on his way.*) Not before dinner, Shalva!

THE AIDE-DE-CAMP: (*while the procession disappears into the palace and only two soldiers of the palace guard remain at the gate; to the rider.*) The Governor 175
does not wish to be molested with military reports before dinner, and his excellency is devoting the afternoon to a conference with eminent architects who have also been invited to dinner. Here they come. (*Three gentlemen have entered. While the rider* 180
goes off, the Aide-de-camp welcomes the architects.) Gentlemen, his excellency is expecting you for dinner. He will devote the whole afternoon to you. And your great new plans! Come quickly!

ONE OF THE ARCHITECTS: We are filled with 185
admiration that his excellency should think of building despite the alarming reports about the Persian war.

THE AIDE-DE-CAMP: "Because of them" would be more accurate. It's nothing. Persia is far away! The 190
garrison here would let themselves be hacked to pieces for the Governor.

(*Noise from the palace. A woman's shrill scream. Cries of command. Aghast, the Aide-de-camp goes toward the archway. An Ironshirt steps out and stops him with his pike.*)

THE AIDE-DE-CAMP: What's going on? Put down that pike, you dog! (*Furiously to the palace guard.*) Disarm this man! Don't you see this is a plot 195
against the Governor's life?

(*The soldiers of the guard do not obey. They look coldly and indifferently at the Aide-de-camp and watch the following scene without interest. The Aide-de-camp fights his way into the palace.*)

ONE OF THE ARCHITECTS: The princes! The princes met in the capital last night. They are opposed to the grand duke and his Governors. Gentlemen, we'd better clear out. 200

(*They go off quickly.*)

THE SINGER:
O blindness of the great! They live like gods on high
Great over bended backs, trusting
In hired fists, confident

Of their power that has already endured so long.
But long is not forever. 205
O passage of time, o hope of the poor.

(*Out through the archway comes the Governor, in chains, between two soldiers armed to the teeth. His face is gray.*)

Forever good-bye, great lord. Deign to walk with head erect.
From your palace windows hostile eyes look down upon you.
You will need no more architects. A plain carpenter is all you'll need.
You will not be moving to a new palace, but to a 210
small hole in the ground.
Look round you one last time, blind man.

(*The arrested man looks around.*)

Are you pleased with what you had? Between Easter mass and Easter meal
You will go to the place whence no one returns.

(*He is led away. The palace guard falls in behind. A horn sounds the alarm. Noise behind the archway.*)

When the house of a great man collapses
Many small folk will be crushed under the ruins. 215
Those who never shared the fortune of the mighty
Will often share their downfall. The
Swift-plunging wagon
Drags the sweating draft horses
Down to the abyss. 220

(*Panic-stricken servants come rushing out of the archway.*)

THE SERVANTS: (*all at once.*) The baskets! All into the third courtyard! Provisions for five days.—The mistress has fainted.—Carry her downstairs, somebody, she can't stay here.—What about us?— They'll slaughter us like chickens. They always 225
do.—Mother of God, what's going to happen?— They say there's been bloodshed in the city.— Nonsense, the Governor has only been politely requested to attend a meeting of the princes. Everything will be settled peaceably, I have it from 230
a reliable source.

(*The two doctors rush into the courtyard.*)

FIRST DOCTOR: (*trying to hold back the other.*) Niko Mikadze, it is your duty as a physician to stay with Natella Abashvili.

SECOND DOCTOR: My duty? Yours!   235

FIRST DOCTOR: Whose turn is it with the child today, Niko Mikadze, yours or mine?

SECOND DOCTOR: Mikha Loladze, do you really suppose I'm going to spend another minute in a plague-ridden house on account of that brat?   240

(*They start to fight. All that can be heard is: "You're neglecting your duty!" and "Duty be damned!" Then the second doctor strikes the first one down.*)

SECOND DOCTOR: Oh, go to hell! (*Out.*)

THE SERVANTS: Nothing to worry about until tonight, the soldiers won't be drunk before then.— Doesn't anybody know if they've mutinied?—The palace guard has ridden away.—Doesn't anybody   245
know what's happened?

GRUSHA: Meliva the fisherman says a comet with a red tail was seen over the capital; that means calamity.

THE SERVANTS: They say news reached the capital   250
yesterday that the Persian war has been completely lost.—The princes have all risen up. They say the grand duke has fled. All his Governors are going to be executed.—They won't hurt the little people. I've got a brother in the Ironshirts. (*The soldier   255
Simon Chachava appears, looking for Grusha in the crowd.*)

THE AIDE-DE-CAMP: (*appears in the archway.*) Into the third courtyard, all of you! Everybody help with the packing! (*He drives the servants off.*)   260

(*Simon finally finds Grusha.*)

SIMON: There you are, Grusha. What are you going to do?

GRUSHA: Nothing. If the worst comes to the worst, I have a brother with a farm in the mountains. But what about you?   265

SIMON: Me? Nothing. (*Again with formality.*) Grusha Vachnadze, your question about my plans gives me pleasure. I have received orders to escort Lady Natella Abashvili.

GRUSHA: But hasn't the palace guard mutinied?   270

SIMON: (*gravely.*) It has.

GRUSHA: Isn't it dangerous to escort her?

SIMON: In Tiflis they say: is stabbing dangerous for the knife?

GRUSHA: You're not a knife, Simon Chachava, you're   275
only a man. What's the lady to you?

SIMON: The lady is nothing to me, but I've got orders and I'm going.

GRUSHA: Then, you're just stubborn, soldier, running into danger for no reason at all. (*Someone   280
calls her from the palace.*) They want me in the third courtyard, I'm in a hurry.

SIMON: If you're in a hurry, let's not argue. A good argument takes time. May I ask whether the young lady still has her parents?   285

GRUSHA: No. Only my brother.

SIMON: Since the time is short, my second question is: is the young lady as healthy as a fish in water?

GRUSHA: Maybe a stitch in my right shoulder now and then, but otherwise strong enough for every   290
kind of work. No one has ever complained.

SIMON: That is common knowledge. When it's Easter Sunday and someone has to go for the goose nevertheless, she's the one. Third question: is the young lady impatient? Does she want cherries in   295
the winter?

GRUSHA: Not impatient, but when people go off to war for no reason and there's no news, it's bad.

SIMON: There will be news. (*Again Grusha is called from the palace.*) And now the main question …   300

GRUSHA: Simon Chachava, I have to go to the third courtyard and I'm in a big hurry, so the answer is "Yes."

SIMON: (*very much embarrassed.*) They say that haste is the wind that blows the scaffolding down. But   305
they also say that the rich are never in a hurry. I'm from …

GRUSHA: Kutsk …

SIMON: So the young lady has made inquiries? I'm healthy, I have no one to look out for, I get ten   310
piasters a month, it'll be twenty when I'm paymaster, and with all my heart I ask for your hand.[8]

GRUSHA: Simon Chachava, it's all right with me.

---

8 piaster] a silver coin.

SIMON: (*takes from his neck a thin chain with a little cross on it.*) The cross belonged to my mother, Grusha Vachnadze, the chain is silver; please wear it.   315

GRUSHA: Many thanks, Simon.

(*He puts it around her neck.*)

SIMON: I've got to harness the horses, the young lady must understand that. The young lady had better go to the third courtyard now, or there will be trouble.   320

GRUSHA: Yes, Simon.

(*They stand undecided.*)

SIMON: I'm only taking her to the troops who are still loyal. When the war is over, I'll be back. Two or three weeks. I hope the time won't hang heavy on my betrothed until I return.   325

GRUSHA: Simon Chachava, I will be waiting for you.
Never fear. Go off to war, soldier   330
The grim, bloody war, the hard bitter war
From which not every man returns.
But when you return I'll be there.
I will be waiting for you under the green elm tree
I will be waiting for you under the bare elm tree   335
I will be waiting till the last has come home again
And even more.
When you come back from the war
No boots will be standing at the door.
You will find no one in bed but me.   340
And my mouth will be unkissed.
When you come back home
You'll be able to say everything's just the same.

SIMON: I thank you, Grusha Vachnadze. And good-bye! (*He bows low to her. She bows just as low to him. Then she runs away quickly without looking back. The Aide-de-camp steps out of the archway.*)   345

THE AIDE-DE-CAMP: Harness the horses to the big carriage, don't stand around, you stinker!

(*Simon Chachava comes to attention and goes off. Out the archway creep two servants, bowed under the weight of enormous trunks. Behind them stumbles Natella Abashvili [the Governor's Wife] supported by her waiting-women. Following her, a woman carrying the child.*)

THE GOVERNOR'S WIFE: Nobody attends to anything. I'm at my wits' end. Where is Michael? Don't hold him so clumsily. Load the trunks on the carriage. Is there any news of the Governor, Shalva?   350

THE AIDE-DE-CAMP: (*shakes his head.*) You must leave at once.   355

THE GOVERNOR'S WIFE: Any word from the city?

THE AIDE-DE-CAMP: No. It's been quiet so far, but there's no time to be lost. There's no room in the carriage for the trunks. Take out what you need.   360 (*The Aide-de-camp goes out quickly.*)

THE GOVERNOR'S WIFE: Just the barest necessities! Quick! Open the trunks, I'll tell you what's needed.

(*The trunks are put down and opened.*)

THE GOVERNOR'S WIFE: (*pointing to some brocade dresses.*) The green one and of course the one with the fur trimming! Where are the doctors? That terrible migraine is coming on again, it always starts at the temples. The one with the pearl buttons …   365

(*Enter Grusha.*)

THE GOVERNOR'S WIFE: Taking your time, aren't you? Get the hot water bottles.   370

(*Grusha runs out, comes back in a moment with the hot water bottles, and is silently ordered about by the Governor's Wife.*)

THE GOVERNOR'S WIFE: (*watching a young chambermaid.*) Don't tear the sleeve!

THE YOUNG WOMAN: But gracious lady, nothing has happened to the dress.   375

THE GOVERNOR'S WIFE: Because I caught you. I've been watching you for a long time. All you're good for is making eyes at the Aide-de-camp! I'll kill you, you bitch! (*Strikes her.*)

THE AIDE-DE-CAMP: (*comes back.*) You must hurry, Natella Abashvili. There's fighting in the city. (*Off again.*)   380

THE GOVERNOR'S WIFE: (*lets the young woman go.*) Good God! Do you think they'll dare lay hands on me? Why should they? (*All are silent. She begins to rummage in the trunks.*) Find my brocade jacket! Help her! What's Michael doing? Is he asleep?   385

THE NURSE: Yes, gracious lady.

THE GOVERNOR'S WIFE: Then put him down a minute and bring me my red boots from the bedroom, I need them for my green dress. (*The nurse puts the child down and runs. To the young woman.*) Don't stand around, you! (*The young woman runs away.*) Stay right here or I'll have you whipped. (*Pause.*) Look how these things have been packed! Without love, without understanding. If I'm not there standing over them … In times like these you see what kind of servants you've got. Masha! (*With an imperious gesture.*) You know how to fill your bellies, but you never heard of gratitude. I'll remember this.

THE AIDE-DE-CAMP: (*in great agitation.*) Natella, you must come at once. The carpet weavers have revolted, they've just hanged Judge Orbeliani of the superior court.

THE GOVERNOR'S WIFE: Why? I must take the silver one, it cost a thousand piasters. And this one and all the furs, and where's my wine-red dress?

THE AIDE-DE-CAMP: (*trying to pull her away.*) Riots have broken out in the slums. We've got to be going. (*A servant runs off.*) Where is the child?

THE GOVERNOR'S WIFE: (*calling the nurse.*) Maro! Get the child ready! Where are you?

THE AIDE-DE-CAMP: (*on his way out.*) We may have to forget about the carriage and go on horseback.

(*The Governor's Wife rummages among the dresses, throws some on a pile that is to go along, then takes them off again. Sounds are heard. Drums. A red glow appears in the sky.*)

THE GOVERNOR'S WIFE: (*rummaging desperately.*) My wine-red dress, I can't find it. (*Shrugging her shoulders, to the second woman.*) Take the whole pile to the carriage. Why hasn't Maro come back? Have you all gone crazy? I knew it would be on the bottom.

THE AIDE-DE-CAMP: (*returning.*) Quick! Quick!

THE GOVERNOR'S WIFE: (*to the second woman.*) Run! Just throw them in the carriage!

THE AIDE-DE-CAMP: We're not taking the carriage. Come now, or I'll go without you.

THE GOVERNOR'S WIFE: Maro! Bring the child! (*to the second woman.*) Look for her, Masha! No, first take the dresses to the carriage. Nonsense, I wouldn't dream of going on horseback! (*Turning around to see the fiery glow and freezes with fright.*) Fire! (*She rushes off; the Aide-de-camp follows her. Shaking her head, the second woman follows her with the bundle of dresses.*)

(*Servants come out from the archway.*)

THE WOMAN COOK: The east gate must be on fire.

THE MAN COOK: They've gone. They've left the carriage and all the provisions. How are we going to get out of here?

A STABLE HAND: Yes, this house won't be healthy for a while. (*To the third woman.*) Zulika, I'll get a couple of blankets and we'll clear out.

THE NURSE: (*coming out of the archway with a pair of boots.*) Gracious lady!

A FAT WOMAN: She's gone.

THE NURSE: What about the child? (*She runs to the child and picks him up.*) The beasts, they've left him. (*She hands the child to Grusha.*) Hold him a second. (*Lying transparently.*) I'm going to see about the carriage. (*She runs off after the Governor's Wife.*)

GRUSHA: What have they done to our master?

THE STABLE HAND: (*drawing a finger across his throat.*) Fft!

THE FAT WOMAN: (*growing hysterical at his gesture.*) Merciful heavens above! Georgi Abashvili, our master! Hale and hearty at morning mass, and now … take me away. We're lost! We'll die in sin. Like Georgi Abashvili our master.

THE THIRD WOMAN: (*trying to soothe her.*) Calm down, Nina. You're not in danger. You've never hurt anybody.

THE FAT WOMAN: (*while she is being led away.*) Merciful heavens above, we must all get away before they come, before they come.

THE THIRD WOMAN: Nina takes it more to heart than his wife. These people can't even do their own mourning! (*She catches sight of the child that Grusha is still holding.*) The child! What are you doing with the child!

GRUSHA: They left it behind.

THE THIRD WOMAN: She left him? Michael, who was sheltered from every draft!

(*The servants gather around the child.*)

GRUSHA: He's waking up.

THE STABLE HAND: Better put him down! I don't like to think what would happen to anybody they find with that child. I'll get our stuff; wait here, all of you. (*Goes off into the palace.*) 475

THE WOMAN COOK: He's right, once they start fighting each other, they wipe out whole families. I'm getting my things. (*All have gone out except for two maids and Grusha with the child in her arms.*)

THE THIRD WOMAN: Didn't you hear? Put him down. 480

GRUSHA: His nurse gave him to me to hold for a second.

THE WOMAN COOK: You simple soul, she won't be back. 485

THE THIRD WOMAN: Keep away from him.

THE WOMAN COOK: They'll be hunting him more than his mother. He's the Governor's heir. Grusha, you're a good soul, but you're not very bright. Take it from me, if he had leprosy it couldn't be worse. 490 Just save your skin.

(*The stable hand has come back with bundles which he distributes among the women. All except Grusha prepare to leave.*)

GRUSHA: (*obstinately.*) He hasn't got leprosy. He's looking at me. He's somebody.

THE WOMAN COOK: Then stop looking at him. You're the boneheaded kind that falls for anything. 495 Go get the lettuce, they say, you have the longest legs; and you run. We're taking the oxcart, you can come with us if you hurry. Lord, the whole district must be on fire!

THE THIRD WOMAN: Haven't you packed any- 500 thing? There isn't much time, the Ironshirts will be here any minute.

(*The two women and the stable hand go off.*)

GRUSHA: I'm coming.

(*Grusha lays the child down, looks at it for a few moments, takes pieces of clothing from the trunks that are standing around, and covers the sleeping child. Then she runs into the palace to get her things. Hoofbeats and women's screams are heard. Enter the Fat Prince with some drunken Ironshirts. One is carrying the Governor's head on a pike.*)

THE FAT PRINCE: Here in the centre! (*One of the soldiers climbs on the back of another, takes the head* 505 *and holds it tentatively over the archway.*) That's not the centre, further to the right, that's it. When I give orders, I see to it that they're carried out properly. (*While the soldier, with hammer and nail, fastens the head to the wall by the hair.*) This 510 morning at the church door I said to Georgi Abashvili: "I love clear skies," but to tell the truth I prefer the lightning that strikes out of a clear sky. Yes, indeed. The only trouble is they've taken the brat away. I need him badly. Search all Gruznia for 515 him. A thousand piasters.

(*While Grusha, looking cautiously around, comes to the portal, the fat prince goes off with the Ironshirts. Again the sound of hoofbeats is heard. Carrying a bundle, Grusha goes toward the archway. When she has almost reached it, she turns around to see if the child is still there. The singer starts singing. She stands motionless.*)

THE SINGER:

As she stood there between door and archway, she heard
Or thought she heard a faint cry: the child
Called out to her, he didn't whimper, but said quite reasonably
Or so at least it seemed to her. 520
"Woman," he said, "help me."

And he went on, not whimpering, but saying quite reasonably
"Consider, woman, that one who does not hear a cry for help
But passes by with a distracted ear will never
Hear again the hushed call of her lover nor 525
The blackbird in the dawn nor the contented
Sighs of the tired grape pickers at angelus."[9]
Hearing this

(*Grusha takes a few steps toward the child and bends over him.*)

---

9 angelus] in this case, the ringing of a bell at sunset to announce the time for Roman Catholic prayers and the end
of the working day.

She went back for one last look
At the child. Just to stay with him
For a few moments until someone should come—   530
His mother perhaps or someone else—

(*She sits down, leaning against a trunk and facing the child.*)

Until she should have to go, for the danger was
     too great, the city was full
Of flames and lamentation.

(*The light dims as though evening were turning to night. Grusha has gone into the palace and come back with a lamp and some milk which she gives the child to drink.*)

THE SINGER: (*in a loud voice.*)
Terrible is the temptation to do good!

(*All through the night, Grusha sits watching the child. Once she lights the little lamp to look at the child, once she throws a brocade mantle over him. From time to time she listens and looks around to make sure no one is coming.*)

THE SINGER:
Long she sat with the child   535
Till evening came, till night came.
Till the dawn came. Too long she sat
Too long she saw
The quiet breathing, the little fists
Until toward morning the temptation grew too   540
     great
And she stood up, bent down and with a sigh
     picked up the child
And carried him away.

(*She does as the singer says.*)

Like something stolen she took him
Like a thief she crept away.

3. THE FLIGHT TO THE
NORTHERN MOUNTAINS
THE SINGER:
When Grusha Vachnadze left the city
On the Gruznian military highway
On the way to the northern mountains
She sang a song, she bought milk.

THE MUSICIANS:
How can she, so human, hope   5
To escape the bloodhounds, the setters of snares?
To the deserted mountains she plodded
Along the Gruznian military highway she plodded
She sang a song, she bought milk.

(*Grusha Vachnadze plodding along, carrying the child in a sack on her back, in one hand a bundle, in the other a large stick.*)

GRUSHA: (*sings.*)
Four old commanders   10
Set out for Iran.
The first commander never fought
The second's fighting came to naught
The third one found the weather not right
The fourth one found his soldiers would not fight.   15
Four old commanders
Away they ran.
Sosso Robakidze
Marched off to Iran.
The war he fought was hard and tough   20
He won the battle soon enough

The weather was all right for him
His soldiers hacked away with vim.
Sosso Robakidze
Is our man.   25

(*A peasant hut appears.*)

GRUSHA: (*to the child.*) Noon, time to eat. So we'll sit in the grass and wait impatiently while good old Grusha buys a cup of milk. (*She sets the child on the ground and knocks on the door of the hut; an old peasant opens.*) Could you give me cup of milk, 30 grandfather, and a millet cake perhaps?
THE OLD MAN: Milk? We haven't got any milk. The high and mighty soldiers from the city have taken our goats. Go to the high and mighty soldiers if you want milk.   35
GRUSHA: But you must have a cup of milk left for a child, grandfather?
THE OLD MAN: For a "God-reward-you," I suppose?
GRUSHA: Who said anything about God rewarding 40 you? (*Takes out her purse.*) We pay like princes. Our

heads in the clouds, our behinds in the water! (*Grumbling, the peasant brings milk.*) And what is the price of this cup of milk?

THE OLD MAN: Three piasters. Milk has gone up. 45

GRUSHA: Three piasters? For a thimbleful? (*Without a word the old man slams the door in her face.*) Michael, did you hear that? Three piasters! We can't afford it. (*She goes back and sits down and gives the child her breast.*) We'll just have to try it this 50 way. Suck hard, think of those three piasters! There's nothing there, but you think you're drinking, and that's something. (*She sees that the child has stopped sucking, and shakes her head. She stands up, goes back to the door and knocks again.*) 55 Grandfather, open up, we'll pay! (*In an undertone.*) I hope you drop dead. (*When the old man opens the door again.*) I expected to pay half a piaster, but the child needs it. How about one piaster?

THE OLD MAN: Two. 60

GRUSHA: Don't close the door again. (*She rummages a long while in her purse.*) Here are two piasters. But this milk had better be filling, we have a long way to go. It's highway robbery and a sin.

THE OLD MAN: Kill the soldiers if you want milk. 65

GRUSHA: (*giving the child milk to drink.*) It's an expensive treat. Drink, Michael, it's half a week's wages. The people around here think we've made our money sitting on our asses. Michael, Michael, I've certainly let myself in for something. (*Looking* 70 *at the brocade mantle in which the child is wrapped.*) A brocade mantle worth a thousand piasters, and not one piaster for milk. (*She looks back.*) Now there's a carriage full of rich refugees. Let's try and get a ride. 75

(*Outside a caravanserai.*)[10]

(*Grusha, wearing the brocade mantle, is seen approaching two fine ladies. She is holding the child in her arms.*)

GRUSHA: Oh, do the ladies wish to spend the night here too? It's so dreadfully crowded everywhere, and not a carriage to be had! My coachman simply took it into his head to go back. I've come at least half a mile on foot. Barefoot! My Persian shoes—you 80 know those heels. But why doesn't somebody come?

OLDER LADY: The landlord is taking his time. Ever since the events in the capital, the whole country has lost its manners. (*Out comes the landlord, a very dignified old man with a long beard, followed by his* 85 *house servant.*)

THE LANDLORD: Forgive an old man for making you wait, my ladies. My little grandson was showing me a peach tree in blossom, over there on the slope, beyond the corn fields. We have a few 90 fruit trees over there, a few cherry trees. Further west (*he points.*) the ground is stonier, the peasants drive their sheep there to graze. You ought to see the peach blossoms, such an exquisite pink.

OLDER LADY: You have a fertile region here. 95

THE LANDLORD: God has blessed it. How are the fruit blossoms coming along further south, my ladies? You're from the south, aren't you?

YOUNGER LADY: I must admit I didn't pay much attention to the landscape. 100

THE LANDLORD: (*politely.*) I understand. The dust. On our highway it's best to proceed at a moderate pace, provided one isn't in too much of a hurry.

OLDER LADY: Put your veil around your neck, dearest. The evening breezes here seem rather cool. 105

THE LANDLORD: They come from the Yanga-Tau glaciers, my ladies.

GRUSHA: Oh, I'm so afraid my son will catch cold.

OLDER LADY: It's a good sized caravanserai. Shall we go in? 110

THE LANDLORD: Oh, the ladies desire rooms? But my caravanserai is overcrowded and the servants have run away. I'm dreadfully sorry but I can't accommodate any more people, not even with references … 115

YOUNGER LADY: But we can't spend the night on the road.

OLDER LADY: (*dryly.*) How much is it?

THE LANDLORD: My ladies, surely you must understand that a landlord must be extremely careful in 120 times like these with so many refugees looking for a place to stay. Perfectly respectable persons of course, but frowned on by the authorities. And so …

---

10 *caravanserai*] a Middle Eastern inn, with a large central court for caravans to camp.

OLDER LADY: My dear man, we are not refugees. We are on our way to our summer residence in the mountains, and that's all there is to it. It would never occur to us to ask your hospitality if we … if we needed it *that* badly.

THE LANDLORD: (*nodding agreement.*) Of course not. Still, I doubt whether the one tiny room I have available would suit the ladies. I am obliged to charge sixty piasters per person. Are the ladies together?

GRUSHA: In a way. I, too, am in need of lodging.

YOUNGER LADY: Sixty piasters! The man's a cutthroat!

THE LANDLORD: (*coldly.*) My ladies, I have no desire to cut anyone's throat, and so … (*Turns to go.*)

OLDER LADY: Must we talk about throats? Come along. (*Goes in, followed by the house servant.*)

YOUNGER LADY: (*in despair.*) A hundred and eighty piasters for one room. (*Looking around at Grusha.*) But not with a child! That's impossible! Suppose it cries!

THE LANDLORD: The price of the room is a hundred and eighty piasters, for two persons or for three.

YOUNGER LADY: (*changed on hearing this, to Grusha.*) On the other hand, my dear, I couldn't bear to think of you out on the road. Do come in.

(*They go into the caravanserai. On the other side of the stage the house servant enters from the rear with baggage. Behind him the elderly lady, then the second lady and Grusha with the child.*)

YOUNGER LADY: A hundred and eighty piasters! I haven't been so upset since they brought poor Igor home.

OLDER LADY: Must you talk about Igor?

YOUNGER LADY: Actually there are four of us, the child is a person, isn't it? (*To Grusha.*) Couldn't you pay at least half?

GRUSHA: That is impossible. You see, I had to leave in a great hurry and the Aide-de-camp forgot to give me enough money.

OLDER LADY: Maybe you haven't even got the sixty?

GRUSHA: I will pay that.

YOUNGER LADY: Where are the beds?

THE HOUSE SERVANT: No beds. There are blankets and sacks. You'll just have to make do. Be glad you're not being lowered into the ground, like plenty of others. (*Goes out.*)

YOUNGER LADY: Did you hear that? I'm going straight to the landlord. The man must be flogged.

OLDER LADY: Like your husband?

YOUNGER LADY: You're so cruel. (*She bursts into tears.*)

OLDER LADY: How will we ever make anything resembling beds out of this?

GRUSHA: Leave it to me. (*She puts the child down.*) It's always easier when there's more than one. And there's still your carriage. (*Sweeping the floor.*) I was taken utterly by surprise! "My dear Anastasia Katarinovska," my husband said to me before dinner, "lie down a while, you know how those migraine headaches will come over you." (*She drags sacks into place, makes up beds; the ladies watch her at work and exchange glances.*) "Georgi," I said to the Governor, "with sixty guests for dinner I can't lie down, the servants aren't to be trusted, and Michael Georgivitch won't eat without me." (*To Michael.*) You see, Michael, everything's going to be all right, didn't I tell you? (*She suddenly notices that the ladies are looking at her strangely and whispering.*) There. At least we won't be lying on the bare ground. I've folded the blankets double.

OLDER LADY: (*in a tone of command.*) You're very clever at bed-making, my dear. Show me your hands!

GRUSHA: (*frightened.*) What do you mean?

YOUNGER LADY: You've been told to show your hands.

(*Grusha shows the ladies her hands.*)

YOUNGER LADY: (*triumphantly.*) Cracks! A domestic!

OLDER LADY: (*goes to the door, calls out.*) Servants!

YOUNGER LADY: We've caught you, you hussy. What have you been up to? Confess.

GRUSHA: (*confused.*) I haven't been up to anything. I thought maybe you'd take us with you in your carriage, just a little way. Please don't make a fuss. I'll go of my own accord.

YOUNGER LADY: (*while the older lady continues to call for servants.*) You'll go all right, but with the police. In the meantime stay here. Don't move!

GRUSHA: But I was even going to pay the sixty piasters. Here. (*shows her purse.*) See for yourself, 210 I've got them. Four tens and a five, no it's a ten, that makes sixty. I only wanted the child to ride in the carriage, that's the truth.

YOUNGER LADY: Oh, you wanted to ride in the carriage! No it comes out. 215

GRUSHA: Gracious lady, I confess, I'm of lowly descent, please don't call the police. The child is of high station, look at his linen, he's a refugee like yourselves.

YOUNGER LADY: Of high station, we've heard that 220 one. His father's a prince, isn't he?

GRUSHA: (*wildly to the elderly lady.*) Stop screaming! Haven't you any heart?

YOUNGER LADY: (*to the elderly lady.*) Be careful, she's going to attack you. She's dangerous! Help! 225 Murder!

THE HOUSE SERVANT: (*entering.*) What's wrong?

ELDERLY LADY: This person has wormed her way in here by playing the lady. Probably a thief.

YOUNGER LADY: And dangerous too. She wanted 230 to kill us. Call the police. I feel my migraine coming on, oh heavens!

THE HOUSE SERVANT: There isn't any police right now. (*To Grusha.*) Pack up your belongings, sister, and make yourself scarce. 235

GRUSHA: (*angrily picking up the child.*) You monsters! At a time when they're nailing your heads to the walls!

THE HOUSE SERVANT: (*pushing her out.*) Shut your mouth. Or the old man will come, and then I pity 240 you.

OLDER LADY: (*to the younger lady.*) Look and see if she hasn't stolen something!

(*While the ladies on the right search feverishly to see whether something has been stolen, the house servant steps out the door left with Grusha.*)

THE HOUSE SERVANT: I always say: Don't buy a pig in a poke. Next time take a look at people 245 before you trust them.

GRUSHA: I thought they'd be decent if they thought I was one of them.

THE HOUSE SERVANT: That was silly of you. Believe me, nothing is harder than imitating lazy, 250 useless people. Once they suspect you of being able to wipe your own ass or of ever in all your life working with your hands, you're done for. Wait a second, I'll get you some millet bread and a few apples. 255

GRUSHA: Better not. I'd better go before the landlord comes. If I walk all night, I'll be out of danger, I think. (*Goes.*)

THE HOUSE SERVANT: (*calls softly after her.*) Keep to the right at the next crossing. 260

(*She disappears.*)

THE SINGER:
When Grusha Vachnadze went northward
Prince Kazbeki's guards followed her.

THE MUSICIANS:
How can a barefoot girl escape from the Ironshirts?
The bloodhounds, the setters of snares?
Even at night they hunt. Pursuers 265
Never get tired. Butchers
Never sleep long.

(*Two Ironshirts are trotting along the highway.*)

THE CORPORAL: Blockhead, you'll never amount to anything. Your heart isn't in it. A superior can tell that by the little things. When I laid that fat 270 woman the other day, you carried out my orders, you held her husband, you kicked him in the stomach, but did you take pleasure in it like a good soldier, or did you just go through the motions? I watched you, Blockhead. You're dead wood, you're 275 a tinkling cymbal, you'll never get a promotion. (*They go on a while in silence.*) Don't think I won't remember that every move you make is a display of insubordination. I forbid you to limp. You only do it because I sold the horses because I'd never 280 get such a good price again. By limping you wish to intimate that you don't care for hiking, I know you. It won't do you any good, it will make things worse for you. Sing!

THE TWO IRONSHIRTS: (*sing.*)
To the war my weary way I'm wending 285
While my sweetheart stays to mind the cattle.
Loyal friends her honour are defending
Till I come back from the bloody battle.

THE CORPORAL: Louder!

THE TWO IRONSHIRTS:

As into my grave instead I travel   290
See my sweetheart throwing in the gravel
Hear her say: "There go the feet with which he
    chased me
There the arms that many times embraced me."

(*Again they walk for a while in silence.*)

THE CORPORAL: A good soldier has to put his heart
and soul in it. He'll let himself be torn to pieces   295
for a superior. With his dying glance he takes in
his corporal's nod of approval. That's all the reward
he wants. There won't be any nod for you, and
you'll have to kick in all the same. Damnation,
how am I going to find the Governor's brat with   300
a subordinate like you, just tell me that.

(*They go on.*)

THE SINGER:

When Grusha Vachnadze came to the Sirra River
Her flight became too much for her, the helpless
    child to heavy.

THE MUSICIANS:

In the corn fields the rosy dawn
Is merely cold to one who has not slept. To the   305
    fugitive
The merry clatter of milk pails from the farm
    where the smoke rises
Sounds menacing. Carrying the child, she
Feels its weight and little else.

(*Grusha stops outside a farm.*)

GRUSHA: Now you've wet yourself again and you
know I have no diapers for you. Michael, I'll have   310
to leave you now. We're far enough from the city.
They can't care enough about a little nothing like
you to follow you all this way. That peasant
woman looks friendly, and get a whiff of the milk!
So good-bye, Michael, I'll forget how you kicked   315
me in the back all night to keep me on the move,
and you forget the short rations. I did my best. I'd
have like to keep you longer because your nose is
so little, but it can't be done. I'd have liked to show
you your first bunny and—teach you to stop   320
wetting yourself, but I've got to go back, because
my sweetheart the soldier ought to be back soon,

too, and what if he didn't find me? You can't ask
that of me, Michael.

(*A fat peasant woman carries a milk pail in through
the door. Grusha waits until she is inside, then she goes
cautiously toward the house. She steals up to the door
and sets the child down in front of it. Then she hides
behind a tree and waits until the peasant woman
comes out again and finds the bundle.*)

THE PEASANT WOMAN: Heavens above, what's   325
this? Husband!
THE PEASANT: (*coming out.*) Now what? Let me eat
my soup.
THE PEASANT WOMAN: (*to the child.*) Where's your
mother? Haven't you got one? It's a boy, I believe.   330
And he's got fine linen, this is a noble child. And they
just drop it on the doorstep. What terrible times!
THE PEASANT: If they think we're going to feed him,
they're mistaken. Take it to the priest in the village,
and that's the end of it.   335
THE PEASANT WOMAN: What would the priest do
with him? He needs a mother. There, he's waking
up. Don't you think we could keep him?
THE PEASANT: (*shouting.*) No!
THE PEASANT WOMAN: If I bed him down in the   340
corner beside the armchair, I'll only need a basket,
and I'll take him out to the fields with me. Look,
he's laughing. Husband, we have a roof over our
heads, we can do it, I'm not listening.

(*She carries him in, the peasant follows protesting.
Grusha comes out from behind a tree, laughs and
hurries away in the direction from which she came.*)

THE SINGER:

Why so happy, woman returning homeward?   345
THE MUSICIANS:

Because with a smile, the helpless child has
Got himself new parents, I am happy. Because the
    dear child
Is off my hands, I am glad.

THE SINGER:

And why so sad?
THE MUSICIANS:

Because I am free and unburdened, I am sad   350
As one who has been robbed
As one who has been made poor.

(*She has only gone a little way when she meets the two Ironshirts who bar the way with their pikes.*)

THE CORPORAL: Young lady, you have bumped into the armed forces. Where have you come from? And why? Have you illicit relations with the enemy? Where are they? What movements are they making in your rear? What about the hills, what about the valleys, how are your stockings fastened? 355

(*Grusha stands stock still in fright.*)

GRUSHA: They are well-fortified, you'd better stop short. 360

THE CORPORAL: I always stop short, you can count on me for that. Why are you gaping at my pike? "A soldier in the field never lets his pike out of his hand." That's regulation, Blockhead, learn it by heart. Well, young lady, where are you going? 365

GRUSHA: To meet my sweetheart, soldier, a certain Simon Chachava, of the palace guard in Nukha. If I write him a letter, he'll break every bone in your body.

THE CORPORAL: Simon Chachava, of course, I know him. He gave me the key, said to look in on you now and then. Blockhead, we're getting unpopular. We'd better tell her our intentions are honourable. Young lady, I may seem to make jokes, but I'm serious underneath. So here you have it officially: I want a child from you. 370 375

(*Grusha lets out a little scream.*)

THE CORPORAL: Blockhead, she catches our meaning. A sweet shock isn't it? "But first I must take the buns out of the oven, lieutenant. First I must change my torn shirt, colonel!" Joking aside, poking aside, young lady: we're combing the region for a certain child. Have you heard anything about such a child, that's turned up from the city, a noble child in fine linen? 380

GRUSHA: No, I haven't heard a thing.

THE SINGER:
Run, kind-hearted girl, the killers are coming! 385
You who are helpless, help the helpless child! And so she runs.

(*She turns suddenly and runs away in panic fear, toward the peasant's house. The Ironshirts exchange glances and follow her cursing.*)

THE MUSICIANS:
In the bloodiest times
There are kindly people.

(*In the peasant's house the fat peasant woman is bending over the child in its basket when Grusha Vachnadze rushes in.*)

GRUSHA: Hide him, quick. The Ironshirts are coming. I left him on the doorstep, but he's not mine, he comes from a noble family. 390

THE PEASANT WOMAN: Who's coming? What Ironshirts?

GRUSHA: Don't waste time. The Ironshirts are looking for him. 395

THE PEASANT WOMAN: They've no business in my house. But it looks like I'll want a word with you.

GRUSHA: Take off his fine linen, it will give us away.

THE PEASANT WOMAN: Don't bother me with linen. In my house I give the orders. And don't throw up on my furniture. Why did you leave it? That's a sin. 400

GRUSHA: (*looking out.*) They'll be coming out from behind the trees any minute. I shouldn't have run away, that made them angry. Oh, what should I do? 405

THE PEASANT WOMAN: (*also peers out and is suddenly scared stiff.*) Mother of God, the Ironshirts!

GRUSHA: They're looking for the child.

THE PEASANT WOMAN: But what if they come in here? 410

GRUSHA: You mustn't give it to them. Say it's yours.

THE PEASANT WOMAN: Yes.

GRUSHA: They'll run it through if you give it to them.

THE PEASANT WOMAN: But suppose they ask me for it? I've got silver for the harvesters in the house. 415

GRUSHA: If you give it to them, they'll run it through, right here in your house. You've got to tell them it's yours.

THE PEASANT WOMAN: Yes. But suppose they don't believe me? 420

GRUSHA: If you say it like you mean it …

THE PEASANT WOMAN: They'll burn the roof over our heads.

GRUSHA: That's why you have to say it's yours. His name is Michael. I shouldn't have told you that. 425

(*The peasant woman nods.*)

GRUSHA: Don't nod your head like that. And don't tremble, they'll notice.

THE PEASANT WOMAN: Yes.

GRUSHA: Stop saying "yes." I can't stand it. (*Shakes her.*) Haven't you got one of your own? 430

THE PEASANT WOMAN: (*mumbling.*) Gone to war.

GRUSHA: Then maybe he's an Ironshirt himself. Would you expect him to run babies through? Wouldn't *you* give him a piece of your mind! "Stop poking your pike into my house, is that how I raised you? Wash your neck before you talk to your mother." 435

THE PEASANT WOMAN: That's a fact. I wouldn't let him do that.

GRUSHA: Promise to tell them he's yours.

THE PEASANT WOMAN: Yes. 440

GRUSHA: They're coming now.

(*Knocking at the door. The women do not answer. Enter the Ironshirts. The peasant woman bows low.*)

THE CORPORAL: That's her all right. What did I tell you? I've got a nose on me. I could smell her. I've got a question to ask you, young lady: Why did you run away? What did you think? That I wanted something from you? I bet it was something indecent. Admit it! 445

GRUSHA: (*while the peasant woman keeps bowing.*) I left milk on the stove. I suddenly remembered it.

THE CORPORAL: I thought it was because I was looking at you indecently. As if I had some idea about you and me. Kind of a sensual look, see what I mean? 450

GRUSHA: I didn't see anything like that.

THE CORPORAL: But it's possible, don't deny it. After all, I could be a swine. I'll be perfectly frank with you: I could get all sorts of ideas if we were alone. (*To the peasant woman.*) Haven't you something to do in the yard? Feed the chickens? 455

THE PEASANT WOMAN: (*falling suddenly on her knees.*) Mr. Soldier, I didn't know a thing. Don't burn the roof over my head! 460

THE CORPORAL: What are you talking about?

THE PEASANT WOMAN: It's got nothing to do with me, Mr. Soldier. She left it on my doorstep, I swear it. 465

THE CORPORAL: (*sees the child and whistles.*) Oho, there's a little fellow in the basket, Blockhead, I smell a thousand piasters. Take the old woman

outside and hold her fast. Seems to me I've got a little interrogation on my hands. 470

(*Without a word the peasant woman lets the soldier lead her away.*)

THE CORPORAL: So here's the baby I wanted of you. (*He goes to the basket.*)

GRUSHA: Mr. Officer, it's mine. It's not the one you're looking for.

THE CORPORAL: Let's have a look. (*He bends over the basket.*) 475

(*Grusha looks in despair.*)

GRUSHA: It's mine, it's mine.

THE CORPORAL: Fine linen.

(*Grusha rushes at him to pull him away. He flings her off and again bends down over the basket. She looks about desperately, sees a big log, lifts it and brings it down on the Corporal's head from behind. He collapses. Quickly picking up the child, she runs out.*)

THE SINGER:
And fleeing from the Ironshirts
After twenty-two days of flight
At the foot of the Yanga-Tau glacier 480
Grusha Vachnadze adopted the child.

THE MUSICIANS:
The helpless one adopted the helpless one.

(*Grusha leans over a half-frozen stream and scoops up water for the child in the hollow of her hand.*)

GRUSHA: (*sings.*)
Since no one wants to take you, child
I shall have to take you.
Black the day as black can be 485
If you're satisfied with me
I will not forsake you.

I have carried you so far
Sore, my feet, and bleeding
Spent such fortunes buying milk 490
You've grown dear to me
(Fondness comes from feeding.)

I will throw your linen out
Swaddle you in tatters 495

I will wash you and baptize
You in glacier water.
(You'll just have to stand it.)

(*She has taken off the child's fine linen and wrapped him in a rag.*)

THE SINGER:
When Grusha Vachnadze, pursued by the
Ironshirts
Came to the footbridge leading over the glacier to   500
the village on the eastern slope
She sang the Song of the Shaky Bridge and risked
two lives.

(*A wind has come up. The footbridge appears in the half-light. One cable is broken and the bridge is slanting over the abyss. Peddlers, two men and a woman, are standing undecided at the end of the bridge when Grusha arrives. One of the men is fishing with a pole for the dangling cable.*)

FIRST MAN: Take your time, young lady, you won't
get across the pass anyway.
GRUSHA: But I have to take my baby to my brother's
place on the east side.   505
THE WOMAN: Have to! What do you mean have
to! I have to get across because I have two carpets
in Atum, which a woman has to sell because her
husband died. But can I do what I have to do; can
she? Audrey has been fishing for the cable for two   510
hours, but even if he catches it how are we going
to make it fast? Tell me that.
FIRST MAN: (*listening.*) Sh-sh, I think I hear
something.
GRUSHA: (*in a loud voice.*) The bridge isn't all that   515
shaky. I think I'll try to cross it.
THE WOMAN: I wouldn't try it if the devil himself
were after me. Why, it's suicide.
FIRST MAN: (*shouting.*) Ho!
GRUSHA: Don't shout! (*To the woman.*) Tell him not   520
to shout.
FIRST MAN: But somebody's shouting down there.
Maybe they've lost their way down there.
THE WOMAN: Why shouldn't he shout? Is there
something shady about you? Are they after you?   525
GRUSHA: I guess I'd better tell you. The Ironshirts
are after me. I hit one of them on the head.

SECOND MAN: Hide the stuff.

(*The woman hides a sack behind a rock.*)

FIRST MAN: Why didn't you tell us right away? (*To
the others.*) If they catch her, they'll make hash out   530
of her!
GRUSHA: Get out of the way, I've got to cross that
bridge.
SECOND MAN: You can't! The chasm is two
thousand feet deep!   535
FIRST MAN: Even if we could catch the cable, there
wouldn't be any sense in it. We could hold it in
our hands, but the Ironshirts could cross the same
way.
GRUSHA: Out of my way!   540

(*Not very distant cries: "She's up there!".*)

THE WOMAN: They're coming close. But you can't
take your child on the bridge. It's almost sure to
collapse. And look down there.

(*Grusha looks into the chasm. More cries from the Ironshirts below.*)

SECOND MAN: Two thousand feet.
GRUSHA: But those men are worse.   545
FIRST MAN: You can't do it. Think of the child. Risk
your own life if they're out to get you, but not the
child's.
SECOND MAN: Besides, she'll be heavier with the
child.   550
THE WOMAN: Maybe she really has to get across.
Give it to me, I'll hide it, and you'll try the bridge
by yourself.
GRUSHA: No. Where he goes, I go. (*To the child.*)
We're in this together, son. (*Sings.*)   555

Deep is the chasm, son
See the bridge sway
Not of our choosing, son
Is our way.

You must go the way that   560
I have picked for you
You must eat the bread that
I have saved for you

Share the two, three morsels
Taking two of three.   565
How big or how little
Better not ask me.

I'll try it.
THE WOMAN: It's tempting God.

(*Cries from below.*)

GRUSHA: I beg you, throw your pole away, or they'll   570
fish up the cable and come after me.

(*She goes out on the swaying bridge. The peddler
woman screams when the bridge threatens to break.
But Grusha goes on and reaches the other side.*)

FIRST MAN: She's across.
THE WOMAN: (*who had fallen on her knees and
prayed, angrily.*) It was a sin all the same.

(*The Ironshirts appear from below. The corporal's head
is bandaged.*)

THE CORPORAL: Have you seen a woman with a   575
child?
FIRST MAN: (*while the second man throws the pole
into the chasm.*) Yes. There she is. And the bridge
won't carry you.
THE CORPORAL: Blockhead, you're going to pay for   580
this.

(*Grusha on the opposite side laughs and shows the Ironshirts the child. She goes on, the bridge stays behind. Wind.*)

GRUSHA: (*looking around at Michael.*) Never be
afraid of the wind, it's only a poor devil like us.
His job is pushing the clouds and he gets colder
than anybody.   585

(*Snow begins to fall.*)

The snow isn't so bad either, Michael. Its job is
covering the little fir trees so the winter won't kill
them. And now I'll sing a song for you. Listen!
(*Sings.*)

Your father is a bandit
And your mother is a whore   590
Every noble man and honest
Will bow as you pass.

The tiger's son will
Feed the little foals his brothers
The child of the serpent   595
Bring milk to the mothers.

4. IN THE NORTHERN MOUNTAINS

THE SINGER:
The sister trudged for seven days.
Across the glacier, down the slopes she trudged.
"When I come to my brother's house," she thought,
"He will stand up and embrace me."
"Is it you, sister?" he will say.   5
"I've long been expecting you. This is my beloved
wife.
And this my farm, mine by marriage.
With eleven horses and thirty-one cows. Be seated!
Sit down at our table with your child and eat."
Her brother's house was in a smiling valley.   10
When the sister came to the brother's house, she
was ill from her journey.
The brother stood up from the table.

(*A stout peasant couple who have sat down to eat.
Lavrenti Vachnadze already has his napkin around his
neck when Grusha, supported by a hired hand and
very pale, enters with the child.*)

LAVRENTI VACHNADZE: Where have you come
from, Grusha?
GRUSHA: (*feebly.*) I've come across the Yanga-Tau   15
pass, Lavrenti.
HIRED HAND: I found her outside the hay shed. She
has a child with her.
THE SISTER-IN-LAW: Go and curry the bay.[11] (*The
hired hand goes out.*)   20
LAVRENTI: This is my wife, Aniko.
THE SISTER-IN-LAW: We thought you were working
in Nukha.
GRUSHA: (*who can hardly stand up.*) Yes, I was.
THE SISTER-IN-LAW: Wasn't it a good position? We   25
heard it was.
GRUSHA: The Governor has been killed.
LAVRENTI: Yes, we heard there was trouble. Your
aunt told us, don't you remember, Aniko?

---

11 curry] groom; bay] a reddish-brown horse.

THE SISTER-IN-LAW: It's perfectly quiet here. City people are always looking for trouble. (*Goes to the door and calls.*) Sosso, Sosso, don't take the cake out of the oven yet, do you hear? Where are you anyway? (*Goes out, calling.*) 30

LAVRENTI: (*quickly, in an undertone.*) Have you a father for it? (*When she shakes her head.*) Just as I thought. We've got to think up something. She's very religious. 35

THE SISTER-IN-LAW: (*coming back.*) Those servants! (*To Grusha.*) You have a child? 40

GRUSHA: It's mine. (*She slumps over. Lavrenti raises her up.*)

THE SISTER-IN-LAW: Saints alive, she's got some disease. What will we do?

(*Lavrenti starts leading Grusha to the bench by the stove. Aniko, horrified, gestures him to stop and points to a sack by the wall.*)

LAVRENTI: (*takes Grusha to the wall.*) Sit down. Sit down. It's only weakness. 45

THE SISTER-IN-LAW: What if it's scarlet fever!

LAVRENTI: There would be spots. It's weakness, Aniko, nothing to worry about. (*To Grusha, who has sat down.*) Are you feeling better now? 50

THE SISTER-IN-LAW: Is the child hers?

GRUSHA: Mine.

LAVRENTI: She's going to join her husband.

THE SISTER-IN-LAW: Oh. Your meat is getting cold. (*Lavrenti sits down and begins to eat.*) It doesn't agree with you cold, the fat is no good when it's cold. You know you have a delicate stomach. (*To Grusha.*) If your husband's not in the city, where on earth is he? 55

LAVRENTI: He lives across the mountains, she says. 60

THE SISTER-IN-LAW: Oh. Across the mountains.

(*Sits down to eat.*)

GRUSHA: I think you'll have to take me somewhere to lie down, Lavrenti.

THE SISTER-IN-LAW: (*continues her interrogation.*) If it's consumption, we'll all get it. Has your husband a farm? 65

GRUSHA: He's a soldier.

LAVRENTI: But he's inherited a farm from his father, a small farm.

THE SISTER-IN-LAW: Hasn't he gone to war? Why not? 70

GRUSHA: (*with difficulty.*) Yes, he's gone to war.

THE SISTER-IN-LAW: Then why are you going to the farm?

LAVRENTI: When he comes back from the war, he'll go to the farm. 75

THE SISTER-IN-LAW: But you're going there right away?

LAVRENTI: Yes, to wait for him.

THE SISTER-IN-LAW: (*screams.*) Sosso, the cake! 80

GRUSHA: (*mumbles feverishly.*) A farm. Soldier. Wait. Sit down, eat.

THE SISTER-IN-LAW: It's scarlet fever.

GRUSHA: (*starting up.*) Yes, he has a farm.

LAVRENTI: I think it's weakness, Aniko. Don't you want to see about the cake, my love? 85

THE SISTER-IN-LAW: But when will he come back if what you're saying is true and the war has broken out again? (*Waddles out, calling.*) Sosso, where are you? Sosso! 90

LAVRENTI: (*stands up quickly, goes to Grusha.*) We'll put you to bed right away. She's a good soul, but not until after dinner.

GRUSHA: (*holds out the child to him.*) Take it! (*He takes it, looking around.*) 95

LAVRENTI: But you can't stay long. She's religious, you see. (*Grusha collapses. Her brother catches her.*)

THE SINGER:
The sister was too sick.
The cowardly brother had to take her in.
The autumn went, the winter came. 100
The winter was long
The winter was short.
The people mustn't find out.
The rats mustn't bite.
The spring mustn't come. 105

(*Grusha sitting at the loom in the storeroom. The child is huddled on the floor. They are wrapped in blankets.*)

GRUSHA: (*sings while weaving.*)
The loved one prepared to go
And his betrothed ran after him pleading
Pleading and in tears, tearfully admonishing:

Dearest love, dearest love
If you must go off to war 110

If you must fight in the hard battle
Don't run ahead of the war
And don't lag behind the war
Up in front there is red fire
In the rear there is red smoke.
Keep in the middle of the war
Stay close to the banner bearer.
The first are always sure to die
The last are sure to be struck down as well
Those in the middle come home again.

Michael, we must be very clever. If we make ourselves as small as cockroaches, my sister-in-law will forget that we're in the house. We'll be able to stay until the snow melts. And don't cry because it's cold. If you're poor and suffer from the cold besides, people won't like you.

(*Lavrenti comes in. He sits down beside his sister.*)

LAVRENTI: Why are you sitting here bundled up like coachmen? Is the room too cold?

GRUSHA: (*hastily removing her shawl.*) It's not cold, Lavrenti.

LAVRENTI: If it's too cold, you shouldn't be sitting here with the child. Aniko would never forgive herself. (*Pause.*) I hope the priest didn't ask you questions about the child.

GRUSHA: He asked, but I didn't tell him anything.

LAVRENTI: That's good. I wanted to talk to you about Aniko. She's a good soul, but she's so very, very sensitive. If people say the least thing about the farm, she gets upset. You see, she takes everything to heart. One time the milkmaid had a hole in her stocking in church, and my dear Aniko has been wearing two pairs of stockings to church ever since. You won't believe it, but it's in the family. (*He listens.*) Are you sure there are no rats here? You can't stay here if there are. (*A sound is heard as of dripping from the roof.*) What's that dripping?

GRUSHA: It must be a leaky barrel.

LAVRENTI: Yes, it must be a barrel.—You've been here for six months now. Was I talking about Aniko? Of course I didn't tell her about that Ironshirt, she has a weak heart. So she doesn't know you can't look for work, and that's why she spoke the way she did yesterday. (*They listen again to the dripping of the melting snow.*) You can't imagine how worried she is about your soldier. "Suppose he comes home and doesn't find her?" she says, and lies awake at night. "He can't be home before spring," I say. The good soul. (*The drops fall faster.*) When do you suppose he'll come, what do you think? (*Grusha is silent.*) Not before spring. Don't you agree? (*Grusha says nothing.*) I see, you've given up expecting him. (*Grusha says nothing.*) But when spring comes and the snow thaws here and on the passes, you can't stay here any longer, they're likely to come looking for you, and people are talking about an illegitimate child.

(*The glockenspiel of the falling drops has become loud and steady.*)

LAVRENTI: Grusha, the snow is melting on the roof; it's spring.

GRUSHA: Yes.

LAVRENTI: (*with enthusiasm.*) I'll tell you what we'll do. You need a place to go, you've got a child (*he sighs.*), so you need a husband to make people stop gossiping. I've been asking around—oh, very cautiously—about a husband for you. I've found one, Grusha. I've spoken to a woman who has a son just across the mountain, with a small farm, she's willing.

GRUSHA: But I can't marry anybody, I've got to wait for Simon Chachava.

LAVRENTI: Of course. I've thought of all that. You don't need a husband in bed, only on paper. I've found the right man. This woman I've made arrangements with—her son is dying. Isn't that perfect? He's at his last gasp. It will be just like we said: "A husband across the mountains." And when you got there, he breathed his last and you were a widow. What do you say?

GRUSHA: I could use an official document for Michael.

LAVRENTI: An official document makes all the difference in the world. Without an official document even the shah of Persia wouldn't dare to call himself the shah. And you'll have a roof over your head.

GRUSHA: What does the woman want for it?

LAVRENTI: Four hundred piasters.

GRUSHA: Where did you get them?

LAVRENTI: (*guiltily.*) Aniko's milk money.

GRUSHA: Over there nobody will know us.—All right, I'll do it. 200

LAVRENTI: (*stands up.*) I'll let the woman know right away.

(*Goes out quickly.*)

GRUSHA: Michael, you certainly mess things up. I came by you as a pear tree comes by sparrows. And because a Christian bends down and picks up a crust of bread to make sure that nothing is wasted. Michael, I ought to have left in a hurry that Easter Sunday in Nukha. Now I'm the ninny. 205

THE SINGER:

The bridegroom lay on his deathbed when the bride appeared. 210

The bridegroom's mother was waiting at the door and pressed her to make haste.

The bride brought a child with her, the witness hid it during the wedding.

(*A room divided by a partition: on one side a bed. Under the mosquito netting a very sick man lies motionless. The mother-in-law comes running in on the other side, pulling Grusha by the hand. After them Lavrenti with the child.*)

THE MOTHER-IN-LAW: Hurry, hurry, or he'll kick in on us before the wedding. (*To Lavrenti.*) You didn't tell me she had a child already. 215

LAVRENTI: What difference does it make? (*With a gesture toward the dying man.*) It can't matter to him, not in his condition.

THE MOTHER-IN-LAW: Not to him! But I'll never outlive the disgrace. We're honest folk. (*She starts to cry.*) My Yussup doesn't have to marry a woman that has a child already. 220

LAVRENTI: All right. I'll throw in another two hundred piasters. You have it in writing that the farm goes to you, but she is entitled to live here for two years. 225

THE MOTHER-IN-LAW: (*drying her tears.*) That will hardly cover the funeral expenses. I hope she'll really give me a hand with the work. But where has the monk gone now? He must have crawled 230

out the kitchen window. Now we'll have the whole village on our necks if they hear that Yussup is giving up the ghost. Oh my goodness! I'll go get him, he mustn't see the child.

LAVRENTI: I'll make sure he doesn't see it. But why a monk and not a priest? 235

THE MOTHER-IN-LAW: It's just as good. Except I made the mistake of giving him half his fee before the ceremony, so now he's gone off to the tavern. I only hope … (*She runs off.*) 240

LAVRENTI: The priest was too expensive for her, the skinflint. She's hired a cheap monk.

GRUSHA: Send Simon Chachava over here if he turns up.

LAVRENTI: Yes. (*Indicating the sick man.*) Don't you want to take a look at him? 245

(*Grusha, who has picked up Michael, shakes her head.*)

LAVRENTI: He doesn't even move. I hope we're not too late.

(*They listen. On the other side neighbours enter, look around and line up along the walls. They begin to mumble prayers. The mother-in-law comes in with the monk.*)

THE MOTHER-IN-LAW: (*after a moment's surprise and irritation, to the monk.*) There you have it. (*She bows to the guests.*) Please be patient just a minute. My son's fiancée has just arrived from the city and there's to be an emergency marriage. (*Goes into the bedroom with the monk.*) I knew you'd spread it far and wide. (*To Grusha.*) The marriage can take place right away. Here's the contract. Me and the bride's brother … (*Lavrenti tries to hide in the background after quickly recovering Michael from Grusha. The mother-in-law waves him away.*) Me and the bride's brother are the witnesses. 250 255 260

(*Grusha has bowed to the monk. They go to the bedside. The mother-in-law pushes back the mosquito netting. The monk begins to reel off his lines in Latin. Meanwhile Lavrenti tries to prevent the child from crying by showing him the ceremony and the mother-in-law keeps motioning him to put the child down. Once Grusha looks around toward the child and Lavrenti waves the child's hand at her.*)

THE MONK: Are you prepared to be a faithful, obedient, and good wife to this man and to cleave to him until death you do part?

GRUSHA: (*looking at the child.*) Yes.

THE MONK: (*to the dying man.*) And are you prepared to be a good husband and provider to this woman until death you do part? 265

(*When the dying man does not answer, the monk repeats his question and looks around.*)

THE MOTHER-IN-LAW: Of course he is. Didn't you hear him say yes?

THE MONK: All right, we declare this marriage concluded. But how about extreme unction? 270

THE MOTHER-IN-LAW: Nothing doing. The marriage cost enough. Now I've got to attend to the mourners. (*To Lavrenti.*) Did we say seven hundred?

LAVRENTI: Six hundred. (*He gives her the money.*) I 275 won't sit down with the guests. I might make friends with somebody. So good-bye Grusha, and if my widowed sister comes to see me one of these days, my wife will bid welcome, or she'll hear from me. 280

(*He goes. The mourners look after him indifferently as he passes through.*)

THE MONK: And may one ask who this child is?

THE MOTHER-IN-LAW: A child? I don't see any child. And you don't see one either. Understand? Or maybe I'll have seen certain goings-on behind 285 the tavern. Come along now.

(*They go into the other room, after Grusha has set the child on the floor and told him to keep quiet. She is introduced to the neighbours.*)

THE MOTHER-IN-LAW: This is my daughter-in-law. She was just in time to find our dear Yussup alive.

ONE OF THE WOMEN: He's been lying abed a whole year now, hasn't he? When my Vassili went 290 off to the army, he came to the farewell party.

ANOTHER WOMAN: A thing like this is terrible for a farm, the corn ready to reap and the farmer in bed. A good thing for him if he doesn't have to suffer much longer is what I say. 295

FIRST WOMAN: (*confidentially.*) At first we thought he took to his bed to keep out of the army. And now he's dying!

THE MOTHER-IN-LAW: Do sit down and have a few cakes. 300

(*The mother-in-law beckons to Grusha and they both go into the bedroom where they take pans of cake from the floor. The guests, including the monk, sit down on the floor and start a muffled conversation.*)

A PEASANT: (*the monk has taken a bottle from his cassock and passed it to him.*) There's a child you say? How can that have happened to Yussup?

THIRD WOMAN: She was certainly lucky to swing it, with him so sick. 305

THE MOTHER-IN-LAW: Now they've started gossiping; and they'll be eating up the funeral cakes and if he doesn't die today, I'll have to bake more tomorrow.

GRUSHA: I'll bake them. 310

THE MOTHER-IN-LAW: Last night some men rode by and I went out to see who it was. When I came back he was lying there like a corpse. That's why I sent for you. He can't last long now. (*She listens.*)

THE MONK: Dear wedding guests and mourners! 315 Deeply moved, we stand before a death bed and a marriage bed, for a woman has been married and a man is soon to be buried. The groom has been washed and the bride is hot. For in the marriage bed there lies a last will, which arouses the lusts 320 of the flesh. Dearly beloved, how various are the paths of humankind! One dies to get a roof over his head, another marries in order that flesh may return to the dust whence it was made. Amen.

THE MOTHER-IN-LAW: (*who has listened.*) He's 325 getting even. I shouldn't have taken such a cheap one, he's no better than I paid for. An expensive one behaves. In Sura there's a priest who's even said to be a saint, but naturally he costs a fortune. A fifty-piaster priest like this has no dignity, he's got 330 just enough religion for fifty piasters, no more. When I went to get him out of the tavern, he was making a speech and yelling: "The war is over! Beware of peace!" We'd better go in.

GRUSHA: (*gives Michael a cake.*) Here's a cake for 335 you, be nice and quiet, Michael. We're respectable people now.

(*They take the cake pans out to the guests. The dying man sits up under the mosquito net, sticks his head out, and looks after the two women. Then he sinks back. The monk has taken two bottles from his cassock and passed them to the peasant who is sitting beside him. Three musicians have entered; the monk grins and waves to them.*)

THE MOTHER-IN-LAW: (*to the musicians.*) What are you doing here with your instruments?

A MUSICIAN: Brother Anastasius here (*indicating the monk.*) said there was a wedding. 340

THE MOTHER-IN-LAW: What's this? Three more people on my neck? Don't you know there's a dying man in there?

THE MONK: A fascinating problem for a musician. 345 Shall it be a muffled wedding march or a dashing funeral dance?

THE MOTHER-IN-LAW: Play something at least, we know nothing can stop you from eating.

(*The musicians play a mixture of genres. The women pass cakes.*)

THE MONK: The trumpet sounds like a whimpering 350 baby, and you, little drum, what is your message to the world?

THE PEASANT: (*beside the monk.*) Couldn't the bride give us a little dance?

THE MONK: With a skeleton? 355

THE PEASANT: (*beside the monk, sings.*)
Mistress Roundass thought it was time to wed
She took an elderly man to bed
To frolic and to dandle.
Next morning she had changed her mind:
I'd rather have a candle. 360

(*The mother-in-law throws the drunken man out. The music breaks off. The guests are embarrassed. Pause.*)

THE GUESTS: (*loudly.*) Did you hear that? The grand duke is back.—But the princes are against him.—Oh, it seems the shah of Persia has lent him a big army to restore order in Gruznia.—How can that be? The shah of Persia hates the grand duke!—But 365 he also hates disorder.—Anyway the war is over. Our soldiers are coming back. (*Grusha drops the cake pan.*)

A WOMAN: (*to Grusha.*) Aren't you feeling well? It's the excitement over our dear Yussup. Sit down and 370 rest, my dear.

(*Grusha stands tottering.*)

THE GUESTS: Now everything will be the same as before.—Except there will be more taxes, because we'll have to pay for the war.

GRUSHA: (*feebly.*) Did someone say the soldiers are 375 coming home?

A MAN: I said so.

GRUSHA: That can't be.

THE MAN: (*to a woman.*) Show her your shawl! We bought it from a soldier. It's from Persia. 380

GRUSHA: (*looks at the shawl.*) They're here.

(*A long pause. Grusha kneels down as though to pick up the cakes. She takes the silver cross and chain from her blouse, kisses the cross and begins to pray.*)

THE MOTHER-IN-LAW: (*seeing that the guests are silently looking at Grusha.*) What's got into you? Can't you pay attention to our guests? What do we care about these fool rumours from the city? 385

THE GUESTS: (*loudly resuming their conversation while Grusha kneels with her forehead to the floor.*) You can buy Persian saddles from the soldiers, some are exchanging them for crutches.—Only the bigwigs on one side can win a war, the soldiers on 390 both sides lose it.—At least the war's over. It's something if they can't drag you off to the army any more. (*The peasant in the bed has sat up. He is listening.*)—What we need is two more weeks of good weather.—Our pear trees are hardly bearing 395 at all this year.

THE MOTHER-IN-LAW: (*passing the cake.*) Have a little more cake. Help yourselves. There's more.

(*The mother-in-law goes into the bedroom with the empty cake pan. She does not see the sick man. She is bending over a full cake pan on the floor when he begins to speak in a hoarse voice.*)

YUSSUP: How much more cake are you going to stuff into their bellies? Do you think I shit money? (*The mother-in-law turns abruptly and stares at him aghast. He climbs out from behind the mosquito net.*) Did they say the war was over? 400

THE FIRST WOMAN: (*in the other room, amiably to Grusha.*) Has the young lady someone in the army? 405

THE MAN: It's good news that they're coming home, isn't it?

YUSSUP: Stop goggling. Where is this woman you've saddled me with?

(*Receiving no answer, he gets out of bed in his night-gown and staggers past the mother-in-law into the other room. She follows him trembling, with the cake pan.*)

THE GUESTS: (*seeing him and exclaim.*) Jesus, Mary 410 and Joseph! Yussup!

(*All spring up in alarm, the women rush toward the door. Grusha, still on her knees, turns her head and stares at Yussup.*)

YUSSUP: A funeral supper. Wouldn't that suit you! Get out before I take a whip to you.

(*The guests leave the house in haste.*)

YUSSUP: (*grimly to Grusha.*) Upsets your little game, eh? 415

(*She says nothing; he takes a millet cake from the pan the mother-in-law is holding.*)

THE SINGER:
Oh, confusion. The wife discovers she has a husband!
By the day she has the child. At night she has the husband.
Day and night her beloved is on his way.
The couple look each other over. The room is small.

(*Yussup sits naked in a tall wooden bathtub and the mother-in-law adds water out of a pitcher. In the bedroom Grusha is sitting huddled over with Michael who is playing at mending straw mats.*)

YUSSUP: She should be doing this, not you. Where 420 has she gone now?

THE MOTHER-IN-LAW: (*calls.*) Grusha! Yussup wants you.

GRUSHA: (*to Michael.*) Here are two more holes for you to mend. 425

YUSSUP: (*as Grusha enters.*) Scrub my back!

GRUSHA: Can't the farmer do it himself?

YUSSUP: "Can't the farmer do it himself?" Take the brush, damn it! Are you my wife or are you a stranger? (*To the mother-in-law.*) Too cold! 430

THE MOTHER-IN-LAW: I'll get some hot water right away.

GRUSHA: Let me go.

YUSSUP: You stay right here! (*The mother-in-law runs out.*) Rub harder. And don't put on airs like you'd 435 never seen a naked man before. Who made your kid? The Holy Ghost?

GRUSHA: The child wasn't conceived in joy, if that's what the farmer means.

YUSSUP: (*looks around at her and grins.*) I wouldn't 440 say that, to look at you. (*Grusha stops scrubbing him and shrinks back. The mother-in-law enters.*) Nice work. You've married me to a cold fish.

THE MOTHER-IN-LAW: She just doesn't try.

YUSSUP: Pour, but be careful. Ouch! Careful, I said. 445 (*To Grusha.*) I wouldn't be surprised if you'd got yourself in trouble in the city. Or what would you be doing here? But I won't go into that. I haven't said anything about the bastard you've brought into my house, but with you my patience is 450 running out. It's not natural. (*To the mother-in-law.*) More! (*To Grusha.*) Even if your soldier comes back, remember, you're married.

GRUSHA: Yes.

YUSSUP: But your soldier won't come back any more, 455 it's no use thinking he will.

GRUSHA: No.

YUSSUP: You're cheating me. You're my wife and you're not my wife. Where you lie, there's nothing, but nobody else can lie there. When I go out to the fields 460 in the morning, I'm dead tired; when I lie down at night, I'm as spry as the devil himself. God made you a woman, and what do you do? My farm doesn't bring in enough for me to buy a woman in the city, and besides, there's the trip to think of. A woman 465 hoes the fields and spreads her legs, that's what it says in our almanac. Do you hear me?

GRUSHA: Yes. (*Softly.*) I'm sorry to be cheating you.

YUSSUP: She's sorry! More water! (*The mother-in-law pours more water.*) Ouch! 470

THE SINGER:
As by the brook she sat washing the linen
She saw his face in the water. And his face grew paler

With each passing moon.
When she stood up to wring out the linen
She heard his voice from the murmuring maple   475
  and his voice grew softer
With each passing moon.
Sighs and excuses multiplied, salt tears and sweat
  were shed.
With each passing moon the child grew up.

(*Grusha is kneeling by a small brook, dipping clothes in the water. A little way off some children are standing. Grusha is talking to Michael.*)

GRUSHA: You may play with them, Michael, but
  don't let them order you around because you're the   480
  smallest.

(*Michael nods and goes to the other children. They start to play.*)

THE BIGGEST BOY: Today we're going to play Heads
  Off. (*To a fat boy.*) You're the prince, you're
  supposed to laugh. (*To Michael.*) You're the
  Governor. (*To a little girl.*) You're the Governor's   485
  Wife, you're supposed to cry when his head is
  chopped off. And I'm going to chop his head off.
  (*He shows a wooden sword.*) With this. First the
  Governor is brought into the yard. The prince
  leads the procession, the Governor's Wife comes   490
  last. (*The procession forms, the fat boy goes first,
  laughing. Then come Michael and the biggest boy,
  then the little girl who is crying.*)
MICHAEL: (*stops still.*) Me chop head off too.
THE BIGGEST BOY: That's my job. You're the littlest.   495
  Governor is easiest. Get down on your knees and
  let your head be chopped off. It's easy.
MICHAEL: Want sword too.
THE BIGGEST BOY: It's mine. (*Gives him a kick.*)
THE LITTLE GIRL: (*calls to Grusha.*) He won't play   500
  right.
GRUSHA: (*laughs.*) They say the smallest duckling
  knows how to swim.
THE BIGGEST BOY: You can be the prince if you
  can laugh.   505

(*Michael shakes his head.*)

THE FAT BOY: I laugh best. Let him chop your head
  off once, then you chop his off and then me.

(*Reluctantly the biggest boy gives Michael the wooden sword and kneels down. The fat boy has sat down, slapping his thighs and laughing loudly. The little girl is wailing. Michael swings the big sword and cuts the other boy's head off; he falls down in the process.*)

THE BIGGEST BOY: Ouch! I'll show you the right
  way.

(*Michael runs off, the children after him. Grusha looks after them laughing. When she turns back, Simon Chachava, in a ragged uniform, is standing on the other side of the brook.*)

GRUSHA: Simon!   510
SIMON: Am I addressing Grusha Vachnadze?
GRUSHA: Simon!
SIMON: (*formally.*) God bless the young lady. I hope
  she is well.
GRUSHA: (*stands up happily and bows low.*) God bless   515
  you, soldier. And thank heaven you have returned
  in good health.
SIMON: As the haddock said, they have found better
  fishes, so they didn't eat me.
GRUSHA: Bravery, said the kitchen helper; luck said   520
  the hero.
SIMON: How have things been? Was the winter
  bearable, were the neighbours kind?
GRUSHA: The winter was rather hard, Simon, and
  the neighbours as usual.   525
SIMON: May I ask whether a certain person is still
  in the habit of putting her legs in the water when
  she washes clothes?
GRUSHA: The answer is no because of the eyes in
  the bushes!   530
SIMON: The young lady is speaking about soldiers.
  A paymaster is standing before you.
GRUSHA: Doesn't that mean twenty piasters?
SIMON: And lodging.
GRUSHA: (*tears coming to her eyes.*) Behind the   535
  barracks under the date palms.
SIMON: Exactly. I see the young lady has taken a look
  around.
GRUSHA: So she has.
SIMON: And she hasn't forgotten. (*Grusha shakes her   540
  head.*) Then the door is still on its hinges, as they say?
  (*Grusha looks at him in silence and shakes her head
  again.*) What do you mean? Is something wrong?

GRUSHA: Simon Chachava, I can never go back to Nukha again. Something has happened. 545

SIMON: What has happened?

GRUSHA: It has happened that I hit an Ironshirt on the head.

SIMON: Grusha Vachnadze must have had good reason. 550

GRUSHA: Simon Chachava, my name isn't the same as before.

SIMON: (*after a pause.*) I don't understand.

GRUSHA: When do women change their names, Simon? Let me explain. Nothing has come 555 between us, everything is the same, you've got to believe me.

SIMON: Nothing has come between us, but something has changed?

GRUSHA: How can I explain it so quickly with the 560 brook between us? Can't you take the bridge and come over?

SIMON: Perhaps it's no longer necessary.

GRUSHA: It's very necessary. Come over, Simon. Hurry! 565

SIMON: Does the young lady mean the soldier has come too late?

(*Grusha looks at him despairingly, her face bathed in tears. Simon stares straight ahead. He has picked up a piece of wood and is whittling.*)

THE SINGER:
So many words are said, so many words are left unsaid.
The soldier has come. Where he has come from he does not say.
Hear what he thought and did not say: 570

The battle began at gray of dawn, blood flowed at noon.
The first fell before me, the second fell behind me, the third fell next to me.
On the first I trampled, the second I left behind, the third was run through by the captain.
My first brother perished by iron, my second brother perished by smoke.
They struck flame from my head, my hands were 575 frozen in my gloves, my toes in my stockings.
To eat I had aspen buds, to drink I had maple broth, I slept at night on stones, or in water.

SIMON: I see a cap in the grass. Can there be a child so soon?

GRUSHA: Yes, Simon, there is. How could I hide it? But you mustn't fret, it's not mine. 580

SIMON: They say: Once the wind starts blowing, it blows through every crack and cranny. The lady need say no more.

(*Grusha bows her head and says nothing.*)

THE SINGER:
Yearning there was, but no waiting.
Broken the oath. The reason is not reported. 585
Hear what she thought and did not say:

Soldier, when you were fighting in battle
The bloody battle, the bitter battle
I found a child who was helpless.
I hadn't the heart to leave it. 590
I had to care for what would have perished
I had to bend down for bread crumbs on the ground
I had to tear myself to pieces for what was not mine
A stranger.
Someone must help 595
For a sapling needs water.
The baby calf strays when the cowherd sleeps
And the cry goes unheard!

SIMON: Give me back the cross I gave you. No, throw it in the brook. 600

(*He turns to go.*)

GRUSHA: Simon Chachava, don't go away, it's not mine, it's not mine! (*She hears the children calling.*) What is it, children?

VOICES: Soldiers!—They're taking Michael away!

(*Grusha stands horrified. Two Ironshirts come toward her, leading Michael.*)

IRONSHIRTS: Are you Grusha? (*She nods.*) Is this 605 your child?

GRUSHA: Yes. (*Simon goes away.*) Simon!

IRONSHIRTS: We have a court order to take this child, found in your care, to the city. There is reason to believe that it is Michael Abashvili, son 610 of Governor Georgi Abashvili and his wife Natella Abashvili. Here is the order, duly signed and sealed. (*They lead the child away.*)

GRUSHA: (*runs after them shouting.*) Leave him, please, he's mine! 615

THE SINGER:

The Ironshirts took the cherished child away. The unhappy woman followed them to the perilous city.

The mother who had borne him demanded the child's return. His foster-mother appeared in court.

Who will decide the case, to whom will the child be given?

Who will the judge be? A good one? A bad one?

The city was in flames. On the seat of justice sat Azdak. 620

5. THE STORY OF THE JUDGE

THE SINGER:

Hear now the story of the judge:

How he became judge, how he passed judgement, what manner of judge he is.

That Easter Sunday when the great uprising took place and the grand duke was overthrown

And Abashvili, his Governor, our child's father, lost his head

Azdak the village scribe found a fugitive in the thicket and hid him in his hut. 5

(*Ragged and tipsy, Azdak helps a fugitive disguised as a beggar into his hut.*)

AZDAK: Stop panting. You're not a horse. And running like snot in April won't save you from the police. Stop, I tell you. (*He catches the fugitive, who has kept going as though to run through the opposite wall of the hut.*) Sit down and eat, here's a piece of cheese. (*He rummages through a chest full of rags and fishes out a cheese; the fugitive starts eating avidly.*) Haven't eaten in some time, huh? (*The fugitive grumbles.*) What were you running for, you asshole? The policemen wouldn't even have seen you. 10 15

THE FUGITIVE: Had to.

AZDAK: Shits? (*The fugitive looks at him uncomprehendingly.*) Jitters? Scared? Hm. Stop smacking your lips like a grand duke or a pig! I can't stand it. We've got to take blue-blooded stink- 20

ers the way God made them. Not you. I once heard of a chief justice who was so independent he farted at dinner. When I watch you eating, horrible thoughts come to me. Why don't you say something? (*Sharply.*) Let's see your hand! Can't you hear me? I want to see your hand. (*Hesitantly the fugitive holds out his hand.*) White. So you're not a beggar at all. A phony, a walking swindle! And me hiding you like you were a self-respecting citizen. What are you running for if you're a landowner? That's what you are, don't deny it, I can tell by your guilty look! (*Stands up.*) Get out! (*The fugitive looks at him uncertainly.*) What are you waiting for, you peasant-flogger? 25 30 35

THE FUGITIVE: Looking for me. Request undivided attention, have proposition.

AZDAK: What's that? A proposition? That's the height of insolence. He wants to make a proposition! The victim scratches till his fingers are bloody, and the leech makes a proposition. Get out, I say! 40

THE FUGITIVE: Understand point of view, convictions. Pay hundred thousand piasters one night. Well?

AZDAK: What? You think you can buy me? For a hundred thousand piasters? A rundown estate. Let's say a hundred and fifty thousand. Where are they? 45

THE FUGITIVE: Not on me naturally. Will send. Hope no doubts.

AZDAK: Deep doubts. Get out! 50

(*The fugitive stands up and trots to the door. A voice from outside.*)

VOICE: Azdak!

(*The fugitive turns around and trots to the opposite corner, where he stops still.*)

AZDAK: (*shouts.*) I'm busy. (*Steps into the doorway.*) Are you nosing around again, Shauva?

SHAUVA THE POLICEMAN: (*outside, reproachfully.*) You've caught another rabbit, Azdak. You promised it wouldn't happen again. 55

AZDAK: (*sternly.*) Don't talk about things you don't understand, Shauva. The rabbit is a dangerous and harmful animal that eats plants, especially the varieties known as weeds, and must therefore be exterminated. 60

SHAUVA: Azdak, don't be so mean to me. I'll lose my job if I'm not severe with you. I know you've got a good heart.

AZDAK: I haven't got a good heart. How often do I have to tell you I'm an intellectual? 65

SHAUVA: (*slyly.*) I know, Azdak. You're a superior man, you say so yourself. All right, I'm only an uneducated Christian and I ask you: If one of the prince's rabbits is stolen and I'm a policeman, what 70 am I supposed to do about the guilty party?

AZDAK: Shauva, Shauva, you ought to be ashamed. There you stand asking me a question when a question is the worst of all temptations. Suppose you were a woman—Nunovna, for instance, the 75 wicked slut—and you show me the upper reaches of your leg—Nunovna's I mean—and ask me: "what should I do about my leg, it itches?"—Is she innocent, behaving like that? No. I catch rabbits, but you catch men. A man is made in God's image, 80 a rabbit isn't, you know that. I'm a rabbit-eater, but you're a cannibal, Shauva, and God will judge you. Go home, Shauva, and repent. No, wait a minute, maybe I've got something for you. (*He looks around at the fugitive who stands there trembling.*) No, never 85 mind. Go home and repent. (*He slams the door in his face. To the fugitive.*) You're surprised, aren't you? That I didn't hand you over. But I couldn't even hand a bedbug over to that dumb-ox policeman, it goes against my grain. Never be afraid of a 90 policeman. So old and such a coward. Eat up your cheese like a poor man, or they're sure to catch you. Do I have to show you how a poor man behaves? (*He pushes him down in his chair and puts the piece of cheese back in his hand.*) The chest is the table. 95 Put your elbows on the table, surround the cheese on the plate as if it might be snatched away at any moment, can you ever be sure? Hold your knife like a small sickle and don't look at the cheese so greedily, your expression should be more on the 100 sorrowful side, because it is already vanishing, like all beauty. (*Watches him.*) They're looking for you, that's in your favour, but how can I know they're not mistaken about you? In Tiflis one time they hanged a landowner, a Turk. He was able to prove 105 that he didn't just cut his peasants in half the usual way, but quartered them. He gouged out twice as much taxes as anybody else, his zeal was above suspicion, but they hanged him as a criminal all the same, just because he was a Turk, which he 110 couldn't help. That was an injustice. He found himself on the gallows the way Pontius Pilate found himself in the Creed. To make a long story short, I don't trust you.

THE SINGER:
And so Azdak lodged the old beggar for the night. 115
When he found out that he was the grand duke in
    person, the butcher
He was ashamed. He denounced himself, he
    ordered the policeman
To take him to Nukha, to court, to be tried.

(*In the courthouse yard three Ironshirts are sitting drinking. From a column hangs a man in a judge's robe. Enter Azdak bound, dragging Shauva behind him.*)

AZDAK: (*cries out.*) I helped the grand duke, the grand thief, the grand butcher, to escape. In the 120 name of justice I demand a public trial and a severe sentence!

THE FIRST IRONSHIRT: Who's this bird?

SHAUVA: It's Azdak, our scribe.

AZDAK: I'm a contemptible traitor, a marked man! 125 Report, flatfoot, how I insisted on being taken to the capital in chains because I sheltered the grand duke, grand scoundrel, by mistake, which was only made clear to me later by this document that I found in my hut. (*The Ironshirts study the 130 document. To Shauva.*) They can't read. See, the marked man denounces himself! Tell them how I made you run with me half the night to clear everything up.

SHAUVA: By threatening me. That wasn't nice of you, 135 Azdak.

AZDAK: Shut up, Shauva, you don't understand. A new era has dawned, it will rumble over you like thunder, you're through, policemen will be exterminated, pfft. Everything will be investigated, 140 brought to light. A man with any sense will turn himself in, he can't escape from the people. Report how I yelled all the way down Shoemaker Lane. (*He acts it out with sweeping gestures, squinting at the Ironshirts.*) "I let the grand scoundrel escape out 145 of ignorance. Tear me to pieces, brothers!" To forestall any questions.

THE FIRST IRONSHIRT: And what was their answer?

SHAUVA: They comforted him on Butcher Lane and laughed themselves sick on Shoemaker Lane, that's all. 150

AZDAK: But you're different, I know that, you're men of iron. Where's the judge, brothers, I want to be questioned.

THE FIRST IRONSHIRT: (*points to the hanged man.*) 155 There's the judge. And stop bothering us. We're touchy about that kind of thing right now.

AZDAK: "There's the judge." Such an answer has never been heard in Gruznia. Townspeople, where is his excellency the Governor? (*He points to the* 160 *gallows.*) There's his excellency, stranger. Where is the chief tax collector? The chief recruiting officer? The patriarch? The chief of police? Here, here, here, all here. Brothers, that's what I was expecting of you. 165

THE SECOND IRONSHIRT: That's enough! What did you expect, you clown?

AZDAK: What happened in Persia, brothers, what happened in Persia?

THE SECOND IRONSHIRT: What happened in 170 Persia?

AZDAK: Forty years ago. Hanged, the whole lot of them. Viziers, tax collectors. My grandfather, a remarkable man, saw it. Three whole days, all over the country. 175

THE SECOND IRONSHIRT: But who governed if the vizier was hanged?

AZDAK: A peasant.

THE SECOND IRONSHIRT: And who commanded the army? 180

AZDAK: A soldier, soldier,

THE SECOND IRONSHIRT: And who gave them their pay?

AZDAK: A dyer, a dyer gave them their pay.

THE SECOND IRONSHIRT: Are you sure it wasn't a 185 carpet weaver?

THE FIRST IRONSHIRT: But why did all that happen, you Persian?

AZDAK: Why it all happened? Do you need a special reason? Why do you scratch yourself, brother? War! 190 Too much war! And no justice! My grandfather

brought back a song that tells the way it was. My friend the policeman and I will sing it for you. (*To Shauva.*) And keep a good hold on the rope, that goes with it. (*He sings, while Shauva holds the rope.*) 195

Why are our sons not bleeding any more, and our daughters weep no more?
Why is it that only the calves in the slaughterhouse have any blood left?
Why is it that only the willows on Lake Urmi are shedding tears?

The emperor stands in need of a new province, the peasant must hand over his savings.
So that the roof of the world may be conquered, 200 the roofs of all the huts are carted off.
Our men are taken away, scattered to all four winds so that the noble lords at home may feast and revel.
And the soldiers kill one another, the generals salute one another.
They bite the widow's tax farthing to see if it is real.
The lances are broken.
The battle has been lost. But the helmets have 205 been paid for.
Is it so? Is it so?

SHAUVA: Yes, yes, yes, yes, it is so.

AZDAK: Do you want to hear the rest?

(*The first Ironshirt nods.*)

THE SECOND IRONSHIRT: (*to the policeman.*) Didn't he teach you the song? 210

SHAUVA: Oh yes, but my voice is no good.

THE SECOND IRONSHIRT: No. (*To Azdak.*) Go on, go on.

AZDAK: The second stanza is about the peace. (*Sings.*)

Public offices overcrowded, officials sitting all the 215 way out to the street.
Rivers overflow the banks and devastate the fields
Men who can't take their own pants down are ruling empires.
They can't count to four but they eat eight courses.
The corn growers look round for buyers, find only starvelings

The weavers go home from their looms in rags. 220
Is it so? Is it so?

SHAUVA: Yes, yes, yes, yes, it is so.

AZDAK:

That's why our sons are not bleeding any more,
and our daughters weep no more

Why only the calves in the slaughterhouse have
any blood left.

Why it is that only the willows on Lake Urmi are 225
shedding tears.

THE FIRST IRONSHIRT: (*after a pause.*) Are you
going to sing that song here in town?

AZDAK: What's wrong with it?

THE FIRST IRONSHIRT: Do you see that red glow
over there? (*Azdak looks around. There is a fiery glow* 230
in the sky.) That's out in the slums. When Prince
Kazbeki had Governor Abashvili beheaded this
morning, our carpet weavers caught the "Persian
disease" too and asked if Prince Kazbeki didn't eat
too many courses. And at noon today they strung 235
up the city judge. But we took care of them for
two piasters a weaver. See what I mean?

AZDAK: (*after a pause.*) I see. (*He looks around
fearfully, slinks off to one side and sits down on the
ground with his head in his hands.*) 240

THE FIRST IRONSHIRT: (*after all have taken a drink,
to the third.*) Now we're going to have a little fun.

(*The first and second Ironshirt go toward Azdak,
blocking his retreat.*)

SHAUVA: I don't think he's really bad, gentlemen.
Steals a few chickens, maybe a rabbit now and
then. 245

THE SECOND IRONSHIRT: (*stepping up to Azdak.*)
You came here to fish in troubled waters, didn't
you?

AZDAK: (*looking up at him.*) I don't know why I came
here. 250

THE SECOND IRONSHIRT: Are you the kind that
sides with the carpet weavers? (*Azdak shakes his
head.*) What about that song?

AZDAK: Got it from my grandfather. A stupid,
ignorant man. 255

THE SECOND IRONSHIRT: Right. And what about
the dyer that handed out the pay?

AZDAK: That was in Persia.

THE FIRST IRONSHIRT: And what about your
denouncing yourself for not hanging the grand 260
duke with your own hands?

AZDAK: Didn't I tell you I let him go?

SHAUVA: I'll vouch for that. He let him go.

(*The Ironshirts drag the screaming Azdak to the
gallows. Then they let him go and laugh uproariously.
Azdak joins in the laughter and laughs loudest. Then
he is untied. All begin to drink. Enter the Fat Prince
with a young man.*)

THE FIRST IRONSHIRT: (*to Azdak.*) Here comes
your new era. 265

(*More laughter.*)

THE FAT PRINCE: And what might there be to laugh
about, my friends? Permit me to put in a serious
word. Yesterday morning the princes of Gruznia
overthrew the grand duke's bellicose government
and liquidated his Governors. Unfortunately the 270
grand duke himself escaped. In this fateful hour
our carpet weavers, those eternal agitators, have
had the audacity to revolt and hang the city judge,
a man whom everyone loved, our dear Illo
Orbeliani. Ts, ts, ts. My friends, what we need here 275
in Gruznia is peace, peace, peace. And justice! Here
I've brought you my dear nephew, Bizergan
Kazbeki, an able man, to be the new judge. I say:
The decision rests with the people.

THE FIRST IRONSHIRT: You mean we're to elect the 280
judge?

THE FAT PRINCE: Exactly. The people will elect an
able man. Talk it over my friends. (*While the
Ironshirts put their heads together.*) Don't worry,
duckling, the job is yours. And once they nab the 285
grand duke, we can stop sucking up to the rabble.

THE IRONSHIRTS: (*among themselves.*) They're scared
shitless because they haven't caught the grand
duke.—We can thank this village scribe for letting
him go.—They're not sure of themselves yet, that's 290
why they're saying "my friends" and "the decision
rests with the people."—Now he's even talking
about justice for Gruznia.—But fun is fun, and
this is going to be fun.—We'll ask the village
scribe, he knows all about justice. Hey, stinko … 295

AZDAK: Do you mean me?

THE FIRST IRONSHIRT: (*continues.*) … would you want this nephew for a judge?

AZDAK: Are you asking me? You're not asking me, are you? 300

THE SECOND IRONSHIRT: Why not? Anything for a laugh.

AZDAK: The way I see it, you want to put him to the test. Am I right? Haven't you got some criminal handy, so the candidate can show his ability? One 305 who knows the ropes.

THE THIRD IRONSHIRT: Let's see. We've got the Governor's bitch's two doctors down in the cellar. Let's take them.

AZDAK: No, that's no good. You can't take real crimi- 310 nals when the judge hasn't been confirmed in office. It's all right for him to be a jackass, but he's got to be confirmed in office, or it's an offense against the law, which is a very sensitive organ, something like the spleen, which must never be punched or death sets 315 in. You can hang them both, that won't be an offense against the law, because no judge was present. The law must be administered with perfect gravity, because it's so stupid. For instance if a judge jails a woman for stealing a piece of millet bread for her 320 child, and he hasn't got his robe on or he scratches himself while handing down the sentence, so that more than a third of him is naked, I mean, suppose he has to scratch the upper part of his leg, then his judgement is a scandal and the law has been flouted. 325 A judge's robe and a judge's hat can hand down a better sentence than a man without them. Justice goes up in smoke if you're not careful. You wouldn't test a jug of wine by giving it to a dog to drink; hell, your wine would be gone. 330

THE FIRST IRONSHIRT: So what do you suggest, you hairsplitter?

AZDAK: I'll play the defendant for you. I already know who he'll be. (*He whispers something in their ears.*) 335

THE FIRST IRONSHIRT: You?

(*All laugh uproariously.*)

THE FAT PRINCE: What have you decided?

THE FIRST IRONSHIRT: We've decided to give it a try. Our good friend here will play the accused, and here's a seat of justice for the candidate. 340

THE FAT PRINCE: It's unusual, but why not? (*To his nephew.*) A mere formality, duckling. What have you learned? Who won the race, the slow runner or the fast one?

THE NEPHEW: The stealthy runner, Uncle Arsen. 345

(*The Nephew sits down on the seat of justice, the Fat Prince stands behind him. The Ironshirts sit down on the steps. Azdak enters with the unmistakable gait of the grand duke.*)

AZDAK: Is there anybody here who knows me? I am the Grand Duke.

THE FAT PRINCE: What is he?

THE SECOND IRONSHIRT: The Grand Duke. He really knows him. 350

THE FAT PRINCE: Good.

THE FIRST IRONSHIRT: Start the trial.

AZDAK: Hear I'm accused inciting war. Ridiculous. Repeat: ridiculous! Sufficient? If not sufficient, brought lawyers, believe five hundred. (*He motions* 355 *behind him, as though there were many lawyers around him.*) Need all available seats for lawyers.

(*The Ironshirts laugh; the Fat Prince joins in.*)

THE NEPHEW: (*to the Ironshirts.*) Do you wish me to try the case? I must say it seems rather unusual—in poor taste, I mean. 360

THE FIRST IRONSHIRT: Get started.

THE FAT PRINCE: (*smiling.*) Throw the book at him, duckling.

THE NEPHEW: Very well. People of Gruznia versus the Grand Duke. Accused, what have you to say 365 for yourself?

AZDAK: Plenty. Naturally read war lost. Declared war only on advice patriots like Uncle Kazbeki. Demand Uncle Kazbeki as witness. (*The Ironshirts laugh.*) 370

THE FAT PRINCE: (*good-naturedly to the Ironshirts.*) Quite a character, isn't he?

THE NEPHEW: Motion overruled. Obviously you can't be prosecuted for declaring war, every ruler has to do that now and then, but only for 375 conducting it incompetently.

AZDAK: Nonsense. Didn't conduct at all. Had it conducted. Had it conducted by princes. Naturally fouled it up.

THE NEPHEW: Do you mean to deny that you were 380
in supreme command?

AZDAK: Certainly not. Always in supreme command. When born, bellowed at nurse. Raised to drop shit in privy. Accustomed to command. Always commanded officials to rob my treasury. 385 Officers flog soldiers, only my command; landowners sleep with peasants' wives only my strict command. Uncle Kazbeki here has big belly only by my command.

THE IRONSHIRTS: (*applauding*.) He's rich. Hurrah 390
for the Grand Duke!

THE FAT PRINCE: Answer him duckling! I'm with you.

THE NEPHEW: I will answer him as befits the dignity of the court. Accused, respect the dignity 395
of the court.

AZDAK: Right. Command you proceed with trial.

THE NEPHEW: Not taking commands from you. You claim forced by princes declare war. How then can you claim princes fouled up war? 400

AZDAK: Not sending enough men, embezzling funds, delivering sick horses, drinking in whorehouse during attack. Move call Uncle Kaz witness.

(*The Ironshirts laugh.*)

THE NEPHEW: Do you mean to make the monstrous assertion that the princes of this country did 405
not fight?

AZDAK: No. Princes fought. Fought for war contracts.

THE FAT PRINCE: This is too much. The man talks like a carpet weaver. 410

AZDAK: Indeed? Only tell truth!

THE FAT PRINCE: Hang him! Hang him!

THE FIRST IRONSHIRT: Take it easy. Go on, Excellency!

THE NEPHEW: Silence! Pronounce sentence: must 415
be hanged. By neck. Lost war. Sentence pronounced. Irrevocable. Take him away.

THE FAT PRINCE: (*hysterically*.) Take him away! Take him away!

AZDAK: Young man, earnestly advise not fall into 420
clipped, military delivery in public. Can't be employed watchdog if howl like wolf. Get me?

THE FAT PRINCE: Hang him!

AZDAK: If people notice princes talk same as grand duke, they will hang grand duke and princes. 425
Moreover annul sentence. Reason: war lost, but not for princes. Princes won their war. Collected three million eight hundred sixty-three piasters for horses not delivered.

THE FAT PRINCE: Hang him! 430

AZDAK: Eight million two hundred forty thousand piasters for army provisions not supplied.

THE FAT PRINCE: Hang him!

AZDAK: Therefore victorious. War only lost for Gruznia, not present in this court. 435

THE FAT PRINCE: I think that will do, my friends. (*To Azdak*.) You can step down, gallowsbird. (*To the Ironshirts*.) My friends, I think you can now confirm the new judge.

THE FIRST IRONSHIRT: I guess we can. Bring down 440
the judge's robe. (*One of them climbs on another's back and takes off the hanged man's robe.*) And now (*to the nephew*.) beat it, so the right ass can sit in the right seat. (*To Azdak*.) Step forward, take the seat. (*Azdak hesitates*.) Sit down on it, man. (*Azdak* 445
is forced into the seat of justice by the Ironshirts.) The judge was always a blackguard, so now let a blackguard be judge. (*The robe is put on him, a basket is set on his head*.) Look at our judge!

THE SINGER:

There was civil war, the ruler was insecure. 450
Azdak was made judge by the Ironshirts.
For two years Azdak was judge.

THE SINGER AND HIS MUSICIANS:

When with flame the skies were glowing and with blood the gutters flowing
Bugs and roaches rose from every crack.
Lances were replaced by cleavers, sermons made 455
by unbelievers
And upon the seat of justice sat Azdak.

(*Azdak is sitting on the seat of justice, peeling an apple. Shauva is sweeping the courtroom. On one side an invalid in a wheelchair, a doctor who is the defendant, and a lame man in rags. On the other side a young man accused of blackmail. An Ironshirt bearing the banner of the Ironshirts corps, stands at the door.*)

AZDAK: Today, in view of the large number of cases pending, the court will hear two cases at once.

Before I begin, a brief announcement: I take. (*He holds out his hand. Only the blackmailer takes out money and gives it to him.*) I reserve the right to punish one of the parties here present (*He looks at the invalid.*) for contempt of court. (*To the doctor.*) You are a doctor, and you (*To the invalid.*) are the plaintiff. Is the doctor to blame for your condition? 465

THE INVALID: He is. I had a stroke on account of him.

AZDAK: That would be professional negligence.

THE INVALID: Worse than negligence. I loaned him money for his studies. He's never repaid a cent, so when I heard he was treating patients for nothing, 470 I had a stroke.

AZDAK: You had every right. (*To the lame man.*) And what are you doing here?

THE LAME MAN: I'm the patient, your worship.

AZDAK: I gather he treated your leg? 475

THE LAME MAN: Not the right one. My rheumatism was in my left leg, he operated on the right leg, that's why I limp.

AZDAK: And he did it for nothing?

THE INVALID: A five-hundred piaster operation for 480 nothing! Gratis! For a mere thank you. And I staked him to his studies! (*To the doctor.*) Did your professors teach you to operate for nothing?

THE DOCTOR: Your worship, it is indeed customary to ask for a fee before operating, because the 485 patient pays more willingly before an operation than afterward. In the present case I believed at the moment of operating that my assistant had already collected my fee. I was mistaken.

THE INVALID: He was mistaken! A good doctor 490 doesn't make mistakes! He examines the patient before operating.

AZDAK: That is correct. (*To Shauva.*) What's the other case, Mr. Public Prosecutor?

SHAUVA: (*zealously sweeping.*) Blackmail. 495

THE BLACKMAILER: Your worship, I'm innocent. I simply wanted to ask a certain landowner whether he had really raped his niece. He informed me most amiably that he had not; if he gave me money, it was only because my uncle wishes to take 500 music lessons.

AZDAK: Aha! (*To the doctor.*) Whereas you, doctor, can cite no extenuating circumstance for your offense?

THE DOCTOR: The most I can say is that to err is 505 human.

AZDAK: Don't you realize that a good doctor must have a sense of financial responsibility? I once heard of a doctor who made a thousand piasters out of a sprained finger by discovering it had 510 something to do with the circulation, which an incompetent doctor might have overlooked, and another time by careful treatment, he turned a gall bladder into a gold mine. There's no excuse for you, doctor. Uxu, the grain dealer, had his son 515 study medicine to learn business methods, which gives you an idea of the high standards of our medical schools. (*To the blackmailer.*) What's this landowner's name?

SHAUVA: He doesn't wish to be named. 520

AZDAK: Then I'll hand down the verdicts. The court holds that blackmail has been proved, and you (*to the invalid.*) are fined one thousand piasters. If you have another stroke, the doctor is ordered to treat you free of charge and amputate if necessary. (*To* 525 *the lame man.*) You are accorded a bottle of cognac in lieu of damages. (*To the blackmailer.*) You will assign half your fee to the public prosecutor inasmuch as the court does not divulge the landowner's name, furthermore you are advised to 530 study medicine because you're cut out for that profession. And you, doctor, for unpardonable professional error, you are acquitted. Next cases!

THE SINGER WITH HIS MUSICIANS:

Every pleasure costs full measure, funds are rarely come by squarely
Justice has no eyes in front or back. 535
That is why we ask a genius to decide and judge between us
Which is done for half a penny by Azdak.

(*From a caravanserai on the Gruznian military highway comes Azdak, followed by the landlord, the old man with the long beard. Behind them the hired hand and Shauva carry the seat of justice. An Ironshirt takes his stance with the banner of the Ironshirts corps.*)

AZDAK: Put it here. Here at least we get some air and a bit of a breeze from that lemon grove over there. It's a good thing for justice to be conducted 540 in the open. The wind picks up her skirts and you can see what she's got on underneath. Shauva, we've had too much to eat. These inspection trips are strenuous. (*To the landlord.*) It's about your daughter-in-law? 545

THE LANDLORD: Your worship, it's about the honour of my family. I wish to make a complaint on behalf of my son who has gone across the mountains on business. Here is the guilty hired hand, and here is my unfortunate daughter-in-law. 550

(*Enter the daughter-in-law, a voluptuous type. She is veiled.*)

AZDAK: (*sits down.*) I take. (*With a sigh the landlord gives him money.*) Good. So much for the formalities. A case of rape?

THE LANDLORD: Your worship, I caught the fellow in the stable, pushing our Ludovika into the straw. 555

AZDAK: Yes, yes, the stable. Splendid horses. That little bay struck my fancy.

THE LANDLORD: Naturally, on behalf of my son, I raked Ludovika over the coals.

AZDAK: (*gravely.*) I said it struck my fancy. 560

THE LANDLORD: (*coldly.*) Really?—Ludovika confessed that the hired man had taken her against her will.

AZDAK: Remove your veil, Ludovika. (*She does so.*) Ludovika, the court has taken a fancy to you. Tell us what happened. 565

LUDOVIKA: (*who has learned her part by rote.*) When I entered the stable to look at the new foal, the hired hand said to me without provocation: "Warm weather we're having," and placed his hand 570 on my left breast. I said to him: "Stop that," but he continued to touch me in an immoral manner, which aroused my anger. Before I could discern his sinful intentions, he had overstepped the bounds. The deed was done when my father-in-law entered 575 and kicked me by mistake.

THE LANDLORD: (*explaining.*) On my son's behalf.

AZDAK: (*to the hired hand.*) Do you admit that you started it?

HIRED HAND: Yes, sir. 580

AZDAK: Ludovika, do you like sweets?

LUDOVIKA: Yes, sunflower seeds.

AZDAK: Do you like to sit for a long time in the bathtub?

LUDOVIKA: Half an hour or so. 585

AZDAK: Mr. Public Prosecutor, put your knife on the ground over there. (*Shauva does so.*) Ludovika, go pick up the public prosecutor's knife.

(*Swaying her hips, Ludovika goes over to the knife and picks it up.*)

AZDAK: (*pointing at her.*) Did you see that? The wiggle on her. The guilty party is discovered. Rape is 590 proved. By eating too much, especially sweet things, by prolonged sitting in warm water, by indolence and soft skin, you have raped that poor man. Do you think you can display a rear end like that in court and get away with it? It's premedi- 595 tated assault with a dangerous weapon. You are sentenced to assign to the court the little bay that your father-in-law rides on his son's behalf. And now, Ludovika, you will accompany me to the stable, because the court wished to inspect the scene 600 of the crime.

(*Over the Gruznian military highway Azdak on his seat of justice is carried from place to place by his Ironshirts. Behind him Shauva carrying the gallows and the hired hand leading the little bay.*)

THE SINGER WITH HIS MUSICIANS:
Times when master fights with master for the
poor are no disaster
Chaos gets the tax collector off their back.
Bearing weights and measures phony, leading
someone else's pony
Through the country rode the poor man's judge, 605
Azdak.
And he took away from Croesus and distributed
gold pieces
To their rightful owners gave them back.
By a bodyguard protected of the humble and
neglected
Rode Gruznia's good-bad judge, Azdak.

(*The little procession moves off.*)

When you go to judge your neighbours leave at 610
home your legal papers
Take a good sharp ax and you'll be on the track.
Never mind about God's thunders, axes often will
do wonders.

[V]

Such a wonder worker is the judge Azdak.

(*Azdak's seat of justice is set up in a tavern. Three kulaks are standing before Azdak, to whom Shauva brings wine. In the corner stands an old peasant woman. In the open doorway and outside, the audience of villagers. An Ironshirt stands at the entrance with the banner of the Ironshirts corps.*)

AZDAK: The public prosecutor has the floor.

SHAUVA: It's about a cow. For five weeks the defendant has had in her barn a cow belonging to the kulak Suru. She has also been found in the possession of a stolen ham, and some cows belonging to the kulak Shutev were killed after he had asked the defendant to pay the rent on a field. 615 620

THE KULAKS: It's my ham, your worship.—It's my cow, your worship.—It's my field, your worship.

AZDAK: What do you have to say to all this, little mother?

THE OLD WOMAN: Your worship, one night five weeks ago, just before morning, somebody knocked on my door, and outside there was a man with a beard, holding a cow. "Dear lady," he said to me, "I am St. Banditus, the worker of miracles, and because your son was killed in the war I'm bringing you this cow as a souvenir. Take good care of her." 625 630

THE KULAKS: Irakli, the bandit, your worship.— Her brother-in-law, your worship! The cow-thief, the firebug!—He should have his head cut off! 635

(*A woman's scream is heard from outside. The crowd grows uneasy and moves back. Enter Irakli the bandit with an enormous ax.*)

THE KULAKS: Irakli! (*They cross themselves.*)

THE BANDIT: A very good evening to you, dear friends! A glass of wine!

AZDAK: Public prosecutor, a jug of wine for our guest. Who are you? 640

THE BANDIT: I'm a wandering hermit, your worship, and thank you for the charitable gift. (*He drains the glass that Shauva has brought him.*) Another.

AZDAK: I'm Azdak. (*He stands up and bows; the Bandit bows likewise.*) The court bids the visiting hermit welcome. Continue, little mother. 645

THE OLD WOMAN: Your worship, the first night I didn't know St. Banditus could perform miracles; it was only a cow. But a few days later the kulak's hired men came and wanted to take the cow away. Outside my door they turned around and went home without my cow and great big bumps sprouted on their heads. Then I knew St. Banditus had moved their hearts and changed them into kindly men. 650 655

(*The Bandit laughs loudly.*)

THE FIRST KULAK: I know what changed them.

AZDAK: That's fine. You'll tell us later. Continue!

THE OLD WOMAN: Your worship, the next to be changed into a good man was the kulak Shutev, a devil as everyone knows. But St. Banditus got him to remit the rent on my little field. 660

THE SECOND KULAK: Because somebody cut my cows' throats in the field.

(*The Bandit laughs.*)

THE OLD WOMAN: (*at a sign from Azdak.*) And then one morning the ham came flying through the window. It hit me in the small of my back, I'm still lame, see, your worship. (*She takes a few steps. The bandit laughs.*) I ask you, your worship: When did a poor woman ever get a whole ham without a miracle? 665 670

(*The Bandit begins to sob.*)

AZDAK: (*coming down from his seat.*) Little mother, that question goes straight to the heart of this court. Kindly be seated. (*Hesitantly the Old Woman sits down on the judge's chair. Azdak sits on the floor with his glass of wine.*) 675

AZDAK: Little mother, I almost called you Mother
    Gruznia, the Sorrowful
The Bereft, whose sons are in the war
Beaten with fists, hopeful
Weeping when she gets a cow. 680
Surprised when she is not beaten.
Little mother, deign to sit in merciful judgement
    upon us, the damned.
(*Bellows at the kulaks.*) Admit you don't believe in miracles, you godless scum! Each of you is fined five hundred piasters for godlessness. Get out! 685

(*The kulaks slink out.*)

AZDAK: And you, little mother, and you, pious man, share a jug of wine with the public prosecutor and Azdak.

THE SINGER AND HIS MUSICIANS:
So he bent the regulations to his own interpretations
And he took the law and stretched it on a rack.   690
And they found out with a shock, it's men with nothing in their pockets
Who alone are able to corrupt Azdak.

Seven hundred days and twenty, he dealt justice to the gentry
And he dealt them every joker in the pack.
On the woolsack you could find him with the gallows close behind him   695
Passing judgements worthy of Azdak.

THE SINGER:
Then the days of disorder were over, the Grand Duke returned.
The Governor's Wife returned, vengeance was taken.
Many died, again the slums were in flames, Azdak was seized with fear.

(*Azdak's seat of justice in the courthouse yard. Azdak is sitting on the ground, mending his shoe and talking with Shauva. Noise from outside. Behind the wall the Fat Prince's head is carried past on a pike.*)

AZDAK: Shauva, the days of your bondage are   700
numbered, the minutes for all I know. For a long time now I've led you by the iron bit of reason till you bled at the mouth, spurred you on with syllogisms and abused you with logic. You're weak by nature; if an argument is slyly tossed your way,   705
you gobble it up, you can't control yourself. It is your nature to lick the hand of a higher being, but there are very different kinds of higher beings. Now you are going to be set free, and soon you'll be able to follow your bent, which is low, and your   710
unerring instinct which teaches you to plant your heavy boot in human faces. For the days of confusion and disorder are past and it's too soon for the great day that I find described in the Song of Chaos, which we shall now sing one last time   715

in memory of those glorious times. Sit down and don't tangle with the tune. Don't be afraid, let it be heard, the refrain is loved by all. (*Sings.*)

Sister, veil your face, brother, go get your knife, the times are out of joint.
The masters are filled with lamentation and the   720
little men with joy.
The city says: Let us drive the powerful from our midst.
The offices are invaded, the lists of serfs are destroyed.
The masters are harnessed to the millstones.
Those who have never seen daylight come out.
The ebony poor-boxes are shattered, the sesame wood is cut up for beds.
Those who had no bread have granaries now, those   725
who begged for grain, now distribute grain.

SHAUVA: Oh, oh, oh, oh.

AZDAK: Where are you, general? Please, please, please make order.
The son of the respected lord can no longer be known. The child of the mistress becomes the son of the slave-girl.
Rich aldermen look for refuge in cold barns, and the paupers who could scarcely find ditches to sleep in loll in soft beds.
The former boatman now owns many ships.   730
When the owner looks for them, they are no longer his.
Five men are sent out by their masters. They say: Go yourselves, we have already arrived.

SHAUVA: Oh, oh, oh, oh.

AZDAK: Where are you general? Please, please, please make order!
Yes, that's what our country might have come   735
to if law and order had been neglected any longer.
But now the grand duke, whose life I saved like a dumb ox, has returned to the capital and the Persians have lent him an army to restore order with. Already the slums are in flames. Bring me   740
the thick book I always sit on. (*Shauva takes the book from the seat of justice and Azdak opens it.*)
This is the book of the law, I've always used it, you can testify to that.

SHAUVA: Yes, to sit on.   745

AZDAK: Now I'd better look and see what they can pin on me. I've connived with paupers, that will cost me dearly. I've helped poverty up on its rickety legs, they'll hang me for drunkenness; I've looked into rich men's pockets, they'll get me for blasphemy. And there's nowhere I can hide, everybody knows me, because I've helped everybody. 750

SHAUVA: Someone's coming.

AZDAK: (*stands up in a fright, then goes trembling to the chair.*) Finished! But I won't do anybody the favour of behaving like a great man. I beg you on my knees for mercy, don't go away, I'm drooling at the mouth. I'm afraid of death. (*Enter Natella Abashvili, the Governor's Wife, with the Aide-de-camp and an Ironshirt.*) 755 760

THE GOVERNOR'S WIFE: Who is this fellow, Shalva?

AZDAK: A fellow who knows his place, your excellency, and yours to command.

THE AIDE-DE-CAMP: Natella Abashvili, the late Governor's Wife, has just returned. She is looking for her two-year-old son, Michael Abashvili. She has received word that the child was carried off to the mountains by a former servant. 765

AZDAK: The child will be brought back, your highness. Yours to command. 770

THE AIDE-DE-CAMP: They say the woman calls the child her own.

AZDAK: She will be beheaded, your highness. Yours to command. 775

THE AIDE-DE-CAMP: That will be all.

THE GOVERNOR'S WIFE: (*on her way out.*) I don't like that man.

AZDAK: (*follows her to the door, bowing low.*) It will all be taken care of, your highness. Yours to command. 780

6. THE CHALK CIRCLE

THE SINGER:
Hear now the story of the lawsuit over Governor
    Abashvili's child
And how the true mother was identified
By the famous test of the chalk circle.

(*In the yard of the courthouse in Nukha. Ironshirts bring in Michael, lead him across the courtyard and out behind. An Ironshirt holds Grusha back in the archway with his pike until the child has been led away. Then she is admitted. With her is the woman Cook from the former Governor's household. Tumult and fiery glow in the distance.*)

GRUSHA: He's a brave boy, he can already wash himself. 5

THE COOK: You're in luck, it's not a real judge, it's Azdak. He drinks like a fish and he doesn't know a thing, the biggest thieves have got off free. He gets everything mixed up and the rich people never bribe him enough, that makes it better for our kind of people. 10

GRUSHA: I need luck today.

THE COOK: Don't say it! (*She crosses herself.*) I'd better say another rosary for the judge to be drunk. (*She moves her lips in silent prayer while Grusha tries in vain to get a glimpse of the child.*) The only thing I don't understand is why you're so intent on keeping him if he isn't yours. In times like these. 15

GRUSHA: He's mine, I've brought him up.

THE COOK: Didn't you ever stop to think what would happen if she came back? 20

GRUSHA: At first I thought I'd give him back, and then I thought she wouldn't come after him any more.

THE COOK: And even a borrowed coat keeps a body warm, is that it? (*Grusha nods.*) I'll swear to anything you say, because you're a good girl. (*Refreshes her memory.*) I was boarding the child for five piasters and then on Easter Sunday evening when the trouble broke out, Grusha came and took him. (*She sees the soldier Chachava approaching.*) But you haven't done right by Simon, I've talked with him, he doesn't understand. 25 30

GRUSHA: (*who doesn't see him.*) I can't worry my head about him now if he doesn't understand. 35

THE COOK: He understands that the child isn't yours, but your being married and not free till death you do part is too much for him to understand.

(*Grusha sees Simon and greets him.*)

SIMON: (*gloomily.*) I wish to inform the lady that I am ready to swear. I am the father of the child. 40

GRUSHA: (*softly.*) That's all right, Simon.

SIMON: At the same time I wish to state that this obligates me in no way. Nor the lady either.

THE COOK: You didn't have to say that. You know she's married.

SIMON: That's her affair, no need to rub it in.

(*Two Ironshirts come in.*)

THE IRONSHIRTS: Where's the judge?—Has anyone seen the judge?

GRUSHA: (*who has turned away and covered her face.*) Stand in front of me. I shouldn't have come to Nukha. If I run into the Ironshirt I hit on the head …

ONE OF THE IRONSHIRTS: (*who have brought the child steps forward.*) The judge isn't here.

(*The two Ironshirts go on looking.*)

THE COOK: I hope nothing has happened to him. With another you won't stand any more chance than a snowball in hell.

(*Another Ironshirt enters.*)

THE IRONSHIRT: (*who has inquired about the judge, reports.*) Nobody there but two old people and a child. The judge has taken a powder.

THE OTHER IRONSHIRT: Keep looking!

(*The first two Ironshirts go out quickly, the third stops still. Grusha lets out a scream. The Ironshirt turns around. It is the corporal, he has a scar across his whole face.*)

THE IRONSHIRT IN THE ARCHWAY: What's the matter, Shotta? Do you know her?

THE CORPORAL: (*after staring at her at length.*) No.

THE IRONSHIRT IN THE ARCHWAY: They say she kidnapped the Abashvili child. If you know anything about it, you can make a pile of money, Shotta.

(*The corporal goes off cursing.*)

THE COOK: Is he the one? (*Grusha nods.*) He'll button up if you ask me. Or he'll have to admit he was after the child.

GRUSHA: (*relieved.*) I'd almost forgotten I saved the child from them …

(*The Governor's Wife comes in with the Aide-de-camp and two lawyers.*)

THE GOVERNOR'S WIFE: Thank goodness the populace haven't come. I can't stand the smell. It gives me a migraine.

THE FIRST LAWYER: Please, gracious lady, be careful what you say until we get another judge.

THE GOVERNOR'S WIFE: I haven't said a thing, Illo Shuboladze. I love the common people and their simple, straightforward ways, it's only the smell that gives me migraine.

THE SECOND LAWYER: There won't be much of an audience. Most of the people have shut themselves up in their houses on account of fighting in the slums.

THE GOVERNOR'S WIFE: Is that the creature?

THE FIRST LAWYER: My dear Natella Abashvili, please refrain from invective until it's definite that the Grand Duke has appointed a new judge and we're rid of the present judge who is just about the lowest individual ever seen in a judge's robe. Look, things seem to be moving.

(*Ironshirts enter the yard.*)

THE COOK: The mistress would be tearing your hair out if she didn't know that Azdak is a friend of the poor. One look at a face is enough for him.

(*Two Ironshirts have started fastening a rope to a column. Azdak is brought in in chains. Behind him, also in chains, Shauva. After him come the three kulaks.*)

AN IRONSHIRT: Thought you'd make a getaway, did you? (*He strikes Azdak.*)

A KULAK: Take off his robe before you string him up!

(*Ironshirts and kulaks pull the judge's robe off Azdak. His ragged underwear becomes visible. One gives him a push.*)

AN IRONSHIRT: (*pushing him to another.*) Want a lump of justice? Here it is!

(*Amid cries of "You take it!" and "I don't need it!" they push Azdak from one to the other until he collapses. Then he is pulled to his feet and dragged under the noose.*)

THE GOVERNOR'S WIFE: (*who has been clapping hysterically during the "ball game".*) I disliked that man the moment I laid eyes on him. 105

AZDAK: (*covered with blood, panting.*) I can't see. Give me a rag.

THE OTHER IRONSHIRT: What do you want to see?

AZDAK: You, you dogs. (*He wipes the blood from his eyes with his shirt sleeve.*) Greetings, dogs! How are you, dogs? How's the dog pack, stinking nicely? Licking the old boot again? Back at each other's throats, dogs? (*A dust-covered rider has entered with the corporal. He has taken papers from a leather pouch and looked through them. Now he intervenes.*) 110 115

THE DUST-COVERED RIDER: Stop! Here's the grand duke's decree concerning the new appointments.

THE CORPORAL: (*roaring.*) Attention! (*All come to attention.*) 120

THE DUST-COVERED RIDER: Here's what it says about the new judge: We hereby appoint a man who distinguished himself by saving a life that is of the utmost importance to our country—a certain Azdak of Nukha. Who's he? 125

SHAUVA: (*pointing to Azdak.*) The one under the gallows, your excellency.

THE CORPORAL: (*bellowing.*) What's going on here?

THE IRONSHIRT: Beg leave to report that his worship was already his worship and was denounced by these kulaks as an enemy of the grand duke. 130

THE CORPORAL: (*indicating the kulaks.*) Take them away! (*They are led off, bowing without interruption.*) See to it that his worship suffers no further annoyance. (*Goes out with the dust-covered rider.*) 135

THE COOK: (*to Shauva.*) She clapped before. I hope he saw her.

THE FIRST LAWYER: This is disastrous.

(*Azdak has fainted. He is brought down, revives, and is again clothed in the robe of justice. He staggers out of the group of Ironshirts.*)

THE IRONSHIRTS: No offense, your worship!— What does your worship wish? 140

AZDAK: Nothing, fellow dogs. An occasional boot to lick. (*To Shauva.*) You're pardoned. (*He is unbound.*) Get me some red wine, sweet. (*Shauva goes out.*) Beat it, I've got a case to try. (*The* 145 Ironshirts go off. Shauva comes back with a jug of wine. Azdak drinks copiously.*) Something for my ass! (*Shauva brings the law book and puts it on the seat of justice. Azdak sits down.*) I take!

(*The plaintiffs who have been holding a worried conference smile with relief. They whisper among themselves.*)

THE COOK: Oh dear! 150

SIMON: They say "You can't fill a well with dew."

THE LAWYERS: (*approach Azdak, who looks up expectantly.*) A perfectly ridiculous case, your worship.—The defendant has abducted the child and refuses to return it. 155

AZDAK: (*holds out his open hand, looking at Grusha.*) A very attractive young lady. (*They give him more.*) I open the proceedings and demand the strict truth. (*To Grusha.*) Especially from you.

THE FIRST LAWYER: High court of justice! As the people say, "Blood is thicker than water." This venerable wisdom … 160

AZDAK: The court wishes to know what counsel's fee is.

THE FIRST LAWYER: (*astonished.*) I beg your pardon? (*Azdak amiably rubs his thumb and forefinger together.*) Oh! Five hundred piasters, your worship, to answer the high court's unusual question. 165

AZDAK: Did you hear that? The question is unusual. I ask you because I listen with a very different ear if I know you're good. 170

THE FIRST LAWYER: (*bows.*) Thank you, your worship. High court of justice! Of all human ties, the ties of blood are the strongest. Mother and child: can there be any closer relationship? May a child be taken from its mother? High court of justice! She conceived it in the sacred ecstasies of love, she carried it in her womb, fed it with her blood, bore it in pain. High court of justice! It is common knowledge that even the ferocious tigress, robbed of her cubs, goes ranging through the mountains without rest, shrunk to a shadow. Nature itself— 175 180

AZDAK: (*interrupting, to Grusha.*) What's your answer to that and all the rest of what counsel is going to say? 185

GRUSHA: It's mine.

AZDAK: Is that all? I hope you can prove it. In any case, I suggest that you tell me why you think I should award you the child. 190

GRUSHA: I brought him up the best I knew how, I always found him something to eat. He had a roof over his head most of the time, I let myself in for all kinds of trouble for his sake, and expenses too. I didn't worry about my own convenience. I taught 195 the child to be friendly to everyone and right from the start to work as best he could, he's still so little.

THE FIRST LAWYER: Your worship, it is significant that the defendant herself alleges no blood tie between the child and herself. 200

AZDAK: The court takes note.

THE FIRST LAWYER: Thank you, your worship. Permit a sorely bereaved woman, who has lost her husband and must now fear to lose her child, to address a few words to you. Gracious Natella 205 Abashvili ...

THE GOVERNOR'S WIFE: (softly.) A cruel fate, sir, compels me to plead with you to return my beloved child. It is not for me to describe the torments of a bereaved mother, the sleepless nights, 210 the—

THE SECOND LAWYER: (erupting.) It is unspeakable how this woman has been treated. She is barred from entering her husband's palace, the income from his estates is withheld from her. Without an 215 iota of feeling they tell her the income is entailed to the legal heir, she can't do a thing without the child, she can't pay her lawyers! (To the first lawyer, who in despair over this outburst, is motioning him frantically to keep quiet.) My dear, Illo Shuboladze, 220 why should it not be made known that the Abashvili estates are at stake?

THE FIRST LAWYER: Honoured Sandro Oboladze, please! We agreed we ... (To Azdak.) It is true, of course, that the outcome of this trial will also de- 225 termine whether our noble client obtains possession of the sizable Abashvili estates; "also," I say, and by design, for the paramount considera- tion, as Natella Abashvili justly pointed out in the first words of her moving plea, is the tragedy of a 230 mother. Even if Michael Abashvili were not heir to the estates, he would still be my client's dearly beloved child.

AZDAK: Enough! The court looks upon your mention of the estates as proof that we're all 235 human.

THE SECOND LAWYER: Thank you, your worship. My dear Illo Shuboladze, we can prove in any event that the woman who seized the child is not the child's mother! Allow me to set the hard facts 240 before the court. By an unfortunate concatenation of circumstances, this child, Michael Abashvili, was left behind when his mother fled the city. Grusha, a kitchen maid in the palace, was present that Easter Sunday and was seen busying herself with 245 the child—

THE COOK: While the lady was busy worrying which dresses to take with her!

THE SECOND LAWYER: (impassive.) Almost a year later Grusha appeared with the child in a mountain 250 village and concluded a marriage with—

AZDAK: How did you get to this mountain village?

GRUSHA: On my feet, your worship, and he was mine.

SIMON: I am the father, your worship. 255

THE COOK: He was boarding with me, your worship, for five piasters.

THE SECOND LAWYER: This man is Grusha's betrothed, your worship, his testimony is therefore untrustworthy. 260

AZDAK: Are you the man she married in the mountain village?

SIMON: No, your worship. She married a peasant.

AZDAK: (motions Grusha over to him.) Why? (Indicating Simon.) No good in bed? I want the 265 truth.

GRUSHA: We didn't get that far. I married on account of the child. To give him a roof over his head. (Indicating Simon.) He was in the war, your worship. 270

AZDAK: And now he wants to get back with you, is that it?

SIMON: I wish to state—

GRUSHA: (angrily.) I'm no longer free, your worship.

AZDAK: And the child, you claim, comes from 275 whoring? (When Grusha does not answer.) Let me ask you one question: What kind of child is it? A ragged little bastard off the streets or the child of a noble, well-to-do family?

GRUSHA: (*angrily.*) An ordinary child. 280

AZDAK: I mean: did he show refined features at an early age?

GRUSHA: He showed a nose in his face.

AZDAK: He showed a nose in his face. I regard that as a significant answer. There's a story they tell 285 about me; it seems that once before pronouncing a verdict I went out and sniffed at a rosebush. Little tricks like that are necessary nowadays. Now I'm going to make it short, I'm not going to listen to any more of you people's lies—(*to Grusha.*) 290 especially yours. I can imagine how you (*to the group around the defendant.*) cooked all this up to pull the wool over my eyes. I know you, you're crooks.

GRUSHA: (*suddenly.*) I can imagine you'd want to 295 make it short, I saw what you took.

AZDAK: Shut up! Did I take anything from you?

GRUSHA: (*in spite of the cook who is trying to restrain her.*) Because I haven't got anything.

AZDAK: Perfectly right. I don't get a thing from you 300 down-and-outers, I could starve. You want justice, but you don't want to pay. When you go to the butcher's, you know you'll have to pay, but you go to the judge like you'd go to a wake.

SIMON: (*in a loud voice.*) "When the horse was to 305 be shod, the horse-fly held out his legs." As the saying goes.

AZDAK: (*takes up the challenge with enthusiasm.*) "Better a treasure from the manure pile than a pebble from a mountain spring." 310

SIMON: "A fine day, let's go fishing, said the angler to the worm."

AZDAK: "I'm my own master, said the hired man and cut off his foot."

SIMON: "I love you like a father, said the Tsar to the 315 peasants and chopped the Tsarevitch's head off."

AZDAK: "A fool's worst enemy is himself."

SIMON: But "a fart has no nose!"

AZDAK: You're fined ten piasters for indecent language in court, that'll teach you what justice is. 320

GRUSHA: Some justice! You throw the book at us because we don't talk refined like her with her lawyers.

AZDAK: Right. You're too dumb. You deserve to be sat on. 325

GRUSHA: Because you want to hand the child over to that woman who's so refined she wouldn't know how to change its diapers! You don't know any more about justice than I do, put that in your pipe!

AZDAK: You've got something there. I'm ignorant, 330 the pants under my robe are full of holes, see for yourself. With me it all goes into eating and drinking, I was raised in a monastery. Come to think of it, I'm fining you ten piasters too, for contempt of court. What's more, you're stupid, 335 antagonizing me instead of making eyes at me and wiggling your ass a little to put me in a good humour. Twenty piasters.

GRUSHA: You can make it thirty and I'll still tell you what I think of your justice, you drunken turnip. 340 How dare you talk to me like the cracked Isaiah on the church window—big shot![12] When they pulled you out of your mother, they didn't expect you to rap her knuckles if she stole a cup of millet some place, and aren't you ashamed of yourself to 345 see me trembling like this on account of you? You serve these people so their houses won't be taken away—because they stole them; since when do houses belong to bedbugs? But you take care of them, or they couldn't drag our men off to their 350 wars, you flunky!

(*Azdak has stood up. He is beaming. Halfheartedly he strikes the table with his little gavel as though to obtain order, but when Grusha goes on reviling him, he merely beats time for her.*)

GRUSHA: I have no respect for you. No more than I have for a thief and a murderer with a knife, he does what he pleases. It's a hundred to one you can take the child away from me, but I'll tell you one 355 thing: for a job like yours they should only pick rapists and usurers, to punish them by making them sit in judgement over their fellow men, which is worse than hanging on the gallows.

AZDAK: That makes thirty, and I'm not going to 360 wrangle with you any more, this isn't a tavern. I'm a judge and I've got my dignity to think of. To tell

---

12 Isaiah] The prophet Isaiah is known for inveighing against his own people, showing particular intolerance for immorality in the wealthy.

you the truth, I've lost interest in your case. Where are those two who wanted a divorce? (*To Shauva.*) Bring them in. I'm adjourning this case for fifteen minutes. 365

THE FIRST LAWYER: (*as Shauva leaves.*) We can rest our case, gracious lady, it's in the bag.

THE COOK: (*to Grusha.*) You've rubbed him the wrong way. Now he'll take the child away from you. 370

(*Enter a very aged couple.*)

THE GOVERNOR'S WIFE: Shalva, my smelling salts.

AZDAK: I take. (*The old people do not understand.*) I hear you want a divorce. How long have you been together? 375

THE OLD MAN: Forty years, your worship.

AZDAK: Why do you want a divorce?

THE OLD MAN: We don't like each other, your worship.

AZDAK: Since when? 380

THE OLD WOMAN: The whole time, your worship.

AZDAK: I will take your request under deliberation and give my decision when I'm through with the other case. (*Shauva leads them to the rear.*) I need the child. (*Motions to Grusha to come over to him and bends down in a not unfriendly manner.*) 385 Woman, I've seen you have a soft spot for justice. I don't believe he's your child, but supposing he were, wouldn't you want him to be rich? You'd only have to say he's not yours. One two three he'd have a palace, and plenty of horses in his stable and 390 plenty of beggars on his doorstep, plenty of soldiers in his service and plenty of petitioners in his courtyard. See? What's your answer to that? Don't you want him to be rich? (*Grusha is silent.*) 395

THE SINGER: Hear now what the angry woman thought and did not say: (*Sings.*)
If he walked in golden shoes
Cold his heart would be and stony.
Humble folk he would abuse 400
He wouldn't know me.

Oh, it's hard to be hard-hearted
All day long from morn to night.
To be mean and high and mighty
Is a hard and cruel plight. 405

Let him be afraid of hunger
Not of the hungry man's spite
Let him be afraid of darkness
But not fear the light.

AZDAK: Woman, I think I understand you. 410

GRUSHA: I won't give him up. I've raised him and he knows me.

(*Shauva brings the child in.*)

THE GOVERNOR'S WIFE: He's in rags!

GRUSHA: That's not true. They didn't give me time to put on his good shirt. 415

THE GOVERNOR'S WIFE: He's been in a pigsty!

GRUSHA: (*furious.*) I'm not a pig but I know someone who is. Where did you leave your child?

THE GOVERNOR'S WIFE: I'll show you, you vulgar slut. (*She is about to fling herself on Grusha but is 420 restrained by the lawyers.*) She's a criminal! She ought to be flogged! This minute!

THE SECOND LAWYER: (*stops her mouth.*) Gracious Natella Abashvili! You promised … Your worship, the plaintiff's nerves … 425

AZDAK: Plaintiff and defendant: the court has heard your case, but has not yet ascertained who this child's real mother is. It is my duty as judge to pick a mother for the child. I'm going to give you a test. Shauva, take a piece of chalk. Draw a circle on the 430 floor. (*Shauva draws a chalk circle on the floor.*) Put the child in the circle! (*Shauva places Michael, who is smiling at Grusha, in the circle.*) Plaintiff and defendant, stand just outside the circle, both of you! (*The Governor's Wife and Grusha step close to 435 the circle.*) Each of you take the child by one hand. The true mother will have the strength to pull the child out of the circle.

THE SECOND LAWYER: (*quickly.*) High court of justice, I object to making the fate of the large 440 Abashvili estates, which are entailed to the child as heir, hinge on the outcome of so dubious a contest. Furthermore, my client is not as strong as this person who is accustomed to physical labor.

AZDAK: She looks well fed to me. Pull! 445

(*The Governor's Wife pulls the child out of the circle. Grusha has let go, she stands aghast.*)

THE FIRST LAWYER: (*congratulates the Governor's*

Wife.) What did I say? The ties of blood.

AZDAK: (*to Grusha.*) What's the matter with you? You didn't pull.

GRUSHA: I didn't hold onto him. (*She runs to Azdak.*) Your worship, I take back what I said against you, I beg your forgiveness. If only I could keep him until he knows all his words. He knows just a few. 450

AZDAK: Don't try to influence the court! I bet you don't know more than twenty yourself. All right, I'll repeat the test to make sure. 455

(*Again the two women take their places.*)

AZDAK: Pull!

(*Again Grusha lets the child go.*)

GRUSHA: I raised him! Do you want me to tear him to pieces? I can't. 460

AZDAK: (*stands up.*) The court has now ascertained who the true mother is. (*To Grusha.*) Take your child and clear out. I advise you not to stay in the city with him. (*To the Governor's Wife.*) And you get out of here before I convict you of fraud. The estates devolve to the city, they will be turned into a park for the children, they need it; and the park shall be named "Azdak Park" after me. 465

(*The Governor's Wife has fainted and is led away by the Aide-de-camp; the lawyers have already gone.*)

(*Grusha stands motionless. Shauva brings her the child.*)

AZDAK: Because I'm taking off the robe of justice, it's got too hot for me. I'm nobody's hero. But I invite you all to a little farewell dance out there in the meadow. Oh, I almost forgot something, too much wine. The divorce. (*Using the seat of justice as a table, he writes something on a piece of paper and starts to leave.*) 470

475

(*The dance music has started up.*)

SHAUVA: (*has read the paper.*) But this is all wrong. You haven't divorced the two old people, you've divorced Grusha from her husband.

AZDAK: Divorced the wrong people? That's too bad, but it sticks, I retract nothing, the law's the law. (*To the very old couple.*) I invite you to my celebration instead, I'll bet you still like each other enough to dance together. (*To Grusha and Simon.*) And from you two I want forty piasters. 480

SIMON: (*takes out his purse.*) Fair enough, your worship. And many thanks. 485

AZDAK: (*putting the money away.*) I'm going to need it.

GRUSHA: We'd better leave the city tonight, hadn't we, Michael? (*Starts to lift the child on her back. To Simon.*) Do you like him? 490

SIMON: (*lifts the child on his back.*) Beg to report: I like him.

GRUSHA: Now I can tell you: I took him because I betrothed myself to you that Easter Sunday. So it's a child of love. Michael, let's dance. 495

(*She dances with Michael. Simon dances with the cook. The old couple dance too. Azdak stands in thought. Soon the dancing couples hide him. He is seen from time to time, more and more seldom as more couples come in and dance.*)

THE SINGER:
    And that night Azdak disappeared and was never
      seen again.
    But the people of Gruznia did not forget him,
      they long remembered
    The days of his judging as a brief
    Golden Age when there was almost justice. 500

(*The dancers dance off the stage. Azdak has vanished.*)

    And you who have heard the story of the chalk circle
    Bear in mind the wisdom of our fathers:
    Things should belong to those who do well by
      them
    Children to motherly women that they may thrive
    Wagons to good drivers that they may be well
      driven 505
    And the valley to those who water it, that it may
      bear fruit.

TENNESSEE WILLIAMS

Cat on a Hot Tin Roof

One of the most successful playwrights of the twentieth century, Tennessee Williams brought a new kind of poetic theatre to the American stage. At the heart of most of his plays lies a dark confrontation between, on the one hand, the delicate elements of his characters' fragile inner lives and desires and, on the other, the brutal external circumstances in which they find themselves. In itself, the confrontation was hardly a new theme in literature, but Williams was able to find such compelling means of dramatizing the situation that his work quickly entered and altered the mythological framework of American popular culture.

Tennessee was born Thomas Lanier Williams, in Columbus, Mississippi, to Cornelius Coffin Williams, a travelling shoe salesman, and Edwina Dakin, the daughter of an Episcopalian minister. The family was not well off, so, as is so often the case, fights between the couple were frequent. These were especially troubling to Thomas because of the anxiety they caused his delicate sister, Rose. After spending a few years in Clarksdale, Mississippi, the family moved to St. Louis in 1918, where Thomas was nicknamed "Tennessee" by his classmates because of his strong southern accent. He began writing early in life, publishing his first works—an essay and a short story—while still a teenager. In 1929, he entered the University of Missouri, but the Great Depression was at hand; in 1931 he was forced to leave school and begin work in the same shoe company in which his father was employed. There Williams continued to write, often secretly.

After a few years in the shoe factory, Tennessee moved to live with his grandparents in Memphis, where he began to write more intensively. In 1935, his first play, *Cairo, Shanghai, Bombay,* was produced there; two years later, when he was back in St. Louis, two more of his plays, *Candles to the Sun* and *The Fugitive Kind,* were produced by the St. Louis Mummers troupe. He returned to university and was awarded a B.A. from the University of Iowa in 1938. Not long after graduating, Williams achieved some important recognition when a collection of his short plays, *American Blues* (1939), was produced by the Group Theater in New York, and he also won two awards: one was a special commendation and a $100 prize which he won in a contest supposedly limited to playwrights under twenty-five (Williams was then twenty-seven) and the other, more importantly, was a $1000 grant from the Rockefeller Foundation. The money allowed him to quit his job as a shoe clerk and turn his attentions back to writing his next play, *Battle of Angels,* which was produced in Boston in 1940.

Williams had a few years of relative quiet before he began what was to prove the most fruitful period of his career. In 1944, Williams' most popular play, *The Glass Menagerie,* was produced first in Chicago and then on Broadway, where it was given an extended run. In the play, the protagonist Tom, who works in a shoe factory, lives with his mother, Amanda, and his anxious and disabled sister, Laura. The family's hopes are all pinned on a "gentleman caller" who will take Laura away into a better life. There is little question that Williams was drawing on elements of his own life for this play. By then, the anxious fits of his sister, Rose, had worsened considerably, and Williams' mother had consented to having a frontal lobotomy performed on the girl—an incident that deeply disturbed Williams for the rest of his life, and that would haunt many of his plays in one disguised form or another.

Williams followed *The Glass Menagerie* with an extraordinary string of successful plays: *A Streetcar Named Desire* (1947), which won the Pulitzer Prize for drama; *Summer and Smoke* (1948); *The Rose Tattoo* (1951); *Camino Real* (1953); *Cat on a Hot Tin Roof* (1955), for which he won a second Pulitzer; *Orpheus Descending* (1957), a reworking of his earlier play, *Battle of Angels*; *Sweet Bird of Youth* (1959); and *Night of the Iguana* (1961). The release of films of *The Glass Menagerie* and *A Streetcar Named Desire* in 1950 and 1951 helped make Williams famous, and by the early 1960s, almost all of his other plays written in the fifteen years since *Glass Menagerie* had been filmed too, along with one original screenplay, *Baby Doll* (1956), another screenplay based on one of his short stories, *Suddenly, Last Summer* (1959), and a further screenplay based on his novel, *The Roman Spring of Mrs. Stone* (1961).

In 1961, however, Williams' astonishingly prodigious flow of creativity came to a halt. While living in New Orleans in 1947, Williams had met and fallen in love with a man named Frank Merlo, who brought a good measure of stability to Williams' personal life. When Merlo died of lung cancer in 1961, Williams was devastated and slid into a deep depression, which was worsened by alcoholism and drug use, and from which he would only emerge, somewhat uncertainly, in the 1970s. He was eventually to produce more than a dozen more plays, many of them interesting, though none ever matched the success of his celebrated work of the 1940s and 1950s. Williams died in 1983, having choked on the bottle-cap of some prescription drugs after a night of drinking.

One of the central themes of *Cat on a Hot Tin Roof* involves Brick's homosexual inclinations toward his dead friend Skipper and the great difficulty he has in either wholly repressing or acknowledging this part of himself. As Williams puts it in an intriguing extended stage direction in the scene between Big Daddy and Brick, this is "the inadmissible thing that Skipper died to disavow between them." So Brick tries to go on living the lie that Skipper tried to preserve, and his disgust at this life of lies—this mendacity—is so strong that he drinks to kill it within himself. But it is significant that the whole question of mendacity is raised in conversation with Big Daddy, whose own condition, like Brick's, is concealed by lies. In the same stage direction, Williams goes on to explain: "The bird that I hope to catch in the net of this play is not the solution of one man's psychological problem. I'm trying to catch the true quality of experience in a group of people, that cloudy, flickering, evanescent—fiercely charged!—interplay of live human beings in the thundercloud of a common crisis." In short, the climate of false appearances and repressed truths pervades the entire play; it hangs in the air oppressively, threatening to stifle some of the characters, to drive them mad. So, while Maggie's frustration is, in part, clearly sexually based, having to live in this unbearable atmosphere of mendacity is also what makes her feel like a "cat on a hot tin roof."

Perhaps it was because he was looking for a sensually based catharsis for this feeling that Elia Kazan, the first director of the play, and a collaborator whom Williams greatly trusted, felt the need to insert a massive storm into the third act of the play: to metaphorically clear the air. Williams followed Kazan's advice in revising the play, but though he admitted the theatrical power of what he and Kazan had done, he was never fully satisfied with the third act as it was originally performed. For later productions and for publication, he never fully returned to his original version—the published versions marked "original" are not exactly that (see Brian Parker, "A Preliminary Stemma for Drafts of Tennessee Williams's *Cat on a Hot Tin Roof* [1955]" [*Publications of Bibliographical Society of America 90:4* (December 1996), pp. 475–96]). Williams even went on tinkering with the text when the play was remounted at the Lincoln Center in 1974, trying to tell his story in the most dramatic way possible, without falling into what he calls "pat conclusions, facile definitions which make a play just a play, not a snare for the truth of human experience."

[C.S.W.]

TENNESSEE WILLIAMS
Cat on a Hot Tin Roof

CHARACTERS
  MARGARET
  BRICK
  MAE, sometimes called Sister Woman
  BIG MAMA
  DIXIE, a little girl
  BIG DADDY
  REVEREND TOOKER
  GOOPER, sometimes called Brother Man
  DOCTOR BAUGH, pronounced "Baw"
  LACEY, a Negro servant
  SOOKEY, another
  CHILDREN

NOTES FOR THE DESIGNER

The set is the bed-sitting-room of a plantation home in the Mississippi Delta. It is along an upstairs gallery which probably runs around the entire house; it has two pairs of very wide doors opening onto the gallery, showing white balustrades against a fair summer sky that fades into dusk and night during the course of the play, which occupies precisely the time of its performance, excepting, of course, the fifteen minutes of intermission.

Perhaps the style of the room is not what you would expect in the home of the Delta's biggest cotton-planter. It is Victorian with a touch of the Far East. It hasn't changed much since it was occupied by the original owners of the place, Jack Straw and Peter Ochello, a pair of old bachelors who shared this room all their lives together. In other words, the room must evoke some ghosts; it is gently and poetically haunted by a relationship that must have involved a tenderness which was uncommon. This may be irrelevant or unnecessary, but I once saw a reproduction of a faded photograph of the verandah of Robert Louis Stevenson's home on that Samoan Island where he spent his last years, and there was a quality of tender light on weathered wood, such as porch furniture made of bamboo and wicker, exposed to tropical suns and tropical rains, which came to mind when I thought about the set for this play, bringing also to mind the grace and comfort of light, the reassurance it gives, on a late and fair afternoon in summer, the way that no matter what, even dread of death, is gently touched and soothed by it. For the set is the background for a play that deals with human extremities of emotion, and it needs that softness behind it.

The bathroom door, showing only pale-blue tile and silver towel racks, is in one side wall; the hall door in the opposite wall. Two articles of furniture need mention: a big double bed which staging should make a functional part of the set as often as suitable, the surface of which should be slightly raked to make figures on it seen more easily; and against the wall space between the two huge double doors upstage: a monumental monstrosity peculiar to our times, a huge console combination of radio-phonograph (hi-fi with three speakers) TV set and liquor cabinet, bearing and containing many glasses and bottles, all in one piece, which is a composition of muted silver tones, and the opalescent tones of reflecting glass, a chromatic link, this thing, between the sepia (tawny gold) tones of the interior and the cool (white and blue) tones of the gallery and sky. This piece of furniture (?!), this monument, is a very complete and compact little shrine to virtually all the comforts and illusions behind which we hide from such things as the characters in the play are faced with . . . .

The set should be far less realistic than I have so far implied in this description of it. I think the walls below the ceiling should dissolve mysteriously into air; the set should be roofed by the sky; stars and moon suggested by traces of milky pallor, as if they were observed through a telescope lens out of focus. Anything else I can think of? Oh, yes, fanlights (transoms shaped like an open glass fan) above all the doors in the set, with panes of blue and amber, and above all, the designer should take as many pains to give the actors room to move about freely (to show their restlessness, their passion for breaking out) as if it were a set for a ballet.

An evening in summer. The action is continuous, with two intermissions.

ACT I

At the rise of the curtain someone is taking a shower in the bathroom, the door of which is half open. A pretty young woman, with anxious lines in her face, enters the bedroom and crosses to the bathroom door.

MARGARET (*shouting above roar of water*): One of those no-neck monsters hit me with a hot buttered biscuit so I have t' change!

[*MARGARET's voice is both rapid and drawling. In her long speeches she has the vocal tricks of a priest delivering a liturgical chant, the lines are almost sung, always continuing a little beyond her breath so she has to gasp for another. Sometimes she intersperses the lines with a little wordless singing, such as "Da-da-daaaa!"*

Water turns off and BRICK calls out to her, but is still unseen. A tone of politely feigned interest, masking indifference, or worse, is characteristic of his speech with MARGARET.]

BRICK: Wha'd you say, Maggie? Water was on s' loud I couldn't hearya   5
MARGARET: Well, I!—just remarked that!—one of th' no-neck monsters messed up m' lovely lace dress so I got t'—cha-a-ange . . . .

[*She opens and kicks shut drawers of the dresser.*]

BRICK: Why d'ya call Gooper's kiddies no-neck monsters?   10
MARGARET: Because they've got no necks! Isn't that a good enough reason?
BRICK: Don't they have any necks?
MARGARET: None visible. Their fat little heads are set on their fat little bodies without a bit of   15
connection.
BRICK: That's too bad.
MARGARET: Yes, it's too bad because you can't wring their necks if they've got no necks to wring! Isn't that right, honey?   20

[*She steps out of her dress, stands in a slip of ivory satin and lace.*]

Yep, they're no-neck monsters, all no-neck people are monsters . . .

[*Children shriek downstairs.*]

Hear them? Hear them screaming? I don't know where their voice boxes are located since they don't have necks. I tell you I got so nervous at that table   25
tonight I thought I would throw back my head and utter a scream you could hear across the Arkansas border an' parts of Louisiana an' Tennessee. I said to your charming sister-in-law, Mae, honey, couldn't you feed those precious little things at a separate   30
table with an oilcloth cover?[1] They make such a mess an' the lace cloth looks *so* pretty! She made enormous eyes at me and said, "Ohhh, noooooo! On Big Daddy's birthday? Why, he would never

---

[1] oilcloth] a water-repellent covering made of canvas coated with hardened oil.

forgive me!" Well, I want you to know, Big Daddy hadn't been at the table two minutes with those five no-neck monsters slobbering and drooling over their food before he threw down his fork an' shouted, "Fo' God's sake, Gooper, why don't you put them pigs at a trough in th' kitchen?"—Well, I swear, I simply could have di-ieed!

Think of it, Brick, they've got five of them and number six is coming. They've brought the whole bunch down here like animals to display at a county fair. Why, they have those children doin' tricks all the time! "Junior, show Big Daddy how you do this, show Big Daddy how you do that, say your little piece fo' Big Daddy, Sister. Show your dimples, Sugar. Brother, show Big Daddy how you stand on your head!"—It goes on all the time, along with constant little remarks and innuendos about the fact that you and I have not produced any children, are totally childless and therefore totally useless!—Of course it's comical but it's also disgusting since it's so obvious what they're up to!

BRICK (*without interest*): What are they up to, Maggie?

MARGARET: Why, you know what they're up to!

BRICK (*appearing*): No, I don't know what they're up to.

[*He stands there in the bathroom doorway drying his hair with a towel and hanging onto the towel rack because one ankle is broken, plastered and bound. He is still slim and firm as a boy. His liquor hasn't started tearing him down outside. He has the additional charm of that cool air of detachment that people have who have given up the struggle. But now and then, when disturbed, something flashes behind it, like lightning in a fair sky, which shows that at some deeper level he is far from peaceful. Perhaps in a stronger light he would show some signs of deliquescence, but the fading, still warm, light from the gallery treats him gently.*]

MARGARET: I'll tell you what they're up to, boy of mine!—They're up to cutting you out of your father's estate, and—

[*She freezes momentarily before her next remark. Her voice drops as if it were somehow a personally embarrassing admission.*]

—Now we know that Big Daddy's dyin' of—cancer . . . .

[*There are voices on the lawn below: long-drawn calls across distance. MARGARET raises her lovely bare arms and powders her armpits with a light sigh. She adjusts the angle of a magnifying mirror to straighten an eyelash, then rises fretfully saying:*]

There's so much light in the room it—

BRICK (*softly but sharply*): Do we?

MARGARET: Do we what?

BRICK: Know Big Daddy's dyin' of cancer?

MARGARET: Got the report today.

BRICK: Oh . . .

MARGARET (*letting down bamboo blinds which cast long, gold-fretted shadows over the room*): Yep, got th' report just now . . . it didn't surprise me, Baby . . . .

[*Her voice has range, and music; sometimes it drops low as a boy's and you have a sudden image of her playing boy's games as a child.*]

I recognized the symptoms soon's we got here last spring and I'm willin' to bet you that Brother Man and his wife were pretty sure of it, too. That more than likely explains why their usual summer migration to the coolness of the Great Smokies was passed up this summer in favour of—hustlin' down here ev'ry whipstitch with their whole screamin' tribe![2] And why so many allusions have been made to Rainbow Hill lately. You know what Rainbow Hill is? Place that's famous for treatin' alcoholics an dope fiends in the movies!

BRICK: I'm not in the movies.

MARGARET: No, and you don't take dope. Otherwise you're a perfect candidate for Rainbow Hill, Baby, and that's where they aim to ship you—over my dead body! Yep, over my dead body they'll ship you there, but nothing would please them better. Then Brother Man could get a-hold of the purse strings and dole out remittances to us, maybe get power of attorney and sign checks for us and cut off our credit wherever, whenever he wanted! Son-of-a-bitch!—How'd you like that, Baby?—

---

2 whipstitch] (slang) every other moment (literally: a quickly sewn diagonal stitch overlaying a seam).

Well, you've been doin' just about ev'rything in your power to bring it about, you've just been doin' ev'rything you can think of to aid and abet them in this scheme of theirs! Quittin' work, devoting yourself to the occupation of drinkin'!—Breakin' your ankle last night on the high school athletic field: doin' what? Jumpin' hurdles? At two or three in the morning? Just fantastic! Got in the paper. *Clarksdale Register* carried a nice little item about it, human interest story about a well-known former athlete stagin' a one-man track meet on the Glorious Hill High School athletic field last night, but was slightly out of condition and didn't clear the first hurdle! Brother Man Gooper claims he exercised his influence t' keep it from goin' out over AP or UP or every goddam "P."[3]

But, Brick? You still have one big advantage!

[During the above swift flood of words, BRICK has reclined with contrapuntal leisure on the snowy surface of the bed and has rolled over carefully on his side or belly.]

BRICK (*wryly*): Did you *say* something, Maggie?

MARGARET: Big Daddy dotes on you, honey. And he can't stand Brother Man and Brother Man's wife, that monster of fertility, Mae. Know how I know? By little expressions that flicker over his face when that woman is holding fo'th on one of her choice topics such as—how she refused twilight sleep!—when the twins were delivered![4] Because she feels motherhood's an experience that a woman ought to experience fully!—in order to fully appreciate the wonder and beauty of it! HAH!—and how she made Brother Man come in an' stand beside her in the delivery room so he would not miss out on the "wonder and beauty" of it either!—producin' those no-neck monsters . . . .

[A speech of this kind would be antipathetic from almost anybody but MARGARET; she makes it oddly

funny, because her eyes constantly twinkle and her voice shakes with laughter which is basically indulgent.]*

—Big Daddy shares my attitude toward those two! As for me, well—I give him a laugh now and then and he tolerates me. In fact!—I sometimes suspect that Big Daddy harbours a little unconscious "lech" fo' me . . . .

BRICK: What makes you think that Big Daddy has a lech for you, Maggie?

MARGARET: Way he always drops his eyes down my body when I'm talkin' to him, drops his eyes to my boobs an' licks his old chops! Ha ha!

BRICK: That kind of talk is disgusting.

MARGARET: Did anyone ever tell you that you're an ass-aching Puritan, Brick?

I think it's mighty fine that that ole fellow, on the doorstep of death, still takes in my shape with what I think is deserved appreciation!

And you wanta know something else? Big Daddy didn't know how many little Maes and Goopers had been produced! "How many kids have you got?" he asked at the table, just like Brother Man and his wife were new acquaintances to him! Big Mama said he was jokin', but that ole boy wasn't jokin', Lord, no!

And when they infawmed him that they had five already and were turning out number six!—the news seemed to come as a sort of unpleasant surprise . . .

[Children yell below.]

Scream, monsters!

[Turns to BRICK with a sudden, gay, charming smile which fades as she notices that he is not looking at her but into fading gold space with a troubled expression. It is constant rejection that makes her humour "bitchy."]

Yes, you should of been at that supper-table, Baby.

[Whenever she calls him "baby" the word is a soft caress.]

Y'know, Big Daddy, bless his ole sweet soul, he's the dearest ole thing in the world, but he does hunch over his food as if he preferred not to notice anything else. Well, Mae an' Gooper were side by side at the table, direckly across from Big Daddy,

---

3   AP, UP] Associate Press and United Press International, news agencies or wire services which once distributed news to member organizations by telegraph.

4   twilight sleep] scopolamine and morphine, an analgesic-amnesiac technique used to provide painless birth from 1902 until the 1960s.

watchin' his face like hawks while they jawed an' jabbered about the cuteness an' brilliance of th' no-neck monsters! 165

[She giggles with a hand fluttering at her throat and her breast and her long throat arched. She comes downstage and recreates the scene with voice and gesture.]

And the no-neck monsters were ranged around the table, some in high chairs and some on th' *Books of Knowledge*, all in fancy little paper caps in honour of Big Daddy's birthday, and all through dinner, well, I want you to know that Brother Man an' his partner 170 never once, for one moment, stopped exchanging pokes an' pinches an' kicks an' signs an' signals!5— Why, they were like a couple of cardsharps fleecing a sucker.—Even Big Mama, bless her ole sweet soul, she isn't th' quickest an' brightest thing in the world, 175 she finally noticed, at last, an' said to Gooper, "Gooper, what are you an' Mae makin' all these signs at each other about?"—I swear t' goodness, I nearly choked on my chicken!

[MARGARET, back at the dressing table, still doesn't see BRICK. He is watching her with a look that is not quite definable—Amused? shocked? contemptuous?—part of those and part of something else.]

Y'know—your brother Gooper still cherishes the 180 illusion he took a giant step up on the social ladder when he married Miss Mae Flynn of the Memphis Flynns.

But I have a piece of Spanish news for Gooper.6 The Flynns never had a thing in this world but 185 money and they lost that, they were nothing at all but fairly successful climbers. Of course, Mae

---

5 *Books of Knowledge*] encyclopaedia volumes.
6 piece of Spanish news] (slang) a startling piece of information. The origins of this old Southern expression are obscure. It may have originated in the sensationalistic tendencies of certain Latin-American newspapers, or possibly in the lurid, yellow journalism of William Randolph Hearst's *Morning Journal*, which published a series of anti-Spanish stories that fomented the Spanish-American War in 1898 and thereby massively increased Hearst's circulation.

Flynn came out in Memphis eight years before I made my debut in Nashville, but I had friends at Ward-Belmont who came from Memphis and they 190 used to come to see me and I used to go to see them for Christmas and spring vacations, and so I know who rates an' who doesn't rate in Memphis society. Why, y'know ole Papa Flynn, he barely escaped doing time in the Federal pen for shady 195 manipulations on th' stock market when his chain stores crashed, and as for Mae having been a cotton carnival queen, as they remind us so often, lest we forget, well, that's one honour that I don't envy her for!—Sit on a brass throne on a tacky float an' ride 200 down Main Street, smilin', bowin', and blowin' kisses to all the trash on the street—

[She picks out a pair of jeweled sandals and rushes to the dressing table.]

Why, year before last, when Susan McPheeters was singled out fo' that honour, y' know what happened to her? Y'know what happened to poor 205 little Susie McPheeters?

BRICK (*absently*): No. What happened to little Susie McPheeters?

MARGARET: Somebody spit tobacco juice in her face. 210

BRICK (*dreamily*): Somebody spit tobacco juice in her face?

MARGARET: That's right, some old drunk leaned out of a window in the Hotel Gayoso and yelled, "Hey, Queen, hey, hey, there, Queenie!" Poor Susie 215 looked up and flashed him a radiant smile and he shot out a squirt of tobacco juice right in poor Susie's face.

BRICK: Well, what d'you know about that.

MARGARET (*gaily*): What do I know about it? I 220 was there, I saw it!

BRICK (*absently*): Must have been kind of funny.

MARGARET: Susie didn't think so. Had hysterics. Screamed like a banshee. They had to stop th' parade an' remove her from her throne an' go on 225 with—

[She catches sight of him in the mirror, gasps slightly, wheels about to face him. Count ten.]

—Why are you looking at me like that?

BRICK (*whistling softly, now*): Like what, Maggie?

MARGARET (*intensely, fearfully*): The way y' were lookin' at me just now, befo' I caught your eye in the mirror and you started t' whistle! I don't know how t' describe it but it froze my blood!—I've caught you lookin' at me like that so often lately. What are you thinkin' of when you look at me like that?

BRICK: I wasn't conscious of lookin' at you, Maggie.

MARGARET: Well, I was conscious of it! What were you thinkin'?

BRICK: I don't remember thinking of anything, Maggie.

MARGARET: Don't you think I know that—? Don't you—?—Think I know that—?

BRICK (*coolly*): Know *what*, Maggie?

MARGARET (*struggling for expression*): That I've gone through this—*hideous!*—*transformation*, become—*hard! Frantic!*

[Then she adds, almost tenderly:]

—*cruel!!*

That's what you've been observing in me lately. How could y' help but observe it? That's all right. I'm not—thin-skinned any more, can't afford t' be thin-skinned any more.

[She is now recovering her power.]

—But Brick? Brick?

BRICK: Did you say something?

MARGARET: I was *goin'* t' say something: that I get—lonely. Very!

BRICK: Ev'rybody gets that . . .

MARGARET: Living with someone you love can be lonelier—than living entirely *alone!*—if the one that y'love doesn't love you . . . .

[There is a pause. BRICK hobbles downstage and asks, without looking at her:]

BRICK: Would you like to live alone, Maggie?

[Another pause: then—after she has caught a quick, hurt breath:]

MARGARET: *No!—God!—God!—I wouldn't!*

[Another gasping breath. She forcibly controls what must have been an impulse to cry out. We see her deliberately, very forcibly, going all the way back to the world in which you can talk about ordinary matters.]

Did you have a nice shower?

BRICK: Uh-huh.

MARGARET: Was the water cool?

BRICK: No.

MARGARET: But it made y' feel fresh, huh?

BRICK: Fresher . . .

MARGARET: I know something would make y' feel *much* fresher!

BRICK: What?

MARGARET: An alcohol rub. Or cologne, a rub with cologne!

BRICK: That's good after a workout but I haven't been workin' out, Maggie.

MARGARET: You've kept in good shape, though,

BRICK (*indifferently*): You think so, Maggie?

MARGARET: I always thought drinkin' men lost their looks, but I was plainly mistaken.

BRICK (*wryly*): Why, thanks, Maggie.

MARGARET: You're the only drinkin' man I know that it never seems t' put fat on.

BRICK: I'm gettin' softer, Maggie.

MARGARET: Well, sooner or later it's bound to soften you up. It was just beginning to soften up Skipper when—

[She stops short.]

I'm sorry. I never could keep my fingers off a sore—I wish you *would* lose your looks. If you did it would make the martyrdom of Saint Maggie a little more bearable. But no such goddam luck. I actually believe you've gotten better looking since you've gone on the bottle. Yeah, a person who didn't know you would think you'd never had a tense nerve in your body or a strained muscle.

[There are sounds of croquet on the lawn below: the click of mallets, light voices, near and distant.]

Of course, you always had that detached quality as if you were playing a game without much concern over whether you won or lost, and now that you've lost the game, not lost but just quit playing, you have that rare sort of charm that usually only happens in very old or hopelessly sick people, the charm of the defeated.—You look so cool, so cool, so enviably cool.   300

REVEREND TOOKER (*off stage right*): Now looka here, boy, lemme show you how to get outa that!

MARGARET: They're playing croquet. The moon has appeared and it's white, just beginning to turn   305
a little bit yellow . . . .

Such a wonderful person to go to bed with, and I think mostly because you were really indifferent to it. Isn't that right? Never had any anxiety about   310
it, did it naturally, easily, slowly, with absolute confidence and perfect calm, more like opening a door for a lady or seating her at a table than giving expression to any longing for her. Your indifference made you wonderful at lovemaking—*strange?*—   315
but true . . . .

REVEREND TOOKER: Oh! That's a beauty.

DOCTOR BAUGH: Yeah. I got you boxed.

MARGARET: You know, if I thought you would never, never, *never*, make love to me again—I   320
would go downstairs to the kitchen and pick out the longest and sharpest knife I could find and stick it straight into my heart, I swear that I would!

REVEREND TOOKER: Watch out, you're gonna miss it.   325

DOCTOR BAUGH: You just don't know me, boy!

MARGARET: But one thing I don't have is the charm of the defeated, my hat is still in the ring, and I am determined to win!

[There is the sound of croquet mallets hitting croquet balls.]

REVEREND TOOKER: Mmm—You're too slip-   330
pery for me.

MARGARET: —What is the victory of a cat on a hot tin roof?—I wish I knew . . . .

Just staying on it, I guess, as long as she can . . . .

DOCTOR BAUGH: Jus' like an eel, boy, jus' like   335
an eel!

[More croquet sounds.]

MARGARET: Later tonight I'm going to tell you I love you an' maybe by that time you'll be drunk enough to believe me. Yes, they're playing croquet. . . .   340

Big Daddy is dying of cancer . . . .

What were you thinking of when I caught you looking at me like that? Were you thinking of Skipper?

[BRICK takes up his crutch, rises.]

Oh, excuse me, forgive me, but laws of silence   345
don't work! No, laws of silence don't work . . . .

[BRICK crosses to the bar, takes a quick drink, and rubs his head with a towel.]

Laws of silence don't work . . . .

When something is festering in your memory or your imagination, laws of silence don't work, it's just like shutting a door and locking it on a house   350
on fire in hope of forgetting that the house is burning. But not facing a fire doesn't put it out. Silence about a thing just magnifies it. It grows and festers in silence, becomes malignant . . . .

[He drops his crutch.]

BRICK: Give me my crutch.   355

[He has stopped rubbing his hair dry but still stands hanging onto the towel rack in a white towel-cloth robe.]

MARGARET: Lean on me.

BRICK: No, just give me my crutch.

MARGARET: Lean on my shoulder.

BRICK: *I don't want to lean on your shoulder, I want my crutch!*   360

[This is spoken like sudden lightning.]

Are you going to give me my crutch or do I have to get down on my knees on the floor and—

MARGARET: *Here, here, take it, take it!*

[She has thrust the crutch at him.]

BRICK (*hobbling out*): Thanks . . .

MARGARET: We mustn't scream at each other, the   365
walls in this house have ears . . . .

[He hobbles directly to liquor cabinet to get a new drink.]

—but that's the first time I've heard you raise your voice in a long time, Brick. A crack in the wall?—

Of composure?

—I think that's a good sign 370

A sign of nerves in a player on the defensive!

[BRICK turns and smiles at her coolly over his fresh drink.]

BRICK: It just hasn't happened yet, Maggie.

MARGARET: What?

BRICK: The click I get in my head when I've had enough of this stuff to make me peaceful 375

Will you do me a favour?

MARGARET: Maybe I will. What favour?

BRICK: Just, just keep your voice down!

MARGARET (*in a hoarse whisper*): I'll do you that favour, I'll speak in a whisper, if not shut up 380 completely, if *you* will do *me* a favour and make that drink your last one till after the party.

BRICK: What party?

MARGARET: Big Daddy's birthday party.

BRICK: Is this Big Daddy's birthday? 385

MARGARET: You know this is Big Daddy's birthday!

BRICK: No, I don't, I forgot it.

MARGARET: Well, I remembered it for you . . . .

[They are both speaking as breathlessly as a pair of kids after a fight, drawing deep exhausted breaths and looking at each other with faraway eyes, shaking and panting together as if they had broken apart from a violent struggle.]

BRICK: Good for you, Maggie. 390

MARGARET: You just have to scribble a few lines on this card.

BRICK: You scribble something, Maggie.

MARGARET: It's got to be your handwriting; it's your present, I've given him my present; it's got 395 to be your handwriting!

[The tension between them is building again, the voices becoming shrill once more.]

BRICK: I didn't get him a present.

MARGARET: I got one for you.

BRICK: All right. You write the card, then.

MARGARET: And have him know you didn't 400 remember his birthday?

BRICK: I didn't remember his birthday.

MARGARET: You don't have to prove you didn't!

BRICK: I don't want to fool him about it.

MARGARET: Just write "Love, Brick!" for God's— 405

BRICK: No.

MARGARET: You've *got* to!

BRICK: I don't have to do anything I don't want to do. You keep forgetting the conditions on which I agreed to stay on living with you. 410

MARGARET (*out before she knows it*): I'm not living with you. We occupy the same cage.

BRICK: You've got to remember the conditions agreed on.

SONNY (*off stage*): Mommy, give it to me. I had it 415 first.

MAE: Hush.

MARGARET: They're impossible conditions!

BRICK: Then why don't you—?

SONNY: I want it, I want it! 420

MAE: Get away!

MARGARET: HUSH! Who is out there? Is somebody at the door?

[There are footsteps in hall.]

MAE (*outside*): May I enter a moment?

MARGARET: Oh, *you!* Sure. Come in, Mae. 425

[MAE enters bearing aloft the bow of a young lady's archery set.]

MAE: Brick, is this thing yours?

MARGARET: Why, Sister Woman—that's my Diana Trophy.[7] Won it at the intercollegiate archery contest on the Ole Miss campus.[8]

MAE: It's a mighty dangerous thing to leave exposed 430 round a house full of nawmal rid-blooded children attracted t'weapons.

MARGARET: "Nawmal rid-blooded children attracted t'weapons" ought t'be taught to keep their hands off things that don't belong to them. 435

MAE: Maggie, honey, if you had children of your own you'd know how funny that is. Will you please lock this up and put the key out of reach?

---

7 Diana Trophy] named after the Roman goddess of the hunt.

8 Ole Miss] affectionate name for the University of Mississippi.

MARGARET: Sister Woman, nobody is plotting the destruction of your kiddies.—Brick and I still have our special archers' license. We're goin' deer-huntin' on Moon Lake as soon as the season starts. I love to run with dogs through chilly woods, run, run leap over obstructions— 440

[She goes into the closet carrying the bow.]

MAE: How's the injured ankle, Brick? 445
BRICK: Doesn't hurt. Just itches.
MAE: Oh, my! Brick—Brick, you should've been downstairs after supper! Kiddies put on a show. Polly played the piano, Buster an' Sonny drums, an' then they turned out the lights an' Dixie an' Trixie 450 puhfawmed a toe dance in fairy costume with *spahkluhs!* Big Daddy just beamed! He just beamed!
MARGARET (*from the closet with a sharp laugh*): Oh, I bet. It breaks my heart that we missed it!

[She reenters.]

But Mae? Why did y'give dawgs' names to all your 455 kiddies?
MAE: *Dogs'* names?
MARGARET (*sweetly*): Dixie, Trixie, Buster, Sonny, Polly!—Sounds like four dogs and a parrot . . .
MAE: Maggie? 460

[MARGARET turns with a smile.]

Why are you so catty?
MARGARET: Cause I'm a cat! But why can't *you* take a joke, Sister Woman?
MAE: Nothin' pleases me more than a joke that's funny. You know the real names of our kiddies. 465 Buster's real name is Robert. Sonny's real name is Saunders. Trixie's real name is Marlene and Dixie's—

[GOOPER downstairs calls for her. "Hey, Mae! Sister Woman, intermission is over!"—She rushes to door, saying:]

Intermission is over! See ya later!
MARGARET: I wonder what Dixie's real name is? 470
BRICK: Maggie, being catty doesn't help things any . . .
MARGARET: I know! *WHY!*—Am I so catty?— Cause I'm consumed with envy an' eaten up with

longing?—Brick, I'm going to lay out your 475 beautiful Shantung silk suit from Rome and one of your monogrammed silk shirts.[9] I'll put your cuff links in it, those lovely star sapphires I get you to wear so rarely . . . .
BRICK: I can't get trousers on over this plaster cast. 480
MARGARET: Yes, you can, I'll help you.
BRICK: I'm not going to get dressed, Maggie.
MARGARET: Will you just put on a pair of white silk pajamas?
BRICK: Yes, I'll do that, Maggie. 485
MARGARET: *Thank* you, thank you so *much!*
BRICK: Don't mention it.
MARGARET: *Oh, Brick!* How long does it have t' go on? This punishment? Haven't I done time enough, haven't I served my term, can't I apply for 490 a—pardon?
BRICK: Maggie, you're spoiling my liquor. Lately your voice always sounds like you'd been running upstairs to warn somebody that the house was on fire! 495
MARGARET: Well, no wonder, no wonder. Y'know what I feel like, Brick?

[Children's and grown-up's voices are blended, below, in a loud but uncertain rendition of "My Wild Irish Rose."]

I feel all the time like a cat on a hot tin roof!
BRICK: Then jump off the roof, jump off it, cats can jump off roofs and land on their four feet 500 uninjured.
MARGARET: Oh, yes!
BRICK: Do it!—fo' God's sake, do it . . .
MARGARET: Do what?
BRICK: Take a lover! 505
MARGARET: I can't see a man but you! Even with my eyes closed, I just see you! Why don't you get ugly, Brick, why don't you please get fat or ugly or something so I could stand it?

[She rushes to hall door, opens it, listens.]

The concert is still going on. Bravo, no-necks, 510 bravo!

[She slams and locks door fiercely.]

---

9 Shantung silk] a type of soft silk that originated in China.

BRICK: What did you lock the door for?

MARGARET: To give us a little privacy for a while.

BRICK: You know better, Maggie.

MARGARET: No, I don't know better   515

[She rushes to gallery doors, draws the rose-silk drapes across them.]

BRICK: Don't make a fool of yourself.

MARGARET: I don't mind makin' a fool of myself over you!

BRICK: I mind, Maggie. I feel embarrassed for you.

MARGARET: Feel embarrassed! But don't continue   520
my torture. I can't live on and on under these circumstances.

BRICK: You agreed to—

MARGARET: I know but—

BRICK: —Accept that condition!   525

MARGARET: I CAN'T! CAN'T! CAN'T

[She seizes his shoulder.]

BRICK: Let go!

[He breaks away from her and seizes the small boudoir chair and raises it like a lion-tamer facing a big circus cat. Count five. She stares at him with her fist pressed to her mouth, then bursts into shrill, almost hysterical laughter. He remains grave for a moment, then grins and puts the chair down.]

[BIG MAMA calls through closed door.]

BIG MAMA: Son? Son? Son?

BRICK: What is it, Big Mama?

BIG MAMA (*outside*): Oh, son! We got the most   530
wonderful news about Big Daddy. I just had t'run up an' tell you right this—

[She rattles the knob.]

—What's this door doin', locked, faw? You all
think there's robbers in the house?

MARGARET: Big Mama, Brick is dressin', he's not   535
dressed yet.

BIG MAMA: That's all right, it won't be the first time I've seen Brick not dressed. Come on, open this door!

[MARGARET, with a grimace, goes to unlock and open the hall door, as BRICK hobbles rapidly to the

bathroom and kicks the door shut. BIG MAMA has disappeared from the hall.]

MARGARET: Big Mama?   540

[BIG MAMA appears through the opposite gallery doors behind MARGARET, huffing and puffing like an old bulldog. She is a short, stout woman; her sixty years and 170 pounds have left her somewhat breathless most of the time; she's always tensed like a boxer, or rather, a Japanese wrestler. Her "family" was maybe a little superior to BIG DADDY's, but not much. She wears a black or silver lace dress and at least half a million in flashy gems. She is very sincere.]

BIG MAMA (*loudly, startling* MARGARET):
Here—I come through Gooper's and Mae's gall'ry
door. Where's Brick? *Brick*—Hurry on out of
there, son, I just have a second and want to give
you the news about Big Daddy.—I hate locked   545
doors in a house . . . .

MARGARET (*with affected lightness*): I've noticed
you do, Big Mama, but people have got to have
some moments of privacy, don't they?

BIG MAMA: No, ma'am, not in *my* house. (*without   550
pause*) Whacha took off you' dress faw? I thought
that little lace dress was so sweet on yuh, honey.

MARGARET: I thought it looked sweet on me, too,
but one of m' cute little table-partners used it for
a napkin so—!   555

BIG MAMA (*picking up stockings on floor*): What?

MARGARET: You know, Big Mama, Mae and
Gooper's so touchy about those children—thanks,
Big Mama . . .

[BIG MAMA has thrust the picked-up stockings in MARGARET's hand with a grunt.]

—that you just don't dare to suggest there's any   560
room for improvement in their—

BIG MAMA: Brick, hurry out!—Shoot, Maggie, you
just don't like children.

MARGARET: I do so like children! Adore them!—
well brought up!   565

BIG MAMA (*gentle—loving*): Well, why don't you
have some and bring them up well, then, instead
of all the time pickin' on Gooper's an' Mae's?

GOOPER (*shouting up the stairs*): Hey, hey, Big

Mama, Betsy an' Hugh got to go, waitin' t' tell yuh g'by! 570

BIG MAMA: Tell 'em to hold their hawses, I'll be right down in a jiffy!

GOOPER: Yes ma'am!

[She turns to the bathroom door and calls out.]

BIG MAMA: Son? Can you hear me in there? 575

[There is a muffled answer.]

We just got the full report from the laboratory at the Ochsner Clinic, completely negative, son, ev'rything negative, right on down the line![10] Nothin' a-tall's wrong with him but some little functional thing called a spastic colon. Can you 580 hear me, son?

MARGARET: He can hear you, Big Mama.

BIG MAMA: Then why don't he say something? God Almighty, a piece of news like that should make him shout. It made *me* shout, I can tell you. 585 I shouted and sobbed and fell right down on my knees!—Look!

[She pulls up her skirt.]

See the bruises where I hit my kneecaps? Took both doctors to haul me back on my feet!

[She laughs—she always laughs like hell at herself.]

Big Daddy was furious with me! But ain't that 590 wonderful news?

[Facing bathroom again, she continues:]

After all the anxiety we been through to git a report like that on Big Daddy's birthday? Big Daddy tried to hide how much of a load that news took off his mind, but didn't fool *me*. He was mighty close to 595 crying about it *himself!*

[Goodbyes are shouted downstairs, and she rushes to door.]

GOOPER: Big Mama!

BIG MAMA: *Hold those people down there, don't let them go!*—Now, git dressed, we're all comin' up to

this room fo' Big Daddy's birthday party because 600 of your ankle.—How's his ankle, Maggie?

MARGARET: Well, he broke it, Big Mama.

BIG MAMA: I know he broke it.

[A phone is ringing in hall. A Negro voice answers: "Mistuh Polly's res'dence."]

I mean does it hurt him much still.

MARGARET: I'm afraid I can't give you that 605 information, Big Mama. You'll have to ask Brick if it hurts much still or not.

SOOKEY (*in the hall*): It's Memphis, Mizz Polly, it's Miss Sally in Memphis.

BIG MAMA: Awright, Sookey. 610

[BIG MAMA rushes into the hall and is heard shouting on the phone:]

Hello, Miss Sally. How are you, Miss Sally?—Yes, well, I was just gonna call you about it. *Shoot!*—

MARGARET: Brick, don't!

[BIG MAMA raises her voice to a bellow.]

BIG MAMA: *Miss Sally? Don't ever call me from the Gayoso Lobby, too much talk goes on in that hotel lobby,* 615 *no wonder you can't hear me!* Now listen, Miss Sally. They's nothin' serious wrong with Big Daddy. We got the report just now, they's nothin' wrong but a thing called a—spastic! *SPASTIC!*—colon . . .

[She appears at the hall door and calls to MARGARET.]

—Maggie, come out here and talk to that fool on 620 the phone. I'm shouted breathless!

MARGARET (*goes out and is heard sweetly at phone*): Miss Sally? This is Brick's wife, Maggie. So nice to hear your voice. Can you hear *mine?* Well, *good!*—Big Mama just wanted you to know that 625 they've got the report from the Ochsner Clinic and what Big Daddy has is a spastic colon. Yes. Spastic colon, Miss Sally. That's right, spastic colon. *G'bye, Miss Sally, hope I'll see you real soon!*

[Hangs up a little before MISS SALLY was probably ready to terminate the talk. She returns through the hall door.]

She heard me perfectly. I've discovered with deaf 630 people the thing to do is not shout at them but

---

[10] Ochsner Clinic] a highly respected physician-owned clinic based in Louisiana.

just enunciate clearly. My rich old Aunt Cornelia
was deaf as the dead but I could make her hear
me just by sayin' each word slowly, distinctly, close
to her ear. I read her the *Commercial Appeal* ev'ry   635
night, read her the classified ads in it, even, she
never missed a word of it.[11] But was she a mean
ole thing! Know what I got when she died? Her
unexpired subscriptions to five magazines and the
Book-of-the-Month Club and a LIBRARY full of   640
ev'ry dull book ever written! All else went to her
hellcat of a sister . . . meaner than she was, even!

[*BIG MAMA has been straightening things up in the
room during this speech.*]

BIG MAMA (*closing closet door on discarded clothes*):
Miss Sally sure is a case! Big Daddy says she's always
got her hand out fo' something. He's not mistaken.   645
That poor ole thing always has her hand out fo'
somethin'. I don't think Big Daddy gives her as
much as he should.
GOOPER: Big Mama! Come on now! Betsy and
Hugh can't wait no longer!   650
BIG MAMA (*shouting*): I'm comin'!

[*She starts out. At the hall door, turns and jerks a
forefinger, first toward the bathroom door, then toward
the liquor cabinet, meaning: "Has Brick been
drinking?" MARGARET pretends not to understand,
cocks her head and raises her brows as if the
pantomimic performance was completely mystifying to
her. BIG MAMA rushes back to MARGARET:*]

Shoot! Stop playin' so dumb!—I mean has he been
drinkin' that stuff much yet?
MARGARET (*with a little laugh*): Oh! I think he had
a highball after supper.   655
BIG MAMA: Don't laugh about it!—Some single
men stop drinkin' when they git married and
others start! Brick never touched liquor before
he—!
MARGARET (*crying out*): THAT'S NOT FAIR!   660
BIG MAMA: Fair or not fair I want to ask you a
question, one question: D'you make Brick happy
in bed?

MARGARET: Why don't you ask if he makes *me*
happy in bed?   665
BIG MAMA: Because I know that—
MARGARET: *It works both ways!*
BIG MAMA: Something's not right! You're childless
and my son drinks!
GOOPER: Come on, Big Mama!   670

[*GOOPER has called her downstairs and she has
rushed to the door on the line above. She turns at the
door and points at the bed.*]

—When a marriage goes on the rocks, the rocks
are *there*, right *there*!
MARGARET: *That's*—

[*BIG MAMA has swept out of the room and slammed
the door.*]

—not—*fair* . . .

[*MARGARET is alone, completely alone, and she feels
it. She draws in, hunches her shoulders, raises her arms
with fists clenched, shuts her eyes tight as a child about
to be stabbed with a vaccination needle. When she
opens her eyes again, what she sees is the long oval
mirror and she rushes straight to it, stares into it with a
grimace and says: "Who are you?"—Then she crouches
a little and answers herself in a different voice which is
high, thin, mocking: "I am Maggie the Cat!"—
Straightens quickly as bathroom door opens a little and
BRICK calls out to her.*]

BRICK: Has Big Mama gone?   675
MARGARET: She's gone.

[*He opens the bathroom door and hobbles out, with his
liquor glass now empty, straight to the liquor cabinet.
He is whistling softly. MARGARET's head pivots on
her long, slender throat to watch him. She raises a hand
uncertainly to the base of her throat, as if it was
difficult for her to swallow, before she speaks:*]

You know, our sex life didn't just peter out in the
usual way, it was cut off short, long before the
natural time for it to, and it's going to revive again,
just as sudden as that. I'm confident of it. That's   680
what I'm keeping myself attractive for. For the time
when you'll see me again like other men see me.
Yes, like other men see me. They still see me, Brick,

---

11 *Commercial Appeal*] a major Memphis daily newspaper.

and they like what they see. Uh-huh. Some of them would give their—Look, Brick! 685

[She stands before the long oval mirror, touches her breast and then her hips with her two hands.]

How high my body stays on me!—Nothing has fallen on me—not a fraction . . . .

[Her voice is soft and trembling: a pleading child's. At this moment as he turns to glance at her—a look which is like a player passing a ball to another player, third down and goal to go—she has to capture the audience in a grip so tight that she can hold it till the first intermission without any lapse of attention.]

Other men still want me. My face looks strained, sometimes, but I've kept my figure as well as you've kept yours, and men admire it. I still turn heads 690 on the street. Why, last week in Memphis everywhere that I went men's eyes burned holes in my clothes, at the country club and in restaurants and department stores, there wasn't a man I met or walked by that didn't just eat me up with his 695 eyes and turn around when I passed him and look back at me. Why, at Alice's party for her New York cousins, the best-lookin' man in the crowd— followed me upstairs and tried to force his way in the powder room with me, followed me to the 700 door and tried to force his way in!

BRICK: Why didn't you let him, Maggie?

MARGARET: Because I'm not that common, for one thing. Not that I wasn't almost tempted to. You like to know who it was? It was Sonny Boy 705 Maxwell, that's who!

BRICK: Oh, yeah, Sonny Boy Maxwell, he was a good end-runner but had a little injury to his back and had to quit.

MARGARET: He has no injury now and has no wife 710 and still has a lech for me!

BRICK: I see no reason to lock him out of a powder room in that case.

MARGARET: And have someone catch me at it? I'm not that stupid. Oh, I might sometime cheat on 715 you with someone, since you're so insultingly eager to have me do it!—But if I do, you can be damned sure it will be in a place and a time where no one but me and the man could possibly know. Because

I'm not going to give you any excuse to divorce 720 me for being unfaithful or anything else . . . .

BRICK: Maggie, I wouldn't divorce you for being unfaithful or anything else. Don't you know that? Hell. I'd be relieved to know that you'd found yourself a lover. 725

MARGARET: Well, I'm taking no chances. No, I'd rather stay on this hot tin roof.

BRICK: A hot tin roof's 'n uncomfo'table place t' stay on . . . .

[He starts to whistle softly.]

MARGARET (*through his whistle*): Yeah, but I can 730 stay on it just as long as I have to.

BRICK: You could leave me, Maggie.

[He resumes his whistle. She wheels about to glare at him.]

MARGARET: *Don't want to and will not!* Besides if I did, you don't have a cent to pay for it but what you get from Big Daddy and he's dying of cancer! 735

[For the first time a realization of BIG DADDY's doom seems to penetrate to BRICK's consciousness, visibly, and he looks at MARGARET.]

BRICK: Big Mama just said he *wasn't*, that the report was okay.

MARGARET: That's what she thinks because she got the same story that they gave Big Daddy. And was just as taken in by it as he was, poor ole things 740
    But tonight they're going to tell her the truth about it. When Big Daddy goes to bed, they're going to tell her that he is dying of cancer.

[She slams the dresser drawer.]

—It's malignant and it's terminal.

BRICK: Does Big Daddy know it? 745

MARGARET: Hell, do they *ever* know it? Nobody says, "You're dying." You have to fool them. They have to fool *themselves*.

BRICK: Why?

MARGARET: *Why?* Because human beings dream of 750 life everlasting, that's the reason! But most of them want it on earth and not in heaven.

[He gives a short, hard laugh at her touch of humour.]

Well . . . . (*She touches up her mascara.*) That's how

it is, anyhow . . . . (*She looks about.*) Where did I put down my cigarette? Don't want to burn up the home-place, at least not with Mae and Gooper and their five monsters in it! 755

[*She has found it and sucks at it greedily. Blows out smoke and continues:*]

So this is Big Daddy's last birthday. And Mae and Gooper, they know it, oh, *they* know it, all right. They got the first information from the Ochsner Clinic. That's why they rushed down here with their no-neck monsters. Because. Do you know something? Big Daddy's made no will? Big Daddy's never made out any will in his life, and so this campaign's afoot to impress him, forcibly as possible, with the fact that you drink and I've borne no children! 760 765

[*He continues to stare at her a moment, then mutters something sharp but not audible and hobbles rather rapidly out onto the long gallery in the fading, much faded, gold light.*]

MARGARET (*continuing her liturgical chant*): Y'know, I'm *fond* of Big Daddy, I am genuinely fond of that old man, I really *am*, you know 770
BRICK (*faintly, vaguely*): Yes, I know you are . . . .
MARGARET: I've always sort of admired him in spite of his coarseness, his four-letter words and so forth. Because Big Daddy *is* what he *is*, and he makes no bones about it. He hasn't turned gentleman farmer, he's still a Mississippi redneck, as much of a redneck as he must have been when he was just overseer here on the old Jack Straw and Peter Ochello place. But he got hold of it an' built it into th' biggest an' finest plantation in the Delta.—I've always *liked* Big Daddy 775 780

[*She crosses to the proscenium.*]

Well, this is Big Daddy's last birthday. I'm sorry about it. But I'm facing the facts. It takes money to take care of a drinker and that's the office that I've been elected to lately. 785
BRICK: You don't have to take care of me.
MARGARET: Yes, I do. Two people in the same boat have got to take care of each other. At least you want money to buy more Echo Spring when this

supply is exhausted, or will you be satisfied with a ten-cent beer?[12] 790

Mae an' Gooper are plannin' to freeze us out of Big Daddy's estate because you drink and I'm childless. But we can defeat that plan. We're *going* to defeat that plan! 795

Brick, y'know, I've been so God damn disgustingly poor all my life!—That's the *truth*, Brick!
BRICK: I'm not sayin' it isn't.
MARGARET: Always had to suck up to people I couldn't stand because they had money and I was poor as Job's turkey. You don't know what that's like. Well, I'll tell you, it's like you would feel a thousand miles away from Echo Spring!—And had to get back to it on that broken ankle . . . without a crutch! 800 805

That's how it feels to be as poor as Job's turkey and have to suck up to relatives that you hated because they had money and all you had was a bunch of hand-me-down clothes and a few old moldy three-per-cent government bonds.[13] My daddy loved his liquor, he fell in love with his liquor the way you've fallen in love with Echo Spring!—And my poor Mama, having to maintain some semblance of social position, to keep appearances up, on an income of one hundred and fifty dollars a month on those old government bonds! 810 815

When I came out, the year that I made my debut, I had just two evening dresses! One Mother made me from a pattern in *Vogue*, the other a hand-me-down from a snotty rich cousin I hated! 820

—The dress that I married you in was my grandmother's weddin' gown . . . .

So that's why I'm like a cat on a hot tin roof!

[*BRICK is still on the gallery. Someone below calls up to him in a warm Negro voice, "Hiya, Mistuh Brick, how yuh feelin?" BRICK raises his liquor glass as if that answered the question.*]

MARGARET: You can be young without money, but you can't be old without it. You've got to be old *with* money because to be old without it is just too 825

---

12 Echo Spring] a Kentucky bourbon whiskey.
13 as poor as Job's turkey] an old expression referring to the biblical Job, whose name is a byword for misfortune.

awful, you've got to be one or the other, either *young* or *with money*, you can't be old and *without* it.—That's the *truth*, Brick . . . .

[BRICK whistles softly, vaguely.]

Well, now I'm dressed, I'm all dressed, there's   830
nothing else for me to do.

[Forlornly, almost fearfully.]

I'm dressed, all dressed, nothing else for me to
do . . . .

*[She moves about restlessly, aimlessly, and speaks, as if
to herself.]*

What am I—? Oh!—my bracelets . . . .

*[She starts working a collection of bracelets over her
hands onto her wrists, about six on each, as she talks.]*

I've thought a whole lot about it and now I know   835
when I made my mistake. Yes, I made my mistake
when I told you the truth about that thing with
Skipper. Never should have confessed it, a fatal
error, tellin' you about that thing with Skipper.
BRICK: Maggie, shut up about Skipper. I mean it,   840
Maggie; you got to shut up about Skipper.
MARGARET: You ought to understand that Skipper
and I—
BRICK: You don't think I'm serious, Maggie? You're
fooled by the fact that I am saying this quiet? Look,   845
Maggie. What you're doing is a dangerous thing
to do. You're—you're—you're—foolin' with
something that—nobody ought to fool with.
MARGARET: This time I'm going to finish what I
have to say to you. Skipper and I made love, if love   850
you could call it, because it made both of us feel a
little bit closer to you. You see, you son of a bitch,
you asked too much of people, of me, of him, of all
the unlucky poor damned sons of bitches that happen to love you, and there was a whole pack of them,   855
yes, there was a pack of them besides me and Skipper, you asked too goddam much of people that
loved you, you—superior creature!—you godlike
being!—And so we made love to each other to
dream it was you, both of us! Yes, yes, yes! Truth,   860
truth! What's so awful about it? I like it, I think the
truth is—yeah! I shouldn't have told you . . . .

BRICK (*holding his head unnaturally still and uptilted
a bit*): It was Skipper that told me about it. Not
you, Maggie.   865
MARGARET: I told you!
BRICK: After he told me!
MARGARET: What does it matter who—?
DIXIE: I got your mallet, I got your mallet.
TRIXIE: Give it to me, give it to me. It's mine.   870

[BRICK turns suddenly out upon the gallery and calls:]

BRICK: Little girl! Hey, little girl!
LITTLE GIRL (*at a distance*): What, Uncle Brick?
BRICK: Tell the folks to come up!—Bring everybody
upstairs!
TRIXIE: It's mine, it's mine.   875
MARGARET: I can't stop myself! I'd go on telling
you this in front of them all, if I had to!
BRICK: Little girl! Go on, go on, will you? Do what
I told you, call them!
DIXIE: Okay.   880
MARGARET: Because it's got to be told and you,
you!—you never let me!

*[She sobs, then controls herself, and continues almost
calmly.]*

It was one of those beautiful, ideal things they tell
about in the Greek legends, it couldn't be anything
else, you being you, and that's what made it so sad,   885
that's what made it so awful, because it was love
that never could be carried through to anything
satisfying or even talked about plainly.
BRICK: Maggie, you gotta stop this.
MARGARET: Brick, I tell you, you got to believe   890
me, Brick, I *do* understand all about it! I—I think
it was—*noble!* Can't you tell I'm sincere when I say
I respect it? My only point, the only point that I'm
making, is life has got to be allowed to continue
even after the *dream* of life is—all—over   895

*[BRICK is without his crutch. Leaning on furniture,
he crosses to pick it up as she continues as if possessed by
a will outside herself:]*

Why, I remember when we double-dated at
college, Gladys Fitzgerald and I and you and
Skipper, it was more like a date between you and
Skipper. Gladys and I were just sort of tagging

along as if it was necessary to chaperone you!—to make a good public impression— 900

BRICK (*turns to face her, half lifting his crutch*): Maggie, you want me to hit you with this crutch? Don't you know I could kill you with this crutch?

MARGARET: Good Lord, man, d'you think I'd care 905 if you did?

BRICK: One man has one great good true thing in his life. One great good thing which is true!—I had friendship with Skipper.—You are naming it dirty!

MARGARET: I'm not naming it dirty! I am naming 910 it clean.

BRICK: Not love with you, Maggie, but friendship with Skipper was that one great true thing, and you are naming it dirty!

MARGARET: Then you haven't been listenin', not 915 understood what I'm saying! I'm naming it so damn clean that it killed poor Skipper!—You two had something that had to be kept on ice, yes, incorruptible, yes!—and death was the only icebox where you could keep it 920

BRICK: I married you, Maggie. Why would I marry you, Maggie, if I was—?

MARGARET: Brick, let me finish!—I know, believe me I know, that it was only Skipper that harboured even any *unconscious* desire for anything not 925 perfectly pure between you two!—Now let me skip a little. You married me early that summer we graduated out of Ole Miss, and we were happy, weren't we, we were blissful, yes, hit heaven together ev'ry time that we loved! But that fall you 930 an' Skipper turned down wonderful offers of jobs in order to keep on bein' football heroes—pro-football heroes. You organized the Dixie Stars that fall, so you could keep on bein' teammates forever! But somethin' was not right with it!—*Me* 935 *included!*—between you. Skipper began hittin' the bottle . . . you got a spinal injury—couldn't play the Thanksgivin' game in Chicago, watched it on TV from a traction bed in Toledo. I joined Skipper. The Dixie Stars lost because poor Skipper 940 was drunk. We drank together that night all night in the bar of the Blackstone and when cold day was comin' up over the Lake an' we were comin' out drunk to take a dizzy look at it, I said, "SKIPPER! STOP LOVIN' MY HUSBAND OR 945

TELL HIM HE'S GOT TO LET YOU ADMIT IT TO HIM!"—one way or another!

HE SLAPPED ME HARD ON THE MOUTH! —then turned and ran without stopping once, I am sure, all the way back into his room at the 950 Blackstone . . . .

—When I came to his room that night, with a little scratch like a shy little mouse at his door, he made that pitiful, ineffectual little attempt to prove that what I had said wasn't true 955

[BRICK *strikes at her with crutch, a blow that shatters the gem-like lamp on the table.*]

—In this way, I destroyed him, by telling him truth that he and his world which he was born and raised in, yours and his world, had told him could not be told?

—From then on Skipper was nothing at all but 960 a receptacle for liquor and drugs . . . .

—*Who shot cock robin? I with my*—

[*She throws back her head with tight shut eyes.*]

—*merciful arrow!*[14]

[BRICK *strikes at her; misses.*]

Missed me!—Sorry,—I'm not tryin' to whitewash my behaviour, Christ, no! Brick, I'm not good. I 965 don't know why people have to pretend to be good, nobody's good. The rich or the well-to-do can afford to respect moral patterns, conventional moral patterns, but I could never afford to, yeah, but—I'm honest! Give me credit for just that, will 970 you *please*?—Born poor, raised poor, expect to die poor unless I manage to get us something out of what Big Daddy leaves when he dies of cancer! But Brick?!—*Skipper is dead! I'm alive!* Maggie the cat is— 975

[BRICK *hops awkwardly forward and strikes at her again with his crutch.*]

---

14 Who shot . . . arrow] allusion to the nursery rhyme, which begins: "Who shot [or: did kill] Cock Robin? / I, said the sparrow / with my bow and arrow / I shot Cock Robin. / Who saw him die / I, said the fly / with my lit-tle eye..." etc.

—alive! I am alive, alive! I am . . .

[He hurls the crutch at her, across the bed she took refuge behind, and pitches forward on the floor as she completes her speech.]

—alive!

[A little girl, DIXIE, bursts into the room, wearing an Indian war bonnet and firing a cap pistol at MARGARET and shouting: "Bang, bang, bang!" Laughter downstairs floats through the open hall door. MARGARET had crouched gasping to bed at child's entrance. She now rises and says with cool fury:]

Little girl, your mother or someone should teach you—(*gasping*)—to knock at a door before you come into a room. Otherwise people might think that you—lack—good breeding   980
DIXIE: Yanh, yanh, yanh, what is Uncle Brick doin' on th' floor?
BRICK: I tried to kill your Aunt Maggie, but I failed—and I fell. Little girl, give me my crutch so I can get up off th' floor.   985
MARGARET: Yes, give your uncle his crutch, he's a cripple, honey, he broke his ankle last night jumping hurdles on the high school athletic field!
DIXIE: What were you jumping hurdles for, Uncle Brick?   990
BRICK: Because I used to jump them, and people like to do what they used to do, even after they've stopped being able to do it . . . .
MARGARET: That's right, that's your answer, now go away, little girl.   995

[DIXIE fires cap pistol at MARGARET three times.]

Stop, you stop that, monster! You little no-neck monster!

[She seizes the cap pistol and hurls it through gallery doors.]

DIXIE (*with a precocious instinct for the cruelest thing*): You're *jealous*!—You're just jealous because you can't have babies!   1000

[She sticks out her tongue at MARGARET as she sashays past her with her stomach stuck out, to the gallery. MARGARET slams the gallery doors and leans panting against them. There is a pause. BRICK has replaced his spilt drink and sits, faraway, on the great four-poster bed.]

MARGARET: You see?—they gloat over us being childless, even in front of their five little no-neck monsters!

[Pause. Voices approach on the stairs.]

Brick?—I've been to a doctor in Memphis, a—a   1005
gynecologist . . . .
    I've been completely examined, and there is no reason why we can't have a child whenever we want one. And this is my time by the calendar to conceive. Are you listening to me? Are you? Are   1010
you LISTENING TO ME!
BRICK: Yes. I hear you, Maggie.

[His attention returns to her inflamed face.]

—But how in hell on earth do you imagine—that you're going to have a child by a man that can't stand you?   1015
MARGARET: That's a problem that I will have to work out.

[She wheels about to face the hall door.]

MAE (*off stage left*): Come on, Big Daddy. We're all goin' up to Brick's room.

[From off stage left, voices: REVEREND TOOKER, DOCTOR BAUGH, MAE.]

MARGARET: *Here they come!*   1020

[The lights dim.]

CURTAIN

ACT II

There is no lapse of time. MARGARET and BRICK are in the same positions they held at the end of Act I.

MARGARET (*at door*): *Here they come!*

[BIG DADDY appears first, a tall man with a fierce, anxious look, moving carefully not to betray his weakness even, or especially, to himself.]

GOOPER: I read in the *Register* that you're getting a new memorial window.

[*Some of the people are approaching through the hall, others along the gallery: voices from both directions. GOOPER and REVEREND TOOKER become visible outside gallery doors, and their voices come in clearly. They pause outside as GOOPER lights a cigar.*]

REVEREND TOOKER (*vivaciously*): Oh, but St. Paul's in Grenada has three memorial windows, and the latest one is a Tiffany stained-glass window that cost twenty-five hundred dollars, a picture of Christ the Good Shepherd with a Lamb in His arms.

MARGARET: Big Daddy.

BIG DADDY: Well, Brick.

BRICK: Hello Big Daddy.—Congratulations!

BIG DADDY: —Crap . . . .

GOOPER: Who give that window, Preach?

REVEREND TOOKER: Clyde Fletcher's widow. Also presented St. Paul's with a baptismal font.

GOOPER: Y'know what somebody ought t' give your church is a *coolin'* system, Preach.

REVEREND TOOKER: Yes, siree, Bob! And y'know what Gus Hamma's family gave in his memory to the church at Two Rivers? A complete new stone parish-house with a basketball court in the basement and a—

BIG DADDY (*uttering a loud barking laugh which is far from truly mirthful*): Hey, Preach! What's all this talk about memorials, Preach? Y' think somebody's about t' kick off around here? 'S that it?

[*Startled by this interjection, REVEREND TOOKER decides to laugh at the question almost as loud as he can. How he would answer the question we'll never know, as he's spared that embarrassment by the voice of GOOPER's wife, MAE, rising high and clear as she appears with "DOC" BAUGH, the family doctor, through the hall door.*]

MAE (*almost religiously*): —Let's see now, they've had their tyyy-phoid shots, and their tetanus shots, their diphtheria shots and their hepatitis shots and their polio shots, they got *those* shots every month from May through September, and—Gooper? Hey! Gooper!—What all have the kiddies been shot faw?

MARGARET (*overlapping a bit*): Turn on the hi-fi, Brick! Let's have some music t' start off th' party with!

BRICK: You turn it on, Maggie.

[*The talk becomes so general that the room sounds like a great aviary of chattering birds. Only BRICK remains unengaged, leaning upon the liquor cabinet with his faraway smile, an ice cube in a paper napkin with which he now and then rubs his forehead. He doesn't respond to MARGARET's command. She bounds forward and stoops over the instrument panel of the console.*]

GOOPER: We gave 'em that thing for a third anniversary present, got three speakers in it.

[*The room is suddenly blasted by the climax of a Wagnerian opera or a Beethoven symphony.*]

BIG DADDY: *Turn that dam thing off!*

[*Almost instant silence, almost instantly broken by the shouting charge of BIG MAMA, entering through hall door like a charging rhino.*]

BIG MAMA: *Wha's my Brick, wha's mah precious baby!!*

BIG DADDY: *Sorry! Turn it back on!*

[*Everyone laughs very loud. BIG DADDY is famous for his jokes at BIG MAMA's expense, and nobody laughs louder at these jokes than BIG MAMA herself, though sometimes they're pretty cruel and BIG MAMA has to pick up or fuss with something to cover the hurt that the loud laugh doesn't quite cover. On this occasion, a happy occasion because the dread in her heart has also been lifted by the false report on BIG DADDY's condition, she giggles, grotesquely, coyly, in BIG DADDY's direction and bears down upon BRICK, all very quick and alive.*]

BIG MAMA: Here he is, here's my precious baby! What's that you've got in your hand? You put that liquor down, son, your hand was made fo' holdin' somethin' better than that!

GOOPER: Look at Brick put it down!

[*BRICK has obeyed BIG MAMA by draining the glass and handing it to her. Again everyone laughs, some high, some low.*]

BIG MAMA: Oh, you bad boy, you, you're my bad little boy. Give Big Mama a kiss, you bad boy, you!—Look at him shy away, will you? Brick never liked bein' kissed or made a fuss over, I guess because he's always had too much of it!

Son, you turn that thing off!

[BRICK has switched on the TV set.]

I can't stand TV, radio was bad enough but TV has gone it one better, I mean—(*plops wheezing in chair*) —one worse, ha, ha! Now what'm I sittin' down here faw? I want t' sit next to my sweetheart on the sofa, hold hands with him and love him up a little!

[BIG MAMA has on a black and white figured chiffon. The large irregular patterns, like the markings of some massive animal, the luster of her great diamonds and many pearls, the brilliants set in the silver frames of her glasses, her riotous voice, booming laugh, have dominated the room since she entered. BIG DADDY has been regarding her with a steady grimace of chronic annoyance.]

BIG MAMA (*still louder*): Preacher, Preacher, hey, Preach! Give me you' hand an' help me up from this chair!

REVEREND TOOKER: None of your tricks, Big Mama!

BIG MAMA: What tricks? You give me you' hand so I can get up an'—

[REVEREND TOOKER extends her his hand. She grabs it and pulls him into her lap with a shrill laugh that spans an octave in two notes.]

Ever seen a preacher in a fat lady's lap? Hey, hey, folks! Ever seen a preacher in a fat lady's lap?

[BIG MAMA is notorious throughout the Delta for this sort of inelegant horseplay. MARGARET looks on with indulgent humour, sipping Dubonnet "on the rocks" and watching BRICK, but MAE and GOOPER exchange signs of humourless anxiety over these antics, the sort of behavior which MAE thinks may account for their failure to quite get in with the smartest young married set in Memphis, despite all.[15]

---

[15] *Dubonnet*] a French wine-based aperitif.

One of the Negroes, LACY or SOOKEY, peeks in, cackling. They are waiting for a sign to bring in the cake and champagne. But BIG DADDY's not amused. He doesn't understand why, in spite of the infinite mental relief he's received from the doctor's report, he still has these same old fox teeth in his guts. "This spastic condition is something else," he says to himself, but aloud he roars at BIG MAMA:]

BIG DADDY: *BIG MAMA, WILL YOU QUIT HORSIN'?*—You're too old an' too fat fo' that sort of crazy kid stuff an' besides a woman with your blood pressure—she had two hundred last spring!—is riskin' a stroke when you mess around like that . . . .

[MAE blows on a pitch pipe.]

BIG MAMA: *Here comes Big Daddy's birthday!*

[Negroes in white jackets enter with an enormous birthday cake ablaze with candles and carrying buckets of champagne with satin ribbons about the bottle necks. MAE and GOOPER strike up song, and everybody, including the NEGROES and CHILDREN, joins in. Only BRICK remains aloof.]

EVERYONE:
Happy birthday to you.
Happy birthday to you.
Happy birthday, Big Daddy—

[Some sing: "Dear, Big Daddy!"]

Happy birthday to you.

[Some sing: "How old are you?"]

MAE has come down center and is organizing her children like a chorus. She gives them a barely audible: "One, two, three!" and they are off in the new tune.]

CHILDREN:
Skinamarinka—dinka—dink
Skinamarinka—do
We love you.
Skinamarinka—dinka—dink
Skinamarinka—do.

[All together, they turn to BIG DADDY.]

Big Daddy, you!

[*They turn back front, like a musical comedy chorus.*]

We love you in the morning;
We love you in the night.
We love you when we're with you,   90
And we love you out of sight.
Skinamarinka—dinka—dink
Skinamarinka—do.

[*MAE turns to BIG MAMA.*]

Big Mama, too!

[*BIG MAMA bursts into tears. The NEGROES leave.*]

BIG DADDY: Now Ida, what the hell is the matter   95
with you?
MAE: She's just so happy.
BIG MAMA: I'm just so happy, Big Daddy, I have
to cry or something.

[*Sudden and loud in the hush:*]

Brick, do you know the wonderful news that Doc   100
Baugh got from the clinic about Big Daddy? Big
Daddy's one hundred per cent!
MARGARET: Isn't that wonderful?
BIG MAMA: He's just one hundred per cent. Passed
the examination with flying colors. Now that we   105
know there's nothing wrong with Big Daddy but
a spastic colon, I can tell you something. I was
worried sick, half out of my mind, for fear that
Big Daddy might have a thing like—

[*MARGARET cuts through this speech, jumping up
and exclaiming shrilly:*]

MARGARET: Brick, honey, aren't you going to give   110
Big Daddy his birthday present?

[*Passing by him, she snatches his liquor glass from him.
She picks up a fancily wrapped package.*]

Here it is, Big Daddy, this is from Brick!
BIG MAMA: This is the biggest birthday Big
Daddy's ever had, a hundred presents and bushels
of telegrams from—   115
MAE (*at the same time*): What is it, Brick?
GOOPER: I bet 500 to 50 that Brick don't *know*
what it is.
BIG MAMA: The fun of presents is not knowing

what they are till you open the package. Open your   120
present, Big Daddy.
BIG DADDY: Open it you'self. I want to ask Brick
somethin! Come here, Brick.
MARGARET: Big Daddy's callin' you, Brick.

[*She is opening the package.*]

BRICK: Tell Big Daddy I'm crippled.   125
BIG DADDY: I see you're crippled. I want to know
how you got crippled.
MARGARET (*making diversionary tactics*): Oh, look,
oh, look, why, it's a cashmere robe!

[*She holds the robe up for all to see.*]

MAE: You sound surprised, Maggie.   130
MARGARET: I never saw one before.
MAE: That's funny.—*Hah!*
MARGARET (*turning on her fiercely, with a brilliant
smile*): Why is it funny? All my family ever had was
family—and luxuries such as cashmere robes still   135
surprise me!
BIG DADDY (*ominously*): Quiet!
MAE (*heedless in her fury*): I don't see how you could
be so surprised when you bought it yourself at
Loewenstein's in Memphis last Saturday. You know   140
how I know?
BIG DADDY: I said, Quiet!
MAE: —I know because the salesgirl that sold it to
you waited on me and said, Oh, Mrs. Pollitt, your
sister-in-law just bought a cashmere robe for your   145
husband's father!
MARGARET: Sister Woman! Your talents are wasted
as a housewife and mother, you really ought to be
with the FBI or—
BIG DADDY: QUIET!   150

[*REVEREND TOOKER's reflexes are slower than the
others'. He finishes a sentence after the bellow.*]

REVEREND TOOKER (*to DOC BAUGH*): —the
Stork and the Reaper are running neck and neck!

[*He starts to laugh gaily when he notices the silence
and BIG DADDY's glare. His laugh dies falsely.*]

BIG DADDY: Preacher, I hope I'm not butting in
on more talk about memorial stained-glass
windows, am I, Preacher?   155

[*REVEREND TOOKER laughs feebly, then coughs dryly in the embarrassed silence.*]

Preacher?

BIG MAMA: Now, Big Daddy, don't you pick on Preacher!

BIG DADDY (*raising his voice*): You ever hear that expression all hawk and no spit? You bring that expression to mind with that little dry cough of yours, all hawk an' no spit 160

[*The pause is broken only by a short startled laugh from MARGARET, the only one there who is conscious of and amused by the grotesque.*]

MAE (*raising her arms and jangling her bracelets*): I wonder if the mosquitoes are active tonight?

BIG DADDY: What's that, Little Mama? Did you make some remark? 165

MAE: Yes, I said I wondered if the mosquitoes would eat us alive if we went out on the gallery for a while.

BIG DADDY: Well, if they do, I'll have your bones pulverized for fertilizer! 170

BIG MAMA (*quickly*): Last week we had an airplane spraying the place and I think it done some good, at least I haven't had a —

BIG DADDY (*cutting her speech*): Brick, they tell me, 175 if what they tell me is true, that you done some jumping last night on the high school athletic field?

BIG MAMA: Brick, Big Daddy is talking to you, son. 180

BRICK (*smiling vaguely over his drink*): What was that, Big Daddy?

BIG DADDY: They said you done some jumping on the high school track field last night.

BRICK: That's what they told me, too. 185

BIG DADDY: Was it jumping or humping that you were doing out there? What were you doing out there at three A.M., layin' a woman on that cinder track?

BIG MAMA: Big Daddy, you are off the sick-list, 190 now, and I'm not going to excuse you for talkin' so—

BIG DADDY: Quiet!

BIG MAMA: —*nasty* in front of Preacher and—

BIG DADDY: *QUIET!*—I ast you, Brick, if you was 195 cuttin' you'self a piece o' poon-tang last night on that cinder track? I thought maybe you were chasin' poon-tang on that track an' tripped over something in the heat of the chase—'sthat it?

[*GOOPER laughs, loud and false, others nervously following suit. BIG MAMA stamps her foot, and purses her lips, crossing to MAE and whispering something to her as BRICK meets his father's hard, intent, grinning stare with a slow, vague smile that he offers all situations from behind the screen of his liquor.*]

BRICK: No, sir, I don't think so 200

MAE (*at the same time, sweetly*): Reverend Tooker, let's you and I take a stroll on the widow's walk.

[*She and the preacher go out on the gallery as BIG DADDY says:*]

BIG DADDY: Then what the hell were you doing out there at three o'clock in the morning?

BRICK: Jumping the hurdles, Big Daddy, runnin' 205 and jumpin' the hurdles, but those high hurdles have gotten too high for me, now.

BIG DADDY: Cause you was drunk?

BRICK (*his vague smile fading a little*): Sober I wouldn't have tried to jump the *low* ones 210

BIG MAMA (*quickly*): Big Daddy, blow out the candles on your birthday cake!

MARGARET (*at the same time*): I want to propose a toast to Big Daddy Pollitt on his sixty-fifth birthday, the biggest cotton planter in— 215

BIG DADDY (*bellowing with fury and disgust*): *I told you to stop it, now stop it, quit this—!*

BIG MAMA (*coming in front of BIG DADDY with the cake*): Big Daddy, I will not allow you to talk that way, not even on your birthday, I— 220

BIG DADDY: I'll talk like I want to on my birthday, Ida, or any other goddam day of the year and anybody here that don't like it knows what they can do!

BIG MAMA: You don't mean that! 225

BIG DADDY: What makes you think I don't mean it?

[*Meanwhile various discreet signals have been exchanged and GOOPER has also gone out on the gallery.*]

BIG MAMA: I just know you don't mean it.

BIG DADDY: You don't know a goddam thing and you never did! 230

BIG MAMA: Big Daddy, you don't mean that.

BIG DADDY: Oh, yes, I do, oh, yes, I do, I mean it! I put up with a whole lot of crap around here because I thought I was dying. And you thought I was dying and you started taking over, well, you 235 can stop taking over now, Ida, because I'm not gonna die, you can just stop now this business of taking over because you're not taking over because I'm not dying, I went through the laboratory and the goddam exploratory operation and there's 240 nothing wrong with me but a spastic colon. And I'm not dying of cancer which you thought I was dying of. Ain't that so? Didn't you think that I was dying of cancer, Ida?

[Almost everybody is out on the gallery but the two old people glaring at each other across the blazing cake. BIG MAMA's chest heaves and she presses a fat fist to her mouth. BIG DADDY continues, hoarsely:]

Ain't that so, Ida? Didn't you have an idea I was 245 dying of cancer and now you could take control of this place and everything on it? I got that impression, I seemed to get that impression. Your loud voice everywhere, your fat old body butting in here and there! 250

BIG MAMA: Hush! The Preacher!

BIG DADDY: Fuck the goddam preacher!

[BIG MAMA gasps loudly and sits down on the sofa which is almost too small for her.]

Did you hear what I said? I said fuck the goddam preacher!

[Somebody closes the gallery doors from outside just as there is a burst of fireworks and excited cries from the children.]

BIG MAMA: I never seen you act like this before 255 and I can't think what's got in you!

BIG DADDY: I went through all that laboratory and operation and all just so I would know if you or me was the boss here! Well, now it turns out that I am and you ain't—and that's my birthday 260 present—and my cake and champagne!—because

for three years now you been gradually taking over. Bossing. Talking. Sashaying your fat old body around the place I made! I made this place! I was overseer on it! I was the overseer on the old Straw 265 and Ochello plantation. I quit school at ten! I quit school at ten years old and went to work like a nigger in the fields. And I rose to be overseer of the Straw and Ochello plantation. And old Straw died and I was Ochello's partner and the place got 270 bigger and bigger and bigger and bigger and bigger! I did all that myself with no goddam help from you, and now you think you're just about to take over. Well, I am just about to tell you that you are not just about to take over, you are not 275 just about to take over a God damn thing. Is that clear to you, Ida? Is that very plain to you, now? Is that understood completely? I been through the laboratory from A to Z. I've had the goddam exploratory operation, and nothing is wrong with 280 me but a spastic colon—made spastic, I guess, by *disgust!* By all the goddam lies and liars that I have had to put up with, and all the goddam hypocrisy that I lived with all these forty years that we been livin' together! 285

Hey! Ida!! Blow out the candles on the birthday cake! Purse up your lips and draw a deep breath and blow out the goddam candles on the cake!

BIG MAMA: Oh, Big Daddy, oh, oh, oh, Big Daddy! 290

BIG DADDY: What's the matter with you?

BIG MAMA: *In all these years you never believed that I loved you??*

BIG DADDY: Huh?

BIG MAMA: *And I did, I did so much, I did love* 295 *you!*—I even loved your hate and your hardness, Big Daddy!

[She sobs and rushes awkwardly out onto the gallery.]

BIG DADDY (*to himself*): *Wouldn't it be funny if that was true . . . .*

[A pause is followed by a burst of light in the sky from the fireworks.]

BRICK! HEY, BRICK! 300

[He stands over his blazing birthday cake. After some moments, BRICK hobbles in on his crutch, holding his

glass. MARGARET follows him with a bright, anxious smile.]

I didn't call you, Maggie. I called Brick.
MARGARET: I'm just delivering him to you.

[She kisses BRICK on the mouth which he immediately wipes with the back of his hand. She flies girlishly back out. BRICK and his father are alone.]

BIG DADDY: Why did you do that?
BRICK: Do what, Big Daddy?
BIG DADDY: Wipe her kiss off your mouth like she'd spit on you. 305
BRICK: I don't know. I wasn't conscious of it.
BIG DADDY: That woman of yours has a better shape on her than Gooper's but somehow or other they got the same look about them. 310
BRICK: What sort of look is that, Big Daddy?
BIG DADDY: I don't know how to describe it but it's the same look.
BRICK: They don't look peaceful, do they?
BIG DADDY: No, they sure in hell don't. 315
BRICK: They look nervous as cats?
BIG DADDY: That's right, they look nervous as cats.
BRICK: Nervous as a couple of cats on a hot tin roof?
BIG DADDY: That's right, boy, they look like a couple of cats on a hot tin roof. It's funny that you and Gooper being so different would pick out the same type of woman. 320
BRICK: Both of us married into society, Big Daddy.
BIG DADDY: Crap . . . I wonder what gives them both that look? 325
BRICK: Well. They're sittin' in the middle of a big piece of land, Big Daddy, twenty-eight thousand acres is a pretty big piece of land and so they're squaring off on it, each determined to knock off a bigger piece of it than the other whenever you let it go. 330
BIG DADDY: I got a surprise for those women. I'm not gonna let it go for a long time yet if that's what they're waiting for.
BRICK: That's right, Big Daddy. You just sit tight and let them scratch each other's eyes out 335
BIG DADDY: You bet your life I'm going to sit tight on it and let those sons of bitches scratch their eyes out, ha ha ha . . . .

But Gooper's wife's a good breeder, you got to admit she's fertile. Hell, at supper tonight she had them all at the table and they had to put a couple of extra leafs in the table to make room for them, she's got five head of them, now, and another one's comin'. 340 345
BRICK: Yep, number six is comin' . . . .
BIG DADDY: Six hell, she'll probably drop a litter next time. Brick, you know, I swear to God, I don't know the way it happens?
BRICK: The way what happens, Big Daddy? 350
BIG DADDY: You git you a piece of land, by hook or crook, an' things start growin' on it, things accumulate on it, and the first thing you know it's completely out of hand, completely out of hand!
BRICK: Well, they say nature hates a vacuum, Big Daddy. 355
BIG DADDY: That's what they say, but sometimes I think that a vacuum is a hell of a lot better than some of the stuff that nature replaces it with.
    Is someone out there by that door? 360
GOOPER: Hey Mae.
BRICK: Yep.
BIG DADDY: Who?

[He has lowered his voice.]

BRICK: Someone int'rested in what we say to each other. 365
BIG DADDY: Gooper?—*GOOPER!*

[After a discreet pause, MAE appears in the gallery door.]

MAE: Did you call Gooper, Big Daddy?
BIG DADDY: Aw, it was you.
MAE: Do you want Gooper, Big Daddy?
BIG DADDY: No, and I don't want you. I want some privacy here, while I'm having a confidential talk with my son Brick. Now it's too hot in here to close them doors, but if I have to close those fuckin' doors in order to have a private talk with my son Brick, just let me know and I'll close 'em. Because I hate eavesdroppers, I don't like any kind of sneakin' an' spyin'. 370 375
MAE: Why, Big Daddy—
BIG DADDY: You stood on the wrong side of the moon, it threw your shadow! 380
MAE: I was just—

BIG DADDY: You was just nothing but *spyin'* an' you *know* it!

MAE (*begins to sniff and sob*): Oh, Big Daddy, you're so unkind for some reason to those that really love you! 385

BIG DADDY: Shut up, shut up, shut up! I'm going to move you and Gooper out of that room next to this! It's none of your goddam business what goes on in here at night between Brick an' Maggie. 390 You listen at night like a couple of rutten peekhole spies and go and give a report on what you hear to Big Mama an' she comes to me and says they say such and such and so and so about what they heard goin' on between Brick an' Maggie, and 395 Jesus, it makes me sick. I'm goin' to move you an' Gooper out of that room, I can't stand sneakin' an' spyin', it makes me puke . . . .

[*MAE throws back her head and rolls her eyes heavenward and extends her arms as if invoking God's pity for this unjust martyrdom; then she presses a handkerchief to her nose and flies from the room with a loud swish of skirts.*]

BRICK (*now at the liquor cabinet*): They listen, do they? 400

BIG DADDY: Yeah. They listen and give reports to Big Mama on what goes on in here between you and Maggie. They say that—

[*He stops as if embarrassed.*]

—You won't sleep with her, that you sleep on the sofa. Is that true or not true? If you don't like 405 Maggie, get rid of Maggie!—What are you doin' there now?

BRICK: Fresh'nin' up my drink.

BIG DADDY: Son, you know you got a real liquor problem? 410

BRICK: Yes, sir, yes, I know.

BIG DADDY: Is that why you quit sports-announcing, because of this liquor problem?

BRICK: Yes, sir, yes, sir, I guess so.

[*He smiles vaguely and amiably at his father across his replenished drink.*]

BIG DADDY: Son, don't guess about it, it's too 415 important.

BRICK (*vaguely*): Yes, sir.

BIG DADDY: And listen to me, don't look at the damn chandelier . . . .

[*Pause. BIG DADDY's voice is husky.*]

—Somethin' else we picked up at th' big fire sale 420 in Europe.

[*Another pause.*]

Life is important. There's nothing else to hold onto. A man that drinks is throwing his life away. Don't do it, hold onto your life. There's nothing else to hold onto 425
    Sit down over here so we don't have to raise our voices, the walls have ears in this place.

BRICK (*hobbling over to sit on the sofa beside him*): All right, Big Daddy.

BIG DADDY: Quit!—how'd that come about? Some 430 disappointment?

BRICK: I don't know. Do you?

BIG DADDY: I'm askin' you, God damn it! How in hell would I know if you don't?

BRICK: I just got out there and found that I had a 435 mouth full of cotton. I was always two or three beats behind what was goin' on on the field and so I—

BIG DADDY: Quit!

BRICK (*amiably*): Yes, quit.

BIG DADDY: Son? 440

BRICK: Huh?

BIG DADDY (*inhales loudly and deeply from his cigar; then bends suddenly a little forward, exhaling loudly and raising his forehead*): —Whew!—ha ha!—I took in too much smoke, it made me a little 445 lightheaded . . . .

[*The mantel clock chimes.*]

Why is it so damn hard for people to talk?

BRICK: Yeah . . . .

[*The clock goes on sweetly chiming till it has completed the stroke of ten.*]

—Nice peaceful-soundin' clock, I like to hear it all night 450

[*He slides low and comfortable on the sofa; BIG DADDY sits up straight and rigid with some unspoken anxiety. All his gestures are tense and jerky as he talks. He wheezes and pants and sniffs through his nervous speech, glancing quickly, shyly, from time to time, at his son.]*

BIG DADDY: We got that clock the summer we wint to Europe, me an' Big Mama on that damn Cook's Tour, never had such an awful time in my life, I'm tellin' you, son, those gooks over there, they gouge your eyeballs out in their grand hotels. And Big Mama bought more stuff than you could haul in a couple of boxcars, that's no crap. Everywhere she wint on this whirlwind tour, she bought, bought, bought. Why, half that stuff she bought is still crated up in the cellar, under water last spring!

That Europe is nothin' on earth but a great big auction, that's all it is, that bunch of old wornout places, it's just a big fire sale, the whole fuckin' thing, an' Big Mama wint wild in it, why, you couldn't hold that woman with a mule's harness! Bought, bought, bought!—lucky I'm a rich man, yes siree, Bob, an' half that stuff is mildewin' in th' basement. It's lucky I'm a rich man, it sure is lucky, well, I'm a rich man, Brick, yep, I'm a mighty rich man.

[His eyes light up for a moment.]

Y'know how much I'm worth? Guess, Brick! Guess how much I'm worth!

[BRICK smiles vaguely over his drink.]

Close on ten million in cash an' blue-chip stocks, outside, mind you, of twenty-eight thousand acres of the richest land this side of the valley Nile.

But a man can't buy his life with it, he can't buy back his life with it when his life has been spent, that's one thing not offered in the Europe fire-sale or in the American markets or any markets on earth, a man can't buy his life with it, he can't buy back his life when his life is finished . . . .

That's a sobering thought, a very sobering thought, and that's a thought that I was turning over in my head, over and over and over—until today . . . .

I'm wiser and sadder, Brick, for this experience which I just gone through. They's one thing else that I remember in Europe.

BRICK: What is that, Big Daddy?

BIG DADDY: The hills around Barcelona in the country of Spain and the children running over those bare hills in their bare skins beggin' like starvin' dogs with howls and screeches, and how fat the priests are on the streets of Barcelona, so many of them and so fat and so pleasant, ha ha!— Y'know I could feed that country? I got money enough to feed that goddam country, but the human animal is a selfish beast and I don't reckon the money I passed out there to those howling children in the hills around Barcelona would more than upholster the chairs in this room, I mean pay to put a new cover on this chair!

Hell, I threw them money like you'd scatter feed corn for chickens, I threw money at them just to get rid of them long enough to climb back into th' car and—drive away . . . .

And then in Morocco, them Arabs, why, I remember one day in Marrakech, that old walled Arab city, I set on a broken-down wall to have a cigar, it was fearful hot there and this Arab woman stood in the road and looked at me till I was embarrassed, she stood stock still in the dusty hot road and looked at me till I was embarrassed. But listen to this. She had a naked child with her, a little naked girl with her, barely able to toddle, and after a while she set this child on the ground and give her a push and whispered something to her.

The child come toward me, barely able t' walk, come toddling up to me and—

Jesus, it makes you sick t' remember a thing like this!

It stuck out its hand and tried to unbutton my trousers!

That child was not yet five! Can you believe me? Or do you think that I am making this up? I wint back to the hotel and said to Big Mama, Git packed! We're clearing out of this country . . . .

BRICK: Big Daddy, you're on a talkin' jag tonight.

BIG DADDY (*ignoring this remark*): Yes, sir, that's how it is, the human animal is a beast that dies but the fact that he's dying don't give him pity for others, no, sir, it—

—Did you say something?

BRICK: Yes.   535

BIG DADDY: What?

BRICK: Hand me over that crutch so I can get up.

BIG DADDY: Where you goin'?

BRICK: I'm takin' a little short trip to Echo Spring.

BIG DADDY: To where?   540

BRICK: Liquor cabinet . . . .

BIG DADDY: Yes, sir, boy—

[He hands BRICK the crutch.]

—the human animal is a beast that dies and if he's
got money he buys and buys and buys and I think
the reason he buys everything he can buy is that   545
in the back of his mind he has the crazy hope that
one of his purchases will be life everlasting!—
Which it never can be . . . . The human animal is
a beast that—

BRICK (*at the liquor cabinet*): Big Daddy, you sure   550
are shootin' th' breeze here tonight.

[There is a pause and voices are heard outside.]

BIG DADDY: I been quiet here lately, spoke not a
word, just sat and stared into space. I had
something heavy weighing on my mind but
tonight that load was took off me. That's why I'm   555
talking.—The sky looks diff'rent to me . . . .

BRICK: You know what I like to hear most?

BIG DADDY: What?

BRICK: Solid quiet. Perfect unbroken quiet.

BIG DADDY: Why?   560

BRICK: Because it's more peaceful.

BIG DADDY: Man, you'll hear a lot of that in the
grave.

[He chuckles agreeably.]

BRICK: Are you through talkin' to me?

BIG DADDY: Why are you so anxious to shut me up?   565

BRICK: Well, sir, ever so often you say to me, Brick,
I want to have a talk with you, but when we talk,
it never materializes. Nothing is said. You sit in a
chair and gas about this and that and I look like I
listen. I try to look like I listen, but I don't listen,   570
not much. Communication is—awful hard
between people an'—somehow between you and
me, it just don't—happen.

BIG DADDY: Have you ever been scared? I mean
have you ever felt downright terror of something?   575

[He gets up.]

Just one moment.

*[He looks off as if he were going to tell an important
secret.]*

BIG DADDY: Brick?

BRICK: What?

BIG DADDY: Son, I thought I had it!

BRICK: Had what? Had what, Big Daddy?   580

BIG DADDY: Cancer!

BRICK: Oh . . .

BIG DADDY: I thought the old man made out of
bones had laid his cold and heavy hand on my
shoulder!   585

BRICK: Well, Big Daddy, you kept a tight mouth
about it.

BIG DADDY: A pig squeals. A man keeps a tight
mouth about it, in spite of a man not having a pig's
advantage.   590

BRICK: What advantage is that?

BIG DADDY: Ignorance—of mortality—is a
comfort. A man don't have that comfort, he's the
only living thing that conceives of death, that
knows what it is. The others go without knowing   595
which is the way that anything living should go,
go without knowing, without any knowledge of it,
and yet a pig squeals, but a man sometimes, he can
keep a tight mouth about it. Sometimes he—

[There is a deep, smoldering ferocity in the old man.]

—can keep a tight mouth about it. I wonder if—   600

BRICK: What, Big Daddy?

BIG DADDY: A whiskey highball would injure this
spastic condition?

BRICK: No, sir, it might do it good.

BIG DADDY (*grins suddenly, wolfishly*): Jesus, I can't   605
*tell you! The sky is open! Christ, it's open again! It's
open, boy, it's open!*

[BRICK looks down at his drink.]

BRICK: You feel better, Big Daddy?

BIG DADDY: Better? Hell! I can breathe!—All of
my life I been like a doubled up fist   610

[He pours a drink.]

—Poundin', smashin', drivin'!—now I'm going to loosen these doubled-up hands and touch things *easy* with them . . . .

[He spreads his hands as if caressing the air.]

You know what I'm contemplating?

BRICK (*vaguely*): No, sir. What are you contemplating? 615

BIG DADDY: Ha ha!—*Pleasure!*—pleasure with women!

[BRICK's smile fades a little but lingers.]

—Yes, boy. I'll tell you something that you might not guess. I still have desire for women and this is 620 my sixty-fifth birthday.

BRICK: I think that's mighty remarkable, Big Daddy.

BIG DADDY: Remarkable?

BRICK: *Admirable*, Big Daddy.

BIG DADDY: You're damn right it is, remarkable 625 and admirable both. I realize now that I never had me enough. I let many chances slip by because of scruples about it, scruples, convention—crap . . . . All that stuff is bull, bull, bull!—It took the shadow of death to make me see it. Now that 630 shadow's lifted, I'm going to cut loose and have, what is it they call it, have me a—ball!

BRICK: A ball, huh?

BIG DADDY: That's right, a ball, a ball! Hell!—I slept with Big Mama till, let's see, five years ago, 635 till I was sixty and she was fifty-eight, and never even liked her, never did!

[The phone has been ringing down the hall. BIG MAMA enters, exclaiming:]

BIG MAMA: Don't you men hear that phone ring? I heard it way out on the gall'ry.

BIG DADDY: There's five rooms off this front gall'ry 640 that you could go through. Why do you go through this one?

[BIG MAMA makes a playful face as she bustles out the hall door.]

Hunh!—Why, when Big Mama goes out of a room, I can't remember what that woman looks like—

645

BIG MAMA: Hello.

BIG DADDY: —But when Big Mama comes back into the room, boy, then I see what she looks like, and I wish I didn't!

[Bends over laughing at this joke till it hurts his guts and he straightens with a grimace. The laugh subsides to a chuckle as he puts the liquor glass a little distrustfully down the table.]

BIG MAMA: Hello, Miss Sally. 650

[BRICK has risen and hobbled to the gallery doors.]

BIG DADDY: Hey! Where you goin'?

BRICK: Out for a breather.

BIG DADDY: Not yet you ain't. Stay here till this talk is finished, young fellow.

BRICK: I thought it was finished, Big Daddy. 655

BIG DADDY: It ain't even begun.

BRICK: My mistake. Excuse me. I just wanted to feel that river breeze.

BIG DADDY: Set back down in that chair.

[BIG MAMA's voice rises, carrying down the hall.]

BIG MAMA: Miss Sally, you're a case! You're a 660 caution, Miss Sally.

BIG DADDY: Jesus, she's talking to my old maid sister again.

BIG MAMA: Why didn't you give me a chance to explain it to you? 665

BIG DADDY: Brick, this stuff burns me.

BIG MAMA: Well, goodbye, now, Miss Sally. You come down real soon. Big Daddy's dying to see you.

BIG DADDY: Crap!

BIG MAMA: Yaiss, goodbye, Miss Sally 670

[She hangs up and bellows with mirth. BIG DADDY groans and covers his ears as she approaches. Bursting in:]

Big Daddy, that was Miss Sally callin' from Memphis again! You know what she done, Big Daddy? She called her doctor in Memphis to git him to tell her what that spastic thing is! Ha-HAAAA!—! And called back to tell me how 675 relieved she was that—Hey! Let me in!

[BIG DADDY has been holding the door half closed against her.]

BIG DADDY: Naw I ain't. I told you not to come and go through this room. You just back out and go through those five other rooms.

BIG MAMA: Big Daddy? Big Daddy? Oh, Big Daddy!—You didn't mean those things you said to me, did you? 680

[He shuts door firmly against her but she still calls.]

Sweetheart? Sweetheart? Big Daddy? You didn't mean those awful things you said to me?—I know you didn't. I know you didn't mean those things 685 in your heart . . . .

[The childlike voice fades with a sob and her heavy footsteps retreat down the hall. BRICK has risen once more on his crutches and starts for the gallery again.]

BIG DADDY: All I ask of that woman is that she leave me alone. But she can't admit to herself that she makes me sick. That comes of having slept with her too many years. Should of quit much sooner but 690 that old woman she never got enough of it—and I was good in bed . . . I never should of wasted so much of it on her . . . . They say you got just so many and each one is numbered. Well, I got a few left in me, a few, and I'm going to pick me a good 695 one to spend 'em on! I'm going to pick me a choice one, I don't care how much she costs, I'll smother her in—minks! Ha ha! I'll strip her naked and smother her in minks and choke her with diamonds! Ha ha! I'll strip her naked and choke her with dia- 700 monds and smother her with minks and hump her from hell to breakfast. *Ha aha ha ha ha!*

MAE (*gaily at door*): Who's that laughin' in there?

GOOPER: Is Big Daddy laughin' in there?

BIG DADDY: Crap!—them two—*drips* 705

[He goes over and touches BRICK's shoulder.]

Yes, son, Brick, boy.—I'm—*happy!* I'm happy, son, I'm happy!

[He chokes a little and bites his under lip, pressing his head quickly, shyly against his son's head and then, coughing with embarrassment, goes uncertainly back to the table where he set down the glass. He drinks and makes a grimace as it burns his guts. BRICK sighs and rises with effort.]

What makes you so restless? Have you got ants in your britches?

BRICK: Yes, sir . . . 710

BIG DADDY: Why?

BRICK: —Something—hasn't—happened . . . .

BIG DADDY: Yeah? What is that!

BRICK (*sadly*): —the click . . . .

BIG DADDY: Did you say click? 715

BRICK: Yes, click.

BIG DADDY: What click?

BRICK: A click that I get in my head that makes me peaceful.

BIG DADDY: I sure in hell don't know what you're 720 talking about, but it disturbs me.

BRICK: It's just a mechanical thing.

BIG DADDY: What is a mechanical thing?

BRICK: This click that I get in my head that makes me peaceful. I got to drink till I get it. It's just a me- 725 chanical thing, something like a—like a—like a—

BIG DADDY: Like a—

BRICK: Switch clicking off in my head, turning the hot light off and the cool night on and—

[He looks up, smiling sadly.]

—all of a sudden there's—peace! 730

BIG DADDY (*whistles long and soft with astonishment; he goes back to Brick and clasps his son's two shoulders*): Jesus! I didn't know it had gotten that bad with you. Why, boy, you're—*alcoholic!*

BRICK: That's the truth, Big Daddy. I'm alcoholic. 735

BIG DADDY: This shows how I—let things go!

BRICK: I have to hear that little click in my head that makes me peaceful. Usually I hear it sooner than this, sometimes as early as—noon, but—
      —Today it's—dilatory 740
      —I just haven't got the right level of alcohol in my bloodstream yet!

[This last statement is made with energy as he freshens his drink.]

BIG DADDY: Uh—huh. Expecting death made me blind. I didn't have no idea that a son of mine was turning into a drunkard under my nose. 745

BRICK (*gently*): Well, now you do, Big Daddy, the news has penetrated.

BIG DADDY: UH-huh, yes, now I do, the news has—penetrated . . . .

BRICK: And so if you'll excuse me— 750

BIG DADDY: No, I won't excuse you.

BRICK: —I'd better sit by myself till I hear that click in my head, it's just a mechanical thing but it don't happen except when I'm alone or talking to no one . . . .

BIG DADDY: You got a long, long time to sit still, 755 boy, and talk to no one, but now you're talkin' to me. At least I'm talking to you. And you set there and listen until I tell you the conversation is over!

BRICK: But this talk is like all the others we've ever had together in our lives! It's nowhere, nowhere!— 760 it's—it's *painful*, Big Daddy . . . .

BIG DADDY: All right, then let it be painful, but don't you move from that chair!—I'm going to remove that crutch . . . .

[He seizes the crutch and tosses it across the room.]

BRICK: I can hop on one foot, and if I fall, I can 765 crawl!

BIG DADDY: If you ain't careful you're gonna crawl off this plantation and then, by Jesus, you'll have to hustle your drinks along Skid Row!

BRICK: That'll come, Big Daddy. 770

BIG DADDY: Naw, it won't. You're my son and I'm going to straighten you out; now that *I'm* straightened out, I'm going to straighten out you!

BRICK: Yeah?

BIG DADDY: Today the report came in from 775 Ochsner Clinic. Y'know what they told me?

[His face glows with triumph.]

The only thing that they could detect with all the instruments of science in that great hospital is a little spastic condition of the colon! And nerves torn to pieces by all that worry about it. 780

[A little girl bursts into room with a sparkler clutched in each fist, hops and shrieks like a monkey gone mad and rushes back out again as BIG DADDY strikes at her. Silence. The two men stare at each other. A woman laughs gaily outside.]

I want you to know I breathed a sigh of relief almost as powerful as the Vicksburg tornado![16]

---

16 Vicksburg tornado] One of the worst tornados in Mississippi history, it struck in 1953.

[There is laughter outside, running footsteps, the soft, plushy sound and light of exploding rockets. BRICK stares at him soberly for a long moment; then makes a sort of startled sound in his nostrils and springs up on one foot and hops across the room to grab his crutch, swinging on the furniture for support. He gets the crutch and flees as if in horror for the gallery. His father seizes him by the sleeve of his white silk pajamas.]

Stay here, you son of a bitch!—till I say go!

BRICK: I can't.

BIG DADDY: You sure in hell will, God damn it. 785

BRICK: No, I can't. We talk, you talk, in—circles! We get no where, no where! It's always the same, you say you want to talk to me and don't have a fuckin' thing to say to me!

BIG DADDY: Nothin' to say when I'm tellin' you 790 I'm going to live when I thought I was dying?!

BRICK: Oh—*that!*—Is that what you have to say to me?

BIG DADDY: Why, you son of a bitch! Ain't that, ain't that—*important?!* 795

BRICK: Well, you said, that, that's said, and now I—

BIG DADDY: Now you set back down.

BRICK: You're all balled up, you—

BIG DADDY: I ain't balled up!

BRICK: You are, you're all balled up! 800

BIG DADDY: Don't tell me what I am, you drunken whelp! I'm going to tear this coat sleeve off if you don't set down!

BRICK: Big Daddy—

BIG DADDY: Do what I tell you! I'm the boss here, 805 now! I want you to know I'm back in the driver's seat now!

[BIG MAMA rushes in, clutching her great heaving bosom.]

BIG MAMA: Big Daddy!

BIG DADDY: What in hell do you want in here, Big Mama?

BIG MAMA: Oh, Big Daddy! Why are you shouting 810 like that? I just cain't stainnnnnnnd—it . . . .

BIG DADDY (raising the back of his hand above his head): GIT!—outa here.

[She rushes back out, sobbing.]

BRICK (*softly, sadly*): Christ   815
BIG DADDY (*fiercely*): Yeah! Christ!—is right . . .

[*BRICK breaks loose and hobbles toward the gallery.
BIG DADDY jerks his crutch from under BRICK so
he steps with the injured ankle. He utters a hissing cry
of anguish, clutches a chair and pulls it over on top of
him on the floor.*]

Son of a—tub of—hog fat . . . .
BRICK: Big Daddy! Give me my crutch.

[*BIG DADDY throws the crutch out of reach.*]

Give me that crutch, Big Daddy.
BIG DADDY: Why do you drink?   820
BRICK: Don't know, give me my crutch!
BIG DADDY: You better think why you drink or
give up drinking!
BRICK: Will you please give me my crutch so I can
get up off this floor?   825
BIG DADDY: First you answer my question. Why
do you drink? Why are you throwing your life
away, boy, like somethin' disgusting you picked up
on the street?
BRICK (*getting onto his knees*): Big Daddy, I'm in   830
pain, I stepped on that foot.
BIG DADDY: Good! I'm glad you're not too numb
with the liquor in you to feel some pain!
BRICK: You—spilled my—drink . . .
BIG DADDY: I'll make a bargain with you. You tell   835
me why you drink and I'll hand you one. I'll pour
you the liquor myself and hand it to you.
BRICK: Why do I drink?
BIG DADDY: Yea! Why?
BRICK: Give me a drink and I'll tell you.   840
BIG DADDY: Tell me first!
BRICK: I'll tell you in one word.
BIG DADDY: What word?
BRICK: DISGUST!

[*The clock chimes softly, sweetly. BIG DADDY gives it
a short, outraged glance.*]

Now how about that drink?   845
BIG DADDY: What are you disgusted with? You got
to tell me that, first. Otherwise being disgusted
don't make no sense!
BRICK: Give me my crutch.

BIG DADDY: You heard me, you got to tell me what   850
I asked you first.
BRICK: I told you, I said to kill my disgust.
BIG DADDY: DISGUST WITH WHAT!
BRICK: You strike a hard bargain.
BIG DADDY: What are you disgusted with?—an'   855
I'll pass you the liquor.
BRICK: I can hop on one foot, and if I fall, I can
crawl.
BIG DADDY: You want liquor that bad?
BRICK (*dragging himself up, clinging to bedstead*):   860
Yeah, I want it that bad.
BIG DADDY: If I give you a drink, will you tell me
what it is you're disgusted with, Brick?
BRICK: Yes, sir, I will try to.

[*The old man pours him a drink and solemnly passes it
to him. There is silence as BRICK drinks.*]

Have you ever heard the word "mendacity"?   865
BIG DADDY: Sure. Mendacity is one of them five
dollar words that cheap politicians throw back and
forth at each other.
BRICK: You know what it means?
BIG DADDY: Don't it mean lying and liars?   870
BRICK: Yes, sir, lying and liars.
BIG DADDY: Has someone been lying to you?
CHILDREN (*chanting in chorus offstage*):
We want Big Dad-dee!
We want Big Dad-dee!   875

[*GOOPER appears in the gallery door.*]

GOOPER: Big Daddy, the kiddies are shouting for
you out there.
BIG DADDY (*fiercely*): Keep out, Gooper!
GOOPER: 'Scuse *me*!

[*BIG DADDY slams the doors after GOOPER.*]

BIG DADDY: Who's been lying to you, has   880
Margaret been lying to you, has your wife been
lying to you about something, Brick?
BRICK: Not her. That wouldn't matter.
BIG DADDY: Then who's been lying to you, and
what about?   885
BRICK: No one single person, and no one lie . . . .
BIG DADDY: Then what, what then, for Christ's
sake?

BRICK: —The whole, the whole—thing . . . .

BIG DADDY: Why are you rubbing your head? You got a headache? 890

BRICK: No, I'm tryin' to—

BIG DADDY: —Concentrate, but you can't because your brain's all soaked with liquor, is that the trouble? Wet brain! 895

[He snatches the glass from BRICK's hand.]

What do you know about this mendacity thing? Hell! I could write a book on it! Don't you know that? I could write a book on it and still not cover the subject? Well, I could, I could write a goddam book on it and still not cover the subject 900 anywhere near enough!!—Think of all the lies I got to put up with!—Pretenses! Ain't that mendacity? Having to pretend stuff you don't think or feel or have any idea of? Having for instance to act like I care for Big Mama!—I 905 haven't been able to stand the sight, sound, or smell of that woman for forty years now!—even when I *laid* her!—regular as a piston . . . .

Pretend to love that son of a bitch of a Gooper and his wife Mae and those five same screechers 910 out there like parrots in a jungle? Jesus! Can't stand to look at 'em!

Church!—it bores the bejesus out of me but I go!—I go an' sit there and listen to the fool preacher! Clubs!—Elks! Masons! Rotary!—*crap!* 915

[A spasm of pain makes him clutch his belly. He sinks into a chair and his voice is softer and hoarser.]

You I *do* like for some reason, did always have some kind of real feeling for—affection—respect— yes, always . . . .

You and being a success as a planter is all I ever had any devotion to in my whole life!—and that's 920 the truth . . . .

I don't know why, but it is!

I've lived with mendacity!—Why can't *you* live with it? Hell, you *got* to live with it, there's nothing *else* to *live* with except mendacity, is there? 925

BRICK: Yes, sir. Yes, sir there is something else that you can live with!

BIG DADDY: What?

BRICK (*lifting his glass*): This!—Liquor . . . .

BIG DADDY: That's not living, that's dodging away from life. 930

BRICK: I want to dodge away from it.

BIG DADDY: Then why don't you kill yourself, man?

BRICK: I like to drink 935

BIG DADDY: Oh, God, I can't talk to you . . . .

BRICK: I'm sorry, Big Daddy.

BIG DADDY: Not as sorry as I am. I'll tell you something. A little while back when I thought my number was up— 940

[This speech should have torrential pace and fury.]

—before I found out it was just this—spastic—colon. I thought about you. Should I or should I not, if the jig was up, give you this place when I go— since I hate Gooper an' Mae an' know that they hate me, and since all five same monkeys are little Maes 945 an' Goopers.—And I thought, No!—Then I thought, Yes!—I couldn't make up my mind. I hate Gooper and his five same monkeys and that bitch Mae! Why should I turn over twenty-eight thousand acres of the richest land this side of the valley Nile to 950 not my kind?—But why in hell, on the other hand, Brick—should I subsidize a goddam fool on the bottle?—Liked or not liked, well, maybe even— *loved!*—Why should I do that?—Subsidize worthless behavior? Rot? Corruption? 955

BRICK (*smiling*): I understand.

BIG DADDY: Well, if you do, you're smarter than I am, God damn it, because I don't understand. And this I will tell you frankly. I didn't make up my mind at all on that question and still to this 960 day I ain't made out no will!—Well, now I don't *have* to. The pressure is gone. I can just wait and see if you pull yourself together or if you don't.

BRICK: That's right, Big Daddy.

BIG DADDY: You sound like you thought I was 965 kidding.

BRICK (*rising*): No, sir, I know you're not kidding.

BIG DADDY: But you don't care—?

BRICK (*hobbling toward the gallery door*): No, sir, I don't care 970

[He stands in the gallery doorway as the night sky turns pink and green and gold with successive flashes of light.]

BIG DADDY: *WAIT!*—Brick . . . .

[*His voice drops. Suddenly there is something shy, almost tender, in his restraining gesture.*]

Don't let's—leave it like this, like them other talks we've had, we've always—talked around things, we've—just talked around things for some fuckin' reason, I don't know what, it's always like something was left not spoken, something avoided because neither of us was honest enough with the—other 980

BRICK: I never lied to you, Big Daddy.

BIG DADDY: Did I ever to *you?*

BRICK: No, sir . . . .

BIG DADDY: Then there is at least two people that never lied to each other. 985

BRICK: But we've never *talked* to each other.

BIG DADDY: We can *now.*

BRICK: Big Daddy, there don't seem to be anything much to say.

BIG DADDY: You say that you drink to kill your 990 disgust with lying.

BRICK: You said to give you a reason.

BIG DADDY: Is liquor the only thing that'll kill this disgust?

BRICK: Now. Yes. 995

BIG DADDY: But not once, huh?

BRICK: Not when I was still young an' believing. A drinking man's someone who wants to forget he isn't still young an' believing.

BIG DADDY: Believing what? 1000

BRICK: Believing . . . .

BIG DADDY: Believing *what?*

BRICK (*stubbornly evasive*): Believing . . . .

BIG DADDY: I don't know what the hell you mean by believing and I don't think you know what you 1005 mean by believing, but if you still got sports in your blood, go back to sports announcing and—

BRICK: Sit in a glass box watching games I can't play? Describing what I can't do while players do it? Sweating out their disgust and confusion in 1010 contests I'm not fit for? Drinkin' a coke, half bourbon, so I can stand it? That's no goddam good any more, no help—time just outran me, Big Daddy—got there first . . .

BIG DADDY: I think you're passing the buck. 1015

BRICK: You know many drinkin' men?

BIG DADDY (*with a slight, charming smile*): I have known a fair number of that species.

BRICK: Could any of them tell you why he drank?

BIG DADDY: Yep, you're passin' the buck to things 1020 like time and disgust with "mendacity" and—crap!—if you got to use that kind of language about a thing, it's ninety-proof bull, and I'm not buying any.

BRICK: I had to give you a reason to get a drink! 1025

BIG DADDY: You started drinkin' when your friend Skipper died.

[*Silence for five beats. Then BRICK makes a startled movement, reaching for his crutch.*]

BRICK: What are you suggesting?

BIG DADDY: I'm suggesting nothing.

[*The shuffle and clop of BRICK's rapid hobble away from his father's steady, grave attention.*]

—But Gooper an' Mae suggested that there was 1030 something not right exactly in your—

BRICK (*stopping short downstage as if backed to a wall*): "Not right"?

BIG DADDY: Not, well, exactly *normal* in your friendship with— 1035

BRICK: They suggested that, too? I thought that was Maggie's suggestion.

[*BRICK's detachment is at last broken through. His heart is accelerated; his forehead sweat-beaded; his breath becomes more rapid and his voice hoarse. The thing they're discussing, timidly and painfully on the side of BIG DADDY, fiercely, violently on BRICK's side, is the inadmissible thing that SKIPPER died to disavow between them. The fact that if it existed it had to be disavowed to "keep face" in the world they lived in, may be at the heart of the "mendacity" that BRICK drinks to kill his disgust with. It may be the root of his collapse. Or maybe it is only a single manifestation of it, not even the most important. The bird that I hope to catch in the net of this play is not the solution of one man's psychological problem. I'm trying to catch the true quality of experience in a group of people, that cloudy, flickering, evanescent—fiercely charged!—interplay of live human beings in the thundercloud of a common crisis. Some mystery should be left in the revelation of character in a play, just as a great deal of mystery is always left in the revelation of character in life, even in one's own character to himself. This does not absolve the playwright of his duty to observe and probe as clearly and deeply as he legitimately can: but it should steer him away from "pat" conclusions, facile definitions which make a play just a play, not a snare for the truth of human experience. The following scene should be played with great concentration, with most of the power leashed but palpable in what is left unspoken.]*

Who else's suggestion is it, is it *yours?* How many others thought that Skipper and I were—

BIG DADDY (*gently*): Now, hold on, hold on a minute, son.—I knocked around in my time.   1040

BRICK: What's that got to do with—

BIG DADDY: I said "Hold on!"—I bummed, I bummed this country till I was—

BRICK: Whose suggestion, who else's suggestion is it?   1045

BIG DADDY: Slept in hobo jungles and railroad Y's and flophouses in all cities before I—

BRICK: Oh, *you* think so, too, you call me your son and a queer. Oh! Maybe that's why you put Maggie   1050
and me in this room that was Jack Straw's and Peter Ochello's, in which that pair of old sisters slept in a double bed where both of 'em died!

BIG DADDY: *Now just don't go throwing rocks at—*

[Suddenly REVEREND TOOKER appears in the gallery doors, his head slightly, playfully, fatuously cocked, with a practised clergyman's smile, sincere as a bird call blown on a hunter's whistle, the living embodiment of the pious, conventional lie. BIG DADDY gasps a little at this perfectly timed, but incongruous, apparition.]

—What're you lookin' for, Preacher?   1055

REVEREND TOOKER: The gentleman's lavatory, ha ha!—heh, heh . . .

BIG DADDY (*with strained courtesy*): —Go back out and walk down to the other end of the gallery, Reverend Tooker, and use the bathroom connected   1060
with my bedroom, and if you can't find it, ask them where it is!

REVEREND TOOKER: Ah, thanks.

[He goes out with a deprecatory chuckle.]

BIG DADDY: It's hard to talk in this place . . .

BRICK: Son of a—!   1065

BIG DADDY (*leaving a lot unspoken*): —I seen all things and understood a lot of them, till 1910. Christ, the year that—I had worn my shoes through, hocked my—I hopped off a yellow dog freight car half a mile down the road, slept in a   1070
wagon of cotton outside the gin—Jack Straw an' Peter Ochello took me in. Hired me to manage this place which grew into this one.—When Jack Straw died—why, old Peter Ochello quit eatin' like a dog does when its master's dead, and died, too!   1075

BRICK: Christ!

BIG DADDY: I'm just saying I understand such—

BRICK (*violently*): Skipper is dead. I have not quit eating!

BIG DADDY: No, but you started drinking.   1080

[BRICK wheels on his crutch and hurls his glass across the room shouting.]

BRICK: YOU THINK SO, TOO?

[Footsteps run on the gallery. There are women's calls. BIG DADDY goes toward the door. BRICK is transformed, as if a quiet mountain blew suddenly up in volcanic flame.]

BRICK: You think so, too? You think so, too? You think me an' Skipper did, did, did!—*sodomy!*— together?

BIG DADDY: Hold—!   1085

BRICK: That what you—

BIG DADDY: —ON—a minute!

BRICK: You think we did dirty things between us, Skipper an'—

BIG DADDY: Why are you shouting like that? Why   1090
are you—

BRICK: —Me, is that what you think of Skipper, is that—

BIG DADDY: —so excited? I don't think nothing. I don't know nothing. I'm simply telling you   1095
what—

BRICK: You think that Skipper and me were a pair of dirty old men?

BIG DADDY: Now that's—

BRICK: Straw? Ochello? A couple of—   1100

BIG DADDY: Now just—

BRICK: —fucking sissies? Queers? Is that what you—
BIG DADDY: Shhh.
BRICK: —think?   1105

[He loses his balance and pitches to his knees without noticing the pain. He grabs the bed and drags himself up.]

BIG DADDY: Jesus!—Whew . . . . Grab my hand!
BRICK: Naw, I don't want your hand . . . .
BIG DADDY: Well, I want yours. Git up!

[He draws him up, keeps an arm about him with concern and affection.]

You broken out in sweat! You're panting like you'd run a race with—   1110
BRICK (*freeing himself from his father's hold*): Big Daddy, you shock me, Big Daddy, you, you—*shock* me! Talkin' so—

[He turns away from his father.]

—casually!—about a—thing like that . . .
—Don't you know how people *feel* about things   1115
like that? How, how *disgusted* they are by things like that? Why, at Ole Miss when it was discovered a pledge to our fraternity, Skipper's and mine, did a, *attempted* to do a, unnatural thing with—
We not only dropped him like a hot rock!—We   1120
told him to git off the campus, and he did, he got!—All the way to—

[He halts, breathless.]

BIG DADDY: —Where?
BRICK: —North Africa, last I heard!
BIG DADDY: Well, I have come back from further   1125
away than that, I have just now returned from the other side of the moon, death's country, son, and I'm not easy to shock by anything here.

[He comes downstage and faces out.]

Always, anyhow, lived with too much space around me to be infected by ideas of other people. One   1130
thing you can grow on a big place more important than cotton!—is *tolerance!*—I grown it.

[He returns toward BRICK.]

BRICK: Why can't exceptional friendship, *real, real, deep, deep friendship!* between two men be respected as something clean and decent without   1135
being thought of as—
BIG DADDY: It can, it is, for God's sake.
BRICK: —*Fairies* . . . .

[In his utterance of this word, we gauge the wide and profound reach of the conventional mores he got from the world that crowned him with early laurel.]

BIG DADDY: I told Mae an' Gooper—
BRICK: Frig Mae and Gooper, frig all dirty lies and 1140
liars!—Skipper and me had a clean, true thing between us!—had a clean friendship, practically all our lives, till Maggie got the idea you're talking about. Normal? No!—It was too rare to be normal, any true thing between two people is too rare to   1145
be normal. Oh, once in a while he put his hand on my shoulder or I'd put mine on his, oh, maybe even, when we were touring the country in pro-football an' shared hotel-rooms we'd reach across the space between the two beds and shake hands   1150
to say goodnight, yeah, one or two times we—
BIG DADDY: Brick, nobody thinks that's not normal!
BRICK: Well, they're mistaken, it was! It was a pure an' true thing an' that's not normal.   1155
MAE (*off stage*): Big Daddy, they're startin' the fireworks.

[They both stare straight at each other for a long moment. The tension breaks and both turn away as if tired.]

BIG DADDY: Yeah, it's—hard t'—talk . . . .
BRICK: All right, then, let's—let it go . . . .
BIG DADDY: Why did Skipper crack up? Why have   1160
you?

[BRICK looks back at his father again. He has already decided, without knowing that he has made this decision, that he is going to tell his father that he is dying of cancer. Only this could even the score between them: one inadmissible thing in return for another.]

BRICK (*ominously*): All right. You're asking for it, Big Daddy. We're finally going to have that real true talk you wanted. It's too late to stop it, now, we got to carry it through and cover every subject.   1165

[He hobbles back to the liquor cabinet.]

Uh-huh.

[He opens the ice bucket and picks up the silver tongs with slow admiration of their frosty brightness.]

Maggie declares that Skipper and I went into pro-football after we left "Ole Miss" because we were scared to grow up . . .

[He moves downstage with the shuffle and clop of a cripple on a crutch. As MARGARET did when her speech became "recitative," he looks out into the house, commanding its attention by his direct, concentrated gaze—a broken, "tragically elegant" figure telling simply as much as he knows of "the Truth":]

—Wanted to—keep on tossing—those long, long!—high, high!—passes that—couldn't be intercepted except by time, the aerial attack that made us famous! And so we did, we did, we kept it up for one season, that aerial attack, we held it high!—Yeah, but— 1170 1175

—that summer, Maggie, she laid the law down to me, said, Now or never, and so I married Maggie . . . .
BIG DADDY: How was Maggie in bed?
BRICK (*wryly*): Great! the greatest! 1180

[BIG DADDY nods as if he thought so.]

She went on the road that fall with the Dixie Stars. Oh, she made a great show of being the world's best sport. She wore a—wore a—tall bearskin cap! A shako, they call it, a dyed moleskin coat, a moleskin coat dyed red!—Cut up crazy! Rented hotel ballrooms for victory celebrations, wouldn't cancel them when it—turned out—defeat 1185
MAGGIE THE CAT! Ha ha!

[BIG DADDY nods.]

—But Skipper, he had some fever which came back on him which doctors couldn't explain and I got that injury—turned out to be just a shadow on the X-ray plate—and a touch of bursitis 1190

I lay in a hospital bed, watched our games on TV, saw Maggie on the bench next to Skipper when he was hauled out of a game for stumbles, 1195 fumbles!—Burned me up the way she hung on his arm!—Y'know, I think that Maggie had always felt sort of left out because she and me never got any closer together than two people just get in bed, which is not much closer than two cats on a— 1200 fence humping . . . .

So! She took this time to work on poor dumb Skipper. He was a less than average student at Ole Miss, you know that, don't you?!—Poured in his mind the dirty, false idea that what we were, him 1205 and me, was a frustrated case of that ole pair of sisters that lived in this room, Jack Straw and Peter Ochello!—He, poor Skipper, went to bed with Maggie to prove it wasn't true, and when it didn't work out, he thought it *was* true!—Skipper broke 1210 in two like a rotten stick—nobody ever turned so fast to a lush—or died of it so quick . . . .
—Now are you satisfied?

[BIG DADDY has listened to this story, dividing the grain from the chaff. Now he looks at his son.]

BIG DADDY: Are *you* satisfied?
BRICK: With what? 1215
BIG DADDY: That half-ass story!
BRICK: What's half-ass about it?
BIG DADDY: Something's left out of that story. What did you leave out?

[The phone has started ringing in the hall.]

GOOPER (*off stage*): Hello. 1220

[As if it reminded him of something, BRICK glances suddenly toward the sound and says:]

BRICK: Yes!—I left out a long-distance call which I had from Skipper—
GOOPER: Speaking, go ahead.
BRICK: —In which he made a drunken confession to me and on which I hung up! 1225
GOOPER: No.
BRICK: —Last time we spoke to each other in our lives . . .
GOOPER: No, sir.
BIG DADDY: You musta said something to him 1230 before you hung up.
BRICK: What could I say to him?
BIG DADDY: Anything. Something.

BRICK: Nothing.

BIG DADDY: Just hung up?   1235

BRICK: Just hung up.

BIG DADDY: Uh-huh. Anyhow now!—we have tracked down the lie with which you're disgusted and which you are drinking to kill your disgust with, Brick. You been passing the buck. This   1240 disgust with mendacity is disgust with yourself.

    You!—dug the grave of your friend and kicked him in it!—before you'd face truth with him!

BRICK: *His* truth, not *mine!*

BIG DADDY: His truth, okay! But you wouldn't face   1245 it with him!

BRICK: Who *can* face truth? Can *you?*

BIG DADDY: Now don't start passin' the rotten buck again, boy!

BRICK: How about these birthday congratulations,   1250 these many, many happy returns of the day, when ev'rybody knows there won't be any except you!

[*GOOPER, who has answered the hall phone, lets out a high, shrill laugh; the voice becomes audible saying: "No, no, you got it all wrong! Upside down! Are you crazy?"*]

BRICK *suddenly catches his breath as he realized that he has made a shocking disclosure. He hobbles a few paces, then freezes, and without looking at this father's shocked face, says:*]

    Let's, let's—go out, now, and—watch the fireworks. Come on, Big Daddy.

[*BIG DADDY moves suddenly forward and grabs hold of the boy's crutch like it was a weapon for which they were fighting for possession.*]

BIG DADDY: Oh, no, no! No one's going out! What   1255 did you start to say?

BRICK: I don't remember.

BIG DADDY: "Many happy returns when they know there won't be any"?

BRICK: Aw, hell, Big Daddy, forget it. Come on out   1260 on the gallery and look at the fireworks they're shooting off for your birthday . . . .

BIG DADDY: First you finish that remark you were makin' before you cut off. "Many happy returns when they know there won't be any"?—Ain't that   1265 what you just said?

BRICK: Look, now. I can get around without that crutch if I have to but it would be a lot easier on the furniture an' glassware if I didn' have to go swinging along like Tarzan of th'—   1270

BIG DADDY: *FINISH! WHAT YOU WAS SAYIN'!*

[*An eerie green glow shows in sky behind him.*]

BRICK (*sucking the ice in his glass, speech becoming thick*): Leave th' place to Gooper and Mae an' their five little same little monkeys. All I want is—

BIG DADDY: "LEAVE TH' PLACE," did you say?   1275

BRICK (*vaguely*): All twenty-eight thousand acres of the richest land this side of the valley Nile.

BIG DADDY: Who said I was "leaving the place" to Gooper or anybody? This is my sixty-fifth birthday! I got fifteen years or twenty years left in   1280 me! I'll outlive *you!* I'll bury you an' have to pay for your coffin!

BRICK: Sure. Many happy returns. Now let's go watch the fireworks, come on, let's—

BIG DADDY: Lying, have they been lying? About   1285 the report from th'— clinic? Did they, did they— find something?—*Cancer.* Maybe?

BRICK: Mendacity is a system that we live in. Liquor is the one way out an' death's the other . . . .

[*He takes the crutch from BIG DADDY's loose grip and swings out on the gallery leaving the doors open. A song, "Pick a Bale of Cotton," is heard.*]

MAE (*appearing in door*): Oh, Big Daddy, the field   1290 hands are singin' fo' you!

BRICK: I'm sorry, Big Daddy. My head don't work any more and it's hard for me to understand how anybody could care if he lived or died or was dying or cared about anything but whether or not there   1295 was liquor left in the bottle and so I said what I said without thinking. In some ways I'm no better than the others, in some ways worse because I'm less alive. Maybe it's being alive that makes them lie, and being almost *not* alive makes me sort of   1300 accidentally truthful—I don't know but— anyway—we've been friends . .

    —And being friends is telling each other the truth . . . .

[*There is a pause.*]

You told *me!* I told *you!*   1305
BIG DADDY (*slowly and passionately*): CHRIST—
    DAMN—
GOOPER (*off stage*): Let her go!

[*Fireworks off stage right.*]

BIG DADDY: —ALL—LYING SONS OF—
    LYING BITCHES!   1310

[*He straightens at last and crosses to the inside door.
At the door he turns and looks back as if he had some
desperate question he couldn't put into words. Then he
nods reflectively and says in a hoarse voice:*]

Yes, all liars, all liars, all lying dying liars!

[*This is said slowly, slowly, with a fierce revulsion. He
goes on out.*]

   —Lying! Dying! Liars!

[*BRICK remains motionless as the lights dim out and
the curtain falls.*]

CURTAIN

ACT III

*There is no lapse of time. BIG DADDY is seen leaving
as at the end of Act II.*

BIG DADDY: ALL LYIN'—DYIN'!—LIARS!
    LIARS!—LIARS!

[*MARGARET enters.*]

MARGARET: Brick, what in the name of God was
    goin' on in this room?

[*DIXIE and TRIXIE enter through the doors and circle
around MARGARET shouting. MAE enters from the
lower gallery window.*]

MAE: Dixie, Trixie, you quit that!   5

[*GOOPER enters through the doors.*]

   Gooper, will y' please get these kiddies to bed right
   now!
GOOPER: Mae, you seen Big Mama?
MAE: Not yet.

[*GOOPER and kids exit through the doors.
REVEREND TOOKER enters through the windows.*]

REVEREND TOOKER: Those kiddies are so full   10
    of vitality. I think I'll have to be starting back to
    town.
MAE: Not yet, Preacher. You know we regard you
    as a member of this family, one of our closest an'
    dearest, so you just got t' be with us when Doc   15
    Baugh gives Big Mama th'actual truth about th'
    report from the clinic.
MARGARET: Where do you think you're going?
BRICK: Out for some air.
MARGARET: Why'd Big Daddy shout "Liars"?   20
MAE: Has Big Daddy gone to bed, Brick?
GOOPER (*entering*): Now where is that old lady?
REVEREND TOOKER: I'll look for her.

[*He exits to the gallery.*]

MAE: Cain'tcha find her, Gooper?
GOOPER: She's avoidin' this talk.   25
MAE: I think she senses somethin'.
MARGARET (*going out on the gallery to* BRICK):
    Brick, they're goin' to tell Big Mama the truth
    about Big Daddy and she's goin' to need you.
DOCTOR BAUGH: This is going to be painful.   30
MAE: Painful things caint always be avoided.
REVEREND TOOKER: I see Big Mama.
GOOPER: Hey, Big Mama, come here.
MAE: Hush, Gooper, don't holler.
BIG MAMA (*entering*): Too much smell of burnt   35
    fireworks makes me feel a little bit sick at my
    stomach.—Where is Big Daddy?
MAE: That's what I want to know, where has Big
    Daddy gone?
BIG MAMA: He must have turned in, I reckon he   40
    went to baid . . .
GOOPER: Well, then, now we can talk.
BIG MAMA: What *is* this talk, *what* talk?

[*MARGARET appears on the gallery, talking to
DOCTOR BAUGH.*]

MARGARET (*musically*): My family freed their
    slaves ten years before abolition. My great-great-   45
    grandfather gave his slaves their freedom five years
    before the War between the States started!

[III]

MAE: Oh, for God's sake! Maggie's climbed back up in her family tree!

MARGARET (*sweetly*): What, Mae?   50

[The pace must be very quick: great Southern animation.]

BIG MAMA (*addressing them all*): I think Big Daddy was just worn out. He loves his family, he loves to have them around him, but it's a strain on his nerves. He wasn't himself tonight, Big Daddy wasn't himself, I could tell he was all worked up.   55

REVEREND TOOKER: I think he's remarkable.

BIG MAMA: Yaisss! Just remarkable. Did you all notice the food he ate at that table? Did you all notice the supper he put away? Why he ate like a hawss!

GOOPER: I hope he doesn't regret it.   60

BIG MAMA: What? Why that man—ate a huge piece of cawn bread with molasses on it! Helped himself twice to hoppin' John.[17]

MARGARET: Big Daddy loves hoppin' John.—We had a real country dinner.   65

BIG MAMA (*overlapping* MARGARET): Yaiss, he simply adores it! an' candied yams? Son? That man put away enough food at that table to stuff a *field* hand!

GOOPER (*with grim relish*): I hope he don't have to pay for it later on . . .   70

BIG MAMA (*fiercely*): What's *that*, Gooper?

MAE: Gooper says he hopes Big Daddy doesn't suffer tonight.

BIG MAMA: Oh, shoot, Gooper says, Gooper says! Why should Big Daddy suffer for satisfying a normal appetite? There's nothin' wrong with that man but nerves, he's sound as a dollar! And now he knows he is an' that's why he ate such a supper. He had a big load off his mind, knowin' he wasn't doomed t'—what he thought he was doomed to . . .   75   80

MARGARET (*sadly and sweetly*): Bless his old sweet soul . . .

BIG MAMA (*vaguely*): Yais, bless his heart, where's Brick?   85

MAE: Outside.

GOOPER: —Drinkin' . . .

BIG MAMA: I know he's drinkin'. Cain't I see he's drinkin' without you continually tellin' me that boy's drinkin'?   90

MARGARET: Good for you, Big Mama!

[She applauds.]

BIG MAMA: Other people *drink* and *have* drunk an' will *drink*, as long as they make that stuff an' put it in bottles.

MARGARET: That's the truth. I never trusted a man that didn't drink.   95

BIG MAMA: *Brick? Brick!*

MARGARET: He's still on the gall'ry. I'll go bring him in so we can talk.

BIG MAMA (*worriedly*): I don't know what this mysterious family conference is about.   100

[Awkward silence. BIG MAMA looks from face to face, then belches slightly and mutters, "Excuse me . . ." She opens an ornamental fan suspended about her throat. A black lace fan to go with her black lace gown, and fans her wilting corsage, sniffing nervously and looking from face to face in the uncomfortable silence as MARGARET calls "Brick?" and BRICK sings to the moon on the gallery.]

MARGARET: Brick, they're gonna tell Big Mama the truth an' she's gonna need you.

BIG MAMA: I don't know what's wrong here, you all have such long faces! Open that door on the hall and let some air circulate through here, will you please, Gooper?   105

MAE: I think we'd better leave that door closed, Big Mama, till after the talk.

MARGARET: Brick!   110

BIG MAMA: Reveren' Tooker, will *you* please open that door?

REVEREND TOOKER: I sure will, Big Mama.

MAE: I just didn't think we ought t' take any chance of Big Daddy hearin' a word of this discussion.   115

BIG MAMA: *I swan!*[18] Nothing's going to be said in Big Daddy's house that he caint hear if he wants to!

GOOPER: Well, Big Mama, it's—

---

17 hoppin' John] a traditional Southern dish of rice and cowpeas, the name of which is probably derived from a similar Creole dish, using *pois pigeon* (pigeon peas, common in Africa).

18 I swan] i.e., "I have sworn."

[MAE gives him a quick, hard poke to shut him up. He glares at her fiercely as she circles before him like a burlesque ballerina, raising her skinny bare arms over her head, jangling her bracelets, exclaiming:]

MAE: *A breeze! A breeze!*

REVEREND TOOKER: I think this house is the   120
coolest house in the Delta.—Did you all know that
Halsey Banks's widow put air-conditioning units
in the church and rectory at Friar's Point in
memory of Halsey?

[General conversation has resumed; everybody is chatting so that the stage sounds like a bird cage.]

GOOPER: Too bad nobody cools your church off   125
for you. I bet you sweat in that pulpit these hot
Sundays, Reverend Tooker.

REVEREND TOOKER: Yes, my vestments are
drenched. Last Sunday the gold in my chasuble
faded into the purple.   130

GOOPER: Reveren', you musta been preachin' hell's
fire last Sunday.

MAE (*at the same time to* DOCTOR BAUGH): You
reckon those vitamin B12 injections are what
they're cracked up t' be, Doc Baugh?   135

DOCTOR BAUGH: Well, if you want to be stuck
with something I guess they're as good to be stuck
with as anything else.

BIG MAMA (*at the gallery door*): *Maggie, Maggie,
aren't you comin' with Brick?*   140

MAE (*suddenly and loudly, creating a silence*): *I have
a strange feeling, I have a peculiar feeling!*

BIG MAMA (*turning from the gallery*): What feeling?

MAE: That Brick said somethin' he shouldn't of said
t' Big Daddy.   145

BIG MAMA: Now what on earth could Brick of said
t' Big Daddy that he shouldn't say?

GOOPER: Big Mama, there's somethin'—

MAE: NOW, WAIT!

[She rushes up to BIG MAMA and gives her a quick hug and kiss. BIG MAMA pushes her impatiently off.]

DOCTOR BAUGH: In my day they had what they   150
call the Keeley cure for heavy drinkers.[19]

BIG MAMA: Shoot!

DOCTOR BAUGH: But now I understand they just
take some kind of tablets.

GOOPER: They call them "Annie Bust" tablets.[20]   155

BIG MAMA: *Brick* don't need to take *nothin'*.

[BRICK and MARGARET appear in gallery doors, BIG MAMA unaware of his presence behind her.]

That boy is just broken up over Skipper's death. You
know how poor Skipper died. They gave him a big,
big dose of that sodium amytal stuff at his home and
then they called the ambulance and give him   160
another big, big dose of it at the hospital and that
and all of the alcohol in his system fo' months an'
months just proved too much for his heart . . .[21] I'm
scared of needles! I'm more scared of a needle than
the knife . . . I think more people have been needled   165
out of this world than—

[She stops short and wheels about.]

Oh—here's Brick! My precious baby—

[She turns upon BRICK with short, fat arms extended, at the same time uttering a loud, short sob, which is both comic and touching. BRICK smiles and bows slightly, making a burlesque gesture of gallantry for MARGARET to pass before him into the room. Then he hobbles on his crutch directly to the liquor cabinet and there is absolute silence, with everybody looking at BRICK as everybody has always looked at BRICK when he spoke or moved or appeared. One by one he drops ice cubes in his glass, then suddenly, but not quickly, looks back over his shoulder with a wry, charming smile, and says:]

BRICK: I'm sorry! Anyone else?

---

teenth century, Doctor Leslie Keeley's so-called cure involved injections of "double chloride of gold"—in fact,
a useless medical procedure. This was, however, accompanied by a sort of group therapy, which was of some
actual benefit.

[20] "Annie Bust"] i.e., Antabuse, a drug that causes nausea
when alcohol is consumed.

[21] sodium amytal] a sedative (most frequently used to create a hypnotic state in which the causes of dissociative
disorders can be diagnosed).

---

[19] Keeley cure] Popular in the United States in the late nine-

BIG MAMA (*sadly*): No, son, I *wish* you wouldn't!

BRICK: I wish I didn't have to, Big Mama, but I'm 170
still waiting for that click in my head which makes
it all smooth out!

BIG MAMA: Ow, Brick, you—BREAK MY HEART!

MARGARET (*at the same time*): *Brick, go sit with Big
Mama!* 175

BIG MAMA: I just cain't staiiiiii-nnnnnnnd-it . . .

[*She sobs.*]

MAE: Now that we're all assembled—

GOOPER: We kin talk . . .

BIG MAMA: Breaks my heart . . .

MARGARET: Sit with Big Mama, Brick, and hold 180
her hand.

[*BIG MAMA sniffs very loudly three times, almost like
three drumbeats in the pocket of silence.*]

BRICK: You do that, Maggie. I'm a restless cripple.
I got to stay on my crutch.

[*BRICK hobbles to the gallery door; leans there as if
waiting. MAE sits beside BIG MAMA, while GOOPER
moves in front and sits on the end of the couch, facing
her. REVEREND TOOKER moves nervously into the
space between them; on the other side, DOCTOR
BAUGH stands looking at nothing in particular and
lights a cigar. MARGARET turns away.*]

BIG MAMA: Why're you all *surroundin'* me—like
this? Why're you all starin' at me like this an' 185
makin' signs at each other?

[*REVEREND TOOKER steps back startled.*]

MAE: Calm yourself, Big Mama.

BIG MAMA: Calm you'self, *you'self*, Sister Woman.
How could I calm myself with everyone starin' at
me as if big drops of blood had broken out on 190
m'face? What's this all about, annh! What?

[*GOOPER coughs and takes a center position.*]

GOOPER: Now, Doc Baugh.

MAE: Doc Baugh?

GOOPER: Big Mama wants to know the complete
truth about the report we got from the Ochsner 195
Clinic.

MAE (*eagerly*): —on Big Daddy's condition!

GOOPER: Yais, on Big Daddy's condition, we got
to face it.

DOCTOR BAUGH: Well . . . 200

BIG MAMA (*terrified, rising*): Is there? Something?
Something that I? Don't—know?

[*In these few words, this startled, very soft, question,
BIG MAMA reviews the history of her forty-five years
with BIG DADDY, her great, almost embarrassingly
true-hearted and simple-minded devotion to BIG
DADDY, who must have had something BRICK has,
who made himself loved so much by the "simple
expedient" of not loving enough to disturb his charming
detachment, also once coupled, like BRICK, with virile
beauty. BIG MAMA has a dignity at this moment; she
almost stops being fat.*]

DOCTOR BAUGH (*after a pause, uncomfortably*):
Yes?—Well—

BIG MAMA: I!!!—want to—*knowwwwww* . . . 205

[*Immediately she thrusts her fist to her mouth as if to
deny that statement. Then for some curious reason, she
snatches the withered corsage from her breast and hurls
it on the floor and steps on it with her short, fat feet.*]

Somebody must be lyin'!—I want to know!

MAE: Sit down, Big Mama, sit down on this sofa.

MARGARET: Brick, go sit with Big Mama.

BIG MAMA: *What is it, what is it?*

DOCTOR BAUGH: I never have seen a more 210
thorough examination than Big Daddy Pollitt was
given in all my experience with the Ochsner
Clinic.

GOOPER: It's one of the best in the country.

MAE: It's THE best in the country—bar *none*! 215

[*For some reason she gives GOOPER a violent poke as
she goes past him. He slaps at her hand without
removing his eyes from his mother's face.*]

DOCTOR BAUGH: Of course they were ninety-
nine and nine-tenths per cent sure before they even
started.

BIG MAMA: Sure of what, sure of what, sure of—
what?—what? 220

[*She catches her breath in a startled sob. MAE kisses
her quickly. She thrusts MAE fiercely away from her,
staring at the DOCTOR.*]

MAE: Mommy, be a brave girl!

BRICK (*in the doorway, singing softly*): "By the light, by the light, Of the sil-ve-ry mo-oo-n . . ."

GOOPER: Shut up!—Brick.

BRICK: Sorry . . .   225

[He wanders out on the gallery.]

DOCTOR BAUGH: But now, you see, Big Mama, they cut a piece off this growth, a specimen of the tissue and—

BIG MAMA: Growth? You told Big Daddy—

DOCTOR BAUGH: Now wait.

BIG MAMA (*fiercely*): You told me and Big Daddy there wasn't a thing wrong with him but—   230

MAE: Big Mama, they always—

GOOPER: Let Doc Baugh talk, will yuh?

BIG MAMA: —little spastic condition of—   235

[Her breath gives out in a sob.]

DOCTOR BAUGH: Yes, that's what we told Big Daddy. But we had this bit of tissue run through the laboratory and I'm sorry to say the test was positive on it. It's—well—malignant . . .

[Pause]

BIG MAMA: —Cancer?! Cancer?!   240

[DOCTOR BAUGH nods gravely. BIG MAMA gives a long gasping cry.]

MAE AND GOOPER: Now, now, now, Big Mama, you had to know . . .

BIG MAMA: WHY DIDN'T THEY CUT IT OUT OF HIM? HANH? HANH?

DOCTOR BAUGH: Involved too much, Big Mama, too many organs affected.   245

MAE: Big Mama, the liver's affected and so's the kidneys, both! It's gone way past what they call a—

GOOPER: A surgical risk.

MAE: —Uh-huh . . .   250

[BIG MAMA draws a breath like a dying gasp.]

REVEREND TOOKER: Tch, tch, tch, tch, tch!

DOCTOR BAUGH: Yes it's gone past the knife.

MAE: *That's why he's turned yellow, Mommy!*

BIG MAMA: *Git away from me, git away from me, Mae!*   255

[She rises abruptly.]

I want Brick! Where's Brick? Where is my only son?

MAE: Mama! Did she say "*only* son"?

GOOPER: What does that make *me*?

MAE: A sober responsible man with five precious children!—*Six!*   260

BIG MAMA: I want Brick to tell me! Brick! Brick!

MARGARET (*rising from her reflections in a corner*): Brick was so upset he went back out.

BIG MAMA: *Brick!*

MARGARET: Mama, let *me* tell you!   265

BIG MAMA: No, no, leave me alone, you're not my blood!

GOOPER: *Mama, I'm your son!* Listen to *me!*

MAE: Gooper's your son, he's your first-born!

BIG MAMA: Gooper never liked Daddy.   270

MAE (*as if terribly shocked*): *That's not TRUE!*

[There is a pause. The minister coughs and rises.]

REVEREND TOOKER (*to* MAE): I think I'd better slip away at this point.

[Discreetly]

Good night, good night, everybody, and God bless you all . . . on this place . . .   275

[He slips out. MAE coughs and points at BIG MAMA.]

GOOPER: Well, Big Mama . . .

[He sighs.]

BIG MAMA: It's all a mistake, I know it's just a bad dream.

DOCTOR BAUGH: We're gonna keep Big Daddy as comfortable as we can.   280

BIG MAMA: Yes, it's just a bad dream, that's all it is, it's just an awful dream.

GOOPER: In my opinion Big Daddy is having some pain but won't admit that he has it.

BIG MAMA: Just a dream, a bad dream.   285

DOCTOR BAUGH: That's what lots of them do, they think if they don't admit they're having the pain they can sort of escape the fact of it.

GOOPER (*with relish*): Yes, they get sly about it, they get real sly about it.   290

MAE: Gooper and I think—

GOOPER: Shut up, Mae! Big Mama, I think—Big Daddy ought to be started on morphine.

BIG MAMA: Nobody's going to give Big Daddy morphine. 295

DOCTOR BAUGH: Now, Big Mama, when that pain strikes it's going to strike mighty hard and Big Daddy's going to need the needle to bear it.

BIG MAMA: I tell you, nobody's going to give him morphine. 300

MAE: Big Mama, you don't want to see Big Daddy suffer, you know you—

[GOOPER, standing beside her, gives her a savage poke.]

DOCTOR BAUGH (*placing a package on the table*): I'm leaving this stuff here, so if there's a sudden attack you all won't have to send out for it. 305

MAE: I know how to give a hypo.

BIG MAMA: Nobody's gonna give Big Daddy morphine.

GOOPER: Mae took a course in nursing during the war. 310

MARGARET: Somehow I don't think Big Daddy would want Mae to give him a hypo.

MAE: You think he'd want *you* to do it?

DOCTOR BAUGH: Well . . .

[DOCTOR BAUGH rises.]

GOOPER: Doctor Baugh is goin'. 315

DOCTOR BAUGH: Yes, I got to be goin'. Well, keep you chin up, Big Mama.

GOOPER (*with jocularity*): She's gonna keep *both* chins up, aren't you, Big Mama?

[BIG MAMA sobs.]

Now stop that, Big Mama. 320

GOOPER (*at the door with* DOCTOR BAUGH): Well, Doc, we sure do appreciate all you done. I'm telling you, we're surely obligated to you for—

[DOCTOR BAUGH has gone out without a glance at him.]

—I guess that doctor has got a lot on his mind but it wouldn't hurt him to act a little more human 325 . . . *[BIG MAMA sobs.]*

Now be a brave girl, Mommy.

BIG MAMA: It's not true, I know that it's just not true!

GOOPER: Mama, those tests are infallible! 330

BIG MAMA: Why are you so determined to see your father daid?

MAE: Big Mama!

MARGARET (*gently*): I know what Big Mama means. 335

MAE (*fiercely*): Oh, do you?

MARGARET (*quietly and very sadly*): Yes, I think I do.

MAE: For a newcomer in the family you sure do show a lot of understanding. 340

MARGARET: Understanding is needed on this place.

MAE: I guess you must have needed a lot of it in your family, Maggie, with your father's liquor problem and now you've got Brick with his! 345

MARGARET: Brick does not have a liquor problem at all. Brick is devoted to Big Daddy. This thing is a terrible strain on him.

BIG MAMA: Brick is Big Daddy's boy, but he drinks too much and it worries me and Big Daddy, and, 350 Margaret, you've got to co-operate with us, you've got to co-operate with Big Daddy and me in getting Brick straightened out. Because it will break Big Daddy's heart if Brick don't pull himself together and take hold of things. 355

MAE: Take hold of *what* things, Big Mama?

BIG MAMA: The place.

[There is a quick and violent look between MAE and GOOPER.]

GOOPER: Big Mama, you've had a shock.

MAE: Yais, we've all had a shock, but . . .

GOOPER: Let's be realistic— 360

MAE: —Big Daddy would never, would *never*, be foolish enough to—

GOOPER: —put this place in irresponsible hands!

BIG MAMA: Big Daddy ain't going to leave the place in anybody's hands; Big Daddy is *not* going 365 to die. I want you to get that in your heads, all of you!

MAE: Mommy, Mommy, Big Mama, we're just as hopeful an' optimistic as you are about Big Daddy's prospects, we have faith in *prayer*—but nevertheless 370 there are certain matters that have to be discussed an' dealt with, because otherwise—

GOOPER: Eventualities have to be considered and now's the time . . . Mae, will you please get my brief case out of our room?

MAE: Yes, honey.

[She rises and goes out through the hall door.]

GOOPER (*standing over* BIG MAMA): Now, Big Mom. What you said just now was not at all true and you know it. I've always loved Big Daddy in my own quiet way. I never made a show of it, and I know that Big Daddy has always been fond of me in a quiet way, too, and he never made a show of it neither.

[MAE returns with GOOPER's brief case.]

MAE: Here's your brief case, Gooper, honey.

GOOPER (*handing the brief case back to her*): Thank you . . . Of cou'se, my relationship with Big Daddy is different from Brick's.

MAE: You're eight years older'n Brick an' always had t' carry a bigger load of th' responsibilities than Brick ever had t' carry. He never carried a thing in his life but a football or a highball.

GOOPER: Mae, will y' let me talk, please?

MAE: Yes, honey.

GOOPER: Now, a twenty-eight-thousand-acre plantation's a mighty big thing t' run.

MAE: Almost singlehanded.

[MARGARET has gone out onto the gallery and can be heard calling softly to BRICK.]

BIG MAMA: You never had to run this place! What are you talking about? As if Big Daddy was dead and in his grave, you had to run it? Why, you just helped him out with a few business details and had your law practice at the same time in Memphis!

MAE: Oh, Mommy, Mommy, Big Mommy! Let's be fair!

MARGARET: Brick!

MAE: Why, Gooper has given himself body and soul to keeping this place up for the past five years since Big Daddy's health started failing.

MARGARET: Brick!

MAE: Gooper won't say it, Gooper never thought of it as a duty, he just did it. And what did Brick do?

Brick kept living in his past glory at college! Still a football player at twenty-seven!

MARGARET (*returning alone*): Who are you talking about now? Brick? A football player? He isn't a football player and you know it. Brick is a sports announcer on T.V. and one of the best-known ones in the country!

MAE: I'm talking about what he was.

MARGARET: Well, I wish you would just stop talking about my husband.

GOOPER: I've got a right to discuss my brother with other members of MY OWN family, which don't include *you*. Why don't you go out there and drink with Brick?

MARGARET: I've never seen such malice toward a brother.

GOOPER: How about his for me? Why, he can't stand to be in the same room with me!

MARGARET: This is a deliberate campaign of vilification for the most disgusting and sordid reason on earth, and I know what it is! It's *avarice, avarice, greed, greed!*

BIG MAMA: *Oh, I'll scream! I will scream in a moment unless this stops!*

[GOOPER has stalked up to MARGARET with clenched fists at his sides as if he would strike her. MAE distorts her face again into a hideous grimace behind MARGARET's back.]

BIG MAMA (*sobs*): Margaret. Child. Come here. Sit next to Big Mama.

MARGARET: Precious Mommy. I'm sorry, I'm sorry, I—!

[She bends her long graceful neck to press her forehead to BIG MAMA's bulging shoulder under its black chiffon.]

MAE: How beautiful, how touching, this display of devotion! Do you know why she's childless? She's childless because that big, beautiful athlete husband of hers won't go to bed with her!

GOOPER: You jest won't let me do this in a nice way, will yah? Aw right—I don't give a goddam if Big Daddy likes me or don't like me or did or never did or will or will never! I'm just appealing to a sense of common decency and fair play. I'll tell you the truth. I've resented Big Daddy's partiality to Brick ever since Brick was born, and the way I've been treated like I was just barely good enough to spit on and sometimes not even good enough for that. Big Daddy is dying of cancer, and it's spread all through him and it's attacked all his vital organs including the kidneys and right now he is sinking into uremia, and you all know what uremia is, it's poisoning of the whole system due to the failure of the body to eliminate its poisons.

MARGARET (*to herself, downstage, hissingly*): *Poisons, poisons! Venomous thoughts and words! In hearts and minds!—That's poisons!*

GOOPER (*overlapping her*): I am asking for a square deal, and, by God, I expect to get one. But if I don't get one, if there's any peculiar shenanigans going on around here behind my back, well, I'm not a corporation lawyer for nothing, I know how to protect my own interests.

[BRICK enters from the gallery with a tranquil, blurred smile, carrying an empty glass with him.]

BRICK: Storm coming up.

GOOPER: Oh! A late arrival!

MAE: Behold the conquering hero comes!

GOOPER: The fabulous Brick Pollitt! Remember him?—Who could forget him!

MAE: He looks like he's been injured in a game!

GOOPER: Yep, I'm afraid you'll have to warm the bench at the Sugar Bowl this year, Brick!

[MAE laughs shrilly.]

Or was it the Rose Bowl that he made that famous run in?—

[Thunder]

MAE: The punch bowl, honey. It was in the punch bowl, the cut-glass punch bowl!

GOOPER: Oh, that's right, I'm getting the bowls mixed up!

MARGARET: Why don't you stop venting your malice and envy on a sick boy?

BIG MAMA: *Now you two hush, I mean it, hush, all of you, hush!*

DAISY, SOOKEY: Storm! Storm comin'! Storm! Storm!

LACEY: Brightie, close them shutters.

GOOPER: Lacey, put the top up on my Cadillac, will yuh?

LACEY: Yes, suh, Mistah Pollitt!

GOOPER (*at the same time*): Big Mama, you know it's necessary for me t' go back to Memphis in th' mornin' t' represent the Parker estate in a lawsuit.

[MAE sits on the bed and arranges papers she has taken from the brief case.]

BIG MAMA: Is it, Gooper?

MAE: Yaiss.

GOOPER: That's why I'm forced to—to bring up a problem that—

MAE: Somethin' that's too important t' be put off!

GOOPER: If Brick was sober, he ought to be in on this.

MARGARET: Brick is present; we're present.

GOOPER: Well, good. I will now give you this outline my partner, Tom Bullitt, an' me have drawn up—a sort of dummy—trusteeship.

MARGARET: Oh, that's it! You'll be in charge an' dole out remittances, will you?

GOOPER: This we did as soon as we got the report on Big Daddy from th' Ochsner Laboratories. We did this thing, I mean we drew up this dummy outline with the advice and assistance of the Chairman of the Boa'd of Directors of th' Southern Plantahs Bank and Trust Company in Memphis, C. C. Bellowes, a man who handles estates for all th' prominent fam'lies in West Tennessee and th' Delta.

BIG MAMA: Gooper?

GOOPER (*crouching in front of* BIG MAMA): Now this is not—not final, or anything like it. This is just a preliminary outline. But it does provide a basis—a design—a—possible, feasible—*plan!*

MARGARET: Yes, I'll bet it's a plan.

[Thunder]

MAE: It's a plan to protect the biggest estate in the Delta from irresponsibility an'—

BIG MAMA: Now you listen to me, all of you, you listen here! They's not goin' to be any more catty talk in my house! And Gooper, you put that away before I grab it out of your hand and tear it right up! I don't know what the hell's in it, and I don't want to know what the hell's in it. I'm talkin' in

Big Daddy's language now; I'm his *wife*, not his
widow, I'm still his *wife*! And I'm talkin' to you in   530
his language an'—

GOOPER: Big Mama, what I have here is—

MAE (*at the same time*): Gooper explained that it's
just a plan . . .

BIG MAMA: I don't care what you got there. Just   535
put it back where it came from, an' don't let me
see it again, not even the outside of the envelope
of it! Is that understood? Basis! Plan! Preliminary!
Design! I say—what is it Big Daddy always says
when he's disgusted?   540

BRICK (*from the bar*): Big Daddy says "crap" when
he's disgusted.

BIG MAMA (*rising*): That's right—CRAP! I say
CRAP too, like Big Daddy!

[*Thunder rolls.*]

MAE: Coarse language doesn't seem called for in   545
this—

GOOPER: Somethin' in me is *deeply outraged* by
hearin' you talk like this.

BIG MAMA: *Nobody's goin' to take nothin'!*—till Big
Daddy lets go of it—maybe, just possibly, not—   550
not even then! No, not even then!

[*Thunder.*]

MAE: Sookey, hurry up an' git that po'ch furniture
covahed; want th' paint to come off?

GOOPER: Lacey, put mah car away!

LACEY: Caint, Mistah Pollitt, you got the keys!   555

GOOPER: Naw, you got 'em, man. [*Calls to MAE.*]
Where th' keys to th' car, honey?

MAE: You got 'em in your pocket!

[*GOOPER exits R.*]

BRICK: [*singing*] "You can always hear me singin'
this song, Show me the way to go home."   560

[*Thunder distantly*]

BIG MAMA: Brick! Come here, Brick, I need you.
Tonight Brick looks like he used to look when he
was a little boy, just like he did when he played
wild games and used to come home when I
hollered myself hoarse for him, all sweaty and pink   565
cheeked and sleepy, with his—red curls shining . . .

[*She comes over to him and runs her fat, shaky hand
through his hair. BRICK draws aside as he does from
all physical contact and continues the song in a
whisper, opening the ice bucket and dropping in the ice
cubes one by one as if he were mixing some important
chemical formula. Distant thunder.*]

Time goes by so fast. Nothin' can outrun it. Death
commences too early—almost before you're half
acquainted with life—you meet the other . . . Oh,
you know we just got to love each other an' stay   570
together, all of us, just as close as we can, especially
now that such a *black* thing has come and moved
into this place without invitation.

[*Awkwardly embracing BRICK, she presses her head to
his shoulder. A dog howls off stage.*]

Oh, Brick, son of Big Daddy, Big Daddy does so
love you. Y'know what would be his fondest dream   575
come true? If before he passed on, if Big Daddy
has to pass on . . .

[*A dog howls.*]

. . . you give him a child of yours, a grandson as
much like his son as his son is like Big Daddy.

MARGARET: I know that's Big Daddy's dream.   580

BIG MAMA: That's his dream.

MAE: Such a pity that Maggie and Brick can't oblige.

BIG DADDY (*off down stage right on the gallery*):
Looks like the wind was takin' liberties with this
place.   585

SERVANT (*off stage*): Yes, sir, Mr. Pollitt.

MARGARET (*crossing to the right door*): Big Daddy's
on the gall'ry.

[*BIG MAMA has turned toward the hall door at the
sound of BIG DADDY's voice on the gallery.*]

BIG MAMA: I can't stay here. He'll see somethin'
in my eyes.   590

[*BIG DADDY enters the room from up stage right.*]

BIG DADDY: Can I come in?

[*He puts his cigar in an ash tray.*]

MARGARET: Did the storm wake you up, Big
Daddy?

BIG DADDY: Which stawm are you talkin' about—
th' one outside or th' hullaballoo in here?   595

[*GOOPER squeezes past BIG DADDY.*]

GOOPER: 'Scuse me:

[*MAE tries to squeeze past BIG DADDY to join GOOPER, but BIG DADDY puts his arm firmly around her.*]

BIG DADDY: I heard some mighty loud talk. Sounded like somethin' important was bein' discussed. What was the powwow about?

MAE (*flustered*): Why—nothin', Big Daddy . . . 600

BIG DADDY (*crossing to extreme left center, taking MAE with him*): What is that pregnant-lookin' envelope you're puttin' back in your brief case, Gooper?

GOOPER (*at the foot of the bed, caught, as he stuffs papers into envelope*): That? Nothin', suh—nothin' 605
much of anythin' at all . . .

BIG DADDY: Nothin'? It looks like a whole lot of nothin'!

[*He turns up stage to the group.*]

You all know th' story about th' young married couple— 610

GOOPER: Yes, sir!

BIG DADDY: Hello, Brick—

BRICK: Hello, Big Daddy.

[*The group is arranged in a semicircle above BIG DADDY, MARGARET at the extreme right, then MAE and GOOPER, then BIG MAMA, with BRICK at the left.*]

BIG DADDY: Young married couple took Junior out to th' zoo one Sunday, inspected all of God's 615
creatures in their cages, with satisfaction.

GOOPER: Satisfaction.

BIG DADDY (*crossing to up stage center, facing front*): This afternoon was a warm afternoon in spring an' that ole elephant had somethin' else on his mind 620
which was bigger'n peanuts. You know this story, Brick?

[*GOOPER nods.*]

BRICK: No, sir, I don't know it.

BIG DADDY: Y'see, in th' cage adjoinin' they was a young female elephant in heat! 625

BIG MAMA (*at BIG DADDY's shoulder*): Oh, Big Daddy!

BIG DADDY: What's the matter, preacher's gone, ain't he? All right. That female elephant in the next cage was permeatin' the atmosphere about her with 630
a powerful and excitin' odor of female fertility! Huh! Ain't that a nice way to put it, Brick?

BRICK: Yes, sir, nothin' wrong with it.

BIG DADDY: Brick says th's nothin' wrong with it!

BIG MAMA: Oh, Big Daddy! 635

BIG DADDY (*crossing to down stage center*): So this ole bull elephant still had a couple of fornications left in him. He reared back his trunk an' got a whiff of that elephant lady next door!—began to paw at the dirt in his cage an' butt his head against 640
the separatin' partition and, first thing y'know, there was a conspicuous change in his *profile*—very *conspicuous*! Ain't I tellin' this story in decent language, Brick?

BRICK: Yes, sir, too fuckin' decent! 645

BIG DADDY: So, the little boy pointed at it and said, "What's that?" His mama said, "Oh, that's—nothin'!"—His papa said, "She's spoiled!"

[*BIG DADDY crosses to BRICK at left.*]

You didn't laugh at that story, Brick.

[*BIG MAMA crosses to down stage right crying. MARGARET goes to her. MAE and GOOPER hold up stage right center.*]

BRICK: No, sir, I didn't laugh at that story. 650

BIG DADDY: What is the smell in this room? Don't you notice it, Brick? Don't you notice a powerful and obnoxious odor of mendacity in this room?

BRICK: Yes, sir, I think I do, sir.

GOOPER: Mae, Mae . . . 655

BIG DADDY: There is nothing more powerful. Is there, Brick?

BRICK: No, sir. No, sir, there isn't, an' nothin' more obnoxious.

BIG DADDY: Brick agrees with me. The odor of 660
mendacity is a powerful and obnoxious odor an' the stawm hasn't blown it away from this room yet. You notice it, Gooper?

GOOPER: What, sir?

BIG DADDY: How about you, Sister Woman? You 665
notice the unpleasant odor of mendacity in this room?

MAE: Why, Big Daddy, I don't even know what that is.

BIG DADDY: You can smell it. Hell it smells like death! 670

[BIG MAMA sobs. BIG DADDY looks toward her.]

What is wrong with that fat woman over there, loaded with diamonds? Hey, what's-you-name, what's the matter with you?

MARGARET (crossing toward BIG DADDY): She had a slight dizzy spell, Big Daddy. 675

BIG DADDY: You better watch that, Big Mama. A stroke is a bad way to go.

MARGARET (crossing to BIG DADDY at center): Oh, Brick, Big Daddy has on your birthday present to him, Brick, he has on your cashmere 680 robe, the softest material I have ever felt.

BIG DADDY: Yeah, this is my soft birthday, Maggie . . . Not my gold or my silver birthday, but my soft birthday, everything's got to be soft for Big Daddy on this soft birthday. 685

[MAGGIE kneels before BIG DADDY at center.]

MARGARET: Big Daddy's got on his Chinese slippers that I gave him, Brick. Big Daddy, I haven't given you my big present yet, but now I will, now's the time for me to present it to you! I have an announcement to make! 690

MAE: What? What kind of announcement?

GOOPER: A sports announcement, Maggie?

MARGARET: Announcement of life beginning! A child is coming, sired by Brick, and out of Maggie the Cat! I have Brick's child in my body, an' that's my 695 birthday present to Big Daddy on this birthday!

[BIG DADDY looks at BRICK who crosses behind BIG DADDY to down stage portal, left.]

BIG DADDY: Get up, girl, get up off your knees, girl.

[BIG DADDY helps MARGARET to rise. He crosses above her, to her right, bites off the end of a fresh cigar, taken from his bathrobe pocket, as he studies MARGARET.]

Uh-huh, this girl has life in her body, that's no lie!

BIG MAMA: BIG DADDY'S DREAM COME TRUE! 700

BRICK: JESUS!

BIG DADDY (crossing right below wicker stand): Gooper, I want my lawyer in the mornin'.

BRICK: Where are you goin', Big Daddy?

BIG DADDY: Son, I'm goin' up on the roof, to the 705 belvedere on th' roof to look over my kingdom before I give up my kingdom—twenty-eight thousand acres of th' richest land this side of the valley Nile!

[He exits through right doors, and down right on the gallery.]

BIG MAMA (following): Sweetheart, sweetheart, sweetheart—can I come with you? 710

[She exits down stage right. MARGARET is down stage center in the mirror area. MAE has joined GOOPER and she gives him a fierce poke, making a low hissing sound and a grimace of fury.]

GOOPER (pushing her aside): Brick, could you possibly spare me one small shot of that liquor?

BRICK: Why, help yourself, Gooper boy.

GOOPER: I will.

MAE (shrilly): Of course we know that this is—a lie. 715

GOOPER: Be still, Mae.

MAE: I won't be still! I know she's made this up!

GOOPER: Goddam it, I said shut up!

MARGARET: Gracious! I didn't know that my little announcement was going to provoke such a storm! 720

MAE: That woman isn't pregnant!

GOOPER: Who said she was?

MAE: She did.

GOOPER: The doctor didn't. Doc Baugh didn't.

MARGARET: I haven't gone to Doc Baugh. 725

GOOPER: Then who'd you go to, Maggie?

MARGARET: One of the best gynecologists in the South.

GOOPER: Uh huh, uh huh!—I see . . .

[He takes out a pencil and notebook.]

—May we have his name, please? 730

MARGARET: No, you may not, Mister Prosecuting Attorney!

MAE: He doesn't have any name, he doesn't exist!

MARGARET: Oh, he exists all right, and so does my child, Brick's baby! 735

MAE: You can't conceive a child by a man that won't sleep with you unless you think you're—

[*BRICK has turned on the phonograph. A scat song cuts MAE's speech.*]

GOOPER: *Turn that off!*

MAE: We know it's a lie because we hear you in here; he won't sleep with you, we hear you! So don't imagine you're going to put a trick over on us, to fool a dying man with a— 740

[*A long drawn cry of agony and rage fills the house. MARGARET turns the phonograph down to a whisper. The cry is repeated.*]

MAE: Did you hear that, Gooper, did you hear that?

GOOPER: Sounds like the pain has struck.

GOOPER: Come along and leave these lovebirds together in their nest! 745

[*He goes out first. MAE follows but turns at the door, contorting her face and hissing at MARGARET.*]

MAE: *Liar!*

[*She slams the door. MARGARET exhales with relief and moves a little unsteadily to catch hold of BRICK's arm.*]

MARGARET: Thank you for—keeping still . . .

BRICK: O.K., Maggie.

MARGARET: It was gallant of you to save my face! 750

[*He now pours down three shots in quick succession and stands waiting, silent. All at once he turns with a smile and says:*]

BRICK: *There!*

MARGARET: What?

BRICK: The *click* . . .

[*His gratitude seems almost infinite as he hobbles out on the gallery with a drink. We hear his crutch as he swings out of sight. Then, at some distance, he begins singing to himself a peaceful song. MARGARET holds the big pillow forlornly as if it were her only companion, for a few moments, then throws it on the bed. She rushes to the liquor cabinet, gathers all the bottles in her arms, turns about undecidedly, then runs out of the room with them, leaving the door ajar on the dim yellow hall. BRICK is heard hobbling back along the gallery, singing his peaceful song. He comes back in, sees the pillow on the bed, laughs lightly, sadly, picks it up. He has it under his arm as MARGARET returns to the room. MARGARET softly shuts the door and leans against it, smiling softly at BRICK.*]

MARGARET: Brick, I used to think that you were stronger than me and I didn't want to be overpowered by you. But now, since you've taken to liquor—you know what?—I guess it's bad, but now I'm stronger than you and I can love you more truly! Don't move that pillow. I'll move it right back if you do!—Brick? 755

760

[*She turns out all the lamps but a single rose-silk-shaded one by the bed.*]

I really have been to a doctor and I know what to do and—Brick?—this is my time by the calendar to conceive?

BRICK: Yes, I understand, Maggie. But how are you going to conceive a child by a man in love with his liquor? 765

MARGARET: By locking his liquor up and making him satisfy my desire before I unlock it!

BRICK: Is that what you've done, Maggie?

MARGARET: Look and see. The cabinet's mighty empty compared to before! 770

BRICK: Well, I'll be a son of a—

[*He reaches for his crutch but she beats him to it and rushes out on the gallery, hurls the crutch over the rail and comes back in, panting.*]

MARGARET: And so tonight we're going to make the lie true, and when that's done, I'll bring the liquor back here and we'll get drunk together, here, tonight, in this place that death has come into . . .— What do you say? 775

BRICK: I don't say anything. I guess there's nothing to say.

MARGARET: Oh, you weak people, you weak, beautiful people!—who give up with such grace. What you want is someone to— 780

[*She turns out the rose-silk lamp.*]

—take hold of you.—Gently, gently with love hand your life back to you, like somethin' gold you let go of. I *do* love you, Brick, I *do!* 785

BRICK (*smiling with charming sadness*): Wouldn't it be funny if that was true?

THE END

SAMUEL BECKETT

Play

~

Culturally speaking, eras seldom seem to pass in neat round figures corresponding precisely with the turning of the calendar. Hence 1989, the year in which the political face of Europe was decisively altered by the collapse of communism, may well be seen in the future as marking the critical point at which the Western culture of the twentieth century effectively ended and that of the twenty-first began. Within the context of world drama, 1989 is already crucial, because it is the year of the death of Samuel Beckett (1906–1989), who has been called "the last modernist" by his biographer, Anthony Cronin, and whose importance to drama and literature in the latter half of the twentieth century can scarcely be overstated.

Samuel Beckett's international fame began to grow in 1952, with the French publication and production of his play *Waiting for Godot* (Beckett pronounced the name with the emphasis on the first syllable: GOD-oh). However, his writing career had really begun in 1929, with the publication of an essay on the novelist James Joyce, a fellow Irish exile whom he had met in Paris the year before and who became a mentor of sorts for the young Beckett. Beckett had at first intended to become an academic, but after having had a taste of teaching, he decided that his forté was writing. His early work extended over a number of genres, including essays—"Dante . . . Bruno . Vico . . Joyce" (1928) (the irregular ellipses represent the centuries separating the writers) and *Proust* (1931); poetry—*Whoroscope* (1930) and *Echo's Bones* (1935); and fiction—a book of short stories called *More Pricks Than Kicks* (1934) and a novel, *Murphy* (1938). Conspicuous by its absence in this list of early works, considering Beckett's later reputation as a dramatist, is any writing for the theatre. However, as Beckett's notebooks have revealed recently, he began to think seriously about drama during the 1930s, though he let his ideas percolate for about fifteen years.

When the Second World War broke out, Beckett joined the French Resistance, but he was forced underground when the Gestapo arrested several members of his group. While still in hiding, he completed another novel, *Watt* (not published until 1953), and as soon as the war was over he began an immensely fruitful period which included the completion of his great trilogy of novels (not published until 1951–53), *Molloy*, *Malone Dies* and *The Unnameable*, an unproduced play, *Eleutheria*, and, of course, *Waiting for Godot*.

Although *Waiting for Godot*, a play about two tramps who pass the time pointlessly waiting for an important acquaintance who, famously, never appears, was recognized by some people to be a play of great importance, it was not widely understood at the time of its first productions. Indeed, it still remains a difficult work for many people—and few of these would claim to find many of Beckett's subsequent works any more accessible, as a few brief descriptions will demonstrate. *Endgame* (1957), which is set in a possibly post-apocalyptic world, features a partially crippled man attending to a blind tyrant who is confined to a makeshift wheelchair, and whose ancient parents live in two garbage cans. In *Krapp's Last Tape* (1960), a single, clown-like character pores over years of his recorded audio diaries, adding his wry comments about his various younger incarnations. In *Happy Days* (1962), a middle-aged woman buried up to her chest (and later her neck) keeps up a stream of mainly optimistic chatter directed at her husband's fading presence. *Breath* (1969) is a thirty-second play that begins with the cry of a newborn and ends with a dying gasp. *Not I* (1971) features a disembodied mouth that chatters desperately and only semi-coherently while a shadowy figure gestures weakly in despair.

It seems that, in many of Beckett's plays, one is looking at something approximating the furthest reach of a certain kind of use of the stage. But contrary to a common misunderstanding, Beckett's work never perversely embraces obscurity for its own sake. He is essentially a poetic playwright, whose unusual style of figurative expression embraces not only poetic speech, but a figurative use of stage and action—what Jean Cocteau described as "the plastic expression of poetry." It is Beckett's unusual use of figurative dramaturgy in an age in which realism is regarded as the norm that causes many of the difficulties in comprehending his work. However, there is another aspect to this problem. Beckett is often called an "absurdist," and thus lumped in with playwrights like Eugene Ionesco. Perhaps nothing has served to occlude a clear view of Beckett's work so much as this "absurdist" label. For where Ionesco's response to modern life was itself a celebration of absurdity, Beckett remained troubled by the absurd elements of the modern human condition, and met the tyranny of existential despair by transforming it into coherent artistic form. Beckett's works are peculiar, rich, complex creations that challenge our preconceptions about the meaning of our own lives; while they often seem to be *about* absurdity, they are not themselves absurd.

While *Play* (1963) may not be Beckett's single most important work for the theatre (that honour still belongs to *Waiting for Godot*, which Beckett's publishers decline to have anthologized), in certain ways it provides a better introduction to Beckett because it is more typical of his work and vision than the more famous play. For example, the run-on speech and the placement of characters in large urns are devices Beckett uses elsewhere—most notably in his novel trilogy. Furthermore, if *Waiting for Godot* has been called, in an oft-repeated quip, the play in which "nothing happens—twice," *Play* manages to embrace the concept suggested by that half-joke by making the description almost literally true. Three characters, rendered immobile by their placement in large urns, are forced by an unseen mobile light source to tell in fragments their interconnected stories; then, near the end of the text, when they admit their weariness and ask for the light to go off, following a brief suggestion of peace, comes the stage direction: *[Repeat play.]*

In other words, the play is to be performed through twice, with the second performance duplicating the first as closely as possible. This is one effect that needs to be experienced in the theatre for its full impact to be felt; but taking the trouble to read the play through twice is at least some help. It seems likely that this double repetition represents eternal repetition, which perhaps evokes the afterlife punishments conceived by Dante in *Inferno*: characters forced to tell their sins over and over as they suffer in the afterlife. It may also recall the philosopher Friedrich Nietzsche's suggestion of a "doctrine of eternal recurrence," whereby all the moments of one's life would be replayed endlessly in eternity, no matter how petty and trivial and thoughtless one's choices may have been. And indeed, a good deal of what is unique in Beckett may be revealed by a comparison of *Play* with a drama on a similar theme, Jean-Paul Sartre's *No Exit* (*Huis clos*).

What is untypical of Beckett's usual practice in *Play* is the basic situation and class of the characters, which almost seem to have been borrowed from some middle-class comedy or melodrama—

one of the several possible meanings contained in the title. Another meaning is the implicit command made by the presence behind the light, the character addressed by the speakers as "you." Who or what this figurative presence may be is left to—as so often in Beckett—the inference of the reader. Is it the author? Is it the reader? Is it God, or some supernatural agent? We aren't told. But, while this aspect of *Play* is left up to us to interpret, in reading Beckett one should always keep in mind his own warning about interpreting the more complex writings of his mentor, the novelist James Joyce: "The danger is in the neatness of identifications."

[C.S.W.]

SAMUEL BECKETT
Play[1]
A play in one act

Front centre, touching one another, three identical grey urns about one yard high. From each a head protrudes, the neck held fast in the urn's mouth. The heads are those, from left to right as seen from auditorium, of W2, M, and W1. They face undeviatingly front throughout the play. Faces so lost to age and aspect as to seem almost part of urns. But no masks.

Their speech is provoked by a spotlight projected on faces alone.

The transfer of light from one face to another is immediate. No blackout, i.e. return to almost complete darkness of opening, except where indicated.

The response to light is immediate.

Faces impassive throughout. Voices toneless except where an expression is indicated.

Rapid tempo throughout.

The curtain rises on a stage in almost complete darkness. Urns just discernible. Five seconds.

Faint spots simultaneously on three faces. Three seconds. Voices faint, largely unintelligible.

W1: Yes, strange, darkness best, and the darker the worse, till all dark, then all well, for the time, but it will come, the time will come, the thing is there, you'll see it, get off me, keep off me, all dark, all still, all over, wiped out — 5

W2: *[Together.]* Yes, perhaps a shade gone, I suppose, some might say, poor thing, a shade gone, just a shade, in the head — 10 *[Faint wild laugh.]* — just a shade, but I doubt it, *I* doubt it, not really, I'm all right, still all right, do my best, all I can —

M: Yes, peace, one assumed, all out, all 15 the pain, all as if ... never been, it will come — *[Hiccup]* — pardon, no sense in this, oh I know ... none the less, one assumed, peace ... I mean ... not merely all over, but as if ... 20 never been —

[Spots off. Blackout. Five seconds. Strong spots simultaneously on three faces. Three seconds. Voices normal strength.]

---

[1] *Play* was written in English in late 1962–3, but was first produced and published in 1963 as *Spiel*, in a German translation by Erika and Elmar Tophoven. It received its first performance in English in 1964.

W1:   I said to him, Give her up —
W2: *[Together]* One morning I was sitting —
M: We were not long together —

[Spots off. Blackout. Five seconds. Spot on W1.]

W1: I said to him, Give her up. I swore by all I held   25
    most sacred —

[Spot from W1 to W2.]

W2: One morning as I was sitting stitching by the
    open window she burst in and flew at me. Give
    him up, she screamed, he's mine. Her photographs
    were kind to her. Seeing her now for the first time   30
    full length in the flesh I understood why he
    preferred me.

[Spot from W2 to M.]

M: We were not long together when she smelled the
    rat. Give up that whore, she said, or I'll cut my
    throat — *[Hiccup.]* pardon — so help me God. I   35
    knew she could have no proof. So I told her I did
    not know what she was talking about.

[Spot from M to W2.]

W2: What are you talking about? I said, stitching
    away. Someone yours? Give up whom? I smell you
    off him, she screamed, he stinks of bitch.   40

[Spot from W2 to W1.]

W1: Though I had him dogged for months by a first-
    rate man, no shadow of proof was forthcoming.
    And there was no denying that he continued as …
    assiduous as ever. This, and his horror of the
    merely Platonic thing, made me sometimes won-   45
    der if I were not accusing him unjustly.[2] Yes.

[Spot from W1 to M.]

M: What have you to complain of? I said. Have I
    been neglecting you? How could we be together
    in the way we are if there were someone else?

---

2 Platonic] an intimate relationship in which sexual desire
    does not exist or has been suppressed (from Plato's de-
    scription in *Symposium* of a love that transcends the in-
    dividual to embrace a universal ideal).

Loving her as I did, with all my heart, I could not   50
but feel sorry for her.

[Spot from M to W2.]

W2: Fearing she was about to offer me violence I rang
    for Erskine and he had her shown out. Her parting
    words, as he could testify, if he is still living, and
    has not forgotten, coming and going on the earth,   55
    letting people in, showing people out, were to the
    effect that she would settle my hash. I confess this
    did alarm me a little, at the time.

[Spot from W2 to M.]

M: She was not convinced. I might have known. I
    smell her off you, she kept saying. There was no   60
    answer to this. So I took her in my arms and
    swore I could not live without her. I meant it,
    what is more. Yes, I am sure I did. She did not
    repulse me.

[Spot from M to W1.]

W1: Judge then of my astonishment when one fine   65
    morning, as I was sitting stricken in the morning
    room, he slunk in, fell on his knees before me,
    buried his face in my lap and … confessed.

[Spot from W1 to M.]

M: She put a bloodhound on me, but I had a little
    chat with him. He was glad of the extra money.   70

[Spot from M to W2.]

W2: Why don't you get out, I said, when he started
    moaning about his home life, there is obviously
    nothing between you any more. Or is there?

[Spot from W2 to W1.]

W1: I confess my first feeling was one of wonder-
    ment. What a male!   75

*[Spot from W1 to M. He opens his mouth to speak. Spot
from M to W2.]*

W2: Anything between us, he said, what do you take
    me for, a something machine? And of course with
    him no danger of the … spiritual thing. Then why
    don't you get out? I said. I sometimes wondered if
    he was not living with her for her money.   80

[Spot from W2 to M.]

M: The next thing was the scene between them. I can't have her crashing in here, she said, threatening to take my life. I must have looked incredulous. Ask Erskine, she said, if you don't believe me. But she threatens to take her own, I said. 85 Not yours? she said. No, I said, hers. We had fun trying to work this out.

[Spot from M to W1.]

W1: Then I forgave him. To what will love not stoop! I suggested a little jaunt to celebrate, to the Riviera or our darling Grand Canary.3 He was looking 90 pale. Peaked. But this was not possible just then. Professional commitments.

[Spot from W1 to W2.]

W2: She came again. Just strolled in. All honey. Licking her lips. Poor thing. I was doing my nails, by the open window. He has told me all about it, 95 she said. Who he, I said filing away, and what it? I know what torture you must be going through, she said, and I have dropped in to say I bear you no ill-feeling. I rang for Erskine.

[Spot from W2 to M.]

M: Then I got frightened and made a clean breast of 100 it. She was looking more and more desperate. She had a razor in her vanity-bag. Adulterers, take warning, never admit.

[Spot from M to W1.]

W1: When I was satisfied it was all over I went over to have a gloat. Just a common tart. What he could 105 have found in her when he had me —

[Spot from W1 to W2.]

W2: When he came again we had it out. I felt like death. He went on about why he had to tell her. Too risky and so on. That meant he had gone back to her. Back to that! 110

3 Riviera] the popular resort area of the Mediterranean coast between France and Italy; Grand Canary] Gran Canaria, the most fertile of Spain's Canary Islands, located in the Atlantic off the coast of Morocco.

[Spot from W2 to W1.]

W1: Pudding face, puffy, spots, blubber mouth, jowls, no neck, dugs you could —

[Spot from W1 to W2.]

W2: He went on and on. I could hear a mower. An old hand mower. I stopped him and said that whatever I might feel I had no silly threats to offer 115 — but not much stomach for her leavings either. He thought that over for a bit.

[Spot from W2 to W1.]

W1: Calves like a flunkey — 4

[Spot from W1 to M.]

M: When I saw her again she knew. She was looking — *[Hiccup.]* — wretched. Pardon. Some fool was 120 cutting grass. A little rush, then another. The problem was how to convince her that no … revival of intimacy was involved. I couldn't. I might have known. So I took her in my arms and said I could not go on living without her. I don't believe 125 I could have.

[Spot from M to W2.]

W2: The only solution was to go away together. He swore we should as soon as he had put his affairs in order. In the meantime we were to carry on as before. By that he meant as best we could. 130

[Spot from W2 to W1.]

W1: So he was mine again. All mine. I was happy again. I went about singing. The world —

[Spot from W1 to M.]

M: At home all heart to heart, new leaf and bygones bygones. I ran into your ex-doxy, she said one night, on the pillow, you're well out of that. Rather 135 uncalled for, I thought. I am indeed, sweetheart, I said, I am indeed. God what vermin women. Thanks to you, angel, I said.

[Spot from M to W1.]

4 flunkey] a menial servant.

W1: Then I began to smell her off him again. Yes.

[Spot from W1 to W2.]

W2: When he stopped coming I was prepared. More 140
or less.

[Spot from W2 to M.]

M: Finally it was all too much. I simply could no
longer —

[Spot from M to W1.]

W1: Before I could do anything he disappeared.
That meant she had won. That slut! I couldn't 145
credit it. I lay stricken for weeks. Then I drove
over to her place. It was all bolted and barred. All
grey with frozen dew. On the way back by Ash
and Snodland — [5]

[Spot from W1 to M.]

M: I simply could no longer — 150

[Spot from M to W2.]

W2: I made a bundle of his things and burnt them.
It was November and the bonfire was going.[6] All
night I smelt them smouldering.

*[Spot off W2. Blackout. Five seconds. Spots half
previous strength simultaneously on three faces. Three
seconds. Voices proportionately lower.]*

W1:   Mercy, mercy —
W2: *[Together.]* To say I am — 155
M: When first this change —

[Spots off. Blackout. Five seconds. Spot on M.]

M: When first this change I actually thanked God. I
thought, It is done, it is said, now all is going
out —

[Spot from M to W1.]

W1: Mercy, mercy, tongue still hanging out for 160

---

5 Ash and Snodland] villages in West Kent, England.
6 November … bonfire] probably a bonfire for Guy
Fawkes Day, celebrated with bonfires and fireworks on
November 5th.

mercy. It will come. You haven't seen me. But you
will. Then it will come.

[Spot from W1 to W2.]

W2: To say I am not disappointed, no, I am. I had
anticipated something better. More restful.

[Spot from W2 to W1.]

W1: Or you will weary of me. 165

[Spot from W1 to M.]

M: Down, all going down, into the dark, peace is
coming, I thought, after all, at last, I was right,
after all, thank God, when first this change.

[Spot from M to W2.]

W2: Less confused. Less confusing. At the same time
I prefer this to … the other thing. Definitely. 170
There are endurable moments.

[Spot from W2 to M.]

M: I thought.

[Spot from M to W2.]

W2: When you go out — and I go out. Some day
you will tire of me and go out … for good.

[Spot from W2 to W1.]

W1: Hellish half-light. 175

[Spot from W1 to M.]

M: Peace, yes, I suppose, a kind of peace, and all that
pain as if … never been.

[Spot from M to W2.]

W2: Give me up, as a bad job. Go away and start
poking and pecking at someone else. On the other
hand— 180

[Spot from W2 to W1.]

W1: Get off me! Get off me!

[Spot from W1 to M.]

M: It will come. Must come. There is no future in
this.

[Spot from M to W2.]

W2: On the other hand things may disimprove, there   185
 is that danger.

[Spot from W2 to M.]

M: Oh of course I know now —

[Spot from M to W1.]

W1: Is it that I do not tell the truth, is that it, that
 some day somehow I may tell the truth at last and
 then no more light at last, for the truth?

[Spot from W1 to W2.]

W2: You might get angry and blaze me clean out of   190
 my wits. Mightn't you?

[Spot from W2 to M.]

M: I know now, all that was just … play. And all this?
 When will all this —

[Spot from M to W1.]

W1: Is that it?

[Spot from W1 to W2.]

W2: Mightn't you?   195

[Spot from W2 to M.]

M: All this, when will all this have been … just play?

[Spot from M to W1.]

W1: I can do nothing … for anybody … any more
 … thank God. So it must be something I have to
 say. How the mind works still!

[Spot from W1 to W2.]

W2: But I doubt it. It would not be like you   200
 somehow. And you must know I am doing my
 best. Or don't you?

[Spot from W2 to M.]

M: Perhaps they have become friends. Perhaps
 sorrow —

[Spot from M to W1.]

W1: But I have said all I can. All you let me. All I —   205

[Spot from W1 to M.]

M: Perhaps sorrow has brought them together.

[Spot from M to W2.]

W2: No doubt I make the same mistake as when it
 was the sun that shone, of looking for sense where
 possibly there is none.

[Spot from W2 to M.]

M: Perhaps they meet, and sit, over a cup of that   210
 green tea they both so loved, without milk or sugar
 not even a squeeze of lemon —

[Spot from M to W2.]

W2: Are you listening to me? Is anyone listening to
 me? Is anyone looking at me? Is anyone bothering
 about me at all?   215

[Spot from W2 to M.]

M: Not even a squeeze of —

[Spot from M to W1.]

W1: Is it something I should do with my face, other
 than utter? Weep?

[Spot from W1 to W2.]

W2: Am I taboo, I wonder. Not necessarily, now that
 all danger is averted. That poor creature — I can   220
 hear her — that poor creature —

[Spot from W2 to W1.]

W1: Bite off my tongue and swallow it? Spit it out?
 Would that placate you? How the mind works still
 to be sure!

[Spot from W1 to M.]

M: Meet, and sit, now in the one dear place, now in   225
 the other, and sorrow together, and compare—
 [Hiccup.] pardon — happy memories.

[Spot from M to W1.]

W1: If only I could think, There is no sense in this
 … either, none whatsoever. I can't.

[Spot from W1 to W2.]

W2: That poor creature who tried to seduce you, what ever became of her, do you suppose? — I can hear her. Poor thing. 230

[Spot from W2 to M.]

M: Personally I always preferred Lipton's.[7]

[Spot from M to W1.]

W1: And that all is falling, all fallen, from the beginning, on empty air. Nothing being asked at all. No one asking me for anything at all. 235

[Spot from W1 to W2.]

W2: They might even feel sorry for me, if they could see me. But never so sorry as I for them.

[Spot from W2 to W1.]

W1: I can't.

[Spot from W1 to W2.]

W2: Kissing their sour kisses. 240

[Spot from W2 to M.]

M: I pity them in any case, yes, compare my lot with theirs, however blessed, and —

[Spot from M to W1.]

W1: I can't. The mind won't have it. It would have to go. Yes.

[Spot from W1 to M.]

M: Pity them. 245

[Spot from M to W2.]

W2: What do you do when you go out? Sift?

[Spot from W2 to M.]

M: Am I hiding something? Have I lost —

[Spot from M to W1.]

W1: She had means, I fancy, though she lived like a pig.

[Spot from W1 to W2.]

_____

7 Lipton's] a brand of tea.

W2: Like dragging a great roller, on a scorching day. The strain ... to get it moving, momentum coming— 250

[Spot off W2. Blackout. Three seconds. Spot on W2.]

W2: Kill it and strain again.

[Spot from W2 to M.]

M: Have I lost ... the thing you want? Why go out? Why go— 255

[Spot from M to W2.]

W2: And you perhaps pitying me, thinking, Poor thing, she needs a rest.

[Spot from W2 to W1.]

W1: Perhaps she has taken him away to live ... somewhere in the sun.

[Spot from W1 to M.]

M: Why go down? Why not— 260

[Spot from M to W2.]

W2: I don't know.

[Spot from W2 to W1.]

W1: Perhaps she is sitting somewhere, by the open window, her hands folded in her lap, gazing down out over the olives—

[Spot from W1 to M.]

M: Why not keep on glaring at me without ceasing? I might start to rave and — [Hiccup.] — bring it up for you. Par— 265

[Spot from M to W2.]

W2: No.

[Spot from W2 to M.]

M: —don.

[Spot from M to W1.]

W1: Gazing down out over the olives, then the sea, wondering what can be keeping him, growing cold. Shadow stealing over everything. Creeping. Yes. 270

[Spot from W1 to M.]

M: To think we were never together.

[Spot from M to W2.]

W2: Am I not perhaps a little unhinged already?   275

[Spot from W2 to W1.]

W1: Poor creature. Poor creatures.

[Spot from W1 to M.]

M: Never woke together, on a May morning, the first
to wake to wake the other two. Then in a little
dinghy —

[Spot from M to W1.]

W1: Penitence, yes, at a pinch, atonement, one was   280
resigned, but no, that does not seem to be the
point either.

[Spot from W1 to W2.]

W2: I say, Am I not perhaps a little unhinged already?
[Hopefully.] Just a little? *[Pause.]* I doubt it.

[Spot from W2 to M.]

M: A little dinghy—   285

[Spot from M to W1.]

W1: Silence and darkness were all I craved. Well, I
get a certain amount of both. They being one.
Perhaps it is more wickedness to pray for more.

[Spot from W1 to M.]

M: A little dinghy, on the river, I resting on my oars,
they lolling on air-pillows in the stern … sheets.   290
Drifting. Such fantasies.

[Spot from M to W1.]

W1: Hellish half-light.

[Spot from W1 to W2.]

W2: A shade gone. In the head. Just a shade. I doubt it.

[Spot from W2 to M.]

M: We were not civilized.

[Spot from M to W1.]

W1: Dying for dark — and the darker the worse.   295
Strange.

[Spot from W1 to M.]

M: Such fantasies. Then. And now —

[Spot from M to W2.]

W2: *I* doubt it.

*[Pause. Peal of wild low laughter from W2 cut short as
spot from her to W1.]*

W1: Yes, and the whole thing there, all there, staring
you in the face. You'll see it. Get off me. Or weary.   300

[Spot from W1 to M.]

M: and now, that you are … mere eye. Just looking.
At my face. On and off.

[Spot from M to W1.]

W1: Weary of playing with me. Get off me. Yes.

[Spot from W1 to M.]

M: Looking for something. In my face. Some truth.
In my eyes. Not even.   305

*[Spot from M to W2. Laugh as before from W2 cut
short as spot from her to M.]*

M: Mere eye. No mind. Opening and shutting on
me. Am I as much —

[Spot off M. Blackout. Three seconds. Spot on M.]

Am I as much as … being seen?

*[Spot off M. Blackout. Five seconds. Faint spots
simultaneously on three faces. Three seconds. Voices,
faint, largely unintelligible.]*

W1:   Yes, strange, etc.
W2: *[Together.]* Yes, perhaps, etc.   310
M: Yes, peace, etc.

[Repeat play.]

M: *[Closing repeat.]* Am I as much as … being seen?

*[Spot off M. Blackout. Five seconds. Strong spots
simultaneously on three faces. Three seconds. Voices
normal strength.]*

W1:	I said to him. Give her up —
W2:	*[Together.]* One morning as I was sitting —
M:	We were not long together —

315

[Spots off. Blackout. Five seconds. Spot on M.]

M: We were not long together —

[Spot off M. Blackout. Five seconds.]

CURTAIN.

LIGHT

The source of light is single and must not be situated outside the ideal space (stage) occupied by its victims.

The optimum position for the spot is at the centre of the footlights, the faces being thus lit at close quarters and from below.

When exceptionally three spots are required to light the three faces simultaneously, they should be as a single spot branching into three.

Apart from these moments a single mobile spot should be used, swivelling at a maximum speed from one face to another as required.

The method consisting in assigning to each face a separate fixed spot is unsatisfactory in that it is less expressive of a unique inquisitor than the single mobile spot.

URNS

In order for the urns to be only one yard high, it is necessary either that traps be used, enabling the actors to stand below stage level, or that they kneel throughout the play, the urns being open at the back.

Should traps be not available, and the kneeling posture found impracticable, the actors should stand, the urns be enlarged to full length and moved back from front to mid-stage, the tallest actor setting the height, the broadest the breadth, to which the three urns should conform.

The sitting posture results in urns of unacceptable bulk and is not to be considered.

CHORUS

W1:	Yes strange	darkness best	and the darker	the worse
W2:	Yes perhaps	a shade gone	I suppose	some might say
M:	Yes peace	one assumed	all out	all the pain
W1:	till all dark	then all well	for the time	but it will come
W2:	poor thing	a shade gone	just a shade	in the head
M:	all as if	never been	it will come	*[Hiccup.]* pardon
W1:	the time will come	the thing is there		you'll see it
W2:	*[Laugh —]*	just a shade		but I doubt it
M:	no sense in this	oh I know		none the less
W1:	get off me	keep off me	all dark	all still
W2:	*I* doubt it	not really	I'm all right	still all right
M:	one assumed	peace I mean	not merely	all over
W1:	all over	wiped out —		
W2:	do my best	all I can —		
M:	but as if	never been —		

MICHEL TREMBLAY

Les Belles Soeurs

Arguably the most important playwright in Canada, Michel Tremblay has seen his work regularly produced and praised internationally to an extent that few other Canadian playwrights have ever known. Through his plays and novels, he has exerted a profound influence not merely on the nation's theatre, but on Canadian culture taken as a whole—particularly on the mythology and collective identity of Quebecois culture. Indeed, he has become one of the most influential living voices speaking for Quebec to the world at large.

Tremblay's early life, however, was somewhat humble. Born in 1942, he was raised in the then working-class Plateau district of Montreal. His mother, Rhéauna Rathier, had been born in Manitoba to a Métis (i.e., of mixed Native and French ancestry) family; his father, Armand, was a Quebec-born linotype operator, a trade into which Tremblay followed his father for a time, entering the Institut des arts graphiques in 1959 and then working as a linotypist from 1963 to 1966. However, Tremblay had been writing from an early age—as a teenager, he had written a series of fantasy stories that later formed the basis of a collection published as *Contes pour buveurs attardés* (1966; published in English in 1977 as *Stories for Late Night Drinkers*)—and during his training and his work as a linotypist, he continued to write. In 1959 came the first of his works to appear publicly: a short story called "Les loups se mangent entre eux"; he also wrote a short play that year, *Le Train*, which won first prize in a CBC competition for young writers in 1964, and which was staged in Montreal in 1965 and 1968. In 1966 another play, *Cinq* (later reworked to become *En pièces détachées)*, was staged, as well as a dramatization of some of the stories from *Contes pour buveurs attardés*. The latter performance was directed by the man who was to become Tremblay's long-time collaborator, André Brassard. Following this flush of success, Tremblay received a Canada Council grant with which he went to Mexico to write his first novel, *La cité dans l'oeuf* (published in 1969). Tremblay's name became much more widely known, however, when *Les Belles Soeurs* opened at Théâtre du Rideau Vert in August 1968. The play created an instant sensation and gave momentum to what has turned out to be one of the most prolific careers in Canadian letters.

The plays that followed over the next decade seemed to be more or less split between domestic dramas which, like *Les Belles Soeurs* and *En pièces detachées*, were mostly set in the world of the residential street, "rue Fabre"—e.g., *Toujour a toi, Marie Lou (Forever Yours, Marie Lou)* (1971) and *Bonjour, la, bonjour* (1974) —and those which featured the gay transvestite characters who frequent the bars of "Le Main" (as in "the main street," not "the hand")—e.g., a musical (written with composer François Dompierre), *Demain matin, Montréal m'attend* (1972); *Le Duchesse de Langeais* and *Hosanna* (both 1973); and *Sainte Carmen de la Main* (1976). However, this division of characters into two separate worlds effectively ended with *Damnée Manon, Sacrée Sandra* (1977), in which monologues by the drag queen, Sandra, and the prudish Manon are interleaved until they are revealed to be united in their creator, "Michel."

Since then, Tremblay's main attention has been given to completing a vast project called "Le Chroniques du Plateau Royal": a series of novels and connected plays (as well as a group of autobiographies) that chronicle the lives of a group of interrelated characters. The novels include: *La grosse femme d'à côté est enceinte (The Fat Woman Next Door is Pregnant)* (1978), *Thérèse et Pierette à l'école des Saints-Anges (Thérèse and Pierette and the Little Hanging Angel)* (1980), *La duchesse et le roturier (The Duchess and the Commoner)* (1982), *Des Nouvelles d'Edouard (News From Edouard)* (1984), *Le coeur decouvert (The Heart Laid Bare)* (1986), *Le premier quartier de la lune (The First Quarter of the Moon)* (1989), and *Un objet de beauté (A Thing of Beauty)* (1997). As subsequent work has revealed further relations among the characters, all of these novels have proved to be related not only to one another, but also to the plays. The latter include: *Les Anciennes Odeurs (Remember Me)* (1981), *Albertine, en cinq temps (Albertine, in Five Times)* (1984), *Le vrai monde? (The Real World?)* (1987), *La Maison Suspendue* (1990), *Marcel poursivi par les chiens (Marcel Pursued by the Hounds)* (1992) and *Encore une fois, si vous permettez (For the Pleasure of Seeing Her Again)* (1998). However, in Tremblay's most recent works, such as the novel *Hotel Bristol* (1999) and the play *L'État des lieux (Impromptu on Nun's Island)* (2002), he seems to be moving away from the characters of the "Plateau Royal Chronicles." This is not the first transformation his work has undergone over the years, and is unlikely to be the last.

Despite the high regard in which virtually all of Tremblay's works are held, it remains his early hit, *Les Belles Soeurs,* for which he is best known. In Quebec, the play is historically important for two main reasons. First, the play was regarded (as, indeed, much of Tremblay's work in Quebec has been), as a political allegory, and one that was appearing at a time of great political change: the period of the "Quiet Revolution." Second, *Les Belles Soeurs* broke through the formal conventions in which Quebec theatre had confined itself for decades. Whereas the working class had been previously portrayed by playwrights such as Gratien Gelinas and Marcel Dubé, Tremblay had his characters speak *"joual"*—the Quebecois dialect peppered with Anglicisms and blasphemies which takes its name from the alleged pronunciation of the French word for horse, *"cheval."* Through his use of this dialect, Tremblay was able to represent these characters more fully than he could have using a more formal style of French, for the cultural history of Quebec inheres in *joual,* just as, for example, the history of the Israelites may be traced in the etymology of the Hebrew language. The choice seems logical to us now. However, at the time, the language of *Les Belles Soeurs* startled the critics and public and became the subject of a prolonged public debate. In retrospect, it appears that *Les Belles Soeurs* transformed the face of theatre in Quebec almost overnight, not only by spawning numerous imitators, but also by encouraging a spirit of experimentation that has made contemporary Quebec theatre among the most innovative in the world.

But, of course, this description of the importance of *Les Belles Soeurs* within Quebec does not explain its immense success in English Canada, or indeed, the rest of the world—for the play has been produced all over the world in more than 20 languages. The story could hardly be more simple: Germain Lauzon wins a million trading stamps and invites a group of relatives and friends over for a "stamp-pasting party," but she eventually discovers that the women have been stealing her stamps throughout the evening. In other hands, the story might have been mildly humorous but ultimately tedious. But the strength of Tremblay's characterizations—which emerge most vividly in the many monologues that interrupt the action—and the sophistication of his dramaturgical technique—such as the use of choral speech: "this stupid rotten life," "Goddamn Johnny," "A club: the fastest road to hell" and, most spectacularly, the "Ode to Bingo"—make the play extremely compelling even for those who have never set foot in a working-class kitchen in Quebec. Like Euripides' *Trojan Women* or Chekhov's *Three Sisters* (or, of course, like Tomson Highway's *The Rez Sisters*) the *belles-soeurs* (sisters-in-law) of Tremblay are powerless within the larger terms of society: they are neither male nor rich, nor do they belong to a conquering nation or class (i.e., they are not Anglophones). So, in a sense, though they have formed their own tight-knit community, they are effectively imprisoned outside the powerful core of society, left hopelessly wishing for some external release from their fate. But far from instilling a more mutually supportive and gentler sense of community, the hothouse circumstances in which they live appears to make them more intensely representative of the values, the affectations, the intolerance, the envy, and the aggression of the very society that has disenfranchised them. *Les Belles Soeurs* offers us, then, in concentrated form, a portrait of humanity in the contemporary materialist world.

[C.S.W.]

MICHEL TREMBLAY
Les Belles Soeurs[1]
Translated by John Van Burek and Bill Glassco

CHARACTERS

GERMAINE LAUZON
LINDA LAUZON, Germaine's daughter
ROSE OUIMET, Germaine's sister
GABRIELLE JODOIN, another sister

LISETTE DE COURVAL,
MARIE-ANGE BROUILLETTE   } neighbours
YVETTE LONGPRÉ
DES-NEIGES VERRETTE

THÉRÈSE DUBUC, Germaine's sister-in-law
OLIVINE DUBUC, Thérèse's mother-in-law

ANGÉLINE SAUVÉ,   } neighbours
RHÉAUNA BIBEAU

LISE PAQUETTE,   } Linda's friends
GINETTE MENARD

PIERRETTE GUÉRIN, Germaine's youngest sister

SCENE

The kitchen of a Montreal tenement, 1965.
Four enormous boxes occupy centre stage.

ACT ONE

LINDA LAUZON enters. She sees the four boxes in the middle of the kitchen.

LINDA: God, what's that? Ma!
GERMAINE: Is that you, Linda?
LINDA: Yeah! What are all these boxes in the kitchen?

---

[1] *Les Belles Soeurs* was written in French in 1965; it premiered at Théâtre du Rideau Vert in Montreal on August 28, 1968, directed by André Brassard; the English translation by Bill Glassco and John van Burek premiered at the St. Lawrence Centre in 1973.

GERMAINE: They're my stamps.[2]

LINDA: Already? Jeez, that was fast.

GERMAINE LAUZON enters.

GERMAINE: Yeah, it surprised me too. They came this morning right after you left. The door-bell rang. I went to answer it and there's this big fellow standing there. Oh, you'd have liked him, Linda. Just your type. About twenty-two, twenty-three, dark curly hair. Nice little moustache. Real handsome. Anyway, he says to me, "Are you the lady of the house, Mme. Germaine Lauzon?" I said, "yes that's me." And he says, "Good, I've brought your stamps." Linda, I was so excited. I didn't know what to say. Next thing I knew, two guys are bringing in the boxes, and the other one's giving me this speech. Linda, what a talker. And such manners. I'm sure you would have liked him.

LINDA: So, what did he say?

GERMAINE: I can't remember. I was so excited. He told me the company he works for was real happy I'd won the million stamps. That I was real lucky .... Me, I was speechless. I wish your father had been here, he could have talked to him. I don't even know if I thanked him.

LINDA: That's a lot of stamps to glue. Four boxes! One million stamps, that's no joke!

GERMAINE: There's only three boxes. The other one's booklets. But I had an idea, Linda. We're not gonna do all this alone! You going out tonight?

LINDA: Yeah, Robert's supposed to call me . . .

GERMAINE: You can't put it off till tomorrow? Listen, I had an idea. I phoned my sisters, your father's sister and I went to see the neighbours. And I've invited them all to come and paste stamps with us tonight. I'm gonna give a stamp-pasting party. Isn't that a great idea? I bought some peanuts, and your little brother went out to get some Coke . . . .

LINDA: Ma, you know I always go out on Thursdays! It's our night out. We're gonna go to a show.

GERMAINE: You can't leave me alone on a night like this. I've got fifteen people coming . . .

LINDA: Are you crazy! You'll never get fifteen people in this kitchen! And you can't use the rest of the house. The painters are here. Jesus, Ma! Sometimes you're really dumb.

GERMAINE: Sure, that's right, put me down. Fine, you go out, do just as you like. That's all you ever do anyway. Nothing new. I never have any pleasure. Someone's always got to spoil it for me. Go ahead Linda, you go out tonight, go to your goddamned show. Jesus Christ Almighty, I'm so fed up.

LINDA: Come on, Ma, be reasonable . . . .

GERMAINE: I don't want to be reasonable, I don't want to hear about it! I kill myself for you and what do I get in return? Nothing! A big fat nothing! You can't even do me a little favour! I'm warning you, Linda, I'm getting sick of waiting on you, you and everyone else. I'm not your servant, you know. I've got a million stamps to paste and I'm not about to do it myself. Besides, those stamps are for the whole family, which means everybody's gotta do their share. Your father's working tonight but if we don't get done he says he'll help tomorrow. I'm not asking for the moon. Help me for a change, instead of wasting your time with that jerk.

LINDA: Robert is not a jerk.

GERMAINE: Sure, he's a genius! Boy, I knew you were stupid, but not that stupid. When are you going to realize your Robert is a bozo? He doesn't even make sixty bucks a week. All he can do is take you to the local movie house Thursday nights. Take a mother's advice, Linda, keep hanging around with that dope and you'll end up just like him. You want to marry a shoe-gluer and be a strapper all your life?

LINDA: Shut up, Ma! When you get sore, you don't know what you're saying. Anyway, forget it . . . . I'll stay home . . . Just stop screaming, okay? And by the way, Robert's due for a raise soon and he'll be making lots more. He's not as dumb as you think. Even the boss told me he might start

---

2 stamps] not postage stamps, but "trading" stamps, a fixed number of which would ordinarily be awarded for every dollar of merchandise purchased by a customer. The stamp system of the 1960s has mostly been replaced today by the various "point" systems, in which a customer carries a card to register points for every purchase at specified businesses.

making big money 'cause they'll put him in charge of something. You wait. Eighty bucks a week is nothing to laugh at. Anyway . . . I'm gonna go phone him and tell him I can't go to the show . . . Hey, why don't I tell him to come and glue stamps with us?

GERMAINE: Mother of God, I just told you I can't stand him and you want to bring him home tonight. Where the hell are your brains? What did I do to make God in heaven send me such idiots? Just this afternoon, I send your brother to get me a bag of onions and he comes home with a quart of milk. It's unbelievable! You have to repeat everything ten times around here. No wonder I lose my temper. I told you, Linda. The party's for girls. Just girls. Your Robert's not queer, is he?

LINDA: Okay Ma, okay, just don't flip your wig. I'll tell him not to come. Jesus, you can't do a thing around here. You think I feel like gluing stamps after working all day. (*She starts to dial a number.*) Why don't you go dust in the living room, eh? You don't have to listen to what I'm going to say . . . . "Hello, may I speak to Robert? . . . . When do you expect him? . . . . Okay, will you tell him Linda phoned? . . . Fine, Mme. Bergeron, and you? . . . That's good . . . Okay, thanks a lot. Bye." (*She hangs up. The phone rings right away.*) "Hello?" . . . Ma, it's for you.

GERMAINE: Twenty years old and you still can't say "One moment please" when you answer a phone.

LINDA: It's only Aunt Rose. Why should I be polite to her?

GERMAINE: (*putting her hand over the receiver*) Will you be quiet! What if she heard you?

LINDA: Who gives a shit?

GERMAINE: "Hello? Oh, it's you, Rose . . . Yeah, they're here . . . How 'bout that? A million of 'em! They're sitting right in front of me and I still can't believe it. One million! One million! I don't know how much that is, but who cares. A million's a million . . . . Sure, they sent a catalogue. I already had one but this one's for this year, so it's a lot better. The old one was falling apart . . . They've got the most beautiful stuff, wait till you see it. It's unbelievable! I think I'll be able to take everything they've got. I'll re-furnish the whole house. I'm gonna get a new stove, new fridge, new kitchen table and chairs. I think I'll take the red one with the gold stars. I don't think you've seen that one . . . . Oh, it's so beautiful, Rose. I'm getting new pots, new cutlery, a full set of dishes, salt and pepper shakers . . . Oh, and you know those glasses with the "caprice" design.[3] Well, I'm taking a set of those, too. Mme. de Courval got a set last year and she paid a fortune for them, but mine will be free. She'll be mad as hell . . . What? . . . Yeah, she'll be here tonight. They've got those chrome tins for flour and sugar, coffee and stuff . . . . I'm taking it all. I'm getting a Colonial bedroom suite with full accessories. There's curtains, dresser-covers, one of those things you put on the floor beside the bed . . . No, dear, not that . . . New wallpaper . . . Not the floral, Henri can't sleep with flowers . . . I'm telling you Rose, it's gonna be one beautiful bedroom. And the living room! Wait till you hear this . . . . I've got a big TV with a built-in stereo, a synthetic nylon carpet, real paintings . . . You know those Chinese paintings I've always wanted, the ones with the velvet? . . . Aren't they though? Oh, and get a load of this . . . I'm gonna have the same crystal platters as your sister-in-law, Aline! I'm not sure, but I think mine are even nicer. There's ashtrays and lamps . . . I guess that's about it for the living room . . . there's an electric razor for Henri to shave with, shower curtains. So what? We'll put one in. It all comes with the stamps. There's a sunken bathtub, a new sink, bathing suits for everyone . . . No, Rose, I am not too fat. Don't get smart. Now listen, I'm gonna re-do the kid's room, completely. Have you seen what they've got for kids' bedrooms? Rose, it's fabulous! They've got Mickey Mouse all over everything. And for Linda's room . . . Okay, sure, you can just look at the catalogue. But come over right away, the others will be here any minute. I told them to come early. I mean it's gonna take forever to paste all those stamps."

MARIE-ANGE BROUILLETTE enters.

---

3 "caprice" design] a ridged pattern resembling water ripples which first began to appear on glassware in the 1940s.

GERMAINE: "Okay, I've gotta go. Mme. Brouillette's just arrived. Okay, yeah . . . . Yeah . . . Bye!"

MARIE-ANGE: Mme. Lauzon, I just can't help it, I'm jealous. 175

GERMAINE: Well, I know what you mean. It's quite an event. But excuse me for a moment, Mme. Brouillette, I'm not quite ready. I was talking to my sister, Rose. We can see each other across the alley, it's handy. 180

MARIE-ANGE: Is she gonna be here?

GERMAINE: You bet! She wouldn't miss this for love nor money. Here, have a seat and while you're waiting look at the catalogue. You won't believe all the lovely things they've got. And I'm getting them 185 all, Mme. Brouillette. The works! The whole catalogue. (*She goes into her bedroom.*)

MARIE-ANGE: You wouldn't catch me having luck like that. Fat chance. My life is shit and it will always be. 190 A million stamps! A whole house. If I didn't bite my tongue, I'd scream. Typical. The ones with all the luck least deserve it. What did Mme. Lauzon do to deserve this, eh? Nothing. Absolutely nothing! She's no better looking than me. In fact, she's no better 195 period. These contests shouldn't be allowed. The priest the other day was right. They ought to be abolished. Why should she win a million stamps and not me? Why? It's not fair. I work too, I've got kids, too, I have to wipe their asses, just like her. If any- 200 thing, my kids are cleaner than hers. I work like a slave, it's no wonder I'm all skin and bones. Her, she's as fat as a pig. And now, I'll have to live next door to her and the house she gets for free. It burns me up, I can't stand it. What's more, there'll be no 205 end to her smart-assed comments 'cause it'll all go straight to her head. She's just the type, the loud-mouthed bitch. We'll be hearing about her god-damned stamps for years. I've a right to be angry. I don't want to die in this shit while madame Fatso 210 here goes swimming in velvet! It's not fair! I'm sick of knocking myself out for nothing! My life is noth-ing. A big fat zero. And I haven't a cent to my name. I'm fed up. I'm fed up with this stupid, rotten life.

During the monologue, GABRIELLE JODOIN, ROSE OIMET, YVETTE LONGPRÉ and LISETTE DE COURVAL have entered. They take their places in the kitchen without paying attention to MARIE-ANGE. The five women get up and turn to the audience. The lighting changes.

THE FIVE WOMEN: (*together*) This stupid, rotten 215 life! Monday!

LISETTE: When the sun with his rays starts caressing the little flowers in the fields and the little birdies open wide their little beaks to send forth their little cries to heaven . . . 220

THE OTHERS: I get up and I fix breakfast. Toast, coffee, bacon, eggs. I nearly go nuts trying to get the others out of bed. The kids leave for school, my husband goes to work.

MARIE-ANGE: Not mine, he's unemployed. He stays 225 in bed.

THE FIVE WOMEN: Then I work. I work like a demon. I don't stop till noon. I wash . . . Dresses, shirts, stockings, sweaters, pants, underpants, bras. The works. I scrub it, wring it out, scrub it again, 230 rinse it . . . My hands are chapped. My back is sore. I curse like hell. At noon, the kids come home. They eat like pigs, they wreck the house, they leave. In the afternoon I hang out the wash, the biggest pain of all. When that's finished, I start the supper. They all 235 come home. They're tired and grumpy. We all fight. But at night, we watch TV. Tuesday.

LISETTE: When the sun with his rays . . .

THE OTHERS: I get up and I fix breakfast. The same goddamned thing. Toast, coffee, bacon, eggs. I 240 drag the others out of bed and I shove them out the door. Then it's the ironing. I work, I work, I work and I work. It's noon before I know it and the kids are mad because lunch isn't ready. I make 'em baloney sandwiches. I work all afternoon. 245 Suppertime comes, we all fight. But at night, we watch TV. Wednesday . . . Shopping day. I walk all day, I break my back carrying parcels this big, I come back home exhausted. But I've still got to make supper. When the others get home I look like 250 I'm dead. I am. My husband bitches, the kids scream. We all fight. But at night, we watch TV. Thursday and Friday . . . Same thing . . . I work. I slave. I kill myself for my pack of morons. Then I spend the day Saturday tripping over the kids and 255 we all fight. But at night, we watch TV. Sunday we go out, the whole family, we get on the bus and go for supper with the mother-in-law. I have to watch the kids like a hawk, laugh at the old man's jokes, eat the old lady's food, which everyone says is better than mine . . . At night, we watch TV. I'm fed up with this stupid, rotten life! This stupid, rotten life! This stupid, rotten life. This stup . . . .

The lights return to normal. They sit down suddenly.

LISETTE: On my last trip to Europe . . . .

ROSE: There she goes with her Europe again. We're in for it now. Once she gets started, there's no shutting her up!

DES-NEIGES VERRETTE comes in. Discreet little greetings are heard.

LISETTE: I only wished to say that in Europe they don't have stamps. I mean, they have stamps, but not like these ones. Only letter stamping stamps.

DES-NEIGES: That's no fun! So they don't get presents like us? Sounds pretty dull to me, Europe.

LISETTE: Oh no, it's very nice despite that . . .

MARIE-ANGE: Mind you, I've got nothing against stamps, they're useful. If it weren't for the stamps, I'd still be waiting for that thing to grind my meat with. What I don't like is the contests.

LISETTE: But why? They can make families happy.

MARIE-ANGE: Maybe, but they're a pain in the ass for the people next door.

LISETTE: Mme. Brouillette, your language! I speak properly, and I'm none the worse for it.

MARIE-ANGE: I like the way I talk, and I say what I got to say. I never went to Europe, so I can't afford to talk like you.

ROSE: Hey, you two, cut it out! We didn't come here to fight. You keep it up, I'm crossing the alley and going home.

GABRIELLE: What's taking Germaine so long? Germaine!

GERMAINE: (*from the bedroom*) Be there in a minute. I'm having a hard time getting into my . . . Well, I'm having a hard time . . . Is Linda there?

GABRIELLE: Linda! Linda! No, she's not here.

MARIE-ANGE: I think I saw here go out a while ago.

GERMAINE: Don't tell me she's snuck out, the little bugger.

GABRIELLE: Can we start pasting stamps in the meantime?

GERMAINE: No wait! I'm going to tell you what to do. Don't start yet, wait till I get there. Chat for a bit.

GABRIELLE: "Chat for a bit?" What are we going to chat about . . .

The telephone rings.

ROSE: My God, that scared me! Hello . . . No, she's out but if you want to wait I think she'll be back in a few minutes. (*She puts the receiver down, goes out on the balcony and shouts*) Linda! Linda, telephone!

LISETTE: So, Mme. Longpré how does marriage agree with your daughter Claudette?

YVETTE: Oh, she loves it. She's having a ball. She told me about her honeymoon, you know.

GABRIELLE: Where did they go to?

YVETTE: Well, he won a trip to the Canary Islands, eh? So you see, they had to put the wedding ahead a bit . . .

ROSE: (*laughing*) The Canary Islands! A honeymoon in bird shit, eh?

GABRIELLE: Come on, Rose!

ROSE: What?

DES-NEIGES: The Canary Islands, where's that?

LISETTE: We stopped by there, my husband and I, on our last trip to Europe. It's real . . . It's a very pleasant country. The women only wear skirts.

ROSE: The perfect place for my husband!

LISETTE: And I'm afraid the natives are not very clean. Of course, in Europe, people don't wash.

DES-NEIGES: It shows too. Look at those Italians next door to me. You wouldn't believe how that woman stinks.

They all burst out laughing.

LISETTE: (*insinuating*) Did you ever notice her clothesline, on Monday?

DES-NEIGES: No, why?

LISETTE: Well, all I know is this . . . . Those people don't have any underwear.

MARIE-ANGE: You're kidding!

ROSE: I don't believe it!

YVETTE: You gotta be joking!

LISETTE: It's the God's truth! Take a look for 340
yourselves next Monday. You'll see.

YVETTE: No wonder they stink.

MARIE-ANGE: Maybe she's too modest to hang them
outside.

The others laugh.

LISETTE: Modest! A European? They don't know 345
what it means. Just look at their movies you see
on TV. It's appalling. They stand right in the
middle of the street and kiss. On the mouth, too!
It's in their blood, you know. Take a look at that
Italian's daughter when she brings her friends 350
around . . . . Her boyfriends, that is . . . It's
disgusting what she does, that girl. She has no
shame! Which reminds me, Mme. Ouimet. I saw
your Michael the other day . . .

ROSE: Not with that slut, I hope! 355

LISETTE: I'm afraid so.

ROSE: You must be mistaken. It couldn't have been
him.

LISETTE: I beg your pardon, but the Italians are my
neighbours, too. The two of them were on the 360
front balcony . . . I suppose they thought no one
could see them . . .

DES-NEIGES: It's true, Mme. Ouimet, I saw them
myself. I tell you, they were necking like crazy.

ROSE: The little bastard! As if one pig in the family's 365
not enough. By pig I mean my husband. Can't
even watch a girl on TV without getting a . . . .
Without getting worked up. Goddamn sex! They
never get enough, those Ouimets. They're all alike,
they . . . 370

GABRIELLE: Rose, you don't have to tell the whole
world . . .

LISETTE: But we're very concerned . . .

DES-NEIGES and MARIE-ANGE: Yes, we are . . .

YVETTE: To get back to my daughter's honeymoon . . . 375

GERMAINE: (*entering*) Here I am, girls! (*Greetings,
"how are you's," etc.*) So, what have you all been
talking about?

ROSE: Oh, Mme. Longpré was telling us about her
daughter Claudette's honeymoon 380

GERMAINE: Really? (*to* YVETTE) Hello, dear . . . (*to*
ROSE) And what was she saying?

ROSE: Sounds like they had a great trip. They met

all these people. They went on a boat. They were
visiting islands, of course, The Canary Islands . . . 385
They went fishing and they caught fish this big.
They ran into some couples they knew . . . . Old
friends of Claudette's. Then they came back together and, oh yes, they stopped over in New York.
Mme. Longpré was giving us all the details . . . 390

YVETTE: Well . . .

ROSE: Eh, Mme. Longpré, isn't that right?

YVETTE: Well, as a matter of fact . . .

GERMAINE: You tell your daughter, Mme. Longpré,
that I wish her all the best. Or course we weren't 395
invited to the wedding, but we wish her well
anyway.

There is an embarrassed silence.

GABRIELLE: Hey! It's almost seven! The rosary![4]

GERMAINE: Dear God, my novena for Ste.-Thérèse.[5]
I'll get Linda's radio. (*She goes out.*) 400

ROSE: What does she want with Ste.-Thérèse,
especially after winning all that?

DES-NEIGES: Maybe she's having trouble with her
kids . . . .

GABRIELLE: No, she would have told me 405

GERMAINE: (*from the bedroom*) Goddamn it! Where
did she put that frigging radio?

ROSE: I don't know, Gaby. Our sister usually keeps
things to herself.

GABRIELLE: Not with me. She tells me everything. 410
You, you're such a blabbermouth . . . .

ROSE: You've got a lot of nerve! What do you mean,
blabbermouth? Gabrielle Jodoin! My mouth's no
bigger than yours.

GABRIELLE: Come off it, you know you can't keep 415
a secret!

---

4 rosary] in Roman Catholicism, a sequence of prayers,
which are usually marked with the aid of a chaplet
(which is also called a rosary), a string of beads to which
a small crucifix is attached. The sequence of prayers usually involves five decades (each decade is a group of ten)
of "Hail Marys" (a prayer addressed to the Virgin Mary),
with each decade preceded by the Lord's Prayer, followed
by the Gloria Patri (Glory be to the Father). In this instance, the prayer is being led by a priest on the radio.

5 novena] a period of religious devotion normally lasting
nine days.

ROSE: Well, I never . . . If you think . . .

LISETTE: Wasn't it you, Mme. Ouimet, who just said we didn't come here to quarrel?

ROSE: Hey, you mind your own business. Besides, I didn't say "quarrel." I said "fight." 420

GERMAINE comes back in with a radio.

GERMAINE: What's going on? I can hear you at the other end of the house!

GABRIELLE: Nothing, it's our sister again . . .

GERMAINE: Settle down, Rose. You're supposed to be the life of the party . . . No fighting tonight. 425

ROSE: You see! In our family we say "fight."

GERMAINE turns on the radio. We hear a voice saying the rosary. All the women get down on their knees. After a few "Hail Marys" a great racket is heard outside. The women scream and run to the door.

GERMAINE: Oh my God! My sister-in-law Thérèse's mother-in-law just fell down three flights of stairs!

ROSE: Did you hurt yourself, Mme. Dubuc? 430

GERMAINE: Rose, shut up! She's probably dead!

THÉRÈSE: (*from a distance*) Are you all right, Mme. Dubuc? (*A faint moan is heard.*) Wait a minute. Let me get the wheelchair off you. Is that better? Now I'm gonna help you get back in your chair. 435 Come on, Mme. Dubuc, make a little effort. Don't be so limp! Ouch!

DES-NEIGES: Here, Mme. Dubuc. Let me give you a hand.

THÉRÈSE: Thanks Mlle. Verrette. You're so kind. 440

The other women come back into the room.

ROSE: Germaine, shut off the radio. I'm a nervous wreck!

GERMAINE What about my novena?

ROSE: How far have you gotten?

GERMAINE: I'm only up to seven, but I promised 445 to do nine.

ROSE: So, pick it up tomorrow and you'll be finished on Saturday.

GERMAINE: It's not for nine days, it's for nine weeks.

THÉRÈSE DUBUC and DES-NEIGES VERRETTE enter with OLIVINE DUBUC, who is in a wheelchair.

GERMAINE: My God, she wasn't hurt bad, I hope. 450

THÉRÈSE: No, no, she's used to it. She falls out of her chair ten times a day. Whew! I'm all out of breath. It's no joke, hauling this thing up three flights of stairs. You got something to drink, Germaine? 455

GERMAINE: Gaby, give Thérèse a glass of water. (*She approaches* OLIVINE DUBUC.) And how are you today, Mme. Dubuc?

THÉRÈSE: Don't get too close, Germaine. She's been biting lately. 460

In fact, OLIVINE DUBUC tries to bite GERMAINE's hand.

GERMAINE: My god, you're right! She's dangerous! How long has she been doing that?

THÉRÈSE: Shut off the radio, Germaine, it's getting on my nerves. I'm too upset after what's happened.

GERMAINE: (*reluctantly shuts off the radio*) It's alright, 465 Thérèse, I understand.

THÉRÈSE: Honestly, you don't know, what it's like, I'm at the end of my tether! You can't imagine my life since I got stuck with my mother-in-law. It's not that I don't love her, the poor woman, I pity 470 her. But she's sick, and so temperamental. I've gotta watch her like a hawk!

DES-NEIGES: How come she's out of the hospital?

THÉRÈSE: Well, you see, Mlle. Verrette, three months ago my husband got a raise, so welfare 475 stopped paying for his mother. If she'd stayed there, we would have had to pay all the bills ourselves.

MARIE-ANGE: My, my, my . . .

YVETTE: That's awful.

DES-NEIGES: Dreadful! 480

During THÉRÈSE's speech, GERMAINE opens the boxes and distributes the stamps and books.

THÉRÈSE: We had to bring her home. It's some cross to bear, believe me! Don't forget, that woman's ninety-three years old. It's like having a baby in the house. I have to dress her, undress her, wash her 485

DES-NEIGES: God forbid!

YVETTE: You poor thing.

THÉRÈSE: No, it's fun. Why only this morning, I said to Paul . . . he's my youngest . . . "Maman's going shopping, so you stay here and take good 490 care of Granny." Well, when I got home, Mme. Dubuc had dumped a quart of molasses all over herself and was playing in it like a kid. Of course, Paul was nowhere to be seen. I had to clean the table, the floor, the wheelchair . . . 495

GERMAINE: What about Mme. Dubuc?

THÉRÈSE: I left her like that for the rest of the afternoon. That'll teach her. If she's gonna act like a baby, I'll treat her like one. Do you realize I have to spoon feed her? 500

GERMAINE: My poor Thérèse. How I feel for you.

DES-NEIGES: You're too good, Thérèse.

GABRIELLE: Much too good, I agree.

THÉRÈSE: What can you do, we all have our crosses to bear. 505

MARIE-ANGE: If you ask me, Thérèse, you've got a heavy one!

THÉRÈSE: Oh well, I don't complain. I just tell myself that our Lord is good and He's gonna help me get through. 510

LISETTE: I can't bear it, it makes me want to weep.

THÉRÈSE: Now, Mme. de Courval, don't overdo it.

DES-NEIGES: All I can say, Mme. Dubuc, is you're a real saint.

GERMAINE: Well, now that you've got stamps and booklets, I'll put a little water in some saucers and we can get started, eh? We don't want to spend the night yacking. 515

She fills a few saucers and passes them around. The women start pasting stamps in the books. GERMAINE goes out on the balcony.

GERMAINE: If Linda were here, she could help me! Linda! Linda! Richard, have you seen Linda? I don't believe it! She's got the nerve to sit and drink Coke while I'm slaving away! Be an angel, will you, and tell her to come home right away? Come see Mme. Lauzon tomorrow and she'll give you some peanuts and candy, if there's any left, okay? Go on, sweetie, and tell her to get home this minute! (*She comes back inside.*) The little bitch. She promised to stay home. 520 525

MARIE-ANGE: Kids are all the same.

THÉRÈSE: You can say that again! They got no respect. 530

GABRIELLE: You're telling me. At our house, it's

unbearable. Ever since my Raymond started his *cours classique* he's changed something awful . . . We don't recognize him! He walks around with his nose in the air like he's too good for us. He speaks Latin, at the table! We have to listen to his awful music. Can you imagine, classical music in the middle of the afternoon? And when we don't want to watch his stupid TV concerts, he throws a fit. If there's one thing I hate it's classical music. 535 540

ROSE: Ah! You're not the only one.

THÉRÈSE: I agree. It drives me crazy. Clink! Clank! Bing, Bang, Bong!

GABRIELLE: Of course, Raymond says we don't understand it. As if there's something to understand! Just because he's learning all sorts of nonsense at school, he thinks he can treat us like dirt. I've got half a mind to yank him out and put him to work. 545

ALL THE WOMEN: Kids are so ungrateful! Kids are so ungrateful! 550

GABRIELLE: Be sure to fill those books, eh, girls? Stamps on every page.

ROSE: Relax, Germaine, you'd think we'd never done it before. 555

YVETTE: Isn't it getting a little warm in here? Maybe we could open the window a bit . . .

GERMAINE: No, no, not with the stamps. It'll make a draft.

ROSE: Come on, Germaine, they're not birds. They won't fly away. Oh, speaking of birds, last Sunday I went to see Bernard, my oldest. Well, you've never seen so many birds in one house. The house is one big bird cage. And it's her doing, you know. She's nuts about birds! And she doesn't want to kill any. Too soft-hearted, but surely to God there's a limit. Listen to this, it's a scream. 560 565

Spotlight on ROSE OUIMET.

ROSE: I'm telling you the woman's nuts. I joke about it but really it's not funny. Anyway, last Easter, Bernard picked up this bird cage for the two kids. Some guy at the tavern needed money, so he sold it to him cheap . . . . Well, the minute he got it in the house, she went bananas. Fell head over heels in love with his birds. No kidding. She took better care of them than she did her kids. Of course, in no time at all the females were laying eggs . . . And 570 575 when they started to hatch, Manon thought they were so cute. She didn't have the heart to get rid of them. You've got to be crazy, eh? So she kept them! The whole flock! God knows how many she's got. I never tried to count 'em . . . But, believe me, every time I set foot in the place I nearly go out of my mind! But wait, you haven't heard anything yet. Every day around two, she opens up the cage and out come her stupid birds. What happens? They fly all over the house. They shit all over everything, including us, and we run after them cleaning it all up. Of course, when it's time to get them back in the cage, they don't want to go. They're having too much fun! So Manon starts screaming at the kids, "Catch Maman's little birdies, Maman's too tired." So the kids go charging after the birds and the place is a frigging circus. Me, I get the hell out! I go sit on the balcony and wait till they've all been caught. (*The women laugh.*) And those kids! God, what brats! Oh, I like them okay, they're my grandchildren. But Jesus, do they drive me nuts. Our kids weren't like that. Say what you like. Young people today, they don't know how to bring up their kids.

GERMAINE: You said it!

YVETTE: That's for sure.

ROSE: I mean, take the bathroom. Now we wouldn't let our kids play in there. Well, you should have seen it on Sunday. The kids went in there like they were just going about their business and in no time flat they'd turned the place upside down. I didn't say a word! Manon always says I talk too much. But I could hear them alright and they were getting on my nerves. You know what they were doing? They took the toilet paper and they unrolled the whole goddamned thing. Manon just yelled "Look, you kids, Maman's gonna get angry." A lot of good that did. They didn't pay any attention. They kept right on going. I would've skinned them alive, the little buggers. And were they having a ball! Bruno, they youngest . . . Can you imagine calling a kid "Bruno"? . . . Anyway, Bruno climbed into the bathtub fully dressed and rolled up in toilet paper and turned on the water. Listen, he was laughing so hard he nearly drowned! He was making boats out of soggy paper and the water was running all over the place. A real flood! Well, I had to do something. I mean, enough is enough, so I gave them a licking and sent them off to bed.

YVETTE: That's exactly what they needed!

ROSE: Their mother raised a stink, of course, but I'll be damned if I was gonna let them carry on like that. Manon, the dim-wit, she just sits there peeling potatoes and listening to the radio. Oh, she's a winner, that one! But I guess she's happy. The only thing she worries about is her birds. Poor Bernard! At times I really feel sorry for him, being married to that. He should have stayed home with me. He was a lot better off . . . (*She bursts out laughing.*)

Lights return to normal.

YVETTE: Isn't she a riot! There's no stopping her.

GABRIELLE: Yeah, there's never a dull moment with Rose.

ROSE: I always say, when it's time to laugh, might as well have a good one. Every story has a funny side, you know? Even the sad ones . . . .

THÉRÈSE: You're damn lucky if you can say that, Mme. Ouimet. It's not everyone . . .

DES-NEIGES: We understand, dear. It must be hard for you to laugh with all your troubles. You're far too good, Mme. Dubuc! You're always thinking of others.

ROSE: That's right, you should think of yourself sometimes. You never go out.

THÉRÈSE: I don't have time! When would you have me go out? I have to take care of her . . . Ah! If only that was all . . .

GERMAINE: Thérèse, don't tell me there's more.

THÉRÈSE: If you only knew! Now that my husband's making some money the family thinks we're millionaires. Why only yesterday, a sister-in-law of my sister-in-law's came to the door with her hand out. Well, you know me. When she told me her story it just broke my heart. So I gave her some old clothes I didn't need anymore . . . Ah, she was so happy . . . . weeping with gratitude . . . she even kissed my hands.

DES-NEIGES: I'm not surprised. You deserve it!

MARIE-ANGE: Mme. Dubuc, I really admire you.

THÉRÈSE: Oh, don't say that . . . .

DES-NEIGES: No, no, no. You deserve it.

LISETTE: You certainly do, Mme. Dubuc. You deserve our admiration and I assure you, I shan't forget you in my prayers. 670

THÉRÈSE: Well, I always say, "If God put poor people on this earth, they gotta be encouraged."

GERMAINE: When you're through filling your books there, instead of piling them on the table, why don't we put them back in the box? . . . Rose, give me a hand. We'll take out the empty books and put in the full ones. 675

ROSE: Good idea. My God! Look at all these books. We gotta fill all them tonight? 680

GERMAINE: Sure, why not? Besides, everyone's not here yet, so we . . .

DES-NEIGES: Who else is coming, Mme. Lauzon?

GERMAINE: Rhéauna Bibeau and Angéline Sauvé are supposed to come by after the funeral parlour. One of Mlle. Bibeau's old girlfriends has a daughter whose husband died. His name was . . . Baril, I think . . . 685

YVETTE: Not Rosaire Baril.

GERMAINE: Yeah, I think that's it . . . 690

YVETTE: But I knew him well! I used to go out with him for Godsake. How do you like that! I'd have been a widow today.

GABRIELLE: Guess what, girls? I got the eight mistakes in last Saturday's newspaper. It's the first time I ever got 'em all and I've been trying for six months . . . I sent in the answer . . . 695

YVETTE: Did you win anything yet?

GABRIELLE: Do I look like someone who's ever won anything? 700

THÉRÈSE: Hey, Germaine, what are you going to do with all these stamps?

GERMAINE: Didn't I tell you? I'm going to redecorate the whole house. Wait a minute . . . Where did I put the catalogue? . . . Ah, here it is. Look at that, Thérèse. I'm gonna have all that for nothing. 705

THÉRÈSE: For nothing! You mean it's not going to cost you a cent?

GERMAINE: Not a cent! Aren't these contests wonderful? 710

LISETTE: That's not what Mme. Brouillette said a while ago . . .

GERMAINE: What do you mean?

MARIE-ANGE: Mme. de Courval, really!

ROSE: Well, come on, Mme. Brouillette. Don't be afraid to say what you think. You said earlier you don't like these contests because only one family wins. 715

MARIE-ANGE: Well, it's true! All these lotteries and contests are unfair. I'm against them. 720

GERMAINE: Just because you never won anything.

MARIE-ANGE: Maybe, maybe, but they're still not fair.

GERMAINE: Not fair, my eye! You're jealous, that's all. You said so yourself the minute you walked in. Well, I don't like jealous people, Mme. Brouillette. I don't like them one bit! In fact, if you really want to know, I can't stand them! 725

MARIE-ANGE: Well! In that case, I'm leaving!

GERMAINE: No, no don't go! Look I'm sorry . . . I'm all nerves tonight, I don't know what I'm saying. We'll just forget it, okay? You have every right to your opinions. Every right. Just sit back down and keep pasting. 730

ROSE: Our sister's afraid of losing one of her workers. 735

GERMAINE: Shut up, Rose! You're always sticking your nose where it don't belong.

ROSE: What's eating you? I can't even open my mouth?

MARIE-ANGE: Alright, I'll stay. But I still don't like them. 740

From this point on, MARIE-ANGE BROUILLETTE will steal all the books she fills. The others will see what she's doing right from the start, except for GERMAINE, obviously, and they will decide to follow suit.

LISETTE: Well, I figured out the mystery charade in last month's *Chatelaine*.[6] It was very easy . . . My first syllable is a Persian king . . .

ROSE: Onassis?[7] 745

LISETTE: No, a *Persian* king . . . It's a "shah" . . .

---

6 *Chatelaine*] a Canadian women's magazine.

7 Onassis] Aristotle Onassis, a multi-millionaire Greek shipping magnate, who lived in a lavish style and was famous in the 1960s for his relationships with opera singer Maria Callas and Jackie Kennedy, widow of the President of the United States.

ROSE: That's a Persian?

LISETTE: Why, of course . . .

ROSE: (*laughing*) That's his tough luck!

LISETTE: My second is for killing bugs . . . No one? 750
. . . Oh, well, "Raid" . . . .

ROSE: My husband's a worm, do you think it would
work on him? . . . She's really nuts with all this
stuff, eh?

LISETTE: And the whole thing is a social game . . . 755

ROSE: Spin the bottle!

GABRIELLE: Rose, will you shut up for Godsake! (*To*
LISETTE) Scrabble?

LISETTE: Oh, come on now, it's simple . . . Shah-
raid . . . Charade! 760

YVETTE: Ah . . . what's a charade?

LISETTE: Of course, I figured it out in no time . . .
It was so easy . . .

YVETTE: So, did you win anything?

LISETTE: Oh, I didn't bother to send it in. I just did 765
it for the challenge . . . Besides, do I look like I
need to win things?

ROSE: Well, I like mystery words, hidden words,
crosswords, turned-around words, bilingual words.
All that stuff with words. It's my specialty. I'm a 770
champ, you know, I've broken all the records!
Never miss a contest . . . Costs me two bucks a
week just for stamps!

YVETTE: So did you win yet?

ROSE: (*looking at* GERMAINE) Do I look like 775
somebody who's ever won anything?

THÉRÈSE: Mme. Dubuc, will you let go of my
saucer? . . . There, now you've done it! You've
spilled it! That's the last straw!

*She socks her mother-in-law on the head and the latter
settles down a little.*

GABRIELLE: Wow! You don't fool around! Aren't you 780
afraid you'll hurt her?

THÉRÈSE: No, no. She's used to it. It's the only way
to shut her up. My husband figured it out. If you
give her a good bash on the head, it seems to
knock her out a while. That way she stays in her 785
corner and we get some peace.

Blackout. Spotlight on YVETTE LONGPRÉ.

YVETTE: When my daughter Claudette got back
from her honeymoon, she gave me the top part of
her wedding cake. I was so proud! It's such a lovely
piece. A miniature sanctuary all made of icing. It's 790
got a red velvet stairway leading up to a platform
and on top of the platform stand the bride and
groom. Two little dolls all dressed up like newly-
weds. There's even a priest to bless them and
behind them there's an altar. It's all icing. I've never 795
seen anything so beautiful. Of course we paid a lot
for the cake. After all, six levels! It wasn't all cake
though. That would have cost a fortune. Just the
first two levels were cake. The rest was wood. But
it's amazing, eh? You'd never have guessed. Anyway, 800
when my daughter gave me the top part, she had
put it under this glass bell. It looked so pretty, but
I was afraid it would spoil . . . you know, without
air. So I took my husband's glass knife . . . He's got
a special knife for cutting glass . . . And I cut a hole 805
in the top of the bell. Now the air will stay fresh
and the cake won't go bad.

Lights up.

DES-NEIGES: Me too. I took a stab at a contest a
few weeks ago. You had to find a slogan for some
bookstore . . . I think it was Hachette or something 810
. . . Anyway, I gave it a try . . . I came up with
"Hachette will chop the cost of your books." Not
bad, eh?

YVETTE: Yeah, but did you win anything?

DES-NEIGES: Do I look like somebody who's ever 815
won anything?

GERMAINE: By the way, Rose, I saw you cutting your
grass this morning. You should buy a lawn-mower.

ROSE: What for? I get along fine with scissors.
Besides it keeps me in shape. 820

GERMAINE: You were puffing away like a steam
engine.

ROSE: But I'm telling you, it's good for me. Anyway,
I can't afford a lawn-mower. Even if I could, that's
the last thing I'd buy. 825

GERMAINE: I'll be getting a lawn-mower with my
stamps . . .

DES-NEIGES: Her and her stamps, she's starting to
get on my nerves! (*She hides a booklet in her purse.*)

ROSE: What are you going to do with a lawn-mower 830
on the third floor?

GERMAINE: You never know, it might come in handy. And who knows, we might move someday.

DES-NEIGES: I suppose she's going to tell us she needs a new house for all the stuff she's gonna get with her lovely stamps. 835

GERMAINE: You know, we probably will need a bigger place for all the stuff I'm gonna get with my stamps.

DES-NEIGES VERRETTE, MARIE-ANGE BROUILLETTE and THÉRÈSE DUBUC all hide two or three books each.

GERMAINE: Rose, if you want, you can borrow my lawn-mower. 840

ROSE: No way! I might bust it. I'd be collecting stamps for the next two years just to pay you back.

The women laugh.

GERMAINE: Don't be smart.

MARIE-ANGE: Isn't she something! Can you beat that! 845

THÉRÈSE: Hey, I forgot to tell you. I guessed the mystery voice on the radio . . . It was Duplessis . . .[8] My husband figured it out 'cause it was an old voice. I sent in twenty-five letters just to be sure they'd get 850 it. And for extra luck, I signed my youngest boy's name, Paul Dubuc . . . .

YVETTE: Did you win anything yet?

THÉRÈSE: (*looking to* GERMAINE) Do I look like someone who's ever won anything? 855

GABRIELLE: Say, do you know what my husband's gonna get me for my birthday?

ROSE: Same as last year. Two pairs of nylons.

GABRIELLE: No sir-ee! A fur coat. Of course, it's not real fur, but who cares? I don't think real fur's 860 worth buying anymore. The synthetics they make nowadays are just as nice. In fact, sometimes nicer.

LISETTE: Oh, I disagree . . .

ROSE: Sure, we all know who's got a fat mink stole!

LISETTE: Well, if you ask me, there's no substitute 865 for authentic, genuine fur. Incidentally, I'll be getting a new stole for autumn. The one I have

now is three years old and it's starting to look . . . . Well, a bit ratty. Mind you, it's still mink, but . . . .

ROSE: Shut your mouth, you bloody liar! We know 870 goddamn well your husband's up to his ass in debt because of your mink stoles and trips to Europe! She's got no more money than the rest of us and she thinks her farts smell like perfume!

LISETTE: Mme. Jodoin, if your husband wants to 875 buy my stole, I'll sell it to him cheap. Then you'll have real mink. After all, between friends . . . .

YVETTE: You know the inflated objects game in the paper, the one where you're supposed to guess what the objects are? Well, I guessed them. There was a 880 screw, a screw-driver and some kind of bent up hook.

THE OTHERS: So . . .

YVETTE sits down.

GERMAINE: You know Daniel, Mme. Rotitaille's little boy? He fell off the second floor balcony the other day. Not even a scratch! How 'bout that? 885

MARIE-ANGE: Don't forget he landed on Mme. Turgeon's hammock. And Monsieur Turgeon was in it at the time . . .

GERMAINE: That's right. He's in hospital for three months. 890

DES-NEIGES: Speaking of accidents, I heard a joke the other day . . .

ROSE: Well, aren't you gonna tell us?

DES-NEIGES: Oh, I couldn't. It's too racy . . .

ROSE: Come on, Mlle. Verrette! We know you've got 895 a stack of them . . .

DES-NEIGES: No. I'm too embarrassed. I don't know why, but I am . . . .

GABRIELLE: Don't be such a tease, Mlle. Verrette. You know darn well you're gonna tell us anyway . . . 900

DES-NEIGES: Well . . . Alright . . . There was this nun who got raped in an alley . . .

ROSE: Sounds good!

DES-NEIGES: And the next morning they found her lying in the yard, a real mess, her habit pulled over 905 her head, moaning away . . . so this reporter comes running over and he says to her, "Excuse me, Sister, but could you tell us something about this terrible thing that's happened to you?" Well, she opens her eyes, looks up at him and in a very small voice she 910 says, "Again, please."

---

8 Duplessis] Maurice Duplessis, premier of Quebec 1936–39 and 1944–59, known as "Le Chef" for the autocratic manner in which he ruled the province.

All the women burst out laughing except for LISETTE DE COURVAL who appears scandalized.

ROSE: Christ Almighty, that's hysterical! I haven't heard such a good one for ages. I'm gonna pee my pants! Mlle. Verrette, where in the world do you get them? 915

GABRIELLE: You know where, from her travelling salesman . . .

DES-NEIGES: Mme. Jodoin, please!

ROSE: That's right too. Her travelling salesman . . .

LISETTE: I don't understand. 920

GABRIELLE: Mlle. Verrette has a travelling salesman who comes to sell her brushes every month.[9] I think she likes him more than his brushes.

DES-NEIGES: Mme. Jodoin, honestly!

ROSE: One thing's for sure, Mlle. Verrette has more 925 brushes than anyone in the parish. Hey, I saw your boyfriend the other day . . . He was sitting in the restaurant . . . He must have been to see you, eh?

DES-NEIGES: Yes, he was—but I assure you, there's nothing between us. 930

ROSE: That's what they all say.

DES-NEIGES: Really, Mme. Ouimet, you're always twisting things to make people look bad. Monsieur Simard is a very nice man.

ROSE: Yeah, but who's to say you're a nice lady? Now, 935 now, Mlle. Verrette, don't get angry. I'm only pulling your leg.

DES-NEIGES: Then don't say things like that. Of course, I'm a nice lady, a thoroughly respectable one too. By the way, the last time he was over, 940 Henri . . . er . . . Monsieur Simard was telling me about a project he has in mind . . . And he asked me to extend you all an invitation. He wants me to organize a demonstration next week . . . At my house. He chose me because he knows my house 945 . . . It'd be for a week Sunday, right after the rosary. I need at least ten people if I'm gonna get my gift . . . You know, they give away those fancy cups to the one who holds the demonstration . . . Fantasy Chinaware . . . You should see them, they're 950

gorgeous. They're souvenirs he brought back from Niagara Falls . . . They must have cost a fortune.

ROSE: You bet, we'll go, eh, girls? I love demonstrations! Any door prizes?

DES-NEIGES: I don't know. I suppose. Maybe . . . 955 Anyway, I'll provide snacks . . .

ROSE: That's more than you get around here. We'll be lucky to see a glass of water!

OLIVINE DUBUC tries to bite her daughter-in-law.

THÉRÈSE: Mme. Dubuc, if you don't stop that I'm gonna lock you in the bathroom and you can stay 960 there for the rest of the evening.

Blackout. Spotlight on DES-NEIGES VERRETTE.

DES-NEIGES: The first time I saw him I thought he was ugly . . . it's true. He's not good-looking. When I opened the door he took off his hat and said, "Would you be interested in buying some brushes, 965 Madame?" I slammed the door in his face. I never let a man in the house! Who knows what might happen . . . . The only one who gets in is the paper boy. He's still too young to get any wrong ideas. Well, a month later my friend with the brushes 970 came back. There was a terrible snowstorm outside, so I let him stand in the hall. Once he was in the house, I was frightened, but I told myself he didn't look dangerous, even if he wasn't good looking . . . He's always well-dressed . . . Not a hair 975 out of place . . . He's a real gentleman . . . . And so polite! Well, he sold me a couple of brushes and then he showed me his catalogue. There was one that I wanted, but he didn't have it with him, so he said I could place an order. Ever since then, he's 980 come back once a month. Sometimes I don't buy a thing. He just comes in and we chat for a while. He's such a nice man. When he speaks, you forget he's ugly. And he knows so many interesting things! The man must travel all over the province! I think 985 . . . . I think I'm in love with him . . . I know it's crazy. I only see him once a month, but it's so nice when we're together. I'm so happy when he comes. I've never felt this way before. Never. Men never paid much attention to me. I've always been . . . 990 unattached. But he tells me about his trips, and all kinds of stories . . . Sometimes they're a bit

---

9 salesman ... brushes] in the 1960s, door-to-door sales-men from the Fuller Brush Company were common throughout North America.

risqué, but honestly, they're so funny! I must admit, I've always liked stories that are a bit off-colour . . . And it's good for you to tell them sometimes. Not all his jokes are dirty, mind you. Lots of them are clean. And it's only lately that he's been telling me the spicy ones. Sometimes they're so dirty I blush! The last time he came he took my hand when I blushed. I nearly went out of my mind. My insides went all funny when he put his big hand on mine. I need him so badly! I don't want him to go away! Sometimes, just sometimes, I dream about him. I dream . . . that we're married. I need him to come and see me. He's the first man that ever cared about me. I don't want to lose him! I don't want to! If he goes away, I'll be all alone again, and I need . . . someone to love . . . (*She lowers her eyes and murmurs.*) I need a man.

The lights come on again. LINDA LAUZON, GINETTE MENARD *and* LISE PAQUETTE *enter.*

GERMAINE: Ah, there you are!

LINDA: I was at the restaurant.

GERMAINE: I know you were at the restaurant. You keep hanging around there, you're gonna end up like your Aunt Pierrette . . . In a whorehouse.

LINDA: Lay off, Ma! You're making a stink over nothing.

GERMAINE: I asked you to stay home . . .

LINDA: Look, I went to get cigarettes and I ran into Lise and Ginette . . .

GERMAINE: That's no excuse. You knew I was having company, why didn't you come right home. You do it on purpose, Linda. You do it just to make my blood boil. You want me to blow my stack in front of my friends? Is that it? You want me to swear in public? Well, Jesus Christ Almighty, you've succeeded! But don't think you're off the hook yet, Linda Lauzon. I'll take care of you later.

ROSE: This is no time to bawl her out, Germaine!

GABRIELLE: Rose, mind your own business.

LINDA: So, I'm a little late, my God, it's not the end of the world!

LISE: It's our fault, Mme. Lauzon.

GINETTE: Yeah, it's our fault.

GERMAINE: I know it's your fault. And I've told Linda a hundred times not to run around with tramps. But you think she gives a damn? Sometimes I'd like to strangle her!

ROSE: Now, Germaine . . .

GABRIELLE: Rose, I told you, stay out of this! You got that? It's their business. It's nothing to do with you.

ROSE: Hey, get off my back! What's with you anyway. Linda's getting bawled out and she hasn't done a goddamn thing!

GABRIELLE: It's none of our business!

LINDA: Leave her alone, Aunt Gaby. She's only trying to defend me.

GABRIELLE: Don't you tell me what to do! I'm your Godmother!

GERMAINE: You see what she's like! Day in and day out! I never brought her up to act this way.

ROSE: Now that you mention it, how do you bring up your kids?

GERMAINE: Hah! You should talk! . . . . Your kids . . .

LINDA: Go on, Aunt Rose, tell her. You're the only one who can give it to her good.

GERMAINE: So, you're siding with your Aunt Rose now are you? You've forgotten what you said when she phoned a while ago, eh? You've forgotten about that? Come on, Linda, tell Aunt Rose what you said about her.

LINDA: That was different . . .

ROSE: Why, what did she say?

GERMAINE: Well, she answered the phone when you called, right? And she was too rude to say, "One moment, please," so I told her to be more polite with you . . . .

LINDA: Will you shut up, Ma! That has nothing to do with it.

ROSE: I want to know what you said, Linda.

LINDA: It's not important, I was mad at her.

GERMAINE: She said, "It's only Aunt Rose. Why should I be polite to her?"

ROSE: I don't believe it . . . You said that?

LINDA: I told you, I was mad at her!

ROSE: I never thought that of you, Linda. There, you've let me down. You've really let me down.

GABRIELLE: Let them fight it out themselves, Rose.

ROSE: You bet I'll let 'em fight. Go on, Germaine. Knock her silly, the little brat! You wanna know something, Linda? Your mother's right. If you're not careful, you'll end up like your Aunt Pierrette. I've got a good mind to slap your face!

GERMAINE: You just try it! You don't lay a hand on my kids! If they need a beating, I'll do it. Nobody else! 1085

THÉRÈSE: Will you please stop bickering. I'm tired!

DES-NEIGES: Lord, yes, you're wearing us out.

THÉRÈSE: You'll wake up my mother-in-law and get her going again. 1090

GERMAINE: She's your problem, not mine! Why didn't you leave her at home?

THÉRÈSE: Germaine Lauzon!

GABRIELLE: Well, she's right. You don't go out to parties with a ninety-three year old cripple. 1095

LISETTE: Mme. Jodoin, didn't I just hear you tell your sister to mind her own business?

GABRIELLE: Keep your big nose out of this, you stuck up bitch! Shut your yap and keep pasting or I'll shut it for you. 1100

LISETTE: (*getting up*) Gabrielle Jodoin!

OLIVINE DUBUC spills the saucer she has been playing with.

THÉRÈSE: Mme. Dubuc, for Godsake!

GERMAINE: Aw, shit, my tablecloth!

ROSE: She's soaked me, the old bag!

THÉRÈSE: That's not true! You weren't even close! 1105

ROSE: Sure, call me a liar right to my face!

THÉRÈSE: Rose Ouimet, you are a liar!

GERMAINE: Look out, she's falling out of her chair!

DES-NEIGES: Oh, no, she's on the floor, again!

THÉRÈSE: Somebody give me a hand. 1110

ROSE: Not me, no way!

GABRIELLE: Pick her up yourself.

DES-NEIGES: Here, I'll help you, Mme. Dubuc.

THÉRÈSE: Thank you, Mlle. Verrette.

GERMAINE: And you, Linda, you watch your step for the rest of the evening. 1115

LINDA: I feel like going back to the restaurant.

GERMAINE: Do that and you won't set foot in this house again, you hear?

LINDA: Sure, I've heard it a thousand times. 1120

LISE: Can it, Linda . . .

THÉRÈSE: For Godsake, Mme. Dubuc, make a little effort. You go limp like that on purpose.

MARIE-ANGE: I'll hold the chair.

THÉRÈSE: Thank you 1125

ROSE: If it was me, I'd take that lousy chair and . . .

GABRIELLE: Rose, don't start again!

THÉRÈSE: Whew! What I go through . . . .

GABRIELLE: Hey, will you get a load of de Courval, still pasting her stamps . . . The bloody snob. As if nothing happened! I guess we're not good enough for her. 1130

Blackout. Spotlight on LISETTE DE COURVAL.

LISETTE: It's like living in a barnyard. Léopold told me not to come and he was right. I should have stayed home. We don't belong with these people. 1135 Once you've tasted life on an ocean liner and have to return to this, well . . . . It's enough to make you weep . . . I can still see myself, stretched out on the deck chair, a Book-of-the-Month in my lap . . . And that lieutenant who was giving me the eye . . . 1140 My husband says he wasn't, but he didn't see what I saw . . . Mmmmm . . . . That was some man. Maybe I should have encouraged him a little more . . . (*She sighs.*) . . . And Europe! Everyone there is so refined! So much more polite than here. You'd 1145 never meet a Germaine Lauzon in Europe. Never! Only people of substance. In Paris, you know, everyone speaks so beautifully and there they talk real French . . . Not like here. . . I despise every one of them. I'll never set foot in this place again! 1150 Léopold was right about these people. These people are cheap. We shouldn't mix with them. Shouldn't talk about them . . . They should be hidden away somewhere. They don't know how to live! We broke away from this and we must never, 1155 ever go back. Dear God, they make me so ashamed!

The lights come back up.

LINDA: I've had it. I'm leaving . . .

GERMAINE: The hell you are! I'm warning you Linda! . . . 1160

LINDA: "I'm warning you, Linda!" Is that all you know how to say?

LISE: Linda, don't be stupid.

GINETTE: Let's stay.

LINDA: No, I'm leaving. I've listened to enough crap for one night. 1165

GERMAINE: Linda, I forbid you to leave!

VOICE OF A NEIGHBOUR: Will you stop screaming up there. We can't hear ourselves think!

ROSE: (*going out on the balcony*) Hey, you! Get back in your house. 1170

NEIGHBOUR: I wasn't talking to you!

ROSE: Oh yes, you were. I'm just as loud as the rest of them!

GABRIELLE: Rose, get in here! 1175

DES-NEIGES: (*referring to the neighbour*) Don't pay any attention to her.

NEIGHBOUR: I'm gonna call the cops!

ROSE: Go right ahead, we need some men up here.

GERMAINE: Rose Ouimet, get back in this house! 1180 And you, Linda . . .

LINDA: I'm leaving. See ya! (*She goes out with* GINETTE *and* LISE.)

GERMAINE: She's gone! Gone! Walked right out! I don't believe it! That kid will be the death of me. 1185 I'm gonna smash something. I'm gonna smash something!

ROSE: Germaine, control yourself.

GERMAINE: Making a fool of me in front of everyone! (*She starts sobbing.*) My own daughter . . . 1190 I'm so ashamed!

GABRIELLE: Come on, Germaine. It's not that bad . . .

LINDA'S VOICE: Hey, if it isn't Mlle. Sauvé. How are you doing? 1195

ANGÉLINE'S VOICE: Hello, sweetheart, how are you?

ROSE: Germaine, they're here. Blow your nose and stop crying.

LINDA'S VOICE: Not bad, thanks.

RHÉAUNA'S VOICE: Where are you off to? 1200

LINDA'S VOICE: I was gonna go to the restaurant, but now that you're here, I think I'll stay.

LINDA, GINETTE and LISE enter with ANGÉLINE and RHÉAUNA.

ANGÉLINE: Hello, everybody.

RHÉAUNA: Hello.

THE OTHERS: Hello, hello. Come on in, how have 1205 you been . . . etc.

RHÉAUNA: What an awful climb, Mme. Lauzon. I'm all out of breath.

GERMAINE: Well, have a seat . . .

ROSE: You're out of breath? Don't worry, my sister's 1210 getting an elevator with her stamps.

They all laugh except RHÉAUNA and ANGÉLINE who don't understand.

GERMAINE: Very funny, Rose! Linda, go get some more chairs . . .

LINDA: Where? There aren't any more.

GERMAINE: Go ask Mme. Bergeron if she'll lend us 1215 some . . .

LINDA: (*to the girls*) Come on, guys . . .

GERMAINE: (*low to* LINDA) We make peace for now, but wait till the others have gone . . .

LINDA: I'm not scared of you. If I come back it's 1220 because Mlle. Sauvé and Mlle. Bibeau showed up, not because of you. (LINDA *goes out with her friends.*)

DES-NEIGES: Here, take my seat, Mlle. Bibeau . . .

THÉRÈSE: Yes, come sit next to me . . . 1225

MARIE-ANGE: Sit down here, Mlle. Bibeau . . .

ANGÉLINE *and* RHÉAUNA: Thank you. Thanks very much.

RHÉAUNA: I see you're pasting stamps.

GERMAINE: We sure are. A million of 'em! 1230

RHÉAUNA: Dear God, a million! How are you getting on?

ROSE: Not bad . . . But my tongue's paralyzed.

RHÉAUNA: You've been doing it with your tongue?

GABRIELLE: Of course not, she's just being smart. 1235

ROSE: Good old Bibeau. Sharp as a tack!

ANGÉLINE: Why don't we give you a hand?

ROSE: Okay. As long as you don't give us some tongue! (*She bursts out laughing.*)

GABRIELLE: Rose, don't be vulgar! 1240

GERMAINE: So, how was the funeral parlour?

Blackout. Spotlight on ANGÉLINE and RHÉAUNA.

RHÉAUNA: I tell you, it came as a shock . . .

ANGÉLINE: But I thought you hardly knew him.

RHÉAUNA: I knew his mother. So did you. Remember, we went to school together. I watched that 1245 man grow up . . .

ANGÉLINE: Such a shame. Gone, just like that. And us, we're still here.

RHÉAUNA: Ah, but not for long . . .

ANGÉLINE: Rhéauna, please . . . 1250

RHÉAUNA: I know what I'm talking about. You can tell when the end is near. I've suffered. I know.

ANGÉLINE: Ah, when it comes to that, we've both had our share. I've suffered, too.

RHÉAUNA: I've suffered a lot more than you, Angéline. Seventeen operations! A lung, a kidney, one of my breasts . . . Gone! I'm telling you, there's not much left. 1255

ANGÉLINE: And me with my arthritis that won't let up. But Mme. . . . What was her name . . . You know, the wife of the deceased . . . She gave me a recipe . . . She says it works wonders. 1260

RHÉAUNA: But you've tried everything. The doctors have all told you, there's nothing you can do. There's no cure for arthritis. 1265

ANGÉLINE: Doctors, doctors! . . . I've had it with doctors. All they think about is money. They bleed you to death and go to California for the winter. You know, Rhéauna, the doctor said he'd get well, Monsieur . . . What was his name again? The one who died? 1270

RHÉAUNA: Monsieur Baril . . .

ANGÉLINE: That's it. I can never remember it. It's easy enough, too. Anyhow, the doctor told Monsieur Baril that he had nothing to worry about 1275 . . . And look what happened . . . Only forty years old . . .

RHÉAUNA: Forty years old! That's too young to die.

ANGÉLINE: He sure went fast . . .

RHÉAUNA: She told me how it happened. It's so sad . . . 1280

ANGÉLINE: Really? I wasn't there. How did it happen?

RHÉAUNA: When he got home from work on Monday night, she thought he was looking a bit 1285 strange. He was white as a sheet, so she asked him how he felt. He said he felt okay and they started supper . . . Well, now, the kids were making a fuss at the table and Monsieur Baril got mad and had to punish Rolande. That's his daughter . . . Of 1290 course, after that, he looked like he was ready to drop . . . she didn't take her eyes off him for a second . . . But she told me later that it happened so fast she didn't have time to do a thing. All of a sudden he said he felt funny and over he went . . . 1295 His face right in the soup. That was it!

ANGÉLINE: Lord, have mercy. So sudden! I tell you, Rhéauna, it's frightening. It gives me the shivers.

RHÉAUNA: Isn't it the truth? We never know when God's going to come for us. He said it Himself, 1300 "I'll come like a thief."

ANGÉLINE: Don't talk like that, it scares me. I don't want to die that way. I want to die in my bed . . . have time to make my confession . . . .

RHÉAUNA: Oh, God forbid that I should die before 1305 confessing! Angéline, promise me you'll call the priest the minute I'm feeling weak. Promise me that.

ANGÉLINE: You know I will. You've asked me a hundred times. Didn't I get him there for your last 1310 attack? You had Communion and everything.

RHÉAUNA: I'm so afraid to die without the last rites.

ANGÉLINE: But what do you have to confess, Rhéauna?

RHÉAUNA: Don't say that, Angéline. Don't ever say 1315 that! We're never too old to sin.

ANGÉLINE: If you ask me, Rhéauna, you'll go straight to heaven. You've got nothing to worry about. Hey! Did you notice Baril's daughter? The way she's changed! She looks like a corpse. 1320

RHÉAUNA: Isn't it the truth. Poor Rolande. She's telling everyone that she killed her father. It's because of her that he got mad, you see, at supper . . . Oh I feel so sorry for her . . . And her mother. What a tragedy! Such a loss for everyone. They'll 1325 miss him so . . . .

ANGÉLINE: You're telling me . . . The father. Mind you, it's not as bad as the mother, but still . . .

RHÉAUNA: True. Losing the mother is worse. You can't replace a mother. 1330

ANGÉLINE: Did you see how nice he looked? . . . Like a young man. He was even smiling . . . . I could have sworn he was asleep. But I still think he's better off where he is . . . You know what they say, it's the ones who stay behind who most deserve 1335 the pity. Him, he's fine now . . . Ah, I still can't get over how good he looked. Almost like he was breathing.

RHÉAUNA: Yeah! But he wasn't.

ANGÉLINE: But I can't imagine why they put him 1340 in that suit . . .

RHÉAUNA: What do you mean?

ANGÉLINE: Didn't you notice? He was wearing a blue suit. You don't do that when you're dead. A blue suit is much too light. Now, navy blue would be okay, but powder blue . . . Never! When you're dead, you wear a black suit. 1345

RHÉAUNA: Maybe he didn't have one. They're not that well off, you know.

ANGÉLINE: Dear God, you can rent a black suit! And look at Mme. Baril's sister! In green! At a funeral parlour! And did you notice how much she's aged? She looks years older than her sister . . . 1350

RHÉAUNA: She is older.

ANGÉLINE: Don't be silly, Rhéauna, she's younger. 1355

RHÉAUNA: No she isn't.

ANGÉLINE: Why sure, Rhéauna, listen! Mme. Baril is at least thirty-seven, but her sister . . .

RHÉAUNA: She's well over forty!

ANGÉLINE: Rhéauna, she isn't! 1360

RHÉAUNA: She's at least forty-five . . .

ANGÉLINE: That's what I'm telling you. She's aged so much, she looks a lot older than she is . . . Listen, my sister-in-law, Rose-Aimée, is thirty-six and the two of them went to school together 1365

RHÉAUNA: Well, anyway, it doesn't surprise me she's aged so fast . . . What with the life she leads . . .

ANGÉLINE: I'm not sure they're true, all those stories.

RHÉAUNA: They must be! Mme. Baril tries to hide it 'cause it's her sister . . . But the truth always comes out. It's like Mme. Lauzon and her sister, Pierrette. Now, if there's one person I can't stand, it's Pierrette Guérin. A shameless hussy! Nothing but shame to her whole family. I tell you, Angéline, I wouldn't want to see her soul. It must be black as coal. 1370 1375

ANGÉLINE: You know, Rhéauna, deep down inside, Pierrette isn't all bad.

Spotlight on GERMAINE LAUZON.

GERMAINE: My sister, Pierrette, I've had nothing to do with her for a long time. Not after what she did. When she was young, she was so good, and so pretty. But now, she's nothing but a whore. My sisters and I were nuts about her. We spoiled her rotten. And look what it got us . . . I don't understand. I don't understand. Papa used to call her his pepper pot. He was so crazy about his little 1380 1385

Pierrette. When he'd put her on his knee, you could tell he was happy. And the rest of us weren't even jealous. . .

ROSE: We'd say, "She's the youngest. It's always that way, it's the youngest who gets the attention." When she started school, we dressed her like a princess. I was already married, but I remember as if it were yesterday. Oh, she was so pretty! Like Shirley Temple! And so quick at school. A lot better than me, that's for sure. I was lousy at school . . . I was the class clown, that's all I was ever good for . . . But her, the little bugger, always coming home with prizes. First in French, first in Arithmetic, first in Religion . . . Yeah, Religion! She was pious as a nun, that kid. I tell you, the Sisters were nuts about her! But to see her today . . . . I almost feel sorry for her. She must need help sometimes . . . She must get so lonely 1390 1395 1400

GABRIELLE: When she finished school, we asked her what she wanted to do. She wanted to be a teacher. She was all set to begin her training . . . . And then she met her Johnny. 1405

THE THREE SISTERS: Goddamn Johnny! He's a devil out of hell! It's all his fault she turned out the way she did. Goddamn Johnny! Goddamn Johnny! 1410

RHÉAUNA: What do you mean, not all bad! You've got to be pretty low to do what she did. Do you know what Mme. Longpré told me about her? 1415

ANGÉLINE: No, what?

THÉRÈSE: Ow!!!

The lights come back up. THÉRÈSE DUBUC gives her mother-in-law a sock on the head.

GERMAINE: Beat her brains out if you have to, Thérèse, but do something!

THÉRÈSE: Sure, beat her brains out! Look, I'm doing all I can to keep her quiet. I'm not about to kill her just to make you happy. 1420

ROSE: If it was up to me, I'd shove her off the balcony . . .

THÉRÈSE: What? Say that again, Rose. I didn't hear you! 1425

ROSE: I was talking to myself.

THÉRÈSE: You're scared, eh?

ROSE: Me, scared?

THÉRÈSE: Yes, Rose. Scared! 1430

MARIE-ANGE: Don't tell me there's gonna be another fight.

ANGÉLINE: Has there been a fight?

RHÉAUNA: Oh, who was fighting?

ANGÉLINE: We should have come sooner. 1435

THÉRÈSE: I won't stand for that. She insulted my mother-in-law! My husband's mother!

LISETTE: There they go again!

ROSE: She's so old! She's useless!

GERMAINE: Rose! 1440

GABRIELLE: Rose, that's cruel! Aren't you ashamed?

THÉRÈSE: Rose Ouimet, I'll never forgive you for those words! Never!

ROSE: Ah, piss off!

ANGÉLINE: Who had a fight? 1445

ROSE: You want to know everything, eh, Mademoiselle Sauvé? You want all the gory details?

ANGÉLINE: Mme. Ouimet!

ROSE: So you can blab it all over town, eh? Isn't that it? 1450

RHÉAUNA: Rose Ouimet, I don't lose my temper often, but I will not allow you to insult my friend.

MARIE-ANGE: (*to herself*) I'll just grab a few more while no one's looking.

GABRIELLE: (*who has seen her*) What are you doing 1455 there, Mme. Brouillette?

ROSE: Fine, I've said enough. I'll shut up.

MARIE-ANGE: Shhhh! Take these and keep quiet!

LINDA, GINETTE and LISE arrive with the chairs. There is a great hullabaloo. All the women change places, taking advantage of the occasion to steal more stamps.

MARIE-ANGE: Don't be afraid, take them!

DES-NEIGES: Aren't you overdoing it? 1460

THÉRÈSE: Hide these in your pocket, Mme. Dubuc . . . No! Damn it! Hide them!

GERMAINE: You know that guy who runs the meat shop, what a thief!

The door opens suddenly and PIERRETTE GUÉRIN comes in.

PIERRETTE: Hi, everybody! 1465

THE OTHERS: Pierrette!

LINDA: Great! It's Aunt Pierrette!

ANGÉLINE: Oh my God, Pierrette!

GERMAINE: What are you doing here? I told you I never wanted to see you again. 1470

PIERRETTE: I heard that my big sister, Germaine, had won a million stamps, so I decided to come over and have a look. (*She sees* ANGÉLINE.) Well, I'll be goddamned! Angéline! What are you doing here? 1475

Everyone looks at ANGÉLINE. Blackout.

ACT TWO

The second act begins with PIERRETTE's entrance. Hence the last six speeches of Act One are repeated now. The door opens suddenly and PIERRETTE GUÉRIN comes in.

PIERRETTE: Hi, everybody!

THE OTHERS: Pierrette!

LINDA: Great! It's Aunt Pierrette!

ANGÉLINE: Oh my God, Pierrette!

GERMAINE: What are you doing here? I told you I 5 never wanted to see you again.

PIERRETTE: I heard that my big sister, Germaine, had won a million stamps, so I decided to come over and have a look. (*She sees* ANGÉLINE.) Well, I'll be goddamned! Angéline! What are you doing here? 10

Everyone looks at ANGÉLINE.

ANGÉLINE: My God! I'm caught.

GERMAINE: What do you mean, Angéline?

GABRIELLE: How come you're talking to Mlle. Sauvé?

ROSE: You oughta be ashamed! 15

PIERRETTE: Why? We're real good friends, eh, Géline?

ANGÉLINE: Oh! I think I'm going to faint! (*She pretends to faint.*)

RHÉAUNA: Good heavens, Angéline! 20

ROSE: She's dead!

RHÉAUNA: What?

GABRIELLE: Don't be ridiculous! Rose, you're getting carried away again.

PIERRETTE: She hasn't even fainted. She's only 25 pretending. (PIERRETTE *approaches* ANGÉLINE.)

GERMAINE: Don't you touch her!

PIERRETTE: Mind your own business! She's my friend.

RHÉAUNA: What do you mean, your friend? 30

GERMAINE: Don't try to tell us Mlle. Sauvé is a friend of yours!

PIERRETTE: Of course she is! She comes to see me at the club almost every Friday night.

ALL THE WOMEN: What! 35

RHÉAUNA: That's impossible.

PIERRETTE: Ask her! Hey, Géline, isn't it true what I'm saying? Come on, stop playing dead and answer me. Angéline, we all know you're faking! Tell them. Isn't it true you come to the club? 40

ANGÉLINE: (*after a silence*) Yes, it's true.

RHÉAUNA: Oh, Angéline! Angéline!

SOME OF THE WOMEN: Dear God, this is dreadful!

SOME OTHER WOMEN: Dear God, this is horrible!

LINDA, GINETTE *and* LISE: Holy shit, that's great! 45

The lights go out.

RHÉAUNA: Angéline! Angéline!

Spotlight on ANGÉLINE and RHÉAUNA.

ANGÉLINE: Rhéauna, you must understand . . .

RHÉAUNA: Don't you touch me! Get away!

THE WOMEN: Who would have thought . . . Such a horrible thing! 50

RHÉAUNA: I'd never have thought this of you. You, in a club. And every Friday night! It's not possible. It can't be true.

ANGÉLINE: I don't do anything wrong, Rhéauna. All I have is a Coke. 55

THE WOMEN: In a club! In a night club!

GERMAINE: God only knows what she does there.

ROSE: Maybe she tries to get picked up.

ANGÉLINE: But I tell you, I don't do anything wrong! 60

PIERRETTE: It's true. She doesn't do anything wrong.

ROSE, GERMAINE *and* GABRIELLE: Shut up, you demon. Shut up!

RHÉAUNA: You're no longer my friend, Angéline. I don't know you. 65

ANGÉLINE: Listen to me, Rhéauna, you must listen! I'll explain everything and then you'll see!

ROSE, GERMAINE *and* GABRIELLE: A club! The fastest road to hell!

ALL THE WOMEN: (*except the girls*) The road to hell, the road to hell! If you go there, you'll lose your soul! Cursed drink, cursed dancing! That's the place where our men go wrong and spend their money on women of sin! 70

ROSE, GERMAINE *and* GABRIELLE: Women of sin like you, Pierrette! 75

ALL THE WOMEN: (*except the girls*) Shame on you, Angéline Sauvé, to spend your time in this sinful way!

RHÉAUNA: But Angéline, a club! It's worse than hell! 80

PIERRETTE: (*laughing heartily*) If hell's anything like the club I work in, I wouldn't mind eternity there!

ROSE, GERMAINE *and* GABRIELLE: Shut up, Pierrette. The devil had your tongue!

LINDA, GINETTE *and* LISE: The devil? Come on! Get with the times! The clubs are not the end of the world! They're no worse than any place else. They're fun! They're lots of fun. The clubs are lots of fun. 85

THE WOMEN: Ah! Youth is blind! Youth is blind! You're gonna lose yourselves and then you'll come crying to us. But it'll be too late! It'll be too late! Watch out! You be careful of these cursed places! We don't always know when we fall, but when we get back up, it's too late! 90 95

LISE: Too late! It's too late! Oh my God, it's too late!

GERMAINE: I hope at least you'll go to confession, Angéline Sauvé!

ROSE: And to think that every Sunday I see you at Communion . . . Communion with a sin like that on your conscience! 100

GABRIELLE: A mortal sin!

ROSE, GERMAINE *and* GABRIELLE: How many times have we been told . . . It's a mortal sin to set foot in a club! 105

ANGÉLINE: That's enough. Shut up and listen to me!

THE WOMEN: Never! You've no excuse!

ANGÉLINE: Rhéauna, will you listen to me! We're old friends. We've been together for thirty-five years. You mean a lot to me, but there are times when I want to see other people. You know how I am. I like to have fun. I grew up in church basements and I want to see other things. Clubs aren't all bad, you know. I've been going for four years and I never did anything wrong. And the people who 110 115 work there, they're no worse than us. I want to meet people, Rhéauna! Rhéauna, I've never laughed in my life!

RHÉAUNA: There are better places to laugh. Angéline, you're going to lose your soul. Tell me you won't go back.

ANGÉLINE: Listen, Rhéauna, I can't! I like to go there, don't you understand. I like it!

RHÉAUNA: You must promise or I'll never speak to you again. It's up to you. It's me or the club. If you only knew how much that hurts, my best friend sneaking off to a night club. How do you think that looks, Angéline? What will people say when they see you going there? Especially where Pierrette works. It's the lowest of them all! You must never go back, Angéline, you hear? If you do, it's finished between us. Finished! You ought to be ashamed!

ANGÉLINE: Rhéauna, you can't ask me not to go back . . . Rhéauna, answer me!

RHÉAUNA: Until you promise, not another word!

The lights come up. ANGÉLINE sits in a corner. PIERRETTE joins her.

ANGÉLINE: Why did you have to come here tonight?

PIERRETTE: Let them talk. They love to get hysterical. They know damn well you don't do anything wrong at the club. In five minutes, they'll forget all about it.

ANGÉLINE: You think so, eh? Well, what about Rhéauna? You think she'll ever forgive me just like that? And Mme. de Courval who's in charge of recreation at the parish, also President of the Altar Society at Our Lady of Perpetual Help! You think she'll continue speaking to me? And your sisters who can't stand you because you work in a club! I'm telling you it's hopeless! Hopeless!

GERMAINE: Pierrette!

PIERRETTE: Listen, Germaine, Angéline feels bad enough. So let's not fight, eh? I came here to see you and paste stamps and I want to stay. And I don't have the plague, okay? Just leave us alone. Don't worry. The two of us'll stay out of your way. After tonight, if you want, I'll never come back again. But I can't leave Angéline alone.

ANGÉLINE: You can leave if you want, Pierrette . . .

PIERRETTE: No, I want to stay.

ANGÉLINE: Okay, then I'll go.

LISETTE: Why don't they both leave!

ANGÉLINE gets up.

ANGÉLINE: (*to* RHÉAUNA) Are you coming? (RHÉAUNA *doesn't answer.*) Okay. I'll leave the door unlocked . . .

She goes towards the door. The lights go out. Spotlight on ANGÉLINE SAUVÉ.

It's easy to judge people. It's easy to judge them, but you have to look at both sides of the coin. The people I've met in that club are my best friends. No one has ever treated me so well . . . Not even Rhéauna. I have fun with those people. I can laugh with them. I was brought up by nuns in the parish halls who did the best they could, poor souls, but knew nothing. I was fifty-five years old when I learned to laugh. And it was only by chance. Because Pierrette took me to her club one night. Oh, I didn't want to go. She had to drag me there. But, you know, the minute I got in the door, I knew what it was to go through life without having any fun. I suppose clubs aren't for everyone, but me, I like them. And of course, it's not true that I only have a Coke. Of course, I drink liquor! I don't have much, but still, it makes me happy. I don't do anyone any harm and I buy myself two hours of pleasure every week. But this was bound to happen someday. I knew I'd get caught sooner or later. I knew it. What am I going to do now? Dear God, what am I going to do? (*Pause.*) Damn it all! Everyone deserves to get some fun out of life! (*Pause.*) I always said that if I got caught I'd stop going . . . But I don't know if I can . . . And Rhéauna will never go along with that. (*Pause.*) Ah, well, I suppose Rhéauna is worth more than Pierrette. (*She gives a long sigh.*) I guess the party's over . . . .

She goes off. Spotlight on YVETTE LONGPRÉ.

YVETTE: Last week, my sister-in-law, Fleur-Ange, had a birthday. They had a real nice party for her. There was a whole gang of us there. First there was her and her family, eh? Oscar David, her husband,

Fleur-Ange David, that's her, and their seven kids: Raymonde, Claude, Lisette, Fernand, Réal, Micheline, and Yves. Her husband's parents, Aurèle David and his wife, Ozéa David, were there too. Next, there was my sister-in-law's mother, Blanche Tremblay. Her father wasn't there 'cause he's dead . . . Then there were the other guests: Antonio Fournier, his wife Rita, Germaine Gervais, also Wilfred Gervais, Armand Campeau, Daniel Lemoyne and his wife Rose-Aimée, Roger Joly, Hormidas Guay, Simone Laflamme, Napoleon Gauvin, Anne-Marie Turgeon, Conrad Joanette, Léa Liasse, Jeanette Landreville, Nona Laplante, Robertine Portelance, Gilbert Morrissette, Lilianne Beaupré, Virginie Latour, Alexandre Thibodeau, Ovila Gariépy, Roméo Bacon and his wife Juliette, Mimi Bleau, Pit Cadieux, Ludger Champagne, Rosaire Rouleau, Roger Chabot, Antonio Simard, Alexandrine Smith, Philemon Langlois, Eliane Meunier, Marcel Morel, Grégoire Cinq-Mars, Théodore Fortier, Hermine Héroux and us, my husband, Euclide, and me. And I think that's just about everyone . . . .

The lights come back up.

GERMAINE: Okay, now let's get back to work, eh?

ROSE: On your toes, girls. Here we go!

DES-NEIGES: We're not doing badly, are we? Look at all I've pasted . . .

MARIE-ANGE: What about all you've stolen . . .

LISETTE: You want to hand me some more stamps, Mme. Lauzon.

GERMAINE: Sure . . . coming right up . . . Here's a whole bunch.

RHÉAUNA: Angéline! Angéline! It can't be true!

LINDA: (*to* PIERRETTE) Hi, Aunt Pierrette.

PIERRETTE: Hi! How're you doing?

LINDA: Oh, not too hot. Ma and I are always fighting and I'm really getting sick of it. She's always bitching about nothing, you know? I'd sure like to get out of here.

GERMAINE: The retreats will be starting pretty soon, eh?

ROSE: Yeah! That's what they said last Sunday.

MARIE-ANGE: I hope we won't be getting the same priest as last year . . . .

GERMAINE: Me too! I didn't like him either. What a bore.

PIERRETTE: Well, what's stopping you? You could come and stay with me . . . .

LINDA: Are you kidding? They'd disown me on the spot!

LISETTE: No, we've got a new one coming this year.

DES-NEIGES: Oh yeah? Who's it gonna be?

LISETTE: A certain Abbé Rochon. They say he's excellent. I was talking to l'Abbé Gagné the other day and he tells me he's one of his best friends . . . .

ROSE: (*to* GABRIELLE) There she goes again with her l'Abbé Gagné. We'll be hearing about him all night! You'd think she was in love with him. L'Abbé Gagné this, l'Abbé Gagné that. Well, if you want my opinion, I don't like l'Abbé Gagné.

GABRIELLE: I agree. He's too modern for me. It's okay to take care of parish activities, but he shouldn't forget he's a priest! A man of God!

LISETTE: Oh, but the man is a saint . . . You should get to know him, Mme. Dubuc. I'm sure you'd like him . . . When he speaks, you'd swear it was the Lord himself talking to us.

THÉRÈSE: Don't overdo it . . .

LISETTE: And the children! They adore him. Oh, that reminds me, the children in the parish are organizing a variety night for next month. I hope you can all make it because it should be very impressive. They've been practising for ages . . .

DES-NEIGES: What's on the programme?

LISETTE: Well, it's going to be very good. There'll be all sorts of things. Mme. Gladu's little boy is going to sing . . .

ROSE: Again! I'm getting sick of that kid. Besides, since he went on television, his mother's got her nose in the air. She thinks she's a real star!

LISETTE: But the child has a lovely voice.

ROSE: Oh yeah? Well, he looks like a girl with his mouth all puckered up like a turkey's ass.

GABRIELLE: Rose!

LISETTE: Diane Aubin will give a demonstration of aquatic swimming . . . We'll be holding the event next door to the city pool, it will be wonderful . . .

ROSE: Any door prizes?

LISETTE: Oh yes, lots. And the final event of the evening will be a giant bingo.

THE OTHER WOMEN: (*except the girls*) A bingo!

Blackout. When the lights come back up, the women are all at the edge of the stage.

LISETTE: Ode to Bingo!

While ROSE, GERMAINE, GABRIELLE, THÉRÈSE and MARIE-ANGE recite the Ode to Bingo, the four other women call out bingo numbers in counterpoint.

ROSE, GERMAINE, GABRIELLE, THÉRÈSE and 290
MARIE-ANGE: Me, there's nothing in the world I like more than bingo. Almost every month we have one in the parish. I get ready two days ahead of time; I'm all wound up, I can't sit still, it's all I can think of. And when the big day 295 arrives, I'm so excited, housework's out of the question. The minute supper's over, I get all dressed up, and a team of wild horses couldn't hold me back. I love playing bingo! I adore playing bingo! There's nothing in the world can 300 beat bingo! When we arrive at the apartment where we're going to play we take off our coats and head straight for the tables. Sometimes it's the living room the lady's cleared, sometimes it's the kitchen. Sometimes it's even the bedroom. 305 We sit at the tables, distribute the cards, set up the chips and the game begins!

The women who are calling the numbers continue alone for a moment.

I'm so excited, I go bananas. I get all mixed up, I sweat like a pig, screw up the numbers, put my chips in the wrong squares, make the caller repeat 310 the numbers, I'm in an awful state! I love playing bingo! I adore playing bingo! There's nothing in the world can beat bingo! The game's almost over. I've got three more tries. Two down and one across. I'm missing the B14! I need the B14! I want the 315 B14! I look at the others. Shit, they're as close as I am. What am I gonna do? I've gotta win! I've gotta win! I've gotta win!

LISETTE: B14!

THE OTHERS: Bingo! Bingo! I've won! I knew it! I 320
knew I couldn't lose! I've won! Hey, what did I win?

LISETTE: Last month we had Chinese dog door

stops. But this month, this month, we've got ashtray floor lamps! 325

THE OTHERS: I love playing bingo! I adore playing bingo! There's nothing in the world beats bingo! What a shame they don't have 'em more often. The more they have, the happier it makes me! Long live the Chinese dogs! Long live the ashtray floor 330 lamps! Long live bingo!

Lights to normal.

ROSE: I'm getting thirsty.

GERMAINE: Oh, God, I forgot the drinks! Linda, get out the Cokes.

OLIVINE: Coke . . . Coke . . . Yeah . . . Yeah, Coke. 335

THÉRÈSE: Relax, Mme. Dubuc. You'll get your Coke like everyone else. But drink it properly! No spilling it like last time.

ROSE: She's driving me up the wall with her mother-in-law . . . 340

GABRIELLE: Forget it, Rose. There's been enough fighting already.

GERMAINE: Yeah! Just keep quiet and paste. You're not doing a thing!

Spotlight on the refrigerator. The following scene takes place by the refrigerator door.

LISE: (*to* LINDA) I've got to talk to you, Linda . . . 345

LINDA: I know, you told me at the restaurant . . . But it's hardly a good time . . .

LISE: It won't take long and I've got to tell somebody, I can't hide it much longer. I'm too upset. And Linda, you're my best friend . . . Linda, I'm going 350 to have a baby.

LINDA: What! But that's crazy! Are you sure?

LISE: Yes, I'm sure. The doctors told me.

LINDA: What are you gonna do?

LISE: I don't know. I'm so depressed! I haven't told 355 my parents yet. My father'll kill me, I know he will. When the doctor told me, I felt like jumping off the balcony . . .

PIERRETTE: Listen, Lise . . .

LINDA: You heard? 360

PIERRETTE: Yeah! I know you're in a jam, kid but . . . I might be able to help you . . .

LISE: Yeah? How?

PIERRETTE: Well, I know a doctor . . .

LINDA: Pierrette, she can't do that!¹⁰   365

PIERRETTE: Come on, it's not dangerous . . . He does it twice a week, this guy.

LISE: I've thought about it already, Linda . . . But I didn't know anyone . . . And I'm scared to try it alone.   370

PIERRETTE: Don't ever do that! It's too dangerous! But with this doctor . . . I can arrange it, if you like. A week from now you'll be all fixed up.

LINDA: Lise, you can't do that!

LISE: What else can I do? It's the only way out. I   375 don't want the thing to be born. Look what happened to Manon Belair. She was in the same boat and now her life's all screwed up because she's got that kid on her hands.

LINDA: What about the father? Can't he marry you?   380

LISE: Are you kidding? I don't even know where he is. He just took off somewhere. Sure, he promised me the moon. We were gonna be happy. He was raking it in, I thought everything was roses. One present after another. No end to it. It was great   385 while it lasted . . . but Goddamn it, this had to happen. It just had to. Why is it always me who ends up in the shit? All I ever wanted was a proper life for myself. I'm sick of working at Kresges. I want to make something of myself, you know, I   390 want to be somebody. I want a car, a decent place to live, nice clothes. My uniforms for the restaurant are all I own, for Chrissake. I never have any money, I always have to scrounge, but I want that to change. I don't want to be cheap anymore. I   395 came into this world by the back door, but by Christ I'll go out by the front! Nothing's gonna stop me. Nothing. You watch, Linda, you'll see I was right. Give me two or three years and you'll see that Lise Paquette is a somebody. And money,   400 she's gonna have it, okay?

LINDA: You're off to a bad start.

LISE: That's just it! I've made a mistake and I want to correct it. After this I'll start fresh. You understand, don't you, Pierrette?   405

PIERRETTE: Sure, I do. I know what it is to want to be rich. Look at me. When I was your age, I left home because I wanted to make some money. But I didn't start by working in a dime store. Oh, no! I went straight to the club. Because that's where   410 the money was. And it won't be long now before I hit the jackpot. Johnny's promised me . . .

ROSE, GERMAINE *and* GABRIELLE: Goddamn Johnny! Goddamn Johnny!

GINETTE: What's going on over here?   415

LISE: Nothing, nothing. (*to* PIERRETTE) We'll talk about it later . . .

GINETTE: Talk about what?

LISE: Forget it. It's nothing!

GINETTE: Can't you tell me?   420

LISE: Look, will you leave me alone?

PIERRETTE: Come on, we can talk over here . . .

GERMAINE: What's happening to those Cokes?

LINDA: Coming, coming . . .

The lights come back up.

GABRIELLE: Hey, Rose, you know that blue suit of   425 yours? How much did you pay for it?

ROSE: Which one?

GABRIELLE: You know, the one with the white lace around the collar?

ROSE: Oh, that one . . . I got it for $9.98.   430

GABRIELLE: That's what I thought. Imagine, today I saw the same one at Reitman's for $14.98.

ROSE: No kidding! I told you I got it cheap, eh?

GABRIELLE: I don't know how you do it. You always find the bargains.   435

LISETTE: My daughter Micheline just found a new job. She's started to work with those F.B.I. machines.

---

10 Abortion was totally illegal in Canada from 1869 (when it was made punishable by life imprisonment) until 1969, when Section 251 of the Criminal Code was revised to decriminalize contraception and permit abortion, though only under extremely restricted conditions. At this time, it was estimated that between 35,000 and 120,000 illegal abortions were taking place in Canada every year. The legal situation effectively remained at this stalemate until 1988, when, after several jury acquittals, the case against Dr. Henry Morgentaler was brought to the Supreme Court of Canada, which struck down the abortion law as unconstitutional in that it was deemed to infringe upon a woman's "right to life, liberty, and security of the person" as guaranteed under section 7 of the Charter of Rights and Freedoms (1982).

MARIE-ANGE: Oh yeah! I hear those things are tough on the nerves. The girls who work them have to change jobs every six months. My sister-in-law, Simonne's daughter, had a nervous breakdown over one. Simonne just called today to tell me about it. 440

ROSE: Oh my God, I forgot, Linda, you're wanted on the phone! 445

Linda runs to the phone.

LINDA: "Hello? Robert? How long have you been waiting?"

GINETTE: Tell me.

LISE: No. Beat it, will you? I want to talk to Pierrette . . . Go on, get lost! 450

GINETTE: Okay, I get the message! You're happy to have me around when there's nobody else, eh? But when someone more interesting comes along . . .

LINDA: "Listen, Robert, how many times do I have to tell you, it's not my fault! I just found out!" 455

THÉRÈSE: Here, Mme. Dubuc, hide these!

ROSE: How are things at your place, Ginette?

GINETTE: Oh, same as usual, they fight all day long . . . Nothing new. My mother still drinks . . . And my father gets mad . . . And they go on fighting . . . 460

ROSE: Poor kid . . . And your sister?

GINETTE: Suzanne? Oh, she's still the brainy one. She can't do anything wrong, you know? "Now there's a girl who uses her head. You should be more like her, Ginette. She's making something of her life" . . . Nobody else even counts, especially me. But they always did like her best. And, of course, now she's a teacher, you'd think she was a saint or something. 465 470

ROSE: Hey, come on, Ginette. Isn't that a bit much?

GINETTE: No, I'm serious . . . my mother's never cared about me. It's always, "Suzanne's the prettiest. Suzanne's the nicest" . . . Day in, day out till I'm sick of it! Even Lise doesn't like me anymore! 475

LINDA: (*on the phone*) "Oh, go to hell! If you're not gonna listen, why should I talk? Call me back when you're in a better mood!" (*She hangs up.*) For Chrissake, Aunt Rose, why didn't you tell me I was wanted on the phone? Now he's pissed off at me! 480

ROSE: Isn't she polite! You see how polite she is?

Spotlight on PIERRETTE GUÉRIN.

PIERRETTE: When I left home, I was head over heels in love, I couldn't even see straight. No one existed for me but Johnny. He made me waste ten years of my life, the bastard. I'm only thirty now and I feel like sixty. The things that guy got me to do! And me, the idiot, I listened to him. Did I ever. Ten years I worked his club for him. I was a looker, I brought in the customers, and that was fine as long as it lasted . . . But now . . . now I'm fucked. I feel like jumping off a bridge. All I got left is the bottle. And that's what I've been doing since Friday. Poor Lise, she thinks she's done for just 'cause she's pregnant. She's young, I'll give her my doctor's name . . . He'll fix her up. It'll be easy for her to start over. But not me. Not me. I'm too old. A girl who's been at it for ten years is washed up. Finished. And try telling that to my sisters. They'll never understand. I don't know what I'm gonna do now. I don't know. 485 490 495 500

LISE: I don't know what I'm gonna do now. I don't know. An abortion, that's serious. I've heard enough stories to know that. But I guess I'm better off going to see Pierrette's doctor than trying to do it myself. Ah, why do these things always happen to me? Pierrette, she's lucky. Working in the same club for ten years, making a bundle . . . And she's in love! I wouldn't mind being in her shoes. Even if her family can't stand her, at least she's happy on her own. 505 510

PIERRETTE: He dumped me, just like that! "It's finished," he said. "I don't need you anymore. You're too old and too ugly. So pack your bags and beat it." That son-of-a-bitch! He didn't leave me a nickel! Not a goddamn nickel! After all I did for him. Ten years! Ten years for nothing. That's enough to make anyone pack it in. What am I gonna do now, eh? What? Become a waitress at Kresge's like Lise?[11] No thanks! Kresge's is fine for kids and old ladies, but not for me. I don't know what I'm gonna do. I just don't know. And here I've gotta pretend everything's great. But I can't tell Linda and Lise I'm washed up. (*Silence.*) Yeah . . . 515 520

---

11 Kresge's] a chain of department stores, which became K-Mart in 1976.

I guess there's nothing left but booze . . . good thing I like that . . . 525

LISE: (*interspersed throughout* PIERRETTE's *last speech*) I'm scared, dear God, I'm scared! (*She approaches* PIERRETTE.) Are you sure this'll work, Pierrette? If you only knew how scared I am!

PIERRETTE: (*laughing*) 'Course it will. It'll be fine, kid. You'll see . . . 530

The lights come back up.

MARIE-ANGE: It's not even safe to go to the show anymore. I went to the Rex the other day to see Belmondo in something, I forget what. I went alone, cause my husband didn't wanna go. Well, 535 all of a sudden, right in the middle of the show this smelly old bum sits down next to me and starts grabbing my knee. You can imagine how embarrassed I was but that didn't stop me. I stood up, took my purse and smashed him right in his ugly 540 face.

DES-NEIGES: Good for you, Mme. Brouillette! I always carry a hat pin when I go to the show. You never know what will happen. And the first one who tries to get fresh with me . . . But I've never 545 used it yet.

ROSE: Hey, Germaine, these Cokes are pretty warm.

GERMAINE: When are you gonna stop criticizing, eh? When?

LISE: Linda, you got a pencil and paper? 550

LINDA: I'm telling you, Lise, don't do it!

LISE: I know what I'm doing. I've made up my mind and nothing's gonna make me change it.

RHÉAUNA: (*to* THÉRÈSE) What are you doing there?

THÉRÈSE: Shh! Not so loud! You should take some, 555 too. Two or three books, she'll never know.

RHÉAUNA: I'm not a thief!

THÉRÈSE: Come on, Mlle. Bibeau, it's not a question of stealing. She got these stamps for nothing and there's a million of 'em. A million! 560

RHÉAUNA: Say what you will, she invited us here to paste her stamps and we've got no right to steal them!

GERMAINE: (*to* ROSE) What are those two talking about? I don't like all this whispering . . . 565

She goes over to RHÉAUNA *and* THÉRÈSE.

THÉRÈSE: (*seeing her coming*) Oh . . . Yeah . . . You add two cups of water and stir.

RHÉAUNA: What? (*Noticing* GERMAINE) Oh! Yes! She was giving me a recipe.

GERMAINE: A recipe for what? 570

RHÉAUNA: Doughnuts!

THÉRÈSE: Chocolate pudding!

GERMAINE: Well, which is it? Doughnuts or chocolate pudding? (*She comes back to* ROSE.) Listen, Rose, there's something fishy going on 575 around here.

ROSE: (*who has just hidden a few books in her purse*) Don't be silly . . . You're imagining things . . . .

GERMAINE: And I think Linda's spending too much time with Pierrette. Linda, get over here! 580

LINDA: In a minute, Ma . . . .

GERMAINE: I said come here! That means now. Not tomorrow!

LINDA: Okay! Don't get in a flap . . . so, so what do you want? 585

GABRIELLE: Stay with us a bit . . . You've been with your Aunt long enough.

LINDA: So what?

GERMAINE: What's going on between her and Lise there? 590

LINDA: Oh . . . Nothing . . .

GERMAINE: Answer when you're spoken to!

ROSE: Lise wrote something down a while ago.

LINDA: It was just an address . . .

GERMAINE: Not Pierrette's, I hope! If I ever find out 595 you've been to her place, you're gonna hear from me, got that?

LINDA: Will you lay off! I'm old enough to know what I'm doing! (*She goes back to* PIERRETTE.)

ROSE: Maybe it's none of my business, Germaine, 600 but . . .

GERMAINE: Why, what's the matter now?

ROSE: Your Linda's picking up some pretty bad habits . . .

GERMAINE: You can say that again! But don't worry, 605 Rose, I can handle her. She's gonna straighten out fast. And as for Pierrette, it's the last time she'll set foot in this house. I'll throw her down the goddamn stairs!

MARIE-ANGE: Have you noticed Mme. Bergeron's 610 daughter lately? Wouldn't you say she's been putting on weight?

LISETTE: Yes, I've noticed that . . .

THÉRÈSE: (*insinuating*) Strange, isn't it? It's all in her middle.

ROSE: I guess the sap's running a bit early this year.

MARIE-ANGE: She tries to hide it too. It's beginning to show, though.

THÉRÈSE: And how! I wonder who could have done it?

LISETTE: It's probably her step-father . . .

GERMAINE: Wouldn't surprise me in the least. He's been after her ever since he married her mother.

THÉRÈSE: It must be awful in that house. I feel sorry for Monique. She's so young . . .

ROSE: Maybe so, but you must admit, she's been looking for it, too. Maybe so, but look how she dresses. Last summer, I was embarrassed to look at her! And you know me, I'm no prude. Remember those red shorts she had on, those short shorts? Well, I said it then, and I'll say it again, "Monique Bergeron is gonna turn out bad." She's got the devil in her, that girl, a real demon. Besides, she's a redhead . . . No, you can say what you like, those unwed mothers deserve what they get and I got no sympathy for 'em.

LISE starts to get up.

PIERRETTE: Take it easy, kid!

ROSE: It's true! It's their own damn fault! I'm not talking about the ones who get raped. That's different. But an ordinary girl who gets herself knocked up, uh! uh! . . . She gets no sympathy from me. It's too goddamn bad! I tell you, if my Carmen ever came home like that, she'd go sailing right through the window! Not that I'm worried about her, mind you. She's not that kind of girl . . . Nope, for me unwed mothers are all the same. A bunch of depraved sluts. You know what my husband calls 'em, eh? Cockteasers!

LISE: I'll kill her if she doesn't shut up!

GINETTE: Why? If you ask me, she's right.

LISE: You shut your trap and get out of here!

PIERRETTE: Isn't that a bit much, Rose?

ROSE: Listen, Pierrette, we know you're an expert on these matters. We know you can't be shocked. Maybe you think it's normal, but we don't. There's one way to prevent it . . .

PIERRETTE: (*laughing*) There's lots of ways. Ever heard of the pill?

ROSE: It's no use talking to you! That's not what I meant! I'm against free love! I'm a Catholic! So leave us alone and stay where you belong, filthy whore!

LISETTE: I think perhaps you exaggerate, Mme. Ouimette. There are occasions when girls can get themselves in trouble and it's not entirely their fault.

ROSE: You! You believe everything they tell you in those stupid French movies!

LISETTE: What have you got against French movies?

ROSE: Nothing. I like English ones better, that's all. French movies, they're too realistic, too far-fetched. You shouldn't believe what they say. They always make you feel sorry for the girl who gets pregnant. It's never anyone else's fault. Well, do you feel sorry for tramps like that? I don't! A movie's a movie and life's life!

LISE: I'll kill her, the bitch! Stupid fucking jerk! She goes around judging everyone and she's got the brains of a . . . And as for her Carmen. Well, I happen to know her Carmen and believe me, she does a lot more than tease! She oughta clean her own house before she shits on everyone else.

Spotlight on ROSE OUIMET.

ROSE: That's right. Life is life and no goddamn Frenchman ever made a movie about that! Sure, any old actress can make you feel sorry for her in a movie. Easy as pie! And when she's finished work, she can go home to her big fat mansion and climb into her big fat bed that's twice the size of my bedroom, for Chrissake! But the rest of us, when we get up in the morning . . . when I wake up in the morning he's lying there staring at me . . . Waiting. Every morning, I open my eyes and there he is, waiting! He's always there, always after me, always hanging over me like a vulture. Goddamn sex! It's never that way in the movies, is it? Oh no, in the movies it's always fun! Besides, who cares about a woman who's gotta spend her life with a pig just 'cause she said yes to him once? Well, I'm telling you, no fucking movie was ever this sad. Because movies don't last a lifetime! (*Silence.*) Why did I ever do it? Why? I should have said no. I should have yelled no at the top of my lungs and stayed an old maid. At least I'd have had some peace. I was so ignorant in those days. Christ, I didn't know what I was in for. All I could think of was "the Holy State of Matrimony!" You gotta be stupid to bring up your kids like that, knowing nothing. My Car- 705 men won't get caught like that. Because I've been telling her for years what men are really worth. She won't be able to say I didn't warn her! (*On the verge of tears.*) She won't end up like me, forty-four years old, with a two year old kid and another one on the 710 way, with a stupid slob of a husband who can't understand a thing, who demands his "rights" at least twice a day, three hundred and sixty-five days a year. When you get to be forty and you realize you got nothing behind you and nothing ahead of you, it 715 makes you want to dump everything and start all over . . . But women . . . women can't do that . . . They get grabbed by the throat, and they stay that way, right to the end!

The lights come back up.

GABRIELLE: Well, I like French movies. They sure 720 know how to make 'em good and sad. They make me cry every time. And you must admit, Frenchmen are a lot better looking than Canadians. They're real men!

GERMAINE: Now wait just a minute! That's not true. 725

MARIE-ANGE: Come on! The little peckers don't even come up to my shoulder. And they act like girls! Of course, what do you expect? They're all queer!

GABRIELLE: I beg your pardon. Some of them are 730 men! And I don't mean like our husbands.

MARIE-ANGE: After our husbands anything looks good.

LISETTE: You don't mix serviettes with paper napkins. 735

GERMAINE: Okay, so our husbands are rough but our actors are just as good and just as good looking as any one of those French fairies from France.

GABRIELLE: Well, I wouldn't say no to Jean Marais.[12] Now there's a real man! 740

---

12 Jean Marais] (1913–1998) a French star known chiefly for his appearances in the films of director-playwright Jean Cocteau (1889–1963), his long-time lover.

OLIVINE: Coke . . . Coke . . . More . . . Coke . . .

ROSE: Hey, can't you shut her up? It's impossible to work! Shove a Coke in her mouth, Germaine. That'll keep her quiet.

GERMAINE: I think I've run out. 745

ROSE: Jesus, you didn't buy much, did you? Talk about cheap!

RHÉAUNA: (*as she steals some more stamps*) Oh, what the heck. Three more books and I can get my chrome dustpan. 750

ANGÉLINE comes in.

ANGÉLINE: Hello . . . (*to* RHÉAUNA) I've come back . . .

THE OTHERS: (*coldly*) Hello . . .

ANGÉLINE: I went to see Father Castelneau . . .

PIERRETTE: She didn't even look at me! 755

MARIE-ANGE: What does she want with Mlle. Bibeau?

DES-NEIGES: I'm sure it's to ask forgiveness. After all, Mlle. Sauvé is a good person and she knows what's right. It'll all work out for the best, you'll 760 see.

GERMAINE: While we're waiting, I'm gonna see how many books we've filled.

The women sit up in their chairs. GABRIELLE hesitates, then speaks.

GABRIELLE: Oh, Germaine, I forgot to tell you. I found a corsetmaker. Her name's Angélina Giroux. 765 Come over here, I'll tell you about her.

RHÉAUNA: I knew you'd come back to me, Angéline. I'm very happy. You'll see, we'll pray together and the Good Lord will forget all about it. God's not stupid, you know. 770

LISE: That's it, Pierrette, they've made up.

PIERRETTE: I'll be goddamned!

ANGÉLINE: I'll just say goodbye to Pierrette and explain . . .

RHÉAUNA: No, you'd best not say another word to 775 her. Stay with me and leave her alone. That chapter's closed.

ANGÉLINE: Whatever you say.

PIERRETTE: Well, that's that. She's won. Makes me want to puke. Nothing left for me to do here. I'm 780 getting out of here.

GERMAINE: Gaby, you're terrific. I'd almost given up hope. It's not everyone can make me a corset. I'll go see her next week. (*She goes over to the box that is supposed to hold the completed books. The women follow her with their eyes.*) My God, there isn't much here! Where are all the booklets? There's no more than a dozen in the box. Maybe they're . . . No, the table's empty! (*Silence. GERMAINE looks at all the women.*) What's going on here? 785–790

THE OTHERS: Well . . . Ah . . . I don't know . . . Really . . .

They pretend to search for the books. GERMAINE stations herself in front of the door.

GERMAINE: Where are my stamps?

ROSE: I don't know, Germaine. Let's look for them.

GERMAINE: They're not in the box and they're not on the table. I want to know what's happened to my stamps! 795

OLIVINE: (*pulling stamps out from under her clothes*) Stamps? Stamps . . . Stamps . . . (*She laughs.*)

THÉRÈSE: Mme. Dubuc, hide that . . . Goddamn it, Mme. Dubuc! 800

MARIE-ANGE: Holy Ste.-Anne!

DES-NEIGES: Pray for us!

GERMAINE: But her clothes are full of them! What the . . . She's got them everywhere! Here . . . And here . . . Thérèse . . . Don't tell me it's you. 805

THÉRÈSE: Heavens, no! I swear, I had no idea!

GERMAINE: Let me see your purse.

THÉRÈSE: Really, Germaine, if that's all the faith you have in me. 810

ROSE: Germaine, don't be ridiculous!

GERMAINE: You too, Rose. I want to see your purse. I want to see all your purses. Every one of them!

DES-NEIGES: I refuse! I've never been so insulted!

YVETTE: Me neither. 815

LISETTE: I'll never set foot in here again!

GERMAINE grabs THÉRÈSE's bag and opens it. She pulls out several books.

GERMAINE: Ahah! I knew it! I bet it's the same with all of you! You bastards! You won't get out of here alive! I'll knock you to kingdom come!

PIERRETTE: I'll help you, Germaine. Nothing but a pack of thieves! And they look down their noses at me! 820

GERMAINE: Show me your purses. (*She grabs ROSE's purse.*) Look at that . . . And that! (*She grabs another purse.*) More here. And look, still more! You too, Mlle. Bibeau? There's only three, but even so! 825

ANGÉLINE: Oh, Rhéauna, you too!

GERMAINE: All of you, thieves! The whole bunch of you, you hear me? Thieves!

MARIE-ANGE: You don't deserve all those stamps. 830

DES-NEIGES: Why you more than anyone else?

ROSE: You made us feel like shit with your million stamps!

GERMAINE: But those stamps are mine!

LISETTE: They ought to be for everyone! 835

THE OTHERS: Yeah, everyone!

GERMAINE: But they're mine! Give them back to me!

THE OTHERS: No way!

MARIE-ANGE: There's lots more in the boxes. Let's help ourselves. 840

DES-NEIGES: Good idea.

YVETTE: I'm filling my purse.

GERMAINE: Stop! Keep your hands off!

THÉRÈSE: Here, Mme. Dubuc, take these! Here's some more. 845

MARIE-ANGE: Come on, Mlle. Verrette. There's tons of them. Here. Give me a hand.

PIERRETTE: Let go of that!

GERMAINE: My stamps! My stamps!

ROSE: Help me, Gaby, I've got too many! 850

GERMAINE: My stamps! My stamps!

A huge battle ensues. The women steal all the stamps they can. PIERRETTE and GERMAINE try to stop them. LINDA and LISE stay seated in the corner and watch without moving. Screams are heard as some of the women begin fighting.

MARIE-ANGE: Give me those, they're mine!

ROSE: That's a lie, they're mine!

LISETTE: (*to GABRIELLE*) Will you let go of me! Let me go! 855

They start throwing stamps and books at one another. Everybody grabs all they can get their hands on, throwing stamps everywhere, out the door, even out the window. OLIVINE DUBUC starts cruising around her wheelchair singing "O Canada." A few women go out with their loot of stamps. ROSE and GABRIELLE stay a bit longer than the others.

GERMAINE: My sisters! My own sisters!

GABRIELLE and ROSE go out. The only ones left in the kitchen are GERMAINE, LINDA and PIERRETTE. GERMAINE collapses into a chair.

GERMAINE: My stamps! My stamps!

PIERRETTE puts her arms around GERMAINE's shoulders.

PIERRETTE: Don't cry, Germaine.

GERMAINE: Don't talk to me. Get out! You're no better than the rest of them! 860

PIERRETTE: But . . .

GERMAINE: Get out! I never want to see you again!

PIERRETTE: But I tried to help you! I'm on your side, Germaine!

GERMAINE: Get out and leave me alone! Don't speak 865 to me. I don't want to see anyone!

PIERRETTE goes out slowly. LINDA also heads towards the door.

LINDA: It'll be some job cleaning all that up!

GERMAINE: My God! My God! My stamps! There's nothing left! Nothing! Nothing! My beautiful new home! My lovely furniture! Gone! My stamps! My 870 stamps!

She falls to her knees beside the chair, picking up the remaining stamps. She is crying very hard. We hear the others outside singing "O Canada." As the song continues, GERMAINE regains her courage. She finishes "O Canada" with the others standing at attention, with tears in her eyes. A rain of stamps falls slowly from the ceiling . . .

END

WALLACE SHAWN

Aunt Dan and Lemon

W allace Shawn (1943–) has been best known as a film actor since 1979, when he made his first onscreen appearances in two of the most popular movies of that year, Woody Allen's *Manhattan* and Bob Fosse's *All That Jazz*. His many subsequent film appearances have included *Atlantic City* (1980); *Hotel New Hampshire* (1984); Vizzini, the "inconceivable" villain in *The Princess Bride* (1987); *Prick Up Your Ears* (1987); Uncle Vanya in *Vanya on 42nd Street*, a film adaptation of Chekhov's play (1994); several other movies by Woody Allen—*Radio Days* (1987), *Shadows and Fog* (1992), and *The Curse of the Jade Scorpion* (2001)—and the voice of Rex the Dinosaur in the *Toy Story* movies (1995 and 1999). He has also often appeared on television (despite not owning a television set himself), as recurring characters in "Taxi," "The Cosby Show," "Murphy Brown," and "Star Trek: Deep Space Nine." To generalize about the roles he has played, he seems to specialize in portraying characters who are endearingly ineffectual, nervously self-conscious and (his own word) "cute" even while being vaguely pompous—a portrait that is evident even in his portrayal of himself in the unusual semi-autobiographical film, *My Dinner with André* (1981).

Yet the self-deprecatory quality of Shawn's public persona conceals an incisive and uncompromising mind, one that evinces a forensic interest in the dark side of human nature. Indeed, Shawn has gone so far as to describe his own life as if he were two separate people: "Person A," the actor in movies, is a cheerful character the public thinks of as "cute"; Person B, the somewhat less famous writer, is heavily preoccupied with exposing the injustices and hypocrisy of the world. He claims to feel this dichotomy strongly enough that, when asked why he doesn't write movies for himself to star in, he explains that "it is because the only one of the two of us who can write is Person B, and he doesn't want Person A in his movie!" (*Interview* magazine, March 1989). To put these two aspects of Shawn's character in another light, we can say that his intellect is as ferociously committed to truth-seeking as his charm is beguiling.

This disarming dual nature—an iron fist within a velvet glove—neatly characterizes the *modus operandi* of his more recent plays. The effect is probably most clearly evident in *The Fever* (1990), a one-person show that Shawn initially performed himself in private living rooms, where he would entertain intimate groups as if he were simply making interesting conversation after dinner. (Subsequently, the play has been performed internationally, often in similarly intimate settings, most notably by Canadian actress Claire Coulter.) But if the circumstances in which *The Fever* was performed seem warm and charming, the content of the play was brutally confrontational: a mesmerizing account of a personal crisis arising from a nauseating awakening to the culpability that comfortable middle-class people living in the so-called "First World" share for the misery and oppression of the oppressed classes of the "Third." Like *Aunt Dan and Lemon*, the play is at once greatly entertaining, deeply disturbing, and intellectually challenging in a lingering way. This combination of amusement and provocation suggests that Shawn is, in some ways, the aesthetic son of Bernard Shaw, whose *Major Barbara* (also included in this anthology) offers a similarly open-ended argument to its audience.

Still, it is perhaps more to the point to compare Shawn's work to that of his real father, William Shawn, the highly respected editor of *The New Yorker* from 1952 to 1987 (and, if we are to believe contributor James Thurber, doing much of the job for founding editor Harold Ross for the decade before that). William Shawn was celebrated above all else for his lofty standards. Under his editorship, *The New Yorker* established a benchmark for journalistic excellence with a great number of long, probing articles on serious topics of international interest; at the same time, the magazine was equally celebrated for its cartoons and witty shorter pieces. In short, through his editorship of *The New Yorker* William Shawn seemed to provide a model of a highly accomplished, urbane, liberal intellectual who was known to despise sentimentality even as he was not above a little fun. Intelligent, literate middle-class Americans embraced the companionship provided by *The New Yorker* because it spoke to their better selves without ever really assaulting their personal sense of entitled bourgeois comfort.

Wallace Shawn's early plays, by contrast, seemed almost deliberately calculated to shock and outrage the sort of people who read his father's magazine. Apparently, father and son always maintained a cordial and respectful relationship (William Shawn died in 1992), but, perhaps out of a sense of guilt about his own privileged upbringing, Wallace Shawn felt compelled to delve beneath the modern urbane civility for which *The New Yorker* provided a sort of touchstone, to expose the desperation and rapaciousness he believed was hidden under the surface of the bourgeoisie. For example, *The Hospital Play* (1971), a grim parable which uses a nightmarish hospital ward as an allegorical substitute for an America embroiled in the war in Vietnam, is characterized by (in Shawn's own words) "a lot of weeping and vomiting" (*Contemporary Dramatists*, 1977). Even W.D. King, whose *Writing Wrongs* (Philadelphia: Temple UP, 1997) is the most extended and sympathetic study of Shawn's work to date, calls the play "incredibly gruesome and unbearable" (p. 61). *Our Late Night* (1975) and *A Thought in Three Parts* (1976) are both predominantly about sex—brutal, mutually abusive sex. The former is centred on a couple who seem to be living out a nightmare projected by an unleashed, hostile, sexually-obsessed unconscious. The latter uses three short plays to show a series of characters attempting to fill the emptiness of their meaningless lives with sexual acts (portrayed so explicitly, brutally, and at such length in the second part that its English premiere incited outraged debate in the House of Lords). *Marie and Bruce* (1979), though less graphically repellent, is still deliberately unpleasant in many respects, portraying a married couple whose mutual frustration and hostility erupt through the surface of their mechanically civil lives to alarming effect. Frankly, even those early plays of Shawn's that are less obviously intended to assault the sensibilities of the audience, such as *Four Meals in May* and *The Old Man* (both 1969) or *The Family Play* and *The Hotel Play* (both 1970), would be distressing for an average middle-class audience to watch, not only because of their tendency to brood on incoherent or violent thoughts, but because each of these plays is written in an enigmatic—indeed, nearly impenetrable—dramatic form.

A decisive shift in Shawn's writing style seems to have occurred in 1981 with the film *My Dinner with André*. The screenplay was created by Shawn with and about his friend, theatre director André Gregory, who had left the theatre in 1975 to begin a long process of self-examination. Shawn distilled the text down from many hours of conversation with Gregory that embraced a broad array of themes, such as the purpose of art and the neurotic elements inherent in modern culture. Much of the interest derives from the friction between the men's characters: the pragmatic and rather cynical Shawn pitted against the flighty and incorrigibly optimistic Gregory. Louis Malle, who was to direct the film, urged the two friends to perform the script on stage first, so that they would develop a sense of how audiences might respond. The success of this theatrical experiment (as well as, perhaps, the new awakening to the broader possibilities of life and art implied for "Wally" in *My Dinner with André*) set Shawn on a new course. From this point on, however disturbing the content he chose, his audience would be addressed, disarmingly, in a far more gentle and charming manner than anything found in his plays up to that point. Shawn used this technique in *The Fever* (discussed above) and, more recently, in *The Designated Mourner* (1996), a play in which three related characters address the audience across time from a totalitarian state sometime in the future, providing accounts of their moral crises and self-justifications for their compromises. But the first fruit of this new approach was *Aunt Dan and Lemon* (1985).

To be sure, as *Aunt Dan and Lemon* demonstrates, Shawn's new approach can hardly be seen as a way of "going easier" on his audience. The very fact that Lemon is, in many respects, a rather charming and interesting character is one of the most challenging aspects of *Aunt Dan and Lemon*. Lemon disarms us with her gentle humour and her frankness and then leads us through a seemingly casual sequence of reminiscences and arguments to a monstrous conclusion. The apparent randomness of the stories she recounts is, of course, illusory. Each scene in the play forms part of a composite representation of the process by which moral conscience and liberal humanism may be disavowed in modern life. Aunt Dan's defence of Henry Kissinger's foreign policies, her stories about Mindy, her explanations for refusing the entangling complications of love, and Lemon's own discussion of the Nazis, as well as her final distaste for Aunt Dan, are all interrelated. But, like a magician, Shawn keeps us distracted and charmed, so that we are not wholly sure how it was that we found ourselves having passively followed an argument that led to such shocking and abhorrent conclusions. Lemon's supposition that each of us desires the comfort and security of "a certain way of life" seems benign enough, but if we tacitly assent to her subsequent arguments—whereby this "certain way of life" is defined as the greatest good, and the elimination of any inconvenient or untidy threat to the purity of that way of life is therefore justified—we find ourselves in the alarming position of having accepted that moral conscience is nothing more than an odious inconvenience, with which we can happily dispense.

Naturally, we are used to the villains of drama presenting such arguments, but hearing them from characters we have been encouraged to befriend is a new and disturbing experience for most audiences. And perhaps what troubles people most of all is the play's lack of moral closure, for Shawn has declined to provide within his play any articulate liberal response to Lemon's calm, logical progression toward horror. He provokes his audiences, drawing them into complicity with Lemon, and then, once she has invited their assent to propositions which only hours before they would have dismissed as morally repugnant, Shawn forces his audiences to leave the theatre and muster their own counter-arguments to Lemon's reasoning. This is an unusual enough experience in the theatre that, whenever the play is performed, there are some people who mistake Lemon's position for Shawn's own, a misunderstanding that the playwright says he has always found painful. It was, in part, to counteract this erroneous impression that Shawn wrote the essay "On the Context of the Play," which is reprinted here, at the end of the play. "If there had been an uplifting ending to the play in which the evil views had been roundly trounced and defeated," Shawn explained in an interview, "then the audience would leave satisfied and the play wouldn't have much impact. But these questions have been raised, and I, as a private citizen, like anyone else, I have my views on these issues, and I began to think, 'Well, I had no desire to put my responses into the play, but why shouldn't I put them down in a little essay?' … I saw no reason to keep my personal position mysterious" (*Wall Street Journal*, November 20, 1985, p. 30). The play and essay are now nearly twenty years old, but Shawn's insistence on confronting us with difficult arguments is perhaps of even more urgent importance to us today than it was when these works first appeared in 1985.

[C.S.W.]

WALLACE SHAWN
Aunt Dan and Lemon[1]

CHARACTERS:
LEMON
MOTHER
FATHER
AUNT DAN
MINDY
ANDY
FREDDIE
MARTY
RAIMONDO
FLORA
JUNE
JASPER

1 *Aunt Dan and Lemon* was produced by the Royal Court Theatre and the New York Shakespeare Festival (Joseph Papp, producer) and received its world premiere at the Royal Court Theatre, London, on August 27, 1985 with the following cast: Lemon: Kathryn Pogson; Mother/Flora/June: Linda Bassett; Father/Freddie/Jasper: Wallace Shawn; Aunt Dan: Linda Hunt; Mindy: Lynsey Baxter; Andy/Marty: Larry Pine; Raimondo: Mario Arrambide. The production was directed by Max Stafford-Clark and designed by Peter Hartwell.

Note: The action of this play is continuous. There should be no pauses at all, except where indicated, despite the fact that the setting changes.

*   *   *

London. A dark room. A woman named Lemon, born in 1960. She sits in an armchair, weak and sick.

LEMON. Hello, dear audience, dear good people who have taken yourselves out for a special treat, a night at the theatre. Hello, little children. How sweet you are, how innocent. If everyone were just like you, perhaps the world would be nice again, perhaps we all would be happy again. *(Pause.)* Dear people, come inside into my little flat, and I'll tell you everything about my life. *(Pause.)* Maybe you're wondering about all these glasses, all these drinks? They're all sweet fruit and vegetable juices, my friends. I spend all my money on these wonderful drinks — lime and celery and lemon and grape — because I'm a very sick girl, and these juices are almost all I can take to sustain this poor little body of mine. Bread and juices, and rolls, of course.

(Pause.) I've always had a problem with regular meals — I mean, regular food at regular hours. Maybe it's only a psychological problem, but it's destroyed my body all the same. *(Pause.)* My parents both died in their early fifties, and it wouldn't surprise me if I were to die even younger than that. It wouldn't surprise me, and it wouldn't bother me. My father was an American who lived most of his life over here, in England. He worked very hard at his job, and he made some money, which I inherited, but it's very, very little with today's prices. It allows me to live, but not much more. *(Pause.)* Maybe because I have nothing to do all day, I sleep very little, and I make a lot of effort just trying to sleep. I used to read mysteries — detective novels — to put myself to sleep, but I don't any more. Lately I've been reading about the Nazi killing of the Jews instead. There are a lot of books about the Nazi death camps. I was reading one last night about the camp called Treblinka.[2] In Treblinka, according to the book, they had these special sheds where the children and women undressed and had their hair taken off, and then they had a sort of narrow outdoor passageway, lined by fences, that led from these sheds all the way out to the gas chambers, and they called that passageway the Road to Heaven. And when the children and women were undressing in the sheds, the guards addressed them quite politely, and what the guards said was that they were going to be taken outside for a shower and disinfection — which happens to be a phrase you read so often in these books, again and again, "a shower and disinfection." "A shower and disinfection." The guards told them that they didn't need to be worried about their clothes at all, because very soon they would be coming back to this very same room, and no one would touch their clothes in the meanwhile. But then once the women and children stepped out of the sheds onto the Road to Heaven, there were other guards waiting for them, and those guards used whips, and the women and children were made to run rapidly down the road and all the way into the chambers, which were tiled with orange and white tiles and looked like showers, but which were really killing chambers. And then the doors would be slammed shut, and the poison would be pumped in until everyone was dead, twenty minutes later, or half an hour later. So apparently the Nazis had learned that it was possible to keep everyone calm and orderly when they were inside the sheds, but that as soon as they found themselves outside, naked, in that narrow passageway, they instinctively knew what was happening to them, and so guards were stationed there with whips to reduce the confusion to a sort of minimum. The strategy was to deal with them politely for as long as possible, and then to use whips when politeness no longer sufficed. Today, of course, the Nazis are considered dunces, because they lost the war, but it has to be said that they managed to accomplish a great deal of what they wanted to do. They were certainly successful against the Jews. *(Pause.)* The simple truth about my life is that I spend an awful lot of time in this room just doing nothing, or looking at the wall. I can't stand the noise of television or even the radio. I don't have visitors, I don't do crossword puzzles, I don't follow sporting events, and I don't follow the news. I hate reading the daily papers, and actually people who *do* read them in a way seem like idiots to me, because they get wildly excited about every new person or thing that comes along, and they think that the world is about to enormously improve, and then a year later they're shocked to learn that that new thing or that new person that was going to make everything wonderful all of a sudden was in fact just nothing or he was just a crook like everyone else, which is exactly what I would probably have guessed already. So the fact is that I spend a lot of time just staring into space. And you know, when you do that, all of your memories come right back to you, and each day you remember a bit more about

2 Treblinka] located 50 miles northeast of Warsaw, Poland. There were actually two "Treblinkas": the first was established in 1941 as a forced labour camp; in 1942, a secret second site, Treblinka II or B, a death camp, was added less than a mile away. Treblinka II would became one of the main Nazi extermination centres, the site of the murder of some 870,000 Jews.

them. Of course I haven't lived much of a life, and I would never say I had. Most of my "sex," if you can call it that, has been with myself. And so many of my experiences have had to do with being sick, like visiting different doctors, falling down on my face in public buildings, throwing up in hallways in strange places, and things like that. So in a way I'm sitting here living in the past, and I don't really have much of a past to live in. And also, of course, I should say that I'm not a brilliant person, and I've never claimed to be one. And actually most of the people I've known as an adult haven't been that brilliant either, which happens to suit me fine, because I don't have the energy to deal with anybody brilliant today. But it means that I'm really thrown back on my childhood, because my most intense memories really go back to my childhood, but not so much to things that I did: instead I remember things I was told. And one of the times that was most intense for me — and that I've been thinking about especially in the last few days — is a certain summer I want to tell you about. And to describe that summer I have to tell you a little about my background and go a bit farther back into things. And you know, people talk about life as if the only things that matter are your own experiences, the things *you* savour the things *you* did or the things that happened to *you*. But you see, to me that's not true. It's not true at all. To me what matters really is the people you knew, the things you learned from them, the things that influenced you deeply and made you what you are. So I may not have done very much in my life. And yet I really feel I've had a *great* life, because of what I've learned from the people I knew.

Lemon drinks. A long silence. Very faintly in the darkness three seated figures begin to be visible.

How far do your memories go back? Mine start when I was three: A lawn. The sun. Mother. Father. And Aunt Dan.

The seated figures stand and form another picture. Mother and Father have their arms around each other. Aunt Dan is slightly apart.

Then a little later, sort of at twilight, everyone walking, then suddenly stopping to look at the sky. Mother. Father. And Aunt Dan.

Mother points at something in the sky. Father and Aunt Dan look.

And then there are the things that happened to other people, but they're mine now. They're my memories.

Raimondo, a Hispanic man in his forties, and Mindy, an English woman in her twenties, are seated at a table. Music in the background.

RAIMONDO. *(to Mindy)* What absolutely wonderful music really delightful —
MINDY. Yes — isn't it?
RAIMONDO. It reminds me of — er — Brasilia Chantelle — you know that group?[3]
MINDY. No, I don't.
RAIMONDO. Oh, it's one of my favourites. They have a vibraphone, a banjo, a sax, and a harp. Ha ha ha!

They both laugh. Now, with Mindy, we see June, an English woman in her twenties, Jasper, an American man in his forties, and Andy, an American man in his early thirties, seated in the midst of a conversation.

MINDY. No, Jasper.
JASPER. What do you mean? Are you totally nuts?
MINDY. Give me all of it!
JASPER. Get lost!
ANDY. Everybody, please! Let's try to approach our problems sensibly, all right?

These figures fade, as Lemon speaks.

LEMON. *(to the audience)* But to tell you about myself, I have to tell you something about my father. I can't avoid it. And the first thing he'd want me to tell you about him is that he loved England. That's what he always said. He came here to study at Oxford University — French literature. And at one of his lectures he met my mother, an English girl. And then Father got a job in an English company that made parts for cars. Jack and Susie. My father and mother. *(Pause.)* But poor Father

---

3 Brasilia Chantelle] a fictitious group.

always felt that his old friends, the people he'd known when he was a student, had no understanding of the work he did. He would always tell us they didn't have a clue. He used to say that over and over and over again.

Father smiles at the audience, finally speaks.

FATHER. I love England. It's a beautiful place. The gardens are lovely. Those English roses. The way they have strawberry jam and that clotted cream with their high teas. And crumpets particularly are very wonderful, I think. There's no American equivalent to crumpets at all — the way they seem to absorb butter like some living creature — the way they get richer and richer as you add all that butter. Well you can't get anything like that in America at all. But you know, it's interesting that there are some fantastic misconceptions about English life, and one of them is the amazing idea that economic life in England is somehow relaxed — not very intense. Well! Ha! When I hear that, I have a big reaction, I have to tell you. And when I tell people about economic life in England today, the first thing I say is, it's *very* intense. It's *very* intense. You see, to begin with, it is very, very hard to get a really good job over here. And then, if you get one, it's really very hard to keep *hold* of it. Because people don't realize that if you *have* a good job, then to *keep* that job, you have to *perform*. You really have to *perform*! If you're on the executive level, you have to perform. I always say, if you don't think I'm right, try sitting in my office for just one week. You'll know what I'm talking about then, you see. That's just what I say to all my old friends when they ask me about it, in that somewhat awkward way that they have. They're all academics, they're scholars, they're writers — they think *they're* using their brains every day and *I'm* somehow using — well, what? — my feet? And that's why I say, I wish you would sit in my office for just one week and do my job and then see whether you need your brains to do it or not. Well, maybe you're so smart you won't *need* your brains — I really don't know. Maybe I'm stupid! But just try it out. Try it for a week and give me a report. Those lazy bastards would drop to their knees with exhaustion after a single day of the work I do. Because the amazing thing about the work *I* do is that you don't just do your work and then say to yourself, "Well done, my boy. That was very well done!" You see, that's what scholars do. That's what writers do. And if you're a scholar or a writer — great — fine — no one in the world can say, "No, no, but your work was bad. Or they can say it, maybe, but then *you* can say, "Oh no, you're wrong, it really was good." But in *my* work there's an actual test, a very simple test which tells you without any doubt or question or debate at all whether your work was in fact "good", or whether it was actually very very "bad". — And the test is, How did your product do in the market? Did people buy it? Well, your work was good. What? They didn't? Well, I'm very, very sorry, your work was *bad*. It was *very bad*. You did a *bad job*. You see, it's no good saying, "But the public doesn't understand me, in twenty years they'll know I was right." Because in twenty years the product won't be on the shelves, you see, so it will be perfectly irrelevant in twenty years. In twenty years that product will be out of date — it will be worthless garbage. So the judgement that's passed on the work I do is extremely harsh, and the punishment for doing badly is very simple: you have to leave. So at the executive level, you can't relax. You work hard. You work hard, you pay attention, and the next day you go in and you work hard again and pay attention again. And if you miss a day — if you go in one day and you just don't feel like working hard, and you just don't feel like paying attention — well, that could very well be the day when you make the mistake that costs you your job, the whole thing. I've seen it happen to a lot of people. I've seen it happen about a thousand times.

LEMON. Some people have warm memories of their family table. I can't say I do! There was a problem about that family table for me.

At the dinner table, Mother, Father and Lemon are silent. Mother and Father eat. Lemon just plays with her food.

MOTHER. What's wrong, my love?
LEMON. Mummy, it's raw.

MOTHER. That lamb? — Raw? — But it's *over-cooked,* darling — I was trying — please — I wanted — 255

LEMON. I'm sorry, Mummy.

MOTHER. But you have to eat — if you don't eat — please — *(to Father)* I can't stand this — 260

LEMON. May I be excused? *(She leaves the table, but stands near by, where her parents can't see her. To the audience)* Father was sure that my problem was caused by the very anxiety which my mother expressed when I didn't eat. *(She eavesdrops on her parents' conversation.)* 265

FATHER. Susie. Susie. I know how you feel! I know how you feel! But you've got to get yourself under control! Yes, it's a *terrible, terrible situation* — but *you're causing* it! 270

MOTHER. Oh no — please —

FATHER. Yes! Yes! I am right about this! I am right about this! You've got to get yourself under control! Because if you don't, we're going to have a really sick girl around here! And I mean *really sick*! Do 275 you hear what I'm saying? I'm saying that doctors will have to come here and *take her away* from us. Do you understand me? When she's out of the room, when she can't hear you, *then* you can cry, you can scream — and I'll cry too, I'll cry right 280 along with you — but when she's *in* the room, you *keep quiet*! We're dealing here with a sick child, a helpless child, *she* can't help feeling *sick*! Don't you *know* that? She would like to be well! She would like to be well! 285

MOTHER. Love — please — you mustn't — don't — darling — you're becoming —

FATHER. No. You leave me alone. You leave me alone right now. Don't you start telling me what I'm becoming. Don't you dare. What the hell do you 290 think I'm becoming? What? Are you trying to say I'm becoming nothing? Is that it? Is that the word you want?

LEMON. *(to the audience)* I listened in the way that children listen. I didn't actually hear the points they 295 were making, point for point. It was more of a sound I heard. There was a certain sort of sound she made, and a certain sort of sound from him. My mother was a saint — she loved him very dearly. But my father was a kind of caged animal, 300

he'd been deprived of everything that would keep him healthy. His life was unsanitary in every way. His entire environment — his cage — was unclean. He was never given a thorough washing. So no wonder — his fur was falling out, he was growing thinner and thinner every day. His teeth were rotten, his shit was rotten, and of course he stank. He stank to hell. When we sat at the table, as if everything was normal, everything was fine, there was an overpowering stench that was coming from my father. My mother ignored it, but you have to say, she did get sick and die at the age of fifty. 305 310

Lemon, as a young child, is in bed. Mother is talking to her.

MOTHER. There was a whole winter when every morning I got up at dawn. I'd brush my teeth, I'd make myself a big pot of coffee and bring it over to my desk, and then I'd sit down, and I'd start reading. Around noon or so I'd finally stand up, and the room would be spinning and sort of shining around me. I'd grab a square of chocolate and a hard-boiled egg, and then I'd run out the door. And that same winter I'd discovered this huge meadow near the edge of town where I used to take walks. And one afternoon as I walked along I saw another girl who was walking also, and as I was looking at her, she looked over at me. And then a few days later, I saw her again, and we found ourselves staring at each other. Finally it happened again a few days later, and the other girl decided to introduce herself. She marched up with a sort of mischievous grin, extended her hand, and announced in a forthright American accent, "My name's Danielle." And you know, Dan in those days used to wear these Victorian blouses and sort of nineteenth-century men's caps — I'd never met anyone like her in my life. So then we walked together for a little while, and then I asked her back to my room for tea. So she came along, and we drank a lot of tea and got very excited, and we drank some sherry that I'd put away somewhere, and we were screaming with laughter into the middle of the night. And then very quietly we went out my door and ran back to that meadow and walked around and around in it, and there was 315 320 325 330 335 340 unbelievably bright moonlight falling on us. And then, the next week, she came back again. And a few weeks later she brought over one of her friends — another American — and it was your father, of course.

LEMON. My parents had named me Leonora, but when I was very little Aunt Dan started calling me Lemon, and then I called myself that, and it became my name. And when I was still very little, five or six or seven or eight, I remember how close Aunt Dan and my parents were.

Mother, Father, Aunt Dan and Lemon are at the table.

AUNT DAN. Dear God, thank you for this meal we are about to eat. Thank you for this table, thank you for these knives, and forks and these plates and glasses. Thank you for giving us all each other, and thank you for giving us not only life, but the ability to know that we *are alive*. May we never spend any moment of these hours together ungrateful for the — *(She hesitates.)* — for the splendours which you have given us — here — in this garden of life. *(Pause for a moment; she looks around.)* Now, let's have lunch.

LEMON. *(to the audience)* My father had romantic feeling about the English countryside. But the spot he chose for our house, not too far from London, was, I always felt, strangely un-English. Particularly in the summer, it seemed to me like a bit of swamp near the Mississippi which had somehow been transported into the English landscape. The air was sticky and hot, the grass and the weeds were as sharp as knives, and as far as the eye could see, a thick scum of tiny insects formed a sort of solid haze between us and the sun. You could hear their noise even inside the house, and when you were outside they were like a storm of tiny pebbles striking your face. All the same, we had a small garden, and when I was five or six or seven or eight, I remember that Aunt Dan and my parents would spend long, long evenings talking in the garden, and I would sit in the grass and listen.

The garden. Night.

They used to agree about everything then.

Mother, Father and Aunt Dan are laughing. Lemon is apart.

FATHER. Did you read that review?

MOTHER. Well, isn't it just the sort of book that Williams *would* love? He doesn't know a thing about those people himself, but he assumes Antonescu has got it all right.

AUNT DAN. And when Antonescu reads the review, he'll say to himself, "Well then I *did* get it right!"

They all laugh.

LEMON. And they used to play these hilarious games.

The garden. Night. Mother, Father and Aunt Dan are playing a game. Aunt Dan is slowly circling around, imitating some animal, and meanwhile tearing some strips of paper. Mother and Father also hold sheets of paper. Lemon is apart, watching.

MOTHER. A cat!
FATHER. No, it's sort of a *sea* monster — isn't it?
MOTHER. A sea *lion*!
FATHER. No — a lion! A lion! *(He rips up pieces of paper.)*
AUNT DAN. Right! A lion!
FATHER. Lion! Lion!

Mother crumples her sheets of paper and throws them at Father and Aunt Dan. They are all laughing.

LEMON. And then there was a time when they stopped playing. And I don't think anyone said, "We shouldn't do this again. We don't enjoy it any more." I think that even a year later or two years later if you'd asked one of them about it they would have said without any hesitation, "Oh yes, we *love* those games. We play them all the time." *(Pause.)* And then there were wonderful evenings when Aunt Dan and my father and I would listen to my mother reading out loud.

The garden. Night. Mother is reading out loud inaudibly. Listening are Father, Lemon and Aunt Dan. Lemon speaks to the audience over the reading.

The sound of her voice was so beautiful. It was so soothing. It made everyone feel calm and at peace.

As Lemon pauses, the reading becomes audible.

MOTHER. Across the dark field the shepherd strode,
    His pipe gripped tightly in his gnarled hand,
    Heedless of the savage winter rain
    Which smote the desolate, barren land.   415
    The sheep had gone; he knew that much,
    And out across the tangled wood he struck.[4]

LEMON. *(as Mother continues reading inaudibly)* And
    then there was a time when she stopped reading.
    I suppose it was like the games, in a way. There   420
    was one evening, some evening, which was the very
    last time she read to us all, but no one remembered
    that evening or even noticed it. *(Pause.)* Well,
    across the garden from the main house was a little
    house which was also ours. My father had built it   425
    to use as a study, but it turned out that he never
    went near it. And so, somehow, over the years,
    little by little, I found that I was moving all of my
    things from my own room in the main house
    across the garden to this little house, till finally I   430
    asked to have my bed moved as well, and so the
    little house became mine. And it was in that little
    house, whenever Aunt Dan would come to visit
    our family, that she and I would have our evening
    talks, and when I look back on my childhood, it   435
    was those talks which I remember more than
    anything else that ever happened to me. And
    particularly the talks we had the summer I was
    eleven years old, which was the last time my
    parents and Aunt Dan were friends, and Aunt Dan   440
    stayed with us for the whole summer, and she came
    to visit me every night. And in a way it was an
    amazing thing that a person like Aunt Dan would
    spend all that time talking to an eleven-year-old
    child who wasn't even that bright, talking about   445
    every complicated subject in the world, but
    listening to Aunt Dan was the best, the happiest,
    the most important experience I'd ever had.
    (Pause.) Of course, Aunt Dan wasn't really my
    aunt. She was one of the youngest Americans ever   450
    to teach at Oxford University, and she was my
    father's best friend, and my mother's too, and she
    was always at our house, so to me she was an aunt.

---

4 Across … struck] Apparently this passage is by Shawn
    himself, though it is written in imitation of a Romantic
    pastoral poem such as Wordsworth's "Michael."

Aunt Dan. But my mother and father had other
    friends, and they had their own lives, and they had   455
    each other, and they had me. But I had only Aunt
    Dan. *(Silence.)* The days that summer were awful
    and hot. I would sit in the garden with Aunt Dan
    and Mother, squinting up at the sun to see if it
    had made any progress in its journey toward the   460
    earth. Then, eventually, I would wolf down some
    tea and bread, and by six o'clock I'd be in my little
    house, waiting for Aunt Dan to come and visit.
    Because Aunt Dan didn't spend her evenings
    talking in the garden with my parents any more.   465
    And as I waited, my mind would already be filling
    with all the things she'd told me, the people she'd
    described. *(Pause.)* Usually there'd still be some
    light in the sky when I would hear her steps
    coming up to the little house. And then she would   470
    very ceremoniously knock on the door. "Come in!"
    I'd shout. I'd already be in my pajamas and tucked
    in under the covers. There'd be a moment's pause.
    And then she'd come in and sit on my bed.

*Night. The little house. Lemon and Aunt Dan are
laughing.*

AUNT DAN. *(to Lemon)* You see, the thing was,   475
    Geoffrey was the most fantastic liar — I mean, he
    was so astonishingly handsome, with those
    gorgeous eyes and those thick, black eyebrows —
    he just had to look at a woman, with those eyes
    of his, and she immediately believed every word   480
    that he said. And he didn't mind lying to his wife
    at all, because she'd trapped him into the marriage
    in the first place, in the most disgusting way, and
    she just lived off his money, you know — she just
    lay in bed all day long in a pink housecoat, talking   485
    on the telephone and reading magazines and
    ordering the servants around like slaves. But he
    knew she'd go mad if he left for the week, so he
    went to her looking totally tragic, and he said,
    "Sadie, I've *got* to go to Paris for a conference for   490
    at least three days, and I'm so upset, I just hate to
    leave you, but some professors over there are
    attacking my theories, and if I don't defend myself
    my entire reputation will be just destroyed." So she
    cried and wailed — she was just like a baby — and   495
    he promised to bring her lots of presents — and,

the next thing was, I heard a little knock on my tiny door, and in came Geoffrey into my basement room. I mean, you can't imagine — this tiny room with nothing in it except all my laundry hanging out to dry — and here was this gigantic prince, the most famous professor in the whole university, a great philosopher, coming to see me, a starving second-year student who was living on a diet of brown bread and fruit and occasionally cheese. Well, for the first two days we didn't *move* from bed — I mean, we occasionally reached across to the table and grabbed a pear or an apple or something — and then on the third day we called a taxi, and we went all the way into London to this extraordinary shop — I'd never seen anything like it in my life — and while the taxi waited we simply filled basket after basket with all this incredible food — I mean, outrageous things like hams from Virginia and asparagus from Brussels and pâté from France and olives and caviar and boxes of marrons glacés, and then we just piled it all into the taxi, along with bottles and bottles of wine and champagne, and back we went to my tiny basement and spent the rest of the week just living like pigs. [5]

LEMON. The light from the window — the purplish light of the dusk — would fall across her face.

AUNT DAN. Now, Lemon, I'm going to tell you something very important about myself. And there aren't many things I'm truly sure of about myself, but this is one. It is that I never — no matter how angry I may be — I never, ever shout at a waiter. And as a matter of fact, I never shout at a porter or a clerk in a bank or anybody else who is in a weaker position in society than me. You see, a lot of people, if they're angry with a *powerful* person, will still speak to that person very politely and nicely, but if they're angry at someone *weaker*, they'll shout, they'll be nasty, they'll actually try to humiliate the person. Now isn't that horrible, Lemon? It's just so *cowardly!* But it's more than that — it shows that these people have no understanding about how the world works. It's as if they thought we could all sort of afford to have no

respect for waiters now, or secretaries, or maids, because we've somehow reached a point where we can just do without them! Well, maybe there's some kind of fantasy in these people's minds that we're already living in some society of the future in which these incredible robots are going to be doing all the work, and every actual citizen will be some kind of concert pianist or a sculptor or a president or something. But I mean, where *are* these robots? Have you ever seen one? Have they even been invented? Well, maybe we'll all see them *some* day. But they're not here now. The way things are now, everybody just can't *be* a president. I mean — I mean, if there's no one around to cook the president's lunch, he's going to have to cook it himself. Do you know what I'm saying? But if no one has put any food in his kitchen, he's going to have to go out and buy it himself. And if no one is waiting in the shop to sell it, he's going to have to go out into the countryside and *grow* it himself, and, you know, that's going to be a full-time job. I mean, he's going to have to resign as president in order to grow that food. It's as simple as that. If all the shop clerks and maids and farmers were to quit their jobs today because they wanted to become painters or nuclear physicists, then within about two weeks everyone in society, even people who used to *be* painters or nuclear physicists, would be out in the woods foraging for berries and roots. Society would completely break down. Because regular work, ordinary work, is no less necessary today than it ever was. And yet almost *everyone* now actually feels *ashamed* of what they do, as if each one felt he'd been unfairly singled out for some degrading punishment. Each one feels, I shouldn't be a labourer, I shouldn't be a clerk, I shouldn't be a minor official! I'm better than that! So naturally the next thing is, they're saying, "Well, I'll show them all — I'll just refuse, I *won't* work, I'll do nothing, or I'll do *almost* nothing, and I'll do it badly." So what's going to happen? We're going to start seeing these embittered typists typing up their documents incorrectly — and then passing them on to these embittered contractors who will misinterpret them to these huge armies of embittered carpenters and

---

5 marrons glacés] glazed chestnuts—an expensive delicacy.

embittered mechanics, and a year later or two years later, we're going to start seeing these ten-story buildings in every city collapsing to the ground, because each one of them is missing some crucial 590 screw in some crucial girder. Buildings will collapse. Planes will come crashing out of the sky. Babies will be poisoned by bad baby food. How can it happen any other way?

LEMON. I would watch the wind gently playing with 595 her hair.

AUNT DAN. Well, that same theatre showed vampire films all night long on Saturday nights, and of course all the students would bring these huge bottles of wine into the theatre with them, and by 600 the time we got out at dawn on Sunday, your parents and I would be absolutely *mad*. We'd sort of crawl out — dripping with blood — and we'd walk through that freezing town, with everyone asleep, to your father's rooms, and then we'd just 605 close the door and put on some record like Arnold Schoenberg's *Transfigured Night*, as loud as we could.[6] I mean, Lemon, you know, that *Transfigured Night* could just make you squeal, it was just as if Arnold Schoenberg was inside your dress 610 and running his hands over your entire body. And then when we'd drunk about twenty cups of coffee we'd all bicycle out to see some other friends of ours called Phyllis and Ned who lived in a kind of abandoned monastery way out of town, and we 615 would sit outside, and Ned would read us these weird items from the week's papers — you know, he collected horrible stories like "Mother Eats Infant's Head While Father Laughs" and things like that — and Phyllis would serve these gigantic 620 salads out on the grass.

LEMON. And then, as we were talking, night would fall.

AUNT DAN. Well, the telephone thing we worked out was great. Alexander could call me right from 625 his office at the laboratory, no matter who was there, or even from a cozy Sunday afternoon by the fire with his wife, and he'd just say something like, "I need to speak with Dr Cunningham, please," and that would mean we would meet at 630 Conrad's, a place we used to go to, and then he'd say, "Oh hi, Nat," and that would mean we would meet at nine. Or of course, if I called *him* and his wife answered, I'd just say something like, "I'm awfully sorry, Mrs Wojwodski, it's Dr Vetzler's 635 office again," and then he'd get on, and I'd say whatever I had to say, and then he'd say something jaunty like, "Oh hi, Bob! No, that's all right, I don't mind a bit!"

LEMON. But her friends were the best. The people 640 she'd known when she was young and wild and living in London. Amazing people. I felt I knew those people myself.

Andy appears next to Lemon.

ANDY. *(to Lemon)* Do you remember Mindy? Do you remember June? Do you remember the night 645 that Mindy introduced us to *Jasper*?

LEMON. There was nothing Aunt Dan didn't tell me about them.

ANDY. *(to Lemon)* Well, June was nice. How could anyone not like June? She was always good- 650 tempered. A wonderful girl. Now, Mindy — Mindy was another story. Mindy could really be sort of annoying, but there were some awfully good reasons for liking her too. For one thing, frankly, she was very, very funny when we were having sex, 655 and that's not nothing. I mean, you know, she thought the whole thing was basically a joke. She just thought bodies were funny, and their little parts were funny, and what they did together was ridiculous and funny. There was just no pressure 660 to make it all work with Mindy, because she really didn't care whether it worked or not. Well, that might have been because she used to spend half her day in bed just playing with herself, and she was going out with about six other men as well as 665 me at the time, but from my point of view, I didn't care *why* she was so relaxed about it all, it was just a pleasure, because that was the time when everyone was madly serious about sex, and it was like some kind of terrible hell we all had to go 670 through at the end of each day before we were allowed to go to sleep. And Mindy was different.

6 *Transfigured Night*] a startling and emotionally wild Expressionist classic that Schoenberg composed for sextet in 1899, revising the score for orchestra in 1917.

Mindy thought it was all funny. And you know something else? I really enjoyed giving money to Mindy, because she didn't have it, and she really wanted it, and she loved to get it.

LEMON. Usually Aunt Dan didn't care about politics. In fact, I remember her saying, "When it comes to politics, I'm an ignoramus." But there were certain people Aunt Dan really loved, and one of them was the diplomat Henry Kissinger, who was working for the American government at the time I was eleven.[7] And it reached a kind of point that she was obsessed with Kissinger. When people would criticize him, she would really become extremely upset. Well, this was the time the Americans were fighting in Vietnam, and people even used to attack Kissinger because while all sorts of awful things were happening over there in the war, he was leading the life of a sort of cheerful bachelor in Washington and Hollywood and going out with lots of different girls. People used to say he was an arrogant person. But Aunt Dan defended him.

AUNT DAN. You see, I don't *care* if he's vain or boastful-maybe he is! I don't *care* if he goes out with beautiful girls or likes to ride around on a yacht with millionaires and sheikhs. All right — he enjoys life! Is that a bad thing? Maybe the fact that he enjoys life inspires all his efforts to *preserve* life, to do what he does every day to make *our* lives possible. I mean, you can hardly call him a frivolous man. Look at his face! Look at that face! He can stay up night after night having a wonderful time with beautiful girls, but he will always have that look on his face, my Lemon, that look of *melancholy*, because he has seen the power of evil in the world.

LEMON. But despite the pain it often caused her, it seemed to me that Aunt Dan just couldn't resist combing every newspaper and every magazine, English *and* American, to see what they were saying about Kissinger every day.

AUNT DAN. I mean, all right now, Lemon, you know, let's face it — we all know there are countries in this world that are not ideal. They're poor. They're imperfect. Their water is polluted. And yes, their governments may be corrupt. But the people in some of these countries are very happy — they have their own farms, they have their own shops, their own newspapers, their own lives that they're leading quietly day by day. And in a lot of these countries the leaders have always been friendly to us, and we've been friendly to them and helped them and supported them. But then what often happens is that there are always some young intellectuals in all of these countries, and they've studied economics at the Sorbonne or Berkeley, and they come home, and they decide to become rebels, and they, take up arms, and they eventually throw out the leaders who were friendly to us, and they take over the whole country.[8] Well, pretty soon they start closing the newspapers, and they confiscate the farms, and they set up big camps way out in the country, and before you know it they're starting to execute all of our friends! Well, what do these journalists think Kissinger should do in a situation like that? It's unbelievable! If he tries for one minute to defend our friends, to stand beside them, they accuse him of being a bully! — a — a *thug*, some kind of swaggering gangster who's brutally mistreating those poor little rebels!

---

7 Kissinger] Dr. Henry Alfred Kissinger (1923–), a German-born Jewish immigrant to the United States (1938) became Assistant to the President (Richard Nixon) for National Security Affairs 1969–1975 and Secretary of State 1973–1977; also a professor at Harvard University and the author of many books and articles on international affairs and foreign policy. He won many awards, including, for example, the Hope Award for International Understanding (1973), the Presidential Medal of Freedom (1977), and, in 1973, the Nobel Peace Prize, awarded jointly to Kissinger and Le Duc Tho of Vietnam, who declined the prize. In recent years there has been a growing movement to have Kissinger indicted as a war criminal, led most notably by the British journalist Christopher Hitchens: see "The Case Against Henry Kissinger," *Harper's Magazine* (February and March 2001); *The Trial of Henry Kissinger* (Verso Press, 2001). Kissinger has replied to these accusations in *Ending the Vietnam War* (Touchstone, 2003).

8 Sorbonne, Berkeley] Université de Paris-Sorbonne and University of California at Berkeley, both hotbeds of radicalism during the wars in Indochina.

LEMON. And she loved to explain Kissinger's strategies to me.

AUNT DAN. He's trying to get the North Vietnamese into a corner, Lemon, so they'll have to give up. And so he goes to the President of North Vietnam, and he says, "Do you know what? You don't have any friends any more. Your friends are dead. I killed them all." And the President of North Vietnam is pretty surprised at first, but then he says to Kissinger, "But what about the President of China? Isn't he my friend?" And Kissinger says, "Oh no, not any more. — He's *my* friend now, I just had dinner with him over at my house, and he told me himself he *hates* you." So what can the President of North Vietnam do? He *has* to give up. But if he still insists that he can do what he likes — well, all the better — we'll bomb his villages, we'll bomb the farms, we'll bomb the harbours, we'll bomb the cities, and it will be a very long while before North Vietnam can bother us again.

LEMON. And there was a story she told me more than once.

AUNT DAN. It was utterly amazing. I could hardly believe it, my little Lemon. It was last winter, and I had a date to have lunch one day at this club in Washington. Well, as I entered the rather formal room where one waited for one's luncheon partner in this rather disgusting, rather unbearable club — and I was waiting to meet a rather unbearable old schoolmate, a member of the club — I suddenly saw, sitting in an overstuffed armchair, Henry Kissinger. At first I couldn't believe it was really Kissinger — why in the world would he be there in this terrible place? But of course, it *was* him, and he undoubtedly had come for the very same reason that I had — a sense of loyalty, a sense of obligation to some old but now perhaps rather stupid friend. And it was possible that Kissinger was early, but it was also possible that that friend of Kissinger's was indeed so stupid that he actually was late to his own lunch with Henry Kissinger. Of course I tried not to stare. I took a seat far across the room. But every now and then I would just peep over and look. And the most striking thing was that, seated in an uncomfortable position in this uncomfortable chair, reading a large report

of some kind, Kissinger was utterly immobile. Each time I looked over, his position was exactly the same as it had been before. And to me that downward-looking angle of his entire head, so characteristic of Kissinger, expressed the habitual humility of a man whose attitude to life was almost prayerful, a man, perhaps, who was living in fear of an all-knowing God. The boastful exuberance of the public Kissinger was nowhere to be seen in this private moment. Kissinger's thoughts were not on himself. No — they were focused on what was written in that large document — and from that same downward look I could tell that the document was not some theoretical essay, not some analysis of something that had happened a hundred years ago, but a document describing some crucial problem which had to be dealt with by Kissinger soon; and in Kissinger's heart I felt I could see one and only one question nervously beating — would he make the right decision about that problem? Would he have the wisdom to do the thing that would help to resolve it, or would he be misled, would he make an error in judgement and act, somehow, so as to make things worse? Let me tell you, there was no arrogance in the man who sat in that uncomfortable, ridiculous armchair, waiting for his stupid friend to come to lunch; that was a man saddened, almost *terrified,* by the awful thought that he might just possibly do something wrong, that he might just possibly make some dreadful mistake. Then, suddenly, Kissinger's friend arrived — stupid, just as I'd predicted, but so much *more* stupid than I would have ever imagined — a huge, vulgar, crew-cutted, red-faced, overgrown baby who greeted Kissinger with a twanging voice and pumped his hand about twenty times. But my God, the warmth with which Kissinger leapt up and greeted this man! I was just utterly stunned by the sheer *joy* which turned Kissinger's face as red as his friend's and seemed to banish from his mind all thought of that heavy manuscript which he still clutched mechanically in his left hand. And as I stayed behind to wait for my old schoolmate, who got from me a greeting that was so much less generous, so much less kind, I watched Kissinger and his ignorant, brutal, pig-like friend walking happily off toward their lunch. And even from far away in the dining-room I still could hear the jolly laugh of Henry Kissinger. A simple man, Lemon. A simple, warm, affectionate man.

LEMON. Naturally, at that time, I often used to dream about running away from my parents and going to live with Aunt Dan in London, and I must admit I often pictured that Kissinger would be dropping in on us fairly regularly there. At least, I imagined, he would never think of missing Sunday breakfast, Aunt Dan's favourite meal. For Kissinger, I imagined, she'd always prepare something very special, like some wonderful little tarts, or eggs done up with brandy and cream. And Kissinger, I felt, would be at his very most relaxed around Aunt Dan. He would stretch himself out on the big couch with a sleepy sort of smile on his face, and he and Aunt Dan would gossip like teenagers, both of them saying outrageous things and trying their best to shock each other. As for myself, the truth was that I was quite prepared to serve Kissinger as his personal slave — I imagined he would like that sort of thing. Well, he could have his pleasure with me, I'd decided long ago, if the occasion ever arose. Few formalities would need to be observed — he didn't have the time, and I knew that very well. An exchange of looks, then right to bed — that would be fine with me. It wasn't how I planned to live as a general rule, but for Kissinger, I thought, I would make an exception. He served humanity. I would serve him. (Pause.) But a lot of people didn't feel about Kissinger the way we did, and after a while we realized something that we both found rather surprising. As it turned out, one of the people who didn't like Kissinger was actually Mother! In fact, Mother didn't like him even at all — just not one bit — and throughout that summer, when Mother and Aunt Dan would chat in the garden in the afternoons, whenever the conversation turned to the subject of Kissinger, as it often did — and more and *more* often, it seemed to me — things would suddenly become extremely tense.

The garden. A silence before Aunt Dan speaks.

AUNT DAN. Susie, do you think he *likes* to bomb a village full of poor peasants?

MOTHER. *(after a brief pause)* Well, I really don't know, Dan. I don't know him.

AUNT DAN. Susie! My God! What a horrible thing to say!

MOTHER. Well, after all, there *are* people who for one reason or another just can't control their lust for blood, or they just give in totally to that side of their nature. . .

AUNT DAN. Susie, really —

MOTHER. — they make up some reason why it has to be done —

AUNT DAN. And you think that Kissinger ? —

MOTHER. I'm sure he says to himself, "I can't avoid this. I'm defending everyone against a terrible danger, this is the only way — " But what if the danger is a fantasy, Dan?

AUNT DAN. But darling, he assesses that! He assesses that! He studies the information. That's exactly what he's doing all day long!

MOTHER. Sure, but sometimes people don't assess things carefully enough, because they've really already made up their minds about them a long time ago.

LEMON. And so the hot afternoons in the garden got worse and worse, and the cool, blessed evenings in the little house, where Aunt Dan would tell me about her friends, by contrast, seemed nicer and nicer. And the amazing thing is that still, in my memory, the afternoons and evenings of that long summer keep following each other, on and on, in an endless alternation.

Mindy appears next to Lemon.

And as the early days of August grew into the late days, Aunt Dan told me more and more about her friend Mindy.

MINDY. *(to Lemon)* I was living a sort of dog's life at that time, quite frankly — making love on ugly bedspreads with strange men and then taking these awful showers with them.

AUNT DAN. *(to Mother)* Look, Susie, he has to make a choice. He has to fight or not fight. One or the other. One or the other.

MOTHER. Well, I —

AUNT DAN. *(interrupting)* Can you imagine a world —

MOTHER. *(interrupting)* Dan —

AUNT DAN. *(interrupting)* Can you imagine a world in which one country after another is suddenly ruled by people who — Has anyone ever looked at you with hatred, Susie? Do you know what that's like? Someone who *really* doesn't enjoy you, someone who *really* doesn't find your jokes funny *at all?* Someone who would actually like to see you beaten, hurt, crying out in pain? Picture countries filled with people like that. Picture a world filled with countries where the people feel like that. Picture those countries *surrounding* us. How would you feel?

MOTHER. You're making —

AUNT DAN. And if you're *going* to put up a fight against that, then does it really make sense to wait till the number of countries you're going to have to fight has become twice the number you'd have to fight now?

MOTHER. You're making a prediction about things that *might* happen.

AUNT DAN. Yes. A prediction. I'm making a prediction.

MINDY. *(to Lemon)* And it would be late at night, and I'd be sitting in some quiet flat with the clock ticking gently, and I'd be looking at some man whom I'd caressed, whom I'd kissed, whose beautiful presents I'd opened excitedly, and he'd be sitting beside me in some sort of endearing underwear, and he'd be telling me about the secrets of his life, and suddenly something would come over me, and a cold sweat would break out on my face, and the most incredible lies, or strange insults, would come out of my mouth, and I would rush to the door and go out into the street. And it was a wonderful thing, on a night like that, to find a telephone and call Andy. And he would always tell me to come right over. And it was really nice on those particular nights to just stick my hand in the air and hail a taxi and go over and play with Andy and his friends.

AUNT DAN. *(to Mother)* Susie, he's not just an individual like you and me — he works for the *government*. The *government*. It's as if you were saying that you and I are so nice every day and why can't our governments be just like us! But you know the whole thing, Susie — you and I are only *able* to be nice because our governments — our governments are *not* nice! You *know* that. I mean, the state? — policemen? — what's it all for? The only point of it all is to save you and me from spending our lives fighting each other with our bare hands in some pile of dirt by the side of the road —

MOTHER. But —

AUNT DAN. — so that if you see me putting this spoon in my purse, you don't have to wrestle me to get the spoon back, you can just pick up the phone and call the police. And if there are people attacking our friends in Southeast Asia, you and I don't have to go over there and fight them with rifles — we just get Kissinger to fight them for us.

MOTHER. But Dan —

AUNT DAN. *We* don't use force. All these *other* people use force, so we don't have to, so we can sit here in this garden and be incredibly nice.

MOTHER. But are you saying that governments can do anything, or Kissinger can do anything, and somehow it's never proper for us to say, Well we don't like this, we think this is wrong? Do you mean to say that we don't have the right to criticize this person's decisions? That no one has the right to criticize them?

AUNT DAN. Oh no, go right ahead. Criticize his decisions all you like. I don't know. Go ahead and criticize everything he does.

MOTHER. I don't —

AUNT DAN. Particularly if you have no idea what you I would do in his place.

MOTHER. Dan, I'm not. . .

Silence.

AUNT DAN. Look, I'm simply saying that it's terribly easy for us to criticize. It's terribly easy for us to sit here and give our opinions on the day's events. And while we sit here in the sunshine and have our discussions about what we've read in the morning papers, there are these certain *other* people, like Kissinger, who happen to have the very bad luck to be society's leaders. And while we sit here chatting, they have to do what has to be done. And so *we* chat, but *they* do what they *have* to do. *They* do what they *have* to do. And if they have to do something, they're prepared to do it. Because I'm very sorry, if you're in a position of responsibility, that means you're responsible for doing whatever it is that has to be done. If you're on the outside, you can complain all day long about what these people are doing. Go ahead. That's fine. That's your right. That's your privileged position. But if you're on the *inside,* if you're in power, if you're responsible, if you're a leader, you don't have that privilege. It's your job to do it. Just to do it. Do it. Don't complain, don't agonize, don't moan, don't wail. Just — do it. Everyone will hate you. Fine. That's their right. But you have to do it. And of course what's so funny is that what you're doing is defending *them. They're* the ones you're defending — it's *so funny!* All day long you're defending them — defending, defending, defending, defending: and your reward is, they spit in your face! All right — so be it. That's the way it is. The joy of leadership. But you can bet that what Kissinger says when he goes to bed at night is, Dear God, I wish I were nothing. Dear God, I wish I were a little child. I wish I were a bird or a fish or a deer living quietly in the woods I wish I were anything but what I am. I am a slave, but they see me as a master. I'm sacrificing my life for them, but they think I'm trying to win power for myself. For myself! Myself! *None* of it is for myself. I *have* no self. I am a leader — that means, I am a slave, I am less than dirt. *They* think of themselves. *I* don't. They think, what would *I* like? What would be nice for *me?* I think, what has to be done? What is the thing I *must* do? I don't think, what would be nice for *me* to do? No. No. Never. Never. Never that. Only, what is the thing I *must* do? What is the thing I *must* do? *(Silence.)* And then these filthy, slimy worms, the little journalists, come along, and it is so far beyond their comprehension — and in a way it's so unacceptable to them — that anyone could possibly be motivated by dreams that are loftier than their own pitiful hopes for a bigger byline, or a bigger car, or a girlfriend with a bigger bust, or a house with a bigger game-room in the basement, that, far from feeling gratitude to this man who has taken the responsibility for making the most painful, difficult decisions we face, they feel they can't rest till they make it impossible for him to continue! *This* is what makes them feel so important: defying the father figure, the big daddy! Worms! Worms! How *dare* they attack him for killing peasants? What decisions did *they* make today? What did *they* have to decide, the little journalists? What did *they* decide? Did they decide between writing one nice long article or instead perhaps writing two tiny little articles? Did they decide between being really extravagant and having dinner at their favourite French restaurant or maybe alternatively saving a little money by going to their second-favourite French restaurant instead? Cowards! Cowards! Can you imagine them confronting a decision that involved human life? Where people would die whatever they decided? They would run just as fast as their little legs would carry them! God! My God! I would *love* to see these cowards face up to some of the consequences of their murder of our leaders! I would *love* to see them face some of the little experiences our leaderless soldiers face when they suddenly meet the North Vietnamese in the middle of the jungle. That might make the little journalists understand what it means to need a bit of support, to long for a government, a strong government standing behind them — those little cowards. Have they ever felt a bayonet go right through their chest? Have they ever felt a knife rip right through their guts? Would they be sneering then, would they be thinking up clever ways to mock our leaders? No, they'd be squealing like pigs, they'd be begging, begging, "Please save me! Please help me!" I would love to be hiding behind a tree watching those little cowards screaming and bleeding and shitting in their pants! I would love to be watching!

Silence.

MOTHER. Dan, I was only —

AUNT DAN. Those slimy cowards. Don't you see how easy it is to do what they do? Sitting in their offices writing their little columns. And when you think of Kissinger — what he does every day —

making those decisions — do you think he makes those decisions lightly?

MOTHER. Dan, I'm sure he's very thoughtful. I'm sure he weighs all the lives in the balance carefully against whatever large objective he's considering. But I was asking, has he weighed them, actually, at — at what I would consider to be their correct measure? Does he have a heart which is capable of weighing them correctly?

AUNT DAN. Oh my God! Really! I don't believe this! I don't believe what I'm hearing from you! Look, I'm sorry, Susie, but all I can say to you is that if he — if he sat at his desk weeping and sobbing all day, I don't think he'd be able to do his job. That's all I can say. He has just as much of a heart as anyone else, you can be sure of that, but how can your heart tell you what you ought to do in a situation of the kind that we're talking about? Your heart just responds to what it finds in front of it, the present moment — the innocent people killed by the bomb. But what about the things that would have happened the next day if the bomb hadn't been dropped? What about the machine guns and the grenades that were neatly stored in that nice little barn? What about the attack that would have been made on the village next door — the houses blown up, the women raped, the tortures, the deaths? What about *those* horrendous events? Well, the heart doesn't care about any of *that,* because those things can't be seen — because those things aren't happening *now.* But the things that will happen tomorrow are real too, Susie. When it is tomorrow, they'll be just as real as the things that are happening now. So I mean — I mean, I'm just asking you, Susie, here is Kissinger. Here is the man who must make the decisions. What do you want this man to do? I'm only asking what you want him to do. What is it that you want him to do?

MOTHER. *(after a long pause)* Do you want more tea, Dan? I don't know. I really don't know. I suppose I do want him to weep and sob at his desk. Yes. Then let him make his decisions.

LEMON. There were times when Aunt Dan just stared at Mother. She just sat and stared.

Andy appears next to Lemon.

ANDY. Well, Mindy would do almost anything, you know, to get hold of money, but with all the good will in the world she still ended up at times without a penny in her purse. And it was at times like that that the phone would ring in the middle of the night, and there would be Mindy asking what I was up to. Well, I was usually flat on my back being fucked by some girl, if you'll pardon my French, or maybe two, but that didn't bother Mindy a bit. She'd come by for some money, and half the time she'd stay to have sex with the rest of us as well. The one thing the girls I liked seemed to have in common was they all liked Mindy — but I mean, who wouldn't? She was so thin she never took up any room, and she never asked anyone for anything but money. In my book, she was okay. Well, you see, they say the English are stuffy, but that's not my experience.

Andy's flat. Late night. Mindy and Jasper are coming in the door, amidst hilarity. Andy, June and Aunt Dan — in her early thirties — are hastily putting on dressing-gowns or long sweaters.

ANDY. Well, well, well — hello, Mindy. What's this?

MINDY. Hello, Andy. I've brought you Jasper.

Mindy presents him with a grand gesture. Whoops from everyone. Andy makes introductions.

ANDY. Delighted, Jasper. June and Dan.

Everyone mock-formally shakes hands, murmuring loudly.

MINDY. *(to Andy)* You see, Jasper's new in town, passing through, a countryman of yours.

ANDY. What, mine?

MINDY. Say hello, Jasper. Show Andy how you talk like him.

ANDY. Now don't be rude, Mindy — he may be shy! Don't make him talk like a puppet. I think he *is* shy. Let him take his time. Shall we have some drinks? June, help me, dear, ask Jasper what he'd like — what about you, Mindy?

MINDY. Vodka, please.

ANDY. A beer for me —

AUNT DAN. Bourbon for me.

JASPER. Oh, can I help?

June and Jasper exit.

ANDY. So who's this Jasper?

MINDY. Well I just met him. He's got a hundred thousand pounds in his trouser pocket.

ANDY. What? Really? 1185

MINDY. He won it. Gambling.

AUNT DAN. My, my.

ANDY. Yes, good for you. I hope you get twenty off him at least.

MINDY. Jesus Christ, I'd really like it all. 1190

ANDY. Well, not *all*. That's not fair, Mindy. Leave him a little.

MINDY. If the poor guy would only have a heart attack and die on your floor, we could keep every penny and no one would know. I mean, he's here 1195 as a tourist, all by himself. We met in the park. He's been wandering around since he won the money. He's lived a good life! And he's a worthless person, I promise you no one would miss him. He's already told me, his wife hates his guts. 1200

ANDY. Why don't you tell him you need the money?

MINDY. I tried that — it didn't work.

Jasper and June return.

JUNE. Jasper's telling me the most amazing story. I think he's frightfully clever.

JASPER. Look, Andy, I won a hundred thousand 1205 pounds tonight, from about six guys in a gambling casino. I don't know how it happened, unless they rigged the deck, and somehow it worked out wrong — I mean, they made some mistake and instead of them getting the cards it turned out to 1210 be me. I mean, I just kept winning — I'd win one hand, and then I'd win again, and then I'd win again, and each time the stakes kept getting bigger — I think they must have thought that each time it would go against me, but it never did. God 1215 damn — my mother would have loved to hear this story — she never saw money in her whole life.

JUNE. God damn — neither did *my* mother, come to think of it.

MINDY. Mine neither. 1220

ANDY. Well, since you ask, *my* mother is quite all right. And how about yours, Dan — is she doing all right?

AUNT DAN. Oh, not too badly.

JASPER. I mean, I'll tell you, Andy, these British men 1225 really like to spend money. They're wild as hell.

ANDY. I've found that myself, I must admit.

JUNE. Where have I been all my life?

ANDY. Oh come on, June, now what about that fellow you were telling me about just last week? A 1230 Member of Parliament, Jasper, who was on his way to Africa on an important commission about something or other and just took June along. He used to buy elephants' tusks as if they were pencils — he gave you so many presents you had to hire 1235 a little boat to carry them all through the swamps, you told me.

JUNE. Not the swamps, dear, that was the *vaal*.[9]

ANDY. Well pardon me, the *vaal* then.

JUNE. I can't stand how these Yankees can't speak the 1240 language.

ANDY. Oh we do all right, we know the major phrases.

JASPER. Yeah, like, "Place your bets," "Let's try another hand" — 1245

ANDY. Yes, right, exactly, things like that —

JUNE. But what part of America do you come from, Jasper?

JASPER. Oh, I'm from Chicago —

AUNT DAN. Aha — 1250

JUNE. Great. I've heard they make the most marvellous steaks. It's just like being a cave man again, a friend of mine said.

ANDY. I think you're thinking of Poughkeepsie, dear.[10] 1255

JUNE. No, that's where they make that white cheese that you put on top of fish.

AUNT DAN. Philadelphia.

JUNE. No, that sounds Greek. Wait — it's a Greek island! Yes, I went there once with a big fisherman. 1260 I didn't understand a word he said, but he certainly knew how to catch fish.

AUNT DAN. That's *not* Philadelphia.

ANDY. Well it *might* be, somehow. Is that where you

---

9 *vaal*] the wetlands around the Vaal river in South Africa.

10 Poughkeepsie] (pronounced "puh-KIP-see") a town on the Hudson river, north of New York City. Steakhouses are popular throughout the whole region.

learned how to mend nets? Didn't you once tell me you could mend nets? 1265

JUNE. Who, me?

MINDY. Look, Jasper, you're neglecting that Scotch.

JASPER. God you're pretty — you know, I really like you. 1270

MINDY. I told you, Jasper — I have a serious boyfriend, you're not allowed to think of me like that — don't look at me like that, I'm telling you, Jasper, or I'm just going to send you home in a cab. 1275

ANDY. She's serious, Jasper — it's hopeless, my friend, I've tried for years.

JASPER. *(to Mindy)* What? — do you think I'm an idiot? You don't have a boyfriend! I don't see him! If you have a boyfriend, then where is he? He 1280 doesn't exist. Does he, Andy?

ANDY. Well, I must admit, *I've* never met him. But she's sure been faithful to the guy, I'll say that much.

JASPER. But is there really a guy, or are you just a 1285 tease?

MINDY. What? What is this, Jasper? Are you calling me a liar?

JASPER. Yes, I am. You know you'll have me if I give you money. 1290

MINDY. Hey, wow — now don't insult me.

JASPER. Well, I'd love to have you without the money, but you told me no. So now I'm asking you *with* the money.

MINDY. Do you really think I would *do* that? 1295

JASPER. Oh — well — for a thousand pounds, no. That would be too cheap — just prostitution. But *ten* thousand pounds — that would be more like marriage. That would be like an intensely serious, permanent relationship, except it wouldn't last 1300 beyond tomorrow morning.

MINDY. No, Jasper.

JASPER. What do you mean? Are you totally nuts?

MINDY. Give me all of it!

JASPER. Get lost! 1305

JUNE. I think this discussion is going in circles.

ANDY. Everyone, please! Let's try to approach our problems sensibly, all right? Now Jasper, you're asking very little of Mindy, in my opinion. You merely want to strip her clothes off for a few hours 1310

and probably fuck her twice at the most, and for this you are offering her ten thousand pounds. Mindy, *my* opinion is, the exchange would be worth it. June, don't you think so? Tell us your opinion. 1315

JUNE. It makes sense.

JASPER. *(to Mindy)* So? What do you say? Ten thousand pounds.

MINDY. For ten thousand pounds you can see my tits. 1320

ANDY. Please, Mindy, let's not turn my flat into an oriental market. Either go to bed with the nice man or send him home, but please don't sit on my sofa and sell different parts of yourself. Besides, if you start dividing yourself into pieces, how do you 1325 know we won't each take a section and end up tearing you to bits?

MINDY. I don't want your money — I want his.

JUNE. I notice she doesn't mention mine. I'll bet she's guessed I don't *have* any. 1330

A pause.

AUNT DAN. I'll throw in five pounds just to watch.

ANDY. Well, I'll pay a hundred pounds *not* to watch, and here it is. *(He puts it on the table and gets up.)* Come on, June.

AUNT DAN. *(to Lemon)* Well, Mindy was a terribly 1335 clever girl, and she managed to get an awful lot of money from poor Jasper. She really did get ten thousand for taking off her shirt, and by the time he'd screwed her she'd got sixty thousand. Meanwhile, he was trying to pay *me* just to leave 1340 the room, but I wouldn't budge. Finally he was so drunk and exhausted he fell asleep, and Mindy sat there on that sofa stark naked and told me stories about her life. Outside the window the city was sleeping, but Mindy's eyes sparkled as she talked 1345 on and on. There wasn't much that she hadn't done, and there were things she didn't tell anyone about, but she told me.

Mindy is seen with Freddie, an American man.

MINDY. *(to Freddie)* All right, I'll do it. Sure. Why not. But you're giving me the money now, right? 1350

FREDDIE. Sure. Of course. I'll see you at Morley's tomorrow evening at nine o'clock. We'll work it

so when we come in you'll have a date already —
it's more fun that way. And we'll call you Rosa.

MINDY. Okay, Freddie. Whatever you like.   1355

*Morley's, a night club. Raimondo, Freddie and Flora
enter. Mindy and Marty are already at a table. Marty
is an American man. Flora is a young American
woman.*

MARTY. Hey! Freddie!

FREDDIE. Marty! Rosa! How unexpected!

MARTY. Hey — what's going on? — you know Rosa?

FREDDIE. I've known her for years. A marvellous girl
— what's she doing with a guy like you, Marty?   1360

They all laugh.

Marty, Rosa, this is Flora Mansfield, and this is my
very good friend Raimondo Lopez. Marty Flora.
Raimondo.

RAIMONDO. Delighted. Señorita —

MINDY. Enchantée, I'm sure.   1365

MARTY. Say, but where the hell is your wife, Freddie?

FREDDIE. My what? No, no, just kidding, Marty,
Corrine's in the country with all the boys —

MARTY. Great. Great. But — er — listen, Freddie,
why don't you and your friends join Rosa and me —   1370

FREDDIE. Oh we'd hate to break in on your quiet
little evening —

MARTY. No, really — We'd love it —

FREDDIE. Really? Do you think? — Well — I don't
know — Raimondo? — er —   1375

RAIMONDO. Well, yes, yes — Certainly — yes.

*Music. They sit down. They all listen to the music for a
while.*

(*to Mindy*) What absolutely wonderful music —
really delightful —

MINDY. Yes — isn't it?

RAIMONDO. It reminds me of — er — Brasilia   1380
Chantelle — do you know that group?

MINDY. No, I don't —

RAIMONDO. Oh, it's one of my favourites. They
have a vibraphone, a banjo, a sax, and a harp. Ha
ha ha! You know, I'm afraid I didn't catch your last   1385
name.

MINDY. Er — Gatti.

RAIMONDO. Oh — are you Italian?

MINDY. Er — on my father's side, yes. But my
mother was English.   1390

RAIMONDO. She's no longer living?

MINDY. No — she died last winter. A terrible illness.

RAIMONDO. I'm very sorry.

MINDY. (*pause*) Oh — thank you, really. So — do
you like this wine?   1395

RAIMONDO. It's very delicious.

MINDY. Yes, it's from Umbria!

RAIMONDO. I love a good wine. You know, someone
said, "When the wine is good, the company is
charming."   1400

MINDY. Oh no no no! When the company is
charming, then *any* wine is good! Ha ha ha —

They laugh.

RAIMONDO. You're single then, Miss Gatti? In
Spanish, you know, we say 'gato' for cat, just like
the Italians.   1405

MINDY. Oh yes, you can call me Miss Cat if you like.

RAIMONDO. Yes — yes — I'll call you Miss Cat.

They laugh.

And with that wonderful necklace — it's just like
a collar — you look like one too! And really, I
think your smile is the *smile* of a cat!   1410

They continue laughing.

MINDY. You've just got the idea in your head, Mr
Lopez.

RAIMONDO. What idea? Now what idea do I have
in my head? Are you telling me what ideas I have
in my head now?   1415

They are both laughing loudly.

You know, I'll bet you can put any idea you like
in a person's head —

MINDY. Oh, what in the world are you talking
about? Eh?

RAIMONDO. If you could only see what's in *my*   1420
head, Miss Cat — Aha ha ha —

A roar of laughter from the other side of the table.

MINDY. Say — it looks like Marty is flirting with
your date!

RAIMONDO. My date? Are you crazy? That's not my

date! That woman's just a friend of Freddie's wife, 1425
a very close friend of Freddie's family!
MINDY. Oh, she is, is she?
RAIMONDO. Yes! — she is!
MINDY. Really!
RAIMONDO. Yes! 1430
MINDY. Well — then I think Marty's flirting with a
very close friend of Freddie's family.

Outside of Morley's. The same group.

MARTY. Well, Rosa, let me take you home. Ha ha —
we've hardly had a chance to talk all evening! Now
— you live on the South Side, don't you, Rosa? 1435
FREDDIE. Well, why don't we all share a cab? Flora
lives on the South Side too —
FLORA. Yes — good —
MARTY. That's fine — great —
MINDY. Well, Freddie, actually, I live on the North 1440
Side, actually —
MARTY. Oh — you do? —
RAIMONDO. So Marty — why don't you drop
Freddie and Flora, and I'll take Rosa along with
me — 1445
MARTY. Oh well, really — oh no — *(to Mindy)* are
you sure you wouldn't mind?
MINDY. No no — not at all —
MARTY. Well then — er — all right — well then,
come along, Flora — you come along with us — 1450
FLORA. Oh — fine — all right —
RAIMONDO. *(to Mindy)* And you come with me.

*Mindy's apartment. Raimondo and Mindy are
standing at different sides of the room. They have come
in a few minutes before. A silence.*

Do you know the first glimpse I had of you
tonight?
MINDY. No — what was it? 1455
RAIMONDO. I was standing in the entrance to the
restaurant, and Flora was checking her coat, and I
looked into the room, and I mostly saw these men
in their boring jackets and ties and these dull-
looking women — and just through a crack 1460
between all those people I suddenly saw a pair of
lavender stockings, and I wondered, who is the
person who belongs to those stockings?

They both laugh.

You know, from a woman's clothing, you can see
everything. Because some clothing is inert and 1465
dead, just dead cloth, like dead skins. And some
clothing is alive. *Some* clothing is there just to cover
the body. And some is there to — to describe the
body, to tell you about it — like a beautiful
wrapping on something sweet. 1470

*There is a silence. He walks toward her. Then he
crouches on the floor in front of her and slides his
hands along her stockings. He puts his head up her
skirt.*

Oh — so warm.

*She stays absolutely still, neither encouraging nor
resisting. After a moment, he removes his head and
looks at her. Then he helps her take off her shoes, and
he removes her stockings. He puts them over the back of
a chair.*

MINDY. Would you like a drink?
RAIMONDO. Well — would you?
MINDY. Thank you. Yes. There's some brandy —
there — 1475

*She points to the brandy. He gets up, gets them both a
drink. He sips his.*

Won't you take off that jacket?
RAIMONDO. Oh — thank you — yes. *(He takes off
his jacket and tie.)*
MINDY. Sit down, why don't you.

He sits. There is a silence.

RAIMONDO. You're so gorgeous — so sweet. You 1480
know, when I get hungry, I'm just like a bear. I
start to sweat till I get to the honey.
MINDY. Finish your brandy. There's plenty of time.

*She wipes his forehead with a napkin as he sips his
drink. As he finishes, she lowers herself to the floor in
front of him, unzips his trousers and starts to kiss his
crotch.*

RAIMONDO. Oh God — yes — yes — oh, please —

After another moment, she looks up.

MINDY. It's chilly in here. And you're still sweating. 1485
Come lie down.

Raimondo starts to stand.

RAIMONDO. I feel dizzy.
MINDY. Just relax.

They head toward the bed. She turns back for her stockings.

RAIMONDO. I feel dizzy. *(In the darkness, his cries of ecstasy.)* Oh, beautiful. Oh, my God —   1490

Now, light from a window falls on the stockings. Mindy is standing by the bed, dressed in a robe, looking down at Raimondo, who is out cold. She shakes him roughly, and he groans slightly but doesn't wake up. Then she opens a drawer, pulls on a pair of jeans, takes out some pieces of rope, and loops them around the knobs at the head of the bed and the knobs at the foot. She slips the nooses around Raimondo's wrists and ankles. She picks up the pair of stockings, and he suddenly speaks. His voice is indistinct.

　　Rosa? Rosa?

She freezes. After a moment, he feels the ropes, then speaks again, a bit louder.

　　What are you doing? Rosa?

She steps onto the bed behind him.

　　Rosa! Please! No! No!

She puts her feet on his shoulders, leans back against the headboard, puts the stockings around his neck and starts to strangle him. She looks straight ahead of her, not at his face, as he struggles and gags.

AUNT DAN. *(to Lemon)* She had to put the guy in this plastic sack, kick him down her back stairs,   1495
haul him outside, and sort of roll him into the trunk of a car that was parked in an alley. Apparently he'd been working with the police for some time against her friend, Freddie. *(A silence.)* Well. My teeth were chattering as I listened to the   1500
words of this naked goddess, whose lipstick was the dreamiest, loveliest shade of rose. Then she fell silent for a long time, and we just looked at each other. And then she sort of winked at me, I think you would call it, and I wanted to touch that   1505
lipstick with my fingers, so I did. And she sort of

grabbed my hand and gave it a big kiss, and my hand was all red. And then we just sat there for another long time. And then, to the music of Jasper snoring on the couch, I started to kiss her   1510
beautiful neck. I was incredibly in love. She kissed me back. I felt as if stars were flying through my head. She was gorgeous, perfect. We spent the rest of the night on the couch, and then we went out and had a great breakfast, and we spent a   1515
wonderful week together.

Pause.

LEMON. *(to Aunt Dan)* Why only a week?
AUNT DAN. What?
LEMON. Why only a week?

Pause.

AUNT DAN. Well, Lemon, you know, it's because. . .   1520
(Pause.) because love always cries out to be somehow expressed. *(Pause.)* But the expression of love leads somehow — nowhere. *(A silence.)* You're living somewhere — situated, you know, on some particular map. Something happens — you express   1525
love — and suddenly you've — you've dropped off the map you were living on, and you're on some other one — unrelated — like a bug that's been brushed from the edge of a table and has fallen off onto the rug below. The beauty of a face makes   1530
you touch a hand, and suddenly you're in a world of actions, of experiences, unrelated to the beauty of that face, unrelated to that face at all, unrelated to beauty. You're doing things and saying things that you never wanted to say or do. *(Pause.)* What   1535
you felt was love. What you felt was that the face was beautiful. And it was not enough for you just to feel love, just to sit in the presence of beauty and enjoy it. Something about your feeling itself made that impossible. And so you just didn't ask,   1540
Well, what will happen when I touch that hand? What will happen between that person and me? You simply did it, you walked off the map, and there was that person, with all their qualities, and there was you, with all *your* qualities, and there you   1545
were together. And it's always, of course, extremely fascinating for as long as you can stand it, but it has nothing to do with the love you originally felt.

Every time, in a way, you think it will have *something* to do with the love you felt. But it never does. It never has anything to do with love.

Silence.

LEMON. *(to the audience)* My father didn't know about my mother's conversations with Aunt Dan in the garden. He had other things on his mind. The friendship ended, it faded away, and it didn't bother him. Aunt Dan never came back to visit us after the summer I was eleven, but a couple of times a year I would take the train into London and visit her, and she would take me out to dinner at some beautiful restaurant, and we'd sit together and have a lovely meal and talk for hours. When I was just eighteen, Aunt Dan got sick, and then when I was nineteen she finally died. *(Pause.)* In the year or two before Aunt Dan got sick there would sometimes be some odd moments, some crazy moments, in those beautiful restaurants. Some moments when both of us would just fall silent. Well, it was really quite straightforward, I suppose. I think there were crazy moments, sitting at those restaurant tables, when both of us were thinking, Well, why not? We adore each other. We always have. There you are sitting right next to me, and isn't this silly? Why don't I just lean over and give you a kiss? But of course Dan would never have touched me first. I would have to have touched her. Well, neither of us really took those moments seriously at all. But sure, there were moments, there were silences, when I could feel her thinking, Well, here I am sitting on this nice lawn, under this lovely tree, and there's a beautiful apple up there that I've got my eye on, and maybe if I just wait, if I just sit waiting here very quietly, maybe the apple will fall right into my lap. I could feel her thinking it, and I could feel how simple and natural it would be just to do it, just to hold her face and kiss her on the lips, but I never did it. It never happened. So there was me and Aunt Dan in the little house, and then there was me and Aunt Dan not touching each other in all those restaurants, and finally there was one last visit to Aunt Dan just before she died, in her own flat, when she was too sick to touch anybody.

Music. Aunt Dan's flat.

There's a nice melody playing on her record-player when I go in. She's smiling. My dress surprises her. Well, I thought it would be right to wear a dress. Who is she now? Is she someone I've ever known? I can't tell. Filthy from the train, I go into her bathroom to wash my hands. And in the bathroom there are a thousand things I don't want to see — what pills she takes, what drops, what medicines — with labels I don't want to read — how many, how often to be taken each day. Have there ever been so many things to hide my eyes from in one small room? Soap that has touched her hands, her face; the basin over which she has bent; the well-worn towel, bearer of the imprint of her nose, her mouth — I feel no need now ever to see her again.

The music has ended. Lemon sits down by Aunt Dan.

It was the nurse's day off. *(A silence; then to Aunt Dan)* Er — umn — does she clean the flat as well, Aunt Dan?

A silence.

AUNT DAN. She's a wonderful woman. I can't tell you. Her kindness. She serves me — she serves me, as if she were a nun. . .

LEMON. A nun?

AUNT DAN. Going to the toilet. My meals. She knows me. We know each other. No talking. She hears my thoughts. She hears all the things that are happening here. *(Pause.)* We listen together. The insects, the wind, the water in the pipes. Sharing these things. Literally everything. The whole world.

The dark room, as at the beginning of the play.

LEMON. *(to the audience)* There's something that people never say about the Nazis now. *(She drinks.)* By the way, how can anybody like anything better than lime and celery juice? It is the best! The thing is that the Nazis were trying to create a certain way of life for themselves. That's obvious if you read these books I'm reading. They believed that the primitive society of the Germanic tribes had created a life of wholeness and meaning for each person. They blamed the sickness and degeneracy of society as *they* knew it — before they came to power, of course — on the mixture of races that had taken place since that tribal period. In their opinion, all the destructive values of greed, materialism, competitiveness, dishonesty, and so on, had been brought into their society by non-Germanic races. They may have been wrong about it, but that was their belief. So they were trying to create a certain way of life. They were trying to create, or re-create, some sort of society of brothers, bound together by a certain code of loyalty and honour. So to make that attempt, they had to remove the non-Germans, they had to eliminate interbreeding. They were trying to create a certain way of life. Now today, of course, everybody says, 'How awful! How awful!' And they were certainly ruthless and thorough in what they did. But the mere fact of killing human beings in order to create a certain way of life is not something that exactly distinguishes the Nazis from everybody else. That's just absurd. When any people feels that its hopes for a desirable future are threatened by some other group, they always do the very same thing. The only question is the degree of the threat. Now for us, for example, criminals are a threat, but they're only a small threat. Right now, we would say about criminals that they're a serious annoyance. We would call them a problem. And right now, the way we deal with that problem is that we take the criminals and we put them in jail. But if those criminals became so vicious, if there got to be so many of them, that our most basic hopes as a society were truly threatened by them — if our whole system of prisons and policemen had fallen so far behind the problem that the streets of our cities were actually controlled and dominated by violent criminals — then we would find ourselves forgetting the prisons and just killing the criminals instead. It's just a fact. Or when the Europeans first came to America, well, the Indians were there. The Indians fought them for every scrap of land. How could they build the kind of society they wanted? If they'd tried to catch all the Indians and put them in jail, they would have had to put all their effort into finding the Indians and building the jails, and then, when the Indians came out, they would undoubtedly have started fighting all over again as

hard as before. And so they decided to kill the Indians. So it becomes absurd to talk about the Nazis as if the Nazis were unique. That's a kind of hypocrisy. Because the fact is, no society has ever considered the taking of life an unpardonable crime or even, really, a major tragedy. It's something that's done when it has to be done, and it's as simple as that. It's no different from the fact that if I have harmful or obnoxious insects — let's say, cockroaches — living in my house, I probably have to do something about it. Or at least, the question I have to ask is: How many are there? If the cockroaches are small, and I see a few of them now and then, that may not be very disturbing to me. But if I see big ones, if I start to see them often, then I say to myself, they have to be killed. Now some people simply hate to kill cockroaches, so they'll wait much longer. But if the time comes when there are hundreds of them, when they're suddenly crawling out of every drawer, when they're in the oven, when they're in the refrigerator, when they're in the toilet, when they're in the bed, then even the person who hates to kill them will go to the shop and get some poison and start killing, because the way of life that that person had wanted to lead is now really being threatened. And yes, the fact is, it's very unpleasant to kill another creature — let's admit it. Each one of us has his own fear of pain and his own fear of death. It's true for people and for every type of creature that lives. I remember once squashing a huge brown roach — I slammed it with my shoe, but it wasn't dead, and I sat and watched it — and it's an awful period just before any creature dies — any insect or animal — when you're watching the stupid, ignorant things that that creature is doing to try to fight off its death — whether it's moving its arms or its legs, or it's kicking, or it's trying to crawl to another part of the floor, or it's trying to lift itself off the ground — those things can't prevent death! — but the creature is trying out every gesture it's capable of, hoping, hoping that something will help it. And I remember how I felt as I watched that big brown roach squirming and crawling, and yet it was totally squashed, and I could see its insides slowly come oozing out. And of course, the bigger a creature is, the harder it is to kill it, and that's awful to see. We know it takes at least ten minutes to hang a person. Even if you shoot them in the head, it's not instantaneous — they still make those squirming movements at least for a moment. And people in gas chambers rush to the doors which they know very well are firmly locked. They fight each other to get to the doors. So killing is always very unpleasant. Now when people say, "Oh, the Nazis were different from anyone, the Nazis were different from anyone," well, maybe that's true in at least one way, which is that I imagine they observed themselves very frankly, perhaps, in the act of killing, and admitted how they really *felt* about the whole process. I imagine that they said, of course it's very unpleasant, and if we didn't have to do it in order to create a way of life that we want for ourselves, we would never be involved in killing at all. But since we *do* have to do it, why not be truthful about it, and why not admit that yes, yes, there's something inside us that likes to kill. Some *part* of us. Why *wouldn't* that be so? Our nature is derived from the nature of animals, and of course there's a part of animal nature that likes to kill. If killing were totally repugnant to animals, they couldn't survive. So an enjoyment of killing is there inside us. In polite society, people don't discuss it, but the fact is that it's enjoyable — it's enjoyable — to make plans for killing, and it's enjoyable to learn about killing that is done by other people, and it's enjoyable to think about killing, and it's enjoyable to read about killing, and it's even enjoyable actually to kill, although when we ourselves are actually killing, an element of unpleasantness always comes in. That unpleasant feeling starts to come in. But even there, one has to say, even though there's an unpleasant side at first to watching people die, we have to admit that after watching for awhile — maybe after watching for a day or maybe for a week or a year — it's still in a way unpleasant to watch, but on the other hand we have to admit that, after we've watched it for all that time — well, we don't really actually care any more. We have to admit that we don't really care. And I think that that last admission is what

really makes people go mad about the Nazis, because in our own society we have this kind of cult built up around what people call the feeling of "compassion." I remember my mother screaming all the time, "Compassion! Compassion! You have to have compassion for other people! You have to have compassion for other human beings!" And I must admit, there's something I find refreshing about the Nazis, which is partly why I enjoy reading about them every night, because they sort of had the nerve to say, "Well, what *is* this compassion? Because I don't know really what it is." And so they must have sort of *asked* each other, you know, "Well, say, Heinrich, have *you* ever felt it?" "Well no, Adolf, what about you?"[11] And they all had to admit that they really didn't know what the hell it was. And I find it sort of relaxing to read about those people, because I have to admit that I don't know either. I mean, I think I've felt it reading a novel, and I think I've felt it watching a film — "Oh how sad, that child is sick! That mother is crying!" — but I can't ever remember feeling it in life. I just don't remember feeling it about something that was happening in front of my eyes. And I can't believe that other people are that different from me. In other words, it was unpleasant to watch that pitiful roach scuttling around on my floor dying, but I can't say I really felt *sad* about it. I felt revolted or sickened I guess I would say but I can't really say I felt sorry for the roach. And plenty of people have cried in my presence or seemed to be suffering and I remember wishing that they'd *stop* suffering and *stop* crying and leave me alone but I don't remember frankly that I actually cared. So you have to say finally, Well, fine if there are all these people like my mother who want to go around talking about compassion all day well, fine, that's their right. But it's sort of refreshing to admit every once in a while that they're talking about something that possibly doesn't exist. And it's sort of an ambition of mine to go around some day and ask each person I meet, Well here is something you've heard about to the

---

11 Heinrich, Adolf] presumably, Heinrich Himmler, who organized the extermination of the Jews, and Adolf Hitler.

point of nausea all of your life, but do you personally actually remember feeling it and if you really do, could you please describe the particular circumstances in which you felt it and what it actually felt *like*? Because if there's one thing I learned from Aunt Dan, I suppose you could say it was a kind of honesty. It's easy to say we should all be loving and sweet, but meanwhile we're enjoying a certain way of life — and we're actually living — due to the existence of certain other people who are willing to take the job of killing on their own backs, and it's not a bad thing every once in awhile to admit that that's the way we're living, and even to give to those certain people a tiny, fractional crumb of thanks. You can be very sure that it's more than they expect, but I think they'd be grateful, all the same.

The lights fade as she sits and drinks.

APPENDIX:

ON THE CONTEXT OF THE PLAY

by Wallace Shawn

When I was around thirteen, I was sitting on a sofa with an older woman, and she said to me rather fiercely, "You don't understand this now, but when you get older, you'll come to appreciate the importance of comfort." This did turn out to be true. At that time I really didn't have much to be comforted about or comforted from, so naturally comfort didn't matter to me then. And now it does. And the older I get, the more I long to feel really comfortable. But I've also come to realize that an awful lot of preparatory work must be undertaken before that particular feeling can begin to exist, and I've learned, too, how all that effort can count for nothing if even one tiny element of the world around me refuses to fit into its necessary place. Yes, I'm at home in my lovely apartment, I'm sitting in my cozy rocking chair, there are flowers on the table, tranquil colors of paint on the walls. But if I've caught a fever and I'm feeling sick, or if a nearby faucet has developed a leak, or if a dog in the courtyard six floors below me is barking, the unity of my peaceful scene is spoiled, and comfort flies out the window. And unfortunately, what in fact prevents me more than anything else from feeling really comfortable — whether I'm leaning back against a soft banquette in a pleasant restaurant or spending a drowsy morning in bed propped up on three or four pillows — is actually the well-intentioned ethical training I received as a child.

My parents brought me up to believe that there was something terribly important called morality — an approach towards life which was based on the paradoxical concept of self-restraint (or the restraint of one part of the self by another part). Instead of teaching me merely to be alert to the threat of potential enemies outside myself, I was instructed to practice, in addition, a sort of constant vigilance over my own impulses — even, at times, a subjugation of them, when certain abstract criteria of justice (which lived in my own mind) determined that someone else's interests should be allowed to prevail over my own desires. Morality, this fantastic and complicated system (which a good many of my friends were taught by their parents as well), was, as we first encountered it, a set of principles and laws. But these principles and laws were really nothing more than a description of how a person would behave if he cared equally about all human beings, even though one of them happened, in fact, to be himself — if he cared about them equally and deeply, so that their suffering actually caused him to suffer as well. And there were such people — there were people who experienced a sense of awe, of humility, before the miracle of life — people who had a gift for morality the way some people had a gift for music or pleasure. But we, for the most part, lacked that gift, so we were taught laws and principles, the simplest of which was just that each other person was as real as we were. Almost all of the rest of morality followed from that. If I could learn to believe that someone, a stranger, was just as real as I was, I could easily see how badly it would hurt him if I treated him cruelly, if I lied to him, if I betrayed him.

But the world is in a constant turmoil of conflict and struggle, I learned, and so morality was not merely a way of looking at life; it was also a guide to action. And its teaching in regard to action was that I should love all the people in the world equally, and that I should take the action prompted by that love.

Of course, I myself was one of those people, and in saying that all people should be equally loved, morality was also saying that I, too, like others, had a rightful place in the world, and so in following the teachings of morality I might even find myself at times acting in defense of my own interests. I might even find myself fighting or killing in their defense. But this would only be so if I had first stepped outside myself, if I had approached myself as merely one among all the human creatures on the earth for whom I cared, and if I, out of my equal love, had solemnly decided to send myself into battle on the side of myself, because this was necessary for everyone's sake.

My daily obligation, then, was certainly not to refrain from action. On the contrary, passivity was seen, from this point of view, as merely a lazy, indifferent, and cowardly form of actionless action. Nor was my obligation to refrain from all activity on my own behalf. No, my daily obligation was, first and foremost, to learn how to make a correct and careful study of the world.

Perhaps I had long ago rejected self-love and self-interest as guides to action. Perhaps I had sworn to myself that I would always act only for everyone's sake, out of love for everyone. But if I didn't know what the world was like, how could I know what action to take? Perhaps it was permissible to kill a person in order to prevent a terrible evil. But if I acted impulsively, heedlessly, and blindly — if I killed the wrong person because I relied on an erroneous suspicion or an intuition, or I based my action on some erroneous theory of the world which I'd accepted for years because it happened to be flattering to someone like me — would I still have behaved in a permissible way? Obviously not. How, then, could I act at all unless, for a moment, for an hour, for a day, I had ruthlessly stripped from my mind all those prejudices and preconceptions which my own particular situation and my own particular history had forced upon me — unless I had cast all these from me and looked at the world for what it was? Who really threatened me? Who really threatened you? What would be the effect on me if you did this? What would be the effect on you if I did that? I had to learn how to examine the world and then to re-examine it, because it changed very fast. And so it turned out that

morality insisted upon accuracy — perpetual, painstaking study and research.

I realize now that this entire training in morality is a jarring element in the life I'm leading, and in my struggle to feel comfortable, to feel at ease, it functions rather like a dog whose barking never stops, a dog whose barking persists throughout the day and then continues regularly all night long. It is a perpetual irritation. Everything visible around me may be perfect and serene, but inside, there is this voice which never stops denouncing me. It does not fit in. Of course I'd be pleased if I could claim that all my relations with other people were in perfect harmony with the laws of morality — and as a matter of fact, in my daily interactions with my friends and colleagues and loved ones, I usually try to follow ethical precepts. But when I draw the curtains of perception a little bit wider and consider the fact that there are thousands and millions of people in the world, all quite real, and that I have some sort of relation to every one of them, I have to admit that it would be hard to insist that all these relations of mine are truly obedient to those solemn laws. I'll say this much — if my relation to each and every peasant in Cambodia is indeed exactly what the principles of morality would demand it to be, it's a miraculous coincidence, because it takes a lot of effort to behave correctly in regard to my friends, and from one end of the year to another I never give those peasants a single thought.

The point I'm making is quite simple. It's that each year I do a certain amount of labour (I personally happen to do something — acting in films — which I find quite amusing), and I'm paid a certain sum of money, and I spend it in certain ways. When I receive my paycheck for the week, I immediately employ groups of people to start making me things, like coffee-grinders and light bulbs and recordings of great violinists, and streams of goods start flowing in my direction from all over the world. In contrast to this, as everyone knows, when a gold miner in South Africa receives the payment for his week's work, he can only set in motion, say, one one-thousandth of that much activity, most of it strictly in the agricultural sector. But even after I've done all the buying that I'm planning to do, half of my money still remains, and I then spend most of that on employing people to do services for me. With some of the money I employ a woman to come on Wednesday morning and clean my apartment, and with most of it I pay the government of my country, the United States of America, to perform a similar service in regard to my environment as a whole. And, of course, one of the most important tasks which my government undertakes is to try to preserve the international structure of the world more or less as it is, so that next year it will not suddenly be I who is working a seventy-hour week in some Godforsaken pit or digging in some field under the burning sun.

Now, as governments go, as governments have gone throughout the course of history, mine has much to recommend it, in my opinion. My view is absolutely that United States society, within its own borders, is less oppressive and less brutal than most, and if given complete sway over the entire world, a United States tyranny would be preferable to many. But as my government happens to be the representative through which I personally conduct my relationships with most of my fellow human beings, I'm obliged to ask, for as long as I continue to be bound by my childhood training, whether my government's actions conform to the laws of morality. Of course, people often say that governments, when dealing with international relations, cannot possibly be responsive to these laws, which appropriately apply only to private life and a government's domestic sphere. The explanation they give is that any government which tried to follow such laws would be at a great disadvantage, because the world's other governments would continue to ignore them. And it is often said, also, that governments have obligations to the people of their own countries, but not to the people of other countries. But, really, to argue in this way is to consider governments to be somehow living beings in their own right, with their own special habits and obligations, whereas from the point of view of the principles of morality, governments are simply organizations established for the convenience of those who control them; they are mere intermediaries, the bearers of messages.

My fellow citizens and I may very well be surrounded by immoral enemies, and we may be tempted to take utterly ruthless actions against them.

We may well feel a profound attachment to one another, combined with a cool indifference towards everyone else on the globe. But the principles of morality do not waver in the face of our particular circumstances; they demand obedience whether obedience is difficult or easy. They rarely insist that a group of people should allow themselves to be trampled upon or destroyed. But they do reject the opinion that those near to me should be treated with love, while those who are distant may be treated with contempt. And they do judge my actions with the same severity whether I perform them with my own hands or through instrumentalities or chains of command. And so of course they do judge my government's actions, and they find that, although I may be a friendly fellow to meet on the street, I have found, through my government, a sneaky way to do some terrible things.

Of course, it is certainly the case that there are crimes which I do not commit against the world's human beings. My boot does not oppress the peoples of Poland or Hungary.[12] The prisoners in the jails of my country are not hung upside down and tortured; our poor do not die of cholera or plague. But my relation to most of the people in the world just cannot be described as exactly the one which morality would demand. And this is why I realize that as long as I preserve my loyalty to my childhood training I will never know what it is to be truly comfortable, and this is why I feel a fantastic need to tear that training out of my heart once and for all so that I can finally begin to enjoy the life that is spread out before me like a feast. And every time a friend makes that happy choice and sets himself free, I find that I inwardly exult and rejoice, because it means there will be one less person to disapprove of me if I choose to do the same.

As I write these words, in New York City in 1985, more and more people who grew up around me are making this decision; they are throwing away their moral chains and learning to enjoy their true situation: Yes, they are admitting loudly and bravely, we live in beautiful homes, we're surrounded by beautiful gardens, our children are playing with wonderful

---

12 Poland or Hungary] Until around 1989, the governments of these countries were strictly controlled by the Soviet Union.

toys, and our kitchen shelves are filled with wonderful food. And if there are people out there who don't seem to like us and who would like to break into our homes and take what we have, well then, part of our good fortune is that we can afford to pay guards to man our gates and keep those people away. And if those who protect us need to hit people in the face with the butts of their rifles, or if they need perhaps even to turn around and shoot, they have our permission, and we only hope they'll do what they do with diligence and skill.

The amazing thing I've noticed about those friends of mine who've made that choice is that as soon as they've made it, they begin to blossom, to flower, because they are no longer hiding, from themselves or anyone else, the true facts about their own lives. They become very frank about human nature. They freely admit that man is a predatory creature, a hunter and a fighter, and they admit that it can warm a human's heart to trick an enemy, to make him cry, to make him do what he doesn't want to do, and even to make him crawl in the mud and die in agony. They admit that to manipulate people can be an art, and that to deceive people can be entertaining. They admit that there's a skill involved in playing life's game, and they admit that it's exciting to bully and threaten and outwit and defeat all the other people who are playing against you. And as they learn to admit these things, and they lose the habit of looking over their shoulders in fear at what exists in their own souls, they develop the charm and grace which shine out from all people who are truly comfortable with themselves, who are not worried, who are not ashamed of their own actions. These are people who are free to love life exuberantly. They can enjoy a bottle of wine or a walk in the garden with unmixed pleasure, because they feel justified in having the bottle of wine, in having the garden. And if, by chance, they run into the laundress who takes care of their clothes, they can chat with her happily and easily, because they accept the fact that some people, themselves, happen to wear beautiful clothes, and others are paid to keep them clean. And, in fact, these people who accept themselves are people whose company everyone enjoys.

So there are those who live gracelessly in a state of discomfort, because they allow themselves to be whipped on an hourly basis by morality's lash, and then there's another group of cheerful, self-confident people who've put morality aside for now, and they're looking happy. But whenever I start dreaming about self-confident people I begin to get terribly nervous, because I always think of the marvelous self-confidence of Hitler, the way he would expound his theories of the world to his aides and orderlies and secretaries at the dining room table night after night with no sense that he needed to keep checking to see if his theories were really true. Hitler's boundless self-confidence enabled him to live each day as a tireless murderer; no weakness, no flagging energy, kept his knife from plunging into his victims hour after hour with mechanical ease. And so, naturally, I ask myself, will I become like him? Yes, of course, I long to be comfortable. But to become a murderer? To murder everyone? If I gave up morality, what would prevent me from murdering everyone?

Hitler was a man who was drawn to murder, to thinking about murder, to dwelling on murder. Particularly to dwelling on murder. Can we not imagine with what eager excitement he must have listened to all of the latest reports from the death camps, the crematoria, which he never in fact visited on a single occasion? But when we speak of dwelling on murder ... that person standing over the daily newspaper — reading about the massacre, reading about the bloodbath, reading about the execution in a room in the prison — that person is me. And am I not in some part of myself identifying with the one in the story who is firing the machine gun at the innocent people, who is pulling the switch that sends the jolts of power through the prisoner strapped in the electric chair? And do I not also enjoy reading about those incredible scientists who are making the preparations for what we might do in some future war that might take place? Do I not join them in picturing, with some small relish, the amazing effects which our different devices would have on possible victims? Is my blood not racing with abnormal speed as I read about these things? Is there not something trembling inside me? I know that these planners, these scientists, are not involved in killing. They're killing no one. But I see what they're doing — they're building the gas chambers, getting together the pellets of poison, assembling the rooms where the clothing and valuables will all be sorted, transporting the victims to convenient camps, and asking them to get undressed for the showers and disinfection which will soon be following. Of course, no one is putting people into the chambers. No one is pumping in the gas.

But wait a minute. Am I crazy now? What am I saying? What does this have to do with Hitler? Of course, I may have insane impulses somewhere inside me, but the difference between Hitler and me is that there was nothing in Hitler which restrained him from following any of his insane impulses to their logical, insane conclusions — he was capable of doing anything at all, if given the chance — because he was utterly without connection to morality.

But I just was thinking about cutting my connection to morality also.

Yes, I was thinking about it. But I didn't do it. At least, I have no memory of doing it. Or was there actually some moment when I did do it, which I've now forgotten?

I don't seem to remember what's happened at all. I know there was a time when I was not like Hitler.

The past feels so terribly close. It's as if I could reach out and touch it. Could I have become like one of those people who remembers, as if it were yesterday, the time when principles of decency grew freshly in his heart, when a love for humanity set him off on his path in life, who still believes that each of his actions is driven and motivated by those very principles and that very love, but who in fact is a coarse and limited brute who buried both love and principles long ago?

How could a person break his attachment to morality without noticing it, without feeling it, without remembering it? Could a perfectly decent person just turn into a cold-hearted beast, a monster, and still feel pretty much the same?

Of course. A perfectly decent person can turn into a monster perfectly easily. And there's no reason why he would feel any different. Because the difference between a perfectly decent person and a monster is just a few thoughts. The perfectly decent person who follows a certain chain of reasoning, ever so slightly and subtly incorrect, becomes a perfect monster at the end of the chain.

Thoughts have extraordinary power in the human world. They can do odd things. Familiar thoughts can lead us by the hand to very strange thoughts. And in a way, we're not as clever as our own thoughts, which have a peculiar habit of developing on their own and taking us to conclusions we never particularly wanted to reach. Even within each thought, other thoughts are hidden, waiting to crawl out.

As the morning begins and I slowly turn my head to look at the clock on my bedside bookcase, my thoughts are already leaping and playing in my brain, ceaselessly spawning other thoughts, changing their shape, dividing in two and then dividing again, merging, dancing together in gigantic clumps. There's no end to the things that the thoughts will do if no one is paying any attention to them.

Our thoughts jump and fly through the pathways of our minds. The world races forward. And meanwhile we're walking slowly around in a daze, trying to remember whether we're still connected to morality or not. False arguments, rapidly expressed, confuse us, seduce us, corrupt us. The chains of reasoning, of thinking, appeared to be sound. What was wrong? But we forget that thinking has its own pathology, and we sit in some room listening to a discussion, and something reasonable and admirable is said, and we nod our heads, and somehow we keep on nodding, and moments later we've agreed to something which would make our former selves turn purple with shame. But we sit there blankly, unaware that anything has happened. Why was it that we failed to notice the first signs of sickness in the argument? At the crucial moment, had our attention wandered? Why would that be? Are we particularly tired right now? Exhausted?

These are the things that happen to us every day. They may happen to you as you read the play you're holding in your hand. And the characters in the play, like you and me, are formed by the chains of reasoning they've followed.

Our lives develop, and our thoughts change, and as our thoughts change, we change. We change each day in small steps, brief conversations, half-conscious moments of reflection, of doubt and resolution.

I stand at the door of my house, ready to defend the loved ones inside from the marauder lurking in the dark. As I steel myself to shoot the marauder, I say to myself, "I must be hard. Cold. Unsentimental." I repeat the litany a hundred times. And the next morning, when the marauder has not come — or the marauder has come and I have shot him — what do I do with my litany? It doesn't disappear from my mind merely because there is no marauder any more. Will I adopt it as a creed? Will I decide to believe that unsentimentality is an important virtue? Will I start to take pleasure in my own coldness? Will I teach myself to be hard now in situations where hardness once would have seemed like a crime?

A friend describes to me the pleasure he took in hitting someone who had insulted him, and I realize that I, too, take pleasure in his story. I recognize in myself a desire for revenge against every person who has ever hurt me. He tells me that he finds it hypocritical to deny that the desire for revenge exists in our hearts. I agree entirely. Will I now decide to adopt revenge as a legitimate motive for my daily actions?

I meet a young woman at a quiet dinner party, and as we sit together she tells me that she sometimes likes to go out with gangsters. She describes in detail the techniques they use in getting other people to do what they want — bribery, violence. I'm shocked and repelled by the stories she tells. A few months later I run into her again at another party and I hear more stories, and this time I don't feel shocked. I'm no longer so aware of the sufferings of those whom the gangsters confront. I'm more impressed by the high style and shrewdness of the gangsters themselves. I begin to understand how difficult it is to be a successful gangster and what extraordinary skill is in fact required to climb to the top of a gangster empire. I find myself listening with a certain enjoyment. By the third time that I encounter this woman I've become a connoisseur of gangster techniques, and the stories she tells now strike me as funny. I consider myself to be, as I always was, a person who entirely disapproves of gangsters, but I still pass on to a friend of mine some of the best stories in the spirit of fun. If my friend now objects that the stories are not really funny, will I find myself somewhat annoyed? Will my friend now seem to me narrow-minded — a humourless prude?

And so every day we encounter the numberless insidious intellectual ploys by which the principle of immorality makes a plausible case for itself, and for every ploy there is a corresponding weakness in our own thinking which causes us not to notice where we're being led until we've already fallen into the trap. Unfortunately, these small intellectual infirmities of ours — our brief lapses of concentration, our susceptibility to slightly inappropriate analogies, the way we tend to forget in what particular contexts the ideas in our heads first made their appearance there, the way our attention can be drawn at the wrong moment by the magician's patter to the hand which does not contain the mysterious coin — just happen to have the power to send history racing off down a path of horror. Morality, if it survived, could protect us from horror, but very little protects morality. And morality, besides, is hard to protect, because morality is only a few thoughts in our heads. And just as we quickly grow accustomed to brutal deeds and make way before them, so we are quickly stunned into foggy submission by the brutal thoughts which, in our striving for comfort, we have allowed into our minds and which can snuff the life out of morality in a matter of moments if we happen to look the other way. And all the time we are operating under the illusion that we, mere individuals, have no power at all over the course of history, when that is in fact (for better or worse) the very opposite of the case.

The shocking truth is that history, too, is at the mercy of my thoughts, and the political leaders of the world sit by their radios waiting to hear whether morality has sickened or died inside my skull. The process is simple. I speak with you, and then I turn out the light and I go to sleep, but, while I sleep, you talk on the telephone to a man you met last year in Ohio, and you tell him what I said, and he hangs up and talks to a neighbor of his, and what I said keeps traveling, farther and farther. And just as a fly can quite blithely and indifferently land on the nose of a queen, so the thought which you mentioned to the man in Ohio can make its way with unimaginable speed into the mind of a president. Because a society is very little more than a network of brains, and a president is no less involved in his society's network than anyone else, and there is almost nothing that he thinks that doesn't come right from that network. In fact, he is virtually incapable of coming up with an attitude to any problem or to any event which has not been nurtured and developed in that network of brains. So as he searches in his mind for a sound approach to the latest cable from the Soviet Premier, what comes to the surface is a thought which he happened to get from me, a thought which first occurred to me one evening thirty years ago when my grandmother turned over a card in a game of canasta with a certain unusual expression on her face.[13]

My grandmother's silence, her manner, affected me. Her gesture, expressive of certain feelings about myself, gave rise in me to a thought, and that thought had nothing to do with the Soviet Union. It was just a thought about daily life. But when it sooner or later becomes necessary for any of us — whether president or ordinary citizen — to come up with thoughts about political affairs, the only raw materials which we have to draw on are the thoughts we've previously formed on the conflicts and dramas of daily life. Our thoughts may be ones we've dreamed up ourselves, or we may have acquired them from our parents, from our lovers, from our Aunt Dan, or from the man in Ohio. But wherever we've found them, they are all we have to work with. Our political attitudes can only come out of what we are — what we were as children, what we've become today, what we've learned in school, at the playground, at the party, at the beach, at home, in bed. And as all of our attitudes flow into action, flow into history, the bedroom and the battlefield soon seem to be one.

My political opinions fly out across the world and determine the course of political events. And political events are determined as well by what I think about the conversation I had with my mother last Saturday when we were having tea. What I say to you about my neighbour's child affects what you feel about the nurse who sits by the side of your friend in the hospital room, and what you say about the nurse affects what your friend's sister thinks about the government of China. Everything you are affects me, and everything I am, all my thoughts — the behavior I

admire or criticize, the way I choose to spend an hour of my time, the things I like to talk about, the stories I like to hear, the jokes I like to tell, the events which delight me and the events which displease me — affect the course of history whether I like it or not, whether I know about it or not, whether I care or not. My power over history is inescapable except through death. Privacy is an illusion. What I do is public, and what I think is public. The fragility of my own thoughts becomes the fragility of the world. The ease with which I could become a swine is the ease with which the world could fall apart, like something rotten.

The uncomfortable and incompetent slaves of morality — those awkward, crippled creatures who insist on believing in a standard which condemns them — are less admirable only than those few perfect beings who perhaps obey morality completely. There are a million possible degrees of obedience, and the person who obeys morality to a higher degree is more admirable than the person who obeys it less, and the person who doesn't struggle to obey it at all is not admirable at all. Of course, almost everyone describes himself as a servant of morality, and even the most outrageous criminals will make such claims, not just publicly but even to themselves, and undoubtedly Hitler himself was no exception. In fact, there is no action so manifestly evil that it cannot be seen and described as a justifiable and purely defensive measure. But none of this should be allowed to confuse us. And it is true also that if we ourselves have any sympathy or any affection for people — if we like people — we will be fond of many who treat morality with utter indifference, including people whose personal histories make their indifference most understandable. But this should not be allowed to confuse us either. Morality happens to be a protection which we need in order to avoid total historical disaster, and so we are obliged to maintain a constant, precise awareness of how morality is faring in the world. Unfortunately or not, we cannot afford to turn our eyes away when our acquaintances, our friends, or we ourselves, drop down a few degrees on the scale of obedience to moral principles. It is obviously foolish and absurd to judge some small decline on the moral scale as if it were a precipitous, lengthy slide. But the temptation is great to be

---

13 canasta] a game that uses two decks of cards and is similar to rummy in that its object is to collect various complete sets.

easy on ourselves, and we've all discovered that it's easier to be easy on ourselves if we're all easy on each other too, and so we are. So when a precipitous slide really does take place, a particular effort is required in order to see it. Sophistries, false chains of reasoning, deception, and self-deception all rush in to conceal the fact that any change has occurred at all. 615

If we live from day to day without self-examination, we remain unaware of the dangers we may pose to ourselves and the world. But if we look into the mirror, we just might observe a rapacious face. Perhaps the face will even show subtle traces, here and there, of hatred and savagery beneath the surface. And maybe most of us look a little bit like Hitler, that ever-present ghost. All right then, we may say in response to the mirror, we are vile, we know it. Everyone is. That's the way people are. Of course we're like Hitler, and we're sick of lacerating ourselves about it, and as a matter of fact, we're even sick of lacerating Hitler — let him be. 620 625 630

This self-pitying response to the unflattering news that we're not quite good means that we've decided, if that's how things are, that we'll accept evil; we'll no longer make any effort to oppose it. This response leads right towards death. 635

But it is utterly ridiculous to say that people are vile. If we step outside and pay a brief visit to the nearest supermarket or the nearest café, we will find ourselves in a position to see, scattered perhaps among scenes of ugliness and greed, examples — some number of examples — of behavior which is thoughtful or kind, moments when someone could easily have been cold or cruel but in fact was not. Perhaps we will see the very same person do something harsh and a moment later something gentle. Everyone knows that this element of goodness exists, that it can grow, or that it can die, and there's something particularly disingenuous and cheap about extricating oneself from the human struggle with the whispered excuse that it's already over. 640 645 650

TOMSON HIGHWAY

The Rez Sisters

Tomson Highway was born in 1951 on his father's trap-line in northern Manitoba, about a thousand kilometres north of Winnipeg, as the eleventh of twelve children. Until he was sent to the Guy Hill Indian Residential School at the age of six, he lived a traditional nomadic life in the wilderness with his family. His only language at that time was Cree; he would not become fluent in English until he was a teenager. At Guy Hill, a Roman Catholic boarding school, Tomson and his younger brother, René (who was to become a renowned dancer and choreographer until his AIDS-related death in 1990), were sexually abused by the priests, an experience that would thereafter haunt the two brothers, as Tomson Highway describes in his semi-autobiographical novel, *The Kiss of the Fur Queen* (1998).

However, if Highway's early life provided unpromising preparation for a career as a celebrated playwright, his extensive natural talents, his diligence, his intelligence and his lively imagination seem to have worked together to provide ample compensation. Following his isolated childhood, Highway lived with a number of white foster families in Winnipeg. At thirteen, he began to play the piano, which led to studies at the University of Manitoba's Faculty of Music and then to London, England, where he studied for a year to become a concert pianist. When he returned to Canada, he enrolled at the University of Western Ontario's Faculty of Music, from which he graduated in 1975. At Western, music had remained Highway's major; it was during his time there, however, that Highway's interest in theatre began to develop. He met and worked with the playwright James Reaney, who was then a member of the faculty at Western and was involved with workshops for his play *Wacousta!* (in the cast of which appeared two young Native actors, Graham Greene and Gary Farmer, who would later star in Highway's *Dry Lips Oughta Move to Kapuskasing*). It was also at this time that Highway saw for the first time a play by Michel Tremblay. Both Reaney and Tremblay were to become significant influences on Highway's own dramatic style.

After graduating from Western, Highway worked for several years as a community worker in various First Nations communities across Canada. He became determined to write about the lives of those who lived on the reserves and began by writing drama for Native audiences, partly because he believed drama effectively complemented Native oral culture. One of his early plays, workshopped at De-ba-jeh-mu-jig Theatre Company (a Native company based on the Wikwemikong Reserve on Manitoulin Island), was *The Rez Sisters* (1986). When the play was remounted in Toronto, it became, to Highway's surprise, a celebrated hit with mainstream audiences. That initial success was further expanded three years later, with what Highway calls "the flip-side" of *The Rez Sisters*: *Dry Lips Oughta Move to Kapuskasing* (1989), his play featuring the men of the Wasy Reserve and a female Nanabush.

For Canadian audiences who had become accustomed over the years to hearing grim accounts about life on the reserves, the enormous vitality, humour and wit of *The Rez Sisters* came as a revela-

tion. Highway doesn't shy away from representing the tragic and dysfunctional aspects of his characters lives, but these are contained within a buoyant and lively vision that allows the characters to emerge as fully rounded human beings rather than as mere sociological statistics. A further revelation was created by Highway's decision to portray his characters as seen from within their own culture, and among their own sex. Whereas most earlier Canadian plays featuring aboriginal characters—such as George Ryga's *The Ecstasy of Rita Joe*—had more or less defined these characters through their relations with white mainstream culture, *The Rez Sisters* offered a more self-defined portrait. As in Tremblay's *Les Belles Soeurs*, the larger mainstream culture and the men affecting these women's lives are mentioned, but they only figure indirectly in the play. And if Highway's sisters are comparable to Chekhov's in their longing for the sort of transcendence they believe may be found in the city (the bingo game in Toronto standing in the place of the Moscow of *Three Sisters*), the city itself remains a sort of phantom, only entering the play in a surrealistic vision based in the women's own imaginations. In a sense, the relation between life on the reserves and the world of mainstream urban culture familiar to most of us is reversed here: Wasy becomes the familiar ground from which Toronto is seen as an exotic and vaguely incomprehensible anomaly.

[C.S.W.]

TOMSON HIGHWAY

The Rez Sisters

A play in two acts

CAST OF CHARACTERS

PELAJIA PATCHNOSE, 53

PHILOMENA MOOSETAIL, 49, sister of Pelajia

MARIE-ADELE STARBLANKET, 39, half-sister of Pelajia & Philomena

ANNIE COOK, 36, sister of Marie-Adele & half-sister of the other two

EMILY DICTIONARY, 32, sister of Annie & ditto

VERONIQUE ST. PIERRE, 45, sister-in-law of all the above

ZHABOONIGAN PETERSON, 24, mentally disabled adopted daughter of Veronique

NANABUSH — who plays the Seagull (the dancer in white feathers), the Nighthawk (the dancer in dark feathers), and the Bingo Master[1]

Time: Late summer, 1986.

beings, and events. Foremost among these beings is the Trickster, as pivotal and important a figure in the Native world as Christ is in the realm of Christian mythology. "Weesageechak" in Cree, "Nanabush" in Ojibway, "Raven" in others, and "Coyote" in still others, this Trickster goes by many names and many guises. In fact, he can assume any guise he chooses. Essentially a comic, clownish sort of character, he teaches us about the nature and the meaning of existence on the planet Earth; he straddles the consciousness of man and that of God, the Great Spirit. Some say that "Nanabush" left this continent when the white man came. We believe he is still here among us—albeit a little the worse for wear and tear—having assumed other guises. Without him—and without the spiritual health of this figure—the core of Indian culture would be gone forever. [T.H]

---

[1] Nanabush] The dream world of North American Indian mythology is inhabited by the most fantastic creatures,

Place: The Wasaychigan Hill Indian Reserve, Manitoulin Island, Ontario. (Note: "Wasaychigan" means "window" in Ojibway.)[2]

ACT ONE

It is mid-morning of a beautiful late August day on the Wasaychigan Hill Indian Reserve, Manitoulin Island, Ontario. Pelajia Patchnose is alone on the roof of her house, nailing shingles on. She wears faded blue denim men's cover-alls and a baseball cap to shade her eyes from the sun. A brightly-colored square cushion belonging to her sister, Philomena Moosetail, rests on the roof beside her. The ladder to the roof is off-stage.

PELAJIA: Philomena, I wanna go to Toronto.
PHILOMENA:

From offstage.

Oh, go on.

PELAJIA: Sure as I'm sitting away up here on the roof of this old house. I kind of like it up here, though. From here, I can see half of Manitoulin Island on a clear day. I can see the chimneys, the tops of apple trees, the garbage heap behind Big Joey's dumpy little house. I can see the seagulls circling over Marie-Adele Starblanket's white picket fence. Boats on the North Channel I wish I was on, sailing away somewhere. The mill at Espanola, a hundred miles away … and that's with just a bit of squinting.[3] See? If I had binoculars, I could see the superstack in Sudbury.[4] And if I were Superwoman, I could see the CN Tower in Toronto. Ah, but I'm just a plain old Pelajia Rosella Patchnose and I'm here in plain, dusty, boring old Wasaychigan Hill … Wasy … waiting … waiting … nailing shining shingles with my trusty silver hammer on the roof of Pelajia Rosella Patchnose's little two-bedroom welfare house. Philomena. I wanna go to Toronto.

Philomena Moosetail comes up the ladder to the roof with one shingle and obviously hating it. She is very well-dressed with a skirt, nylons, even heels, completely impractical for the roof.

PHILOMENA: Oh, go on.
PELAJIA: I'm tired, Philomena, tired of this place. There's days I wanna leave so bad.
PHILOMENA: But you were born here. All your poop's on this reserve.
PELAJIA: Oh, go on.
PHILOMENA: You'll never leave.
PELAJIA: Yes, I will. When I'm old.
PHILOMENA: You're old right now.
PELAJIA: I got a good 30 years to go …
PHILOMENA: … and you're gonna live every one of them right here beside me …
PELAJIA: … maybe 40 …
PHILOMENA: … here in Wasy.

Tickles Pelajia on the breasts.

Chiga-chiga-chiga.
PELAJIA:

Yelps and slaps Philomena's hand away.

Oh, go on. It's not like it used to be.
PHILOMENA: Oh, go on. People change, places change, time changes things. You expect to be young and gorgeous forever?
PELAJIA: See? I told you I'm not old.
PHILOMENA: Oh, go on. You.
PELAJIA: "Oh, go on. You." You bug me like hell when you say that.
PHILOMENA: You say it, too. And don't give me none of this "I don't like this place. I'm tired of it." This place is too much inside your blood. You can't get rid of it. And it can't get rid of you.
PELAJIA: Four thirty this morning, I was woken by …
PHILOMENA: Here we go again.
PELAJIA: … Andrew Starblanket and his brother, Matthew. Drunk. Again. Or sounded like …

2 Wasaychigan Hill Indian Reserve] a mythical location. The word "Reserve" is used in Canada rather than "Reservation," which is used in the United States. Manitoulin Island contains five reserves, the largest of which is the Wikwemikong Unceded Indian Reserve, on the eastern side of the island.

3 mill at Espanola] the Domtar pulp and paper mill, which is the largest employer in Espanola, a town in the North Shore Region of Lake Huron near Manitoulin Island.

4 superstack in Sudbury] the immense smokestack of the Inco mine.

PHILOMENA: Nothing better to do.

PELAJIA: … fighting over some girl. Heard what sounded like a baseball bat landing on somebody's back. My lawn looks like the shits this morning.

PHILOMENA: Well, I like it here. Myself, I'm gonna go to every bingo and I'm gonna hit every jackpot between here and Espanola and I'm gonna buy me that toilet I'm dreaming about at night … big and wide and very white …

PELAJIA: Aw-ni-gi-naw-ee-dick.[5]

PHILOMENA: I'm good at bingo.

PELAJIA: So what! And the old stories, the old language. Almost all gone … was a time Nanabush and Windigo and everyone here could rattle away in Indian as fast as Bingo Betty could lay her bingo chips down on a hot night.[6]

PHILOMENA: Pelajia Rosella Patchnose. The sun's gonna drive you crazy.

And she descends the ladder.

PELAJIA: Everyone here's crazy. No jobs. Nothing to do but drink and screw each other's wives and husbands and forget about our Nanabush.

From offstage Philomena screams. She fell down the ladder.

Philomena!

As she looks over the edge of the roof.

What are you doing down there?

PHILOMENA: What do you think? I fell.

PELAJIA: Bring me some of them nails while you're down there.

PHILOMENA:

Whining and still from offstage, from behind the house.

You think I can race up and down this ladder? You think I got wings?

PELAJIA: You gotta wear pants when you're doing a man's job. See? You got your skirt ripped on a nail and now you can see your thighs. People gonna think you just came from Big Joey's house.

---

5 Aw-ni-gi-naw-ee-dick] Oh, go on. (Ojibway)
6 Windigo] in Native mythology, a spirit associated with cannibalism.

PHILOMENA:

She comes up the ladder in a state of disarray.

Let them think what they want. That old cow Gazelle Nataways … always acting like she thinks she's still a spring chicken. She's got them legs of hers wrapped around Big Joey day and night …

PELAJIA: Philomena. Park your tongue. My old man has to go the hundred miles to Espanola just to get a job. My boys. Gone to Toronto. Only place educated Indian boys can find decent jobs these days. And here I sit all broken-hearted.

PHILOMENA: Paid a dime and only farted.

PELAJIA: Look at you. You got dirt all over your backside.

Turning her attention to the road in front of her house and standing up for the first and only time.

And dirt roads! Years now that old chief's been making speeches about getting paved roads "for my people" and still we got dirt roads all over.

PHILOMENA: Oh, go on.

PELAJIA: When I win me that jackpot next time we play bingo in Espanola …

PHILOMENA:

Examining her torn skirt, her general state of disarray, and fretting over it.

Look at this! Will you look at this! Ohhh!

PELAJIA: … I'm gonna put that old chief to shame and build me a nice paved road right here in front of my house. Jet black. Shiny. Make my lawn look real nice.

PHILOMENA: My rib-cage!

PELAJIA: And if that old chief don't wanna make paved roads for all my sisters around here …

PHILOMENA: There's something rattling around inside me!

PELAJIA: … I'm packing my bags and moving to Toronto.

Sits down again.

PHILOMENA: Oh, go on.

She spies Annie Cook's approach a distance up the hill.

Why, I do believe that cloud of dust over there is

Annie Cook racing down the hill, Pelajia.

PELAJIA: Philomena. I wanna go to Toronto.

PHILOMENA: She's walking mighty fast. Must be 120
excited about something.

PELAJIA: Never seen Annie Cook walk slow since the
day she finally lost Eugene to Marie-Adele at the
church 19 years ago. And even then she was
walking a little too fast for a girl who was supposed 125
to be broken-heart … *(Stopping just in time and
laughing.)* … heart-broken.

Annie Cook pops up the top of the ladder to the roof.

ANNIE:

All cheery and fast and perky.

Halloooo! Whatchyou doing up here?

PELAJIA: There's room for only so much weight up
here before we go crashing into my kitchen, so 130
what do you want?

ANNIE: Just popped up to say hi.

PELAJIA: And see what we're doing?

ANNIE: Well …

PELAJIA: Couldn't you see what we're doing from up 135
where you were?

ANNIE:

Confidentially, to Philomena.

Is it true Gazelle Nataways won the bingo last
night?

PHILOMENA: Annie Cook, first you say you're gonna
come with me and then you don't even bother 140
showing up. If you were sitting beside me at that
bingo table last night you would have seen Gazelle
Nataways win that big pot again with your own
two eyes.

ANNIE: Emily Dictionary and I went to Little 145
Current to listen to Fritz the Katz.

PELAJIA: What in God's name kind of a band might
that be?

ANNIE: Country rock. My favourite. Fritz the Katz
is from Toronto. 150

PELAJIA: Fritzy … ritzy … Philomena! Say something.

PHILOMENA: My record player is in Espanola getting
fixed.

ANNIE: That's nice. 155

PHILOMENA: Good.

ANNIE: Is it true Gazelle Nataways plans to spend
her bingo money to go to Toronto with … with
Big Joey?

PHILOMENA: Who wants to know? Emily Diction- 160
ary?

ANNIE: I guess so.

PELAJIA: That Gazelle Nataways gonna leave all her
babies behind and let them starve to death?

ANNIE: I guess so. I don't know. I'm asking you. 165

PELAJIA and PHILOMENA: We don't know.

ANNIE: I'm on my way to Marie-Adele's to pick her
up.

PELAJIA: Why? Where you gonna put her down?

Pelajia and Philomena laugh.

ANNIE: I mean, we're going to the store together. To 170
the post office. We're going to pick up a parcel. They
say there's a parcel for me. They say it's shaped like
a record. And they say it's from Sudbury. So it must
be from my daughter, Ellen …

PELAJIA and PHILOMENA: … "who lives with this 175
white guy in Sudbury" …

ANNIE: How did you know?

PHILOMENA: Everybody knows.

ANNIE: His name is Ray<u>mond</u>. Not <u>Ray</u>mond. But
Ray<u>mond</u>. Like in Bon Bon. 180

Philomena tries out "bon bon" to herself.

He's French.

PELAJIA: Oh?

ANNIE: Garage mechanic. He fixes cars. And you
know, talking about Frenchmen, that old priest is
holding another bingo next week and when I win … 185

To Philomena.

Are you going?

PELAJIA: Does a bear shit in the woods?

ANNIE: … when I win, I'm going to Espanola and
play the bingo there. Emily Dictionary says that
Fire Minklater can give us a ride in her new car. 190
She got it through Ray<u>mond</u>'s garage. The bingo
in Espanola is bigger. And it's better. And I'll win.
And then I'll go to Sudbury, where the bingos are
even bigger and better. And then I can visit my
daughter, Ellen … 195

PELAJIA: … "who lives with this white guy in Sudbury" …

ANNIE: … and go shopping in the record stores and go to the hotel and drink beer quietly — not noisy and crazy like here — and listen to the live bands. It will be so much fun. I hope Emily Dictionary can come with me.

PHILOMENA: It's true. I've been thinking …

PELAJIA: You don't say.

PHILOMENA: It's true. The bingos here are getting kind of boring …

ANNIE: That old priest is too slow and sometimes he gets the numbers all mixed up and the pot's not big enough.

PHILOMENA: And I don't like the way he calls the numbers. *(Nasally.)* B 12, 0 64.

ANNIE: When Little Girl Manitowabi won last month …

PHILOMENA: She won just enough to take a taxi back to Buzwah.[7]

ANNIE: That's all.

Both Annie and Philomena pause to give a quick sigh of yearning.

PHILOMENA: Annie Cook, I want that big pot.

ANNIE: We all want big pots.

PELAJIA: Start a revolution!

PHILOMENA and ANNIE: Yes!

ANNIE: All us Wasy women. We'll march up the hill, burn the church hall down, scare the priest to death, and then we'll march all the way to Espanola, where the bingos are bigger and better …

PHILOMENA: We'll hold big placards!

ANNIE: They'll say: "Wasy women want bigger bingos!"

PELAJIA: And one will say: "Annie Cook Wants Big Pot!"

PHILOMENA: … and the numbers at those bingos in Espanola go faster and the pots get bigger by the week. Oh, Pelajia Patchnose, I'm getting excited just thinking about it!

ANNIE: I'm going.

PELAJIA: You are, are you?

ANNIE: Yes. I'm going. I'm running out of time. I'm going to Marie-Adele's house and then we'll walk to the store together to pick up the parcel — I'm sure there'll be a letter in it, and Marie-Adele is expecting mail, too — and we'll see if Emily Dictionary is working today and we'll ask her if Fire Minklater has her new car yet so we can go to Espanola for that big pot.

She begins to descend the ladder.

PELAJIA: Well, you don't have much to do today, do you?

ANNIE: Well. Toodle-oo!

And she pops down the ladder and is gone.

PELAJIA: Not bad for someone who was in such a hurry to get her parcel. She talks faster than she walks.

Noticing how dejected and abandoned Philomena looks, she holds up her hammer.

Bingo money. Top quality. $24.95.

PHILOMENA: It's true. Bingos here in Wasy are getting smaller and smaller all the time. Especially now when the value of the dollar is getting lesser and lesser. In the old days, when Bingo Betty was still alive and walking these dirt roads, she'd come to every single bingo and she'd sit there like the Queen of Tonga, big and huge like a roast beef, smack-dab in the middle of the bingo hall.[8] One night, I remember, she brought two young cousins from the city — two young women, dressed real fancy, like they were going to Sunday church — and Bingo Betty made them sit one on her left, with her three little bingo cards, and one on her right, with her three little ones. And Bingo Betty herself sat in the middle with 27 cards. Twenty seven cards! Amazing.

Pelajia starts to descend the ladder, and Philomena, getting excited, steps closer and closer to the edge of the roof.

---

7 Buzwah] a town on Wikwemikong Reserve.

8 Queen of Tonga] Queen Salote Tupou III ruled the Polynesian kingdom of Tonga (a British protectorate) from 1918 to 1965, during which time her title became a byword for a grand monarch enjoying absolute power.

And those were the days when they still used bingo chips, not these dabbers like nowadays, and everyone came with a little margarine container full of these bingo chips. When the game began and they started calling out the numbers, Bingo Betty was all set, like a horse at the race-track in Sudbury, you could practically see the foam sizzling and bubbling between her teeth. Bingo Betty! Bingo Betty with her beady little darting eyes, sharp as needles, and her roly-poly jiggledy-piggledy arms with their stubby little claws would go: chiga-chiga-chiga-chiga-chiga-chiga arms flying across the table smooth as angel's wings chiga-chiga-chiga-chiga-chiga-chiga-woosh! Cousin on the left chiga-chiga, cousin on the right, chiga, chiga-eeee!

She narrowly misses falling off the roof and cries out in terror.

PELAJIA: Philomena!

PHILOMENA:

Scrambling on hands and knees to Pelajia, and coming to rest in this languorous pose, takes a moment to regain her composure and catch her breath.

And you know, to this very day, they say that on certain nights at the bingo here in Wasy, they say you can see Bingo Betty's ghost, like a mist, hovering in the air above the bingo tables, playing bingo like it's never been played before. Or since.

PELAJIA: Amazing! She should have gone to Toronto.

Black-out.

The same day, same time, in Wasaychigan Hill. Marie-Adele Starblanket is standing alone outside her house, in her yard, by her 14-post white picket fence. Her house is down the hill from Pelajia Patchnose's, close to the lake. A seagull watches her from a distance away. He is the dancer in white feathers. Through this whole section, Nanabush (i.e., Nanabush in the guise of the seagull), Marie-Adele, and Zhaboonigan play "games" with each other. Only she and Zhaboonigan Peterson can see the spirit inside the bird and can sort of (though not quite) recognize him for who he is. A doll belonging to a little girl lies on the porch floor. Marie-Adele throws little stones at the seagull.

MARIE-ADELE: Awus! Wee-chee-gis. Ka-tha pu-g'wun-ta oo-ta pee-wee-sta-ta-gu-mik-si. Awus! Neee. U-wi-nuk oo-ma kee-tha ee-tee-thi-mi-soo-yin holy spirit chee? Awus! Hey, maw ma-a oop-mee tay-si-thow u-wu seagull bird. I-goo-ta poo-goo ta-poo. Nu-gu-na-wa-pa-mik. Nu-gu-na-wa-pa-mik.[9]

NANABUSH: As-tum.[10]

MARIE-ADELE: Neee. Moo-tha ni-gus-kee-tan tu-pi-mi-tha-an. Moo-tha oo-ta-ta-gwu-na n'tay-yan. Chees-kwa. *(Pause.)* Ma-ti poo-ni-mee-see i-goo-ta wee-chi-gi-seagull bird come shit on my fence one more time and you and anybody else look like you cook like stew on my stove. Awus![11]

Veronique St. Pierre "passes by" with her adopted daughter Zhaboonigan Peterson.

VERONIQUE: Talking to the birds again, Mare-Adele Starblanket?

MARIE-ADELE: Aha. Veronique St. Pierre. How are you today?

VERONIQUE: Black Lady Halked's sister-in-law Fire Minklater, Fire Minklater's husband, just bought Fire Minklater a car in Sudbury.

MARIE-ADELE: New?

VERONIQUE: Used. They say he bought it from some Frenchman, some garage. Cray-on.

MARIE-ADELE: Raymond.

VERONIQUE: These Frenchmen are forever selling us their used cars. And I'm sure that's why Black Lady Halked has been baring those big yellow teeth of hers, smiling all over the reserve recently. She looks like a hound about to pounce on a mouse, she smiles so hard when she smiles. I'd like to see her

---

9 Awus! … Nu-gu-na-wa-pa-mik] Go away! You stinking thing. Don't be coming messing around here for nothing. Go away! Neee. Who the hell do you think you are, the Holy Spirit? Go away! Hey, but he won't fly away, this seagull bird. He just sits there. And watches me. Watches me. (Cree)

10 As-tum] Come. (Cree)

11 Neee … Awus!] Neee. I can't fly away. I have no wings. Yet. *Pause.* Will you stop shitting all over the place you stinking seagull bird etc. (Cree)

Note: "Neee" is a very common Cree expression with the approximate meaning of, "Oh you." [T.H.]

smile after plastic surgery. Anyway. At the bingo last night she was hinting that it wouldn't be too long before she would be able to go to the bingo in Espanola more frequently. Unfortunately, a new game started and you know how Black Lady Halked has to concentrate when she plays bingo — her forehead looks like corduroy, she concentrates so hard — so I didn't get a chance to ask her what she meant. So. Fire Minklater has a used car. Imagine! Maybe I can make friends with her again. NO! I wouldn't be caught dead inside her car. Not even if she had a brand-new Cadillac. How are your children? All 14 of them.

MARIE-ADELE: Okay, I guess.

VERONIQUE: Imagine. And all from one father. Anyway. Who will take care of them after you … ahem … I mean … when you go to the hospital?

MARIE-ADELE: Eugene.

ZHABOONIGAN: Is he gentle?

MARIE-ADELE: Baby-cakes. How are you?

ZHABOONIGAN: Fine.

Giggles.

VERONIQUE: She's fine. She went berry-picking yesterday with the children.

ZHABOONIGAN: Where's Nicky?

MARIE-ADELE: Nicky's down at the beach.

ZHABOONIGAN: Why?

MARIE-ADELE: Taking care of Rose-Marie.

ZHABOONIGAN: Oh.

MARIE-ADELE: Yup.

ZHABOONIGAN: Me and Nicky, ever lots of blueberries!

MARIE-ADELE: Me and Nicky picked lots of blueberries.

ZHABOONIGAN: I didn't see you there.

MARIE-ADELE: When?

ZHABOONIGAN: Before today.

MARIE-ADELE: How come Nicky didn't come home with any?

ZHABOONIGAN: Why?

Marie-Adele shrugs. Zhaboonigan imitates this, and then pretends she is stuffing her mouth with berries.

MARIE-ADELE: Aw, yous went and made pigs of yourselves.

ZHABOONIGAN: Nicky's the pig.

MARIE-ADELE: Neee.

ZHABOONIGAN: Are you going away far?

MARIE-ADELE: I'm not going far.

ZHABOONIGAN: Oh. Are you pretty?

Marie-Adele, embarrassed for a moment, smiles and Zhaboonigan smiles, too.

MARIE-ADELE: You're pretty, too.

Zhaboonigan tugs at Marie-Adele's shoelaces.

Oh, Zhaboonigan. Now you have to tie it up. I can't bend too far cuz I get tired.

Zhaboonigan tries to tie the shoelaces with great difficulty. When she finds she can't she throws her arms up and screams.

ZHABOONIGAN: Dirty trick! Dirty trick!

She bites her hand and hurts herself.

MARIE-ADELE: Now, don't get mad.

VERONIQUE: Stop it. Stop it right now.

ZHABOONGAN: No! No!

MARIE-ADELE: Zha. Zha. Listen. Listen.

ZHABOONIGAN: Stop it! Stop it right now!

MARIE-ADELE: Come on Zha. You and I can name the koos-koos-suk.[12] All 14 of them.

ZHABOONIGAN: Okay. Here we go.

Marie-Adele leads Zhaboonigan over to the picket fence and Veronique follows them.

ZHABOONIGAN:

To Veronique.

No.

Veronique retreats, obviously hurt.

MARIE-ADELE:

Taking Zhaboonigan's hand and counting on the 14 posts of her white picket fence.

Simon, Andrew, Matthew, Janie, Nicky, Ricky, Ben, Mark, Ron, Don, John, Tom, Pete, and Rose-Marie. There.

---

12 koos-koos-suk] The little pigs. (Cree)

Underneath Marie-Adele's voice, Zhaboonigan has been counting.

ZHABOONIGAN: One, two, three, four, five, six, seven, eight, nine, ten, eleven, twelve, thirteen, fourteen.

Giggles.

MARIE-ADELE: Ever good counter you, Zhaboonigan. 385

ZHABOONIGAN: Yup.

VERONIQUE: This reserve, sometimes I get so sick of it. They laugh at me behind my back, I just know it. They laugh at me and Pierre St. Pierre because we don't have any children of our own. 390 "Imagine, they say, she's on her second husband already and she still can't have children!" They laugh at Zhaboonigan Peterson because she's crazy, that's what they call her. They can't even take care of their own people, they'd rather laugh at them. 395 I'm the only person who would take Zhaboonigan after her parents died in that horrible car crash near Manitowaning on Saturday November 12 1964 may they rest in peace.[13] *(She makes quick sign of the cross without skipping a beat.)* I'm the only one 400 around here who is kind enough. And they laugh at me. Oh, I wish I had a new stove, Marie-Adele. My stove is so old and broken down, only two elements work anymore and my oven is starting to talk back at me. 405

MARIE-ADELE: Get it fixed.

VERONIQUE: You know that Pierre St. Pierre never has any money. He drinks it all up.

She sighs longingly.

Some day! Anyway. Zhaboonigan here wanted to go for a swim so I thought I'd walk her down — 410 drop by and see how you and the children are doing — it will do my weak heart good, I was saying to myself.

MARIE-ADELE: Awus!

As she throws a pebble at the seagull on the stone, Veronique, for a second, thinks it's her Marie-Adele is

---

shooing away. There is a brief silence broken after awhile by Zhaboonigan's little giggle.

VERONIQUE: Anyway, I was walking down by that 415 Big Joey's shameless little shack just this morning when guess who pokes her nose out the window but Gazelle Nataways — the nerve of that woman. I couldn't see inside but I'm sure she was only half-dressed, her hairdo was all mixed up and she said 420 to me: "Did you know, Veronique St. Pierre, that Little Girl Manitowabi told me her daughter, June Bug McLeod, just got back from the hospital in Sudbury where she had her tubes tied and told her that THE BIGGEST BINGO IN THE WORLD 425 is coming to Toronto?"

MARIE-ADELE: When?

VERONIQUE: I just about had a heart attack.

MARIE-ADELE: When?

VERONIQUE: But I said to Gazelle anyway: Is there 430 such a thing as a BIGGEST BINGO IN THE WORLD? And she said: Yes. And she should know about these things because she spends all her waking and sleeping hours just banging about in bed with the biggest thing on Manitoulin Island, 435 I almost said.

MARIE-ADELE: This bingo. When?

VERONIQUE: She didn't know. And now that I think of it, I don't know whether to believe her. After all, who should believe a woman who wrestles 440 around with dirt like Big Joey all night long leaving her poor babies to starve to death in her empty kitchen? But if it's true, Marie-Adele, if it's true that THE BIGGEST BINGO IN THE WORLD is coming to Toronto, I'm going and I want you to 445 come with me.

MARIE-ADELE: Well …

VERONIQUE: I want you to come shopping with me and help me choose my new stove after I win.

MARIE-ADELE: Hang on … 450

VERONIQUE: They have good stoves in Toronto.

MARIE-ADELE: Let's find out for sure. Then we start making plans.

VERONIQUE: Maybe we should go back and ask that Gazelle Nataways about this. If she's sure. 455

MARIE-ADELE: Maybe we should go and ask June Bug MacLeod herself.

---

[13] Manitowaning] a town on Manitoulin Island.

VERONIQUE: We can't walk to Buzwah and I'm too old to hitch-hike.

MARIE-ADELE: There's Eugene's van. He'll be home by six. 460

VERONIQUE: I want to find out NOW. But what if people see us standing at Big Joey's door?

MARIE-ADELE: What do you mean? We just knock on the door, march right in, ask the bitch, and 465 march right out again.

VERONIQUE: Zhaboonigan dear, wait for me over there.

She waits until Zhaboonigan is safely out of earshot and then leans over to Marie-Adele in a conspiratorial whisper.

Anyway. You must know, Marie-Adele, that there's all kinds of women who come streaming out of 470 that house at all hours of the day and night. I might be considered one of them. You know your youngest sister, Emily Dictionary, was seen staggering out of that house in the dead of night two nights ago? 475

MARIE-ADELE: Veronique St. Pierre, what Emily Dictionary does is Emily's business.

Annie Cook enters, walking fast and comes to a screeching halt.

ANNIE: Hallooooo! Whatchyou doin'?

VERONIQUE:

Giving Annie the baleful eye.

How are you?

ANNIE: High as a kite. Just kidding. Hi, Zha. 480

ZHABOONIGAN: Hi.

Giggles. She runs toward Marie-Adele, bumping into Annie en route.

ANNIE: Hey, Marie-Adele.

ZHABOONIGAN: Marie-Adele. How's your cancer?

Giggles and scurries off laughing.

VERONIQUE: Shkanah, Zhaboonigan, sna-ma-bah … [14] 485

MARIE-ADELE: Come on, before that post office closes for lunch.

VERONIQUE: You didn't tell me you were going to the store.

ANNIE: Well, we are. 490

To Marie-Adele.

Hey, is Simon in? I'm sure he's got my Ricky Skaggs album. You know the one that goes *(Sings.)* "Honeee!" [15]

Calling into the house.

Yoo-hoo, Simon!

MARIE-ADELE: He's in Espanola with Eugene. 495

VERONIQUE: Expecting mail, Annie Cook?

ANNIE: A parcel from my daughter, Ellen, who lives with this white guy in Sudbury …

VERONIQUE: So I've heard.

ANNIE: And my sister here is expecting a letter, too. 500

VERONIQUE: From whom?

ANNIE: From the doctor, about her next check-up.

VERONIQUE: When?

MARIE-ADELE: We don't know when. Or where. Annie, let's go. 505

ANNIE: They say it's shaped like a record.

VERONIQUE: Maybe there'll be news in that parcel about THE BIGGEST BINGO IN THE WORLD!

Shouts toward the lake, in a state of great excitement.

Zhaboonigan! Zhaboonigan! We're going to the 510 store!

ANNIE: THE BIGGEST BINGO IN THE WORLD?

VERONIQUE: In Toronto. Imagine! Gazelle Nataways told me. She heard about it from Little Girl 515 Manitowabi over in Buzwah who heard about it from her daughter June Bug McLeod who just got back from the hospital in Sudbury where she had her tubes tied I just about had a heart attack!

ANNIE: Toronto? 520

MARIE-ADELE: We gotta find out for sure.

ANNIE: Right.

---

14 Shkanah … sna-ma-bah] Shush, Zhaboonigan, don't say that. (Ojibway)

15 Ricky Skaggs] a popular country singer; "Honey (Open That Door)" was a hit for Skaggs in the 1980s.

MARIE-ADELE: We could go to Big Joey's and ask Gazelle Nataways except Veronique St. Pierre's too scared of Gazelle. 525

VERONIQUE: I am not.

ANNIE: You are too.

MARIE-ADELE: We could wait and borrow Eugene's van …

VERONIQUE: I am not. 530

ANNIE: … drive over to Buzwah …

MARIE-ADELE: … and ask June Bug McLeod …

ANNIE: … but wait a minute! …

MARIE-ADELE and ANNIE: Maybe there IS news in that parcel about this BIGGEST BINGO IN THE WORLD! 535

MARIE-ADELE: Come on.

VERONIQUE:

Shouting toward the lake.

Zhaboonigan! Zhaboonigan!

ANNIE: And here I was so excited about the next little bingo that old priest is holding next week. Toronto! 540 Oh, I hope it's true!

VERONIQUE: Zhaboonigan! Zhaboonigan! Zhaboonigan! Dammit! We're going to the store!

And the "march" to the store begins, during which Nanabush, still in the guise of the seagull, follows them and continues to play tricks, mimicking their hand movements, the movement of their mouths, etc. The three women appear each in her own spot of light at widely divergent points on the stage area.

ANNIE: When I go to the BIGGEST BINGO IN THE WORLD, in Toronto, I will win. For sure, I 545 will win. If they shout the B 14 at the end, for sure I will win. The B 14 is my lucky number after all. Then I will take all my money and I will go to every record store in Toronto. I will buy every single one of Patsy Cline's records, especially the one that goes 550 *(Sings.)* "I go a-walking, after midnight," oh I go crazy every time I hear that one.[16] Then I will buy a huge record player, the biggest one in the whole world. And then I will go to all the taverns and all the night clubs in Toronto and listen to the live 555 bands while I drink beer quietly — not noisy and crazy like here — I will bring my daughter Ellen and her white guy from Sudbury and we will sit together. Maybe I will call Fritz the Katz and he will take me out. Maybe he will hire me as one of his singers and 560 I can *(Sings.)* "Oooh," in the background while my feet go *(Shuffles her feet from side to side.)* while Fritz the Katz is singing and the lights are flashing and the people are drinking beer and smoking cigarettes and dancing. Ohhh, I could dance all night with that 565 Fritz the Katz. When I win, when I win THE BIGGEST BINGO IN THE WORLD!

MARIE-ADELE: When I win THE BIGGEST BINGO IN THE WORLD, I'm gonna buy me an island. In the North Channel, right smack-dab 570 in the middle — eem-shak min-stik[17] — the most beautiful island in the world. And my island will have lots of trees — great big bushy ones — and lots and lots and lots of sweetgrass. MMMMM! And there's gonna be pine trees and oak trees and 575 maple trees and big stones and little stonelets — neee — and, oh yeah, this real neat picket fence, real high, long and very, very, very white. No bird shit. Eugene will live there and me and all my Starblanket kids. Yup, no more smelly, stinky old 580 pulp and paper mill in Espanola for my Eugene — pooh! — my 12 Starblanket boys and my two Starblanket girls and me and Eugene all living real nice and comfy right there on Starblanket Island, the most beautiful incredible goddamn island in 585 the whole goddamn world. Eem-shak min-stik! When I win THE BIGGEST BINGO IN THE WORLD!

VERONIQUE: Well, when I win the BIGGEST BINGO IN THE WORLD. No! After I win THE 590 BIGGEST BINGO IN THE WORLD, I will go shopping for a brand-new stove. In Toronto. At the Eaton Centre. A great big stove. The kind Madame Benoit has. The kind that has the three different compartments in the oven alone. I'll have the 595 biggest stove on the reserve. I'll cook for all the children on the reserve. I'll adopt all of Marie-Adele Starblanket's 14 children and I will cook for

---

16 Patsy Cline] a popular country singer of the late 1950s and early 1960s. "Walking After Midnight" was one of her biggest hits; "Crazy" was another.

17 A great big island. (Cree)

them. I'll even cook for Gazelle Nataways' poor starving babies while she's lolling around like a pig in Big Joey's smelly, sweaty bed. And Pierre St. Pierre can drink himself to death for all I care. Because I'll be the best cook on all of Manitoulin Island! I'll enter competitions. I'll go to Paris and meet what's-his-name Cordon Bleu![18] I'll write a cookbook called "The Joy of Veronique St. Pierre's Cooking" and it will sell in the millions! And I will become rich and famous! Zhaboonigan Peterson will wear a mink while she eats steak tartare-de-frou-frou! Madame Benoit will be so jealous she'll suicide herself. Oh, when I win THE BIGGEST BINGO IN THE WORLD!

Zhaboonigan comes running in from swimming, "chasing" after the other three women, counting to herself and giggling.

ZHABOONIGAN: One, two, three, four, five, six, seven, eight, nine, ten, eleven, twelve, thirteen, fourteen.

At the store. Annie Cook, Marie-Adele Starblanket, Veronique St. Pierre, and Zhaboonigan Peterson have arrived. Emily Dictionary makes a sudden appearance, carrying a huge bag of flour on her shoulder. She is one tough lady, wearing cowboy boots, tight blue jeans, a black leather jacket — all three items worn to the seams — and she sports one black eye.

EMILY:

In a loud, booming voice that paralyzes all movement in the room while she speaks.

Zhaboonigan Peterson! What in Red Lucifer's name ever possessed you to be hangin' out with a buncha' dizzy old dames like this?

Bag of flour hits floor with a "doof."

MARIE-ADELE: Emily. Your eye.
EMILY: Oh, bit of a tussle.
VERONIQUE: With who?
EMILY: None of your goddamn business.
MARIE-ADELE: Emily, please.

18 Cordon Bleu] not a person, but a chef's school in Paris.

ANNIE:

Following Emily about the store while Veronique tries, in vain, to hear what she can.

I wasn't able to find out from Pelajia Patchnose or Philomena Moosemeat if Gazelle Nataways is going to Toronto this weekend with … Big Joey … they didn't know … Gazelle did win the bingo last night though.

EMILY: Aw shit. Veronique St. Pierre, you old bag. Is it true Gazelle Nataways is takin' off for Toronto with that hunk Big Joey?

VERONIQUE: It WAS you coming out of that house two nights ago. I walked by as quickly as I could …

EMILY: … shoulda come out and nailed your big floppy ears to the door …

VERONIQUE: … and I would have called the police but I was too scared Big Joey might come after me and Zhaboonigan later …

EMILY: … yeah, right.

ZHABOONIGAN: Yeah, right.

VERONIQUE: … and I have a weak heart, you know? Who hit you? Big Joey? Or Gazelle Nataways?

EMILY: The nerve of this woman.

VERONIQUE: Well?

EMILY:

Calls Zhaboonigan, who is behind the counter, on the floor, playing with the merchandise.

Zhaboonigan Peterson! Where in Red Lucifer's name is that dozy pagan?

VERONIQUE: You keep hanging around that house and you're gonna end up in deep trouble. You don't know how wicked and vicious those Nataways women can get. They say there's witchcraft in their blood. And with manners like yours, Emily Dictionary, you'd deserve every hex you got.

EMILY: Do I know this woman? Do I know this woman?

VERONIQUE:

During this speech, Marie-Adele and Annie sing "Honeeee" tauntingly.

I'm sorry I have to say this in front of everyone like this but this woman has just accused my daughter of being a pagan. I didn't call her Zhaboonigan. The people on this reserve, who have nothing better to do with their time than call each other names, they called her that. Her name is Marie-Adele. Marie-Adele Peterson. You should talk. I should ask you where in Red … Red … whatever, you got a circus of a name like Emily Dictionary. 660

Emily grabs Veronique and throws her across the room. Veronique goes flying right into Pelajia, who has entered the store during the latter part of this speech.

PELAJIA: Veronique St. Pierre! Control yourself or I'll hit you over the head with my hammer. 665

VERONIQUE:

Blows a "raspberry" in Pelajia's face.

Bleah!

ANNIE: No, Pelajia, no.

EMILY: Go ahead, Pelajia. Make my day.

ANNIE: Down, put it down.

PHILOMENA:

As she comes scurrying into the store.

I have to use the toilet. 670

Running to Emily.

I have to use your toilet.

And goes scurrying into the toilet.

ANNIE:

To Pelajia.

Remember, that's Veronique St. Pierre and if you get on the wrong side of Veronique St. Pierre she's liable to spread rumors about you all over kingdom come and you'll lose every bit of respect you got on this reserve. Don't let those pants you're wearing go to your head. 675

PELAJIA:

Catching Annie by the arm as she tries to run away.

Annie Cook! You got a mouth on you like a helicopter.

ANNIE: Veronique's mad at you, Emily, because you won't tell her what happened the other night at Big Joey's house. And she's jealous of Gazelle Nataways because Gazelle won the bingo again last night and 680

she hopes you're the one person on this reserve who has the guts to stand up to Gazelle. 685

VERONIQUE:

Making a lunge at Annie, who hides behind Emily.

What's that! What's that! Ohhh! Ohhh!

ANNIE: Leave me alone, you old snoop. All I wanna know is is this big bingo really happening in Toronto.

VERONIQUE: Annie Cook. You are a little suck. 690

EMILY:

To Veronique.

Someday, someone oughta stick a great big piece of shit into that mouth of yours.

PELAJIA:

To Emily.

And someday, someone ought to wash yours out with soap.

PHILOMENA:

Throwing the toilet door open, she sits there in her glory, panties down to her ankles.

Emily Dictionary. You come back to the reserve after all these years and you strut around like you own the place. I know Veronique St. Pierre is a pain in the ass but I don't care. She's your elder and you respect her. Now shut up, all of you, and let me shit in peace. 700

And slams the washroom door. Veronique, scandalized by this, haughtily walks through toward the door, bumping into Pelajia en route.

PELAJIA: Philomena. Get your bum out here. Veronique St. Pierre is about to lose her life.

She raises her hammer at Veronique.

VERONIQUE:

To Pelajia.

Put that hammer away. And go put a skirt on, for heaven's sake, you look obscene in those tight pants. 705

ANNIE: Hit her. Go on. Hit the bitch. One good bang is all she needs.

EMILY: Yeah, right. A gang-bang is more like it.

And a full-scale riot breaks out, during which the women throw every conceivable insult at each other. Emily throws open the toilet door and Philomena comes stomping out, pulling her panties on and joining the riot. All talk at the same time, quietly at first, but then getting louder and louder until they are all screaming.

PHILOMENA: *(To Annie.)* What a slime. Make promises and then you go do something else. And I always have to smile at you. What a slime. *(To Emily.)* All that rough talk. I know what's behind it all. You'll never be big enough to push me around. *(To Marie-Adele.)* Fourteen kids! You look like a wrinkled old prune already. *(To Pelajia.)* At least I'm a woman. *(To Veronique.)* Have you any idea how, just how offensive, how obnoxious you are to people? And that halitosis. Pooh! You wouldn't have it if you didn't talk so much.

EMILY: *(To Philomena.)* So damned bossy and pushy and sucky. You make me sick. Always wanting your own way. *(To Veronique.)* Goddamned trouble-making old crow. *(To Pelajia.)* Fuckin' self-righteous old bitch. *(To Marie-Adele.)* Mental problems, that's what you got, princess. I ain't no baby. I'm the size of a fuckin' church. *(To Annie.)* You slippery little slut. Brain the size of a fuckin' pea. Fuck, man, take a Valium.

VERONIQUE: *(To Emily.)* You have no morals at all. You sick pervert. You should have stayed where you came from, where all the other perverts are. *(To Pelajia.)* Slow turtle. Talk big and move like Jell-o. *(To Annie.)* Cockroach! *(To Philomena.)* You big phony. Flush yourself down that damned toilet of yours and shut up. *(To Marie-Adele.)* Hasn't this slimy little reptile *(Referring to Annie.)* ever told you that sweet little Ellen of hers is really Eugene's daughter? Go talk to the birds in Sudbury and find out for yourself.

PELAJIA: *(To Veronique.)* This reserve would be a better place without you. I'm tired of dealing with people like you. Tired. *(To Marie-Adele.)* You can't act that way. This here's no time to be selfish. You spoiled brat. *(To Philomena.)* You old fool. I thought you were coming back to help me and

here you are all trussed up like a Thanksgiving turkey, putting on these white lady airs. *(To Annie.)* Annie Cook. Move to Kapuskasing! *(To Emily.)* "Fuck, fuck, fuck!" Us Indian women got no business talking like that.

MARIE-ADELE: *(To Pelajia.)* You don't have all the answers. You can't fix everything. *(To Annie.)* White guys. Slow down a minute and see how stupid you look. *(To Emily.)* Voice like a fog-horn. You ram through everything like a truck. You look like a truck. *(To Veronique.)* Some kind of insect, sticking insect claws into everybody's business. *(To Philomena.)* Those clothes. You look like a giant Kewpie doll. You make me laugh.

ANNIE: *(To Marie-Adele.)* You always make me feel so … small … like a little pig or something. You're no better than me. *(To Philomena.)* Why can't you go to bingo by yourself, you big baby? At least I got staying power. Piss off. *(To Veronique.)* Sucking off everybody else's life like a leech because you got nothing of your own. Pathetic old coot. Just buzz off. *(To Emily.)* You call me names. I don't call you names. You think you're too smart. Shut up. *(To Pelajia.)* "Queen of the Indians," you think that's what you are. Well, that stupid hammer of yours doesn't scare me. Go away. Piss me off.

Then Pelajia lifts her hammer with a big loud "Woah"! And they come to a sudden dead stop. Pause. Then one quick final volley, all at once, loudest of all.

PHILOMENA: *(To Annie.)* You slimy buck-toothed drunken worm!

EMILY: *(To Veronique.)* Fuckin' instigator!

VERONIQUE: *(To Marie-Adele.)* Clutching, clinging vine!

PELAJIA: *(To Veronique.)* Evil no-good insect!

MARIE-ADELE: *(To Veronique.)* Maggot-mouthed vulture!

ANNIE: *(To Philomena.)* Fat-assed floozy, get off the pot!

Marie-Adele, stung to the quick, makes a vicious grab for Veronique by the throat. In a split-second, all freeze. Lights out in store interior. Lights on on Zhaboonigan, who has run out in fright during the riot, outside the store. Nanabush, still in his guise as the seagull, makes

*a grab at Zhaboonigan. Zhaboonigan begins talking to
the bird.*

ZHABOONIGAN: Are you gentle? I was not little.
Maybe. Same size as now. Long ago it must be?
You think I'm funny? Shhh. I know who you are.
There, there. Boys. White boys. Two. Ever nice 785
white wings, you. I was walking down the road to
the store. They ask me if I want ride in car. Oh, I
was happy I said, "Yup." Took me far away. Ever
nice ride. Dizzy. They took all my clothes off me.
Put something up inside me here. *(Pointing to her* 790
crotch, underneath her dress.) Many, many times.
Remember. Don't fly away. Don't go. I saw you
before. There, there. It was a. Screwdriver. They
put the screwdriver inside me. Here. Remember.
Ever lots of blood. The two white boys. Left me 795
in the bush. Alone. It was cold. And then.
Remember. Zhaboonigan. Everybody calls me
Zhaboonigan. Why? It means needle. Zhaboonigan. Going-through-thing. Needle Peterson.
Going-through-thing Peterson. That's me. It was 800
the screwdriver. Nice. Nice. Nicky Ricky Ben
Mark. *(As she counts, with each name, feathers on
the bird's wing.)* Ever nice. Nice white birdie you.

*During this last speech, Nanabush goes through agon-
izing contortions. Then lights change instantly back to
the interior of the store. The six women spring back
into action. Philomena stomps back into the toilet.*

MARIE-ADELE: *(To Veronique.)* Fine. And the whole
reserve knows the only reason you ever adopted 805
Zhaboonigan is for her disability cheque.
ANNIE: You fake saint.

*Annie, Marie-Adele, and Emily start pushing
Veronique, round-robin, between the three of them,
laughing tauntingly until Veronique is almost reduced
to tears.*

VERONIQUE: *(Almost weeping.)* Bastards. The three
of you.

*Marie-Adele grabs Veronique by the throat and lifts her
fist to punch her in the face. But the exertion causes her
body to weaken, almost to the point of collapse, from
her illness. At this point, Philomena emerges from the
toilet.*

PHILOMENA: *(Crinkling her nose.)* Emily. Your toilet. 810
WOMEN: Shhhh.
MARIE-ADELE: *(Holding her waist, reeling, barely
audible.)* Oh, shit.
PHILOMENA: I can't get it to flush.
WOMEN: Shhhh. 815
PELAJIA: *(Rushing to Marie-Adele.)* Marie-Adele.
You're not well.
MARIE-ADELE: *(Screams.)* Don't touch me.

*Complete silence from all while Marie-Adele weaves
and struggles to keep herself from collapsing. Annie
scurries offstage, to the back part of the store, where the
post office would be.*

EMILY: *(To Veronique.)* You f'in' bitch!
PHILOMENA: What did I just tell you? Who did that 820
to your eye?
VERONIQUE: Big Joey.
EMILY: *(To Veronique.)* Look here, you old buzzard.
I'll tell you a few things. You see this fist? You see
these knuckles? You wanna know where they come 825
from? Ten years. Every second night for 10 long
ass-fuckin' years that goddamn Yellowknife asshole
Henry Dadzinanare come home to me so drunk
his eyes was spittin' blood like Red Lucifer himself
and he'd beat me purple. 830
VERONIQUE: I wish I'd been there to see it all.
EMILY: Yeah, scumbag. I wish you'd been there to
watch me learn to fight back like you've never seen
a woman fight for her life before. Take a look at
this eye. I earned it, Veronique St. Pierre, I earned 835
it.
PHILOMENA: Henry Dadzinanare, Big Joey. They're
all the same. Emily, use your brains.
EMILY: Use my brains. Yeah, right. I used them
alright the night he came at me with an axe and 840
just about sank it into my spine, I grabbed one
bag, took one last look at the kids and walked out
of his life forever.
ANNIE:

From offstage.

And she took the bus to San Francisco.
PHILOMENA: And gets herself mixed up with a 845
motorcycle gang, for God's sake.

EMILY:

Now addressing all in the room.

Rosabella Baez, Hortensia Colorado, Liz Jones, Pussy Commanda. And me. The best. "Rose and the Rez Sisters," that's us. And man, us sisters could weave knuckle magic. 850
VERONIQUE: So why did you bother coming back?
PHILOMENA: You stay out of this.
EMILY: Come back to the Rez for a visit, get all wedged up with that hunk Big Joey one night…

Grunts.

PHILOMENA: I give up. 855
EMILY: … and I was hooked. Couldn't leave. Settlin' back on a coupla beers with Big Joey the other night when Gazelle Nataways come sashayin' in like she's got half the Rez squished down the crack of her ass. She was high. I was high. Hell, we were 860 all high. Get into a bit of a discussion, when she gets me miffed and I let fly, she let fly, Big Joey let fly, misses that nympho and lands me one in the eye instead.
VERONIQUE: So it was Big Joey. 865
EMILY: Damn rights. And that's as close as he got cuz I put him out for the night right then and there. Just one of these. *(Brandishing her fist.)* One. That's all it took.

Veronique runs off to look for Zhaboonigan.

ANNIE and PHILOMENA: Emily Dictionary. 870

Philomena with exasperation, Annie with adulation, from offstage.

ANNIE: You're amazing!
EMILY: Not Dictionary. Dadzinanare. Henry Dadzinanare. The man who made me learn to fight back. Never let a man raise one dick hair against me since. 875
VERONIQUE:

Calling out to Zhaboonigan.

Zhaboonigan. Don't you be talking to the birds like that again. You're crazy enough as it is.
ANNIE:

As she comes running back in from the post office with her parcel, already unwrapped, and two letters, one for herself, already unfolded, and one still in its envelope.

See? I told you. It's a record. Patsy Cline.
PHILOMENA: Never mind Patsy Cline.
ANNIE:

As she hands Marie-Adele the letter in the envelope.

Hey, Marie-Adele. 880
EMILY: Read your friggin' letter, Annie Cook.
ANNIE: Listen to this.

Zhaboonigan walks back in as Annie reads her own letter very haltingly.

Dear Mom: Here is the record you wanted. I thought you'd like the picture of Patsy Cline on the cover. *(Annie shows off her record.)* See? It's Patsy 885 Cline. *(Returns to her letter.)* I also thought you might like to know that there is a bingo called THE BIGGEST BINGO IN THE WORLD. Can you fu … ture that?
EMILY:

Who has been looking over Annie's shoulder.

Feature. Feature. 890
ANNIE: Can you … feature … that? … that's coming to Toronto. The jackpot is $500,000. It's on Saturday, September 8. Raymond's Mom was in Toronto. Aunt Philomena will hit the roof when she hears this. Much love, your daughter Ellen. 895

Annie announces once more.

There is a brief electric silence followed by an equally electric scream from all the women. Even Zhaboonigan screams. Excitement takes over completely.

VERONIQUE: So it's true! It's true!
PHILOMENA: The Espanola bingo. Piffle. Mere piffle.
VERONIQUE: My new stove!
PHILOMENA: My new toilet! White! Spirit white!
EMILY:

Grabbing Zhaboonigan and dancing around the room with her.

I'd take the money, come back to the Rez, beat the 900 shit out of Gazelle Nataways and take you down to Frisco with me. Whaddaya think?

ZHABOONIGAN: Yup.

MARIE-ADELE:

In the background, where she has been reading her letter quietly to herself.

September 10.

ANNIE:

Taking the letter from Marie-Adele.

Look, Pelajia. Marie-Adele's tests are in Toronto just two days after THE BIGGEST.   905

There is a brief embarrassed silence.

MARIE-ADELE: Kill two birds with one stone.

To Nanabush.

I wanna go.

To Pelajia and Philomena.

I wanna go.

VERONIQUE: Goood!   910

EMILY:

Mimicking Veronique.

Goood! Now how the hell are you guys gonna get down to Toronto? You're all goddamn welfare cases.

ANNIE: Fire Minklater.

VERONIQUE: Mary, mother of Jesus! I refuse, I absolutely refuse to be seen anywhere near that   915
sorceress! We'll chip in and rent a car.

EMILY: Zhaboonigan Peterson here gonna chauffeur you down?

ZHABOONIGAN: Yup.

VERONIQUE: Don't you make fun of my daughter.   920

EMILY: What kind of stove you gonna buy, Veronique St. Pierre? Westinghouse? Electrolux? Yamaha? Kawasaki?

VERONIQUE: Oh my god, Marie-Adele, I never thought about it. They will have so many stoves   925
in Toronto, I'll get confused.

ANNIE: If you go to Toronto and leave Wasy for even one day, Emily, you'll lose Big Joey forever …

VERONIQUE: To that witch!

ANNIE: … and then whose thighs will you have to   930
wrestle around with in the dead of night? You'll dry up, get all puckered up and pass into ancient history.

EMILY: Annie Cook. I don't know what the fuck you're yatterin' on about now but I'd like to hear you say two words of French to that white guy in   935
Sudbury you're so damn proud of.

ANNIE: Oh my god, Marie-Adele, she's right. I won't know what to say to this Raymond. I've never met him. I can't speak French. All I can say in French is Raymond and Bon Bon and I don't even know   940
what that means. I can't go and live with them, not even after I win THE BIGGEST BINGO IN THE WORLD. What am I gonna do?

She collapses on the floor and rolls around for a bit.

EMILY: And Philomena Moosemeat's so fulla shit she'd need five toilets to get it all out.   945

PHILOMENA:

Going at Emily.

And just who do you think you're talking to, Miss Dictionary, just who the hell do you think you're talking to?

With a resounding belly butt from Emily, they begin to wrestle.

PELAJIA:

Banging her hammer on the counter.

Alright, alright. It's obvious we've got a problem here.   950

EMILY:

Throwing Philomena off to the side.

I'll say.

MARIE-ADELE: It's true. None of us has any money.

But Veronique, standing behind Pelajia, winks at the others and makes a hand motion indicating that Pelajia, for one, does have money. All the other women slowly surround Pelajia. But Pelajia catches the drift and quickly collects herself to meet the onslaught. During Pelajia's speech, the women respond at periodic intervals with a "yoah" and "hmmm," etc., as when a chief speaks at a council meeting.

PELAJIA: I say we all march down to the Band Office and ask the Band Council for a loan that will pay for the trip to this bingo. I know how to handle   955 that tired old chief. He and I have been arguing about paved roads for years now. I'll tell him we'll build paved roads all over the reserve with our prize money. I'll tell him the people will stop drinking themselves to death because they'll have paved roads to walk on. I'll tell him there'll be more jobs because the people will have paved roads to drive to work on. I'll tell him the people will stop fighting and screwing around and Nanabush will come back to us because he'll have paved roads to dance on. There's enough money in there for everyone, I'll say. And if he doesn't lend us the money, I'll tell him I'm packing my bags and moving to Toronto tomorrow.

EMILY: That oughta twist his arm but good.

PELAJIA: And if he still says no, I'll bop him over the head with my hammer and we'll attack the accountant and take the money ourselves. Philomena, we're going to Toronto!

The seven women have this grand and ridiculous march to the band office, around the set and all over the stage area, with Pelajia leading them forward heroically, her hammer just a-swinging in the air. Nanabush trails merrily along in the rear of the line. They reach the "band office" — standing in one straight line square in front of the audience. The "invisible" chief "speaks": cacophonous percussion for about seven beats, the women listening more and more incredulously. Finally, the percussion comes to a dead stop.

PELAJIA: No?

Pelajia raises her hammer to hit the "invisible" chief, Nanabush shrugs a "don't ask me, I don't know," Emily fingers a "fuck you, man." Blackout. End of Act One.

ACT TWO

All seven women are holding a meeting in the basement of Pelajia Patchnose's house. This is a collection of chairs and stools off to the side of the stage area. The only light comes from an old, beat-up trilight pole lamp. Some have tea, Emily and Annie a beer.

VERONIQUE: We should have met at the priest's house.

PELAJIA: No! We're gonna work this out on our own. Right here. Emily Dictionary, you chair.

And she lends Emily her hammer.

VERONIQUE: She's good at ordering people around.
PHILOMENA: Shut up.
EMILY: First. When are we leaving?

She bangs the hammer regularly throughout the meeting.

VERONIQUE: How much is the trip going to cost?
EMILY: When are we leaving?
PHILOMENA: How long to Toronto?
ANNIE: Four hours.
EMILY: When are we leaving?
PHILOMENA: The only human being who can make it in four hours is Annie Cook.
VERONIQUE: I'm not dying on the highway.
PHILOMENA: Eight hours.
PELAJIA: No way we're gonna stop at every toilet on the highway.
MARIE-ADELE: Six hours. Eugene's driven there.
VERONIQUE: Maybe we can borrow his van.
ANNIE: Maybe we can borrow Big Joey's van.

A quick little aside to Pelajia.

Hey, can I have another beer?
PELAJIA: No.
VERONIQUE: What about Gazelle Nataways?
EMILY: We're gonna borrow his van, not his buns, for Chris'sakes.
MARIE-ADELE: The only thing we have to pay for is gas.
ANNIE: Philomena's got gas.
EMILY: Right! Six hours. Eugene's van.
MARIE-ADELE: We still don't know when we're leaving.
PHILOMENA: Bingo's on Saturday night.
ANNIE: Leave Saturday morning.
VERONIQUE: Oh! I'll be so tired for the bingo. I'll get confused. Wednesday. Rest on Thursday.
ANNIE: And rest again on Friday? Too much resting. I can't go for that.
PELAJIA: And we can't afford such a long stay.
PHILOMENA: Where are we gonna stay?
EMILY: Whoa!

Pause.

PELAJIA: Friday night.

EMILY: Right. Leave Friday night. Next.

PHILOMENA: Coming home right after the bingo.

MARIE-ADELE: And leave me behind? Remember my   45
tests are Monday morning.

EMILY: Right. Monday noon, we come back. Next.

VERONIQUE: Don't go so fast. My mind is getting
confused.

EMILY: Goood! Next.   50

MARIE-ADELE: Where are we gonna stay?

ANNIE: The Silver Dollar![19]

MARIE-ADELE: You can't stay there.

ANNIE: There's rooms upstairs.

PELAJIA: You wanna sleep in a whorehouse?   55

VERONIQUE: Zhaboonigan! Don't listen to this part.

PELAJIA: There's room at my son's.

PHILOMENA: Two washrooms! He's got a wonderful
education.

EMILY: Next.   60

VERONIQUE: Who's going to drive?

ANNIE: Emily. She can drive anything.

VERONIQUE: I believe it.

ANNIE: But I can drive, too.

VERONIQUE: Oh my god.   65

ANNIE: Long as I don't have to drive in the city. You
drive the city.

VERONIQUE: Me?

ANNIE and MARIE-ADELE: No!

PELAJIA: Long as you don't drive too fast, Annie   70
Cook.

PHILOMENA: And we'll pack a lunch for the trip and
then eat in restaurants. Chinese.

PELAJIA: Can't afford it. We chip in, buy groceries
and cook at my son's.   75

VERONIQUE: I'll give $10.

EMILY: You old fossil. You want us to starve?

PHILOMENA: $50 a day. Each.

EMILY: Philomena Moosemeat! That's $50 times
seven people times four days. That's over $1000   80
worth of groceries.

VERONIQUE: Imagine!

MARIE-ADELE: Okay. Veronique St. Pierre. You cook.
$20 apiece. Right?

EMILY: Right. Next.   85

PHILOMENA: Anybody writing this down?

ANNIE: I'm gonna go to Sam the Recordman.

MARIE-ADELE: I'll make the grocery list.

PELAJIA: How much for gas?

VERONIQUE:

Still in dreamland over the groceries.

$1,000!   90

PHILOMENA:

Flabbergasted.

Nooo! You goose.

ANNIE: $40.

EMILY: $150. Period. Next.

PELAJIA: We got 10 days to find this money.

MARIE-ADELE: What's it cost to get into the bingo?   95

VERONIQUE: All the Indians in the world will be
there!

PHILOMENA: $50.

ANNIE: And we're gonna be the only Indians there.

PELAJIA: Silence.   100

*There is a long, thoughtful silence, broken only after
awhile by a scream from Zhaboonigan. Nanabush has
knocked her off her stool. The women laugh.*

Can't think of anything else.

PHILOMENA: Add it up.

She hands a pencil to Emily.

EMILY:

Calculates.

$1,400. You guys need $200 each.

VERONIQUE: Where am I going to get $400?

EMILY: Make it. End of meeting.   105

*And the women start their fundraising activities with a
vengeance. The drive is underlined by a wild rhythmic
beat from the musician, one that gets wilder and
wilder with each successive beat, though always
underpinned by this persistent, almost dance-like pulse.
The movement of the women covers the entire stage
area, and like the music, gets wilder and wilder, until*

---

[19] Silver Dollar] a night club attached to the Waverly Hotel, on Spadina Avenue in Toronto.

by the end it is as if we are looking at an insane eight-ring circus, eight-ring because through all of this, Nanabush, as the seagull, has a holdiay, particularly with Marie-Adele's lines of laundry, as Marie-Adele madly strings one line of laundry after another all over the set, from Pelajia's roof to Emily's store, etc. For the garage sale, Annie sells off Pelajia's lamp, chairs, etc. so that Pelajia's "basement" simply dissolves into the madness of the fundraising drive.

Beat one.

Pelajia is hammering on the roof.
Emily is at the store cash register and rings up each sale as Annie, Philomena, Marie-Adele, Zhaboonigan, and Veronique stand shoulder to shoulder and pass the following from one side of the stage to the other:
seven large sacks marked "FLOUR"
two giant tubs marked "LARD"
one bushel of apples

Beat two.

Zhaboonigan brings small table on and puts it stage left.
Annie brings table on and puts it stage right.
Philomena brings a basket full of beer bottles to center and empties it. She has a baby attached to her.
Veronique comes on with cloth and Windex and starts "cleaning windows" rhythmically, listening to whatever gossip she can hear.
Marie-Adele strings two lines of clothing across the stage.
Pelajia hammers on her roof.
Emily brings on several empty beer cases and fills them with Philomena's bottles.

Beat three.

Zhaboonigan brings in six quarts of blueberries and then takes over window cleaning from Veronique.
Annie brings on basket of old clothes and a broken kitchen chair.
Philomena brings on another basket full of beer bottles, empties it. She now has two babies attached to her, like a fungus.
Emily fills beer cases rapidly, expertly.
Pelajia gets down off roof, hammering everything until she is on hands and knees, hammering the floor.
Marie-Adele strings third and fourth lines of laundry across the stage.

Veronique comes in burdened with seven apple pies and puts them on Annie's table.

Beat four.

Pelajia hammers as she crawls across the floor.
Zhaboonigan washes windows like a person possessed.
Emily runs and rings up a sale on the cash register and then brings on more empty beer cases and loads them up.
Philomena brings on a third load of bottles. Three babies are now attached to her.
Annie brings on an old trilight pole lamp and an old record player, which she opens and stacks alongside the rest of her stuff.
Annie and Emily sing a line of their song with very bad harmony.
Marie-Adele strings fifth and sixth lines of laundry across stage.
Veronique comes on with seven loaves of bread and puts them neatly by the pies.

Beat five.

Pelajia hammers as she crawls across the floor, hammering everything in sight. The women protect their poor feet.
Zhaboonigan washes windows even faster; she's starting to cry.
Emily and Philomena work together filling the empty beer cases as fast as they can. Emily runs to the register, rings in seven sales and sings a bit of song with Annie, better this time. Philomena now has four kids attached to her body.
Annie comes on with a small black and white TV with rabbit ears and an old toaster.
Veronique comes on with six dozen buns and dumps them out of their tins all over the table.
Pelajia hammers faster and faster.
Zhaboonigan is now working like a maniac and is sobbing.
Marie-Adele strings seventh and eighth lines of laundry across stage.

Beat six.

Emily goes to cash register and tallies their earnings; she works the register with tremendous speed and efficiency all this beat.
Zhaboonigan continues washing windows.

Philomena sticks a sign in beer bottles: World's Biggest Bottle Drive. She now has five babies attached to her. Veronique sticks a sign on her table: World's Biggest Bake Sale.
Annie sticks a sign up around her stuff: World's Biggest Garage Sale.
Marie-Adele sticks a sign up on Zha's table: Big Blueberries and Laundry While You Wait.
Pelajia begins hammering the air. She may have lost her marbles.

Beat Seven.

EMILY: Whoa!

The "music" comes to a sudden stop. The women all collapse. The women look at each other. They then quickly clear the stage of everything they've brought on as Pelajia speaks, consulting her list. By the end of Pelajia's speech, the stage area is clear once more, except for a microphone stand that one of the women has brought on as part of the "clean-up" activities.

PELAJIA: Bottle drive. Ten cents a bottle, 24 bottles in a case, equals two dollars and 40 cents. 777 bottles collected divided by 24 is 32 cases and nine singles and that's 32 times $2.40 equals $77.70. 110 Blueberries equals $90. Good pickin' Zha and the Starblanket kids. Washing windows at $5.00 a house times 18 houses. Five eights are 40, carry the four and add the five is 90 bucks less two on account of that cheap Gazelle Nataways only gave 115 three dollars. That's $88. Household repair is four roofs including the Chief's and one tiled floor is $225. Garage sale brung in $246.95, the bake sale equals $83 after expenses, we make 110 bucks on doing laundry, 65 bucks babysitting, 145 from 120 Emily doing a double shift at the store and I have generously donated $103 from my savings. That brings us to a grand total of $1233.65. So!

Emily and Annie move forward as the music starts up. They are lit only by tacky floor flood-lighting, and are, in effect, at the Anchor Inn, Little Current.[20] Emily speaks into the microphone.

---

[20] *Little Current*] a town on the northeastern shore of Manitoulin Island.

EMILY: Thank-you. Thank-you, ladies and gentlemen. I thank you very much. And now for the last song of 125 the night, ladies and gents, before we hit the road. A song that's real special to me in my heart. A song I wrote in memory of one Rosabella Baez, a Rez Sister from way back. And Rose baby, if you're up there tonight, I hope you're listenin' in. Cuz it's called: 130 "I'm thinkin' of You." Here goes …

Emily and Annie grab their microphones; Emily sings lead, Annie sings backup. And it's "country" to the hilt.

I'm thinkin' of you every moment,
As though you were here by my side;
I'll always remember the good times,
So darlin' please come back to me. 135

I'm dreamin' of you every night,
That we were together again;
If time can heal up our partin'
Then love can remove all this pain.

Instrumental — dance break

If love is the secret of livin', 140
Then give me that love, shinin' light;
When you are again by my side,
Then livin' will once more be right.

The audience claps. Emily says, "Thank-you." And then she and Annie join the other women, who have, during the song, loaded themselves, their suitcases, and their lunches into the "van." This van consists of three battered old van seats stuck to the walls of the theatre, on either side and up high. The back seat is on the "stage left" side of the theatre and the other two are on the other side, the middle seat of the van towards the back of the theatre, the front seat, complete with detachable steering wheel, just in front and "stage right" of the stage area. Each seat is lit by its own light.

EMILY: How much did me and Annie take in singin' at the Anchor Inn? 145
PELAJIA: $330 at the door.
MARIE-ADELE: Solid packed house, eh? Shoulda charged more.
ANNIE: Fifty bucks for the oom-chi-cha machine. Twenty bucks for Ronnie's guitar. That's our only 150 costs.

EMILY: Ha! We're laughin'.

A capella reprise of a verse of their song, which fades into highway sounds, and they drive, for a few moments, in silence.

In the van, driving down the highway to Toronto, at night. The women have intimate conversations, one on one, while the rest are asleep or seated at the other end of the van. Annie is driving. Emily sits beside her listening to her Walkman, while Marie-Adele is "leaning" over Annie's shoulder from her place in the middle seat. Veronique sits beside Marie-Adele, sleeping. Pelajia and Philomena are in the very back seat with Zhaboonigan between them.

MARIE-ADELE: Nee, Annie, not so fast.

Pause. Annie slows down.

So. You couldn't get Ellen and <u>Ray</u><u>mond</u> to come along? I'd like to meet this <u>Ray</u>mond someday.   155
ANNIE:

Angrily insisting on the correct pronunciation.

Ray<u>mond</u>! Ellen says he's got a whole library full of cassette tapes.
MARIE-ADELE: Annie. You ever think about getting married again?
ANNIE: Not really. I can hear the band at the Silver   160
Dollar already.
MARIE-ADELE: Do you still think about … Eugene?
ANNIE: What're you talkin' about? Of course, I think about him, he's my brother-in-law, ain't he?
MARIE-ADELE: He made his choice.   165
ANNIE: Yeah. He picked you.
MARIE-ADELE: Annie. I never stole him off you.
ANNIE: Drop dead. Shit! I forgot to bring that blouse. I mean. In case I sing. Shit.
MARIE-ADELE: If I'm gone and Eugene if he starts   170
drinkin' again. I see you going for him.
ANNIE: Why would I bother? I had my chance 20 years ago. Christ!
MARIE-ADELE: Twenty years ago, I was there.
ANNIE: Why would I want 14 kids for?   175
MARIE-ADELE: That's exactly what I'm scared of. I don't want them kids to be split up. You come near Eugene you start drinking messing things up me not here I come back and don't matter where you are …

ANNIE: I don't want him. I don't want him. I don't   180
want him. I don't want him. I don't want him.
EMILY: Put us all in the fuckin' ditch!
PELAJIA: Hey, watch your language up there.
ANNIE: Shit! I don't care. There's nothing more to say about it. Why don't you take your pills and go   185
to sleep.

Pelajia and Philomena begin talking.

PHILOMENA: September 8 again.
PELAJIA: Hmmm? What about September 8?
PHILOMENA: You don't remember?
PELAJIA: What?   190
PHILOMENA: How could you?
PELAJIA: Mama died?
PHILOMENA: No! Remember?
PELAJIA: I can't remember. Got so much on my mind. So many things to forget.   195
ZHABOONIGAN:

To Philomena.

You like me?
PHILOMENA: Yes, Zhaboonigan. I like you.
ZHABOONIGAN: I like the birdies.
PHILOMENA: You like talking to the birdies?
ZHABOONIGAN: Yup.   200

She falls asleep.

PHILOMENA: Zhaboonigan … sometimes I wonder …
PELAJIA: It's dark … warm … quiet …
PHILOMENA: Toronto. Had a good job in Toronto. Yeah. Had to give it all up. Yeah. Cuz mama got   205
sick. Philomena Margaret Moosetail. Real live secretary in the garment district. He'd come in and see my boss. Nice man, I thought. That big, red, fish-tail Caddy. Down Queen Street. He liked me. Treated me like a queen. Loved me. Or I thought   210
he did. I don't know. Got pregnant anyway. Blond, blue-eyed, six foot two. And the way he smelled. God! His wife walks in on us.

Long silence.

He left with her.

Long silence.

I don't even know to this day if it was a boy or a girl. I'm getting old. That child would be … 28 … 28 years old. September 8. You now what I'm gonna do wit that money if I win? I'm gonna find a lawyer. Maybe I can find that child. Maybe I wouldn't even have to let him … her … know who I am. I just … want to see … who …

PELAJIA: I hope you win.

Annie and Emily, at the front of the van with Annie driving, are laughing and singing, "I'm a little Indian who loves fry bread." From time to time, they sneak each other a sip of this little bottle of whiskey Annie has hidden away inside her purse.

I'm a little Indian who loves fry bread,[21]
Early in the morning and when I go to bed;
Some folks say I'm crazy in the head,
Cuz I'm a little Indian who loves fry bread.

Now, some folks say I've put on a pound or two,
My jeans don' fit the way they used to do;
But I don't care, let the people talk,
Cuz if I don't get my fry bread, you'll hear me
     squawk.

ANNIE: So tell me. What's it like to go to a big bar like … I mean like … the Silver Dollar.

EMILY: Lotta Nishnawbs.[22]

ANNIE:

Disappointed.

Yeah? Is the music good?

EMILY: Country rock.

ANNIE:

Screams gleefully.

Yee-haw! Maybe the band will ask me up to sing, eh? I'll sing something fast.

EMILY: You would, too.

ANNIE:

Sings real fast.

"Well, it's 40 below and I don't give a fuck, got a

heater in my truck and I'm off to the rodeo. Woof!"[23] Something like that.

EMILY: Yup. That's pretty fast.

ANNIE: Hey. Maybe Fritz the Katz will be there. Never know. Might get laid, too, eh? Remember Room 20 at the Anchor Inn? Oh, that Fritz! Sure like singin' with him. Crazy about the way …

EMILY:

Starts singing Patsy Cline's famous "Crazy … crazy for feelin' so lonely …" all the way through Annie's next speech.

ANNIE: … he stands there with his guitar and his 10-gallon hat. Is that what you call them hats? You know the kind you wear kind of off to the side like this? That's what he does. And then he winks at me. *(Sings.)* "Crazy …" Oooh, I love, just love the way the lights go woosh woosh in your eyes and kinda' wash all over your body. Me standing there shuffling my feet side to side, dressed real nice and going *(Sings.)* "Ooooh darlin' …" with my mike in my hand just so. Oh! And the sound of that band behind me. And Fritz. *(Sings.)* "Crazy, crazy for feelin' so lonely…"

EMILY: Yeah. You look good on stage.

ANNIE: Yeah?

EMILY: How come you're so keen on that guy anyway?

ANNIE: Sure Veronique St. Pierre isn't just pretending to be asleep back there?

Emily and Marie-Adele check Veronique in the middle seat.

MARIE-ADELE: Nah. Out like a lamp.

EMILY: Hey! We'll get her drunk at the Silver Dollar and leave her passed out under some table. Take two beers to do that.

ANNIE: Hey. Too bad Big Joey had to come back from Toronto before we got there, eh?

EMILY: Man! That dude's got buns on him like no other buns on the face of God's entire creation.

---

21 fry bread] a traditional Native food.
22 Nishnawbs] Indians. (Ojibway)

23 40 below …] From "The Rodeo Song," by Gaye Delorme, performed by Gary Lee and Showdown, an Alberta-based band.

Whooo! Not to mention a dick that's bigger than a goddamn breadbox.

Annie screams gleefully.

How about Fritz? What's his look like?   275

ANNIE:

After an awkward pause.

He's Jewish, you know.

EMILY:

Laughing raucously.

World's first Jewish country singer!

ANNIE: Don't laugh. Those Jews make a lot of money, you know.

EMILY: Not all of them.   280

ANNIE: Fritz buys me jeans and things. I'm gonna be one of them Jewish princesses.

EMILY: What's wrong with being an Indian princess?

ANNIE: Aw, these white guys. They're nicer to their women. Not like Indian guys. Screw you, drink   285
all your money, and leave you flat on your ass.

EMILY: Yeah, right. Apple Indian Annie. Red on the outside. White on the inside.

ANNIE: Emily!

EMILY: Keep your eye on the road.   290

ANNIE: Good ol' highway 69.[24]

EMILY: Hey. Ever 69 with Fritz?

MARIE-ADELE: Neee.

ANNIE: White guys don't make you do things to them. You just lie there and they do it all for you.   295
Ellen's real happy with her Raymond. You can tell the way she sounds on the phone. Maybe someday I'll just take off with a guy like Fritz.

EMILY: Then what? Never come back to the rez?

Annie is cornered. Emily then slaps her playfully on the arm.

Hey. Know what?   300

Sings.

When I die, I may not go to heaven.
I don't know if they let Indians in;

If they don't, just let me go to Wasy, lord,
Cuz Wasy is as close as I've been.[25]

ANNIE: Lots of white people at this Silver Dollar?   305

EMILY: Sometimes. Depends.

ANNIE: How much for beer there?

EMILY: Same as up here. Nah! Don't need money, Annie Cook. You just gotta know how to handle men. Like me and the Rez sisters down in Frisco.   310

ANNIE: Yeah?

EMILY: I'll take care of them.

ANNIE: Maybe we can find a party, eh? Maybe with the band.

EMILY: Whoa! Slow down, Annie Cook! Easy on the   315
gas!

MARIE-ADELE: Annie!

Pow. Black-out. They have a flat tire.

The flat tire. Everything now happens in complete darkness.

VERONIQUE: Bingo!

PHILOMENA: What was that? What happened?

ANNIE: I don't know. Something just went "poof"!   320

EMILY: Alright. Everybody out. We got a fuckin' flat.

They all climb out of the van.

VERONIQUE: Oh my god! We'll never get to the bingo.

ZHABOONIGAN: Pee pee.

PELAJIA: I can't fix a flat tire.

ANNIE: Emily can.   325

PELAJIA: Get the jack. Spare tire.

ANNIE: Philomena's wearing one.

ZHABOONIGAN: Pee pee.

PHILOMENA: This is all your fault, Annie Cook.

MARIE-ADELE: It's in the back.   330

ANNIE: So what do we do?

PELAJIA: What's the matter with Zha?

PHILOMENA: Gotta make pee pee.

VERONIQUE: I knew there was something wrong with this van the moment I set eyes on it. I should   335
have taken the bus.

PHILOMENA: Oh shut up. Quack, quack, quack.

ANNIE: Don't look at me. It's not my fault the tires are all bald.

---

24 highway 69] the main highway running south from Sudbury through Parry Sound.

25 A parody of a Tanya Tucker song, "Texas (When I Die)."

PHILOMENA: Nobody's blaming you. 340
ANNIE: But you just did.
PHILOMENA: Quack, quack, quack.
VERONIQUE: Where are we?
ANNIE: The Lost Channel.[26] This is where you get off. 345
VERONIQUE:

Groans.

Ohhh!
EMILY: Yeah, right.
PHILOMENA: Shhh!
PELAJIA: Jack's not working too well.
EMILY: Okay. Everybody. Positions. 350
VERONIQUE: Not me. My heart will collapse.
EMILY: You wanna play bingo?
VERONIQUE:

Groans.

Ohhhh!
ANNIE: Hurry up! Hurry up!
EMILY: Okay. One, two, three lift. 355

Everybody lifts and groans.

PELAJIA: Put the jack in there.

All lift, except Marie-Adele and Zha, who wander off into the moonlit darkness. Dim light on them.

ZHABOONIGAN: Ever dark.
MARIE-ADELE: You'll be fine, Zhaboonigan.

Suddenly, a nighthawk — Nanabush, now in dark feathers — appears, darting in the night.

ZHABOONIGAN: The birdies!
MARIE-ADELE: Yes, a birdie. 360
ZHABOONIGAN: Black wings!

Marie-Adele begins talking to the bird, almost if she were talking to herself. Quietly, at first, but gradually — as the bird begins attacking her — growing more and more hysterical, until she is shrieking, falling, and thrashing about insanely.

---

26 Lost Channel] a ghost town off Highway 69, north of Parry Sound.

MARIE-ADELE: Who are you? What do you want? My children? Eugene? No! Oh no! Me? Not yet. Not yet. Give me time. Please. Don't. Please don't. Awus! Get away from me. Eugene! Awus! You 365 fucking bird! Awus! Awus! Awus! Awus! Awus!

And she has a total hysterical breakdown.

Zhaboonigan, at first, attempts to scare the bird off by running and flailing her arms at it. Until the bird knocks her down and she lies there on the ground, watching in helpless astonishment and abject terror. Underneath Marie-Adele's screams, she mumbles to herself, sobbing.

ZHABOONIGAN: One, two, three, four, five, six, seven ... Nicky Ricky Ben Mark ... eight, nine, ten, eleven, twelve ...

Until the other women come running. Total darkness again.

EMILY: What the ... 370
ANNIE: Marie-Adele!
PELAJIA: Stop her! Hold her!
VERONIQUE: What's happening?
PHILOMENA: Marie Adele. Now, now ... come ... come ... 375
EMILY:

In the background.

Stop that fucking screaming will ya, Marie-Adele!
PHILOMENA: Emily. There's no need to talk to her like that now.
PELAJIA: Help us get her in the van.
PHILOMENA: Come ... come, Marie-Adele ... 380 everything's fine ... you'll be fine ... come ... shhh ... shhh ...

And they ease Marie-Adele back into the van. Once all is beginning to settle down again:

PELAJIA: Everything okay now?
PHILOMENA: Yes. She's fine now.
PELAJIA: Emily, take over. 385
VERONIQUE: Yes. I don't trust that Annie Cook. Not for one minute.
EMILY: All set?
MARIE-ADELE: What time is it?

PELAJIA: Twenty after four. 390

ANNIE: Oh! We're over two hours behind schedule. Hurry up. Hurry up.

VERONIQUE: I'll be exhausted for the bingo tomorrow night. Maybe I should just take 15 cards. 395

EMILY: You can rest your heart. And your mouth. All day tomorrow. All set?

And she starts up the van. The van lights come back on.

The dialogues resume. Marie-Adele now sits in the front with Emily, who is driving. Zhaboonigan sits between them, Pelajia and Philomena are now in the middle seat, Annie and Veronique in the back.

EMILY: You scared the shit out of me out there.

Silence.

Don't do that again.

Silence.

Feeling better now? 400

Silence.

MARIE-ADELE: I could be really mad, just raging mad just wanna tear his eyes out with my nails when he walks in the door and my whole body just goes "k-k-k-k" … He doesn't talk, when something goes wrong with him, he doesn't talk, 405 shuts me out, just disappears. Last night he didn't come home. Again, it happened. I couldn't sleep. You feel so ugly. He walks in this morning. Wanted to be alone, he said. The curve of his back, his breath on my neck, "Adele, ki-sa-gee-ee-tin oo- 410 ma,"[27] making love, always in Indian, only. When we still could. I can't even have him inside me anymore. It's still growing there. The cancer. Pelajia, een-pay-seek-see-yan.[28]

PELAJIA: You know one time, I knew this couple 415 where one of them was dying and the other one was angry at her for dying. And she was mad because he was gonna be there when she wasn't and she had so much left to do. And she'd lie there in bed and tell him to do this and do that and he'd 420 say "Okay, okay." And then he'd go into the kitchen and say to me, "She's so this and she's so that and she's so damned difficult." And I watched all this going on. That house didn't have room for two such angry people. But you know, I said to 425 her, "You gotta have faith in him and you gotta have faith in life. He loves you very much but there's only so much he can do. He's only human." There's only so much Eugene can understand, Marie-Adele. He's only human. 430

EMILY: Fuckin' right. Me and the Rez sisters, okay? Cruisin' down the coast highway one night. Hum of the engine between my thighs. Rose. That's Rosabella Baez, leader of the pack. We were real close, me and her. She was always thinkin' real 435 deep. And talkin' about bein' a woman. An Indian woman. And suicide. And alcohol and despair and how fuckin' hard it is to be an Indian in this country. *(Marie-Adele shushes her gently.)* No goddamn future for them, she'd say. And why, why, 440 why? Always carryin' on like that. Chris'sakes. She was pretty heavy into the drugs. Guess we all were. We had a fight. Cruisin' down the coast highway that night. Rose in the middle. Me and Pussy Commanda off to the side. Big 18-wheeler come 445 along real fast and me and Pussy Commanda get out of the way. But not Rose. She stayed in the middle. Went head-on into that truck like a fly splat against a windshield. I swear to this day I can still feel the spray of her blood against my neck. I 450 drove on. Straight into daylight. Never looked back. Had enough gas money on me to take me far as Salt Lake city. Pawned my bike off and bought me a bus ticket back to Wasy. When I got to Chicago, that's when I got up the nerve to wash 455 my lover's dried blood from off my neck. I loved that woman, Marie-Adele, I loved her like no man's ever loved a woman. But she's gone. I never wanna go back to San Francisco. No way, man.

MARIE-ADELE:

Comforting the crying Emily.

You should get some rest. Let Annie take over. 460

EMILY: I'll be fine. You go to sleep. Wake you up when we get to Toronto.

---

27 Adele, I love you. (Cree)
28 Pelajia, I'm scared to death. (Cree)

Emily puts her Walkman on and starts to sing along quietly to "Blue Kentucky Girl" by Emmylou Harris with its "I swear I love you ..." while Marie-Adele leans her head against the "window" and falls asleep.

After a few moments, Zhaboonigan, who has been dozing off between Emily and Marie-Adele in the front seat, pokes her head up and starts to sing along off-key. Then she starts to play with Emily's hair.

EMILY:

Shrugging Zhaboonigan's hand off.

Don't bug me. My favorite part's coming up.

Initiated by Zhaboonigan, they start playing "slap." The game escalates to the point where Emily almost bangs Zhaboonigan over the head with her elbow.

EMILY: Yeah, right. You little retard.

Mad at this, Zhaboonigan hits Emily in the stomach.

Don't hit me there, you little ... Hey, man, like   465
ummm ... I'm sorry, Zha.
ZHABOONIGAN: Sorry.
EMILY:

Emily feels her belly thoughtfully. After a brief silence:

You gonna have kids someday, Zha?
ZHABOONIGAN: Ummm ... buy one.
EMILY: Holy! Well, kids were alright. Aw geez, Zha,   470
that man treated me real bad. Ever been tied to a
bed post with your arms up like this? Whoa!

Grabbing the steering wheel.

Maybe you should drive.
ZHABOONIGAN: Scary.
EMILY: Aw, don't be scared. Fuck.   475
ZHABOONIGAN: Fuck.
EMILY: Zhaboonigan Peterson! Your ma'll give me a
black eye.

Zhaboonigan turns her head toward the back seat, where Veronique sits sleeping, and says one more time, really loud.

ZHABOONIGAN: Fuck!
EMILY: Shhh! Look, Zha. You don't let any man   480
bother you while we're down in T.O. You just stick
close to me.

ZHABOONIGAN: Yup.
EMILY: We're sisters right? Gimme five.

They slap hands.

Alright. Bingo!!!   485

Instantly, the house lights come on full blast. The Bingo Master — the most beautiful man in the world — comes running up center aisle, cordless mike in hand, dressed to kill: tails, rhinestones, and all. The entire theatre is now the bingo palace. We are in: Toronto!!!!

BINGO MASTER: Welcome, ladies and gentlemen, to
the biggest bingo the world has ever seen! Yes, ladies
and gentlemen, tonight, we have a very, very special
treat for you. Tonight, ladies and gentlemen, you
will be witness to events of such gargantuan propor-   490
tions, such cataclysmic ramifications, such masterly
and magnificent manifestations that your minds will
reel, your eyes will nictitate, and your hearts will
palpitate erratically.

Because tonight, ladies and gentlemen, you will   495
see the biggest, yes, ladies and gentlemen, the very
biggest prizes ever known to man, woman, beast,
or appliance. And the jackpot tonight? The
jackpot, ladies and gentlemen, is surely the biggest,
the largest, the hugest, and the most monstrous   500
jackpot ever conceived of in the entire history of
monstrous jackpots as we know them. $500 000!
Yes, ladies and gentlemen, $500 000 can be yours
this very night! That's half a million — A HALF
MILLION SMACKEROOS!!! IF you play the   505
game right.

And all you have to do, ladies and gentlemen,
is reach into your programs and extract the single
bingo card placed therein. Yes, ladies and gentlemen, the single bingo card placed therein, which   510
bingo card will entitle you to one chance at winning the warm-up game for a prize of $20. $20!
And all you have to do is poke holes in that single
bingo card. Yes, ladies and gentlemen, just poke
holes in that single bingo card and bend the num-   515
bers backward as the numbers are called. And don't
forget the free hole in the middle of the card.
Twenty dollars, ladies and gentlemen, that's one
line in any direction. That means, of course, ladies and gentlemen, that the first person to form   520

one line, just one straight line in any direction on their card, will be the very lucky winner of the $20 prize. $20! Are you ready, ladies and gentlemen? Are you ready? Then let the game begin! Under the G 56. Etc.... 525

The audience plays bingo, with the seven women, who have moved slowly into the audience during the Bingo Master's speech, playing along. Until somebody in the audience shouts, "Bingo!"

BINGO MASTER: Hold your cards, ladies and gentlemen, bingo has been called.

The Bingo Master and the assistant stage manager check the numbers and the prize money is paid out.

BINGO MASTER: And now for the game you've been waiting for, ladies and gentlemen. Now for the big game. Yes, ladies and gentlemen, get ready for 530 THE BIGGEST BINGO IN THE WORLD! For the grand jackpot prize of $500, 000! Full house, ladies and gentlemen, full house! Are you ready? Are you ready? Then let the game begin!

The house lights go out. And the only lights now are on the bingo balls bouncing around in the bingo machine — an eery, surreal sort of glow — and on the seven women who are now playing bingo with a vengeance on centrestage, behind the Bingo Master, where a long bingo table has magically appeared with Zhaboonigan at the table's center banging a crucifix Veronique has brought along for good luck. The scene is lit so that it looks like "The Last Supper."

The women face the audience. The bingo table is covered with all the necessary accoutrements: bags of potato chips, cans of pop, ashtrays (some of the women are smoking), etc. The Bingo Master calls out number after number — but not the B 14 — with the women improvising responses. These responses — Philomena has 27 cards! — grow more and more raucous: "B 14? Annie Cook? One more number to go! The B 14! Where is that B 14?! Gimme that B14! Where the fuck is that B14?!!!" etc. Until the women have all risen from the table and come running downstage, attacking the bingo machine and throwing the Bingo Master out of the way. The women grab the bingo machine with shouts of: "Throw this fucking machine

into the lake! It's no damn good!" *etc. And they go running down center aisle with it and out of the theatre. Bingo cards are flying like confetti. Total madness and mayhem. The music is going crazy.*

And out of this chaos emerges the calm, silent image of Marie-Adele waltzing romantically in the arms of the Bingo Master. The Bingo Master says "Bingo" into her ear. And the Bingo Master changes, with sudden bird-like movements, into the nighthawk, Nanabush in dark feathers. Marie-Adele meets Nanabush.

During this next speech, the other women, one by one, take their positions around Marie-Adele's porch, some kneeling, some standing. The stage area, by means of "lighting magic," slowly returns to its Wasaychigan Hill appearance.

MARIE-ADELE: U-wi-nuk u-wa? U-wi-nuk u-wa? 535 Eugene? Neee. U-wi-nuk ma-a oo-ma kee-tha? Ka. Kee-tha i-chi-goo-ma so that's who you are ... at rest upon the rock ... the master of the game ... the game ... it's me ... nee-tha ... come ... come ... don't be afraid ... as-tum ... come ... to ... 540 me ... ever soft wings ... beautiful soft ... soft ... dark wings ... here ... take me ... as-tum ... as-tum ... pee-na-sin ... wings ... here ... take me ... take ... me ... with ... pee-na-sin ...[29]

As Nanabush escorts Marie-Adele into the spirit world, Zhaboonigan, uttering a cry, makes a last desperate attempt to go with them. But Emily rushes after and catches her at the very last split second. And the six remaining women begin to sing the Ojibway funeral song. By the beginning of the funeral song, we are back at the Wasaychigan Hill Indian Reserve, at Marie-Adele's grave.

---

[29] U-wi-nuk ... pee-na-sin ...] Who are you? Who are you? Eugene? Nee. then who are you really? Oh. It's you, so that's who you are ... at rest upon the rock ... the master of the game ... the game ... it's me ... me ... come ... come ... don't be afraid ... come ... come ... to ... me ... ever soft wings ... beautiful soft ... soft ... darkwings ... here ... take me ... come ... come ... come and get me ... wings here ... take me ... take ... me ... with ... come and get me ... (Cree)

WOMEN: Wa-kwing, wa-kwing,   545
    Wa-kwing nin wi-i-ja;
    Wa-kwing, wa-kwing,
    Wa-kwing, nin wi-i-ja.[30]

*At Marie-Adele's grave. During Pelajia's speech, the
other women continue humming the funeral song until
they fade into silence. Pelajia drops a handful of earth
on the grave.*

PELAJIA: Well, sister, guess you finally hit the big
    jackpot. Best bingo game we've ever been to in our   550
    lives, huh? You know, life's like that, I figure. When
    all is said and done. Kinda' silly, innit, this business
    of living? But. What choice do we have? When
    some fool of a being goes and puts us Indians
    plunk down in the middle of this old earth, dishes   555
    out this lot we got right now. But. I figure we gotta
    make the most of it while we're here. You certainly
    did. And I sure as hell am giving it one good try.
    For you. For me. For all of us. Promise. Really. See
    you when that big bird finally comes for me.   560

*Whips out her hammer one more time, holds it up in
the air and smiles.*

    And my hammer.

*Back at the store in Wasaychigan Hill. Emily is tearing
open a brand-new case of the small cans of Carnation
milk, takes two cans out and goes up to Zhaboonigan
with them.*

EMILY: See, Zha? The red part of here and the white
    part down here and the pink flowers in the middle?
ZHABOONIGAN: Oh.
EMILY: Carnation milk.   565
ZHABOONIGAN: Carnation milk.
EMILY: And it goes over here where all the other red
    and white cans are, okay?
ZHABOONIGAN: Yup.

*Zhaboonigan rushes to Emily and throws her arms
around her affectionately. Emily is embarrassed and
struggles to free herself. Just then, Annie enters. She's lost*

___

30 Wa-kwing … nin wi-i-ja] Heaven, heaven, heaven, I'm
    going there; Heaven, heaven, heaven, I'm going there.
    (Ojibway)

*some of her speed and frenetic energy. There's obviously
something wrong with her.*

ANNIE: Hallooo! Whatchyou doing.   570
EMILY: Red Lucifer's whiskers! It's Annie Cook.
ANNIE: Well, we seem to have survived the biggest
    bingo in the world, eh? Well … ummm … not
    all of us … not Marie-Adele … but she knew she
    was … but we're okay. (*Laughs.*) … us? …   575
EMILY: Annie Cook. Sometimes you can be so
    goddamn ignorant. (*Pause.*) Too bad none of us
    won, eh.
ANNIE: Philomena Moosemeat won $600. That's
    something.   580
EMILY: Yup. That's one helluva jazzy toilet she's got
    there, eh?
ANNIE: She's got eight-ply toilet paper. Dark green.
    Feels like you're wiping your ass with moss!
EMILY: Holy!   585
ANNIE: I'm singing back-up for Fritz weekends. 25
    bucks a gig. That's something, eh?
EMILY: Katz's whore …
ANNIE: What?
EMILY: You heard me.   590
ANNIE: The Katz's what?
EMILY: Chris'sakes. Wake up.
ANNIE: I love him, Emily.
EMILY: You been drinkin'.
ANNIE: Please, come with me tonight.   595
EMILY: Have to wait for the old buzzard to come pick
    up this dozy daughter of hers and that's not 'til
    seven.
ANNIE: Okay?
EMILY: Alright. But we're comin' right back to the   600
    Rez soon as the gig's over. Hear?
ANNIE: Thanks. Any mail today?
EMILY: Sorry.
ANNIE: That's okay. See you at seven.

And she exits.

ZHABOONIGAN: Why … why … why do you call   605
    me that?
EMILY: Call you what?
ZHABOONIGAN: Dozy dotter.

*Awkward silence, broken after awhile by Zhaboonigan's
little giggle.*

EMILY: Look, Zha. Share a little secret with you, okay? 610

ZHABOONIGAN: Yup.

EMILY: Just you and me, promise?

ZHABOONIGAN: Yup.

EMILY: Gazelle Nataways'll see fit to kill … but I'm gonna have a baby. 615

ZHABOONIGAN:

Drops the Carnation milk cans she's been holding all this time and gasps.

Ohhh! Big Joey!

EMILY:

In exasperation.

This business of having babies …

And the last we see of them is Zhaboonigan playfully poking Emily in the belly and Emily slapping Zhaboonigan's hand away.

At Eugene Starblanket's house. Veronique St. Pierre is sitting on the steps, glowing with happiness, looking up at the sky as though looking for seagulls. She sees none so she picks up the doll that lies under her chair and cradles it on her lap as though it were a child. At this point, Annie Cook enters.

ANNIE: Hallooo!

Surprised to see Veronique sitting there.

Veronique St. Pierre. What are you doing here?

VERONIQUE: Annie Cook. Haven't you heard I'm 620 cooking for Eugene and the children these days? It's been four days since the funeral as you know may she rest in peace *(Makes a quick sign of the cross without missing beat.)* but I was the only person on this reserve who was willing to help with these 625 14 little orphans.

ANNIE: That's nice. But I came to see if Simon Star …

VERONIQUE: The stove is so good. All four elements work and there is even a timer for the oven. As I was saying to Black Lady Halked at the bingo last 630 night, "Now I don't have to worry about burning the fried potatoes or serving the roast beef half-raw."

ANNIE: Well, I was about to …

VERONIQUE: Yes, Annie Cook. I bought a roast beef 635 just yesterday. A great big roast beef. Almost 16 pounds. It's probably the biggest roast beef that's been seen on this reserve in recent years. The meat was so heavy that Nicky, Ricky, Ben, and Mark had to take turns carrying it here for me. Oh, it was 640 hard and slippery at first, but I finally managed to wrestle it into my oven. And it's sitting in there at this very moment just sizzling and bubbling with the most succulent and delicious juices. And speaking of succulent and delicious juices, did you 645 come to call on Eugene? Well, Eugene's not home.

ANNIE: Yeah, right. I came to see if Simon had that new record.

VERONIQUE: Why?

ANNIE: I'm singing in Little Current tonight and I 650 gotta practice this one song.

VERONIQUE:

Contemptuously.

That Ritzie Ditzie character.

ANNIE: It's Fritz the Katz, Veronique St. Pierre. FREDERICK STEPHEN KATZ. He's a very fine musician and a good teacher. 655

VERONIQUE: Teacher?! Of what?! As I was saying to Little Girl Manitowabi and her daughter June Bug McLeod at the bingo last night, "You never know about these non-Native bar-room types." I said to them, "We have enough trouble right here on this 660 reserve without having our women come dragging these shady white characters into the picture." Before you know it, you will end up in deep trouble and bring shame and disrespect on the name of Pelajia Pathnose and all your sisters, 665 myself included.

ANNIE: Myself included, my ass! Veronique St. Pierre. I wish you would shut that great big shitty mouth of yours at least once a year!

VERONIQUE:

Stunned into momentary silence. Then.

Simon Starblanket is not home. 670

With this, she bangs the doll down viciously.

ANNIE: Good day, Veronique St. Pierre.

And exits.

Veronique, meanwhile, just sits there in her stunned state, mouth hanging open and looking after the departing Annie.

On Pelajia Patchnose's roof. As at the beginning of the play, Pelajia is alone, nailing shingles on. But no cushion this time.

PELAJIA: Philomena. Where are those shingles?
PHILOMENA:

From offstage.

Oh, go on. I'll be up in just a minute.
PELAJIA:

Coughs.

The dust today. It's these dirt roads. Dirt roads all over. Even the main street. If I were chief around here, that's the very first thing I would do is … 675
PHILOMENA:

Coming up the ladder with one shingle and the most beautiful pink, lace-embroidered, heart-shaped pillow you'll ever see.

Oh, go on. You'll never be chief.
PELAJIA: And why not?
PHILOMENA: Because you're a woman.
PELAJIA: Bullshit! If that useless old chief of ours was 680 a woman, we'd see a few things get done around here. We'd see our women working, we'd see our men working, we'd see our young people sober on Saturday nights, and we'd see Nanabush dancing up and down the hill on shiny black paved roads. 685

Annie Cook pops up at the top of the ladder.

ANNIE: Pelajia for chief! I'd vote for you.
PHILOMENA: Why, Annie Cook. You just about scared me off the edge of this roof.
PELAJIA: Someday, we'll have to find you a man who can slow you down. So what do you want this 690 time, Annie Cook?
ANNIE: Well, to tell you the truth, I came to borrow your record player, Philomena Moosemeat … I mean, Moosetail. I'm going to practice this one song for tonight. Emily Dictionary is coming to 695 Little Current to watch me sing with the band.
PELAJIA: It's back from Espanola.

PHILOMENA:

To Pelajia.

Pelajia Rosella Patchnose!

To Annie.

It's still not working very well. There's a certain screeching, squawking noise that comes out of it 700 every time you try to play it.
PELAJIA: That's okay, Philomena. There's a certain screechy, squawky noise that comes out of Annie Cook every time she opens her mouth to sing anyway. 705
PHILOMENA: Yes, Annie Cook. You can borrow it. But only for one night.
ANNIE: Good. Hey, there's a bingo in Espanola next week and Fire Minklater is driving up in her new car. There might be room. 710

To Philomena:

Would you like to go?
PELAJIA: Does a bear shit in the woods?
PHILOMENA:

Glares at Pelajia first.

Yes.

Then quickly to Annie.

Make … make sure you don't leave me behind.
ANNIE: I'll make sure. Well. Toodle-oo! 715

And she pops down the ladder again, happy, now that she's finally got her record player.

PELAIJIA: That Annie Cook. Records and bingo. Bingo and records.
PHILOMENA: You know, Pelajia, I'd like to see just what this Fritz looks like. Maybe he IS the man who can slow her down, after all. 720
PELAJIA: Foolishness! Annie Cook will be walking fast right up until the day she dies and gets buried beside the two of us in that little cemetery beside the church.
PHILOMENA: Oh, go on. 725

Pause. As Philomena sits down beside her sister, leaning with her elbow on her heart-shaped pillow.

So, Pelajia Patchnose. Still thinking about packing your bags and shipping off to Toronto?

PELAJIA: Well … oh … sometimes. I'm not so sure I would get along with him if I were to live down there. I mean my son Tom. He was telling me not to play so much bingo.

PHILOMENA: His upstairs washroom. Mine looks just like it now.

PELAJIA: Here we go again.

PHILOMENA: Large shining porcelain tiles in hippity-hoppity squares of black and white … so clean you can see your own face, like in a mirror, when you lean over to look into them. It looks so nice. The shower curtains have a certain matching blackness and whiteness to them — they're made of a rich, thick, plasticky sort of material — and they're see-through in parts. The bathtub is beautiful, too. But the best, the most wonderful, my absolute most favorite part is the toilet bowl itself. First of all, it's elevated, like on a sort of … pedestal, so that it makes you feel like … the Queen … sitting on her royal throne, ruling her Queendom with a firm yet gentle hand. And the bowl itself — white, spirit white — is of such a shape, such an exquisitely soft, perfect oval shape that it makes you want to cry. Oh!!! And it's so comfortable you could just sit on it right up until the day you die!

After a long, languorous pause, Philomena snaps out of her reverie when she realizes that Pelajia, all this time, has been looking at her disbelievingly and then contemptuously. Pelajia cradles her hammer as though she'd like to bang Philomena's head with it. Philomena delicately starts to descend the ladder. The last we see of her is her Kewpie-doll face. And beside it, the heart-shaped pillow, disappearing like a setting sun behind the edge of the roof. Once she's good and gone. Pelajia dismisses her.

PELAJIA: Oh, go on!

Then she pauses to look wistfully at the view for a moment.

Not many seagulls flying over Eugene Starblanket's house today.

And returns once more to her hammering on the roof as the lights fade into black-out. Split seconds before complete black-out, Nanabush, back once more in his guise as the seagull, "lands" on the roof behind the unaware and unseeing Pelajia Patchnose. He dances to the beat of the hammer, merrily and triumphantly.

END OF PLAY.

TIMBERLAKE WERTENBAKER

Our Country's Good

based on the novel *The Playmaker* by Thomas Keneally

O ne of the main influences on the revitalization of Western theatre in the 1960s and 1970s was collective creation: the development of a performance script by a company through collaboration rather than leaving the creation of the text to a single author working in isolation. There are many different forms of collective creation, but one of the most sophisticated and successful forms is that known in England as the "Joint Stock Method." In 1974, directors William Gaskill and Max Stafford-Clark and a group of actors had founded Joint Stock Company with the express purpose of bringing playwrights such as David Hare, Howard Brenton, and Caryl Churchill together with actors and a director to collaborate in the early stages of a new script. The theory was that the most accomplished playwrights, such as Molière and Shakespeare, had not created their work in isolation, but in close contact with a particular company. After a few experiments, the mature form of the Joint Stock method had become fairly routine. First, the company would, as a group, undertake research into a particular project (usually, but not invariably, initiated by the director or writer), and then, having gathered the work, spend a few weeks pooling their resources, improvising and looking for ways of theatricalizing the material. Next came a period during which the writer would work alone, taking from the research whatever the writer found most compelling. At an agreed-upon date, a rehearsal script would be delivered, and for the next few weeks, the work would be rehearsed and revised simultaneously until the production was ready.

In the case of *Our Country's Good*, the concept for the play began with Thomas Keneally's exciting novel, *The Playmaker*, about the first theatrical production in Australia, a performance of George Farquhar's *The Recruiting Officer* (1706), which was performed by the first group of convicts in the penal colony in 1789. Keneally (1935–) had made extensive use of historical documents to build the world of his novel, including the diaries of Ralph Clark, a young lieutenant who often recorded his troubling dreams. Only volumes one and three of Clark's diaries have survived; as it happens, the period in which the play was produced would have been covered by the lost second volume. When Keneally decided to take poetic licence and make Ralph the director of the play (the actual director is unknown), the novel began to take form.

Max Stafford-Clark read *The Playmaker* in the summer of 1987, shortly after it was published, and he quickly developed the notion of mounting a dual production, in which a single cast of actors would appear in both Farquhar's *The Recruiting Officer* and an adaptation of Keneally's novel. In January 1988, Stafford-Clark approached Timberlake Wertenbaker, a playwright whose work he knew from his time as Artistic Director of the Royal Court Theatre, to write the adaptation. Wertenbaker was chosen in part because her then most recent play, *The Grace of Mary Traverse* (1985), had successfully managed to be contemporary in its relevance while evoking a compelling image of eighteenth-century London.

Stafford-Clark describes the ensuing rehearsal period in his entertaining and informative book, *Letters to George: The Account of a Rehearsal* (1989). First the entire company read Keneally's novel and *The Fatal Shore* (1986) by Robert Hughes—a brilliant history of the founding of Australia and the first penal colony—and individually read a good number of other books about the period. Then began the improvisations. For example, in one series of exercises, Stafford-Clark assigned the members of his cast playing cards at random, and, based on the colour of the card, required them to assume a position in a debate about the worth of theatre in the new colony, with the intensity of their commitment to their position determined by the number on the card. Thus, a black ten was passionately opposed to the production, a red two very mildly in favour of it, and so on. This work became the basis of Wertenbaker's scene, "The Authorities Discuss the Merits of the Theatre"—which has no direct equivalent in Keneally's novel.

Indeed, that scene is only one of many differences between Keneally's novel and Wertenbaker's play, which is finally less a direct adaptation of the novel than a new work inspired by it. Wertenbaker and Stafford-Clark's decision to take maximum licence in creating a play out of Keneally's story seems to have been a good one, in that it allowed the creation of many of the finest features of *Our Country's Good* as a drama, such as the examination of role-playing on and off the stage, the demonstration of the power of imagination and spoken language to convince listeners, and the thematic use of double-casting to undermine essentialist notions of inherited criminal natures. Imagine, for instance, the effect in the original production of the scene in which Campbell, played by Jim Broadbent, went offstage to flog Arscott, also played by Jim Broadbent; or when Jude Akuwudike, a black actor who had appeared as the Aborigine in the first scene, performed the role of Tench, the racist officer who dismisses the "savages"; or when Lesley Sharp, who played Mary Brenham, opined in the role of Reverend Johnson that "actresses are not famed for their morals."

But perhaps the most powerful effect of *Our Country's Good* is the profound impression it makes upon audiences of the fundamental humanitarian value of the theatre. Through their work on *The Recruiting Officer*, a well-written, albeit very light comedy, we see the convicts discover a sense of dignity. Those who drifted into a life of crime, and hence into imprisonment because it seemed that life offered no other possibilities, find a world of liberty in the imaginative work of inhabiting another role. The collaborative effort required by the production instils a sense of community in them by according an essential value to their voices and efforts, and plants the seeds of hope for a new society built upon generous co-operation and creative exchange of ideas.

Lael Louisiana Timberlake Wertenbaker (that unusual third given name being an old family surname) was born in 1951 in the United States, and was raised there, in Canada, and in France. Her father, Charles Wertenbaker, was a foreign correspondent for *Time* magazine, and her mother, Lael Tucker Wertenbaker, was an author who created a minor sensation with her book *Death of a Man* (1958), about her decision to help her terminally ill husband, Timberlake's father, commit suicide in 1955. The book was made into a play, *A Gift of Time* by Garson Kanin, in which Henry Fonda and Olivia de Havilland played Timberlake's parents on Broadway. The character of Timberlake herself, who was about four years old at the time of her father's death, is a small role in the play.

Timberlake Wertenbaker's next important connection with theatre came while she was teaching English in Greece and wrote a number of plays for children. After moving to England, she began to write for the fringe theatres in London. Her first works, *The Third* (1980), *Case to Answer*

(1980) and *New Anatomies* (1981), were well-regarded minor successes. But after her next play, *Abel's Sister*, played in the smaller Royal Court Theatre space in 1983, she was invited to become playwright-in-residence for the next Royal Court season, during which time she produced *The Grace of Mary Traverse* (1985), for which she won the *Plays and Players* award for the Most Promising New Playwright of 1985. Since then, she has written many plays and translations, including *Our Country's Good* (1988), which won the Laurence Olivier Play of the Year Award and the *Evening Standard* Play of the Year Award. *Our Country's Good* was followed by *The Love of a Nightingale* (1989), a dramatization of the tragic Procne and Philomele myth found in Ovid, about the rape and silencing of a young woman by her brother-in-law, the King of Thrace. In *Three Birds Alighting on a Field* (1991), Wertenbaker forayed into the world of galleries and art collectors, examining the relationship between artistic and commercial values. *The Break of Day* (1995) is a play about three women and their partners examining the choices they've made in life as they face middle age and the new millennium. *After Darwin* (1998) is set in two times. In part, it is a dramatization of the tensions between the inventor of the theory of evolution, nineteenth-century naturalist Charles Darwin, and Captain Robert FitzRoy, the devoutly Christian naval officer on whose ship, *The Beagle*, Darwin was making his paramount voyage of discovery, but it also portrays the lives of a company of actors who are performing this dramatization and who find their sense of these historical tensions disrupting their relationships. Wertenbaker's numerous translations include three plays by Marivaux—*False Admissions*, *Successful Strategies* and *La Dispute*; Anouilh's *Leocadia*; Maeterlink's *Pelleas and Melisande*; Arane Mnouchkine's adaptation of Klaus Mann's *Mephisto*; Sophocles' *Theban Plays*; and Euripides' *Hecuba*.

Thomas Keneally is an Australian writer based in Sydney who is best known for his novels *The Chant of Jimmie Blacksmith* (1972), *Gossip from the Forest* (1975), *Confederates* (1979), *The Playmaker* (1987), a book on Irish history called *The Great Shame* (1998), and, most of all, the novel *Schindler's List* (1982), which won the Booker Prize and was made into an Oscar-winning movie by Steven Spielberg.

[C.S.W.]

TIMBERLAKE WERTENBAKER

Our Country's Good

based on the novel *The Playmaker* by Thomas Keneally

CHARACTERS:
CAPTAIN ARTHUR PHILLIP, RN
  (*Governor-in-Chief of New South Wales*)
MAJOR ROBBIE ROSS, RM
CAPTAIN DAVID COLLINS, RM
  (*Advocate General*)
CAPTAIN WATKIN TENCH, RM
CAPTAIN JEMMY CAMPBELL, RM
REVEREND JOHNSON
LIEUTENANT GEORGE JOHNSTON, RM
LIEUTENANT WILL DAWES, RM
SECOND LIEUTENANT RALPH CLARK, RM
SECOND LIEUTENANT WILLIAM FADDY, RM
MIDSHIPMAN HARRY BREWER, RN
  (*Provost Marshal*)
AN ABORIGINAL AUSTRALIAN
JOHN ARSCOTT
BLACK CAESAR
KETCH FREEMAN
ROBERT SIDEWAY
JOHN WISEHAMMER
MARY BRENHAM
DABBY BRYANT
LIZ MORDEN
DUCKLING SMITH
MEG LONG

The play takes place in Sydney, Australia in 1788-89.

ACT 1

SCENE 1

THE VOYAGE OUT

The hold of a convict ship bound for Australia, 1787. The convicts huddle together in the semi-darkness. On deck, the convict Robert Sideway is being flogged. Second Lieutenant Ralph Clark counts the lashes in a barely audible, slow and monotonous voice.

RALPH CLARK. Forty-four, forty-five, forty-six, forty-seven, forty-eight, forty-nine, fifty.

Sideway is untied and dumped with the rest of the convicts. He collapses. No one moves. A short silence.

JOHN WISEHAMMER. At night? The sea cracks against the ship. Fear whispers, screams, falls silent, hushed. Spewed from our country, forgotten, bound to the dark edge of the earth, at night what is there to do but seek English cunt, warm, moist, soft, oh the comfort, the comfort of the lick, the thrust into the nooks, the crannies of the crooks of England. Alone, frightened, nameless in this stinking hole of hell, take me, take me inside you, whoever you are. Take me, my comfort and we'll remember England together. 10

JOHN ARSCOTT. Hunger. Funny. Doesn't start in the stomach, but in the mind. A picture flits in and out of a corner. Something you've eaten long ago. Roast beef with salt and grated horseradish. 15

MARY. I don't know why I did it. Love, I suppose.

SCENE 2

A LONE ABORIGINAL AUSTRALIAN DESCRIBES
THE ARRIVAL OF THE FIRST CONVICT FLEET IN
BOTANY BAY ON JANUARY 20, 1788[1]

THE ABORIGINE. A giant canoe drifts onto the sea,
clouds billowing from upright oars. This is a dream
which has lost its way. Best to leave it alone.

SCENE 3

PUNISHMENT

*Sydney Cove. Governor Arthur Phillip, Judge David
Collins, Captain Watkin Tench, Midshipman Harry
Brewer. The men are shooting birds.*

PHILLIP. Was it necessary to cross fifteen thousand
miles of ocean to erect another Tyburn?[2]

TENCH. I should think it would make the convicts
feel at home.

COLLINS. This land is under English law. The court
found them guilty and sentenced them accordingly. There: a bald-eyed corella.[3]

PHILLIP. But hanging?

COLLINS. Only the three who were found guilty of
stealing from the colony's stores. And that, over
there on the Eucalyptus, is a flock of "cacatua
galerita"—the sulphur-crested cockatoo. You have
been made Governor-in-Chief of a paradise of
birds, Arthur.[4]

PHILLIP. And I hope not of a human hell, Davey.
Don't shoot yet, Watkin, let's observe them. Could
we not be more humane?

TENCH. Justice and humaneness have never gone
hand in hand. The law is not a sentimental
comedy.

PHILLIP. I am not suggesting they go without
punishment. It is the spectacle of hanging I object
to. The convicts will feel nothing has changed and
will go back to their old ways.

TENCH. The convicts never left their old ways,
Governor, nor do they intend to.

PHILLIP. Three months is not long enough to decide
that. You're speaking too loud, Watkin.

COLLINS. I commend your endeavour to oppose the
baneful influence of vice with the harmonizing arts
of civilization, Governor, but I suspect your edifice
will collapse without the mortar of fear.

PHILLIP. Have these men lost all fear of being
flogged?

COLLINS. John Arscott has already been sentenced
to 150 lashes for assault.

TENCH. The shoulder-blades are exposed at about
100 lashes and I would say that somewhere
between 250 and 500 lashes you are probably
condemning a man to death anyway.

COLLINS. With the disadvantage that the death is
slow, unobserved and cannot serve as a sharp
example.

PHILLIP. Harry?

HARRY. The convicts laugh at hangings, Sir. They
watch them all the time.

TENCH. It's their favourite form of entertainment,
I should say.

PHILLIP. Perhaps because they've never been offered
anything else.

TENCH. Perhaps we should build an opera house for
the convicts.[5]

PHILLIP. We learned to love such things because they
were offered to us when we were children or young

---

1   Botany Bay] The explorer Captain Cook had named and
recorded his landing at Botany Bay in 1770, but when
the first transports of convicts arrived eighteen years later
to found the penal colony, Botany Bay turned out to be a
poor landing place for ships and to have no fresh water.
Hence, the settlement was relocated up the coast to Sydney Cove, although in Britain, it continued to be known
familiarly as "Botany Bay" for many years afterward.

2   Tyburn] a place of execution. The Tyburn is a stream in
London flowing into the Thames, but the name is associated with the Middlesex Gallows, a public gibbet that
stood near the stream in the corner of Hyde Park until
1783.

3   bald-eyed corella] a type of parrot.

4   Governor-in-Chief] Captain Arthur Phillip of the Royal
Navy (1738–1814) served as the first Governor of New

South Wales (then the eastern half of the continent of
Australia, which had not yet been named) from January
1788 to December 1792.

5   opera house] Sydney is, of course, now home to one of
the world's great opera houses.

men. Surely no one is born naturally cultured? I'll have the gun now. 55

COLLINS. We don't even have any books here, apart from the odd play and a few Bibles. And most of the convicts can't read, so let us return to the matter in hand, which is the punishment of the 60 convicts, not their education.

PHILLIP. Who are the condemned men, Harry?

HARRY. Thomas Barrett, age 17. Transported seven years for stealing one ewe sheep.

PHILLIP. Seventeen! 65

TENCH. It does seem to prove that the criminal tendency is innate.

PHILLIP. It proves nothing.

HARRY. James Freeman, age 25, Irish, transported fourteen years for assault on a sailor at Shadwell 70 Dock.

COLLINS. I'm surprised he wasn't hanged in England.

HARRY. Handy Baker, marine and the thieves' ringleader.

COLLINS. He pleaded that it was wrong to put the 75 convicts and the marines on the same rations and that he could not work on so little food. He almost swayed us.

TENCH. I do think that was an unfortunate decision. My men are in a ferment of discontent. 80

COLLINS. Our Governor-in-Chief would say it is justice, Tench, and so it is. It is also justice to hang these men.

TENCH. The sooner the better, I believe. There is much excitement in the colony about the hang- 85 ings. It's their theatre, Governor, you cannot change that.

PHILLIP. I would prefer them to see real plays: fine language, sentiment.

TENCH. No doubt Garrick would relish the prospect 90 of eight months at sea for the pleasure of entertaining a group of criminals and the odd savage.

PHILLIP. I never liked Garrick, I always preferred Macklin. 95

COLLINS. I'm a Kemble man myself. We will need a hangman.[6]

PHILLIP. Harry, you will have to organise the hanging and eventually find someone who agrees to that hideous office. 100

Phillip shoots.

COLLINS. Shot.[7]

TENCH. Shot.

HARRY. Shot, Sir.

COLLINS. It is my belief the hangings should take place tomorrow. The quick execution of justice for 105 the good of the colony, Governor.

PHILLIP. The good of the colony? Oh, look! We've frightened a kangaroo.

They look.

ALL. Ah!

HARRY. There is also Dorothy Handland, 82, who 110 stole a biscuit from Robert Sideway.

PHILLIP. Surely we don't have to hang an 82-year-old woman?

COLLINS. That will be unnecessary. She hanged herself this morning. 115

SCENE 4

THE LONELINESS OF MEN

Ralph Clark's tent. It is late at night. Ralph stands, composing and speaking his diary.

RALPH. Dreamt, my beloved Alicia, that I was walking with you and that you was in your riding-habit—oh my dear woman when shall I be able to hear from you—

All the officers dined with the Governor—I 5 never heard of any one single person having so great a power vested in him as Captain Phillip has by his commission as Governor-in Chief of New

---

6 Garrick, Macklin, Kemble] David Garrick (1717–1779), widely regarded as one of the greatest actors in English history, was actor-manager at the Drury Lane Theatre from 1747; Charles Macklin (1699–1797), an actor-playwright with a violent temper, was especially known for his moving performance as Shylock; John Philip Kemble (1757–1823), a more formal and artificial actor, was known for his declamatory performances of tragedy with his sister, Sarah Siddons.

7 Shot] common abbreviated version of "good shot."

South Wales—dined on a cold collation but the Mutton which had been killed yesterday morning was full of maggots—nothing will keep 24 hours in this dismal country I find— 10

Went out shooting after breakfast—I only shot one cockatoo—they are the most beautiful birds—

Major Ross ordered one of the Corporals to flog 15 with a rope Elizabeth Morden for being impertinent to Captain Campbell—the Corporal did not play with her but laid it home which I was very glad to see—she has long been fishing for it—

On Sunday as usual, kissed your beloved image 20 a thousand times—was very much frightened by the lightning as it broke very near my tent—several of the convicts have run away.

He goes to his table and writes in his journal.

If I'm not made 1st Lieutenant soon …

Harry Brewer has come in.

RALPH. Harry— 25
HARRY. I saw the light in your tent—
RALPH. I was writing my journal.

Silence.

Is there any trouble?
HARRY. No. (*Pause.*) I just came.

Talk, you know. If I wrote a journal about my life 30 it would fill volumes. Volumes. My travels with the Captain—His Excellency now, no less, Governor-in-Chief, power to raise armies, build cities—I still call him plain Captain Phillip. He likes it from me. The war in America and before that, Ralph, my life 35 in London. That would fill a volume on its own. Not what you would call a good life.

Pause.

Sometimes I look at the convicts and I think, one of those could be you, Harry Brewer, if you hadn't joined the navy when you did. The officers may 40 look down on me now, but what if they found out that I used to be an embezzler?
RALPH. Harry, you should keep these things to yourself.
HARRY. You're right, Ralph. 45

Pause.

I think the Captain suspects, but he's a good man and he looks for different things in a man—
RALPH. Like what?
HARRY. Hard to say. He likes to see something unusual. Ralph, I saw Handy Baker last night. 50
RALPH. You hanged him a month ago, Harry.
HARRY. He had a rope—Ralph, he's come back.
RALPH. It was a dream. Sometimes I think my dreams are real—but they're not.
HARRY. We used to hear you on the ship, Ralph, 55 calling for your Betsey Alicia.
RALPH. Don't speak her name on this iniquitous shore!
HARRY. Duckling's gone silent on me again. I know it's because of Handy Baker. I saw him as well as I 60 see you. Duckling wants me, he said, even if you've hanged me. At least your poker's danced its last shindy, I said. At least it's young and straight, he said, she likes that. I went for him but he was gone. But he's going to come back, I know it. I didn't 65 want to hang him, Ralph, I didn't.
RALPH. He did steal that food from the stores.

Pause.

I voted with the rest of the court those men should be hanged, I didn't know His Excellency would be against it. 70
HARRY. Duckling says she never feels anything. How do I know she didn't feel something when she was with him? She thinks I hanged him to get rid of him, but I didn't, Ralph.

Pause.

Do you know I saved her life? She was sentenced 75 to be hanged at Newgate for stealing two candlesticks but I got her name put on the transport lists.[8] But when I remind her of that she says she wouldn't have cared. Eighteen years old, and she didn't care if she was turned off. 80

Pause.

These women are sold before they're ten. The Captain says we should treat them with kindness.

---

8 Newgate] the most famous of London's prisons.

RALPH. How can you treat such women with kindness? Why does he think that?

HARRY. Not all the officers find them disgusting, Ralph—haven't you ever been tempted? 85

RALPH. Never! (*Pause.*) His Excellency never seems to notice me.

Pause.

He finds time for Davey Collins, Lieutenant Dawes. 90

HARRY. That's because Captain Collins is going to write about the customs of the Indians here—and Lieutenant Dawes is recording the stars.

RALPH. I could write about the Indians.

HARRY. He did suggest to Captain Tench that we do 95 something to educate the convicts, put on a play or something, but Captain Tench just laughed. He doesn't like Captain Tench.

RALPH. A play? Who would act in a play?

HARRY. The convicts of course. He is thinking of 100 talking to Lieutenant Johnston, but I think Lieutenant Johnston wants to study the plants.

RALPH. I read *The Tragedy of Lady Jane Grey* on the ship.[9] It is such a moving and uplifting play. But how could a whore play Lady Jane? 105

HARRY. Some of those women are good women, Ralph, I believe my Duckling is good. It's not her fault—if only she would look at me, once, react. Who wants to fuck a corpse!

Silence.

I'm sorry. I didn't mean to shock you, Ralph, I have 110 shocked you, haven't I? I'll go.

RALPH. Is His Excellency serious about putting on a play?

HARRY. When the Captain decides something, Ralph. 115

RALPH. If I went to him—no. It would be better if you did, Harry, you could tell His Excellency how much I like the theatre.

HARRY. I didn't know that Ralph, I'll tell him.

RALPH. Duckling could be in it, if you wanted. 120

HARRY. I wouldn't want her to be looked at by all the men.

RALPH. If His Excellency doesn't like *Lady Jane* we could find something else.

Pause.

A comedy perhaps … 125

HARRY. I'll speak to him, Ralph. I like you.

Pause.

It's good to talk …

Pause.

You don't think I killed him then?

RALPH. Who?

HARRY. Handy Baker. 130

RALPH. No, Harry. You did not kill Handy Baker.

HARRY. Thank you, Ralph.

RALPH. Harry, you won't forget to talk to His Excellency about the play?

SCENE 5

AN AUDITION

Ralph Clark, Meg Long. Meg Long is very old and very smelly. She hovers over Ralph.

MEG. We heard you was looking for some women, Lieutenant. Here I am.

RALPH. I've asked to see some women to play certain parts in a play.

MEG. I can play, Lieutenant, I can play with any part 5 you like. There ain't nothing puts Meg off. That's how I got my name: Shitty Meg.

RALPH. The play has four particular parts for young women.

MEG. You don't want a young woman for your 10 peculiar, Lieutenant, they don't know nothing. Shut your eyes and I'll play you as tight as a virgin.

RALPH. You don't understand, Long. Here's the play. It's called *The Recruiting Officer*.[10]

---

9 *The Tragedy of Lady Jane Grey*] a sentimental piece about the 15-year-old whose reign as Queen of England lasted only nine days in 1553, written by Nicholas Rowe in 1715.

---

10 *The Recruiting Officer*] the 1706 comedy by George Farquhar (1678–1707), which became one of the most popular plays of the eighteenth century.

MEG. Oh, I can do that too.   15
RALPH. What?
MEG. Recruiting. Anybody you like. (*She whispers.*)
You want women: you ask Meg. Who do you
want?
RALPH. I want to try some out.   20
MEG. Good idea, Lieutenant, good idea. Ha! Ha!
Ha!
RALPH. Now if you don't mind—

Meg doesn't move.

Long!
MEG. (*frightened but still holding her ground.*) We   25
thought you was a madge cull.
RALPH. What?
MEG. You know, a fluter, a mollie. (*Impatiently.*) A
prissy cove, a girl![11] You having no she-lag on the
ship.[12] Nor here, neither. On the ship maybe you   30
was seasick. But all these months here. And now
we hear how you want a lot of women, all at once.
Well, I'm glad to hear that, Lieutenant, I am. You
let me know when you want Meg, old Shitty Meg.

*She goes off quickly and Robert Sideway comes straight
on.*

SIDEWAY. Ah, Mr. Clark.   35

He does a flourish.

I am calling you Mr. Clark as one calls Mr. Garrick
Mr. Garrick. We have not had the pleasure of
meeting before.
RALPH. I've seen you on the ship.
SIDEWAY. Different circumstances, Mr. Clark, best   40
forgotten. I was once a gentleman. My fortune has
turned. The wheel … You are doing a play, I hear,
ah, Drury Lane, Mr. Garrick, the lovely Peg
Woffington.[13] (*Conspiratorially.*) He was so cruel
to her. She was so pale—   45

RALPH. You say you were a gentleman, Sideway?
SIDEWAY. Top of my profession, Mr. Clark,
pickpocket, born and bred in Bermondsey.[14] Do
you know London, Sir, don't you miss it? In these
my darkest hours, I remember my happy days in   50
that great city. London Bridge at dawn—hand on
cold iron for good luck. Down Cheapside with the
market traders—never refuse a mince pie.[15] Into
St. Paul's churchyard—I do love a good church—
and begin work in Bond Street.[16] There, I've   55
spotted her, rich, plump, not of the best class,
stands in front of the shop, plucking up courage,
I pluck her. Time for coffee until five o'clock and
the pinnacle, the glory of the day: Drury Lane. The
coaches, the actors scuttling, the gentlemen   60
watching, the ladies tittering, the perfumes, the
clothes, the handkerchiefs.

*He hands Ralph the handkerchief he has just stolen
from him.*

Here, Mr. Clark, you see the skill. Ah, Mr. Clark,
I beg you, I entreat you, to let me perform on your
stage, to let me feel once again the thrill of a play   65
about to begin. Ah, I see ladies approaching: our
future Woffingtons, Siddons.[17]

*Dabby Bryant comes on, with a shrinking Mary
Brenham in tow. Sideway bows.*

Ladies.

---

[11] madge cull, fluter, mollie, prissy cove, girl] all slang for
homosexual.

[12] she-lag] (slang) female convict.

[13] Drury Lane] the most famous theatre in London; Peg
Woffington] (1714–1760), a charismatic actress, who was
for several years Garrick's lover and leading lady. She was
best known for "breeches parts" (roles in which the hero-

ine pretends to be a man), including an acclaimed Silvia
in *The Recruiting Officer* at Drury Lane. The "cruel" comment is more likely meant to allude to Garrick's performance as Hamlet to her Ophelia than to their offstage lives,
in which Woffington was allegedly unkind to Garrick.
In fact, however, it would have been virtually impossible for the real Sideway, who was born in 1759, to have
seen Peg Woffington at all: poor health forced her to retire from the stage in 1757, and she died three years later.

[14] Bermondsey] an area in the docklands, southeast of London Bridge.

[15] Cheapside] a major street in London.

[16] St. Paul's churchyard] the streets just outside St. Paul's
Cathedral; Bond Street] a fashionable shopping district
in London.

[17] Siddons] Sarah Siddons (1755–1831), the most famous
leading lady at Drury Lane from 1782 on.

I shall await your word of command, Mr. Clark, I
shall be in the wings. 70

Sideway scuttles off.

DABBY. You asked to see Mary Brenham, Lieutenant.
Here she is.
RALPH. Yes—the Governor has asked me to put on
a play. (*To Mary.*) You know what a play is?
DABBY. I've seen lots of plays, Lieutenant, so has 75
Mary.
RALPH. Have you, Brenham?
MARY. (*inaudibly.*) Yes.
RALPH. Can you remember which plays you've seen?
MARY. (*inaudibly.*) No. 80
DABBY. I can't remember what they were called, but
I always knew when they were going to end badly.
I knew right from the beginning. How does this
one end, Lieutenant?
RALPH. It ends happily. It's called *The Recruiting* 85
Officer.
DABBY. Mary wants to be in your play, Lieutenant,
and so do I.
RALPH. Do you think you have a talent for acting,
Brenham? 90
DABBY. Of course she does, and so do I. I want to
play Mary's friend.
RALPH. Do you know *The Recruiting Officer*, Bryant?
DABBY. No, but in all those plays, there's always a
friend. That's because a girl has to talk to someone 95
and she talks to her friend. So I'll be Mary's friend.
RALPH. Silvia—that's the part I want to try Brenham
for—doesn't have a friend. She has a cousin. But
they don't like each other.
DABBY. Oh. Mary doesn't always like me. 100
RALPH. The Reverend Johnson told me you can read
and write, Brenham?
DABBY. She went to school until she was ten. She
used to read to us on the ship. We loved it. It put
us to sleep. 105
RALPH. Shall we try reading some of the play?

*Ralph hands her the book. Mary reads silently, moving
her lips.*

I mean read it aloud. As you did on the ship. I'll help
you, I'll read Justice Balance. That's your father.
DABBY. Doesn't she have a sweetheart?

RALPH. Yes, but this scene is with her father. 110
DABBY. What's the name of her lover?
RALPH. Captain Plume.
DABBY. A Captain! Mary!
RALPH. Start here, Brenham.

Mary begins to read.

MARY. "Whilst there is life there is hope, Sir." 115
DABBY. Oh, I like that, Lieutenant. This is a good
play, I can tell.
RALPH. Shht. She hasn't finished. Start again,
Brenham, that's good.
MARY. "Whilst there is life there is hope, Sir; perhaps 120
my brother may recover."
RALPH. That's excellent, Brenham, very fluent. You
could read a little louder. Now I'll read.
"We have but little reason to expect it. Poor Owen!
But the decree is just; I was pleased with the death 125
of my father, because he left me an estate, and now
I'm punished with the loss of an heir to inherit
mine."

Pause. He laughs a little.

This is a comedy. They don't really mean it. It's to
make people laugh. "The death of your brother 130
makes you sole heiress to my estate, which you
know is about twelve hundred pounds a year."
DABBY. Twelve hundred pounds! It must be a
comedy.
MARY. "My desire of being punctual in my obedience 135
requires that you would be plain in your com-
mands, Sir."
DABBY. Well said, Mary, well said.
RALPH. I think that's enough. You read very well,
Brenham. Would you also be able to copy the play? 140
We have only two copies.
DABBY. Course she will. Where do I come in,
Lieutenant? The cousin.
RALPH. Can you read, Bryant?
DABBY. Not those marks in the books, Lieutenant, 145
but I can read other things. I read dreams very
well, Lieutenant. Very well.
RALPH. I don't think you're right for Melinda. I'm
thinking of someone else. And if you can't read …
DABBY. Mary will read me the lines, Lieutenant. 150
RALPH. There's Rose …

DABBY. Rose. I like the name. I'll be Rose. Who is she?

RALPH. She's a country girl …

DABBY. I grew up in Devon, Lieutenant.[18] I'm perfect for Rose. What does she do?   155

RALPH. She—well, it's complicated. She falls in love with Silvia.

Mary begins to giggle but tries to hold it back.

But it's because she thinks Silvia's a man. And she—they—she sleeps with her. Rose. With Silvia. Euh. Silvia too. With Rose. But nothing happens.   160

DABBY. It doesn't? Nothing?

Dabby bursts out laughing.

RALPH. Because Silvia is pretending to be a man, but of course she can't—

DABBY. Play the flute? Ha! She's not the only one around here. I'll do Rose.   165

RALPH. I would like to hear you.

DABBY. I don't know my lines yet, Lieutenant. When I know my lines, you may hear me do them. Come on, Mary—   170

RALPH. I didn't say you could—I'm not certain you're the right—Bryant, I'm not certain I want you in the play.

DABBY. Yes you do, Lieutenant. Mary will read me the lines and I, Lieutenant, will read you your dreams.   175

There's a guffaw. It's Liz Morden.

RALPH. Ah. Here's your cousin.

There is a silence. Mary shrinks away. Dabby and Liz stare at each other, each holding her ground, each ready to pounce.

Melinda. Sylvia's cousin.

DABBY. You can't have her in the play, Lieutenant.

RALPH. Why not?   180

DABBY. You don't have to be able to read the future to know that Liz Morden is going to be hanged.

Liz looks briefly at Dabby, as if to strike, then changes her mind.

---

18 Devon] a county in the southwest of England.

LIZ. I understand you want me in your play, Lieutenant. Is that it?

She snatches the book from Ralph and strides off.

I'll look at it and let you know.   185

SCENE 6

THE AUTHORITIES DISCUSS
THE MERITS OF THE THEATRE

Governor Arthur Phillip, Major Robbie Ross, Judge David Collins, Captain Watkin Tench, Captain Jemmy Campbell, Reverend Johnson, Lieutenant George Johnston, Lieutenant Will Dawes, Second Lieutenant Ralph Clark, Second Lieutenant William Faddy.

It is late at night, the men have been drinking, tempers are high. They interrupt each other, overlap, make jokes under and over the conversation but all engage in it with the passion for discourse and thought of eighteenth-century men.

ROSS. A play! A f—

REVD. JOHNSON. Mmhm.

ROSS. A frippery frittering play!

CAMPBELL. Ahee, aeh, here?[19]

RALPH. (*timidly.*) To celebrate the King's birthday, on June the 4th.   5

ROSS. If a frigating ship doesn't appear soon, we'll all be struck with stricturing starvation—and you—you—a play!

COLLINS. Not putting on the play won't bring us a supply ship, Robbie.   10

ROSS. And you say you want those contumelious convicts to act in this play. The convicts!

CAMPBELL. Eh, kev, weh, discipline's bad. Very bad.

RALPH. The play has several parts for women. We have no other women here.   15

COLLINS. Your wife excepted, Reverend.

REVD. JOHNSON. My wife abhors anything of that nature. After all, actresses are not famed for their morals.   20

COLLINS. Neither are our women convicts.

---

19 Ahee, aeh] Much of Campbell's speech consists of expletives and non-verbal vocatives, which would be delivered on stage in a thick Scottish accent.

REVD. JOHNSON. How can they be when some of our officers set them up as mistresses.

He looks pointedly at Lieutenant George Johnston.

ROSS. Filthy, thieving, lying whores and now we have to watch them flout their flitty wares on the stage! 25

PHILLIP. No one will be forced to watch the play.

DAWES. I believe there's a partial lunar eclipse that night. I shall have to watch that. The sky of this southern hemisphere is full of wonders. Have you looked at the constellations? 30

Short pause.

ROSS. Constellations. Plays! This is a convict colony, the prisoners are here to be punished and we're here to make sure they get punished. Constellations! Jemmy? Constellations!

He turns to Jemmy Campbell for support.

CAMPBELL. Tss, weh, marines, marines: war, phoo, 35 discipline. Eh? Service—His Majesty.

PHILLIP. We are indeed here to supervise the convicts who are already being punished by their long exile. Surely they can also be reformed?

TENCH. We are talking about criminals, often 40 hardened criminals. They have a habit of vice and crime. Many criminals seem to have been born that way. It is in their nature.

PHILLIP. Rousseau would say that we have made them that way, Watkin: "Man is born free, and 45 everywhere he is in chains."[20]

REVD. JOHNSON. But Rousseau was a Frenchman.

ROSS. A Frenchman! What can you expect? We're going to listen to a foraging Frenchman now—

COLLINS. He was Swiss actually. 50

CAMPBELL. Eeh, eyeh, good soldiers, the Swiss.

PHILLIP. Surely you believe man can be redeemed, Reverend?

REVD. JOHNSON. By the grace of God and belief in the true church, yes. But Christ never proposed 55 putting on plays to his disciples. However, he didn't forbid it either. It must depend on the play.

JOHNSTON. He did propose treating sinners, especially women who have sinned, with compassion. Most of the convict women have committed small 60 crimes, a tiny theft—

COLLINS. We know about your compassion, not to say passion, for the women convicts, George.

TENCH. A crime is a crime. You commit a crime or you don't. If you commit a crime, you are a 65 criminal. Surely that is logical? It's like the savages here. A savage is a savage because he behaves in a savage manner. To expect anything else is foolish. They can't even build a proper canoe.[21]

PHILLIP. They can be educated. 70

COLLINS. Actually, they seem happy enough as they are. They do not want to build canoes or houses, nor do they suffer from greed and ambition.

FADDY. (*looking at Ralph.*) Unlike some.

TENCH. Which can't be said of our convicts. But 75 really, I don't see what this has to do with a play. It is at most a passable diversion, an entertainment to wile away the hours of the idle.

CAMPBELL. Ttts, weh, heh, the convicts, bone idle.

DAWES. We're wiling away precious hours now. Put 80 the play on, don't put it on, it won't change the shape of the universe.

RALPH. But it could change the nature of our little society.

FADDY. Second Lieutenant Clark change society! 85

PHILLIP. William!

TENCH. My dear Ralph, a bunch of convicts making fools of themselves, mouthing words written no doubt by some London ass, will hardly change our society. 90

RALPH. George Farquhar was not an ass! And he was from Ireland.

ROSS. An Irishman! I have to sit there and listen to an Irishman!

CAMPBELL. Tss, tt. Irish. Wilde. Wilde.[22] 95

---

20 Rousseau] Jean-Jacques Rousseau (1712–1778), philosopher; the quotation is the opening line of *The Social Contract* (1762).

21 proper canoe] The canoes of the Australian Aborigines were simpler but also more quickly made than their North American counterparts, being made of a single, large, oval piece of eucalyptus bark stitched together at the ends.

22 Wilde] apparently an anachronism; neither Oscar Wilde nor his well-known father, Sir William, was yet born.

REVD. JOHNSON. The play doesn't propagate Catholic doctrine, does it, Ralph?

RALPH. He was also an officer.

FADDY. Crawling for promotion.

RALPH. Of the Grenadiers.[23]

ROSS. Never liked the Grenadiers myself.

CAMPBELL. Ouah, pheuee, grenades, pho. Throw and run. Eh. Backs.[24]

RALPH. The play is called *The Recruiting Officer*.

COLLINS. I saw it in London I believe. Yes. Very funny if I remember. Sergeant Kite. The devious ways he used to serve his Captain …

FADDY. Your part, Ralph.

COLLINS. William, if you can't contribute anything useful to the discussion, keep quiet!

Silence.

REVD. JOHNSON. What is the plot, Ralph?

RALPH. It's about this recruiting officer and his friend, and they are in love with these two young ladies from Shrewsbury and after some difficulties, they marry them.

REVD. JOHNSON. It sanctions Holy Matrimony then?

RALPH. Yes, yes, it does.

REVD. JOHNSON. That wouldn't do the convicts any harm. I'm having such trouble getting them to marry instead of this sordid cohabitation they're so used to.

ROSS. Marriage, plays, why not a ball for the convicts?

CAMPBELL. Euuh. Boxing.

PHILLIP. Some of these men will have finished their sentence in a few years. They will become members of society again, and help create a new society in this colony. Should we not encourage them now to think in a free and responsible manner?

TENCH. I don't see how a comedy about two lovers will do that, Arthur.

PHILLIP. The theatre is an expression of civilisation.

We belong to a great country which has spawned great playwrights: Shakespeare, Marlowe, Jonson, and even in our own time, Sheridan. The convicts will be speaking a refined, literate language and expressing sentiments of a delicacy they are not used to. It will remind them that there is more to life than crime, punishment. And we, this colony of a few hundred will be watching this together, for a few hours we will no longer be despised prisoners and hated gaolers. We will laugh, we may be moved, we may even think a little. Can you suggest something else that will provide such an evening, Watkin?

DAWES. Mapping the stars gives me more enjoyment, personally.

TENCH. I'm not sure it's a good idea having the convicts laugh at officers, Arthur.

CAMPBELL. No. Pheeoh, insubordination, heh, ehh, no discipline.

ROSS. You want this vice-ridden vermin to enjoy themselves?

COLLINS. They would only laugh at Sergeant Kite.

RALPH. Captain Plume is a most attractive, noble fellow.

REVD. JOHNSON. He's not loose, is he Ralph? I hear many of these plays are about rakes and encourage loose morals in women. They do get married? Before, that is, before. And for the right reasons.

RALPH. They marry for love and to secure wealth.

REVD. JOHNSON. That's all right.

TENCH. I would simply say that if you want to build a civilisation there are more important things than a play. If you want to teach the convicts something, teach them to farm, to build houses, teach them a sense of respect for property, teach them thrift so they don't eat a week's rations in one night, but above all, teach them how to work, not how to sit around laughing at a comedy.

PHILLIP. The Greeks believed that it was a citizen's duty to watch a play. It was a kind of work in that it required attention, judgement, patience, all social virtues.

TENCH. And the Greeks were conquered by the more practical Romans, Arthur.

COLLINS. Indeed, the Romans built their bridges, but they also spent many centuries wishing they

---

23 Grenadiers] elite troops nominally trained in the hurling of grenades, though the use of the grenade had declined during the eighteenth century.

24 Backs] another slang term for homosexual, from "man of the back door."

were Greeks. And they, after all, were conquered by barbarians, or by their own corrupt and small spirits.

TENCH. Are you saying Rome would not have fallen if the theatre had been better?

RALPH. (*very loud.*) Why not? (*Everyone looks at him and he continues, fast and nervously.*) In my own small way, in just a few hours, I have seen something change. I asked some of the convict women to read me some lines, these women who behave often no better than animals. And it seemed to me, as one or two—I'm not saying all of them, not at all—but one or two, saying those well-balanced lines of Mr. Farquhar, they seemed to acquire a dignity, they seemed—they seemed to lose some of their corruption. There was one, Mary Brenham, she read so well, perhaps this play will keep her from selling herself to the first marine who offers her bread—

FADDY. (*under his breath.*) She'll sell herself to him, instead.

ROSS. So that's the way the wind blows—

CAMPBELL. Hooh. A tempest. Hooh.

RALPH. (*over them.*) I speak about her, but in a small way this could affect all the convicts and even ourselves, we could forget our worries about the supplies, the hangings and the floggings, and think of ourselves at the theatre, in London with our wives and children, that is, we could, euh—

PHILLIP. Transcend—

RALPH. Transcend the darker, euh—transcend the—

JOHNSTON. Brutal—

RALPH. The brutality—remember our better nature and remember—

COLLINS. England.

RALPH. England.

A moment.

ROSS. Where did the wee Lieutenant learn to speak?

FADDY. He must have had one of his dreams.

TENCH. (*over them.*) You are making claims that cannot be substantiated, Ralph. It's two hours, possibly of amusement, possibly of boredom, and we will lose the labour of the convicts during the time they are learning the play. It's a waste, an unnecessary waste.

REVD. JOHNSON. I'm still concerned about the content.

TENCH. The content of a play is irrelevant.

ROSS. Even if it teaches insubordination, disobedience, revolution?

COLLINS. Since we have agreed it can do no harm, since it might, possibly, do some good, since the only person violently opposed to it is Major Ross for reasons he has not made quite clear, I suggest we allow Ralph to rehearse his play. Does anyone disagree?

ROSS. I—I—

COLLINS. We have taken your disagreement into account, Robbie.

CAMPBELL. Ah, eeh, I—I—(*He stops.*)

COLLINS. Thank you, Captain Campbell. Dawes? Dawes, do come back to earth and honour us with your attention for a moment.

DAWES. What? No? Why not? As long as I don't have to watch it.

COLLINS. Johnston?

JOHNSTON. I'm for it.

COLLINS. Faddy?

FADDY. I'm against it.

COLLINS. Could you tell us why?

FADDY. I don't trust the director.

COLLINS. Tench?

TENCH. Waste of time.

COLLINS. The Reverend, our moral guide, has no objections.

REVD. JOHNSON. Of course I haven't read it.

TENCH. Davey, this is not an objective summing up, this is typical of your high-handed manner—

COLLINS. (*angrily.*) I don't think you're the one to accuse others of a high-handed manner, Watkin.

PHILLIP. Gentlemen, please.

COLLINS. Your Excellency, I believe, is for the play and I myself am convinced it will prove a most interesting experiment. So let us conclude with our good wishes to Ralph for a successful production.

ROSS. I will not accept this. You willy-wally wobbly words—Greeks, Romans, experiment—to get your own way.[25] You don't take anything seriously, but I know this play—this play—order will become

---

25 willy-wally] throw about; wobbly] vague.

disorder. The theatre leads to threatening theory and you, Governor, you have His Majesty's commission to build castles, cities, raise armies, 270 administer a military colony, not fandangle about with a lewdy play!26 I am going to write to the Admiralty about this. (*He goes.*)

PHILLIP. You're out of turn, Robbie.

CAMPBELL. Aah—eeh—a. Confusion. (*He goes.*) 275

DAWES. Why is Robbie so upset? So much fuss over a play.

JOHNSTON. Major Ross will never forgive you, Ralph.

COLLINS. I have summed up the feelings of the 280 assembled company, Arthur, but the last word must be yours.

PHILLIP. The last word will be the play, gentlemen.

SCENE 7

HARRY AND DUCKLING GO ROWING

Harry Brewer, Duckling Smith. Harry is rowing. Duckling is sulking.

HARRY. It's almost beginning to look like a town. Look, Duckling, there's the Captain's house. I can see him in his garden.

Harry waves. Duckling doesn't turn around.

Sydney. He could have found a better name. Mobsbury. Lagtown. Duckling Cove, eh? 5

Harry laughs. Duckling remains morose.

The Captain said it had to be named after the Home Secretary.27 The courthouse looks impressive all in brick. There's Lieutenant Dawes' observatory. Why don't you look, Duckling?

Duckling glances, then turns back.

The trees look more friendly from here. Did you 10 know the Eucalyptus tree can't be found anywhere else in the world? Captain Collins told me that. Isn't that interesting? Lieutenant Clark says the

three orange trees on his island are doing well. It's the turnips he's worried about, he thinks they're 15 going to be stolen and he's too busy with his play to go and have a look. Would you like to see the orange trees, Duckling?

Duckling glowers.

I thought you'd enjoy rowing to Ralph's island. I thought it would remind you of rowing on the 20 Thames. Look how blue the water is. Duckling. Say something. Duckling!

DUCKLING. If I was rowing on the Thames, I'd be free.

HARRY. This isn't Newgate, Duckling. 25

DUCKLING. I wish it was.

HARRY. Duckling!

DUCKLING. At least the gaoler of Newgate left you alone and you could talk to people.

HARRY. I let you talk to the women. 30

DUCKLING. (*with contempt.*) Esther Abrahams, Mary Brenham!

HARRY. They're good women.

DUCKLING. I don't have anything to say to those women, Harry. My friends are in the women's 35 camp—

HARRY. It's not the women you're after in the women's camp, it's the marines who come looking for buttock, I know you, who do you have your eye on now, who, a soldier? Another marine, a 40 Corporal? Who, Duckling, who?

Pause.

You've found someone already, haven't you? Where do you go, on the beach? In my tent, like with Handy Baker, eh? Where, under the trees?

DUCKLING. You know I hate trees, don't be so filthy. 45

HARRY. Filthy, you're filthy, you filthy whore.

Pause.

I'm sorry, Duckling, please. Why can't you?—can't you just be with me? Don't be angry. I'll do anything for you, you know that. What do you want, Duckling? 50

DUCKLING. I don't want to be watched all the time. I wake up in the middle of the night and you're watching me. What do you think I'm going to do

---

26 fandangle] fool; lewdy] corruption of "lewd."

27 Home Secretary] Phillip had named the settlement after the British Home Secretary, Lord Thomas Townshend Sydney.

in my sleep, Harry? Watching, watching, watching. JUST STOP WATCHING ME.   55

HARRY. You want to leave me. All right, go and live in the women's camp, sell yourself to a convict for a biscuit. Leave if you want to. You're filthy, filthy, opening your legs to the first marine—

DUCKLING. Why are you so angry with your   60
Duckling, Harry? Don't you like it when I open my legs wide to you? Cross them over you—the way you like? What will you do when your little Duckling isn't there anymore to touch you with her soft fingertips, Harry, where you like it? First   65
the left nipple and then the right. Your Duckling doesn't want to leave you Harry.

HARRY. Duckling …

DUCKLING. I need freedom sometimes, Harry.

HARRY. You have to earn your freedom with good   70
behaviour.

DUCKLING. Why didn't you let them hang me and take my corpse with you, Harry? You could have kept that in chains. I wish I was dead. At least when you're dead, you're free.   75

Silence.

HARRY. You know Lieutenant Clark's play?

Duckling is silent.

Do you want to be in it?

Duckling laughs.

Dabby Bryant is in it too and Liz Morden. Do you want to be in it? You'd rehearse in the evenings with Lieutenant Clark.   80

DUCKLING. And he can watch over me instead of you.

HARRY. I'm trying to make you happy, Duckling, if you don't want to—

DUCKLING. I'll be in the play.   85

Pause.

How is Lieutenant Clark going to manage Liz Morden?

HARRY. The Captain wanted her to be in it.

DUCKLING. On the ship we used to see who could make Lieutenant Clark blush first. It didn't take   90
long, haha.

HARRY. Duckling, you won't try anything with Lieutenant Clark, will you?

DUCKLING. With that Mollie? No.

HARRY. You're talking to me again. Will you kiss   95
your Harry?

They kiss.

I'll come and watch the rehearsals.

SCENE 8

THE WOMEN LEARN THEIR LINES

Dabby Bryant is sitting on the ground muttering to herself with concentration. She could be counting. Mary Brenham comes on.

MARY. Are you remembering your lines, Dabby?

DABBY. What lines? No. I was remembering Devon. I was on my way back to Bigbury Bay.[28]

MARY. You promised Lieutenant Clark you'd learn your lines.   5

DABBY. I want to go back. I want to see a wall of stone. I want to hear the Atlantic breaking into the estuary. I can bring a boat into any harbour, in any weather. I can do it as well as the Governor.

MARY. Dabby, what about your lines?   10

DABBY. I'm not spending the rest of my life in this flat, brittle burnt-out country. Oh, give me some English rain.

MARY. It rains here.

DABBY. It's not the same. I could recognise English   15
rain anywhere. And Devon rain, Mary, Devon rain is the softest in England. As soft as your breasts, as soft as Lieutenant Clark's dimpled cheeks.

MARY. Dabby, don't!

DABBY. You're wasting time, girl, he's ripe for the   20
plucking. You can always tell with men, they begin to walk sideways. And if you don't—

MARY. Don't start. I listened to you once before.

DABBY. What would you have done without that lanky sailor drooling over you?   25

MARY. I would have been less of a whore.

DABBY. Listen my darling, you're only a virgin once. You can't go to a man and say, I'm a virgin except

---

28 Bigbury Bay] a port on the English Channel.

for this one lover I had. After that, it doesn't matter how many men go through you.

MARY. I'll never wash the sin away.

DABBY. If God didn't want women to be whores he shouldn't have created men who pay for their bodies. While you were with your little sailor, there were women in that stinking pit of a hold who had three men on them at once, men with the pox, men with the flux, men biting like dogs.[29]

MARY. But if you don't agree to it, then you're not a whore, you're a martyr.

DABBY. You have to be a virgin to be a martyr, Mary, and you didn't come on that ship a virgin. "A.H. I love thee to the heart", ha, tattooed way up there—

Dabby begins to lift Mary's skirt to reveal a tattoo high up on the inner thigh. Mary leaps away.

MARY. That was different. That was love.

DABBY. The second difficulty with being a martyr is that you have to be dead to qualify. Well, you didn't die, thanks to me, you had three pounds of beef a week instead of two, two extra ounces of cheese.

MARY. Which you were happy to eat!

DABBY. We women have to look after each other. Let's learn the lines.

MARY. You sold me that first day so you and your husband could eat!

DABBY. Do you want me to learn these lines or not?

MARY. How can I play Silvia? She's brave and strong. She couldn't have done what I've done.

DABBY. She didn't spend eight months and one week on a convict ship. Anyway, you can pretend you're her.

MARY. No. I have to be her.

DABBY. Why?

MARY. Because that's acting.

DABBY. No way I'm being Rose, she's an idiot.

MARY. It's not such a big part, it doesn't matter so much.

DABBY. You didn't tell me that before.

MARY. I hadn't read it carefully. Come on, let's do the scene between Silvia and Rose. (*She reads.*) "I

have rested but indifferently, and I believe my bedfellow was as little pleased; poor Rose! Here she comes"—

DABBY. I could have done something for Rose. Ha! I should play Silvia.

MARY. "Good morrow, my dear, how d'ye this morning?" Now you say: "Just as I was last night, neither better nor worse for you."

Liz Morden comes on.

LIZ. You can't do the play without me. I'm in it! Where's the Lieutenant?

DABBY. She's teaching me some lines.

LIZ. Why aren't you teaching me the lines?

MARY. We're not doing your scenes.

LIZ. Well do them.

DABBY. You can read. You can read your own lines.

LIZ. I don't want to learn them on my own.

Liz thrusts Dabby away and sits by Mary.

I'm waiting.

DABBY. What are you waiting for, Liz Morden, a blind man to buy your wares?

MARY. (*quickly.*) We'll do the first scene between Melinda and Silvia, all right?

LIZ. Yea. The first scene.

Mary gives Liz the book.

MARY. You start.

Liz looks at the book.

You start. "Welcome to town, cousin Silvia"—

LIZ. "Welcome to town, cousin Silvia"—

MARY. Go on—"I envied you"—

LIZ. "I envied you"—You read it first.

MARY. Why?

LIZ. I want to hear how you do it.

MARY. Why?

LIZ. Cause then I can do it different.

MARY. "I envied you your retreat in the country; for Shrewsbury, methinks, and all your heads of shires"—

DABBY. Why don't you read it? You can't read!

LIZ. What?

She lunges at Dabby.

---

[29] pox] syphilis; flux] diarrhea.

MARY. I'll teach you the lines.

DABBY. Are you her friend now, is that it? Mary the holy innocent and thieving bitch—

Liz and Dabby seize each other. Ketch Freeman appears.

KETCH. (*with nervous affability.*) Good morning, ladies. And why aren't you at work instead of at each other's throats?   110

Liz and Dabby turn on him.

LIZ. I wouldn't talk of throats if I was you, Mr. Hangman Ketch Freeman.[30]

DABBY. Crap merchant.[31]

LIZ. Crapping cull. Switcher.   115

MARY. Roper.

KETCH. I was only asking what you were doing, you know, friendly like.

LIZ. Stick to your ropes, my little galler, don't bother the actresses.   120

KETCH. Actresses? You're doing a play?

LIZ. Better than dancing the Paddington frisk in your arms—noser![32]

KETCH. I'll nose on you, Liz, if you're not careful.

LIZ. I'd take a leap in the dark sooner than turn off   125
my own kind. Now take your whirligigs out of our sight, we have lines to learn.[33]

Ketch slinks away as Liz and Dabby spit him off.

DABBY. (*after him.*) Don't hang too many people, Ketch, we need an audience!

---

30 Ketch] not his real name, but slang for hangman, after Jack Ketch, a famous executioner of the seventeenth century.

31 Crap merchant, crapping cull, switcher, roper, galler] all slang for "hangman." "Crap merchant," because bodies involuntarily defecate when hanged; "crapping cull," because a cull is a prostitute's dupe, so a "crapping cull" would be a client who favoured defecation; "switcher," because he "switches" his victims into the afterlife; "roper," for the obvious reason; "galler," because he puts them on the "gallows."

32 Paddington frisk] (slang) the spasms of the hanged (the Middesex gallows at Tyburn were in the parish of Paddington); noser] informer.

33 turn off] execute; whirligigs] testicles.

MARY. "Welcome to town, cousin Silvia." It says you   130
salute.[34]

LIZ. (*giving a military salute.*) "Welcome to town, cousin—Silvia."

SCENE 9

RALPH CLARK TRIES TO KISS HIS DEAR WIFE'S PICTURE

Ralph's tent. Candlelight. Ralph paces.

RALPH. Dreamt my beloved Betsey that I was with you and that I thought I was going to be arrested.

He looks at his watch.

I hope to God that there is nothing the matter with you my tender Alicia or that of our dear boy—   5

He looks at his watch.

My darling tender wife I am reading Proverbs waiting till midnight, the Sabbath, that I might kiss your picture as usual.

He takes his Bible and kneels. Looks at his watch.

The Patrols caught three seamen and a boy in the women's camp.   10

He reads.

"Let thy fountain be blessed: and rejoice with the wife of thy youth."
        Good God what a scene of whoredom is going on there in the women's camp.

He looks at his watch. Gets up. Paces.

Very hot this night.   15
        Captain Shea killed today one of the kangaroos—it is the most curious animal I ever saw.

He looks at his watch.

Almost midnight, my Betsey, the Lord's day—

He reads.

---

34 salute] Some sort of courteous and warm greeting is meant.

"And behold, there met him a woman with the attire of an harlot, and subtle of heart.

...So she caught him, and kissed him with an impudent face."[35]

Felt ill with the toothache my dear wife my God what pain.

Reads.

"So she caught him and kissed him with an impudent face …"

"I have perfumed my bed with myrrh, aloes, cinnamon—"[36]

Sarah McCormick was flogged today for calling the doctor a c—midnight—

This being Sunday took your picture out of its prison and kissed it—God bless you my sweet woman.

He now proceeds to do so. That is, he goes down on his knees and brings the picture to himself. Ketch Freeman comes into the tent. Ralph jumps.

KETCH. Forgive me, Sir, please forgive me, I didn't want to disturb your prayers. I say fifty Hail Marys myself every night, and 200 on the days when— I'll wait outside, Sir.

RALPH. What do you want?

KETCH. I'll wait quietly, Sir, don't mind me.

RALPH. Why aren't you in the camp at this hour?

KETCH. I should be, God forgive me, I should be. But I'm not. I'm here. I have to have a word with you, Sir.

RALPH. Get back to the camp immediately, I'll see you in the morning, Ketch.

KETCH. Don't call me that, Sir, I beg you, don't call me by that name, that's what I came to see you about, Sir.

RALPH. I was about to go to sleep.

KETCH. I understand, Sir, and your soul in peace, I won't take up your time, Sir, I'll be brief.

Pause.

RALPH. Well?

KETCH. Don't you want to finish your prayers? I can be very quiet. I used to watch my mother, may her poor soul rest in peace, I used to watch her say her prayers, every night.

RALPH. Get on with it!

KETCH. When I say my prayers I have a terrible doubt. How can I be sure God is forgiving me? What if he will forgive me, but hasn't forgiven me yet? That's why I don't want to die, Sir. That's why I can't die. Not until I am sure. Are you sure?

RALPH. I'm not a convict: I don't sin.

KETCH. To be sure. Forgive me, Sir. But if we're in God's power, then surely he makes us sin. I was given a guardian angel when I was born, like all good Catholics, why didn't my guardian angel look after me better? But I think he must've stayed in Ireland. I think the devil tempted my mother to London and both our guardian angels stayed behind. Have you ever been to Ireland, Sir? It's a beautiful country. If I'd been an angel I wouldn't have left it either. And when we came within six fields of Westminister, the devils took over. But it's God's judgement I'm frightened of. And the women's. They're so hard. Why is that?

RALPH. Why have you come here?

KETCH. I'm coming to that, Sir.

RALPH. Hurry up, then.

KETCH. I'm speaking as fast as I can, Sir—

RALPH. Ketch—

KETCH. James, Sir, James, Daniel, Patrick, after my three uncles. Good men they were too, didn't go to London. If my mother hadn't brought us to London, may God give peace to her soul and breathe pity into the hearts of hard women— because the docks are in London and if I hadn't worked on the docks on that day, May 23rd, 1785, do you remember it, Sir? Shadwell Dock. If only we hadn't left, then I wouldn't have been there, then nothing would have happened, I wouldn't have become a coal heaver on Shadwell Dock and been there on the 23rd of May when we refused to unload because they were paying us so badly, Sir. I wasn't even near the sailor who got killed. He shouldn't have done the unloading, that was wrong of the sailors, but I didn't kill him, maybe one blow, not to look stupid, you know, just to show I was with the lads, even if I wasn't, but I

35 And behold … impudent face] Proverbs 7:10 and 7:13.
36 I have … cinnamon] Proverbs 7:17.

didn't kill him. And they caught five at random, 100
Sir, and I was among the five, and they found the
cudgel, but I just had that to look good, that's all,
and when they said to me later you can hang or
you can give the names, what was I to do, what
would you have done, Sir? 105

RALPH. I wouldn't have been in that situation,
Freeman.

KETCH. To be sure, forgive me, Sir. I only told on
the ones I saw, I didn't tell anything that wasn't
true, death is a horrible thing, that poor sailor. 110

RALPH. Freeman, I'm going to bed now—

KETCH. I understand, Sir, I understand. And when
it happened again, here! And I had hopes of
making a good life here. It's because I'm so friendly,
see, so I go along, and then I'm the one who gets 115
caught. That theft, I didn't do it, I was just there,
keeping a look out, just to help some friends, you
know. But when they say to you, hang or be
hanged, what do you do? Someone has to do it. I
try to do it well. God had mercy on the whore, 120
the thief, the lame, surely he'll forgive the hang—
it's the women—they're without mercy—not like
you and me, Sir, men. What I wanted to say, Sir,
is that I heard them talking about the play.

Pause.

Some players came into our village once. They 125
were loved like the angels, Lieutenant, like the
angels. And the way the women watched them—
the light of a spring dawn in their eyes.

    Lieutenant—

    I want to be an actor. 130

SCENE 10

JOHN WISEHAMMER AND MARY BRENHAM
EXCHANGE WORDS

Mary is copying The Recruiting Officer *in the
afternoon light. John Wisehammer is carrying bricks
and piling them to one side. He begins to hover over
her.*

MARY. "I would rather counsel than command; I
don't propose this with the authority of a parent,
but as the advice of your friend"—

WISEHAMMER. Friend. That's a good word. Short,
but full of promise. 5

MARY. "That you would take the coach this moment
and go into the country."

WISEHAMMER. Country can mean opposite things.
It renews you with trees and grass, you go rest in
the country, or it crushes you with power: you die 10
for your country, your country doesn't want you,
you're thrown out of your country.

Pause.

I like words.

Pause.

My father cleared the houses of the dead to sell
the old clothes to the poor houses by the Thames. 15
He found a dictionary—Johnson's dictionary—it
was as big as a Bible.[37] It went from A to L. I
started with the A's. Abecedarian: someone who
teaches the alphabet or rudiments of literature.
Abject: a man without hope. 20

MARY. What does indulgent mean?

WISEHAMMER. How is it used?

MARY. (*reads.*) "You have been so careful, so
indulgent to me"—

WISEHAMMER. It means ready to overlook faults. 25

Pause.

You have to be careful with words that begin with
'in'. It can turn everything upside down. Injustice.
Most of that word is taken up with justice, but the
'in' twists it inside out and makes it the ugliest
word in the English language. 30

MARY. Guilty is an uglier word.

WISEHAMMER. Innocent ought to be a beautiful
word, but it isn't, it's full of sorrow. Anguish.

Mary goes back to her copying.

MARY. I don't have much time. We start this in a few
days. 35

---

37 Johnson's dictionary] critic, poet and essayist Samuel
Johnson's *A Dictionary of the English Language*, published
in two volumes in 1755, was the best-written and most
comprehensive English dictionary to have been published to that point.

Wisehammer looks over her shoulder.

I have the biggest part.

WISEHAMMER. You have a beautiful hand.

MARY. There is so much to copy. So many words.

WISEHAMMER. I can write.

MARY. Why don't you tell Lieutenant Clark? He's doing it. 40

WISEHAMMER. No … no … I'm—

MARY. Afraid?

WISEHAMMER. Diffident.

MARY. I'll tell him. Well, I won't. My friend Dabby will. She's— 45

WISEHAMMER. Bold.

Pause.

Shy is not a bad word, it's soft.

MARY. But shame is a hard one.

WISEHAMMER. Words with two L's are the worst. Lonely, loveless. 50

MARY. Love is a good word.

WISEHAMMER. That's because it only has one L. I like words with one L: Luck. Latitudinarian.[38]

Mary laughs.

Laughter. 55

SCENE 11

THE FIRST REHEARSAL

Ralph Clark, Robert Sideway, John Wisehammer, Mary Brenham, Liz Morden, Dabby Bryant, Duckling Smith, Ketch Freeman.

RALPH. Good afternoon, ladies and gentlemen—

DABBY. We're ladies now. Wait till I tell my husband I've become a lady.

MARY. Sshht.

RALPH. It is with pleasure that I welcome you— 5

SIDEWAY. Our pleasure, Mr. Clark, our pleasure.

RALPH. We have many days of hard work ahead of us.

LIZ. Work! I'm not working. I thought we was acting.

---

[38] Latitudinarian] a person with a broad and liberal outlook.

RALPH. Now let me introduce the company— 10

DABBY. We've all met before, Lieutenant, you could say we know each other, you could say we'd know each other in the dark.

SIDEWAY. It's a theatrical custom, the company is formally introduced to each other, Mrs. Bryant. 15

DABBY. Mrs. Bryant? Who's Mrs. Bryant?

SIDEWAY. It's the theatrical form of address, Madam. You may call me Mr. Sideway.

RALPH. If I may proceed—

KETCH. Shhh! You're interrupting the director. 20

DABBY. So we are, Mr. Hangman.

The women all hiss and spit at Ketch.

RALPH. The ladies first: Mary Brenham who is to play Silvia. Liz Morden who is to play Melinda. Duckling Smith who is to play Lucy, Melinda's maid.

DUCKLING. I'm not playing Liz Morden's maid. 25

RALPH. Why not?

DUCKLING. I live with an officer. He wouldn't like it.

DABBY. Just because she lives chained up in that old toss pot's garden.[39]

DUCKLING. Don't you dare talk of my Harry— 30

RALPH. You're not playing Morden's maid, Smith, you're playing Melinda's. And Dabby Bryant, who is to play Rose, a country girl.

DABBY. From Devon.

DUCKLING. (*to Dabby.*) Screw jaws![40] 35

DABBY. (*to Duckling.*) Salt bitch![41]

RALPH. That's the ladies. Now, Captain Plume will be played by Henry Kable.

He looks around.

Who seems to be late. That's odd. I saw him an hour ago and he said he was going to your hut to learn some lines, Wisehammer? 40

Wisehammer is silent.

Sergeant Kite is to be played by John Arscott, who

---

[39] toss pot] (slang) drunkard.

[40] screw jaws] The expression usually means "smart-mouthed," though in this context, the reference may well be to fellatio.

[41] Salt bitch] (salt being another expression for coitus) fucking bitch.

did send a message to say he would be kept at work an extra hour.

DABBY. An hour! You won't see him in an hour! 45

LIZ. (*under her breath.*) You're not the only one with new wrinkles in your arse, Dabby Bryant.[42]

RALPH. Mr. Worthy will be played by Mr. Sideway.

Sideway takes a vast bow.

SIDEWAY. I'm here.

RALPH. Justice Balance by James Freeman. 50

DUCKLING. No way I'm doing a play with a hangman. The words would stick in my throat.

More hisses and spitting. Ketch shrinks.

RALPH. You don't have any scenes with him, Smith. Now if I could finish the introductions. Captain Brazen is to be played by John Wisehammer. 55
    The small parts are still to be cast. Now. We can't do the first scene until John Arscott appears.

DABBY. There won't be a first scene.

RALPH. Bryant, will you be quiet please! The second scene. Wisehammer, you could read Plume. 60

Wisehammer comes forward eagerly.

    No, I'll read Plume myself. So, Act One, Scene Two, Captain Plume and Mr. Worthy.

SIDEWAY. That's me. I'm at your command.

RALPH. The rest of you can watch and wait for your scenes. Perhaps we should begin by reading it. 65

SIDEWAY. No need, Mr. Clark. I know it.

RALPH. Ah, I'm afraid I shall have to read Captain Plume.

SIDEWAY. I know that part too. Would you like me to do both? 70

RALPH. I think it's better if I do it. Shall we begin? Kite, that's John Arscott, has just left—

DABBY. Running.

RALPH. Bryant! I'll read the line before Worthy's entrance: "None at present. 'Tis indeed the picture 75 of Worthy, but the life's departed." Sideway? Where's he gone?

Sideway has scuttled off. He shouts from the wings.

SIDEWAY. I'm preparing my entrance, Mr. Clark, I won't be a minute. Could you read the line again, slowly? 80

RALPH. 'Tis indeed the picture of Worthy, but the life's departed. What, arms-a-cross, Worthy!"

Sideway comes on, walking sideways, arms held up in a grandiose eighteenth-century theatrical pose. He suddenly stops.

SIDEWAY. Ah, yes, I forgot. Arms-a-cross. I shall have to start again.

He goes off again and shouts.

    Could you read the line again louder please? 85

RALPH. "What, arms-a-cross, Worthy!"

Sideway rushes on.

SIDEWAY. My wiper! Someone's buzzed my wiper! There's a wipe drawer in this crew, Mr. Clark.[43]

RALPH. What's the matter?

SIDEWAY. There's a pickpocket in the company. 90

DABBY. Talk of the pot calling the kettle black.

Sideway stalks around the company threateningly.

SIDEWAY. My handkerchief. Who prigged my handkerchief?[44]

RALPH. I'm sure it will turn up, Sideway, let's go on.

SIDEWAY. I can't do my entrance without my handker- 95 chief. (*Furious.*) I've been practising it all night. If I get my mittens on the rum diver I'll—[45]

He lunges at Liz, who fights back viciously. They jump apart each taking threatening poses and Ralph intervenes with speed.

RALPH. Let's assume Worthy has already entered, Sideway. Now, I say: "What arms-a-cross, Worthy! Methinks you should hold 'em open when a friend's 100 so near. I must expel this melancholy spirit."

Sideway has dropped to his knees and is sobbing in a pose of total sorrow.

---

42 new wrinkles in … arse] new information (making one older and wiser).

43 wiper] (slang, as are the next several expressions glossed) handkerchief; wipe drawer] a pickpocket of handkerchiefs.

44 prigged] stole.

45 mittens] hands; rum diver] clever pickpocket.

What are you doing down there, Sideway?

SIDEWAY. I'm being melancholy. I saw Mr. Garrick being melancholy once. That's what he did. Hamlet it was. 105

He stretches his arms to the ground and begins to repeat.

"Oh that this too, too solid flesh would melt. Oh that this too too solid flesh would melt. Oh that this too too—"

RALPH. This is a comedy. It is perhaps a little lighter. Try simply to stand normally and look melancholy. 110 I'll say the line again. (*Sideway is still sobbing.*) The audience won't hear Captain Plume's lines if your sobs are so loud, Sideway.

SIDEWAY. I'm still establishing my melancholy.

RALPH. A comedy needs to move quite fast. In fact, 115 I think we'll cut that line and the two verses that follow and go straight to Worthy greeting Plume.

WISEHAMMER. I like the word melancholy.

SIDEWAY. A greeting. Yes. A greeting looks like this.

He extends his arms high and wide.

"Plume!" Now I'll change to say the next words. 120 "My dear Captain", that's affection isn't it? If I put my hands on my heart, like this. Now, "Welcome." I'm not quite sure how to do "Welcome."

RALPH. I think if you just say the line.

SIDEWAY. Quite. Now. 125

He feels Ralph.

RALPH. Sideway! What are you doing?

SIDEWAY. I'm checking that you're safe and sound returned. That's what the line says: "Safe and sound returned."

RALPH. You don't need to touch him. You can see 130 that!

SIDEWAY. Yes, yes. I'll check his different parts with my eyes. Now, I'll put it together, "Plume! My dear Captain, welcome. Safe and sound returned!"

He does this with appropriate gestures.

RALPH. Sideway—it's a very good attempt. It's very 135 theatrical. But you could try to be a little more— euh—natural.

SIDEWAY. Natural! On the stage! But Mr. Clark!

RALPH. People must—euh—believe you. Garrick after all is admired for his naturalness. 140

SIDEWAY. Of course. I thought I was being Garrick—but never mind. Natural. Quite. You're the director, Mr. Clark.

RALPH. Perhaps you could look at me while you're saying the lines. 145

SIDEWAY. But the audience won't see my face.

RALPH. The lines are said to Captain Plume. Let's move on. Plume says: "I 'scaped safe from Germany," shall we say—America? It will make it more contemporary— 150

WISEHAMMER. You can't change the words of the playwright.

RALPH. Mm, well, "and sound, I hope, from London: you see—I have—"

Black Caesar rushes on.

RALPH. Caesar, we're rehearsing—would you— 155

CAESAR. I see that well, Monsieur Lieutenant. I see it is a piece of theatre, I have seen many pieces of theatre in my beautiful island of Madagascar so I have decided to play in your piece of theatre.

RALPH. There's no part for you. 160

CAESAR. There is always a part for Caesar.

SIDEWAY. All the parts have been taken.

CAESAR. I will play his servant.

He stands next to Sideway.

RALPH. Farquhar hasn't written a servant for Worthy.

DUCKLING. He can have my part. I want to play 165 something else.

CAESAR. There is always a black servant in a play, Monsieur Lieutenant. And Caesar is that servant. So, now I stand here just behind him and I will be his servant. 170

RALPH. There are no lines for it, Caesar.

CAESAR. I speak in French. That makes him a more high up gentleman if he has a French servant, and that is good. Now he gets the lady with the black servant. Very chic. 175

RALPH. I'll think about it. Actually, I would like to rehearse the ladies now. They have been waiting patiently and we don't have much time left. Freeman, would you go and see what's happened to Arscott. Sideway, we'll come back to this scene 180 another time, but that was very good, very good. A little, a little euh, but very good.

Sideway bows out, followed by Caesar.

Now we will rehearse the first scene between Melinda and Silvia. Morden and Brenham, if you would come and stand here. Now the scene is set in Melinda's apartments. Silvia is already there. So, if you stand here, Morden. Brenham, you stand facing her. 185

LIZ. (*very, very fast.*) "Welcome to town cousin Silvia I envied you your retreat in the country for Shrewsbury methinks and all your heads of shires are the most irregular places for living—" 190

RALPH. Euh, Morden—

LIZ. Wait, I haven't finished yet. "Here we have smoke noise scandal affectation and pretension in short everything to give the spleen and nothing to divert it then the air is intolerable—" 195

RALPH. Morden, you know the lines very well.

LIZ. Thank you, Lieutenant Clark.

RALPH. But you might want to try and act them. 200

Pause.

Let's look at the scene.

Liz looks.

You're a rich lady. You're at home. Now a rich lady would stand in a certain way. Try to stand like a rich lady. Try to look at Silvia with a certain assurance.

LIZ. Assurance. 205

WISEHAMMER. Confidence.

RALPH. Like this. You've seen rich ladies, haven't you?

LIZ. I robbed a few.

RALPH. How did they behave?

LIZ. They screamed. 210

RALPH. I mean before you—euh—robbed them.

LIZ. I don't know. I was watching their purses.

RALPH. Have you ever seen a lady in her own house?

LIZ. I used to climb into the big houses when I was a girl, and just stand there, looking. I didn't take anything. I just stood. Like this. 215

RALPH. But if that was your own house, you would think it was normal to live like that.

WISEHAMMER. It's not normal. It's not normal when others have nothing. 220

RALPH. When acting, you have to imagine things. You have to imagine you're someone different. So, now, think of a rich lady and imagine you're her.

Liz begins to masticate.

What are you doing?

LIZ. If I was rich I'd eat myself sick. 225

DABBY. Me too, potatoes.

The convicts speak quickly and over each other.

SIDEWAY. Roast beef and Yorkshire pudding.

CAESAR. Hearts of palm.

WISEHAMMER. Four fried eggs, six fried eggs, eight fried eggs. 230

LIZ. Eels, oysters—

RALPH. Could we get on with the scene, please? Brenham, it's your turn to speak.

MARY. "Oh, Madam, I have heard the town commended for its air." 235

LIZ. "But you don't consider Silvia how long I have lived in't."

RALPH. (*to Liz.*) I believe you would look at her.

LIZ. She didn't look at me.

RALPH. Didn't she? She will now. 240

LIZ. "For I can assure you that to a lady the least nice in her constitution no air can be good above half a year change of air I take to be the most agreeable of any variety in life."

MARY. "But prithee, my dear Melinda, don't put on such an air to me." 245

RALPH. Excellent, Brenham. You could be a little more sharp on the "don't."

MARY. "Don't." (*Mary now tries a few gestures.*) "Your education and mine were just the same, and I remember the time when we never troubled our heads about air, but when the sharp air from the Welsh mountains made our noses drop in a cold morning at the boarding school." 250

RALPH. Good! Good! Morden? 255

LIZ. "Our education cousin was the same but our temperaments had nothing alike."

RALPH. That's a little better, Morden, but you needn't be quite so angry with her. Now go on Brenham. 260

LIZ. I haven't finished my speech!

RALPH. You're right, Morden, please excuse me.

LIZ. (*embarrassed.*) No, no, there's no need for that, Lieutenant. I only meant—I don't have to.

RALPH. Please do. 265

LIZ. "You have the constitution of a horse."

RALPH. Much better, Morden. But you must always remember you're a lady. What can we do to help you? Lucy.

DABBY. That's you, Duckling. 270

RALPH. See that little piece of wood over there? Take it to Melinda. That will be your fan.

DUCKLING. I'm not fetching nothing for Liz.

RALPH. She's not Morden, she's Melinda, your mistress. You're her servant, Lucy. In fact, you 275 should be in this scene. Now take her that fan.

DUCKLING. (*gives the wood to Liz.*) Here.

LIZ. Thank you, Lucy, I do much appreciate your effort.

RALPH. No, you would nod your head. 280

WISEHAMMER. Don't add any words to the play.

RALPH. Now, Lucy, stand behind Morden.

DUCKLING. What do I say?

RALPH. Nothing.

DUCKLING. How will they know I'm here? Why 285 does she get all the lines? Why can't I have some of hers?

RALPH. Brenham, it's your speech.

MARY. "So far as to be troubled with neither spleen, colic, nor vapours—" 290

The convicts slink away and sink down, trying to make themselves invisible as Major Ross, followed by Captain Campbell, come on.

"I need no salt for my stomach, no—"

She sees the officers herself and folds in with the rest of the convicts.

RALPH. Major Ross, Captain Campbell, I'm rehearsing.

ROSS. Rehearsing! Rehearsing!

CAMPBELL. Tssaach. Rehearsing. 295

ROSS. Lieutenant Clark is rehearsing. Lieutenant Clark asked us to give the prisoners two hours so he could rehearse, but what has he done with them? What?

CAMPBELL. Eeeh. Other things, eh. 300

ROSS. Where are the prisoners Kable and Arscott, Lieutenant?

CAMPBELL. Eh?

RALPH. They seem to be late.

ROSS. While you were rehearsing, Arscott and Kable 305 slipped into the woods with three others, so five men have run away and it's all because of your damned play and your so-called thespists.[46] And not only have your thespists run away, they've stolen food from the stores for their renegade 310 escape, that's what your play has done.

RALPH. I don't see what the play—

ROSS. I said it from the beginning. The play will bring down calamity on this colony.

RALPH. I don't see— 315

ROSS. The devil, Lieutenant, always comes through the mind, here, worms its way, idleness and words.

RALPH. Major Ross, I can't agree—

ROSS. Listen to me, my lad, you're a Second Lieutenant and you don't agree or disagree with 320 Major Ross.

CAMPBELL. No discipline, tcchhha.

Ross looks over the convicts.

ROSS. Caesar! He started going with them and came back.

RALPH. That's all right, he's not in the play. 325

CAESAR. Yes I am, please Lieutenant, I am a servant.

ROSS. John Wisehammer!

WISEHAMMER. I had nothing to do with it!

ROSS. You're Jewish aren't you? You're guilty. Kable was last seen near Wisehammer's hut. Liz Morden! 330 She was observed next to the colony's stores late last night in the company of Kable who was supposed to be repairing the door. (*To Liz.*) Liz Morden, you will be tried for stealing from the stores. You know the punishment? Death by 335 hanging. (*Pause.*) And now you may continue to rehearse, Lieutenant.

Ross goes. Campbell lingers, looking at the book.

CAMPBELL. Ouusstta. *The Recruiting Officer*. Good title. Arara. But a play, tss, a play.

He goes. Ralph and the convicts are left in the shambles of their rehearsal. A silence.

---

46 thespists] The word is thespians (after Thespis, the first Greek actor).

ACT 2

SCENE 1

VISITING HOURS

Liz, Wisehammer, Arscott, Caesar all in chains. Arscott is bent over, facing away.

LIZ. Luck? Don't know the word. Shifts its bob when I comes near.[47] Born under a ha'penny planet I was.[48] Dad's a nibbler, don't want to get crapped.[49] Mum leaves. Five brothers, I'm the only tritter.[50] I takes in washing. Then. My own father. Lady's walking down the street, he takes her wiper. She screams, he's shoulder-clapped, says, it's not me, Sir, it's Lizzie, look, she took it.[51] I'm stripped, beaten in the street, everyone watching. That night, I take my dad's cudgel and try to kill him, I prig all his clothes and go to my older brother. He don't want me. Liz, he says, why trine for a make, when you can wap for a winne?[52] I'm no dimber mort, I says.[53] Don't ask you to be a swell mollisher, Sister, men want Miss Laycock, don't look at your mug.[54] So I begin to sell my mother of saints.[55] I thinks I'm in luck when I meet the swell cove.[56] He's a bobcull: sports a different wiper every day of the week.[57] He says to me, it's not enough to sell your mossie face, Lizzie, it don't bring no shiners no more.[58] Shows me how to spice the swells.[59] So. Swell has me up the wall, flashes a pocket watch, I lifts it. But one time, I stir my stumps too slow, the swell squeaks beef, the snoozie hears, I'm nibbled.[60] It's up the ladder to rest, I thinks when I goes up before the fortune teller, but no, the judge's a bobcull, I nap the King's pardon and it's seven years across the herring pond.[61] Jesus Christ the hunger on the ship, sailors won't touch me: no rantum scantum, no food.[62] But here, the Governor says, new life. You could nob it here, Lizzie, I thinks, bobcull Gov, this niffynaffy play, not too much work, good crew of rufflers, Kable, Arscott, but no, Ross don't like my mug, I'm nibbled again and now it's up the ladder to rest for good.[63] Well. Lizzie Morden's life. And you, Wisehammer, how did you get here?

WISEHAMMER. Betrayal. Barbarous falsehood. Intimidation. Injustice.

LIZ. Speak in English, Wisehammer.

WISEHAMMER. I am innocent. I didn't do it and I'll keep saying I didn't.

LIZ. It doesn't matter what you say. If they say you're a thief, you're a thief.

WISEHAMMER. I am not a thief. I'll go back to England to the snuff shop of Rickett and Loads and say, see, I'm back, I'm innocent.

LIZ. They won't listen.

WISEHAMMER. You can't live if you think that way.

Pause.

I'm sorry. Seven years and I'll go back.

LIZ. What do you want to go back to England for? You're not English.

WISEHAMMER. I was born in England. I'm English. What do I have to do to make people believe I'm English?

---

47 Shifts its bob] (slang—as are the subsequent terms glossed in this speech) moves away (like a fisherman moving his line).

48 ha'penny planet] astrologically, an unlucky star.

49 nibbler] petty thief; crapped] hanged.

50 tritter] girl.

51 shoulder-clapped] arrested.

52 trine for a make … wap for a winne] hang for a halfpenny … have sex for a penny (a variation on an expression in the London underworld: "If she won't wap for a Winne, let her trine for a Make").

53 dimber mort] pretty wench.

54 swell mollisher] fashionable woman; Miss Laycock] female genitals; mug] face.

55 mother of saints] vagina.

56 swell cove] fashionable gentleman.

57 bobcull] a sweet-natured man (an expression used chiefly by whores about their kinder clients).

58 mossie] mossy, decrepit; shiners] money, gold coins.

59 spice] rob; swells] fashionable people.

60 squeaks beef] shouts "stop thief"; snoozie] night constable; nibbled] caught.

61 up the ladder to rest] hanging; fortune teller] judge; nap] receive; King's pardon] reprieve from execution; across the herring pond] transported across the ocean.

62 rantum scantum] sexual intercourse.

63 nob it] prosper; niffynaffy] silly; rufflers] vagabonds.

LIZ. You have to think English. I hate England. But I think English. And him, Arscott, he's not said anything since they brought him in but he's thinking English, I can tell.

CAESAR. I don't want to think English. If I think English I will die. I want to go back to Madagascar and think Malagasy.[64] I want to die in Madagascar and join my ancestors. 60

LIZ. It doesn't matter where you die when you're dead. 65

CAESAR. If I die here, I will have no spirit. I want to go home. I will escape again.

ARSCOTT. There's no escape!

CAESAR. This time I lost my courage, but next time I ask my ancestors and they will help me escape. 70

ARSCOTT. (*shouts.*) There's no escape!

LIZ. See. That's English. You know things.

CAESAR. My ancestors will know the way.

ARSCOTT. There's no escape I tell you.

Pause.

You go in circles out there, that's all you do. You go out there and you walk and walk and you don't reach China.[65] You come back on your steps if the savages don't get you first. Even a compass doesn't work in this foreign upside-down desert. Here. You can read. Why didn't it work? What does it say? 75 80

He hands Wisehammer a carefully folded, wrinkled piece of paper.

WISEHAMMER. It says north.

ARSCOTT. Why didn't it work then? It was supposed to take us north to China, why did I end up going in circles?

WISEHAMMER. Because it's not a compass. 85

ARSCOTT. I gave my only shilling to a sailor for it. He said it was a compass.

WISEHAMMER. It's a piece of paper with north written on it. He lied. He deceived you, he betrayed you. 90

Sideway, Mary and Duckling come on.

---

64 Malagasy] the language spoken in Madagascar.
65 you don't reach China] It was the belief of some of the early convicts that New South Wales was connected to the Asian mainland.

SIDEWAY. Madam, gentlemen, fellow players, we have come to visit, to commiserate, to offer our humble services.

LIZ. Get out!

MARY. Liz, we've come to rehearse the play. 95

WISEHAMMER. Rehearse the play?

DUCKLING. The Lieutenant has gone to talk to the Governor. Harry said we could come see you.

MARY. The Lieutenant has asked me to stand in his place so we don't lose time. We'll start with the first scene between Melinda and Brazen. 100

WISEHAMMER. How can I play Captain Brazen in chains?

MARY. It's the theatre. We will believe you.

ARSCOTT. Where does Kite come in? 105

SIDEWAY. (*bowing to Liz.*) Madam, I have brought you your fan. (*He hands her the "fan", which she takes.*)

SCENE 2

HIS EXCELLENCY EXHORTS RALPH

Phillip, Ralph.

PHILLIP. I hear you want to stop the play, Lieutenant.

RALPH. Half of my cast is in chains, Sir.

PHILLIP. That is a difficulty, but it can be overcome. Is that your only reason, Lieutenant? 5

RALPH. So many people seem against it, Sir.

PHILLIP. Are you afraid?

RALPH. No, Sir, but I do not wish to displease my superior officers.

PHILLIP. If you break conventions, it's inevitable you make enemies, Lieutenant. This play irritates them. 10

RALPH. Yes and I—

PHILLIP. Socrates irritated the state of Athens and was put to death for it.

RALPH. Sir— 15

PHILLIP. Would you have a world without Socrates?

RALPH. Sir, I—

PHILLIP. In the *Meno*, one of Plato's great dialogues, have you read it, Lieutenant, Socrates demonstrates that a slave boy can learn the principles of geometry as well as a gentleman. 20

RALPH. Ah—

PHILLIP. In other words, he shows that human beings have an intelligence which has nothing to do with the circumstances into which they are born. 25

RALPH. Sir—

PHILLIP. Sit down, Lieutenant. It is a matter of reminding the slave of what he knows, of his own intelligence. And by intelligence you may read goodness, talent, the innate qualities of human beings. 30

RALPH. I see—Sir.

PHILLIP. When he treats the slave boy as a rational human being, the boy becomes one, he loses his fear, and he becomes a competent mathematician. A little more encouragement and he might become an extraordinary mathematician. Who knows? You must see your actors in that light. 35

RALPH. I can see some of them, Sir, but there are others ... John Arscott— 40

PHILLIP. He has been given 200 lashes for trying to escape. It will take time for him to see himself as a human being again.

RALPH. Liz Morden— 45

PHILLIP. Liz Morden—(*He pauses.*) I had a reason for asking you to cast her as Melinda. Morden is one of the most difficult women in the colony.

RALPH. She is indeed, Sir.

PHILLIP. Lower than a slave, full of loathing, foul mouthed, desperate. 50

RALPH. Exactly, Sir. And violent.

PHILLIP. Quite. To be made an example of.

RALPH. By hanging?

PHILLIP. No, Lieutenant, by redemption. 55

RALPH. The Reverend says he's given up on her, Sir.

PHILLIP. The Reverend's an ass, Lieutenant. I am speaking of redeeming her humanity.

RALPH. I'm afraid there may not be much there, Sir.

PHILLIP. How do we know what humanity lies hidden under the rags and filth of a mangled life? I have seen soldiers given up for dead, limbs torn, heads cut open, come back to life. If we treat her as a corpse, of course she will die. Try a little kindness, Lieutenant. 60 65

RALPH. But will she be hanged, Sir?

PHILLIP. I don't want a woman to be hanged. You will have to help, Ralph.

RALPH. Sir!

PHILLIP. I had retired from His Majesty's Service, Ralph. I was farming. I don't know why they asked me to rule over this colony of wretched souls, but I will fulfil my responsibility. No one will stop me. 70

RALPH. No, Sir, but I don't see—

PHILLIP. What is a statesman's responsibility? To ensure the rule of law. But the citizens must be taught to obey that law of their own will. I want to rule over responsible human beings, not tyrannise over a group of animals. I want there to be a contract between us, not a whip on my side, terror and hatred on theirs. And you must help me, Ralph. 75 80

RALPH. Yes, Sir. The play—

PHILLIP. Won't change much, but it is the diagram in the sand that may remind—just remind the slave boy—Do you understand? 85

RALPH. I think so.

PHILLIP. We may fail. I may have a mutiny on my hands. They are trying to convince the Admiralty that I am mad. 90

RALPH. Sir!

PHILLIP. And they will threaten you. You don't want to be a Second Lieutenant all your life.

RALPH. No, Sir!

PHILLIP. I cannot go over the head of Major Ross in the matter of promotion. 95

RALPH. I see.

PHILLIP. But we have embarked, Ralph, we must stay afloat. There is a more serious threat and it may capsize us all. If a ship does not come within three months, the supplies will be exhausted. In a month, I will cut the rations again. (*Pause.*) Harry is not well. Can you do something? Good luck with the play, Lieutenant. Oh, and Ralph— 100

RALPH. Sir— 105

PHILLIP. Unexpected situations are often matched by unexpected virtues in people, are they not?

RALPH. I believe they are, Sir.

PHILLIP. A play is a world in itself, a tiny colony we could almost say. 110

Pause.

And you are in charge of it. That is a great responsibility.

RALPH. I will lay down my life if I have to, Sir.

PHILLIP. I don't think it will come to that, Lieutenant. You need only do your best. 115

RALPH. Yes, Sir, I will, Sir.

PHILLIP. Excellent.

RALPH. It's a wonderful play, Sir. I wasn't sure at first, as you know, but now—

PHILLIP. Good, Good. I shall look forward to seeing it. I'm sure it will be a success. 120

RALPH. Thank you, Sir. Thank you.

SCENE 3

HARRY BREWER SEES THE DEAD

Harry Brewer's tent. Harry sits, drinking rum, speaking in the different voices of his tormenting ghosts and answering in his own.

HARRY. Duckling! Duckling! "She's on the beach, Harry, waiting for her young Handy Baker." Go away, Handy, go away! "The dead never go away, Harry. You thought you'd be the only one to dance the buttock ball with your trull, but no one owns a whore's cunt, Harry, you rent."[66] I didn't hang you. "You wanted me dead." I didn't. "You wanted me hanged." All right, I wanted you hanged. Go away! (*Pause.*) "Death is horrible, Mr. Brewer, it's dark, there's nothing." Thomas Barrett! You were 10 hanged because you stole from the stores. "I was seventeen, Mr. Brewer." You lived a very wicked life. "I didn't." That's what you said that morning, "I have led a very wicked life." "I had to say something, Mr. Brewer, and make sense of dying. 15 I'd heard the Reverend say we were all wicked, but it was horrible, my body hanging, my tongue sticking out." You shouldn't have stolen that food! "I wanted to live, go back to England, I'd only be twenty-four. I hadn't done it much, not like you." 20 Duckling! "I wish I wasn't dead, Mr. Brewer; I had plans. I was going to have my farm, drink with friends and feel the strong legs of a girl around me—" You shouldn't have stolen. "Didn't you ever steal?" No! Yes. But that was different. Duckling! 25

5

66 dance the buttock ball] have sexual intercourse; trull] whore.

"Why should you be alive after what you've done?" Duckling! Duckling!

Duckling rushes on.

DUCKLING. What's the matter, Harry?

HARRY. I'm seeing them.

DUCKLING. Who? 30

HARRY. All of them. The dead. Help me.

DUCKLING. I heard your screams from the beach. You're having another bad dream.

HARRY. No. I see them.

Pause.

Let me come inside you. 35

DUCKLING. Now?

HARRY. Please.

DUCKLING. Will you forget your nightmares?

HARRY. Yes.

DUCKLING. Come then. 40

HARRY. Duckling …

She lies down and lifts her skirts. He begins to go down over her and stops.

What were you doing on the beach? You were with him, he told me, you were with Handy Baker.

SCENE 4

THE ABORIGINE MUSES ON THE NATURE OF DREAMS

THE ABORIGINE. Some dreams lose their way and wander over the earth, lost. But this is a dream no one wants. It has stayed. How can we befriend this crowded, hungry and disturbed dream?

SCENE 5

THE SECOND REHEARSAL

Ralph Clark, Mary Brenham and Robert Sideway are waiting. Major Ross and Captain Campbell bring the three prisoners Caesar, Wisehammer and Liz Morden. They are still in chains. Ross shoves them forward.

ROSS. Here is some of your caterwauling cast, Lieutenant.

CAMPBELL. The Governor, chht, said, release, tssst. Prisoners.

ROSS. Unchain Wisehammer and the savage, 5
Captain Campbell. (*Points to Liz.*) She stays in chains. She's being tried tomorrow, we don't want her sloping off.

RALPH. I can't rehearse with one of my players in chains, Major. 10

CAMPBELL. Eeh. Difficult. Mmmm.

ROSS. We'll tell the Governor you didn't need her and take her back to prison.

RALPH. No. We shall manage. Sideway, go over the scene you rehearsed in prison with Melinda, please. 15

CAESAR. I'm in that scene too, Lieutenant.

RALPH. No you're not.

LIZ and SIDEWAY. Yes he is, Lieutenant.

SIDEWAY. He's my servant.

Ralph nods and Liz, Sideway and Caesar move to the side and stand together, ready to rehearse, but waiting.

RALPH. The rest of us will go from Silvia's entrance 20
as Wilful. Where's Arscott?

ROSS. We haven't finished with Arscott yet, Lieutenant.

CAMPBELL. Punishment, eeeh, for escape. Fainted. Fifty-three lashes left. Heeeh.

ROSS. (*pointing to Caesar.*) Caesar's next. After 25
Morden's trial.

Caesar cringes.

RALPH. Brenham, are you ready? Wisehammer? I'll play Captain Plume.

ROSS. The wee Lieutenant wants to be in the play too. He wants to be promoted to convict. We'll 30
have you in the chain gang soon, Mr. Clark, haha. (*A pause. Ross and Campbell stand, watching. The Convicts are frozen.*)

RALPH. Major, we will rehearse now.

Pause. No one moves.

We wish to rehearse. 35

ROSS. No one's stopping you, Lieutenant.

Silence.

RALPH. Major, rehearsals need to take place in the utmost euh—privacy, secrecy you might say. The actors are not yet ready to be seen by the public.

ROSS. Not ready to be seen? 40

RALPH. Major, there is a modesty attached to the process of creation which must be respected.

ROSS. Modesty? Modesty! Sideway, come here.

RALPH. Major. Sideway—stay—

ROSS. Lieutenant, I would not try to countermand 45
the orders of a superior officer.

CAMPBELL. Obedience. Ehh, first euh, rule.

ROSS. Sideway.

Sideway comes up to Ross.

Take your shirt off.

Sideway obeys. Ross turns him and shows his scarred back to the company.

One hundred lashes on the Sirius for answering an 50
officer.[67] Remember, Sideway? Three hundred lashes for trying to strike the same officer.

I have seen the white of this animal's bones, his wretched blood and reeky convict urine have spilled on my boots and he's feeling modest? Are 55
you feeling modest, Sideway?

He shoves Sideway aside.

Modesty.
Bryant. Here.

Dabby comes forward.

On all fours.

Dabby goes down on all fours.

Now wag your tail and bark, and I'll throw you a 60
biscuit. What? You've forgotten? Isn't that how you begged for your food on the ship? Wag your tail, Bryant, bark! We'll wait.
Brenham.

Mary comes forward.

Where's your tattoo, Brenham? Show us. I can't see 65
it. Show us.

Mary tries to obey, lifting her skirt a little.

If you can't manage, I'll help you. (*Mary lifts her skirt a little higher.*) I can't see it.

But Sideway turns to Liz and starts acting, boldly, across the room, across everyone.

---

67 Sirius] one of the ships on which the convicts were transported.

SIDEWAY. "What pleasures I may receive abroad are indeed uncertain; but this I am sure of, I shall meet with less cruelty among the most barbarous nations than I have found at home." 70

LIZ. "Come, Sir, you and I have been jangling a great while; I fancy if we made up our accounts, we should the sooner come to an agreement." 75

SIDEWAY. "Sure, Madam, you won't dispute your being in my debt—my fears, sighs, vows, promises, assiduities, anxieties, jealousies, have run on for a whole year, without any payment."

CAMPBELL. Mmhem, good that. Sighs, vows, promises, hehem, mmm. Anxieties. 80

ROSS. Captain Campbell, start Arscott's punishment.

Campbell goes.

LIZ. "A year! Oh Mr. Worthy, what you owe me is not to be paid under a seven years' servitude. How did you use me the year before—" 85

The shouts of Arscott are heard.

"How did you use me the year before—"

She loses her lines. Sideway tries to prompt her.

SIDEWAY. "When taking advantage—"

LIZ. "When taking advantage of my innocence and necessity—"

But she stops and drops down, defeated. Silence, except for the beating and Arscott's cries.

SCENE 6

THE SCIENCE OF HANGING

Harry, Ketch Freeman, Liz, sitting, staring straight ahead of her.

KETCH. I don't want to do this.

HARRY. Get on with it, Freeman.

KETCH. (*to Liz.*) I have to measure you.

Pause.

I'm sorry.

Liz doesn't move.

You'll have to stand, Liz. 5

Liz doesn't move.

Please.

Pause.

I won't hurt you. I mean, now. And if I have the measurements right, I can make it quick. Very quick. Please.

Liz doesn't move.

She doesn't want to get up, Mr. Brewer. I could come back later. 10

HARRY. Hurry up.

KETCH. I can't. I can't measure her unless she gets up. I have to measure her to judge the drop. If the rope's too short, it won't hang her and if the rope's too long, it could pull her head off. It's very difficult, Mr. Brewer, I've always done my best. 15

Pause.

But I've never hung a woman.

HARRY. (*in Tom Barrett's voice.*) "You've hung a boy." (*To Ketch.*) You've hung a boy. 20

KETCH. That was a terrible mess, Mr. Brewer, don't you remember. It took twenty minutes and even then he wasn't dead. Remember how he danced and everyone laughed. I don't want to repeat something like that, Mr. Brewer, not now. Someone had to get hold of his legs to weigh him down and then— 25

HARRY. Measure her, Freeman!

KETCH. Yes, Sir. Could you tell her to get up. She'll listen to you. 30

HARRY. (*shouts.*) Get up, you bitch.

Liz doesn't move.

Get up!

He seizes her and makes her stand.

Now measure her!

KETCH. (*measuring the neck, etc., of Liz.*) The Lieutenant is talking to the Governor again, Liz, maybe he'll change his mind. At least he might wait until we've done the play. 35

Pause.

I don't want to do this.

I know, you're thinking in my place you wouldn't. But somebody will do it, if I don't, and I'll be gentle. I won't hurt you.   40

Liz doesn't move, doesn't look at him.

It's wrong, Mr. Brewer. It's wrong.

HARRY. (*in Tom Barrett's voice.*) "It's wrong. Death is horrible." (*In his own voice to Ketch.*) There's no food left in the colony and she steals it and gives it to Kable to run away.   45

KETCH. That's true, Liz, you shouldn't have stolen that food. Especially when the Lieutenant trusted us. That was wrong, Liz. Actors can't behave like normal people, not even like normal criminals. Still, I'm sorry. I'll do my best.   50

HARRY. "I had plans." (*To Ketch.*) Are you finished?

KETCH. Yes, yes. I have all the measurements I need. No, one more. I need to lift her. You don't mind, do you, Liz?   55

He lifts her.

She's so light. I'll have to use a very long rope. The fig tree would be better, it's higher. When will they build me some gallows, Mr. Brewer? Nobody will laugh at you, Liz, you won't be ashamed, I'll make sure of that.   60

HARRY. "You could hang yourself." Come on, Freeman. Let's go.

KETCH. Goodbye, Liz. You were a very good Melinda. No one will be as good as you.

They begin to go.

LIZ. Mr. Brewer.   65

HARRY. "You wanted me dead." I didn't. You shouldn't've stolen that food!

KETCH. Speak to her, please, Mr. Brewer.

HARRY. What?

LIZ. Tell Lieutenant Clark I didn't steal the food. Tell   70
him—afterwards. I want him to know.

HARRY. Why didn't you say that before? Why are you lying now?

LIZ. Tell the Lieutenant.

HARRY. "Another victim of yours, another body. I   75
was so frightened, so alone."

KETCH. Mr. Brewer.

HARRY. "It's dark. There's nothing." Get away, get away!

LIZ. Please tell the Lieutenant.   80

HARRY. "First fear, then a pain at the back of the neck. Then nothing." I can't see. It's dark. It's dark.

Harry screams and falls.

SCENE 7

THE MEANING OF PLAYS

THE ABORIGINE. Ghosts in a multitude have spilled from the dream. Who are they? A swarm of ancestors comes through unmended cracks in the sky. But why? What do they need? If we can satisfy them, they will go back. How can we satisfy them?   5

Mary, Ralph, Dabby, Wisehammer, Arscott. Mary and Ralph are rehearsing. The others are watching.

RALPH. "For I swear, Madam, by the honour of my profession, that whatever dangers I went upon, it was with the hope of making myself more worthy of your esteem, and if I ever had thoughts of preserving my life, 'twas for the pleasure of dying   10
at your feet."

MARY. "Well, well, you shall die at my feet, or where you will; but you know, Sir, there is a certain will and testament to be made beforehand."

I don't understand why Silvia has asked Plume   15
to make a will.

DABBY. It's a proof of his love, he wants to provide for her.

MARY. A will is a proof of love?

WISEHAMMER. No. She's using will in another sense.   20
He must show his willingness to marry her. Dying is used in another sense, too.[68]

RALPH. He gives her his will to indicate that he intends to take care of her.

DABBY. That's right, Lieutenant, marriage is nothing,   25
but will you look after her?

WISEHAMMER. Plume is too ambitious to marry Silvia.

MARY. If I had been Silvia, I would have trusted Plume.   30

---

68 Dying … another sense] as a euphemism for orgasm (as in *petite mort*).

DABBY. When dealing with men, always have a contract.

MARY. Love is a contract.

DABBY. Love is the barter of perishable goods. A man's word for a woman's body.

WISEHAMMER. Dabby is right. If a man loves a woman, he should marry her.

RALPH. Sometimes he can't.

WISEHAMMER. Then she should look for someone who can.

DABBY. A woman should look after her own interests, that's all.

MARY. Her interest is to love.

DABBY. A girl will love the first man who knows how to open her legs. She's called a whore and ends up here. I could write scenes, Lieutenant, women with real lives, not these Shrewsbury prudes.

WISEHAMMER. I've written something. The prologue of this play won't make any sense to the convicts: "In ancient times, when Helen's fatal charms" and so on. I've written another one. Will you look at it, Lieutenant?

Ralph does so and Wisehammer takes Mary aside.

You mustn't trust the wrong people, Mary. We could make a new life together, here. I would marry you, Mary, think about it, you would live with me, in a house. He'll have to put you in a hut at the bottom of his garden and call you his servant in public, that is, his whore. Don't do it, Mary.

DABBY. Lieutenant, are we rehearsing or not? Arscott and I have been waiting for hours.

RALPH. It seems interesting, I'll read it more carefully later.

WISEHAMMER. You don't like it.

RALPH. I do like it. Perhaps it needs a little more work. It's not Farquhar.

WISEHAMMER. It would mean more to the convicts.

RALPH. We'll talk about it another time.

WISEHAMMER. Do you think it should be longer?

RALPH. I'll think about it.

WISEHAMMER. Shorter? Do you like the last two lines? Mary helped me with them.

RALPH. Ah.

WISEHAMMER. The first lines took us days, didn't they Mary?

RALPH. We'll rehearse Silvia's entrance as Jack Wilful. You're in the scene, Wisehammer. We'll come to your scenes in a minute, Bryant. Now, Brenham, remember what I showed you yesterday about walking like a gentleman? I've ordered breeches to be made for you, you can practise in them tomorrow.

MARY. I'll tuck my skirt in. (*She does so and takes a masculine pose.*) "Save ye, save ye, gentlemen."

WISEHAMMER. "My dear, I'm yours."

He kisses her.

RALPH. (*angrily.*) It doesn't say Silvia is kissed in the stage directions!

WISEHAMMER. Plume kisses her later and there's the line about men kissing in the army. I thought Brazen would kiss her immediately.

RALPH. It's completely wrong.

WISEHAMMER. It's right for the character of Brazen.

RALPH. No it isn't. I'm the director, Wisehammer.

WISEHAMMER. Yes, but I have to play the part. They're equal in this scene. They're both Captains and in the end fight for her. Who's playing Plume in our performance?

RALPH. I will have to, as Kable hasn't come back. It's your line.

WISEHAMMER. Will I be given a sword?

RALPH. I doubt it. Let's move on to Kite's entrance, Arscott has been waiting too long.

ARSCOTT. (*delighted, launches straight in.*) "Sir, if you please—"

RALPH. Excellent, Arscott, but we should just give you our last lines so you'll know when to come in. Wisehammer.

WISEHAMMER. "The fellow dare not fight."

RALPH. That's when you come in.

ARSCOTT. "Sir, if you please—"

DABBY. What about me? I haven't done anything either. You always rehearse the scenes with Silvia.

RALPH. Let's rehearse the scene where Rose comes on with her brother Bullock. It's a better scene for you Arscott. Do you know it?

ARSCOTT. Yes.

RALPH. Good. Wisehammer, you'll have to play the part of Bullock.

WISEHAMMER. What? Play two parts?

RALPH. Major Ross won't let any more prisoners off work. Some of you will have to play several parts. 120

WISEHAMMER. It'll confuse the audience. They'll think Brazen is Bullock and Bullock Brazen.

RALPH. Nonsense, if the audience is paying attention, they'll know that Bullock is a country boy and Brazen a Captain. 125

WISEHAMMER. What if they aren't paying attention?

RALPH. People who can't pay attention should not go to the theatre.

MARY. If you act well, they will have to pay attention.

WISEHAMMER. It will ruin my entrance as Captain Brazen. 130

RALPH. We have no choice and we must turn this necessity into an advantage. You will play two very different characters and display the full range of your abilities. 135

WISEHAMMER. Our audience won't be that discerning.

RALPH. Their imagination will be challenged and trained. Let's start the scene. Bryant?

DABBY. I think *The Recruiting Officer* is a silly play. 140 I want to be in a play that has more interesting people in it.

MARY. I like playing Silvia. She's bold, she breaks rules out of love for her Captain and she's not ashamed. 145

DABBY. She hasn't been born poor, she hasn't had to survive, and her father's a Justice of the Peace. I want to play myself.

ARSCOTT. I don't want to play myself. When I say Kite's lines I forget everything else. I forget the 150 judge said I'm going to have to spend the rest of my natural life in this place getting beaten and working like a slave. I can forget that out there it's trees and burnt grass, spiders that kill you in four hours and snakes. I don't have to think about what 155 happened to Kable, I don't have to remember the things I've done, when I speak Kite's lines I don't hate any more. I'm Kite. I'm in Shrewsbury. Can we get on with the scene, Lieutenant, and stop talking? 160

DABBY. I want to see a play that shows life as we know it.

WISEHAMMER. It doesn't matter when a play is set. It's better if it's set in the past, it's clearer. It's easier to understand Plume and Brazen than some of the 165 officers we know here.

RALPH. Arscott, would you start the scene?

ARSCOTT. "Captain, Sir, look yonder, a-coming this way, 'tis the prettiest, cleanest little tit."

RALPH. Now Worthy—He's in this scene. Where's 170 Sideway?

MARY. He's so upset about Liz he won't rehearse.

RALPH. I am going to talk to the Governor, but he has to rehearse. We must do the play, whatever happens. We've been rehearsing for five months! 175 Let's go on. "Here she comes, and what is that great country fellow with her?"

ARSCOTT. "I can't tell, Sir."

WISEHAMMER. I'm not a great country fellow.

RALPH. Act it, Wisehammer. 180

DABBY. "Buy chickens, young and tender, young and tender chickens." This is a very stupid line and I'm not saying it.

RALPH. It's written by the playwright and you have to say it. "Here, you chickens!" 185

DABBY. "Who calls?"

RALPH. Bryant, you're playing a pretty country wench who wants to entice the Captain. You have to say these lines with charm and euh—blushes.

DABBY. I don't blush. 190

RALPH. I can't do this scene without Sideway. Let's do another scene.

Pause.

Arscott, let's work on your big speeches, I haven't heard them yet. I still need Sideway. This is irresponsible, he wanted the part. Somebody go 195 and get Sideway.

No one moves.

ARSCOTT. I'll do the first speech anyway, Sir. "Yes, Sir, I understand my business, I will say it; you must know, Sir, I was born a gypsy, and bred among that crew till I was ten years old, there I 200 learned canting and lying;—"

DABBY. That's about me!

ARSCOTT. I was bought from my mother Cleopatra by a certain nobleman, for three guineas, who liking my beauty made me his page—" 205

DABBY. That's my story. Why do I have to play a silly milkmaid? Why can't I play Kite?

MARY. You can't play a man, Dabby.

DABBY. You're playing a man: Jack Wilful.

MARY. Yes, but in the play, I know I'm a woman, whereas if you played Kite, you would have to think you were a man. 210

DABBY. If Wisehammer can think he's a big country lad, I can think I'm a man. People will use their imagination and people with no imagination shouldn't go to the theatre. 215

RALPH. Bryant, you're muddling everything.

DABBY. No. I see things very clearly and I'm making you see clearly, Lieutenant. I want to play Kite.

ARSCOTT. You can't play Kite! I'm playing Kite! You can't steal my part! 220

RALPH. You may have to play Melinda.

DABBY. All she does is marry Sideway, that's not interesting.

Dabby stomps off. Ketch comes on.

KETCH. I'm sorry I'm late, Lieutenant, but I know all my lines. 225

RALPH. We'll rehearse the first scene between Justice Balance and Silvia. Brenham.

Arscott stomps off.

MARY. "Whilst there is life there is hope, Sir; perhaps my brother may recover." 230

KETCH. "We have but little reason to expect it—"

MARY. I can't. Not with him. Not with Liz—I can't.

She runs off.

RALPH. One has to transcend personal feelings in the theatre.

Wisehammer runs after Mary.

(*To Ketch.*) We're not making much progress today, let's end this rehearsal. 235

He goes. Ketch is left alone, bewildered.

SCENE 8

DUCKLING MAKES VOWS

Night. Harry, ill. Duckling.

DUCKLING. If you live, I will never again punish you with my silence. If you live, I will never again turn away from you. If you live, I will never again imagine another man when you make love to me. If you live, I will never tell you I want to leave you. 5 If you live, I will speak to you. If you live, I will be tender with you. If you live, I will look after you. If you live, I will stay with you. If you live, I will be wet and open to your touch. If you live, I will answer all your questions. If you live, I will 10 look at you. If you live, I will love you.

Pause.

If you die, I will never forgive you.

She leans over him. Listens. Touches. Harry is dead.

I hate you.
No. I love you.

She crouches into a fetal position, cries out.

How could you do this? 15

SCENE 9

A LOVE SCENE

The beach. Night. Mary, then Ralph.

MARY. (*to herself.*) "Captain Plume, I despise your listing-money; if I do serve, 'tis purely for love— of that wench I mean. For you must know," etc—
"So you only want an opportunity for accomplishing your designs upon her?" 5
"Well, Sir, I'm satisfied to the point in debate; but now let me beg you to lay aside your recruiting airs, put on the man of honour, and tell me plainly what usage I must expect when I'm under your command." 10

She tries that again, with a stronger and lower voice. Ralph comes on, sees her. She sees him, but continues.

"And something tells me, that if you do discharge me 'twill be the greatest punishment you can inflict; for were we this moment to go upon the greatest dangers in your profession, they would be less terrible to me than to stay behind you. And 15 now your hand—this lists me—and now you are my Captain."

RALPH. (*as Plume.*) "Your friend." (*Kisses her.*)
"'Sdeath! There's something in this fellow that
charms me." 20

MARY. "One favour I must beg—this affair will make
some noise—"

RALPH. Silvia—

He kisses her again.

MARY. "I must therefore take care to be impressed
by the Act of Parliament—" 25

RALPH. "What you please as to that. Will you lodge
at my quarters in the meantime? You shall have
part of my bed." Silvia. Mary.

MARY. Am I doing it well? It's difficult to play a man.
It's not the walk, it's the way you hold your head. 30
A man doesn't bow his head so much and never
at an angle. I must face you without lowering my
head. Let's try it again.

RALPH. "What you please as to that.—Will you
lodge at my quarters in the meantime? You shall 35
have part of my bed." Mary!

She holds her head straight. Pause.

Will you?

Pause.

MARY. Yes.

They kiss.

RALPH. Don't lower your head. Silvia wouldn't.

She begins to undress, from the top.

I've never looked at the body of a woman before. 40

MARY. Your wife?

RALPH. It wasn't right to look at her.
Let me see you.

MARY. Yes.
Let me see you. 45

RALPH. Yes.

He begins to undress himself.

SCENE 10

THE QUESTION OF LIZ

Ralph, Ross, Phillip, Collins, Campbell.

COLLINS. She refused to defend herself at the trial.
She didn't say a word. This was taken as an
admission of guilt and she was condemned to be
hanged. The evidence against her, however, is
flimsy. 5

ROSS. She was seen with Kable next to the food
stores. That is a fingering fact.

COLLINS. She was seen by a drunken soldier in the
dark. He admitted he was drunk and that he saw
her at a distance. He knew Kable was supposed to 10
be repairing the door and she's known to be friends
with Kable and Arscott. She won't speak, she won't
say where she was. That is our difficulty.

ROSS. She won't speak because she's guilty.

PHILLIP. Silence has many causes, Robbie. 15

RALPH. She won't speak, Your Excellency, because of
the convict code of honour. She doesn't want to
beg for her life.

ROSS. Convict code of honour. This pluming play
has muddled the muffy Lieutenant's mind.[69] 20

COLLINS. My only fear, Your Excellency, is that she
may have refused to speak because she no longer
believes in the process of justice. If that is so, the
courts here will become travesties. I do not want
that. 25

PHILLIP. But if she won't speak, there is nothing
more we can do. You cannot get at the truth
through silence.

RALPH. She spoke to Harry Brewer.

PHILLIP. But Harry never regained consciousness 30
before he died.

RALPH. James Freeman was there and told me what
she said.

PHILLIP. Wasn't this used in the trial?

COLLINS. Freeman's evidence wasn't very clear and 35
as Liz Morden wouldn't confirm what he said, it
was dismissed.

ROSS. You can't take the word of a crooked crawling
hangman.

---

69 pluming] affected and trivial; muffy] foolish.

PHILLIP. Why won't she speak? 40

ROSS. Because she's guilty.

PHILLIP. Robbie, we may be about to hang the first woman in this colony. I do not want to hang the first innocent woman.

RALPH. We must get at the truth. 45

ROSS. Truth! We have 800 thieves, perjurers, forgers, murderers, liars, escapers, rapists, whores, coiners in this scrub-ridden, dust-driven, thunder-bolted, savage-run, cretinous colony. My marines who are trained to fight are turned to gouly gaolers, fed less 50 than the prisoners—

PHILLIP. The rations, Major, are the same for all, prisoners and soldiers.

ROSS. They have a right to more so that makes them have less. Not a ship shifting into sight, the 55 prisoners are running away, stealing, drinking and the wee ductile Lieutenant talks about the truth.

PHILLIP. Truth is indeed a luxury, but its absence brings about the most abject poverty in a civilisation. That is the paradox. 60

ROSS. This is a profligate prison for us all, it's a hellish hole we soldiers have been hauled to because they blame us for losing the war in America. This is a hateful, hary-scary, topsy-turvy outpost, this is not a civilization. I hate this 65 possumy place.[70]

COLLINS. Perhaps we could return to the question of Liz Morden. (*Calls.*) Captain Campbell.

Campbell brings in Liz Morden.

Morden, if you don't speak, we will have to hang you; if you can defend yourself, His Excellency can 70 overrule the court. We would not then risk a miscarriage of justice. But you must speak. Did you steal that food with the escaped prisoner Kable?

A long silence.

RALPH. She— 75

COLLINS. It is the accused who must answer.

PHILLIP. Liz Morden. You must speak the truth.

COLLINS. We will listen to you.

Pause.

RALPH. Morden. No one will despise you for telling the truth. 80

PHILLIP. That is not so, Lieutenant. Tell the truth and accept the contempt. That is the history of great men. Liz, you may be despised, but you will have shown courage.

RALPH. If that soldier has lied— 85

ROSS. There, there, he's accusing my soldiers of lying. It's that play, it makes fun of officers, it shows an officer lying and cheating. It shows a corrupt justice as well, Collins—

CAMPBELL. Good scene that, very funny, hah, 90 scchhh.

COLLINS. *Et tu*, Campbell?[71]

CAMPBELL. What? Meant only. Hahah. "If he be so good at gunning he shall have enough…he may be of use against the French, for he shoots flying," 95 hahaha. Good, and then there's this Constable ha—

ROSS. Campbell!

PHILLIP. The play seems to be having miraculous effects already. Don't you want to be in it, Liz? 100

RALPH. Morden, you must speak.

COLLINS. For the good of the colony.

PHILLIP. And of the play.

A long silence.

LIZ. I didn't steal the food.

COLLINS. Were you there when Kable stole it? 105

LIZ. No. I was there before.

ROSS. And you knew he was going to steal it?

LIZ. Yes.

ROSS. Guilty. She didn't report it.

COLLINS. Failure to inform is not a hangable 110 offence.

ROSS. Conspiracy.

COLLINS. We may need a retrial.

PHILLIP. Why wouldn't you say any of this before?

ROSS. Because she didn't have time to invent a lie. 115

---

70 hary-scary] corruption of "harum-scarum"—wild, giddy; possumy] stupid(?).

71 *Et tu*] (French) "and you?"—an allusion to the treachery of closest friends: in Shakespeare's *Julius Caesar*, Caesar's last words as his friend, Brutus, stabs him along with the other conspirators (historically, Caesar is said to have spoken the words in Greek).

COLLINS. Major, you are demeaning the process of law.

PHILLIP. Why, Liz?

LIZ. Because it wouldn't have mattered.

PHILLIP. Speaking the truth? 120

LIZ. Speaking.

ROSS. You are taking the word of a convict against the word of a soldier—

COLLINS. A soldier who was drunk and uncertain of what he saw. 125

ROSS. A soldier is a soldier and has a right to respect. You will have revolt on your hands, Governor.

PHILLIP. I'm sure I will, but let us see the play first. Liz, I hope you are good in your part.

RALPH. She will be, Your Excellency, I promise that. 130

LIZ. Your Excellency, I will endeavour to speak Mr. Farquhar's lines with the elegance and clarity their own worth commands.

SCENE 11

BACKSTAGE

Night. The Aborigine.

THE ABORIGINE. Look: oozing pustules on my skin, heat on my forehead. Perhaps we have been wrong all this time and this is not a dream at all.

The Actors come on. They begin to change and make-up. The Aborigine drifts off.

MARY. Are the savages coming to see the play as well?

KETCH. They come around the camp because they're dying: smallpox. 5

MARY. Oh.

SIDEWAY. I hope they won't upset the audience.

MARY. Everyone is here. All the officers too.

LIZ. (*to Duckling.*) Dabby could take your part. 10

DUCKLING. No. I will do it. I will remember the lines.

MARY. I've brought you an orange from Lieutenant Clark's island. They've thrown her out of Harry Brewer's tent. 15

WISEHAMMER. Why? He wouldn't have wanted that.

DUCKLING. Major Ross said a whore was a whore and I was to go into the women's camp. They've taken all of Harry's things.

She bursts into tears.

MARY. I'll talk to the Lieutenant. 20

LIZ. Let's go over your lines. And if you forget them, touch my foot and I'll whisper them to you.

SIDEWAY. (*who has been practising his own.*) We haven't rehearsed the bow. Garrick used to take his this way: you look up into the circle, to the sides, 25 down, make sure everyone thinks you're looking at them.[72] Get in a line.

They do so.

ARSCOTT. I'll be in the middle. I'm the tallest.

MARY. No, Arscott. (*Mary places herself in the middle.*) 30

SIDEWAY. Dabby, you should be next to Mary.

DABBY. I won't take a bow.

SIDEWAY. It's not the biggest part, Dabby, but you'll be noticed.

DABBY. I don't want to be noticed. 35

SIDEWAY. Let's get this right. If we don't all do the same thing, it will look a mess.

They try. Dabby is suddenly transfixed.

DABBY. Hurray, hurray, hurray.

SIDEWAY. No, they will be shouting bravo, but we're not in a line yet. 40

DABBY. I wasn't looking at the bow, I saw the whole play, and we all knew our lines, and Mary, you looked so beautiful, and after that, I saw Devon and they were shouting bravo, bravo Dabby, hurray, you've escaped, you've sailed thousands and 45 thousands of miles on the open sea and you've come back to your Devon, bravo, Dabby, bravo.[73]

MARY. When are you doing this, Dabby?

DABBY. Tonight.

---

72 circle] the upper balconies.

73 Dabby] The real Dabby Bryant did indeed escape the Australian penal colony by sailing over the sea with several other convicts in an open boat, with Bryant navigating by the stars. Most of those who accompanied her died on the way, but she was recaptured and taken back for trial in London. There her case attracted the attention of the distinguished writer James Boswell, who lobbied on her behalf until she was pardoned and then provided her with a pension for life.

MARY. You can't.   50

DABBY. I'll be in the play till the end, then in the confusion, when it's over, we can slip away. The tide is up, the night will be dark, everything's ready.

MARY. The Lieutenant will be blamed, I won't let you.   55

DABBY. If you say anything to the Lieutenant, I'll refuse to act in the play.

ARSCOTT. When I say my lines, I think of nothing else. Why can't you do the same?

DABBY. Because it's only for one night. I want to   60
grow old in Devon.

MARY. They'll never let us do another play, I'm telling the Lieutenant.

ALL. No, you're not.

DABBY. Please, I want to go back to Devon.   65

WISEHAMMER. I don't want to go back to England now. It's too small and they don't like Jews. Here, no one has more of a right than anyone else to call you a foreigner. I want to become the first famous writer.[74]   70

MARY. You can't become a famous writer until you're dead.

WISEHAMMER. You can if you're the only one.

SIDEWAY. I'm going to start a theatre company.[75] Who wants to be in it?   75

WISEHAMMER. I'll write you a play about justice.

SIDEWAY. Only comedies, my boy, only comedies.

WISEHAMMER. What about a comedy about unrequited love?

LIZ. I'll be in your company, Mr. Sideway.   80

KETCH. And so will I. I'll play all the parts that have dignity and gravity.

SIDEWAY. I'll hold auditions tomorrow.

DABBY. Tomorrow.

DUCKLING. Tomorrow.   85

MARY. Tomorrow.

LIZ. Tomorrow.

---

74 Wisehammer] The real Wisehammer became a farmer and then a successful merchant in Sydney.

75 Sideway] The real Sideway started the first Australian theatre company seven years later.

A long silence. (Un ange passe.)[76]

MARY. Where are my shoes?

Ralph comes in.

RALPH. Arscott, remember to address the soldiers when you talk of recruiting. Look at them: you are   90
speaking to them. And don't forget, all of you, to leave a space for people to laugh.

ARSCOTT. I'll kill anyone who laughs at me.

RALPH. They're not laughing at you, they're laughing at Farquhar's lines. You must expect them to laugh. 95

ARSCOTT. That's all right, but if I see Major Ross or any other officer laughing at me, I'll kill them.

MARY. No more violence. By the way, Arscott, when you carry me off the stage as Jack Wilful, could you be a little more gentle? I don't think he'd be   100
so rough with a young gentleman.

RALPH. Where's Caesar?

KETCH. I saw him walking towards the beach earlier. I thought he was practising his lines.

ARSCOTT. Caesar!   105

He goes out.

WISEHAMMER. (*to Liz.*) When I say "Do you love fishing, Madam?", do you say something then?—

RALPH. (*goes over to Duckling.*) I am so sorry, Duckling. Harry was my friend.

DUCKLING. I loved him. But now he'll never know   110
that. I thought that if he knew he would become cruel.

RALPH. Are you certain you don't want Dabby to take your part?

DUCKLING. No! I will do it. I want to do it.   115

Pause.

He liked to hear me say my lines.

RALPH. He will be watching from somewhere. (*He goes to Mary.*) How beautiful you look.

MARY. I dreamt I had a necklace of pearls and three children.   120

RALPH. If we have a boy we will call him Harry.

---

76 Un ange passe] (French) "an angel passes"—an expression used when there is an unexpected moment of silence and contemplation mid-conversation.

MARY. And if we have a girl?

RALPH. She will be called Betsey Alicia.

Arscott comes in with Caesar drunk and dishevelled.

ARSCOTT. Lying on the beach, dead drunk.

CAESAR. (*to Ralph, pleading.*) I can't. All those people. 125
My ancestors are angry, they do not want me to
be laughed at by all those people.

RALPH. You wanted to be in this play and you will
be in this play—

KETCH. I'm nervous too, but I've overcome it. You 130
have to be brave to be an actor.

CAESAR. My ancestors will kill me.

He swoons. Arscott hits him.

ARSCOTT. You're going to ruin my first scene.

CAESAR. Please, Lieutenant, save me.

RALPH. Caesar, if I were back home, I wouldn't be 135
in this play either. My ancestor's wouldn't be very
pleased to see me here—But our ancestors are
thousands of miles away.

CAESAR. I cannot be a disgrace to Madagascar.

ARSCOTT. You will be more of a disgrace if you don't 140
come out with me on that stage. NOW.

MARY. Think of us as your family.

SIDEWAY. (*to Ralph.*) What do you think of this bow?

RALPH. Caesar, I am your Lieutenant and I
command you to go on that stage. If you don't, 145
you will be tried and hanged for treason.

KETCH. And I'll tie the rope in such a way you'll
dangle there for hours full of piss and shit.

RALPH. What will your ancestors think of that,
Caesar? 150

Caesar cries but pulls himself together.

KETCH. (*to Liz.*) I couldn't have hanged you.

LIZ. No?

RALPH. Dabby, have you got your chickens?

DABBY. My chickens? Yes. Here.

RALPH. Are you all right? 155

DABBY. Yes. (*Pause.*) I was dreaming.

RALPH. Of your future success?

DABBY. Yes. Of my future success.

RALPH. And so is everyone here, I hope. Now, Arscott.

ARSCOTT. Yes. Sir! 160

RALPH. Calm.

ARSCOTT. I have been used to danger, Sir.

SIDEWAY. Here.

LIZ. What's that?

SIDEWAY. Salt. For good luck. 165

RALPH. Where did you get that from?

SIDEWAY. I have been saving it from my rations. I
have saved enough for each of us to have some.

They all take a little salt.

WISEHAMMER. Lieutenant?

RALPH. Yes, Wisehammer. 170

WISEHAMMER. There's—there's—

MARY. There's his prologue.

RALPH. The prologue. I forgot.

Pause.

Let me hear it again.

WISEHAMMER. From distant climes o'er wide- 175
spread seas we come,
Though not with much éclat or beat of drum,
True patriots all; for be it understood,
We left our country for our country's good;
No private views disgraced our generous zeal,
What urg'd our travels was our country's weal, 180
And none will doubt but that our emigration
Has prov'd most useful to the British nation.[77]

Silence.

RALPH. When Major Ross hears that, he'll have an
apoplectic fit.

MARY. I think it's very good. 185

DABBY. So do I. And true.

SIDEWAY. But not very theatrical.

RALPH. It is very good, Wisehammer, it's very well
written, but it's too—too political. It will be
considered provocative. 190

---

77 Wisehammer's prologue] This prologue became somewhat famous in England, having been circulated as the
supposed work of a convict. However, Robert Hughes
reluctantly corrects the record: "Alas, later research has
shown that this was not penned by a convict in Port
Jackson, but by Henry Carter, a hack journalist in London, well after he heard the play had been performed"
(*The Fatal Shore*, New York: Vintage Books, 1988,
p. 340).

WISEHAMMER. You don't want me to say it.

RALPH. Not tonight. We have many people against us.

WISEHAMMER. I could tone it down. I could omit "We left our country for our country's good."

DABBY. That's the best line.   195

RALPH. It would be wrong to cut it.

WISEHAMMER. I worked so hard on it.

LIZ. It rhymes.

SIDEWAY. We'll use it in the Sideway Theatre.

RALPH. You will get much praise as Brazen,   200
Wisehammer.

WISEHAMMER. It isn't the same as writing.

RALPH. The theatre is like a small republic, it requires private sacrifices for the good of the whole. That is something you should agree with,   205
Wisehammer.

Pause.

And now, my actors, I want to say what a pleasure it has been to work with you. You are on your own tonight and you must do your utmost to provide the large audience out there with a pleasurable,   210
intelligible and memorable evening.

LIZ. We will do our best, Mr. Clark.

MARY. I love this!

RALPH. Arscott.

ARSCOTT. (*to Caesar.*) You walk three steps ahead   215
of me. If you stumble once, you know what will happen to you later? Move!

RALPH. You're on.

Arscott is about to go on, then remembers.

ARSCOTT. Halberd! Halberd!

He is handed his halberd and goes upstage and off, preceded by Caesar beating the drum. Backstage, the remaining actors listen with trepidation to Kite's first speech.

ARSCOTT. "If any gentlemen soldiers, or others, have   220
a mind to serve Her Majesty, and pull down the French King; if any prentices have severe masters, any children have undutiful parents; if any servants have too little wages or any husband too much wife; let them repair to the noble Sergeant Kite,   225
at the Sign of the Raven, in this good town of Shrewsbury, and they shall receive present relief and entertainment" …

And to the triumphant music of Beethoven's Fifth Symphony *and the sound of applause and laughter from the First Fleet audience, the first Australian performance of* The Recruiting Officer *begins.*[78]

---

[78] *triumphant … Fifth Symphony*] i.e., from the fourth movement.

CARYL CHURCHILL

Mad Forest

C aryl Churchill was born in London in 1938, to a mother who worked for a time as an actress and model, and a father who was an editorial cartoonist with the *Daily Mail*. But she spent much of her childhood in Montreal, where she had emigrated with her family at the end of the Second World War. In 1956, she returned to England and enrolled at Oxford University, graduating with a B.A. in English in 1960. During her time at Oxford, she wrote three plays that received student productions, and shortly after graduating she began to write radio drama for the BBC. Like other English dramatists, such as Harold Pinter and Tom Stoppard, she credits the experience of writing for radio for developing in her a certain discipline and economy of style; however, she has also said that the freedom from the constraints of working within a specific material setting allowed her imagination to rove further than it might otherwise have done.

In the early 1970s, Churchill returned to writing for the stage, submitting work to the prestigious Royal Court Theatre and eventually becoming resident dramatist there in 1974–75. Among the plays she wrote at this time were *Owners* (1972), a socialist critique of the way property ownership can erode personal relationships, and a feminist exploration of repression and femininity, *Objections to Sex and Violence* (1975). Shortly after completing her residency at the Royal Court she began work with two companies that would have a lasting effect on her approach to playwriting: Joint Stock, which was co-founded by former Royal Court artistic director William Gaskill and would later be led by Max Stafford-Clark, who has directed the premieres of many of Churchill's plays; and Monstrous Regiment, a feminist theatre company. Both of these companies employed an extended workshop process, in Britain often called "the Joint Stock method," which encouraged playwrights to develop work alongside and out of actors' research and improvisations. (For further details about this process, see the introduction to *Our Country's Good*.) In 1976, Churchill was working simultaneously on two plays set in seventeenth-century England: for Monstrous Regiment, she wrote *Vinegar Tom*, a much-admired play about witches, and for Joint Stock, she wrote *Light Shining in Buckinghamshire*, a play about the English Civil War.

The latter project inaugurated a long and fruitful collaboration with the Joint Stock company, resulting in a series of plays that made Churchill famous. These include: *Cloud Nine* (1979), a wickedly funny satire in which sexual and colonial politics overlap; *Top Girls* (1982), a dark satire about a feminist who has achieved success but has become self-absorbed and cruel; *Fen* (1983), a bleak drama about women living in isolated agricultural communities; and, in collaboration with South African playwright David Lan, *A Mouthful of Birds* (1986), a play about women and violence in which scenes based on Euripides' *The Bacchae* are interwoven with scenes set in contemporary London. One of the most successful and unusual of Churchill's plays developed though workshops with Stafford-Clark and an acting ensemble is *Serious Money* (1987), a satire in rhyming couplets about the climate of rampant greed on the London stock market in the 1980s. Its opening on Broadway was timely: just after the stock market crash of October 1987. Thus, topicality, along with warm critical notices, ensured a long and highly successful run for an artistically ambitious play which otherwise surely would have been considered a non-commercial prospect.

Caryl Churchill's *Mad Forest: A Play from Romania* (1990) did not arise directly out of collaboration with Joint Stock, but it was created using a similar workshop process. In January 1990, only a few weeks after the fall of Romanian dictator Nicolae Ceauşescu, Churchill began work with director Mark Wing-Davey and a group of student actors from London's Central School. In March, they travelled as a group to Romania to conduct first-hand research and to work with students at the Caragiale Institute of Theatre and Cinema in Bucharest. In May, they began rehearsals for *Mad Forest* back in London, performing it a few weeks later at Central School, and then returning to Romania in September to perform the play at the Bucharest National Theatre.

Most of the political details that are necessary to understand *Mad Forest* are explained in the footnotes accompanying the text, but some brief additional background may prove helpful. After the First World War, which Romania had entered in 1916 on the side of the Allies, the country was enlarged at the 1919 Paris Peace Conference, when it was awarded the formerly Hungarian territory of Transylvania. In the following years, major democratic reforms made headway until the depression of the 1930s, when Carol II, the son of a former king, returned from exile. During his reign, the Iron Guard, a fascist movement, gained much influence, and Romania came under the control of the Nazis during the Second World War. Accordingly, the country was forced to enter the war on the Axis side, though a revolution near the end of the war reversed Romania's position and the country briefly joined the Allies. At the war's end, Romania fell under the Soviet Union's sphere of influence and for the next twenty years became a Soviet satellite country. In the late 1960s, Nicolae Ceauşescu became president of Romania, and while the country gained some autonomy from the Soviets under his rule, he himself proved a ruthless autocrat, turning the country into a brutal police state. Ceauşescu was overthrown on December 22, 1989. He and his wife, Elena, were captured, hurriedly tried and then executed by firing squad on December 25. Shortly afterwards, the National Salvation Front was founded by former communists, led by Ion Iliescu, and the party gained power. Iliescu, though less brutal than Ceauşescu had been, proved ruthless with dissenters.

Mad Forest begins during the last days of Ceauşescu's reign, and continues over the next few months, up to the time the play was written, in May 1990. In the first part of the play, Churchill shows how the sense of paralysis caused by political disenfranchisement has led to cynicism and apathy, and from there to a gradual erosion of will and identity. The ghost of Flavia's grandmother provides a neat summary of the shift in the Romanian outlook from the mid to the late twentieth century when she says to her granddaughter:

> You're pretending this isn't your life. You think it's going to happen some other
> time. When you're dead you'll realise you were alive now. When I was your age
> the war was starting. I welcomed the Nazis because I thought they'd protect us
> from the Russians and I welcomed the Communists because I thought they'd pro-
> tect us from the Germans. I had no principles. My husband was killed. But at
> least I knew that was what happened to me. There were things I did. I did them.
> Or sometimes I did nothing. It was me doing nothing.

However, at the time in which the play begins, as Flavia puts it, "nobody's living." In other words, because they reside in a world that is thoroughly saturated with habitual deception and hypocrisy, no one in Romania experiences any essential connection between what they do and who they are. They have effectively foresworn personal agency, and so have no sense that they are living meaningful lives. If they tried to make the connection, to exercise personal agency—in short, to start living—they know that, as Flavia succinctly says, "it would hurt." *Mad Forest* is a drama about the suffering involved in that difficult struggle to regain one's self and start living again.

If Romania's political history since 1990, when *Mad Forest* was first produced, is any indication, her people are still involved in that struggle. In 1992, Ceauşescu's successor, Ion Iliescu, and his party composed of former communists, the National Salvation Front, were re-elected. Then, in the 1996 elections, they lost power to a centre-right five-party alliance. However, internal squabbles destroyed the precarious governing alliance, and in 2000, Iliescu was once again re-elected, in preference to the far-right Party of Greater Romania, which, at the time of writing remains the main opposition party.

[C.S.W.]

CARYL CHURCHILL

Mad Forest[1]

A play from Romania

On the plain where Bucharest now stands there used to be "a large forest crossed by small muddy streams ... It could only be crossed by foot and was impenetrable to the foreigner who did not know the paths ...The horsemen of the steppe were compelled to go round it, and this difficulty, which irked them so, is shown by the name ... Teleorman—Mad Forest."
— *A Concise History of Romania*,
Otetea and MacKenzie

CHARACTERS:
VLADU FAMILY:
    BOGDAN, an electrician
    IRINA, a tramdriver
    THEIR CHILDREN:
        LUCIA, a primary school teacher
        FLORINA, a nurse
        GABRIEL, an engineer
    RODICA, Gabriel's wife
    WAYNE, Lucia's bridegroom
    GRANDFATHER, Bogdan's father
    GRANDMOTHER, Bogdan's mother
    OLD AUNT, Bogdan's aunt
ANTONESCU FAMILY:
    MIHAI, an architect
    FLAVIA, a teacher
    RADU, an art student, their son
    GRANDMOTHER, Flavia's grandmother who
        is dead

---

1 *Mad Forest* was first staged by students in their final year of training at the Central School of Speech and Drama, London, on June 25, 1990. It was subsequently performed at the National Theatre, Bucharest, from September 17, and opened at the Royal Court Theatre, London on October 9, 1990 with the same cast.

OTHERS:
IANOŞ
SECURITATE MAN
DOCTOR
PRIEST
ANGEL
VAMPIRE
DOG
SOMEONE WITH SORE THROAT
PATIENT
TWO SOLDIERS
TOMA, age 8
GHOST
WAITER
PAINTER
GIRL STUDENT
2 BOY STUDENTS
TRANSLATOR
BULLDOZER DRIVER
SECURITATE OFFICER
SOLDIER
STUDENT DOCTOR
FLOWERSELLER
HOUSEPAINTER
PEOPLE IN QUEUES AND WEDDING GUESTS.

Notes on Layout

A speech usually follows the one immediately before it BUT:

(1) When one character starts speaking before the other has finished, the point of interruption is marked / and the first character continues talking regardless:
e.g.

GABRIEL. They came to the office yesterday and gave us one of their usual pep talks and at the end one of them took me aside / and said we'd like to see
IRINA. Wait.
GABRIEL. you tomorrow. So I know what that meant …

(2) Sometimes two speakers interrupt at once while the first speaker continues: *
e.g.

FLAVIA. Why don't the Front tell the truth and admit they're communists? / *Nothing to be
MIHAI. Because they're not.
RADU. *I don't care what they're called, it's the same people.
FLAVIA. ashamed of in communism …

Here both MIHAI and RADU interrupt FLAVIA at the same point.

I. LUCIA'S WEDDING

The company recite, smiling, a poem in Romanian in praise of Elena Ceauşescu.[2]

Stirring Romanian music.

Each scene is announced by one of the company reading from a phrasebook as if an English tourist, first in Romanian, then in English, and again in Romanian.

1. Lucia are patru ouă. Lucia has four eggs.

Music continues. BOGDAN and IRINA VLADU sit in silence, smoking Romanian cigarettes.
BOGDAN turns up the music on the radio very loud.
He sits looking at IRINA.
IRINA puts her head close to BOGDAN's and talks quickly and quietly, to convince him.
He argues back, she insists, he gets angry. We can't hear anything they say.
They stop talking and sit with the music blaring.
BOGDAN is about to speak when FLORINA and LUCIA come in, laughing.
They stop laughing and look at BOGDAN and IRINA.
IRINA turns the radio down low.

---

2 Elena Ceauşescu] the wife of Nicolae Ceauşescu, dictator of Romania 1965 to 1989.

LUCIA produces four eggs with a flourish. IRINA kisses her.
BOGDAN ignores her.
LUCIA produces a packet of American cigarettes.
FLORINA laughs.
LUCIA opens the cigarettes and offers them to IRINA.
She hesitates, then puts out her cigarette and takes one.
FLORINA takes one.
BOGDAN ignores them.
LUCIA offers a cigarette to BOGDAN, he shakes his head.
LUCIA takes a cigarette. They sit smoking.
BOGDAN finishes his cigarette. He sits without
smoking. Then he takes a cigarette.
LUCIA and FLORINA laugh.
BOGDAN picks up an egg and breaks it on the floor.
IRINA gathers up the other eggs to safety.
LUCIA and FLORINA keep still.
IRINA turns the radio up loud and is about to say
something.
BOGDAN turns the radio completely off. IRINA ignores
him and smokes.
FLORINA gets a cup and spoon and scrapes up what she
can of the egg off the floor.
LUCIA keeps still.

2. Cine are un chibrit? Who has a match?

ANTONESCU family, noticeably better off than the
VLADUS. MIHAI thinking and making notes, FLAVIA
correcting exercise books, RADU drawing.
They sit in silence for some time. When they talk they
don't look up from what they're doing.

MIHAI. He came today.

FLAVIA. That's exciting.

RADU. Did he make you change it?

MIHAI. He had a very interesting recommendation.
   The arch should be this much higher.   5

RADU. And the columns?

MIHAI. We will make an improvement to the spacing
   of the columns.

FLAVIA. That sounds good.

They go on working.

The lights go out. They are resigned, almost indifferent.
RADU takes a match and lights a candle.
They sit in candlelight in silence.

RADU. I don't see why.   10

FLAVIA. We've said no.

RADU. If I leave it a year or two till after the
   wedding, I / could —

FLAVIA. No.

RADU. It's not her fault if her sister —   15

MIHAI. The whole family. No. Out of the question.

Pause.

   There are plenty of other girls, Radu.

They sit in silence.
The lights come on.
FLAVIA blows out the candle and snuffs it with her
fingers.
They all start reading again.

RADU. So is that the third time he's made you change
   it?

MIHAI doesn't reply. They go on working.

3. Ea are o scrisoare din Statele Unite.
She has a letter from the United States.

LUCIA is reading an airmail letter, smiling. She kisses
the letter. She puts it away. FLORINA comes in from
work.

LUCIA. Tired?

Pause. FLORINA is taking off her shoes.

   I'm sorry.

FLORINA smiles and shrugs.

LUCIA. No but all of you … because of me and
   Wayne.

FLORINA. You love him.   5

LUCIA takes out the letter and offers it to FLORINA.
FLORINA hesitates. LUCIA insists.
FLORINA reads the letter, she is serious. LUCIA watches
her.
FLORINA gives the letter back.

LUCIA. And Radu? Have you seen him lately?

FLORINA shrugs.

4. Elevii ascultă lectia.
The pupils listen to the lesson.

FLAVIA speaks loudly and confidently to her pupils.

FLAVIA. Today we are going to learn about a life dedicated to the happiness of the people and noble ideas of socialism.

The new history of the motherland is like a great river with its fundamental starting point in the bi-ography of our general secretary, the president of the republic, Comrade Nicolae Ceauşescu, and it flows through the open spaces of the important dates and problems of contemporary humanity. Because it's evident to everybody that linked to the personality of this great son of the nation is eve-rything in the country that is most durable and harmonious, the huge transformations taking place in all areas of activity, the ever more vigorous and ascendant path towards the highest stages of progress and civilisation. He is the founder of the country. More, he is the founder of man. For everything is being built for the sublime develop-ment of man and country, for their material and spiritual wellbeing.

He started his revolutionary activity in the ear-liest years of his adolescence in conditions of danger and illegality, therefore his life and strug-gle cannot be detached from the most burning moments of the people's fight against fascism and war to achieve the ideals of freedom and aspira-tions of justice and progress.

We will learn the biography under four headings.
1. village of his birth and prison
2. revolution
3. leadership
4. the great personality of Comrade Nicolae Ceauşescu.

5. Cumpărăm carne. We are buying meat.

RADU is in a queue of people with shopping bags. They stand a long time in silence.
Someone leaves a bag with a bottle in it to mark the place and goes.
They go on standing.

RADU whispers loudly.

RADU. Down with Ceauşescu.

The woman in front of him starts to look around, then pretends she hasn't heard. The man behind pretends he hasn't heard and casually steps slightly away from RADU.
Two people towards the head of the queue look round and RADU looks round as if wondering who spoke.
They go on queueing.

6. Doi oameni stau la soare.
Two men are sitting in the sun.

BOGDAN and a SECURITATE MAN.[3]

SECURITATE. Do you love your country?

BOGDAN nods.

And how do you show it?

Pause.

You love your country, how do you show it?

BOGDAN is about to speak. He stops. He is about to speak.

You encourage your daughter to marry an American.
BOGDAN. No.
SECURITATE. She defies you?

Silence.

Your daughter was trained as a primary school teacher, she can no longer be employed. Romania has wasted resources that could have benefited a young woman with a sense of duty.

Silence.

I understand your wife works as a tramdriver and has recently been transferred to a depot in the south of the city which doubles the time she has to travel to work. You are an electrician, you have been a foreman for some time but alas no longer.

---

3 Securitate] the central agency of the Romanian security network, engaged in the detection and suppression of alleged political dissidents.

Your son is an engineer and is so far doing well. Your other daughter is a nurse. So far there is nothing against her except her sister.

Pause.

I'm sure you are eager to show that your family are patriots. 20

Silence. BOGDAN looks away.

When they know your daughter wants to marry an American, people may confide their own shameful secrets. They may mistakenly think you are someone who has sympathy with foreign regimes. Your other children may make undesirable friends who think you're prepared to listen to what they say. They will be right. You will listen. 25

Pause. BOGDAN is about to say something but doesn't.

What?

Pause.

Your colleagues will know you have been demoted and will wrongly suppose that you are short of money. As a patriot you may not have noticed how anyone out of favour attracts the friendship of irresponsible bitter people who feel slighted. Be friendly. 30

35

Pause.

What a beautiful day. What a beautiful country.

Silence. BOGDAN looks at him.

You will make a report once a week.

7. Ascultaţi? Are you listening?

LUCIA and a DOCTOR.
While they talk the DOCTOR writes on a piece of paper, pushes is over to LUCIA, who writes a reply, and he writes again.

DOCTOR. You're a slut. You've brought this on yourself. The only thing to be said in its favour is that one more child is one more worker.

LUCIA. Yes, I realise that.

DOCTOR. There is no abortion in Romania. I am shocked that you even think of it. I am appalled 5

that you dare suggest I might commit this crime.

LUCIA. Yes, I'm sorry.

LUCIA gives the doctor an envelope thick with money and some more money.

DOCTOR. Can you get married?

LUCIA. Yes. 10

DOCTOR. Good. Get married.

The DOCTOR writes again, LUCIA nods.

DOCTOR. I can do nothing for you. Goodbye.

LUCIA smiles. She makes her face serious again.

LUCIA. Goodbye.

8. Sticla cu vin este pe masă.
The bottle of wine is on the table.

RADU, GABRIEL and IANOŞ with a bottle of wine.
They are in public so they keep their voices down.

IANOŞ. He died and went to heaven and St. Peter says, God wants a word with you. So he goes in to see God and God says, "I hear you think you're greater than me." And he says, "Yes, I am." And God says, "Right, who made the sun?" "You did." "Who made the stars?" "You did." "Who made the earth?" "You did." "Who made all the people and all the animals and all the trees and all the / plants and —" 5

RADU. And all the wine.

IANOŞ. And everything?" And he said, "You did, God." And God says, "Then how could you possibly be greater than me?" And he says, "All these things, what did you make them from?" And God said, "Chaos, I made it all out of Chaos." "There you are," he said, "I made chaos." 10

15

RADU. A cosmonaut leaves a message for his wife. "Gone to Mars, back in two weeks." Two weeks later he comes back and his wife has left him a message. "Gone shopping, don't know when I'll be back." 20

GABRIEL. A man wants a car and he saves up his money and at last he's able to buy a Trabant. He's very proud of it. And he's driving along in his little Trabant and he stops at the traffic lights and bang, a car crashes into the back of it. So he leaps out very angry, and it's a black car with a short 25 numberplate, but he's so angry he doesn't care and he starts banging on the bonnet. Then a big dumper truck stops behind the black car and the driver gets out and he takes a crowbar and he starts smashing the back of the black car. And the Securitate man gets out of his battered black car and he says to the truck driver, "What's going on? I can understand him being upset because I hit his car, but what's the matter with you?" And the driver says, "Sorry, I thought it had started."

9. Cerul este albastru. The sky is blue.

An ANGEL and a PRIEST.

ANGEL. Don't be ashamed. When people come into church they are free. Even if they know there are Securitate in church with them. Even if some churches are demolished, so long as there are some churches standing. Even if you say Ceauşescu, Ceauşescu, because the Romanian church is a church of freedom. Not outer freedom of course but inner freedom.

Silence. The PRIEST sits gazing at the ANGEL.

PRIEST. This is so sweet, like looking at the colour blue, like looking at the sky when you're a child lying on your back, you stare out at the blue but you're going in, further and further in away from the world, that's what it's like knowing I can talk to you. Someone says something, you say something back, you're called to a police station, that happened to my brother. So it's not safe to go out to people and when you can't go out sometimes you find you can't go in, I'm afraid to go inside myself, perhaps there's nothing there, I just keep still. But I can talk to you, no one's ever known an angel work for the Securitate, I go out into the blue and I sink down and down inside myself, and yes then I am free inside, I can fly about in that blue, that is what the church can give people, they can fly about inside that blue.

ANGEL. So when the Romanian church writes a letter to the other Christian churches apologising for not taking a stand / against —

PRIEST. Don't talk about it. I'd just managed to forget.

ANGEL. Don't be ashamed. There was no need for them to write the letter because there's no question of taking a stand, it's not the job of the church / to—

PRIEST. Everyone will think we're cowards.

ANGEL. No no no. Flying about in the blue.

PRIEST. Yes. Yes.

Pause.

You've never been political?

ANGEL. Very little. The Iron Guard used to be rather charming and called themselves the League of the Archangel Michael and carried my picture about.[4] They had lovely processions. So I dabbled.

PRIEST. But they were fascists.

ANGEL. They were mystical.

PRIEST. The Iron Guard threw Jews out of windows in '37, my father remembers it. He shouted and they beat him up.

ANGEL. Politics, you see. Their politics weren't very pleasant. I try to keep clear of the political side. You should do the same.

Pause.

PRIEST. I don't trust you any more.

ANGEL. That's a pity. Who else can you trust?

Pause.

Would you rather feel ashamed?

Pause.

Or are you going to take some kind of action, surely not?

Silence.

PRIEST. Comfort me.

---

4 Iron Guard, League of ... Michael] The Legion or League of the Archangel Michael was a fascist organization founded in 1927 to promote the "Christian and racial" reformation of Romania. Out of this anti-Semitic and mystical nationalist group, a militant sub-organization, the Iron Guard, emerged to become the main political force in Romania from 1930 to 1941.

10. Acesta este fratele nostru. This is our brother.

BOGDAN, IRINA, LUCIA, FLORINA, sitting in the dark with candles. IRINA is sewing LUCIA's wedding dress. GABRIEL arrives, excited.

GABRIEL. Something happened today. / They came to

IRINA. Wait.

IRINA moves to turn on the radio, then remembers it isn't working.

GABRIEL. the office yesterday and gave us their usual pep talk and at the end one of them took me aside / and said we'd like to see you

IRINA. Wait.

GABRIEL. tomorrow. So I knew what that meant, they were going to ask me / to do something for

IRINA. Wait, stop, there's no power.

GABRIEL. them. I prayed all night I'd be strong enough to say no, I was so afraid I'd be persuaded, / I've never been brave. So I went in and they said …

IRINA. Gaby, stop, be quiet.

FLORINA. No, what if they do hear it, they know what they did.

GABRIEL. And they said, "What is patriotism?" I said, "It's doing all you can, working as hard as possible." And they said, / "We thought you might

BOGDAN. Gabriel.

FLORINA. No, let him.

IRINA puts her hands over her ears. But after a while she starts to listen again.

GABRIEL. not understand patriotism because your sister and this and this, but if you're a patriot you'll want to help us." And I said, "Of course I'd like to help you," and then I actually remembered, listen to this, "As Comrade Ceaușescu says, 'For each and every citizen work is an honorary and fundamental duty. Each of us should demonstrate high professional probity, competence, creativity, devotion and passion in our work.' And because I'm a patriot I work so hard that I can't think of anything else, I wouldn't be able to listen to what my colleagues talk about because I have to concentrate. I work right through the lunch hour." And I stuck to it and they couldn't do anything.

And I'm so happy because I've put myself on the other side, I hardly knew there was one. They made me promise never to tell anyone they'd asked me, and they made me sign something, I didn't care by then, I'd won, so I signed it, not my wife or my parents it said that specifically because they know what the first thing is you'd do, and course I'm doing it because I don't care, I'm going straight home to Rodica to tell her. I'm so happy, and I've come to share it with you because I knew you'd be proud of me.

IRINA. But you signed. You shouldn't tell us. I didn't hear.

FLORINA kisses GABRIEL.

FLORINA. But Radu's right to keep away from us.

Pause.

BOGDAN. You're a good boy.

GABRIEL. I was shaking. The first thing when I went in they said —

BOGDAN holds up his hand and GABRIEL stops. Pause.

LUCIA. What if I don't get my passport?

11. Uite! Look!

A SOLDIER and a WAITER stand smoking in the street. Suddenly one of them shouts "Rat!" and they chase it. RADU, IANOȘ and GABRIEL pass and join in. The rat is kicked about like a football. Then RADU, IANOȘ and GABRIEL go on their way and the SOLDIER and the WAITER go back to smoking.

12. Eu o vizitez pe nepoata mea. I am visiting my granddaughter.

FLAVIA and MIHAI sitting silently over their work. FLAVIA'S GRANDMOTHER, who is dead. She is an elegant woman in her 50s.

GRANDMOTHER. Flavia, your life will soon be over. You're nearly as old as I was when you were a little girl. You thought I was old then but you don't think you're old.

FLAVIA. Yes I do. I look at my children's friends and I know I'm old.

GRANDMOTHER. No, you still think your life hasn't started. You think it's ahead.

FLAVIA. Everyone feels like that.

GRANDMOTHER. How do you know? Who do you talk to? Your closest friend is your grandmother and I'm dead, Flavia, don't forget that or you really will be mad.

FLAVIA. You want me to live in the past? I do, I remember being six years old in the mountains, isn't that what old people do?

GRANDMOTHER. You remember being a child, Flavia, because you're childish. You remember expecting a treat.

FLAVIA. Isn't that good? Imagine still having hope at my age. I admire myself.

GRANDMOTHER. You're pretending this isn't your life. You think it's going to happen some other time. When you're dead you'll realise you were alive now. When I was your age the war was starting. I welcomed the Nazis because I thought they'd protect us from the Russians and I welcomed the Communists because I thought they'd protect us from the Germans. I had no principles. My husband was killed. But at least I knew that was what happened to me. There were things I did. I did them. Or sometimes I did nothing. It was me doing nothing.

Silence.

FLAVIA. Mihai.

MIHAI. Mm?

FLAVIA. Do you ever think … if you think of something you'll do … do you ever think you'll be young when you do it? Do you think I'll do that next time I'm twenty? Not really exactly think it because of course it doesn't make sense but almost … not exactly think it but …

MIHAI shakes his head and goes back to his work.

FLAVIA. Yes, my life is over.

GRANDMOTHER. I didn't say that.

FLAVIA. I don't envy the young, there's nothing ahead for them either. I'm nearer dying and that's fine.

GRANDMOTHER. You're not used to listening. What did I say?

Pause.

FLAVIA. But nobody's living. You can't blame me.

GRANDMOTHER. You'd better start.

FLAVIA. No, Granny, it would hurt.

GRANDMOTHER. Well.

Silence.

FLAVIA. Mihai.

MIHAI goes on working.

Mihai.

He looks up.

Silence.

13. Ce oră este? What's the time?

LUCIA and IANOŞ standing in silence with their arms round each other.
She looks at her watch, he puts his hand over it.
They go on standing.

14. Unde este troleibuzul? Where is the trolleybus?

People waiting for a bus, including RADU.
FLORINA joins the queue. She doesn't see him.
He sees her. He looks away.
She sees him without him noticing, she looks away.
He looks at her again, they see each other and greet each other awkwardly. They look away.
RADU goes up to her.

RADU. How are you?

FLORINA. Fine.

RADU. And your family?

FLORINA. Fine, and yours?

RADU. So when's Lucia's wedding?

FLORINA. You know when it is.

They stand apart waiting for the bus.

15. Pe Irina o doare capul. Irina has a headache.

LUCIA is trying on her wedding dress, helped by IRINA.

16. Lucia are o coroană de aur.
Lucia has a golden crown.

The wedding. LUCIA and WAYNE are being married by the PRIEST. BOGDAN, IRINA, FLORINA, GABRIEL and RODICA. Other guests.

Two wedding crowns. The PRIEST crosses WAYNE with a crown, saying:

PRIEST. The servant of God Wayne is crowned for the handmaid of God Lucia, in the name of the father, and of the son, and of the holy spirit.
ALL. (*sing.*) Amen.

This is repeated three times, then the PRIEST puts the crown on WAYNE's head. He crosses LUCIA with a crown saying

PRIEST. The handmaid of God Lucia is crowned for the servant of God Wayne, in the name of the father, and of the son, and of the holy spirit.
ALL. (*sing.*) Amen.

This is repeated three times, then the PRIEST puts the crown on LUCIA's head.

Music.

II. DECEMBER

None of the characters in this section are the characters in the play that began in part I. They are all Romanians speaking to us in English with Romanian accents. Each behaves as if the others are not there and each is the only one telling what happened.

PAINTER. My name is Valentin Bărbat, I am a painter, I hope to go to the Art Institute. I like to paint horses. Other things too but I like horses. On December 20 my girlfriend got a call, go to the Palace Square. People were wearing black armbands for Timişoara.[5] There was plenty of

---

[5] Timişoara] a city in Western Romania occupied by many ethnic Hungarians. On the 16th and 17th of December, 1989, there were anti-government demonstrations in the city in support of a Hungarian priest, Lazlo Tokeş. Nicolae Ceauşescu ordered the demonstrators shot, prompting widespread outrage among the Romanian people.

people but no courage. Nothing happened that day and we went home.

GIRL STUDENT. My name's Natalia Moraru, I'm a student. On the 21st of December I had a row with my mother at breakfast about something trivial and I went out in a rage. There was nothing unusual, some old men talking, a few plainclothes policemen, they think they're clever but everyone knows who they are because of their squashed faces.

TRANSLATOR. I'm Dimitru Constantinescu, I work as a translator in a translation agency. On the 21st we were listening to the radio in the office to hear Ceauşescu's speech. It was frightfully predictable. People had been brought from factories and institutes on buses and he wanted their approval for putting down what he called the hooligans in Timişoara. Then suddenly we heard boos and the radio went dead. So we knew something had happened. We were awfully startled. Everyone was shaking.

BOY STUDENT 1. My name is Cornel Drăgan, I am a student and I watch the speech on TV. The TV went dead, I was sure at last something happens so I go out to see.

GIRL STUDENT. I went into a shop and heard something had been organised by Ceauşescu and the roads were blocked by traffic. I thought I'd walk to the People's Palace.

BULLDOZER DRIVER. My name is Illie Barbu. I can work many machines. I work in all the country to build hospitals and schools. Always build, never pull down. In December I work at the People's Palace, I drive a bulldozer. There are always many Securitate and today they make us scared because they are scared.

BOY STUDENT 1. I see people running away and I try to stop them to ask what is happening but nobody has courage to talk. At last someone says, Let's hope it has started.

BOY STUDENT 2. Well, I'm Stefan Rusu, in fact I come from Craiova, I only live in Bucharest since September to study. On the 21 no one in our zone knew what was going on. My uncle had just come back from Iran so my sister and I went to meet him and my mother. In the Callea Vittoria I saw

Securitate who were upset, they were whispering. Well in fact Securitate have come to me when I was working and asked me to write reports on my colleagues. I agreed because I would get a passport and go to America, but I never wrote anything bad to get someone in trouble. Nobody knew I did this with Securitate. Now I could see the Securitate in the street was scared. Cars were breaking the rules and driving the wrong way up the road. We went to the Intercontinental Hotel but we were not allowed to have a meal. We were whispering, my mother told us she had been in the square and heard people booing.

STUDENT 1. I got to the square and people are shouting against Ceauşescu, shouting "Today in Timişoara, tomorrow in all the country." I look at their lips to believe they say it. I see a friend and at first I don't know him, his face has changed, and when he looks at me I know my face is changed also.

DOCTOR. My name is Illeana Chiriţa. I'm a student doctor, I come to this hospital from school, we must get six months' practical. The 21 was a normal day on duty, I didn't know anything.

GIRL STUDENT. On my way to the People's Palace I saw people queueing for a new thriller that had just been published, so as I was feeling guilty about my mother I decided to try and buy one, thrillers are her favourite books. So I queued to get the book, and at about one o'clock I went home.

BULLDOZER DRIVER. I leave work to get my son from school and I don't go back to work, I go to the Palace Square.

STUDENT 1. There were two camps, army and people, but nobody's shooting. Some workers from the People's Palace come with construction material to make barricades. More and more people come, we are pushed together.

DOCTOR. On my way home in the afternoon there was a woman crying because she lost her handbag, the other women comfort her saying, "It could be worse, people were crushed and lost their shoes, don't cry for such a small thing."

SECURITATE. Claudiu Brad, I am an officer in Securitate. In everything I did I think I was right, including 21. I went to military high school

because I like uniforms. My family has no money for me to study but I did well. I went to the Officers School of Securitate and got in the external department, which is best, the worst ones go in the fire service. Nobody knows I am in Securitate except one friend I have since I am three years old. I have no other friends but I like women and recruit them sometimes with clothes. On December 21 I am taking the pulse of the street in plain clothes with a walkie-talkie hidden. My district is Rossetti Place. I report every three hours if the crowd move their position, how could they be made calm, what they want.

SOLDIER. My name is Gheorghe Marin. I am in the army from September. My mother is in house, my father mechanic in railway. December I am near the airport. They say Hungarians come from Hungary into Romania, we must shoot them. They give us four magazines. Before, we work in the fields, we have one lessons to shoot. 21 we are in trenches, we have spades to dig. We wait something, we don't know what. We don't know Ceauşescu speak, we don't know what happen in Bucharest.

GIRL STUDENT. I'd planned to go see a film with a friend but in the afternoon my father said I must ring up and pretend to be ill, then my friend rang and said that she is ill. I wanted to go out and my father said I couldn't go alone. I thought of an excuse — we had to have some bread, so we went out together. There were a lot of people moving from Union Place towards University Place and I heard someone shout, "Down with the Dictator." I was very confused. This was opposed to the policy of the leading forces. A man came up and asked what was happening but my father pulled me away because he realised the man was a provoker who starts arguments and then reports the people who get involved. My father insisted we go home, I said he was a coward and began to cry. He said if he was single he would behave differently.

BULLDOZER DRIVER. In the square there is much army and tanks. My son is six years old, I am scared for him. I take him home and we watch what happens on TV with my wife and daughter.

STUDENT 2. About five o'clock we heard people

shouting "Jos Ceauşescu."[6] My uncle wanted to go home to Cluj. Walking back I noticed it was 99% young people in the square with police and soldiers near them and I thought "That's the end for them." At home we tried to avoid the topic and get it out of our minds.

STUDENT 1. There are vans bringing drink and I tell people not to drink because Securitate wants to get us drunk so we look bad. In the evening we tried to make a barricade in Rossetti Place. We set fire to a truck.

SECURITATE. There are barricades and cars burning in my district, I report it. Later the army shoot the people and drive tanks in them. I go off duty.

HOUSEPAINTER. My name is Margareta Antoniu, my work is a housepainter. I paint the windows on the big apartment blocks. I come back to work just now because I have a baby. The 21, the evening, I come home from a village with my children and my husband says it is happening. We expect it because of Timişoara. He hear tanks and shooting like an earthquake. We are happy someone fight for our people.

DOCTOR. My husband was away to visit his parents and I felt lonely. My mother phoned and warned me to stay home and said, "Listen to the cassette"—this is our code for Radio Free Europe.[7]

FLOWERSELLER. My name is Cordelia Dediliuc. I am a flowerseller, 22 years. Three children, 7, 4 and 2. I have a great pain because my mother die three weeks. My husband is very good, we meet when I am 14, before him I know only school and home. Before I tell you December I tell you something before in my family. My son who is 4 is 2, we live in a small room, I cook, I go out and my child pull off the hot water and hurt very bad. I come in and see, I my big child 5 my hands on his neck because he not take care. Now I have illness, I have headache, and sometimes I don't know what to do. When the revolution start I am home with

my children. The shooting is very big. I hold my children and stay there.

PAINTER. When we heard shooting we went out, and we stayed near the Intercontinental Hotel till nearly midnight. I had an empty soul. I didn't know who I was.

STUDENT 1. They shot tracer bullets with the real bullets to show they were shooting high. At first people don't believe they will shoot in crowd again after Timişoara.

PAINTER. I saw a tank drive into the crowd, a man's head was crushed. When people were killed like that more people came in front of the tanks.

FLOWERSELLER. My husband come home scared, he has seen dead people. I say him please not go out again because the children.

GIRL STUDENT. At about 11 my family began to argue so I went to my room. I heard shooting and called my father. He wouldn't let me open the shutter but through the crack I saw a wounded army officer running across the street screaming.

PAINTER. It's enough to see one person dead to get empty of feeling.

FLOWERSELLER. But I sleep and he goes out. I can't see something because the window of the apartment is not that way but I hear the shooting.

STUDENT 2. My mother, sister and I all slept in the same room that night because we were scared.

DOCTOR. The block of flats was very quiet. Lights were on very late. I could hear other people listening to the radio.

GIRL STUDENT. I sat up till four in the morning. I wanted to go out but my father had locked the door and hidden the key.

STUDENT 1. At four in the morning I telephone my mother and tell her peoples are being killed.

PAINTER. That night it seems it must be all over. I hope it will go on tomorrow but don't know how.

SECURITATE. In the night the army cleaned the blood off the streets and painted the walls and put tar on the ground where there were stains from the blood so everything was clean.

STUDENT 1. At six in the morning there is new tar on the road but I see blood and something that is a piece of skin. Someone puts down a white cloth on the blood and peoples throw money, flowers,

---

6 Jos Ceauşescu] Down with Ceauşescu.
7 Radio Free Europe] a radio network based in Munich and funded by the United States to broadcast pro-Western propaganda to Communist countries in Europe.

candles, that is the beginning of the shrines.

DOCTOR. On my way to work on the morning of the 22 there were broken windows and people washing the street.

BULLDOZER DRIVER. On the 22 I go back to work. I am afraid I am in trouble with Securitate because I leave work the day before but nobody says nothing.

DOCTOR. At the hospital no one knew what had happened but there were 14 dead and 19 wounded. There were two kinds of wounds, normal bullet wounds and bullets that explode when they strike something and break bones in little pieces, there is no way of repairing them.

HOUSEPAINTER. About 7 o'clock I take a shower. I hear a noise in the street. I look out, I see thousands of workers from the Industrial Platforms. I am wet, I have no clothes, I stay to watch. There are more and more, two three kilometres. Now I know Ceauşescu is finish.

DOCTOR. At about 8 I saw out the window people going towards University Square holding flags. They pass a church and suddenly they all knelt down in silence. My colleagues began to say, He will fall. An old doctor, 64 years old, climbed to a dangerous place to get down Ceauşescu's picture and we all cheered. We heard on the radio the General in charge of the Army had killed himself and been announced a traitor. We kept treating patients and running back to the radio.

STUDENT 2. We heard that the General committed suicide and there was a state of emergency declared. I thought everything is lost.

GIRL STUDENT. I insisted we go out. My father dressed like a bride taking a long time.

FLOWERSELLER. I go to the market to get food and many people are going to the centre. I watch them go by. I am sorry I get married so young.

TRANSLATOR. I went to work as usual but there was only one colleague in my office. We heard shots so we went out. I've noticed in films people scatter away from gunfire but here people came out saying, "What's that?" People were shouting, "Come with us," so we went in the courtyard and shouted too.

GIRL STUDENT. We hadn't gone far when we saw a crowd of people with banners with Jos Ceauşescu, shouting, "Come and join us." They were low class men so we didn't know if we could trust them. I suggested we cross the road so no one could say we were with them.

TRANSLATOR. I heard people shouting, "Down with Ceauşescu," for the first time. It was a wonderful feeling to say those words, Jos Ceauşescu.

GIRL STUDENT. Suddenly there was a huge crowd with young people. For the first time I saw the flag with the hole cut out of it. I began to cry, I felt ashamed I hadn't done anything. My father agreed to go on but not with the crowd.

STUDENT 2. Then I saw students singing with flags with holes in them and I thought, "Surely this is the end." I walked on the pavement beside them, quickly looking to the side for an escape route like a wild animal.

TRANSLATOR. I had promised my wife to take care. We were walking towards the tanks and I was in a funk. But when you're with other people you keep walking on.

GIRL STUDENT. We came to University Place. For the first time I saw blood, it was smeared on a wooden cross. It's one thing to hear shooting but another to see blood. There were police in front of the Intercontinental Hotel. But in a crowd you disappear and feel stronger.

TRANSLATOR. Then I saw there were flowers in the guns.

GIRL STUDENT. I saw a tank with a soldier holding a red carnation.

TRANSLATOR. Everyone was hugging and kissing each other, you were kissing a chap you'd never seen before.

GIRL STUDENT. And when I looked again the police had vanished.

STUDENT 2. I saw people climbing on army vehicles, I thought they'd taken them from the soldiers, then I realised the soldiers were driving and I heard people shouting, "The army is with us." Then I started to cry and I shouted too, "The army is with us."

TRANSLATOR. There were no words in Romanian or English for how happy I was.

SECURITATE. On the 22 the army went over to the

side of the people. I gave my pistol to an army officer and both magazines were full. That's why I'm here now. I had no more superiors and I wanted to get home. I caught the train and stayed in watching what happened on TV.

HOUSEPAINTER. We leave our six children with my mother and we follow some tanks with people on them. They are go to the TV station. We are there with the first people who make revolution.

BULLDOZER DRIVER. I work till half past ten or eleven, then I see tanks not with army, with men on them. I think I will take the bulldozer. But when I get to the gates my boss says, "There is no need, Ceauşescu is no more, Ceauşescu nu mai e." I see no Securitate so I go home to my family.

DOCTOR. Out of the window I saw a silver helicopter and pieces of paper falling—we thought the people had won and they were celebration papers.

GIRL STUDENT. There were leaflets thrown down from helicopters saying, "Go home and spend Christmas with your family."

DOCTOR. A boo went up outside when people say what they had said.

GIRL STUDENT. Suddenly I heard bangbang and I thought my heart would explode, but it was small children throwing celebration crackers against the walls. My father had an attack of cramp and couldn't move any further.

STUDENT 1. In the Palace Square when the tanks turn round we are afraid they will fire on us again. But they turn towards Ceauşescu's balcony.

STUDENT 2. I saw books and papers thrown down from the balcony and I thought I must do something so I went to the radio station. I heard people singing "Wake Up Romanian" and realised it was a victory.

DOCTOR. About 12.30 I heard on the radio "Wake Up Romanian," the anthem which used to be banned, and announcers who apologise for not telling the truth, they had been made to lie. Everyone began to cry and laugh. The doctors and the orderlies were equal.

GIRL STUDENT. We saw an appeal on TV at a friend's house for blood so I went to the hospital with our friend's son-in-law. There were hundreds of people waiting to give blood but only fifty bottles, luckily I was able to give blood.

STUDENT 2. I bought some champagne and went home to my family to celebrate.

DOCTOR. I went home about 3 and my husband has bought 6 bottles of champagne and we called our neighbours in. For the first time in my life I felt free to laugh.

GIRL STUDENT. We went to the TV station, it was surrounded by cars beeping, soldiers wearing armbands to show they were with the people. We were told the water was poisoned by Securitate so I ran to buy some milk so my doggie could have something to drink.

STUDENT 1. In the afternoon I go to meet my mother when she comes out of the school. Everyone is shouting "Ole ole ole ole" and cars hoot their horns. Then I go to see my grandmother to show her I am all right.

Pause.

PAINTER. That night the terror shooting started. There was no quiet place.

TRANSLATOR. When the terror shooting started, I was at home and heard it. My legs buckled, I vomited, I couldn't go out. It took me weeks to get over that.

STUDENT 1. About 7 o'clock we heard on the radio, "Help, our building is being attacked." So I went out again.

HOUSEPAINTER. At the radio station I am scared, my husband says, "Why you come then?" Terroristi shoot from a building and my husband goes with men inside and catch them. There are many wounded and I help. I am the only woman.

SOLDIER. They say us it is not Hungarians. It is terroristi. We guard the airport. We shoots anything, we shoots our friend. I want to stay alive.

PAINTER. They are asking on TV for people to defend the TV station. My girlfriend and I go out. We stop a truck of young people and ask where they're going, they say, "We are going to die." They say it like that. We can do nothing there, everyone knows it.

STUDENT 1. There was a gypsy who had a gun and he says, "Come with me, I want people strong with courage." He says we must go to the factory of August 23 where they have guns for the guards.[8] The Romanian people are cowards and have no courage to get in the truck, but at last we go to the factory. There are more than one hundred people but only 28 get guns, I get one, they say, "Be careful and come back with the gun." Then we go to a police station because we know they are on the side of the people and we ask for bullets. At first they don't want to give them, they say "We need them to defend the building." We say, "Give us at least one bullet each to be of some use."

STUDENT 2. People were shouting, "Come with us," but I thought, "It's a romantic action, it's useless to go and fight and die." I thought I was a coward to be scared. But I thought, "I will die like a fool protecting someone I don't know. How can I stop bullets with my bare hands? It's the job of the army, I can do nothing, I will just die." So I went home.

BOY STUDENT 1. At the TV station I am behind the wall of a house and they shoot across me from both sides. I go into a house, the terroristi are gone, I telephone my mother to tell her where I am. If I stay ten minutes longer I am dead because they shoot that house. In the road a boy stands up and is shot. A month later is his eighteenth birthday. I ask myself if he is shot by our soldiers. I am standing looking round, bullets are flying. After a while you don't feel scared.

PAINTER. My girlfriend and I were at the TV station. I didn't know who we were fighting with or how bad it was. I was just acting to save our lives. It is terrible to hate and not to be able to do something real.

GIRL STUDENT. That evening I wanted to put on my army clothes and go out and shoot—I got three out of three in the shooting test when I was

---

8 August 23] On August 23, 1944, the German-supported fascist government of Romania was overthrown by democratic forces led by King Michael and Iuliu Maniu; this, however, opened the door to the occupation of Romania by the Soviet Red Army, and so the date came to be celebrated as the inauguration of the communist era in Romania.

in the army. But my father had locked the door again and hidden the key.

HOUSEPAINTER. At ten o'clock we go back to the TV station with some bread.

STUDENT 1. A lot of people bring tea and food though they didn't know if there will be better days and more to eat. They bring things they save for Christmas. Some people say the food is poisoned so that people who bring it must eat and drink first.

PAINTER. I was with my girlfriend so I felt I should act as a man and be confident. I was curious to know what I would feel in difficult moments.

STUDENT 1. There are children of 12 or 13 moving everywhere, they are harder to see, bringing us bullets saying, "What do you need? What shall I bring you?"

PAINTER. A man was shot in the throat in front of me. Some people couldn't look but I was staring, trying not to forget. I had an insane curiosity. It was like an abattoir. He was like an animal dying with no chance. He had an expression of confusedness. It was incredible he had so much blood. I felt empty.

HOUSEPAINTER. At half-past eight we go to buy some bread, then home to sleep. My mother ask where I was and I say I go out to buy some bread, just that.

DOCTOR. On the 23 I went to work. Two boys came in with a young man on a stretcher, which they put down, one of them fell to the ground and began to scream—he sees the wounded man is his older brother. His friend takes him down the hall to get a tranquiliser, it is very dark and when they come back the friend trips over something, it is the body of the older brother, who is dead waiting for surgery. The younger brother was only 14. He threw himself on the corpse and won't move, he said he wants to die with his brother.

STUDENT 1. On the morning of the 23 I went home and I slept for two hours. I kept the gun with me in bed.

GIRL STUDENT. I was about to go out to defend my school when my grandmother began to panic and we thought she would have a heart attack, so I promised to stay in, and I spent the day passing messages to people on the phone. Some people don't like me because of my father.

STUDENT 2. The train didn't go that day so I stayed at home. I thought, "This is not my town. I will go to my own town and act there." 500

DOCTOR. I stayed in the hospital without going home till the 28. We had enough medicine for immediate cases. Once or twice we had to use out of date anaesthetic and the patient woke up during 505 the operation, not often but it happened. We had no coffee or food. When my husband came to see me, more than seeing him I was pleased he had 30 packets of cigarettes. We ate what the patients left and people brought some bread and some jam 510 so on Christmas day we had jam sandwiches.

SECURITATE. When I heard about the execution on the 25 I came at night with my father to the authorities to certify what I was doing during the event. I was detained three days by the army, then 515 told to remain at home. I will say one thing. Until noon on the 22 we were law and order. We were brought up in this idea. I will never agree with unorder. Everyone looks at me like I did something wrong. It was the way the law was then and the 520 way they all accepted it.

STUDENT 1. On the 25 we hear about the trial and their deaths. It is announced that people must return their weapons so we go to the factory and give back our guns. Of the 28 who had guns only 525 4 are alive.

BULLDOZER DRIVER. I stay home with my family till the 28, then I go to work. They say the time I was home will be off my holidays. There is no more work on the People's Palace, nobody knows 530 if they finish it.

PAINTER. Painting doesn't mean just describing, it's a state of spirit. I didn't want to paint for a long time then.

III.   FLORINA'S WEDDING

1. Cîinelui îi e foame. The dog is hungry.

Night, outside. A shrine. A DOG is lying asleep. A man approaches. He whistles. The DOG gets up and approaches, undecided between eagerness and fear. The

man is a VAMPIRE.[9]

VAMPIRE. Good dog. Don't be frightened.

DOG approaches, then stops. Growls. Retreats, advances. Growls.

No no no no no. You can tell of course. Yes, I'm not a human being, what does that matter? It means you can talk to me.

DOG. Are you dead? 5

VAMPIRE. No, no I'm not unfortunately. I'm undead and getting tired of it. I'm a vampire, you may not have met one before, I usually live in the mountains and you look like a dog who's lived on scraps in the city. How old are you? 10

DOG. Five, six.

VAMPIRE. You look older but that's starvation. I'm over five hundred but I look younger, I don't go hungry.

DOG. Do you eat dogs? 15

VAMPIRE. Don't be frightened of me, I'm not hungry now. And if I was all I'd do is sip a little of your blood, I don't eat. I don't care for dogs' blood.

DOG. People's blood?

VAMPIRE. I came here for the revolution, I could 20 smell it a long way off.

DOG. I've tasted man's blood. It was thick on the road. I gobbled it up quick, then somebody kicked me.

VAMPIRE. Nobody knew who was doing the killing, 25 I could come up behind a man in a crowd.

DOG. Good times.

VAMPIRE. There's been a lot of good times over the years.

DOG. Not for me. 30

VAMPIRE. Do you belong to anyone?

DOG. I used to but he threw me out. I miss him. I hate him.

VAMPIRE. He probably couldn't feed you.

DOG. He beat me. But now nobody talks to me. 35

VAMPIRE. I'm talking to you.

DOG. Will you keep me?

---

9 Vampire] Transylvania, the fifteenth-century home of Vlad the Impaler, prototype of Dracula, lies in Romania; accordingly, vampire legends abound in the country.

VAMPIRE. No, I'm just passing the time.

DOG. Please. I'm nice. I'm hungry.

VAMPIRE. Vampires don't keep pets. 40

DOG. You could feed me.

DOG approaches VAMPIRE carefully.

VAMPIRE. I've no money to buy food for you, I don't buy food, I put my mouth to a neck in the night, it's a solitary—get off.

As the DOG reaches him he makes a violent gesture and the DOG leaps away.

DOG. Don't throw stones at me, I hate it when they 45 throw stones, I hate being kicked, please please I'd be a good dog, I'd bite your enemies. Don't hurt me.

VAMPIRE. I'm not hurting you. Don't get hysterical.

DOG approaches again.

DOG. I'm hungry. You're kind. I'm your dog. 50

DOG is licking his hands.

VAMPIRE. Stop it, go away. Go. Go. Go away.

DOG slinks a little further off then approaches carefully.

DOG. I'm your dog. Nice. Yes? Your dog? Yes?

VAMPIRE. You want me to make you into a vampire? A vampire dog?

DOG. Yes please, yes yes. 55

VAMPIRE. It means sleeping all day and going about at night.

DOG. I'd like that.

VAMPIRE. Going about looking like anyone else, being friendly, nobody knowing you. 60

DOG. I'd like that.

VAMPIRE. Living forever, / you've no idea. All that

DOG. I'd—

VAMPIRE. happens is you begin to want blood, you try to put it off, you're bored with killing, but you 65 can't sit quiet, you can't settle to anything, your limbs ache, your head burns, you have to keep moving faster and faster, that eases the pain, seeking. And finding. Ah.

DOG. I'd like that. 70

VAMPIRE. And then it's over and you wander around looking for someone to talk to. That's all. Every night. Over and over.

DOG. You could talk to me. I could talk to you. I'm your dog. 75

VAMPIRE. Yes, if you like, I don't mind. Come here. Good dog.

VAMPIRE puts his mouth to the DOG's neck.

2. Toată lumea speră ca Gabriel să se însănătoşească repede.
Everyone hopes Gabriel will feel better soon.

i.

GABRIEL is in bed in hospital.
FLORINA, working there as a nurse, passes his bed.

FLORINA. I see less of you working here than if I came for a visit.

GABRIEL. Wait.

FLORINA. I can't.

GABRIEL. We won. Eh? Ole ... Yes? 5

FLORINA. Yes but don't talk. Wait for your visitors.

GABRIEL. Rodica?

FLORINA. Mum and dad.

GABRIEL. Something wrong with Rodica?

FLORINA. No. 10

GABRIEL. You'd tell me / if she was hurt.

FLORINA. Don't talk, Gabriel, rest. She's not hurt.

GABRIEL. Do nurses tell the truth?

FLORINA. I do to you.

She goes.
IRINA and BOGDAN arrive with food.

IRINA. Eggs in the shops. We're getting the benefit 15 already. I'll ask Florina who I should give it to. Keep the apples here. Make sure you get it all, you fought for it.

GABRIEL. Where's Rodica?

IRINA. She couldn't come. 20

GABRIEL. I want her.

IRINA. Don't, don't, you're not well, I'll never forgive her, she's perfectly all right.

GABRIEL. What?

IRINA. She's frightened to go out. Now when there's 25 nothing happening. She sends her love.

BOGDAN has a bottle of whisky.

BOGDAN. This is for the doctor. / Which doctor
GABRIEL. No need.
BOGDAN. do I give it to?
GABRIEL. No.   30
IRINA. Yes, a little present for the doctor so he's gentle
with you.
GABRIEL. That was before. Not now.
BOGDAN. When your mother had her operation,
two bottles of whisky and then it was the wrong   35
doctor.
IRINA. They can't change things so quickly, Gaby.
BOGDAN. You do something for somebody, he does
something for you. Won't change that. Give my
father a cigarette, he puts it behind his ear. Because 40
you never know.
GABRIEL. Different now.
BOGDAN. Who shall I give it to? I'll ask Florina.

*MIHAI, FLAVIA and RADU arrive. RADU takes
GABRIEL's hand.*

MIHAI. Radu wanted to visit his friend Gabriel so
we thought we'd come with him.   45
FLAVIA. We've brought a few little things.
MIHAI. To pay our respects to a hero.

They stand awkwardly. Then FLAVIA embraces IRINA.

IRINA. Radu's a hero too.
FLAVIA. The young show us the way,
BOGDAN. We're glad you're safe, Radu.   50
FLAVIA. And Florina's here?
IRINA. Yes, she's working.
MIHAI. You must be proud of her.
BOGDAN. She worked for five days without
stopping.   55
RADU. I'll go and find her.
FLAVIA. Yes, find her, Radu.

RADU goes.

MIHAI. We're so glad the young people no longer
have a misunderstanding. We have to put the past
behind us and go forward on a new basis.   60
BOGDAN. Yes, nobody can be blamed for what
happened in the past.
IRINA. Are you warm enough, Gaby? I can bring a
blanket from home.

ii.

*Evening in the hospital. Patient(s) in dressing-gown(s).
Someone comes looking for a doctor.*

SORE THROAT. I'm looking for the doctor. I have a   65
sore throat. I need to get an antibiotic.

*A patient shuffles slowly about, taking the person down
corridors and opening doors, looking for a doctor.
Different sounds come from the rooms—a woman
crying, a man muttering (it's the patient from III, we
barely hear what he's saying, just get the sound of
constant questions), a priest chanting. They go off, still
looking.*

iii.

*A couple of weeks after I. Sunlight. GABRIEL is much
better, sitting up. RODICA is sitting beside him holding
his hand. Flowers. A PATIENT in a dressing-gown
comes to talk to them.*

PATIENT. Did we have a revolution or a putsch?
Who was shooting on the 21st? And who was
shooting on the 22nd? Was the army shooting on
the 21st or did some shoot and some not shoot   70
or were the Securitate disguised in army uniforms?
If the army were shooting, why haven't they been
brought to justice? And were they still shooting on
the 22nd? Were they now disguised as the
Securitate? Most important of all, were the   75
terrorists and the army really fighting or were they
only pretending to fight? And for whose benefit?
And by whose orders? Where did the flags come
from? Who put loudhailers in the square? How
could they publish a newspaper so soon? Why did 80
no one turn off the power at the TV? Who got
Ceauşescu to call everyone together? And is he
really dead? How many people died at Timişoara?
And where are the bodies? Who mutilated the
bodies? And were they mutilated after they'd been 85
killed specially to provoke a revolution? By whom?
For whose benefit? Or was there a drug in the food
and water at Timişoara to make people more
aggressive? Who poisoned the water in Bucharest?
GABRIEL. Please stop.   90
PATIENT. Why weren't we shown the film of the

execution?

GABRIEL. He is dead.

PATIENT. And is the water still poisoned?

GABRIEL. No.   95

PATIENT. And who was shooting on the 22nd?

GABRIEL. The army, which was on the side of the people, was fighting the terrorists, who were supporting Ceauşescu.

PATIENT. They changed clothes.   100

GABRIEL. Who changed clothes?

PATIENT. It was a fancy dress party. Weren't you there? Didn't you see them singing and dancing?

GABRIEL. My sister's coming from America.

PATIENT. Does she know what happened?   105

GABRIEL. She'll have read the newspapers.

PATIENT. Then you must tell her. Do you know?

GABRIEL. I can't talk about it now.

PATIENT. Are you a Communist?

GABRIEL. No but my sister's / coming now.   110

PATIENT. Communist. I hope you die.

FLORINA, RADU and LUCIA.
LUCIA embraces GABRIEL and RODICA.

LUCIA. All the way over on the plane I was terrified of what I was going to see. But you look beautiful. In America everyone's thrilled. I told my friends, "My brother was there, he was wounded, he's a   115
hero." I watched TV but they never showed enough, I kept playing it and stopping when there was a crowd, I thought I must know somebody, I was crying all the time, I was so ashamed not to be here. I've brought you some chocolate, and   120
oranges.

GABRIEL. How's America?

LUCIA. If you mean how's Wayne he's fine, he has an allergy but let's forget that, he has a lot of meetings so he can't be here. But America. There   125
are walls of fruit in America, five different kinds of apples, and oranges, grapes, pears, bananas, melons, different kinds of melon, and things I don't know the name—and the vegetables, the aubergines are a purple they look as if they've been   130
varnished, red yellow green peppers, white onions red onions, bright orange carrots somebody has shone every carrot, and the greens, cabbage spinach broad beans courgettes, I still stare every time I go

shopping.[10] And the garbage, everyone throws   135
away great bags full of food and paper and tins, every day, huge bags, huge dustbins, people live out of them. Eat some chocolate.

They eat the chocolate.
PATIENT comes back again.

PATIENT. Have they told you who was shooting on the 22nd? / And why was it necessary to kill   140

GABRIEL. Please, not now.

PATIENT. Ceauşescu so quickly?

LUCIA. Have some chocolate.

PATIENT takes some chocolate and puts it in his pocket.

PATIENT. Who has taken the supplies we were sent from the west? Nurse?   145

FLORINA. I'm not on duty.

PATIENT. Did we have a revolution? Or what did we have?

RADU. Come on, let's find your bed.

RADU takes him off still talking.

PATIENT. Why did they close the schools a week   150
early? Why did they evacuate the foreigners from the geriatric hospital? Who were the men in blue suits who appeared on the streets before the 21st?

Silence.

LUCIA. They have mental patients in here with the wounded? That's not very good.   155

FLORINA. He was wounded on the head. / He has

LUCIA. That explains a lot.

FLORINA. headaches and gets upset. Yes, he's a bit crazy.

Pause.

LUCIA. Hungarians were fighting beside us they said   160
on TV. And Ianoş wasn't hurt, that's good. I think Americans like Hungarians.

GABRIEL. The poor Hungarians have a bad time because they're not treated better than everyone else. How did they treat us when they had a   165
chance? They go abroad and insult Romania to make people despise us.

---

10 aubergines] eggplants; courgettes] zucchinis.

LUCIA. This is what we used to say before? Don't we say something different?

GABRIEL. Ask granny about Hungarians. 170

LUCIA. It's true, in America they even like the idea of gypsies, they think how quaint. But I said to them you don't like Blacks here, you don't like Hispanics, we're talking about lazy greedy crazy people who drink too much and get rich on the 175 black market. That shut them up.

GABRIEL. But Ianoş doesn't count as Hungarian.

RADU comes back.

LUCIA. So you got rid of the lunatic all right? Have some more chocolate.

RADU shakes his head.

Go on, there's plenty more. 180

RADU. We're not greedy, Lucia. We don't just think about food.

LUCIA. It's a celebration, it's fun to have chocolate, can't you have fun?

RADU. No I can't. Celebrate what? 185

FLORINA. Radu, not now.

RADU. Who was shooting on the 22nd? That's not a crazy question.

FLORINA. Lucia's just arrived. Gabriel's still not well.

RADU. The only real night was the 21st. After that, 190 what was going on? It was all a show.

LUCIA. No, it was real, Radu, / I saw it on television.

FLORINA. I don't want to hear / all this now.

RADU. Were they fighting or pretending to fight? Who let off firecrackers? Who brought loudhailers? 195

Pause.
LUCIA looks at FLORINA.

FLORINA. At the Municipal Hospital the head doctor gave medical supplies for the west to police to sell on the black market. / And

LUCIA. That I can believe.

RADU. he locked the wounded in a room with no 200 one to take care of them so he could hand them over / to the Securitate and some of them died.

LUCIA. But that's just him. It's not a plot.

Pause.

FLORINA. How many people were killed at Timişoara? Where are the bodies? There were 205 bodies found in a sandpit for the long-jump. / Where are the rest?

LUCIA. But what does that mean?

RADU. Why did no one turn off the power at the TV station? 210

Pause.

LUCIA. Gabriel? Rodica?

GABRIEL. I'm too tired.

RODICA turns her head away.

iv.

Some time later. IRINA helping GABRIEL to walk. He reaches a chair and falls into it laughing.

IRINA. Good. Good.

Silence.

I used to say more with the radio on.

GABRIEL. Have you heard people say that by the 215 22nd / the revolution had been stolen?[11]

IRINA. No no no no no. I've no time for all that nonsense.

GABRIEL. But—

IRINA. No. No no no. Now. Walk. 220

3. Rodica mai are coşmare.
Rodica is still having nightmares.

RODICA is wearing a cloak and a big fur hat with dollars and flowers on it. Two soldiers come in.

SOLDIER 1. We're the last soldiers, your Majesty. The rest of the army's on the side of the people.

SOLDIER 2. The helicopter's going to rescue you.

She takes a telephone from under her cloak and dials endlessly.

---

[11] by the 22nd … revolution … stolen] December 22nd, the day the Romanian army defected from the government to join the people, also marked the foundation of the National Salvation Front, a coalition of people who declared themselves hostile to Ceauşescu and intent on forming a new government, but which turned out to be composed primarily of former Communist Party officials.

The SOLDIERS take off their uniforms and get dressed again in each other's identical clothes. Meanwhile GABRIEL comes in wearing a huge Romanian flag, his head through the hole. He gives RODICA a box of matches and goes.

SOLDIER 2. Why doesn't anyone love you after all you've done for them? 5

SOLDIER 1. Have you enough money to pay for the helicopter?

She gives them money from her hat. They pocket each thing she gives them and hold out their hands for more till she has nothing left on her hat. She gives them the hat. They hold out their hands for more.

SOLDIER 1. Give us your hands.

Her hands disappear under her cloak.

SOLDIER 2. Give us your feet.

Her feet disappear under her cloak and she sinks down till she is kneeling.

SOLDIER 1. There's no helicopter. You'll have to run. 10

The SOLDIERS go.
RODICA opens the matchbox—"ole ole ole ole" chanted by huge crowd. She opens and closes it several times and the song continues each time. Sound of gunfire. She looks round in a panic for somewhere to hide the matchbox. She puts it under her cloak, then changes her mind and takes it out. It is now a pill, which she swallows.

A SOLDIER comes in and searches, kicking at anything in the way.
He goes to her and opens her mouth.
"Ole ole ole ole" chanted by huge crowd.
He opens and closes her mouth several times, the chant continues each time.

4. Cînd am fost să ne vizităm bunicii la ţară, era o zi însorită. When we went to visit our grandparents in the country it was a sunny day.

FLORINA, LUCIA, RADU and IANOŞ are visiting FLORINA and LUCIA's GRANDPARENTS in the country, so they can meet RADU before the wedding. The GRANDPARENTS are peasants. IANOŞ has a child with him, a boy of about 8, TOMA. The following things happen in the course of a long sunny afternoon, out of doors, immediately outside the GRANDPARENTS' house where there is a bench, and nearby.

i.

THE GRANDPARENTS embrace LUCIA and FLORINA, greet RADU warmly, IANOŞ more formally. TOMA clings shyly to IANOŞ.

ii.

IANOŞ has a ball and tries to interest TOMA in playing with him and RADU. They go off.

GRANDMOTHER. That young man's a Hungarian.

LUCIA. He's a friend of Radu and Gabriel's, Granny.

GRANDMOTHER. I knew a woman married a Hungarian. His brother killed her and ripped the child out of her stomach. 5

FLORINA. He's just a friend of Gabriel's, Granny.

GRANDMOTHER. Radu seems a nice young man. He's Romanian. What's wrong with that child?

FLORINA. He's been in an orphanage.

GRANDMOTHER. Is it a gypsy? 10

LUCIA. Of course not.

GRANDMOTHER. They wouldn't let him adopt a Romanian.

iii.

LUCIA with IANOŞ and TOMA.

LUCIA. Do we have to have him with us all the time?

IANOŞ. He likes me. 15

LUCIA. I like you but I'm not getting much chance to show it.

IANOŞ. He'll settle down.

LUCIA. Can he talk?

IANOŞ. Yes of course. 20

LUCIA. I haven't heard him.

IANOŞ. He doesn't know you.

LUCIA. I think your parents are remarkable. What if it goes wrong? Can you give him back?

IANOŞ. We don't want to give him back. We're adopting him. 25

LUCIA. Your parents are adopting him.

IANOŞ. Yes but me too.

LUCIA rolls the ball.

LUCIA. Don't you want to play with the ball, Toma?

She goes and gets it herself.

   Ball. Ball. Can you say ball, Toma?   30

TOMA buries himself in IANOŞ.

LUCIA. I think your parents are sentimental.
IANOŞ. Are you going back to America?

LUCIA shrugs.

   I still owe your husband money.
LUCIA. Did you borrow money from him?
IANOŞ. He paid for the abortion.   35
LUCIA. But he didn't know. It was money he gave
   me, it was my money. You can't pay him back, he'd
   want to know what it was for.
IANOŞ. I haven't got the money anyway.

Pause.

   Aren't you ashamed?   40
LUCIA. What of? No.
IANOŞ. Not the abortion.
LUCIA. What?
IANOŞ. I don't know. The wedding?
LUCIA. No, why?   45
IANOŞ. I'm ashamed.
LUCIA. Why?

Pause.

IANOŞ. I'm ashamed of loving you when I think
   you're probably not very nice.

Silence.

LUCIA. Shall I stay here and marry you?   50

Silence.

   This is the last of the chocolate.

*As she gets it out, TOMA pounces on it and runs a little
way off, stuffing it all into his mouth.*

   You horrible child. I hate you.
IANOŞ. Don't shout at him. How can he help it?
   You're so stupid.

LUCIA. Don't shout at me.   55

*TOMA whimpers. He starts to shake his head
obsessively.*

IANOŞ. Toma. Come here.

*TOMA goes on.
IANOŞ goes to him.*

   Toma.

*TOMA hits IANOŞ and starts to bellow with panic.
IANOŞ holds him, he subsides into whimpering.
IANOŞ sits on the ground holding him.*

LUCIA. Did you tell anyone about us after I left?
IANOŞ. No.
LUCIA. It might be better if we're seen as something   60
   new.

Silence.

LUCIA. Is he very naughty?
IANOŞ. Not yet. Most of the time he's so good it's
   frightening. The babies there don't cry.
LUCIA. He's going to be terrible. I won't be much   65
   use.

Silence.

IANOŞ. I'd like to go to America. I've got a passport.
LUCIA. Just for a holiday. I don't like America.
IANOŞ. So is that the only reason you want to stay
   here? I hoped you loved America.   70

Pause.

   Would your family let you marry a Hungarian?

iv.

RADU and FLORINA. RADU drawing.

RADU. Iliescu's going to get in because the workers
   and peasants are stupid.[12]

Pause.

---

12 Iliescu] Ion Iliescu, head of the National Salvation Front,
   a former member of the Communist Party, who remained mostly resistant to Western economic and democratic reforms.

Not stupid but they don't think. They don't have
the information.   75

Pause.

I don't mean your family in particular.

FLORINA. You're a snob like your father. You'd have
joined the party.

RADU. Wouldn't you?

Silence.
He touches her face.

FLORINA. I used to feel free then.   80

RADU. You can't have.

FLORINA. I don't now and I'm in a panic.

RADU. It's because the Front tricked us. / When
we've got rid—13

FLORINA. It's because I could keep everything out.   85

Pause.

RADU. But you didn't have me then.

FLORINA. No but I thought you were perfect.

RADU. I am perfect.

Silence.

RADU. What?

FLORINA. Sometimes I miss him.   90

RADU. What? Why?

FLORINA. I miss him.

RADU. You miss hating him.

FLORINA. Maybe it's that.

RADU. I hate Iliescu.   95

FLORINA. That's not the same.

RADU. I hate him worse. Human face. And he'll get
in because they're stupid and do what they're told.
Ceauşescu Ceauşescu. Iliescu Iliescu.

FLORINA. I don't have anyone to hate. You some-   100
times.

RADU. Me?

FLORINA. Not really.

RADU. Me?

---

13 the Front] National Salvation Front.

v.

*The GRANDPARENTS are sitting side by side on the
bench, the others around them. The GRANDPARENTS
speak slowly, the others fast.*

GRANDFATHER. He was killed while he was putting   105
up posters.

RADU. You see? they're murderers. / It's the same

LUCIA. For which party, grandpa?

RADU. tactics / of intimidation.

IANOŞ. Who killed him?   110

GRANDFATHER. Posters for the Peasants Party.

FLORINA. Is that / who you support?

RADU. The Front claim the country supports them
but it's only / because of intimidation.

IANOŞ. So did they find out who killed him?   115

GRANDMOTHER. Yes, it was gypsies killed him.

RADU. Gypsies? / They were probably paid by the

FLORINA. How did they know it was them?

RADU. Front.

IANOŞ. They'd hardly need paying to murder   120
somebody.

RADU. Or it could have been Front supporters /

LUCIA. Or Securitate.

RADU. and they put the blame on the gypsies.

GRANDFATHER. It was two gypsies, a father and son,   125
who used to work in his garden. They had a
quarrel with him. He used to beat them.

LUCIA. So was it just a quarrel, / not politics at all?

FLORINA. Did anyone see them?

GRANDMOTHER. But that quarrel was years ago.   130

GRANDFATHER. A lot of people didn't like him
because he used to be a big landowner. The
Peasants Party would give him back his land.

FLORINA. So he was killed because / the rest of the

LUCIA. I thought the Peasants Party was for peasants.   135

IANOŞ. No, they're millionaires the leaders of it.

FLORINA. village didn't want him to get all the land?

LUCIA. He should get it / if it's his.

FLORINA. No after all this time working on it /
everyone—   140

RADU. Never mind that, he was against the Front,
that's why they killed him. He was against the
Communists.

GRANDFATHER. He was a party member. He was
very big round here. He was a big Securitate man.   145

LUCIA. So whose side was he on?
GRANDMOTHER. He wasn't a very nice man. Nobody liked him.

vi.

GRANDFATHER is sitting on the bench, the others lying on the grass, each separately except that TOMA is near IANOŞ. Long silence.

IANOŞ. I want to go to Peru.
RADU. Rome. And Pompeii.   150
LUCIA. A holiday by the sea.

Pause.

FLORINA. Sleep late in the morning.

Pause.

RADU. Paint what I see in my head.
FLORINA. Go into work tomorrow and everyone's better.   155
LUCIA. Gabriel walking.
IANOŞ. Rodica talking.

They laugh.

FLORINA. New shoes.
RADU. Paintbrushes with fine points.

Pause.

FLORINA. Drive a fast car.   160
LUCIA. Be famous.
IANOŞ. Toblerone.

Pause.

RADU. Make money.

Pause.

IANOŞ. Learn everything in the world by the end of the week.   165

Pause.

LUCIA. Not be frightened.

The pauses get longer.

RADU. Make Florina happy.

Long pause.

IANOŞ. Make Toma happy.

Silence.

FLORINA. Live forever.

Longer silence.

LUCIA. Die young.   170

Very long silence.

FLORINA. Go on lying here.

Very long silence.

5. Mai doreşti puţină brînză?
Would you like some more cheese?

MIHAI and FLAVIA eating cheese and salami.

FLAVIA. You know when Radu was born and they said he'd be born dead. Three days, no hope. And then Radu. The pain stops just like that. And then joy. I felt the same the morning of the 22nd. Did you ever feel joy before?   5
MIHAI. I'm not sure I did.
FLAVIA. All those years of pain forgotten. You felt that?
MIHAI. It was certainly a remarkable experience.
FLAVIA. It can't last of course. Three days after he   10
was born I was crying. But I still loved Radu. And what have we still got from the 22nd?
MIHAI. The work on the People's Palace will probably continue as soon as its new function has been determined.   15
FLAVIA. What?
MIHAI. I'm not sure they'll find me some other work. I'm not in any way compromised, I was on the streets, I'm clearly a supporter of the Front. And in any case—   20
FLAVIA. I wasn't talking about you.
MIHAI. Good, I had the impression you might be worried.

Pause.

FLAVIA. All I was trying to do was teach correctly. Isn't history what's in the history book? Let them   25
give me a new book, I'll teach that.
MIHAI. Are you losing your job?

FLAVIA. I didn't inform on my pupils, I didn't accept bribes. Those are the people whose names should be on the list.

MIHAI. Are they not on the list?

FLAVIA. They are on the list but why am I with them? The new head of department doesn't like me. He knows I'm a better teacher than he is. I can't stop teaching, I'll miss the children.

Silence during which RADU comes in.

Why are you always out, Radu? Come and eat.

RADU is already making sandwiches.

MIHAI. I hope you're going to join us for a meal.

RADU goes on making sandwiches.

RADU. Have you noticed the way Iliescu moves his hands? And the words he uses?

MIHAI. He comes from a period when that was the style.

RADU. Yes, he does, doesn't he.

MIHAI. Not tonight, Radu. Your mother's had bad news at work about her job.

FLAVIA. The new head of department—

RADU. There you are. It's because of me. No one who's opposed to the Front / will get anywhere.

MIHAI. Radu, I don't know what to do with you. Nothing is on a realistic basis.

RADU. Please don't say that.

MIHAI. What's the matter now?

RADU. Don't say "realistic basis."

FLAVIA. It's true, Mihai, you do talk in terrible jargon from before, it's no longer correct.

MIHAI. The head of department is in fact a supporter of the Liberals.

RADU. Is he?

FLAVIA. It may not come to anything.

RADU. You mean it's because of what you did before? What did you do?

MIHAI. Radu, this is not a constructive approach.

RADU. It won't come to anything, don't worry. It's five weeks since we made our list of bad teachers. Nobody cares that the students and staff voted. It has to go to the Ministry.

FLAVIA. Do you want me to lose my job?

RADU. If you deserve to.

FLAVIA slaps RADU.
Silence.

RADU. Do you remember once I came home from school and asked if you loved Elena Ceauşescu?

FLAVIA. I don't remember, no. When was that?

RADU. And you said yes. I was seven.

FLAVIA. No, I don't remember.

Pause.

But you can see now why somebody would say what they had to say to protect you.

RADU. I've always remembered that.

FLAVIA. I don't remember.

RADU. No, you wouldn't.

Pause.

FLAVIA. Why are you saying this, Radu? Are you making it up? You're manipulating me to make me feel bad. I told you the truth about plenty of things.

RADU. I don't remember.

FLAVIA. No, you wouldn't.

Silence.

Now. We have some dried apples.

RADU. I expect dad got them from someone with a human face.

RADU is about to leave.

MIHAI. Radu, how do you think you got into the Art Institute?

RADU. The still life with the green vase was the one / they particularly—

MIHAI. Yes your work was all right. I couldn't have managed if it was below average.

RADU leaves MIHAI with the sandwiches and goes.
Silence.

MIHAI. Who do we know who can put in a word for you?

FLAVIA. We don't know who we know. Someone who put in a word before may be just the person to try and keep clear of.

Pause.

But Radu's painting is exceptional.

MIHAI. Yes, in fact I didn't do anything.

FLAVIA. You must tell him. 100

MIHAI. He won't believe me.

Pause.

FLAVIA. Twenty years marching in the wrong direction. I'd as soon stop. Twenty years' experience and I'm a beginner. Yes, stop. There, I feel better. I'm not a teacher. 105

MIHAI. They might just transfer you to the provinces.

Pause.

It won't happen. Trust me.

Silence. MIHAI goes on with his meal.

FLAVIA. Granny. Granny?

Her GRANDMOTHER doesn't come. Silence. FLAVIA goes on with her meal.

6. Gabriel vine acasă diseară.
Gabriel is coming home tonight.

Downstairs in the block of flats where GABRIEL and RODICA live. GABRIEL, with a crutch, is arriving home from hospital with RADU, FLORINA, LUCIA, IANOŞ, and other friends. They have been for a drink on the way and have some bottles with them.

ALL. The lift's broken.
　How do we get Gaby up the stairs?
　We'll have the party here.
　Rodica's waiting in the flat.
　We shouldn't have stayed so long at the Berlin. 5
　We can carry him up.
　We need a drink first.
　Let's do it here.
　Do it, I've never seen it.
　Yes, Radu, to celebrate Gaby coming home. 10

Someone announces:

The trial and execution of Nicolae and Elena Ceauşescu.

RADU and FLORINA are the Ceauşescus.

IANOŞ. Hurry up. Move along.

RADU. Where are they taking us, Elena?

FLORINA. I don't know, Nicu. He's a very rude man. 15

RADU. Don't worry we'll be rescued in a minute. This is all part of my long-term plan.

CEAUŞESCU (RADU) keeps looking at his watch and up at the sky.

IANOŞ. Sit down.

FLORINA. Don't sit down.

RADU. My legs are tired. 20

FLORINA. Stand up.

IANOŞ. Sit down.

RADU. The Securitate will get in touch with my watch.

IANOŞ. Answer the questions of the court. 25

RADU. What court? I don't see any court. Do you Elena?

FLORINA. No court anywhere here.

RADU. The only judges I recognise are ones I've appointed myself. 30

SOMEONE. You're on trial for genocide.

FLORINA. These people are hooligans. They're in the pay of foreign powers. That one's just come back from America.

ALL. Who gave you the order to shoot at Timişoara? 35
　What did you have for dinner last night?
　Why have you got gold taps in your bathroom?
　Do you shit in a gold toilet?
　Shitting yourselves now.
　Why did you pull down my uncle's house? 40
　etc.

FLORINA. Where's the helicopter?

RADU. On its way.

FLORINA. Have these people arrested and mutilated.

RADU. Maybe just arrested and shot. They are our 45
　children.

FLORINA. After all we've done for them. You should kiss my hands. You should drink my bathwater.

ALL. That's enough trial.
　We find you guilty on all counts. 50
　Execution now.

FLORINA. You said there'd be a helicopter, Nicu.

IANOŞ. Stand up.

FLORINA. Sit down.

They are roughly pushed to another place.

RADU. You can't shoot me. I'm the one who gives   55
   the orders to shoot.
FLORINA. We don't recognise being shot.
ALL. Gypsy.
   Murderer.
   Illiterate.   60
   We've all fucked your wife.
   We're fucking her right now.
   Let her have it.

They all shoot ELENA (FLORINA), who falls dead at
once. GABRIEL, who is particularly vicious throughout
this, shoots with his crutch. All make gun noises, then
cheer. CEAUŞESCU (RADU) runs back and forth. They
shout again.

ALL. We fucked your wife.
   Your turn now.
   Murderer.   65
   Bite your throat out.

Meanwhile CEAUŞESCU (RADU) is pleading.

RADU. Not me, you've shot her that's enough. I've
   money in Switzerland, I'll give you the number of
   my bank account, you can go and get my   70
   money—
IANOŞ. In his legs.

They shoot and he falls over, still talking and crawling
about.

RADU. My helicopter's coming, you'll be sorry, let
   me go to Iran—
IANOŞ. In the belly.   75

They shoot, he collapses further but keeps talking.

RADU. I'll give you the People's Palace—
IANOŞ. In the head.

They shoot again. He lies still.
They all cheer and jeer.
CEAUŞESCU (RADU) sits up.

RADU. But am I dead?
ALL. Yes.

He falls dead again.
More cheering, ole ole ole etc.
RADU and FLORINA get up, everyone's laughing.

IANOŞ hugs LUCIA lightly.
GABRIEL suddenly hits out at IANOŞ with his crutch.

GABRIEL. Get your filthy Hungarian hands off her.   80
IANOŞ. What?
GABRIEL. Just joking.

A MAN looks out of one of the doors of the flats to see
what the noise is. They go quiet. He shuts the door.

7. Abia terminase lucrul, cînd a venit Radu.
She had just finished work when Radu came.

Hospital at night. A corridor. FLORINA has just come
off duty. RADU is meeting her. They hug.

FLORINA. Someone died tonight. It was his fifth
   operation. Whey they brought him in all the
   nurses were in love with him. But he looked like
   an old man by the time he died.
RADU. Was he one of the ones shot low in the back   5
   and out through the shoulder?
FLORINA. He was shot from above in the shoulder
   and it came out low down in his back.
RADU. No, all those wounds are / from being—
FLORINA. You don't know anything about it. I was   10
   nursing him.
RADU. A doctor told me.
FLORINA. What does it matter? / He's dead anyway.
RADU. They were in the crowd with us shooting
   people in the back.   15

Pause.

   And where are they now?

Pause.

FLORINA. So what have you done today? Sat in the
   square and talked?
RADU. I know you're tired.
FLORINA. I like being tired, I like working, I don't   20
   like listening to you talk.
RADU. People are talking about a hunger strike.
FLORINA. Fine, those of you who weren't killed can
   kill yourselves.

Pause.

RADU. Do you want to know what it's for?   25

FLORINA. No.

Pause.

I hope you're not thinking of it.

RADU. Someone's been getting at you, haven't they?

FLORINA. Because if you do / the wedding's off.

RADU. Someone's threatened you. Or offered you   30
something.

FLORINA. It's what I think. / Did you really say that?

RADU. I don't like what you think.

FLORINA. I don't like what you think. You just want
to go on playing hero, / you're weak, you're lazy—   35

RADU. You're betraying the dead. Aren't you
ashamed? Yes, I'm a hooligan. Let's forget we know
each other. / Communist.

FLORINA. You don't know me.

RADU goes.
FLORINA is alone.
She is joined by the GHOST of a young man.

GHOST. I'm dead and I never got married. So I've   40
come to find somebody. I was always looking at
you when I was ill. But you loved Radu then. I
won't talk like he does. I died, that's all I want to
know about it. Please love me. It's lonely when
you're dead. I have to go down a secret road. Come   45
with me. It's simple.

8. Multă fericire. We wish you happiness.

*FLORINA and RADU's wedding party at a hotel. Both
families are there, and old peasant AUNT of Bogdan's
and a WAITER. Music in background. The following
conversations take place, sometimes overlapping or
simultaneously.*

i.

*It's some time into the party so everyone's had a few
drinks without being drunk yet.*

1.

FLAVIA. What's so wonderful about a wedding is
everyone laughs and cries and it's like the
revolution again. Because everyone's gone back
behind their masks. Don't you think so?

BOGDAN. I don't know. Perhaps. You could say that.   5

2.

MIHAI. I forgot to take my windscreen wipers off last
night so of course they were stolen. Still, my son
doesn't get married every day.

3.

IRINA. She and her followers talk without speaking,
they know each other's thoughts. She just looks at   10
you and she knows your troubles. I told her all
about Gaby.

LUCIA. So you told her your troubles. No wonder
she knows.

IRINA. When they send him to Italy for his operation   15
maybe we won't need a clairvoyant. She said I
could take him to see her.

LUCIA. He'll just laugh.

IRINA. She says we have no soul. We've suffered for
so many years and we don't know how to live. Are   20
people very different in other countries, Lucia?

LUCIA. Cheer up, have a drink. It's Florina's wedding
day.

IRINA. I'll miss Florina.

4.

LUCIA is talking to a smiling WAITER.

WAITER. I remember your wedding last year. That   25
was a very different time. We had bugs in the vases.
Mind you. Can I help you change some dollars?

LUCIA. No thank you.

WAITER. I used to help your husband. It's easier now.
My brother's gone to Switzerland to buy a   30
Mercedes. You're sure I can't help you? Top rate,
high as Everest.

LUCIA. Thank you but I've no dollars left.

The WAITER's smile disappears.

5.

BOGDAN. I know someone at work killed his son-
in-law. He put an axe in his head. Then he put a   35
knife in the dead man's hand to make out it was
self-defence, and said anyway he wasn't there, it
was his son. And he got away with it. Clever eh?

RADU. What happened to the son?

BOGDAN. Luckily he had some money, he only got   40
six years.

RADU. What's he going to do to his dad when he
gets out?

They laugh.

6.

FLAVIA. How's your little brother?

IANOŞ. He wakes up in the night now and cries. 45

FLAVIA. How's your mother?

They laugh.

7.

FLORINA. I thought I was going to get the giggles.

RADU. It was good though.

FLORINA. It was lovely.

8.

IANOŞ. Lucia and I are going to start a newspaper. 50

LUCIA. A friend's sending us magazines from
   America and we'll translate interesting articles.

IANOŞ (*to* LUCIA.) Do people really dress like in
   Vogue?

9.

IRINA. I bought these shoes in the street. 55

FLAVIA. Did they want dollars?

IRINA. Yes, Lucia's last dollars went on the wedding.

FLAVIA. Black market prices have shot up.

IRINA. It's not black market, it's free market.

10.

IANOŞ. A French doctor told me 4000 babies / have 60
   it.

GABRIEL. I hate the French, they're so superior.

IANOŞ. Yes, they do like to help.

GABRIEL. Merci, merci.

IANOŞ. Can you really sterilise infected needles with 65
   alcohol?

GABRIEL. I'm sterilising myself with alcohol.

11. *Old peasant AUNT shouts ritual chants at
   FLORINA.*

AUNT. Little bride, little bride,
   You're laughing, we've cried.
   Now a man's come to choose you 70
   We're sad because we lose you.
   Makes you proud to be a wife
   But it's not an easy life.
   Your husband isn't like a brother
   Your mother-in-law's not like a mother. 75
   More fun running free and wild

Than staying home to mind a child.
   Better to be on the shelf
   Only have to please yourself.
   Little bride don't be sad, 80
   Not to marry would be mad.
   Single girls are all in tears,
   They'll be lonely many years.
   Lovely girl you're like a flower, /
   Only pretty for an hour— 85

BOGDAN. Hush, auntie, you're not in the country
   now.

FLORINA. No, I like it. Go on.

ii.

*Later. People have had more to drink and are more
cheerful, emotional, aggressive.*

1.

IRINA. If only he'd stayed in University Square.

LUCIA. He could have been shot there. 90

IRINA. The bullets missed Ianoş.

LUCIA. Do you wish they'd hit him?

IRINA. No but of course anyone else.

2.

FLORINA. Be nice to your mum and dad.

RADU. I am nice. 95

3.

BOGDAN. Whinge whinge. Gaby was shot, all right.
   Everyone whinges. Layabout students. Radu and
   Ianoş never stop talking, want to smack them in
   the mouth. "Was it a revolution?" Of course it was.
   / My son was shot for it and we've got 100

MIHAI. Certainly.

BOGDAN. This country needs a strong man.

MIHAI. And we've got one.

BOGDAN. We've got one. Iliescu's a strong man. We
   can't have a traffic jam forever. Are they going to 105
   clear the square or not?

MIHAI. The government has to avoid any action that
   would give credibility to the current unsubstanti-
   ated allegations.

BOGDAN. They're weak, aren't they. 110

4.

FLAVIA. I'm going to write a true history, Florina,

so we'll know exactly what happened. How far do
you think Moscow was involved / in planning the
coup?

FLORINA. I don't know. I don't care. I'm sorry.   115

FLAVIA. What did you vote? Liberal?

FLORINA. Yes of course.

FLAVIA. So did I, so did I.

She hugs FLORINA.

Mihai doesn't know. And next time we'll win. Jos
Iliescu.   120

5.

RADU. Look at Gaby, crippled for nothing. They've
voted the same lot in.

IRINA. It's thanks to Gaby you can talk like this.

6.

IANOŞ. Have another drink.

LUCIA. I've had another drink.   125

IANOŞ. Have another drink.

They laugh.

7.

IRINA. Ceauşescu shouldn't have been shot.

RADU. Because he would have exposed people / in
the Front.

IRINA. He should have been hung up in a cage and   130
stones thrown at him.

They laugh.

8.

BOGDAN (*to* MIHAI.) If Radu had been hurt instead
of Gaby, he'd be in hospital in Italy by now.

9.

GABRIEL. I can't work. Rodica can't work. What's
going to happen to us? I wish I'd been killed.   135

FLORINA. You're going to Italy.

GABRIEL. When? Can't you do something to hurry
things up, Florina? Sleep with a doctor? Just
joking.

10.

IRINA. I don't like seeing you with Ianoş.   140

LUCIA. He's Gabriel's friend.

IRINA. I was once in a shop in Transylvania and they
wouldn't serve me because I couldn't speak
Hungarian. / In my own country.

LUCIA. Yes, but—   145

IRINA. And what if the doctor only spoke Hungarian
/ and someone wanted a doctor?

BOGDAN. Stuck up bastards.

IRINA. Are you going back to America? You're not
going back.   150

LUCIA. Didn't you miss me?

IRINA. Aren't you ashamed? Two years of hell to get
your precious American and you don't even want
him. Did he beat you?

LUCIA. I got homesick.   155

IRINA. Was Ianoş going on before?

LUCIA. Of course not. You didn't think that?

IRINA. I don't know what I thought. I just made the
wedding dress.

LUCIA. You like Ianoş.   160

IRINA. Go back to America, Lucia, and maybe we
can all go. You owe us that.

BOGDAN. You're a slut, Lucia.

11.

FLAVIA. Where are the tapes they made when they
listened to everyone talking? All that history   165
wasted. I'd like to find someone in the Securitate
who could tell me. Bogdan, do you know anyone?

BOGDAN. Why me?

FLAVIA. I used to know someone but she's disappeared.   170

BOGDAN. They should be driven into the open and
punished. Big public trials. The Front aren't doing
their job.

FLAVIA. There wouldn't be enough prisons.

BOGDAN. (*to* MIHAI.) There's a use for your People's   175
Palace.

12.

MIHAI. I was in the British Embassy library reading
the Architect's Journal and there's a building in
Japan forty stories high with a central atrium up
to twenty stories. So the problem is how to get   180
light into the central volume. The German
engineer has an ingenious solution where they've
installed computerised mirrors angled to follow the
sun so they reflect natural light into the atrium
according to the season and the time of day, so you   185
have sunlight in a completely enclosed space.

13.

FLORINA. I'm glad about you and Ianoş.

They kiss.

Tell me something.

LUCIA. Don't ask.

FLORINA. No, tell me.   190

LUCIA. Two years is a long time when you hardly
know somebody. I'd lost my job, I had to go
through with it, I wanted to get away.

FLORINA. But you loved Wayne at first? If you didn't
I'll kill you.   195

LUCIA. Of course I did. But don't tell Ianoş.

14.

PRIEST. You can't blame anybody. Everyone was
trying to survive.

BOGDAN. Wipe them out. Even if it's the entire
population. We're rubbish. The Front are stuck-up   200
bastards. They'd have to wipe themselves out too.

PRIEST. We have to try to love our enemies.

BOGDAN. Plenty of enemies. So we must be the
most loving people in the world. Did you love
him? Give him a kiss would you?   205

PRIEST. When I say love. It's enough not to hate.

BOGDAN. Handy for you having God say be nice
to Ceauşescu.

PRIEST. You're your own worst enemy, Bogdan.

BOGDAN. So I ought to love myself best.   210

PRIEST. Don't hate yourself anyway.

BOGDAN. Why not? Don't you? You're a smug
bugger.

iii.

*Later. Two simultaneous conversations develop so that
there are two distinct groups. Everyone has drunk a lot
by now. BOGDAN, who is too drunk to care if anyone
listens, puts remarks at random to either group.*

1.

BOGDAN. a. Private schools, private hospitals. I've
seen what happens to old people. I want to buy   215
my father a decent death.

b. I support the Peasant's Party because my father's
a peasant. I'm not ashamed of that. They should
have their land because their feet are in the earth

and they know things nobody else knows. Birds,   220
frogs, cows, god, the direction of the wind.

c. CIA, KGB, we're all in the hands of foreign
agents. That's one point where I'm right behind
Ceauşescu.

2. MIHAI, RADU *and* FLORINA, *joined by* FLAVIA.

MIHAI. The Front wouldn't fix the vote because they   225
knew they were going to win. Everyone appreciates
the sacrifice made by youth. The revolution is in
safe hands. This isn't a day for worrying, Florina
and Radu, you take too much on yourselves. I wish
you could let it all go for a little while. Please   230
believe me, I want your happiness.

FLORINA. We know you do.

She kisses him.

RADU. Yes, I know. I appreciate that.

MIHAI. After all, I'm not a monster. Most of the
country supports the Front. It's only in my own   235
home it takes courage to say it. We have a
government of reconciliation.

FLAVIA. Why don't the Front tell the truth and admit
they're communists? /*Nothing to be

MIHAI. Because they're not.   240

RADU. *I don't care what they're called, it's the same
people.

FLAVIA. ashamed of in communism, / nothing to be

FLORINA. They should have been banned / from

MIHAI. That's your idea of freedom, banning people?   245

FLORINA. standing in the election.

RADU. We've got to have another revolution.

FLAVIA. ashamed of in planning the revolution if
they'd just admit it. You never dared speak out
against Ceauşescu, Mihai, and you don't dare speak   250
out now. Say it, I'm a communist and so what. /
Say it, I'm a communist.

RADU. Jos comunismul, jos comunismul. / Jos
Iliescu. Jos tiranul.[14] Jos Iliescu. Jos Iliescu.

FLORINA. Radu, don't be childish.   255

*BOGDAN joins in shouting "Jos comunismul," then
turns his attention to the other group.*

---

14 Jos comunismul ... tiranul] Down with communism ...
tyranny.

3. GABRIEL *at first in group with* MIHAI *then with* LUCIA, IANOȘ *and* IRINA.

GABRIEL. The only reason we need an internal security force is if Hungary tried to invade us / we'd need to be sure—

LUCIA. Invade? are you serious?

IANOȘ. When we get Transylvania back it's going to be legally / because it's ours.   260

IRINA. You're not going to marry a Hungarian.

LUCIA. I'm married already.

IANOȘ. Gaby, the Hungarians started the revolution. Without us you'd still be worshipping Ceaușescu.   265
/ And now the

GABRIEL jeers.

LUCIA. We didn't worship him.

IRINA. Gaby's a hero, Ianoș.

IANOȘ. Romanians worship Iliescu. Who's the opposition? Hungarians.   270

GABRIEL. That's just voting for your language.

LUCIA. Why shouldn't they have their own schools?

IRINA. And lock Romanian children out in the street. If it wasn't bad enough you going to America, now a Hungarian, / and Gaby crippled, and Radu's   275
irresponsible, I worry for Florina.

GABRIEL. If they want to live in Romania / they can

LUCIA. In the riots on TV I saw a Hungarian on the

GABRIEL. speak Romanian.

IANOȘ. We can learn two languages, we're not stupid.   280

LUCIA. ground and Romanians kicking him.

GABRIEL. That was a Romanian on the ground, and Hungarians—you think we're stupid?

IANOȘ. You were under the Turks too long, it made you like slaves.   285

LUCIA. You think I'm a slave? I'm not your slave.

GABRIEL pushes IANOȘ, who pushes him back.
BOGDAN arrives.

BOGDAN. Leave my son alone. Hungarian bastard. And don't come near my daughter.

IANOȘ. I'm already fucking your daughter, you stupid peasant.   290

BOGDAN hits IANOȘ.
RADU restrains BOGDAN.
LUCIA attacks BOGDAN.
BOGDAN hits RADU.

MIHAI pushes BOGDAN.
BOGDAN hits MIHAI.
FLAVIA attacks BOGDAN.
IANOȘ pushes GABRIEL.
IRINA protects GABRIEL.
GABRIEL hits IANOȘ.
RADU attacks BOGDAN.
MIHAI restrains RADU.
RADU attacks MIHAI.
FLORINA attacks RADU.
GABRIEL hits out indiscriminately with his crutch and accidentally knocks BOGDAN to the floor.

Stunned silence.

FLAVIA. This is a wedding. We're forgetting our programme. It's time for dancing.

They pick themselves up, see if they are all right. Music—the lambada.[15] Gradually couples form and begin to dance. BOGDAN and IRINA, MIHAI and FLAVIA, FLORINA and RADU, LUCIA and IANOȘ. GABRIEL tries to dance on his crutch.
For some time they dance in silence. The ANGEL and VAMPIRE are there, dancing together. They begin to enjoy themselves.
Then they start to talk while they dance, sometimes to their partner and sometimes to one of the others, at first a sentence or two and finally all talking at once. The sentences are numbered in a suggested order. At 14, every couple talks at once, with each person alternating lines with their partner and overlapping with their partner at the end. So that by the end everyone is talking at once but leaving the vampire's last four or five words to be heard alone. At first they talk quietly then more freely, some angry, some exuberant. They speak Romanian.

BOGDAN. 1. Țara asta are nevoie de un bărbat puternic. (This country needs a strong man.)
5. Sîntem un gunoi. (We're rubbish.)   295
13. Dă-le una peste gură. (Smack them in the mouth.)

---

15   *lambada*] an erotic dance from Brazil, in which couples dance quickly while touching one another at the hips. A song called "Lambada," by Kaoma, made the dance an international fad in the early 1990s.

Ei ştiu lucruri pe care nimeni altcineva nu le ştie, păsări, broaşte, vaci, dumnezeu, direcţia vîntului. (They know things nobody else knows, birds, frogs, cows, god, the direction of the wind.)

IRINA. 3. Ea spune ca noi nu avem suflet. (She says we have no soul.)

12. (El) ar trebui spînzurat într-o cuşcă, să dea lumea cu pietre în el. (He should have been hung up in a cage and stones thrown at him.)

14. Tu n-o să te mariţi cu-n ungur. (You're not going to marry a Hungarian.) Datorită lui Gaby poţi să vorbeşti aşa. (It's thanks to Gaby you can talk like this.)

MIHAI. 8. Nimic nu e pe baze realistice. (Nothing is on a realistic basis.)

Trebuie să lăsăm trecutul în spate. (We have to put the past behind us.)

Frontul doreşte sa înlesnească demorcraţia. (The Front wish to facilitate democracy.)

Ei nu vor aranja votarea, fiindcă ştiu ei că vor învinge. (They wouldn't fix the vote because they knew they were going to win.)

FLAVIA. 2. Nu este istoria ce e în cartea de istorie? (Isn't history what's in the history books?)

14. Vreau să predau corect. (I want to teach correctly.)

Unde sînt casetele? (Where are the tapes?)

Voi scrie o istorie advarată, ca să ştim exact ce s-a întîmplat. (I'm going to write a true history so we'll know exactly what happened.)

Am votat cu liberalii. (I voted Liberal.)

FLORINA. 4. Uneori îmi este dor de el. (Sometimes I miss him.)

14. Doctorul şef a încuiat răniţii într-o cameră. (The head doctor locked the wounded in a room.)

Comuniştii nu trebuie să candideze în alegeri. (The communists shouldn't stand in the election.)

Imi place să fiu obosită, nu-mi place să te aud vorbind. (I like being tired, I don't like listening to you talk.)

RADU. 9. Cine a tras în douazeci şi doi? Nu e o întrebare absurdă. (Who was shooting on the 22nd? That's not a crazy question.)

Cine a aruncat pocnitori? Cine a adus difuzoare? (Who let off firecrackers? Who brought loud-hailers?)

Nu-mi pasă cum se numsec, este acelaşi popor. (I don't care what they're called it's the same people.)

Trădezi morţii. (You're betraying the dead.)

LUCIA. 11. Mi-a fost ruşine ca nu am fost acolo. (I was so ashamed not to be here.)

14. Dar ce inseamna asta? De ce parte a fost el? (But what does it mean? Whose side was he on?)

De ce n-au şcolile lor? (Why shouldn't they have their own schools?)

Nu sint sclava ta. (I'm not your slave.)

IANOŞ. 7. Esti acuzat de genocid. (You're on trial for genocide.)

Cine este opozitia? Ungurii. (Who's the opposition? Hungarians.)

Voi aţi fost prea mult sub turci, sînteţi ca sclavii. (You were under the Turks too long, you're like slaves.)

Vreau sa învăţ tot. (I want to learn everything.)

GABRIEL. 10. Sînt aşa de fericit, ca sînt de cealaltă parte. (I'm so happy I've put myself on the other side.)

14. Diferit acum. (Different now.)

Ii urasc pe francezi. (I hate the French.)

Ungurii îi fac pe oameni să ne dispreţuiască. (The Hungarians make people despise us.)

Aş vrea să fi fost omorît. Glumesc. (I wish I'd been killed. Just joking.)

ANGEL. 6. Să nu-ţi fie ruşine. (Don't be ashamed.)

13. Nu libertatea din afară ci libertatea interioară. (Not outer freedom of course but inner freedom.)

Am încercat sa mă ţin departe de politica. (I try to keep clear of the political side.)

Zburînd în albastru. (Flying about in the blue.)

VAMPIRE. 11. Nu-ţi fie frică. (Don't be frightened.)

14. Nu sînt o fiinţă umană. (I'm not a human being.)

Incepi sa vrei sînge. Membrele to dor, capul îţi arde. Trebuie să te mişti din ce în ce mai repede. (You begin to want blood. Your limbs ache, your head burns, you have to keep moving faster and faster.)

COLLEEN WAGNER

The Monument

B orn in Elk Point, Alberta during a prairie blizzard in 1949, Colleen Wagner has lived much of her life in the city, though she has observed that her work "remains influenced by the plains environment." She studied visual arts at the Ontario College of Art, and Literature and Drama at the University of Toronto and L'Institute du Film et Théâtre in Poland. From 1973 to 1980, she worked as an actress and, occasionally, as a designer. Wagner's writing career began in 1986, and her first play, *Sand*, won the distinction of being short-listed for the award for best international play by the Royal Exchange Theatre in Manchester, England. Since then, she has written two other plays, several screenplays and short stories, and has taught writing at Sheridan College, Centennial College, Ryerson University, the Ontario College of Art and Design, the University of Toronto and the University of New Brunswick. She also served as playwright-in-residence at Necessary Angel Theatre in 1989 and at Canadian Stage Company in 1997. She is currently Assistant Professor of Screenwriting in the Department of Film and Video at York University in Toronto. She is also working on a screenplay adaptation of *The Monument* and has two new stage plays in the works, *Home* and *The Morning Bird*.

From the beginning, Wagner's writing has dealt with the large questions we face where life teeters on the verge of death. *Sand* (1986) is set in a timeless farm country that has degenerated into an enormous desert. When a woman returns to her family home after a long absence, claiming to be able to end the drought because she is a rainmaker, she is met with distrust by those who fear that she must want revenge. Wagner's next play, *Eclipsed* (1991), used the parallel stories of a young man who has been diagnosed with a fatal auto-immune disease and a gardener whose precious plants are suffering from blight to pose questions not only about nature and free will, but about how the fear of death itself can impinge on freedom. Wagner's starkest treatment of our confrontation with death, however, is her best known play, *The Monument*, which won the 1996 Canadian Governor General's Award for Drama and has been produced not only in Toronto, Winnipeg and Edmonton, but in Berlin, Beijing, and Melbourne, Australia. That the play has been successfully produced on four continents in three languages suggests something of the universality of its themes.

Yet, wherever we find the so-called "universal" in literature, it always seems to be founded on the exploration of something much more specific. In this case, although the story could (alas) be understood as happening anywhere (perhaps even in some purgatorial afterlife), when the play was first produced in 1995, the names of the characters and the nature of the war crimes described inevitably evoked the terrible civil war in Bosnia-Herzegovina. In 1995, any hope that, as the bloodiest century in world history drew to a close and the Cold War ended, the brutality of war might also become a thing of the past was badly shaken as the details of the atrocities routinely committed in Bosnia came to light. The Bosnian War showed just how close below the surface of modern civilization barbarism still lay. Archaic tribal hatreds that had seemed largely obsolete erupted onto the surface of ordinary life in a modernized, educated society, and brought motiveless savagery, violence, lawlessness and bloodlust. The despair and bewilderment felt by many people is expressed by Mejra in *The Monument* when she says: "We all know soldiers don't do that to women and children. Men don't do that sort of thing. We all know that. Isn't that the 'truth'?" Bosnia showed that it wasn't; the veil of comforting notions that many in the West had begun to take for the "truth" had been torn away, revealing a much grimmer prospect.

That grimmer prospect is perhaps summed up by another of Mejra's questions: "Is war fate?" This second question is not merely rhetorical. It haunts this play as, indeed, it has lingered just beneath the surface of any serious discussion of the future of civilization over the past century. Wisely, Wagner does not presume to provide any certain resolution to this problem. Instead, she insists on using her play to look for a deeper truth by shaming all facile answers to the question into silence. We are forced to acknowledge the terrible idea that violence and vengeance may be every bit as essential a part of our humanity as are (we hope) mercy and compassion. Certainly, history offers little comfort, for the problem may be said to extend as far back as Genesis, as we find implied when Mejra asks Stetko, "Do you think the first lie ever told was to protect another?"and Stetko reluctantly admits that "Probably the first person to tell a lie did it to save himself."

The earliest play in this two-volume anthology, *The Oresteia* of Aeschylus, and the most famous play, Shakespeare's *Hamlet*, are both concerned with the theme of vengeance and whether the imperative it seems to hold over human nature is an absolute one or not. Any question about human nature that has lingered for two-and-a-half-thousand years is unlikely to be resolved easily or quickly, so Wagner offers an ending that, under the circumstances, is perhaps the most attractive one that is, realistically, available to us: *"the monument of Mejra and Stetko in a moment of possibilities."*

[C.S.W.]

﹏﹏

COLLEEN WAGNER
The Monument[1]

In memory of my mother,
Lucille Anne Wagner (née Caskey)

CHARACTERS
STETKO, 19
MEJRA, 50

"A voice was heard in Ramah,
Sobbing and lamenting
Rachel weeping for her children,
refusing to be comforted
because they were no more."
Jeremiah 31:15

SCENE 1

STETKO is strapped to an electric chair. A single bulb above him provides the only light. He appears small in the vast darkness. He speaks to spectators sitting in a gallery behind or around him. We cannot see the gallery or the spectators.

STETKO: The one I like the best was 17, maybe 18.
And pretty. With watery eyes.
Like a doe's.
She was like that.

I was her first.   5
I mean, she was a virgin.
A man can tell.
She said she wasn't, but the way she bled —
and cried —

I knew.   10

I didn't mean to hurt her.
Every time she cried out I pulled back.
I wanted it to last.

Pause.

I don't care for orgasm like some men.
They only think about coming. They rush   15
    through
like they're pumping iron
just wanting to come.
Not me.
Once you come that's it.
It's over.   20
And there you are facing the same old things that
    were
there before you started.

I don't care for the world much.

(*laughs*) 'Course it doesn't care much for me either.
So big deal, eh?   25
It don't care for me, I don't care for it…
Big deal.

The doctors — make me laugh — they're trying to
figure me out.
Why I'm like this.   30
Nobody agrees.
Dr. Casanova — Yeah! Casanova! I think he's joking
when he tells me his name. I laugh in his face.
He stares back.
He's got eyes like a chicken's.   35
Beady.
And small.

---

1 "The Monument" premiered in January, 1995 at Canadian Stage Company, Toronto, in co-production with Necessary Angel Theatre and the Manitoba Theatre Centre. It was directed by Richard Rose and featured Rosemary Dunsmore as Mejra and Tom Barnett as Stetko.

So I don't say nothing.
We have one-hundred and six sessions and I don't say
anything. Not a word. We stare at each other for one   40
hour, one-hundred and six times.
He thinks I'm a "passive aggressive".
I think he's fucking nuts.

They bring in another doctor.
A woman.   45
She comes with a body guard.
'Cause I'm dangerous.
That's what the body guard said.
"Dangerous."
I say to her, "wanna fuck?"   50
She says, "and then go to the forest?"
I know what she's doing — egging me on.
Trying to trick me.
Get me to talk.
I look at her and I think, this doctor has never   55
    done it
except in a nice soft bed and she doesn't do it much,
and she doesn't like it when she does do it.
She's got a tight puckered mouth.
I said to her "Is your ass like your mouth?"
She says, "No. One exhales, the other inhales. Don't   60
yours?"
She's funny. So I talk to her.
Except,
I don't tell her where the bodies are.

I don't remember.   65

Pause.

I tell her about my girlfriend.
My girlfriend's a virgin.
She wants to do it but there's no place.
She lives at home.
Whenever we'd go into her room her mother would   70
listen at the door and open it all of a sudden and
    poke
her head in. "It's too quiet in here," she'd say. "If you
got nothing to say then you can join us in the living
room. If you do have something to say, say it and
come out here. It's not good for people to spend too   75
much time alone together when they've got nothing

to say." She should talk. I don't think she's said two
words to her husband since "I do" at the wedding.

We couldn't do it at my place 'cause I was in the army.
Some men would bring their girlfriends to the camp   80
and would do it while others watched.
I can't come when people are watching. And the men
never let you forget it when you don't come.
So I never brought my girlfriend.

I never took her to the forest.   85

I think she's watching.
I don't want her to think I'm nervous.
I didn't eat or drink since yesterday.
I don't want to mess my pants in front of her.

After I was arrested she went to the camps where the   90
women were held.
They told her that I'd been there and raped 23 girls.
At first I told her it wasn't true.
It wasn't really.
I mean I had to.   95
The other men forced me.
First time I said no they stripped me naked and
laughed at me — said I had no dick, said I turned
    into
a girl all of a sudden, that maybe they should do it to
me.   100

So I did it.

I couldn't come.
So they rubbed my face in shit and made me do it
'til I came.

I faked it.   105

She just laid there looking at me.
She didn't care. She gave up.
She didn't even blink when I was doing it to her.
Just laid there like she was dead.

After it was over they told me to kill her.   110
I had to. I had lowest rank.
We took her to the forest and I shot her with my

machine gun and hid her body under a log. It'd been
raining and she was covered in mud. Somebody
   might
have mistaken her for a dead pig.   115

That was the first time I did it.
Sex.

I didn't mind killing her 'cause she knew I faked it
   and
I didn't want her telling anyone.
It was like that.   120

We went to the prison camps about every 3 days
   after
that and would pick out women and we'd all do it
   then
drive them out to the forest. We'd rape them again
then kill them.

Everybody was doing it.   125
I don't know why.

That's where I saw the one I liked.
In one of the camps.
I was the first.

I got nothing against those "people" personally.   130
I was 17.
I had to enlist. If I didn't they'd think I was a
sympathizer and they'd kill my family.
Only soldiers were getting paid.
My brothers and I were the only ones in the family   135
making any money.
I drove a cab before but with the war nobody was
taking them. Besides, only the army could buy gas.

So you do what comes up.

Who knows what that will be, eh? — what life brings?   140
You're born.
You die.
And in between you try to live a little.

Maybe it's fate, eh? — our lives.

Pause.

I'm not proud of what I did and I'm sorry my   145
   girlfriend found out.
I'm sorry we couldn't do it before I die.

Pause.

I did to the one I like what I wanted to do to my
girlfriend because I knew my girlfriend wouldn't let
me do it to her.

It was getting harder and harder to get it up.   150
I knew one day I'd get caught faking it.
So I took this girl to the forest after we raped her.
I got to drive alone.
The others thought I was taking her there to kill her.
I tied her up to a tree so she was just off the ground   155
and started talking to her.
I told her about my girlfriend, about me driving a
   cab,
and about my uncle, who has a still out back of his
house, and how he's always dodging the authorities
and selling to them at the same time.   160
I tell her she's pretty
that she reminds me of my girlfriend.
My girlfriend's studying to be a nurse.
She says she wants to put some good back into the
world.   165

I would too.
If I knew how.
Who wouldn't, eh?
If they knew how.

Pause.

So I take all her clothes off and she's crying and   170
begging me not to do it.
I want to
but I don't.
Her crying doesn't stop me.
I can't get it up.   175
I can't do it anymore.

That's what I really regret.
That I didn't do it with my girlfriend before I got caught. I think I could have come with her.

The woman doctor, Nika, Dr. Nika — she wouldn't 180
tell me her first name — said that was reserved for friends. Obviously I wasn't one of them.
I don't know what she told the authorities but next thing you know I'm being tried for war crimes.
Makes me laugh. 185
If war is a crime why do we keep having them?
Why isn't everybody arrested?
They show us porno films and tell us doing it to women is good for morale and they bring women in and then after the war is over they tell us what we did 190
is a crime.
After it's over you find out there were rules.
Like no raping women.
(*ironic*) No massacres.
Just good clean fighting — as if it were a duel, as 195
    if it
were honourable.
As if you were brave.

Men aren't brave. We're all so scared we're going to die we do anything to stay alive. We'll shoot a guy
    in
the back. We'll creep into his bedroom in the middle 200
of the night and shoot him in his sleep.

And we'll rape his wife and daughters.
Nobody's going to stop you.

Some of the men said we shouldn't kill the women.
We should get them all pregnant with our babies and 205
that's how we'd win the war.
Create a new race.

I heard some men were keeping women 'til after they got them pregnant. Seven, eight months. Too late
    for
them to do anything about it. 210

It's a very good way to wipe out a race. Take away their women and get them pregnant. Their own husbands don't even want them after that. And what's

she going to do, kill her own baby and be completely alone? 215

They're doing it to our women too!

I never did that.

I don't care who wins the war.
It was just a job.

I guess rape is just part of it. 220

MEJRA enters. She's dressed in black and stands to STETKO'S right which makes it difficult for him to see her. She looks at him impassively.

Long, long silence.

STETKO: Are you the executioner?

No response.

I guess it's only fitting that a woman do it.

Silence.

Women can't rape men.
Too bad, eh?
There's probably a lot of women who would if they 225
could.

Silence.

I'm as ready as I'll ever be.
I guess.

I suppose going for a piss before we begin is out of the question. 230

He laughs. She remains silent.

STETKO: I'm not going to say I'm sorry if that's
    what you're waiting for.
What difference would it make?
It won't bring them back.
It won't undo what I did.

It won't make me a better man.   235

MEJRA: Won't it?

STETKO: Ah, she has a tongue.

Pause. He strains to see her.

(derisive) I'm sorry.
Feel better?

MEJRA: Should I?   240

STETKO: Isn't that what forgiveness is all about?
I say sorry and the world forgives me.

I'M SORRY.

Silence.

I don't mean it, of course, and so how can I expect
forgiveness.   245

MEJRA: Is that what you want?

STETKO: I want to do it with my girlfriend.
And I want to take a leak.
My life is simple.

MEJRA: So take a leak.   250

Do you think we haven't seen a man pee his pants
    before?
If you were a dog you could pee down your leg quite
easily.
But you're not a dog are you? And so you can't pee
your own pants.   255
You're too dignified for that.
You may think other people act like animals but not
you. You're a good person.
A good dog, who has only had a bad owner.

STETKO: Are you a doctor?   260

MEJRA: No.

STETKO: Missionary?

MEJRA: No.

STETKO: A mother?

MEJRA: …no.   265

Silence.

STETKO: And you're not the executioner…?

MEJRA: I'm your saviour.

STETKO: Oh yeah?

MEJRA: Yes.

STETKO: Maybe I don't want to be saved.   270

MEJRA: That's up to you.

STETKO: What do you mean?

MEJRA: I can have you released.

STETKO: Is this a joke?

MEJRA: No joke.   275

STETKO: You can set me free?!

MEJRA: On condition.

STETKO: What condition?

MEJRA: You must do as I say for the rest of your life.

STETKO: Do as — just do whatever you say?   280

MEJRA: Yes.

STETKO: Like…anything?

MEJRA: Everything.

STETKO: No deal.

MEJRA: As you wish. (*begins to exit*)   285

STETKO: Wait!
   What if you asked me to kill myself?

MEJRA: Then you would have to do it.

   Silence.

STETKO: Would you?
   Is that it? The State's too bankrupt to do it? It's a new   290
   way to save money — get the prisoners to do it
   themselves.
   That's it, isn't it?
   They're too cheap.
   Maybe the power's been cut off, eh.   295
   What a laugh!

   Silence.

MEJRA: It's up to you.

STETKO: What kind of choice is that?

MEJRA: The only one you have.

STETKO: One choice is no choice.   300

MEJRA: You have two.

STETKO: I do it or they do it.

MEJRA: They do it or you obey me for the rest of
   your life.

   Silence.

STETKO: Why would they do that?

MEJRA: If you want to find out you'll have to postpone   305
   your death.

STETKO: What if I don't do as you tell me?

MEJRA: What do you think — that you'll get away
   with it?
   Run and hide
   — like a frightened dog?

   Where can you go?   310
   Everyone knows your face.

   You're the most hated man in the world.

STETKO: Is that true?

MEJRA: What do you think?
   You kill twenty-three young girls and people will   315
   love you for it?

STETKO: So why do you want to save me?

MEJRA: You'll have to agree to the conditions if you
   want to find out.

   (*checking her watch*) It's time.

   STETKO experiences a few frantic moments.
   MEJRA begins to leave.

STETKO: Sure!   320
   Okay.
   What have I got to lose.

   Lights out.

SCENE 2

That night. STETKO fingers the last morsels of food
from a bowl and sucks his fingers clean.

STETKO: (*after a satisfying burp*) Very good.
   Prison food is the worst.
   Sometimes I wouldn't eat it.
   I left some in a corner once. Even the rats wouldn't
   touch it.   5
   But today I might have.

MEJRA: Freedom makes everything look good?

STETKO: Even makes you and your scowling face
 look good.

 So, you live here?

MEJRA: Yes.

STETKO: No husband about?

MEJRA: Killed.

STETKO: I lost a brother.
 And sister.
 Do you have any beer?

MEJRA: Yes, but none of it is for you.

STETKO: Aah. I see.

MEJRA: What do you see?

STETKO: Nothing.

MEJRA: Then why do you say "I see" when you in
 fact see nothing?

STETKO: It's just a phrase.

MEJRA: It's also a lie.

STETKO: Truth. Lie. What difference does it make?

MEJRA: Don't you know?

 Pause.

STETKO: What do you want me to say?

MEJRA: Tell the truth.

STETKO: Everybody said what I did was wrong.
 That I should
 die for what I did. Bad people are punished. Isn't that
 the truth? Bad people go to jail.

Good people, innocent people go free.
I'm free.
So tell me, am I bad or good?
What's the truth?

MEJRA: You're not free.

STETKO: From my shoes, things look different.

 *MEJRA swiftly picks up a small farm sickle which has
 been stuck in the ground, and with a single smooth
 motion deliberately slices off his ear. As he falls to the
 ground she clamps a collar and chain around his neck
 and fastens it to a bolt in the ground. He gasps for air.*

MEJRA: Get up.

 *She kicks him sharply. He cries and gasps on the
 ground.*

MEJRA: Get up!

 He rises slowly, realizing, as he rises, that he is bound.

STETKO: What is this — ?!

 She strikes him across the face and chest.

 What are you doing?!

 She slaps his mouth.

MEJRA: (*ordering*) You will be silent.

STETKO: Why are you doing this?

 She strikes his mouth again.

MEJRA: You will be silent.

 STETKO goes to speak but thinks better of it.

 *MEJRA begins to beat him, methodically,
 dispassionately, one open-handed slap after another.*

 STETKO rages, straining to fight back.

STETKO: STOP IT!

She stops.

MEJRA: You will be silent and you will take your
beating like a man.

STETKO: Why should I? 45

MEJRA: Because that's the deal.

STETKO: Are you going to beat me to death?

MEJRA: I am going to beat you until you fall to the
ground or until I'm unable to beat you any
longer.

She strikes him and STETKO immediately falls.

Get up.

STETKO: I've fallen. 50

MEJRA: Get up you coward.

Pause.

Last time.

STETKO reluctantly, but obediently, rises.

Stand up tall.

*He leans into the collar and prepares himself for the
beating. MEJRA stands in front of him and begins the
beating, a beating which seems to last forever.*

*The lighting changes to indicate a passing of time into
night and a slivered moon. In this light we only see
her back and her arms swinging back and forth as
she strikes him.*

MEJRA stops for breath.

MEJRA: Get down.

*He goes to his knees, shakily. She takes off a scarf and
bandages his ear. They both fight back tears.*

STETKO: Why did you do that? 55

MEJRA: Because you don't know the difference
between the truth and a lie.

STETKO: I don't even know you.
Do I?
Have we ever met?
Have I — have I ever done anything to you? 60

MEJRA: You don't know me.
We've never met before.
(*finishing the bandaging*) Not like a nurse would do
it, not like your girlfriend, but it will serve its
purpose. 65

STETKO: Do you know my girlfriend?

MEJRA: I know of her.

STETKO: Because of me?

MEJRA: Of course.

STETKO: She was there, wasn't she? 70
At the jail?
She must know I'm here.
I'd like to see her.
…can I?

MEJRA: She's dead. 75

Silence.

STETKO: I know she was there.

MEJRA: You saw her?

STETKO: She said she'd come.
She said she'd see if she could come in with me —
near the end. 80

MEJRA: She was shot on her way to the jail.

STETKO: (*on his feet*) You're lying!

MEJRA: If that's what you choose to believe.

STETKO: Tell me you're lying!

Silence.

STETKO: Is it true?   85

MEJRA: Don't you know?

STETKO: (*stunned*) Is she really dead?

MEJRA: You tell me.

STETKO: Show me proof!
   The police report!   90

MEJRA: Why should I?
   Why should I tell you, prove to *you?*
   Who are you to ask for anything?

STETKO: I have a right to know the truth!

Long silence.

STETKO: She's alive.   95
   I know it.
   You're playing games with my mind.
   I know about mind games.

MEJRA: Time for bed.
   You sleep out here.   100

STETKO: Outside?

MEJRA: Outside.

She exits. He stands stubbornly.

STETKO: Fuck you.
   Fuck you.

Blackout.

SCENE 3

STETKO, shackled, is yoked to a wooden plough.
MEJRA is behind guiding it. The plough is stuck.

MEJRA: Can't you pull harder, Stinko?

STETKO: It's Stetko.
   Stet-ko.

MEJRA: I prefer Stinko.

STETKO: I prefer not to pull harder.   5

MEJRA: You have no say in the matter.

Silence.
He leans into the yoke.

STETKO: It won't budge.

MEJRA: If we can't make something of this land we'll
   starve.

They look at the charred remains of the land.

STETKO: Sometimes I think we should all starve.
   We'd be better off.   10

MEJRA: (*laughing*) Stinko, you are so stupid you're
   funny.

STETKO: Don't call me Stinko okay?
   Please.

Pause.

MEJRA: Okay.

Silence.

He tries again. It won't budge.

STETKO: Maybe nothing will grow anyway.   15
   It's probably been poisoned.
   We sometimes sprayed.

MEJRA: There are landmines also.

STETKO: Here?!

MEJRA: Afraid to die?   20

STETKO: Everybody is afraid to die.

MEJRA: Is that so?

STETKO: Sure.
   Except when living looks worse. Then they want
      to die.

MEJRA: Were the women you killed like that?   25

STETKO: Some.

MEJRA: All?

STETKO: Some.

MEJRA: Who?

STETKO: I don't remember.   30

MEJRA: What were their names?

STETKO: I don't know.
   Why?

   Silence.

MEJRA: Pull.

STETKO: It won't budge.   35

MEJRA: We have to dig it out.

STETKO: (*in the yoke*) How can I?

   Long silence.

STETKO grins. MEJRA begins to dig with her hands.
STETKO leans against the plough and whistles a light
tune. MEJRA, angry, digs harder, faster.

STETKO: (*looking up*) Sunstroke weather.

She looks up at him in anger. He grins back.

Take the yoke off, Mejra.

She resumes digging.

I've met people like you before.   40
Stubborn.
So stubborn they don't know when they're beat.
When they need the help of others. Even if they don't
like those others.

MEJRA: This rock was never here before!   45

STETKO: Maybe it's not a rock.
   Maybe it is a landmine.

   MEJRA weeps.

Hey, it's a joke.
It's a rock.
It's obvious it's a rock. I'm joking.   50

You have to laugh at life sometimes.
Otherwise you go mad.

MEJRA: That's your remedy is it?

STETKO: (*shrugs*) Got a better idea?

   MEJRA swiftly unhooks him from the yoke, cuffs his
   hands in front of him, and drags him by his chains
   to the rock.

MEJRA: Dig it out.   55

STETKO: How?

MEJRA: With your feet. Your mouth. Your nose.
   I don't care.
   Just do it.

   STETKO assesses the rock for a moment then proceeds
   to poke with one foot. He whistles a long note.

STETKO: She's a big one.   60

MEJRA: Dig.

He works harder, using both feet. This motion develops a kind of Russian jig or march. He sings and kicks at the dirt until he tires.

STETKO: This is sunstroke weather.

MEJRA: For idiots, yes.

STETKO: What's life, eh?
Drudgery, and a few dances in between.   65
Care to dance, madam?

MEJRA: Dig.

STETKO: Take off my shirt.

It's hot.

I like the sun.   70
I never saw daylight in prison.
It's the first hot day of the year.

MEJRA strikes him

MEJRA: Stinko, you are nothing.
No one.
A dog.   75
A slave.
A murderer.

STETKO: I know what I am.
I know I'm a murderer
and a dog   80
and a slave.
I don't care.
I'm not proud.
I can be those things.

MEJRA: You *are* those things.   85

STETKO: So what?
So what do we do with that?

Kill me?
You went to a lot of trouble to save me.
Why? Eh?   90
What do you want?
I'm your dog and slave.
I'm Stinko the murderer.
So what?

She sits on the rock.

MEJRA: So what.   95
Right.
So what.
What do we do with dogs and slaves and murderers.

What would you do?

STETKO: Shoot them probably.   100

MEJRA: Shoot them.

STETKO: Yeah.
It's simple.

MEJRA: Maybe I should shoot you.

STETKO: You like me.   105

MEJRA: Understand one thing if you can stupido —
I despise you.

STETKO: So shoot me.

Silence.

STETKO: So use me like a dog and a slave 'til it's
time to shoot me.
Do you think I care. Eh?
What do I have to care about?   110

MEJRA: Don't look for pity!
Dig!

Pause.

He begins, furious at first, then grins and switches

again to his manic dance, singing at the top of his lungs, kicking dirt everywhere until the rock is exposed. He clasps his handcuffed arms around the boulder and heaves with all his might and lifts the rock triumphantly to his chest. He turns as if he would hurl the rock at her, but it's impossible.

MEJRA: Go ahead.
Show me what you're really made of.
Smash my face with it.   115

STETKO laughs at his own impotence.

Drop it on your foot.

STETKO: (*suddenly serious*) I can't.

MEJRA: Why not?

STETKO: I don't know.

MEJRA puts her foot beneath the rock.

MEJRA: Drop it on mine.   120

He releases the rock immediately. She pulls her foot away in time.

Try again.

STETKO: (*laughs*) It's too heavy.

MEJRA: Pick it up.

STETKO: You are one strange woman.

MEJRA: Who are you to judge?   125
Pick it up.

STETKO attempts to pick it up but can't.

STETKO: Impossible.

MEJRA: A moment ago it was possible.
Pick it up now or I'll bury you in this field.

STETKO: I can't pick it up now.   130
I had strength then.
I don't now.
I used it all up.
Who do you think I am — Hercules? I can lift mountains on command?   135

MEJRA: Didn't you kill on command?

No response.

Which is harder? Killing someone or lifting a mountain?
Is that where your strength is Stinko?
In hatred?
If you hate enough you can lift a mountain and   140
kill a people, on command.

STETKO: I don't hate them.

MEJRA: You kill people you like?

Silence.

STETKO: I wish you'd never come to save me.

MEJRA: I never came to save you.

STETKO: You said you were my saviour.   145

MEJRA: I lied.

You know all about lies don't you?
Haven't you ever said to a young girl, I'll show you the forest.

STETKO: I never!   150

MEJRA: Someday you'll take me to this forest.

STETKO: What do you mean?

MEJRA: You look nervous.
We all know about the forest.
Dead bodies.   155

Not your girlfriend though.
She died on the street.
A virgin.

STETKO weeps.

You're right, Stetko.
I am your saviour.   160
Now pick up that rock because you owe me.
Pick it up out of gratitude instead of hate.

Go on.

He tries, but in vain.

Hate works best for you.

STETKO: For you too.   165
   You hate me.

MEJRA: Yes.

STETKO: Why?

MEJRA: I might kill you before I could finish my
   sentence.

   Pause.

STETKO: You're one of "them", aren't you?   170

MEJRA: What if I am?

STETKO: My aunt is one.
   My father's brother married one.
   I used to see them a lot.
   Before.   175

   Now everybody fights.
   The whole family.

   Everyone thinks they're right.
   That's why people need someone to take charge.
   Keep people in line. Make them shut up and do   180
      as they're told.

MEJRA: You?

STETKO: Not me
   but somebody.

MEJRA: Then you'll like our arrangement.
   It's a dictatorship.   185
   I'm the dictator.
   I tell you what to do and you do it.

STETKO: Sure.
   I don't care.
   People don't care who's in charge just so long as they   190
   don't have to take responsibility.

MEJRA: I'll take responsibility.
   Pick up the rock and drop it on your foot.

STETKO: It's not normal to injure yourself.

MEJRA: It's normal to harm someone else?   195

STETKO: I've done nothing to you.

MEJRA: (*suddenly angry*) Pick up the rock.

STETKO: I can't.

   He grins.

   Funny thing about "dictators" eh?
   What happens when nobody does as they're told?   200
   What's the dictator to do? Kill them all?
   Then there'd be nobody left to do all the dirty
      work.
   Then the dictator isn't a dictator anymore.
   Maybe everybody is pretending to be who they are.
   Maybe everybody has to believe a lie.   205

MEJRA: And what lie do you want to believe — that
   I'm here
   to save you, or to bury you alive?

STETKO: (*grins*) I believe you like me.
   But you're too old and ugly for a young guy like me.

MEJRA: Too ugly to be raped, too old to be 210
    impregnated.
  Just right for killing.

STETKO: For sure. We would have just shot you.

MEJRA: I would have considered myself lucky.

STETKO: Strange world, eh?

MEJRA: What will it be? 215
  Choose.

Pause.

  Pick it up.

STETKO: No.

Pause.

MEJRA starts digging STETKO'S grave with her hands.

  What are you doing?

MEJRA: Guess. 220

STETKO: You stupid bitch fucking cunt —

He heaves the rock to his chest.

MEJRA: *(slaps him across the face)* Don't ever call me
  that again.

STETKO: What's with you?
  I lift it.
  I drop it. 225
  Doesn't matter what I do I get slapped down.
  You wouldn't touch me if I wasn't tied up.

MEJRA: You wouldn't rape girls if they were armed.

STETKO: *(laughs)* Guess not.
  You think I'm stupid?
  I know they don't like it. 230

MEJRA: No they don't.

STETKO: You been raped?

MEJRA: None of your business.

STETKO: I take that for a yes. 235

MEJRA: I don't care how you take it, just understand
  this, the military is not the only one with power.

STETKO: *(grins)* Untie me, Mejra.

MEJRA: *(grins)* Not yet, Stinko.

STETKO: This rock is too fucking heavy. 240

MEJRA: Drop it — except on your foot —
  and I bury you alive.

STETKO: What is the point of this?

MEJRA: The right to choose.

STETKO: Hold it, break my foot, or be buried alive?! 245

MEJRA: I knew you had some potential, Stinko.

She exits.

STETKO: Don't call me Stinko!
  It's Stetko.
  Stet-ko Tef-te-dar-i-ja.
  Stupid — 250

He stops short just in case she hears him. He holds the rock as the lights indicate the coming of night. He sings a marching tune, badly, defiantly.

Blackout.

SCENE 4

*MEJRA is bandaging STETKO'S foot. He shivers from
cold and shock.*

MEJRA: Papa cut his tail off and he howled and
    wailed through
the night and in the morning the poison was out
    of his system.
The shock drove it out of his body.
He was my father's favourite dog.
He used to say "I loved that dog enough to chop   5
    its tail off —
which is more than I could do for my children."

STETKO: What if he had died?

MEJRA: Who knows.
    We only ever know what does happen.

STETKO: I wouldn't have done that.   10
    I probably would have just watched, to see if he'd
    make it on his own.
    See if he was meant to live.

MEJRA: Who decides that?
    Who decides who will live and who won't?   15

STETKO: (*shrugs*) I don't know.

MEJRA: My father loved that dog.

STETKO: (*grins*) Like you love me?

MEJRA: I don't love you.

STETKO: You sure?   20

MEJRA: Positive.

STETKO: You live out here alone.
    No neighbours.
    Nothing.
    You see me. Young —   25

MEJRA: (*bursts out laughing*) You are so arrogant and
    stupid—
    I think all your brains must be in your cock.
    And you're impotent!

STETKO: Not anymore.
    Last night I had a hard on.   30
    That's why I dropped the rock.
    So I could masturbate.

MEJRA: You lie.

Pause.

STETKO: Yeah.
    I couldn't hold it any longer.   35
    My back was killing me.
    In a way I was relieved when it fell.

MEJRA: Nothing like pain to stop…everything.

    I have something for you.

STETKO: A gift?   40

MEJRA: Sort of.
    I found it.

STETKO: What is it?

MEJRA: A rabbit.
    It had been caught in a snare and chewed its front   45
    paw off to escape.
    I was going to kill it for dinner but it snarled at me.
    I thought anything that wants to live that badly
    deserves a chance. So I brought it home.

STETKO: I had a pet rabbit when I was seven.
    Where is it?   50

MEJRA: There, in the basket.

STETKO limps to the basket, opens it, and looks in.

STETKO: It hissed at me!

MEJRA: Maybe it doesn't want our help.
Maybe it wants to die.

STETKO: Nobody wants to die.   55

MEJRA: How do you know?

STETKO: …I saw lots of people die.

MEJRA: The girls?

STETKO: Yeah. Some of them didn't seem to care.
But they probably knew it was for the best. Nobody   60
wants a woman who's been raped.
Husbands walk away.

MEJRA: Mothers never walk away.

Silence. STETKO considers this statement.

That's where men become confused.
They don't know what to do about mothers.   65

STETKO: It bit me!

He sucks his finger and closes the basket.

Look at me.
No ear.
Crushed foot.
Bit finger.   70

MEJRA: Should we kill it?

STETKO: — no.

MEJRA: Why not?

STETKO: It doesn't know any different.
It doesn't know I'm a friend.   75

What are you smiling about?

MEJRA: I'm not. I'm musing.
We forgive an animal but not a people.

Well, it's yours then.

She gives him dinner.

This is all there is.   80

STETKO: What is this?

MEJRA: It was growing near the marsh.

STETKO: A man can't live on this.

MEJRA: Eat the rabbit then. That's all there is.

She exits.

STETKO: And what did you have, eh?!   85
Beer?
Potatoes with gravy?
Some cabbage?
Stewed beef and cabbage with potatoes and paprika,
and carrots.   90
Dumplings.
I'll die on this!
She's going to starve me to death.

*The rabbit scratches at the basket. He opens it and
looks in.*

Where do you think you're going, eh? With 3 feet.
What a pair.   95
Maybe if we team up we'll have enough feet between
us to escape.
Maybe I ought to eat you instead.
Stay and eat — run and —
and what?   100
Be eaten?
What a life, eh?
Eat or be eaten.
What a fucking life.
That's it though, isn't it.   105
At least for you.
I'm a man.
I'm supposed to be above that.

(starting to eat) But I'm not.

He shares some of his greens with the rabbit.

I'm not.   110

Blackout.

SCENE 5

*STETKO is bent over looking closely at a small green
growth in the ploughed field. The rabbit is beside him
in the basket. He straightens up suddenly and runs, still
shackled, as far as the chain leash permits.*

STETKO: MEJRAA!
  Something is growing!

He runs back to the growth and examines it further.

  A green thing.
  What though?
  It's not even in the row.   5
  Maybe it's a weed.
  (*grins*) Maybe it's — rabbit food!
  That's what you wish, eh?
  Is that what you wish?
  A big green salad?   10
  Even if it's a weed?
  MEJRAAAA.

  It must be a weed.
  Nothing else is growing except it.
  Do you like weeds, eh?   15
  Would you like to try a leaf or two?

STETKO plucks a leaf but the whole plant comes up.

STETKO: Oh shit! The whole thing's come up.
  Maybe it was dying anyway.
  What do you think?
  A plant comes up that easy — can't be meant to live,   20
  eh?

He dangles it over the opened basket.

  Feast your eyes on that.

Do you want it?
Roll over.
(*laughs*) You're no dummy.   25
Only dogs roll over for their dinner.
And play dead.
Because you're so smart you can have it.
Don't bite my fingers.
Gently.   30
You see, even a stupid animal can learn.
Yes, you'll let me pet you as long as I feed you.
It's nice, eh?
Feels good.

MEJRA enters with cut flowers.

MEJRA: Look what I found.   35
  Growing.
  Wild flowers.

STETKO: They're nice.
  Pretty.

MEJRA: They're weeds but who names the rose?[2]   40

STETKO: Huh?

MEJRA: Never mind.
  Why were you shouting?

STETKO: Something was growing here too.

MEJRA: Of course.   45
  I planted it this morning.
  It's a wild bean plant.
  I found it by the marsh.
  A lone survivor.

STETKO: Lone?   50
  The only one?

---

2 who names the rose] "by whose authority are some plants
  named weeds and others, roses." Cf. "What's in a name?
  A rose by any other name would smell as sweet" (Shakespeare, *Romeo and Juliet*, II, ii).

MEJRA: I don't know how it grew, but there it was, so I
uprooted it and brought it here.

STETKO: I don't think it will make it.

MEJRA: Why not?   55

STETKO: Too hot.

MEJRA: It's not too hot.

STETKO: Too dry.

MEJRA: We'll carry water from the mountains if we
have to.
It'll grow.   60
It has to.
That's all there is.

What's the matter?

What have you done, Stinko?
You look — ridiculous.   65

She pushes him aside and can't see the plant.

Where is it?!

Did you eat it, you pig?!

STETKO: No.

MEJRA: Did you feed it to that damn rabbit!

STETKO: No.   70

MEJRA: Then where is it?

STETKO shrugs and looks confused.

Don't you realize that was our chance to grow
something?

STETKO: I'll do without.

MEJRA: You idiot!   75

We'll all do without!

She sees the rabbit.

MEJRA: You fed it to the rabbit.
(*snatching it*) Give me that.

It is a gnawed nub.

Nothing.
Chewed the vital part first.   80

She strikes STETKO.

Shit for brains.

STETKO: I thought it was a weed.

MEJRA: It was!
One we could eat.

STETKO: We'll find something else.   85

MEJRA: What?

STETKO: — flowers.
Mix them with something.
Grass!
Roast them.   90

MEJRA: I can't believe you!

STETKO: I didn't know!
I wouldn't have done it if I'd known.
Why didn't you tell me?

MEJRA: I don't have to report to you.   95

STETKO: No, but if you'd told me — if you'd said
"Hey, Stinko, I planted a wild bean in the field, don't
feed it to the rabbit —"

*She realizes his attachment to the rabbit and makes
a step toward it.*

MEJRA: Give me the rabbit.

[V]

STETKO: (*steps between it and her*) No.   100

MEJRA: Get out of my way.

STETKO: — no.

MEJRA: Move, or I'll beat you purple.

STETKO: Please, Mejra.
   She's mine.   105

MEJRA: She's not yours any more than the sun is yours.
   The air
   the water
   this land.
   You own nothing!   110

STETKO: Then why did you give her to me?

MEJRA: I heard something about your girlfriend.
   She was raped.

STETKO: You lie!

MEJRA: She was shot first.   115
   Killed.
   Then raped.
   She was lucky, wouldn't you say?
   She didn't have to endure the — what —
   indignity?   120
   Pain?
   A lucky girl.

STETKO: You lie.

MEJRA: Yes. I lie.
   We all lie.   125
   Why do we do that, Stetko?
   Why do you lie?

STETKO: I don't know.

MEJRA: Think!

STETKO: Depends on the lie.   130

MEJRA: You lied about the rabbit.
   You said she didn't eat the green.
   Why?

STETKO: I was afraid you'd hurt her.

MEJRA: Do you think the first lie ever told was to   135
   protect another?

STETKO: …maybe.

MEJRA: You think we're that noble?

STETKO: Probably the first person to tell a lie did it
   to save himself.

MEJRA: From what?
   What are we saving ourselves from?   140

STETKO: I don't know.

MEJRA: Think!
   What are you afraid of Stetko?

Silence.

STETKO: What do you want to hear?
   I'll say anything.   145
   I don't care.
   Whatever you want.
   Do you think just because somebody says
      something
   they mean it?

MEJRA: You lie to make life easier for yourself?   150
   It's more convenient to go along with the others?

STETKO: Sure.

MEJRA: You raped and killed girls because it was
   easier than disobeying orders.

STETKO: Yes!
   Yesyesyes!   155
   It's easier to obey.
   I obey authority.

I obey you.
It's easier.

MEJRA: I guess that's why the soldiers killed your   160
girlfriend first.
It's easier to rape them when they're dead.

STETKO: She wasn't raped!

MEJRA: Yes she was.
Gang raped.
From the back.   165

He covers his ears and sings wildly fighting tears.
MEJRA exits.

Lights indicate night and a lambent moon.
STETKO stops singing and sobs.

Lights out.

SCENE 6

The same lambent moon. MEJRA enters with a jar.
STETKO stands defeated.

MEJRA: I brought you a beer.

He looks at it, at her, then takes it.

STETKO: (*ironic, tasting*) To life. (*and swallows a*
large mouthful)
It's warm.

MEJRA: Yes.

STETKO: Who cares, eh?   5
To life!

He drinks.

MEJRA: To life.
To children.
To love.

STETKO: To love.   10
Who knows about love.

MEJRA: I do.

STETKO: You are the cruellest woman I know.

MEJRA: Kindness is not love.
Besides, I don't love you.   15

STETKO: You hate me.

MEJRA: Yes.

STETKO: Why do you hate me so much?

Silence.

Why did you bring me here?

MEJRA: Drink up Stetko.   20

STETKO: Thank you.
For not calling me Stinko.

Is it late?

MEJRA: Almost morning.

STETKO: You couldn't sleep.   25

MEJRA: No.

STETKO: Me either.

MEJRA: I know.

STETKO: You watch me?

MEJRA: I just know.   30

STETKO: Was she really raped?
Tell me the truth Mejra.

MEJRA: What is the truth?
    I tell you your girlfriend is dead.
    Raped.   35
    I can't show you the body.
    There is no body to be found.
    People tell you one thing.
    The military tells another.

    We'll read about the war in the papers — new   40
    territories divided among the victors.
    New leaders.
    Economic decisions determined by outside interests.
    There will be medals for the dead soldiers on all sides.
    Plaques for the brave and foolhardy.   45
    Monuments for the Generals.

    What will anyone know about you and your
    girlfriend?
    About me?
    About the girls in the forest?   50

    What is the truth?

    The truth.
    is like love.
    It defies words.
    It's known without "facts".   55

STETKO: Was she or wasn't she?

MEJRA: She's missing.
    That's all we know.
    That's the "facts."
    Now, what is the truth?   60
    You're a soldier. You know how a soldier's mind
    works.
    Is she alive?
    A virgin?

STETKO: Maybe she's hiding.   65

MEJRA: Yes, maybe she's hiding.

    Silence.

STETKO: Things happen in war.

We're trained to follow orders. Our lives depend
    on it.
    It's automatic.
    Soldiers aren't supposed to think.   70
    Only obey.

MEJRA: I guess you'll bear the "other side" no ill if
    they've captured your girlfriend.

    STETKO drinks.

STETKO: Warm beer is better than no beer.

MEJRA: (*ironic*)
    "Facts" are better than truth.   75
    Revenge is better than sorrow.

STETKO: I hope I never grow old and bitter like you.

MEJRA: Then chances are you'll die young.

STETKO: (*shrugs*) What can I do?
    I'm a prisoner.   80
    I do nothing.
    I think nothing.

MEJRA: Right.
    You're helpless.
    I'm helpless.   85
    We're all victims of fate.

    She can see STETKO thinking about the issue of fate.

    Is war fate?

STETKO: I don't know.

MEJRA: And the girls?

STETKO: (*shrugs*) A girl walks by   90
    and —
    In a war
    you can get away with it.

    Everybody's doing it.
    Rape is just part of war.   95

That's how some men pump themselves up.
Get their adrenaline going.
Makes them reckless.
Fearless.
I've seen men run into the open afterwards, spraying   100
bullets.
Most of them get shot down, but some don't and
they come back looking like heroes.
Everyone cheers.
They get first pick of the women.   105

I never did it.
Run in the open.

MEJRA: You only shot women.

STETKO: Yeah.
That's how it was.   110

He drinks.

That was their fate.

MEJRA: They cut her tongue out
and slit her open from her vagina to her navel
and filled the hole with dirt
and pissed on it.   115

STETKO: I don't believe you anymore.

MEJRA: That's right.
We all know soldiers don't do that to women and
children.
Men don't do that sort of thing.   120
We all know that.
Isn't that the "truth"?

Tomorrow we go to the forest.

She exits.

A pale light of dawn.

Blackout.

SCENE 7

They stand in the forest.

STETKO: It's gone.

MEJRA: She.
She is not an it.

STETKO: She.
She's gone.   5
Animals must have got her.

MEJRA: This was the first one you killed?

STETKO: Yeah.

MEJRA: Where's the log? You said you put a log over
her body.

STETKO: Someone must have taken it for firewood.   10

MEJRA: No evidence.

STETKO: No.

MEJRA: No one is going to know the truth.
That's the plan isn't it?
Keep it secret.   15
No reminders.

Maybe you're lying.
Maybe this isn't the right place.

STETKO: This is the right place.

Silence.

MEJRA: Did you know her name?   20

STETKO: I didn't ask.

MERJA: Missing.
That's her epitaph.
Missing.

[VII]

Where are the others?   25

STETKO: I don't know.

MEJRA: You knew where she was, where are the others?

STETKO: I don't know.
  This was the first one I killed.
  The first always sticks in the mind.   30
  After that it was —
  I don't know —

MEJRA: Routine?

STETKO: Sort of.

MEJRA: What about the girl you liked best?   35
  The virgin.
  What was her name.

STETKO: I don't know.

MEJRA: Think!

STETKO: I don't remember.   40

MEJRA: You don't remember or *won't* remember?

STETKO: I *don't* remember.

  Silence.

MEJRA: Where is she?

  Pause.

STETKO: A different place.

MEJRA: Where?   45

STETKO: In a grave.

MEJRA: You buried her?

STETKO: We dug a big grave and put lots of them in it.

MEJRA: Where is it?

STETKO: I don't remember!   50

MEJRA: Take me there.

STETKO: How can I when I don't know where it is?!

MEJRA: What will make you remember?

STETKO: What?

MEJRA: What do I have to do to make you remember?   55

STETKO: Some things are just gone from memory.
  Blocked out.

MEJRA: (*hands him a shovel*) Start digging.

STETKO: It's not here!

MEJRA: Your own grave.   60
  Start digging.

STETKO: Things have changed!
  The markings are different.
  Trees have been cut
  and —   65
  (*looking up, remembering*)
  It was west
  the sun was in my eyes
  it was late afternoon.

MEJRA: Find it.

STETKO: There was a tree   70
  a large tree
  there were bullet holes in the bark
  and a strong branch hung low —
  the one I tied her up to
  I see it   75
  but I don't know where it is now.

MEJRA: Then dig.

STETKO: I'm not sure where it is!

MEJRA: Then dig!

STETKO: Come on, Mejra.   80

MEJRA: (*strikes him*) Find her.

Pause.

*STETKO wanders in one direction, stops, shakes his
head and then wanders in another direction.*

STETKO: No.

*He wanders, thinks he's getting close, stops, uncertain.
He takes a few steps further. MEJRA stands impassive
and watches.*

*Meanwhile, the lighting has gradually changed to
indicate the passing of time and a change of location.
They are now deeper in the forest; it is darker, the
shadows are longer.*

STETKO stops and looks down.

STETKO: This is it.

MEJRA comes to the spot.

MEJRA: Here?

STETKO: Yes.   85

MEJRA: Are you sure?

STETKO: I'm sure.

MEJRA: How do you know?

STETKO: I can tell.
  I can feel it.   90

MEJRA: Feel what?

STETKO: I don't know.

STETKO remembers.

MEJRA: Tell me.

Silence.

Tell me, Stetko.
They mustn't be forgotten.   95
Same as your girlfriend.
They must not be forgotten.

Pause.

You like her best.

Tell me.

Pause.

STETKO: I was driving the jeep.   100
  I was laughing.
  Finally I was alone.
  I got to drive on my own — with her,
  this girl.
  I felt really good.   105
  The sun was shining the whole time.
  I was singing
  I'm finally alone with this girl.
  And I'm singing —

He sings a popular song.

I look over at her   110
  and she's not smiling
  just looking straight ahead.
  I'd forgot you see,
  I forgot what I was supposed to be doing —
  killing them.   115
  I forgot.
  I was suddenly a free man going for a ride with my
  girl.

Then everything got serious.
  I don't remember anything until we get here   120
  and I tell her to lift her arms up over her head.
  And she does.
  I tie her hands together and throw the rope over the
  tree branch.

It's gone now.   125
Somebody has cut it down.

I pull the rope 'til she's stretched as far as she can go
and then I pull 'til she's just off the ground.
She looks so pretty.
Big watery eyes   130
like a doe's.
I cut her dress —
because her hands are tied and I can't get it off
otherwise.
I use my hunting knife.   135
She's got very white skin.
It's never seen the sun.
She's got a thin line of black hairs that run up to her
belly button.
I think it's quite sexy.   140
I tell her so.
I go up to her
and
put my arms around her
and kiss her neck.   145
I figure I can do it with her.
I feel her shiver.
I ask her if she's cold.
She says "no".
I ask her if she's afraid.   150
She shakes her head
but I think she's lying.
I ask her if she wants me to undress —
maybe she hasn't seen a man before
naked.   155
She closes her eyes
tight.
So I tell her I won't take my clothes off
and she opens them again
and I can see she's crying.   160
So I stop
and sit down on a log
or rock
and I tell her about myself
and my uncle.   165
I tell her about my girlfriend.

I ask her what she wants to be when she grows up.
She says she wants to be a teacher.

I tell her she's just like my girlfriend
wanting to put some good back into the world.   170
I tell her I would too
if I knew how.

I tell her she's beautiful.
I tell her I want to do it with her.

I figure maybe I can come with her.   175

She begs me not to
but I try anyway.

Only I can't.
I can't get hard.
It won't go in.   180
I can't do it anymore.

It's all over.

Pause.

I don't know what to do.

She begs me to set her free.
And I'm thinking "what if I do?"   185
What if I set her free. What will happen?
I'm scared — in case the others find out —
they'd kill me for letting the enemy go.

She says she won't tell anyone.
I notice her hands are swollen and white.   190
It's getting late
the sun's going down
I have to return the jeep.

So I leave it to fate.
I say, "Let's see if she's meant to live."   195

I back away
and
close my eyes
and aim the gun
and I say to myself   200
if I miss,
no matter what,

I let her go.

Pause.

It hit her in the face.

Silence.

I cut her down and dragged her to a grave we'd dug   205
before but hadn't covered over
and I put her into it
and buried her.

Long, long silence.

MEJRA: Dig it open.

STETKO: What!?   210

MEJRA: Dig the grave open.

STETKO: She's dead!

MEJRA: Dig it open!

STETKO: I can't.
   I'll be sick.   215

MEJRA: Be sick, but dig.

STETKO: What's the point!

MEJRA: Proof.
   We want the "facts".

STETKO: I did it like I said!   220

MEJRA: Stetko you will dig open that grave or you
   will dig your own and lie in it.
   Choose.

Pause.

STETKO takes the shovel and digs.

STETKO: It's been a while.
   There might not be anything left.   225

MEJRA: Dig.

He digs.

STETKO: I hear corpses carry diseases.

MEJRA: None worse than any the living carry.

He digs deeper.

STETKO: Maybe this is the wrong spot.

MEJRA: It'll be the right one for you.   230

He digs even deeper.

STETKO: There were a lot of bodies.
   How will I know which is her?

MEJRA: Because her spirit will return and shriek her
   name.

*He drops the shovel and scrambles out. MEJRA blocks
his way.*

   Afraid of spirits?

STETKO: We shouldn't be doing this!   235

MEJRA: Why?
   Afraid to revisit?
   Do you feel graves are haunted —
   that the spirits of the dead linger on if their bodies
   have been brutalized?   240
   Murdered?

   Dig.

STETKO: It was a war!
   I only did as I was told!

MEJRA: Such a good boy.   245
   What if you'd said no.

[VII]

STETKO: They would have killed me.

MEJRA: Me or you.
  It comes to that.
  Me.
  or you.   250

STETKO: War changes everything.
  Once you're in it —
  there are no choices.

MEJRA: Yes there are.   255
  Dig.

STETKO: Right.
  "Dig."
  Obey or die.
  People will always rather obey than die.   260

MEJRA: Dig.

STETKO: Sure.
  I'm not proud.
  I'm no hero.
  I'll dig.   265

He digs furiously.

  I don't know about life.
  I'm no great thinker.
  What am I supposed to know that would change
  things.

MEJRA: You should look at every woman as if she   270
    were your daughter.

He stops.

  Every woman
  as if she were your daughter.

  Dig.

STETKO: I can't.

MEJRA: You can   275

and you will.

STETKO: (*digs*) Okay.
  Big deal.
  Big f'ing deal.

  I've hit something.   280

MEJRA: Keep digging.

STETKO: I think — (*looking closely, leaping out*) — it's a
  head!

MEJRA: Pull it out.

He looks frantic.

  Pull it out.   285

STETKO: I can't.

Long silence.

STETKO walks into the grave and pulls at the corpse.

  Okay!
  It's out!

MEJRA: Bring her here.

STETKO: Oh god —   290

He hauls it up and tosses the small corpse at her feet.

MEJRA: Who is she?

STETKO: I don't know.

MEJRA: What was her name?

STETKO: I don't know!

Pause.

MEJRA: Dig up the rest.   295

STETKO: Oh god!
Fucking hell —

He stomps into the grave and digs.

MEJRA looks at the corpse and brushes off the decomposing skull.

MEJRA: How old child?
You will not be forgotten.

STETKO tosses another decomposed body on the ground. MEJRA goes to it and puts a finger through a hole in the breast bone.

Was it quick   300
or did you suffocate in the grave?

Another body, and another are unceremoniously tossed out. MEJRA goes to one and bends low.

Is it you?
(*kneeling*) Is it you?

She cradles the body in her arms, and rocks, and begins to keen.

STETKO climbs out and observes. When MEJRA finally sees him she stops.

A long, long silence.

MEJRA: Come here.

He does.

On your knees.   305

He hesitates but obeys.

Hold her.

She offers the body to him.

Hold her.

STETKO reluctantly holds out his arms to receive the corpse.

Her name is Ana.
She was 19.
Young looking for her age.   310
She wanted to be a teacher — of philosophy.
She respected all religions.
She was brave and kind all at once.

She had a thin line of black hair that ran up to her navel.   315
And watery eyes
like a doe's.

She felt every person had dignity regardless of their race.

She believed love was the answer.   320
Patience was the teacher.
Compassion was the mirror.
She would say, "I am the reflection of love and trust and joy — all that you are
but haven't yet recognized   325
in yourself."

Silence.

I felt her adjust her shoulder before she entered this world. A world not yet ready for grace and beauty.

I never taught her about evil.
I thought I could protect her by hiding the truth.   330

Pause.

Give her back to me.

Pause.

STETKO returns the corpse with as much grace and reverence as he can. MEJRA stands. Silence.

You can get up now.

He doesn't.

[VII]

No longer "missing".

Get up.

STETKO: I can't.   335

MEJRA: You are going to dig up the rest
  and then you have one more task.

You are going to tell the story of the missing ones.
The women and children you killed.
You are going to name them.   340
We are going to build a monument to the truth
  about war.
We are going to let the mothers reclaim their
  daughters.

STETKO: They'll kill me.
  Then the truth will never be out.

MEJRA: The truth has a way of emerging.   345
  Nothing can stop it
  once it's started.
  I may be gagged
  my husband tortured
  my house burned down   350
  my land stolen
  my children savaged
  but the wind will speak my name
  the waters will tell the fish
  the fish will tell the hunter   355
  "I am."
  I am.

Blackout.

SCENE 8

*A monument of the dead bodies has been built. The
corpses have been seated, stacked in a circle, looking
out.*

*MEJRA is standing by the monument holding the corpse
of Ana in her arms. The basket with the rabbit is near
the monument. STETKO stands centre stage holding one*

of the corpses in his arms. He is uncertain and nervous.

STETKO: Uh…

He looks at MEJRA.

MEJRA: Name them.

STETKO: I don't know who they are.

MEJRA: It's time.

STETKO: (*looking at the monument*) I don't know.   5
  It's a blur.
  You just did it.

MEJRA: "I." "I" did it.

STETKO: "I" just did it.
  I…   10
  killed them.

Silence.

STETKO: My girlfriend is missing.
  She has dark shoulder-length hair.
  She wears it in a pony-tail.

  She has green eyes.   15
  Her name
  is Ini.
  Ini Herak.

Pause.

MEJRA: Name all the girls you killed, Stetko.

STETKO: I didn't always ask their name.   20

Silence.

MEJRA: Describe them.

STETKO: I can't.

Pause.

MEJRA: Begin with the first.

STETKO: I don't know who she was.

MEJRA: What did she look like?   25

STETKO: …She was older.
  Maybe 40.

After I shot her I hid her body under a log.

MEJRA: Remember her.

*He sets the corpse he is holding with the others. It
triggers a memory.*

STETKO: She had had children. I saw stretch marks   30
  on her belly.
  She had a birth mark near her left shoulder — a
  purple
  one shaped like a kidney bean.

Long silence.

I killed a girl named Mini. Fifteen.
  She had a sun-burned face.
  Luba, maybe 21.   35
  And a young girl with reddish hair. Long. Down to
  her waist.
  A girl named Sara. She wore glasses. She was short
  and chubby.
  A married woman. She had a wedding ring with a   40
  tiny diamond set into the band.
  Monica. She had a gap between her two front teeth.

A girl with one brown eye and one green one.
  Carol. I think she was pregnant.
  Eva. She was a swimmer in training for the   45
  Olympics.
  A girl who said she was a waitress. She dyed her hair
  blonde.
  Dark roots were showing.
  Misa. Sixteen.
  Her older sister.   50
  Twins. Thirteen. They looked identical.
  A mother of 2 boys.

A girl with a scar on her right side.
  An older woman who wore a copper bracelet on each   55
  wrist.
  A girl with a mole beside her left nipple.
  A girl with pimples.
  A girl with black lace-up boots.
  A girl with big soft lips.   60

He has trouble continuing.

STETKO: Ana.
  Ana.

*MEJRA, in a rage, rushes at STETKO with the shovel
and strikes him on the back. He falls against the
bodies and scrambles behind the monument. MEJRA
pursues him and strikes him a single hard blow to
the head. He falls still and silent, his feet extending
beyond the bodies.*

Silence.

*MEJRA realizes she has killed him and is horrified.
She fights back retching. She looks up and out and
realizes her deed has been witnessed. She starts to flee,
but can't. It's pointless. She's been seen and the deed
too horrible to run from. She wants to scream but
can't. She is like a caught animal. She runs back to
STETKO.*

*She decides to bury him, and after glancing around
for a suitable spot, proceeds to drag him out by his
feet. She begins to dig a hole when STETKO groans.
She hears him and rushes to him, grabbing his head
in her hands.*

Stetko?
Stetko!
Are you — ?!   65

*She checks his breathing and unconsciously, ecstatic,
hugs him to her chest.*

*STETKO stirs. MEJRA, aware of her compromise,
abruptly drops his head, stands up, apart, and resumes
a hardness. STETKO sits up and rubs his head.*

[VIII]

Silence.

STETKO: So, you're glad I'm alive, eh?

You're just like me, Mejra.
A murderer.
A slave and a dog.

MEJRA: Don't you compare us!   70

STETKO: "If you hate enough you can kill a people on
command?"
Who commanded you?
You think you're above it all, eh?
Once you got what you wanted from me then you   75
were going to do me in. Just like we do to prisoners.
You'd make a good soldier, Mejra.

MEJRA: I did it for my daughter!

STETKO: I had no daughter.
Only me.   80
Who are you to say who's more important?

MEJRA: I was doing it for love.

STETKO: That's what the soldiers say.
"Love for my country."

MEJRA: It's not the same!   85

STETKO: We all have our reasons, eh?
We all think we're right.

So what's the answer
eh, Mejra?

MEJRA: She was innocent!   90

STETKO: War is no place for the innocent.

MEJRA: How dare you!

STETKO: Going to kill me again?

MEJRA stops.

Silence.

Me or you.
Isn't that what you said?   95
Me
or you.

Who's it going to be?

Why don't you look at every man as if he were
your son?

Silence.

MEJRA: Would you have died to save your girlfriend?   100

STETKO: I don't know.
How do we ever know that?

MEJRA: I would have cut my own throat to save Ana.
I would have endured rape by every last soldier.
They could have flayed me alive and dragged my wet   105
body through the streets.

STETKO: And you would kill for her too.

You can't win a war by dying for the enemy.

Pause.

You willing to die for me, Mejra?

She is outraged at the idea. STETKO laughs at her.

STETKO: So much for ideals, eh?   110

It's easy to hate.
Easy to kill once you feed that hate.

Isn't that right, Mejra?

MEJRA: You make life unendurable.

STETKO: But we're here.
You're here.
I'm here.
We made it.

MEJRA: Yes.
There is no justice in this world.

STETKO: No.
Dogs and slaves.

MEJRA: Dogs and slaves.

Long silence.

Get out of here.

She tosses him the keys to his chains.

You're free to go.

STETKO does not go.

Go.

MEJRA turns to leave.

STETKO: Where will you go?

MEJRA: Back to the land.

STETKO: Can I go with you?

MEJRA: No.

STETKO: You need someone.

MEJRA: Not you.

STETKO: Who then?

There is no one, is there?
You're alone.

MEJRA: Go home to your family.

STETKO: They might take me back.

MEJRA: So go.

STETKO: Mejra?

No response.

I'm sorry.
I'm sorry for what I did.

Pause.

Forgive me.

MEJRA: How?

STETKO: Pardon?

MEJRA: How can I forgive you?
Show me.
Show me how to forgive.
I don't know how.

STETKO takes an uncertain step toward MEJRA.

STETKO: (*almost a whisper*) I'm sorry.

He unconsciously reaches out a finger to touch MEJRA'S hand.

Forgive me.

MEJRA unconsciously makes a movement in his direction.

Slow fade on the monument of MEJRA and STETKO in a moment of possibilities.

The end.

Glossary of Dramatic Terms

absurdism, VOL. II: 8, 145, 277, 440. Associated with the minimalist style and bleak worldview of twentieth-century plays of the post-World-War-Two period (especially those of Ionesco, Pinter, and, problematically, Beckett). Such works seem set in a world stripped of faith in god or a rational cosmos, in which idealism has been lost, and human action and communication are futile. Absurdist characters are often portrayed as trapped in a pointless round of trivial, self-defeating acts of comical repetitiveness. For this reason, absurdism can verge on **farce** or **black comedy**. Connected with the shock and disillusionment that followed World War Two, absurdism was anticipated in parts of Büchner's *Woyzeck* (in this volume). See also **existentialism**.

act [of a play], VOL. I: 438, VOL. II: 390. The sections into which a play or other theatrical work have been divided, either by the playwright or a later editor. Dividing plays into five acts became popular during the Renaissance in imitation of Roman tragedy; modern works are sometimes divided into three.

aestheticism, VOL. II: 108. Or "art for art's sake." A reaction to the **realism** and socially reforming agendas of late-nineteenth-century art. Associated in the theatre chiefly with Oscar Wilde, aestheticism asserted art's freedom to be separate and different from ordinary life and practical uses.

agōn, VOL. I: 3. Greek for contest or competition, from which we get prot*agon*ist, the first or main actor/character, as well as related words like agony, antagonize, etc. Plays were originally performed in competition, for prizes.

alexandrine couplets, VOL. I: 469. A rhymed verse form based on six-beat measures in which every second line rhymes with the one before. Alexandrines were used in French tragedy and comedy throughout the seventeenth and into the eighteenth century. They require highly skilled actors for their proper delivery.

"alienation effect," VOL. II: 170. Also known by the German term *verfremdungseffekt*, it is a Russian concept popularized by Bertolt Brecht to refer to any technique used in the theatre to distance spectators from the performance to the point where they can view it critically and ask questions about it. To alienate a phenomenon is to "make it strange," to make it seem odd or surprising. Actors do this when they keep their character at a distance rather than merging with it, or deliver their lines as if in quotation marks; directors use the "A-effect" when they interrupt the action or call attention to its artificiality with music, slides, or lighting. The opposite of "to alienate" is "to naturalize." See also **epic drama**.

allegory, VOL. I: xiii, 202, 240, VOL. II: xiii, 450. From the Greek for "speaking otherwise," allegories are generally **didactic** stories that consist of an accessible literal narrative that is meant to be taken symbolically as well. They often represent large-scale religious or political struggles in disguise. Allegorical characters frequently personify abstract values (Love, Charity, Greed, Big Business). Anima, the central figure in *The Play of the Virtues*, represents the human soul in general; see also *Everyman* (both in Volume I).

allusion, VOL. I: 208, 469. A more or less veiled reference, within one work of art, to the ideas, words, images or even simply to the existence of another work of art or its creator.

anachronism, VOL. I: 208. Accidentally or intentionally attributing people, things, ideas and events to historical periods in which they do not and could not possibly belong.

antiquarianism, VOL. II: 4. The desire, particularly in nineteenth-century theatre, to avoid the above (**anachronism**) by meticulously researching the clothing, décor, music and architecture of various historical periods. Its goal is to ensure that the sets and costumes for a given play are accurate for the time and place in which the story is set.

apron, VOL. I: 500. The part of a stage that extends into the auditorium or audience beyond the **proscenium** arch; sometimes called a **forestage** or a thrust stage.

artistic director, VOL. I: 502, 771, VOL. II: 66, 167, 547, 588. The creative and administrative head of a theatre company, responsible for selecting plays and determining the style and mandate of the troupe. Before the twentieth century, this role was sometimes taken by the playwright, as in Molière's case, or by the leading actor, as in dozens of "actor-managers" of the English theatre.

asides, VOL. I: 147. Words delivered by actors to the audience, or by characters to themselves, which by **convention** are treated as if they were inaudible to the other characters on stage.

aulos, VOL. I: 5. The double-reeded pipe used on the ancient Greek stage as musical accompaniment for tragedy and comedy.

autos sacramentales, VOL. I: 258. Spanish religious plays. See also **Bible-cycle plays,** *carros,* and **mystery play.**

Bible-cycle plays, VOL. I: 186, 189. Medieval religious plays, usually performed outdoors, often on wheeled carts, dramatizing stories from the Bible. See also **mystery play** and **pageant-wagons.**

black comedy, VOL. II: 8. Humour based on death, horror, or any incongruously macabre subject matter.

"book," VOL. II: 169. The non-musical, verbal component of a musical (see **musical theatre**); in opera and **operetta,** the non-musical text is called the "libretto."

Boulevard, VOL. I: 498, VOL. II: 2. After the French Revolution, the largest theatre district in Paris, and for years the home of its **illegitimate theatre.** Sometimes called the "Boulevard of Crime" for its sensational true-crime stories and **melodrama.**

box-set, VOL. II: 4. A stage set consisting of three contiguous walls and a ceiling, realistic floor coverings, light fixtures, and practical windows and doors through which actors make their entrances and exits as if into a real room or building (see **realism**). Developed in the nineteenth century, it is still used occasionally by **scenographer**s today.

breeches roles, VOL. I: 552. Roles written or adapted for female actors in which they portray men or dress in male attire; especially popular during the English Restoration and throughout the eighteenth century, when men's trousers, or breeches, were form-fitting and reached only to the knee.

burlesque, VOL. II: 169. A comical imitation of an existing work which affectionately ridicules its sillier qualities, usually through exaggeration, substitution, and incongruity. The term is also used, in an unrelated sense, for a twentieth-century genre of American variety entertainment featuring music, pairs of comedians, and a succession of female striptease acts.

caricature, VOL. II: 277. An exaggerated and simplified depiction of character; the reduction of a personality to one or two telling traits at the expense of all other nuances and contradictions.

carros, VOL. I: 258. The wheeled parade floats on which religious plays were performed in Spain; similar mobile stages were called **pageant-wagons** in England.

catharsis, VOL. I: 92, VOL. II: 390. The infamously obscure medical term used by Aristotle in his *Poetics* to describe the purpose of **tragedy:** to stimulate pity and fear in the audience, and then bring about the purgation or purification (*catharsis*) of these and similar emotions. Since Aristotle, the term has been widely adopted to refer to the healthy and pleasurable effects of releasing strong emotions, not only by watching a play, but in life generally.

choral lyric, VOL. I: 1. A poem performed by a singing, dancing chorus; one of the early genres of Greek poetry out of which drama developed. See also **dithyramb.**

choral speech, VOL. II: 451. Text in a drama that is spoken simultaneously by a group of characters in a manner comparable to that of the ancient Greek **chorus.**

chorus, VOL. I: I, 92. Originally, the choir of singing, dancing, masked young men who performed in ancient Greek tragedy and comedy. Treated in tragedy as a "character" within the story, the chorus often represents aggrieved groups (old men, foreign slaves, victims of the plague). The chorus berates, implores, advises, harasses, pursues, and sometimes even helps and commiserates with the main characters, but mostly bears witness to their doings and sayings. In **Old Comedy**, the chorus serves at times as the mouthpiece for the poet. It gradually disappeared from tragedy and comedy, but many attempts have been made to revive some version of it, notably during the Italian and English Renaissance, under **Weimar Classicism**, and by such twentieth-century playwrights as Jean Anouilh, T.S. Eliot, and Michel Tremblay. The singing and dancing chorus appears today most commonly in **musical theatre**, opera, and **operetta**.

collective creation, VOL. II: 172, 547. A theatrical work not written in isolation by a single author but jointly created through the rehearsal process by a group of performers, with or without the help of a writer to record and synthesize their ideas.

comedia capa y espada, VOL. I: 258. Spanish "cape and sword" plays, popular during the seventeenth century. Often featuring macho heroes who must sacrifice their love to preserve their honour, such works combined comedy, violence and adventure in a mix not unlike that of contemporary action films.

Comédie Française, VOL. I: 498, 501. The oldest state-funded theatre company still in existence. Formed in 1680, at the command of King Louis XIV, through the amalgamation of the two remaining French-language troupes in Paris, one of which was Molière's. Called the *Comédie Française* to distinguish it from the Italian company then resident in the capital (see *commedia dell'arte*), it was granted a monopoly on the performance of French drama. A symbol today of national conservatism.

comédies rosses, VOL. II: 4. Plays most closely associated with André Antoine's *Théâtre Libre* in late-nineteenth-century Paris. *Comédies rosses* featured sordid revelations of the depravity and bestiality of outwardly respectable but hypocritical upper- or middle-class characters.

comedy, VOL. I: xii, 2, 118–19, 190, 296, 366, 437-38, 468, 501, 504, 552, 605, VOL. II: xii, 66, 109, 168, 174, 440, 548. A play written to induce joy or laughter in the audience. Unlike **tragedy**, which generally takes characters from a condition of prosperity to a state of destruction or loss, comedy usually begins with a problem, and ends with its happy resolution. Comedy ranges from laughing genres like **satire** and **comedy of manners**, **parody**, **farce** and **burlesque**, to such weepy genres as sentimental and romantic comedy (see also **situation comedy**).

comedy of manners, VOL. I: xiii, 501, VOL. II: xiii. A type of comic play that flourished in the late seventeenth century in London, and elsewhere since, which bases its humour on the sexual and marital intrigues of "high society." It is sometimes contrasted with "comedy of character" as its **satire** is directed at the social habits and conventional hypocrisy of the whole leisured class. Also called **Restoration comedy**; exemplified by the plays of Behn, Wycherley and Congreve.

commedia dell'arte, VOL. I: 146, 257, 259, 502, 684, VOL. II: 7. A species of partly masked, highly physical, and almost completely improvised comic performance that emerged in Renaissance Italy and remained popular all across Europe for the next three hundred years. Its name, which essentially means "professional acting," distinguishes it from the scholarly amateur theatre that emerged at the same time (*commedia erudita*). Its characters were few in number and always more or less the same (see **stock characters**), but some remain in use today: Harlequin, Pierrot, Pulchinella, and others. See also *lazzi*.

commedia erudita, VOL. I: 257–58. The theatre of the scholarly academies that flourished in Renaissance Italy. Its practitioners, who were "erudite" or well-read, wrote plays in imitation of Greek and Roman **tragedies**, **satyr plays**, and **comedies**, staged them in new experimental indoor theatres, and in the process invented many aspects of post-classical theatre: the **proscenium** arch, illusionistic, changeable scenery, theatrical lighting, **pastoral drama**, and opera.

company, VOL. I: 295, 437, 468, VOL. II: 549, 588. Used to refer both to the members of a theatre-producing organization (including all creative and technical personnel), either travelling or resident in its own theatre building, and to the cast of an individual play.

convention, VOL. II: 206, 342. A device, technique, habit or practice that, through long usage, has come to be accepted as normal and expected regardless of how illogical or inappropriate it might otherwise seem. See, for example, **asides**.

corrales, VOL. I: 258. Name for the outdoor courtyard theatres of Spain during the Renaissance and beyond; similar in many ways to the public theatres of Elizabethan England.

cross-dressing, VOL. I: 184. The wearing of the clothing of the opposite sex, either on stage or in life, is typical of many single-gender theatrical traditions, such as those of ancient Greece and Shakespearean England, in which only men performed. See also **breeches roles**.

Dada, VOL. II: 169. A modernist "anti-art" art movement initially associated with Tristan Tzara, Zurich, and the first World War, but taken up by others elsewhere as well. Informed by a disgusted rejection of the civilization that produced that war, Dadaist artworks and cabaret-style performances attacked all the traditional values of European art by aggressively championing nonsense, randomness, vulgarity and anarchy. Along with the Italian Futurists, Dada expanded the language of modern theatre with its use of noise, chaos, spontaneity, and simultaneous, multi-media "happenings" in unconventional venues. See **modernism**.

determinism, VOL. II: 171. The idea that behaviour is shaped in advance, especially by the laws of heredity (genetics and the family) and environment (social and political factors). In contrast to a belief in **personal agency**, determinism implies that humans are not completely responsible for their actions.

Determinism in drama is associated particularly with nineteenth-century writers like Emile Zola, who argued, against the moralism of **melodrama**, for an objectively scientific study of humanity. See also **Naturalism**.

dialect, VOL. II: 450. A local variation of a given spoken language, such as Cockney English or Cajun French.

dialectic argument, VOL. II: 206. A mode of thought, associated with Socrates and with the nineteenth-century philosophers Hegel and Marx, in which terms are understood to contain their opposites, so that each one, being partial and only half the truth, should be annulled into a higher synthesis. The opposite of binary thinking (right or wrong, on or off), a dialectical argument has three terms (thesis, antithesis, synthesis), and says "yes, but also…, and therefore…" Brecht's "**alienation effect**" was based on and intended to induce dialectic thinking.

dialogue, VOL. II: 2, 67, 109, 170, 205–06, 277. Words spoken by actors, usually implying the exchange of language between two or more speakers.

didactic theatre, VOL. I: 189. Dramatic performances intended to teach a particular moral, political or religious lesson to the audience.

director, VOL. II: 170, 173, 390, 547. The individual or team responsible for interpreting, casting, and rehearsing a play, and making creative decisions regarding its staging. Before the twentieth century, these functions were performed not by a person who specialized in direction but by the leading actor in a troupe or by the playwright. See also *mise en scène*.

dithyramb, VOL. I: 1. A type of poem sung and danced in ancient Greece to celebrate the wine-god, Dionysus, and from which tragedy seems in some sense to have emerged. Dithyrambs performed by 50-member men's and boys' choirs competed for prizes during the Athenian theatre festivals (see also **choral lyric**).

double-casting, VOL. II: 548. Giving an actor two (or more) parts to play within a given production.

double entendre, VOL. I: 498. An utterance meant to be heard in two ways, one innocently literal and the other obscene or sexually suggestive. It is an important technique in comedy, especially **comedy of manners**.

downstage-centre, VOL. II: 167. A position on stage near the audience and halfway between each side wing. In order to aid the perspective illusion of painted scenery, theatre stages used to be raked upwards, with the horizon-line higher at the back of the stage than at the front. To move "downstage" is therefore to come closer to the audience.

dramaturgy, VOL. II: 341. The art or principles of playwriting.

dumb-show, VOL. I: 186. The silent representation of an action through physical mimicry and gestures only.

epic drama, VOL. II: 8. A term popularized by Bertolt Brecht (though invented by Erwin Piscator) to describe a style of theatrical storytelling that, for political reasons, pits itself against the conventional rules of **dramaturgy** as outlined by Aristotle, who distinguished "epic" from "dramatic" writing. Whereas traditional drama is supposed to make audiences empathize with the struggle of a single, psychologically self-contained protagonist, epic drama places characters against the backdrop of the largest possible historical and political context in order that their actions do not seem inevitable, or determined by private "human nature," but are revealed as part of a public, man-made, and therefore alterable set of historical facts. To prevent spectators from lapsing into an unthinking emotional stupor, epic theatre uses short, **episodic**, self-contained scenes, multi-media projections, written text, and music to interrupt and "alienate" the action rather than to emphasize its emotions. See "alienation effect," **epic poetry**, and **dialectic argument**.

epic poetry, VOL. I: 1. A form of oral verse, originally sung from memory to musical accompaniment by specialist bards, containing a vast panorama of human life in war and peace. The epics of ancient Greece, each tens of thousands of lines long, are known to us mainly through the works of Homer, the *Iliad* and the *Odyssey*. The stories of humans and gods contained in such poems provided most of the narrative material of Athenian **tragedy** and the **satyr play**.

epilogue, VOL. I: 365. A short, topical, often comic poem appended the end of a play and delivered directly to the audience by a popular actor.

episodic plot, VOL. II: 3. A play or literary work composed of a series of separate and to some degree interchangeable incidents (rather than of a single, unified, and continuously unfolding narrative) is said to have an episodic **plot**.

existentialism, VOL. II: 8. A kind of philosophy in which the meaning of human life is derived from the actual experience of the living individual. First detectable in the anti-systematic thinking of Kierkegaard in the nineteenth century, existentialism came to be associated with the playwrights, novelists and philosophers of post-World-War-Two France (especially Jean-Paul Sartre and Albert Camus). The existential worldview, in which life is assumed to have no essential or pre-existing meanings other than those we personally choose to endow it with, can produce an absurdist sensibility (see **absurdism**).

Expressionism, VOL. II: 8, 168, 170, 277. An influential art movement of the early twentieth century, c. 1907–1920s (see **modernism**). Associated with Germany, it was strongly visual in orientation; indeed, some of its pioneers in drama were visual artists (Kandinsky, Kokoschka). It aimed to give external expression to internal psychological states, usually of an extreme, nightmarish, or otherwise violent kind. Expressionist characters are often tormented by a hostile, overly mechanized, dehumanizing urban environment. Their paranoid or fearsome inner visions are represented visually on stage through distorted perspectives and uncanny colours, menacing lighting, unrealistic and exaggerated costumes, and confusing discontinuities of time and space. Expressionist plays can have a tendency to **allegory**.

fairytale, VOL. I: xiii, 684, VOL. II: xiii. An old and traditionally oral story, often assumed to be suitable only for children, in which the ordinary laws of nature are superseded by fantasy and the fulfillment of wishes. Fairytales are often surprisingly violent and typically composed of **conventional** elements such as handsome princes and sleeping beauties, enchanted forests, talking animals, wicked mothers and witches, and trials or enchanted objects that come in threes. Fairytale characters often use magic or guile to defeat rivals, marry a rich monarch, and live happily ever after.

farce, VOL. I: xiii, 186–87, 209, 222, 649, VOL. II: xiii, 174. Sometimes classed as the "lowest" form of **comedy**. Its humour depends not on verbal wit, but on physicality and sight gags: pratfalls, beatings, peltings with pies, malfunctioning equipment, unpleasant surprises, and sudden necessities to hide in boxes and closets. However, most comedy contains *some* elements of farce, which requires highly skilled actors for its effects. Also called "slapstick" in honour of the double-shafted baton carried by Arlecchino in *commedia dell'arte*, which when struck against another actor in a simulated beating made a loud slap.

folio edition, VOL. I: 365. A large-format printed version of a manuscript, often used in connection with Shakespeare's plays. After Shakespeare's death, two of his former partners in the King's Company, John Heminges and Henry Condell, collected thirty-six of his plays (excluding *Pericles* and *Two Noble Kinsmen*) and in 1623 published the collection in a volume that has since been called the First Folio. "Folio" refers to the size obtained when a sheet of paper of standard size is folded once, making two leaves or four pages, which can then be sewn together along the fold to make a book. When the sheet is folded twice—creating four leaves or eight pages—it is called a "**quarto**."

forestage, VOL. I: 500. See **apron**, above.

fringe theatre, VOL. II: 548. The production of plays and performance pieces outside or "on the margins" of mainstream theatre institutions.

Furies, VOL. I: 9. In the *Oresteia* trilogy, the spirits of vengeance. They were conceived in Greek mythology as underworld goddesses who punish murderers or incite the victim's surviving relatives to do so. Euphemistically called the Eumenides, "the kindly ones," out of fear of offending them as their cruelty was notorious, these frightful goddesses comprise the chorus of the final **tragedy** in Aeschylus's trilogy (see Volume I).

gallery, VOL. I: 501. Used in several senses to refer to an upper balcony in a theatre. In the Elizabethan public theatre, musicians sat in a "musicians' gallery" above the stage; indoor London theatre auditoriums of the next few centuries were divided in pit, boxes, and gallery, the last being the uppermost and least expensive seats. To "play to the gallery" is to pitch the level of one's performance to (what was assumed to be) the least discerning members of the audience, originally servants of those sitting below.

harlequinades, VOL. I: 501, 649. A form of theatrical entertainment popular in England in the eighteenth century, consisting of English versions of the **stock characters** of Italian *commedia dell'arte*. See also **pantomime**.

history play, VOL. I: 295, 366. A dramatic re-imagining of real people and events drawn from the annals of the past. Shakespeare and Schiller are considered among the greatest writers of history plays; Büchner and Strindberg are also noted for them. From time to time, such works have played important roles in the establishment of a nation's self-image and founding myths. Some degree of **anachronism** tends to be considered acceptable in historical dramas.

humorous comedy, VOL. I: 649. A play emphasizing laughter and used in the context of eighteenth-century theatre in contrast with sentimental **comedy**. (Sentimental comedy was meant to induce "a joy too exquisite for laughter." Advanced by writers such as Richard Steele in the early eighteenth century, it was a wholesome, anti-aristocratic, middle-class alternative to the sex-and-adultery comedy of the Restoration.)

iambic dialogue, VOL. I: 2. Speech in a poetic drama that, with its unstressed/stressed rhythm (or short/long accent), most closely approximates the rhythm of everyday speech. Iambics were first used in Greek poetry in abusive poems that attacked particular individuals.

illegitimate theatre, VOL. II: 2. A historical term, now often used in quotation marks, to describe the many types of musical, variety, spectacular, and non-literary entertainment that exist alongside, or are seen as imperiling the survival of, more elevated and challenging forms. It derives from the monopolistic laws that regulated English and French theatre until the mid-nineteenth century, and which gave "licenses" to one or two companies only, along with protection from competition from other upstart enterprises. Known for their literary drama, serious opera and ballet, such theatres were called the legitimate houses; all others, technically illegal and therefore "illegitimate," avoided prosecution by steering clear of regular or classical plays, sometimes inventing new genres in the process (see, for example, **melodrama**).

improvisation, VOL. II: 548. The seemingly spontaneous invention of dramatic dialogue and/or a dramatic plot by actors without the assistance of a written text. All performers must generally be able do this in short bursts—to cover a mistake on stage, or to plumb the depths of a character during rehearsals. But improvisation is also a highly specialized art-form with its own rules and **conventions**. The actors of the *commedia dell'arte* tradition, who could extemporize on stage for hours on the basis of only a bare-bones scenario posted backstage, were said to be expert in it.

interlude, VOL. I: 186, 202. A short and often comical play or other entertainment performed between the **acts** of a longer or more serious work, particularly during the later Middle Ages and early Renaissance.

irony, VOL. I: 69, 93, VOL. II: 174. A contrast between what is said and what is known. Some speakers use it intentionally, as when Socrates feigned ignorance of things he knew quite well, to draw out other "philosophers." By contrast, dramatic irony occurs when characters utter statements whose full meaning is not understood by them (although it is clear to those who hear it, such as the audience or the other characters on stage). Many of Oedipus's remarks, which are true in ways he does not yet grasp, exemplify dramatic irony. Tragic irony, on the other hand, is said to occur when events turn out in an opposite way to what was expected and desired, yet so strangely fittingly that, in retrospect, it seems as if this outcome should have been predicted or known all along (see **tragedy**, with its "reversal and recognition"). Some forms of **satire** may also rely on irony.

jeu, VOL. I: 187. French for "play," as in a game; used in the titles of some French dramas (although not in the sense of "a theatrical play" in general, which is *une pièce*).

lazzi, VOL. I: 684. Italian for "turn" or "trick." Used of the comical gags, jokes, acrobatics, and **stock** gestures for which the servant characters of the *commedia dell'arte* were famous. Whenever the actors ran dry in their **improvisation**, Arlecchino or one of the other *zanni* (comic servants) would jump-start the action, drawing on a pre-perfected repertoire of tumbles, flips, beatings or other (usually physical) stage business.

legitimate theatre, VOL. II: 2. Historically, a state-licensed and legally protected monopoly theatre; metaphorically, by extension, the "high art" theatre world. See **illegitimate theatre**.

liturgical drama, VOL. I: 185–86. A play or playlet based on the text of the Catholic religious service that is performed as part of the service itself, originally staged in Latin by clerics, and eventually in various vernaculars. they were first documented in the tenth century, when Benedictine monks used gestures to act out the lines of the Easter Mass known as the "Quem Quaeritis" trope—a section of sung text depicting an exchange between an angel and the Marys who are looking for Jesus' body at the sepulchre. Over the next three centuries, such illustrations of key moments of the church service blossomed into semi-autonomous plays.

Liturgical drama declined after the Reformation, but can still be found today in some places, especially in Spain and South America.

make-up, VOL. I: 184. Any substance, usually in liquid, cream or powder form, that is used to disguise, transform, age, or decorate an actor's face. It includes the white lead reportedly used by Thespis in the sixth century B.C.E., as well as the "pancake," "powder," and "grease-paint" of later periods. In theatre traditions that do not use **masks**, and where distances or artificial lighting can impair visibility, make-up is sometimes used for the practical purpose of helping the audience to see the actors' features.

mansion, VOL. I: 188. Used in the Medieval period to describe the various locations represented, as part of the outdoor set, in some types of religious plays (see **passion play** and **miracle play**). For a piece about the Passion of Christ, for example, structures would be built to depict such locales as Heaven, Bethlehem, Jerusalem, Limbo, and Hell. Often elaborately decorated and equipped with sophisticated special-effects machines, such mansions were simultaneously visible throughout the play; the action advanced not through set changes but through the movement of actors from one mansion to the next.

mask, VOL. I: 2. Any removable and reusable material used to disguise, transform, obscure or decorate all or part of an actor's face. Many Western theatre traditions use masks as a **convention**. Greek and Roman actors always wore full masks with large, gaping mouth-holes (except in mimes); Italian actors of the *commedia dell'arte* wore coloured leather half-masks that covered their eyes, nose and upper cheeks. With the return of non-realistic performance styles in the twentieth century, the use of masks has become widespread again.

masques, VOL. I: 259. Spectacular entertainments performed at royal courts as part of special celebrations such as weddings and feast-days, chiefly during the Renaissance. Consisting of music, dance, technical wizardry, and extravagantly opulent costumes, masques celebrated the virtues of the reigning monarch in terms, images and allegories drawn from Classical mythology. Members of the royal family and their entourage took part by joining in the dancing or allowing themselves to be carried aloft on "clouds" animated by hidden machines. In England, Ben Jonson provided the poetry for famous masques created in collaboration with architect and **scenographer** Inigo Jones.

melodrama, VOL. I: xii, xiii, 499, 770, VOL. II: xii, xiii, 1–3, 26, 66, 168, 206, 440. A type of storytelling that emerged in France and Germany in the wake of the French Revolution, and that is marked by many features of that event: a clear division of characters into the poor, weak, and good hero on one hand, often a child, woman, mute or slave; and a rich, powerful, and evil villain on the other, who schemes to exploit or harm the victim but who is triumphantly overthrown at the last possible minute, usually in a sensational fire, fight, avalanche, or other violent cataclysm. Literally "music-drama," melodrama originally used background music throughout the action, much like film soundtracks do, to emphasize the characters' emotions, warn of approaching danger, and shape the spectator's emotional response (especially at the ends of acts and scenes, when actors assumed particularly pathetic or frightening postures and held them, frozen, in **tableaux**). Melodrama was the most popular narrative genre in Europe and North America in the nineteenth century. It still retains its popularity today, but it has long since left the theatre, taking up residence in the Hollywood film.

minstrel show, VOL. II: 26. A type of musical variety entertainment consisting of racist **burlesque**s of African-American performance styles. Hugely popular in the United States from the mid-nineteenth to the early-twentieth century, minstrel shows were generally performed by white singers in "blackface" (black **make-up** with highlights applied to emphasize the lips and eyes), and were based on grotesquely exaggerated stereotypes. Minstrelsy developed elaborate **convention**s and achieved such wide mainstream acceptance that it attracted contributions from respectable composers such as Stephen Foster. There were even some instances in which African-American performers themselves adopted blackface and **caricature**-based mannerisms in order to appeal to popular taste. Long after minstrelsy's racist foundations were themselves recognized and denounced, variations on the minstrel show continued to appear, for example on British television (the BBC's "Black and White Minstrel Show" ran from 1958 to 1978).

miracle play, VOL. I: 185, 190. A type of medieval religious drama based on material drawn from stories and legends about the lives, works, suffering and martyrdom of Christian saints. Also called a **saint's play**.

mise en scène, VOL. II: 4, 168. French expression, literally meaning "the putting on stage," which has been adopted in other languages to describe the sum total of creative choices made in the staging of a play. Because these are nowadays usually made by a **director**, *mise en scène* can be used interchangeably with "direction," but the French term conveys a greater sense of the artistry involved, particularly with respect to the visual, stylistic, and conceptual aspects of a production that are not explicitly covered by the English term.

modernism, VOL. I: 241, VOL. II: 167ff, 439. A widespread movement in Western culture, datable perhaps to the Paris Exposition of 1889, which sought to sever all ties with the past and invent new modes of art, thought, and life that were consistent with (what was believed to be) an unprecedented new age of machines, speed, new possibility and change. Like the unadorned steel of the Eiffel Tower, like the architectural adage that "form follows function," like Futurist symphonies written for typewriter and vacuum cleaner, modernism rejected all ornamental beauty, challenged all recognizable artistic **conventions**, and tried to reinvent painting, music, theatre, architecture and other arts from scratch. Modernist sub-movements, such as **Symbolism**, Futurism, Constructivism, **Expressionism**, **Dada**, and **Surrealism**, advanced their own styles; but they all shared a desire to use artistic materials—light, colour, sound, space, time, bodies—in boldly new ways. From the early 1970s, the austerity and radicalism of modernism was rejected by many artists in favour of **postmodernism**.

monologue, VOL. II: 449–50. Used to refer to text that is spoken by an actor on stage alone, or to the audience, but not to another character. Can also be used in the sense of "a long uninterrupted speech."

morality play, VOL. I: xii, xiii, 185–89, 202, VOL. II: xii, xiii. A type of religious drama that flourished in the Middle Ages, usually cast in the form of an **allegory**, and intended to teach a clear moral lesson to the audience. *Everyman* (in volume I) is one of the most famous of all morality plays.

mumming, VOL. I: 187. The practice of disguising oneself in costume and, with other mummers, going door to door to entertain one's neighbours, usually in connection with an ancient seasonal festival or holiday. Modern-day Halloween approximates the practices of the earliest known mummers, who seem to have been common in England in the Middle Ages.

musical theatre, VOL. II: 169. Virtually all theatre, in all periods and places, features music. But the term "musical theatre" refers to a specific, often American genre of entertainment that dominated the commercial theatre districts of New York, London, and other cities through the twentieth century. Divided into songs, dances, and unsung spoken sections, and frequently featuring large dancing choruses, musicals can be hard to distinguish from some kinds of opera and **operetta**; but whereas the vocal parts of opera can usually be handled only by professional musicians, musical theatre **scores** are generally intended for actors (who happen to be able to sing). Very great musicals will tend to "cross over" and be taken into the **repertoires** of serious opera companies eventually.

mystery play, VOL. I: 185, 187–88, 208–09. A type of religious drama popular in the Middle Ages, based on narrative material taken from the Old and New Testaments. In England, mystery plays, also called **Bible-cycle plays**, were performed by the members of trade and craft guilds in the streets of market towns, often on Corpus Christi day. See **pageant-wagons**, *carros*, and *autos sacramentales*.

Naturalism, VOL. I: xiii, 685, VOL. II: xiii, 1, 4, 5, 8, 277. The term used by Emile Zola in the late nineteenth century to describe a new, scientific method of novel-writing and playwriting. Influenced by medical science—and a few naturalist playwrights were actually doctors—Naturalism aimed to diagnose human crimes and evils as dispassionately as a doctor would a disease. Like specimens in an experiment, Naturalist characters are placed within specific biological, political, and social conditions, conditions that are often referred to collectively as "heredity" and "environment." The goal is to observe, as objectively and unmoralistically as possible, what kind of behaviour results (see **determinism**). Naturalist works can be grim in tone and detailed in their **realism**, often focusing on the ugly or "pathological" side of life (suicide, infanticide, poverty, venereal disease, prostitution).

neoclassical dramaturgy, VOL. I: 259. The principles, rules and **conventions** of writing plays according to the precepts and ideals of **neoclassicism**. Often based on the so-called **unities** of time, place, and action.

neoclassicism, VOL. I: 469, 498–99, 501–02. Literally the "new classicism," the aesthetic style in drama and other art-forms that dominated high culture in Europe through the seventeenth and eighteenth centuries, and in some places into the nineteenth century, or until it was swept away by **Romanticism**. Its subject matter was often taken from Greek and Roman myth and history; but more important than its subject matter was its *style*, which was based on a selective and often downright false image of the ancient world. It valued order, reason, clarity and moderation; it rejected strong contrasts in tone as well as, usually, the supernatural and anything that cannot be rationally motivated within the plot of a play (such as the appearance of gods, witches, or a dancing chorus). Racine's *Phèdre* (in Volume I) is considered one of the most perfectly realized neoclassical dramas. See also **unities**.

New Comedy, VOL. I: 5, 92, 146, 257, 438. A type of comic play that flourished in ancient Greece from the fourth century B.C.E., particularly under such playwrights as Menander. It was later imported into Rome, where its plots and characters were reworked in Latin. Replacing **Old Comedy** after Athens' defeat in the Peloponnesian War, it focused on private, everyday domestic situations involving parent-child disharmony, money, neighbours, and parental obstacles to love and marriage. Its young lovers, bad-tempered parents, scheming slaves and golden-hearted prostitutes quickly achieved the status of **stock characters**. Also known as **situation comedy**.

Old Comedy, VOL. I: 5, 92, 119, 147. The type of dramatic **satire** practiced in fifth-century Athens and equated today with the works of Aristophanes (see *Frogs* in this volume). The genre is known for its fantastical and unrealistic **episodic** plots, its frequent use of animal choruses (frogs, birds, wasps, horse-mounted knights), and particularly for its brilliant verbal wit, free obscenity, and fearless attacks on living Athenian politicians and other public figures (e.g., Euripides and Socrates). See also **chorus**.

operetta, VOL. II: 169. Also known as "light opera." A theatrical work that is mostly sung and intended to be performed by professional singers. Associated with the works of Franz Lehar and Johann Strauss II, operetta differs from opera in three ways: it features longer unsung spoken scenes, tends to treat lighter, frothier subjects, and uses less challenging and more popular musical idioms. See also **musical theatre**.

orchestra, VOL. I: 3. Lit., "the dancing place." In the ancient world it was the lower, flat, circular surface-area of the outdoor theatre where the **chorus** danced and sang. It was also used by fifty-member choirs in the performance of **dithyrambs**, which were danced in a circular formation. As the dancing chorus disappeared from drama, the orchestra shrank to a semi-circle below a raised stage; over the centuries, it was eventually given over to musicians. The term is mainly used in the theatre today to refer to this orchestra-pit, or to the ground-floor seats of the auditorium, also called the *parterre* or stalls.

pageant-wagons, VOL. I: 188. Wheeled and elaborately decorated parade floats used as mobile stages in England for the performance of **Bible-cycle plays,** or **mystery plays.** They were sometimes built on two levels, with trap doors and mechanical devices for raising angels or thrones up to heaven. Actors drew them through the streets of market towns along a prearranged route, either by hand or horse, stopping intermittently at fixed performance locations to enact their portion of the Biblical narrative. Many wagons were stored through the year in covered sheds and brought out on Corpus Christi day.

Panathenaia, VOL. I: 3. Lit., "all-Athenian," a large ancient Greek summer festival featuring contests, prizes, and religious rituals, specializing in the competitive recitation of **epic poetry.**

pantomime, VOL. I: 501, 649, VOL. II: 169. Originally a genre of virtuoso solo performance invented by the ancient Romans. It is usually used today to refer to a type of spectacular entertainment that emerged in London at the beginning of the eighteenth century, featuring *commedia dell'arte* characters, magical special-effects wizardry, music, dance, and fantastical **episodic** plots. It remained very popular into the nineteenth century, when it picked up certain features of **melodrama** and developed into the form it usually takes today, the "Christmas Panto," which involves some audience participation, often of children. Also used in the sense of "to enact silently," or mime (see **dumb-show**).

parable, VOL. I: 684, VOL. II: 482. A short story told to illustrate a moral principle. It differs from **allegory** in being shorter and simpler: parables do not generally function on two levels simultaneously.

parody, VOL. I: 208. A comic play or other work in which an institution, phenomenon, person, or artistic genre is ridiculed, usually through exaggeration, debasement, substitution, and incongruity. Unlike **burlesque,** which tends to target a specific work and imitate its tone, style, or oddities perfectly and even affectionately, parody is loose, general, and critical.

passion play, VOL. I: 188. A type of late medieval religious drama based on episodes from the life of Christ as related in the New Testament, similar to the **saint's play** or **miracle play** insofar as it dramatizes the persecution, suffering, and death of a martyr revered by Christians. Sometimes staged over many days, usually on an outdoor **mansion** set featuring Heaven on the left and a prominent and spectacularly equipped Hell Mouth on the right.

pastoral drama, VOL. I: 258. A type of play invented during the Renaissance by members of Italian scholarly academies in an attempt to revive the **satyr play** of ancient Greece (see *commedia erudita*). Filtering the lusty, drunken goat-men, ecstatic maenads, and rustic settings of the satyr play though their Christian worldview, such writers created a new theatrical genre in which innocent shepherds, nymphs, and shepherdesses gambol in an idealized natural landscape free from the pressures of city life and the corruptions of civilization.

personal agency, VOL. II: 171, 590. The power, as exercised by an individual, to originate and carry out his or her desires from sources within the self, free from or against the **determinism** of external forces.

playwright-in-residence, VOL. II: 549, 622. A writer or creator of plays who is engaged by a theatre company to work within their midst for a period of time, either for the purpose of nurturing a young talent, or gaining prestige from association with an established writer, and usually in the hope that he or she will produce new work for the company to perform.

plot, VOL. II: 205, 277. Not to be confused with the "story," the plot of a play or other literary work is the precise arrangement of incidents used to tell the story. The same story can give rise to countless plots, depending on the point at which the writer chooses to begin (at Oedipus's birth? or on the last day of his reign?), what he or she chooses to dramatize (the wedding night of Oedipus and Jocasta? the murder of Hamlet's father?), and how he chooses to bring the events about (a messenger? a lost letter? an epiphany? a gun-battle?).

poetic prose dramas, VOL. II: 67. Plays that employ symbolism, metaphor and heightened language to a degree normally associated with poetry, but that are written in prose rather than verse.

postmodernism, VOL. I: 241, 685. A movement in art and culture during the last quarter of the twentieth century named for its rejection of **modernism.** Characterized by its re-embrace of tradition, postmodern art incorporates styles and conventions from previous historical periods, usually in eclectic combinations that reveal new aspects of each one. Noted for its playfulness and ironic detachment (see **irony**), postmodernism has been accused of lacking political seriousness; but its tendency to bring different media, periods, and cultural values into contact with one another (Western and Eastern theatre traditions, puppets and live actors, classical sculptures and computers, etc.) suggests that it is committed to seeing the world "globally" and resisting the domination of imagery and ideas by any one group or ideology.

proagon, VOL. I: 93. Greek for "pre-contest." Refers to the point in the Athenian theatre festivals at which playwrights appeared before the public with their actors to advertise their upcoming play. Functioned like the "trailer" of contemporary movies in generating audience interest. At first performed outdoors, such events came to be held in the Odeon, or music-hall. See *agōn*.

proscenium, VOL. I: 258, 259, 500, 501, VOL. II: 298. A Latin architectural term derived from the Greek *proskenion*, the front-most section of the theatre building (*skēnē*) as it developed in the post-Classical, Hellenistic period. During the Renaissance, when theatres were built indoors, artificial lighting, perspective painting, and changeable scenery were adopted in **scenography**. To hide the scene-shifting equipment and lighting instruments from view of the spectators, a single archway was constructed at the front of the acting area. (The first proscenium of this type was built for the Teatro Farnese in 1618.) Stages on which a pictorial illusion is created with the help of a three- or four-sided border or frame are called "proscenium arch," or "picture-frame" theatres, and they reached their heyday during the nineteenth century, the age of **realism**.

protagonist, VOL. II: 1, 2, 170, 296, 298, 389. The central character in a drama or other literary work; see *agōn*.

quarto, VOL. I: 316, 318, 503, 552, 605. Refers to the size of a published book created from sheets of paper that have been folded twice. When sewn together along the second fold and ripped along the first, eight pages are produced. In the case of Shakespeare, the word is used of certain printed copies of his plays that appeared during his lifetime, usually in "bootleg" versions (see by contrast the **folio** edition). Before the advent of copyright laws, publication of plays during the author's life was strongly resisted, as this would have made the works available to rival companies. When such plays did appear, usually against the wishes of the playwright, they often did so in badly corrupted versions. For example, the first edition of *Hamlet* (1603) is believed to be a reconstruction of the play from memory by the actor who played Marcellus. Much of the text seems merely paraphrased, but the **stage directions** are probably authentic. The second edition of *Hamlet* (1604) is more reliable. These two editions of the play are known as the First and Second Quarto (or Q1 and Q2).

realism, VOL. I: 685, 713, VOL. II: 1, 4, 5, 8, 144, 167. The attempt to so faithfully duplicate the appearance of the real world in art that viewers might conceivably be fooled into accepting the imitation for the thing itself. In the theatre, realism usually refers to a style of production perfected in the nineteenth century, when vast expense and labour were devoted to achieving the kinds of all-consuming illusions that today are more commonly associated with movies. Because the theatre's technical equipment, and the audience, must be hidden from view to achieve such illusions, theatrical realism is often associated with darkened auditoriums and picture-frame or **proscenium**-arch stages.

repertoire, VOL. I: 437, 468, 503, VOL. II: 1, 66, 169, 205. Used to refer either, in general, to the sum total of plays that are considered stage-worthy at a given time, or to the particular list of plays that can be readied for performance by an individual theatre company (or performer).

repertory, VOL. II: 205. A system of scheduling plays non-consecutively by alternating them with other plays from a company's current **repertoire**. The repertory or "rep" system is very rare in North American commercial theatre.

Restoration comedy, VOL. I: 501, 605–06. A genre of witty and sexually uninhibited drama associated with the London theatres in the decades after 1660, when King Charles II was "restored" to the English throne. It was known for its pungent **satire**, obsession with the habits of the upper classes, and cynical depiction of human customs, particularly the institution of marriage. Also see **comedy of manners.**

role-playing, VOL. I: xiii, 146, 184, 190, VOL. II: xiii, 548. The pretended adoption of the identity or function of another person. All acting, of course, is a type of role-playing. The impersonation of others is a common theme in drama and appears within the plots of countless plays.

romance, VOL. I: xiii, 296, 366, VOL. II: xiii, 168. A dreamlike genre of fiction or storytelling in which the ordinary laws of nature are suspended, in which statues come to life, shipwrecked men emerge from the sea unharmed, and troubled or broken worlds are magically healed at the end, often by daughters, and often in **pastoral** settings.

Romanticism, VOL. I: 770, VOL. II: 1, 5. A widespread movement in art and culture, beginning in the later eighteenth century, that aimed to throw off the shackles of **neoclassicism.** Rejecting all rules and rational principles, Romantic art emphasized feeling, stark contrasts, extreme or abnormal psychological states, as well as the inner world of dreams, fantasies, and the supernatural. Natural and untutored "genius" was prized over technical mastery, untamed and "sublime" nature over civilization. Some Romantic poets did produce works for the stage, such as Goethe and Schiller, and Byron and Shelley, but Romanticism in the theatre

more often took the form of violently emotional acting, particularly the kind made famous by Edmund Kean. Romanticism also manifested itself throughout nineteenth-century theatre in **melodrama** and Gothic plays, with their intense villains, brooding heroes, spooky vampires, and dark medieval castles.

saint's play, VOL. I: xii, 185, 189, 190–91, VOL. II: xii. See **miracle play**.

satire, VOL. I: xiii, 119, VOL. II: xiii, 8, 341, 588. A humorous play or other work in which people, attitudes, or types of behaviour are ridiculed for the purpose of correcting their blameworthy qualities. Satirists differ from other types of comic writers in that they are often morally outraged by the follies and vices they depict. Of all types of **comedy**, satire is the most critical. It can also, paradoxically, be the most subtle, for satirists may mask their fury with humour so effectively that they can seem to be condoning the faults they abhor. Satire often makes use of **irony** and frequently targets politicians and other public figures. For this reason, satire tends to flourish in liberal societies where free speech is prized. See also **Old Comedy** and **comedy of manners**.

satyr play, VOL. I: 2, 258. Ancient Athenian genre of comical drama, usually a mythological **burlesque,** which was performed by a singing and dancing chorus dressed in satyr costume (a furry loincloth to which a goat's tail and artificial penis were attached, plus a mask depicting an ugly snubbed nose, high forehead, and goat's ears). In Greek myth, satyrs were the drunken, randy, rabble-rousing attendants of Dionysus, in whose honour all theatre was performed in ancient Greece. Satyr plays were staged as part of the Greek **tragic tetralogy**, either as the first or the last play of the four. See also **pastoral drama**.

scenography, VOL. I: 3. Also called "set design" or "stage design," scenography is often preferred today as a term to describe the visual and spatial aspects of a theatrical production. This is because many artists working in the theatre do not design only the sets, but also the costumes and sometimes even the lighting, too, for a unified effect. Scenography also implies that the creation of a beautiful and functional environment on stage is a specialized art-form, not merely a variant of other types of design.

score, VOL. II: 169. The musical text of an opera, **operetta** or **musical**, as written by a composer, containing parts for singers and musicians.

screenplay, VOL. II: 341, 390, 482, 622. The written text used in the making of a movie. It describes the sequence of shots and camera angles that will be used in the telling of the story, as well as what the characters do and say. Screenplays are often based on pre-existing stage-plays and novels.

set design, VOL. II: 3. See **scenography**.

situation comedy, VOL. I: xiii, 5, 146, 190, 500, 713. VOL. II: xiii. Humorous play or other performed story concerning everyday domestic trials and tribulations within families and/or between friends and neighbours. Love, marriage, wealth, and family or neighbourhood harmony are usually the focus of sitcoms. The jokes are generated by awkward or complex situations involving false assumptions, mistaken identities, and attempts to trick others out of money, prestige, or lovers. Sitcoms often feature **stock characters** such as the braggart, the parasite, the clever servant, the stupid servant, the violent cook, and so on. See also **New Comedy** and **convention**.

skēnē, VOL. I: 3. Greek for "scene house." Used of the covered, indoor portion of the Theatre of Dionysus in ancient Athens that was used by the actors for entrances, exits, and changes of costumes and **masks**. The *skēnē* also housed the theatre's special-effects machinery. In fifth-century tragedy, the scene house generally represented a palace or temple with its large central doors. In later centuries, scene buildings were constructed with new architectural features such as multiple openings and rows of pillars for receiving painted scenery; in such Hellenistic theatres, the *skēnē* was expanded and divided into an upper and a lower stage (or *proskenion*; see **proscenium**).

"social problem" plays, VOL. II: 66–67. Dramas, usually from the late nineteenth and early twentieth centuries, that focused on specific topical and controversial issues such as prostitution, slum landlordism, venereal disease, and other malaises of modern society. Associated with Shaw and Ibsen in particular, and often closely related to the plays of **Naturalism**.

sound-scape, VOL. II: 170. Named by analogy with "landscape," a sound-scape is the totality of sound-effects, ambient noises and music used by a sound-designer or **director** as the aural background for a production.

stage design, VOL. II: 3. See **scenography**.

stage directions, VOL. I: 189, VOL. II: 390, 440. The written but unspoken parts of a play text, sometimes provided by the playwright and sometimes by later editors, that describe gestures, stage action or technical effects (set changes, music cues, etc.). It was very rare until the nineteenth century, when detailed staging instructions became routine. With the rise of the **director** in the twentieth century, the freedom of theatre artists to determine the stage action for themselves has been energetically asserted, and for this reason stage directions are considered nonessential parts of the play by many theatre practitioners today.

stichomythia, VOL. I: 2. One of the meters of Greek dramatic poetry, used for the rapid exchange of short lines of **dialogue** between two speakers, approximating the effect of a witness under cross-examination. Of all Greek verse forms, it is the most definitive of drama and most strongly contrasted with its long **monologue** passages, which remain closer to earlier forms of **epic poetry** and **choral lyric**. See also **iambic dialogue**.

stock characters, VOL. I: 684. Personality types in dramatic literature that recur so often that their particular collection of character traits, their professions, and sometimes even their names and costumes have become fixed. Some genres of theatre consist almost entirely of stock characters, such as the *commedia dell'arte*. Since this **convention** is much more typical of **comedy** than **tragedy**, great comic actors will often devote their entire careers to perfecting, developing, and even radically re-interpreting one of these stock characters, which are sometimes called "masks" in honour of the masked improvisers of the Italian comedy tradition. See also **caricature, New Comedy,** and **situation comedy.**

Sturm und Drang, VOL. I: 502, 770. German for "Storm and Stress." A literary movement that took its name from the title of an F.M. von Klinger play of 1776, and which was one of the earliest mani-festations of **Romanticism,** it is associated particu-larly with the work of Goethe and Schiller (see *The Robbers* in Volume I).

subplot, VOL. I: 7, 405, 469, 552. A secondary narra-tive embedded within the main one that usually comments on, contrasts with, or in some other way illuminates the primary line of action in a play or other literary work. Subplots usually mirror the events related in the main **plot,** except transposed to a different and often lower social plane or tone.

Surrealism, VOL. II: 169, 277. One of the many influ-ential schools within **modernism.** Like **realism,** to which it obviously refers, surrealism incorporates elements of the true appearance of life and nature; but unlike realism, it combines these elements ac-cording to a logic more typical of dreams than waking life. Isolated aspects of surrealist art may create powerful illusions of reality, but the effect of the whole is to disturb or question our sense of reality rather than to confirm it.

symbolism, VOL. II: 5, 67, 168, 277. The use of signs, visible images or other sensuous effects to repre-sent invisible or intangible ideas.

Symbolist theatre, VOL. II: 5, 144. A movement based in late-nineteenth-century Paris in which play-wrights, following the lead of Symbolist poets and painters, tried to convey invisible emotional or spiritual truths through a careful orchestration of atmosphere and **symbolism.** Most of the works of the Symbolist theatre were presented at either Paul Fort's *Théâtre d'Art* or Aurélien Lugné-Poë's *Théâtre de l'Oeuvre.*

tableaux, VOL. I: 713. Plural of *tableau,* French for painting or picture. It is used in drama to refer to a visually pleasing and emotionally compelling ar-rangement of actors' bodies on stage. First recom-mended for wide use by theorist and playwright Denis Diderot in the eighteenth century, such con-sciously contrived stage pictures did gain promi-nence in the centuries that followed, particularly in **melodrama,** which often called for them in the **stage directions.**

theatron, VOL. I: 3. Greek word for theatre, literally "the viewing place."

tragedy, VOL. I: xiii, 2, 92, 118–19, 187, 296, 366, 468, 501, VOL. II: xiii, 1, 174. A Greek word believed to mean "song of the goat-singers" (see **satyr play** and **dithyramb**). Originating in the sixth century B.C.E., tragedy is the oldest dramatic genre and remains for many the "highest" form of poetry. Our knowl-edge of it derives mainly from the plays of Aeschylus, Sophocles, and Euripides, as well as from the little we know about the manner of its performance (see ***agōn,* chorus, mask, orchestra,** *skēnē,* and **tragic tetralogy**). Our understanding of it has also been shaped by Aristotle, whose de-scription of Athenian tragedy in his *Poetics* remains a touchstone for tragic theory and practice to this day. According to Aristotle, tragedy is the imita-tion of an organically unified, serious action in which the **plot,** or arrangement of incidents, elic-its the audience's pity and fear and then effects a **catharsis,** or purgation, of these and similar emo-tions. Tragic plots generally take the **protagonist** from a condition of good fortune to bad, often to his or her destruction, involve mental and/or physical suffering, and ideally take place within families, usually of a socially elevated or prominent type (royal families, for example). In Aristotle's view the most effective tragic plots also involve a simultaneous "reversal and recognition," a moment when the character's fortune turns for the worse and he or she is suddenly able to grasp a truth that was unavailable before. Tragedy has been recon-ceived by every subsequent age that has practiced it, beginning in the Renaissance. In the seven-teenth century it was reinvented according to the principles of **neoclassicism**; in the eighteenth according to those of the Enlightenment ("middle-class" or "bourgeois tragedy"). **Romanticism** in turn created its own tragic forms, often inspired by Shakespeare. Notable re-thinkings of tragedy in the modern age include Arthur Miller's essay "Tragedy and the Common Man." See also **working-class tragedy**.

tragic tetralogy, VOL. I: 2, 8. A four-part **tragedy**. Mostly associated with the (non-comic) plays of Athens in the fifth-century B.C.E., it consisted of one **satyr play** and three tragedies written on related themes. Another famous tragic tetralogy, *The Ring of the Nibelung*, was written in the nineteenth century by composer Richard Wagner. This four-part "music drama," created in imitation of Greek tragedy, is based on the heroes and gods of Germanic myth.

tragi-comedy, VOL. I: xiii, VOL. II: xiii. A genre of drama in which many elements of **tragedy** are present, but which generally has a happy end. Corneille's *The Cid* is an excellent example of this genre, which was sometimes preferred to straight tragedy under **neoclassicism**. See *Fuenteovejuna* (in Volume I).

unities [of action, time and place], VOL. I: 257. A doctrine invented by the theorists of **neoclassicism**, who considered "the three unities" an essential rule of proper **tragedy**. It stipulates that the plot, the span of time it represents, and the amount of physical terrain it covers must together approximate the true unity of real space/time conditions (i.e., the single location and continuous two-hour time-period that prevails on stage during performance, during which one can realistically represent only so much action and no more). The concept was based on a misreading of Aristotle, and was soon ridiculed almost out of existence by writers such as G.E. Lessing and Samuel Johnson. But it did succeed in determining the form taken by tragedy during the seventeenth and eighteenth centuries. It also ensured that the *un*-unified plays of Shakespeare would remain beneath the contempt of many for over a hundred years. Despite their poor grounding in ancient theatre practice and the rigidity with which their (mostly French) advocates enforced them, the unities remain a useful concept in drama. Works of theatrical **realism** and **Naturalism**, for example, tend to observe them instinctively.

vomitorium, VOL. I: 7. In theatrical contexts, used to describe a ramp or raked hallway under the seats of the auditorium that allows spectators to ascend to their seats, or actors to the playing area, from below. The ancient Romans, who built their poured-concrete theatres on flat ground rather than nestled into naturally occurring hillsides, were the first to use "voms."

Weimar Classicism, VOL. I: 502. The style of playwriting, acting, and **scenography** associated with the Weimar Court Theatre during the late eighteenth century, when Schiller and Goethe were **playwright**s-in-residence and **artistic director**s there. Following their *Sturm und Drang* periods, both adopted an approach to writing and staging plays that was noted for its greater fidelity to Classical Greek culture than was common in **neoclassicism**. See also **antiquarianism**.

word-scenery, VOL. I: 498. The use of language alone, when spoken by actors on stage, to convey the locations depicted in a play without the help of sets, lighting, or other theatrical effects. It is typical of bare-stage traditions like those of Shakespeare. Superb examples of the effectiveness of word-scenery can be found in Shakespeare's Prologues to *Henry V*.

working-class tragedy, VOL. II: 8. A **tragedy** whose **protagonist** is drawn from the "proletarian" or working class. The genre does not appear until the nineteenth century (see Büchner's *Woyzeck* in Volume II), and is based on an implicit rejection of the traditional, Aristotelian assumption that only the "best" of a society's citizens were suitable for serious dramatic treatment.

workshop, VOL. II: 515, 588. The process of developing and improving a play through a collaboration between a playwright and a group of theatre artists with the goal of producing a script deemed ready for performance.